Fodor's

THE COMPLETE GUIDE TO
NATIONAL PARKS
OF THE WEST

Welcome to
The National Parks of the West

Awe-inspiring, often remote landscapes and unlimited recreational opportunities make a trip to any western national park a grand adventure. You can raft the raging Colorado River as it pushes through the Grand Canyon, view wildlife in Yosemite while you hike, or watch Yellowstone's Old Faithful geyser in action. Places such as Mesa Verde also preserve the long history of life in the West. Wherever you explore in the parks, these sprawling treasures invite you to discover nature's stunning variety and reconnect with the great outdoors.

TOP REASONS TO GO

★ **Wildlife:** From bison to bald eagles to bears, the parks shelter amazing species.

★ **Hiking:** Countless scenic trails for all levels inspire and challenge walkers.

★ **Geology:** Unique formations like Oregon's Crater Lake and Utah's Arches astound.

★ **Great Views:** Mountain peaks and scenic overlooks reward climbers and drivers alike.

★ **History:** Monuments and outposts trace the settling of the former Wild West.

★ **Luxury Lodges:** Famous hotels pair old-school grandeur with splendid surroundings.

Contents

Fodor's Features

Contents

Contents

MAPS

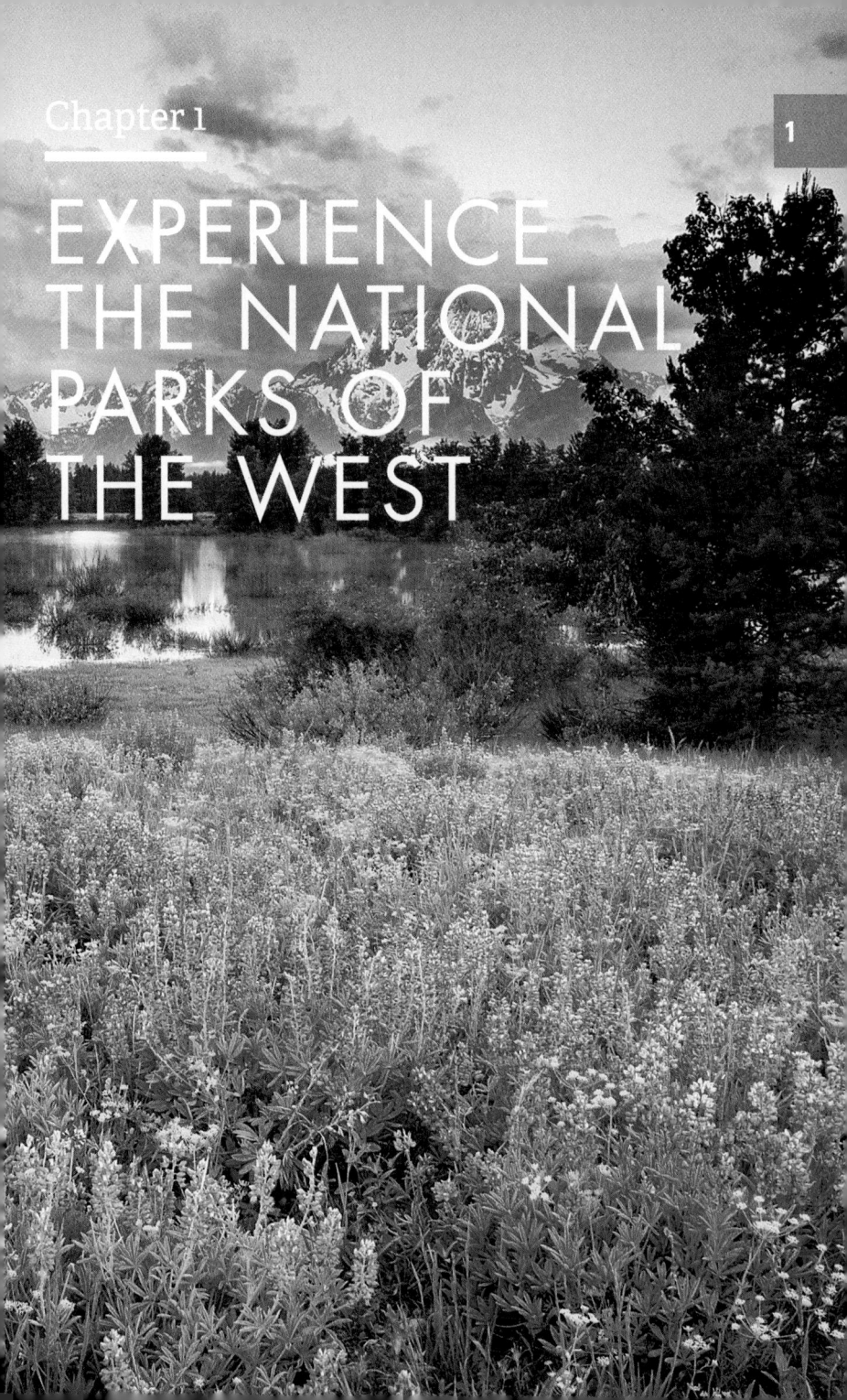

EXPERIENCE THE NATIONAL PARKS OF THE WEST

35 ULTIMATE EXPERIENCES

The National Parks of the West offer terrific experiences that should be on every traveler's list. Here are Fodor's top picks for a memorable trip.

1 Day climb in the Tetons

Grand Teton National Park, Wyoming

Known for having some of the country's best rock climbing, the gold standard at this park is a trip 13,770 feet up the Grand Teton which, if you go with one of the park's two approved outfitters, is open to beginners but may be better suited for those with some climbing experience. *(Ch. 17)*

2 Witness the beauty of the Big Room

Carlsbad Caverns National Park, New Mexico
The massive cavern's most beautiful section is a softly lit ballroom of sparkling speleothems called the Big Room, ringed with a paved path. *(Ch. 11)*

3 Visit all four distinct districts of the park

Canyonlands National Park, Utah
The Green and Colorado Rivers divide the park into districts of canyons, mesas, arches, and hoodoos. Most accessible is Island in the Sky, a sandstone mesa. *(Ch. 9)*

4 See unusual boxwork cave formations

Wind Cave National Park, South Dakota
This is the sixth-longest cave system in the world, with over 140 miles of underground passageways. It's the densest "maze cave" on Earth. *(Ch. 34)*

5 See Delicate Arch and the Windows Section

Arches National Park, Utah
The sandstone arches here, famous symbols of the American Southwest, have been carved by thousands of years of wind, water, and ice. *(Ch. 4)*

6 Discover extinct creatures

Badlands National Park, South Dakota
This landscape of eroded rock formations preserves the remains of mammals 33 million years old. See replicas of some of the fossils discovered here. *(Ch. 5)*

7 Ogle General Sherman

Sequoia National Park, California
The General Sherman tree is the largest living tree in the world, at 275 feet tall and 36 feet in diameter at its roots. *(Ch. 32)*

8 | Hike to the top of Half Dome

Yosemite National Park, California
The 16-mile round-trip trail to the top of Half Dome climbs nearly 5,000 feet. The challenge rewards hikers with unparalleled views of the Yosemite Valley. *(Ch. 36)*

9 | Investigate coastal tide pools

Olympic National Park, Washington
Along the park's rocky coastal outcroppings are tidepools full of giant green anemone, sea stars and other intertidal species. *(Ch. 26)*

10 | See the town where mail arrives by mule

Grand Canyon National Park, Arizona
The Havasupai people have lived in Supai for centuries, 8 miles from the nearest road. Accessible only by foot, it's last town in the country to receive mail by mule. *(Ch. 16)*

11 | Drive the Going-to-the-Sun Road

Glacier National Park, Montana
Construction began in 1921 on the 53-mile long road, which spans the width of the park. See the park's most famous features and wildlife. *(Ch. 15)*

12 Hike to the Santa Elena Canyon

Big Bend National Park, Texas
The sheer cliffs of the dramatic Santa Elena Canyon flank the Rio Grande, forming the boundary between Mexico and Texas in Big Bend National Park. *(Ch. 6)*

13 See volcanic erosion

Pinnacles National Park, California
More than 70 condors live in this moonscape of eroded volcanic detritus. See them at High Peaks or from the Peaks View scenic overlook. *(Ch. 28)*

14 Explore Wizard Island

Crater Lake National Park, Oregon
At the west end of Crater Lake, an extinct volcano and the deepest lake in the United States, is Wizard Island, which is capped with a 100-foot deep crater. *(Ch. 13)*

15 Look into the past

Petrified Forest National Park, Arizona
Thousands of years of human history is scattered across the desert landscape; over 600 archaeological and petroglyph sites have been found. *(Ch. 27)*

16 See one of the world's oldest organisms

Great Basin National Park, Nevada
Pine trees make up Nevada's ancient forest. The Bristlecone pine is the world's longest-living tree and likely its oldest living organism. *(Ch. 18)*

17 Watch hoodoos change color

Bryce Canyon National Park, Utah
Bryce Canyon has the largest concentration of hoodoos in the world. At sunset they are ablaze with pinks, oranges, yellows, and reds. *(Ch. 8)*

18 See the country's largest cactus

Saguaro National Park, Arizona
The Saguaro cactus, the largest succulent in the United States, grows in abundance in this slice of the Sonoran Desert. The plants can grow up to 40 feet. *(Ch. 31)*

19 See the South Rim Drive's 12 unique views

Black Canyon of the Gunnison National Park, Colorado
The 7-mile South Rim Drive has 12 separate overlooks, each offering a different view of the park's famous gorge. *(Ch. 7)*

20 Explore a geologic wrinkle in the Earth

Capitol Reef National Park, Utah
Utah's Waterpocket Fold is a geological wrinkle in the Earth's crust where shifting tectonic plates sent sedimentary rocks upwards into a spiny plateau. *(Ch. 10)*

21 Trek to the summit of the Lassen Peak

Lassen Volcanic National Park, California
Lassen Peak is the world's largest "plug dome" volcano. Though dormant, it's the southernmost active volcano in the Cascade Range. *(Ch. 22)*

22 Hike one of the most dangerous volcanoes

Mount Rainier National Park, Washington
Mount Rainier is considered one of the most dangerous volcanoes in the world due to its large film of glacial ice. *(Ch. 24)*

23 Explore desertscapes and ghost towns

Death Valley National Park, California
Mining towns sprang up in Death Valley when there was gold in the Panamint Mountains, but were abandoned once the riches ran out in the late 1800s. *(Ch. 14)*

24 Kayak around Santa Cruz Island

Channel Islands National Park, California
Due to thousands of years of isolation, these islands are inhabited by plants and animals found nowhere else on Earth. Rent a kayak and explore. *(Ch. 12)*

25 Explore Cliff Palace

Mesa Verde National Park, Colorado
Cliff Palace was inhabited by 100 people for over a century before it was abandoned during 13th-century droughts. *(Ch. 23)*

26 Watch the goings on at Prairie Dog Town

Theodore Roosevelt National Park, North Dakota
The official "Prairie Dog Town" is less than a mile down the Buckhorn Trail from the Caprock Coulee Trailhead. *(Ch. 33)*

27 Hike the Pacific Crest Trail

Kings Canyon National Park, California
Through the High Sierra, a landscape of steep peaks and deep valleys, the trail hits its formidable highest point at Forester Pass, 13,153 above sea level. *(Ch. 32)*

28 Explore Fern Canyon

Redwood National and State Parks, California
In this 325 million-year-old stream canyon, cliff walls with ancient ferns frame the gorge. *(Ch. 29)*

29 Hike to the "Top of Texas"

Guadalupe Mountains National Park, Texas
Guadalupe Peak is the highest point in the state of Texas, a whopping 8,749 feet above sea level. If you're game enough to make it to the top, you'll climb 3,000 feet. *(Ch. 20)*

30 Hike The Narrows

Zion National Park, Utah
The only way to pass through The Narrows, a gorge so slim that it's less than 30 feet wide at some points, is by walking in the Virgin River. *(Ch. 37)*

31 Backpack beneath mountain glaciers

North Cascades National Park, Washington
Envisioned as an undeveloped backcountry, 94% of North Cascades National Park remains untouched, dotted with alpine lakes, forests, and 300 glaciers. *(Ch. 25)*

32 See the desert in bloom

Joshua Tree National Park, California
This rocky park is known for its unusual Joshua Tree, a tall, stately yucca plant. In the springtime, cacti, succulents, and the Joshua Trees are in full bloom. *(Ch. 21)*

33 Sand sled down dunes

Great Sand Dunes National Park, Colorado
The sand dunes, the steepest in North America, are made up of 5 billion cubic meters of sand once found at the bottom of mountain lakes. *(Ch. 19)*

34 See Grand Prismatic

Yellowstone National Park, Wyoming
Grand Prismatic Spring is the largest hot spring in the United States, and third largest in the world. *(Ch. 35)*

35 Ride across the park on horseback

Rocky Mountain National Park, Colorado
Ride on horseback through 415 square miles of incredible alpine beauty. Two stables offer guided tours in the summer. *(Ch. 30)*

WHAT'S WHERE

Parks in this section are organized by state.

WASHINGTON

24 Mount Rainier. The fifth-highest mountain in the Lower 48, Mount Rainier is so massive that the summit is rarely visible—but when conditions are right, the image of the entire mountain is unforgettable. Hikes cover temperate rain forest, old-growth forests of hemlock and fir, high meadows, and tundra—not to mention hot springs, glaciers, lakes, and waterfalls. **Best Paired With:** North Cascades and Olympic

25 North Cascades. Hiking on a real glacier is a memorable experience—especially if you add in marmots, golden eagles, and coyotes—and North Cascades is home to several hundred of them. **Best Paired With:** Mount Rainier and Olympic

26 Olympic. Centered on Mount Olympus and framed on three sides by water, this park is known for its temperate rain forests, rugged coastal expanses, Sol Duc hot springs, and hiking (or skiing) at Hurricane Ridge. **Best Paired With:** North Cascades and Mount Rainier

OREGON

13 Crater Lake. Crater Lake is a geological marvel—the 21-square-mile sapphire-blue lake inside a caldera is the nation's deepest. The park itself includes about 90 miles of trails. **Best Paired With:** Mount Rainier and Olympic or Redwood and Lassen Volcanic

MONTANA

15 Glacier–Waterton Lakes. The rugged mountains that weave their way through the Continental Divide in northwest Montana are the backbone of Glacier and its sister park in Canada, Waterton Lakes. The park's Going-to-the-Sun Road is a spectacular drive that crosses the crest of the Continental Divide.

NORTH DAKOTA

33 Theodore Roosevelt. Theodore Roosevelt is known for chunks of badlands on the Little Missouri River and the 26th president's beloved Elkhorn Ranch. This is one of the most isolated parks in the Lower 48.

WYOMING

17 Grand Teton. With no foothills, the unimpeded view of the Teton Range rising out of Jackson Hole is stunning. Wildlife from short-tailed weasels to grizzly bears abounds. **Best Paired With:** Yellowstone

35 Yellowstone. Best known for Old Faithful, the world's most famous geyser, flowing hot springs, and mud pots, Yellowstone is the oldest national park in the world. Spotting the abundant wildlife, like bison, elk, moose, and bears, is the other main draw. **Best Paired With:** Grand Teton

SOUTH DAKOTA

5 Badlands. The park's eroded buttes and spires cast amazing shades of red and yellow across the South Dakota prairie. In addition to scenery, it has some of the world's richest mammal fossil beds. **Best Paired With:** Wind Cave

34 Wind Cave. One of the largest caves in the world, with beautiful cave formations including boxwork (3-D calcite honeycomb patterns on cave walls and ceilings), Wind Cave is the place to go spelunking. **Best Paired With:** Badlands

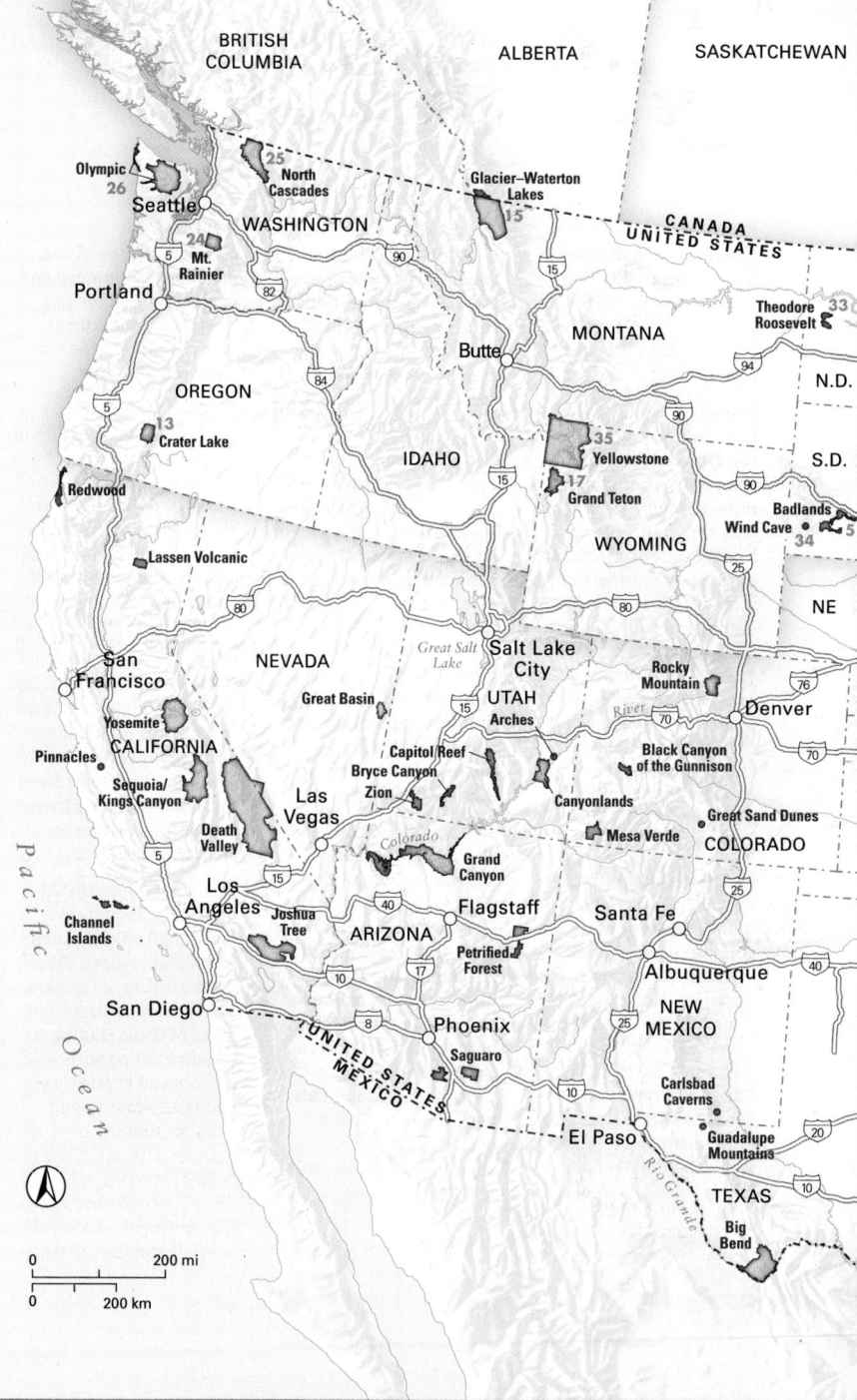

WHAT'S WHERE

NEVADA

18 Great Basin. It may be one of the nation's least visited national parks, but the stalactites, stalagmites, and popcorn in Lehman Caves and the solitude of backcountry treks are big draws.

UTAH

4 Arches. Four hours (235 miles) from Salt Lake City, this park has the world's largest concentration of natural sandstone arches, including that most-famous symbol of Utah, Delicate Arch. Nearby is Moab, an adventure hot spot, with world-class white-water rafting on the Colorado River, rock climbing, four-wheeling, and mountain biking. **Best Paired With:** Canyonlands

8 Bryce Canyon. Exploring the hoodoos (spectacular columns of rock) at this park is like wandering through a giant maze. Bryce is within a few hours of Utah's other national parks and near Kodachrome Basin State Park and Grand Staircase–Escalante National Monument. **Best Paired With:** Capitol Reef and Zion

9 Canyonlands. Biking on White Rim Road, white-water rafting in Cataract Canyon—plus spires, pinnacles, cliffs, and mesas as far as the eye can see—are the top reasons to go. **Best Paired With:** Arches

10 Capitol Reef. Seven times larger than nearby Bryce Canyon and much less crowded, Capitol Reef is known for its 100-mile-long Waterpocket Fold, a monocline (or "wrinkle" in the Earth's crust). It has many options for day hikes as well as backcountry trips into slot canyons, arches, cliffs, domes, and slickrock. **Best Paired With:** Bryce Canyon and Zion

37 Zion. Sheer 2,000-foot cliffs and river-carved canyons are what Zion is all about, and hiking the Narrows and the Subway are on many an adventurer's bucket list. Zion is right next to hospitable Springdale, which is full of amenities and charm. **Best Paired With:** Bryce Canyon and Grand Canyon

COLORADO

7 Black Canyon of the Gunnison. This steep and narrow river gorge has sheer cliffs and a drop twice as high as the Empire State Building.

19 Great Sand Dunes. The roughly 30 square miles of landlocked dune fields are an impressive sight. Aside from the dunes there are eight different life zones to explore, ranging from salty wetlands to alpine peaks.

23 Mesa Verde. Located in the Four Corners region—the junction of Utah, Colorado, New Mexico, and Arizona—this park houses an amazing collection of Ancestral Puebloan dwellings, some carved directly into cliff faces, and ancient artifacts.

30 Rocky Mountain. Alpine lakes, mountain peaks, and wildlife such as elk and bighorn sheep draw visitors to the park. There are more than 350 miles of trails leading to meadows filled with wildflowers and crystal lakes and 14,259-foot Long's Peak to summit.

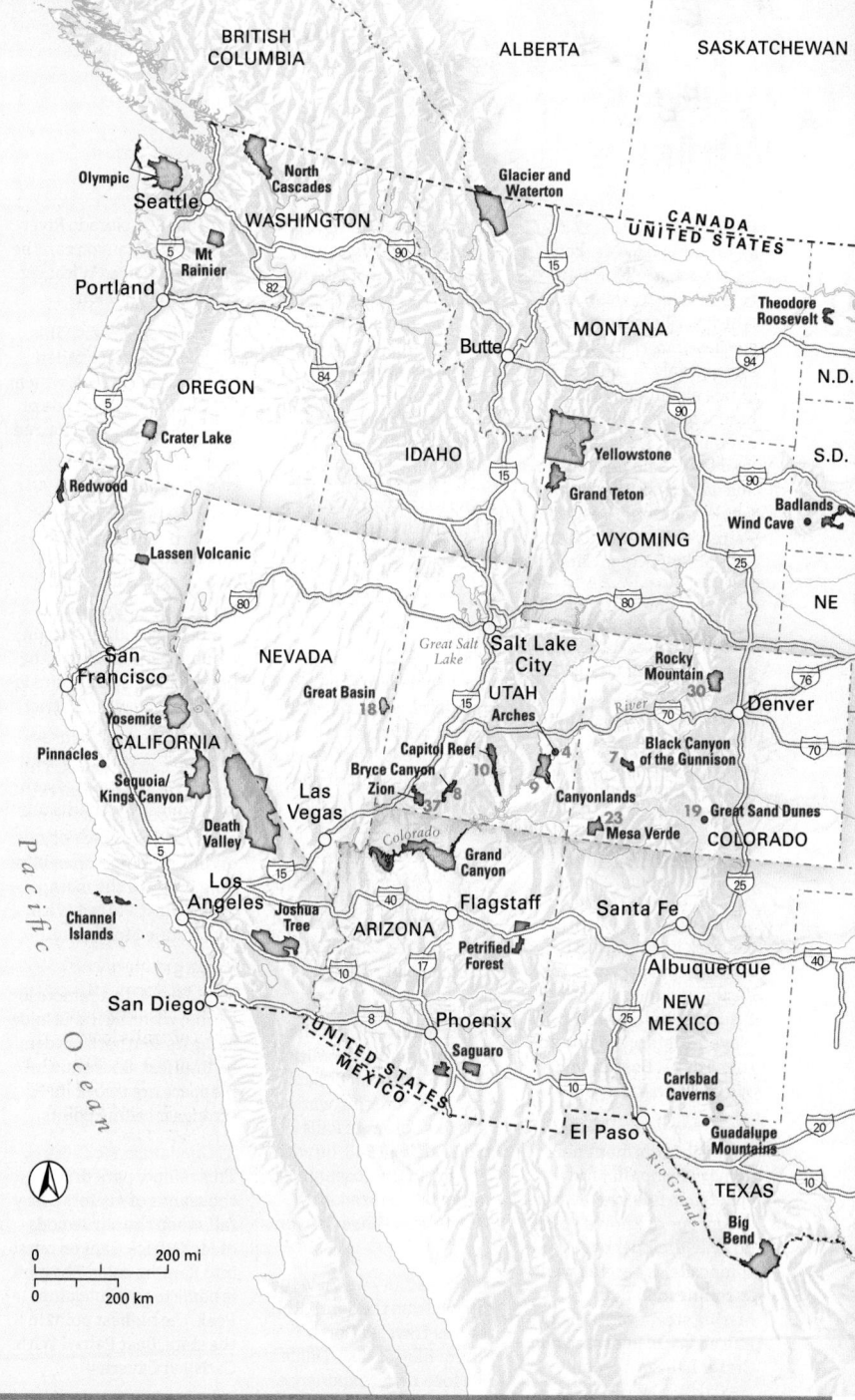

WHAT'S WHERE

CALIFORNIA

12 Channel Islands. You must take a boat or plane to reach the five islands, which are home to many species of terrestrial plants and animals found nowhere else on Earth. You're bound to see wildlife such as dolphins, sea lions, island foxes, and pelicans and can kayak, dive, and go whale-watching. **Best Paired With:** Yosemite and Sequoia and Kings Canyon

14 Death Valley. This is a vast, lonely, beautiful place with breathtaking vistas, blasting 120-degree heat, and mysterious moving rocks. The desert landscape is surrounded by majestic mountains, dry lakebeds, spring wildflowers, and Wild West ghost towns. **Best Paired With:** Joshua Tree and Zion

21 Joshua Tree. Large stands of Joshua trees gave the park its name, but it's also a great spot for bouldering and rock climbing. Brilliant wildflower displays and starry nights add to the draw. **Best Paired With:** Death Valley

22 Lassen Volcanic. Lassen Peak, a dormant plug dome volcano that last erupted in 1915, and every other type of known volcano (shield, cinder cone, and composite) is here, as well as roiling mud pots and hissing steam vents. **Best Paired With:** Redwood and Crater Lake or Yosemite

28 Pinnacles. Hiking among rugged volcanic spires is the most popular activity at Pinnacles, and the best chance you'll have at encountering one of the extremely rare California condors that make their home here. **Best Paired With:** Yosemite

29 Redwood. Redwood is home to the world's tallest trees: giant coast redwoods, which grow to more than 300 feet tall. **Best Paired With:** Lassen Volcanic and Crater Lake

32 Sequoia and Kings Canyon. Sequoias are the big trees here, which have monstrously thick trunks and branches. The Generals Highway, which connects the two parks, features many of these natural marvels. The Kings Canyon Scenic Byway offers views into a canyon deeper than the Grand Canyon. **Best Paired With:** Yosemite National Park

36 Yosemite. Dozens of famed features, from the soaring granite monoliths of Half Dome and El Capitan, to shimmering waterfalls like Yosemite Falls and Bridalveil Fall, lie within reach in the Yosemite Valley. **Best Paired With:** Sequoia and Kings Canyon

ARIZONA

16 Grand Canyon. View the canyon from the South Rim, the less-traveled North Rim, or hike or take a mule ride for a richer experience. Rafting the Colorado River through the canyon can't be beat. **Best Paired With:** Petrified Forest or Zion

27 Petrified Forest. This park is known for fallen and fossilized trees, which look like they are made of colorful stone. **Best Paired With:** Grand Canyon

31 Saguaro. The park takes its name from the saguaro cactus, the largest of its kind in the United States, found here. The park is split into two districts bookending Tucson (about 30 miles apart); the better collection of cacti is found in the west district.

NEW MEXICO

11 Carlsbad Caverns. The park's 119 caves, bizarre underground rock formations, and roughly 400,000 diving, dipping, sonar-blipping bats are the main draws. **Best Paired With:** Guadalupe Mountains

TEXAS

6 Big Bend. In a remote location, with the Rio Grande along its southern border, its limitless skies and ample space are two of its strongest selling points.

20 Guadalupe Mountains. This remote park draws thousands of visitors every fall, when the hardwoods of McKittrick Canyon burst into flaming color. The park is home to the Guadalupe Peak, the highest point in the state. **Best Paired With:** Carlsbad Caverns

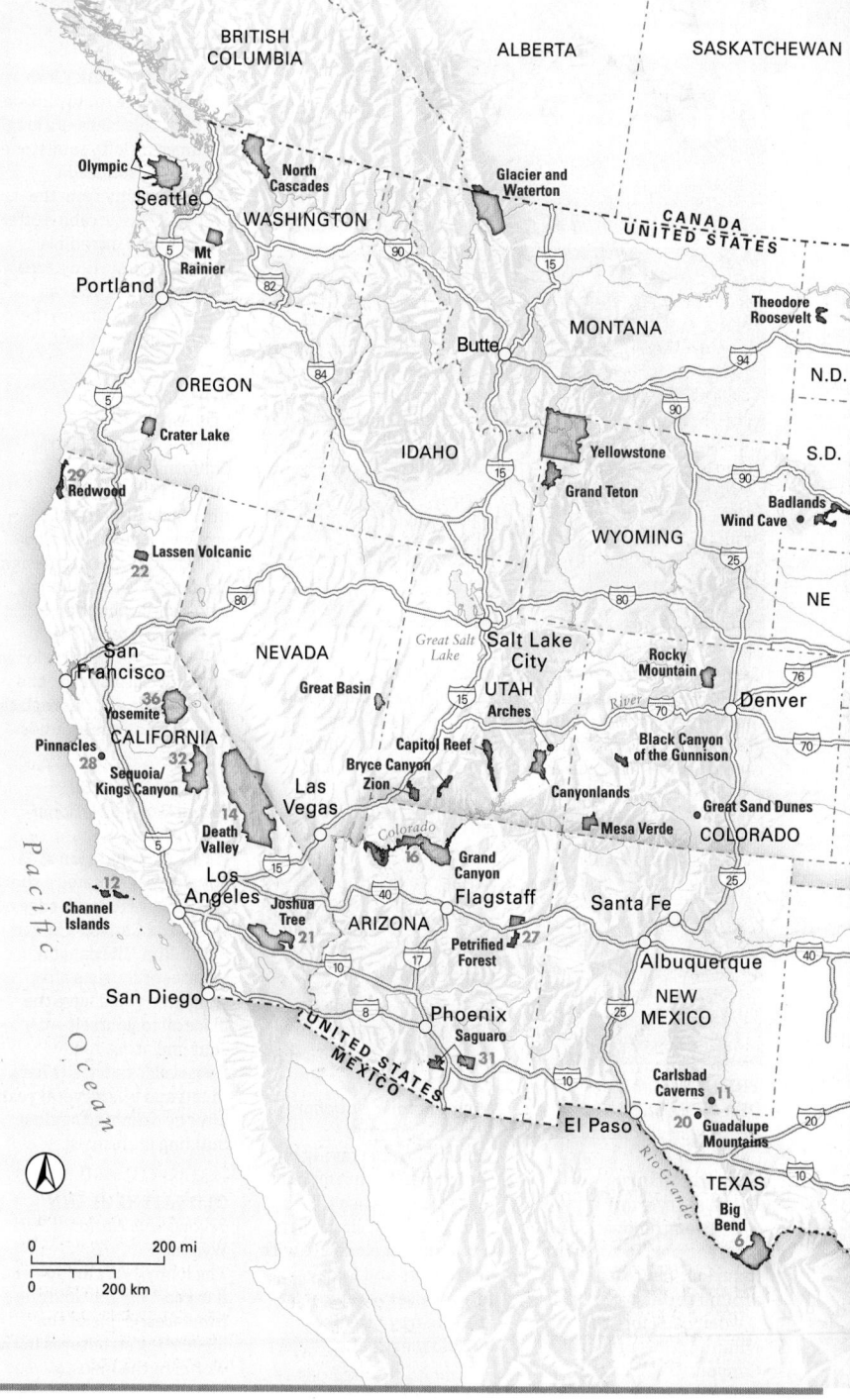

BRITISH COLUMBIA

ALBERTA

SASKATCHEWAN

Olympic

North Cascades

Glacier and Waterton

Seattle

WASHINGTON

CANADA
UNITED STATES

Portland

Mt Rainier

Theodore Roosevelt

MONTANA

Butte

N.D.

OREGON

Crater Lake

IDAHO

S.D.

29
Redwood

Yellowstone

Grand Teton

WYOMING

NE

22
Lassen Volcanic

San Francisco

NEVADA

Great Salt Lake

Salt Lake City

UTAH

Rocky Mountain

Denver

36
Yosemite

Great Basin

Arches

River

28
Pinnacles

CALIFORNIA

32

Capitol Reef

Black Canyon of the Gunnison

Sequoia/ Kings Canyon

Bryce Canyon

Zion

Canyonlands

Great Sand Dunes

14

Las Vegas

Mesa Verde

COLORADO

Death Valley

Colorado

16

Grand Canyon

12
Channel Islands

Los Angeles

Joshua Tree

Flagstaff

Santa Fe

21

ARIZONA

San Diego

UNITED STATES
MEXICO

8

Petrified Forest

27

Albuquerque

Phoenix

NEW MEXICO

Saguaro

31

Carlsbad Caverns

11

El Paso

20
Guadalupe Mountains

Rio Grande

TEXAS

Big Bend

6

Pacific Ocean

0   200 mi

0   200 km

The 12 Best National Parks of the West Lodges

JENNY LAKE LODGE
Grand Teton National Park, Wyoming
East Coast "dudes" began this homestead in 1922, back when there were just two cabins. Hiking trails accessible from the grounds offer views of Grand Teton and Mt. Moran, and guests can ride horses and cruiser-style bikes around the grounds.

THE INN AT DEATH VALLEY
Death Valley National Park, California
This 1927 Spanish Mission–style inn underwent renovations and reopened in 2018 with luxurious new casitas around the historic Oasis Gardens. Explore the winding trails of Mosaic Canyon.

PARADISE INN
Mount Rainier National Park, Washington
Visitors began staying at the timber-frame inn here in 1917, and it hasn't changed much since then. A restaurant complete with park views and a cozy fireplace serves appropriately hearty fare like buffalo meatloaf.

ZION LODGE
Zion National Park, Utah
The only place to stay inside the park, this 1920s-era lodge is framed by lofty sandstone cliffs, with trailheads leading directly from the property. Rustic cabins offer porches with incredible views and stone fireplaces. Bonus: at night, you can watch deer grazing on the lawn in the moonlight.

THE MAJESTIC YOSEMITE HOTEL
Yosemite National Park, California
Built in 1927 as the Ahwahnee Hotel, the property blends Art Deco and Native American design elements—some of which inspired the fictional Overlook Hotel in *The Shining*. Stay in a main lodge room for classic decor, or a cozy cottage with a fireplace elsewhere on the grounds.

EL TOVAR HOTEL
Grand Canyon National Park, Arizona
It's all about location at El Tovar Hotel, situated a short stroll away from the edge of the Grand Canyon's famed South Rim. The canyon empties of tourists after sunset, so you'll have the place all to yourself—try contemplating Teddy Roosevelt's two visits here, in 1911 and 1913, several years after he'd advised against building in the park.

OLD FAITHFUL INN
Yellowstone National Park, Wyoming
The lobby, built in 1904 and flanked by gigantic stone fireplaces, is one of the biggest log structures in the world. In the 1950s, a

The Majestic Yosemite Hotel

printing press in the basement supplied nightly dinner menus. Comfortably furnished rooms here face the famous geyser.

MANY GLACIER HOTEL
Glacier National Park, Montana
Glacial peaks provide a grand backdrop for this rustic lodge beside Swiftcurrent Lake in

Glacier National Park's northeastern section. The series of Swiss chalet–style buildings house modestly decorated guest rooms.

KALALOCH LODGE
Olympic National Park, Washington
Come to this serene oceanfront setting to explore rainforests, glaciers, and protected coastline.

ROSS LAKE RESORT
North Cascades National Park, Washington
Hike or take a ferry to this secluded resort. Cabins sit along the lake shore overlooking the Pacific Northwest landscape of blue water and rolling evergreen Cascades. Guests must bring their own food, and all cabins have full kitchens.

Spend a day at Ruby Beach or Lake Crescent, before enjoying sustainable seafood and Washington State wines at Creekside Restaurant back at the lodge.

CRATER LAKE LODGE
Crater Lake National Park, Oregon
Gaze on the deepest lake in the U.S. from this rustic lodge perched on the southwest rim of the caldera. The vivid blue water is due to the lake's depth—nearly 2,000 feet—and the surrounding volcanic peaks only add to the dramatic beauty.

DRAKESBAD GUEST RANCH
Lassen Volcanic National Park, California
Electricity here is scarce, so guests use kerosene lamps, and showers are in a shared bathhouse. A hot spring pool turns into a giant hot tub at night. Free meals are provided.

The Best Campgrounds in the National Parks of the West

JENNY LAKE CAMPGROUND
Grand Teton National Park, Wyoming
Just a short walk from glacial Jenny Lake, framed by the craggy Teton range at the edge of the Cascade Canyon, this campground is a favorite among kayakers and canoers, anglers in search of lake trout, hikers, climbers, and bikers.

WHITE RIVER CAMPGROUND
Mount Rainier National Park, Washington
Three thousand feet into a glacial canyon, 112 campsites (tent only) make up Mount Rainier National Park's White River Campground. White River is nestled in a forest with soaring pine-laden slopes.

JUMBO ROCKS CAMPGROUND
Joshua Tree National Park, California
This campground is woven among the stacked and strewn oversized volcanic boulders unique to Joshua Tree National Park, which change color in the shifting evening light. Several hiking trails begin here.

CHISOS BASIN CAMPGROUND
Big Bend National Park, Texas
Surrounded by rugged cliffs high in the Chisos Mountains, this campground is a picturesque slice of montane scrubland, all Arizona cypress and desert-hearty mesquite trees. It's perfectly positioned close to the park's most popular trails.

SLOUGH CREEK CAMPGROUND
Yellowstone National Park, Wyoming
There are just 16 sites at Slough Creek, 14 of which are large enough to accommodate an RV. It's located in the heart of the Lamary Valley, one of the best places for wildlife viewing in the park.

FRUITA CAMPGROUND
Capitol Reef National Park, Utah
Fed by the Fremont River, which meanders along the campground's edge, Fruita is literally an oasis in the desert, surrounded by the cool, green shade of historic orchards.

NORTH RIM CAMPGROUND
Grand Canyon National Park, Arizona
The fairly quiet North Rim Campground sits at 8,200 feet in elevation bordering the Transept Canyon, an offshoot of the main canyon. Many campsites have fantastic views.

Fruita Campground

MORAINE PARK CAMPGROUND
Rocky Mountain National Park, Colorado
This beautiful campground is spread out through a Douglas fir and pine forest, surrounded by a meadow of tall grasses and wildflowers and sheltered by craggy peaks rising up to 14,000 feet.

KINTLA LAKE CAMPGROUND
Glacier National Park, Montana
Just south of the Canadian border, Kintla Lake is the park's most remote developed campground. Perched on the edge of the pristine lake, this 13-site, RV-free campground offers campers serene solitude.

AZALEA CAMPGROUND
Kings Canyon National Park, California
Azalea is sheltered by towering pines and sequoias. The campground is hilly and dotted with massive boulders, creating a sense of privacy among its 110 first-come, first-served sites.

KALALOCH CAMPGROUND
Olympic National Park, Washington
For truly epic sunset views, the Kalaloch Campground can't be beat. Perched on the edge of a cliff overlooking the Pacific Ocean, this 166-site campground is right on the edge of North America.

TEXAS SPRINGS CAMPGROUND
Death Valley National Park, California
The massive size of this place, the quickly shifting shades of the desert, will take your breath away.

WATCHMAN CAMPGROUND
Zion National Park, Utah
This massive 176-site campground, a quarter of a mile from the south entrance and visitor center, sits in the shadow of the famous Zion rock formation. Reserve well in advance.

Field Guide: Geology and Terrain

MESAS AND CUESTAS

A mesa is an isolated hill with a smooth, flat top and steeply sloping sides. Its topmost layer is composed of rock that protects the lower layers from erosion. A cuesta is essentially a mesa that dips slightly to one side. A single mesa or cuesta may cover hundreds of square miles.

VOLCANOES AND VOLCANISM

Volcanoes are openings in Earth's crust where magma reaches the surface. Volcanic activity, or volcanism, can create many geologic formations like batholiths (large, rounded domes), or dikes and sills (banded, sheetlike formations).

GLACIERS AND GLACIAL FEATURES

Heavy snow compacted by centuries of pressure forms the slow-moving river of ice known as a glacier. Although most of the glaciers of North America have retreated, you can still see them in some of the Western parks.

GEOTHERMAL FEATURES

Hissing geysers, gurgling mud pots, and steaming hot springs have fascinated travelers ever since mountain man John Coulter described them to an unbelieving public in 1810. Today, these "freaks of a fiery nature," as Rudyard Kipling described them, are created when superheated water rises to Earth's surface from a magma chamber below. In the case of geysers, the water is trapped under the surface until the pressure is so great that it bursts through. Mud pots, also known as paint pots, are a combination of hot water, hydrogen sulfide gas, and dissolved volcanic rock.

CRATERS AND CALDERAS

A crater is a bowl-shape depression that's left behind when a volcano erupts. A caldera (Spanish for "cooking pot" or "cauldron") is essentially a big, sunken crater in which the volcano's inner magma chamber has also collapsed.

MONUMENT

This general term applies to two distinct geologic formations: those that are much taller than they are wide, and those that resemble man-made structures.

Geothermal Features

BUTTES AND SPIRES
Buttes are isolated hills with very steep sides and flat tops (they're defined as a hill that's higher than it is wide). They are formed in sedimentary (layered) rock by erosion, when wind or water wear away softer layers to leave a section of harder rock behind. As a butte erodes, it may become one or more spires, which look like giant stone columns (with a uniform thickness and smooth profile that tapers slightly at the top).

DESERT VARNISH
This reddish-brown or black coating, sometimes called rock varnish, drips down arid canyon walls. Windblown dust or rain containing iron and manganese, along with microorganisms living on the rock's surface, create the color. Ancestral Puebloans and other ancient Native Americans scratched petroglyphs into it.

PLAYAS
Shallow lake beds known as playas ("beaches" in Spanish) commonly lie in the low points of arid Southwestern valleys. These sedimentary basins often fill with rainwater, then dry again as the water evaporates.

ARCHES AND BRIDGES
An arch is a window in a rock wall that typically forms through erosion, when wind and/or water wear away the surface to create a hole all the way through. A natural bridge is a type of arch created by rushing water. Together, they are called windows.

Wildlife in the Parks

EAGLES
With a wingspan of up to 7½ feet, the adult golden eagle has dark plumage, except for a golden head. Golden eagles are seen in Mount Rainier, Redwood, Sequoia and Kings Canyon, Theodore Roosevelt, and Yellowstone; you might see a bald eagle, distinguished by their white heads, in North Cascades, Olympic, Redwood, Sequoia and Kings Canyon, Yellowstone, and Zion.

BISON
Yellowstone is the only place in the country where bison have lived continuously since prehistoric times; currently, between 2,300 and 4,500 animals make up the park's two herds. They can also be seen at Badlands, Grand Teton, Great Sand Dunes, Theodore Roosevelt, and Wind Cave.

BIGHORN SHEEP
Clambering along rocky ledges, bighorn sheep fascinate with their ability to travel so easily where the rest of us can't. In winter the docile herd animals descend to lower elevations. Many of the national parks of the West are home to a few varieties of bighorn sheep. They rut in autumn, when antlered males fight each other dramatically over mates.

GRAY WOLF
These impressive canines, listed as threatened or endangered in parts of the United States, communicate with each other through body language, barks, and howls. Wolves are wary of humans, but you might spot one at Grand Teton, Mount Rainier, North Cascades, and Yellowstone National Parks.

MOOSE
Feeding on fir, willows, and aspens, the moose is the largest member of the deer family: the largest bulls stand 7 feet tall at the shoulders and weigh up to 1,600 pounds. Look for moose in Glacier, Grand Teton, Rocky Mountain, and Yellowstone National Parks.

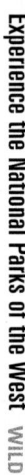

GRIZZLY BEAR

A male grizzly can weigh 700 pounds and reach a height of 8 feet when standing on its hind legs. After hibernation (November to March), they emerge hungry, sometimes prompting trail closures.

MOUNTAIN GOAT

Not really goats at all (they're actually related to antelope), these woolly mountaineers live in high elevations throughout the northwestern United States. Look for them in Glacier, Mount Rainier, North Cascades, and Yellowstone National Parks.

ELK

Elk congregate where forest meets meadows. In September and October, bulls attract mating partners by bugling, a loud whistling. Elk are residents of many national parks.

MOUNTAIN LION

Although mountain lions live throughout the American West, from northern Canada through the South American Andes, chances are you won't see them at most of the parks due to their elusive nature. Also called cougars, these enormous carnivores can be 8 feet long and weigh up to 200 pounds. They're capable of taking down a mule deer or elk.

COYOTE

Coyotes are highly intelligent animals. As big as a mid-size dog, they thrive throughout the western United States and at many national parks. They travel most often alone or in pairs, but occasionally form small packs for hunting. Although they pose little threat to humans, never approach one.

What You Need to Know Before You Visit America's National Parks of the West

SEASONS AND WEATHER WORK DIFFERENTLY HERE
National parks are places of extremes—extreme beauty and extreme weather. In May, for example, you'll see snow at Yellowstone and North Cascades; while down at Guadalupe Mountains on the Texas/New Mexico border, the unrelenting sun has already dried out the landscape; and in Death Valley, average temperatures are already in the 90s. No matter which park you visit, prepare for both excessive heat and brutal cold.

PLAN AHEAD FOR THE MOST ADVENTUROUS PARK EXPERIENCES
National park rangers protect the parks' ecologies from the millions of tourists who visit annually. This means that for some of the most popular adventures in the park—kayaking up-bay at Glacier Bay or exploring Slaughter Canyon Cave at Carlsbad Caverns—there are only a handful of spots open and they fill up well in advance, so be sure to reserve early on the park's website. In some places, like at Yosemite's Half Dome, the required permit is only accessible via a lottery system, with just 300 winners a day.

LEAVE NO TRACE
Anything you bring into the park must be carried back out or put in the appropriate garbage or recycling receptacle. Don't pick up any rocks or artifacts or fossils; don't collect flowers or firewood; and never touch or interact with a wild animal.

SOME CAMPSITES ARE RESERVED FOR WALK-UPS
Most parks reserve campsites for first-come, first-served walk-ups. As long as you get there as early in the morning as possible, you're likely to get a spot, even on weekends. They aren't always the most desirable campgrounds in the park, though—at Yosemite, for example, most of the walk-up sites are located in high country and not in the Yosemite Valley—but it's much better than staying home.

RECOGNIZE AND RESPECT THE PARK'S INDIGENOUS HISTORY
Yellowstone, our oldest national park, was established in 1872, and visitation has grown steadily since. In the first eight months of 2018, 3.8 million people visited Yellowstone. For many centuries, however, the only visitors to these places were the indigenous peoples of North America. Evidence of settlement and exploration by natives in the national parks dates back more than 10,000 years. Thanks to a mandate that enforces management of cultural and ecological resources in the parks, artifacts left behind have been well preserved. For some of the best insight into Native American history, plan a visit to Mesa Verde, the Grand Canyon, Badlands, or the Utah triad—Arches, Zion, and Canyonlands. If you find an artifact while hiking or backpacking in a national park, never pick it up; artifacts are useless to archaeologists unless they are found within their original context.

FIRES ARE A HUGE CONCERN
Hot, dry conditions, overgrown forests, and unhealthy trees have turned the West into a tinderbox, and wildfires ravage the landscape year-round. In 2018 Yosemite closed for the first time since 1990 due to the nearby Ferguson Fire, and the burning of more than 12,000 acres of Glacier National Park by the Howe Ridge Fire. Most national parks still allow campfires in designated fire pits, however, while others have charcoal grills. Outside of these designated areas, fires are both illegal and incredibly dangerous. If you plan to camp in the backcountry and need fire for cooking, bring a small camp stove or propane burner.

Saguaro National Park

DON'T SKIP THE VISITOR CENTER

At most national parks, the visitor center is more than just a place to get information on the best hiking trails. Here you'll often find museum-quality displays on the park's ecology, geology, and biology; some even have archaeological artifacts on view.

TAKE WARNING SIGNS AND RANGER ADVICE SERIOUSLY

National parks are one of the few remaining places in the United States that have not been sanitized for your safety; in some cases the only thing that stands between you and certain death is a sign. Visitors die every year in climbing and hiking accidents and animal encounters in America's national parks. Always take precautionary signs and ranger advice seriously.

FIND BEAUTY AND SOLITUDE AWAY FROM THE FAMOUS SITES

It's kind of a catch-22: you go to a national park to experience the beauty and solitude of the natural world only to discover that everyone else had the same plan. Rather than visiting the most popular sites, hit the trails (or water), particularly routes that are longer than 3 miles and can't be traversed by baby carriages and large tour groups. They may not be listed as the park's top must-see locations but they're almost guaranteed to be just as spectacular, yet apart from the crowds.

GET A GOOD LOOK AT WHAT WE COULD LOSE AS CLIMATE CHANGE PROGRESSES

National parks are ground zero for the environmental havoc wrought by climate change. These extreme environments are seeing rapid change as glaciers melt (Glacier Bay) and wildfires rage (Yosemite and Glacier). While this is devastating to watch, visiting the national parks reminds us what we have to lose.

NATIONAL PARKS OF THE WEST BEST BETS

Fodor's writers and editors have chosen our favorites to help you plan. Search individual chapters for more recommendations.

👁 SIGHTS

BEACHES
Channel Islands, *Ch. 12*
Olympic, *Ch. 26*
Redwood, *Ch. 29*

BIRDS
Big Bend, *Ch. 6*
Carlsbad Caverns, *Ch. 11*
Great Sand Dunes, *Ch. 19*
Guadalupe Mountains, *Ch. 20*
Joshua Tree, *Ch. 21*
Mount Rainier, *Ch. 24*
Pinnacles, *Ch. 28*
Rocky Mountain, *Ch. 30*
Theodore Roosevelt, *Ch. 33*

BISON
Grand Teton, *Ch. 17*
Great Sand Dunes, *Ch. 19*
Theodore Roosevelt, *Ch. 33*
Yellowstone, *Ch. 35*

BOATING
Big Bend, *Ch. 6*
Channel Islands, *Ch. 12*
Glacier-Waterton, *Ch. 15*
Grand Canyon, *Ch. 16*
Grand Teton, *Ch. 17*
Lassen Volcanic, *Ch. 22*
North Cascades, *Ch. 25*
Olympic, *Ch. 26*
Redwood, *Ch. 29*
Theodore Roosevelt, *Ch. 33*
Yellowstone, *Ch. 35*
Yosemite, *Ch. 36*

CAVES AND CAVERNS
Carlsbad Caverns, *Ch. 11*
Channel Islands, *Ch. 12*
Great Basin, *Ch. 18*

Sequoia and Kings Canyon, *Ch. 32*
Wind Cave, *Ch. 34*

FISHING
Big Bend, *Ch. 6*
Black Canyon of the Gunnison, *Ch. 7*
Capitol Reef, *Ch. 10*
Channel Islands, *Ch. 12*
Glacier-Waterton, *Ch. 15*
Grand Canyon, *Ch. 16*
Grand Teton, *Ch. 17*
Great Basin, *Ch. 18*
Mount Rainier, *Ch. 24*
North Cascades, *Ch. 25*
Olympic, *Ch. 26*
Redwood, *Ch. 29*
Rocky Mountain, *Ch. 30*
Sequoia and Kings Canyon, *Ch. 32*
Theodore Roosevelt, *Ch. 33*
Yellowstone, *Ch. 35*
Yosemite, *Ch. 36*

GEOLOGICAL GREATS
Arches, *Ch. 4*
Bryce Canyon, *Ch. 8*
Canyonlands, *Ch. 9*
Carlsbad Caverns, *Ch. 11*
Crater Lake, *Ch. 13*
Grand Canyon, *Ch. 16*
Lassen Volcanic, *Ch. 22*
Petrified Forest, *Ch. 27*
Yellowstone, *Ch. 35*

GEYSERS
Death Valley, *Ch. 14*
Lassen Volcanic, *Ch. 22*
Mount Rainier, *Ch. 24*
Olympic, *Ch. 26*
Yellowstone, *Ch. 35*

GLACIERS AND ICE FIELDS
Glacier-Waterton, *Ch. 15*
Grand Teton, *Ch. 17*
Mount Rainier, *Ch. 24*
North Cascades, *Ch. 25*
Olympic, *Ch. 26*

HORSEBACK RIDING
Glacier, *Ch. 15*
Lassen Volcanic, *Ch. 22*
Mount Rainier, *Ch. 24*
Olympic, *Ch. 26*
Rocky Mountain, *Ch. 30*
Yosemite, *Ch. 36*

MOUNTAINS
Big Bend, *Ch. 6*
Capitol Reef, *Ch. 10*
Glacier, *Ch. 15*
Grand Teton, *Ch. 17*
Guadalupe Mountains, *Ch. 20*
Lassen Volcanic, *Ch. 22*
North Cascades, *Ch. 25*
Olympic, *Ch. 28*
Rocky Mountain, *Ch. 30*
Sequoia and Kings Canyon, *Ch. 32*
Yosemite, *Ch. 36*

TREES AND FORESTS
Joshua Tree, *Ch. 21*
North Cascades, *Ch. 25*
Olympic, *Ch. 26*
Petrified Forest, *Ch. 27*
Redwood, *Ch. 29*
Sequoia and Kings Canyon, *Ch. 32*
Yosemite, *Ch. 36*

VOLCANOES
Crater Lake, *Ch. 13*
Death Valley, *Ch. 14*
Lassen Volcanic, *Ch. 22*
Mount Rainier, *Ch. 24*
Yellowstone, *Ch. 35*

WATERFALLS
Crater Lake, *Ch. 13*
Great Sand Dunes, *Ch. 19*
Lassen Volcanic, *Ch. 22*
Mount Rainier, *Ch. 24*
Olympic, *Ch. 26*
Rocky Mountain, *Ch. 30*
Yellowstone, *Ch. 35*
Yosemite, *Ch. 36*

WINTER SPORTS
Bryce Canyon, *Ch. 8*
Joshua Tree, *Ch. 21*
Mount Rainier, *Ch. 24*
Olympic, *Ch. 26*
Rocky Mountain, *Ch. 30*
Yellowstone, *Ch. 35*
Yosemite, *Ch. 36*
Zion, *Ch. 37*

⑪ RESTAURANTS

ARCHES
Desert Bistro, *Ch. 4*
Eklekticafe, *Ch. 4*
Moab Garage, Arches, *Ch. 4*
Sweet Cravings Bakery + Bistro, *Ch. 4*

BIG BEND
Cedar Coffee Supply, *Ch. 6*
Reata, *Ch. 6*
Stellina, *Ch. 6*
12 Gage Restaurant, *Ch. 6*

BRYCE CANYON
Bryce Canyon Lodge, *Ch. 8*
Centro Woodfired Pizzeria, *Ch. 8*
Stone Hearth Grille, *Ch. 8*

CAPITOL REEF
Cafe Diablo, *Ch. 10*
Hell's Backbone Grill, *Ch. 10*

CARLSBAD CAVERNS
Milton's Taproom and Brewery, *Ch. 11*
Red Chimney Pit Bar-B-Q, *Ch. 11*
Trinity Hotel, Carlsbad Caverns, *Ch. 11*

CRATER LAKE
Crater Lake Lodge Dining Room, *Ch. 13*
Morning Glory, *Ch. 13*

DEATH VALLEY
Inn at Death Valley Dining Room, *Ch. 14*

GLACIER AND WATERTON LAKES
Belton Chalet Grill Dining Room, *Ch. 15*

GRAND CANYON
El Tovar Dining Room, Grand Canyon, *Ch. 16*
Grand Canyon Lodge Dining Room, *Ch. 16*
Red Raven Restaurant, *Ch. 16*

GRAND TETON
Snake River Grill, *Ch. 17*
Teton Thai, *Ch. 17*

GREAT BASIN
Kerouac's, *Ch. 18*

JOSHUA TREE
Pappy & Harriet's Pioneer-town Palace, *Ch. 21*

LASSEN VOLCANIC
Highlands Ranch Restaurant and Bar, *Ch. 22*
Lassen Ale Works Boardroom, *Ch. 22*

MESA VERDE
Metate Room Restaurant, *Ch. 23*
Ore House, *Ch. 23*

NORTH CASCADES
Dining Room at Sun Mountain Lodge, *Ch. 25*

OLYMPIC
Blondie's Plate, *Ch. 26*
Oak Table Café, *Ch. 26*

REDWOOD
Cafe Brio, *Ch. 29*
SeaQuake Brewing, *Ch. 29*
Brick & Fire Bistro, *Ch. 29*

ROCKY MOUNTAIN
Fat Cat Cafe, *Ch. 30*
Sagebrush BBQ & Grill, *Ch. 30*

SAGUARO
Beyond Bread, *Ch. 31*
Café Poca Cosa, *Ch. 31*
Mi Nidito, *Ch. 31*

SEQUOIA AND KINGS CANYON
The Vintage Press, *Ch. 32*

THEODORE ROOSEVELT
Theodore's, *Ch. 33*

WIND CAVE
Old Style Saloon No. 10, *Ch. 34*
Deadwood Social Club, *Ch. 34*

YELLOWSTONE
Lake Hotel Dining Room, *Ch. 35*
Old Faithful Snow Lodge Obsidian Dining Room, *Ch. 35*

YOSEMITE
The Majestic Yosemite Hotel Dining Room, *Ch. 36*
Mountain Room, *Ch. 36*
Erna's Elderberry House, *Ch. 36*
South Gate Brewing Company, *Ch. 36*

ZION
Kanab Creek Bakery, *Ch. 37*
King's Landing Bistro, *Ch. 37*
Sego, Zion, *Ch. 37*

🛏 HOTELS

ARCHES
Best Western Canyonlands Inn, *Ch. 4*
Cali Cochitta Bed & Breakfast, *Ch. 4*
Red Cliffs Lodge, *Ch. 4*
Sunflower Hill Luxury Inn, *Ch. 4*

BIG BEND
Chisos Mountains Lodge, *Ch. 6*
Gage Hotel, *Ch. 6*
Holland Hotel, *Ch. 6*
Hotel Saint George, *Ch. 6*

BRYCE CANYON
Bryce Canyon Lodge, *Ch. 8*
Entrada Escalante Lodge, *Ch. 8*
Stone Canyon Inn, *Ch. 8*

CANYONLANDS
Desert Rose Inn and Cabins, *Ch. 9*

CAPITOL REEF
Boulder Mountain Lodge, *Ch. 10*
Lodge at Red River Ranch, *Ch. 10*

CARLSBAD CAVERNS
Trinity Hotel, *Ch. 11*

CHANNEL ISLANDS
Four Seasons Resort The Biltmore Santa Barbara, *Ch. 12*
The Ritz-Carlton Bacara, Santa Barbara, *Ch. 12*

CRATER LAKE
Crater Lake Lodge, *Ch. 13*
Winchester Inn, *Ch. 13*

DEATH VALLEY
Inn at Death Valley, *Ch. 14*

GLACIER-WATERTON
Lake McDonald Lodge, *Ch. 15*

GRAND CANYON
El Tovar Hotel, *Ch. 16*
Grand Canyon Lodge, *Ch. 16*

GRAND TETON
Jenny Lake Lodge, *Ch. 17*
The Wildflower Lodge at Jackson Hole, *Ch. 17*
The Wort Hotel, *Ch. 17*

GREAT BASIN
Hidden Canyon Retreat, *Ch. 18*

JOSHUA TREE
Orbit In Hotel, *Ch. 21*
29 Palms Inn, *Ch. 21*

LASSEN VOLCANIC
Drakesbad Guest Ranch, *Ch. 22*
Highlands Ranch Resort, *Ch. 22*

MESA VERDE
Far View Lodge, *Ch. 23*
Strater Hotel, *Ch. 23*

MOUNT RAINIER
Paradise Inn, *Ch. 24*
Stormking Spa and Cabins, *Ch. 24*

NORTH CASCADES
Freestone Inn, *Ch. 25*
Sun Mountain Lodge, *Ch. 25*

OLYMPIC
Kalaloch Lodge, *Ch. 26*
Colette's Bed & Breakfast, *Ch. 26*
Sea Cliff Gardens Bed & Breakfast, *Ch. 26*
Seabrook Cottage Rentals, *Ch. 26*

PETRIFIED FOREST
La Posada Hotel, *Ch. 27*

PINNACLES
Inn at the Pinnacles, *Ch. 28*

REDWOOD
Elk Meadow Cabins, *Ch. 29*
Carter House Inns, *Ch. 29*
Historic Requa Inn, *Ch. 29*

ROCKY MOUNTAIN
Stanley Hotel, *Ch. 30*
Historic Rapids Lodge & Restaurant, *Ch. 30*

SAGUARO
Arizona Inn, *Ch. 31*
Hacienda del Sol Guest Ranch Resort, *Ch. 31*
Hotel Congress, Saguaro, *Ch. 31*
White Stallion Ranch, Saguaro, *Ch. 31*

SEQUOIA AND KINGS CANYON
Wuksachi Lodge, *Ch. 32*
Rio Sierra Riverhouse, *Ch. 32*

THEODORE ROOSEVELT
Rough Riders Hotel, *Ch. 33*

WIND CAVE
Audrie's and Abend House Cottage, *Ch. 34*

YOSEMITE
The Majestic Yosemite Hotel, *Ch. 36*
Château du Sureau, *Ch. 36*
Rush Creek Lodge, *Ch. 36*

ZION
Zion Lodge, *Ch. 37*
Cable Mountain Lodge, *Ch. 37*
Canyon's Lodge, *Ch. 37*
Desert Pearl Inn, *Ch. 37*

Did You Know?

One of the world's best examples of arid-land erosion, the Grand Canyon provides a record of three of the four eras of geological time.

What to Read and Watch Before Your Trip

OUR NATIONAL PARKS BY JOHN MUIR

As a naturalist, environmentalist, and early advocate for the protection of America's Western forests, John Muir has become synonymous with America's national parks. This collection of essays celebrates the beauty of America's untamed wilderness and will no doubt inspire readers to strike out on their own.

YOSEMITE AND THE RANGE OF LIGHT BY ANSEL ADAMS

This collection features more than 150 black-and-white photos that capture the jaw-dropping majesty of the High Sierras as only a master photographer can. Ansel Adams's camera is able to capture both the grandeur of Yosemite's mountains and valleys and the intimate nature of the relationship between people and the natural world.

YELLOWSTONE HAS TEETH BY MARJANE AMBLER

It's one thing to visit Yellowstone; it's another to call it home. In this memoir, Marjane Ambler recounts the time she and her husband spent living in a remote section of the park among a small community of rangers.

DESERT SOLITAIRE BY EDWARD ABBEY

Arches National Park serves as the stunning backdrop of Edward Abbey's account as a park ranger. The essays describe both the hostility and the beauty of the American southwest with funny, poetic, and often elegiac prose. Although first published in 1968, Abbey's advocacy on behalf of the country's natural wonders is as prescient today as it was 50 years ago.

GLORYLAND BY SHELTON JOHNSON

When Yellowstone was first established, the park was patrolled by a regiment of Buffalo Soldiers. This historical novel by Shelton Johnson (a Yosemite park ranger himself) tells the story of one soldier who finds a home among the mountains and rivers of Yosemite when his regiment is assigned to guard the park.

BUTCH CASSIDY AND THE SUNDANCE KID

George Roy Hill's 1969 Western tells the (mostly) real-life story of outlaws Robert Leroy Parker (a.k.a. Butch Cassidy) and Harry Alonzo Longabaugh (a.k.a. the Sundance Kid). Over the course of the film Paul Newman and Robert Redford are chased by lawmen, rob trains, and banter against the backdrop of Zion National Park and in the ghost town of Grafton, a few miles south of Zion.

THE RIVER WILD

Meryl Streep and Kevin Bacon star in this 1994 thriller about a family's whitewater rafting vacation going awry when they cross paths with a pair of on-the-lam criminals. It was shot on the Middle Fork of the Flathead River, which forms part of the southern boundary of Glacier National Park.

THELMA AND LOUISE

The quintessential road trip movie, *Thelma and Louise* follows the titular friends as they make their way from Arkansas to the Grand Canyon. Parts of the film were shot in Arches and Canyonlands National Park. But that iconic final scene was actually filmed at Dead Horse Point State Park in Utah.

STAR WARS: A NEW HOPE

You could be forgiven for thinking that the arid Death Valley National Park looks like something from a galaxy far, far away. It did, after all, serve as the location for the desert planet of Tatooine in *Star Wars: A New Hope* and *Return of the Jedi*. And while it's still possible to film in Death Valley you can no longer film to the same extent as George Lucas and Co. once did.

Chapter 2

PLANNING YOUR VISIT

Park Passes

NATIONWIDE PASSES

Although not all national parks charge admission—and children under age 16 always enter free—many do. If you're visiting several American national parks in one vacation or over the course of a year, you can save money with one of the America the Beautiful (all called Interagency) passes, which generally cover the cardholder and all others in a single vehicle (or the cardholder and up to three other passengers age 16 and older at places that charge per person).

What's more, the passes are valid for entry to more than 2,000 federal recreation sites managed by six participating agencies. These include the NPS as well as the Bureau of Land Management, Bureau of Reclamation, Fish and Wildlife Service, U.S. Army Corps of Engineers, and USDA Forest Service.

Although the NPS (⊕ www.nps.gov/planyourvisit/passes.htm) has pass details, and you can buy passes on location at some participating sites, the United States Geological Survey (USGS) is the primary source for information and purchase (☎ 888/275–8747, Ext. 3 ⊕ store.usgs.gov/recreational-passes). Another good source is Recreation.gov (☎ 877/444–6777 reservations ☎ 888/448–1474 customer service ☎ 518/885–3639 international ⊕ www.recreation.gov).

Although USGS phone and online orders incur a $5 or $10 handling charge, they do include a free brochure and vehicle hang tags (if you're driving a motorcycle or an open-top vehicle, inquire about free decals). All passes are nontransferable and nonrefundable (lost or stolen passes must be repurchased), and you must show photo ID with your pass at entrances.

Access Pass. United States citizens or permanent residents with disabilities medically determined to be permanent (documentation required) can acquire this free, lifetime pass. At some locations, it might also allow for discounts on camping, tour, and other amenities.

Annual Pass. Available to anyone age 16 or older, this pass costs $80 and is valid for a year from the date of purchase. It can be shared by two "owners," who need not be related or married (both must sign the back of the pass).

Every Kid in a Park Pass. This free pass (⊕ www.everykidinapark.gov) is available to U.S. students in their fourth-grade school year (i.e., it's valid Sept.–Aug.) and covers three accompanying family members or friends.

Senior Pass. If you're 62 or older and are a U.S. citizen or permanent resident, you can buy an annual $20 pass or a lifetime $80 pass. At some sites, this pass might also allow for amenity discounts. In addition, senior citizens can acquire passes via a mail-in application (wstore.usgs.gov/s3fs-public/senior_pass_application.pdf); additional fees apply.

Volunteer Pass. Look into this free, annual pass if you've logged 250 volunteer hours at recreation sites or lands overseen by one of the six federal pass-program agencies.

Military Pass. This pass is free to current members (and members' dependents) of the Army, Navy, Air Force, Marines, and Coast Guard, as well as the Reserves and National Guard.

OTHER PASSES

Most national parks offer individual annual passes. Prices vary but hover around $35 to $70 (⊕ *www.nps.gov/ aboutus/entrance-fee-prices.htm*). If you might visit a particular park more than once in a year, look into its annual pass. Sometimes, there's only a small difference between a single day's and a year's admission.

If you're planning to travel to Canadian national parks, Parks Canada (☎ *877/737–3783 in North America* ☎ *519/826–5391 elsewhere* ⊕ *www. pc.gc.ca*), the Canadian equivalent of the NPS, issues an annual Discovery Pass (⊕ *www.commandesparcs-parksorders. ca*) that allows free entry to 80 parks and other sites. Prices range from about US$45 to US$105.

OTHER ANNUAL PASSES

Most individual national parks also offer an annual pass for unlimited access to that particular park. Prices vary, but hover around $30 to $50. In a few cases these passes include admission to two parks that are near each other, such as Grand Teton and Yellowstone. If you think you might be back to a park within a year, ask the gate attendant how much the annual pass is. In some parks, there's only a small difference between a single day's and a year's admission.

PETS IN THE PARKS

2

Generally, pets are allowed only in developed areas of the national parks, including drive-in campgrounds and picnic areas. They must be kept on a leash at all times. With the exception of guide dogs, pets are not allowed inside buildings, on most trails, on beaches, or in the backcountry. They also may be prohibited in areas controlled by concessionaires, such as restaurants. Some national parks have kennels; call ahead to learn the details and to see if there's availability. Some of the national forests (⊕ *www.fs.fed.us*) surrounding the parks have camping and are more lenient with pets, although you should not plan to leave your pet unattended at the campsite.

Planning Your Visit PARK PASSES

Family Fun

TOP 5 TIPS

1. Plan ahead. At many parks, rooms and campsites fill up fast, so make your reservations as early as you can. Many parks will have every room and campsite booked several months in advance (weekends are especially popular). We recommend booking at least six months ahead, and more if you plan to visit one of the more popular parks, such as Grand Canyon, Grand Teton, Rocky Mountain, Yellowstone, or Yosemite. If you plan on staying outside the park, check with the hotels you're considering as far ahead as you can, as these places can fill up fast as well. You also can go online. All the national parks have websites—links to all of them are at the National Park Service page (⊕ *www.nps.gov*).

2. Get the kids involved. It might seem easier to do the planning yourself, but you'll probably have a better time—and your kids definitely will—if you involve them. No matter how old they are, children ought to have a good idea of where you're going and what you're about to experience. It will help get them excited beforehand and will likely make them feel like they have a say and a stake in the trip. Discuss the park's attractions and give your kids a choice of two or three options (that are all amenable to you, of course). Many of the parks' sites have links with advice on family travel or info on children's activities.

3. Know your children. Consider your child's interests. This will help you plan a vacation that's both safe and memorable (for all the right reasons). For starters, if you have kids under four, be honest with yourself about whether the national park itself is an appropriate destination. Parents are notorious for projecting their awe for majestic scenery and overall enthusiasm for

sightseeing on their younger kids, who might be more interested in cataloging the snacks in the hotel room's minibar. Likewise, be realistic about your child's stamina and ability. If your children have never been hiking, don't expect them to be able to do a long hike at a higher altitude than they are used to. Remember: Children's first experience hiking can make them a lover or a hater of the activity, so start off slowly and try some practice hikes near home.

4. Pack wisely. Be sure you're bringing kid-size versions of the necessities you'll pack for yourself. Depending on the park you're visiting (and the activities you're planning), that will probably include sturdy sandals or hiking shoes, sunglasses, sunscreen, and insect repellent. You'll almost certainly need a few layers of clothing and plenty of water and snacks. In terms of hydration, the American Academy of Pediatrics recommends giving children ages 9 to 12 about 3 to 8 ounces of water or another beverage every 20 minutes during strenuous exercise; adolescents should drink 24 to 50 ounces every hour.

5. Develop a Plan B. National parks are natural places, meaning they change dramatically with the seasons and the weather, so you should plan on alternate activities if Mother Nature isn't cooperative. And if you've already talked with your kids about your options, you can pick a new plan that appeals to everyone.

BUDGETING YOUR TRIP

Like most vacations, a trip to a national park can be as frugal, or as fancy, as you like. Here are a few things to consider:

Getting in. Individual admission to the national parks ranges from free to $30, depending on the park. You also can buy an America the Beautiful Pass for $80,

SAMPLE BUDGET FOR A FAMILY OF FOUR

Here is an idea of what a family of four might spend on a three-day trip to Grand Canyon National Park, during which they stay and eat all their meals within the park. Depending on your accommodations and dining-out options, the total you spend can vary dramatically.

Admission: $35 per car; admission covers seven days in the park

Lodging: A standard double room in one of the in-park lodges on the popular South Rim ranges from approximately $95 to $250 a night. Total for three nights: $285 to $750; double that ($570 to $1,500) if you have older children in a separate room.

Meals: Dining options in the park range from no-frills snack bars to upscale restaurants. Per-meal costs run from $10 to $40 or more, per person (you might be able to spend less if you're cooking meals over your campfire or packing bag lunches). Total (three meals per person, per day for three days): $360 to $1,440.

Souvenirs: Budget $5 to $10 per person per day for souvenirs so that everybody can get something small each day, or one or two larger items per trip. Total: $60 to $120.

TOTAL COST: $490 to $3,100

Most parks have several accommodation options outside the park, as well.

Eating. In each of the parks, all the in-park concessions are run by companies under contract with the National Park Service, meaning their prices are set by the government. Generally speaking, prices are a bit higher than what you'd pay outside the park, but not significantly so. You also can bring in your own food and eat at one of the park's picnic areas.

Entertainment. Just looking at the wonders of the park is entertainment enough for many youngsters, but the many sports and outdoor activities—from hiking and bicycling to horseback riding and cave touring, depending on the park—help children stay active while exploring. Many park visitor centers also have films; some parks, such as Grand Canyon and Zion, even have IMAX movies. Cost for these offerings varies, ranging from free to a couple hundred dollars for more involved programs, such as a white-water rafting trip.

Souvenirs. All the parks have gift shops, and many stock items that are actually useful. For example, you'll find things like kid-size binoculars, fanny packs, and magnifying glasses, all of which can make your child's visit even more enjoyable. Budget $5 or $10 to cover one item (maybe something you might have bought for your child anyway, like a new sun hat).

KIDS' PROGRAMS

More than half of the 417 U.S. National Park Service units (national parks as well as historic sites, national monuments, preserves, and other significant places) are part of the Junior Ranger Program, which offers kids the opportunity to learn about individual parks by filling out a short workbook or participating in an activity such as taking a hike with a park

which will get you and three other adults (kids 15 and under are free) into any national park (as well as other designated federal lands) for one year.

Sleeping. Fewer than half of the parks charge for camping; the cost is typically less than $20 per night. In many parks, you also can stay at a lodge, where prices run from $100 to $500 a night.

ranger. After completing the program, kids get a badge (or a pin or patch, depending on the park). For availability, check with the ranger station or visitor center when you arrive. Kids can also complete Junior Ranger activities online (⊕ *www.nps.gov/kids/jrrangers.cfm*).

In addition to the Junior Ranger Program, kids can find a variety of activities in the parks designed just for them. Some parks, such as Olympic and Grand Teton, loan "Discovery Packs," backpacks filled with kid-friendly tools like magnifying glasses. Call ahead for availability.

Many ongoing general-interest or park-specific programs—stargazing in Bryce Canyon, say, or rock-climbing in Yosemite—will also be of interest to kids.

When you're through with the organized activities and are ready to head off on your own, remember that kids often take a shorter view of things than adults do, meaning they may need to be reminded once in a while of why you're there and what lies ahead (especially if it's a cool waterfall or swimming hole). Singing camp songs, playing games like I Spy, or staging scavenger hunts will help kids refocus if they get bored or whiny.

WEBSITES FOR KIDS

- wwww.smokeybear.com
- wwww.nationalparks.org/connect/npf-kids
- wwww.nps.gov/kids/jrrangers.cfm
- wwww.doi.gov/public/teachandlearn

What to Pack

TOP 10 ESSENTIALS

Packing lists for any trip vary according to the individual and his or her needs, of course, but here are 10 essential things to include in your luggage for a national parks vacation.

1. Binoculars. Many of the parks are a bird- (and animal-) watcher's dream. A pair of binos will help you spot feathered friends as well as larger creatures. Binoculars are sold according to power, or how much the objects you're viewing are magnified (i.e., 7x, 10x, 12x), and the diameter of objective lens, which is the one on the fat end of the binoculars; 10x is a good choice for magnification, field of view, and steadiness.

2. Clothes that layer. In much of the West (especially at higher elevations), days are often warm while nights turn chilly. The weather also can change quickly, with things going from dry and sunny to windy and wet in a matter of minutes. This means you need to pack with both warm and cold (as well as wet and dry) weather in mind. The easiest solution is to dress in layers. Experts suggest synthetics such as polyester (used in Coolmax and other "wicking" fabrics that draw moisture away from your skin, and fleece, which is an insulator) and lightweight merino wool. Look for socks in wicking wool or polyester. Don't forget a waterproof poncho or jacket.

3. Long pants and long-sleeve shirts. It's wise to minimize exposed skin when hiking, especially in areas with poison ivy and/or ticks and at higher elevations, where the sun's radiation is much stronger. Convertible pants (the bottom portion zips off, leaving you in a pair of shorts) are another good option—they're often made of quick-drying and rugged material and allow you the flexibility of pants or shorts at a moment's notice.

MAPS

If you plan to do a lot of hiking or mountaineering, especially in the backcountry, invest in detailed maps and a compass. Topographical maps are sold in well-equipped outdoor stores (REI and Cabela's, for example). Maps in different scales are available from the U.S. Geological Survey. To order, go to ⊕ *www.usgs.gov/pubprod/ maps.html* or call ☎ *888/275–8747.*

4. Sturdy shoes or sandals. If you plan to do any hiking, be sure your footwear has rugged soles, a necessity on unpaved trails. Be sure to break in your shoes before the trip.

5. Insect repellent. If you're hiking or camping in an area with lots of mosquitoes, a good bug spray can help keep your trip from being a swatting marathon. A repellent also helps deter ticks. Most experts recommend repellents with DEET (N,N-diethyl-m-toluamide); the higher the level of DEET, the longer the product will be effective. Just be sure to use a separate sunscreen, not a single product with both ingredients (this is because you're supposed to reapply sunscreen every few hours, but doing so with DEET could deliver a dangerous dose of the chemical).

6. Skin moisturizer, sunscreen, and lip balm. In the parks, you're likely to be outside for longer—and in higher altitudes and drier climates—than you're used to. All of this can leave your skin and lips parched and burned. Sunscreen should provide both UVA and UVB protection, with an SPF of at least 15; look for a lotion marked "sweatproof" or "sport" and be sure to reapply throughout the day.

7. Sunglasses and hat. Higher elevation means more ultraviolet radiation; research shows there's an 8% to 10% increase in UV intensity for every 1,000 feet in elevation gain. Look for sunglasses that provide 100% UV protection.

8. Journal and camera. When your jaw drops at the glorious vistas and your head clears from all the fresh air, you may want to try your hand at sketching what you see or jotting down your thoughts. And of course, you'll want to get photographs.

9. Snacks and water. National parks by their nature are remote, and some are lacking in services. Bring plenty of water and healthy snacks (or meals, depending on how long you plan to be out and what you're likely to find in the park). When hiking in hot weather, experts recommend ½ to 1 quart of water (or another fluid) per person, per hour, to prevent potentially dangerous dehydration. The risk of dehydration is greater at elevations above 8,000 feet. Even if you're not hiking, have water and food in the car for long drives where facilities might be scarce.

10. First-aid kit. A solid kit should contain a first-aid manual, aspirin (or ibuprofen), razor blades, tweezers, a needle, scissors, adhesive bandages, butterfly bandages, sterile gauze pads, 1-inch-wide adhesive tape, an elastic bandage, antibacterial ointment, antiseptic cream or spray, antihistamines, calamine lotion, and moleskin (for blisters).

HIKING ITEMS

For vacations where you'll be hiking for longer than an hour or two at a time, consider investing in the following:

■ a **compass and map**

■ a **daypack** with enough room for everybody's essentials

■ **energy bars** (they may not be five-star dining, but they do give you energy and keep your kids—and you—from getting cranky)

■ a **hiking stick or poles**, especially if you've got bad knees

■ a **water filter** to treat water

■ **bear bells** if you're in bear country

■ **reusable water bottles**

CAMPING GEAR

Planning on roughing it on your national parks vacation? In addition to a working tent (check the zipper before you go!), sleeping bags and pillows, and, of course, the ingredients for s'mores (graham crackers, chocolate bars, and marshmallows), here are some things veteran campers recommend be among your gear:

■ **camping chairs** (folding or collapsible)

■ **camp stove and fuel**

■ **cooking utensils, plates, and cups**

■ **duct tape** (great for covering tears)

■ **flashlight, headlamp, and lantern**

■ **matches**

■ **paper towels, napkins, wet wipes**

■ **a multipurpose knife and cutting board**

■ a **rope** (for laundry or to help tie things down; pack clothespins, too)

■ a **sleeping pad or air mattress**

■ a **tarp** (will help keep the bottom of your tent—and you—dry)

■ a **cooler**

■ **toilet paper**

■ a **shovel** (to bury waste) or **plastic bags** (to haul it out)

Photography Tips

Today's digital cameras make it difficult to take a truly lousy picture, but there are still some things even the best models can't do on their own. The tips here (some of them classic photography techniques) won't turn you into the next Ansel Adams, but they might prevent you from being upstaged by your eight-year-old with her smartphone.

The Golden Hours. The best photos are taken when most of us are either snoozing or eating dinner: about an hour before and after sunrise and sunset. When the light is gentle and golden, your photos are less likely to be overexposed or filled with harsh shadows and squinting people.

Divide to Conquer. You can't go wrong with the Rule of Thirds: When you're setting up a shot, mentally divide your picture area into thirds, horizontally and vertically, which will give you nine squares. Any one of the four places where the lines intersect (the four corners of the center square) represents a good spot to place your primary subject. (If all this talk of imaginary lines makes your head spin, just remember not to automatically plop your primary focal point in the center of your photos.)

Lock Your Focus. To get a properly focused photo using a camera with auto-focus, press the shutter button down halfway and wait a few seconds before pressing down completely. (On most cameras, a light or a beep will indicate that you're good to go.)

Circumvent Auto-Focus. If your camera isn't homing in on your desired focal point, center the primary subject smack in the middle of the frame and depress the shutter button halfway, allowing the camera to focus. Then, without lifting your finger, compose your photo properly (moving your camera so the focal point isn't in the center of the shot), and press the shutter all the way down.

Jettison the Jitters. Shaky hands are among the most common causes of out-of-focus photos. If you're not good at immobility, invest in a tripod or rest the camera on something steady—such as a wall, a bench, or a rock—when you shoot. If all else fails, lean against something sturdy to brace yourself.

Consider the Imagery. Take a moment or two to consider why you're shooting what you're shooting. Once you've determined this, start setting up your photo. Look for interesting lines that curve into your image—such as a path, the shoreline, or a fence—and use them to create the impression of depth. You can do the same thing by photographing people with their bodies or faces positioned at an angle to the camera.

Ignore All the Rules. Sure, thoughtful contemplation and careful execution are likely to produce brilliant images, but there are times when you just need to capture the moment. If you see something wonderful, grab your camera and just get the picture. If the photo turns out to be blurry, off-center, or over- or underexposed, you can always Photoshop it later.

Smartphone Tips: When possible, don't use the zoom tool. This reduces the picture's resolution and can lead to fuzzy photos. Instead, it's best to crop your photos manually. Also, it's helpful to turn on the grid feature, which helps you compose your shots.

Special Considerations. If you're going to any Indian reservations (many are near national parks), check the rules before you take photographs. In many cases you must purchase a permit.

Staying Healthy, Playing It Safe

ALTITUDE SICKNESS

Altitude sickness can result when you've moved to high elevations without having time to adjust. When you're at a mile (5,280 feet) or more above sea level, and especially when you're higher than 8,500 feet, you may feel symptoms of altitude sickness: shortness of breath, light-headedness, nausea, fatigue, headache, and insomnia. To help your body adjust, drink lots of water, avoid alcohol, and wait a day or two before attempting vigorous activity. If your symptoms are severe, last several days, or worsen, seek medical attention.

ANIMAL BITES

Although animals abound in the national parks, the odds of your meeting one face to face, let alone sustaining a bite, are slim (especially if you follow the rules about not feeding them). But if you are bitten or scratched by any wild animal—even a small one—seek medical attention. You may need stitches and antibiotics, or a rabies or tetanus shot. If that animal is a snake, stay calm (if the snake is venomous, a lot of movement can spread the poison). Have someone else get medical help for you right away.

DEHYDRATION

If your body doesn't have the fluids it needs, you're dehydrated. Symptoms can range from minor (a dull headache) to life-threatening (seizures, coma). Dehydration is often caused by excessive sweating coupled with inadequate fluid intake, and is a real concern in the national parks, where visitors are generally active (hiking, climbing) but not good at carrying and drinking water. Dehydration is a particular problem for children and seniors and for anyone exercising in dry climates; it's also more likely at high altitudes. To counter a mild case, drink water or another beverage. Take small sips over a period of time instead of trying to force down a large amount. A serious case requires immediate medical attention. To prevent dehydration, be sure to bring and consume enough water: ½ to 1 quart per person for each hour of exercise.

DON'T FEED THE ANIMALS

It's dangerous—and illegal (you'll be fined). Animals in many national parks are used to humans being around and may not flee at your presence. But feeding wild animals habituates them to humans and teaches them to look to us for food. When that happens, they lose the ability to hunt or forage on their own, meaning they might starve to death or be hit by cars when looking for handouts. Feeding animals also causes them to be more aggressive, and thus more dangerous, to future visitors. Aggressive animals are removed from areas where they'll have contact with people; in some cases, they're relocated, but in others, they're put down.

HEAT-RELATED ILLNESS

Typically caused by excessive exertion in high temperatures such as a strenuous hike in the desert, heat exhaustion or more serious heatstroke can cause nausea, headaches, and dizziness— and even seizures, unconsciousness, and death. If you suspect heat-related illness, rest in a cool, shady place and drink water. Dehydration is often a factor in heat exhaustion and heatstroke. Apply cool compresses to the head, forehead, and trunk. If the victim is unconscious or confused, seek medical help immediately.

Chapter 3

GREAT ITINERARIES

Updated by
Laura M. Kidder

Great Itineraries

Due to their grand size and endless recreation opportunities, visitors can easily spend an entire trip exploring just one national park. But adventurous travelers looking to discover more of the West can take on a bigger itinerary involving several parks, plus a couple of other destinations (national monuments, state parks, scenic byways, and the like) that show off some of the most impressive scenery America has to offer. We've put together a collection of these itineraries, aimed at the most popular (and feasible) routes taken by curious explorers.

Most of the national parks are so large you need a vehicle to properly explore, so planning a driving trip to visit them is a no-brainer. Whether you fly into the nearest airport and rent a car or drive all the way in your own vehicle, these itineraries can help you plan your route—and your time in the parks—to give you the best experience possible. Each itinerary is meant to be used for inspiration in planning your own trip, tailored to your interests and your travel style. We suggest you pick the parks that most appeal to you and linger a little longer there. That being said, those who want to see more in less time will prefer the tours just as they are.

We've developed these itineraries based on the idea that you'll be traveling during the summer, when you'll find most roads and facilities open in the parks. If you'll be traveling at another time of year, be sure to check with the park(s) you'll be visiting about road conditions and closures. Many parks are in remote and/or mountainous areas, accessible by roads that are subject to seasonal closures.

You should also note that "summer" can mean something different in different parts of the West; warm weather typically arrives much later in the year in the northern United States than it does in

Arizona and New Mexico. Additionally, we're assuming you'll be traveling in a passenger car. If you're driving an RV (or pulling a trailer), check with the park(s) ahead of time to see if they have any restrictions on these vehicles.

Washington State National Parks Road Trip Itinerary, 8 Days

A trip to Washington's three national parks—plus a visit to Mount St. Helen's National Volcanic Monument—takes you through rugged Pacific coastline and high alpine terrain as well as lush temperate rain forest, glaciers, waterfalls, and some of the largest remnants of ancient forests in the U.S.

DAY 1: WELCOME TO WASHINGTON STATE

For those coming from out of state, the nearest airport is Seattle-Tacoma International, where you can start your journey by picking up a rental car. Depending on when your flight gets in, you can rest up at a nearby hotel for the night or make the 85-mile, 1½-hour drive to Sedro-Woolley, Washington, where you can spend the night.

DAY 2: NORTH CASCADES NATIONAL PARK

46 miles or about an hour drive from Sedro-Woolley.

From Sedro-Woolley, drive east for 46 miles along Route 20, also known as the North Cascades Highway, to the entrance of North Cascades National Park. Take your first stroll through an old-growth forest on the Skagit River Loop (1.8 miles), which starts at the visitor center near the town of Newhalem, about 9 miles from the entrance, then devote the rest

of the day to driving through the park on Route 20, stopping at various overlooks. Exit the park and continue through the scenic Methow Valley and on to Chelan (about 190 miles from the park's western boundary) to stay the night.

DAYS 3 AND 4: MOUNT RAINIER NATIONAL PARK

205 miles or a 3-hour, 45-minute drive from Chelan; 136 miles or a 2-hour, 45-minute drive from Arlington.

From Chelan, get an early start to drive to Ohanapecosh, the southeastern entrance to Mount Rainier National Park. When you arrive, take a drive on the spectacular Sunrise Road (about 30 miles round-trip), which reveals the "back" (northeast) side of Rainier. Book a room in nearby Ashford (about 19 miles east of the park's Nisqually entrance) and make that your base for the next two nights.

The next day, energetic hikers will want to tackle one of the four- to six-hour trails that scale the park's many peaks. Less ambitious visitors can take one of the shorter hikes in the Paradise Inn area or join a ranger-led walk through wildflower meadows. Another option is to hike to Panorama Point (a strenuous 4-mile round-trip), near the foot of the Muir Snowfield, for breathtaking views of the glaciers and high ridges of Rainier. Finish your day with dinner at the Paradise Inn, where you can watch the sunset on the peak.

DAY 5: MOUNT ST. HELENS AND THE OLYMPIC FOOTHILLS

120 miles or a 2½-hour drive from Mount Rainier.

Today, drive south to spend the day visiting the Mount St. Helens National Volcanic Monument, where you can enter from the west side via Route 504 and

Great Itineraries

see the destruction caused by the 1980 eruption. After leaving the monument, follow Route 504 back to Interstate 5 and head north to Olympia, winding through scenic Puget Sound countryside, skirting the Olympic foothills, and periodically dipping down to the waterfront en route to Port Angeles, where you'll spend the night.

DAYS 6 AND 7: OLYMPIC NATIONAL PARK
212 miles or a 4-hour drive from Mount St. Helens to Port Angeles.

The next morning, launch into a full day at Olympic National Park. From the Port Angeles entrance, drive 17 miles south to Hurricane Ridge, where you'll find several trails taking you through meadows and subalpine forest. The Hurricane Hill Trail (3.2 miles round-trip) delivers panoramic views of the mountains and ocean. Afterward, head back to Port Angeles for the night.

On Day 7, follow U.S. 101 west to La Push, a skinny satellite of coastal land that's part of the national park (69 miles from Port Angeles). From La Push, hike 1.4 miles to Third Beach for a taste of the wild Pacific coastline. Back on U.S. 101, head south to the town of Forks and then east to the Hoh Rain Forest, also part of Olympic National Park. Explore the moss-covered alders and big-leaf maples, then follow a circular route on U.S. 101 to Lake Quinault, winding west toward the coast, then back to the lake and the national park. Check into the Lake Quinault Lodge, then drive up the river to access one of several trails—the Graves Creek Trail is a popular choice—through the lush Quinault Valley.

DAY 8: HEADING HOME
Catch your flight back home from Seattle–Tacoma International, about 130 miles (a 2½-hour drive) from Olympic via I-5.

Yellowstone and Grand Teton National Parks Road Trip Itinerary, 7 Days

A visit to these two parks takes you through one of the last remaining natural ecosystems in this region of the world. Here, you'll see wildlife ranging from beavers, bison, and bears to weasels and wolves, plus pristine mountain lakes, bubbling mud pots, and the world's biggest collection of geysers.

DAY 1: WELCOME TO YELLOWSTONE
If you'll be flying, the Jackson Hole Airport in Jackson, Wyoming, is probably the best place to start, as it's only an hour from the southern entrance of Yellowstone. You'll find plenty of lodging options in Jackson for your first night, or you can book a room at one of the park's nine lodges—the centrally located Lake Hotel or the iconic Old Faithful Inn.

DAYS 2–4: YELLOWSTONE NATIONAL PARK
Dedicate the next three days to Yellowstone National Park, which, because of its sheer size and incredible diversity of wildlife and scenery, could take a lifetime to explore. Spend your first day on the park's 140-mile Grand Loop Road. This road forms a big figure-eight as it passes nearly every major Yellowstone attraction, and offers interpretive displays, overlooks, and short trails along the way.

On your second day in the park, visit Old Faithful and take a short hike (about 2½ miles round-trip) around Mystic Falls, then head up to the Canyon Village section of the park for a look at the Grand Canyon of Yellowstone, with its two separate waterfalls. For a more strenuous option, hike from Dunraven Pass to the

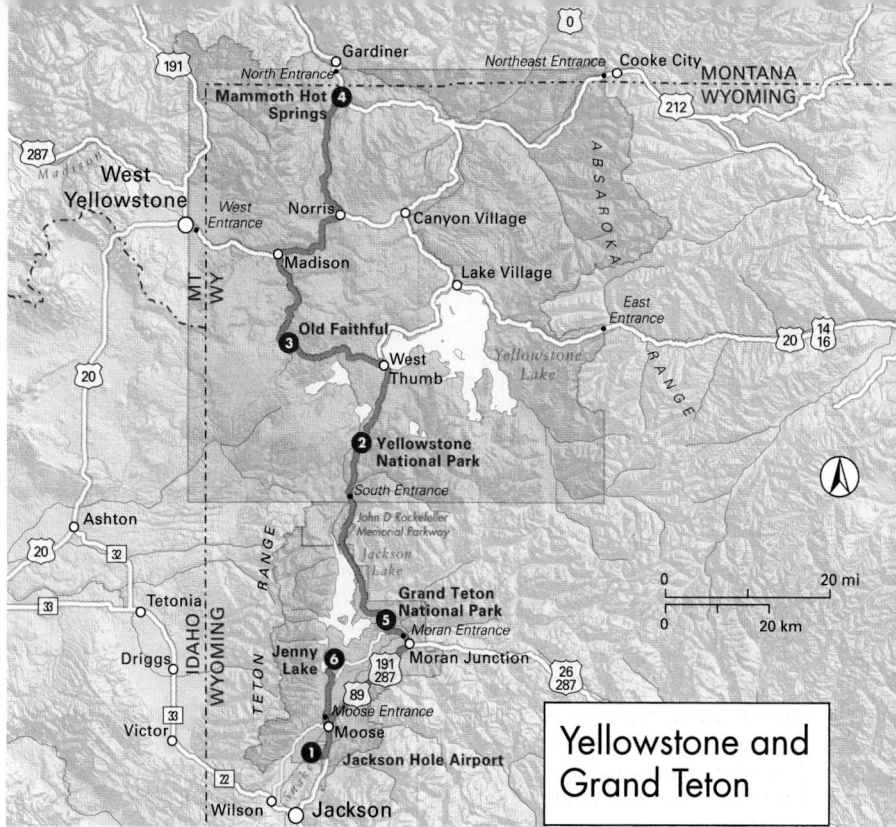

summit of Mount Washburn for wildflowers, wildlife, and panoramic views (6.2 miles round-trip).

For your third day, explore the northern part of the park, starting with the Mammoth Hot Springs area, with its terraced limestone formations. From there, head past Tower-Roosevelt to the Lamar Valley in the far northeast corner of the park for gorgeous mountain views, enormous herds of bison, and your best chance to spot wolves. Then check out the Mud Volcano and Sulphur Caldron in the Hayden Valley area, just south of Canyon Village.

DAYS 5 AND 6: GRAND TETON NATIONAL PARK

7 miles from Yellowstone's southern entrance to the northern boundary of Grand Teton.

Leaving Yellowstone, drive south into Grand Teton National Park. The sheer ruggedness of the Tetons makes them seem imposing and unapproachable, but a drive on Teton Park Road, with frequent stops at scenic turnouts, will get you up close and personal with the peaks. The Jenny Lake Scenic Drive delivers fantastic views as well; just north of Jenny Lake, pull over to the Leigh Lake Trailhead for a hike. You can take the 3.7-mile loop around String Lake, or head north, then take the right-hand branch of the trail and follow the eastern shore of the lake (turn around at the campground on Trapper Lake) for a 9-mile hike. Spend your two nights at any of the excellent lodges or cabins in the park.

Your second day in the park, head back to Jenny Lake and catch a shuttle boat across to the western side, where you can take either a short hike along the Cascade Canyon Trail (2 miles round-trip) or hike the Forks of Cascade Canyon, a

Great Itineraries

9.6-mile trip that's well worth the effort. If you'd rather explore Jenny Lake from the water, rent a canoe or kayak or take a guided tour.

DAY 7: HEAD HOME

When your visit to Grand Teton is complete, getting back to the Jackson Hole Airport couldn't be simpler: it's actually inside the park boundary, about 4 miles from the southern entrance.

Black Hills and Badlands National Parks Road Trip Itinerary, 6 Days

The national parks of southwestern South Dakota—along with the state park and two national memorials nearby—deliver a surprising variety of sights: the swaying grasses and abundant wildlife of one of the country's few remaining intact prairies, the complex labyrinth of passages and unique geologic formations in one of the world's longest caves, and some of the richest fossil beds on Earth.

DAY 1: WIND CAVE NATIONAL PARK

The closest commercial airport is Rapid City Regional Airport, about 70 miles from Wind Cave. Arrive in the morning to pick up your rental car and make the 1½-hour drive to Wind Cave National Park, with more than 33,000 acres of wildlife habitat above ground (home to bison, elk, pronghorn, and coyotes) and one of the world's longest caves below. Take an afternoon cave tour and a short drive through the park. Spend the night in Hot Springs, about 7 miles from the park's southern boundary.

DAY 2: CUSTER STATE PARK

20 miles or a 40-minute drive from Hot Springs.

Spend today at Custer State Park, which is adjacent to Wind Cave. The 71,000-acre park has exceptional drives, lots of wildlife (including a herd of 1,300 bison), and fingerlike granite spires rising from the forest floor (they're the reason this is called the Needles region of South Dakota). While you're in the park, be sure to visit Limber Pine Natural Area, a National Natural Landmark containing spectacular ridges of granite. If you have time, check out the Cathedral Spires trail, 3 miles round-trip. Overnight in one of five mountain lodges at the Custer State Park Resort.

DAY 3: JEWEL CAVE NATIONAL MONUMENT AND CRAZY HORSE MEMORIAL

About 16 miles from Custer State Park to Jewel Cave; 19 miles from Jewel Cave to Crazy Horse Memorial.

Today, venture down U.S. 16 to Jewel Cave National Monument, 13 miles west of the town of Custer, an underground wilderness where you can see beautiful nailhead and dogtooth spar crystals lining its more than 195 miles of passageways.

After visiting Jewel Cave, head back to Custer and take U.S. 16/385 to Crazy Horse Memorial (about 5 miles north of Custer), home to a colossal mountain carving of the legendary Lakota leader and the Indian Museum of North America. Afterward, head 10 miles north to the former gold and tin mining town of Hill City, where you'll spend the night.

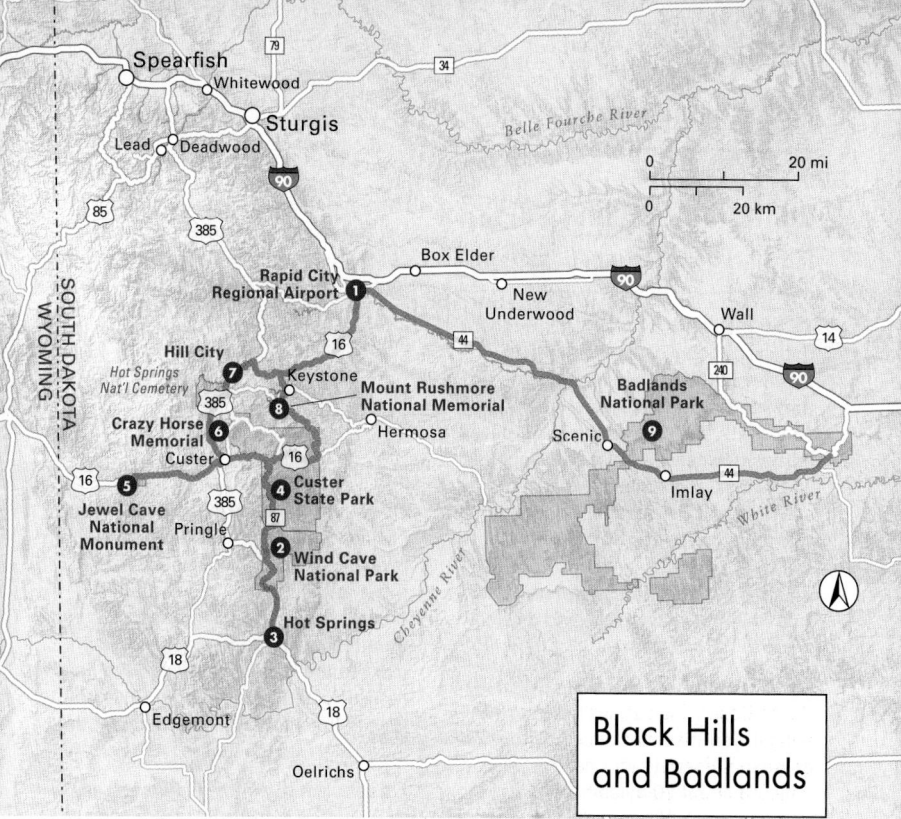

Black Hills and Badlands

DAY 4: MOUNT RUSHMORE NATIONAL MEMORIAL

12 miles or about a 30-minute drive from Hill City.

This morning, travel to Mount Rushmore National Memorial, where you can view the huge carved renderings of presidents Washington, Jefferson, Theodore Roosevelt, and Lincoln. Afterward, head northwest for 23 miles back to Rapid City, the eastern gateway to the Black Hills. Spend the night here.

DAY 5: BADLANDS NATIONAL PARK

75 miles or a 1-hour, 15-minute drive from Rapid City to the northeast entrance of Badlands.

Begin your day early and drive west (via Interstate 90) to Badlands National Park, a 244,000-acre geologic wonderland. The

Badlands Highway Loop Road (Highway 240) wiggles through the moonlike landscape of the park's north unit for 32 miles. Stop in at the Ben Reifel Visitor Center, at the far eastern edge of the park, to pick up a trail map and head out on a hike. The Notch Trail, 1.5 miles round-trip, offers spectacular views of the White River Valley, but is definitely not for anyone with a fear of heights. The Cliff Shelf trail, 0.5 mile round-trip, is a more mellow option that showcases rock formations and juniper forest as well as occasional wildlife sightings.

After you leave the park, head back to Rapid City to spend the night.

DAY 6: HEADING HOME

The airport in Rapid City is about 10 minutes southeast of town.

Great Itineraries

California National Parks Road Trip Itinerary, 9 Days

This trip takes you to California's most popular national parks. Yosemite is a nearly 1,200-square-mile expanse in the western Sierras filled with meadows, waterfalls, and spectacular granite domes and canyons. Nearby Sequoia and Kings Canyon national parks deliver spectacular alpine scenery along with the world's largest trees. And Death Valley is a land of extremes, with its impossibly dry (and hot) below-sea-level basin alongside high mountain peaks and diverse wildlife.

DAY 1: WELCOME TO CALIFORNIA

If you're planning to start this trip with a flight, your best bet would be to arrive at Fresno Yosemite International Airport, which is about 70 miles from the southern entrance to Yosemite (your first stop) and 80 miles from the northern entrance to Sequoia and Kings Canyon (your last).

From the airport, head north toward Yosemite National Park and its Mariposa/Wawona Entrance, following Highway 41. Depending on how much time you've got, either do some exploring (head for the Yosemite Valley Visitor Center, about 32 miles from the Wawona entrance) or look for lodging. You can stay in the park (there are several options, from primitive camping to luxury rooms at the Majestic Yosemite Hotel) or in Mariposa, about 43 miles (1 hour) west of the Wawona Entrance on Route 140.

DAYS 2–4: YOSEMITE NATIONAL PARK

70 miles or about a 1½-hour drive from the airport.

Early in the morning of Day 2, head into Yosemite Valley, near the center of the

park, and take a hike on Lower Yosemite Fall Trail, an easy 1.1-mile loop. If you've got more time and ambition, continue on for the first mile of the Upper Fall Trail to Columbia Rock, where you'll be rewarded with spectacular views of both the upper and lower sections of the highest waterfall in North America. Afterward, stop in at the historic Majestic Yosemite Hotel, then attend one of the ranger programs or a presentation at Yosemite Theater.

On your second day in the park, head back to the Yosemite Valley area and take an easy hike around Mirror Lake (5 miles round-trip) or a more strenuous trek to Vernal Fall (2.5 miles round-trip), then drop in at the Yosemite Museum (next to the visitor center) and the nearby reconstructed Indian Village. Drive up to Glacier Point for a valley-wide view, timing your arrival for sunset.

On your last day in the park, head east to Tuolumne Meadows, where you can stretch your legs with a hike (an easy option is the 1.5-mile round-trip trail to Soda Springs and historic Parsons Lodge). Then take a drive on Tioga Road (check ahead to make sure it is not closed), a 59-mile stretch through the high country that takes you over Tioga Pass (9,941 feet) and along the highest stretch of road in California. Leave the park through the Tioga Pass Entrance, then drive southeast 134 miles (about 2 hours, 15 minutes) to the town of Lone Pine, where you'll spend the night.

DAYS 5 AND 6: DEATH VALLEY NATIONAL PARK

38 miles or a 40-minute drive from Lone Pine to the park's western entrance.

On Day 5, drive to Death Valley National Park, known as the lowest, driest, and hottest place in North America. Covering more than 5,300 square miles, it's also the biggest national park in the lower

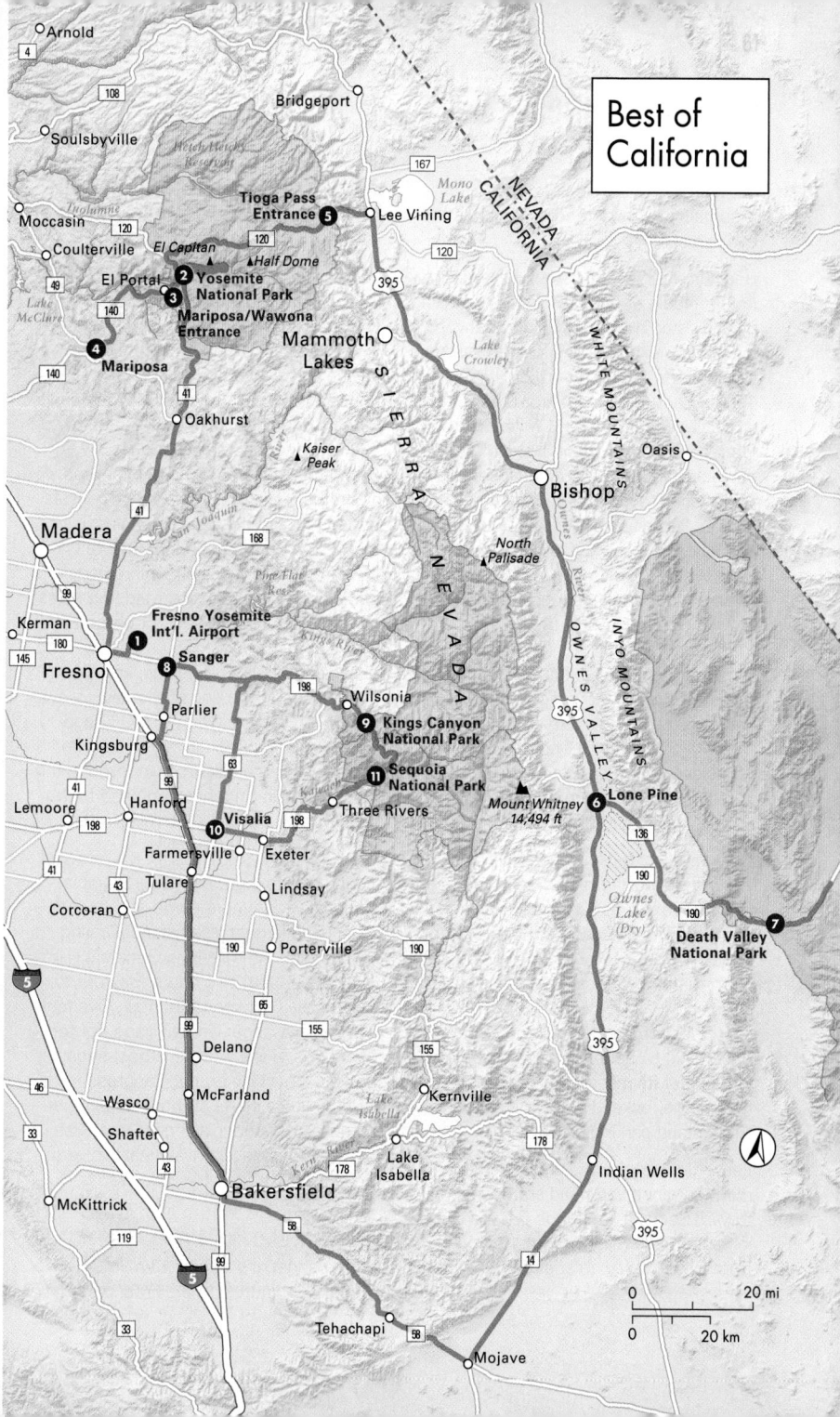

Great Itineraries

48, with vast expanses of desert and mountain ranges extending as far as the eye can see.

Begin in the Furnace Creek area, roughly in the middle of the park. If you're getting an early start, hike into Golden Canyon by taking the 1-mile-long interpretive trail, which starts 2 miles south of Highway 190 on Badwater Road. From there, head to Devil's Golf Course (11 miles south of Furnace Creek) to see millions of tiny salt pinnacles and, if you get up close, a mass of perfectly round holes. Badwater Basin, 8 miles farther south, has expansive saltwater flats and the lowest point in the park, which is 282 feet below sea level. Then go to the highest spot—Dante's View, 5,000 feet above the valley floor—for the best views and blessedly cooler temperatures (the lookout is about 20 miles southeast of Furnace Creek). If you want to hike, there's a trail leading from the parking area onto Dante's Ridge that offers even more spectacular vistas (it's ½ mile to the first summit, then another 4 miles to Mount Perry).

On your second day in Death Valley, explore the northern section of the park, near Grapevine Canyon (about 52 miles north of Furnace Creek). Uhebe Crater is visible from a turnout on the road. From there, if your car has high clearance and good tires, you can drive 27 miles southwest on a rough dirt road to the Racetrack, a phenomenal dry lake bed famous for its mysterious moving rocks (to see the rocks, drive 2 miles past the Grandstand parking area).

Leave the park via the western (Panamint) entrance and head southwest toward Sequoia and Kings Canyon. Stop in Sanger, 280 miles (about 4½ hours) from Death Valley, to spend the night.

DAYS 7 AND 8: SEQUOIA AND KINGS CANYON NATIONAL PARKS
41 miles or a 55-minute drive from Sanger.

From Sanger, drive east to the Big Stump Entrance of Kings Canyon National Park. Inside the park, head to Grant Grove Village and stop at the visitor center there, then take the Kings Canyon Scenic Byway (Route 180) along the Kings River and its giant granite canyon that is well over a mile deep at some points. Stop along the way at pull-outs for long vistas of some of the highest mountains in the United States. Hike the Zumwalt Meadow Trail (1.5 miles), which starts just before the end of the road, 4.5 miles from Cedar Grove Village, for gorgeous views of the park's largest meadow, plus high granite walls, talus, and the river below. At the end of the day, follow Route 180 back to Grant Grove Village and take Generals Highway south into Sequoia National Park. Leave through the Ash Mountain Entrance and head to the nearby town of Visalia (35 miles, about 46 minutes away) for the night.

Spend the next day exploring Sequoia National Park, where some of the world's oldest and largest trees stand. Driving the winding, 40-mile-long Generals Highway takes about two hours. Be sure to stop at the Redwood Mountain Overlook, just outside Cedar Grove Village, for terrific views of the world's largest sequoia grove. Take a hike on the Congress Trail (2 miles), which starts at the General Sherman Tree, the world's largest tree, just off the Generals Highway near Wolverton Road. At the end of the day, head back to Sanger for the night.

DAY 9: HEADING HOME
From Sanger, it's a short 13-mile drive (about 20 minutes) to the Fresno airport.

Best of
Utah and Arizona

Utah and Arizona National Parks Road Trip Itinerary, 9 Days

This itinerary takes you through Zion's massive sandstone cliffs and narrow slot canyons, the hoodoos (odd-shape pillars of rock left by erosion) of Bryce Canyon, and the overwhelming majesty of the Grand Canyon, close to 300 river miles long, 18 miles wide, and a mile deep.

DAY 1: WELCOME TO CANYON COUNTRY

Plan to fly into and out of St. George Municipal Airport in St. George, Utah. It's close to all three parks, with Zion a little more than an hour away.

From the airport, head east toward Zion National Park, about 46 miles. Depending on how much daylight you've got, you can start exploring the park—enter at the south entrance and head to the Zion Canyon Visitor Center—or find a room for the next three nights in Springdale, the bustling town just outside the park (1.1 miles from the south entrance).

DAYS 2 AND 3: ZION NATIONAL PARK

46 miles or about a 1-hour drive from the airport to the south entrance of Zion National Park.

Start your day at the visitor center, just inside the south entrance, south of the junction of the Zion–Mount Carmel Highway and the Zion Canyon Scenic Drive. Then explore the Drive, either in your own vehicle or via the park's free shuttle, which runs February or March through

Great Itineraries

October or November (a round-trip ride takes about 80 minutes; private vehicles are not allowed in the summer). Intrepid hikers will want to tackle the Narrows, Zion's infamous 16-mile-long gorge cut by the Virgin River, which requires hikers to spend more than half of their time walking, wading, or swimming in the fast-flowing river. For everyone else, Zion offers plenty of other hiking options. The Emerald Pool trails (about 1 mile each) take you on a fairly easy hike from Zion Lodge, about 3 miles from Canyon Junction, to Lower and Upper Emerald Pool and waterfalls.

Spend the next day exploring the Kolob Canyons, in the northwestern corner of the park about 40 miles from Canyon Junction. Take the Kolob Canyons Road 5 miles to its end at the Kolob Canyons Viewpoint, where you'll get fabulous views of the surrounding red rock canyons. For a spectacular 5-mile hike, drive about 2 miles back on the Kolob Canyons Road to the Taylor Creek Trail, which takes you past historic homesteaders' cabins and through a narrow box canyon to the Double Arch Alcove, a large arched grotto.

At the end of the day, leave the park via the beautiful Zion–Mount Carmel Highway and its historic mile-long tunnel. You'll pass through slickrock country, with huge, petrified sandstone dunes etched by ancient waters, and head to Bryce Canyon, where you'll spend the night (you've got a few lodging options, both inside and just outside the park in the town of Bryce Canyon).

DAY 4: BRYCE CANYON NATIONAL PARK

74 miles or about a 1-hour, 25-minute drive from the east entrance of Zion.

Start your tour of Bryce Canyon National Park at the visitor center, about 1 mile past the park entrance. Central to your tour of Bryce Canyon is the 18-mile-long main park road, where numerous scenic turnouts reveal vistas of bright red-orange rock. IIf you're visiting from mid-April to late October, the free Bryce Canyon Shuttle will take you to many of the park's most popular attractions. Trails worth exploring include the 1-mile Bristlecone Loop Trail and the 1.3-mile Navajo Loop Trail, both of which will get you into the heart of the park.

At the end of the day, leave the park and head toward Kanab, 78 miles (about 1 hour, 25 minutes) away, to spend the night en route to the Grand Canyon.

DAY 5: EN ROUTE TO THE GRAND CANYON

284 miles or a 5-hour, 25-minute drive from Bryce Canyon to the South Rim of ˊ the Grand Canyon.

Today, you'll drive from Kanab to Grand Canyon National Park, about 210 miles away. Check into a hotel in Grand Canyon Village on the South Rim or in Tusayan, a few miles to the south, for the next two nights. If you've got time, hike (or take the shuttle) to Yavapai Point, just west of the visitor center in the South Rim Village, to catch the sunset.

DAYS 6–8: GRAND CANYON NATIONAL PARK

If you didn't make it yesterday, begin today's tour with a stop at the Grand Canyon Visitor Center, near Mather Point in the South Rim Village, for the latest maps and information. While you're there, check out the Historic District, with its early-19th-century train depot and other buildings, many built by the Santa Fe Railroad. Get your bearings with a drive (or, if you're visiting early spring–late fall, a free shuttle ride) on the 7-mile-long Hermit Road. Take a hike on the Rim Trail, a nearly flat path (much of

which is paved) that hugs the edge of the canyon from the Village to Hermit's Rest, 2.8 miles to the west.

On your second day in the park, tackle the upper section of one of the "Corridor Trails"—South Kaibab or Bright Angel—which start at the South Rim and meet in the Bright Angel Campground at the bottom of the canyon (the third Corridor Trail, North Kaibab, connects the bottom of the canyon to the North Rim). Bright Angel, the easier of the two, is one of the most scenic paths into the canyon; the trailhead is near Kolb Studio, at the western end of the Village.

For your last day in the park, sign up for an interpretive ranger-led program; they cover a wide variety of subjects, including geology, history, and wildlife, so pick up a list at the Grand Canyon Visitor Center. Afterward, you can spend the

night in (or near) the park again, or start your drive back toward the airport in St. George. The town of Fredonia, Arizona (200 miles; 3 hours, 40 minutes from the South Rim) would be a good stopping point for the night.

DAY 9: HEADING HOME
The St. George Municipal Airport is 74 miles (1 hour, 22 minutes) from Fredonia.

Utah and Colorado National Parks Road Trip Itinerary, 6 Days

With this itinerary, you'll get to experience two of Utah's best parks. There's Arches, famous for its spectacular colors and unique landforms—natural stone arches, soaring pinnacles, plus giant fins

Great Itineraries

and balanced rocks—and Canyonlands, with a wilderness of canyons and buttes carved by the Colorado River and its tributaries. A few hours away, Colorado's Mesa Verde offers a peek into the lives of the Ancestral Puebloan people, who made it their home from AD 600 to 1300.

DAY 1: WELCOME TO UTAH

The closest airport to your first two destinations is Canyonlands Field, also known as Moab Airport, where you can get flights to and from Denver. After you land and get your rental car, head into Moab (18 miles; 25 minutes away), where you'll find plenty of options for food and lodging. Book yourself a room for the next three nights.

DAYS 2 AND 3: ARCHES NATIONAL PARK
5 miles from Moab.

Your trip begins at Arches National Park, which holds the world's largest concentration of natural rock windows or "arches." Start with a guided hike in the Fiery Furnace, a maze of sandstone canyons and fins that is considered one of the most spectacular hikes in the park. On your second day, explore the Devil's Garden and Windows sections of the park. Head back to Moab for the night.

DAYS 4 AND 5: CANYONLANDS
30 miles or about a 35-minute drive from Moab.

From Moab, head to Canyonlands National Park. Start at the park's Island in the Sky District, at the northern end of the park (about 30 miles from Moab). Explore the area from the road, which has many overlooks, or hike the first section of the Upheaval Dome Trail, an 8.3-mile loop that starts at Whale Rock, about 11 miles from the visitor center and spotlights an enormous syncline, or downward fold in the Earth's crust (there are overlooks

½ mile and 1 mile from the trailhead). At the end of the day, on your way back to Moab, take a detour into Dead Horse Point State Park, about 11 miles from the Canyonlands entrance, and head up to the top of the mesa for magnificent views of the Colorado River as it goosenecks through the canyons below.

On Day 5, head to the Needles District, at the southwest corner of the park, and hike the Slickrock Trail (2.4 miles roundtrip), keeping an eye out for bighorn sheep. At the end of the day, drive east about 110 miles (2 hours) to Cortez, where you can find a hotel for the night.

DAY 6: MESA VERDE NATIONAL PARK
120 miles or a 2-hour, 12-minute drive from Canyonlands.

From Coretz, drive about 11 miles east to Mesa Verde National Park, with 5,000 archaeological sites (including 600 cliff dwellings) left behind by the Ancestral Puebloan people, who lived here more than 1,000 years ago. Begin your visit at the visitor center, just before the entrance station, to get the latest park information and purchase tour tickets for some of the more popular tours (to get the most out of your visit, plan to take at least one ranger-led tour). Inside the park, stop at the Chapin Mesa Museum.

After exploring Mesa Verde, you can spend the night at the Far View Lodge inside the park or head back to Cortez. Or, if you've got an early flight in the morning, you can drive back to Moab.

From Mesa Verde, it's a 143-mile (2½-hour) drive to Canyonlands Field airport.

Chapter 4

ARCHES NATIONAL PARK

Updated by
Andrew Collins

4

UTAH

WELCOME TO ARCHES NATIONAL PARK

TOP REASONS TO GO

★ **Arch appeal:** Nowhere in the world has as large an array or quantity of natural arches.

★ **Legendary landscape:** A photographer's dream—no wonder it's been the chosen backdrop for many Hollywood films.

★ **Treasures hanging in the balance:** Landscape Arch and Balanced Rock look like they might topple any day. And they could—the features in this park erode and evolve constantly.

★ **Fins and needles:** Fins are parallel vertical shafts of eroding rock that slowly disintegrate into tower-like "needles." The spaces around and between them will carve their way into your memories like the wind and water that formed them.

★ **Moab:** Known as Utah's "adventure capital," this small town is a great base from which to explore by foot, bicycle, balloon, watercraft, and four-wheeler.

Southeastern Utah's Arches National Park boasts some of the most unimaginable rock formations in the world. Off U.S. 191, Arches (along with Canyonlands National Park) is in Moab, 236 miles southeast of Salt Lake City and 27 miles south of Interstate 70.

1 Devils Garden. 18 miles from the visitor center, this is the end of the paved road in Arches. It has the park's only campground, a picnic area, and access to drinking water. Trails in Devils Garden lead to Landscape Arch and several other noteworthy formations.

2 Fiery Furnace. About 14 miles from the visitor center this area is so labeled because its orange spires of rock look much like tongues of flame. Reservations are required, often weeks in advance, to join the twice-daily ranger-guided treks, or you can obtain a permit to visit Fiery Furnace on your own, but only experienced, well-prepared hikers should attempt this option.

3 Delicate Arch/Wolfe Ranch. A spur road about 11.7 miles from the visitor center leads to the moderately strenuous 3-mile round-trip trail and viewpoints for the park's most famous feature—Delicate Arch. To see it from below, follow the road to the viewpoint, then walk to either easily accessible viewing area.

4 The Windows. Reached on a spur 9.2 miles from the visitor center, here you can see many of the park's natural arches from your car or on an easy rolling trail.

5 Balanced Rock. This giant rock teeters atop a pedestal, creating a 128-foot formation of red rock grandeur right along the roadside, about 9 miles from the visitor center.

6 Petrified Dunes. Just a tiny pull-out about 5 miles from the visitor center, it's a memorable stop for pictures of acres and acres of petrified sand dunes.

7 Courthouse Towers. The Three Gossips, Sheep Rock, and Tower of Babel are all here. Enter this section of the park 3 miles past the visitor center. The Park Avenue Trail winds through the area.

8 Moab. A river-running, mountain-biking, canyoneering hub, Moab—whose small downtown lies 5 miles south of the park—is the can't-miss base for all of your adventures.

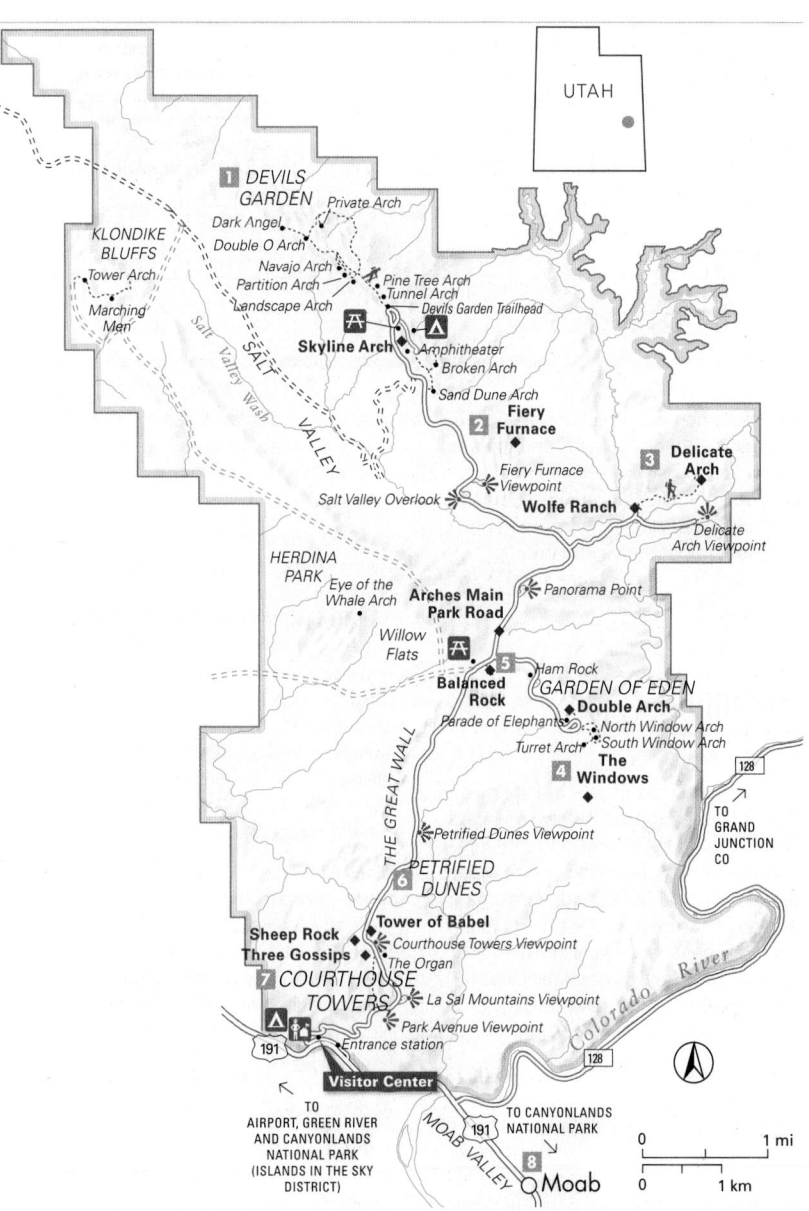

UTAH

1 DEVILS GARDEN
Private Arch
Dark Angel
Double O Arch
KLONDIKE BLUFFS
Navajo Arch
Pine Tree Arch
Partition Arch
Tunnel Arch
Tower Arch
Landscape Arch
Devils Garden Trailhead
Marching Men
Skyline Arch
Amphitheater
Broken Arch
Sand Dune Arch
2 Fiery Furnace
3 Delicate Arch
Fiery Furnace Viewpoint
Salt Valley Overlook
Wolfe Ranch
SALT VALLEY
Salt Valley Wash
Delicate Arch Viewpoint
HERDINA PARK
Eye of the Whale Arch
Arches Main Park Road
Panorama Point
Willow Flats
5 Ham Rock
Balanced Rock
GARDEN OF EDEN
Double Arch
Parade of Elephants
North Window Arch
Turret Arch
South Window Arch
4 The Windows
128
TO GRAND JUNCTION CO
THE GREAT WALL
Petrified Dunes Viewpoint
6 PETRIFIED DUNES
Tower of Babel
Sheep Rock
Courthouse Towers Viewpoint
Three Gossips
The Organ
7 COURTHOUSE TOWERS
La Sal Mountains Viewpoint
Park Avenue Viewpoint
191
Entrance station
Colorado River
128
Visitor Center
TO AIRPORT, GREEN RIVER AND CANYONLANDS NATIONAL PARK (ISLANDS IN THE SKY DISTRICT)
MOAB VALLEY
191
TO CANYONLANDS NATIONAL PARK
8 Moab

| 0 | | 1 mi |
| 0 | | 1 km |

More than 1 million visitors come to Arches annually, drawn by the red rock landscape and its wind- and water-carved rock formations. The park is named for the 2,000-plus sandstone arches that frame horizons, cast precious shade, and are in a perpetual state of gradual transformation, the result of constant erosion.

Fancifully named attractions like Three Penguins, Queen Nefertiti, and Tower of Babel stir curiosity, beckoning visitors to stop and marvel. Immerse yourself in this spectacular landscape, but don't lose yourself entirely—summer temperatures frequently exceed 100°F, and water is hard to come by inside the park boundaries.

Planning

WHEN TO GO

The busiest times of year are spring and fall. In the spring blooming wildflowers herald the end of winter, and temperatures in the 70s and 80s bring the year's largest crowds. The crowds remain steady in summer as the thermostat often exceeds 100°F and above in July and August. Sudden dramatic cloudbursts create rainfalls over red rock walls in late-summer "monsoon" season.

Fall means clear, warm days and crisp, cool nights. The park is much quieter in winter, and from December through February you can hike many of the trails in relative solitude. Snow occasionally falls in the valley beneath La Sal Mountains,

and when it does, Arches is a photographer's paradise, as snow drapes slickrock mounds and natural rock windows.

FESTIVALS AND EVENTS

★ Moab Arts Festival

Every Memorial Day weekend, artists from across the West gather at Moab's Swanny City Park to show their wares, including pottery, photography, and paintings. This fun, free festival is small enough to be manageable and sells a variety of affordable artworks. Soundtracked by live music, they also have activities for kids and lots of food. ✉ Moab ☎ 435/259–2742 ⊕ www. moabartsfestival.org.

Moab Art Walk

Moab galleries and shops celebrate the perfect weather of spring and fall with a series of exhibits. Art Walks are held the second Saturday of the month from April through June and September through November. Stroll the streets (5–8 pm) to see and purchase original works by Moab and regional artists. ✉ Moab ☎ 435/259–6272 ⊕ www.moabartwalk.com.

Canyonlands PRCA Rodeo

Cowboys come to the Old Spanish Trail Arena (just south of Moab) for three days

AVERAGE HIGH/LOW TEMPERATURES					
JAN.	**FEB.**	**MAR.**	**APR.**	**MAY**	**JUNE**
44/22	52/28	64/35	71/42	82/51	93/60
JULY	**AUG.**	**SEPT.**	**OCT.**	**NOV.**	**DEC.**
100/67	97/66	88/55	74/42	56/30	45/23

in late May or early June to try their luck on thrashing bulls and broncs at this annual Western tradition. ⊠ *3641 S. U.S. 191, Moab* ⊕ *www.moabcanyonlands-rodeo.com.*

★ **Moab Folk Festival**
Some of America's top folk artists converge in Moab each November to perform on indoor and outdoor stages. Past artists have included Richard Thompson, Shawn Colvin, Bruce Cockburn, Loudon Wainwright III, and Ferron. ⊠ *Moab* ☎ *435/259–3198* ⊕ *www.moabfolkfestival.com.*

Moab Music Festival
Moab's red rocks resonate with world-class music—classical, jazz, and traditional—during this annual festival held at indoor and outdoor venues including the city park, local auditoriums, private homes, and a natural stone grotto along the Colorado River. Musicians from all over the globe perform, and it's one of the West's top music showcases. The festival starts the Thursday before Labor Day and runs about two weeks. ⊠ *Moab* ☎ *435/259–7003* ⊕ *www.moabmusicfest.org.*

PLANNING YOUR TIME
There's no food service in the park, so pack snacks, lunch, and plenty of water before you head into Arches. Also plan ahead to get tickets to the daily ranger-led Fiery Furnace walks, held spring through fall. It's a highlight for those who are adventurous and in good shape (see Ranger Programs Overview, below, for details). The one-day itinerary below is based on what to do on a day that you can't visit Fiery Furnace. If you do take a Fiery Furnace walk, you should also have

time to drive the park road and perhaps walk on the Park Avenue trail. If you have a third day, take a rafting trip on the nearby Colorado River.

ARCHES IN ONE DAY
Start as early as sunrise for cool temperatures and some of the best natural light, and head out on the 3-mile round-trip hike on the **Delicate Arch Trail.** The route is strenuous but extremely rewarding. Next head to **Devils Garden,** another great spot for morning photography, where you'll also find the easy, primarily flat trail to **Landscape Arch,** the second of the park's two must-see arches. If you're a fairly experienced hiker, continue on to **Double O,** but note that this portion of the trail is somewhat strenuous. Along the way, picnic in the shade of a juniper or in a rock alcove. By the time you return you'll be ready to see the rest of the park by car, with some short strolls on easy paths.

In the mid- to late afternoon, drive to **Balanced Rock** for photos, then on to the **Windows.** Depending on what time the sun is due to set, go into town for dinner before or after you drive out to Delicate Arch or along the park road to watch the sun set the rocks aglow.

GETTING HERE AND AROUND
AIR TRAVEL
Moab is served by tiny Canyonlands Field Airport, which has daily service to Denver on United Airlines and a couple of car rental agencies. The nearest mid-size airport is Grand Junction Regional Airport in Grand Junction, Colorado, which is approximately 110 miles from Moab and is served by most major airlines.

4

Arches National Park PLANNING

CAR TRAVEL

The park entrance is just off U.S. 191 on the north side of downtown Moab, 28 miles south of Interstate 70 and 130 miles north of the Arizona border. Arches is also about 30 miles from the Island in the Sky section and 80 miles from the Needles District of Canyonlands National Park. If you're driving to Arches from points east on Interstate 70, consider taking Exit 214 in Utah (about 50 miles west of Grand Junction, CO), and continuing south on picturesque Highway 128, the Colorado River Scenic Byway, about 50 miles to Moab. Bear in mind that services can be sparse on even major roads in these parts.

Branching off the main, 18-mile park road—officially known as Arches Scenic Road—are two spurs, one 2½ miles to the Windows section and one 1.6 miles to Delicate Arch trailhead and viewpoint. There are several four-wheel-drive roads in the park; always check at the visitor center for conditions before attempting to traverse them. The entrance road into the park can back up mid-morning to early afternoon during busy periods. You'll encounter less traffic early in the morning or at sunset.

PARK ESSENTIALS
ACCESSIBILITY

Not all park facilities meet federally mandated accessibility standards, but as visitation to Arches increases, the park continues efforts to increase accessibility. Visitors with mobility impairments can access the visitor center, all park restrooms, and one campsite (#7) at the Devils Garden Campground. The Park Avenue Viewpoint is a paved path with a slight decline near the end, and both Delicate Arch and Balanced Rock viewpoints are partially hard-surfaced.

PARK FEES AND PERMITS

Admission to the park is $30 per vehicle, $25 per motorcycle, and $15 per person entering on foot or bicycle, valid for seven days. To encourage visitation to the park during less busy times, a $50 local park pass grants you admission to both Arches and Canyonlands parks as well as Natural Bridges and Hovenweep national monuments for one year.

PARK HOURS

Arches National Park is open year-round, seven days a week, around the clock. It's in the Mountain time zone.

CELL PHONE RECEPTION

Cell phone reception is spotty in the park. There's a pay phone at the visitor center.

EDUCATIONAL OFFERINGS
RANGER PROGRAMS

As you explore Arches, look for sandwich boards announcing "Ranger Sightings" and stop for a 3- to 10-minute program led by park staff. Topics range from geology and desert plants to mountain lions and the Colorado River. Most nights, spring through fall, more in-depth campfire programs are available at Devils Garden Campground amphitheater. You may also find guided walks (in addition to the beloved Fiery Furnace walk) during your visit. For information on current schedules and locations of park programs, contact the visitor center or check the bulletin boards throughout the park.

★ Fiery Furnace Walk

NATIONAL/STATE PARK | Join a park ranger on a 2½-hour scramble through a labyrinth of rock fins and narrow sandstone canyons. You'll see arches and other eye-popping formations that can't be viewed from the road. You should be very fit and not afraid of heights or confined spaces for this moderately strenuous experience. Wear sturdy hiking shoes, sunscreen, and a hat, and bring at least a liter of water. Guided walks into the Fiery Furnace are offered mid-April through September, usually a few times a day (hours vary), and leave from Fiery Furnace Viewpoint, about 15 miles from the park visitor center. Tickets for the morning walks must be reserved (at

⊕ *www.recreation.gov*) and are available beginning six months in advance and up to four days before the day of the tour. Tickets for afternoon Fiery Furnace walks must be purchased in person at the park visitor center, ideally as soon as you arrive in Moab and as far ahead as seven days before your hike. Children ages 5–12 are charged half-price; kids under 5 are not allowed. Book early as the program usually fills months prior to each walk. ⊠ *Arches National Park* ⚓ *Trailhead: on Arches Scenic Dr.*☞ *$16.*

Junior Ranger Program

NATIONAL/STATE PARK | FAMILY | Kids 2–12 can pick up a Junior Ranger booklet at the visitor center. It's full of activities, word games, drawings, and thought-provoking material about the park and the wildlife. To earn your Junior Ranger badge, you must complete several activities in the booklet, attend a ranger program, or watch the park film and pick up some trash in the park. ⊠ *Arches National Park.*

LEARNING RESOURCES
Red Rock Explorer Pack

NATIONAL/STATE PARK | FAMILY | Families can check out a youth backpack filled with tools for learning about both Arches and Canyonlands national parks. A guide for naturalists, a three-ring binder of activities, hand lens magnifier, and binoculars are just some of the loaner items. Backpacks can be returned to either Arches or Island in the Sky visitor center. Use of the backpack is free. ⊠ *Arches National Park.*

RESTAURANTS

Whether you select an award-winning continental restaurant in Moab, a nearby resort, or the tavern in Green River, you can dress comfortably in shorts or jeans. But don't let the relaxed attire fool you: culinary surprises await, with spectacular views as a bonus.

In the park itself, there are no dining facilities and no snack bars. Supermarkets, bakeries, and delis in downtown Moab will be happy to make you food to go. If you bring a packed lunch, there are several picnic areas from which to choose.

HOTELS

Though there are no hotels or cabins in the park itself, in the surrounding area every type of lodging is available, from economy chain motels to B&Bs and high-end, high-adventure resorts. It's important to know when popular events are held, however, as accommodations can, and do, fill up weeks ahead of time. *Hotel reviews have been shortened. For full information, visit Fodors.com.*

What It Costs			
$	$$	$$$	$$$$
RESTAURANTS			
under $13	$13–$20	$21–$30	over $30
HOTELS			
under $101	$101–$150	$151–$200	over $200

VISITOR INFORMATION
PARK CONTACT INFORMATION Arches
National Park ⊠ *N. U.S. 191* ☎ *435/719–2299* ⊕ *www.nps.gov/arch.*

VISITOR CENTER
★ Arches Visitor Center

With well-designed hands-on exhibits about the park's geology, wildlife, and history; helpful rangers; a water station, and a bookstore; the center is a great way to start your park visit. ⊠ *N. U.S. 191* ☎ *435/719–2299* ⊕ *nps.gov/arch.*

 Sights

SCENIC DRIVES
★ Arches Main Park Road

NATIONAL/STATE PARK | The main park road and its two short spurs are extremely scenic and allow you to enjoy many park sights from your car. The main road leads through Courthouse Towers, where

Plants and Wildlife in Arches

As in any desert environment, the best time to see wildlife in Arches is early morning or evening. Summer temperatures keep most animals tucked away in cool places, though ravens and lizards are exceptions. If you happen to be in the right place at the right time, you may spot one of the beautiful turquoise-necklace-collared lizards. It's more likely you'll see the western whiptail. Mule deer, jackrabbits, and small rodents are usually active in cool morning hours or near dusk. You may spot a lone coyote foraging day or night. The park protects a small herd of desert bighorns, and some of their tribe are sometimes seen early in the morning grazing beside U.S. 191 south of the Arches entrance. Never approach bighorns, which have been known to charge people who attempt to get too close, or any other animals in the park. Ravens, mule deer, and small mammals such as chipmunks are very used to seeing people and will get close to you, but don't feed them.

you can see Sheep Rock and the Three Gossips, then alongside the Great Wall, the Petrified Dunes, and Balanced Rock. A drive to the Windows section takes you to attractions like Double Arch, and you can see Skyline Arch along the roadside as you approach the Devils Garden campground. The road to Delicate Arch allows hiking access to one of the park's main features. Allow about two hours to drive the 45-mile round-trip, more if you explore the spurs and their features and stop at viewpoints along the way. ✉ *Arches National Park.*

HISTORIC SITES

Wolfe Ranch

HISTORIC SITE | Civil War veteran John Wesley Wolfe and his son started a small ranch here in 1888. He added a cabin in 1906 when his daughter Esther and her family came west to live. Built out of Fremont cottonwoods, the rustic one-room cabin still stands on the site. Look for remains of a root cellar and a corral as well. Even older than these structures is the nearby Ute rock-art panel by the Delicate Arch trailhead. About 150 feet past the footbridge and before the trail starts to climb, you can see images of bighorn sheep and figures on horseback, as well as some smaller images believed to be dogs. ✉ *Off Delicate Arch Rd.*

SCENIC STOPS

It's easy to spot some of the arches from your car, but take the time to step outside and walk beneath the spans and giant walls of orange rock. This gives you a much better idea of their proportion. You may feel as writer Edward Abbey did when he awoke on his first day as a park ranger in Arches: that you're walking in the most beautiful place on Earth.

It's especially worthwhile to visit as the sun goes down. At sunset, the rock formations glow, and you'll often find photographers behind their tripods waiting for magnificent rays to descend on Delicate Arch or other popular sites. The Fiery Furnace earns its name as its narrow fins glow red just before the sun dips below the horizon. Full-moon nights are particularly dramatic in Arches as the creamy white Navajo sandstone reflects light, and eerie silhouettes are created by towering fins and formations.

Balanced Rock

NATURE SITE | One of the park's favorite sights, 9¼ miles from the park entrance, this rock is visible for several minutes as you approach—and just gets more impressive and mysterious as you get closer. The formation's total height is 128 feet, with the huge balanced rock rising 55 feet above the pedestal. Be sure to hop out of the car and walk the short (⅓-mile) loop around the base. ⊠ *Arches Scenic Dr.*

★ Delicate Arch

NATURE SITE | The iconic symbol of the park and the state (it appears on many of Utah's license plates), Delicate Arch is tall and prominent compared to many of the spans in the park— it's big enough that it could shelter a four-story building. The arch is a remnant of an Entrada Sandstone fin; the rest of the rock has eroded and it now frames La Sal Mountains in the background. Drive 2.2 miles off the main road to the viewpoint to see the arch from a distance, or hike right up to it from the trailhead that starts near Wolfe Ranch. The trail, 13 miles from the park entrance and 1.2 miles off the main road, is a moderately strenuous 3-mile round-trip hike with no shade or access to water. It's especially picturesque shortly after sunrise or before sunset. ⊠ *Delicate Arch Rd.*

Double Arch

NATURE SITE | In the Windows section of the park, 11¾ miles from the park entrance, Double Arch has appeared in several Hollywood movies, including *Indiana Jones and the Last Crusade*. From the parking lot you can also take the short and easy Window Trail to view North Window, South Window, and Turret Arch. ⊠ *The Windows Rd.*

Fiery Furnace

NATURE SITE | Fewer than 10% of the park's visitors ever descend into the chasms and washes of Fiery Furnace (a permit or a ranger-led hike is the only way to go), but you can gain an appreciation for this twisted, unyielding landscape from the Overlook, 14 miles from the park entrance. At sunset, the rocks glow a vibrant flamelike red, which gives the formation its daunting moniker. ⊠ *Off Arches Scenic Dr.*

Skyline Arch

NATURE SITE | A quick walk from the parking lot at Skyline Arch, 16½ miles from the park entrance, gives you closer views and better photos. The short trail is less than a half mile round-trip and only takes a few minutes to travel. ⊠ *Devils Garden Rd.*

The Windows

NATURE SITE | **FAMILY** | As you head north from the park entrance, turn right at Balanced Rock to find this concentration of natural windows, caves, and needles 11¾ miles from the park entrance. Stretch your legs on the easy paths that wind between the arches and soak in a variety of geological formations. ⊠ *The Windows Rd.*

🏃 Activities

Arches lies in the middle of one of the adventure capitals of the United States. Deep canyons and towering walls are everywhere you look. Thousand-foot sandstone walls draw rock climbers from across the globe. Hikers can choose from shady canyons or red rock ridges that put you in the company of the West's big sky. The Colorado River forms the southeast boundary of the park and can give you every grade of white-water adventure.

Moab-based outfitters can set you up for any sport you may have a desire to try: mountain biking, ATVs, dirt bikes, four-wheel-drive vehicles, kayaking, climbing, stand-up paddleboarding, and even skydiving. Within the park, it's best to stick with basics such as hiking, sightseeing, and photography. Climbers and other adventure seekers should always inquire at the visitor center about restrictions.

MULTISPORT OUTFITTERS

Adrift Adventures

BOATING | **FAMILY** | This outfitter takes pride in well-trained guides who can take

Good Reads

Arches Visitor Center Bookstore Operated by Canyonlands Natural History Association, this bookstore at the park entrance is the place in the park to buy maps, guidebooks, driving tours on CD, and material about the park's natural and cultural history. ⊠ *N. U.S. 191* ☎ *435/259–6003.*

■ *127 Hours: Between a Rock and a Hard Place* by Aron Ralston. This true story—made into a movie of the same name starring James Franco—took place southeast of Arches and is a modern-day survivor story of solitary man in nature.

■ *A Naturalist's Guide to Canyon Country*, by David Williams and Gloria Brown, is an excellent, compact field guide for both Arches and Canyonlands national parks.

■ *Desert Solitaire.* Eminent naturalist Edward Abbey's first ranger assignment was Arches; this classic is a must-read.

■ *Road Guide to Arches National Park*, by Peter Anderson, has basic information about the geology and natural history in the park.

■ *Moab Classic Hikes*, by Damian Fagan, succinctly gives the skinny on 40 area hikes and includes maps and photos.

you via foot, raft, kayak, 4X4, jet boat, stand-up paddleboard, and more, all over the Moab area, including the Colorado and Green rivers and Arches Jeep and hiking adventures. They also offer history, movie, and rock-art tours. They've been in business since 1977 and have a great reputation around town. ⊠ *378 N. Main St., Moab* ☎ *435/259–8594, 800/874–4483* ⊕ *www.adrift.net* ⚓ *From $49.*

Dual Sport Utah

FOUR-WHEELING | If you're into dirt biking, this is the only outfitter in Moab specializing in street-legal, off-road dirt-bike tours and rentals. Follow the Klondike Bluffs trail to Arches, or negotiate the White Rim Trail in Canyonlands in a fraction of the time you would spend on a mountain bike. You can also rent Jet Skis here. ⊠ *197 W. Center. St., Moab* ☎ *435/260–2724* ⊕ *www.dualsportutah.com* ⚓ *From $225.*

Moab Adventure Center

BOATING | FAMILY | At the prominent storefront on Main Street you can schedule most any type of local adventure experience you want, including rafting, 4X4 tours, scenic flights, hikes, balloon rides, and a couple of excellent bus overview tours of Arches highlights. You can also purchase clothing and outdoor gear for your visit. ⊠ *225 S. Main St., Moab* ☎ *435/259–7019, 866/904–1163* ⊕ *www.moabadventurecenter.com* ⚓ *From $85.*

NAVTEC

BOATING | Doc Williams was the first doctor in Moab in 1896, and some of his descendants never left, sharing his love for the area through this rafting, canyoneering, and 4X4 company. Whether you want to explore the region by boat, boots, or wheels, you'll find a multitude of one-day and multiday options here. ⊠ *321 N. Main St., Moab* ☎ *435/259–7983, 800/833–1278* ⊕ *www.navtec.com* ⚓ *From $85.*

BICYCLING

There's world-class biking all around Arches National Park, but the park proper is not the best place to explore on two wheels. Bicycles are allowed only on established roads, and because there are no shoulders cyclists share the roadway with drivers and pedestrians. If you do want to take a spin in the park, try the dirt-and-gravel Willow Flats Road, the old entrance to the park. The road is about 6½ miles one-way and starts across from Balanced Rock parking lot. It's a pretty mountain-bike ride on dirt and sand through slickrock, pinyon, and juniper country. You must stay on the road with your bicycle or chance steep fines.

Chile Pepper Bike Shop

BICYCLING | For mountain bike rentals, sales, service, and gear, plus espresso, stop here before you set out. ⊠ 702 S. Main St., Moab 🕾 435/259–4688 ⊕ www.chilebikes.com.

★ Poison Spider Bicycles

BICYCLING | In a town of great bike shops, this fully loaded shop is one of the best. Poison Spider serves the thriving road-cycling community as well as mountain bikers. Rent, buy, or service your bike here. You can also arrange for shuttle and guide services and purchase merchandise. Want to ship your bike to Moab for your adventure? Poison Spider will store it until you arrive and the staff will reassemble it for you and make sure everything is in perfect working order. ⊠ 497 N. Main St., Moab 🕾 435/259–7882, 800/635–1792 ⊕ www.poisonspiderbicycles.com.

Rim Tours

BICYCLING | Reliable, friendly, and professional, Rim Tours has been taking guests on guided one-day or multiday mountain-bike tours, including Klondike Bluffs (which enters Arches) and the White Rim Trail (inside Canyonlands) since 1985. Road-bike tours as well as bike rentals are also available. Bike skills a little rusty? Rim Tours also offers mountain-bike instructional tours and skill clinics. ⊠ 1233 S. U.S. 191, Moab 🕾 435/259–5223, 800/626–7335 ⊕ www.rimtours.com ⚏ Tours from $149.

Western Spirit Cycling Adventures

BICYCLING | Head here for fully supported, go-at-your-own-pace, multiday mountain-bike and road-bike tours throughout the western states, including trips to Canyonlands, Trail of the Ancients, and the 140-mile Kokopelli Trail, which runs from Grand Junction, Colorado, to Moab. Guides versed in the geologic wonders of the area cook up meals worthy of the scenery each night. Ask about family rides, and road bike trips, too. There's also the option to combine a Green River kayak trip with the three-night White Rim Trail ride. ⊠ 478 S. Mill Creek Dr., Moab 🕾 435/259–8732, 800/845–2453 ⊕ www.westernspirit.com ⚏ From $950.

BIRD-WATCHING
Within the park you'll definitely see plenty of the big, black, beautiful ravens. Look for them perched on top of a picturesque juniper branch or balancing on the bald knob of a rock. Noisy black-billed magpies populate the park, as do the more melodic canyon and rock wrens. Lucky visitors may spot a red-tailed hawk and hear its distinctive call.

Serious birders will have more fun visiting the Nature Conservancy's **Scott M. Matheson Wetlands Preserve,** 5 miles south of the park. The wetlands is home to more than 200 species of birds including the wood duck, western screech owl, indigo bunting, and plumbeous vireo.

BOATING AND RIVER EXPEDITIONS
Although the Colorado River runs along the border of the park, there is no boating within the park proper. You can, however, enjoy a splashy ride nearby on the Fisher Towers stretch of the river north of Moab, and there are plenty of outfitters in Moab that can set you up for expeditions.

★ Canyon Voyages Adventure Co.

BOATING | FAMILY | This is an excellent choice for rafting or kayaking adventures on the Colorado River—including the

Fisher Towers section—or Green River. Don and Denise Oblak run a friendly, professional company with a retail store and rental shop that's open year-round. Most customers take one-day trips, but they also offer multiday itineraries, guided tours, and rentals. They also operate a great kayak school. Ask about stand-up paddleboarding, biking, and horseback riding, too. ⊠ *211 N. Main St., Moab* ☎ *435/241–3846, 866/377–3216* ⊕ *www. canyonvoyages.com* ⊡ *From $65.*

Holiday River Expeditions

BOATING | Since 1966, this outfitter has offered one- to eight-day adventures on the San Juan, Green, and Colorado rivers, including inside Canyonlands National Park. They also offer multisport trips, women's retreats, and bike adventures, including the White Rim Trail. ⊠ *2075 E. Main St., Green River* ☎ *435/564–3273, 800/624–6323* ⊕ *www.bikeraft.com* ⊡ *From $190.*

FOUR-WHEELING

With thousands of acres of nearby Bureau of Land Management lands to enjoy, it's hardly necessary to use the park's limited trails for four-wheel adventures. You can, however, go backcountry in Arches on the Willow Flats Road and the Salt Valley Road—just don't set out for this expedition without first stopping at the visitor center to learn of current conditions. Salt Valley Road is very sandy and requires experience to drive on it.

Coyote Land Tours

FOUR-WHEELING | Imposing Mercedes Benz Unimog trucks (which dwarf Hummers) take you to parts of the backcountry where you could never wander on your own. Technical tours challenge drivers with imposing rock formations, washes, and assorted obstacles, and there are tamer sunset excursions and camp-style ride-and-dine trips. They stand by their money-back "great time" guarantee. ⊠ *Moab* ☎ *435/260–6056* ⊕ *www. coyotelandtours.com* ⊡ *From $59.*

Taking Dogs to the Park

Dogs aren't allowed on national park trails and must be on leash in the Devils Garden Campground. However, canines can join you on Bureau of Land Management trails. The heat can be stifling, so remember to bring enough water for you and your four-legged friend and hit the trails in the early morning hours.

High Point Hummer & ATV

FOUR-WHEELING | You can rent vehicles, including ATVs, UTVs, and Jeeps, or get a guided tour of the backcountry in open-air Hummer vehicles or ATVs, or dune buggy–like "side-by-sides" that seat up to six people. The enthusiastic owners love families and small, intimate groups, and offer hiking and canyoneering as well. ⊠ *281 N. Main St., Moab* ☎ *435/259–2972, 877/486–6833* ⊕ *www. highpointhummer.com* ⊡ *From $69.*

HIKING

Getting out on any one of the park trails will surely cause you to fall in love with this Mars-like landscape. But remember, you are hiking in a desert environment and approximately 1 mile above sea level. Many people succumb to heat and dehydration because they do not drink enough water. Park rangers recommend a gallon of water per day per person.

Balanced Rock Trail

HIKING/WALKING | **FAMILY** | You'll want to stop at Balanced Rock for photo ops, so you may as well walk the easy, partially paved trail around the famous landmark. This is one of the most accessible trails in the park and is suitable even for small children. The 15-minute stroll is only about ⅓ mile round-trip. *Easy.* ⊠ *Arches*

National Park ⊹ Trailhead: approximately 9¼ miles from park entrance.

Broken Arch Trail

HIKING/WALKING | An easy walk across open grassland, this loop trail passes Broken Arch, which is also visible from the road. The arch gets its name because it appears to be cracked in the middle, but it's not really broken. The trail is 1¼ miles round-trip, but you can extend your adventure to about 2 miles round-trip by continuing north past Tapestry Arch and through Devils Garden Campground. *Easy. ⊠ Arches National Park ⊹ Trailhead: off Devils Garden Rd., 16½ miles from park entrance.*

★ Delicate Arch Trail

HIKING/WALKING | FAMILY | To see the park's most famous freestanding arch up close takes effort and won't offer you much solitude—but it's worth every step. The 3-mile round-trip trail ascends via steep slickrock, sandy paths, and along one narrow ledge (at the very end) that might give pause to anyone afraid of heights. Plus, there's almost no shade. First-timers should start early to avoid the midday heat in summer. Still, at sunrise, sunset, and every hour in between, it's the park's busiest trail. Heat mixed with lack of shade makes this a strenuous hike in the summer. Bring plenty of water as heatstroke is a very real possibility. Allow two to three hours, depending on your fitness level and how long you care to linger at the arch. If you go at sunset or sunrise, bring a headlamp or flashlight. Don't miss Wolfe Ranch and some ancient rock art near the trailhead. *Moderate–Difficult. ⊠ Arches National Park ⊹ Trailhead: on Delicate Arch Rd., 13 miles from park entrance.*

★ Devils Garden Trail

HIKING/WALKING | Landscape Arch is a highlight of this trail but is just one of several arches within reach, depending on your ambitions. It's an easy ¾-mile one-way (mostly gravel, relatively flat) trip to Landscape Arch, one of the longest stone spans in the world. Beyond Landscape Arch the scenery changes dramatically and the hike becomes more strenuous, as you must climb and straddle slickrock fins and negotiate some short, steep inclines. Finally, around a sharp bend, the stacked spans that compose Double O Arch come suddenly into view. Allow up to three hours for this round-trip hike of just over 4 miles. For a still longer (6-mile round-trip) and more rigorous hike, venture on to see a formation called Dark Angel and then return to the trailhead on the primitive loop, making the short side hike to Private Arch. The hike to Dark Angel is a difficult route through fins. Other possible (and worthwhile) detours lead to Navajo Arch, Partition Arch, Tunnel Arch, and Pine Tree Arch. Allow about five hours for this adventure, take plenty of water, and watch your route carefully. Pick up the park's useful guide to Devils Garden, or download it from the website before you go. *Moderate–Difficult. ⊠ Arches National Park ⊹ Trailhead: on Devils Garden Rd., end of main road, 18 miles from park entrance.*

Double Arch Trail

HIKING/WALKING | If it's not too hot, it's a simple walk to here from Windows Trail. This relatively flat trek leads to two massive arches that make for great photo opportunities. The ½-mile round-trip gives you a good taste of desert flora and fauna. *Easy. ⊠ Arches National Park ⊹ Trailhead: 2½ miles from main road, on Windows Section spur road.*

Fiery Furnace

HIKING/WALKING | This area of the park has taken on a near-mythical lure for park visitors, who are drawn to challenging yet breathtaking terrain. Rangers strongly discourage inexperienced hikers from entering here—in fact, you can't enter without watching a video about how to help protect this very special section of the park and obtaining a permit ($6). Up to one month's advance reservations are required to get a spot on the 2-mile round-trip ranger-led hikes ($16), offered mid-April–September, through this unique formation. A hike through these rugged rocks and sandy washes is challenging but fascinating. Hikers will need to use their hands at times to scramble up and through narrow cracks and along vertigo-inducing ledges above drop-offs, and there are no trail markings. If you're not familiar with the Furnace you can easily get lost or cause damage, so watch your step and use great caution. For information about reservations, see Ranger Programs Overview above. The less intrepid can view Fiery Furnace from the Overlook off the main road. *Difficult.* ⊠ *Arches National Park* ⊹ *Trailhead: off main road, about 14 miles from park entrance.*

Landscape Arch

HIKING/WALKING | This natural rock opening, which measures 306 feet from base to base and looks like a delicate ribbon of rock bending over the horizon, is the longest geologic span in North America. In 1991, a slab of rock about 60 feet long, 11 feet wide, and 4 feet thick fell from the underside, leaving it even thinner. You reach it via a rolling, gravel, 1.6-mile-long trail. *Easy–Moderate.* ⊠ *Arches National Park* ⊹ *Trailhead: at Devils Garden Rd., at end of main road, 18 miles north of park entrance.*

Park Avenue Trail

HIKING/WALKING | The first named trail that park visitors encounter, this is a relatively easy, 2-mile round-trip walk (with only one small hill but a somewhat steep descent into the canyon) amid walls and towers that vaguely resemble a New York City skyline. You'll walk under the gaze of Queen Nefertiti, a giant rock formation that some observers think has Egyptian-looking features. If you are traveling with companions, make it a one-way, 1-mile downhill trek by having them pick you up at the Courthouse Towers Viewpoint. Allow about 45 minutes for the one-way journey. *Easy–Moderate.* ⊠ *Arches National Park* ⊹ *Trailhead: 2 miles from park entrance on main park road.*

Sand Dune Arch Trail

HIKING/WALKING | **FAMILY** | You may return to the car with shoes full of bright red sand from this giant sandbox in the desert—it's fun exploring in and around the rock. Set aside five minutes for this shady, 530-yard walk and plenty of time if you have kids, who will love playing amid this dramatic landscape. Never climb on this or any other arch in the park, no matter how tempting—it's illegal, and it could result in damage to the fragile geology or personal injury. The trail intersects with the Broken Arch Trail—you can visit both arches with an easy 1½-mile round-trip walk. *Easy.* ⊠ *Arches National Park* ⊹ *Trailhead: off Arches Scenic Dr., about 16½ miles from park entrance.*

Tower Arch Trail

HIKING/WALKING | Check with park rangers before attempting the dirt road through Salt Valley to Klondike Bluffs parking area. If rains haven't washed out the road, a trip to this seldom-visited area provides a solitude-filled hike culminating in a giant rock opening. Allow from two to three hours for this 3½-mile round-trip hike, not including the drive. *Moderate.* ⊠ *Arches National Park* ⊹ *Trailhead: at Klondike Bluffs parking area, 24½ miles from park entrance, 7¾ miles off main road.*

The Windows

HIKING/WALKING | **FAMILY** | An early stop for many visitors to the park, a trek through the Windows gives you an opportunity to get out and enjoy the desert air. Here you'll see three giant openings in the rock and walk on a trail that leads right through the holes. Allow about an hour on this gently inclined, 1-mile round-trip hike. As most visitors don't follow the "primitive" trail around the backside of the two windows, take advantage if you want some desert solitude. The primitive trail adds an extra half hour to the hike.

People in the Park

Old Doc Williams

A commemorative site in the park is named for Dr. John Williams, a dedicated local doctor and outdoorsman who loved to hike in Arches. Doc Williams, who lived to 103, was the first doctor to set up shop in Moab, back in 1896. So appreciated was his presence that area health commissioners named him county health officer. Locals, especially Native Americans, who came to his office and drugstore would often receive a treat—sugar or a bit of hard candy. If the store was closed, folks gathered around his house and watched through the windows until Mrs. Williams brought out a loaf of home-baked bread.

Easy. ⊠ *Arches National Park* ✛ *Trailhead: on the Windows Rd., 12 miles from park entrance.*

ROCK CLIMBING AND CANYONEERING

Rock climbers travel from across the country to scale the sheer red rock walls of Arches National Park and surrounding areas. Most climbing routes in the park require advanced techniques. Permits are not required, but climbers are encouraged to register for a free permit, either online or at a kiosk outside the visitor center. Climbers are responsible for knowing park regulations, temporary route closures, and restricted routes. Two popular routes ascend Owl Rock in the Garden of Eden (about 10 miles from the visitor center); the well-worn route has a difficulty of 5.8, while a more challenging option is 5.11 on a scale that goes up to 5.13-plus. Many climbing routes are available in the Park Avenue area, about 2.2 miles from the visitor center. These routes are also extremely difficult climbs. No commercial outfitters are allowed to lead rock-climbing excursions in the park, but guided canyoneering (which involves ropes, rappelling, and some basic climbing) is allowed, and permits are required for canyoneering. Before climbing, it's imperative that you stop at the visitor center and check with a ranger about climbing regulations.

Desert Highlights

CLIMBING/MOUNTAINEERING | This guide company takes adventurous types on descents and ascents through canyons (with the help of ropes), including those found in the Fiery Furnace at Arches National Park. Full-day and multiday canyoneering treks are available to destinations both in and near the national parks. Desert Highlights does not offer guided rock climbing. ⊠ *50 E. Center St., Moab* ☎ *435/259–4433, 800/747–1342* ⊕ *www. deserthighlights.com* ✍ *From $105.*

★ **Moab Cliffs & Canyons**

CLIMBING/MOUNTAINEERING | In a town where everyone seems to offer rafting and 4X4 expeditions, Moab Cliffs & Canyons focuses exclusively on canyoneering, climbing, and rappelling—for novice and veteran adventurers. Prices vary according to how many people sign up. This is the outfitter that provided technical assistance to the crew on the movie *127 Hours*. ⊠ *253 N. Main St., Moab* ☎ *435/259–3317, 877/641–5271* ⊕ *www. cliffsandcanyons.com* ✍ *From $72.*

Did You Know?

"I happened to catch this beautiful light on the back side of Pine Tree Arch on the Devils Garden Trail." —*photo by Merryl Edelstein, Fodors. com member*

Nearby Towns

Moab is the primary gateway to both Arches and Canyonlands national parks. Don't let its outsize image and status as Grand County seat fool you: only about 5,200 people live here year-round— compared with the 1.5 million who visit annually. Near the Colorado River in a beautiful valley between red rock cliffs, Moab is an interesting, eclectic place to visit, and it's home to a mix of both super-casual and hip restaurants, plus Southwestern-inspired souvenirs, art galleries, tour operators, recreation outfitters, and a growing selection of lodging options.

The next-closest town to Arches, about 50 miles to the northwest, is **Green River,** a fairly sleepy little town with some less expensive—but also less noteworthy—dining and lodging options and the excellent John Wesley Powell River History Museum. Each September the fragrance of fresh cantaloupe, watermelon, and honeydew fills the air, especially during Melon Days, a family-fun harvest celebration on the third weekend of September. As Moab hotels have become more expensive and crowded spring through fall, many park visitors have taken to staying farther south in the small southeastern Utah towns of **Monticello, Blanding,** and **Bluff** (see the Canyonlands National Park chapter for more on these three towns), and even 110 miles away up in **Grand Junction, Colorado,** a lively and attractive small city of about 62,000 with a bustling historic downtown and some great, reasonably priced dining and lodging options and close proximity to gorgeous Colorado National Monument.

VISITOR INFORMATION
Discover Moab Information Center ⊠ *25 E. Center St., Moab* ☎ *435/259–8825* ⊕ *www.discovermoab.com.*

Visit Grand Junction Information Center ⊠ *740 Horizon Dr., Grand Junction* ☎ *970/244–1480* ⊕ *www.visitgrandjunction.com.*

 Sights

Canyonlands by Night & Day
ENTERTAINMENT CRUISE | Since 1963 this outfitter has been known for its two-hour, after-dark boat ride on the Colorado River (March–October). While illuminating the canyon walls with 40,000 watts, the trip includes music and narration highlighting Moab's history, Native American legends, and geologic formations along the river. You can also combine the boat trip with a Dutch-oven dinner. Daytime jet boat tours are offered, too, as well as tours by Hummer, airplane, and helicopter (land and air tours are offered year-round). ⊠ *1861 U.S. 191, Moab* ☎ *435/259–2628, 800/394–9978* ⊕ *www.canyonlandsbynight.com* 🍴 *Dinner and boat tour $69.*

Courthouse Wash
NATURE SITE | Although this rock-art panel fell victim to an unusual case of vandalism in 1980, when someone scoured the petroglyphs and pictographs that had been left by four cultures, you can still see ancient images if you take a short walk from the parking area on the left-hand side of the road, heading south. ⊠ *U.S. 191, about 2 miles south of Arches entrance.*

★ John Wesley Powell River History Museum
MUSEUM | FAMILY | Learn what it was like to travel down the Green and Colorado rivers in the 1800s in wooden boats. A series of displays tracks the Powell Party's arduous, dangerous 1869 journey, and visitors can watch the award-winning film *Journey Into the Unknown* for a cinematic taste of the white-water adventure. The center also houses the River Runner's Hall of Fame, a tribute to those who have followed in Powell's wake. River-themed art occupies a gallery

and there's a dinosaur exhibit on the lower level. ⊠ *1765 E. Main St., Green River* ☎ *435/564-3427* ⊕ *www.johnwesleypowell.com* 🎫 *$6* ⊘ *Closed Mon. in winter.*

La Sal Mountains

MOUNTAIN—SIGHT | If you want a break from the desert heat, wander up to this snowcapped mountain range about 30 miles from Arches National Park. At 12,726 feet, Mount Peale is the tallest peak you'll see—it's also southern Utah's highest point. You don't need to go nearly that high to picnic in a meadow or take one of many alpine hikes in this largely unvisited area. There's also a scenic drive that gives you some great vistas of the valley. The roads can be impassable in winter, but the cross-country skiing is great. ⊠ *La Sal Mountain Loop Rd., Moab* ✛ *Begins off U.S. 191, about 10 miles south of Moab* ☎ *435/637-2817* ⊕ *www. fs.usda.gov/mantilasal.*

Moab Arts and Recreation Center

ARTS CENTERS | Offering a slice of Moab's arts scene, from "Quick Draw Sales" where artists have three hours to create pieces during the annual Red Rock Arts Festival, to dance, crafts, and fitness classes, this has been the spirited hub of arts activities in Moab since 1997. ⊠ *111 E. 100 N, Moab* ☎ *435/259-6272* ⊕ *www.moabrecreation.com.*

Museum of Moab

MUSEUM | **FAMILY** | Exhibits on the history, geology, and paleontology of the Moab area include settler-era antiques, and ancient and historic Native Americans are remembered in displays of baskets, pottery, sandals, and other artifacts. Displays also chronicle early Spanish expeditions into the area, regional dinosaur finds, and the history of uranium discovery. ⊠ *118 E. Center St., Moab* ☎ *435/259-7985* ⊕ *www.moabmuseum.org* 🎫 *$5.*

 Shopping

ART GALLERIES

Lema's Kokopelli Gallery

ART GALLERIES | The Lema family has built a reputation for fair prices on a large selection of Native American and Southwest-themed jewelry, art, pottery, rugs, and more. Everything sold here is authentic. ⊠ *70 N. Main St., Moab* ☎ *435/259-5055* ⊕ *www.kokopellioutlet. com.*

★ Tom Till Gallery

ART GALLERIES | Stop here to buy stunning original photographs of the area's parks by one of the nation's best-loved landscape photographers. ⊠ *61 N. Main St., Moab* ☎ *435/259-9808* ⊕ *www.tomtill. com.*

BOOKS

Back of Beyond Books

BOOKS/STATIONERY | **FAMILY** | A Main Street treasure, this comprehensive bookstore features the American West, environmental studies, Native American cultures, water issues, and Western history, as well as rare antiquarian books on the Southwest. There's also a nice nook for kids. ⊠ *83 N. Main St., Moab* ☎ *435/259-5154, 800/700-2859* ⊕ *www. backofbeyondbooks.com.*

 Sights

★ Colorado River Scenic Byway—Highway 128

SCENIC DRIVE | One of the most scenic drives in the Four Corners region, Highway 128 intersects U.S. 191, 3 miles south of Arches. The 44-mile highway runs along the Colorado River with 2,000-foot red rock cliffs rising on both sides. This gorgeous river corridor is home to a winery, orchards, and a couple of luxury lodging options. It also offers a spectacular view of world-class climbing destination Fisher Towers before winding north to Interstate 70. Give yourself an hour to 90 minutes to drive it. ✉ *Hwy. 128, Moab.*

🍴 Restaurants

IN THE PARK

PICNIC AREAS

Balanced Rock

TOUR—SIGHT | The view is the best part of this picnic spot opposite Balanced Rock parking area. There's no water, but there are tables. If you sit just right you might find some shade under a small juniper; otherwise, this is an exposed site. Pit toilets are nearby. ✉ *9¼ miles from park entrance on main road.*

★ Devils Garden

RESTAURANT—SIGHT | There are grills, water, picnic tables, and restrooms here and, depending on the time of day, some shade from junipers and rock walls. It's a good place for lunch before or after a hike. ✉ *End of main road, 18 miles from park entrance.*

GREEN RIVER

Ray's Tavern

$ | AMERICAN | In little downtown Green River, Ray's is something of a Western legend and a favorite hangout for river runners. The bar that runs the length of this 1940s restaurant reminds you this is still a tavern and a serious watering hole—but all the photos and rafting memorabilia make it comfortable for families as well. **Known for:** legendary burgers; great people-watching; homemade apple pie. [$] *Average main: $10* ✉ *25 S. Broadway, Green River* ☎ *435/564–3511* 🌐 *www.raystavern.com.*

MOAB

Antica Forma

$$ | ITALIAN | Moab's best pizza joint, which has a wildly popular original location in the northeastern Utah town of Vernal, opened here in 2018, offering an extensive list of thin-crust wood-fired pizzas with interesting toppings, plus plenty of classic antipasto (mussels in white wine, homemade burrata, arancini) and pasta options. Have a seat at one of the granite-top tables in the high-ceilinged dining room, peruse the well-curated wine and beer list, and tuck into one of the specialty pies, perhaps the white pie with pistachio pesto, Italian sausage, homemade mozzarella, pecorino romano, basil, and olive oil. **Known for:** regular and gluten-free pizza crusts; extensive craft beer selection; creative pizza toppings. [$] *Average main: $15* ✉ *267 N. Main St., Moab* ☎ *435/355–0167* 🌐 *www.anticaforma.com.*

★ Desert Bistro

$$$$ | MODERN AMERICAN | Long one of Moab's most sophisticated dining options, Desert Bistro occupies a 19th-century dance hall off Main Street where the appealing ambience matches the cuisine. The kitchen innovates seasonally with cosmopolitan, artfully presented fare like gyoza stuffed with smoked tofu and Anasazi bean hummus, and ancho-lime-rubbed pork tenderloin with a roasted green chili–epazote sauce. **Known for:** plenty of vegan and vegetarian options; house-baked breads and desserts; "flown in daily" rotating fish special. [$] *Average main: 34* ✉ *36 S. 100 W, Moab* ☎ *435/259–0756* 🌐 *www.desertbistro.com* 🕒 *No lunch. Closed Nov.–Mar.*

★ Eklecticafe

$ | ECLECTIC | This place is easy to miss, but worth finding for one of the more creative, healthy menus in Moab. Breakfast and lunch items include a variety of burritos and wraps, scrambled tofu, salmon cakes, Indonesian satay kebabs, and many fresh, organic salads. **Known for:** first-rate coffee; creative menu; funky, artsy setting. [$] *Average main: $9* ✉ *352 N. Main St., Moab* ☎ *435/259–6896* 🕒 *No dinner.*

La Sal House

$$ | MODERN AMERICAN | Named for the soaring mountain range southeast of town, this stylish dinner house with

exposed timber, tile floors, and leather banquettes has elevated Moab's culinary and cocktail scene to unprecedented heights. Both classic and new elixirs (consider the sumac lemonade with local gin and mint) prime diners for the extraordinary seasonally inspired dishes, which might include a farmers salad of Utah greens, tomatoes, shishito peppers, feta, and bourbon-peach vinaigrette, followed by Colorado lamb with Ethiopian-spiced and braised sweet potato, cauliflower, and chickpeas. **Known for:** stellar craft cocktails; innovate food with global influences; relatively reasonable prices. $ *Average main: $20* ⊠ *11 E. 100 N, Moab* ☎ *435/259–5725* ⊕ *www. lasalhouse.com* ⊘ *Closed Sun. and Mon. No lunch.*

Miguel's Baja Grill

$$ | **MEXICAN** | Great southern Baja food, including freshly prepared Pacific seafood and massive flour tortillas, is served in this colorful alleyway and restaurant in the heart of downtown Moab. Try the Mariscos a la Paz, featuring shrimp, scallops, mahimahi, and clams in a spicy tomato sauce bursting with arbol chilies. **Known for:** ceviche; potent margaritas; Baja-style fish tacos. $ *Average main: $18* ⊠ *51 N. Main St., Moab* ☎ *435/259–6546* ⊕ *www.miguelsbajagrill.com.*

Moab Brewery

$$ | **AMERICAN** | Moab's first microbrewery is known for its Scorpion Pale Ale, Squeaky Bike Nut Brown Ale, and an assortment of other brews from light to dark. The on-site restaurant is spacious and comfortable and decorated with kayaks, bikes, and other adventure paraphernalia. **Known for:** lively crowd; house-made gelato; very good craft beer. $ *Average main: $14* ⊠ *686 S. Main St., Moab* ☎ *435/259–6333* ⊕ *www.themoabbrewery.com.*

Moab Diner

$ | **AMERICAN** | **FAMILY** | For breakfast (served all day), plus lunch and dinner, this neon-lighted retro diner and ice cream shop is a favorite place of old-time Moabites who appreciate the reasonable prices and good-size portions of reliably tasty American fare, from caramelized-pecan pancakes to green-chili cheeseburgers. Friendly servers whisk quickly amid the bustling dining room, and kids love the banana splits, milk shakes, and other sweet treats for dessert. **Known for:** opens at 6 am; malted milk shakes; green chili served on or as a side with many dishes. $ *Average main: $9* ⊠ *189 S. Main St., Moab* ☎ *435/259–4006* ⊕ *www.moabdiner.com* ⊘ *Closed Sun.*

★ Moab Garage

$ | **ECLECTIC** | Set in a vintage redbrick storefront on downtown Moab's busiest block, this urbane café and ice-cream shop also offers enough hearty savory dishes throughout the day—plus a well-curated selection of beer and wine—to serve as a legit breakfast, lunch, or dinner option. Consider the Liege-style waffles with fresh berries or avocado toast early in the day, or a veggie "meatball" or fancy grilled cheese sandwich (the preparation of the latter changes daily), Cobb salad, or street tacos later in the day. **Known for:** nitro-infused ice cream; superb coffee; grilled cheese sandwiches. $ *Average main: $9* ⊠ *78 N. Main St., Moab* ☎ *435/554–8467* ⊕ *www.facebook.com/moabgarageco* ⊘ *Closed Tues.*

Ray's Tavern

$ | **AMERICAN** | In little downtown Green River, Ray's is something of a Western legend and a favorite hangout for river runners. The bar that runs the length of this 1940s restaurant reminds you this is still a tavern and a serious watering hole—but all the photos and rafting memorabilia make it comfortable for families as well. **Known for:** legendary burgers; great people-watching; homemade apple pie. $ *Average main: $10* ⊠ *25 S. Broadway, Green River* ☎ *435/564–3511* ⊕ *www.raystavern.com.*

Quesadilla Mobilla

$ | MEXICAN FUSION | Opened by a young, outdoorsy couple with a passion for southeastern Utah, this food truck permanently moored on a prominent downtown corner serves prodigious, delicious—if not necessarily authentic—quesadillas. Order at the window and dine at one of the outdoor tables in the pretty landscaped courtyard, or take your meal with you on an outdoor adventure. **Known for:** huge portions; great food for picnics or hikes; very affordable. $ *Average main: $9 ⊠ 95 N. Main St., Moab ☎ 435/260–0289 ⊕ www.quesadillamobilla.com ⊗ No dinner.*

Sabaku Sushi

$$ | JAPANESE | Sushi in the desert may seem surprising, but the chefs here know what they're doing. The fish is flown in fresh several times a week, the veggies are crisp, and the sauces are spicy—locals particularly love the spicy tuna roll with cucumber and avocado served with sriracha and eel sauce. **Known for:** fresh and artfully prepared sushi; friendly service; good sake selection. $ *Average main: $17 ⊠ 90 E. Center St., Moab ☎ 435/259–4455 ⊕ www.sabakusushi.com ⊗ Closed Mon. No lunch.*

Sunset Grill

$$$ | AMERICAN | This cliffside home of former uranium kingpin Charlie Steen offers the best views of any restaurant in town, especially at sunset—the dining room's big windows take in the Colorado River and surrounding red rocks. The traditional American fare—including filet mignon, prime rib, sautéed Idaho trout, and shrimp scampi—is generally well-prepared if not especially inventive. **Known for:** historical setting; stunning view; slow-roasted prime rib. $ *Average main: $25 ⊠ 900 N. Main St., Moab ☎ 435/259–7146 ⊕ www.moabsunsetgrill.com ⊗ Closed Sun. No lunch.*

★ Sweet Cravings Bakery + Bistro

$ | BAKERY | FAMILY | In addition to doling out some of the largest and most delicious cookies and cinnamon rolls you've ever tried, this cheerful and informal bakery café presents a terrific roster of breakfast and lunch panini, wraps, and sandwiches, and daily comfort foods like potpies and soups. Baked goods are all from scratch, gluten-free options abound, produce is local, meats are preservative-free, and coffee is 100% Rainforest Alliance and organic. **Known for:** hefty cinnamon rolls; many gluten-free options; local produce and ingredients. $ *Average main: $10 ⊠ 397 N. Main St., Moab ☎ 435/259–8983 ⊕ www.cravemoab.com ⊗ No dinner.*

Hotels

OUTSIDE THE PARK

MOAB

Accommodations Unlimited

$$$ | RENTAL | Some of the best nightly lodging values in the area are rental condominiums and homes. **Pros:** in-town units are convenient to everything; with full kitchens you can dine in. **Cons:** no free coffee and breakfast in the lobby. $ *Rooms from: $169 ⊠ 9 N. Main St., Moab ☎ 435/259–6575, 866/937–6622 ⊕ www.moabcondorentals.com ⟿ 63 condos, 15 homes.*

★ Best Western Canyonlands Inn

$$$$ | HOTEL | FAMILY | The confluence of Main and Center streets is the epicenter of Moab, and this comfortable, contemporary, impeccably clean hotel anchors the intersection, providing a perfect base for families. **Pros:** steps from many restaurants; sparkling, contemporary rooms; complimentary breakfast alfresco on outdoor patio. **Cons:** central location can feel a bit crowded at busy times; books up far in advance; pool is closed in winter (but hot tub is open year-round). $ *Rooms from: $252 ⊠ 16 S. Main St., Moab ☎ 435/259–2300, 800/649–5191 ⊕ www.bestwestern.com ⟿ 80 rooms ⦿| Breakfast.*

Best Campgrounds In and Around Arches

Campgrounds in and around Moab range from sprawling RV parks with myriad amenities to quaint, shady retreats near a babbling brook. The Devils Garden Campground in the park is a wonderful spot to call home for a few days, though it is often full and lacks an RV dump station. More than 350 campsites are operated in the vicinity by the Bureau of Land Management—their sites on the Colorado River and near the Slickrock Trail are some of the nicest (and most affordable, at just $15/night) in the area. The most centrally located campgrounds in Moab generally accommodate RVs.

In the Park

Devils Garden Campground. This campground is one of the most unusual—and gorgeous—in the West, and in the national park system, for that matter. ✉ *End of main road, 18 miles from park entrance* ☎ *435/719–2299, 877/444–6777 for reservations* 🌐 *www.recreation.gov.*

Outside the Park

Bureau of Land Management Campgrounds. Most of the 350 sites at 26 different BLM campgrounds are in the Moab area, including some stunning sites along the Colorado River (Highway 128 and Highway 279), Sand Flats Recreation Area (near the Slickrock Trail), and Canyon Flats Recreation Area (outside Needles District of Canyonlands). ☎ *435/259–2100* 🌐 *www.blm.gov/utah/moab.*

Canyonlands RV Resort and Campground. Although this camping park is in downtown Moab, the campground is astride Pack Creek and has many shade trees. ✉ *555 S. Main St., Moab* ☎ *435/259–6848 or 877/415–3991* 🌐 *www.canyonlandsrv.com.*

Moab Valley RV Resort and Campground. Near the Colorado River, this campground with an expansive view feels more like a mall than a campground with its abundant space, activities, and services. ✉ *1773 N. U.S. 191, Moab* ☎ *435/259–4469 or 877/418–8535* 🌐 *www.moabvalleyrv.com.*

Slickrock Campground. At one of Moab's older campgrounds you'll find lots of mature shade trees and all the basic amenities—plus three hot tubs where adults have priority. ✉ *1301½ N. U.S. 191, Moab* ☎ *435/259–7660 or 800/448–8873* 🌐 *www.slickrockcampground.com.*

Up the Creek Campground. Perhaps the quietest of the in-town campgrounds, Up the Creek lies under big cottonwoods on the banks of Mill Creek. ✉ *210 E. 300 S, Moab* ☎ *435/260–1888* 🌐 *www.moabupthecreek.com.*

★ **Cali Cochitta Bed & Breakfast**

$$$ | **B&B/INN** | One of the first homes built in Moab, this 19th-century Victorian in the heart of town, two blocks from Main Street shops and restaurants, has been restored to its classic style. **Pros:** the two cottages allow pets; easy walk to the hub of town; breakfast in the garden from accomplished chef. **Cons:** the least expensive rooms are a bit small; in slightly busy location; no pool. [$] *Rooms from: $175* ✉ *110 S. 200 E, Moab* ☎ *435/259–4961* 🌐 *www.moabdreaminn.com* 🛏 *6 rooms* 🍴 *Breakfast.*

Castle Creek B&B

$$ | **B&B/INN** | This attractive, contemporary five-room inn makes an appealing and reasonably priced base for visiting Arches and Canyonlands from Grand Junction, which itself offers much to see and do. **Pros:** spacious rooms; gas fireplaces and whirlpool tubs in each room; very reasonable rates. **Cons:** nearly a two-hour drive from Moab; on a busy road; no pets. [$] *Rooms from: $125* ✉ *638 Horizon Dr., Grand Junction* ☎ *970/241–9105* 🌐 *www.castlecreekbandb.com* 🛏 *5 rooms* 🍴 *Free Breakfast.*

Fairfield Inn & Suites Grand Junction Downtown

$$ | **HOTEL** | This modern, spotless, and contemporary midrange chain option is steps from the many restaurants, galleries, and shops in downtown Grand Junction. **Pros:** handy location in historic downtown Grand Junction; well-kept rooms and facilities; pet-friendly. **Cons:** nearly a two-hour drive from Moab; cookie-cutter decor; downtown location is less appealing for nature lovers. [$] *Rooms from: $117* ✉ *225 Main St., Grand Junction* ☎ *970/242–2525* 🌐 *www.marriott.com* 🛏 *70 rooms* 🍴 *Free Breakfast.*

Gonzo Inn

$$$ | **HOTEL** | This eclectic inn stands out for its design, color, art, and varnished adobe construction. **Pros:** unique, spotless, and hip; steps to Main Street; pool and hot tub. **Cons:** interior hallways can be dark; no elevator; not all rooms have a good view. [$] *Rooms from: $199* ✉ *100 W. 200 S, Moab* ☎ *435/259–2515* 🌐 *www.gonzoinn.com* 🛏 *43 rooms* 🍴 *Breakfast.*

Hampton Inn

$$$ | **HOTEL** | This property features a huge lobby with plenty of room to spread out. **Pros:** reliably clean; walking distance from downtown; hot breakfast included. **Cons:** no pets; noise insulation could be improved. [$] *Rooms from: $229* ✉ *488 N. Main St., Moab* ☎ *435/259–3030* 🌐 *hamptoninn.hilton.com* 🛏 *79 rooms* 🍴 *Breakfast.*

Moab Rustic Inn

$$ | **HOTEL** | One of the best values amid Moab's increasingly pricey lodging landscape, this homey downtown sister property to Red Cliffs Lodge is, as the name suggests, rustic, but the 35 rooms are all clean and comfortable, and provide ample room for families or friends traveling together. **Pros:** most rooms sleep at least four guests; terrific value; nice pool and barbecue area. **Cons:** simple (but comfortable) furnishings; downtown location can be a little busy at times; the two apartments with kitchens often book far ahead. [$] *Rooms from: $139* ✉ *120 E. 100 S, Moab* ☎ *435/259–6177* 🌐 *www.moabrusticinn.com* 🛏 *35 rooms* 🍴 *Free Breakfast.*

Moab Springs Ranch

$$$$ | **RENTAL** | **FAMILY** | First developed by William Granstaff in the late 19th century, this 18-acre property about 3 miles from Arches and 2 miles from downtown Moab features comfortable hotel rooms, town houses, and brand-new bungalows set by a meandering spring and decades-old sycamores, mulberries, and cottonwoods. **Pros:** scenic setting; along bike path to town; all have kitchens or kitchenettes. **Cons:** about a 30-minute walk from downtown; some U.S. 191 traffic noise; most units have two-night minimum stays. [$] *Rooms from: $235* ✉ *1266 N. Main St., Moab* ☎ *435/259–7891* 🌐 *www.moabspringsranch.com* 🛏 *23 units* 🍴 *No meals.*

★ Red Cliffs Lodge

$$$$ | **RESORT** | There are few settings in Utah that match this gorgeous, classically Western lodge where the Colorado River rolls by right outside your door and canyon walls reach for the sky in all their red glory. **Pros:** stunning setting on the river; a smorgasbord of adventures; complimentary afternoon tasting at on-site winery. **Cons:** 14 miles from town from Moab; Wi-Fi is weak

in spots; restaurant is adequate but not exceptional. $ *Rooms from: $234* ✉ *Hwy. 128, Moab* ✛ *Mile marker 14* ☎ *435/259–2002, 866/812–2002* ⊕ *www.redcliffslodge.com* ⌁ *110 units* ❍| *Breakfast.*

Moab Red Stone Inn

$$ | HOTEL | One of the best bargains in town, this timber-frame motel offers small, clean rooms at the south end of the Moab strip near restaurants and shops. **Pros:** walking distance to Moab restaurants and shops; the price is right. **Cons:** pool is at sister property across busy Main Street; no frills. $ *Rooms from: $130* ✉ *535 S. Main St., Moab* ☎ *435/259–3500, 800/772–1972* ⊕ *www.moabredstone.com* ⌁ *52 rooms* ❍| *No meals.*

River Terrace Hotel

$$ | HOTEL | The peaceful setting, on the bank of the Green River, is conducive to a good night's rest, and this nicely maintained hotel is conveniently less than 2 miles off Interstate 70, although nearly an hour's drive from Arches. **Pros:** shady riverside location (be sure to request a river-view room); very reasonable rates; on-site restaurant. **Cons:** in a sleepy town with few attractions; not within distance of downtown Green River; about 50 miles north of Moab. $ *Rooms from: $141* ✉ *1740 E. Main St., Green River* ☎ *435/564–3401, 877/564–3401* ⊕ *www.river-terrace.com* ⌁ *50 rooms* ❍| *Breakfast.*

Sorrel River Ranch Resort & Spa

$$$$ | RESORT | One of the premier luxury resorts in the Southwest, this lodge on the banks of the Colorado River, 17 miles north of Moab, is the ultimate destination for a relaxing and plush getaway, especially if you enjoy spa treatments. **Pros:** swanky spa and restaurant; luxurious rooms; red rock setting along the Colorado River. **Cons:** about 17 miles from Moab; steep rates; restaurant quality a bit uneven for the prices. $ *Rooms from: $489* ✉ *Hwy. 128, Moab* ✛ *Mile marker*

17.5 ☎ *435/259–4642, 877/317–8244* ⊕ *www.sorrelriver.com* ⌁ *59 rooms* ❍| *No meals.*

SpringHill Suites by Marriott Moab

$$$ | HOTEL | Views of the Colorado River are sure to wow guests at this all-suites hotel that shares a large pool area and hot tub with the neighboring sister property, the similarly excellent (and usually a bit more affordable) Fairfield Inn & Suites. **Pros:** attractive pool area; views of river and red rocks; extensive hot breakfast included. **Cons:** not within walking distance of downtown; expensive during busy periods; pleasant but generic decor. $ *Rooms from: $190* ✉ *1865 N. U.S. 191, Moab* ☎ *435/259–5350, 888/236–2427* ⊕ *www.marriott.com* ⌁ *99 rooms* ❍| *Breakfast.*

★ Sunflower Hill Luxury Inn

$$$ | B&B/INN | Near the heart of old downtown Moab, this thriving turn-of-the-20th-century inn is all about comfort and the guest experience. **Pros:** just blocks from town; beautifully appointed rooms; friendly hosts. **Cons:** children younger than 10 not allowed; room decor is a little frilly for some tastes; not ideal if you prefer a larger property. $ *Rooms from: $179* ✉ *185 N. 300 E, Moab* ☎ *435/259–2974, 800/662–2786* ⊕ *www.sunflowerhill.com* ⌁ *12 rooms* ❍| *Breakfast.*

Chapter 5

BADLANDS NATIONAL PARK

Updated by
Laura M. Kidder

SOUTH
DAKOTA

WELCOME TO BADLANDS NATIONAL PARK

TOP REASONS TO GO

★ **Fossils:** From the mid-1800s, the fossil-rich Badlands area has welcomed paleontologists, research institutions, and fossil hunters who have discovered the fossil remnants of numerous species from ancient days.

★ **A world of wildlife:** Badlands National Park is home to a wide array of wildlife: bison, pronghorn, deer, black-footed ferrets, prairie dogs, rabbits, coyotes, foxes, and badgers.

★ **Stars aplenty:** Due to its remote location and vastly open country, Badlands National Park contains some of the clearest and cleanest air in the country, which makes it perfect for viewing the night sky.

★ **Moonscape:** With hundreds of square miles of ragged ridgelines and sawtooth spires, Badlands National Park touts a landscape that is otherworldly.

The park is divided into three units: the North Unit and the southern Stronghold and Palmer units. The two southern units are within Pine Ridge Indian Reservation and are jointly managed by the National Park Service and the Oglala Sioux Tribe. Much of the southern park is accessible only on foot, horseback, or a high-clearance four-wheel-drive vehicle.

1 North Unit. This is the most accessible unit and includes the Badlands Wilderness Area.

2 Palmer Creek Unit. This is the most isolated section of the park—no recognized roads pass through its borders. You must obtain permission from private landowners to pass through their property (contact the White River Visitor Center). Allot one day to hike in and one day to hike out.

3 Stronghold Unit. This was used as a gunnery range for the United States Air Force and the South Dakota National Guard from 1942 until the late 1960s. Discarded remnants and unexploded ordnance make this area potentially dangerous. Do not handle fragments; report the location to a ranger instead.

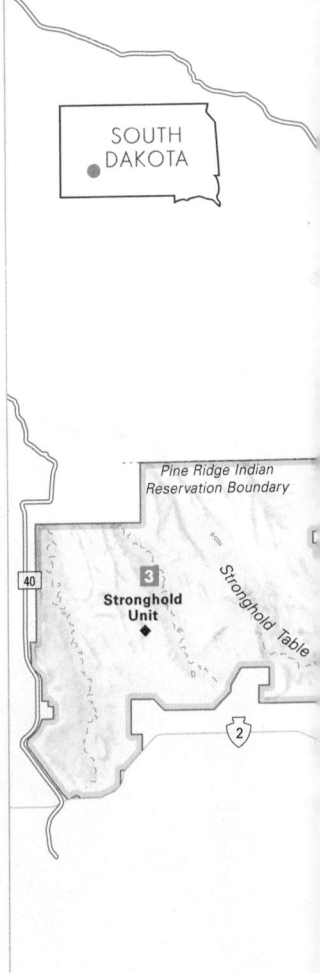

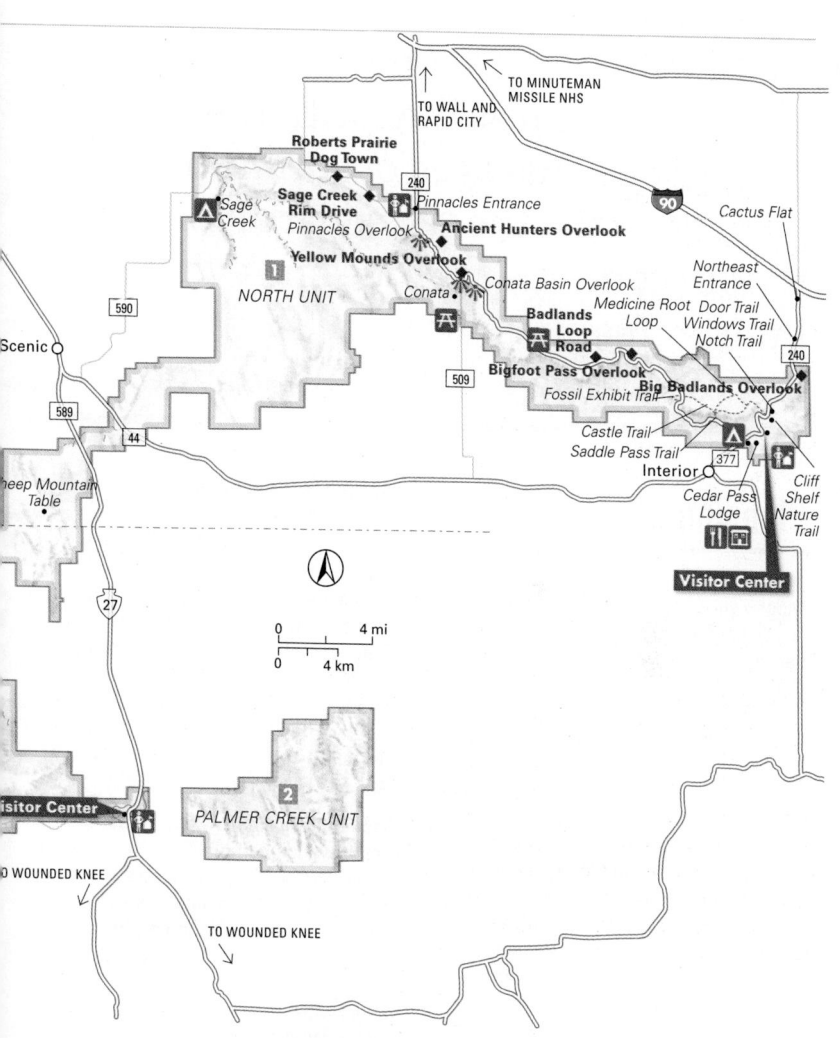

TO MINUTEMAN
MISSILE NHS

TO WALL AND
RAPID CITY

Roberts Prairie
Dog Town

Sage Creek
Rim Drive

Pinnacles Entrance

Pinnacles Overlook

Ancient Hunters Overlook

Yellow Mounds Overlook

Cactus Flat

NORTH UNIT

Conata

Conata Basin Overlook

Northeast
Entrance

Badlands
Loop
Road

Medicine Root
Loop

Door Trail
Windows Trail
Notch Trail

Scenic

Bigfoot Pass Overlook

Fossil Exhibit Trail

Big Badlands Overlook

Castle Trail

Saddle Pass Trail

Interior

Sheep Mountain
Table

Cedar Pass
Lodge

Cliff
Shelf
Nature
Trail

Visitor Center

Sage
Creek

590

589

44

27

0   4 mi

0   4 km

Visitor Center

PALMER CREEK UNIT

TO WOUNDED KNEE

TO WOUNDED KNEE

240

90

240

509

377

So stark and forbidding are the chiseled spires, ragged ridgelines, and deep ravines of South Dakota's badlands that Lieutenant Colonel George Custer described them as "hell with the fires burned out." Ravaged over time by wind and rain, the 380 square miles of terrain continue to erode and evolve. Prairie creatures thrive on the untamed territory, and animal fossils abound.

Planning

WHEN TO GO

Most visitors see the park between Memorial Day and Labor Day. The park's vast size and isolation prevent it from ever being too packed—though it is usually crowded the first week of August, when hundreds of thousands of motorcycle enthusiasts flock to the Black Hills for the annual Sturgis Motorcycle Rally. In summer, temperatures typically hover around 90°F—though it can get as hot as 116°F—and sudden mid-afternoon thunderstorms are not unusual. Storms put on a spectacular show of thunder and lightning, but it rarely rains for more than 10 or 15 minutes (the average annual rainfall is 16 inches). Autumn weather is generally sunny and warm. Snow usually appears by late October. Winter temperatures can be as low as −40°F. Early spring is often wet, cold, and unpredictable. By May the weather usually stabilizes, bringing pleasant 70°F days.

FESTIVALS AND EVENTS

Badlands Quilters Weekend Getaway

A display of the region's finest hand- and machine-made quilts, plus quilting classes by expert quilters, demonstrations, and sales are held in Wall's community center the second weekend in March. A local church hosts the Saturday night banquet. A group makes patriotic quilts that are then donated to local VA hospitals. ⊠ *Wall Community Center, 5th and Main St., Wall* ☎ *605/279–2889.*

Black Hills Stock Show and Rodeo

Watch world-champion wild-horse races, bucking horses, timed sheepdog trials, draft-horse contests, and steer wrestling during this two-week-long professional rodeo at the Rushmore Plaza Civic Center in Rapid City and Central States Fairgrounds (the festival's headquarters). Don't miss the stockman's banquet and ball. ⊠ *Rushmore Plaza Civic Center, 444 Mt. Rushmore Rd., Rapid City* ☎ *605/355–3861 festival, 605/394–4115 civic center* ⊕ *www.blackhillsstockshow. com.*

AVERAGE HIGH/LOW TEMPERATURES					
JAN.	**FEB.**	**MAR.**	**APR.**	**MAY**	**JUNE**
34/11	40/16	48/24	62/33	72/44	82/56
JULY	**AUG.**	**SEPT.**	**OCT.**	**NOV.**	**DEC.**
91/60	92/55	81/46	65/34	48/21	39/17

Red Cloud Indian Art Show

Native American paintings and sculptures by both emerging and professional artists are the focus of this 11-week-long exhibition, beginning on the first Sunday in June, at the Red Cloud Indian School in Pine Ridge. ⊠ *Drexel Hall, 100 Mission Dr., Pine Ridge* 🕾 *605/867–8257* ⊕ *www. redcloudart.show.*

PLANNING YOUR TIME
BADLANDS IN ONE DAY

With a packed lunch and plenty of water, arrive at the park via the northeast entrance (off I–90 at Exit 131) and follow Badlands Loop Road (Route/Highway 240) southwest toward the **Ben Reifel Visitor Center.** You can pick up park maps and information here, and also pay the park entrance fee (if the booth at the entrance was closed).

Next, stop at the **Big Badlands Overlook,** just south of the northeast entrance, to get a good feel for the landscape. As you head toward the visitor center, hike any one of several trails you'll pass, or if you prefer guided walks, arrive at the visitor center in time to look at the exhibits and talk with rangers before heading over to the **Fossil Exhibit Trail.** The badlands are one of the richest fossil fields in the world, and along the trail are wayside exhibits describing creatures that once lived here. After your walk, drive a couple of miles to the **Big Foot Pass Overlook,** up on the right. Picnic tables here let you enjoy a packed lunch amid grassy prairies, with the rocky badland formations all around you.

After lunch, continue driving along Badlands Loop Road, stopping at the various overlooks for views and a hike or two. Near the Conata Picnic Area, you'll find the **Big Pig Dig,** a fossil site that was excavated by paleontologists through the summer of 2008. When you reach the junction with **Sage Creek Rim Road,** turn left and follow it along the northern border of the 100-square-mile **Badlands Wilderness Area,** which is home to hundreds of bison.

Provided the road is dry, take a side trip 5 miles down Sage Creek Rim Road to **Roberts Prairie Dog Town,** inhabited by a huge colony of the chattering critters. Children will love to watch these small rodents, which bark warning calls and dive underground if you get too close to their colony. The animals built burrow networks that once covered the Great Plains, but since European settlers established ranches in the region during the late 19th century, prairie dogs have become a far rarer sight. The park is less developed the farther you travel on Sage Creek Rim Road, allowing you to admire the sheer isolation and untouched beauty of badlands country. Hold out for a glorious sunset over the shadows of the nearby Black Hills, and keep your eyes open for animals stirring about.

GETTING HERE AND AROUND
CAR TRAVEL

The North Unit of Badlands National Park is 75 miles east of Rapid City and about 140 miles northeast of Wind Cave National Park in western South Dakota. It's accessed via Exit 110 or 131 off I–90, or Route 44 east to Route 377. Few roads, paved or otherwise, pass within the park. Badlands Loop Road (Route 240) is the most traveled and the only one that intersects I–90. It's well maintained and rarely crowded. Parts of Route 44 and Route 27 run at the fringes of the badlands, connecting the visitor centers and Rapid City. Unpaved roads should be traveled with care when wet. Sheep Mountain Table Road, the only public road into the Stronghold Unit, is impassable when wet, with deep ruts—sometimes only high-clearance vehicles can get through. Off-road driving is prohibited. There's free parking at visitor centers, overlooks, and trailheads.

PARK ESSENTIALS
ACCESSIBILITY
Cedar Pass Lodge, the visitor centers, and most overlooks are wheelchair accessible. The Fossil Exhibit Trail and the Window Trail have reserved parking and are accessible by ramp, although they are quite steep in places. The Door and Cliff Shelf trails are accessible by boardwalk. Cedar Pass Campground has two fully accessible sites, plus many other sites that are sculpted and easily negotiated by wheelchair users; its office and amphitheater also are accessible. The Bigfoot Picnic Area has reserved parking, ramps, and an accessible pit toilet. Other areas of the park can be difficult or impossible to navigate by those with limited mobility.

PARK FEES AND PERMITS
The entrance fee is $12 per person or $25 per vehicle, and is good for seven days. An annual park pass is $50. A backcountry permit isn't required for hiking or camping in Badlands National Park, but it's a good idea to check in at park headquarters before setting out on a backcountry journey. Backpackers may set up camps anywhere except within a half mile of roads or trails. Open fires are prohibited.

PARK HOURS
The park is open 24/7 year-round and is in the Mountain time zone. Ranger programs are offered late May to early September. For offerings and times, check at the Ben Reifel Visitor Center

and the Cedar Pass Lodge; a schedule might also be posted at the Cedar Pass Campground kiosk.

CELL PHONE RECEPTION
Cell phone service has improved measurably over the last decade in western South Dakota, but you may not get a signal in much of the park. The closest pay phone you'll find will likely be in Wall.

EDUCATIONAL OFFERINGS
RANGER PROGRAMS
Evening Program and Night Sky Viewing
TOUR—SIGHT | Watch a 45-minute presentation on the wildlife, natural history, paleontology, or another aspect of the badlands. Shows typically begin around 9 pm; confirm time and topics at the visitor center or park website. Stick around afterward for the Night Sky Viewing, a star-gazing interpretive program complete with telescopes. ⊠ *Cedar Pass Campground amphitheater, 20681 Hwy. 240* ⊕ *www.nps.gov/badl.*

Fossil Talk
TOUR—SIGHT | What were the badlands like many years ago? This 20-minute talk about protected fossil exhibits will inspire and answer all your questions. It's held at 10:30 and 1:30 daily at the Fossil Exhibit Trail. Check at the visitor center or on the park website for details. ⊠ *Badlands National Park ⊹ Fossil Exhibit Trail, Badlands Loop Rd., 5 miles northwest of the Ben Reifel Visitor Center* ⊕ *www. nps.gov/badl.*

Geology Walk
TOUR—SIGHT | Learn the geologic story of the White River badlands in a 45-minute walk, generally departing from the Door Trailhead daily at 8:30 am (check at the visitor center or on the park website). The terrain can be rough in places, so be sure to wear hiking boots or sneakers. A hat is a good idea, too. ⊠ *Badlands National Park ⊹ Door and Window trails parking area, Badlands Loop Rd., 2 miles south of the northeast entrance* ⊕ *www.nps. gov/badl.*

Junior Ranger Program

TOUR—SIGHT | FAMILY | Children ages 7–12 can join in this daily, 30-minute adventure, typically a short hike, game, or other hands-on activity focused on badlands wildlife, geology, or fossils. Parents are welcome. Meet at the visitor center at 11:30, and wear closed-toe shoes. ⊠ *Ben Reifel Visitor Center, 25216 Hwy. 240* ☎ *605/433–5361* ⊕ *www.nps.gov/badl.*

RESTAURANTS

Dining on the prairies of South Dakota has always been a casual and family-oriented experience, and in that sense little has changed in the past century. Even the fare, which consists largely of steak and potatoes, has stayed consistent (in fact, in some towns, "vegetarian" can be a dirty word). But for its lack of comparative sophistication, the grub in the restaurants surrounding Badlands National Park is typically very good. You'll probably never have a better steak—beef or buffalo—outside this area. You should also try cuisine influenced by Native American cooking. In the park itself there's only one restaurant. The food is quite good, but don't hesitate to explore other options farther afield. You'll find the most choices in Wall.

HOTELS

Badlands National Park is often visited by families on a vacation to see the American West, but few opt to stay overnight here, especially when there's a profusion of accommodations in the Black Hills, situated a mere 50 miles east. As a result, there are few lodging options in and around the park, and if you're determined to bed down within park boundaries, you have only one choice: Cedar Pass Lodge. Though rustic, it's comfortable, inexpensive, and has eco-friendly cabins.

The rustic-but-comfy formula is repeated by the area's few motels, hotels, and inns. Most are chain hotels in Wall, grouped around the interstate. Whether you stay inside or outside the park, you shouldn't have to worry about making reservations very far in advance, except during the first full week of August, when the entire region is inundated with more than half a million motorcyclists for the annual Sturgis Motorcycle Rally. Rooms for miles around book up more than a year in advance.

Hotel reviews have been shortened. For full information, visit Fodors.com.

What It Costs			
$	**$$**	**$$$**	**$$$$**
RESTAURANTS			
under $13	$13–$20	$21–$30	over $30
HOTELS			
under $101	$101–$150	$151–$200	over $200

TOURS

Affordable Adventures Badlands and Wall Drug Tour

TOUR—SIGHT | Take a seven-hour narrated tour through the park and surrounding badlands, with a stop at the famous Wall Drug Store for lunch (not included in the fee). Tours can easily be customized and are available year-round; there's hotel pick up in Rapid City. ⊠ *5542 Meteor St., Rapid City* ☎ *605/342–7691, 888/888–8249* ⊕ *www.affordableadventuresbh.com* ☞ *From $135.*

Fort Hays and Mount Rushmore Tours

TOUR—SIGHT | FAMILY | This nine-hour tour amid the Black Hills begins at Fort Hays on the *Dances with Wolves* film set and visits Mount Rushmore, Custer State Park, and the Crazy Horse Memorial. Guests are responsible for their own lunches at the State Game Lodge; a pre-trip breakfast and a post-trip cowboy dinner show are add-on options. ⊠ *2255 Fort Hayes Dr., Rapid City* ☎ *605/343–3113* ⊕ *www.mountrushmoretours.com* ☞ *From $80.*

VISITOR INFORMATION

PARK CONTACT INFORMATION Badlands
National Park ☎ *605/433–5361* ⊕ *www.nps.gov/badl.*

VISITOR CENTERS
Ben Reifel Visitor Center

INFO CENTER | Open year-round, the park's main information hub has brochures, maps, and information on ranger programs. Check out exhibits on geology and wildlife, and watch paleontologists at work in the Fossil Prep Lab (June–September). View the film, *Land of Stone and Light,* in the 95-seat theater, and shop in the Badlands Natural History Association Bookstore. The facility is named for a Sioux activist and the first Lakota to serve in Congress. Born on the nearby Rosebud Indian Reservation, Ben Reifel also served in the Army during World War II. ⊠ *Badlands National Park* ✛ *Badlands Loop Rd., near Hwy. 377 junction, 8 miles from northeast entrance* ☎ *605/433–5361.*

White River Visitor Center

INFO CENTER | Open in summer, this small center serves almost exclusively serious hikers and campers venturing into the Stronghold or Palmer unit. If that's you, stop here for maps and details about road and trail conditions. The center is on the Pine Ridge Indian Reservation. While you're here you can see fossils and Lakota artifacts, and learn about Sioux culture. ⊠ *Badlands National Park* ✛ *25 miles south of Hwy. 44 via Hwy. 27* ☎ *605/455–2878* ⊕ *www.nps.gov/badl.*

◉ Sights

SCENIC DRIVES

For the average visitor, a casual drive is the essential means by which to see Badlands National Park. To do the scenery justice, drive slowly, and don't hesitate to get out and explore on foot when the occasion calls for it.

★ Badlands Loop Road

SCENIC DRIVE | The simplest drive is on two-lane Badlands Loop Road (Route/Highway 240). The drive circles from exit 110 off I–90 through the park and back to the interstate at Exit 131. Start from either end and make your way around to the various overlooks along the way. Pinnacles and Yellow Mounds overlooks are outstanding places to examine the sandy pink- and brown-toned ridges and spires distinctive to the badlands. At a certain point the landscape flattens out slightly to the north, revealing spectacular views of mixed-grass prairies. The Cedar Pass area of the drive has some of the park's best trails. ⊠ *I–90, Exit 110* ⊕ *www.nps.gov/badl.*

Sage Creek Rim Drive

SCENIC DRIVE | This gravel route near the Pinnacles entrance follows the road less traveled and covers rougher terrain than Badlands Loop Road. Sage Creek Rim Road is completely negotiable by most vehicles, but should be avoided during a thunderstorm when the sudden rush of water may cause flooding. It might also close temporarily after snowstorms. The road follows the northern border of the park for 13 miles, passing at least three overlooks. Only a third of this area is composed of the eroded rocky spires and sharp ridges distinctive to the park. A vast mixed-grass prairie covers the rest. Keep an eye out for free-roaming bison. ⊠ *Badlands National Park* ⊕ *www.nps.gov/badl.*

HISTORIC SITES
Ancient Hunters Overlook

VIEWPOINT | Perched above a dense fossil bed, this overhang, adjacent to the Pinnacles overlook, is where prehistoric bison hunters drove herds of buffalo over the edge. ⊠ *Badlands National Park* ✛ *22 miles northwest of the Ben Reifel Visitor Center* ⊕ *www.nps.gov/badl.*

Big Pig Dig

ARCHAEOLOGICAL SITE | Until 2008, paleontologists dug for fossils at this site near

Peter Norbeck's Park

Much of the credit for setting aside South Dakota's badlands as public lands is owed to Peter Norbeck, a powerful politician who was also largely responsible for establishing nearby Custer State Park and obtaining federal funding for Mount Rushmore National Memorial. Convinced that the state's badlands formations were more distinctive than those in other parts of the American West, Norbeck began lobbying for a new national park almost immediately after he was elected a U.S. senator in 1920. Political maneuvering tied up the proposal in Congress for nearly 10 years, and land issues delayed the measure for another decade. Finally, on March 4, 1939, the region was declared Badlands National Monument by President Calvin Coolidge. It was re-designated as a national park in 1978.

the Conata Picnic Area. It was named for a large fossil originally thought to be of a prehistoric pig (it actually turned out to be a small, hornless rhinoceros). Wayside signs and exhibits, including a mural, provide context on the area and its fossils. ⊠ *Badlands National Park* ✛ *17 miles northwest of the Ben Reifel Visitor Center.*

Stronghold Unit

HISTORIC SITE | With few paved roads and no campgrounds, the park's southwest section is difficult to access without a four-wheel-drive vehicle. If you're willing to trek, its isolation provides a rare opportunity to explore badlands rock formations and prairies completely undisturbed. From 1942 to 1968, the U.S. Air Force and South Dakota National Guard used much of the area as a gunnery range. Hundreds of fossils were destroyed by bomber pilots, who frequently targeted the large fossil remains of an elephant-size titanothere (an extinct relative of the rhinoceros). Beware of unexploded bombs, shells, rockets, and other hazardous materials. Steer clear of it and find another route.

Within the Stronghold Unit, the **Stronghold Table,** a 3-mile-long plateau, can be reached only by crossing a narrow land bridge just wide enough to let a wagon pass. It was here, just before the Massacre at Wounded Knee in 1890, that some 600 Sioux gathered to perform one of the last known Ghost Dances, a ritual in which the Sioux wore white shirts that they believed would protect them from bullets. ⊠ *Badlands National Park* ✛ *North and west of White River Visitor Center; entrance off Hwy. 27* ⊕ *www. nps.gov/badl.*

SCENIC STOPS
★ Badlands Wilderness Area

NATURE PRESERVE | Covering about a quarter of the park, this 100-square-mile area is part of the country's largest prairie wilderness. About two-thirds of the Sage Creek region is mixed-grass prairie, making it the ideal grazing grounds for bison, pronghorn, and many of the park's other native animals. The Hay Butte Overlook (2 miles northwest on Sage Creek Rim Road) and the Pinnacles Overlook (1 mile south of the Pinnacles entrance) are the best places to get an overview of the wilderness area. Feel free to park at an overlook and hike your own route into the untamed, unmarked prairie. ⊠ *Badlands National Park* ✛ *25 miles northwest of Ben Reifel Visitor Center* ⊕ *www.nps. gov/badl.*

Big Badlands Overlook

VIEWPOINT | From this spot just south of the park's northeast entrance, the vast majority of the park's 1 million annual visitors get their first views of the White River Badlands. ⊠ *Badlands National Park* ✛ *5 miles northeast of the Ben Reifel Visitor Center.*

Big Foot Pass Overlook

VIEWPOINT | See where Sioux chief Big Foot and his band traveled through the badlands on their way to the battle at Wounded Knee, December 29, 1890. ⊠ *Badlands National Park* ✛ *7 miles northwest of the Ben Reifel Visitor Center.*

Roberts Prairie Dog Town

NATURE PRESERVE | **FAMILY** | Once a homestead, the site today contains one of the country's largest (if not the largest) colonies of black-tailed prairie dogs. ⊠ *Sage Creek Rim Rd.* ✛ *5 miles west of Badlands Loop Rd.*

Yellow Mounds Overlook

VIEWPOINT | Contrasting sharply with the whites, grays, and browns of the badlands pinnacles, the mounds viewed from here greet you with soft yet vivid yellows, reds, and purples. ⊠ *Badlands National Park* ✛ *16 miles northwest of Ben Reifel Visitor Center.*

 Activities

Pure, unspoiled, empty space is the greatest asset of Badlands National Park, and it can only be experienced to its highest degree if you're on foot. Spring and autumn are the best times of the year to do wilderness exploring, because the brutal extremes of summer and winter can—and do—kill. In fact, the two biggest enemies to hikers and bicyclists in the badlands are heat and lightning.

Before you venture out, make sure you have at least one gallon of water per person per day, and be prepared to take shelter from freak thunderstorms, which often strike in the late afternoon with little warning.

AIR TOURS

Black Hills Balloons

TOUR—SPORTS | Based in Custer, Black Hills Balloons has more than 30 years of experience providing bird's-eye views of some of the Black Hills' most picturesque locations. Tours meet up at Custer's Buffalo Ridge Theater. Reservations are essential. ⊠ *Buffalo Ridge Theater, 370 W. Mount Rushmore Rd., Custer* ☎ *605/673–2520* ⊕ *www.blackhillsballoons.com* ⊑ *From $295.*

BICYCLING

Bicycles are permitted only on designated roads, which may be paved or unpaved. They are prohibited from closed roads, trails, and the backcountry. Flat-resistant tires are recommended.

Sheep Mountain Table Road

BICYCLING | This 7-mile dirt road in the Stronghold Unit is ideal for mountain biking, but should be attempted only when dry. The terrain is level for the first 3 miles, then it climbs and levels out again. At the top you can take in great views of the area. ⊠ *Badlands National Park* ✛ *About 14 miles north of White River Visitor Center.*

Two Wheeler Dealer Cycle and Fitness

BICYCLING | Family-owned and-operated Two Wheeler Dealer Cycle and Fitness, based in Spearfish, stocks hundreds of bikes for sale and plenty of them to rent. The service is exceptional. Get trail and route information for Badlands National Park and the Black Hills at the counter. ⊠ *305 Main St., Spearfish* ☎ *605/642– 7545* ⊕ *www.twowheelerdealer.com.*

BIRD-WATCHING

Especially around sunset, get set to watch the badlands come to life. More than 215 bird species have been

Plants and Wildlife in Badlands

The park's sharply defined cliffs, canyons, and mesas are near-deserts with little plant growth. Most of the park, however, is made up of mixed-grass prairies, where more than 460 species of hardy grasses and wildflowers flourish in the warmer months. Prairie coneflower, yellow plains prickly pear, pale-green yucca, buffalo grass, and sideoats grama are just a few of the plants on the badlands plateau. Trees and shrubs are rare and usually confined to dry creek beds. The most common trees are Rocky Mountain junipers and plains cottonwoods.

It's common to see pronghorn antelope and mule deer dart across the flat plateaus, bison grazing on the buttes, prairie dogs and sharp-tailed grouse, and, soaring above, golden eagles, turkey vultures, and hawks. Also present are coyotes, swift foxes, jackrabbits, bats, gophers, porcupines, skunks, bobcats, horned lizards, bighorn sheep, and prairie rattlers. The latter are the only venomous reptiles in the park—watch for them near rocky outcroppings and in prairie-dog towns. Backcountry hikers might consider heavy boots and long pants reinforced with leather or canvas. Although rarely seen, weasels, mountain lions, and the endangered black-footed ferret roam the park.

recorded in the area, including herons, pelicans, cormorants, egrets, swans, geese, hawks, golden and bald eagles, falcons, vultures, cranes, doves, and cuckoos. Established roads and trails are the best places from which to watch for nesting species. The Cliff Shelf Nature Trail and the Castle Trail, which both traverse areas with surprisingly thick vegetation, are especially good locations. You may even catch sight of a rare burrowing owl at the Roberts Prairie Dog Town. Be sure to bring along a pair of binoculars.

HIKING

The isolation and otherworldliness of the badlands are best appreciated with a walk through them. Take time to examine the dusty rock beneath your feet, and be on the lookout for fossils and animals. Fossil Exhibit Trail and Cliff Shelf Nature Trail are must-dos, but even these popular trails tend to be primitive. You'll find bathrooms at Fossil Exhibit Trail. Both trails feature boardwalks, so you won't be shuffling through dirt and gravel.

Because the weather here can be so variable, rangers suggest that you be prepared for anything. Wear sunglasses, a hat, and long pants, and have rain gear available. It's illegal to interfere with park resources, which includes everything from rocks and fossils to plants and artifacts. Stay at least 100 yards away from wildlife. Due to the dry climate, open fires are never allowed. Tell friends, relatives, and the park rangers if you're going to embark on a multiday expedition. Assume that your cell phone, if you've brought one, won't get a signal in the park. But most important of all, be sure to bring your own water. Sources of water in the park are few and far between, and none of them are drinkable. All water in the park is contaminated by minerals and sediment, and park authorities warn that it's untreatable. If you're backpacking into the wilderness, bring at least a gallon of water per person per day. For day hikes, rangers suggest you drink at least a quart per person per hour.

Badlands Wilderness Area

HIKING/WALKING | If you want a challenge, you might consider trekking this 100-square-mile parcel of grassy steppes and rocky canyons east of the highway and south of Sage Creek Rim Road, near the Pinnacles entrance. There are no services here and very few visitors, even in summer. Before venturing out, check in with park staff at one of the visitor centers. *Difficult.* ✉ *Badlands National Park* ✢ *Trailhead: 25 miles northwest of Ben Reifel Visitor Center, off Hwy. 240.*

Castle Trail

HIKING/WALKING | The park's longest hike runs 5 miles one-way between the Fossil Exhibit trailhead on Badlands Loop Road and the parking area for the Door and Windows trails. Although the Castle Trail is fairly level, allow at least three hours to cover the entire 10 miles out and back. If you choose to follow the Medicine Root Loop, which detours off the Castle Trail, you'll add ½ mile to the trek. Experienced hikers will do this one more quickly. *Moderate.* ✉ *Badlands National Park* ✢ *Trailhead: 5 miles north of Ben Reifel Visitor Center, off Hwy. 240.*

Cliff Shelf Nature Trail

HIKING/WALKING | This ½-mile loop winds through a wooded prairie oasis in the middle of dry, rocky ridges and climbs 200 feet to a peak above White River Valley for an incomparable view. Look for chipmunks, squirrels, and red-winged blackbirds in the wet wood, and eagles, hawks, and vultures at hilltop. Even casual hikers can complete this trail in far less than an hour, but if you want to observe the true diversity of wildlife present here, stay longer. *Moderate.* ✉ *Badlands National Park* ✢ *Trailhead: 1 mile east of Ben Reifel Visitor Center, off Hwy. 240.*

Door Trail

HIKING/WALKING | The ¾-mile round-trip trail leads through a natural opening, or door, in a badlands rock wall. The eerie sandstone formations and passageways beckon, but it's recommended that you stay on the trail. The first 100 yards of the trail are on a boardwalk. Even a patient and observant hiker will take only an hour here. *Easy.* ✉ *Badlands National Park* ✢ *Trailhead: 2 miles east of Ben Reifel Visitor Center, off Hwy. 240.*

★ Fossil Exhibit Trail

HIKING/WALKING | **FAMILY** | The trail, in place since 1964, has fossil replicas of early mammals displayed at wayside exhibits along its ¼-mile length, which is completely wheelchair accessible. Give yourself at least an hour to fully enjoy this popular hike. *Easy.* ✉ *Badlands National Park* ✢ *Trailhead: 5 miles northwest of Ben Reifel Visitor Center, off Hwy. 240.*

Notch Trail

HIKING/WALKING | One of the park's more interesting hikes, this 1½-mile round-trip trail takes you over moderately difficult terrain and up a ladder. Winds at the notch can be fierce, but it's worth lingering for the view of the White River Valley and the Pine Ridge Indian Reservation. If you take a couple of breaks and enjoy the views, you'll probably spend a little more than an hour on this hike. *Moderate–Difficult.* ✉ *Badlands National Park* ✢ *Trailhead: 2 miles north of Ben Reifel Visitor Center, off Hwy. 240.*

Saddle Pass Trail

HIKING/WALKING | This route, which connects with Castle Trail and Medicine Root Loop, is a steep, ¼-mile round-trip route up and down the side of "The Wall," an impressive rock formation. Plan on spending about an hour on this climb. *Difficult.* ✉ *Badlands National Park* ✢ *Trailhead: 2 miles west of Ben Reifel Visitor Center, off Hwy. 240* ⊕ *www.nps. gov/badl.*

Window Trail

HIKING/WALKING | This ¼-mile round-trip trail ends at a natural hole, or window, in a rock wall. You'll see more of the distinctive badlands pinnacles and spires. *Easy.* ✉ *Badlands National Park* ✢ *Trailhead: 2* *miles north of Ben Reifel Visitor Center, off Hwy. 240.*

HORSEBACK RIDING

The park has one of the largest and most beautiful territories in the state in which to ride a horse. Riding is allowed in most of the park except for some marked trails, roads, and developed areas. The mixed-grass prairie of the Badlands Wilderness Area is especially popular with riders. However, note that the weather in the Badlands Wilderness Area can be unpredictable. Only experienced riders or people accompanied by experienced riders should venture far from more developed areas.

There are several restrictions and regulations that you must be aware of if you plan to ride your own horse. Potable water for visitors and animals is a rarity. Riders must bring enough water for themselves and their stock. Only certified weed-free hay is approved in the park. Horses are not allowed to run free within the borders of the park.

📩 Shopping

A free park newspaper, *Badlands Visitor Guide,* is available at the park's visitor centers and by email request at Badl_Information@nps.gov. Several park brochures on such topics as geology, photography, and horseback riding in the park are free at the visitor centers and from ⊕ *www.nps.gov/badl.*

Badlands Natural History Association Bookstore

MUSEUM | The Badlands Natural History Association Bookstore sells a full line of printed materials related to the region, from books on geology and paleontology to postcards and posters. ⊠ *Ben Reifel Visitor Center, Badlands Loop Rd.* ✛ *Near Hwy. 377 junction, 8 miles from northeast entrance* ☎ *605/433–5489* ⊕ *www. badlandsnha.org.*

Gear Up!

Scheels All Sport In the Rushmore Crossing Mall, off I–90 at East-North Street or Lacrosse Street exit, the enormous Scheels All Sport carries a wide selection of all-weather hiking gear, footwear, and clothes as well as binoculars suitable for bird-watchers. ⊠ *1225 Eglin St., Rapid City* ☎ *605/342–9033* ⊕ *www.scheels.com.*

Cedar Pass Gift Store

GIFTS/SOUVENIRS | This shop at the Cedar Pass Lodge carries a small selection of handmade gifts and Native American crafts. ⊠ *1 Cedar St.* ☎ *605/433–5460* ⊗ *Closed Nov.–mid-Apr.*

Nearby Towns

Badlands National Park is off I–90 with two separate entrances. Badlands can be a one- or two-day stop for visitors who are traveling through the area or a place of frequent visits to locals. Located 50 miles east of the edge of the Black Hills (and Rapid City, the largest community on this side of the state), Badlands allows travelers a unique stop in a highly dense area of national parks, monuments, and memorials. Its close proximity to national treasures such as Mount Rushmore National Memorial, Wind Cave National Park, Jewel Cave National Monument, Devils Tower National Monument, and Custer State Park allows visitors to take in a wealth of sightseeing excursions in a relatively small area. The Black Hills provide a wonderful backdrop for the dry canyon and dusty buttes of the badlands.

Built against a steep ridge of badland rock, **Wall** was founded in 1907 as a railroad station, and is among the closest towns to Badlands National Park, 8 miles from the Pinnacles entrance to the North

Wounded Knee Massacre

In late December 1890 the men of the Seventh Cavalry, armed with a federal mandate (and some light artillery), intercepted a group of 350 Lakota in southwest South Dakota with the intention of disarming them and marching them to Nebraska, where they would be forced onto scattered reservations. The disarming process was remarkably peaceful—that is, until soldiers approached a warrior named Black Coyote. According to several accounts, Black Coyote wouldn't relinquish his weapon without compensation, since he had bought the firearm himself. Somehow, a weapon was discharged, and at least one soldier ordered the troops to open fire. Fearful of an impending attack, the cavalry did so, even bringing their artillery to bear on the Lakota camp. Warriors scrambled to retrieve their seized rifles to re-arm themselves. By the time the smoke had cleared, about 150 Lakota and 25 U.S. soldiers lay dead. Although most of the remaining Lakota managed to escape, the majority perished in the elements, the victims of a sudden blizzard. When a burial party returned to the site after the storm, they found the frozen and contorted bodies of nearly 300 Lakota, mostly women and children, which they placed in a common grave.

In the following days, newspapers and government officials referred to the confrontation as a "battle," but it was none other than wholesale slaughter. Within a year, the army had awarded 23 Medals of Honor to members of the Seventh Cavalry for "valor" shown in the carnage (modern-day activists are seeking to have them rescinded). Even so, there was no cover-up of this affair. The American people were incensed, and from this point on, any government-led extermination of the Indian people ended. The blood in the snow at Wounded Knee melted in the spring of 1891, and as it thawed and ran across the prairie in a thousand rivulets, it carried with it a way of life for the American Indian.

In 1890, the men of the Seventh Cavalry opened fire on a group of 350 Lakota in southwest South Dakota. A few managed to escape, but nearly 300 Lakota, mostly women and children, were buried in a common grave. Although the army awarded 23 Medals of Honor to members of the Seventh Cavalry, the American people were incensed. From this point on, any government-led extermination of Native Americans ended.

Unit. Wall is home to about 850 residents and the world-famous Wall Drug Store, best known for its fabled jackalopes and free ice water.

Pine Ridge, about 35 miles south of the Stronghold Unit, is on the cusp of Pine Ridge Indian Reservation. The town was established in 1877 as an Indian agency for Chief Red Cloud and his band of

followers. With 2,800 square miles, the reservation, home, and headquarters of the Oglala Sioux, is second in size only to Arizona's Navajo Reservation. **Rapid City,** in the eastern buttes of the Black Hills, is South Dakota's second-largest city and a good base from which to explore the treasures of the state's southwestern corner, including the neighboring Black Hills National Forest, the badlands 75 miles to the east, and Mount Rushmore and Wind Cave National Park, 25 miles and 140 miles to the southwest respectively.

VISITOR INFORMATION
Oglala Sioux Tribe (Pine Ridge)
The Pine Ridge Reservation is home to more than 40,000 Oglala Lakota, members of a major Sioux division known as the Western or Teton Sioux, who live in nine tribal districts on 1.4 million acres of land. They are led by a Tribal Council President who is advised by an executive committee and a tribal council. ✉ *Pine Ridge* ☎ *605/867–5821* ⊕ *www.oglala-lakotanation.info.*

Rapid City Convention and Visitors Bureau
✉ *512 Main St., Suite 240, Rapid City* ☎ *605/718–8484, 800/487–3223* ⊕ *www.visitrapidcity.com.*

Wall–Badlands Area Chamber of Commerce
✉ *501 Main St., Wall* ☎ *605/279–2665, 888/852–9255* ⊕ *www.wall-badlands.com.*

 Sights

Main Street Square
PLAZA | FAMILY | This attractive plaza in downtown Rapid City is a focal point for a wide array of special events throughout the year, including movies under the stars, food festivals, a farmers' market, musical performances, and ice skating. At various times of the year, the square features interactive fountains, gardens, a large oval lawn, and a fire pit. ✉ *Destination Rapid City, 526 Main St., Suite 980, Rapid City* ☎ *605/716–7979* ⊕ *www.mainstreetsquarerc.com.*

★ Mount Rushmore National Memorial
MEMORIAL | One of the nation's most iconic attractions, the giant likenesses of Washington, Jefferson, Lincoln, and Theodore Roosevelt, lies just 65 miles west of Badlands. An excellent interpretive center, self-guided audio tours, a trail network, and a Youth Exploration Center

make a visit even more memorable. You can also learn about the creation of the monument in the refurbished Sculptor's Studio. The site is illuminated at night year-round; in warmer months, a patriotic lighting ceremony is held nightly. ✉ *13000 Rte. 244, Keystone* ☎ *605/574–2523* ⊕ *www.nps.gov/moru* 🚗 *Parking $12.*

Outdoor Campus West
INFO CENTER | A project of South Dakota Game, Fish, and Parks, this attractive education center opened in 2011. It couples a hands-on museum featuring native habitats—including a freshwater aquarium—and wildlife with a 32-acre outdoor campus offering outdoor activity classes year-round. Nearby are 1½ miles of hiking trails. ✉ *4130 Adventure Trail, Rapid City* ☎ *605/394–2310* ⊕ *gfp.sd.gov/toc-west* ☉ *Closed Sun. Nov.–Apr.*

Red Cloud Indian School Heritage Art Museum
MUSEUM | Changing exhibits highlight Native American culture and art; the permanent collection has 10,000 contemporary and historical pieces. The gift shop sells locally made Lakota crafts and fine or decorative works of art. ✉ *100 Mission Dr., Pine Ridge* ☎ *605/867–8257* ⊕ *www.redcloudschool.org/museum* 🚗 *Free.*

★ Wall Drug Store
STORE/MALL | FAMILY | This South Dakota original got its start in 1931 by offering free ice water to road-weary travelers. Today its four dining rooms seat 530 visitors at a time. A life-size mechanical Cowboy Orchestra and Chuckwagon Quartet greet you inside, and, in the back, you'll find an animated T. rex, a replica of Mount Rushmore, and a panning and mining experience. The attached Western Mall has 14 shops selling all kinds of keepsakes from cowboy hats, boots, and Black Hills gold jewelry to T-shirts and fudge. Just don't skip the donuts. ✉ *510 Main St., Wall* ☎ *605/279–2175* ⊕ *www.walldrug.com* 🚗 *Free.*

Wounded Knee Historical Site
NATIVE SITE | A stone obelisk commemorates the site of the 1890 massacre at Wounded Knee, the last major conflict between the U.S. military and Native Americans. Only a handful of visitors make pilgrimages to the remote site today, which is simple and largely unchanged from its 1890 appearance. ✉ *U.S. 18, Pine Ridge* ✢ *12 miles northwest of Pine Ridge* 🎟 *Free.*

Wounded Knee: The Museum
MUSEUM | This modern facility interprets the history of the December 29, 1890, Wounded Knee Massacre through interactive exhibits with historical photos and documents. Although a tour of the museum is an excellent companion to a visit to the actual site of the massacre, many visitors choose to stop at this convenient location off I–90 in lieu of a stop at the isolated battleground 80 miles to the south. ✉ *207 10th Ave., Wall* ☎ *605/279–2573* 🌐 *www.woundedkneemuseum.org* 🎟 *$6* 🕓 *Closed Mon. and early Oct.–late May.*

SHOPPING

Cedar Pass Lodge Gift Store
GIFTS/SOUVENIRS | The shop's extensive collection includes locally made bead and quillwork, Black Hills gold, and silver and turquoise jewelry, as well as postcards, pottery, books, and films. Drinks and snack are available. ✉ *20681 Hwy. 240, Interior* ☎ *605/433–5460* 🌐 *www.cedarpasslodge.com* 🕓 *Closed Nov.–mid-Apr.*

🍴 Restaurants

IN THE PARK

Cedar Pass Lodge Restaurant
$ | **AMERICAN** | **FAMILY** | Cool off within dark, knotty-pine walls under an exposed-beam ceiling, and enjoy a hearty meal of steak or tacos and fry bread. **Known for:** locally sourced fish, meat, and produce; fresh fry bread; decent selection of vegetarian and gluten-free dishes. [$] *Average main: $9* ✉ *20681 Hwy. 240, Interior* ☎ *605/433–5460* 🌐 *www.cedarpasslodge.com* 🕓 *Closed Nov.–mid-Apr.*

PICNIC AREAS

Bigfoot Pass Overlook
RESTAURANT—SIGHT | There is only a handful of tables here and no water, but the incredible view makes it a lovely spot to have lunch. ✉ *Badlands Loop Rd.* ✢ *7 miles northwest of Ben Reifel Visitor Center.*

Conata Picnic Area
RESTAURANT—SIGHT | A half-dozen or so covered picnic tables are scattered over this area, which rests against a badlands wall ½ mile south of Badlands Loop Road. There's no potable water, but there are bathroom facilities and you can enjoy your lunch in peaceful isolation at the threshold of the Badlands Wilderness Area. The Conata Basin area is to the east, and Sage Creek area is to the west. ✉ *Conata Rd.* ✢ *15 miles northwest of Ben Reifel Visitor Center* 🌐 *www.nps.gov/badl.*

White River Visitor Center
RESTAURANT—SIGHT | Directly behind this visitor center are four covered tables, where you can picnic simply and stay protected from the wind. There are also bathroom facilities here. ✉ *Rte. 27* ✢ *25 miles south of Rte. 44.*

OUTSIDE THE PARK

WALL

Cactus Family Restaurant and Lounge
$ | **AMERICAN** | Delicious hotcakes and pies await you at this restaurant in downtown Wall. In summer you'll find a buffet large enough to satisfy any appetite. **Known for:** downhome flavor; good value for money; central location. [$] *Average main: $10* ✉ *519 Main St., Wall* ☎ *605/279–2561.*

Western Art Gallery Restaurant
$ | **AMERICAN** | More than 200 original oil paintings, all with a Western theme, line the dining room of this eatery in the Wall Drug building. For a tasty meal, try a hot

Best Campgrounds in Badlands

Pitching a tent and sleeping under the stars is one of the greatest ways to fully experience the sheer isolation and unadulterated empty spaces of Badlands National Park. You'll find two relatively easy-access campgrounds within park boundaries, but only one has any sort of amenities. The second is little more than a flat patch of ground with some signs. Unless you desperately need a flush toilet to have an enjoyable camping experience, you're just as well off hiking into the wilderness and choosing your own campsite. The additional isolation will be well worth the extra effort. You can set up camp anywhere that's at least a half mile from a road or trail and is not visible from any road or trail.

Cedar Pass Campground. With tent sites and 20 RV sites as well as coin-operated showers, this is the most developed campground in the park, and it's near the Ben Reifel Visitor Center, Cedar Pass Lodge, and a half-dozen hiking trails. ✉ *Rte. 377, ¼ mile south of Badlands Loop Rd.* ☎ *605/433–5361* 🌐 *www.cedarpasslodge.com.*

Sage Creek Primitive Campground. If you want to get away from it all, this lovely, isolated spot surrounded by nothing but fields and crickets is the right camp for you. ✉ *Sage Creek Rim Rd., 25 miles west of Badlands Loop Rd.* ☎ *No phone.*

beef sandwich or a buffalo burger. **Known for:** road-trip classic; Western memorabilia; friendly service. $ *Average main: $12* ✉ *510 Main St., Wall* ☎ *605/279–2175* 🌐 *www.walldrug.com* ⏲ *No dinner.*

Hotels

IN THE PARK

Cedar Pass Lodge

$$$ | **HOTEL** | Besides impressive views of the badlands, these cabins include modern touches like flat-screen TVs and Wi-Fi connections. **Pros:** new cabins; the best stargazing in South Dakota. **Cons:** remote location; long drive to other restaurants. $ *Rooms from: $176* ✉ *20681 Hwy. 240, Interior* ☎ *605/433–5460, 877/386–4383* 🌐 *www.cedarpasslodge.com* ⏲ *Closed Nov.–mid-Apr.* 🛏 *26 cabins* 🍴 *No meals.*

OUTSIDE THE PARK

INTERIOR

Badlands Budget Host Motel

$ | **HOTEL** | Every room in this motel has views of the nearby Buffalo Gap National Grasslands. **Pros:** clean and comfortable; close to the national park. **Cons:** standard rooms with no frills. $ *Rooms from: $83* ✉ *900 SD Hwy. 377, Interior* ☎ *605/433–5335, 800/388–4643* 🌐 *www.badlandsbudgethostmotel.com, www.badlandsinteriorcampground.com (for camping only)* ⏲ *Closed Oct.–Mar.* 🛏 *21 rooms, 70 campsites* 🍴 *No meals.*

Badlands Inn

$$ | **HOTEL** | At this inn where every room faces Badlands National Park, you can awaken to a panoramic view of sunrise over Vampire Peak and the rest of the rugged landscape, 1½ miles from the park's visitor center. **Pros:** exceptional views; affordable rates; friendly staff. **Cons:** basic rooms; often fills up by early afternoon. $ *Rooms from: $130* ✉ *20615 Hwy. 377, Interior* ☎ *605/433–5401, 877/386–4383* 🌐 *www.badlandsinn.com* ⏲ *Closed mid-Sept.–mid-May* 🛏 *20 rooms* 🍴 *Free Breakfast.*

Best Western Plains

$$ | HOTEL | FAMILY | A couple blocks from downtown Wall and just 8 miles from Badlands National Park, this pleasant motel has both standard hotel rooms as well as two-bedroom family suites that sleep up to six people. **Pros:** continental breakfast; great indoor and outdoor pools; good location for families. **Cons:** chain motel; no restaurant on-site. Ⓢ *Rooms from: $150* ✉ *712 Glenn St., Wall* ☎ *605/279–2145, 800/528–1234* ⊕ *www.bestwestern.com* 74 rooms, 8 family suites* |○| *Breakfast.*

Circle View Guest Ranch

$$ | B&B/INN | FAMILY | Located in the heart of the badlands, this B&B has spectacular views. **Pros:** friendly people; beautiful views; great for groups. **Cons:** small and isolated. Ⓢ *Rooms from: $150* ✉ *20055 Hwy. 44 E, Interior* ☎ *605/433–5582* ⊕ *www.circleviewranch.com* 8 rooms, 3 cabins* |○| *Breakfast.*

RAPID CITY

Coyote Blues Village B&B

$$$ | B&B/INN | This European-style lodge on 30 acres displays an unusual mix of antique furnishings and contemporary art. **Pros:** tucked away from the highway; exceptional food. **Cons:** not within walking distance of other restaurants. Ⓢ *Rooms from: $195* ✉ *23165 Horseman's Ranch Rd., Rapid City* ☎ *605/574–4477* ⊕ *www. coyotebluesvillage.com* 10 rooms* |○| *Breakfast.*

Chapter 6

BIG BEND NATIONAL PARK

6

Updated by
Andrew Collins

TEXAS

WELCOME TO BIG BEND NATIONAL PARK

TOP REASONS TO GO

★ **Varied terrain:** Visit thorny desert, a fabled international-border river, bird-abundant woods, and mountain spirals all in the same day.

★ **Wonderful wildlife:** Catch sight of the park's extremely diverse animals, including bands of swarthy javelinas, reclusive mountain lions, and lumbering black bears.

★ **Bird-watching:** Spy a pied-billed grebe or another member of the park's more than 450 bird species, including the Lucifer hummingbird and the unique-to-this-area pato mexicano (Mexican duck).

★ **Hot spots:** Dip into the natural hot springs (105°F) near Rio Grande Village.

★ **Mile-high mountains:** Lace up those hiking boots and climb the Chisos Mountains, reaching almost 8,000 feet skyward in some places and remaining relatively cool except May–October, when temperatures reach into the upper 90s even at high elevations.

1 Chisos Basin. This bowl-shape canyon amid the Chisos Mountains is at the heart of Big Bend. It's a trailhead for numerous hikes and a prime place to watch a sunset through a "fracture" in the bowl known as the Window.

2 Castolon. Just east of Santa Elena Canyon, this cluster of adobe dwellings was once used by ranchers and the U.S. military, earning it a spot on the National Register of Historic Places.

3 Rio Grande Village. Tall, shady cottonwoods highlight the park's eastern fringe along the Mexican border and Rio Grande. It's popular with RVers and bird-watchers.

4 North Rosillos. Dinosaur fossils have been found in this remote, northern portion of the park that sees very few visitors. Comprising primarily back roads, this is where nomadic warriors traveled into Mexico via the Comanche Trail.

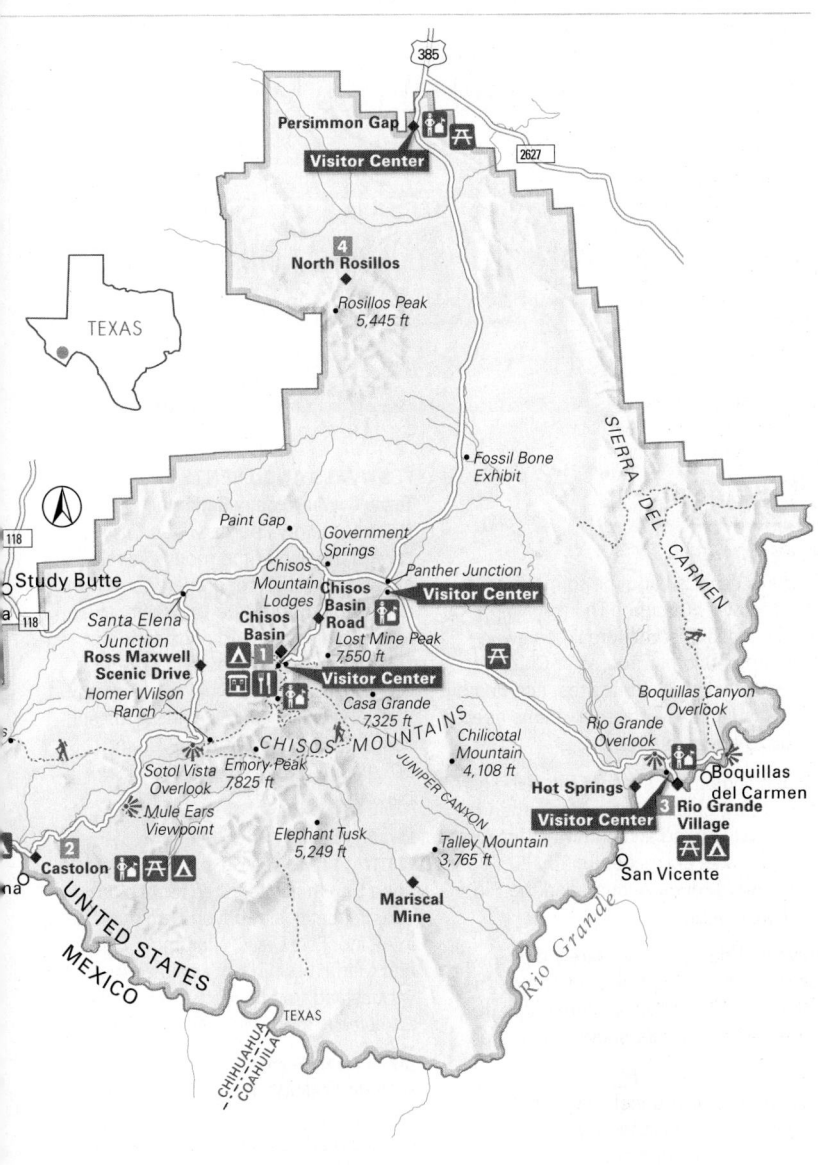

385

Persimmon Gap
Visitor Center
2627

TEXAS

4
North Rosillos

Rosillos Peak
5,445 ft

Fossil Bone
Exhibit

SIERRA DEL CARMEN

118

Paint Gap
Government
Springs
Panther Junction

Study Butte

118

Chisos
Mountain
Lodges
Chisos
Basin
Road
Visitor Center

Santa Elena
Junction
Ross Maxwell
Scenic Drive

Chisos
Basin

Lost Mine Peak
• 7,550 ft

1
Visitor Center

Boquillas Canyon
Overlook

Homer Wilson
Ranch

Casa Grande
7,325 ft
Chilicotal
Mountain
4,108 ft

Rio Grande
Overlook

CHISOS MOUNTAINS

Sotol Vista
Overlook
Emory Peak
7,825 ft

JUNIPER CANYON

Hot Springs

Boquillas
del Carmen

Mule Ears
Viewpoint

Elephant Tusk
5,249 ft

Talley Mountain
3,765 ft

3 **Rio Grande**
Village
Visitor Center

San Vicente

2
Castolon

UNITED STATES

Mariscal
Mine

Rio Grande

MEXICO

CHIHUAHUA
COAHUILA

TEXAS

Cradled in the southwestern elbow of Texas, the 801,163 acres of Big Bend National Park hang suspended above the deserts of northern Mexico. From the craggy, forested Chisos Mountains to the flat, stark plains of the Chihuahuan Desert, Big Bend is one of the nation's most geographically diverse parks, with a dramatic backdrop that inspired Hollywood's first Western sets.

Planning

WHEN TO GO

There is never a bad time to make a Big Bend foray—but during Thanksgiving, Christmas, and spring break, be aware that competition for rooms at Chisos Mountains Lodge, campsites, and nearby hotels is fierce—with reservations needed up to a year in advance.

Depending on the season, Big Bend can be hot, dry, cold, or rainy. Many shun the park in late spring and summer, because temperatures skyrocket (up to 120°F) from May through August, and the Rio Grande lowers.

In winter, temperatures rarely dip below 30°F. During those few times the mercury takes a dive, visitors might be rewarded with a rare snowfall at upper elevations.

The mountains routinely are 5 to 20 degrees cooler than the rest of the park, while the sweltering stretches of the Rio Grande are 5 to 10 degrees warmer.

FESTIVALS AND EVENTS

Texas Cowboy Poetry Gathering

FESTIVAL | Every February, generally toward the end of the month, ranchers and cowboys congregate for three days at Sul Ross State University to regale audiences with original poetry and washtub-bass tributes to singers like Bob Wills. The idea is to preserve the traditions of the West in words and song. ⊠ *Sul Ross State University, U.S. 90, Alpine* ☎ *432/837–2326* ⊕ *www. cowboy-poetry.org.*

Viva Big Bend

FESTIVAL | This West Texas showcase of Lone Star music features rock, blues, country, Latin, and beyond, on stages in Alpine, Fort Davis, Marathon, Lajitas, and Marfa, both in large paid-admission venues and free concerts on hotel patios. ⊠ *Alpine* ⊕ *www.vivabigbend.com.*

Marfa Lights Festival

FESTIVAL | FAMILY | This Labor Day weekend gathering celebrates the mysterious multicolored lights that appear at night in the Chinati Mountains east of U.S. 67 and south of U.S. 90, generally 10 to 20 times a year. Do they result from pockets of atmospheric gas? The spirits of dead Apaches? Overactive imaginations? Whatever they are, they draw curious visitors to Marfa for a parade, live music, and food. ✉ *Presidio County Courthouse lawn, N. Highland Ave., Marfa* ☎ *432/295–1804* ⊕ *www.marfachamber. org.*

Alpine Gallery Night Artwalk

FESTIVAL | For two days each November, the peculiar mix of ranching and artist culture that inhabits Alpine overflows the galleries and seeps into the town's main drag, Holland Avenue. Musicians play at the train depot, barbecue vendors crowd the streets, and local artists display their works in many downtown businesses. ✉ *Holland Ave., Alpine* ☎ *432/837–3067* ⊕ *www.artwalkalpine.com.*

Terlingua International Chili Championship

FESTIVAL | On the first Saturday of November, top chefs spice up cooling weather with chili cooking, bragging, and partying at this spicy chili cook-off held behind the Terlingua Store in Terlingua ghost town. Some of the prize-winning cooks dole out samples. And this is Texas, pardner: no beans allowed. ✉ *229–70 FM 170, Terlingua* ⊕ *www.abowlofred.com.*

PLANNING YOUR TIME

BIG BEND IN ONE DAY

Big Bend is the seventh largest park in the Continental United States. The westside and east-side routes to its storied attraction branch apart at the foot of **Chisos Basin Road** in the heart of the park. Attempting both in one day, covering an aggregate 110 miles, could be hectic and ultimately frustrating, and you'll miss the striking details that bring the park and its history to life. Whichever side you decide to focus on, do spend half your day amid the mountain peaks of **Chisos Basin.** To the west, the goal is **Santa Elena Canyon,** carved by the Rio Grande. From Chisos Mountains Lodge, drive 7 miles north on **Chisos Basin Road,** turn west on Route 118 and connect with **Ross Maxwell**

Scenic Drive, which curls past silent homesteads, stunning overlooks, and the Castolon Historic District (old adobe buildings and a working general store) near the Rio Grande. Explore as many overlooks and historical sites as time allows on this 30-mile stretch, then hike the spectacular **Santa Elena Canyon Trail** (1.6 miles round-trip). During rainy periods, you might need to wade Terlingua Creek before ascending a short but moderately steep trail cut into the canyon, which eventually steps down to a sandy riverside clearing. The majestic canyon is framed by gargantuan 1,500-foot-tall cliffs flanking the Rio Grande. Back at the trailhead, return to Chisos Basin Ross Maxwell Scenic Drive or the slower but picturesque unpaved Old Maverick Road (12.8 miles; high-clearance and four-wheel-drive vehicles only).

A second one-day option is to explore the east side of the park: head east from **Chisos Basin** toward **Rio Grande Village,** along the way exploring Panther Junction Visitor Center, Dugout Wells, Mariscal Mine, Hot Springs, Daniels Ranch, and Boquillas Canyon. At Rio Grande Village, stroll through cottonwoods by the river, home to many birds. There's also a well-stocked convenience store and gas station for a midday snack. If you have time and a passport, cross the river at nearby Boquillas Crossing and while away a few hours in the rustic village of Boquillas del Carmen, Mexico. Return to Chisos Basin by the same route, hopefully in time to hike the short Window View Trail, where prime-time hues are captured at sunset.

GETTING HERE AND AROUND

AIR TRAVEL

The nearest major airport is in Midland, four hours north of the park, but many visitors fly into El Paso, five hours northwest, which is served by more flights and airlines.

AVERAGE HIGH/LOW TEMPERATURES					
JAN.	**FEB.**	**MAR.**	**APR.**	**MAY**	**JUNE**
62/38	68/42	75/48	84/56	89/63	95/70
JULY	**AUG.**	**SEPT.**	**OCT.**	**NOV.**	**DEC.**
93/71	92/71	86/65	81/57	71/47	63/39

CAR TRAVEL

It can take 90 minutes to cross this huge park, but you'll be treated to gorgeous scenery. Big Bend's northern entrance is 39 miles south of Marathon via U.S. 385, but it's another 45 minutes drive to reach central Chisos Basin. To the western entrance, it's 80 miles from Alpine via Highway 118 and 70 miles from Presidio on Highway FM 170. Paved park roads have twists and turns, some very extreme in higher elevations; if you have an RV longer than 24 feet or a trailer longer than 20 feet, you should avoid Chisos Basin Road into higher terrain in the park's center. Four-wheel-drive vehicles are needed for many backcountry roads. Don't leave valuables in your car at remote parking areas.

PARK ESSENTIALS

ACCESSIBILITY

Visitor centers and some campsites at Rio Grande Village and Chisos Basin are wheelchair accessible. The Founder's Walk and Panther Path at Panther Junction, Window View Trail at Chisos Basin, and Rio Grande Village Nature Trail boardwalk are wheelchair-accessible trails. The Rio Grande and Chisos Basin amphitheaters also are accessible.

PARK FEES AND PERMITS

It costs $30 to enter at the gate by car, and your pass is good for seven days. Entry on foot, bicycle, or commercial vehicle is $15; entry by motorcycle is $25. A Big Bend Annual Pass is $55. Camping fees in developed campgrounds are $14 per night, while backcountry camping is $12 for up to 14 days. Mandatory backcountry camping, boating, and fishing permits are available at visitor centers.

PARK HOURS

Big Bend National Park never closes. Visitor centers at Rio Grande Village, Persimmon Gap, and the Castolon Historic District close in summer. The park is in the Central time zone.

CELL PHONE RECEPTION

Cell phone reception is spotty in much of the park, though service is generally more reliable in flat, open country. The visitor centers have pay phones.

EDUCATIONAL OFFERINGS
RANGER PROGRAMS
Birding Talks
INFO CENTER | FAMILY | When staffing allows, rangers lead two-hour birding tours; bring binoculars. ⊠ *Chisos Basin Visitor Center, End of Chinos Basin Rd.* ☎ *432/477–2264* ⊕ *www.nps.gov/bibe.*

★ **Interpretive Activities**
INFO CENTER | FAMILY | Ranger-guided activities are held throughout the park, indoors and outdoors, and include slideshows, talks, and walks on natural and cultural history. Check visitor centers and campground bulletin boards for event postings, which are usually updated every two weeks. ⊠ *Panther Junction Visitor Center, 1 Panther Dr.* ☎ *432/477–2251* ⊕ *www.nps.gov/bibe.*

Junior Ranger Program
INFO CENTER | FAMILY | This self-guided program for kids of all ages is taught through a free booklet of nature-based activities (available at visitor centers). Upon completion of the course, kids are given a Junior Ranger badge or patch. ⊠ *Panther*

Junction Visitor Center, 1 Panther Dr.
☎ *432/477–2251* ⊕ *www.nps.gov/bibe.*

RESTAURANTS

Although the park itself has just one casual and fairly basic restaurant, albeit with stunning views, little Terlingua—just outside the park entrance, has a few more interesting options. And the towns along the U.S. 90 corridor north of the park, including Marathon, Alpine, and Marfa, have a growing mix of excellent eateries, ranging from historic steak-focused hotel dining rooms to hip Austin-style contemporary bistros and mod coffeehouses.

HOTELS

At the Chisos Mountains Lodge, the only hotel in the park, you can select from a freestanding stone cottage or a motel-style room, both within a pace or two of popular trailheads and spectacular views—Chisos sunsets and sunrises are not to be missed. The region flanking Big Bend retains its grand historic hotels, such as the glamorous Hotel Paisano in Marfa (which also has a few hip design hotels), Gage Hotel in Marathon, Holland Hotel in Alpine, and Hotel El Capitan in Van Horn. But you'll also find the well-outfitted Lajitas Golf Resort and some funky, moderately priced options near the park in Terlingua.

Hotel reviews have been shortened. For full information, visit Fodors.com.

What It Costs			
$	$$	$$$	$$$$
RESTAURANTS			
under $13	$13–$20	$21–$30	over $30
HOTELS			
under $101	$101–$150	$151–$200	over $200

VISITOR INFORMATION
PARK CONTACT INFORMATION
Big Bend National Park

There are five visitor centers in Big Bend: Panther Junction, considered park headquarters, at the intersection of Western Entrance Road (which Hwy. 118 becomes) and Persimmon Road (which U.S. 385 becomes); Persimmon Gap at the park's northern entrance at U.S. 385; Rio Grande Village, on the eastern border near Boquillas Canyon and Mexico; the Castolon Historic District on Ross Maxwell Scenic Drive, near Santa Elena Canyon in the southwestern corner of the park; and up high in Chisos Basin, by Chisos Mountains Lodge. Rio Grande Village, Castolon, and Persimmon Gap are closed May–October. Cost for vehicles entering the park (from the north and west gates) is $30, good for one week. ✉ *Big Bend National Park* ☎ *432/477–2251* ⊕ *www.nps.gov/bibe.*

VISITOR CENTERS
Castolon Visitor Center

HISTORIC SITE | FAMILY | Here along the road to Santa Elena Canyon you'll find some of the most hands-on exhibits the park has to offer, with fossils, plants, and implements used by the farmers and miners who settled here in the 1800s and early 1900s. Nearby is an old adobe gallery displaying poster boards explaining the U.S.–Mexico "transparent border." ✉ *Castolon Historic District, Ross Maxwell Scenic Dr.* ☎ *432/477–2666* ⊕ *www.nps.gov/bibe* ⊙ *Closed May–Oct.*

Chisos Basin Visitor Center

INFO CENTER | The small but informative center, by the park's only lodge, is one of the better equipped, with an interactive computer exhibit and a bookstore. An adjacent general store has camping supplies and basic groceries. There are nods to the wild, with natural resource and geology exhibits, a map of bear and mountain lion sightings, and a larger-than-life representation of a mountain lion. The center sponsors educational activities here and at the nearby Chisos Basin Amphitheater. ⊠ *End of Chisos Basin Rd.* ☎ *432/477–2264* ⊕ *www.nps.gov/bibe.*

★ Panther Junction Visitor Center

INFO CENTER | FAMILY | The park's main visitor center, near the base of the Chisos Mountains, contains a bookstore and impressive exhibits on the park's mountain, river, and desert environments. An elegantly produced 22-minute film detailing the wonders of the park shows on request in the theater, and there's a sprawling replica of the park's topographical folds. Nearby, a gas station offers limited groceries. ⊠ *1 Panther Junction Dr.* ☎ *432/477–2251* ⊕ *www. nps.gov/bibe.*

Persimmon Gap Visitor Center

INFO CENTER | Complete with exhibits and a bookstore, this seasonal visitor center is the northern gateway into miles of flatlands that surround the more scenic heart of Big Bend. Dinosaur fossils have been found here; the **Fossil Discovery Exhibit** is on the road between Persimmon Gap and Panther Junction. ⊠ *Big Bend National Park* ✛ *On Main Park Rd. (U.S. 385), 2 miles south of the park's northern entrance* ☎ *432/477–2251* ⊕ *www.nps.gov/bibe* ✆ *Closed May–Oct.*

Rio Grande Village Visitor Center

INFO CENTER | At this seasonal center you take in the videos of Big Bend's geological and natural features at the minitheater and view exhibits on the Rio Grande. ⊠ *End of Rio Grande Village Rd.* ☎ *432/477–2251* ⊕ *www.nps.gov/bibe* ✆ *Closed May–Oct.*

 Sights

SCENIC DRIVES

★ Chisos Basin Road

MOUNTAIN—SIGHT | FAMILY | This 7-mile road climbs majestically from Chisos Basin Junction to Chisos Mountains Lodge, with a spur leading to a campground. In these higher elevations (the heart of Big Bend), you're slightly more likely to spot lions and bears as well as white-tailed deer amid juniper trees and pinyon pines. You'll also see lovely, red-barked Texas madrone along with some Chisos oaks and Douglas fir trees. Several roadside exhibits along the way explain the various ecosystems. Because of sharp curves and switchbacks, this drive is not suitable for RVs longer than 24 feet. ⊠ *Big Bend National Park* ✛ *3 miles west of Panther Junction* ⊕ *www. nps.gov/bibe.*

★ Ross Maxwell Scenic Drive

HISTORIC SITE | FAMILY | Although it extends only 30 miles, you can easily spend a full day on this aptly named route admiring the views, visiting historic sites, taking short hikes, and getting a Big Bend education. There are scenic overlooks, a backside perspective of the Chisos Mountains, exhibits, and the ruins of old homesteads. If you don't mind a little grate in your gait from the gravel that blankets the road, you can make this drive a loop by reconnecting with West Entrance Road (near Highway 118) from Santa Elena Canyon via unpaved Old Maverick Road for 12.8 miles. If you're in an RV or a low-clearance car, don't attempt rough Old Maverick Road. ⊠ *Big Bend National Park* ✛ *Off West Entrance Rd., about 12 miles west of Panther Junction.*

HISTORIC SITES

Castolon Historic District

HISTORIC SITE | FAMILY | Adobe buildings and wooden shacks serve as reminders of the farming and military community of Castolon, near the banks of the Rio Grande. The Magdalena House has historical exhibits. A general store, housed in an old adobe building and fronted by shaded picnic tables, is good for drinks and snacks. The nearby Castolon Visitor Center closes May–October. ⊠ *Castolon Historic District* ✛ *Ross Maxwell Scenic Dr.* ☎ *432/477–2225.*

Hot Springs

HOT SPRINGS | **FAMILY** | Hikers soak themselves in the 105°F waters alongside the Rio Grande, where petroglyphs coat the canyon walls nearby. The remains of a post office, motel, and bathhouse point to the old commercial establishment operating here in the early 1900s. The 1.6-mile dirt road leading to the Hot Springs trailhead from Rio Grande Village Road cannot accommodate RVs and is best avoided after rainstorms. Also, don't leave valuables in your car, especially during the slow season. ✉ *Big Bend National Park ✛ Off Rio Grande Village Rd.*

Mariscal Mine

MINE | Hard-working men and women once coaxed cinnabar, or mercury ore, from the Mariscal Mine, located at the north end of Mariscal Mountain. They abandoned the mines and surrounding stone buildings in the 1940s. If you stop here, take care not to touch the timeworn stones, as they may contain poisonous mercury residue. You need a high-clearance vehicle to navigate the road here from Rio Grande Village. ✉ *River Rd. E ✛ 5 miles west of Rio Grande Village.*

SCENIC STOPS

★ Chisos Basin

NATURE SITE | **FAMILY** | Panoramic vistas, a restaurant with an up-close view of jagged mountain peaks, and glimpses of the Colima warbler (which summers in Big Bend) await in the forested Chisos Basin. Considered the spiritual heart of Big Bend, at an elevation of 5,400 feet, it's ringed by taller peaks and also has hiking trails, a lodge, a campground, a grocery store, a gift shop, an amphitheater, the famous Window rock formation, and one of five park visitor centers. Winter sometimes brings snow, but in summer this is where you can find a little relief from the desert heat below. ✉ *Big Bend National Park ✛ End of Chisos Mountain Rd.*

★ Santa Elena Canyon

BODY OF WATER | **FAMILY** | The finale of a short but vigorous hike (1.6 miles round-trip) over a steep slope is a spectacular view of the Rio Grande and sheer limestone cliffs that rise 1,500 feet to create a narrow, natural box with the U.S. on one side, and Mexico on the other. Summer can feel like a sauna, but you might have this secluded place to yourself. ✉ *End of Maxwell Scenic Dr.*

Activities

Spectacular and varied scenery plus more than 300 miles of road spell adventure for hikers, bikers, horseback riders, or those simply in need of a ramble on foot or by Jeep. A web of dusty, unpaved roads lures adventuresome drivers and experienced hikers deep into the backcountry, while paved roads make shorter trails and scenic overlooks more accessible. Because the park has nearly half of the bird species in North America, birding ranks high. Boating is also popular, because some of the park's most striking features are accessible only via the Rio Grande.

MULTISPORT OUTFITTERS

Angell Expeditions

TOUR—SPORTS | A smaller outfitter based between Lajitas and Presidio in tiny Redford, Charlie Angell customizes river- and land-based tours, meeting his clients on-site in both Big Bend National Park and Big Bend Ranch State Park—or at regional destinations beyond park boundaries. ✉ *Redford* ☎ *432/384–2304* ⊕ *www.angellexpeditions.com* 🖼 *From $140.*

Big Bend River Tours

TOUR—SPORTS | **FAMILY** | Exploring the Rio Grande is this outfitter's specialty. Custom tours can be half a day up to 10 days and include rafting, canoeing, and hiking and horseback trips combined with a river float. ✉ *23331 FM 170, Terlingua*

West Texas fauna include prairie dogs, jackrabbits, and roadrunners, while its flora include yuccas.

☎ *800/545–4240, 432/371–3033* ⊕ *www.bigbendrivertours.com* ⊠ *From $75.*

Desert Sports

TOUR—SPORTS | From rentals—mountain bikes, boats, and inflatable kayaks—to experienced guides for mountain-bike touring, boating, and hiking, this outfitter has it covered. The company prides itself on its small size and personal touch. ⊠ *22937 FM 170, Terlingua* ☎ *432/371–2727, 888/989–6900* ⊕ *www.desert-sportstx.com* ⊠ *From $95.*

Far Flung Outdoor Center

TOUR—SPORTS | FAMILY | Call these pros for personalized nature, historical, and geological trips via rafts, ATVs, and 4X4s. Trips include gourmet rafting tours with cheese and wine served on checkered tablecloths alongside the river, and sometimes spectacular star viewing at night. The property offers overnight "casitas" with kitchenettes and a full range of amenities. ⊠ *FM 170, Terlingua* ⊹ *½ mile west of Jct. of FM 170–Hwy. 118* ☎ *800/839–7238, 432/371–2633* ⊕ *www.bigbendfarflung.com* ⊠ *From $59.*

BICYCLING

Mountain biking the backcountry roads can be so solitary that you're unlikely to encounter another human being; note that bikes are not permitted off-road or on trails. The solitude also means you should be extraordinarily prepared for the unexpected with ample supplies, especially water and sun protection (summer heat is brutal, and you're unlikely to find shade except in forested areas of Chisos Basin). Biking is recommended only during the cooler months (October–April).

On paved roads, a regular road bike should suffice, but you'll have to bring your own—outfitters tend to stock only mountain bikes. For an easy ride on mostly level ground, try the 13-mile (one-way) unpaved **Old Maverick Road** on the west side of the park, connecting Santa Elena Canyon Road and West Entrance roads. For a challenge, take the unpaved **Old Ore Road** for 27 miles from the park's north area to near Rio Grande Village on the east side.

Plants and Wildlife in Big Bend

Because Big Bend contains habitats as diverse as spent volcanoes, slick-sided canyons, and the Rio Grande, it follows that species here are extremely diverse, too. Among the park's most notable residents are endangered species like the Mexican long-nosed bat (which feasts on the nectar of agave and cacti), shadow-dappled peregrine falcon, swarthy javelina, and fat-bellied horned lizard (Texans call them "horny toads"). More than 450 species of birds wing throughout the park, including the black-capped vireo and the turkey vulture, which boasts a 6-foot wingspan.

In the lower desert, be aware of scorpions and rattlesnakes, especially in the summer at dusk and dawn. The vipers aren't normally aggressive, so try to refrain from sudden movement and give them a wide berth.

In the highlands mountain lions lurk, while black bears loll in the crags and valleys. Your chances of spotting the reclusive creatures are slim, though greater at dusk and dawn. If you do encounter either, don't run away. Instead, stand tall, shout, throw rocks if necessary, and look as scary as possible.

If the winged, furred, and legged denizens of Big Bend are watch-worthy, so, too, are the plants populating the region. Supremely adapted to the arroyos, valleys, and slopes, the plants range from the endangered Chisos Mountains hedgehog cactus (found only in the park) to the towering rasp of the giant dagger yucca. Also here are 60 types of cacti—so be careful where you tread.

BIRD-WATCHING

Situated on north–south migratory pathways, Big Bend is home to approximately 450 species of birds—more than any other national park. In fact, the birds that flit, waddle, soar, and swim in the park represent more than half the bird species found in North America, including the Colima warbler, found nowhere else in the United States. To glimpse darting hummingbirds, turkey vultures, golden eagles, and the famous Colima, look to the Chisos Mountains. To spy woodpeckers and scaled quail (distinctive for dangling crests), look to the desert scrub. And for cuckoos, cardinals, and screech owls, you must prowl along the river. Rangers often lead birding talks.

★ Chisos Basin

BIRD WATCHING | Known as a "sky island" towering over the surrounding desert "sea," Chisos Basin shelters the only lodge in the park and is etched by numerous hiking trails of varying difficulty. One takes you to the top of Emory Peak, the highest point in Big Bend. You'll have to hike the high country (above 5,400 feet elevation) to spy the Colima warbler and Lucifer hummingbird, but bear, deer, javelina, and even mountain lions have been known to range closer to the lodge grounds. Your chances of encountering them are rather small, especially during the day. If you do, the animals will likely shy away. At more than a mile high, the basin floor is an especially inviting destination May–October. ⊠ *End of Chisos Basin Rd.* ☎ *432/477–2264.*

★ Rio Grande Village

BIRD WATCHING | Considered the best birding habitat in Big Bend, this river wetland has summer tanagers and vermilion flycatchers among many other species. This is a good trail for kids, and a portion of it is wheelchair accessible. ⊠ *End of Rio Grande Village Rd.* ☎ *432/477–2251.*

BOATING AND RAFTING

Much is made of the park's hiking trails and the exquisite views they offer. Likewise, the watery pathway that is the Rio Grande should be mentioned for the spectacular views it affords. The 118 miles of the Rio Grande that border the park form its backbone, defining the vegetation, landforms, and animals found at the park's southern rim. By turns shallow and deep, the river flows through stunning canyons and picks up speed over small and large rapids.

Alternately soothing and exciting (Class II and III rapids develop here, particularly after the summer rains), the river can be traversed in several ways, from guided rafting tours to more strenuous kayak and canoe expeditions. In general, rafting trips spell smoother sailing for families, though thrills are inherent when soaring over the river's meringue-like tips and troughs. Be cautious, however, for fatalities have occurred. ■TIP➔ **Be sure to check the river levels before planning an outing—many times during the year the river's too low to get a decent rafting experience. Conversely, during an especially wet monsoon season, the river rises to levels that even guides won't challenge.**

You can bring your own raft to the boat launch at the Rio Grande, but you must obtain a $12 river-use permit (which allows you to camp along the river) from a visitor center. Leave the Jet Skis at home; no motorized vehicles are allowed on the Rio Grande. For less fuss, go with a tour guide or outfitter on trips that range from a few hours to several days. Most outfitters are in the communities of Study Butte, Terlingua, and Lajitas, just west of the park boundary off FM 170. They rent rafts, canoes, kayaks, and inflatable kayaks (nicknamed "duckies") for when the river is low. Their guided trips cost in the tens to thousands of dollars. Personalized river tours are available

all year, and they might include gourmet rafting tours that end with beef Wellington and live country music. Though many of the rafting trips are relatively smooth, thus safe for younger boaters, always check with tour operators.

FISHING

You can cast a line into the Rio Grande all year for free, as long as you obtain a permit from one of the park's visitor centers. You cannot use jug lines, traps, or other nontraditional fishing methods.

HIKING

Each of the park's zones has its own appeal. The east side offers demanding mountain hikes, border canyons, limestone aplenty, and sandy washes with geographic spectacles. Westside trails go down into striking scenery in the Santa Elena Canyon and up into towering volcanic landforms. Descend into gorges, arroyos, and springs or ascend into the must-see scenic windows of Grapevine Hills. The heart of the park has abandoned mines, pine-topped vistas, scrub vegetation around the Chisos, and deserts lying just below soaring Chisos Mountain aeries. ■TIP➔ **Carry enough drinking water—a gallon per person daily (more when extremely hot).**

While Big Bend certainly has "expedition level" trails to test the most veteran backpacker, many are very demanding and potentially dangerous—attempt these only if you're quite experienced. The trails we've included here are best suited to moderately active hikers, but a few easy ones are appropriate even for novices and young kids.

Boquillas Canyon Trail

HIKING/WALKING | After climbing over a rocky bluff with sweeping views of the Rio Grande and the desert in Mexico beyond it, this picturesque trek drops into a lush sandy canyon and parallels the river. Soaring cliffs rise on either side, and the trail ends at a scenic point where the canyon narrows dramatically.

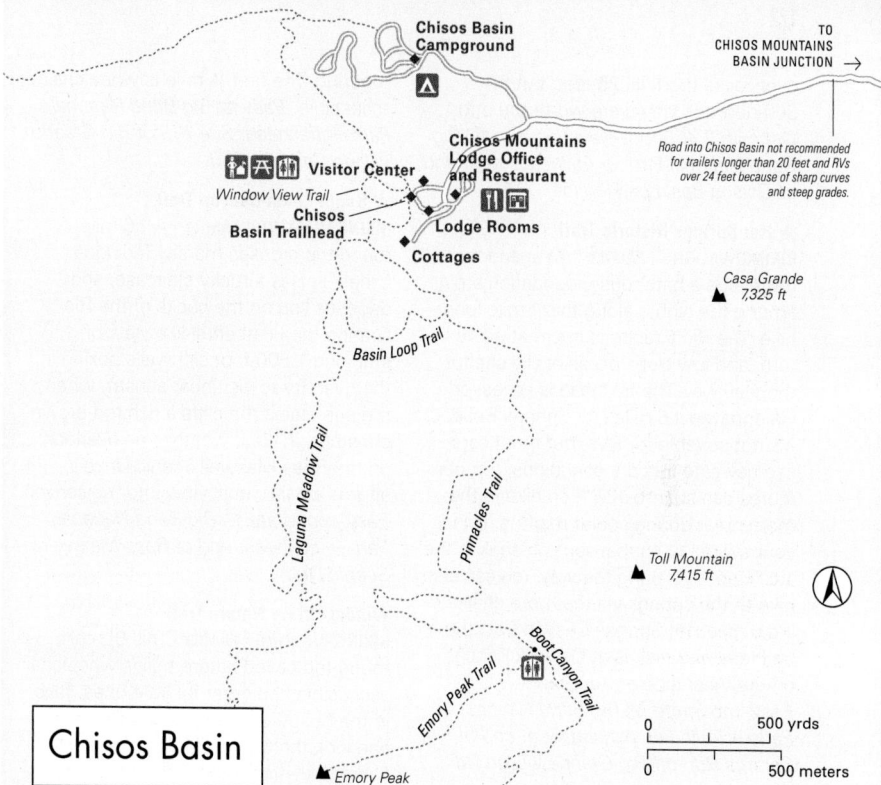

Chisos Basin

Easy–Moderate. ☒ *Big Bend National Park* ⊹ *Trailhead: parking lot at end of Boquillas Canyon Spur Rd., near Rio Grande Village.*

Chihuahuan Desert Nature Trail

HIKING/WALKING | FAMILY | A windmill and spring form a desert oasis, a refreshing backdrop to a ½-mile round-trip, hot and flat nature trail; wild doves are abundant, the hike is pleasant, and kids will do just fine. While you're there, keep an eye out for the elf owl, one of the sought-after birds on the Big Bend's "Top 10" list. *Easy.* ☒ *Hwy. 118* ⊹ *Trailhead: Dugout Wells, 6 miles southeast of Panther Junction.*

Chisos Basin Loop Trail

HIKING/WALKING | FAMILY | A forested area and higher elevations give you some sweeping views of the lower desert and distant volcanic mountains on this 1.6-mile round-trip. The loop intersects with a few longer trails. The elevation at the trailhead is 5,400 feet. Set aside about an hour. *Moderate, elevation gain 500 feet.* ☒ *Big Bend National Park* ⊹ *Trailhead: west end of Chisos Basin parking lot.*

★ Emory Peak Trail

HIKING/WALKING | Give yourself about six hours to complete this rugged 10.5-mile round-trip alpine trek to the park's highest peak, at 7,832 feet. The initial 3.5-mile stretch follows the Pinnacles Trail, which eventually leads to the South Rim—a rewarding 12- to 14.5-mile round-trip adventure that can be done in a very long full day but is more easily managed with a night of camping. For Emory Peak, you pick up a 1-mile spur that affords some dazzling vistas as it zigzags up to the summit. Note there's a bit of scrambling over rocks the final 25 feet, but the 360-degrees views are worth the effort. *Difficult, 2,400-foot elevation gain.* ⊠ *Big Bend National Park* ⊹ *Trailhead: west end of Chisos Basin parking lot.*

★ **Hot Springs Historic Trail**

HIKING/WALKING | FAMILY | An abandoned motel and a bathhouse foundation are among the sights along this 1-mile loop hike. The Rio Grande is heard at every turn, and low trees occasionally shelter the walkway. The trailhead is accessed via unpaved 1.6-mile Hot Springs Road. It's not suitable for RVs, but most cars can navigate it in dry conditions. Temperatures can soar to 120°F, so hike in the morning or during cooler months. Bring your swimsuit so that you can soak in the 105°F springs along the way. You can also hike to the springs via the more challenging 6-mile Hot Springs Canyon Trail, the trailhead of which is at Daniel's Ranch, on the west side of Rio Grande Village. *Easy–moderate.* ⊠ *Big Bend National Park* ⊹ *Trailhead: parking lot at end of Hot Springs Rd., off Rio Grande Village Rd.*

★ **Lost Mine Trail**

HIKING/WALKING | Set aside about three hours to leisurely explore the nature of the Chisos Mountains along this 4.8-mile round-trip trail. It starts at 5,700 feet and climbs 1,100 feet to an even loftier vantage point. The breathtaking view at marker 10, about halfway up, is a worthy destination in itself. *Moderate–difficult.* ⊠ *Big Bend National Park* ⊹ *Trailhead: mile marker 5 on the Chisos Basin Rd.*

Rio Grande Village Nature Trail

HIKING/WALKING | FAMILY | Down by the Rio Grande, this short, ¾-mile loop trail packs a powerful wildlife punch. The village is one of the best spots in the park to see rare birds, and other wildlife isn't in short supply either. Keep a lookout for coyotes, javelinas (they look like wild pigs), and other mammals. This is a good trail for kids, so expect higher traffic. Restrooms are nearby, and the trail can be done in less than an hour, even when

lingering. The first ¼ mile is wheelchair accessible. *Easy.* ⊠ *Big Bend National Park* ⊹ *Trailhead: Site #18 of Rio Grande Village Campground.*

★ **Santa Elena Canyon Trail**

HIKING/WALKING | FAMILY | A 1.6-mile round-trip crosses marshy Terlingua Creek, scales a rocky staircase, and deposits you on the banks of the Rio Grande for a cathedral-like view of stunning 1,500-foot cliff walls boxing in the river. Try to visit near sunset, when the sun stains the cliffs a rich red-brown chestnut. In clear weather, an overlook on the Ross Maxwell Scenic Drive affords a panoramic view into the canyon. *Easy–moderate.* ⊠ *Big Bend National Park* ⊹ *Trailhead: end of Ross Maxwell Scenic Dr.*

Window View Nature Trail

HIKING/WALKING | FAMILY | This 0.3-mile round-trip paved nature trail is wheelchair accessible and great for little ones. Take in the beautiful, craggy-sided Chisos and look through the V-shape rock-sided "Window" framing the desert below (you can hike to this very point via the quite rewarding, moderately difficult 5.6-mile round-trip Window Trail, which is accessed from the same trailhead). This self-guided trail, which is especially captivating at sunset, is easily accomplished in 20 minutes. Be on the lookout for wild javelina, which occasionally root through here. They're not normally aggressive, but give them a respectful distance. *Easy.* ⊠ *Big Bend National Park* ⊹ *Trailhead: west end of Chisos Basin parking lot.*

JEEP TOURS

Wheeled traffic is welcome in the park, up to a point. RVs, trucks, cars, and Jeeps are allowed on designated paved and dirt roads, though personal ATV use is prohibited. Jeep rental isn't available inside the park, but Jeep, SUV, and ATV tours just outside the park are possible through outfitters. Jeep tours can cost as little as $79 for a three-hour tour, while

Good Reads

■ *Naturalist's Big Bend*, by Roland H. Wauer and Carl M. Fleming, paints a picture of the park's diverse plants and animals.

■ *Big Bend: The Story Behind the Scenery*, by Carol E. Sperling and Mary L. Van Camp, is rife with colorful photos illustrating the park's history and geology.

■ For gleeful and awestruck thoughts on the Big Bend wilderness, check out *God's Country or Devil's Playground*, which collects the writing of nearly 60 authors.

■ The Natural History Association's *Road Guide* gives in-depth information on the web of paved and improved dirt roads running through the park—and the views you can see from them. Find it on sale at park visitor centers.

6

Big Bend National Park

ATV tours ring up at about $170 for the first person, with reduced rates for a second rider.

SWIMMING

Though it might be tempting to doff sweat-drenched T-shirts in favor of bathing suits, be careful where you take your dips. The Rio Grande has ample waters, but swimming isn't recommended due to dangerous currents and high pollution levels.

Performing Arts

Most of the art in the park can be found on canyon walls—pictographs line the cliffs in the southern area of Big Bend—and inside the walls of the park visitor centers. Movies about the park's wildlife and geology are often shown at Persimmon Gap, Panther Junction, and Rio Grande Village visitor centers.

If you're looking to socialize, try the Rio Grande Village. Chances are, people will be grilling and shooting the breeze in this 100-site campground. Or, head to Hot Springs if you're in the mood to view the Milky Way with a few other folks (depending on the season). The bulk of

the area's fine-arts, festivals, live music, dancing, and other entertainment options lies in towns outside the park's borders.

While the park doesn't have specific entertainment events set up, the crystal-clear nighttime skies, breathtaking from Hot Springs, make for some stellar (literally) entertainment. Taking in the park's gorgeous sunsets, which range from deep, flamingo-tongue red to indigo to butter yellow, isn't a bad pastime either.

Nearby Towns

Marathon, just a 45-minute drive from the northern entrance, is one of the closest towns to Big Bend. Once a shipping hub, the population-430 town still contains reminders of its Old West railroad days, including the iconic Gage Hotel. **Alpine,** a town of about 6,000, hunkers down among the Davis Mountains 80 miles north of the park's western entrance. It's known for Sul Ross State University, with its excellent Museum of the Big Bend, and you'll find a few notable eateries, galleries, and hotels here. About 25 miles west is **Marfa,** a population-1,800, middle-of-nowhere West Texas hamlet with a world-renowned contemporary arts scene and an increasingly hip and stylish clutch of restaurants, art galleries, hotels, and boutiques. Its spooky, unexplained "Marfa lights" are attributed to everything from atmospheric disturbances to imagination.

Once the headquarters of quicksilver mining (now defunct), the barely populated **Terlingua ghost town** is 7 miles from the park's west entrance on Highway 118. Just east of Terlingua is **Study Butte,** which also has its roots in the old quicksilver-mining industry. The combined Terlingua–Study Butte population is about 265, many of them iconoclasts and big-city refugees. Follow FM 170 west from Terlingua for 13 miles to the flat-rock formations of tiny **Lajitas.** Once a U.S. Cavalry outpost, Lajitas, which means "little flat stones," has been converted into a resort area offering golf and equestrian activities. The border town of **Presidio,** 70 miles from the park's western entrance, is regarded as a key gateway to northern Mexico. Across the border from Presidio is a spring-break favorite, **Ojinaga, Mexico,** famous for its partylike atmosphere. It's also a springboard to Copper Canyon, a striking series of canyons that run down the west side of the Sierra Tarahumara.

Boquillas del Carmen, Mexico Crossing
NATIONAL/STATE PARK | Big Bend residents and visitors were thrilled when Boquillas Crossing into Mexico, closed since 9/11, reopened in 2013. Residents of both countries can now use the crossing, about 2 miles east of Rio Grande Village. Check the park website for current hours, but generally the crossing is open summer from 9 am to 6 pm, Friday through Monday, and in winter from 8 am to 5 pm, Wednesday through Sunday. A passport is required. Once a mining boomtown that fed off rich minerals and silver, Boquillas has shrunk to a small pool of families, partly as a result of when the crossing had closed. But

there is a restaurant and bar on the other side, plus some shopping. U.S. citizens are allowed to bring back up to $200 in merchandise duty-free. Drive to the crossing past Rio Grande Village, from which you can access a $5 round-trip row boat across the Rio Grande. The remaining ¾-mile to the village can be made on foot, by donkey ($5 round-trip), pickup truck ($5), or horseback ($8). **If you do not return to the border in time, you may be stuck in Mexico for two or three days.** ⌖ *Off Boquillas Canyon Rd., near Rio Grande Village* ⊕ *www.nps.gov/bibe.*

VISITOR INFORMATION
Alpine Chamber of Commerce ✉ *106 N. 3rd St., Alpine* ☏ *432/837–4144, 800/561–3712* ⊕ *www.alpinetexas.com.* **Big Bend Chamber of Commerce** ⊕ *bigbendchamberofcommerce.org.* **Fort Davis Chamber of Commerce** ✉ *100 Memorial Sq., No. 4, Fort Davis* ☏ *432/426–3015, 800/524–3015* ⊕ *www.fortdavis.com.* **Marfa Visitor Center** ✉ *302 S. Highland Ave., Marfa* ☏ *432/729–4772* ⊕ *www. visitmarfa.com.* **Presidio Convention & Visitors Bureau** ✉ *507 W. O'Reilly St., Presidio* ☏ *432/229–3517* ⊕ *www.presidiotx.us.*

Best Bets for Families

■ **Cowboy Poetry.** Cowboys and cowgirls regale audiences with tales at Sul Ross State University's annual event.

■ **McDonald Observatory's Star Parties.** Guides lead observers on a tour of the celestial bodies.

■ **Overnight Rafting Trips.** Far Flung Outdoor Center sometimes offers spring-break trips for families with kids under 12. Trips include short hikes, goggles for stargazing, and canoeing.

⊙ Sights

Barton Warnock Visitor Center

INFO CENTER | Affiliated with Big Bend Ranch State Park of Texas, this visitor center offers a self-guided walking tour through a 2½-acre landscaped desert garden. It's a good way to get acquainted with the Trans-Pecos region before adventuring to either the national or state park. Also on the grounds are an interpretive center, a covered picnic area, a bookstore, and a gift shop. ⊠ FM 170, Lajitas ✛ 1 mile east of Lajitas ☎ 432/424–3327 ⊕ www.tpwd.state. tx.us/state-parks/barton-warnock ⊠ $5 Oct.–Apr.; $3 May–Sept.

★ Big Bend Ranch State Park

NATIONAL/STATE PARK | FAMILY | As a western buffer to Big Bend National Park, this rugged desert wilderness extends along the Rio Grande across more than 300,000 acres from east of Lajitas to Presidio. It's less developed than the national park (if that seems possible), but you can hike, mountain bike, backpack, raft, and ride horseback. A collection of hiking trailheads spoke off from FM 170 across from the Barton Warnock Visitor Center at Lajitas, which serves as the park's eastern information post. The western visitor center is at Fort Leaton State Historical Site near Presidio. ⊠ Presidio ☎ 432/358–4444 ⊕ www.tpwd. state.tx.us/state-parks/big-bend-ranch ⊠ $5 peak; $3 non-peak.

★ Chinati Foundation

ART GALLERIES—ARTS | This internationally renowned contemporary art museum, which occupies 15 buildings on a 340-acre campus, is in the vanguard of the minimalist movement that defines the Marfa aesthetic. Chinati emphasizes large installations and changes its exhibits regularly, and it has a well-attended annual open house. The foundation conducts guided tours Wednesday through Sunday of its huge contemporary-art holdings, and some installations can be visited on self-guided tours. Tours often book up quickly; it's highly recommended that you book online in advance. ⊠ 1 Cavalry Row, Marfa ☎ 432/729–4362 ⊕ www.chinati.org ⊠ From $10.

★ Fort Davis National Historic Site

HISTORIC SITE | FAMILY | Fort Davis (also the city's namesake) provides a history lesson on this late 1800s region, with exhibits and many original buildings preserved. You can spend hours touring the sprawling grounds, which include barracks, the post hospital, the visitor center, and servants' quarters. ⊠ 101 Lt. Henry Flipper Dr., Fort Davis ☎ 432/426–3224 ⊕ www.nps.gov ⊠ $10 per person, $20 per vehicle.

Fort Leaton State Historic Site

HISTORIC SITE | The 23-acre site in Presidio County contains a thick-walled adobe fort and trading post that dates back to pioneer days. There are exhibits, a ½-mile nature trail, picnic sites, guided tours, and a store. The park is day-use only. The fort also doubles as the western visitor center for Big Bend Ranch State Park. ⊠ FM 170, Presidio ✛ 4 miles southeast of Presidio ☎ 432/229–3613 ⊕ www. tpwd.state.tx.us/state-parks/fort-leaton ⊠ $5 peak; $3 non-peak.

★ McDonald Observatory Visitors Center

INFO CENTER | FAMILY | Check out exhibits, examine sunspots and flares safely via film, or peer into the workings of giant research telescopes. Guided bus tours of the domed observatories depart daily following programs at 11 and 2. After nightfall, the observatory offers star parties. Online reservations in advance are required for all public programs. The beautiful 15-mile drive from Fort Davis to the visitor center, at 6,235 elevation, is worth the trip. ⊠ 3640 Dark Sky Dr., Fort Davis ☎ 432/426–3640, 877/984–7827 ⊕ www.mcdonaldobservatory.org ⊠ Programs $8, star parties $12.

Border Crossing at Big Bend

Once upon a time, Big Bend visitors could splash across the Rio Grande and into the confines of Boquillas and Santa Elena, small Mexican towns that buttered their bread by selling Americans handicrafts. Now, if you want to visit one of the border towns, you must do so by entering official checkpoints in Texas; closed after 9/11, the Boquillas Crossing, at the park's southeastern edge, reopened in 2013 and is open during the day, Friday–Monday in summer and Wednesday–Sunday in winter.

You'll take a row boat the short distance across the Rio Grande to reach Boquillas ($5 round-trip), then walk, take a burro ($5), the back of a pickup ($5), or ride a horse ($8) the remaining ¾-mile to town, where you'll find a few bars, restaurants, and shops. To reenter the United States, you'll need a passport.

Once you get to Mexico, don't fret about language difficulties or money incompatibility. Boquillas is very tourist-friendly, and most there speak English. U.S. currency is accepted.

★ **Museum of the Big Bend**

INFO CENTER | FAMILY | With 5,000 square feet of space, this history-lover's haven has exhibits representing the life and cultures of the region and sponsors an annual show on ranching handiwork (such as saddles, reins, and spurs) held in conjunction with the Cowboy Poetry Gathering each February. The map collection is renowned. ⊠ *Sul Ross State University, 400 N. Harrison St., Alpine* ⊹ *following campus signs from U.S. 90* ☏ *432/837–8143* ⊕ *www.sulross.edu/museum* ✆ *Free* ⊗ *Closed Mon.*

Nightlife Outside the Park

While recreation and outdoor adventures are alive inside the park, the arts are vibrant outside it, especially in Marfa, where you'll also find some lively bars. Activities include live poetry readings, gallery-hopping, and several annual art and music festivals.

Ballroom Marfa

ART GALLERIES—ARTS | This hip, modern, and undeniably cool gallery and performance space presents edgy rotating contemporary exhibits as well as occasional live music and film, especially on weekends. ⊠ *108 E. San Antonio St., Marfa* ☏ *432/729–3600* ⊕ *www.ballroommarfa.org.*

Railroad Blues

MUSIC CLUBS | A cool live-music venue, Railroad Blues is a magnet for local performers and Austin-style sounds that stray out to West Texas on a regular basis. The cozy wooden bar thick with atmosphere and characters weaves an after-dark tapestry that is certifiably Lone Star hip, and the beer and wine selection is impressive. ⊠ *504 W. Holland Ave., Alpine* ☏ *432/837–3103* ⊕ *www.railroad-blues.com.*

🍴 Restaurants

IN THE PARK

Chisos Mountains Lodge Restaurant

$$ | AMERICAN | FAMILY | The decor of this comfy and casual eatery is unassuming, likely because the star attraction is the signature view through three walls of windows that bring the craggy Chisos Mountains to your table. They serve decent, tried-and-true American food, with a few Mexican specialties; the staff is friendly and efficient. **Known**

for: astounding views from dining room and patio; nice selection of Texas craft beers; tasty soups of the day. $ *Average main: $16* ⊠ *End of Chisos Mountain Rd.* ☎ *432/477–2291* ⊕ *www.chisosmountainslodge.com.*

PICNIC AREAS
Dugout Wells Area
NATIONAL/STATE PARK | There is a picnic table under the shady cottonwoods off the Dugout Wells Trail loop, plus a vault toilet, but no running water to wash your hands. ⊠ *Rio Grande Village Rd.* ✦ *6 miles southeast of Panther Junction* ⊕ *www.nps.gov/bibe.*

Persimmon Gap Area
INFO CENTER | Quiet and remote, this peaceful picnic area has tables shaded by metal roofs called ramadas. There are no grills, but there is a pit toilet. ⊠ *Big Bend National Park* ✦ *North entrance to Big Bend, on U.S. 385 from Marathon* ⊕ *www.nps.gov/bibe.*

Rio Grande Village Area
NATIONAL/STATE PARK | FAMILY | Half a dozen picnic tables are scattered under cottonwoods south of the convenience store. Half a mile away at Daniels Ranch there are two tables and a grill. Wood fires aren't allowed (charcoal and propane are). ⊠ *Hwy. 118* ✦ *22 miles southeast of Panther Junction* ⊕ *www.nps.gov/bibe.*

Santa Elena Canyon Area
NATIONAL/STATE PARK | FAMILY | Two tables sit in the shade next to the parking lot at the trailhead. There is a vault toilet. ⊠ *Big Bend National Park* ✦ *8 miles west of Castolon, accessible via Ross Maxwell Scenic Dr.* ⊕ *www.nps.gov/bibe.*

OUTSIDE THE PARK
Brick Vault Brewery and Barbecue
$ | **BARBECUE** | Opened by the owners of the iconic Gage Hotel just down the street, this lively microbrewery serves reliably good Texas-style barbecue, including brisket, turkey, ribs, and sausages with a nice selection of sides (pineapple slaw, jalapeño mac and cheese). Set in an 1880s building that once housed a mercantile and later a service station, the space has a fun retro-funky vibe and turns out interesting craft beer. **Known for:** tender brisket; Capt. Shepard's Pecan Porter; attractive outdoor patio. $ *Average main: $12* ⊠ *103 1st St., Marathon* ☎ *432/386–4205* ⊕ *www.facebook.com/brickvaultbrewery* ☾ *Closed Mon.–Wed. No dinner Sun.*

★ Cedar Coffee Supply
$ | **CAFÉ** | Coffee connoisseurs and java junkies flock from nearby towns to this minimalist third wave café that turns out some of the finest single-origin sips in West Texas, from straightforward macchiatos to lattes with organic honey-lavender syrup. On Friday, Saturday, and Tuesday, Cedar Coffee also serves up a limited selection of exceptionally tasty breakfast and lunch items, including savory and sweet crepes and Belgian waffles with berries. **Known for:** potent cold brew (it's available bottled, too, so you can stock up); house-made horchata; matcha lattes. $ *Average main: $6* ⊠ *103 West Ave. E, Alpine* ⊕ *www.cedarcoffeesupply.com* ☾ *Closed Sun.*

Espresso y Poco Mas
$ | **CAFÉ** | For some of the tastiest breakfast fare close to the park, try this funky down-home spot in Terlingua ghost town, which makes everything from scratch, including the flour tortillas used for hearty breakfast burritos. The coffee is the best in town, and the desserts are homemade. **Known for:** several types of breakfast burritos; overstuffed sandwiches; organic coffee from Big Bend Roasters. $ *Average main: $7* ⊠ *La Posada Milagro Guesthouse & Casitas, 100 Milagro Rd., Terlingua* ☎ *432/371–3044* ⊕ *www.laposadamilagro.net.*

LaVenture
$$$ | **MODERN AMERICAN** | The urbane restaurant just off the lobby at Marfa's design-driven Hotel Saint George wouldn't feel out of place in Austin or Brooklyn, its softly illuminated brick

walls hung with bold contemporary local art. The seasonal, market-inspired cuisine, from lighter flatbread pizzas and cheese-charcuterie boards, to more substantial plates of grass-fed bone-in rib eye and pappardelle pasta with garlic-fennel sausage, is accompanied by one of the better curated wine lists in West Texas, plus a first-rate cocktail selection. **Known for:** locally sourced seasonal ingredients; house-made desserts; Texas wagyu beef tartare. [$] *Average main: $26* ✉ *Hotel Saint George, 105 S. Highland Ave., Marfa* ☎ *432/729–3700* 🌐 *www.marfasaint-george.com.*

Pizza Foundation

$ | **PIZZA** | **FAMILY** | Set in a sleekly industrial warehouse-style building on the east edge of downtown Marfa, Pizza Foundation appeals to families with its casual atmosphere and the quality thin-crust pizza the native Rhode Island owners turn out. They close for the evening when they run out of pizza, so you might call ahead to see if they're still making pies. **Known for:** Jarritos Mexican soft drinks; Big Bend Brewery beers on tap; white pizza with ricotta, spinach, and olive oil. [$] *Average main: $10* ✉ *305 S. Spring St., Marfa* ☎ *432/729–3377* 🌐 *www.facebook.com/Pizza-Foundation-8521289278* 🕒 *Closed Mon.–Thurs.*

★ Reata

$$$ | **SOUTHWESTERN** | A favorite of many West Texans spending the day in Alpine, Reata ("rope" in Spanish) feels both welcoming and upscale, with big, wooden tables and a pleasant rancher/cowboy vibe. It's a "howdy"-type place with prompt but down-home service and a menu that emphasizes creative Southwestern and Tex-Mex fare, such as tortilla soup, calf fries with cream gravy, and beef tamales with pecan mash, plus generously portioned steaks from a legendary ranch in the nearby Davis Mountains. [$] *Average main: $22* ✉ *203 N. 5th St., Alpine* ☎ *432/837–9232* 🌐 *www.reata.net* 🕒 *Closed Sun.*

Starlight Theatre

$$ | **SOUTHWESTERN** | This convivial restaurant-saloon with live-music is ground zero for all the ghosts and other characters of Terlingua. The menu includes plenty of local flavor, such as Terlingua chili and the chicken-fried wild boar with Terlingua gold beer gravy. **Known for:** the mixed grill of wild boar–venison sausage, grilled quail, and steak; mesquite-smoked brisket; Sunday brunch. [$] *Average main: $19* ✉ *631 Ivey Rd., Terlingua* ☎ *432/371–3400* 🌐 *www.thestarlighttheatre.com* 🕒 *No lunch.*

★ Stellina

$$ | **MEDITERRANEAN** | In both value and quality, this high-ceilinged wine bar and Mediterranean bistro anchored by a long central bar ranks among the top culinary experiences in the Big Bend region. Best known for its superb wines from around the world, Stellina also turns out exquisitely plated, vegetable-intensive meals based on what's available in season, from roasted-corn gazpacho in summer to baked orecchiette pasta with Brussels sprouts, cauliflower, leeks, and fontina cheese. **Known for:** well-curated and-priced international wine list; house-made pastas with seasonal sauces and accompaniments; knowledgeable, friendly service. [$] *Average main: $16* ✉ *103 N. Highland St., Marfa* ☎ *432/729–2030* 🌐 *www.stellinamarfa.com* 🕒 *Closed Sun. and Mon. No lunch.*

★ 12 Gage Restaurant

$$$$ | **MODERN AMERICAN** | When the sun sets, this intimate, fireplace-warmed indoor–outdoor restaurant is the best place to eat and socialize in Marathon. The innovative menu, featuring fresh produce from the Gage Hotel Garden across the railroad tracks, changes with the season but maintains a Southwestern flair. [$] *Average main: $35* ✉ *101 N.W. 1st St., Marathon* ☎ *432/386–4205* 🌐 *www.gagehotel.com.*

Bluebonnets: The Pride of Texas

Ever since men first explored the prairies of Texas, the bluebonnet has been revered. Native Americans wove folktales around this bright bluish-violet flower; early-day Spanish priests planted it thickly around their newly established missions; and the cotton boll and cactus competed fiercely with it for the state flower—the bluebonnet won the title in 1901.

Nearly half a dozen varieties of the bluebonnet, distinctive for flowers resembling pioneers' sunbonnets, exist throughout the state. From mid-January until late March, at least one of the famous flowers carpets the park: the Big Bend (also called Chisos) bluebonnet has been described as the most majestic species, as its deep-blue flower spikes can shoot up to three feet in height. The Big Bend bluebonnets can be found beginning in late winter on the flats of the park as well as along El Camino del Rio (Route 170), which follows the legendary Rio Grande between Lajitas and Presidio, Texas.

Hotels

IN THE PARK

★ Chisos Mountains Lodge

$$ | **HOTEL** | **FAMILY** | With ranger talks just next door at the visitor center, miles of hiking trails to suit all levels of fitness, and plenty of wildlife nearby, these comfortable no-frills rooms—some of which have been nicely remodeled—are a great place for families. **Pros:** sweeping mountain views from many rooms; steps from numerous hiking trailheads; reasonable rates considering the dramatic setting. **Cons:** no phones or TVs; Wi-Fi is either weak or nonexistent in many rooms; small, basic bathrooms. [$] *Rooms from: $145* ✉ *End of Chisos Basin Rd.* ☎ *432/477–2291 desk, 877/386–4383 Forever Resorts* 🌐 *www.chisosmountainslodge.com* 🛏 *72 rooms* 🍴 *No meals.*

OUTSIDE THE PARK

Big Bend Casitas at Far Flung

$$$ | **B&B/INN** | **FAMILY** | Next door to Far Flung Outdoor Center and just 3 miles from the western boundary of Big Bend National Park, the outfitter operates 12 freestanding casitas with hardwood floors, flat-screen TVs, kitchenettes, two pillow-top queen beds, and back porches with rocking chairs. **Pros:** homey atmosphere; activity package deals available with outfitter; grills and a kitchenette for self catering. **Cons:** no restaurant on-site, but there are a couple within walking distance; no pets; two-night minimum stay. [$] *Rooms from: $179* ✉ *23310 FM 170, Terlingua* ☎ *800/839–7238, 432/371–2633* 🌐 *www.bigbendfarflung.com/lodging* 🛏 *12 rooms* 🍴 *No meals.*

El Cosmico

$ | **HOTEL** | An unusual setup that suits Marfa's quirky personality, hipster-approved El Cosmico is a nomadic draw for adventurers, with tents, teepees, campsites, a yurt, and 1950s-style trailers that provide surprising comfort. **Pros:** rugged-chic, laid-back environment; "well-behaved" dogs are welcome; set on 21 scenic acres with great high-desert views. **Cons:** not well-suited to families; when the temperature dips below freezing, which is often in winter, the pipes in the outdoor bath houses can freeze; Wi-Fi can be spotty or slow in some units. [$] *Rooms from: $100* ✉ *802 S. Highland Ave., Marfa* ☎ *432/729–1950, 877/822–1950* 🌐 *www.elcosmico.com* 🛏 *26 rooms* 🍴 *No meals.*

Best Campgrounds in Big Bend

The park's copious campsites are separated, roughly, into two categories—frontcountry and backcountry. Each of its four frontcountry sites, except Rio Grande Village RV Campground, has toilet facilities at a minimum. Inside the park, rates are $14 for tent sites and $33 for the RV sites at Rio Grande Village. Far more numerous are the primitive backcountry sites, which require $12 permits from the visitor center. Primitive campsites with spectacular views are accessed via River Road, Glenn Springs, Old Ore Road, Paint Gap, Old Maverick Road, Grapevine Hills, Pine Canyon, and Croton Springs.

Chisos Basin Campground. Scenic views and cool shade are the highlights here, as well as access to some of the best alpine hiking in the park. About half of these sites can be reserved. ⊠ *End of Chisos Basin Rd.* ☎ *877/444–6777* ⊕ *www.recreation.gov.*

Cottonwood Campground. This 24-site, first-come, first-served spot near Castolon Visitor Center is popular for bird-watching near the Rio Grande. ⊠ *Off Ross Maxwell Scenic Dr.*

Maverick Ranch RV Park. Just outside the park at Lajitas Golf Resort, this layout has 100 RV sites and 18 primitive camping sites. There's a clubhouse, deli, hot showers, laundry facilities, picnic area, and hiking trails. It's also pet-friendly. ⊠ *FM 170* ☎ *432/424–5180* ⊕ *www.lajitasgolfresort.com*

Rio Grande Village Campground. This shady oasis is a popular birding spot. It's also a great site for kids and seniors, due to the ease of accessing facilities. There are 100 campsites with coin-operated showers, restrooms, and laundry. ⊠ *End of Rio Grande Village Rd.* ☎ *877/444–6777* ⊕ *www.recreation.gov.*

Rio Grande Village RV Park. Often full during holidays, this is one of the best sites for families because of the minitheater and proximity to the hot spring, which is fun to soak in at night. There are 25 RV sites with full hookups. ⊠ *End of Rio Grande Village Rd.* ☎ *432/477–2293, 877/386–4383* ⊕ *www.reserveusa.com.*

Eve's Garden B&B

$$$ | B&B/INN | This whimsical, color-saturated property built with recycled building materials and lots of imagination creates an entirely singular lodging experience. **Pros:** one-of-a-kind property; a full breakfast with delicious local, organic ingredients is included; lots of cool design elements. **Cons:** a bit quirky for some travelers; not well-suited to families; no pets. $ *Rooms from: $168* ⊠ *200 N.W. 3rd St., Marathon* ☎ *432/386–4165* ⊕ *www.evesgarden.org* ⤴ *7 rooms* ❧ *Breakfast.*

★ **Gage Hotel**

$$$$ | HOTEL | Cowboy, Native American, and Hispanic cultures are reflected in the furnishings of this gorgeously restored historic hotel, built in the 1920s by renowned architect Henry Trost, facing the life-sustaining railroad tracks. **Pros:** amazing architecture; outstanding restaurant, bar, and coffeehouse; health center, pool, and spa. **Cons:** very popular in spring and fall, so it's often booked well in advance; expensive for the area; busy during weddings and events. $ *Rooms from: $240* ⊠ *102 N.W. 1st St., Marathon* ☎ *432/386–4205, 800/884–4243* ⊕ *www.*

gagehotel.com 🛏 *45 rooms* 🍴 *No meals.*

Holiday Hotel

$$ | **B&B/INN** | The quirky denizens of old Terlingua ghost town have renovated these long-abandoned miners' homes into one-of-a-kind retreats. **Pros:** the funky and fun Starlight Theatre is on-site; artfully appointed accommodations; relatively close to Big Bend western entrance. **Cons:** in a tiny village far from many services; a little too quirky for some; no phones or TVs in the rooms. [$] *Rooms from: $130* ✉ *635 Ivey Rd., Terlingua* ☎ *432/201–1177* 🌐 *www.bigbendholidayhotel.com* 🛏 *8 units* 🍴 *No meals.*

★ **Holland Hotel**

$$ | **HOTEL** | Once just a stop on the transcontinental railroad, the rancher-themed Holland Hotel is now a historic landmark still hung with its original sign on the main, bustling drag in downtown Alpine—just doors down from shops, cafés, and galleries. **Pros:** inviting lobby and courtyard; colorful rooms exude historic charm; swimming pool available at the co-owned Maverick Inn. **Cons:** noise from nearby trains (earplugs provided in rooms); older property with a few quirks; breakfast is on the meager side. [$] *Rooms from: $140* ✉ *209 W. Holland Ave., Alpine* ☎ *432/837–2800, 800/535–8040* 🌐 *thehollandhoteltexas.com* 🛏 *27 rooms* 🍴 *Breakfast.*

Hotel El Capitan

$$ | **HOTEL** | Famed architect Henry Trost designed this Spanish Revival hotel, which takes its place among such other glamorous Trost landmarks as the Hotel Paisano (Marfa), the Holland Hotel (Alpine), and the Gage Hotel (Marathon). **Pros:** lovely, historic architecture; great value; pet-friendly. **Cons:** about 200 miles northwest of Big Bend; close to interstate highway; some rooms are quite small. [$] *Rooms from: $135* ✉ *100 E. Broadway, Van Horn* ☎ *432/283–1220, 877/283–1220* 🌐 *www.thehotelelcapitan.com* 🛏 *36 rooms* 🍴 *Breakfast.*

Hotel Paisano

$$ | **HOTEL** | Once the playground of Liz Taylor, Rock Hudson, and James Dean, who stayed here while filming *Giant*, the Paisano has maintained its glamour with glistening Mediterranean architecture, a fountain in the courtyard dining area, and dress and jewelry shops in downstairs hallways. **Pros:** Hollywood nostalgia; in the center of town; bar and restaurant are great for people-watching. **Cons:** no elevator; some rooms and bathrooms are quite small; not much of a view from most rooms. [$] *Rooms from: $124* ✉ *207 N. Highland Ave., Marfa* ☎ *432/729–3669, 844/476–2732* 🌐 *www.hotelpaisano.com* 🛏 *40 rooms* 🍴 *No meals.*

★ **Hotel Saint George**

$$$$ | **HOTEL** | The region's swankiest lodging, in the heart of downtown Marfa, has an airy lobby and common spaces hung with museum-quality local contemporary artwork, and houses Bar Saint George, LaVenture restaurant, and renowned Marfa Book Company. **Pros:** hip design and muted color palette; beautiful pool and bar; ultracomfy beds and fancy amenities. **Cons:** on the pricey side; the adult vibe isn't conducive to families. [$] *Rooms from: $249* ✉ *105 S. Highland Ave., Marfa* ☎ *432/729–3700* 🌐 *www.marfasaintgeorge.com* 🛏 *55 rooms* 🍴 *No meals.*

Indian Lodge

$$ | **HOTEL** | **FAMILY** | Built of adobe in the 1930s by the Civilian Conservation Corps, the Indian Lodge makes for an old-timey, out-of-the-way Southwestern experience. **Pros:** swimming pool; numerous hiking trails nearby; central air and heat. **Cons:** no pets allowed; nearly 150 miles from Big Bend National Park entrance; decidedly rustic. [$] *Rooms from: $105* ✉ *Davis Mountains State Park, Park Rd. 3, Fort Davis* ☎ *432/426–3254, 800/792–1112* 🌐 *www.tpwd.texas.gov/state-parks/indian-lodge* 🛏 *39 rooms* 🍴 *No meals.*

Lajitas Golf Resort & Spa
$$$$ | **RESORT** | The former cavalry post turned ghost town is now a privately owned collection of Western-themed tourist attractions with a golf resort, spa, riding stables, convenience store, RV park, and hiking trails, adding up to the nicest place to eat, shop, and overnight within 25 miles of the park. **Pros:** resort is a town unto itself, with many activities; the golf course is one of the best in West Texas; good access to western side of Big Bend National Park. **Cons:** pricey rooms for the area; not as much to do in this tiny town; no elevator. [$] *Rooms from: $209* ✉ *FM 170, Lajitas* ☎ *432/424–5000, 877/525–4827* 🌐 *www.lajitasgolfresort.com* 🛏 *102 rooms* 🍴 *No meals.*

La Posada Milagro
$$$ | **B&B/INN** | As rustic, yet comfortable, as Terlingua gets, this cozy compound has all the amenities and views that you could hope for in such a faraway outpost. **Pros:** short drive from Big Bend National Park; some rooms have fireplaces; terrific café. **Cons:** far from many services; shared bathrooms for some rooms are located in separate building; breakfast isn't complimentary. [$] *Rooms from: $185* ✉ *100 Milagro Rd., Terlingua* ☎ *432/371–3044* 🌐 *www.laposadamilagro.net* 🛏 *5 casitas* 🍴 *No meals.*

Chapter 7

BLACK CANYON OF THE GUNNISON NATIONAL PARK

Updated by
Kellee Katagi

COLORADO

WELCOME TO BLACK CANYON OF THE GUNNISON NATIONAL PARK

TOP REASONS TO GO

★ **Sheer of heights:** Play it safe, but edge as close to the canyon rim as you dare and peer over into an abyss that's more than 2,700 feet deep in some places.

★ **Rapids transit:** Experienced paddlers can tackle Class V rapids and 50°F water with the occasional portage past untamable sections of the Gunnison River.

★ **Fine fishing:** Fish the rare Gold Medal Waters of the Gunnison. Of the 9,000 miles of trout streams in Colorado, only 168 miles have this "gold medal" distinction.

★ **Triple-park action:** Check out Curecanti National Recreation Area and Gunnison Gorge National Conservation Area, which bookend Black Canyon.

★ **Cliff-hangers:** Watch experts climb the Painted Wall—Colorado's tallest vertical wall at 2,250 feet—and other challenging rock faces.

Black Canyon of the Gunnison is a park of extremes—great depths, narrow widths, tall cliffs, and steep descents.

1 East Portal. The only way you can get down to the river via automobile in Black Canyon is on the steep East Portal Road. There's a campground and picnic area here, as well as fishing and trail access.

2 North Rim. If you want to access this side of the canyon from the south, expect a drive of up to three hours as you wind around the canyon. The area's remoteness and difficult location mean the North Rim is never crowded; the road is partially unpaved and closes in the winter. There's also a small ranger station here.

3 South Rim. This is the main area of the park. The park's only visitor center is here, along with a campground and a few picnic areas. The South Rim Road closes at Gunnison Point in the winter, when skiers and snowshoers take over.

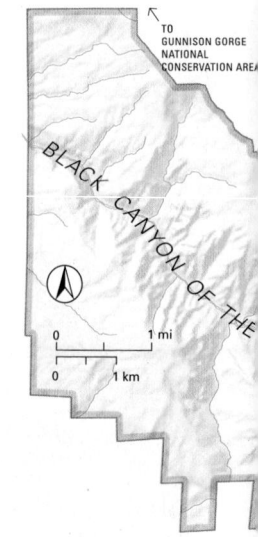

TO
GUNNISON GORGE
NATIONAL
CONSERVATION AREA

BLACK CANYON OF THE

0   1 mi
0   1 km

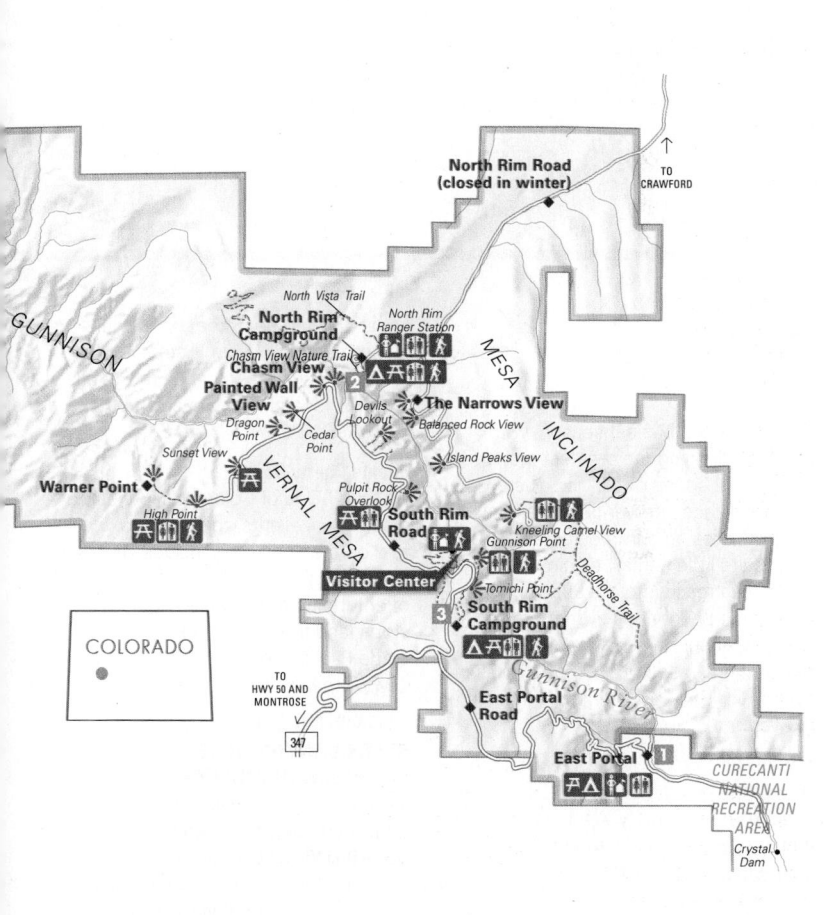

The Black Canyon of the Gunnison River is one of Colorado's most awe-inspiring places. A vivid testament to the powers of erosion, the canyon is roughly 2,000 feet deep. The steep angles of the cliffs allow little sunlight, and ever-present shadows blanket the canyon walls, leaving some of it in almost perpetual darkness.

Planning

WHEN TO GO

Summer is the busiest season, with July experiencing the greatest crowds. However, a spring or fall visit gives you two advantages: fewer people and cooler temperatures. In summer, especially in years with little rainfall, daytime temperatures can reach into the 90s. A winter visit to the park brings even more solitude, as all but one section of campsites are shut down and only about 2 miles of South Rim Road, the park main road, are plowed.

November through March is when the snow hits, with an average of about 3 to 8 inches of it monthly. April through May and September and October are the rainiest, with about an inch of precipitation each month. June is generally the driest month. Temperatures at the bottom of the canyon are about 8 degrees warmer than at the rim.

FESTIVALS AND EVENTS
Main in Motion

FESTIVAL | From 6–8:30 pm every Thursday in the summer, Main Street in Montrose is the place to be. Street performers and other artisans join Historic Downtown Montrose restaurants and shops to make for a pleasant evening stroll. ☎ 970/964–9304.

Paonia Cherry Days

FESTIVAL | One of Colorado's longest-running annual events, this small-town festival on the 4th of July includes a parade, food, crafts, sidewalk sales, and a variety of entertainment celebrating local cherry crops (and the other fruits that have made Paonia famous). ☎ 970/527–3886 ⊕ www.paoniacherrydays.com.

PLANNING YOUR TIME
BLACK CANYON OF THE GUNNISON IN ONE DAY

Pack a lunch and head to the canyon's South Rim, beginning with a stop at the **South Rim Visitor Center.** Before getting back into the car, take in your first view of Black Canyon from **Gunnison Point,** adjacent to the visitor center. Then set out on a driving tour of the 7-mile **South Rim Road,** allowing the rest of the morning to stop at the various viewpoints that overlook the canyon. Don't miss **Chasm View** and **Painted Wall View,** and be sure to stretch your legs along the short (0.4 mile

AVERAGE HIGH/LOW TEMPERATURES					
JAN.	FEB.	MAR.	APR.	MAY	JUNE
37/14	42/16	50/18	47/23	67/37	75/44
JULY	AUG.	SEPT.	OCT.	NOV.	DEC.
84/51	81/50	72/42	62/31	48/23	37/12

round-trip) **Cedar Point Nature Trail.** If your timing is good, you'll reach **High Point,** the end of the road, around lunchtime.

After lunch, head out on **Warner Point Nature Trail** for an hour-long hike (1.5 miles round-trip). Then retrace your drive along South Rim Road back to the visitor center.

GETTING HERE AND AROUND
AIR TRAVEL
The Black Canyon of the Gunnison lies between the cities of Gunnison and Montrose, both of which have small regional airports.

CAR TRAVEL
The park has three roads. South Rim Road, reached by Route 347, is the primary thoroughfare and winds along the canyon's South Rim. From about late November to early April, the road is not plowed past the visitor center at Gunnison Point. North Rim Road, reached by Route 92, is usually open from May through Thanksgiving; in winter, the road is unplowed. On the park's south side, the serpentine East Portal Road descends abruptly to the Gunnison River below. The road is usually open from the beginning of May through the end of November. Because of the grade, vehicles or vehicle-trailer combinations longer than 22 feet are not permitted. The park has no public transportation.

PARK ESSENTIALS
ACCESSIBILITY
South Rim Visitor Center is accessible to people with mobility impairments, as are most of the sites at South Rim Campground. Drive-to overlooks on the South Rim include Tomichi Point, the alternate

gravel viewpoint at Pulpit Rock (the main one is not accessible), Chasm View (gravel), Sunset View, and High Point. Balanced Rock (gravel) is the only drive-to viewpoint on the North Rim. None of the park's hiking trails are accessible by car.

PARK FEES AND PERMITS
Entrance fees are $15 per week per vehicle. Visitors entering on bicycle, motorcycle, or on foot pay $7 for a weekly pass. To access the inner canyon, you must pick up a wilderness permit (no fee).

PARK HOURS
The park is open 24/7 year-round. It's in the Mountain time zone.

CELL-PHONE RECEPTION
Cell-phone reception in the park is unreliable and sporadic. There are public telephones at South Rim Visitor Center and South Rim Campground.

EDUCATIONAL OFFERINGS
RANGER PROGRAMS
Junior Ranger Program. Kids of all ages can participate in this program with an activities booklet to fill in while exploring the park. Inquire at the South Rim Visitor Center.

RESTAURANTS
The park itself has no eateries, but nearby towns have choices ranging from traditional American to an eclectic café and bakery.

HOTELS
Black Canyon is devoid of hotels. Smaller hotels, some excellent B&Bs, and rustic lodges are nearby, as are a few of the larger chains. *Hotel reviews have been shortened. For full information, visit Fodors.com.*

7

Black Canyon of the Gunnison National Park PLANNING

What It Costs

	$	$$	$$$	$$$$
RESTAURANTS				
	under $13	$13–$18	$19–$25	over $25
HOTELS				
	under $121	$121–$170	$171–$230	over $230

VISITOR INFORMATION

PARK CONTACT INFORMATION Black Canyon of the Gunnison National Park ⊕ *7 miles north of U.S. 50 on CO Hwy. 347* ☎ *970/641–2337* ⊕ *www.nps.gov/blca.*

VISITOR CENTERS

North Rim Ranger Station

INFO CENTER | This small facility on the park's North Rim is open only in summer. Rangers can provide information and assistance and can issue permits for wilderness use and rock climbing. If rangers are out in the field, which they often are, guests can find directions for obtaining permits posted in the station. ⊠ *North Rim Rd., 11 miles from Rte. 92 turnoff* ☎ *970/641–2337.*

South Rim Visitor Center

INFO CENTER | The park's only visitor center offers interactive exhibits and introductory films detailing the park's geology and wildlife. Inquire at the center about free guided tours and informational ranger programs. ⊠ *Black Canyon of the Gunnison National Park ⊕ 1½ mile from the entrance station on South Rim Rd.* ☎ *970/249–1914.*

 Sights

SCENIC DRIVES

The scenic South and North Rim roads offer deep and distant views into the canyon. Both also offer several lookout points and short hiking trails along the rim. The trails that go down into the canyon are steep and strenuous, and essentially unmarked, and so are reserved for experienced (and very fit) hikers.

East Portal Road

SCENIC DRIVE | The only way to access the Gunnison River from the park by car is via this paved route, which drops approximately 2,000 feet down to the water in only 5 miles, giving it an extremely steep grade. Vehicles longer than 22 feet are not allowed on the road. If you're towing a trailer, you can unhitch it near the entrance to South Rim campground. The bottom of the road is actually in the adjacent Curecanti National Recreation Area. A tour of East Portal Road, with a brief stop at the bottom, takes about 45 minutes. ☉ *Closed mid-Nov.–mid.-Apr.*

North Rim Road

SCENIC DRIVE | Black Canyon's North Rim is much less frequented, but no less spectacular—the walls here are near vertical—than the South Rim. To reach the 15½-mile-long North Rim Road, take the signed turnoff from Route 92 about 3 miles south of Crawford. The road is paved for about the first 4 miles; the rest is gravel. After 11 miles, turn left at the intersection (the North Rim Campground is to the right). There are six overlooks along the road as it snakes along the rim's edge. Kneeling Camel, at the road's east end, provides the broadest view of the canyon. Set aside about two hours for a tour of the North Rim. ☉ *Closed late Nov.–mid-Apr.*

South Rim Road

SCENIC DRIVE | This paved 7-mile stretch from Tomichi Point to High Point is the park's main road. The drive follows the canyon's level South Rim; 12 overlooks are accessible from the road, most via short gravel trails. Several short hikes along the rim also begin roadside. Allow between two and three hours round-trip.

SCENIC STOPS

The vast depths that draw thousands of visitors each year to Black Canyon have also historically prevented any extensive human habitation from taking root, so cultural attractions are largely absent here. But what the park lacks in historic sites it more than makes up for in scenery.

Chasm and Painted Wall Views

VIEWPOINT | At the heart-in-your-throat Chasm viewpoint, the canyon walls plummet 1,820 feet to the river, but are only 1,100 feet apart at the top. As you peer down into the depths, keep in mind that this section is where the Gunnison River descends at its steepest rate, dropping 240 feet within the span of a mile. A few hundred yards farther is the best place from which to see Painted Wall, Colorado's tallest cliff. Pinkish swaths of pegmatite (a crystalline, granite-like rock) give the wall its colorful, marbled appearance. ⊠ *Black Canyon of the Gunnison National Park* ✥ *Approximately 3½ miles from the Visitor Center on South Rim Rd.*

Narrows View

VIEWPOINT | Look upriver from this North Rim viewing spot and you'll be able to see into the canyon's narrowest section, just a slot really, with only 40 feet between the walls at the bottom. The canyon is also taller (1,725 feet) here than it is wide at the rim (1,150 feet). ⊠ *North Rim Rd., first overlook past the ranger station.*

Warner Point

NATURE SITE | This viewpoint, at the end of the Warner Point Nature Trail, delivers awesome views of the canyon's deepest point (2,722 feet), plus the nearby San Juan and West Elk mountain ranges. ⊠ *End of Warner Point Nature Trail, westernmost end of South Rim Rd.*

🏃 Activities

Recreational activities in Black Canyon run the gamut from short and easy nature trails to world-class (and experts-only) rock climbing and kayaking. The cold waters of the Gunnison River are well-known to trout anglers.

BICYCLING

Bikes are not permitted on any of the trails, but cycling along the South Rim or North Rim Road is a great way to view the park.

BIRD-WATCHING

The sheer cliffs of Black Canyon, though not suited for human habitation, provide a great habitat for birds. Peregrine falcons, white-throated swifts, and other cliff-dwelling birds revel in the dizzying heights, while at river level you'll find American dippers foraging for food in the rushing waters. Canyon wrens, which nest in the cliffs, are more often heard than seen, but their hauntingly beautiful songs are unforgettable. Dusky grouse are common in the sagebrush areas above the canyon, and red-tailed

7

Black Canyon of the Gunnison National Park

and Cooper's hawks and turkey vultures frequent the canyon rims. The best times for birding are spring and early summer.

BOATING AND KAYAKING

With Class V rapids, the Gunnison River is one of the premier kayak challenges in North America. The spectacular 14-mile stretch of the river that passes through the park is so narrow in some sections that the rim seems to be closing up above your head. Once you're downstream from the rapids (and out of the park), the canyon opens up into what is called the Gunnison Gorge. The rapids ease considerably, and the trip becomes more of a quiet float on Class I to Class IV water.

Kayaking the river through the park requires a wilderness use permit (and lots of expertise), and rafting is not allowed. Access to the Gunnison Gorge is only by foot or horseback. However, several outfitters offer guided raft and kayak trips in the Gunnison Gorge and other sections of the Gunnison River.

FISHING

The three dams built upriver from the park in Curecanti National Recreation Area have created prime trout fishing in the waters below. Certain restrictions apply: Only artificial flies and lures are permitted, and a Colorado fishing license is required for people aged 16 and older. Rainbow trout are catch-and-release only, and there are size and possession limits on brown trout (check at the visitor center). Most anglers access the river from the bottom of East Portal Road; an undeveloped trail goes along the riverbank for about three-quarters of a mile.

HIKING

All trails can be hot in summer and most don't receive much shade, so bring water, a hat, and plenty of sunscreen. Dogs are permitted, on leash, on Rim Rock, Cedar Point Nature, and Chasm View Nature trails, and at any overlook. Hiking into the inner canyon, while

Wildlife in Black Canyon

You may spot peregrine falcons nesting in May and June, or other birds of prey such as red-tailed hawks, Cooper's hawks, and golden eagles circling overhead at any time of year. In summer, turkey vultures join the flying corps, and in winter, bald eagles. Mule deer, elk, and the very shy bobcat also call the park home. In spring and fall, you may see a porcupine among pinyon pines on the rims. Listen for the high-pitched chirp of the yellow-bellied marmot, which hangs out on sunny, rocky outcrops. Though rarely seen, mountain lions and black bears also live in the park.

doable, is not for the faint of heart—or slight of step. Six named routes lead down to the river, but they are not maintained or marked. In fact, the park staff won't even call them trails; they refer to them as "controlled slides." These supersteep, rocky routes vary in one-way distance from 1 to 2.75 miles, and the descent can be anywhere from 1,800 to 2,722 feet. Your reward, of course, is a rare look at the bottom of the canyon and the fast-flowing Gunnison. ■ TIP→ Don't attempt an inner-canyon hike without plenty of water (the park's recommendation is one gallon per person, per day). For descriptions of the routes and the necessary permit to hike them, stop at the visitor center at the South Rim or North Rim ranger station. Dogs are not permitted in the inner canyon.

Cedar Point Trail

HIKING/WALKING | FAMILY | This 0.4-mile round-trip interpretive trail leads out from South Rim Road to two overlooks. It's an easy stroll, and signs along the way detail the surrounding plants. *Easy.* ⊠ *Black*

Canyon of the Gunnison National Park ✛ Trailhead: off South Rim Rd., 4¼ miles from South Rim Visitor Center.

Chasm View Nature Trail

HIKING/WALKING | The park's shortest trail (0.3 mile round-trip) starts at North Rim Campground and offers an impressive 50-yard walk right along the canyon rim as well as an eye-popping view of Painted Wall and Serpent Point. This is also an excellent place to spot raptors, swifts, and other birds. *Moderate.* ✉ *Black Canyon of the Gunnison National Park* ✛ *Trailhead: at North Rim Campground, 11¼ miles from Rte. 92.*

Deadhorse Trail

HIKING/WALKING | Despite its name, the 5-mile Deadhorse Trail is actually a pleasant hike, starting on an old service road from the Kneeling Camel View on the North Rim Road. The trail's farthest point provides the park's easternmost viewpoint. From this overlook, the canyon is much more open, with pinnacles and spires rising along its sides. *Easy.* ✉ *Black Canyon of the Gunnison National Park* ✛ *Trailhead: at the southernmost end of North Rim Rd.*

North Vista Trail

HIKING/WALKING | The round-trip hike to Exclamation Point is 3 miles; a more difficult foray to the top of 8,563-foot Green Mountain (a mesa, really) is 7 miles. The trail leads you along the North Rim; keep an eye out for especially gnarled pinyon pines—the North Rim is the site of some of the oldest groves of pinyons in North America, between 400 and 700 years old. *Moderate.* ✉ *Black Canyon of the Gunnison National Park* ✛ *Trailhead: at North Rim ranger station, off North Rim Rd., 11 miles from Rte. 92 turnoff.*

Oak Flat Loop Trail

HIKING/WALKING | This 2-mile loop is the most demanding of the South Rim hikes, as it brings you about 400 feet below the canyon rim. In places, the trail is narrow and crosses some steep slopes, but you

Bridge Over the River Gunnison?

A bridge that would span the canyon's two rims was proposed in the 1930s. The bad news is that it was never built, so it'll take you 2 to 3 hours to drive from one rim around to the other. The good news for the long trek is all the unforgettable scenery along the way.

won't have to navigate any steep drop-offs. Oak Flat is the shadiest of all the South Rim trails; small groves of aspen and thick stands of Douglas fir along the loop offer some respite from the sun. *Difficult.* ✉ *Black Canyon of the Gunnison National Park* ✛ *Trailhead: just west of the South Rim Visitor Center.*

Rim Rock Nature Trail

HIKING/WALKING | The terrain on this 1-mile round-trip trail is primarily flat and exposed to the sun, with a bird's-eye view into the canyon. An interpretive pamphlet, which corresponds to markers along the route, is available at the visitor center and the campground trailhead. *Moderate.* ✉ *Black Canyon of the Gunnison National Park* ✛ *Trailheads: at Tomichi Point overlook or Loop C in South Rim Campground.*

★ Warner Point Nature Trail

HIKING/WALKING | The 1.5-mile round-trip hike starts from High Point. It provides fabulous vistas of the San Juan and West Elk mountains and Uncompahgre Valley. Warner Point, at trail's end, has the steepest drop-off from rim to river: a dizzying 2,722 feet. *Moderate.* ✉ *Black Canyon of the Gunnison National Park* ✛ *Trailhead: at the end of South Rim Rd.*

HORSEBACK RIDING

Although its name might indicate otherwise, Deadhorse Trail is actually the only trail in the park where horses are allowed. The trail is an easy-to-moderate 5-mile loop that begins east of North Rim Road. Horses are not allowed on the South Rim, and can be on the North Rim only on the Deadhorse Trail, in the North Rim Campground, or on the North Rim Road during transport in a trailer.

Black Canyon of the Gunnison has no facilities geared toward horses. If you bring your own horse, go to the end of North Rim Road and park your trailer at Kneeling Camel Overlook to access Deadhorse Trail. No permit is required.

TOURS

Elk Ridge Trail Rides

HORSEBACK RIDING | You can take 90-minute and two-hour rides at this ranch just outside the Black Canyon National Park. ✉ *10203 Bostwick Park Rd., Montrose* ☎ *970/240–6007* ✉ *$85 for 90 min.; $95 for 2 hrs. Reservations required.*

ROCK CLIMBING

For expert rock climbers, the sheer cliffs of the Black Canyon represent one of Colorado's premier big-wall challenges. Some routes can take several days to complete, with climbers sleeping on narrow ledges, or "portaledges." Though there's no official guide to climbing in the park, reports from individual climbers are kept on file at the South Rim Visitor Center. Nesting birds of prey may lead to wall closure at certain times of year.

Rock climbing in the park is for experts only, but you can do some bouldering at the Marmot Rocks area, about 100 feet south of South Rim Road between Painted Wall and Cedar Point overlooks (park at Painted Wall). Four boulder groupings offer a variety of routes rated from easy to very difficult; a pamphlet with a diagrammed map of the area is available at the South Rim Visitor Center.

Irwin Guides

CLIMBING/MOUNTAINEERING | Intermediate and expert climbers can take full-day rock-climbing guided tours in the Black Canyon on routes from 6 to 15 pitches in length. ✉ *330 Belleview Ave., Crested Butte* ☎ *970/349–5430* ⊕ *www.irwinguides.com* ✉ *$395 for one person; $265 for two or more.*

WINTER ACTIVITIES

From late November to early April, South Rim Road is not plowed past the visitor center, offering park guests a unique opportunity to cross-country ski or snowshoe on the road. The Park Service also grooms a cross-country ski trail and marks a snowshoe trail through the woods, both starting at the visitor center. It's possible to ski or snowshoe on the unplowed North Rim Road, too, but it's about 4 miles from where the road closes, through sagebrush flats, to the canyon rim.

Nearby Towns

The primary gateway to Black Canyon is **Montrose,** 15 miles west of the park. The legendary Ute chief, Ouray, and his wife, Chipeta, lived near here in the late 1800s. Today, Montrose straddles the important agricultural and mining regions along the Uncompahgre River, and is the area's main shopping hub. The closest town to Black Canyon's North Rim is **Crawford,** about 3 miles from the entrance to the North Rim Road, a small hillside enclave amid the sheep and cattle ranches of the North Fork Valley with a small downtown area. Northeast on Route 92 (20 miles) is **Paonia,** a unique and charming blend of the old and new West. Here, career environmentalists and hippie types who have escaped the mainstream mingle with longtime ranchers, miners, and fruit growers. Eleven miles northwest of Crawford on Route 92 is the small ranching and mining community of **Hotchkiss.** The trappings and sensibilities of the Old

West are here, from cowboy bars and fields of livestock to the annual summertime rodeo.

ESSENTIALS
VISITOR INFORMATION North Fork Valley Tourism ☎ 970/872–3226 ⊕ www.north-forkvalley.net.

 # Sights

★ Colorado National Monument
MEMORIAL | Sheer red-rock cliffs open to 23 miles of steep canyons and thin monoliths that sprout as high as 450 feet from the floor of Colorado National Monument. This vast tract of rugged, ragged terrain was declared a national monument in 1911 at the urging of an eccentric visionary named John Otto. Now it's popular for rock climbing, horseback riding, cross-country skiing, biking, and camping. Cold Shivers Point is just one of the many dramatic overlooks along **Rim Rock Drive,** a 23-mile scenic route with breathtaking views. The town of Fruita, at the base of Colorado National Monument, is a haven for mountain bikers and hikers. It makes a great center for exploring the area's canyons—whether from the seat of a bike or the middle of a raft, heading for a leisurely float trip. ⊠ Fruita ☎ 970/858–3617 ⊕ www.nps.gov/colm ☜ $15 per wk per vehicle. Visitors entering on motorcycle pay $10; bicycle or foot pay $5 for weekly pass.

Crawford State Park
NATIONAL/STATE PARK | The focus of this 337-acre park is Crawford Reservoir, created in 1963 when a dam was built to increase the supply of irrigated water to the surrounding ranches and farms. Boating and waterskiing are permitted on the reservoir, as are swimming and fishing (the lake is stocked with rainbow trout). The park has a 1-mile wheelchair-accessible hiking trail along with the primitive ½-mile Indian Fire Nature Trail, which runs along the reservoir on the park's west side. ⊠ 1 mile south of Crawford, 40468 Hwy. 92, Crawford ☎ 970/921–5721 ⊕ cpw.state.co.us/placestogo/Parks/crawford ☜ $7.

Curecanti National Recreation Area
BODY OF WATER | This recreation area, part of the National Park Service, encompasses three reservoirs along 40 miles of the Gunnison River. Blue Mesa is the largest body of water in Colorado; Morrow Point and Crystal are fjord-like reservoirs set in the upper Black Canyon of the Gunnison. All three reservoirs provide water-based recreational opportunities, including fishing, boating, and paddling, but only Blue Mesa offers boat ramps. Excellent fly fishing can be found upstream (east) of Blue Mesa Reservoir along the Gunnison River. A variety of camping and hiking opportunities are also available. The Elk Creek Visitor Center on U.S. 50 is available year-round for trip-planning assistance. ⊠ 102 Elk Creek, Gunnison ☎ 970/641–2337 ⊕ www.nps.gov/cure ☜ Free.

 # Activities

BOATING
Lake Fork Marina
BOATING | Located on the western end of Blue Mesa Reservoir off U.S. 92, the Lake Fork Marina rents all types of boats. If you have your own, there's a ramp at the marina and slips for rent. ⊠ Off U.S. 92, near Lake Fork Campground, Gunnison ☎ 970/641–3048 ⊕ www.thebluemesa.com.

Morrow Point Boat Tours
BOATING | Starting in neighboring Curecanti National Recreation Area, these guided tours run twice daily (except Tuesday) in the summer, at 10 am and 12:30 pm. Morrow Point Boat Tours take passengers on a 90-minute tour via pontoon boat, and require a 1-mile walk to the boat dock. Reservations are required. ⊠ Pine Creek Trail and Boat Dock, U.S. 50, milepost 130, 25 miles west of Gunnison, Gunnison ☎ 970/641–2337

Best Campgrounds in Black Canyon of the Gunnison

There are three campgrounds in Black Canyon National Park. The small North Rim Campground is first come, first served, and is closed in the winter. Vehicles longer than 35 feet are discouraged from this campground. South Rim Campground is considerably larger, and has a loop that's open year-round. Reservations are accepted in South Rim Loops A and B. Power hookups only exist in Loop B. The East Portal campground is at the bottom of the steep East Portal Road and is open whenever the road is open. It offers 15 first-come, first-served tent sites in a pretty setting. Water has to be trucked up to the campgrounds, so use it in moderation; it's shut off in mid-to-late September. Generators are not allowed at South Rim and are highly discouraged on the North Rim.

East Portal Campground. Its location next to the Gunnison River makes it perfect for fishing. ⊠ *East Portal Rd., 5 miles from the main entrance.*

North Rim Campground. This small campground, nestled amid pine trees, offers the basics along the quiet North Rim. ⊠ *North Rim Rd., 11¼ miles from Rte. 92.*

South Rim Campground. Stay on the canyon rim at this main campground right inside the park entrance. Loops A and C have tent sites only. The RV hookups are in Loop B, and those sites are priced higher than those in other parts of the campground. It's possible to camp here year-round (Loop A stays open all winter), but the loops are not plowed, so you'll have to hike in with your tent. ⊠ *South Rim Rd., 1 mile from the visitor center.*

⊕ *www.nps.gov/cure* ✉ *$24* ⊙ *Closed mid-Sept.–May.*

🍴 Restaurants

IN THE PARK
PICNIC AREAS
There are a variety of picnic areas at Black Canyon of the Gunnison, all with pit toilets; all are closed when it snows.

East Portal
RESTAURANT—SIGHT | This picnic area, located at the bottom of the canyon, accommodates large groups. There are tables, fire grates, bathrooms, and a large shaded shelter. ⊠ *East Portal Rd. at the Gunnison River.*

High Point
RESTAURANT—SIGHT | When the sun is unforgiving, this overlook offers more

shade than most of the other picnic areas. There are tables and bathrooms but no fire grates. ⊠ *West end of South Rim Rd.*

North and South Rim campgrounds
RESTAURANT—SIGHT | Feel free to use unoccupied camping sites for picnicking. There are tables, fire grates, and bathrooms. ⊠ *North Rim: West end of North Rim Rd.; South Rim: About 1 mile east of South Rim Visitor Center on South Rim Rd.*

Pulpit Rock
RESTAURANT—SIGHT | There are tables and bathrooms at this overlook. ⊠ *2 miles west of the South Rim Visitor Center.*

Sunset View
RESTAURANT—SIGHT | There are tables and bathrooms at this overlook. ⊠ *About 1 mile east of High Point on South Rim Rd.*

OUTSIDE THE PARK

MONTROSE

Camp Robber

$$ | **SOUTHWESTERN** | This simply decorated restaurant serves some of Montrose's most creative cuisine, such as its famous green-chile chicken and potato soup or the house specialty: green-chile pistachio-crusted pork medallions. At lunch, salads with housemade dressings, hearty sandwiches, and blue-corn enchiladas fuel hungry hikers. **Known for:** Sunday brunch; homemade desserts; shaded patio. [$] *Average main: $15* ✉ *1515 Ogden Rd., Montrose* ☎ *970/240–1590* 🌐 *www.camprobber.com* 🕒 *No dinner Sun.*

Hotels

OUTSIDE THE PARK

MONTROSE

Red Arrow Inn & Suites

$ | **HOTEL** | This low-key establishment is a great value, with very reasonable prices for one of the nicest lodgings in the area, mainly because of the large, pretty rooms filled with handsome wood furnishings. **Pros:** complimentary airport shuttle; good breakfast; pleasant pool. **Cons:** motel-style entrances; next to busy street. [$] *Rooms from: $98* ✉ *1702 E. Main St., Montrose* ☎ *970/249–9641* 🌐 *www.redarrowinn.com* 🛏 *59 rooms* 🍴 *Free Breakfast.*

Chapter 8

BRYCE CANYON NATIONAL PARK

8

Updated by
Andrew Collins

UTAH

WELCOME TO
BRYCE CANYON NATIONAL PARK

TOP REASONS TO GO

★ **Hoodoo heaven:** The boldly colored, gravity-defying limestone tentacles reaching skyward—called hoodoos—are Bryce Canyon's most recognizable attraction.

★ **Famous fresh air:** With some of the clearest skies in the nation, the park offers views that, on a clear day, can extend more than 100 miles and into three states.

★ **Spectacular sunrises and sunsets:** The deep orange and crimson hues of the park's hoodoos are intensified by the light of the sun at either end of the day.

★ **Dramatically different zones:** From the highest point of the rim to the canyon base, the park spans 2,000 feet, so you can explore three unique climatic zones: spruce-fir forest, ponderosa-pine forest, and pinyon pine-juniper forest.

★ **Snowy fun:** Bryce gets an average of 87 inches of snowfall a year, and is a popular destination for skiers and snowshoe enthusiasts.

Bryce Canyon National Park isn't a single canyon, but rather a series of natural amphitheaters on the eastern edge of the Paunsaugunt Plateau. The park's scenic drive runs along a formation known as the Pink Cliffs and offers more than a dozen amazing overlooks. One strategy is to drive without stops to the end of the 18-mile road and turn around, stopping at the scenic overlooks—which will then all be conveniently on the right side of the road, on the return drive. From the main park road you can also access the most popular hiking trails down into the canyons. A handful of roads veers east of the scenic drive to access other points of interest. For relief from the frequent heavy traffic and scarce parking during the spring–fall high season, leave your car outside the park and ride the free (once you've paid the park entrance fee) shuttle buses.

1 Bryce Amphitheater. It's the heart of the park. From here you can access historic Bryce Canyon Lodge as well as Sunrise, Sunset, and Inspiration points. Walk to Bryce Point at sunrise to view the mesmerizing collection of massive hoodoos known as Silent City.

2 Under-the-Rim Trail. This rugged, minimally maintained 23-mile trail is the best way to access Bryce Canyon backcountry. It can be a challenging three-day adventure or a half day of fun via one of the four access points from the main road. A handful of primitive campgrounds (permits required) lines the route.

3 Rainbow and Yovimpa Points. The end of the scenic road, but not of the scenery, here you can hike a loop trail through ancient bristlecone pines and look south into Grand Staircase–Escalante National Monument.

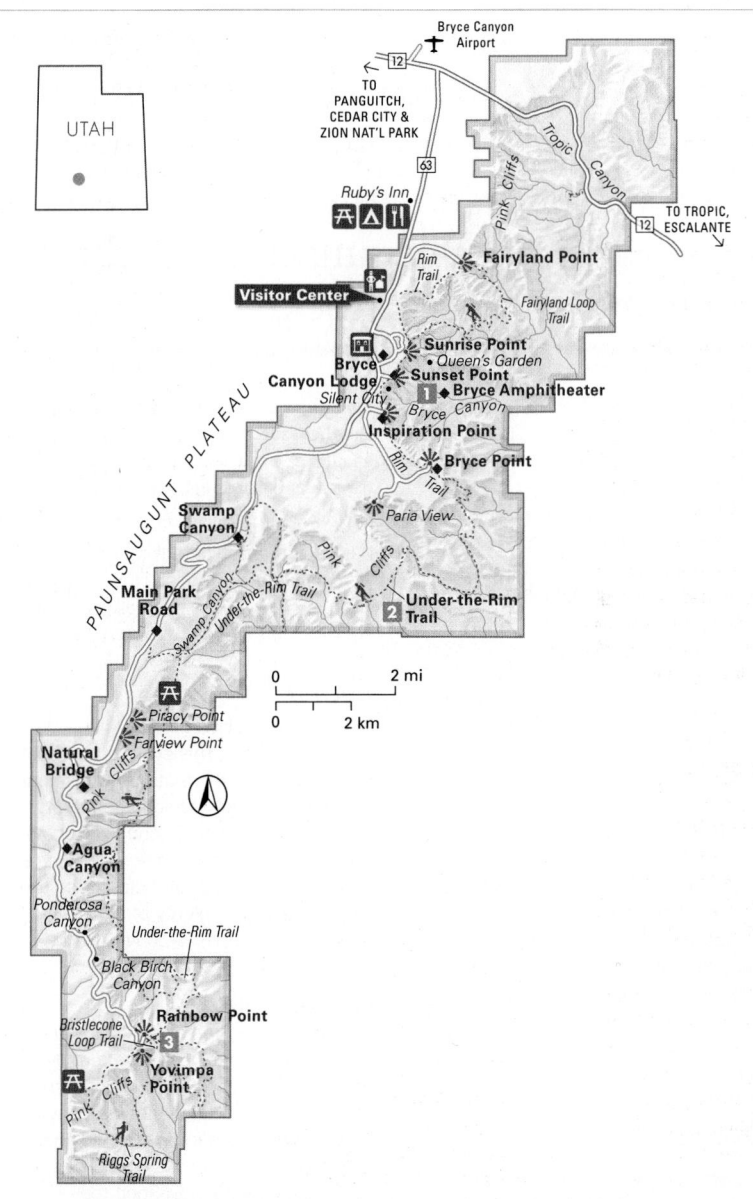

UTAH

Bryce Canyon
Airport

TO
PANGUITCH,
CEDAR CITY &
ZION NAT'L PARK

12

63

Ruby's Inn

TO TROPIC,
ESCALANTE
12

Tropic Canyon

Pink Cliffs

Visitor Center

Rim Trail

Fairyland Point

Fairyland Loop Trail

Sunrise Point
• Queen's Garden
Sunset Point

Bryce
Canyon Lodge
Silent City

1 ♦ **Bryce Amphitheater**

Bryce Canyon

Inspiration Point

♦ **Bryce Point**

Rim Trail

PAUNSAUGUNT PLATEAU

♦ Paria View

Swamp Canyon

Pink Cliffs

Swamp Canyon

Under-the-Rim Trail

2 **Under-the-Rim Trail**

Main Park Road

0   2 mi

0   2 km

Piracy Point

Farview Point

Natural Bridge

Pink Cliffs

♦ **Agua Canyon**

Ponderosa Canyon

Under-the-Rim Trail

Black Birch Canyon

Bristlecone Loop Trail

Rainbow Point

3

Yovimpa Point

Pink Cliffs

Riggs Spring Trail

A land that captures the imagination and the heart, Bryce is a favorite among the Southwest's national parks. Although its splendor has been well-known for decades, Bryce Canyon wasn't designated a national park until 1928. Bryce Canyon is known for its fanciful hoodoos, best viewed at sunrise or sunset, when the light plays off the red rock.

In geological terms, Bryce is actually an amphitheater, not a canyon. The hoodoos in the amphitheater took on their unusual shapes because the top layer of rock—cap rock—is harder than the layers below it. If erosion undercuts the soft rock beneath the cap too much, the hoodoo will tumble. Bryce continues to evolve today, but the hoodoos are a permanent feature; old ones may die, but new ones are constantly forming as the amphitheater rim recedes.

Planning

WHEN TO GO

Around Bryce Canyon National Park and the nearby Cedar Breaks National Monument area, elevations approach and surpass 9,000 feet, making for temperamental weather, intermittent and seasonal road closures due to snow, and downright cold nights well into June. The air is cooler on the rim of the canyon than it is at lower altitudes. ■TIP→ If you choose to see Bryce Canyon April through October, you'll be visiting with the rest of the world. During this period, traffic on the main road can be heavy and parking limited, so consider taking one of the park shuttle buses. RV access is also limited to a handful of lots and camping areas, most of them near the park entrance, during these months.

If it's solitude you're looking for, come to Bryce any time between November and February. The park is open all year long, so if you come during the cooler months you might just have a trail all to yourself.

FESTIVALS AND EVENTS

Bryce Canyon Winter Festival

FESTIVAL | FAMILY | This event at the Best Western Ruby's Inn features cross-country ski races, snow-sculpting contests, ski archery, ice-skating, and kids' snow boot races. Clinics to hone skills such as snowshoeing and photography also take place, and there's plenty of entertainment, too. ☎ 435/834–5341 ⊕ www.rubysinn.com.

Quilt Walk Festival

FESTIVAL | During the bitter winter of 1864, Panguitch residents set out over the mountains to fetch provisions from the town of Parowan, 40 miles away. Legend says the men, frustrated and ready to turn back, laid a quilt on the snow and knelt to pray. Soon they

AVERAGE HIGH/LOW TEMPERATURES					
JAN.	FEB.	MAR.	APR.	MAY	JUNE
39/15	39/17	45/23	54/29	64/37	75/45
JULY	AUG.	SEPT.	OCT.	NOV.	DEC.
80/53	80/50	70/42	58/32	45/23	36/15

realized the quilt had kept them from sinking into the snow. Spreading quilts before them as they walked, leapfrog style, the men traveled to Parowan and back. This four-day event in June commemorates the event with quilting classes, a tour of pioneer homes, tractor pull, dinner-theater, and other events. ☎ *435/690–9228* ⊕ *www.quiltwalk.org.*

★ **Utah Shakespeare Festival**

FESTIVAL | Since 1962, Cedar City has gone Bard-crazy, staging productions of Shakespeare's plays June through October in theaters both indoors and outdoors at Southern Utah University. The Tony award-winning regional theater offers literary seminars, backstage tours, cabarets featuring festival actors, and an outdoor pre-show with Elizabethan performers. Shows are presented in three state-of-the-art theaters. Reserve in advance as many performances sell out. ☎ *435/586–7878* ⊕ *www.bard.org.*

PLANNING YOUR TIME
BRYCE CANYON IN ONE DAY

Begin your day at the **visitor center** to get an overview of the park and to purchase books and maps. Watch the 20-minute film and peruse the excellent exhibits about the natural and cultural history of Bryce Canyon. Then, proceed to the historic **Bryce Canyon Lodge.** From here, stroll along the relaxing **Rim Trail.** If you have the time and stamina to walk into the amphitheater, the portion of the Rim Trail near the lodge gets you to the starting point for either of the park's two essential hikes, the **Navajo Loop Trail** from **Sunset Point** or the **Queen's Garden Trail** that connects Sunset to **Sunrise Point.**

Afterward (or if you skip the hike), drive the 18-mile **main park road,** stopping at the overlooks along the way. Allowing for traffic, and if you stop at all 13 overlooks, this drive will take you between two and three hours.

If you have the time for more walking, a short, rolling hike along the **Bristlecone Loop Trail** at **Rainbow Point** rewards you with spectacular views and a cool walk through a forest of bristlecone pines.

End your day watching the sunset at **Inspiration Point** or dinner at Bryce Canyon Lodge.

GETTING HERE AND AROUND
AIR TRAVEL

The nearest commercial airport to Bryce Canyon, Cedar City Regional Airport is 80 miles west and has daily direct flights from Salt Lake City. The airports in Salt Lake City and Las Vegas are the closest major ones to the park—each is about a four-hour drive.

BUS TRAVEL

A shuttle bus system operates in Bryce Canyon from mid-April through mid-October. Buses start at 8 am and run every 10 to 15 minutes until 8 pm in summer and 6 pm in early spring and October; they're free once you pay park admission. The route begins at Ruby's Inn and Ruby's Campground outside the park entrance and stops at the visitor center, lodge, campgrounds, and all the main overlooks and trailheads.

CAR TRAVEL

The closest major cities to Bryce Canyon are Salt Lake City and Las Vegas, each about 270 miles away. You reach the park via Highway 63, just off of Highway 12, which connects U.S. 89 just south of Panguitch with Torrey, near Capitol Reef National Park. You can see the park's highlights by driving along the well-maintained road running the length of the main scenic area. Bryce has no restrictions on automobiles on the main road, but from spring through fall you may encounter heavy traffic and full parking lots—it's advisable to take the shuttle bus at this time.

PARK ESSENTIALS
ACCESSIBILITY

Most park facilities were constructed between 1930 and 1960. Some have been upgraded for wheelchair accessibility, while others can be used with some assistance. The Sunset campground offers two sites with wheelchair access. Few of the trails, however, can be managed in a standard wheelchair due to the sandy, rocky, or uneven terrain. The section of the Rim Trail between Sunrise and Inspiration points is wheelchair accessible. The 1-mile Bristlecone Loop Trail at Rainbow Point has a hard surface and could be used with assistance, but several grades do not meet standards. Accessible parking is marked at all overlooks and public facilities.

PARK FEES

The entrance fee is $35 per vehicle for a seven-day pass and $20 for pedestrians or bicyclists, and includes unlimited use of the park shuttle. An annual Bryce Canyon park pass, good for one year from the date of purchase, costs $40. If you leave your private vehicle outside the park at the shuttle staging area or Ruby's Inn, the one-time entrance fee is $35 per party and includes transportation on the shuttle.

A $5 backcountry permit, available from the visitor center, is required for camping in the park's interior, allowed only on Under-the-Rim Trail and Rigg's Spring Loop, both south of Bryce Point. Campfires are not permitted.

PARK HOURS

The park is open 24/7, year-round. It's in the Mountain time zone.

CELL PHONE RECEPTION

Cell phone reception is hit-or-miss in the park, with some of the higher points along the main road your best bet. The lodge and visitor center have limited (it can be slow during busy periods) Wi-Fi, and there are pay phones at a few key spots in the park, but these are gradually being removed.

EDUCATIONAL OFFERINGS
RANGER PROGRAMS

★ **Campfire and Auditorium Programs**

TOUR—SIGHT | Bryce Canyon's natural diversity comes alive in the park's North Campground amphitheater, the Visitor Center Theater, or in the Bryce Canyon Lodge Auditorium. Ranger talks, multimedia programs, and guided walks introduce you to geology, astronomy, wildlife, history, and many other topics related to Bryce Canyon and the West. ⊠ *Bryce Canyon National Park.*

★ **Full Moon Hike**

TOUR—SIGHT | Rangers lead guided hikes on the nights around each full moon (two per month May–October). You must wear heavy-traction shoes, and reserve a spot on the day of the hike. In peak season the tickets are distributed through a lottery system. Schedules are posted at the visitor center and on the park's website. ⊠ *Bryce Canyon National Park* ⊕ *www.nps.gov.*

Geology Talk

TOUR—SIGHT | Rangers regularly host free half-hour discussions about the long geological history of Bryce Canyon; they are nearly always held at Sunset Point. ⊠ *Bryce Canyon National Park.*

Junior Ranger Program

TOUR—SIGHT | FAMILY | Kids can sign up to be Junior Rangers at the Bryce Canyon Visitor Center. They have to complete several activities in their free Junior Ranger booklet, as well as collect some

Plants and Wildlife in Bryce Canyon

With elevations approaching 9,000 feet, many of Bryce Canyon's 400 plant species are unlike those you'll see at less lofty places. Look at exposed slopes and you might catch a glimpse of the pygmy pinyon, or the gnarled, 1,000-year-old bristlecone pine. At lower altitudes are the Douglas fir, ponderosa pine, and the quaking aspen, which sit in groves of twinkling leaves. No fewer than three kinds of sagebrush—big, black, and fringed—grow here, as well as the blue columbine.

Mule deer and chipmunks are common companions on the trails and are used to human presence. You might also catch a glimpse of the endangered Utah prairie dog. Give them a wide berth; they may be cute, but they bite (and it's illegal to approach or feed wildlife in any national park). Other animals include elk, black-tailed jackrabbits, and the desert cottontail. More than 210 species of bird live in the park or pass through as a migratory stop. Bird-watchers are often rewarded handsomely for their vigilance: eagles, peregrine falcons, and even the rare California condor have all been spotted in the park.

litter, and attend a ranger program. Allow three to six hours total. Ask a ranger about each day's schedule of events and topics, or look for postings at the visitor center, Bryce Canyon Lodge, and campground bulletin boards. ⊠ *Bryce Canyon National Park.*

★ Night Sky Program

TOUR—SIGHT | City folk are lucky to see 2,500 stars in their artificially illuminated skies, but out here among the hoodoos you see three times as many. The Night Sky Program includes low-key astronomy lectures and multimedia presentations, followed by telescope viewing (weather permitting). The program is typically offered on Tuesday, Thursday, and Saturday from April through September and less frequently the rest of the year. Check the visitor center for details. ⊠ *Bryce Canyon National Park.*

Rim Walk

TOUR—SIGHT | Join a park ranger for a ½-mile, hour-long stroll along the gorgeous rim of Bryce Canyon starting at the Sunset Point overlook. Reservations are not required for the walk, which is usually offered daily from May to September. Check with the visitor center or the park website for details. ⊠ *Bryce Canyon National Park.*

RESTAURANTS

Dining options in the park proper are limited to a few options in or near Bryce Canyon Lodge; you'll also find a handful of restaurants serving mostly standard American fare within a few miles of the park entrance, in Bryce Canyon City. Venture farther afield—to Tropic and Escalante to the east, and Panguitch and Hatch to the west—and the diversity of culinary offerings increases a bit.

HOTELS

Lodgings in and around Bryce Canyon include both rustic and modern options, but all fill up fast in summer. Bryce Canyon Lodge is the only hotel inside the park, but there are a number of options in Bryce Canyon City, just north of the park's entrance. Nearby Panguitch and Tropic, and Escalante a bit farther away, are small towns with a number of additional budget and mid-range hotels, and these places tend to have more last-minute availability. *Hotel reviews have been shortened. For full information, visit Fodors.com.*

What It Costs

	$	$$	$$$	$$$$
RESTAURANTS				
	under $13	$13–$20	$21–$30	over $30
HOTELS				
	under $101	$101–$150	$151–$200	over $200

VISITOR INFORMATION

PARK CONTACT INFORMATION Bryce Canyon National Park ☎ *435/834–5322* ⊕ *www.nps.gov/brca.*

VISITOR CENTER

★ **Bryce Canyon Visitor Center**

INFO CENTER | FAMILY | Even if you're anxious to hit the hoodoos, the visitor center—just to your right after the park entrance station—is the best place to start if you want to know what you're looking at and how it got there. Rangers staff a counter where you can ask questions or let them map out an itinerary of "must-sees" based on your time and physical abilities. There are also multimedia exhibits, Wi-Fi, books, maps, backcountry camping permits for sale, and the Bryce Canyon Natural History Association gift shop, whose proceeds help to support park programs and conversation. ⊠ *Hwy. 63* ☎ *435/834–5322* ⊕ *www.nps.gov/brca.*

 Sights

HISTORIC SITES

Bryce Canyon Lodge

BUILDING | The lodge's architect, Gilbert Stanley Underwood, was a national park specialist, having designed lodges at Zion and Grand Canyon before turning his T-square to Bryce in 1924. The results are worth a visit as this National Historic Landmark has been faithfully restored, right down to the lobby's huge limestone fireplace, and log and wrought-iron chandelier. Inside the historic building, the only remaining hotel built by the

Grand Circle Utah Park Company, are a restaurant and gift shop, as well as information on park activities. The lodge operation includes several historic log cabins and two motels nearby on the wooded grounds, just a short walk from the rim trail. Everything but the Sunset Motel (which is open early March–early January) shuts down from early November through late March. ⊠ *Off Hwy. 63* ☎ *435/834–8700* ⊕ *www.brycecanyon-forever.com.*

SCENIC DRIVES

★ **Main Park Road**

SCENIC DRIVE | Following miles of canyon rim, this thoroughfare gives access to more than a dozen scenic overlooks between the park entrance and Rainbow Point. Major overlooks are rarely more than a few minutes' walk from the parking areas, and many let you see more than 100 miles on clear days. Remember that all overlooks lie east of the road. To keep things simple, proceed to the southern end of the park and stop at the overlooks on your northbound return; they will all be on the right side of the road. Allow two to three hours to travel the entire 36-mile round-trip. The road is open year-round, but may close temporarily after heavy snowfalls. Keep your eyes open for wildlife as you drive. Trailers are not allowed at Bryce Point and Paria View, but you can park them at the parking lot across the road from the visitor center. RVs can drive throughout the park (with limited parking options spring through fall), and vehicles longer than 25 feet are not allowed at Paria View. ⊠ *Bryce Canyon National Park.*

SCENIC STOPS

Agua Canyon

CANYON | This overlook in the southern section of the park, 12 miles south of the park entrance, has a nice view of several standout hoodoos. Look for the top-heavy formation called the Hunter, which actually has a few small hardy trees growing on its cap. As the rock erodes, the park evolves; snap a picture because the Hunter may look different the next time you visit. ⊠ *Bryce Canyon National Park.*

Bryce Point

CANYON | After absorbing views of the Black Mountains and Navajo Mountain, you can follow the Under-the-Rim Trail and go exploring beyond Bryce Amphitheater to the cluster of top-heavy hoodoos known collectively as the Hat Shop. Or, take a left off the Under-the-Rim Trail and hike the challenging Peekaboo Loop Trail with its geological highlight, the **Wall of Windows.** Openings carved into a wall of rock illustrate the drama of erosion that formed Bryce Canyon. ⊠ *Inspiration Point Rd., 5½ miles south of park entrance.*

Fairyland Point

TRAIL | Best visited as you exit the park, this scenic overlook adjacent to Boat Mesa, ½ mile north of the visitor center and a mile off the main park road, has splendid views of Fairyland Amphitheater and its delicate, fanciful forms. The Sinking Ship and other formations stand before the grand backdrop of the Aquarius Plateau and distant Navajo Mountain. Nearby is the Fairyland Loop trailhead—it's a stunning five-hour hike in summer and a favorite of snowshoers in winter. ⊠ *Off Hwy. 63.*

★ **Inspiration Point**

VIEWPOINT | Not far (1½ miles) east along the Rim Trail from Bryce Point is Inspiration Point, site of a wonderful vista on the main amphitheater and one of the best places in the park to see the sunset. (You will have plenty of company and hear a variety of languages as the sun goes down.) ⊠ *Inspiration Point Rd.*

Natural Bridge

VIEWPOINT | Formed over millions of years by wind, water, and chemical erosion, this 85-foot rusty-orange arch formation—one of several rock arches in the park—is an essential photo op. Beyond the parking lot lies a rare stand of aspen trees, their leaves twinkling in the wind. Watch out for distracted drivers at this stunning viewpoint. ⊠ *Main park road, 11 miles south of park entrance.*

★ **Rainbow and Yovimpa points**

TRAIL | Separated by less than half a mile, Rainbow and Yovimpa points offer two fine panoramas facing opposite directions. Rainbow Point's best view is to the north overlooking the southern rim of the amphitheater and giving a glimpse of Grand Staircase–Escalante National Monument; Yovimpa Point's vista spreads out to the south. On an especially clear day you can see all the way to Arizona's highest point, Humphrey's Peak 150 miles away. Yovimpa Point also has a shady and quiet picnic area with tables and restrooms. You can hike between them on the easy Bristlecone Loop Trail or tackle the more strenuous 9-mile Riggs Spring Loop Trail, which passes the tallest point in the park. This is the outermost auto stop on the main road, so visitors often drive here first and make it their starting point, then work their way back to the park entrance. ⊠ *End of main park road, 18 miles south of park entrance.*

★ **Sunrise Point**

TRAIL | Named for its stunning views at dawn, this overlook a short walk from Bryce Canyon Lodge is one of the park's most popular stops. It's also the trailhead for the Queen's Garden Trail and the Fairyland Loop Trail. You have to descend the Queen's Garden Trail to get a glimpse of the regal **Queen Victoria,** a hoodoo that appears to sport a crown and glorious full skirt. The trail is popular and marked clearly, but a bit challenging with 350 feet of elevation change. ⊠ *Off Hwy. 63.*

Sunset Point

TOUR—SIGHT | Watch the late-day sun paint the hoodoos here. You can see **Thor's Hammer,** a delicate formation similar to a balanced rock, from the rim, but when you hike 550 feet down into the

Word of Mouth

"It was early morning when I took this photo looking out across Bryce Canyon. With a chill still in the air we hiked to the edge of the canyon, and were rewarded with this breathtaking view."
—photo by Pete Foley, Fodors.com member

amphitheater on the Navajo Loop Trail you can walk through the famous and very popular Wall Street—a deep, shady "slot" canyon. The point is near Bryce Canyon Lodge. ⊠ *Bryce Canyon National Park.*

Activities

Most visitors explore Bryce Canyon by car, but the hiking trails are far more rewarding. At these elevations, you'll have to stop to catch your breath more often if you're used to being closer to sea level. It gets warm in summer but rarely uncomfortably hot, so hiking farther into the depths of the park is not difficult, so long as you don't pick a hike that is beyond your abilities.

AIR TOURS
Bryce Canyon Airlines & Helicopters
TOUR—SPORTS | For a bird's-eye view of Bryce Canyon National Park, take a dramatic helicopter ride or airplane tour over the fantastic sandstone formations. Longer full-canyon tours and added excursions to sites such as the Grand Canyon, Monument Valley, and Zion are also offered. Flight last from 35 minutes to four hours. ☎ *435/834–8060* ⊕ *www.rubysinn.com/scenic-flights* ⊠ From $110.

BIRD-WATCHING
More than 210 bird species have been identified in Bryce. Violet-green swallows and white-throated swifts are common, as are Steller's jays, American coots, rufous hummingbirds, and mountain bluebirds. Lucky bird-watchers will see golden eagles floating across the skies above the pink rocks of the amphitheater, and experienced birders might spot an osprey nest high in the canyon wall. The best time in the park for avian variety is from May through July.

HIKING
To get up close and personal with the park's hoodoos, set aside a half day to hike into the amphitheater. Remember, after you descend below the rim you'll have to get back up. The air gets warmer

Good Reads

Bryce Canyon Auto and Hiking Guide, by Tully Stroud, has info on the geology and history of the area. Supplement the free park map with the Bryce Canyon Hiking Guide, with an amphitheater hiking map. To prepare kids ages 5 to 10 for a trip to the park, order the Kid's Guide to Bryce Canyon.

Bryce Canyon Natural History Association Both the visitor center and the Bryce Canyon Natural History Association are excellent sources of books on the region. ☎ 435/834–4782, 888/362–2642 ⊕ *www.brycecanyon.org.*

the lower you go, and the altitude will have you huffing and puffing unless you're very fit. The uneven terrain calls for lace-up shoes on even the well-trodden, high-traffic trails and sturdy hiking boots for the more challenging ones. No below-rim trails are paved. For trail maps, information, and ranger recommendations, stop at the visitor center. Bathrooms are at most trailheads but not down in the amphitheater.

Bristlecone Loop Trail
HIKING/WALKING | This 1-mile trail with a modest 200 feet of elevation gain lets you see the park from its highest points of more than 9,000 feet, alternating between spruce and fir forest and wide-open vistas out over Grand Staircase–Escalante National Monument and beyond. You might see yellow-bellied marmots and dusky grouse, critters not found at lower elevations in the park. Plan on 45 minutes to an hour. *Easy.* ⊠ *Bryce Canyon National Park* ✛ *Trailhead: at Rainbow Point parking lot, 18 miles south of park entrance.*

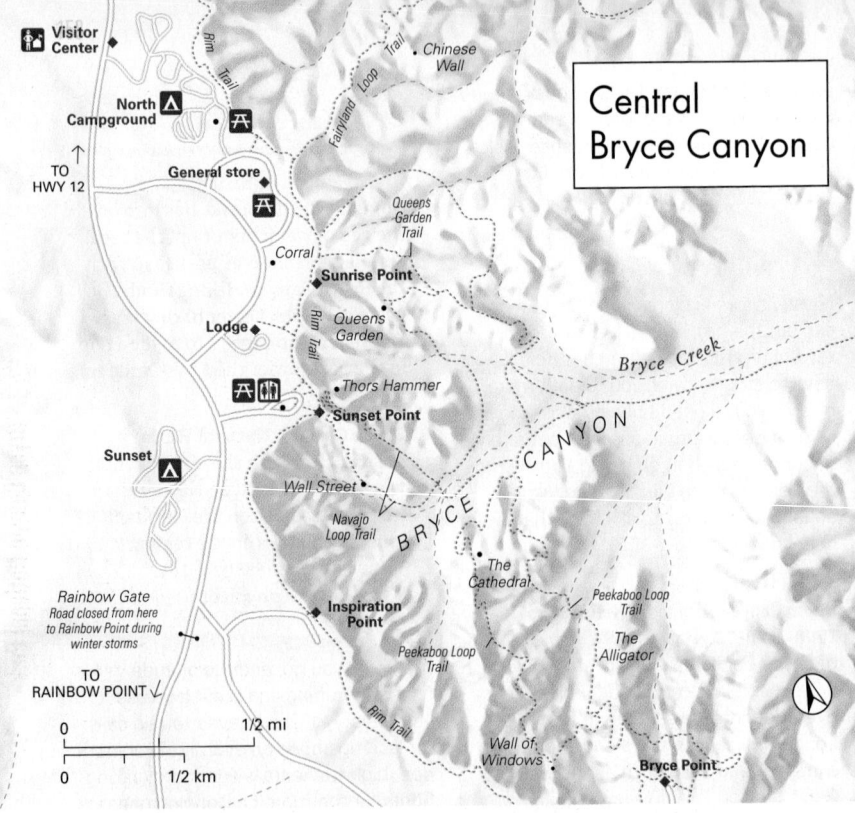

TO
HWY 12

TO
RAINBOW POINT

Visitor Center

North Campground

General store

Corral

Queens Garden Trail

Sunrise Point

Lodge

Queens Garden

Thors Hammer

Sunset Point

Sunset

Wall Street

Navajo Loop Trail

Chinese Wall

Rim Trail

Fairyland Loop Trail

Bryce Creek

BRYCE CANYON

The Cathedral

Peekaboo Loop Trail

The Alligator

Inspiration Point

Peekaboo Loop Trail

Rim Trail

Wall of Windows

Bryce Point

Rainbow Gate
Road closed from here to Rainbow Point during winter storms

0   1/2 mi

0   1/2 km

Central Bryce Canyon

Fairyland Loop Trail

HIKING/WALKING | Hike into whimsical Fairyland Canyon on this trail that gets more strenuous and less crowded as you progress along its 8 miles. It winds around hoodoos, across trickles of water, and finally to a natural window in the rock at Tower Bridge, 1½ miles from Sunrise Point and 4 miles from Fairyland Point. The pink-and-white badlands and hoodoos surround you the whole way. Don't feel like you have to go the whole distance to make it worthwhile. But if you do, allow at least five hours round-trip with 1,700 feet of elevation change. *Difficult.* ☒ *Bryce Canyon National Park* ⚓ *Trailheads: at Fairyland Point and Sunrise Point.*

Hat Shop Trail

HIKING/WALKING | The sedimentary haberdashery sits 2 miles from the trailhead. Hard gray caps balance precariously atop narrow pedestals of softer, rust-color rock. Allow three to four hours to travel this strenuous but rewarding 4-mile round-trip trail, the first part of the longer Under-the-Rim Trail. *Difficult.* ☒ *Bryce Canyon National Park* ⚓ *Trailhead: at Bryce Point, 5½ miles south of park entrance.*

Navajo Loop Trail

HIKING/WALKING | **FAMILY** | One of Bryce's most popular and dramatic attractions is this steep descent via a series of switchbacks leading to Wall Street, a slightly claustrophobic hallway of rock only 20 feet wide in places with walls 100 feet high. After a walk through the Silent City, the northern end of the trail brings Thor's Hammer into view. A well-marked intersection offers a shorter way back via Two Bridges Trail or continuing on the

Queen's Garden Trail to Sunrise Point. For the short version allow at least an hour on this 1½-mile trail with 550 feet of elevation change. *Moderate.* ⊠ *Bryce Canyon National Park ⊹ Trailhead: at Sunset Point, near Bryce Canyon Lodge.*

★ Navajo/Queen's Garden Combination Loop

HIKING/WALKING | FAMILY | By walking this extended 3-mile loop, you can see some of the best of Bryce; it takes a little more than two hours. The route passes fantastic formations and an open forest of pine and juniper on the amphitheater floor. Descend into the amphitheater from Sunrise Point on the Queen's Garden Trail and ascend via the Navajo Loop Trail; return to your starting point via the Rim Trail. *Moderate.* ⊠ *Bryce Canyon National Park ⊹ Trailheads: at Sunset and Sunrise points, 2 miles south of park entrance.*

★ Peekaboo Loop

HIKING/WALKING | The reward of this steep trail is the Wall of Windows and the Three Wise Men. Horses use this trail in spring, summer, and fall and have the right-of-way. Start at Bryce, Sunrise, or Sunset Point and allow four to five hours to hike the 5-mile trail or 7-mile double-loop. *Difficult.* ⊠ *Bryce Canyon National Park ⊹ Trailheads: at Bryce Point, 5½ miles south of park entrance; Sunrise and Sunset points, near Zion Park Lodge.*

Queen's Garden Trail

HIKING/WALKING | FAMILY | This hike is the easiest way down into the amphitheater, with 350 feet of elevation change leading to a short tunnel, quirky hoodoos, and lots of like-minded hikers. It's the essential Bryce "sampler." Allow two hours total to hike the 1½-mile trail plus the ½-mile rim-side path and back. *Easy.* ⊠ *Bryce Canyon National Park ⊹ Trailhead: at Sunrise Point, 2 miles south of park entrance.*

Riggs Spring Loop Trail

HIKING/WALKING | One of the park's two true backpacker's trails, this rigorous

9-mile path has an overnight option at the Yovimpa Pass, Riggs Spring, or Corral Hollow campsites. You'll journey past groves of twinkling aspen trees and the eponymous spring close to the campsite. Start at either Yovimpa or Rainbow point and be prepared for 1,500 feet of elevation change. Campers need to check in at the visitor center ahead of time for backcountry permits. *Difficult.* ⊠ *Bryce Canyon National Park ⊹ Trailheads: at Yovimpa and Rainbow points, 18 miles south of park entrance.*

Under-the-Rim Trail

HIKING/WALKING | Starting at Bryce Point, the trail travels 23 miles to Rainbow Point, passing through the Pink Cliffs, traversing Agua Canyon and Ponderosa Canyon, and taking you by several springs. Most of the hike is on the amphitheater floor, characterized by up-and-down terrain among stands of ponderosa pine; the elevation change totals about 1,500 feet. It's the park's longest trail, but four trailheads along the main park road allow you to connect to the Under-the-Rim Trail and cover its length as a series of day hikes. Allow at least two days to hike the route in its entirety, and although it's not a hoodoo-heavy hike there's plenty to see to make it a more leisurely three-day affair. *Difficult.* ⊠ *Bryce Canyon National Park ⊹ Trailheads: at Bryce Point, Swamp Canyon, Ponderosa Canyon, and Rainbow Point.*

HORSEBACK RIDING

Many of the park's hiking trails were first formed beneath the hooves of cattle wranglers. Today, hikers and riders share the trails. A number of outfitters can set you up with a gentle mount and lead you to the park's best sights. Not only can you cover more ground than you would walking, but equine traffic has the right-of-way at all times. Call ahead to the stables for reservations to find a trip that's right for you, from 90 minutes to all day. The biggest outfitters have more than 100 horses and mules to choose

Hikers in Bryce are rewarded with vistas highlighting the park's colorful landscape.

from. People under the age of seven or who weigh more than 220 pounds are prohibited from riding.

Canyon Trail Rides

HORSEBACK RIDING | Descend to the floor of the Bryce Canyon amphitheater via horse or mule—most visitors have no riding experience so don't hesitate to join in. A two-hour ride ambles along the amphitheater floor through the Queen's Garden before returning to Sunrise Point. The half-day expedition follows Peekaboo Loop Trail, winds past the Fairy Castle, and passes the Wall of Windows before returning to Sunrise Point. Two rides a day of each type leave in the morning and early afternoon. There are no rides in winter. ⊠ *Bryce Canyon Lodge, Off Hwy. 63* ☎ *435/679–8665* ⊕ *www.canyonrides. com* ✉ *From $65.*

Ruby's Horseback Adventures

HORSEBACK RIDING | FAMILY | Ride to the rim of Bryce Canyon, venture through narrow slot canyons in Grand Staircase–Escalante National Monument, or even retrace the trails taken by outlaw Butch Cassidy more than 100 years ago. Rides last from one hour to all day. Kids must be 7 or older to ride, in some cases 10. Wagon rides to the rim of Bryce Canyon are available for all ages, as are sleigh rides in winter. ⊠ *Bryce Canyon National Park* ☎ *866/782–0002* ⊕ *www.horser-ides.net* ✉ *From $55.*

WINTER ACTIVITIES

Unlike most of Utah's other national parks, Bryce Canyon receives plenty of snow, making it a popular cross-country ski area. Rim Trail, Paria Loop, and other paths above the canyon are popular destinations. The visitor center sells shoe-traction devices, and some of the ranger-guided snowshoe activities include snowshoes and poles.

Ruby's Winter Activities Center

SKIING/SNOWBOARDING | FAMILY | This facility grooms miles of private, no-cost trails that connect to the ungroomed trails inside the park. Rental snowshoes, ice skates, and cross-country ski equipment are available. ⊠ *Hwy. 63, 1 mile north of park entrance, Bryce Canyon City*

☏ *435/834–5341* ⊕ *www.rubysinn.com/ winter-activities.*

Nearby Towns

Panguitch calls itself the "Center of Scenic Utah," and it's an accurate moniker. The small town 25 miles northwest of Bryce Canyon has restaurants, motels, gas stations, and trinket shops; you'll find a few more eateries and other businesses in tiny **Hatch,** 15 miles south of Panguitch. Just 10 miles east of the park, little **Tropic** has a handful of noteworthy lodgings and eateries. Continue about 37 miles northeast to reach **Escalante,** a western gateway to the Grand Staircase–Escalante National Monument with several good places to stay and eat. From Interstate 15, **Cedar City** is where you exit to Bryce (it's a 90-minute drive). With a population of 31,200, it's the region's largest city and the home of Southern Utah University and the Utah Shakespeare Festival, which draws theater buffs from all over.

VISITOR INFORMATION Cedar City/Brian Head Tourism Bureau ✉ *581 N. Main St., Cedar City* ☏ *800/354–4849, 435/586– 5124* ⊕ *www.visitcedarcity.com.* **Escalante Interagency Visitor Center** ✉ *755 W. Main St., Escalante* ☏ *435/826–5499* ⊕ *www.blm.gov/visit/escalante-interacgency-visitor-center.* **Garfield County Tourism Office** ✉ *55 S. Main St., Panguitch* ☏ *435/676–1161, 800/468–8660* ⊕ *www. brycecanyoncountry.com.*

◉ Sights

Bryce Museum & Bryce Wildlife Adventure
MUSEUM | FAMILY | Imagine a zoo frozen in time: this 14,000-square-foot private museum contains more than 1,600 butterflies and 1,000 taxidermy animals in tableaux mimicking actual terrain and animal behavior. The animals and birds come from all parts of the world. An African room has baboons, bush pigs,

Cape buffalo, and a lion. There's also a collection of living deer that kids delight in feeding, and ATV and bike rentals for touring Scenic Byway 12 and the Paunsaugunt Plateau. ✉ *1945 W. Scenic Hwy. 12, Bryce Canyon City* ☏ *435/834–5555* ⊕ *www.brycewildlifeadventure.com* ☏ *$8* ⊗ *Closed mid-Nov.–Mar.*

Cedar Breaks National Monument
NATURE SITE | From the rim of Cedar Breaks, 23 miles east of Cedar City and 60 miles west of Bryce, a natural amphitheater plunges a half-mile into the Markagunt Plateau. Short hiking trails along the rim make this landscape a wonderful summer stop, especially if you're headed to Cedar City or the Shakespeare Festival. ✉ *Visitor Center, Hwy. 148, Brian Head* ✛ *3½ miles north of Hwy. 14* ☏ *435/586–9451* ⊕ *www.nps.gov/ cebr* ☏ *$7* ⊗ *Visitor center closed early Sept.–mid-May.*

Escalante Petrified Forest State Park
NATIONAL/STATE PARK | This state park was created to protect a huge repository of petrified wood, easily spotted along two moderate-to-strenuous hiking trails. Of equal interest is the park's Wide Hollow Reservoir at the base of the hiking trails, which has a swimming beach and is good for boating, fishing, and birding. ✉ *710 N. Reservoir Rd., Escalante* ☏ *435/826–4466* ⊕ *www.stateparks. utah.gov* ☏ *$8.*

Grand Staircase–Escalante National Monument
NATURE PRESERVE | In September 1996, President Bill Clinton designated 1.7 million acres in south-central Utah as Grand Staircase–Escalante National Monument. The three distinct sections—the Grand Staircase, the Kaiparowits Plateau, and the Canyons of the Escalante—offer remote backcountry experiences hard to find elsewhere in the Lower 48. Waterfalls, shoulder-width slot canyons, and improbable colors all characterize this wilderness. One of the best access points from Bryce is along Scenic Byway

8

Bryce Canyon National Park

12, which straddles the northern border of the monument—the Hogback section, between the small towns of Escalante and Boulder (which offer outfitters, lodging, and dining), is particularly spectacular. ⊠ *Hwy. 12, Escalante* ✛ *15 miles northeast of Escalante* ☎ *435/644–1200* ⊕ *www.blm.gov* ⚏ *Free.*

★ Kodachrome Basin State Park

NATIONAL/STATE PARK | FAMILY | Yes, it is named after the old-fashioned color photo film, and once you see it you'll understand why the National Geographic Society gave it the name. The stone spires known as "sand pipes" cannot be found anywhere else in the world. Hike any of the trails to spot some of the 67 pipes in and around the park. The short Angels Palace Trail takes you quickly into the park's interior, up, over, and around some of the badlands. ⊠ *Cottonwood Canyon Rd., Cannonville* ☎ *435/679–8562* ⊕ *www.stateparks.utah.gov* ⚏ *$8.*

SCENIC DRIVES

★ Highway 12 Scenic Byway

SCENIC DRIVE | Keep your camera handy and steering wheel steady along this route between Escalante and Loa, near Capitol Reef National Park. Though the highway starts at the intersection of U.S. 89, west of Bryce Canyon National Park, the stretch that begins in Escalante is one of the most spectacular. Be sure to stop at the scenic overlooks; almost every one will give you an eye-popping view, and information panels let you know what you're looking at. Pay attention while driving, though; the paved road is twisting and steep, and at times climbs over a hogback with sheer drop-offs on both sides.

U.S. 89/Utah's Heritage Highway

LOCAL INTEREST | Winding north from the Arizona border all the way to Spanish Fork Canyon, an hour south of Salt Lake City, U.S. 89 is known as the Heritage Highway for its role in shaping Utah history. At its southern end, Kanab (see the Zion National Park chapter) is known

as "Little Hollywood," having provided the backdrop for many famous Western movies and TV commercials. The town has since grown considerably into a major recreation hub and a base for visiting Zion, Bryce, and the North Rim of the Grand Canyon. Other towns north along this famous road may not have the same notoriety in these parts, but they do offer eye-popping scenery as well as some lodging and dining options relatively close to Bryce Canyon.

ACTIVITIES

BICYCLING

Excursions of Escalante

EXCURSIONS | Hiking, backpacking, photography, and canyoneering tours in the Escalante region are custom-fit to your needs and abilities by experienced guides. Canyoneers will be taken into the slot canyons to move through slot chutes or rappel down walls and other obstacles. All gear and provisions are provided whether it's a day hike or multiday adventure. ⊠ *125 E. Main St., Escalante* ☎ *800/839–7567* ⊕ *www.excursionsofescalante.com* ⚏ *From $165.*

Hell's Backbone Road

BICYCLING | For a scenic and challenging mountain-bike ride, follow the 44-mile Hell's Backbone Road from Panguitch to the Escalante region and beyond. The route, also known as Highway 12, gives riders stunning views and a half-dozen quaint townships as a reward for the steep grades. This is also the road you take to reach Highway 63 into Bryce.

🍴 Restaurants

IN THE PARK

★ Bryce Canyon Lodge

$$$ | AMERICAN | With a high-beam ceiling, tall windows, and a massive stone fireplace, the dining room at this historic lodge set among towering pines abounds with rustic western charm. The kitchen serves three meals a day (reservations aren't accepted, so be prepared for a wait), and the dishes—highlights of which include chile-rubbed seared ahi, burgundy-braised bison stew, and almond-and-panko-crusted trout—feature organic or sustainable ingredients whenever possible. **Known for:** good selection of local craft beers; fudge brownie with whipped cream and ice cream; hearty breakfasts. $ *Average main: $27* ✉ *Off Hwy. 63* ☎ *435/834–8700* ⊕ *www.brycecanyonforever.com/dining* ☉ *Closed early Nov.–late Mar.*

Valhalla Pizzeria & Coffee Shop
$ | PIZZA | FAMILY | A quick and casual 40-seat eatery across the parking lot from Bryce Canyon Lodge, this pizzeria and coffee shop is a good bet for an inexpensive meal, especially when the lodge dining room is too crowded. Breakfast choices include homemade pastries and fresh fruit, or kick back on the tranquil patio in the evening and enjoy fresh pizza or salad. **Known for:** light breakfasts; decent beer and wine selection; filling pizzas. $ *Average main: $12* ✉ *Off Hwy. 63* ☎ *435/834–8709* ⊕ *www.brycecanyonforever.com/pizza* ☉ *Closed mid-Oct.–mid-May.*

PICNIC AREAS
North Campground
RESTAURANT—SIGHT | FAMILY | Across the road and slightly east of the Bryce Canyon Visitor Center, this popular campground has a couple of scenic picnic areas plus a general store and easy trail access. ✉ *Main park road* ✛ *½ mile south of visitor center.*

Yovimpa Point
CANYON | At the southern end of the park, this shady, quiet spot has tables and restrooms nearby. A short walk leads to the edge of the Paunsaugunt Plateau and offers long-distance, panoramic views. ✉ *End of main park road.*

OUTSIDE THE PARK
Bryce Canyon Pines Restaurant
$$ | AMERICAN | Inside of the Bryce Canyon Pines Motel, about 6 miles

northwest of Bryce Canyon National Park, this down-home, family-friendly roadhouse decorated with Old West photos and memorabilia serves up reliably good stick-to-your-rib breakfasts, hefty elk burgers, rib-eye steaks, and Utah rainbow trout. But the top draw here is homemade pie, which come in a vast assortment of flavors, from banana-blueberry cream to boysenberry. **Known for:** delectable pies; friendly staff; plenty of kids' options. $ *Average main: $16* ✉ *Hwy. 12, mile marker 10, Bryce Canyon City* ☎ *435/834–5441* ⊕ *www.brycecanyonrestaurant.com.*

Burger Barn
$ | BURGER | FAMILY | You order at the window and sit at one of the outdoor tables when dining at this laid-back burger joint in a little red barn near Panguitch Lake, a great option en route between Bryce and Cedar Breaks National Monument or Cedar City. The one-third Black Angus steak burgers here come with a variety of toppings (the barbecue-bacon variety has lots of fans), and there's fish-and-chips, sweet-potato fries, and shakes and ice cream. **Known for:** two-fisted burgers; pretty setting near a mountain lake; ice cream sundaes. $ *Average main: $7* ✉ *75 S. Hwy. 143, Panguitch* ☎ *435/233–7201.*

★ Centro Woodfired Pizzeria
$ | PIZZA | You can watch your handmade artisanal pizza being pulled from the fires of the brick oven, then sit back and enjoy a seasonal pie layered with ingredients such as house-made fennel sausage and wood-roasted cremini mushrooms. The creamy vanilla gelato layered with a balsamic reduction and sea salt is highly addictive. **Known for:** house-made sausage; good wine and beer list; creative desserts. $ *Average main: $12* ✉ *50 W. Center St., Cedar City* ☎ *435/867–8123* ☉ *Closed Sun.*

Cowboy's Smokehouse Café
$$ | BARBECUE | From the Western-style interior and creaky floors to the smoker

out back, this rustic café has an aura of Texan authenticity—there are cowboy collectibles and game trophies lining the walls. No surprise that barbecue is the specialty here, with ample portions of favorites such as ribs, mesquite-flavored beef and pulled pork, and the restaurant's own house-made sauce, along with lighter sandwiches and salads. **Known for:** cash only (but there's an ATM on premises); prodigious steaks; German sausage platter. [$] *Average main: $20* ✉ *95 N. Main St., Panguitch* ☎ *435/676–8030* 🌐 *www.thecowboysmokehouse.com* 💳 *No credit cards* ⏲ *Closed Sun.*

Escalante Outfitters

$ | **AMERICAN** | This warm and inviting log cabin–style restaurant—part of a popular tour operator, camp store, and cabin and camping compound—is a great place to sit back and relax after a day of hiking, fly-fishing, or road-tripping. Try one of the creatively topped pizzas, a veggie sandwich, or an apple-pecan-arugula salad, or drop in for one of the best cups of (fair trade) coffee in the region. **Known for:** delicious pizzas with interesting toppings; lively and fun dining room; first-rate fair trade coffee. [$] *Average main: $12* ✉ *310 W. Main St., Escalante* ☎ *435/826–4266* 🌐 *www.escalanteoutfitters.com.*

Galaxy Diner

$ | **DINER** | **FAMILY** | This kitschy '50-style diner with a big chrome sign is a popular stop between Bryce and Zion among everyone from motorcyclists to families with young kids. Start the day with a green-chile, bacon, and cheese omelet, or stop in later for a burger or sandwich—and do save room for an old-time banana split or vanilla malt. **Known for:** fun retro decor; old-fashioned ice cream; big breakfast portions. [$] *Average main: $6* ✉ *216 N. Main St., Hatch* ☎ *435/735–4017* 🌐 *www.galaxyofhatch.com* ⏲ *Closed winter.*

★ **Stone Hearth Grille**

$$$ | **MODERN AMERICAN** | With sweeping views toward Bryce Canyon from the back deck, an art-filled dining room with a stone fireplace, and some of the most accomplished modern American fare within an hour's drive of the park, this refined yet unpretentious restaurant on the outskirts of tiny Tropic is well worth a splurge. Favorites here include grilled artichoke with hollandaise sauce, radicchio Caesar salad, and bone-in grilled pork chops with cheddar-potato fondue. **Known for:** breathtaking views; well-curated wine list; great children's menu. [$] *Average main: $29* ✉ *1380 W. Stone Canyon La., Tropic* ☎ *435/679–8923* 🌐 *www.stonehearthgrille.com* ⏲ *Closed Nov.–mid-Mar.*

Hotels

IN THE PARK

★ **Bryce Canyon Lodge**

$$$ | **HOTEL** | This historic, rugged stone-and-wood lodge close to the amphitheater's rim offers motel-style rooms with semiprivate balconies or porches and cozy, beautifully designed lodgepole pine–and–stone cabins, some with cathedral ceilings and gas fireplaces. **Pros:** close proximity to canyon rim and trails; lodge is steeped in history and has loads of personality; cabins have fireplaces and exude rustic charm. **Cons:** closed in winter; books up fast; no TVs. [$] *Rooms from: $171* ✉ *Off Hwy. 63* ☎ *435/834–8700, 877/386–4383* 🌐 *www.brycecanyonforever.com* ⏲ *Closed early Jan.–early Mar.* 🛏 *113 rooms* 🍴 *No meals.*

OUTSIDE THE PARK

Best Western Bryce Canyon Grand Hotel

$$$$ | **HOTEL** | If you appreciate creature comforts but can do without much in the way of local personality, this four-story hotel just outside the park fits the bill—rooms are relatively posh, with comfortable mattresses, pillows, and bedding, spacious bathrooms, and modern appliances, and there's an outdoor pool and pleasant patio. **Pros:** clean, spacious rooms; lots of amenities and activities;

Best Campgrounds in Bryce Canyon

The two campgrounds in Bryce Canyon National Park fill up fast, especially in summer, and are family-friendly. All are drive-in, except for the handful of backcountry sites that only backpackers and gung-ho day hikers ever see.

North Campground. A cool, shady retreat in a forest of ponderosa pines, this is a great home base for your exploration of Bryce Canyon. You're near the general store, trailheads, and the visitor center. ✉ *Main park road, ½ mile south of visitor center* ☎ *435/834–5322.*

Sunset Campground. This serene alpine campground is within walking distance of Bryce Canyon Lodge and many trailheads. All sites are filled on a first-come, first-served basis. ✉ *Main park road, 2 miles south of visitor center* ☎ *435/834–5322.*

short drive or free shuttle ride from Bryce Canyon. **Cons:** no pets allowed; pricey during busy times; standard chain ambience. [$] *Rooms from: $209* ✉ *30 N. 100 E, Bryce Canyon City* ☎ *866/909–8845, 435/834–5700* 🌐 *www.brycecanyongrand.com* 🛏 *164 rooms* 🍴 *Breakfast.*

Best Western Plus Ruby's Inn
$$ | **HOTEL** | **FAMILY** | This bustling Southwestern-themed hotel has expanded over the years to include various wings with rooms that vary widely in terms of size and character. **Pros:** lots of services and amenities; short drive or free shuttle ride into the park; nice indoor pool. **Cons:** can get very busy, especially when the big tour buses roll in; too big for charm or a quiet getaway; uneven quality of restaurants. [$] *Rooms from: $149* ✉ *26 S. Main St., Bryce Canyon City* ☎ *435/834–5341, 866/866–6634* 🌐 *www.rubysinn.com* 🛏 *370 rooms* 🍴 *No meals.*

Bryce Canyon Pines
$$ | **HOTEL** | Most rooms in this motel complex tucked into the woods 6 miles southwest of the park entrance have excellent mountain views. **Pros:** guided horseback rides; pool and hot tub; lively restaurant famed for homemade pies. **Cons:** thin walls; room quality varies widely; furnishings are a bit dated. [$] *Rooms from: $140* ✉ *Hwy. 12, mile marker 10, Bryce Canyon City* ☎ *800/892–7923* 🌐 *www.brycecanyonmotel.com* 🛏 *46 rooms.*

Bybee's Steppingstone Motel
$$ | **HOTEL** | This cheerfully decorated, reasonably priced, and intimate seven-room boutique motel in tiny downtown Tropic is just 15 minutes east of the park and on the way toward Escalante. **Pros:** individually decorated rooms; more reasonably priced than other properties near Bryce; Keurig coffeemakers and tea kettles in every room. **Cons:** check-in office has limited hours; pets not allowed; no breakfast (but oatmeal and granola bars are provided). [$] *Rooms from: $109* ✉ *21 S. Main St., Tropic* ☎ *435/679–8998* 🌐 *www.bybeesteppingstone.com* 🕓 *Closed Nov.–Mar.* 🛏 *7 rooms* 🍴 *No meals.*

★ **Entrada Escalante Lodge**
$$$ | **HOTEL** | Each of the eight rooms in this smart, contemporary lodge in Escalante have patios with expansive views of the surrounding mountains, plus plenty of cushy perks like French presses and fresh-ground coffee, plush bedding, and 50-inch smart TVs. **Pros:** great restaurant; stunning views of Grand Staircase–Escalante National Monument; pets, including horses, are welcome. **Cons:** an

hour from Bryce Canyon National Park; in a very secluded, small town; somewhat high rates for the area. $ *Rooms from: $159* ⊠ *480 W. Main St., Escalante* ☎ *435/826–4000* ⊕ *www.entradaescalante.com* 🛏 *8 rooms* ⦿ *No meals*.

Escalante Outfitters

$ | **HOTEL** | A one-stop shop for planning and buying gear for your outdoor adventure, or if you're traveling on a budget and don't care about amenities, the seven log bunkhouse cabins here share a single bathhouse, and tent sites are also available (there's also one larger family cabin that sleeps four and has its own bath). **Pros:** very good restaurant; pet-friendly; lots of tours available. **Cons:** in a small, secluded town; you may have to wait in line for a shower; an hour's drive from Bryce. $ *Rooms from: $55* ⊠ *310 W. Main St., Escalante* ☎ *435/826–4266* ⊕ *www.escalanteoutfitters.com* 🛏 *8 cabins* ⦿ *No meals*.

SpringHill Suites Cedar City

$$ | **HOTEL** | **FAMILY** | Among the several chain properties in Cedar City, the best gateway to Bryce Canyon from Interstate 15 (though still 80 miles away), this modern and well-maintained all-suites Marriott property has the nicest rooms and best amenities. **Pros:** spacious and spotless rooms; nice mountain views; nice fitness center and indoor pool. **Cons:** not much local character; 90-minute drive from Bryce; some noise from I–15. $ *Rooms from: $119* ⊠ *1477 S. Old Hwy. 91, Cedar City* ☎ *435/586–1685* ⊕ *www.marriott.com* 🛏 *72 rooms* ⦿ *Free Breakfast*.

★ Stone Canyon Inn

$$$ | **B&B/INN** | Although not actually in the park, this stunningly situated luxury inn lies just east of Bryce Canyon, and rooms and the excellent on-site restaurant, Stone Hearth Grille, have astounding views of the park's hoodoos—there's even a trailhead nearby that accesses some of Bryce's best trails. **Pros:** the most stylish rooms in the area (some are tree houses); fantastic restaurant on-site; soaking tubs and fireplaces in some rooms. **Cons:** on the pricey side; not within walking distance of downtown shops and restaurants; no breakfast. $ *Rooms from: $195* ⊠ *1380 W. Stone Canyon La., Tropic* ☎ *435/679–8611, 866/489–4680* ⊕ *www.stonecanyoninn.com* 🛏 *15 rooms* ⦿ *No meals*.

CANYONLANDS NATIONAL PARK

Updated by
Andrew Collins

UTAH

WELCOME TO CANYONLANDS NATIONAL PARK

TOP REASONS TO GO

★ **Endless vistas:** The view from Island in the Sky stretches for miles as you look out over millennia of sculpting by wind and rain.

★ **Seeking solitude:** Needles, an astoundingly beautiful part of the park to explore on foot, sees very few visitors—it can sometimes feel like you have it all to yourself.

★ **Radical rides:** The Cataract Canyon rapids and the White Rim Trail are world-class adventures by boat or bike.

★ **Native American artifacts:** View rock art and Ancestral Puebloan dwellings in the park.

★ **Wonderful wilderness:** Some of the country's most untouched landscapes are within the park's boundaries, and they're worth the extra effort needed to get there.

★ **The night skies:** Far away from city lights, Canyonlands is ideal for stargazing.

Canyonlands National Park, in southeastern Utah, is divided into three distinct land districts and the river district, so it can be a little daunting to visit. It's exhausting, but not impossible, to explore the Island in the Sky and Needles in the same day.

1 Island in the Sky. From any of the overlooks here you can see for miles and look down thousands of feet to canyon floors. Chocolate-brown canyons are capped by white rock, and deep-red monuments rise nearby.

2 Needles. Pink, orange, and red rock is layered with white rock and stands in spires and pinnacles around grassy meadows. Extravagantly red mesas and buttes interrupt the horizon as in a picture postcard of the Old West.

3 The Maze. Only the most intrepid adventurers explore this incredibly remote mosaic of rock formations. There's a reason Butch Cassidy hid out here.

4 Rivers. For many, rafting through the waterways is the best way to see the park. The Green and Colorado, while very different today as a result of man-made dams than when John Wesley Powell explored them in the mid-1800s, are spectacular.

5 Horseshoe Canyon. Plan on several hours of dirt-road driving to get here, but the famous rock-art panel "Great Gallery" is a grand reward at the end of a long hike.

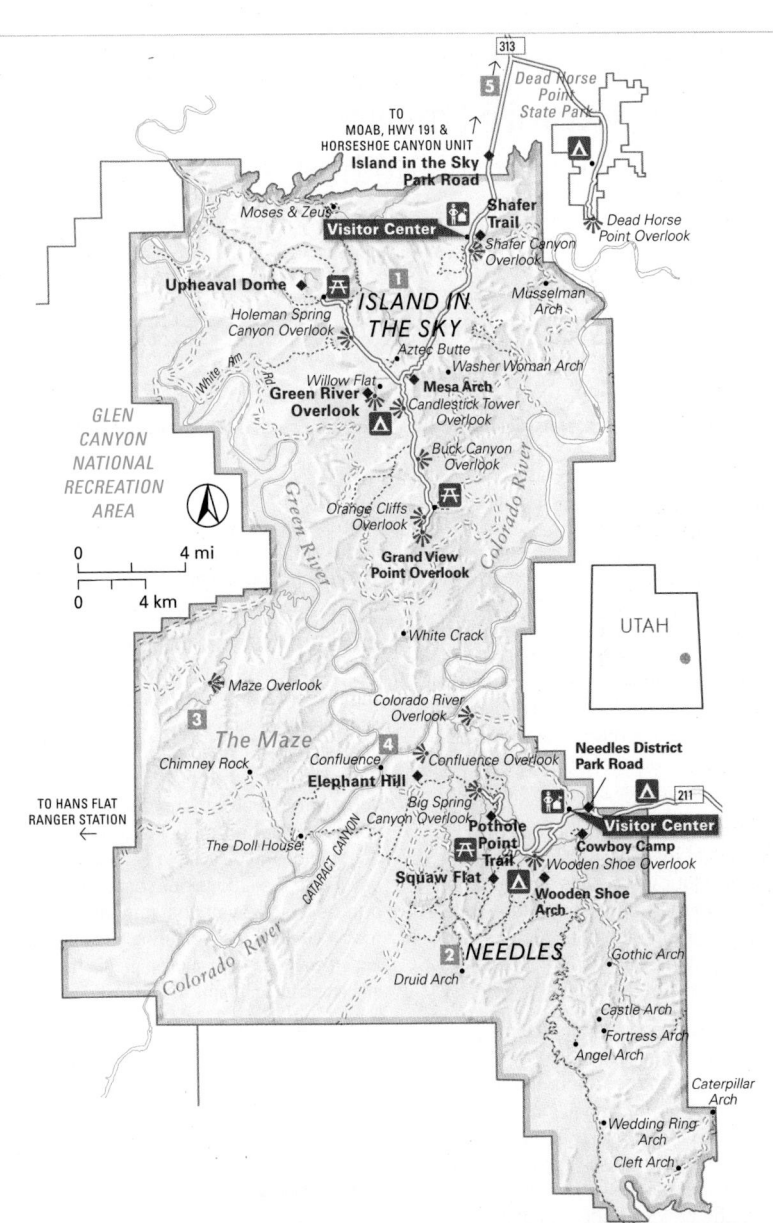

TO
MOAB, HWY 191 &
HORSESHOE CANYON UNIT
Island in the Sky
Park Road

Dead Horse
Point
State Park

Dead Horse
Point Overlook

Moses & Zeus

Visitor Center

Shafer
Trail

Shafer Canyon
Overlook

Musselman
Arch

Upheaval Dome

ISLAND IN
THE SKY

Holeman Spring
Canyon Overlook

White Rim Rd.

Aztec Butte

Washer Woman Arch

Willow Flat

Green River
Overlook

Mesa Arch

Candlestick Tower
Overlook

GLEN
CANYON
NATIONAL
RECREATION
AREA

Buck Canyon
Overlook

Green River

Colorado River

Orange Cliffs
Overlook

0   4 mi
0   4 km

Grand View
Point Overlook

White Crack

UTAH

Maze Overlook

Colorado River
Overlook

The Maze

Confluence

Confluence Overlook

Needles District
Park Road

Chimney Rock

Elephant Hill

Big Spring
Canyon Overlook

Visitor Center

TO HANS FLAT
RANGER STATION

The Doll House

CATARACT CANYON

Pothole
Point
Trail

Cowboy Camp

Wooden Shoe Overlook

Squaw Flat

Colorado River

Wooden Shoe
Arch

NEEDLES

Druid Arch

Gothic Arch

Castle Arch

Fortress Arch

Angel Arch

Caterpillar
Arch

Wedding Ring
Arch

Cleft Arch

Canyonlands is truly four parks in one, but the majority of visitors drive through the panoramic vistas of Island in the Sky and barely venture anywhere else. Plan a day to explore the Needles district and see the park from the bottom up. Float down the Green and Colorado rivers on a family-friendly rafting trip, or take on the white water in the legendary Cataract Canyon.

Planning

WHEN TO GO

Gorgeous weather means that spring and fall are most popular. Canyonlands is seldom crowded, but in spring backpackers and four-wheelers populate the trails and roads. During Easter week, some of the four-wheel-drive trails in the park are used for Jeep Safari, an annual event drawing thousands of visitors to town.

The crowds thin out by July as the thermostat reaches 100°F and higher for about four weeks. It's a great time to get out on the Colorado or Green River winding through the park. October can be a little rainy, but the region receives only 8 inches of rain annually.

The well-kept secret is that winter, except during occasional snow storms, can be a great time to tour the park. Crowds are gone, snowcapped mountains stand in the background, and key roads in Island in the Sky and Needles are well-maintained (although it's wise to check the park website for conditions).

Winter here is one of nature's most memorable shows, with red rock dusted white and low-floating clouds partially obscuring canyons and towers.

PLANNING YOUR TIME
CANYONLANDS IN ONE DAY

Your day begins with a choice: Island in the Sky or Needles. If you want expansive vistas looking across southeast Utah's canyons, head for the island, where you stand atop a giant mesa. If you want to walk among Canyonlands' spires and buttes, Needles is your destination. If you have a second or third day in the area, consider contacting an outfitter to take you on a rafting or 4X4 trip. ■TIP→ **Before venturing into the park, top off your gas tank, pack a picnic lunch, and stock up on plenty of water.**

Make your first stop along the main park road at the visitor center to learn about ranger talks or special programs. Next visit **Shafer Canyon Viewpoint,** where a short walk takes you out on a finger of land with views of the canyon over both sides. From here you can see Shafer

AVERAGE HIGH/LOW TEMPERATURES					
JAN.	FEB.	MAR.	APR.	MAY	JUNE
44/22	52/28	64/35	71/42	82/51	93/60
JULY	AUG.	SEPT.	OCT.	NOV.	DEC.
100/67	97/66	88/55	74/42	56/30	45/23

Trail's treacherous descent as it hugs the canyon walls below.

Then drive to **Mesa Arch.** Grab your camera and water bottle for the short hike out to the arch perched on the cliff's edge. After your excursion, take the spur road to Upheaval Dome, with its picnic spot in the parking lot. A short walk takes you to the first viewpoint of this crater. If you still have energy, 30 more minutes and a little sense of adventure, continue to the second overlook.

Retrace your drive to the main park road and continue to **Grand View Point.** Stroll along the edge of the rim, and see how many landmarks you can spot in the distance. White Rim Overlook is the best of the scenic spots, particularly if you're not afraid of heights and venture all the way out to the end of the rocky cliffs (no guardrail here). On the way back to dinner in Moab, spend an hour in Dead Horse Point State Park.

If you can stay overnight as well, then begin the day by setting up camp at Needles Campground or one of the other wonderful group camping areas in Needles. Then hit the **Joint Trail,** or any of the trails that begin from the campground, and spend the day hiking in the backcountry. Save an hour for the brief but terrific little hike to **Cave Springs,** and be sure to drive to the end of the park road to check out Big Spring Canyon Overlook. Sleep under countless stars.

GETTING HERE AND AROUND
AIR TRAVEL
Moab is served by tiny Canyonlands Field Airport, which has daily service to Denver on United Airlines and a couple of car rental agencies. The nearest mid-sized airport is Grand Junction Regional Airport in Grand Junction, Colorado, which is approximately 110 miles from Moab and is served by most major airlines.

CAR TRAVEL
Off U.S. 191, Canyonlands' Island in the Sky visitor center is 29 miles from Arches National Park and 32 miles from Moab on Highway 313 west of U.S. 191; the Needles District is 80 miles from Moab and reached via Highway 211, 34 miles west of U.S. 191.

Before starting a journey to any of Canyonlands' three districts, make sure your gas tank is topped off, as there are no services inside the large park. The Maze is especially remote, 135 miles from Moab, and actually a bit closer (100 miles) to Capitol Reef National Park. In the Island in the Sky District, it's about 15 miles from the entrance station to Grand View Point, with a 5-mile spur to Upheaval Dome. The Needles scenic drive is 10 miles from the entrance station, with two spurs, about 3 miles each. Roads in the Maze—suitable only for high-clearance, four-wheel-drive vehicles—wind for hundreds of miles through the rugged canyons. Within the parks, it's critical that you park only in designated pull-outs or parking areas.

PARK ESSENTIALS
ACCESSIBILITY
There are currently no trails in Canyonlands accessible to people in wheelchairs, but Grand View Point and Buck Canyon Overlook at Island in the Sky are wheelchair accessible. In Needles, the visitor center, restrooms, Squaw Flat Campground, and Wooden Shoe

Overlook are wheelchair accessible. The visitor centers at the Island in the Sky and Needles districts are also accessible, and the park's pit toilets are accessible with some assistance.

PARK FEES AND PERMITS

Admission is $30 per vehicle, $15 per person on foot or bicycle, and $25 per motorcycle, good for seven days. Your Canyonlands pass is good for all the park's districts. There's no entrance fee to the Maze District of Canyonlands. A $55 local park pass grants you admission to both Arches and Canyonlands as well as Natural Bridges and Hovenweep national monuments for one year.

You need a permit for overnight backpacking, four-wheel-drive camping, river trips, and mountain-bike camping. Online reservations can be made four months in advance on the park website. Four-wheel-drive day use in Salt, Horse, and Lavender canyons and all motorized vehicles and bicycles on the Elephant Hill and White Rim trails also require a permit, which you can obtain online up to 24 hours before your trip or in person at visitor centers.

PARK HOURS

Canyonlands National Park is open 24 hours a day, seven days a week, year-round. It is in the Mountain time zone.

CELL PHONE RECEPTION

Cell phone reception may be available in some parts of the park, but not reliably so. Public telephones are at the park's visitor centers.

EDUCATIONAL OFFERINGS

For more information on current schedules and locations of park programs, contact the visitor centers or check the bulletin boards throughout the park. Programs change periodically and may sometimes be canceled because of limited staffing.

Explorer Pack

TOUR—SIGHT | FAMILY | Just like borrowing a book from a library, kids can check out a backpack filled with tools for learning. The sturdy backpack includes binoculars, a magnifying glass, and a three-ring binder full of activities. These are available at Needles and Island in the Sky visitor centers. ⊠ *Canyonlands National Park.*

RANGER PROGRAMS
Grand View Point Overlook Talk

TOUR—SIGHT | Spring through fall, rangers lead short presentations at Grand View Point about the geology that created Utah's Canyonlands. ⊠ *Grand View Point, Island in the Sky.*

Junior Ranger Program

TOUR—SIGHT | FAMILY | Kids ages of all ages can pick up a Junior Ranger booklet at the visitor centers. It's full of puzzles, word games, and fun facts about the park and its wildlife. To earn the Junior Ranger badge, they must complete several activities in the booklet. ⊠ *Canyonlands National Park* 🆓 *Free.*

RESTAURANTS

There are no dining facilities in the park, although Needles Outpost campground, a mile from Needles Visitor Center, has a small solar-powered store with snacks and drinks. Moab has a multitude of dining options, and there are a few very casual restaurants in Monticello and Blandings (in the latter community, restaurants don't serve alcohol and are typically closed Sunday), plus a couple of excellent eateries a bit farther south in Bluff.

HOTELS

There is no lodging in the park. Most visitors—especially those focused on Island in the Sky—stay in Moab or perhaps Green River, but the small towns of Monticello, Blanding, and Bluff—which have a smattering of motels and inns—are also convenient for exploring the Needles District. *Hotel reviews have been shortened. For full information, visit Fodors.com.*

What It Costs			
$	$$	$$$	$$$$
RESTAURANTS			
under $13	$13–$20	$21–$30	over $30
HOTELS			
under $101	$101–$150	$151–$200	over $200

VISITOR INFORMATION

PARK CONTACT INFORMATION Canyonlands National Park ☎ 435/719–2313 ⊕ www.nps.gov/cany.

VISITOR CENTERS

Hans Flat Ranger Station

INFO CENTER | Only experienced and intrepid visitors will likely ever visit this remote outpost—on a dirt road 46 miles east of Highway 24 in Hanksville. The office is a trove of books, maps, and other documents about the unforgiving Maze District of Canyonlands, but rangers will strongly dissuade any inexperienced off-road drivers and backpackers to proceed into this truly rugged wilderness. Just to get here you must drive 46 miles on a dirt road that is sometimes impassable even to 4X4 vehicles. There's a pit toilet, but no water, food, or services of any kind. If you're headed for the backcountry, permits cost $30 per group for up to 14 days. Rangers offer guided hikes in Horseshoe Canyon on most weekends in spring and fall. ⊠ Jct. of Recreation Rds. 777 and 633, Maze ☎ 435/259–2652.

★ Island in the Sky Visitor Center

INFO CENTER | The gateway to the world-famous White Rim Trail, this visitor center 21 miles from U.S. 191 draws a mix of mountain bikers, hikers, and tourists. Enjoy the orientation film, then browse the bookstore for information about the region. Exhibits help explain animal adaptations as well as some of the history of the park. Check the website or at the center for a daily schedule of ranger-led programs. ⊠ Off Hwy. 313, Island in the Sky ☎ 435/259–4712 ⊗ Closed late Dec.–early Mar.

Needles District Visitor Center

INFO CENTER | This gorgeous building is 34 miles from U.S. 191 via Highway 211, near the park entrance. Needles is remote, so it's worth stopping to inquire about road, weather, and park conditions. You can also watch the interesting orientation film, refill water bottles, and get books, trail maps, and other information. ⊠ off Hwy. 211, Needles ☎ 435/259–4711 ⊗ Closed late Nov.–early Mar.

 ## Sights

SCENIC DRIVES

Island in the Sky Park Road

SCENIC DRIVE | This 15-mile-long main road inside the park is bisected by a 5-mile side road to the Upheaval Dome area. To enjoy dramatic views, including the Green and Colorado river canyons, stop at the overlooks and take the short walks. Once you get to the park, allow at least two hours—and ideally four—to explore. ⊠ Island in the Sky.

Needles District Park Road

SCENIC DRIVE | You'll feel like you've driven into a Hollywood Western as you roll along the park road in the Needles District. Red mesas and buttes rise against the horizon, blue mountain ranges interrupt the rangelands, and the colorful red-and-white needles stand like soldiers on the far side of grassy meadows. Definitely hop out of the car at a few of the marked roadside stops, including both overlooks at Pothole Point. Allow at least two hours in this less-traveled section of the park. ⊠ Needles.

HISTORIC SITES

ISLAND IN THE SKY

Shafer Trail

SCENIC DRIVE | This rough trek that leads to the 100-mile White Rim Road was probably first established by ancient Native Americans, but in the early 1900s

Plants and Wildlife in Canyonlands

Wildlife is not the attraction in Canyonlands, as many of the creatures sleep during the heat of the day. On the bright side, there are fewer people and less traffic to scare the animals away. Cool mornings and evenings are the best time to spot them, especially in summer when the heat keeps them in cool, shady areas. Mule deer are nearly always seen along the roadway as you enter the Needles District, and you'll no doubt see jackrabbits and small rodents darting across the roadway. Approximately 350 bighorn sheep populate the park. If you happen upon one of these regal animals, do not approach it even if it is alone, as bighorn sheep are skittish by nature and easily stressed. Also, report your sighting to a ranger, and note that some areas of the park are closed May–August, which is bighorn sheep lambing season.

ranchers used it to drive cattle into the canyon. Originally narrow and rugged, it was upgraded during the uranium boom, when miners hauled ore by truck from the canyon floor. Check out the road's winding route down canyon walls from Shafer Canyon Overlook before you drive it to see why it's mostly used by daring four-wheelers and energetic mountain bikers. Off the main road, less than 1 mile from the park entrance, it descends 1,400 feet to the White Rim. Check with the visitor center about road conditions before driving the Shafer Trail. It's often impassable after rain or snow. ⊠ *Island in the Sky.*

NEEDLES

Cowboy Camp

HISTORIC SITE | FAMILY | This fascinating stop on the 0.6-mile round-trip **Cave Springs Trail** is an authentic example of cowboy life more than a century ago. You do not need to complete the entire trail (which includes two short ladders and some rocky hiking) to see the 19th-century artifacts at Cowboy Camp. ⊠ *End of Cave Springs Rd., Needles* ✛ *2.3 miles from visitor center.*

SCENIC STOPS

ISLAND IN THE SKY

★ Grand View Point

VIEWPOINT | This 360-degree view is the main event for many visitors to Island in the Sky. Look down on the deep canyons of the Colorado and Green rivers, which have been carved by water and erosion over the millennia. Stretch your legs on the trails along the canyon edge. ⊠ *End of main park road, Island in the Sky* ✛ *12 miles from visitor center.*

Green River Overlook

VIEWPOINT | From the road it's just 100 yards to this stunning view of the Green River to the south and west. It's not far from Island in the Sky campground. ⊠ *About 1 mile off Upheaval Dome Rd., Island in the Sky* ✛ *8 miles from visitor center.*

Mesa Arch

NATURE SITE | If you don't have time for the 2,000 arches in nearby Arches National Park, you should take the easy, half-mile round-trip walk to Mesa Arch. The arch is above a cliff that drops 800 feet to the canyon bottom. Through the arch, views of Washerwoman Arch and surrounding buttes, spires, and canyons make this a favorite photo opportunity.

✉ Off main park road, Island in the Sky ✛ 6 miles from visitor center.

★ Upheaval Dome

NATURE SITE | This mysterious crater is one of the wonders of Island in the Sky. Some geologists believe it's an eroded salt dome, but others think it was made by a meteorite. The trip to the first overlook is about a half-mile; energetic visitors can continue another half-mile to the second overlook for an even better perspective. ✉ End of Upheaval Dome Rd., Island in the Sky ✛ 11 miles from visitor center.

NEEDLES
Pothole Point Trail

TRAIL | Microscopic creatures lie dormant in pools that fill only after rare rainstorms. When the rains do come, some eggs hatch within hours and life becomes visible. If you're lucky, you'll hit Pothole Point after a storm. The dramatic views of the Needles and Six Shooter Peak make this easy, 0.6-mile round-trip worthwhile. Plan for about 45 minutes. There's no shade, so wear a hat and take plenty of water. ✉ Off main road, Needles ✛ 5 miles from visitor center.

Wooden Shoe Arch

NATURE SITE | FAMILY | Kids enjoy looking for the tiny window in the rock that looks like a wooden shoe with a turned-up toe. If you can't find it on your own, there's a marker to help you. ✉ Off main park road, Needles ✛ 2 miles from visitor center.

🏃 Activities

Canyonlands is one of the world's best destinations for adrenaline junkies. You can rock climb, mountain bike treacherous terrain, tackle world-class white-water rapids, and make your 4X4 crawl over steep cliffs along precipitous drops. Compared with other national parks, Canyonlands allows you to enjoy an amazing amount of solitude while having the adventure of a lifetime. *For additional tour operators that cover not just the*

Meet Me At Sunset

Sunset is one of the picture-perfect times in Canyonlands, as the slanting sun shines over the vast network of canyons that stretch out below Island in the Sky. A moonlight drive to Grand View Point can also give you lasting memories as the moon drenches the white sandstone in light. Likewise, late-afternoon color in the spires and towers at the Needles District is a humbling, awe-inspiring scene.

park but the greater Moab region, see Sports and the Outdoors in the Arches National Park Chapter (Chapter tk)

TOURS
Redtail Aviation

TOUR—SPORTS | This company's daily, regional tours give you an eagle's-eye view of the park, and you'll walk away with new respect and understanding of the word "wilderness." The Canyonlands Tour, one of several flightseeing options, lasts for one hour. A two-person minimum applies. ✉ Canyonlands Field Airport, 94 W. Aviation Way, Moab ✛ Off U.S. 191 ☎ 435/259–7421 ⊕ www.redtailaviation.com ✆ From $179 per person.

BICYCLING
Magpie Cycling

BICYCLING | Professional guides and mountain biking instructors lead groups (or lone riders) on daylong and multiday bike trips exploring the Moab region's most memorable terrain, including the White Rim, Needles, and the Maze. If you need to rent a bike, Magpie can meet you at its preferred shop, Poison Spider Bicycles (☎ 435/259–7882 or 800/635–7882 ⊕ poisonspiderbicycles.com). ✉ Moab ☎ 435/259–4464,

Did You Know?

The scenic and rocky 100-mile White Rim Road, which cuts through Island in the Sky near the Green River, is popular with those in Jeeps and on mountain bikes. Day-use permits, available at the park visitor center or up to 24 hours in advance through the park's reservations website, are required for motorized and bicycle trips on White Rim. The number of overnight and day-use permits is limited and in high demand in spring and fall. Reservations for overnight permits are available no more than four months, and no fewer than two days, in advance.

800/546–4245 ⊕ www.magpieadventures.com ☞ Day tours from $150, multiday from $875.

TRAILS
White Rim Road

BICYCLING | Mountain bikers from all over the world like to brag that they've conquered this 100-mile ride. The trail's fame is well deserved: it traverses steep roads, broken rock, and dramatic ledges, as well as long stretches that wind through the canyons and look down onto others. If you're biking White Rim without an outfitter, you'll need careful planning, vehicle support, and much sought-after backcountry reservations. Permits are available no more than four months, and no less than two days, prior to permit start date. There is a 15-person, three-vehicle limit for groups. Day-use permits are also required and can be obtained at the Island in the Sky visitor center or reserved 24 hours in advance through the park's website. ⊠ Off main park road about 1 mile from entrance, then about 11 miles on Shafer Trail, Island in the Sky.

BOATING AND RAFTING

In Labyrinth Canyon, north of the park boundary, and in Stillwater Canyon, in the Island in the Sky District, the river is quiet and calm and there's plenty of shoreside camping. The Island in the Sky leg of the Colorado River, from Moab to its confluence with the Green River and downstream a few more miles to Spanish Bottom, is ideal for both canoeing and for rides with an outfitter in a large, stable jet boat. If you want to take a self-guided flat-water float trip in the park you must obtain a $30 permit, which you have to request by mail or fax. Make your upstream travel arrangements with a shuttle company before you request a permit. For permits, contact the reservation office at park headquarters (☎ 435/259–4351).

Below Spanish Bottom, about 64 miles downstream from Moab, 49 miles from the Potash Road ramp, and 4 miles south of the confluence, the Colorado churns into the first rapids of legendary Cataract Canyon. Home of some of the best white water in the United States, this piece of river between the Maze and the Needles districts rivals the Grand Canyon stretch of the Colorado River for adventure. During spring melt-off these rapids can rise to staggering heights and deliver heart-stopping excitement. The canyon cuts through the very heart of Canyonlands, where you can see this amazing wilderness area in its most pristine form. The water calms down a bit in summer. Outfitters will take you for the ride of your life in this wild canyon, where the river drops more steeply than anywhere else on the Colorado River (in ¾ mile, the river drops 39 feet). You can join an expedition lasting anywhere from one to six days, or you can purchase a $20 permit for a self-guided trip from park headquarters.

Oars

BOATING | This well-regarded outfitter can take you for several days of rafting and/or hiking on the Colorado and Green rivers. Hiking/interpretive trips are available in Canyonlands and Arches, and for those not into white water, they also offer calm-water trips. ⊠ Moab ☎ 435/259–5865, 800/342–5938 ⊕ www.oars.com/utah ☜ From $119.

Sheri Griffith Expeditions

BOATING | In addition to trips through the white water of Cataract, Westwater, and Desolation canyons, on the Colorado and Green rivers, this company also offers specialty expeditions for women, writers, and families. One of their more luxurious expeditions features dinners cooked by a professional chef and served on linen-covered tables. Cots and other sleeping amenities also make roughing it a little more comfortable. ⊠ 2231 S. U.S. 191, Moab ☎ 435/259–8229, 800/332–2439 ⊕ www.griffithexp.com ☜ From $180.

TOURS
FOUR-WHEELING

Nearly 200 miles of challenging back-country roads lead to campsites, trail-heads, and natural and cultural features in Canyonlands. All of the roads require high-clearance, four-wheel-drive vehicles, and many are inappropriate for inexperienced drivers. The 100-mile White Rim Trail, for example, can be extremely challenging, so make sure that your four-wheel-drive skills are well-honed and that you are capable of making basic road and vehicle repairs. Carry at least one full-size spare tire, extra gas, extra water, a shovel, a high-lift jack, and—October through April—chains for all four tires. Double-check to see that your vehicle is in top-notch condition, for you definitely don't want to break down in the interior of the park: towing expenses can exceed $1,000.

Day-use permits, available at the park visitor centers or 24 hours in advance through the park website, are required for motorized and bicycle trips on the Elephant Hill and White Rim trails. For overnight four-wheeling trips you must purchase a $30 permit, which you can reserve no more than four months and no fewer than two days in advance by contacting the Backcountry Reservations Office (☎ 435/259–4351). Cyclists share all roads, so be aware and cautious of their presence. Vehicular traffic traveling uphill has the right-of-way. Check at the visitor center for current road conditions before taking off into the backcountry. You must carry a washable, reusable toilet with you in the Maze District and carry out all waste.

ISLAND IN THE SKY
White Rim Road

FOUR-WHEELING | Winding around and below the Island in the Sky mesa top, the dramatic, 100-mile White Rim Road offers a once-in-a-lifetime driving experience. As you tackle Murphy's Hogback, Hardscrabble Hill, and more formidable obstacles, you will get some fantastic views of the park. Attempting to travel the loop in one day is not recommended—plan instead to camp overnight with advance reservations, which can be made up to four months in advance (book ASAP for busy spring and fall weekends). Day-use permits, which are available at the park visitor center or 24 hours in advance through the park website, are required for motorized and bicycle trips on White Rim Road. Bring plenty of water, a spare tire, and a jack, as no services are available on the road. White Rim Road starts at the end of Shafer Trail. ✉ *Off main park road about 1 mile from entrance, then about 11 miles on Shafer Trail, Island in the Sky.*

THE MAZE
Flint Trail

FOUR-WHEELING | This remote, rugged road is the most popular in the Maze District, but it's not an easy ride. It has 2 miles of switchbacks that drop down the side of a cliff face. You reach Flint Trail from the Hans Flat Ranger Station, 46 miles from the closest paved road. From Hans Flat to the end of the road at the Doll House it's a 41-mile drive that takes at least six hours one-way. The Maze is not recommended as a day trip, so you'll have to purchase an overnight backcountry permit for $30. Despite its remoteness, the Maze District can fill to capacity during spring and fall, so plan ahead. ✉ *Hans Flat Ranger Station, Jct. of Recreation Rds. 777 and 633, Maze.*

NEEDLES
Elephant Hill

FOUR-WHEELING | The first 3 miles of this route are passable by all vehicles, but don't venture out without asking about road conditions. For the rest of the trail, only 4X4 vehicles are allowed. The route is so difficult that many people get out and walk—it's faster than you can drive it in some cases. The trek from Elephant Hill Trailhead to Devil's Kitchen is 3½ miles; from the trailhead to the

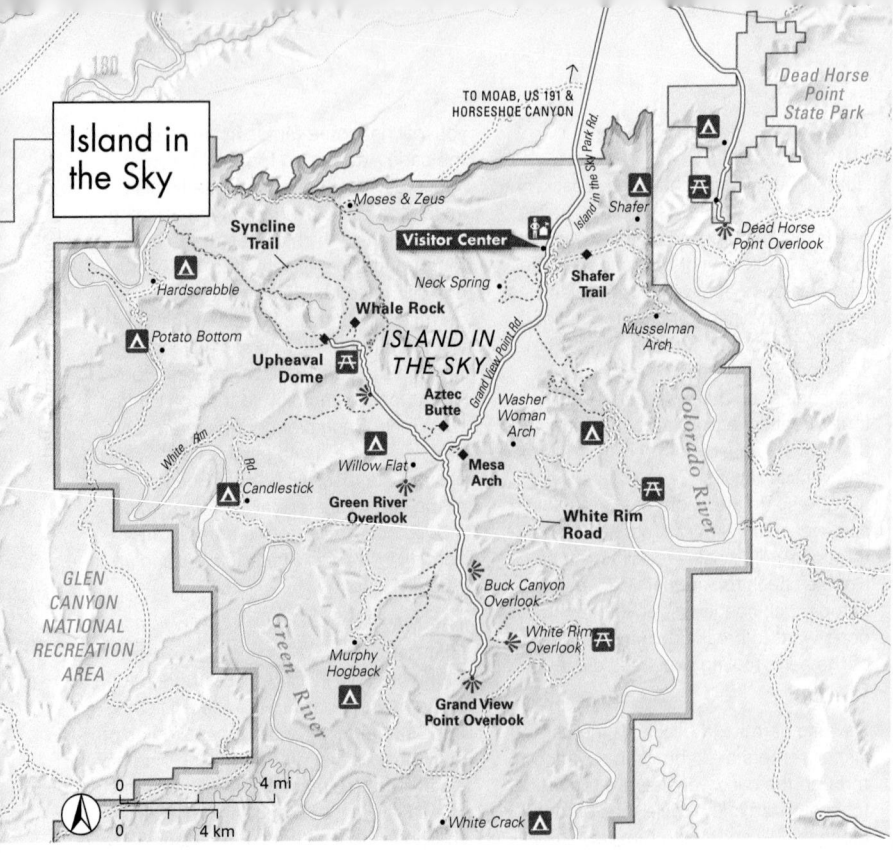

Island in the Sky

TO MOAB, US 191 &
HORSESHOE CANYON

Dead Horse
Point
State Park

Moses & Zeus

Syncline
Trail

Visitor Center

Shafer

Dead Horse
Point Overlook

Hardscrabble

Neck Spring

Shafer
Trail

Potato Bottom

Whale Rock

**ISLAND IN
THE SKY**

Musselman
Arch

Upheaval
Dome

Aztec
Butte

Washer
Woman
Arch

Colorado River

White Rim Rd.

Candlestick

Willow Flat

Mesa
Arch

Green River
Overlook

White Rim
Road

GLEN
CANYON
NATIONAL
RECREATION
AREA

Green River

Buck Canyon
Overlook

Murphy
Hogback

White Rim
Overlook

Grand View
Point Overlook

0   4 mi

0   4 km

White Crack

Confluence Overlook, it's a 14½-mile round-trip and requires at least eight hours. Don't attempt this without a well-maintained 4X4 vehicle and spare gas, tires, and off-road knowledge. A day-use permit, which is available at the park visitor center or 24 hours in advance through the park website, is required for motorized and bicycle trips on the Elephant Hill Trail. ✉ *Off main park road, Needles* ✛ *Turnoff about 3 miles west of visitor center.*

HIKING

At Canyonlands National Park you can immerse yourself in the intoxicating colors, smells, and textures of the desert. Many of the trails are long, rolling routes over slickrock and sand in landscapes dotted with juniper, pinyon, and sagebrush. Interconnecting trails in the Needles District provide excellent

opportunities for weeklong backpacking excursions. The Maze trails are primarily accessed via four-wheel-drive vehicle. In the separate Horseshoe Canyon area, Horseshoe Canyon Trail takes a considerable amount of effort to reach, as it's about 120 miles from Moab, the final 32 miles of which are a bumpy, and often sandy, dirt road.

ISLAND IN THE SKY
Aztec Butte Trail

HIKING/WALKING | The highlight of the 2-mile round-trip hike is the chance to see Ancestral Puebloan granaries. The view into Taylor Canyon is also nice. *Easy–Moderate.* ✉ *Island in the Sky* ✛ *Trailhead: Upheaval Dome Rd., about 7 miles from visitor center.*

★ Grand View Point Trail

HIKING/WALKING | If you're looking for a level walk with some of the best scenery in the West, stop at Grand View Point and wander this 2-mile round-trip trail along the cliff edge. Many people just stop at the paved overlook and drive on, but you'll gain breathtaking perspective by strolling along this flat cliffside trail. On a clear day you can see up to 100 miles to the Maze and Needles districts of the park and each of Utah's major laccolithic mountain ranges: the Henrys, Abajos, and La Sals. *Easy.* ⊠ *Island in the Sky* ✛ *Trailhead: end of main park road, 12 miles from visitor center.*

★ Mesa Arch Trail

HIKING/WALKING | **FAMILY** | After the overlooks, this is the most popular trail in the park, a ½-mile loop that acquaints you with desert plants and terrain and offers vistas of La Sal Mountains. The highlight of this hike is a natural arch window perched over an 800-foot drop, giving a rare downward glimpse through the arch rather than the usual upward view of the sky. It's one of the best spots in the park to enjoy the sunrise. *Easy.* ⊠ *Island in the Sky* ✛ *Trailhead: 6 miles from visitor center.*

Syncline Loop Trail

HIKING/WALKING | If you're up for a strenuous day of hiking, try this 8-mile trail that follows the canyons around Upheaval Dome. You get limited views of the dome itself as you actually make a complete loop around the outside of the crater. This challenging trek—best avoided during the hot summer months—requires some route-finding and scrambling through boulder fields, plus tackling some steep switchbacks—the total elevation gain is 1,300 feet. Carry a map, a flashlight, and extra water and food. You'll get some sheltering afternoon shade if you hike the trail clockwise. *Difficult.* ⊠ *Island in the Sky* ✛ *Trailhead: Upheaval Dome Rd., 12 miles from park entrance.*

Upheaval Dome Trail

HIKING/WALKING | It's fun to imagine that a giant meteorite crashed to earth here, sending shock waves around the planet.

But some geologists believe that salt, collecting and expanding upward, formed a dome and then exploded, causing the crater. Either way, it's worth the steep hike to see it and decide for yourself. You reach the main overlook after just 0.4 mile, but you can double your pleasure by going on to a second overlook for a better view. The trail is steeper and rougher after the first overlook. Round-trip to the second overlook is 2 miles. *Moderate.* ⊠ *Island in the Sky* ✛ *Trailhead: Upheaval Dome Rd., 12 miles from park entrance.*

Whale Rock Trail

HIKING/WALKING | If you've been hankering to walk across some of that pavement-smooth stuff they call slickrock, the hike to Whale Rock will make your feet happy. This 1-mile round-trip adventure, which culminates with a tough final 100-foot climb and features some potentially dangerous dropoffs, takes you to the very top of the whale's back. Once you get there, you are rewarded with great views of Upheaval Dome and Trail Canyon. *Easy–Moderate.* ⊠ *Island in the Sky* ✛ *Trailhead: Upheaval Dome Rd., 10 miles from visitor center.*

THE MAZE

Horseshoe Canyon Trail

HIKING/WALKING | This remote region of the park is accessible by dirt road, and only in good weather. Park at the lip of the canyon and hike 6½ miles round-trip to the Great Gallery, considered by some to be the most significant rock-art panel in North America. Ghostly life-size figures in the Barrier Canyon style populate the amazing panel. The hike is moderately strenuous, with a 750-foot descent. Allow at least six hours for the trip and take a gallon of water per person. There's no camping allowed in the canyon, although you can camp on top near the parking lot. *Difficult.* ⊠ *Maze* ✛ *Trailhead: 32 miles east of Hwy. 24.*

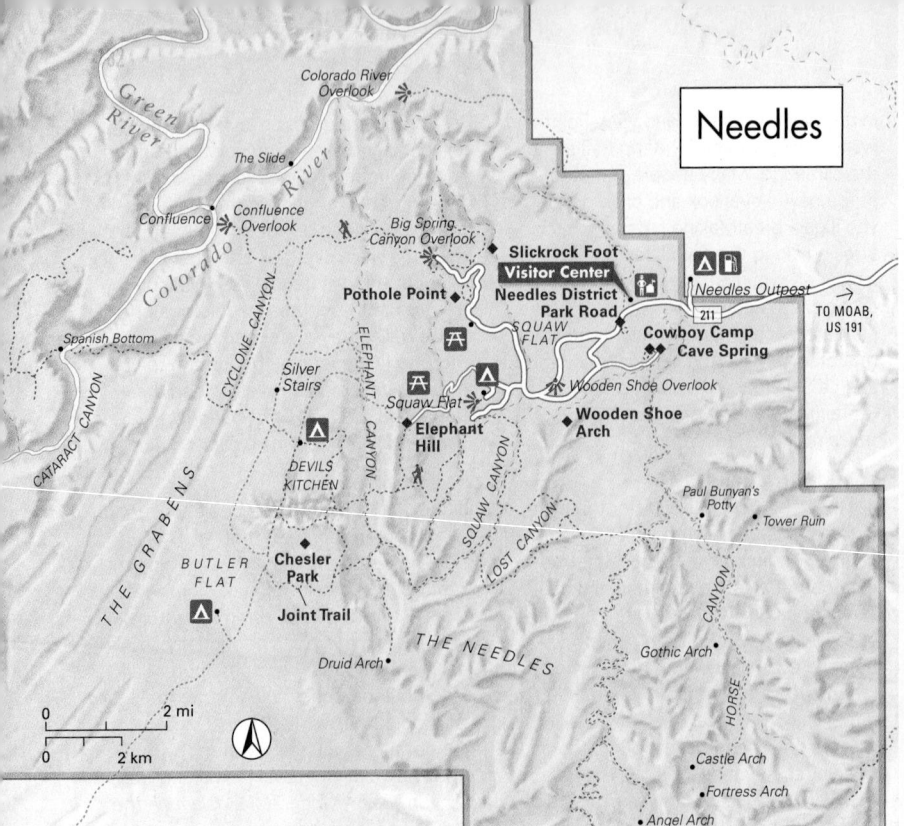

Needles

Colorado River
Overlook

Green
River

The Slide

Colorado River

Confluence
Confluence
Overlook

Big Spring
Canyon Overlook

Slickrock Foot
Visitor Center
Needles District
Park Road

Needles Outpost

Pothole Point

TO MOAB,
US 191

211

SQUAW
FLAT

Cowboy Camp
Cave Spring

Spanish Bottom

CYCLONE CANYON

Silver
Stairs

ELEPHANT CANYON

Wooden Shoe Overlook

Squaw Flat

Wooden Shoe
Arch

CATARACT CANYON

Elephant
Hill

SQUAW CANYON

DEVILS
KITCHEN

LOST CANYON

Paul Bunyan's
Potty

Tower Ruin

THE GRABENS

BUTLER
FLAT

Chesler
Park

Joint Trail

THE NEEDLES

Druid Arch

Gothic Arch

HORSE CANYON

Castle Arch

0   2 mi
0   2 km

Druid Arch

Fortress Arch

Angel Arch

NEEDLES

★ Cave Spring Trail

HIKING/WALKING | FAMILY | One of the best, most interesting trails in the park takes you past a historic cowboy camp, precontact rock art, and great views. Two wooden ladders and one short, steep stretch may make this a little daunting for the extremely young or old, but it's also a short hike (0.6 mile round-trip), features some shade, and has many notable features *Easy–Moderate.* ✉ *Needles* ⊹ *Trailhead: end of Cave Springs Rd., 2.3 miles from visitor center.*

Chesler Viewpoint

HIKING/WALKING | Chesler Park is a grassy meadow dotted with spires and enclosed by a circular wall of colorful "needles." One of Canyonlands' more popular trails leads through the area to the famous Joint Trail. This trek to the viewpoint is

6 miles round-trip. *Moderate–Difficult.* ✉ *Needles* ⊹ *Trailhead: Elephant Hill parking lot, 6 miles from visitor center.*

★ Joint Trail

HIKING/WALKING | Part of the Chesler Park Loop, this trail follows a series of deep, narrow fractures in the rock. A shady spot in summer, it will give you good views of the Needles formations for which the district is named. The loop travels briefly along a four-wheel-drive road and is 11 miles round-trip; allow at least five hours to complete it. *Difficult.* ✉ *Needles* ⊹ *Trailhead: Elephant Hill parking lot, 6 miles from visitor center.*

Slickrock Trail

HIKING/WALKING | Wear a hat and carry plenty of water if you're on this trail—you won't find any shade along the 2.4-mile round-trip trek. This is the rare frontcountry site where you might spot one of the few remaining native herds of bighorn sheep in the national park system. Nice panoramic views. *Easy–Moderate.* ✉ *Needles* ✛ *Trailhead: main park road, 6 miles from visitor center.*

ROCK CLIMBING

Canyonlands and the surrounding area draw climbers from all over the world. Permits are not required, but because of the park's sensitive archaeological nature it's imperative that you stop at the visitor center to pick up regulations pertaining to the park's cultural resources. Popular climbing routes include Moses and Zeus towers in Taylor Canyon, and Monster Tower and Washerwoman Tower on the White Rim Road. Like most routes in Canyonlands, these climbs are for experienced climbers only. Just outside the Needles District, Indian Creek is one of the country's best traditional climbing areas.

Nearby Towns

Moab, the major gateway to both Arches and Canyonlands national parks, abounds with outfitters, shops, restaurants, and lodging options—see the Arches National Park chapter for more on this bustling, free-spirited hub of outdoor recreation. A handful of smaller communities south of Moab along U.S. 191 are closer than Moab to the Needles District and contain a smattering of amenities.

Roughly 55 miles south of Moab, **Monticello** is less than an hour from the Needles District and lies at 7,000 feet elevation, making it a cool summer refuge from desert heat. In winter it gets downright cold and sometimes receives heavy snow; the Abajo Mountains rise to 11,360 feet to the west of town. Monticello has a few basic motels and restaurants and is a good halfway point between Moab and Colorado's Mesa Verde National Park. Tiny **Blanding,** 20 miles south of Monticello, has a few bare-bones motels and prides itself on

Up, Up, and Away

Bluff International Balloon Festival Colorful hot-air balloons—some from as far away as England—take to the skies over Valley of the Gods and the town of Bluff during this mid-January festival. It's always a friendly crowd, and the balloon pilots often will trade a free ride if you help as part of their chase crew. Attend the "glow in" if weather allows, and see balloons illuminated against the night sky by the flame from the propane heaters that fill them with hot air. Bring warm clothing and expect crisp, clear weather. ✉ *Bluff* ☎ *435/672–2341* ⊕ *www.bluffutah.org.*

old-fashioned conservative values—it's a dry town, so alcohol sales are prohibited. It's the gateway to Edge of the Cedars State Park, Hovenweep National Monument, Natural Bridges Natural Monument, Grand Gulch, and the eastern end of Lake Powell. About 25 miles south of Blanding, tiny **Bluff** has a couple of the region's most appealing lodging and dining options and is an excellent gateway for Hovenweep, exploring the San Juan River, and visiting Monument Valley and the northern edge of the Navajo Nation.

VISITOR INFORMATION Blanding Visitor Center ✉ *12 N. Grayson Pkwy., Blanding* ☎ *435/678–3662* ⊕ *www.blanding-ut.gov.* **Southeastern Utah Welcome Center** ✉ *216 S. Main St., Monticello* ✛ *Next to Frontier Museum* ☎ *435/587–3401* ⊕ *www. monticelloutah.org.*

 **Sights**

★ **Dead Horse Point State Park**
NATIONAL/STATE PARK | One of the gems of Utah's state park system, right at the

edge of the Island in the Sky section of Canyonlands, this park overlooks a sweeping oxbow of the Colorado River some 2,000 feet below. Dead Horse Point itself is a small peninsula connected to the main mesa by a narrow neck of land. As the story goes, cowboys used to drive wild mustangs onto the point and pen them there with a brush fence. There's a modern visitor center with a coffee shop and museum. The park's Intrepid Trail System has become popular with mountain bikers and hikers alike. Be sure to walk the 4-mile rim trail loop and drive to the park's eponymous point if it's a nice day. ⊠ *Hwy. 313* 🕾 *435/259–2614, 800/322–3770 camping reservations* ⊕ *www.stateparks.utah.gov* 🖾 *$20 per vehicle.*

Dinosaur Museum

MUSEUM | FAMILY | Skeletons, fossils, footprints, and reconstructed dinosaur skins are all on display at this small museum. Hallways hold a collection of movie posters featuring Godzilla and other monsters dating back to the 1930s. ⊠ *754 S. 200 W, Blanding* 🕾 *435/678–3454* ⊕ *www. dinosaur-museum.org* 🖾 *$4* ⊘ *Closed mid-Oct.–mid-Apr.*

★ Edge of the Cedars State Park Museum

MUSEUM | FAMILY | Behind what is one of the nation's foremost museums dedicated to the Ancestral Puebloan culture, an interpretive trail leads to an ancient village that they once inhabited. Portions have been partially excavated, and visitors can climb down a ladder into a 1,000-year-old ceremonial room called a kiva. The museum displays a variety of pots, baskets, spear points, and rare artifacts—even a pair of sandals said to date back 1,500 years. ⊠ *660 W. 400 N, Blanding* 🕾 *435/678–2238* ⊕ *www.stateparks.utah. gov* 🖾 *$5* ⊘ *Closed Sun. in Nov.–Mar.*

Hovenweep National Monument

MEMORIAL | The best place in southeast Utah to see ancient tower ruins dotting the scenic cliffs, if you're headed south from Canyonlands and have an interest in Ancestral Puebloan culture, a visit to this monument is a must. Park rangers strongly advise following printed maps and signs from U.S. 191 near Blanding, Utah, or County Road G from Cortez, Colorado. GPS is not reliable here. Once you get there, you'll find unusual tower structures (which may have been used for astronomical observation) and ancient dwellings. ⊠ *Hovenweep Rd.* 🕾 *970/562–4282* ⊕ *www.nps.gov/hove.*

Natural Bridges National Monument

NATURE SITE | Stunning natural bridges, ancient Native American ruins, and magnificent scenery throughout make Natural Bridges National Monument a must-see if you have time to make the trip. Sipapu is one of the largest natural bridges in the world, spanning 225 feet and standing more than 140 feet tall. You can take in the Sipapu, Owachomo, and Kachina bridges via an 8.6-mile round-trip hike that meanders around and under them. A 13-site primitive campground is an optimal spot for stargazing. The national monument is 40 miles from Blanding. ⊠ *Hwy. 275, off Hwy. 95, Natural Bridges National Monument* 🕾 *435/692–1234* ⊕ *www.nps.gov/nabr* 🖾 *$15 per vehicle.*

Valley of the Gods

A red fairyland of slender spires and buttes, the Valley of the Gods is a smaller version of Monument Valley. Approximately 12 miles west of Bluff, you can take a pretty, private drive through this relatively unvisited area on the 17-mile-long Valley of the Gods Road, which begins on U.S. 163 and ends on Highway 261. ⊠ *Mexican Hat* 🕾 *435/587–1500* ⊕ *www.bluffutah.org/valley-of-the-gods.*

🛍 Shopping

Thin Bear Indian Arts

CRAFTS | The Hosler family has operated this tiny little trading post in the same location since 1973. Authentic jewelry, rugs, baskets, and pottery are for sale at this friendly spot. ⊠ *1944 S. Main St., Blanding* 🕾 *435/678–2940* ⊘ *Closed Sun.*

Best Campgrounds in Canyonlands

Canyonlands campgrounds are some of the most beautiful in the national park system. At the Needles District, campers will enjoy fairly private campsites tucked against red rock walls and dotted with pinyon and juniper trees. At Island in the Sky, starry nights and spectacular vistas make the small campground an intimate treasure. Hookups are not available in either of the park's campgrounds; however, some sites are long enough to accommodate units up to 28 feet long.

Needles Campground. The defining features of the camp sites at Squaw Flat are house-size red rock formations, which provide some shade, offer privacy from adjacent campers, and make this one of the more unique campgrounds in the national park system. ⊠ *Off main road, about 3 miles from park entrance, Needles* ☎ *435/259–4711.*

Willow Flat Campground. From this little campground on a mesa top, you can walk to spectacular views of the Green River. Most sites have a bit of shade from juniper trees. ⊠ *Off main park road, about 9 miles from park entrance, Island in the Sky* ☎ *435/259–4712.*

Outside the Park

Dead Horse Point State Park Campground. But for the name, this gem of a site has every attribute of a great national park campground: a stunning location and view atop a mesa, well-maintained pads, room for RVs, and a canopy of infinite stars nightly. It fills up at about the same pace as the national park campgrounds. ⊠ *Dead Horse Point State Park, Hwy. 313* ☎ *435/259–2614* ⊕ *www.stateparks.utah.gov.*

🍴 Restaurants

IN THE PARK
PICNIC AREAS
Grand View Point

VIEWPOINT | It's hard to get a better view than from this dramatic spot that looks out toward the Colorado River canyon and Needles District in the distance. There are picnic tables, grills, restrooms, and shade. ⊠ *Grand View Point, Island in the Sky.*

Needles District Picnic Area

CITY PARK | The most convenient picnic spot in the Needles District is a sunny location on the way to Big Spring Canyon Overlook. There are picnic tables, but no other amenities. ⊠ *Needles ⊹ Main park road, 5 miles west of visitor center.*

OUTSIDE THE PARK
Twin Rocks Cafe

$ | SOUTHWESTERN | Part of the appeal of eating at this colorful diner-style eatery in tiny Bluff is that the restaurant sits beneath a striking pair of 150-foot-tall rock spires. There's also an outstanding Navajo trading post inside, and the kitchen turns out tasty and hearty Native American and Southwestern fare, from Navajo frybread French toast with local peaches in the morning to burgers, beef stew, and chili at lunch and dinner. **Known for:** Navajo frybread; locally crafted jewelry and weavings in the trading post; delicious and filling breakfasts. Ⓢ *Average main: $9* ⊠ *913 E. Navajo Twins Dr., Bluff* ☎ *435/672–2341* ⊕ *www.facebook.com/twinrockscafe.*

Hotels

OUTSIDE THE PARK

★ Desert Rose Inn and Cabins

$$$ | **HOTEL** | Bluff's largest and most upscale hotel, which also contains two of the region's best restaurants, is an attractive, wood-sided lodge with a huge two-story front porch. **Pros:** rustic-elegant room furnishings; two terrific restaurants; pool and Jacuzzi. **Cons:** nearly two-hour drive to Needles District; remote town without many amenities; a bit spendy for the area. [$] *Rooms from: $163* ✉ *701 W. Main St., Bluff* ☎ *435/672–2303* 🌐 *www.desertroseinn.com* 🛏 *53 rooms* 🍴 *No meals.*

Inn at the Canyons

$$ | **HOTEL** | One of the largest properties in Monticello, which is just under an hour from Needles District Visitor Center, this is also one of the comfiest, with a heated indoor pool and a hot tub that's just what the doctor ordered for soaking adventure-weary bodies. **Pros:** nicely maintained rooms; year-round indoor pool and hot tub; close to Needles district of Canyonlands. **Cons:** sits near the main road through town, so might be noisy; in a sleepy town; room decor is not memorable. [$] *Rooms from: $125* ✉ *533 N. Main St., Monticello* ☎ *435/587–2458* 🌐 *www.monticellocanyonlandsinn.com* 🛏 *43 rooms* 🍴 *Breakfast.*

Recapture Lodge

$ | **HOTEL** | The knowledgeable longtime owners of this family-operated inn provide detailed tips for exploring the surrounding canyon country. **Pros:** set on shady grounds with riverside walking trails; owner is a wildlife biologist and naturalist happy to share his knowledge; pets and horses welcome. **Cons:** nearly two-hour drive to Needles District; older property with small rooms and basic amenities; no phones in rooms. [$] *Rooms from: $98* ✉ *250 E. Main St., Bluff* ☎ *435/672–2281* 🌐 *www.recapturelodge.com* 🛏 *26 rooms* 🍴 *Breakfast.*

Chapter 10

CAPITOL REEF NATIONAL PARK

10

Updated by
Andrew Collins

UTAH

WELCOME TO CAPITOL REEF NATIONAL PARK

TOP REASONS TO GO

★ **The Waterpocket Fold:** See an excellent example of a monocline—a fold in the Earth's crust with one very steep side in an area that is otherwise horizontal. This one's almost 100 miles long.

★ **Fewer crowds:** Although visitation has nearly doubled (to 1.2 million per year) since 2011, Capitol Reef is less crowded than nearby parks, such as Zion and Bryce Canyon.

★ **Fresh fruit:** Pick apples, pears, apricots, and peaches in season at the pioneer-planted orchards at historic Fruita. These trees still produce plenty of fruit.

★ **Rock art:** View pictographs and petroglyphs left by Native Americans who lived in this area from AD 300 to 1300.

★ **Pioneer artifacts:** Buy tools and utensils similar to those used by Mormon pioneers at the Gifford Homestead.

At the heart of this 378-square-mile park is the massive natural feature known as the Waterpocket Fold, which runs roughly northwest to southeast along the park's spine. Capitol Reef itself is named for a formation along the fold near the Fremont River. A historic pioneer settlement, the green oasis of Fruita is easily accessed by car, and the 8-mile Scenic Drive provides a good overview of the canyons and rock formations that populate the park. Colors here range from deep, rich reds to sage greens to crumbling gray sediments. The absence of large towns nearby ensures that night skies are brilliant starscapes.

1 Fruita. This historic pioneer village is at the heart of what most people see of Capitol Reef. The one and only park visitor center nearby is the place to get travel and weather information and maps. Scenic Drive, through Capitol Gorge, provides a view of the Golden Throne.

2 Cathedral Valley. The views are stunning and the silence deafening in the park's remote northern section. High-clearance vehicles are required, as is crossing the Fremont River. Driving in this valley is next to impossible when the Cathedral Valley Road is wet, so ask at the visitor center about current weather and road conditions.

3 Muley Twist Canyon. At the southern reaches of the park, this canyon is accessed via Notom-Bullfrog Road from the north, and Burr Trail Road from the west and southeast. High-clearance vehicles are required for Upper Muley and Strike Valley Overlook.

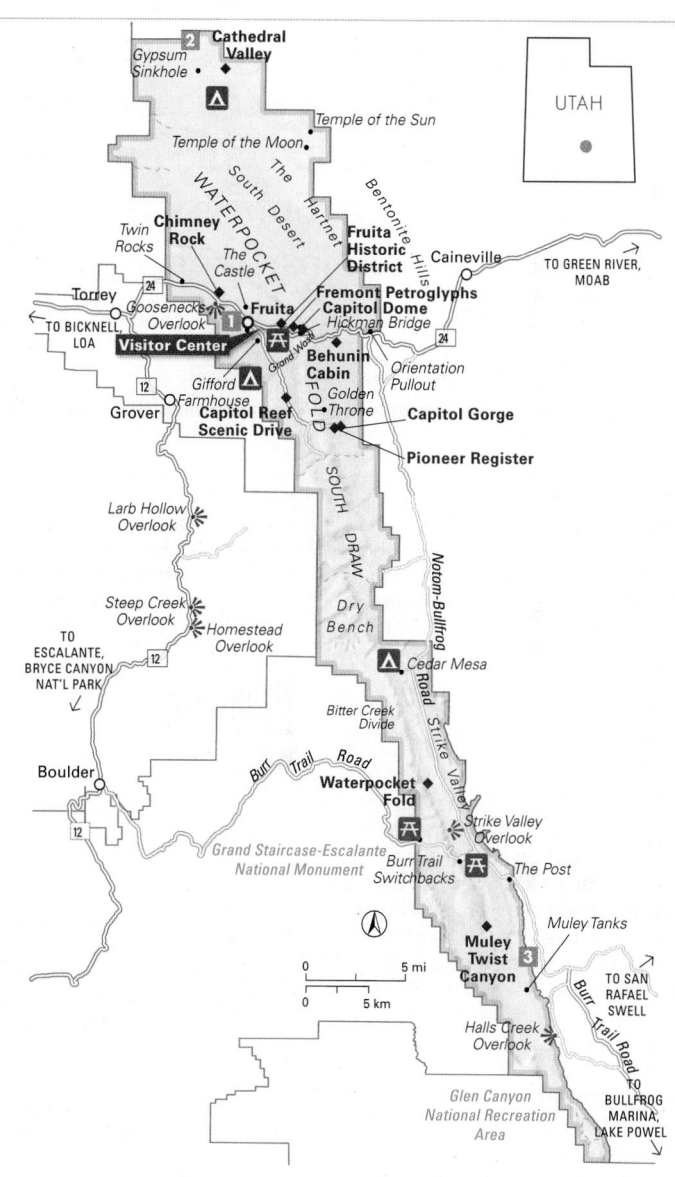

Capitol Reef National Park is a natural kaleidoscopic feast for the eyes, with colors more dramatic than anywhere else in the West. The Moenkopi rock formation is a rich, red-chocolate hue; deep blue-green juniper and pinyon stand out against it. Sunset brings out the colors in an explosion of copper, platinum, and orange, then dusk turns the cliffs purple and blue.

The park preserves the Waterpocket Fold, a giant wrinkle in the earth that extends 100 miles between Thousand Lake Mountain and Lake Powell. When you climb high onto the rocks or into the mountains, you can see this remarkable geologic wonder and the jumble of colorful cliffs, massive domes, soaring spires, and twisting canyons that surround it. It's no wonder early pioneers called this part of the country the "land of the sleeping rainbow."

Beyond incredible sights, the fragrance of pine and sage rises from the earth, and canyon wrens serenade you as you sit by the water. Flowing across the heart of Capitol Reef is the Fremont River, a narrow little creek that can turn into a swollen, raging torrent during desert flash floods. The river sustains cottonwoods, wildlife, and verdant valleys rich with fruit. During the harvest, your sensory experience is complete when you bite into a perfect ripe peach or apple from the park's orchards. Your soul, too, will be gratified here. You can walk the trails in relative solitude and—except during busier periods—enjoy the beauty without confronting significant crowds on the roads or paths. All around you are signs of those who came before: ancient Native Americans of the Fremont culture, Mormon pioneers who settled the land, and other courageous explorers who traveled the canyons.

Planning

WHEN TO GO

Spring and early summer are the most bustling seasons. Some folks clear out in the midsummer heat, and then return for the apple harvest and crisp temperatures of autumn. Although the park is less crowded than nearby Zion, Bryce Canyon, and Arches, visitation has increased dramatically in recent years, and the campground fills quickly (and is by reservation only). Annual rainfall is scant, but when it does rain, flash floods can wipe out park roads. Snowfall is usually light. Sudden, short-lived snowstorms—and thunderstorms—are not uncommon in the spring.

AVERAGE HIGH/LOW TEMPERATURES					
JAN.	FEB.	MAR.	APR.	MAY	JUNE
41/20	47/26	58/33	66/40	74/48	87/58
JULY	AUG.	SEPT.	OCT.	NOV.	DEC.
91/65	89/64	80/54	66/44	51/31	41/22

FESTIVALS AND EVENTS

Women's Redrock Music Festival

FESTIVAL | Held at the Robbers Roost Bookstore, this two-day event has been attracting independent female musicians from all corners of the globe, as well as hundreds of fans, since 2007. Run by the nonprofit Entrada Institute, a regional arts and education organization, the festival benefits Utah women through donations and scholarships. ⊠ *185 W. Main St., Torrey* ☏ *435/425–3265* ⊕ *www.womensredrockmusicfest.com.*

Wayne County Fair

FESTIVAL | **FAMILY** | The great American county fair tradition is at its finest in Loa in mid-August. A demolition derby, rodeo, horse shows, and a parade are all part of the fun. You'll also find crafts such as handmade quilts, agricultural exhibits, children's games, and plenty of good food. ☏ *435/836–1300* ⊕ *waynecountyutah.org.*

★ Harvest Time Scarecrow Festival

FESTIVAL | Events for this month-long celebration marking the end of another busy season are held throughout Wayne County. In addition to a scarecrow contest, there are plenty of family-friendly events, including live music, arts and crafts, pumpkin carving, and a Halloween party. ⊠ *Torrey* ☏ *435/425–3265* ⊕ *www.entradainstitute.org.*

PLANNING YOUR TIME

CAPITOL REEF IN ONE DAY

Pack a picnic lunch, snacks, and cold drinks to take with you (there are no restaurants in the park). As you enter the park from the west, look to your left for Chimney Rock; in a landscape of spires, cliffs, and knobs, this deep-red landmark is unmistakable. Start your journey at the **visitor center,** where you can study a three-dimensional map of the area, peruse exhibits, watch a short film, and browse the many books and maps related to the park. Then, head for Scenic Drive, stopping at the **Fruita Historic District** to see some of the sites associated with the park's Mormon history. Visit **Gifford Homestead** to browse the gift shop. Enjoy that lunch you packed at picnic tables on rolling green lawns lining both sides of the road by the Gifford House.

Check out the **Fremont Indian Petroglyphs,** and if you feel like some exertion, take a hike on the Hickman Bridge Trail. From the trail (or 2 miles east of the visitor center from Highway 24 if you skip the hike), you'll see **Capitol Dome.** Along this stretch of Highway 24 stop to see the old one-room **Fruita Schoolhouse,** the **petroglyphs,** and the **Behunin Cabin.** Next you'll have to backtrack west a few miles on Highway 24 to find the **Goosenecks Trail.** At the same parking lot you'll find the trailhead for **Sunset Point Trail**; take this short hike in time to watch the setting sun hit the colorful cliffs.

GETTING HERE AND AROUND

AIR TRAVEL

The nearest major airports are in Salt Lake City and Las Vegas, about 3½ and 5½ hours away by car, respectively. St. George Regional Airport (3½ hours away) is a handy, smaller airport with direct flights from several major cities in the West, Cedar City Municipal Airport (2¾ hours) has direct daily service on Delta from Salt Lake City, and Canyonlands Field Airport in Moab (2 hours away) has direct daily service on United Airlines from Denver.

CAR TRAVEL

You can approach Capitol Reef country from several approaches, including highways 24 and 72 from Interstate 70 (and Moab), Highway 12 from Bryce Canyon National Park, and Highway 20 to U.S. 89 to Highway 62 from U.S. 15. All are well-maintained, safe roads that bisect rich agricultural communities steeped in Mormon history (especially in the nearby towns of Bicknell and Loa). Highway 24 runs across the middle of Capitol Reef National Park, offering scenic views the entire way.

PARK ESSENTIALS

ACCESSIBILITY

Capitol Reef doesn't have many trails that are accessible to people in wheelchairs. The visitor center, museum, film, and restrooms are all accessible, as is the campground amphitheater where evening programs are held. The Fruita Campground Loop C restroom is accessible; so is the boardwalk to the petroglyph panel on Highway 24, 1.2 miles east of the visitor center.

PARK FEES AND PERMITS

There is no fee to enter the park, but it's $20 per vehicle (or $10 per bicycle and $15 per motorcycle) to travel on Scenic Drive beyond Fruita Campground; this fee is good for one week, paid via the "honor system" at a drop box versus a staffed entry gate. Backcountry camping permits are free; pick them up at the visitor center. An annual pass that allows unlimited access to Scenic Drive is $35.

PARK HOURS

The park is open 24/7 year-round. It's in the Mountain time zone.

CELL PHONE RECEPTION

Cell phone reception is nearly nonexistent in the park, although you may pick up a weak signal in a few spots. Pay phones are at the visitor center and at Fruita Campground.

EDUCATIONAL OFFERINGS

RANGER PROGRAMS

In summer, ranger programs are offered at no charge. You can obtain current information about ranger talks and other park events at the visitor center or campground bulletin boards.

Evening Program

TOUR—SIGHT | FAMILY | Learn about Capitol Reef's geology, Native American cultures, wildlife, and more at the campground amphitheater about a mile from the visitor center. Programs typically begin around sunset. See the schedule at the visitor center. ⊠ *Capitol Reef National Park.*

Junior Ranger Program

TOUR—SIGHT | FAMILY | Each child who participates in this self-guided, year-round program completes a combination of activities in the Junior Ranger booklet, attends a ranger program, or watches the park movie. ⊠ *Capitol Reef National Park.*

Ranger Talks

TOUR—SIGHT | FAMILY | Typically, the park offers a daily morning geology talk at the visitor center and a daily afternoon petroglyph-panel talk. Occasional geology hikes, history tours, and moon and stargazing tours are also sometimes offered. Times vary. ⊠ *Capitol Reef National Park.*

RESTAURANTS

Inside Capitol Reef you won't find any restaurants, though in summer there's a small store selling baked goods and ice cream. More dining options exist close by in Torrey, where you can find everything from creative Southwestern fusion cuisine to basic hamburger joints serving consistently good food.

HOTELS

There are no lodging options within Capitol Reef, but clean and comfortable accommodations for all budgets exist just west in nearby Torrey, and not far beyond in Bicknell and Loa. There are also a couple of options east of the park, in Hanksville. Book well ahead if visiting

Plants and Wildlife in Capitol Reef

The golden rock and rainbow cliffs are at their finest at sunset, when it seems as if they are lighted from within. That's also when mule deer wander through the orchards near the campground. The deer are quite used to people, but it's illegal to feed or even approach them. Many of the park's animals move about only at night to escape the heat, but pinyon jays and black-billed magpies flit around the park all day. The best place to see wildlife is near the Fremont River, where animals are drawn to drink. Ducks and small mammals such as the yellow-bellied marmot live nearby. Desert bighorn sheep also live in Capitol Reef, but they are elusive; your best chance for spotting them is during a long hike deep within the park. If you should encounter a sheep, do not approach it, as they've been known to charge people.

March through October. *Hotel reviews have been shortened. For full information, visit Fodors.com.*

What It Costs

	$	$$	$$$	$$$$
RESTAURANTS				
	under $13	$13–$20	$21–$30	over $30
HOTELS				
	under $101	$101–$150	$151–$200	over $200

VISITOR INFORMATION
PARK CONTACT INFORMATION Capitol Reef National Park ⊠ *Off Hwy. 24* ☎ *435/425–3791* ⊕ *www.nps.gov/care.*

VISITOR CENTERS
Capitol Reef Visitor Center
INFO CENTER | FAMILY | Watch a park movie, talk with rangers, or peruse the many books, maps, and materials for sale in the bookstore. Towering over the center (11 miles east of Torrey) is the Castle, one of the park's most prominent rock formations. ⊠ *Scenic Dr. at Hwy. 24* ☎ *435/425–3791* ⊕ *www.nps.gov/care.*

 Sights

SCENIC DRIVES
Capitol Reef Scenic Drive
SCENIC DRIVE | FAMILY | This 8-mile road, simply called Scenic Drive, starts at the visitor center and winds its way through the Fruita Historic District and colorful sandstone cliffs into Capitol Gorge; a side road, Grand Wash Road, provides access into the canyon. At Capitol Gorge, the canyon walls become steep and impressive but the route becomes unpaved for about the last 2 miles, and road conditions may vary due to weather and usage. Check with the visitor center before setting out. ⊠ *Off Hwy. 24, 11 miles east of Torrey.*

SCENIC STOPS
Behunin Cabin
BUILDING | FAMILY | Elijah Cutlar Behunin used blocks of sandstone to build this cabin in 1882. Floods in the lowlands made life too difficult, and he moved before the turn of that century. The house, 5.9 miles east of the visitor center, is empty, but you can peek through the window to see the interior. ⊠ *Hwy. 24.*

Capitol Dome

NATURE SITE | One of the rock formations that gave the park its name, this giant sandstone dome is visible in the vicinity of the Hickman Bridge trailhead, 1.9 miles east of the visitor center. ⊠ *Hwy. 24.*

★ Capitol Gorge

SCENIC DRIVE | Eight miles south of the visitor center, Scenic Drive ends, at which point you can drive an unpaved spur road into Capitol Gorge. The narrow, twisting road on the floor of the gorge was a route for pioneer wagons traversing this part of Utah starting in the 1860s. After every flash flood, pioneers would laboriously clear the route so wagons could continue to go through. The gorge became the main automobile route in the area until 1962, when Highway 24 was built. The short drive to the end of the road has striking views of the surrounding cliffs and leads to one of the park's most popular walks: the hiking trail to the water-holding "tanks" eroded into the sandstone. ⊠ *Scenic Dr.*

Chimney Rock

NATURE SITE | Even in a landscape of spires, cliffs, and knobs, this deep-red landform, 3.9 miles west of the visitor center, is unmistakable. ⊠ *Hwy. 24.*

Fremont Petroglyphs

NATIVE SITE | Between AD 300 and 1300 the Capitol Reef area was occupied by Native Americans who were eventually referred to by archaeologists as the Fremont, named after the Fremont River that flows through the park. A nice stroll along a boardwalk bridge, 1.1 miles east of the visitor center, allows close-up views of ancient rock art, which can be identified by the large trapezoidal figures often depicted wearing headdresses and ear baubles. ⊠ *Hwy. 24.*

★ Fruita Historic District

HISTORIC SITE | FAMILY | In the 1880s Nels Johnson became the first homesteader in the Fremont River Valley, building his home near the confluence of Sulphur Creek and the Fremont River. Other Mormon settlers followed and established small farms and orchards, creating the village of Junction. The orchards thrived, and by 1900 the name was changed to Fruita. The orchards, less than a mile from the visitor center, are preserved and protected as a Rural Historic District. ⊠ *Scenic Dr.*

Pioneer Register

HISTORIC SITE | Travelers passing through Capitol Gorge in the 19th and early 20th centuries etched the canyon wall with their names and the date. Directly across the canyon from the Pioneer Register and about 50 feet up are signatures etched into the canyon wall by an early United States Geologic Survey crew. Though it's illegal to write or scratch on the canyon walls today, plenty of damage has been done by vandals over the years. You can reach the register via an easy hike from the sheltered trailhead at the end of Capitol Gorge Road, 10.3 miles south of the visitor center; the register is about 10 minutes along the hike to the sandstone "tanks." ⊠ *Off Scenic Dr.*

The Waterpocket Fold

NATURE SITE | A giant wrinkle in the earth extends almost 100 miles between Thousand Lake Mountain and Lake Powell. You can glimpse the fold by driving south on Scenic Drive after it branches off Highway 24, past the Fruita Historic District. For complete immersion enter the park via the 36-mile Burr Trail from Boulder. Roads through the southernmost reaches of the park are largely unpaved. The area is accessible to most vehicles during dry weather, but check with the visitor center for current road conditions. ⊠ *Capitol Reef National Park.*

🎢 Activities

The main outdoor activity at Capitol Reef is hiking. There are trails for all levels. Remember to bring and drink plenty of

Good Reads

- *Capitol Reef: Canyon Country Eden,* by Rose Houk, is an award-winning collection of photographs and lyrical essays on the park.

- *Dwellers of the Rainbow: Fremont Culture in Capitol Reef National Park,* by Rose Houk, offers a brief background of the Fremont culture in Capitol Reef.

- *Capitol Reef National Park: The Complete Hiking and Touring Guide,* by Rich Stinchfield, is an outstanding companion for hiking and exploring.

- *Exploring the Diverse Geology of Capitol Reef National Park,* by Thomas H. Morris, teaches the basic geology of the park.

- *Red Rock Eden,* by George Davidson, tells the story of historic Fruita, its settlements, and its orchards.

---

water and eat salty snacks wherever you go in Capitol Reef.

MULTISPORT OUTFITTER

Hondoo Rivers & Trails

CAMPING—SPORTS-OUTDOORS | This tour company has been providing high-quality backcountry trips into Capitol Reef National Park, Escalante Canyons, and the High Plateaus since the mid-1970s. From April to October, they'll take you on hiking, horseback-riding, and Jeep day tours. Trips are designed to explore the geologic landforms in the area, seek out wildflowers in season, and to encounter free-roaming mustangs, bison, and big-horn sheep when possible. Multiday trips can also be arranged. ⊠ *90 E. Main St., Torrey* ☎ *435/425–3519* ⊕ *www.hondoo. com* ⊇ *From $120.*

BICYCLING

Bicycles are allowed only on established roads in the park. Highway 24 is a state highway and receives a substantial amount of through traffic, so it's not the best place to pedal. Scenic Drive is better, but the road is narrow, and you have to contend with drivers dazed by the beautiful surroundings. In fact, it's a good idea to traverse it in the morning or

evening when traffic is reduced, or in the off-season. Four-wheel-drive roads are certainly less traveled, but they are often sandy, rocky, and steep. You cannot ride your bicycle in washes or on hiking trails.

Cathedral Valley/North District Loop

BICYCLING | Located in the remote north of the park, you can enjoy solitude and a true backcountry ride on this trail. The entire route is about 58 miles long and can be accessed at Caineville, off Highway 24, or at River Ford Road, 5 miles west of Caineville; for a multiday trip, there's a primitive campground about midway through the loop. ⊠ *Off Hwy. 24.*

South Draw Road

BICYCLING | This is a very strenuous but picturesque ride that traverses dirt, sand, and rocky surfaces, and crosses several creeks that may be muddy. It's not recommended in winter or spring because of deep snow at higher elevations. The route starts at an elevation of 8,500 feet on Boulder Mountain, 13 miles south of Torrey, and ends 15¾ miles later at 5,500 feet in the Pleasant Creek parking area at the end of Scenic Drive. ⊠ *Bowns Reservoir Rd. and Hwy. 12.*

FOUR-WHEELING

You can explore Capitol Reef in a 4X4 on a number of exciting backcountry routes, but note that all vehicles must remain on designated roadways. Road conditions can vary greatly depending on recent weather patterns.

Cathedral Valley/North District Loop

FOUR-WHEELING | The north end of Capitol Reef, along this backcountry road, is filled with towering monoliths, panoramic vistas, water crossings, and a stark desert landscape. The area is remote and the road through it unpaved, so do not enter without a high-clearance vehicle, some planning, and a cell phone (although reception is virtually nonexistent). The drive through the valley is a 58-mile loop that you can begin at River Ford Road, 11¾ miles east of the visitor center off Highway 24; allow half a day. If your time is limited, you can tour only the Caineville Wash Road, which takes about two hours. Pick up a self-guided auto tour brochure at the visitor center. ⊠ *River Ford Rd., off Hwy. 24.*

HIKING

Many park trails in Capitol Reef include steep climbs, but there are a few easy-to-moderate hikes. A short drive from the visitor center takes you to a dozen trails.

Capitol Gorge Trail and the Tanks

HIKING/WALKING | Starting at the Pioneer Register, about a ½ mile from the Capitol Gorge parking lot, is a ½-mile trail that climbs to the Tanks—holes in the sandstone, formed by erosion, that hold water after it rains. After a scramble up about ¼ mile of steep trail with cliff drop-offs, you can look down into the Tanks and see a natural bridge below the lower tank. Including the walk to the Pioneer Register, allow an hour or more for this interesting hike, one of the park's most popular. *Moderate.* ⊠ *Capitol Reef National Park* ✛ *Trailhead: at end of Scenic Dr., 10 miles south of visitor center.*

★ Chimney Rock Trail

HIKING/WALKING | You're almost sure to see ravens drifting on thermal winds around the deep-red Mummy Cliff that rings the base of this trail. This loop trail begins with a steep climb to a rim above dramatic Chimney Rock. The trail is 3.6 miles round-trip, with a 590-foot elevation change. No shade. Use caution during monsoon storms due to lightning hazards. Allow three to four hours. *Moderate–Difficult.* ⊠ *Capitol Reef National Park* ✛ *Trailhead: Hwy. 24, about 3 miles west of visitor center.*

Cohab Canyon Trail

HIKING/WALKING | Find rock wrens and Western pipistrelles (canyon bats) on this trail. One end is directly across from the Fruita Campground on Scenic Drive; the other is across from the Hickman Bridge parking lot. The first ¼ mile from Fruita is strenuous, but the walk becomes easier except for turnoffs to the overlooks, which are short. You'll find miniature arches, skinny side canyons, and honeycombed patterns on canyon walls where the wrens make nests. The trail is 3.2 miles round-trip to the Hickman Bridge parking lot (two to three hours). The Overlook Trail adds 1 mile. Allow two hours to overlooks and back. *Moderate.* ⊠ *Capitol Reef National Park* ✛ *Trailheads: Scenic Dr., about 1 mile south of visitor center, or Hwy. 24, about 2 miles east of visitor center.*

Fremont River Trail

HIKING/WALKING | What starts as a quiet little stroll beside the river turns into an adventure. The first ½ mile of the trail wanders past orchards next to the Fremont River. After you pass through a narrow gate, the trail changes personality and you're in for a steep climb on an exposed ledge with drop-offs. The views at the top of the 480-foot ascent are worth it. It's 2 miles round-trip; allow two hours. *Moderate.* ⊠ *Capitol Reef National Park* ✛ *Trailhead: near amphitheater off*

Loop C of Fruita Campground, about 1 mile from visitor center.

Golden Throne Trail

HIKING/WALKING | As you hike to the base of the Golden Throne, you may be lucky enough to see one of the park's elusive desert bighorn sheep, but you're more likely to spot their split-hoof tracks. The trail is about 2 miles of gradual rise with some steps and drop-offs. The Golden Throne is hidden until you near the end of the trail, then suddenly you see the huge sandstone monolith. If you hike near sundown the throne burns gold. The round-trip hike is 4 miles and takes two to three hours. *Difficult.* ⊠ *Capitol Reef National Park* ⊹ *Trailhead: at end of Capitol Gorge Rd., 10 miles south of visitor center.*

Goosenecks Trail

HIKING/WALKING | This nice little walk gives you a good introduction to the land surrounding Capitol Reef. Enjoy the dizzying views from the overlook on this 0.2-mile round-trip jaunt. *Easy.* ⊠ *Capitol Reef National Park* ⊹ *Trailhead: at Hwy. 24, about 3 miles west of visitor center.*

Grand Wash Trail

HIKING/WALKING | At the end of unpaved Grand Wash Road you can continue on foot through the canyon to its end at Highway 24. This flat hike takes you through a wide wash between canyon walls, and is an excellent place to study the geology up close. The round-trip hike is 4.4 miles; allow two to three hours for your walk. Check at the ranger station for flash-flood warnings before entering the wash. *Easy.* ⊠ *Capitol Reef National Park* ⊹ *Trailhead: at Hwy. 24, east of Hickman Bridge parking lot, or at end of Grand Wash Rd., off Scenic Dr. about 5 miles from visitor center.*

Hickman Bridge Trail

HIKING/WALKING | This trail leads to a natural bridge of Kayenta sandstone, with a 133-foot opening carved by intermittent flash floods. Early on, the route climbs a set of steps along the Fremont River. The trail splits, leading along the right-hand branch to a strenuous uphill climb to the Rim Overlook and Navajo Knobs. Stay to your left to see the bridge, and you'll encounter a moderate up-and-down trail. Up the wash on your way to the bridge is a Fremont granary on the right side of the small canyon. Allow about two hours for the 1.8-mile round-trip. Expect lots of company. *Moderate.* ⊠ *Capitol Reef National Park* ⊹ *Trailhead: Hwy. 24, 2 miles east of visitor center.*

Sunset Point Trail

HIKING/WALKING | The trail starts from the same parking lot as the Goosenecks Trail. Benches along this easy hike (0.8 mile round-trip) invite you to sit and meditate surrounded by the colorful desert. At the trail's end you'll be rewarded with broad vistas into the park; it's even better at sunset. *Easy.* ⊠ *Capitol Reef National Park* ⊹ *Trailhead: at Hwy. 24, about 3 miles west of visitor center.*

Nearby Towns

The best home base for exploring Capitol Reef, the pretty town of **Torrey,** just west of the park, has lots of personality. Giant old cottonwood trees make it a shady, cool place to stay, and the townspeople are friendly and accommodating. A little farther west on Highway 24, tiny **Teasdale** is a charming settlement cradled in a cove of the Aquarius Plateau. The homes look out onto brilliantly colored cliffs and green fields. Quiet **Bicknell** lies another few miles west of Torrey. The Wayne County seat of **Loa,** 10 miles west of Torrey, was settled by pioneers in the 1870s. If you head south from Torrey instead of west, you can take a spectacular 32-mile drive along Highway 12 (see the Bryce Canyon National Park chapter for more details) to **Boulder,** a town so remote that its mail was carried on horseback until 1940. Nearby is Anasazi State Park. In the opposite direction, 51 miles east, **Hanksville** is a place to stop

![Temple of the Sun, a monolith in Capitol Reef's Cathedral Valley, is a favorite with photographers.]()

Temple of the Sun, a monolith in Capitol Reef's Cathedral Valley, is a favorite with photographers.

for food and fuel—the small wayside en route to Moab also has a couple of decent budget motels.

VISITOR INFORMATION Garfield County Office of Tourism ☎ *800/444–6689, 435/676–1160* ⊕ *www.brycecanyoncountry.com* **Wayne County Office of Tourism** ☎ *435/425–3365, 800/858–7951* ⊕ *www.capitolreef.org.*

 Sights

Anasazi State Park
BUILDING | FAMILY | This former archaeological site includes portions of an Ancestral Puebloan (Anasazi) village occupied most likely sometime between AD 1050 and 1200, a small but informative museum with artifacts discovered on-site, and a reconstructed pueblo dwelling. ⊠ *460 N. Hwy. 12, Boulder* ☎ *435/335–7308* ⊕ *stateparks.utah.gov* ⌨ *$5.*

★ Goblin Valley State Park
NATURE SITE | FAMILY | Strange-looking "hoodoos" rise up from the desert landscape 12 miles north of Hanksville, making Goblin Valley home to hundreds of strange goblin-like rock formations with a dramatic orange hue. Short, easy trails wind through the goblins making it a fun walk for kids and adults. ⊠ *Hwy. 24* ☎ *435/275–4584* ⊕ *stateparks.utah.gov* ⌨ *$15 per vehicle.*

★ San Rafael Swell Recreation Area
NATURE SITE | Tremendous geological upheavals pushed through the Earth's surface eons ago, forming a giant oval-shape dome of rock about 80 miles long and 30 miles wide, giving rise to the name "swell." Over the years, the harsh climate beat down the dome, eroding it into a wild array of multicolor sandstone and creating buttes, pinnacles, mesas, and canyons that spread across more than 600,000 acres. In the northern Swell, the Wedge Overlook peers into the Little Grand Canyon and the San Rafael River below. The strata at the edges of the southern Swell are angled near vertical, creating the San Rafael Reef. Both are known for fantastic hiking, canyoneering, and mountain biking.

✉ *BLM Field Office, 125 S. 600 W, Price* ☎ *435/636–3600* ⊕ *www.blm.gov/visit/ search-details/2187/2.*

SCENIC DRIVES
Burr Trail Scenic Backway
SCENIC DRIVE | Branching east off Scenic Byway 12 (see the Bryce Canyon National Park chapter) in Boulder, Burr Trail travels through the Circle Cliffs area of Grand Staircase–Escalante National Monument into Capitol Reef. The views are of backcountry canyons and gulches. The road is paved between Boulder and the eastern boundary of Capitol Reef. It leads into a hair-raising set of switchbacks—not suitable for RVs or trailers—that ascend 800 feet in ½ mile. Before attempting to drive this route, check with the Capitol Reef Visitor Center for road conditions—it can be impassable in wet or snowy weather. From Boulder to its intersection with Notom-Bullfrog Road the route is 36 miles long. ✉ *Off Hwy. 12, Boulder* ⊕ *www.nps.gov/glca/plan-yourvisit/driving-the-burr-trail.htm.*

★ Utah Scenic Byway 24
SCENIC DRIVE | For 75 miles between Loa and Hanksville, you'll cut right through Capitol Reef National Park. Colorful rock formations in all their hues of red, cream, pink, gold, and deep purple extend from one end of the route to the other. The closer you get to the park the more colorful the landscape becomes. The vibrant rock finally gives way to lush green hills and the mountains west of Loa.

 Activities

FISHING
Alpine Adventures
FISHING | With a stellar reputation for personalized attention during fly-fishing trips into the high backcountry around Capitol Reef and the Fremont River, Alpine Adventures also leads trophy hunting tours. ✉ *Torrey* ☎ *435/425–3660* ⊕ *alpine-adventuresutah.com* ⊜ *From $225.*

Fishlake National Forest
FISHING | At an elevation of 8,800 feet is Fish Lake, which lies in the heart of its namesake 1.4-million-acre forest. The area has several campgrounds and wonderful lodges. The lake is stocked annually with lake and rainbow trout, mackinaw, and splake. A large population of brown trout is native to the lake. The Fishlake National Forest office (115 E. 900 N, Richfield) can provide all the information you need for fishing, camping, and hiking in the forest. ✉ *Hwy. 25, 8 miles north of Hwy. 24* ☎ *435/836–9233* ⊕ *www. fs.usda.gov/fishlake.*

🎭 Performing Arts

Robbers Roost
MUSIC | This shop, named after Butch Cassidy's hideout, is home base for the Entrada Institute, an alliance of arts and outdoors enthusiasts that holds musical events and talks, usually on Saturday nights, from May through October—there's also a farmers' market on Saturday afternoons. The annual Women's Redrock Music Festival, held each August, attracts more than 600 attendees to hear performance art, blues, rock, jazz, and folk. ✉ *185 W. Main St. (Hwy. 24), Torrey* ☎ *435/425–3265* ⊕ *robbers-roostbooks.com.*

🛍 Shopping

Flute Shop Trading Post
GIFTS/SOUVENIRS | Unique and unexpected, the nifty Flute Shop sells Native American jewelry, rocks, fossils, and flutes, handcrafted by owner Vance Morrill. There's also a quiet and inexpensive four-unit motel. ✉ *1705 S. Hwy. 12, Torrey* ⊹ *4 miles south of Hwy. 24* ☎ *435/425–3144* ⊕ *www.fluteshopmotel.com.*

Gallery 24
ART GALLERIES—ARTS | This pleasing space sells contemporary fine art from southern Utah–based artists that includes paintings, photography, ceramics, and

Did You Know?

The 3.5-mile round-trip trek up to Chimney Rock has some steep switchbacks, but the journey yields panoramic views. The trailhead is 3 miles from the park visitor center, near the entrance. It is forbidden to rock climb on it.

sculpture. ⊠ *135 E. Main St., Torrey* 🕾 *435/425–2124* ⊕ *www.gallery24.biz.*

★ Torrey Gallery

ART GALLERIES—ARTS | In a pioneer home off Main Street, this lovely gallery specializes in regional art. Its offerings include paintings, sculpture, and photographs, as well as antique and contemporary Navajo rugs discovered by the longtime collectors who own the gallery. ⊠ *160 W. Main St., Torrey* 🕾 *435/425–3909* ⊕ *torreygallery.com.*

Torrey Trading Post

CRAFTS | Come here for Native American jewelry and pottery, T-shirts, wood carvings, stone figures, gifts for children, and more. The trading post also rents out a handful of deluxe and camping cabins. ⊠ *25 W. Main St., Torrey* 🕾 *435/425–3716* ⊕ *www.torreytradingpost.com.*

 Restaurants

IN THE PARK
PICNIC AREA
Gifford House Store and Museum

NATIONAL/STATE PARK | One mile south of the visitor center in a grassy meadow with the Fremont River flowing by, this is an idyllic shady spot in the Fruita Historic District for a sack lunch, complete with tables, drinking water, grills, and a convenient restroom. ⊠ *Scenic Dr.*

OUTSIDE THE PARK
★ Cafe Diablo

$$$ | AMERICAN | Nestled in the tiny hamlet of Torrey is one of the better restaurants in the state, with innovative, seasonal Southwestern fusion fare that includes dishes such as lamb shank braised in rioja sauce, and pumpkin-seed trout. The dining room is hung with the work of local artists, and seating on the peaceful patio surrounded by gardens affords views of distant red-rock mountains. **Known for:** produce is sourced from restaurant's own organic farm; delicious desserts; excellent international wine and creative cocktail lists. $ *Average main:*

$27 ⊠ *599 W. Main St. (Hwy. 24), Torrey* 🕾 *435/425–3070* ⊕ *www.cafediablo.com* ◔ *Closed late Oct.–Mar. No lunch.*

Capitol Reef Café

$$ | AMERICAN | Known for its varied selection of reliably good and healthy fare, this unpretentious eatery has a laid-back vibe and is attached to a gift shop that stocks an eclectic selection of Native American and Southwestern books and artwork. Favorites dishes include huevos rancheros in the morning, and smoked-trout salad, wild-mushroom lasagna, and charbroiled New York steaks later in the day. **Known for:** hearty breakfasts; nice mix of vegetarian options; good beer and wine selection. $ *Average main: $16* ⊠ *360 W. Main St. (Hwy. 24), Torrey* 🕾 *435/425–3271* ⊕ *capitolreefinn.com* ◔ *Closed late Oct.–mid-Mar.*

★ Hell's Backbone Grill

$$$ | MODERN AMERICAN | On the stunning grounds of the Boulder Mountain Lodge and a frequent James Beard Award semifinalist, this remote eatery—its creative, oft-changing menu is inspired by Native American, Western range, Southwestern, and Mormon pioneer recipes—is worth the 40-mile drive south of Torrey along scenic Highway 12. The chef-owners have a historical connection to the area, and many of the ingredients they use come directly from their own organic farm. **Known for:** peaceful setting; farm-fresh ingredients; innovative farm-to-bar cocktails. $ *Average main: $26* ⊠ *20 N. Hwy. 12, Boulder* 🕾 *435/335–7464* ⊕ *www.hellsbackbonegrill.com* ◔ *Closed Dec.–mid-Mar.*

Marinia's Country Cafe

$ | DINER | FAMILY | Large portions of home-style cooking draw a steady parade of regulars and visitors to this local favorite, where you'll find jalapeño burgers, fried chicken, homemade soups, and pies. Hearty breakfasts are served all day, and there are always some tasty daily specials. **Known for:** pies filled with seasonal fruits; down-home friendly vibe;

all-day breakfast. $ *Average main: $11* ✉ *289 N. Main St., Loa* ☎ *435/836–2047* ⊘ *Closed Sun.*

Rim Rock Patio

$$ | **AMERICAN** | **FAMILY** | In addition to serving hearty and delicious pizzas, barbecue, pastas, and salads, this casual eatery with a huge, partially covered outdoor deck and patio offers some of the best views toward Capitol Reef, as it's located less than a mile from the park's western entrance. Enjoy a microbrew with your pie and listen to live music most weekends, and if you're in the mood for more substantial fare, check out the neighboring sister establishment, the Rim Rock Restaurant, which specializes in steaks and more upscale American fare. **Known for:** open later than most restaurants in Torrey; astounding patio views; best pizzas in town. $ *Average main: $16* ✉ *2523 Hwy. 24, Torrey* ☎ *435/425–3389* ⊕ *www.therimrock.net.*

Stan's Burger Shak

$ | **BURGER** | This is the traditional pit stop between Lake Powell or Moab and Capitol Reef, featuring great burgers, fries, and the best homemade onion rings around. Shakes, available in such unusual flavors as peach cobbler and root beer freeze, are a specialty. **Known for:** homemade onion rings; thick shakes; home-style burgers. $ *Average main: $8* ✉ *140 S. Hwy. 95, Hanksville* ☎ *435/542–3330* ⊕ *www.stansburgershak.com* ⊘ *Closed Dec.–mid-Feb.*

 **Hotels**

OUTSIDE THE PARK

Austin's Chuck Wagon Motel

$ | **HOTEL** | Foremost at this pleasant complex are friendly service and immaculate rooms, including standard-size in the motel-style lodge or stand-alone cabins that sleep up to six. **Pros:** bargain rates; several restaurants and shops within walking distance; large outdoor pool. **Cons:** family atmosphere might

not please solitary travelers; handful of original rooms a bit rustic for some; breakfast not included (although morning coffee, tea, and cocoa are complimentary). $ *Rooms from: $67* ✉ *12 W. Main St., Torrey* ☎ *435/425–3335, 800/863–3288* ⊕ *austinschuckwagonmotel.com* ⊘ *Closed Nov.–Mar.* ↵ *28 rooms* ⊗ *No meals.*

★ Boulder Mountain Lodge

$$$ | **HOTEL** | If you're traveling scenic Highway 12 between Capitol Reef and Bryce Canyon national parks, don't miss this wonderful lodge with a fireplace in the two-story great room and acclaimed Hell's Backbone restaurant on the premises. **Pros:** a perfect spot for peace and solitude; good deals during the off-season; scenic pond, bird sanctuary, and horses grazing on grounds. **Cons:** remote setting; books up well in advance in summer and fall; about an hour's drive from Capitol Reef National Park. $ *Rooms from: $175* ✉ *20 N. Hwy. 12, Boulder* ☎ *435/335–7460, 800/556–3446* ⊕ *www.boulder-utah.com* ↵ *22 rooms* ⊗ *No meals.*

Capitol Reef Resort

$$ | **HOTEL** | For a relaxing and well-kept home base with some extra perks, try this hilltop motel just minutes from the park, with many rooms opening to patios and balconies that overlook Capitol Reef's not-so-distant sandstone cliffs. **Pros:** on-site restaurant and gift shop; great views; some unusual room options, including a teepee, cabin, and Conestoga wagon. **Cons:** breakfast not included in rates; sometimes books up with weddings; pets not allowed. $ *Rooms from: $119* ✉ *2600 E. Hwy. 24, Torrey* ☎ *435/425–3761* ⊕ *www.capitolreefresort.com* ↵ *100 rooms* ⊗ *No meals.*

★ Lodge at Red River Ranch

$$$$ | **HOTEL** | With its grand main room, high beam ceilings, and fine antiques, this rustic-chic log lodge set against a storybook red-rock landscape where buffalo roam feels like something out of

Best Campgrounds in Capitol Reef

Campgrounds—both the highly convenient Fruita Campground and the backcountry sites—in Capitol Reef fill up fast between March and October. Most of the area's state parks have camping facilities, and the region's two national forests offer many wonderful sites.

Cathedral Valley Campground. This small (just six sites), basic (no water, pit toilet), no-fee campground in the park's remote northern district touts sprawling views, but the bumpy road there is hard to navigate. ✉ *Hartnet Junction, on Caineville Wash Rd.* ☎ *435/425–3791.*

Cedar Mesa Campground. Wonderful views of the Waterpocket Fold and Henry Mountains surround this primitive (pit toilet, no water), no-fee campground with five sites in the park's southern district. ✉ *Notom-Bullfrog Rd., 22 miles south of Hwy. 24* ☎ *435/425–3791.*

Fruita Campground. Near the orchards and the Fremont River, the park's developed (flush toilets, running water), shady campground is a great place to call home for a few days. The sites require a $20 nightly fee and those nearest the Fremont River or the orchards are the most coveted. ✉ *Scenic Dr., about 1 mile south of visitor center* ☎ *435/425–3791* 🌐 *www.recreation.gov.*

a vintage western movie. **Pros:** beautiful views of the dramatic surroundings; staff can help arrange fly-fishing and horseback riding; restaurant can prepare sack lunches for a day of exploring. **Cons:** dining room only open for breakfast (which is not included in rates); no shops or restaurants within walking distance; pricey for the area. [$] *Rooms from: $209* ✉ *2900 W. Hwy. 24, Teasdale* ☎ *435/425–3322, 800/205–6343* 🌐 *redriverranch.com* 🛏 *15 rooms* 🍴 *No meals.*

Muley Twist Inn

$$ | **B&B/INN** | This gorgeous, contemporary B&B sits on 10 acres of pristine wilderness, with expansive views of the colorful landscape in just about every direction. **Pros:** dramatic setting against a beautiful rock cliff; delicious full breakfast included; large wraparound deck to relax on. **Cons:** a bit removed from civilization; closed in winter; intimate property. [$] *Rooms from: $145* ✉ *249 W. 125 South St., Teasdale* ☎ *435/425–3640, 800/530–1038* 🌐 *www.muleytwistinn.com* ⏲ *Closed Nov.–Mar.* 🛏 *5 rooms* 🍴 *Breakfast.*

Rim Rock Inn

$ | **HOTEL** | On a bluff with outstanding views into the desert, this motel with clean, basic, and reasonably priced rooms (breakfast is included) is one of the closest to the western entrance of Capitol Reef National Park. **Pros:** immaculate rooms; very affordable; set on 10 rugged acres. **Cons:** a bit removed from town; rooms don't have much personality; very basic breakfast. [$] *Rooms from: $89* ✉ *2523 E. Hwy. 24, Torrey* ☎ *435/425–3398* 🌐 *www.therimrock.net* ⏲ *Closed Nov.–Mar.* 🛏 *19 rooms* 🍴 *Breakfast.*

SkyRidge Inn Bed and Breakfast

$$$ | **B&B/INN** | Each of this airy, modern inn's windows offers an exceptional year-round view of the desert and mountains surrounding Capitol Reef National Park, while inside, the walls are hung with the works of local artists and unusual furniture—each piece chosen for its look and feel—makes the guest rooms and common areas both stimulating and comfortable. **Pros:** excellent full breakfasts included; close to restaurants and other amenities; local artwork and unique decor. **Cons:** rooms fill quickly in high season; too cozy for some; not the best option for kids. [$] *Rooms from: $155* ✉ *1012 E. Hwy 24, Torrey* ☎ *435/425–3775* 🌐 *skyridgeinn.com* 🛏 *6 rooms* 🍴 *Breakfast.*

Whispering Sands Motel
$$ | **HOTEL** | One of the only lodging options offering eastern access to Capitol Reef, this simple but clean and comfy two-story motel makes a good base if you're on your way to or from Moab or planning to visit nearby Goblin Valley State Park. **Pros:** best option to the east of the park; clean and cheerful rooms; good value. **Cons:** not many good dining options nearby; about a 45-minute drive from the heart of Capitol Reef; pets now allowed. [$] *Rooms from: $109* ✉ *90 S. Hwy. 95, Hanksville* ☎ *435/542–3238* 🌐 *www.whisperingsandsmotel.com* 🛏 *23 rooms* 🍴 *Free Breakfast.*

Chapter 11

CARLSBAD CAVERNS NATIONAL PARK

Updated by
Andrew Collins

NEW
MEXICO

WELCOME TO CARLSBAD CAVERNS NATIONAL PARK

TOP REASONS TO GO

★ **400,000 hungry bats:** From mid-May to late October, bats wing to and from the caverns in a swirling, visible tornado.

★ **Take a self-guided tour through the underworld:** Plummet 75 stories underground and step into enormous caves hung with stalactites and bristling with stalagmites.

★ **Living Desert Zoo and Gardens:** More preserve than zoo, this 1,500-acre park houses scores of rare species, including black bears, Bolson tortoises, and endangered Mexican wolves.

★ **Birding at Rattlesnake Springs:** Nine-tenths of the park's 357 bird species, including roadrunners, golden eagles, and acrobatic cave swallows, visit this green desert oasis with scenic hiking trails.

★ **Pecos River:** A Southwest landmark and recreational oasis, the attractively landscaped Pecos River flows through the heart of nearby Carlsbad.

1 Bat Flight. The 400,000-member Brazilian free-tailed bat colony here snatches up 3 tons of bugs a night. Watch them leave at dusk from the park amphitheater.

2 Carlsbad Caverns Big Room Tour. Travel 75 stories below the surface to visit the Big Room, where you can traipse beneath a 230-foot-tall ceiling and take in immense and eerie cave formations, directly beneath the park visitor center.

3 Living Desert Zoo and Gardens State Park. Western river cooter turtles, javelinas, and Mexican gray wolves reside within naturalistic enclosures in this sprawling hilltop preserve on the west side of Carlsbad, a 40-minute drive north of the park.

4 The Pecos River. Running through downtown Carlsbad, a beautifully landscaped stretch of this 926-mile landmark river gives life to boating, water-skiing, and fishing.

5 Rattlesnake Springs. Nine-tenths of the park's 357 species of birds show up at Rattlesnake Springs as it's one of the few water sources in this area.

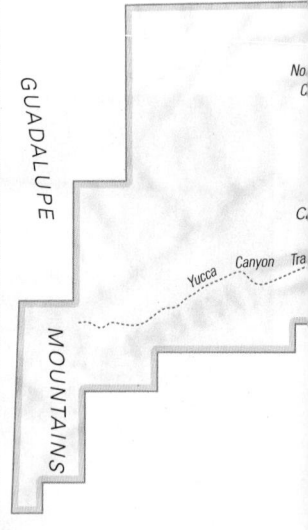

GUADALUPE

MOUNTAINS

Yucca Canyon Tra

NEW
TE

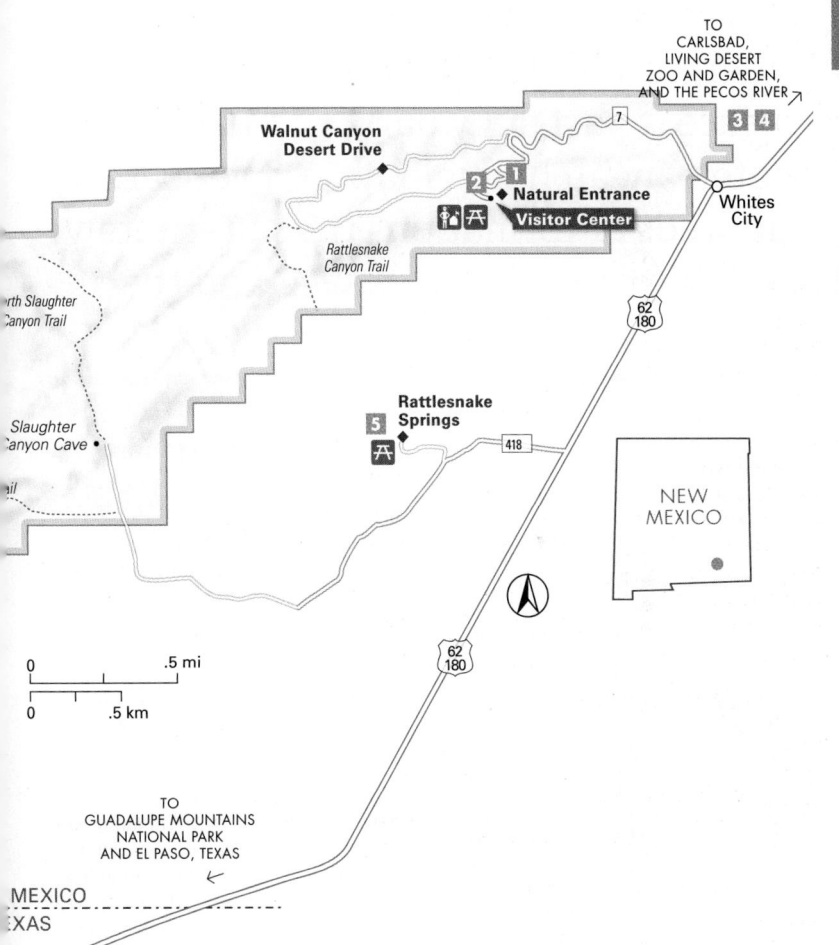

TO
CARLSBAD,
LIVING DESERT
ZOO AND GARDEN,
AND THE PECOS RIVER

3 **4**

7

Whites
City

**Walnut Canyon
Desert Drive**

2 **1**
Natural Entrance

Visitor Center

*Rattlesnake
Canyon Trail*

*rth Slaughter
Canyon Trail*

62
180

*Slaughter
Canyon Cave* •

**Rattlesnake
Springs**

5

418

NEW
MEXICO

il

0 _____ .5 mi

0 _____ .5 km

62
180

TO
GUADALUPE MOUNTAINS
NATIONAL PARK
AND EL PASO, TEXAS

MEXICO
XAS

On the surface, Carlsbad Caverns National Park is deceptively normal—but all bets are off once visitors set foot in the elevator, which plunges 75 stories underground. The hollow beneath the surface is part silky darkness, part subterranean hallucination. There are hundreds of formations that alternately resemble cakes, ocean waves, and the face of a mountain troll.

Planning

WHEN TO GO

While the desert above may alternately bake or freeze, the caverns remain in the mid-50s. If you're coming to see the Brazilian free-tailed bat, arrive between spring and mid-fall.

FESTIVAL AND EVENTS
Star Parties

FESTIVAL | FAMILY | Coinciding with the new or first-quarter moon of every other month, star parties are held outside Living Desert Zoo & Gardens State Park about six times a year. A laser tour and powerful telescope bring the heavens closer. Call for dates. ⊠ *1504 Miehls Dr. N, Carlsbad* ☎ *575/887–5516* ⊕ *www. livingdesertnm.org.*

Native American Heritage Days

FESTIVAL | FAMILY | On the second weekend of May the state park hosts a celebration of Native American history, including vendors, guest speakers, and children's events. ⊠ *1504 Miehls Dr.,*

Carlsbad ☎ *575/887–5516* ⊕ *www. emnrd.state.nm.us.*

Dawn of the Bats

FESTIVAL | FAMILY | The third Saturday in July each year, early risers gather at the cave's entrance to watch tens of thousands of bats return home from their nocturnal search for food. Nature walks and other special ranger programs are offered as well during this free event. ⊠ *727 Carlsbad Cavern Hwy.* ☎ *575/785–2232* ⊕ *www.nps.gov/cave.*

★ Christmas on the Pecos

FESTIVAL | FAMILY | Magical Christmas displays decorate Carlsbad homes along a 3-mile stretch of the Pecos River in a fairyland of seasonal delight. Boat tours ($20 adults Friday and Saturday; $15 adults Sunday–Thursday) run from the day after Thanksgiving through New Year's Eve except Christmas Eve, beginning at 5:30. Vessels depart from the Pecos River Village Conference Center. Purchase tickets there, at the Carlsbad Chamber of Commerce (*302 S. Canal St.*), or online. ⊠ *Pecos River Village Conference Center,*

AVERAGE HIGH/LOW TEMPERATURES					
JAN.	**FEB.**	**MAR.**	**APR.**	**MAY**	**JUNE**
56/33	60/36	66/42	75/50	83/58	91/64
JULY	**AUG.**	**SEPT.**	**OCT.**	**NOV.**	**DEC.**
91/66	89/65	83/60	75/52	64/42	58/35

711 Muscatel Ave., Carlsbad ☎ *575/628–0952* ⊕ *www.christmasonthepecos.com.*

PLANNING YOUR TIME
CARLSBAD CAVERNS IN ONE DAY
In a single day, visitors can easily view both the eerie, exotic caverns and the volcano of bats that erupts from the caverns each evening. Unless you're attending the annual Dawn of the Bats, when visitors view the early-morning bat return, go ahead and sleep past sunrise and then stroll into the caves.

For the full experience, begin by taking the **Natural Entrance Trail,** which allows visitors to trek into the cave from surface level. This tour winds past the Bone-yard, with its intricate ossifications and a massive boulder called the Iceberg. After 1¼ miles, or about an hour, the trail links up with the **Big Room Trail.** If you're not in good health or are traveling with young children, you might want to skip the Natural Entrance and start with the Big Room Trail, which begins at the foot of the elevator. This underground walk extends 1¼ miles on level, paved ground, and takes about 1½ hours to complete. There is a shortcut option that's about half as long. If you have made reservations in advance or chance upon some openings, you also can take the **King's Palace** guided tour for 1 mile and an additional 1½ hours. It leaves from the Big Room near the elevator. At 83 stories deep, the palace is the lowest part of the cavern open to the public. By this time, you will have spent four hours in the cavern. Take the elevator back up to the top. If you're not yet tuckered out, consider a short hike along the sunny, self-guided

½-mile **Desert Nature Walk** by the visitor center.

To picnic by the birds, bees, and water of **Rattlesnake Springs,** take U.S. 62/180 south from Whites City 5½ miles, and turn back west onto Route 418. You'll find old-growth shade trees, grass, picnic tables, restrooms, and water. Many varieties of birds flit from tree to tree. Return to the Carlsbad Caverns entrance road and take the 9½-mile Walnut Canyon Desert Drive loop (sometimes called Desert Loop Road). Leave yourself enough time to return to the **visitor center** for the evening bat flight.

GETTING HERE AND AROUND
AIR TRAVEL
The nearest full-service airports are in the Texas cities of El Paso (150 miles away) and Midland (160 miles away). Cavern City Air Terminal, between Carlsbad and the park, is served by a small regional carrier, Boutique Air, with regularly sched-uled service to both Albuquerque and Dallas/Fort Worth.

CAR TRAVEL
The park entrance is 21 miles southwest of Carlsbad, New Mexico, and 32 miles north of Guadalupe Mountains National Park via U.S. 62/180. The ascending 7-mile Carlsbad Cavern Highway from the turnoff at Whites City is paved with pull-outs, which allow motorists to take in the view. Be alert for wildlife crossing roadways, especially in the early morning and at night. There's a gas station near the entrance to the park.

PARK ESSENTIALS
ACCESSIBILITY

Though the park covers a huge expanse aboveground (and there are paved roads traversing the grounds), most of the parts you'll want to see are below the surface. Trails through the most-visited portion of the main cavern are paved and well maintained, and portions of the paved Big Room trail in Carlsbad Cavern is accessible to wheelchairs. Individuals who have difficulty walking should access the Big Room via elevator. Strollers are not permitted on any trails.

PARK FEES AND PERMITS

No fee is charged for parking or to enter the aboveground portion of the park. It costs $12 to descend into Carlsbad Caverns either by elevator or through the Natural Entrance. Costs for guided tours of other parts of the main cavern or two other caverns in the park, Spider Cave and Slaughter Canyon Cave, range from $7 to $20 plus general admission. For guided-tour reservations go to ⊕ *www. recreation.gov* or call ☎ *877/444–6777.*

Those planning overnight hikes must obtain a free backcountry permit, and all hikers are advised to stop at the visitor center information desk for current information about trails. Trails are marked by cairns (rock piles) and can in some places be tricky to follow; a topographic map is recommended. Dogs are not allowed in the park, but a kennel is available at the park visitor center for a fee.

PARK HOURS

The park is open year-round, except Christmas Day, New Year's Day, and Thanksgiving. From Memorial Day weekend through Labor Day, access to the cavern is from 8:30 to 5; entrance tickets are sold until 4:45, with the last entry via the Natural Entrance at 4. After Labor Day until Memorial Day weekend, cavern access is from 8:30 to 3:30; entrance tickets are sold until 3:15, and the last entry via the Natural Entrance is at 2:30.

Carlsbad Caverns is in the Mountain time zone.

AUTOMOBILE SERVICE STATION
White's City Fuel

This gas station by the park entrance has no attendant, but the self-serve pumps are available 24/7; credit cards only. Expect prices to be slightly higher than those in Carlsbad. ⊠ *19 Carlsbad Cavern Hwy., Whites City* ☎ *575/875–2291.*

CELL PHONE RECEPTION

Cell phone service is spotty in the park. It works best in the parking lots outside the visitor center. There's no Wi-Fi or cell service inside any caverns. Note that cell phones here often pick up signals from the Central time zone—keep that in mind when relying on your phone's clock for the correct time.

EDUCATIONAL OFFERINGS
RANGER PROGRAMS
★ **Evening Bat Flight Program**

CAVE | FAMILY | In the amphitheater at the Natural Entrance (off a short trail from the main parking lot) a ranger discusses the park's batty residents before the creatures begin their sundown exodus. The bats aren't on any predictable schedule, so times are a little iffy. Ideally, viewers will first hear the bats preparing to exit, followed by a vortex of black specks swirling out of the cave mouth in search of dinner against the darkening sky. When conditions are favorable, hundreds of thousands of bats will soar off over the span of half an hour or longer. ⊠ *727 Carlsbad Cavern Hwy.* ☎ *575/236–1374* ⊕ *www.nps.gov/cave.*

RESTAURANTS

Inside the park there are just three dining options—the surface-level dining room, the underground snack bar near the elevator, and picnicking at one of the tables at the east end of the parking lot. Luckily, everything is reasonably priced (especially for national park eateries). Outside the park, skip the mediocre eateries in nearby Whites City and drive into Carlsbad, which has plenty of good options.

HOTELS

Camping in the backcountry, at least a half mile from any trail, is your only lodging option in the park. Backcountry camping permits are required and available at the visitor center.

Outside the park your options expand, but rates in the immediate vicinity are shockingly high because of steep year-round demand by workers in the booming nearby oil-field industry. Whites City, just outside the park's main entrance, has a very basic and relatively affordable Rodeway Inn. Even cookie-cutter chain hotels in the nearest big town, Carlsbad, typically run $300 to $500 nightly. You can find comparable lodgings for a third to half the price in towns farther afield, such as Artesia (an hour away) and even Roswell (a little less than two hours)—this strategy makes sense if you're only visiting the park for a day or two, and at least it's a fairly scenic drive through southeastern New Mexico's high desert. *Hotel reviews have been shortened. For full information, visit Fodors.com.*

What It Costs			
$	**$$**	**$$$**	**$$$$**
RESTAURANTS			
under $13	$13–$20	$21–$30	over $30
HOTELS			
under $150	$151–$250	$251–$350	over $350

VISITOR INFORMATION

PARK CONTACT INFORMATION Carlsbad Caverns National Park ⊠ *3225 National Parks Hwy., Carlsbad* ✢ *7 miles from turnoff at Whites City* ☎ *575/785–2232 park menu options, 877/444–6777 cave tour reservations, 575/875–3012 bat flight schedule* ⊕ *www.nps.gov/cave.*

Notable Quote

"The more I thought of it the more I realized that any hole in the ground which could house such a gigantic army of bats must be a whale of a big cave."

—Jim White, from *Jim White's Own Story: The Discovery and History of Carlsbad Caverns*

VISITOR CENTERS

★ **Carlsbad Caverns National Park Visitor Center**

INFO CENTER | FAMILY | Within this user-friendly facility at the top of an escarpment, a 75-seat theater offers engrossing films and ranger programs about the different types of caves. Exhibits offer a primer on bats, geology, wildlife, and the early tribes and settlers that once lived in and passed through the Carlsbad Caverns area. Friendly rangers staff an information desk, where maps are distributed and tickets are sold. A gift shop, café, and bookstore also are on the premises. ⊠ *727 Carlsbad Cavern Hwy.* ✢ *7 miles west of U.S. 62/180* ☎ *575/785–2232* ⊕ *www.nps.gov/cave* ⊠ *Free admission to the visitor center, from $12 for tours (Natural Entrance and Big Room).*

⦿ Sights

SCENIC DRIVES

Walnut Canyon Desert Drive. This scenic drive begins ½ mile from the visitor center. It travels 9½ miles along the top of a ridge to the edge of Rattlesnake Canyon, which you can access via a marked trail, and sinks back down through upper Walnut Canyon to the main entrance road. The backcountry scenery on this one-way gravel loop is stunning; go late in the afternoon or early in the morning to enjoy the full spectrum of changing light and dancing colors. Along the way,

Plants and Wildlife in Carlsbad Caverns

Without a doubt, the park's most prominent and popular residents are Brazilian free-tailed bats. Their bodies barely span the width of a hand, yet their wingspan is more than 11 inches. Female bats give birth to a single pup each year, which usually weighs more than a quarter of what an adult bat does. Their tiny noses and big ears enable them to search for the many tons of bugs they consume over their lifetime. Numbering nearly a third of a million, these tiny creatures are the park's mascot.

One of New Mexico's best birding areas is at Rattlesnake Springs. Summer and fall migrations give you the best chance of spotting the most varieties of the more than 357 species of birds. Lucky visitors may spot the occasional golden eagle or get the thrill of glimpsing a brilliant, gray-and-crimson vermilion flycatcher.

Snakes are most likely to appear late spring through early fall, especially at dusk and dawn. ■TIP➔ If you're out walking, be wary of different rattle-snake species, such as banded-rocks and diamondbacks. If you see one, don't panic. Rangers say they are more scared of us than we are of them. Just don't make any sudden movements, and slowly walk away or back around the vipers.

This area is also remarkable because of its location in the Chihuahuan Desert, which sprouts unique plant life. There are thick stands of raspy-leaved yuccas, as well as the agave (mescal) plants that were once a food source for early Native American tribes. The leaves of this leggy plant are still roasted in sand pits by tribal elders during traditional celebrations.

In spring, the stands of yucca plants unfold white flowers on their tall stalks. Blossoming cacti and desert wildflowers are among the natural wonders of Walnut Canyon. You'll see bright red blossoms adorning reach-for-the-sky ocotillo plants, and sunny yellow blooms sprouting from prickly pear cactus.

you'll see Big Hill Seep's trickling water, the tall, flowing ridges of the Guadalupe mountain range, and maybe even some robust mule deer. The scenic road is not for RVs or trailers, and it can occasionally be closed for maintenance.

SCENIC STOPS

★ **The Big Room**

CAVE | FAMILY | With a floor space equal to about 14 football fields, this subterrane-an focal point of Carlsbad Cavern clues visitors in to just how large the cavern really is. The White House could fit in one corner of the Big Room, and wouldn't come close to grazing the 230-foot ceiling. Entrance can be accessed by ele-vator or through the Natural Entrance and a 1.25-mile descending trail. Either way,

at 750 feet below the surface you will connect with the self-guided 1.25-mile Big Room loop, a relatively level (it has some steps), paved pathway through the almost hallucinatory wonders of various formations and decorations. You also get a layman's lesson on how the cavern was carved. This self-guided tour costs $12; kids under 15 are admitted for free but must be accompanied by an adult. Reservations are not necessary. An audio guide is available from the visitor center bookstore for $5. Even in summer, long pants and long-sleeved shirts are advised for cave temperatures in the mid-50s. ✉ *Visitor center, 727 Carlsbad Cavern Hwy.* ⊕ *www.nps.gov/cave* ✉ *$12.*

★ Natural Entrance

CAVE | FAMILY | As natural daylight recedes, a self-guided, paved trail twists and turns downward from the yawning mouth of the main cavern, about 100 yards east of the visitor center. The route is winding and sometimes slick from water seepage above ground. A steep descent of about 750 feet, much of it secured by hand rails, takes you about a mile through the main corridor and past dramatic features such as the Bat Cave and the Boneyard. (Despite its eerie name, the formations here don't look much like femurs and fibulae; they're more like spongy bone insides.) Iceberg Rock is a massive boulder that dropped from the cave ceiling millennia ago. After about a mile, you'll link up underground with the 1.25-mile Big Room Trail and can return to the surface via elevator or by hiking back out. Footware with a good grip is recommended. No reservations required. ⊠ *727 Carlsbad Cavern Hwy.* ✛ *7 miles west of U.S. 62/180 at Whites City turnoff* ⊕ *www.nps.gov/cave* ⊠ *$12* ☞ *Children under 16 must be accompanied by an adult.*

Rattlesnake Springs

NATURE PRESERVE | FAMILY | Enormous cottonwood trees shade the picnic and recreation area at this cool, secluded oasis near Black River. The rare desert wetland harbors butterflies, mammals, and reptiles, as well as 90% of the park's 357 bird species. Don't let the name scare you; there may be rattlesnakes here, but no more than at any similar site in the Southwest. Restroom facilities are available, but camping and overnight parking are not allowed. ⊠ *Hwy. 418* ✛ *Take U.S. 62/180 5½ miles south of Whites City and turn right (west) onto Hwy. 418 for 2½ miles* ⊕ *www.nps.gov/cave.*

A Long Way Down ◉

Lechuguilla Cave in Carlsbad Caverns National Park is the deepest limestone cave in the United States. Scientists began mapping the cave network in 1986, and though they've located some 112 miles of caverns extending to a depth of more than 1,600 feet, much more of this area along the park's northern border remains to be investigated. Lechuguilla, named after a spiny native cactus, is not open to the public, but an exhibit describing it can be viewed at the visitor center.

🏃 Activities

BIRD-WATCHING

From redheaded turkey vultures to golden eagles, 357 species of birds have been identified in Carlsbad Caverns National Park. Ask for a checklist at the visitor center and then start looking for greater roadrunners, red-winged blackbirds, white-throated swifts, northern flickers, and pygmy nuthatches.

★ Rattlesnake Springs

BIRD WATCHING | FAMILY | Offering one of the best bird habitats in the Southwest, this is a natural wetland rife with old-growth cottonwoods. Because southern New Mexico is in the northernmost region of the Chihuahuan Desert, you're likely to see birds largely unseen anywhere else in the United States outside extreme southern Texas and Arizona. If you see a flash of crimson, you might have spotted a vermilion flycatcher. Wild turkeys also flap around this oasis, which also has a shaded picnic area. Potable water and permanent toilets are on-site. As elsewhere in the park, you are expected to leave a small footprint. Do not

The Big Room is a limestone chamber in the cavern.

disturb, and if you pack it in, pack it out. ⊠ *Hwy. 418* ✛ *Take U.S. 62/180 5½ miles south of Whites City and turn right (west) onto Hwy. 418 for 2½ miles* ⊕ *www.nps.gov/cave.*

HIKING

Deep, dark, and mysterious, the Carlsbad Caverns are such a park focal point that the 40,000-plus acres of wilderness above them have gone largely undeveloped, perfect for those looking for solitude. What you find are rudimentary trails that crisscross the dry, textured terrain and lead up to elevations of 6,000 feet or more. These routes often take a half day or more to travel; at least one, Guadalupe Ridge Trail, is long enough that it calls for camping overnight. Walkers who just want a little dusty taste of desert flowers and wildlife should try the Chihuahuan Desert Nature Walk.

Finding the older, less well-maintained trails can be difficult, although many are marked by cairns (rock piles). Pick up a topographical map at the visitor center bookstore, and be sure to pack a lot of water. There's none out in the desert, and you'll need at least a gallon per person per day. The high elevation coupled with a potent sunshine punch can deliver a nasty sunburn, so pack SPF 30 (or higher) sunblock and a hat, even in winter. No pets are allowed on the trails. The day hikes are free, but you do have to obtain a free backcountry permit from the visitor center if you're camping.

Chihuahuan Desert Nature Trail

HIKING/WALKING | **FAMILY** | While waiting for the evening bat-flight program, take this ½-mile self-guided loop hike that begins just east of the visitor center. The tagged and identified flowers and plants make this a good place to get acquainted with local desert flora. Part of the trail is an easy stroll even for the littlest ones, and part is wheelchair accessible. The payoff is great for everyone, too: a sweeping, vivid view of the desert basin. *Easy.* ⊠ *Carlsbad Caverns National Park* ✛ *Trailhead: just east of visitor center* ⊕ *www.nps.gov/cave.*

Guadalupe Ridge Trail

HIKING/WALKING | This long, winding ramble follows an old road all the way to the western edge of the park. Because of its length (about 12 miles one-way), an overnight stay in the backcountry is strongly recommended. The hike may be long, but for serious hikers the up-close-and-personal views into Rattlesnake and Slaughter canyons are more than worth it—not to mention the serenity of being miles and miles away from civilization. *Difficult.* ⊠ *Carlsbad Caverns National Park* ✛ *Trailhead: junction of Walnut Canyon Desert Dr. and Ridge Rd.* ⊕ *www.nps.gov/cave.*

Juniper Ridge Trail

HIKING/WALKING | Climb up about 800 feet in elevation as you head north on this nearly 3½-mile one-way trail, which leads to the northern edge of the park and then turns toward Crooked Canyon. While not the most notable trek, it's challenging enough to keep things interesting. Allow yourself half a day, and be sure to bring lots of water, especially when the temperature rises. *Moderate.* ⊠ *Carlsbad Caverns National Park* ✛ *Trailhead: 1 mile past interpretive marker 15 on Walnut Canyon Desert Dr.* ⊕ *www.nps.gov/cave.*

North Slaughter Canyon Trail

HIKING/WALKING | Beginning at the Slaughter Canyon Cave parking lot (four-wheel-drive or high-clearance vehicles are recommended; check with visitor center for road conditions before setting out), the trail traverses a heavily vegetated canyon bottom into a remote part of the park. As you begin hiking, look off to the east (to your right) to see the dun-colored ridges and wrinkles of the Elephant Back formation, the first of many dramatic limestone formations visible from the trail. The route travels 5½ miles one-way, the last 3 miles steeply climbing onto a limestone ridge escarpment. Allow a full day for the round-trip. *Difficult.* ⊠ *Carlsbad Caverns National Park* ✛ *Trailhead: at Slaughter Canyon Cave parking lot, Hwy. 418, 10 miles west of U.S. 62/180.*

Good Read

Jim White's Own Story, by early explorer Jim White, tells of this cowboy's exploits into the heart of Carlsbad Caverns before it was developed as a national park.

Old Guano Road Trail

HIKING/WALKING | Meandering a little more than 3½ miles one-way on mostly flat terrain, the trail dips sharply toward Whites City campground, where it ends. Give yourself about four to five hours to complete the walk. Depending on the temperature, this hike can be a bit taxing, but the high desert sun can be potent any time of the year. *Moderate.* ⊠ *Carlsbad Caverns National Park* ✛ *Trailhead: at Bat Flight Amphitheater* ⊕ *www.nps.gov/cave.*

Rattlesnake Canyon Overlook Trail

HIKING/WALKING | FAMILY | A ¼-mile stroll off Walnut Canyon Desert Drive offers a nice overlook down into verdant Rattlesnake Canyon. *Easy.* ⊠ *Carlsbad Caverns National Park* ✛ *Trailhead: interpretive marker 9 on Walnut Canyon Desert Dr.* ⊕ *www.nps.gov/cave.*

Rattlesnake Canyon Trail

HIKING/WALKING | Small cairns guide you along this picturesque trail, which descends from 4,570 to 3,900 feet as it winds into the canyon, which is lush with greenery from spring through fall. Allow half a day to trek down into the canyon and make the somewhat strenuous climb out; the total trip is about 6 miles. *Moderate.* ⊠ *Carlsbad Caverns National Park* ✛ *Trailhead: at interpretive marker 9 on Walnut Canyon Desert Dr.* ⊕ *www.nps.gov/cave.*

★ Yucca Canyon Trail

HIKING/WALKING | Sweeping views of the Guadalupe Mountains and El Capitan give allure to this challenging but beautiful trail. Drive past Rattlesnake Springs and

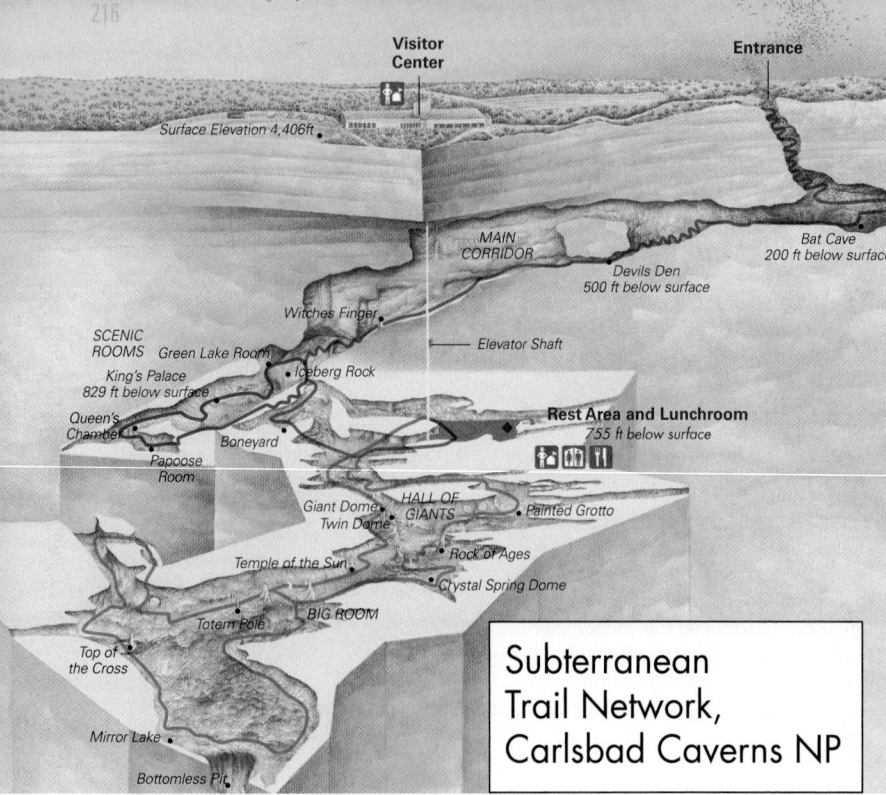

Visitor Center

Surface Elevation 4,406ft

Entrance

MAIN CORRIDOR

Devils Den
500 ft below surface

Bat Cave
200 ft below surface

Witches Finger

Elevator Shaft

SCENIC ROOMS   Green Lake Room

King's Palace
829 ft below surface

Iceberg Rock

Queen's Chamber

Boneyard

Rest Area and Lunchroom
755 ft below surface

Papoose Room

Giant Dome   HALL OF GIANTS
Twin Dome

Painted Grotto

Temple of the Sun

Rock of Ages

Crystal Spring Dome

Totem Pole   BIG ROOM

Top of the Cross

Mirror Lake

Bottomless Pit

Subterranean Trail Network, Carlsbad Caverns NP

stop at the park boundary before reaching the Slaughter Canyon Cave parking lot (four-wheel-drive or high-clearance vehicles are recommended; check with visitor center for road conditions before setting out). Turn west along the boundary fence line to the trailhead. The 7½-mile round-trip begins at the mouth of Yucca Canyon and climbs nearly 1,500 feet up to the top of the escarpment for a panoramic view. Most people turn around at this point; the hardy can continue along a poorly maintained route that follows the top of the ridge for a few more miles. The first part of the hike takes half a day. If you continue on, plan on a full day. *Difficult.* ✉ *Carlsbad Caverns National Park* ⚓ *Trailhead: at Slaughter Canyon Cave parking lot, Hwy. 418, 10 miles west of U.S. 62/180.*

CAVING

Carlsbad Caverns is famous for the beauty and breadth of its inky depths, as well as for the accessibility of some of its largest caves. All cave tours, except for the self-guided Natural Entrance and Big Room, are ranger-led, so safety is rarely an issue in the caves, no matter how remote. Depending on the difficulty of your cave selection (Spider Cave is the hardest to navigate), you'll need at most kneepads, gloves, flashlight batteries, sturdy pants, hiking boots with ankle support, and some water. The fee for the Natural Entrance and Big Room is $12 for ages 16 and up. Guided tours have an additional fee of $7 to $20, and the days and times of these tours vary throughout the year; check with the visitor center or visit the park website for a current tour schedule.

Cave Resources Office

SPELUNKING | Those who want to go it alone outside the more established caverns can get permits and information about 10 backcountry caves from the Cave Resources Office, which you must contact by phone at least a month before of your trip. Heed rangers' advice for these remote, undeveloped, nearly unexplored caves. ✉ *Carlsbad Caverns Visitor Center, 727 Carlsbad Cavern Hwy.* ☎ *575/785–2232* ⊕ *www.nps.gov/cave.*

Ranger-Led Tours

SPELUNKING | **FAMILY** | Cavers who wish to explore both developed and wild caves can go on ranger-led tours, all of which require three AA batteries for headlamps (which will be supplied). Reservations for the six different tours (Hall of the White Giant, Lower Cave, Slaughter Canyon Cave, Left-Hand Tunnel, King's Palace, and Spider Cave) are generally required at least a day in advance. Payment is by credit card over the phone or online, or by mailing a check if you're making reservations 21 days or more in advance; confirm first that space is available. ✉ *Carlsbad Caverns Visitor Center, 727 Carlsbad Cavern Hwy.* ☎ *877/444–6777 for reservations* ⊕ *www.nps.gov/cave* 🎫 *From $7.*

Hall of the White Giant

SPELUNKING | Plan to squirm through some tight passages for long distances to access a very remote chamber, where you'll see towering, glistening white formations that explain the name. This strenuous, ranger-led tour lasts about four hours. Steep climbs and sharp drop-offs might elate you—or make you queasy. Wear sturdy hiking shoes and bring gloves, kneepads, and three AA batteries with you. No kids under 12. ✉ *Carlsbad Caverns Visitor Center, 727 Carlsbad Cavern Hwy.* ☎ *877/444–6777 reservations* ⊕ *www.nps.gov/cave* 🎫 *From $12* 👟 *Reservations essential.*

★ King's Palace

SPELUNKING | **FAMILY** | Throughout this regal room, stunningly handsome and indeed fit for a king, you'll see leggy "soda straws" large enough for a giant to sip, plus bizarre formations that defy reality. The tour also winds through the Queen's Chamber, dressed in ladylike, multitiered curtains of stone. The mile-long walk is on a paved trail, but there's one steep hill toward the end. This ranger-guided tour lasts about 1½ hours and gives you a "look" at the natural essence of a cave—a complete blackout, when artificial lights (and sound) are extinguished. While advance reservations are highly recommended, this is the one tour you might be able to sign up for on the spot. Children younger than four aren't allowed on this tour. ✉ *Carlsbad Caverns Visitor Center, 727 Carlsbad Cavern Hwy.* ⊕ *Departs from underground rest area near elevators* ☎ *877/444–6777 reservations* ⊕ *www.nps.gov/cave* 🎫 *From $8.*

Lower Cave

SPELUNKING | Fifty-foot vertical ladders and a dirt path lead you into undeveloped portions of Carlsbad Caverns. It takes about half a day to negotiate this moderately strenuous side trip led by a knowledgeable ranger. Visitors must bring their own gloves and three AA batteries. No children under 12. ✉ *Carlsbad Caverns Visitor Center, 727 Carlsbad Cavern Hwy.* ☎ *877/444–6777 reservations* ⊕ *www. nps.gov/cave* 🎫 *From $12* 👟 *Reservations essential.*

Slaughter Canyon Cave

SPELUNKING | Discovered in the 1930s by a local goatherd, this cave is one of the most popular secondary sites in the park, about 23 miles southwest of the visitor center. Both the hike to the cave mouth and the tour will take about half a day, but it's worth it to view the deep cavern darkness as it's penetrated only by flashlights and sometimes headlamps. From the Slaughter Canyon parking area, give yourself 45 minutes to make the steep ½-mile climb up a trail leading to the mouth of the cave. You'll find that the cave consists primarily of a single corridor, 1,140 feet long, with numerous side passages.

You can take some worthwhile pictures of this cave. Wear hiking shoes with ankle support, and carry plenty of water. You're also expected to bring three AA batteries. No kids under six. It's a great adventure if you're in shape and love caving. ⊠ *End of Hwy. 418* ⊕ *You'll follow a ranger in your own vehicle from visitor center* ☎ *877/444–6777 reservations* ⊕ *www.nps.gov/cave* ⊠ *From $12* ⚠ *Reservations essential.*

Spider Cave

SPELUNKING | Visitors may not expect to have an adventure in a cavern system as developed and well stocked as Carlsbad Caverns, but serious cavers and energetic types have the chance to crawl on cave floors, clamber up tight tunnels, stoop under overhangs, and climb steep, rocky pitches. This backcountry cave is listed as "wild," a clue that you might need a similar nature to attempt a visit. Plan to wear your warm but least-favorite clothes, as they'll probably get streaked with grime. Bring three AA batteries. It will take you half a day to complete this ranger-led tour noted for being physically demanding and for its continuing role as a living research laboratory. No kids under 12, and this is absolutely not for the claustrophobic. The cave is named after the hordes of daddy long-legs that pulsate on the walls of the opening, but they're harmless. ⊠ *Carlsbad Caverns Visitor Center, 727 Carlsbad Cavern Hwy.* ⊕ *You'll follow a ranger in your own vehicle from visitor center* ☎ *877/444–6777 for reservations* ⊕ *www.nps.gov/cave* ⊠ *From $12* ⚠ *Reservations essential.*

Nearby Towns

On the Pecos River, with 3 miles of beaches, lawns, and picturesque riverside pathways, **Carlsbad, New Mexico,** seems suspended between the past and the present and is the main base for lodging and dining for park visitors. With a few notable attractions of its own, this small city with about 29,000 residents is part–oil boom town, part–Old West, with a decided Mexican-American accent. The town square of mom-and-pop shops, a few short blocks from the river, encircles a Pueblo-style county courthouse designed in the late 1930s by renowned New Mexican architect John Gaw Meem. At the main entrance road into the park, about 7 miles from the visitor center, is **Whites City,** a tiny privately owned village with the nearest lodging, dining, and gas station. It's a sleepy community, however, and most visitors spend their time outside the park in Carlsbad.

VISITOR INFORMATION Carlsbad Chamber of Commerce ⊠ *302 S. Canal St., Carlsbad* ☎ *575/887–6516* ⊕ *www.carlsbadchamber.com.*

Sights

Brantley Lake State Park

BODY OF WATER | FAMILY | In addition to 4,200-acre Brantley Lake and dam, this park 12 miles north of Carlsbad offers primitive camping areas, nature trails, a visitor center, and 51 fully equipped campsites. There's also fishing for largemouth bass, bluegill, and others as well as two boat ramps. ⊠ *33 E. Brantley Lake Rd., Carlsbad* ☎ *575/457–2384* ⊕ *www.emnrd.state.nm.us* ⊠ *$5 per vehicle for day use.*

Carlsbad Museum and Arts Center

MUSEUM | Pueblo pottery, Native American artifacts, and early cowboy and ranch memorabilia fill this downtown cultural center, along with exhibitions of contemporary art. The real treasure, though, is the McAdoo Collection, with works by painters of the Taos Society of Artists. ⊠ *418 W. Fox St., Carlsbad* ☎ *575/887–0276* ⊕ *www.cityofcarlsbadnm.com/museum.cfm* ☉ *Closed Sun. and Mon.*

★ Living Desert Zoo and Gardens State Park
GARDEN | FAMILY | More preserve than traditional zoo, the park contains an impressive collection of plants and animals native to the Chihuahuan Desert. The Desert Arboretum has hundreds of exotic cacti and succulents, and the Living Desert Zoo is home to mountain lions, javelinas, deer, elk, bobcats, bison, and a black bear. Nocturnal exhibits let you view the area's nighttime wildlife, a walk-through aviary houses birds of prey, and there's a reptile exhibit. The park also sponsors some great educational events. Though there are shaded rest areas, restrooms, and water fountains, in summer it's more comfortable to visit in the morning before the desert oven heats up. A self-guided tour takes little more than an hour. The expansive view from here is the best in town. ✉ *1504 Miehls Dr. N, Carlsbad* ☎ *575/887–5516* 🌐 *www.livingdesertnm.org* 🎟 *$5.*

Nightlife

Fiesta Drive-In Theatre
FILM | FAMILY | This throwback offers reasonably current movie selections in an old-school setting. It's generally open most weekends—check their Facebook page for current showings. ✉ *401 W. Fiesta Dr., Carlsbad* ☎ *575/885–4126.*

★ Milton's Taproom and Brewery
BREWPUBS/BEER GARDENS | Opened in 2016 inside a historic downtown warehouse, this first-rate craft brewery has rapidly become one of the top beer makers in southern New Mexico. There's often live music, and a food truck serves tasty barbecue most evenings. ✉ *108 E. Mermod St., Carlsbad* ☎ *575/689–1026* 🌐 *www.miltonsbrewing.com.*

Restaurants

IN THE PARK

Carlsbad Caverns Restaurant
$ | AMERICAN | This comfy, cafeteria-style restaurant adjacent to the gift shop in the visitor center is the only dining option in the caverns' complex other than an underground snack bar. The food—hamburgers, sandwiches, some Mexican dishes—is fine in a pinch. **Known for:** close proximity to the main cavern; no alcohol; takeout options. [$] *Average main: $8* ✉ *Carlsbad Caverns Visitor Center, 727 Carlsbad Cavern Hwy.* ☎ *575/785–2281* 🌐 *www.nps.gov/cave* 🕒 *No dinner.*

Underground Lunchroom
$ | FAST FOOD | At 750 feet underground, near the elevator and entrance to the Big Room, you can grab a snack, soft drink, or club sandwich at this handy snack bar. Service is quick, even when there's a crowd, and although the food doesn't stand out, it's fun dining in this otherworldly setting. **Known for:** unusual setting deep within the park's main cavern. [$] *Average main: $8* ✉ *Carlsbad Caverns Visitor Center, 727 Carlsbad Cavern Hwy.* ☎ *575/785–2232* 🌐 *www.nps.gov/cave* 🕒 *No dinner.*

PICNIC AREAS

★ Rattlesnake Springs
$ | NATIONAL/STATE PARK | Of the several places to picnic in the park, this is the prettiest by far. There are about a dozen picnic tables and grills, many of them tree-shaded, and drinking water and restrooms are available. The seclusion of the site and the oasis-like draw add to the tranquility. Be alert to the presence of wildlife. ✉ *Hwy. 418* ✥ *Take U.S. 62/180 5½ miles south of Whites City and turn right (west) onto Hwy. 418 for 2½ miles* 🌐 *www.nps.gov/cave.*

OUTSIDE THE PARK

CARLSBAD

Blue House Bakery & Cafe
$ | BAKERY | This breakfast nook housed in a charming historic bungalow is a favorite of locals and a treat for travelers weary of so many generic coffee shops. Freshly squeezed juices, inventive breakfast sandwiches, homemade pastries, and arguably the best coffee in town start

the day off right. **Known for:** spacious, umbrella-shaded outdoor patio; gooey cinnamon rolls; breakfast croissants filled with sausage, potatoes, and green chile. [$] *Average main: $7* ✉ *609 N. Canyon St., Carlsbad* ☎ *575/628–0555* ⏲ *Closed Sun. No lunch. No dinner.*

Carniceria San Juan de Los Lagos

$ | **MEXICAN** | Equal parts butcher, bakery, and restaurant, this spacious and colorfully decorated compound turns out some of the most authentic Mexican food in this corner of the state, from burritos and tacos to *chicharrón*. There's a long menu, and although alcohol isn't available, there is a selection of Mexican soft drinks and sweets. **Known for:** carnitas-stuffed tacos and tortas; breakfast burritos; traditional house-baked Mexican pastries. [$] *Average main: $9* ✉ *1200 N. Pate St., Carlsbad* ☎ *575/887–0034.*

Lucky Bull

$$ | **SOUTHWESTERN** | Set inside the city's historic former city hall, this casual tavern serves some of the best upscale pub grub in town, including roasted green chile queso blanco, mammoth burgers with a range of interesting toppings, and hand-cut rib-eye steaks. An upstairs tap room carries a fine selection of craft beers, with an emphasis on New Mexico brewers. **Known for:** Pecos Valley poutine (fries topped with green chile gravy and cheddar); country-fried steak; impressive craft-beer selection. [$] *Average main: $17* ✉ *220 W. Fox St., Carlsbad* ☎ *575/725–5444* ⏲ *Closed Sun.*

No Whiner Diner

$ | **CAFÉ** | **FAMILY** | A no-frills eatery that would make Mom and Pop proud, the No Whiner Diner offers comfort-food favorites like meat loaf, chicken-fried steak, and hot and cold sandwiches stacked on homemade bread. It caters to all cravings, from tuna salad to breaded veal, and includes a kids' menu. [$] *Average main: $9* ✉ *1801 S. Canal St., Carlsbad* ☎ *575/234–2815* 🌐 *www.nowhinerdiner.com* ⏲ *Closed weekends.*

Pecos River Cafe

$ | **AMERICAN** | **FAMILY** | If you're planning a big hike underground or through one of the park's canyons, this casual breakfast and lunch spot is a terrific go-to for its prodigious breakfast burritos, egg dishes, and pancakes, plus burgers and Mexican platters at lunch. Just about anything can be topped with spicy New Mexico green chile sauce, and everything is available for takeout. Alas, it's open only on weekdays. **Known for:** house-made green and red chile; half-pound guacamole burgers; sweet-cream pancakes. [$] *Average main: $9* ✉ *409 S. Canal St., Carlsbad* ☎ *575/887–8882* 🌐 *www.pecosrivercafe.com* ⏲ *Closed weekends. No dinner.*

★ **Red Chimney Pit Bar-B-Q**

$$ | **BARBECUE** | **FAMILY** | If you hanker for sweet-and-tangy pecan wood–smoked barbecue, this homey, log-cabin-style spot serves up consistently tasty fare at reasonable prices. Sauce from an old family recipe is slathered on chicken, pork, beef brisket, turkey, and ham. **Known for:** sides of smoked mac-and-cheese and seasoned corn; charbroiled burgers; spicy jalapeño sausage. [$] *Average main: $13* ✉ *817 N. Canal St., Carlsbad* ☎ *575/885–8744* 🌐 *www.redchimneybbq.com* ⏲ *Closed Sun. and Mon.*

★ **Trinity Hotel**

$$ | **ITALIAN** | The region's top pick for a romantic, elegant meal, this handsome dining room with vaulted ceilings, tall windows, and a long old-fashioned bar is set inside the beautifully restored 1892 Trinity Hotel. The kitchen turns out hearty and flavorful Italian fare, from traditional pastas to halibut with lemon-caper sauce, and a signature dish, chicken bolloco—essentially fettuccine Alfredo with fresh green chilies added. Unwind at the bar, which features excellent local wines, including some from the owner's own vineyards in Deming. **Known for:** local goat cheese with blackberries and habañero sauce;

an excellent selection of acclaimed New Mexico wines; lobster ravioli. $ *Average main: $17* ✉ *201 S. Canal St., Carlsbad* ☎ *575/234–9891* ⊕ *www.thetrinityhotel. com* ⊗ *No dinner Sun.*

YellowBrix

$$ | MODERN AMERICAN | This attractive restaurant set in a former 1920s home has several different dining rooms as well as a breezy courtyard patio where local acoustic musicians sometimes perform. The kitchen serves eclectic fare with sophisticated flourishes, including poached-pear salads, sashimi tuna with a spicy wasabi-soy sauce, pressed Cuban panini sandwiches, and an extensive selection of steaks. **Known for:** Brix bacon-wrapped meat loaf; friendly and efficient service; chocolate lava cake. $ *Average main: $20* ✉ *201 N. Canal St., Carlsbad* ☎ *575/941–2749* ⊕ *www. yellowbrixrestaurant.com.*

 ## Hotels

OUTSIDE THE PARK
CARLSBAD
Days Inn

$$ | HOTEL | An older property that has been largely modernized, Days Inn is on the right side of town for those driving to the caverns and points south. **Pros:** close to regional airport; pool; pet-friendly. **Cons:** no elevator to the second floor; shows its age in places. $ *Rooms from: 139* ✉ *3910 National Parks Hwy., Carlsbad* ☎ *575/887–7800* ⊕ *www.wyndhamhotels.com/days inn/carlsbad* ⇆ *42 rooms, 8 suites* ¶◎¶ *Breakfast.*

Fairfield Inn and Suites

$$$$ | HOTEL | This Marriott hotel is close to all of Carlsbad's major attractions and on the south end of town, toward the caverns; its stylish, modern rooms feature Wi-Fi and Internet hookups. **Pros:** comfortable beds; building is clean and new; exercise room; business center. **Cons:** most rooms don't have a refrigerator, although the suites do; no pets allowed. $ *Rooms from: $209* ✉ *2525*

Camping in Carlsbad Caverns

Backcountry camping is by permit only. No campfires allowed in the park, and all camping is hike-to. Commercial sites can be found in Whites City and Carlsbad.

S. Canal St., Carlsbad ☎ *575/887–8000* ⊕ *www.marriott.com* ⇆ *73 rooms, 18 suites* ¶◎¶ *Breakfast.*

Hampton Inn and Suites

$$$$ | HOTEL | On the south side of downtown leading to the Carlsbad Caverns, this well-maintained chain property lies within walking distance of a few restaurants, a gas station, and a Walmart. **Pros:** staff is very friendly and accommodating; clean, well-kept amenities. **Cons:** some rooms need better soundproofing; among the more pricey hotels in town. $ *Rooms from: $375* ✉ *120 Esperanza Circle, Carlsbad* ☎ *575/725–5700* ⊕ *www.carlsbadsuites.hamptoninn.com* ⇆ *85 rooms* ¶◎¶ *Breakfast.*

Holiday Inn Express

$$$$ | HOTEL | Within walking distance of the only movie theater in Carlsbad, as well as the Carlsbad Mall, the hotel is also close to the Carlsbad hospital and Living Desert Zoo & Gardens State Park. **Pros:** full, hot breakfast; convenient location for the north side of town. **Cons:** a little farther away from the park than other hotels; no pets allowed. $ *Rooms from: $259* ✉ *2210 W. Pierce St., Carlsbad* ☎ *575/234–1252* ⊕ *www.hiexpress. com* ⇆ *56 rooms, 24 suites* ¶◎¶ *Breakfast.*

Hotel Artesia

$ | HOTEL | The most distinctive lodging option in pleasant workaday town Artesia, which is about 60 miles north of the park, this streamlined-looking art deco–style hotel has roomy accommodations with blond-wood furniture and the same in-room amenities you'd find at the several chain hotels in town. **Pros:** within walking distance of several downtown Artesia restaurants and bars; great value; design is more interesting than competing chain properties. **Cons:** about a 75-minute drive to the park visitor center; rooms can feel a little dark. $ *Rooms from: $130* ⊠ *203 N. 2nd St., Artesia* ☎ *575/746–2066, 888/746–2066* ⊕ *www.hotelartesia.com* ⟿ *50 rooms* ¶◎¶ *Free Breakfast.*

La Quinta Inn & Suites

$$$ | HOTEL | Joining new construction of other chain hotels on Carlsbad's south side, this La Quinta continues the brand's transformation from a Southwestern-style motor lodge to multistory hotel. **Pros:** on the closer side of town to the caverns; outdoor pool; 24-hour fitness center; pet-friendly. **Cons:** impersonal "big box" layout; pricey. $ *Rooms from: $200* ⊠ *4020 National Parks Hwy., Carlsbad* ☎ *575/236–1010* ⊕ *www.lq.com* ⟿ *96 rooms, 1 suite* ¶◎¶ *Breakfast.*

Rodeway Inn

$ | HOTEL | This bland but economical two-story motel just outside the entrance to the national park has spacious rooms that have recently undergone a remodel. **Pros:** the closest lodging to Carlsbad Caverns; water park is a welcome splash in summer; rates are cheaper than in Carlsbad. **Cons:** rooms and service are very bare-bones; often books well ahead, especially on summer weekends. $ *Rooms from: $140* ⊠ *6 Carlsbad Cavern Hwy., Whites City* ☎ *575/785–2148* ⊕ *www.choicehotels.com* ⟿ *60 rooms* ¶◎¶ *Breakfast.*

Stevens Inn

$$ | HOTEL | FAMILY | A sprawling local landmark decades old, the Stevens was once Carlsbad's premier motel and entertainment destination for the region, and has kept pace through periodic renovations. **Pros:** decent rates for the area; there's a pool and fitness room; has a full-service restaurant and bar. **Cons:** aging property that could use some updating. $ *Rooms from: $179* ⊠ *1829 S. Canal St., Carlsbad* ☎ *575/887–2851, 800/730–2851* ⊕ *www.stevensinncarlsbad.com* ⟿ *220 rooms* ¶◎¶ *Breakfast.*

TownePlace Suites by Marriott Carlsbad

$$$ | HOTEL | FAMILY | Among the several new and modern chain properties that have opened in town in recent years, this sleek member of Marriott's extended-stay-oriented TownePlace Suites brand has among the largest and best-outfitted accommodations. **Pros:** convenient location; smartly designed rooms; rates, while still often quite high, are often lower than other chain properties in town. **Cons:** it looks like any other TownePlace Suites property; can be very expensive when demand soars. $ *Rooms from: $299* ⊠ *311 Pompa St., Carlsbad* ☎ *575/689–8850* ⊕ *www.marriott.com* ⟿ *94 rooms* ¶◎¶ *Free Breakfast.*

★ Trinity Hotel

$$ | B&B/INN | By far the most elegant and atmospheric lodging option in the region, this graceful 1892 redbrick former bank building has nine luxuriously appointed rooms with high ceilings, plush beds with pillow-top mattresses, hidden flat-screen TVs, and spacious bathrooms with glass walk-in showers. **Pros:** centrally located and steps from several good restaurants; less expensive than comparable hotels in town; terrific bar and restaurant. **Cons:** no elevator; no interior access to the lobby; no pets allowed. $ *Rooms from: $189* ⊠ *201 S. Canal St., Carlsbad* ☎ *575/234–9891* ⊕ *www.thetrinityhotel.com* ⟿ *9 rooms* ¶◎¶ *Breakfast.*

Chapter 12

CHANNEL ISLANDS
NATIONAL PARK

12

Updated by
Cheryl Crabtree

CALIFORNIA

WELCOME TO
CHANNEL ISLANDS NATIONAL PARK

TOP REASONS TO GO

★ **Rare flora and fauna:** The Channel Islands are home to 145 species of terrestrial plants and animals found nowhere else on Earth.

★ **Time travel:** With no cars, phones, or services, these undeveloped islands provide a glimpse of what California was like hundreds of years ago, away from hectic modern life.

★ **Underwater adventures:** The incredibly healthy channel waters rank among the top 10 diving destinations on the planet—but you can also visit the kelp forest virtually via Channel Islands Live, a live underwater program.

★ **Marvelous marine mammals:** More than 30 species of seals, sea lions, whales, and other marine mammals ply the park's waters at various times of year.

★ **Sea-cave kayaking:** Paddle around otherwise inaccessible portions of the park's 175 miles of gorgeous coastline—including one of the world's largest sea caves.

1 Anacapa. Tiny Anacapa is a 5-mile stretch of three islets, with towering cliffs, caves, natural bridges, and rich kelp forests.

2 San Miguel. Isolated, windswept San Miguel, the park's westernmost island (access permit required), has an ancient caliche forest and hundreds of archaeological sites chronicling the Native Americans' 13,000-year history on the islands. More than 30,000 pinnipeds (seals and sea lions) hang out on the island's beaches during certain times of year.

3 Santa Barbara. More than 5 miles of scenic trails crisscross this tiny island, known for its excellent wildlife viewing and native plants. It's a favorite destination for diving, snorkeling, and kayaking.

4 Santa Cruz. The park's largest island offers some of the best hikes and kayaking opportunities, one of the world's largest and deepest sea caves, and more species of flora and fauna than any other park island.

5 Santa Rosa. Campers love to stay on Santa Rosa, with its myriad hiking opportunities, stunning white-sand beaches, and rare grove of Torrey pines. It's also the only island accessible by plane.

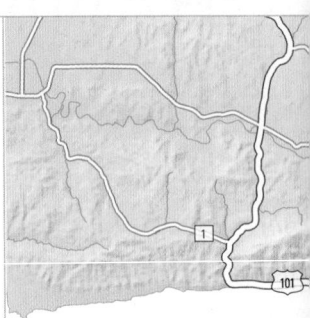

Harris Point

Point Bennett

Cuyler Harbor

Cabrillo Monume
Lester Ranch site

Vai

Tyler Bight

San Miguel Island

San Miguel Passage

Sandy Point

Santa Rosa Island

5

P A C I F I C

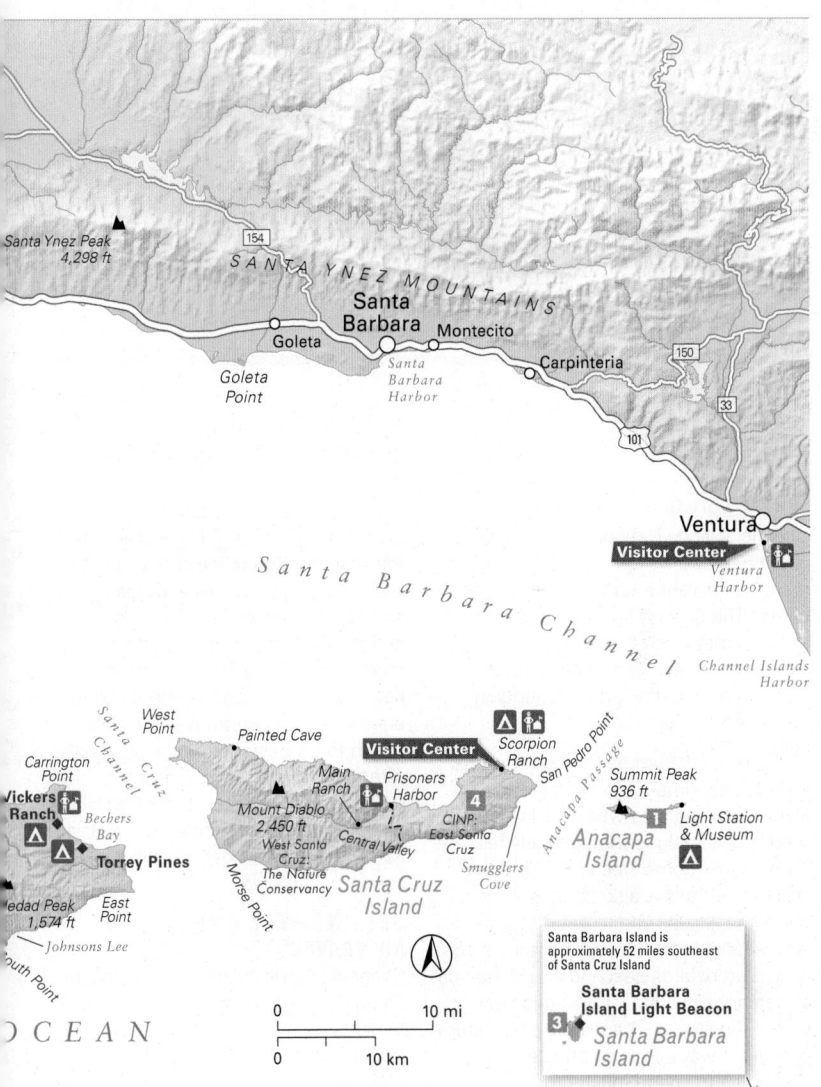

Santa Ynez Peak
4,298 ft

SANTA YNEZ MOUNTAINS

154

Santa Barbara

Goleta

Montecito

Goleta Point

Santa Barbara Harbor

Carpinteria

150

33

101

Ventura

Visitor Center

Ventura Harbor

Santa Barbara Channel

Channel Islands Harbor

Santa Cruz Channel

West Point

Painted Cave

Carrington Point

Vickers Ranch

Bechers Bay

Torrey Pines

Main Ranch

Prisoners Harbor

Visitor Center

Scorpion Ranch

San Pedro Point

Summit Peak
936 ft

Light Station & Museum

Mount Diablo
2,450 ft

Central Valley

CINP:
East Santa Cruz

Anacapa Passage

Anacapa Island

West Santa Cruz:
The Nature Conservancy

Smugglers Cove

Morse Point

Santa Cruz Island

edad Peak
1,574 ft

East Point

Johnsons Lee

outh Point

OCEAN

0   10 mi

0   10 km

Santa Barbara Island is approximately 52 miles southeast of Santa Cruz Island

Santa Barbara Island Light Beacon

Santa Barbara Island

4

1

On crystal-clear days the craggy peaks of Channel Islands are easy to see from the mainland, jutting from the Pacific in sharp detail. A high-speed boat will whisk you to the closest islands in less than an hour, yet very few people ever visit them. Those who do will experience one of the most splendid land-and-sea wilderness areas on the planet.

Planning

WHEN TO GO

Channel Islands National Park records about 620,000 visitors each year, but many never venture beyond the visitor center. The busiest times are holidays and summer weekends; if you're going then, make your transportation and accommodation arrangements in advance.

The warm, dry summer and fall months are the best time to go camping. Humpback and blue whales arrive to feed from late June through early fall. The rains usually come December through March—but this is also the best time to spot gray whales and to get discounts at area hotels. In the late spring, thousands of migratory birds descend on the islands to hatch their young, and wildflowers carpet the slopes. The water temperature is nearly always cool, so bring a wet suit if you plan to spend much time in the ocean, even in the summer. Fog, high winds, and rough seas can happen any time of the year.

PLANNING YOUR TIME
CHANNEL ISLANDS IN ONE DAY
If you have a few hours or a day to visit the Channel Islands, start with viewing the exhibits at the **Channel Islands National Park Visitor Center** in Ventura. Then cruise over to **East Anacapa** for sweeping views of Santa Cruz Island and the mainland—provided it's not too foggy—and hiking, the primary activity here. Wander through western gull rookeries or peer down from steep cliffs and watch the antics of sea lions and seals. Alternatively, zip out to Scorpion Landing or Prisoner's Harbor on **Santa Cruz Island** on a high-speed catamaran run by Island Packers for more extended hiking, snorkeling, or kayaking.

GETTING HERE AND AROUND
AIR TRAVEL
Channel Islands Aviation flies solely to Santa Rosa Island. You can catch a flight to Santa Rosa Island and San Miguel Island from the Camarillo Airport, south of Ventura, and the Santa Barbara Airport.

BOAT TRAVEL
The visitor center for Channel Islands National Park is on California's mainland, in the town of Ventura, off U.S. 101. From

AVERAGE HIGH/LOW TEMPERATURES					
JAN.	FEB.	MAR.	APR.	MAY	JUNE
66/44	66/45	66/46	68/48	69/51	71/55
JULY	AUG.	SEPT.	OCT.	NOV.	DEC.
74/57	75/59	75/57	74/53	70/48	66/44

the harbors at Ventura, Santa Barbara, and Oxnard you can board a boat to one of the islands. If you have your own boat, you can land at any of the park islands without a permit, but you should visit the park website for instructions and information on restricted areas. A permit is required to land on the Nature Conservancy property on Santa Cruz Island. Boaters landing at San Miguel must contact the park ranger beforehand.

Island Packers
Sailing on high-speed catamarans from Ventura or a mono-hull vessel from Oxnard, Island Packers goes to Santa Cruz Island daily most of the year, weather permitting. The boats also go to Anacapa several days a week, and to the outer islands from April through November. They also cruise along Anacapa's north shore on three-hour wildlife tours (no disembarking) several times a week. ⊠ *3550 Harbor Blvd., Oxnard* ☎ *805/642–1393* ⊕ *islandpackers.com* ⌨ *$38*.

CAR TRAVEL
To reach the Ventura harbor, exit U.S. 101 in Ventura at Seaward Boulevard or Victoria Avenue and follow the signs to Ventura Harbor/Spinnaker Drive. To access Channel Islands Harbor in Oxnard, exit U.S. 101 at Victoria Avenue and head south approximately 7 miles to Channel Islands Boulevard. To access dive and whale-watching boats in Santa Barbara, exit U.S. 101 at Castillo Street and head south to Cabrillo Boulevard, then turn right for the harbor entrance. Private vehicles are not permitted on the islands. Pets are also not allowed in the park.

TRAIN TRAVEL
Amtrak makes stops in Santa Barbara, Ventura, and Oxnard; from the Amtrak station, just take a taxi, rideshare service or waterfront shuttle bus to the harbor.

PARK ESSENTIALS
ACCESSIBILITY
The Channel Islands National Park Visitor Center is fully accessible.

The islands themselves have few facilities and are not easy to navigate by individuals in wheelchairs or those with limited mobility. Limited wheelchair access is available on Santa Rosa Island via air transportation.

PARK FEES AND PERMITS
There is no fee to enter Channel Islands National Park, but unless you have your own boat, you will pay $38 or more per person for a ride with a boat operator. The cost of taking a boat to the park varies depending on which operator you choose. Also, there is a $15-per-day fee for staying in one of the islands' campgrounds.

If you take your own boat, landing permits are not required to visit islands administered by the National Park Service. However, boaters who want to land on the Nature Conservancy preserve on Santa Cruz Island must have a permit. Visit ⊕ *www.nature.org/cruzpermit* for permit information; allow 10 business days to process and return your permit application. If you anchor in a nearby cove at any island, at least one person should remain aboard the boat at all times. San Miguel Island is property of the U.S. Navy. Visitors must obtain an access permit to visit the island. Access permits are available at the boat and air concession offices and at a self-registration station on the island. To hike beyond the ranger station on San Miguel you need a reservation and permit; call ☎ 805/658–5711 to be matched up with a ranger, who must accompany you. Anglers must have a state fishing license; for details, call the California Department of Fish and Wildlife at ☎ 916/653–7664 or visit ⊕ www.wildlife.ca.gov. More than a dozen Marine Protected Areas (MPAs) with special resource protection regulations surround the islands, so read the guidelines carefully before you depart.

PARK HOURS

The islands are open every day of the year. Channel Islands National Park Visitor Center in Ventura is closed on Thanksgiving and Christmas. Channel Islands National Park is in the Pacific time zone.

CELL PHONE RECEPTION

In general, cell phone reception is spotty and varies by location and service provider. Public telephones are available on the mainland near the Channel Islands National Park Visitor Center but not on the islands.

EDUCATIONAL OFFERINGS

RANGER PROGRAMS

Ranger programs are held at the Channel Islands National Park Visitor Center in Ventura.

Channel Islands Live Program

NATIONAL/STATE PARK | FAMILY | Want a cool sneak preview of the islands and the colorful sea life below? Experience them virtually through the Channel Islands Live Program, which takes you on interactive tours of the park. In the Live Dive Program, divers armed with video cameras explore the undersea world of the kelp forest off Anacapa Island; images are transmitted to monitors located on the dock at Landing Cove, in the mainland visitor center, and online. The Live Hike Program takes you on a similar interactive virtual tour of Anacapa Island. Live

Transit Times to the Islands

Island	Distance and Time by Boat	Cost (per hiker/camper)
Anacapa Island	14 miles/1 hr from Oxnard	$59/$79
San Miguel Island	58 miles/3 hrs from Ventura	$105/$147
Santa Barbara Island	55 miles/2½–3 hrs from Ventura	$82/$114
Santa Cruz Island	20 miles/1 hr from Ventura	$59/$79
Santa Rosa Island	46 miles/2 hrs from Ventura	$82/$114

webcams also connect you 24/7 with panoramic views of Anacapa Island, bald eagle and peregrine falcon nests, Santa Cruz Island (from Mount Diablo, the island's highest peak) and underwater life in a kelp forest. ⊕ www.nps.gov/chis/planyourvisit/channel-islands-live-nps.htm 🎦 Free.

Tidepool Talk

TOUR—SIGHT | Explore the area's marine habitat without getting your feet wet. Rangers at the Channel Islands Visitor Center demonstrate how animals and plants adapt to the harsh conditions found in tidal pools of the Channel Islands. ✉ Channel Islands National Park Visitor Center, 1901 Spinnaker Rd., Ventura ☎ 805/658–5730 🎦 Free.

RESTAURANTS

Out on the islands, there are no restaurants, no snack bars, and in some cases, no potable water. Instead, pack a fancy picnic or a simple sandwich. For a quick meal before or after your island trip, each of the harbors has a number of decent eateries nearby.

Back on the mainland, though, it's a dining gold mine. Santa Barbara has a long-standing reputation for culinary excellence, and a "foodie" renaissance in recent years has transformed Ventura into a dining destination—with dozens of new restaurants touting nouvelle cuisine made with organic produce and meats. Fresh seafood is a standout, whether it's prepared simply in wharf-side hangouts or incorporated into sophisticated bistro menus. Dining attire is generally casual, though slightly dressy casual wear is the custom at pricier restaurants.

HOTELS

It's easy to choose where to stay in the park—your only option is sleeping in your tent in a no-frills campground. If you hanker for more creature comforts, you can splurge on a bunk and meals on a dive boat.

There's a huge range of lodging options on the mainland, from seaside camping to posh international resorts. The most affordable options are in Oxnard, Ventura, and Carpinteria, a small seaside community between Santa Barbara and Ventura. Despite rates that range from pricey to downright shocking, Santa Barbara's numerous hotels and bed-and-breakfasts attract thousands of patrons year-round. Wherever you stay, be sure to make reservations for the summer and holiday weekends (especially Memorial Day, July 4, Labor Day, and Thanksgiving) well ahead of time; it's not unusual for coastal accommodations to fill completely during these busy times. Also be aware that some hotels double their rates during festivals and other events.

Hot Spots

INFO CENTER | For room reservations for destinations in Ventura and Santa Barbara counties, contact Hot Spots. ☎ 800/793–7666 ⊕ www.hotspotsusa.com.

Hotel reviews have been shortened. For full information, visit Fodors.com.

What It Costs			
$	$$	$$$	$$$$
RESTAURANTS			
under $16	$16–$22	$23–$30	over $30
HOTELS			
under $120	$121–$175	$176–$250	over $250

VISITOR INFORMATION
VISITOR CENTERS
Channel Islands National Park Visitor Center

INFO CENTER | The park's Robert J. Lagomarsino Visitor Center has a museum, a bookstore, and a three-story observation tower with telescopes. The museum's exhibits and a 24-minute film, *Treasure in the Sea,* provide an engaging overview of the islands. In the marine life exhibit, sea stars cling to rocks, and a brilliant orange Garibaldi darts around. Also on display are full-size reproductions of a male northern elephant seal and the pygmy mammoth skeleton unearthed on Santa Rosa Island in 1994.

On weekends and holidays at 11 am and 3 pm, rangers lead various free public programs describing park resources, and from Wednesday through Saturday in summer the center screens live ranger broadcasts of hikes and dives on Anacapa Island. Webcam images of bald eagles and other land and sea creatures are shown at the center and on the park's website. ✉ *1901 Spinnaker Dr., Ventura* ☎ *805/658–5730* ⊕ *www.nps.gov/chis.*

Outdoors Santa Barbara Visitor Center

INFO CENTER | The small office in the Santa Barbara Harbor provides maps and other information about Channel Islands National Park and Channel Islands National Marine Sanctuary; the Santa Barbara Maritime Museum is housed in the same building. Call ahead to verify hours. ✉ *113 Harbor Way, Santa Barbara* ☎ *805/456–8752* ⊕ *outdoorsb.sbmm.org.*

Plants and Wildlife on the Channel Islands

Channel Islands National Park is home to species found nowhere else on Earth: mammals such as the island fox and the island deer mouse and birds like the island scrub jay live forever on the endangered species list. Thousands of western gulls hatch each summer on Anacapa, then fly off to the mainland where they spend about four years learning all their bad habits. Then they return to the island to roost and have chicks of their own. It all adds up to a living laboratory not unlike the one naturalist Charles Darwin discovered off the coast of South America 200 years ago, which is why the Channel Islands are often called the North American Galápagos.

Sights

THE ISLANDS

Anacapa Island

ISLAND | Most people think of Anacapa as an island, but it's actually comprised of three narrow islets. Although the tips of these volcanic formations nearly touch, the islets are inaccessible from one another except by boat. All three have towering cliffs, isolated sea caves, and natural bridges; Arch Rock, on East Anacapa, is one of the best-known symbols of Channel Islands National Park.

Wildlife viewing is the main activity on East Anacapa, particularly in summer when seagull chicks are newly hatched and sea lions and seals lounge on the beaches. Exhibits at East Anacapa's compact **museum** include the original lead-crystal Fresnel lens from the 1932 lighthouse.

On West Anacapa, depending on the season and the number of desirable species lurking about here, boats travel to **Frenchy's Cove.** On a voyage here you might see anemones, limpets, barnacles, mussel beds, and colorful marine algae in the pristine tide pools. The rest of West Anacapa is closed to protect nesting brown pelicans. ⊠ *Channel Islands National Park.*

San Miguel Island

ISLAND | The westernmost of the Channel Islands, San Miguel Island is frequently battered by storms sweeping across the North Pacific. The 15-square-mile island's wild windswept landscape is lush with vegetation. Point Bennett, at the western tip, offers one of the world's most spectacular wildlife displays when more than 30,000 pinnipeds hit its beach. Explorer Juan Rodríguez Cabrillo was the first European to visit this island; he claimed it for Spain in 1542. Legend holds that Cabrillo died on one of the Channel Islands—no one knows where he's buried, but there's a memorial to him on a bluff above Cuyler Harbor. ⊠ *Channel Islands National Park.*

Santa Barbara Island

ISLAND | At about 1 square mile, Santa Barbara Island is the smallest of the Channel Islands and nearly 35 miles south of the others. Triangular in shape, Santa Barbara's steep cliffs—which offer a perfect nesting spot for the Scripps's murrelet, a rare seabird—are topped by twin peaks. In spring you can enjoy a brilliant display of yellow coreopsis. Learn about the wildlife on and around the islands at the island's small museum. ⊠ *Channel Islands National Park.*

★ Santa Cruz Island

ISLAND | Five miles west of Anacapa, 96-square-mile Santa Cruz Island is the largest of the Channel Islands. The National Park Service manages the easternmost 24% of the island; the rest is owned by the Nature Conservancy, which requires a permit to land. When your boat drops you off on a portion of the 70 miles of craggy coastline, you see two rugged mountain ranges with peaks soaring to 2,500 feet and deep canyons traversed by streams. This landscape is the habitat of a remarkable variety of flora and fauna—more than 600 types of plants, 140 kinds of land birds, 11 mammal species, five varieties of reptiles, and three amphibian species live here. Bird-watchers may want to look for the endemic island scrub jay, which is found nowhere else in the world.

One of the largest and deepest sea caves in the world, **Painted Cave** lies along the northwest coast of Santa Cruz. Named for the colorful lichen and algae that cover its walls, Painted Cave is nearly ¼ mile long and 100 feet wide. In spring a waterfall cascades over the entrance. Kayakers may encounter seals or sea lions cruising alongside their boats inside the cave. The Channel Islands hold some of the richest archaeological resources in North America; all artifacts are protected within the park. Remnants of a dozen Chumash villages can be seen on the island. The largest of these villages, at the eastern end, occupied the area now called **Scorpion Ranch.** The Chumash mined extensive chert deposits on the island for tools to produce shell-bead money, which they traded with people on the mainland. You can learn about Chumash history and view artifacts, tools, and exhibits on native plant and wildlife at the interpretive visitor center near the landing dock. Visitors can also explore remnants of the early-1900s ranching era in the restored historic adobe and outbuildings. ⊠ *Channel Islands National Park.*

Santa Rosa Island

ISLAND | Between Santa Cruz and San Miguel, Santa Rosa is the second largest of the Channel Islands. The terrain along the coast varies from broad, sandy beaches to sheer cliffs—a central mountain range, rising to 1,589 feet, breaks the island's relatively low profile. Santa Rosa is home to about 500 species of plants, including the rare Torrey pine, and three unusual mammals, the island fox, the spotted skunk, and the deer mouse. They hardly compare, though, to their predecessors: a nearly complete skeleton of a 6-foot-tall pygmy mammoth was unearthed in 1994.

From 1901 to 1998, cattle were raised at the island's **Vail & Vickers Ranch.** The route from Santa Rosa's landing dock to the campground passes by the historic ranch buildings, barns, equipment, and the wooden pier where cattle were brought onto the island. ⊠ *Channel Islands National Park.*

 **Activities**

DIVING

Some of the best snorkeling and diving in the world can be found in the cool waters surrounding the Channel Islands. In the relatively warm water around Anacapa and eastern Santa Cruz, photographers can get great shots of rarely seen giant black bass swimming among the kelp forests. Here you also find a reef covered with red brittle starfish. If you're an experienced diver, you might swim among five species of seals and sea lions, or try your hand at spearing rockfish or halibut near San Miguel and Santa Rosa. The best time to scuba dive is in summer and fall, when the water is often clear up to a 100-foot depth.

Explorer Diving Adventures

SCUBA DIVING | The 65-foot *Explorer* ferries passengers out to all the islands

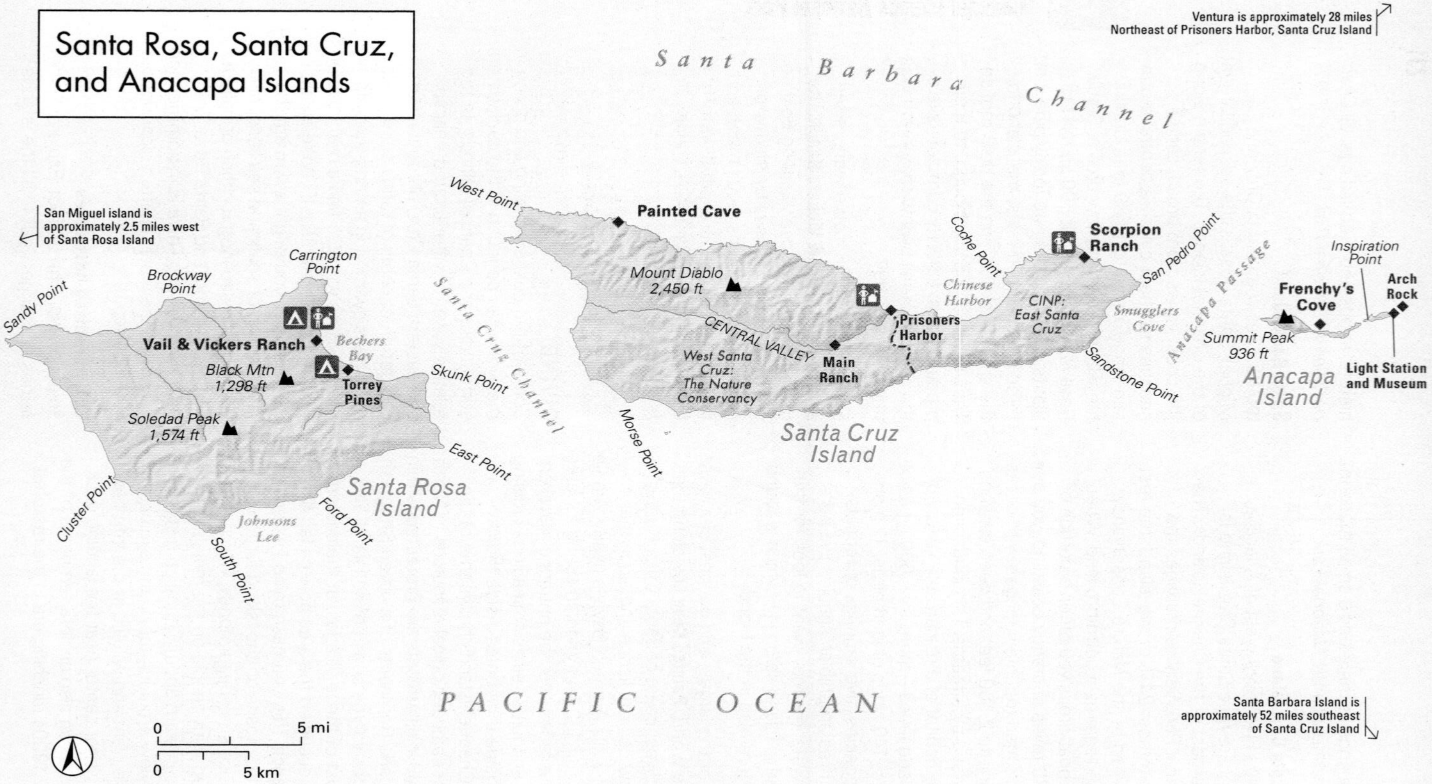

Santa Rosa, Santa Cruz, and Anacapa Islands

Northeast of Prisoners Harbor, Santa Cruz Island
Ventura is approximately 28 miles

Santa Barbara Channel

San Pedro Point

Scorpion Ranch

Smugglers Cove

Coche Point

Sandstone Point

Anacapa Passage

Inspiration Point

Arch Rock

Frenchy's Cove

Summit Peak 936 ft

Light Station and Museum

Anacapa Island

CINP: East Santa Cruz

Chinese Harbor

Prisoners Harbor

Main Ranch

CENTRAL VALLEY

West Santa Cruz: The Nature Conservancy

Painted Cave

▲ *Mount Diablo 2,450 ft*

Santa Cruz Island

Morse Point

West Point

Santa Cruz Channel

Skunk Point

East Point

Santa Rosa Island

Ford Point

Johnsons Lee

South Point

Cluster Point

Carrington Point

Bechers Bay

Torrey Pines

Vail & Vickers Ranch

▲ *Black Mtn 1,298 ft*

▲ *Soledad Peak 1,574 ft*

Brockway Point

Sandy Point

PACIFIC OCEAN

San Miguel Island is approximately 2.5 miles west of Santa Rosa Island

Santa Barbara Island is approximately 52 miles southeast of Santa Cruz Island

0   5 mi
0   5 km

for single- and multiday adventures. Rates include food, snacks, beverages, and air. ✉ *1583 Spinnaker Dr., Ventura* ☎ *805/890–1142* ⊕ *www.explorerdive-boat.com* 💲 *From $125 for day trips.*

Peace Dive Boat

SCUBA DIVING | Ventura Harbor–based Peace Dive Boat runs single- and multiday diving adventures near all the Channel Islands. Travelers sleep aboard the ship. ✉ *1691 Spinnaker Dr., Dock G, Ventura* ☎ *805/650–3483* ⊕ *www.peace-boat.com* 💲 *From $120.*

Raptor Dive Boat

SCUBA DIVING | Ventura Dive & Sport's 46-foot custom boat, the *Raptor,* takes divers on two- and three-tank trips to Anacapa and Santa Cruz islands and is available for private charters, including official open-water swims in the channel. ✉ *Ventura* ☎ *805/650–7700* ⊕ *www.raptordive.com* 💲 *From $120.*

Spectre Dive Boat

SCUBA DIVING | This boat runs single-day diving trips to Anacapa and Santa Cruz. Fees include three dives, air, and food. ✉ *1575 Spinnaker Dr., Suite 105B–75, Ventura* ☎ *805/486–1166* ⊕ *www.calboat-diving.com* 💲 *From $120.*

Truth Aquatics

SCUBA DIVING | Truth runs kayaking, paddleboarding, hiking, snorkeling, and scuba excursions to the National Marine Sanctuary and Channel Islands National Park. ✉ *Departures from SEA Landing, Santa Barbara Harbor* ☎ *805/962–1127* ⊕ *truthaquatics.com* 💲 *From $120.*

HIKING

The terrain on most of the islands ranges from flat to moderately hilly. There are no services on the islands (and no public phones; cell phone reception is dicey). You need to bring all your own food, water (except on Santa Cruz and Santa Rosa, where there are water faucets at campgrounds), and supplies.

Truth Aquatics

HIKING/WALKING | This outfitter is author-ized to land on some of the park's islands for multiday overnight trips that include naturalist-led hikes (you sleep and eat on board the 65-to-90-foot twin-engine vessels). ✉ *301 W. Cabrillo Blvd., Santa Barbara* ☎ *805/962–1127* ⊕ *www.truth-aquatics.com* 💲 *From $340.*

Cavern Point Trail

HIKING/WALKING | **FAMILY** | This moder-ate 2-mile hike takes you to the bluffs northwest of Scorpion harbor on Santa Cruz, where there are magnificent coast-al views and pods of migrating gray whales from December through March. *Moderate.* ✉ *Trailhead: at Scorpion Ranch Campground, Santa Cruz Island.*

Cuyler Harbor Beach Trail

HIKING/WALKING | This easy walk takes you along a 2-mile-long white sand beach on San Miguel. The eastern section is occasionally cut off by high tides. Access permit required. *Easy.* ✉ *Trailhead: at San Miguel Campground, San Miguel Island.*

East Point Trail

HIKING/WALKING | This strenuous 12-mile hike along beautiful white-sand beach-es yields the opportunity to see rare Torrey pines. Some beaches are closed between March and September, so you have to remain on the road for portions of this hike. *Difficult.* ✉ *Trailhead: at Santa Rosa Campground, Santa Rosa Island.*

Elephant Seal Cove Trail

HIKING/WALKING | This moderate to strenu-ous walk takes you across Santa Barbara to a point where you can view magnif-icent elephant seals from steep cliffs. *Moderate.* ✉ *Trailhead: at Landing Cove, Santa Barbara Island.*

Historic Ranch Trail

HIKING/WALKING | **FAMILY** | This easy ½-mile walk on Santa Cruz Island takes you to a historic ranch where you can visit an interpretive center in an 1800s adobe and see remnants of a cattle ranch. *Easy.*

✉ *Trailhead: at Scorpion Beach, Santa Cruz Island.*

Inspiration Point Trail

HIKING/WALKING | FAMILY | This 1½-mile hike along flat terrain takes in most of East Anacapa; there are great views from Inspiration Point and Cathedral Cove. *Easy.* ✉ *Trailhead: at Landing Cove, Anacapa Island.*

Lester Ranch Trail

HIKING/WALKING | This short but strenuous 2-mile hike leads up a spectacular canyon filled with waterfalls and lush native plants. At the end of a steep climb to the top of a peak, views of the historic Lester Ranch and the Cabrillo Monument await. If you plan to hike beyond the Lester Ranch, you'll need a hiking permit; call or visit the park website for details. Access permit required. *Difficult.* ✉ *Trailhead: at San Miguel Campground, San Miguel Island* ☎ *805/658–5730.*

Point Bennett Trail

HIKING/WALKING | Rangers conduct 15-mile hikes across San Miguel to Point Bennett, where more than 30,000 pinnipeds (three different species) can be seen. Access permit required. *Difficult.* ✉ *Trailhead: at San Miguel Campground, San Miguel Island.*

★ Prisoners Harbor/Pelican Cove Trail

HIKING/WALKING | Taking in quite a bit of Santa Cruz, this moderate to strenuous 3-mile trail one-way to Pelican Cove is one of the best hikes in the park. You must be accompanied by an Island Packers naturalist or secure a permit (visit ⊕ *www.nature.org/cruzpermit* ; allow 10 to 15 business days to process and return your application), as the hike takes you through Nature Conservancy property. *Moderate.* ✉ *Trailhead: at Prisoners Harbor, Santa Cruz Island.*

Torrey Pines Trail

HIKING/WALKING | This moderate 5-mile loop climbs up to Santa Rosa's grove of rare Torrey pines and offers stellar views of Becher's Bay and the channel.

Moderate. ✉ *Trailhead: at Santa Rosa Campground, Santa Rosa Island.*

Water Canyon Trail

HIKING/WALKING | Starting at Santa Rosa Campground, this 2-mile walk along a white-sand beach includes some exceptional beachcombing. Frequent strong winds can turn this easy hike into a fairly strenuous excursion, so be prepared. If you extend your walk into Water Canyon, you can follow animal paths to a lush canyon full of native vegetation. *Easy.* ✉ *Trailhead: at Santa Rosa Campground, Santa Rosa Island.*

KAYAKING

The most remote parts of the Channel Islands are accessible only by a sea kayak. Some of the best kayaking in the park can be found on Anacapa, Santa Barbara, and the eastern tip of Santa Cruz. Anacapa has plenty of sea caves, tidal pools, and even natural bridges you can paddle beneath. Santa Cruz has plenty of secluded beaches to explore, as well as seabird nesting sites and seal and sea lion rookeries. One of the world's largest colonies of Scripps's murrelets resides here, and brown pelicans, cormorants, and storm petrels nest in Santa Barbara's steep cliffs.

It's too far to kayak from the mainland out to the islands, but outfitters have tours that take you to the islands. Tours are offered year-round, but high seas may cause trip cancellations between December and March. ■ TIP➔ **Channel waters can be unpredictable and challenging. Don't venture out alone unless you are an experienced kayaker; guided trips are highly recommended. All kayakers should carry proper safety gear and equipment and be prepared for sudden strong winds and weather changes. Also refrain from disturbing wildlife. Visit the park website for kayaking rules and tips.**

The operators listed here hold permits from the National Park Service to conduct kayak tours; if you choose a different

Inspiration Point on Anacapa Island.

company, verify that it holds the proper permits.

Channel Islands Adventure Company
KAYAKING | Full-service outfitter Channel Islands Adventure Company (an arm of Santa Barbara Adventure Company) conducts guided kayaking and snorkeling day trips from its storefront at Scorpion Anchorage on Santa Cruz Island, plus chartered single- and multiday excursions to the Channel Islands. All trips depart from Ventura Harbor and include equipment, guides, and paddling lessons. Transportation with an Island Packers boat is an additional fee. ✉ *32 E. Haley St., Santa Barbara* ☎ *805/884–9283* ⊕ *islandkayaking.com* 🛥 *From $109 plus $59 ferry.*

WHALE-WATCHING
About a third of the world's cetacean species (27 to be exact) can be seen in the Santa Barbara Channel. In July and August, humpback and blue whales feed off the north shore of Santa Rosa. From late December through March, up to 10,000 gray whales pass through the Santa Barbara Channel on their way from Alaska to Mexico and back again, and on a whale-watching trip during this time frame, you should see one or more of them. Other types of whales, but fewer in number, swim the channel June through August.

Island Packers
WHALE-WATCHING | Depending on the season, you can take a three-hour tour or an all-day tour from either Ventura or Channel Islands harbors with Island Packers. From January through March you're almost guaranteed to see gray whales in the channel. ✉ *1691 Spinnaker Dr., Ventura* ☎ *805/642–1393* ⊕ *www. islandpackers.com* 🛥 *From $38.*

Nearby Towns

With a population of nearly 110,000, **Ventura** is the main gateway to Channel Islands National Park. It's a classic California beach town filled with interesting restaurants, a wide range of accommodations, and miles of clean, white beaches. South of Ventura is **Oxnard,** a community of 208,000 boasting a busy harbor and uncrowded beaches. Known for its Spanish ambience, **Santa Barbara** has a beautiful waterfront set against a backdrop of towering mountains—plus glistening palm-lined beaches, white-washed adobe structures with red-tile roofs, and a hip, youthful vibe in the downtown/waterfront area.

VISITOR INFORMATION Oxnard Convention & Visitors Bureau ⊠ *2775 N. Ventura Rd., Suite 204, Oxnard* ☎ *805/385–7545* ⊕ *www.visitoxnard.com.* **Ventura Visitors & Convention Bureau** ⊠ *101 S. California St., Ventura* ☎ *805/648–2075* ⊕ *www.visitventuraca.com.* **Visit Santa Barbara** ⊠ *500 E. Montecito St., Santa Barbara* ☎ *805/966–9222, 800/676–1266* ⊕ *www.santabarbaraca.com.*

 Sights

Mission San Buenaventura
HISTORIC SITE | The ninth of the 21 California missions, Mission San Buenaventura was established in 1782 and the current church was rebuilt and rededicated in 1809. A self-guided tour takes you through a small museum, a quiet courtyard, and a chapel with 250-year-old paintings. ⊠ *211 E. Main St., at Figueroa St., Ventura* ☎ *805/643–4318* ⊕ *www.sanbuenaventuramission.org* ⊠ *$5.*

★ Mission Santa Barbara
RELIGIOUS SITE | Widely referred to as the "Queen of Missions," this is one of the most beautiful and frequently photographed buildings in coastal California. Dating to 1786, the architecture evolved from adobe-brick buildings with thatch roofs to more permanent edifices as the mission's population burgeoned. An earthquake in 1812 destroyed the third church built on the site. Its replacement, the present structure, is still a functioning Catholic church. Mission Santa Barbara has a splendid Spanish/Mexican colonial art collection, as well as Chumash

sculptures and the only Native American–made altar and tabernacle left in the California missions. Docents lead 60-minute tours ($13 adult) Tuesday through Friday at 11 am, and Saturday at 10:30 am. ⊠ *2201 Laguna St., at E. Los Olivos St., Santa Barbara* ☎ *805/682–4149 gift shop, 805/682–4713 tours* ⊕ *www.santabarbaramission.org* ⊠ *$9 self-guided tour.*

★ Santa Barbara County Courthouse
GOVERNMENT BUILDING | Hand-painted tiles and a spiral staircase infuse the courthouse, a national historic landmark, with the grandeur of a Moorish palace. This magnificent building was completed in 1929. An elevator rises to an arched observation area in the tower that provides a panoramic view of the city. Before or after you take in the view, you can (if it's open) visit an engaging gallery devoted to the workings of the tower's original, still operational Seth Thomas clock. The murals in the ceremonial chambers on the courthouse's second floor were painted by an artist who did backdrops for some of Cecil B. DeMille's films. **Join a free guided tour weekdays at 10:30, daily at 2.** ⊠ *1100 Anacapa St., at E. Anapamu St., Santa Barbara* ☎ *805/962–6464* ⊕ *sbcourthouse.org.*

Santa Barbara Maritime Museum
MUSEUM | FAMILY | California's seafaring history is the focus here. High-tech, hands-on exhibits, such as a virtual sport-fishing activity that lets participants haul in a "big one" and a local surfing history retrospective, make this a fun stop for families. The museum's shining star is a rare, 17-foot-tall Fresnel lens from the historic Point Conception Lighthouse. Ride the elevator to the fourth-floor observation area for great harbor views. ⊠ *113 Harbor Way, off Shoreline Dr., Santa Barbara* ☎ *805/962–8404* ⊕ *sbmm.org* ⊠ *$8* ⊙ *Closed Wed.*

Santa Barbara Museum of Natural History
MUSEUM | FAMILY | The gigantic blue whale skeleton greets you at the entrance to this complex whose major draws include

its planetarium, space lab, and gem and mineral display. Startlingly alive-looking stuffed specimens, complete with nests and eggs, roost in the bird hall, and a room of dioramas illustrates Chumash Indian history and culture. Outdoors, nature trails wind through the serene oak-studded grounds. A Nature Pass, available at the museum and the associated Sea Center, is good for discounted admission to both facilities. ✉ *2559 Puesta del Sol Rd., off Mission Canyon Rd., Santa Barbara* ☎ *805/682–4711* 🌐 *sbnature.org* 🎟 *$12; free 3rd Sun. of month Sept.–Apr.*

Santa Barbara Museum of Natural History Sea Center

MUSEUM | FAMILY | A branch of the Santa Barbara Museum of Natural History, the Sea Center specializes in Santa Barbara Channel marine life and conservation. It's a fascinating, hands-on marine science laboratory that lets you participate in experiments, projects, and exhibits. The two-story glass walls open to stunning ocean, mountain, and city views. ✉ *211 Stearns Wharf, Santa Barbara* ☎ *805/962–2526* 🌐 *www.sbnature.org* 🎟 *$9.*

Stearns Wharf

STORE/MALL | Built in 1872, Stearns Wharf is Santa Barbara's most visited landmark. Expansive views of the mountains, cityscape, and harbor unfold from every vantage point on the three-block-long pier. Although it's a nice walk from the Cabrillo Boulevard parking areas, you can also park on the pier and then wander through the shops or stop for a meal at one of the wharf's restaurants. ✉ *Cabrillo Blvd. and State St., Santa Barbara* 🌐 *stearnswharf.org.*

★ **Ventura Oceanfront**

PROMENADE | Four miles of gorgeous coastline stretch from the county fairgrounds at the northern border of the city of San Buenaventura, through San Buenaventura State Beach, down to Ventura Harbor in the south. The main attraction here is the San Buenaventura City Pier, a landmark built in 1872 and restored in 1993. Surfers rip the waves just north of the pier, and sunbathers relax on white-sand beaches on either side. The mile-long promenade and the Omer Rains Bike Trail north of the pier attract scores of joggers, surrey cyclers, and bikers throughout the year. ✉ *California St., at ocean's edge, Ventura.*

🍴 Restaurants

IN THE PARK

Picnic Areas

RESTAURANT—SIGHT | Picnic tables are available on all the islands except San Miguel. You can also picnic on some of the beaches of Santa Cruz, Santa Rosa, and San Miguel; be aware that high winds are always a possibility on Santa Rosa and San Miguel.

OUTSIDE THE PARK

SANTA BARBARA

Brophy Bros.

$$$ | SEAFOOD | The outdoor tables at this casual harborside restaurant have perfect views of the marina and mountains. Staffers serve enormous, exceptionally fresh fish dishes and provide guests with a pager so you can stroll along the waterfront until the beep lets you know your table is ready. **Known for:** seafood salad and chowder; stellar clam bar; long wait times. [$] *Average main: $25* ✉ *119 Harbor Way, off Shoreline Dr., Santa Barbara* ☎ *805/966–4418* 🌐 *brophybros.com.*

La Super-Rica

$ | MEXICAN | This food stand on the east side of town serves some of the spiciest and most authentic Mexican dishes between Los Angeles and San Francisco. Fans (the late chef Julia Child was one) fill up on the soft tacos served with yummy spicy or mild sauces and legendary beans. **Known for:** house-made tortillas; daily specials such as chilaquiles; vegetarian and gluten-free dishes. [$] *Average main: $14* ✉ *622 N. Milpas St., at Alphonse St., Santa Barbara*

☎ 805/963–4940 💳 *No credit cards* 🕓 *Closed Tues. and Wed.*

VENTURA

Andria's Seafood

$ | **SEAFOOD** | The specialties at this casual, family-oriented restaurant in Ventura Harbor Village are fresh fish-and-chips and homemade clam chowder. After placing your order at the counter, you can sit outside on the patio and enjoy the view of the harbor and marina. **Known for:** harbor views; homemade clam chowder. [$] *Average main: $15* ✉ *1449 Spinnaker Dr., Suite A, Ventura* ☎ *805/654–0546* 🌐 *andriasseafood.com.*

Brophy Bros.

$$$ | **SEAFOOD** | The Ventura outpost of the wildly popular Santa Barbara restaurant provides the same fresh seafood-oriented meals in a spacious second-story setting overlooking the harbor. Feast on everything from fish-and-chips and crab cakes to chowder and delectable fish—often straight from the boats moored below. **Known for:** lively atmosphere; harbor views; killer clam bar. [$] *Average main: $25* ✉ *1559 Spinnaker Dr., in Ventura Harbor Village, Ventura* ☎ *805/639–0865* 🌐 *brophybros.com.*

Harbor Cove Café

$ | **CAFÉ** | Waterfront views next to Channel Islands National Park visitor center, hearty, cooked-to-order meals, and boxed picnic lunches make this casual dockside eatery a popular spot for island travelers and beach-goers. Fill up on a breakfast burrito before boarding the boat, take a boxed deli-sandwich along, and refuel with a hefty Angus burger, chowder, or fish-and-chips when you return. **Known for:** hearty breakfasts; harbor views; seafood tacos. [$] *Average main: $15* ✉ *1867 Spinnaker Dr., Ventura* ☎ *805/658–1639* 🕓 *No dinner Sun.–Thurs. in summer, no dinner rest of year.*

Lure Fish House

$$ | **SEAFOOD** | Fresh, sustainably caught seafood charbroiled over a mesquite grill, a well-stocked oyster bar, specialty cocktails, and a wine list heavy on local vintages lure diners into this slick, nautical-themed space downtown. The menu centers on the mostly local catch and organic vegetables, and includes tacos, sandwiches, and salads. **Known for:** shrimp-and-chips; cioppino; citrus crab-cake salad. [$] *Average main: $22* ✉ *60 S. California St., Ventura* ☎ *805/567–4400* 🌐 *lurefishhouse.com.*

Hotels

OUTSIDE THE PARK

OXNARD

Embassy Suites by Hilton Mandalay Beach Hotel & Resort

$$$$ | **HOTEL** | Tropical gardens, small waterfalls, and sprawling pool areas surround this Spanish-Mediterranean complex, set on 8 acres of white-sand beach north of Channel Islands Harbor. **Pros:** on the beach; family-friendly; just a mile to island boats in Channel Islands Harbor. **Cons:** 4 miles from island transportation from Ventura Harbor; fee for parking; no full kitchens. [$] *Rooms from: $289* ✉ *2101 Mandalay Beach Rd., Oxnard* ☎ *805/984–2500* 🌐 *www.embassysuitesmandalay.com* 🛏 *250 suites* 🍴 *Breakfast.*

SANTA BARBARA

★ Four Seasons Resort The Biltmore Santa Barbara

$$$$ | **RESORT** | Surrounded by lush, perfectly manicured gardens and across from the beach, Santa Barbara's grande dame has long been a favorite for quiet, California-style luxury. **Pros:** spa with 11 treatment rooms; access to members-only clubs and restaurant on-site; steps from the beach. **Cons:** back rooms are close to train tracks; expensive; several miles from downtown hub. [$] *Rooms from: $795* ✉ *1260 Channel Dr., Santa Barbara* ☎ *805/969–2261, 805/565–8299 for reservations only* 🌐 *www.fourseasons.com/santabarbara* 🛏 *207 rooms* 🍴 *No meals.*

Best Campgrounds on the Channel Islands

Camping is the best way to experience the natural beauty and isolation of Channel Islands National Park. Unrestricted by tour schedules, you have plenty of time to explore mountain trails, snorkel in the kelp forests, or kayak into sea caves. Campsites are primitive, with no water (except on Santa Rosa and Santa Cruz) or electricity. Campfires are not allowed on the islands, though you may use enclosed camp stoves. Use bear boxes for storing your food. You must carry all your gear and pack out all trash. Campers must arrange transportation to the islands before reserving a campsite (and yes, park personnel do check).

National Park Service Reservation System You can get specifics on each campground and reserve a campsite ($15 per night) by contacting the National Park Service Reservation System up to six months in advance. ☎ 877/444–6777 ⊕ www.recreation.gov.

Del Norte Campground. This remote campground on Santa Cruz offers backpackers sweeping ocean views from its 1,500-foot perch. It's accessed via a 3½-mile hike through a series of canyons and ridges. ⊠ Prisoners Harbor landing.

East Anacapa Campground. You need to walk ½ mile and ascend more than 150 steps to reach this open, treeless camping area above Cathedral Cove. ⊠ East Anacapa landing.

San Miguel Campground. Accessed by a steep, 1½-mile hike across the beach and through a lush canyon, this campground is on the site of the Lester Ranch; the Cabrillo Monument is nearby. Be aware that strong winds and thick fog are common here. ⊠ Cuyler Harbor landing.

Santa Barbara Campground. This seldom-visited campground perched on a cliff above Landing Cove is reached via a challenging ½-mile, uphill climb. ⊠ Landing Cove.

Santa Cruz Scorpion Campground. In a grove of eucalyptus trees, this campground is near the historic buildings of Scorpion Ranch. It's accessed via an easy, ½-mile, flat trail from Scorpion Beach landing. ⊠ Scorpion Beach landing.

Santa Rosa Campground. Backcountry beach camping is available on this island; it's a 1½-mile, flat walk to the campground. There's a spectacular view of Santa Cruz Island across the water and easy access to fantastic hiking trails. ⊠ Bechers Bay landing.

12

Channel Islands National Park

Hilton Santa Barbara Beachfront Resort
$$$$ | **RESORT** | A full-scale resort with seven buildings spread over 24 landscaped acres across from East Beach, the hotel was founded by the late TV actor Fess Parker, best known for playing Davy Crockett and Daniel Boone. **Pros:** numerous amenities; right across from the beach; free shuttle to train station and airport. **Cons:** train noise filters into some rooms; too spread out for some; pricey. Ⓢ Rooms from: $475 ⊠ 633 East Cabrillo Blvd., Santa Barbara ☎ 800/879–2929, 805/564–4333 ⊕ www.hiltonsantabar-barabeachfrontresort.com ⤳ 360 rooms ⦿ No meals.

Hotel Indigo

$$$ | HOTEL | The closest hotel to the train station and across the street from the Funk Zone, artsy Hotel Indigo is a fine choice for travelers who appreciate contemporary art and want easy access to dining, nightlife, and the beach. **Pros:** multilingual staff; a block from Stearns Wharf; great value for location. **Cons:** showers only (no bathtubs); train whistles early morning; rooms on small side. $ *Rooms from: $249* ✉ *121 State St., Santa Barbara* ☎ *805/966–6586* ⊕ *www.indigosantabarbara.com* ↝ *41 rooms* ❍ *No meals.*

Motel 6 Santa Barbara Beach

$$ | HOTEL | A half block from East Beach amid fancier hotels sits this basic but comfortable motel—the first Motel 6 in existence, and the first in the chain to transform into a contemporary Euro-style abode. **Pros:** very close to zoo and beach; friendly staff; clean. **Cons:** no frills; motel-style rooms; no breakfast. $ *Rooms from: $169* ✉ *443 Corona Del Mar Dr., Santa Barbara* ☎ *805/564–1392, 800/466–8356* ⊕ *motel6.com* ↝ *51 rooms* ❍ *No meals.*

★ The Ritz-Carlton Bacara, Santa Barbara

$$$$ | RESORT | A luxury resort with four restaurants and a 42,000-square-foot spa and fitness center with 36 treatment rooms, the Ritz-Carlton Bacara provides a gorgeous setting for relaxing retreats. **Pros:** serene natural setting; three zero-edge pools; three golf courses nearby. **Cons:** pricey; not close to downtown; sand on beach not pristine enough for some. $ *Rooms from: $475* ✉ *8301 Hollister Ave., Goleta* ☎ *805/968–0100* ⊕ *www.ritzcarlton.com/santabarbara* ↝ *358 rooms* ❍ *No meals.*

VENTURA

Four Points by Sheraton Ventura Harbor Resort

$$$ | RESORT | An on-site restaurant, spacious rooms, and a slew of amenities make this 17-acre property—which includes sister hotel Holiday Inn Express—a popular and practical choice for Channel Islands visitors. **Pros:** close to island transportation; quiet location; short drive to historic downtown. **Cons:** not in the heart of downtown; noisy seagulls sometimes congregate nearby; service can be spotty. $ *Rooms from: $199* ✉ *1050 Schooner Dr., Ventura* ☎ *805/658–1212, 800/368–7764* ⊕ *fourpoints.com/ventura* ↝ *106 rooms* ❍ *No meals.*

Holiday Inn Express Ventura Harbor

$$$ | HOTEL | A favorite among Channel Islands visitors, this quiet, comfortable, lodge-inspired property sits right at the Ventura Harbor entrance. **Pros:** quiet at night; easy access to harbor restaurants and activities; five-minute drive to downtown. **Cons:** busy area on weekends; complaints of erratic service; fee for parking. $ *Rooms from: $189* ✉ *1080 Navigator Dr., Ventura* ☎ *805/856–9533, 888/233–9450* ⊕ *hiexpress.com* ↝ *69 rooms* ❍ *Breakfast.*

Ventura Beach Marriott

$$$ | HOTEL | Spacious, contemporary rooms, a peaceful location just steps from San Buenaventura State Beach, and easy access to downtown arts and culture make the Marriott a popular choice. **Pros:** walk to beach and biking/jogging trails; a block from historic pier; great value for location. **Cons:** close to highway; near busy intersection. $ *Rooms from: $239* ✉ *2055 E. Harbor Blvd., Ventura* ☎ *805/643–6000, 888/236–2427* ⊕ *marriottventurabeach.com* ↝ *285 rooms* ❍ *No meals.*

CRATER LAKE NATIONAL PARK

Updated by
Andrew Collins

OREGON

WELCOME TO
CRATER LAKE NATIONAL PARK

TOP REASONS TO GO

★ **The lake:** Cruise inside the caldera basin and gaze into the extraordinary sapphire-blue water of the country's deepest lake, stopping for a ramble around Wizard Island.

★ **Native land:** Enjoy the rare luxury of interacting with totally unspoiled terrain.

★ **The night sky:** Billions of stars glisten in the pitch-black darkness of an unpolluted sky.

★ **Splendid hikes:** Accessible trails spool off the main roads and wind past colorful bursts of wildflowers and cascading waterfalls.

★ **Lake-rim lodging:** Spend the night perched on the lake rim at the rustic yet stately Crater Lake Lodge.

1 Crater Lake. The park's focal point, this scenic destination is known for its deep blue hue.

2 Wizard Island. Visitors can take boat rides to this protruding landmass rising from the western section of Crater Lake; it's a great place for hiking and picnicking.

3 Mazama Village. About 5 miles south of Rim Drive, the village is your best bet for stocking up on snacks, beverages, and fuel.

4 Cleetwood Cove Trail. The only designated trail to hike down the caldera and reach the lake's edge is on the rim's north side off Rim Drive; boat tours leave from the dock at trail's end.

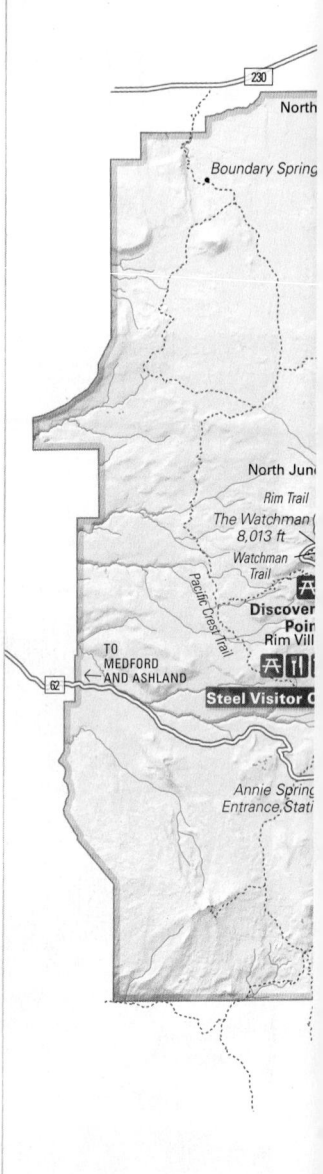

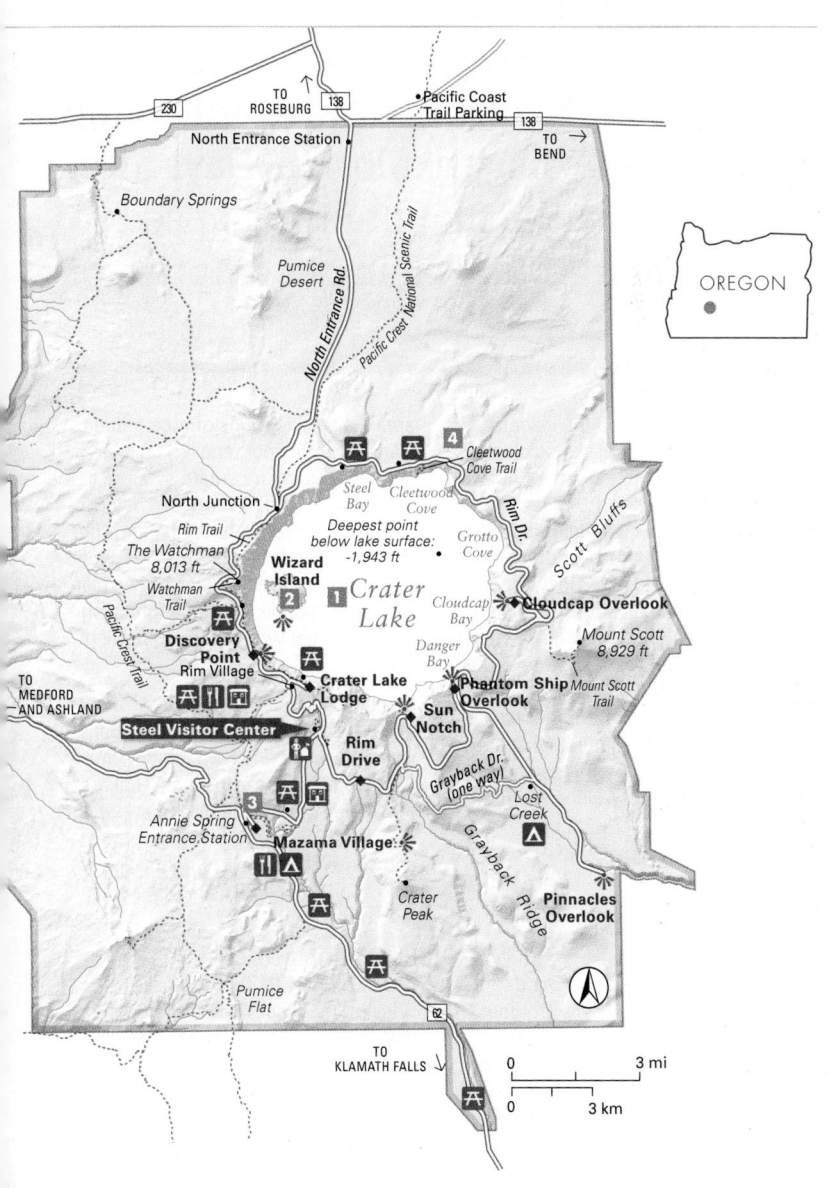

The pure, crystalline blue of Crater Lake astounds visitors at first sight. More than 5 miles wide and ringed by cliffs almost 2,000 feet high, the lake was created approximately 7,700 years ago, following Mt. Mazama's fiery explosion. Days after the eruption, the mountain collapsed on an underground chamber emptied of lava.

Rain and snowmelt filled the caldera, creating a sapphire-blue lake so clear that sunlight penetrates to a depth of 400 feet (the lake's depth is 1,943 feet). Crater Lake is both the clearest and deepest lake in the United States—and the ninth deepest in the world. For most visitors, the star attractions of Crater Lake are the lake itself and the breathtakingly situated Crater Lake Lodge. Although it takes some effort to reach it, Wizard Island is another outstanding draw. Other park highlights include the natural, unspoiled beauty of the forest and the geological marvels you can access along the Rim Drive.

Planning

WHEN TO GO

The park's high season is July and August. September and early October tend to draw smaller crowds. From October until well into June, nearly the entire park closes due to heavy snowfall. The road is kept open just from the South Entrance to the rim in winter, except during severe weather. Early summer snowmelt often creates watery breeding

areas for large groups of mosquitoes. Bring lots of insect repellent in June and July, and expect mosquito swarms in the early morning and at sunset. They can also be a problem later in the summer in campgrounds and on the Cleetwood Cove Trail, so pack repellent if you plan on camping or hiking. You might even consider a hat with mosquito netting.

FESTIVALS AND EVENTS
Oregon Shakespeare Festival
$ | FESTIVAL | More than 400,000 Bard lovers descend on charming downtown Ashland (85 miles from Crater Lake) for this nearly yearlong festival that presents works by Shakespeare and other past and contemporary playwrights. ⊠ *Ashland* ☎ *541/482–4331* ⊕ *www.osfashland.org.*

PLANNING YOUR TIME
CRATER LAKE IN ONE DAY
Begin at the **Steel Visitor Center,** a short drive from Annie Spring, the only park entrance open year-round. The center's interpretive displays and a short video describe the forces that created the lake and what makes it unique. From here, begin circling the crater's rim by heading northeast on **Rim Drive,** allowing an hour

AVERAGE HIGH/LOW TEMPERATURES					
JAN.	**FEB.**	**MAR.**	**APR.**	**MAY**	**JUNE**
34/18	35/18	37/19	42/23	50/28	58/34
JULY	**AUG.**	**SEPT.**	**OCT.**	**NOV.**	**DEC.**
68/41	69/41	63/37	52/31	40/23	34/19

to stop at overlooks—be sure to check out the Phantom Ship rock formation in the lake—before you reach the trailhead of **Cleetwood Cove Trail,** the only safe and legal way to access the lake. If you're game for a good workout, hike down the trail to reach the dock at trail's end and hop aboard a **tour boat** for a two-hour ranger-guided excursion. If you'd prefer to hike on your own, instead take the late-morning shuttle boat to **Wizard Island** for a picnic lunch and a trek to the island's summit.

Back on Rim Drive, continue around the lake, stopping at the **Watchman Trail** for a short but steep hike to this peak above the rim, which affords a splendid view of the lake and a broad vista of the surrounding southern Cascades. Wind up your visit at **Crater Lake Lodge.** Allow time to wander the lobby of this 1915 structure that perches right on the rim. Dinner at the lodge's restaurant, overlooking the lake, caps the day—reservations are strongly advised, although you can enjoy drinks, appetizers, and desserts in the Great Hall or out on the back terrace without having booked ahead.

GETTING HERE AND AROUND
Rogue Valley International–Medford Airport (MFR) is the nearest commercial airport. About 75 miles southwest of the park, it's served by Alaska, Allegiant, Delta, and United Airlines and has rental cars. Amtrak trains stop in downtown Klamath Falls, 50 miles south of the park. Car rentals are available.

Crater Lake National Park's South Entrance, open year-round, is off Highway 62 in southern Oregon. If driving here from California, follow Interstate 5 north to Medford and head east on Highway 62, or take U.S. 97 north past Klamath Falls, exiting northwest on Highway 62. From Portland, Oregon, allow from 5½ to 6 hours to reach the park's South Entrance, by taking Interstate 5 to Medford. In summer, when the North Entrance is open, the drive from Portland takes just 4½ hours via Interstate 5, Highway 58 (through Oakridge), U.S. 97, and Highway 138. If coming from Portland in summer, staying at an Oakridge, Chemult, or Diamond Lake lodging the night before your arrival will get you fairly close to the park the following morning.

Most of the park is accessible only from late June or early July through mid-October. The rest of the year, snow blocks park roadways and entrances except Highway 62 and the access road to Rim Village from Mazama Village. Rim Drive is typically closed because of snow from mid-October to mid-July, and you could encounter icy conditions at any time of year, particularly in the early morning.

PARK ESSENTIALS
ACCESSIBILITY
All the overlooks along Rim Drive are accessible to those with impaired mobility, as are Crater Lake Lodge, the facilities at Rim Village, and Steel Visitor Center. A half dozen accessible campsites are available at Mazama Campground.

PARK FEES AND PERMITS
Admission to the park is $25 per vehicle, good for seven days (the fee will increase to $30 in 2020). For all overnight trips, backcountry campers and hikers must obtain a free wilderness permit at Canfield Ranger Station, which is at the park headquarters adjacent to Steel Visitor

Center and open daily 9–5 from mid-April through early November, and 10–4 the rest of the year.

PARK HOURS

Crater Lake National Park is open 24 hours a day year-round; however, snow closes most park roadways from October to June. Lodging and dining facilities usually are open from late May to mid-October. The park is in the Pacific time zone.

CELL PHONE RECEPTION

Cell phone reception in the park is unreliable, although generally it works around Crater Lake Lodge, which—along with Mazama Village—also has public phones.

EDUCATIONAL OFFERINGS

RANGER PROGRAMS

★ **Boat Tours**

ISLAND | FAMILY | The most popular way to tour Crater Lake itself is on a two-hour ranger-led excursion aboard a 37-passenger launch. The first narrated tour leaves the dock at 9:30 am; the last departs at 3:45 pm. Four of the 10 daily boats stop at Wizard Island, where you can get off and reboard three or six hours later. Two of these trips act as shuttles, with no ranger narration. They're perfect if you just want to get to Wizard Island to hike. The shuttles leave at 8:30 and 11:30 and return to Cleetwood Cove at 12:45 and 3:35, respectively. To get to the dock you must hike down Cleetwood Cove Trail, a strenuous 1.1-mile walk that descends 700 feet in elevation along the way; only those in excellent physical shape should attempt the hike. Bring adequate water with you. Purchase boat-tour tickets at Crater Lake Lodge, Annie Creek Restaurant and gift shop, the top of the trail, and through reservations. Restrooms are available at the top and bottom of the trail. ⊠ *Crater Lake National Park* ✛ *Access Cleetwood Cove Trail off Rim Dr., 11 miles north of Rim Village* ☎ *541/594–2255, 888/774–2728 reservations* ⊕ *www.travelcraterlake.com* 🖾 *From $32.*

Junior Ranger Program

TOUR—SIGHT | FAMILY | Kids ages 6–12 learn about Crater Lake while earning a Junior Ranger patch in daily sessions during summer months at the Rim Visitor Center, and year-round they can earn a badge by completing the Junior Ranger Activity Booklet, which can be picked up at either visitor center. ☎ *541/594–3100* ⊕ *www.nps.gov/crla/learn/kidsyouth.*

TOURS

Main Street Adventure Tours

GUIDED TOURS | This Ashland-based outfitter's guided tours in southern Oregon include seven-hour ones to Crater Lake. During these tours, available year-round, participants are driven around part of the lake and, seasonally, given the chance to take a boat tour. Along the way to the park there are stops at the Cole M. Rivers Fish Hatchery, the Rogue River Gorge, and Lake of the Woods. ⊠ *Ashland* ☎ *541/625–9845* ⊕ *www.ashland-tours.com* 🖾 *From $135.*

RESTAURANTS

There are just a few casual eateries and convenience stores within the park, all near the main (southern) entrance. For fantastic upscale dining on the caldera's rim, head to the Crater Lake Lodge. Outside the park, Klamath Falls has a smattering of good restaurants, and both Medford and Ashland abound with first-rate eateries serving farm-to-table cuisine and local Rogue Valley wines. *Restaurant reviews have been shortened. For full information visit Fodors.com.*

HOTELS

Crater Lake's summer season is relatively brief, and Crater Lake Lodge, the park's main accommodation, is generally booked up a year in advance. If you are unable to get a reservation, check availability as your trip approaches—cancellations do happen on occasion. The other in-park option, the Cabins at Mazama Village, also books up early in summer. Outside the park there are a couple of options in nearby Prospect as well as

Fort Klamath, and Union Creek, and you'll find numerous lodgings a bit farther afield in Klamath Falls, Medford, Ashland, and Roseburg. Additionally, if visiting the park via the North Entrance in summer, you might consider staying in one of the handful of lodgings in Diamond Lake, Oakridge, and Chemult. Even Bend is an option, as it's just a two-hour drive from North Entrance, which is only slightly longer than the drive from Ashland to the main entrance. *Hotel reviews have been shortened. For full information, visit Fodors.com.*

What It Costs			
$	$$	$$$	$$$$
RESTAURANTS			
under $12	$12–$20	$21–$30	over $30
HOTELS			
under $100	$100–$150	$151–$200	over $200

VISITOR INFORMATION

PARK CONTACT INFORMATION Crater Lake National Park ☎ *541/594–3000* ⊕ *www.nps.gov/crla.*

PARK LITERATURE AND INFORMATION Crater Lake Natural History Association ☎ *541/594–3111* ⊕ *www.craterlakeoregon.org.*

VISITOR CENTERS
Rim Visitor Center

INFO CENTER | In summer you can obtain park information at the center, introduce your kids to a number of Junior Ranger activities or stop into the nearby Sinnott Memorial Overlook, which has a small museum and a 900-foot view down to the lake's surface as well as ranger talks three times per day. In winter, snowshoe walks are offered on weekends and holidays. A short walk away, the Rim Village Gift Store and cafeteria are the only services open in winter. ⊠ *Rim Dr.* ⊹ *7 miles north of Annie Spring entrance*

station ☎ *541/594–3000* ⊕ *www.nps.gov/crla.*

Steel Visitor Center

INFO CENTER | Open year-round, the center, part of the park's headquarters, has restrooms, a small post office, and a shop that sells books, maps, and postcards. There are fewer exhibits than at comparable national park visitor centers, but you can view an engaging 22-minute film, *Crater Lake: Into the Deep,* which describes the lake's formation and geology and examines the area's cultural history. ⊠ *Rim Dr.* ⊹ *4 miles north of Annie Spring entrance station* ☎ *541/594–3000* ⊕ *www.nps.gov/crla.*

 ## Sights

SCENIC DRIVES
★ **Rim Drive**

SCENIC DRIVE | Take this 33-mile scenic loop for views of the lake and its cliffs from every conceivable angle. The drive takes two hours not counting frequent stops at overlooks and short hikes that can easily stretch this to a half day. Rim Drive is typically closed due to heavy snowfall from mid-October to mid-June, and icy conditions can be encountered any month of the year, particularly in early morning. ⊠ *Crater Lake National Park* ⊹ *Drive begins at Rim Village, 7 miles from (Annie Spring) South Entrance; from North Entrance, follow North Entrance Rd. south for 10 miles* ⊕ *www.nps.gov/crla.*

HISTORIC SITES
★ **Crater Lake Lodge**

HOTEL—SIGHT | Built in 1915, this regal log-and-stone structure was designed in the classic style of Western national park lodges, and the original lodgepole-pine pillars, beams, and stone fireplaces are still intact. The lobby, fondly referred to as the Great Hall, serves as a warm, welcoming gathering place where you can play games, socialize with a cocktail, or gaze out of the many windows to view spectacular sunrises and sunsets by a crackling fire. Exhibits off the lobby contain historic photographs and memorabilia from throughout the park's history. ⊠ *Rim Village* ⊕ *www.craterlakelodges. com.*

SCENIC STOPS
Cloudcap Overlook
VIEWPOINT | The highest road-access overlook on the Crater Lake rim, Cloudcap has a westward view across the lake to Wizard Island and an eastward view of Mt. Scott, the volcanic cone that is the park's highest point. ⊠ *Crater Lake National Park* ⊹ *2 miles off Rim Dr., 13 miles northeast of Steel Visitor Center.*

Discovery Point
VIEWPOINT | This overlook marks the spot at which prospectors first spied the lake in 1853. Wizard Island is just northeast, close to shore. ⊠ *West Rim Dr.* ⊹ *1½ miles north of Rim Village.*

Mazama Village
INFO CENTER | In summer, a campground, cabin-style motel, restaurant, gift shop, amphitheater, and gas station are open here. No gasoline is available in the park from mid-October to mid-May. Snowfall determines when the village and its facilities open and close for the season. Hours vary; call ahead. ⊠ *Mazama Village Rd.* ⊹ *Off Hwy. 62, near Annie Spring entrance station* ☏ *541/594–2255, 888/774–2728* ⊕ *www.craterlakelodges. com.*

Phantom Ship Overlook
VIEWPOINT | From this point you can get a close look at Phantom Ship, a rock formation that resembles a schooner with furled masts and looks ghostly in fog. ⊠ *East Rim Dr.* ⊹ *7 miles northeast of Steel Visitor Center.*

★ Pinnacles Overlook
VIEWPOINT | Ascending from the banks of Sand and Wheeler creeks, unearthly spires of eroded ash resemble the peaks of fairy-tale castles. Once upon a time, the road continued east to a former

entrance. A path now replaces the old road and follows the rim of Sand Creek (affording more views of pinnacles) to where the entrance sign still stands. ⊠ *Pinnacles Rd.* ⊹ *12 miles east of Steel Visitor Center.*

Sun Notch
VIEWPOINT | It's a relatively easy ½-mile loop hike through wildflowers and dry meadow to this overlook, which has views of Crater Lake and Phantom Ship. Mind the cliff edges. ⊠ *East Rim Dr.* ⊹ *About 4½ miles east of Steel Visitor Center.*

★ Wizard Island
ISLAND | The volcanic eruption that led to the creation of Crater Lake resulted in the formation of this magical island a quarter mile from the lake's western shore. The views at its summit—reached on a somewhat strenuous 2-mile hike—are stupendous.

Getting to the island requires a strenuous 1-mile hike down (and later back up) the steep Cleetwood Cove Trail to the cove's dock. There, board either the shuttle boat to Wizard Island or a Crater Lake narrated tour boat that includes a stop on the island. If you opt for the latter, you can explore Wizard Island a bit and reboard a later boat to resume the lake tour.

The hike to Wizard Summit, 763 feet above the lake's surface, begins at the island's boat dock and steeply ascends over rock-strewn terrain; a path at the top circles the 90-foot-deep crater's rim. More moderate is the 1¾-mile hike on a rocky trail along the shore of Wizard Island, so called because William Steel, an early Crater Lake booster, thought its shape resembled a wizard's hat. ⊠ *Crater Lake National Park* ⊹ *Access Cleetwood Cove Trail off Rim Dr., 11 miles north of Rim Village* ☏ *541/594–2255, 888/774–2728* ⊕ *www.travelcraterlake.com* ⌑ *Shuttle boat $32, tour boat $57.*

Wildlife in Crater Lake

Wildlife in the Crater Lake area flourishes in the water and throughout the surrounding forest.

Salmon and Trout

Two primary types of fish swim beneath the surface of Crater Lake: kokanee salmon and rainbow trout. Kokanees average about 8 inches in length, but they can grow to nearly 18 inches. Rainbow trout are larger than the kokanee but are less abundant in Crater Lake. Trout—including bull, Eastern brook, rainbow, and German brown—swim in the park's many streams and rivers.

Elk, Deer, and More

Remote canyons shelter the park's elk and deer populations, which can sometimes be seen at dusk and dawn feeding at forest's edge. Black bears and pine martens—cousins of the short-tailed weasel—also call Crater Lake home. Birds such as hairy woodpeckers, California gulls, red-tailed hawks, and great horned owls are more commonly seen in summer in forests below the lake.

Activities

FISHING

Fishing is allowed in the lake, but you may find the experience frustrating—in such a massive body of water, the problem is finding the fish. Try your luck near the Cleetwood Cove boat dock, or take poles on the boat tour and fish off Wizard Island. Rainbow trout and kokanee salmon lurk in Crater Lake's aquamarine depths, and some grow to enormous sizes. You don't need a state fishing license, but to protect the lake's pristine waters, the park service prohibits the use of worms, fish eggs, or any other organic bait; only artificial lures are permitted. Private boats are prohibited on the lake.

HIKING

Annie Creek Canyon Trail

HIKING/WALKING | This somewhat challenging 1½-mile hike loops through a deep stream-cut canyon, providing views of the narrow cleft scarred by volcanic activity. This is a good area to look for flowers and deer. *Moderate.* ⊠ *Mazama Campground, Mazama Village Rd.* ⊹ *Trailhead: behind amphitheater between D and E campground loops.*

Boundary Springs Trail

HIKING/WALKING | If you feel like sleuthing, take this moderate 5-mile round-trip hike to the headwaters of the Rogue River. The trail isn't well marked, so a detailed trail guide is necessary. You'll see streams, forests, and wildflowers along the way before discovering Boundary Springs pouring out of the side of a low ridge. *Moderate.* ⊠ *Crater Lake National Park* ⊹ *Trailhead: pullout on Hwy. 230, near milepost 19, about 5 miles west of Hwy. 138.*

★ Castle Crest Wildflower Trail

HIKING/WALKING | This picturesque 1-mile round-trip trek passes through a spring-fed meadow and one of the park's flatter hikes. Wildflowers burst into full bloom here in July. You can also access Castle Crest via a similarly easy half-mile loop trail from East Rim Drive. *Easy.* ⊠ *Crater Lake National Park* ⊹ *Trailhead: either East Rim Dr. or across road from Steel Visitor Center parking lot.*

Cleetwood Cove Trail

HIKING/WALKING | This strenuous 2¼-mile round-trip hike descends 700 feet down nearly vertical cliffs along the lake to the boat dock. Be in very good shape before you tackle this well-maintained trail—it's the hike back up that catches some visitors unprepared. Bring along plenty of water. *Difficult.* ✉ *Crater Lake National Park* ✛ *Trailhead: on Rim Dr., 11 miles north of Rim Village.*

Godfrey Glen Trail

HIKING/WALKING | This 1-mile loop trail is an easy stroll through an old-growth forest with canyon views. Its dirt path is accessible to wheelchairs with assistance. *Easy.* ✉ *Crater Lake National Park* ✛ *Trailhead: Mission Valley Rd., 2½ miles south of Steel Visitor Center.*

Pacific Crest Trail

HIKING/WALKING | You can hike a portion of the Pacific Crest Trail, which extends from Mexico to Canada and winds through the park for 33 miles. For this prime backcountry experience, catch the trail off Highway 138 about a mile east of the North Entrance, where it heads south and then toward the west rim of the lake and circles it for about 6 miles, then descends down Dutton Creek to the Mazama Village area. You'll need a detailed map for this hike; check online or with the PCT association. *Difficult.* ✉ *Crater Lake National Park* ✛ *Trailhead: at Pacific Crest Trail parking lot, off Hwy. 138, 1 mile east of North Entrance* ⊕ *www.pcta.org.*

★ Mt. Scott Trail

HIKING/WALKING | This strenuous 4½-mile round-trip trail takes you to the park's highest point—the top of Mt. Scott, the oldest volcanic cone of Mt. Mazama, at 8,929 feet. The average hiker needs 90 minutes to make the steep uphill trek—and about 60 minutes to get down. The trail starts at an elevation of about 7,679 feet, so the climb is not extreme, but the trail is steep in spots. The views of the lake and the broad Klamath Basin are spectacular. *Difficult.* ✉ *Crater Lake National Park* ✛ *Trailhead: 14 miles east of Steel Visitor Center on Rim Dr., across from road to Cloudcap Overlook.*

★ Watchman Peak Trail

HIKING/WALKING | This is one of the park's best and most easily accessed hikes. Though it's just more than 1½ miles round-trip, the trail climbs more than 400 feet—not counting the steps up to the actual lookout, which has great views of Wizard Island and the lake. *Moderate.* ✉ *Crater Lake National Park* ✛ *Trailhead: at Watchman Overlook, Rim Dr., about 4 miles northwest of Rim Village.*

SKIING

There are no maintained ski trails in the park, although some backcountry trails are marked with blue diamonds or snow poles. Most cross-country skiers park at Rim Village and follow a portion of West Rim Drive toward Wizard Island Overlook (4 miles). The road is plowed to Rim Village, but it can be closed temporarily due to severe storms. Snow tires and chains are essential. Visit ⊕ *www.nps.gov/crla* for a list of additional trails and their length and difficulty.

SWIMMING

Swimming is allowed in the lake, but is at your own risk (there are no lifeguards), and it's generally popular only on hot days and among the hardiest of souls. Made up entirely of snowmelt and rainfall, Crater Lake is very cold—about 45°F to 56°F in summer. The lagoons on Wizard Island and at Cleetwood Cove are your only real choices—but swimming is only advisable when the air temperature rises above 80°F, which is relatively rare.

Nearby Towns

Klamath Falls and Ashland, both south of the park, and Roseburg, to the west, are the three main gateways to Crater Lake National Park. Other practical bases include Medford, 10 miles from Ashland, and (in summer, when Crater Lake's North Entrance is open), the city of Bend, a 2- to 2½-hour drive north. **Klamath Falls** is about an hour's drive from the park. Klamath Lake, the largest freshwater lake in Oregon, is just north of the city, and its acres of parks and marinas provide endless opportunities to enjoy water sports and bird-watching. **Ashland,** one of Oregon's premier arts and recreational destinations, is set in the foothills of the Siskiyou Mountains. One of the city's chief appeals is its famed Oregon Shakespeare Festival. Ashland has fine small inns, shops, and restaurants, and the increasingly acclaimed Rogue Valley wine country is nearby. Crater Lake is about a two-hour drive away. **Roseburg's** location at the western edge of the southern Cascades led to its status as a timber-industry center—still the heart of the town's economy—but its setting along the Umpqua River has drawn fishermen for years. The drive from Roseburg to Crater Lake's North Entrance takes about two hours.

VISITOR INFORMATION Ashland Chamber of Commerce ⊠ *110 E. Main St., Ashland* ☎ *541/482–3486* ⊕ *www.ashlandcham-ber.com.* **Meet Me In Klamath** ⊠ *205 Riverside Dr., Klamath Falls* ☎ *541/882–1501, 800/445–6728* ⊕ *www.discoverklamath. com.* **Roseburg Area Visitors Center** ⊠ *410 S.E. Spruce St., Roseburg* ☎ *541/672–9731, 800/440–9584* ⊕ *www.visitrose-burg.com.*

 Sights

★ **Klamath Basin National Wildlife Refuge Complex**
NATURE PRESERVE | As many as 500 bald eagles make Klamath Basin their rest stop, amounting to the largest wintering concentration of these birds in the contiguous United States. Located along the Pacific Flyway bird migration route, the nearly 40,000 acres of freshwater wetlands in this complex of six different refuges serve as a stopover for nearly 1 million waterfowl in the fall. Any time of year is bird-watching season; more than 400 species of birds—including about 30 types of raptors—have been spotted in the Klamath Basin, along with many

mammals, reptiles, and amphibians. For a leisurely excursion by car, follow the tour routes in the Lower Klamath and Tule Lake refuges—the latter has a superb bookstore and visitor center and is also a short drive from Lava Beds National Monument. ⊠ *Tule Lake Refuge Visitor Center, 4009 Hill Rd., Tulelake* ✛ *27 miles south of Klamath Falls via Hwy. 39* ☎ *530/667–2231* ⊕ *www.fws.gov/refuge/ tule_lake* ☞ *Free.*

Lava Beds National Monument
NATIONAL/STATE PARK | About midway between Crater Lake and Lassen Volcanic national parks, this 47,000-acre tract of lava beds is a popular stop among travelers taking the scenic route between these two parks. The lava beds are just down the road from the Tule Lake and Lower Klamath national wildlife refuges. Many of the top attractions at Lava Beds are underground lava tubes created 32,000 years ago during the eruptions of Mammoth Crater. You can buy lamps and hard hats in the visitor center to tour these fascinating, bat-filled caves. The park has miles of hiking trails above ground as well. ⊠ *1 Indian Well, off Hill Rd., Tulelake* ✛ *45 miles south of Klamath Falls via Hwy. 39* ☎ *530/667–8113* ⊕ *www.nps.gov/labe* ☞ *$20.*

★ **Oregon Caves National Monument**
CAVE | Marble caves, large calcite formations, and huge underground rooms shape this rare adventure in geology. Guided cave tours take place on the hour in late spring and fall, and every half hour in June, July, and August. The 90-minute half-mile tour is moderately strenuous, with low passageways, twisting turns, and more than 500 stairs; children must be at least 42 inches tall to participate. Cave tours aren't given in winter. Above ground, the surrounding valley holds an old-growth forest with some of the state's largest trees. **GPS coordinates for the caves often direct drivers onto a mostly unpaved forest service road meant for four-wheel-drive vehicles. Instead, follow**

well-signed Highway 46 off U.S. 199 at Cave Junction, which is also narrow and twisting in parts; RVs or trailers more than 32 feet long are not advised. ⊠ *19000 Caves Hwy. (Hwy. 46), 20 miles east of U.S. 199, 140 miles southwest of Crater Lake, Cave Junction* ☎ *541/592–2100* ⊕ *www.nps. gov/orca* ⊠ *Park free, tours $10.*

🍴 Restaurants

IN THE PARK
Annie Creek Restaurant
$$ | AMERICAN | FAMILY | This family-friendly dining spot in Mazama Village serves hearty if unmemorable comfort fare, and service can be hit or miss. Blue cheese–bacon burgers, Cobb salads, sandwiches, pizzas, lasagna, and a tofu stir-fry are all on the menu. **Known for:** large portions; convenient to lake and the park's southern hiking trails; several varieties of burgers. $ *Average main: $13* ⊠ *Mazama Village Rd. and Ave. C, near Annie Spring entrance station* ☎ *541/594–2255* ⊕ *www.craterlakelodges.com* ☉ *Closed late Sept.–late May.*

★ Crater Lake Lodge Dining Room
$$$$ | PACIFIC NORTHWEST | The only sophisticated dining option inside the park, the dining room is magnificent, with a large stone fireplace and views of Crater Lake's clear-blue waters. Breakfast and lunch are enjoyable here, but the dinner is the main attraction, with tempting dishes that emphasize local produce and Pacific Northwest seafood—think crostini topped with wild Oregon mushrooms and pan-seared rockfish with seasonal veggies. **Known for:** nice selection of Oregon wines; rustic and historic atmosphere; views of the lake. $ *Average main: $34* ⊠ *Crater Lake Lodge, 1 Lodge Loop Rd.* ☎ *541/594–2255* ⊕ *www.craterlakelodges.com* ☉ *Closed mid-Oct.–mid-May.*

PICNIC AREAS
Godfrey Glen Trail
RESTAURANT—SIGHT | In a small canyon abuzz with songbirds, squirrels, and chipmunks, this picnic area has a south-facing, protected location. The half dozen picnic tables here are in a small meadow; there are also a few fire grills and a pit toilet. ⊠ *Crater Lake National Park* ✛ *2½ miles south of Steel Visitor Center.*

Rim Drive
RESTAURANT—SIGHT | About a half dozen picnic-area turnouts encircle the lake; all have good views, but they can get very windy. Most have pit toilets, and a few have fire grills, but none have running water. ⊠ *Rim Dr.*

★ Rim Village
RESTAURANT—SIGHT | This is the only park picnic area with running water. The tables are set behind the visitor center, and most have a view of the lake below. There are flush toilets inside the visitor center. ⊠ *Rim Dr., Rim Village* ✛ *By Crater Lake Lodge.*

★ Wizard Island
RESTAURANT—SIGHT | The park's best picnic venue is on Wizard Island; pack a lunch and book yourself on one of the early-morning boat tour departures, reserving space on an afternoon return. There are no formal picnic areas and just pit toilets, but you'll discover plenty of sunny and shaded spots where you can enjoy a quiet meal and appreciate the astounding scene that surrounds you. The island is accessible by boat only. ⊠ *Crater Lake* ✛ *Boat dock at end of Cleetwood Cove Trail, off Rim Dr., 11 miles north of Rim Village* ⊕ *www.travelcraterlake.com.*

OUTSIDE THE PARK
Beckie's Cafe
$ | AMERICAN | FAMILY | You can get breakfast, lunch, or dinner at this rustic roadhouse diner 15 miles west of Crater Lake's southern entrance, but no one will fault you for skipping your vegetables and going straight for the dessert. Since

Best Campgrounds in Crater Lake

Tent campers and RV enthusiasts alike enjoy the heavily wooded and well-equipped setting of Mazama Campground. Lost Creek is much smaller, with minimal amenities and a more "rustic" Crater Lake experience. Pack bug repellent and patience if camping in the snowmelt season.

Lost Creek Campground. The 16 small, remote tent sites here are usually available on a daily basis; in summer arrive early to secure a spot (it's open early July–mid-October). The cost is $5 nightly. ✉ *3 miles south of Rim Rd. on Pinnacles Spur Rd. at Grayback Dr.* ☎ *541/594–3100.*

Mazama Campground. This campground is set well below the lake caldera in the pine and fir forest of the Cascades not far from the main access road (Highway 62). Drinking water, showers, and laundry facilities help ensure that you don't have to rough it too much. About half the 214 spaces are pull-throughs, some with electricity and a few with hookups. The best tent spots are on some of the outer loops above Annie Creek Canyon. Tent sites cost $23, RV ones $32. ✉ *Mazama Village, near Annie Spring entrance station* ☎ *541/594–2255, 888/774–2728* 🌐 *www.craterlakelodges.com.*

1926, Beckie's homemade pies have been a must-have treat for travelers on their way to or from the park. **Known for:** fresh-baked fruit pies; hearty breakfasts; barbecue wagon on summer weekends. [$] *Average main: $12* ✉ *Union Creek Resort, 56484 Hwy. 62, Prospect* ☎ *541/560–3563* 🌐 *www.unioncreekoregon.com/beckies-cafe.*

Gathering Grounds Cafe
$ | **CAFÉ** | Although this bustling coffeehouse with comfortable seating and exposed-brick walls is a hot spot for espresso drinks made from house-roasted coffee beans, it's also a great option for grabbing healthful, flavorful picnic items. Fresh-fruit parfaits and croissant and English muffin sandwiches are popular for breakfast. **Known for:** delicious panini sandwiches at breakfast and lunch; best coffee in town, roasted in-house; comfy armchairs. [$] *Average main: $9* ✉ *116 S. 11th St., Klamath Falls* ☎ *541/887–8403* 🌐 *www.gatheringgroundscafe.com* 🕓 *Closed Sun. No dinner.*

★ Morning Glory
$$ | **AMERICAN** | Breakfast reaches new heights in an eclectically furnished, blue Craftsman-style bungalow across the street from Southern Oregon University. The extraordinarily good food emphasizes breakfast fare—omelets filled with crab, artichokes, Parmesan, and smoked-garlic cream; Tandoori tofu scrambles with cherry-cranberry chutney; lemon-poppy waffles with seasonal berries; and cranberry-hazelnut French toast with lemon butter. **Known for:** large portions; long lines; crab omelet and crab melt. [$] *Average main: $13* ✉ *1149 Siskiyou Blvd., Ashland* ☎ *541/488-8636.*

Hotels

IN THE PARK

The Cabins at Mazama Village
$$$ | **HOTEL** | In a wooded area 7 miles south of the lake, this complex is made up of several A-frame buildings and has modest rooms with two queen beds and a private bath. **Pros:** clean and well-kept facility; very close to the lake and plenty of hiking trails; most affordable of the

park lodgings. **Cons:** lots of traffic into adjacent campground; no TVs or phones in rooms; not actually on Crater Lake (but a short drive away). [$] *Rooms from: $165* ✉ *Mazama Village* ⊕ *Near Annie Spring entrance station* ☎ *541/594–2255, 888/774–2728* 🌐 *www.craterlakelodges.com* ⏲ *Closed mid-Oct.–late May* 🛏 *40 rooms* 🍴 *No meals.*

★ Crater Lake Lodge
$$$$ | **HOTEL** | The period feel of this 1915 lodge on the caldera's rim is reflected in its lodgepole-pine columns, gleaming wood floors, and stone fireplaces in the common areas, and the simple guest rooms. **Pros:** ideal location for watching sunrise and sunset reflected on the lake; exudes rustic charm; excellent restaurant. **Cons:** books up far in advance; rooms are small and have tubs only, no shower; no air-conditioning. [$] *Rooms from: $201* ✉ *1 Lodge Loop Rd.* ⊕ *Rim Village, east of Rim Visitor Center* ☎ *541/594–2255, 888/774–2728* 🌐 *www.craterlakelodges.com* ⏲ *Closed mid-Oct.–mid-May* 🛏 *71 rooms* 🍴 *No meals.*

OUTSIDE THE PARK

Prospect Historic Hotel Bed and Breakfast
$$$ | **B&B/INN** | The likes of Theodore Roosevelt, Zane Grey, Jack London, and William Jennings Bryan have stayed here at this quaint, country-style bed-and-breakfast that's just 39 miles southwest of the park entrance on Highway 62. **Pros:** three waterfalls within walking distance; large property with beautiful grounds and creek; one of the nearest lodgings to the park. **Cons:** small, remote town; breakfast is not included for guests staying in motel units; rooms in motel units lack charm of those in main inn. [$] *Rooms from: $160* ✉ *391 Mill Creek Dr., Prospect* ☎ *541/560–3664, 800/944–6490* 🌐 *www.prospecthotel.com* 🛏 *10 main house rooms, 14 motel rooms* 🍴 *Breakfast.*

Running Y Ranch Resort
$$$ | **RESORT** | **FAMILY** | Golfers rave about the Arnold Palmer–designed course at this 3,600-acre resort in a juniper-and-ponderosa–shaded canyon overlooking Upper Klamath Lake. **Pros:** indoor pool; 8 miles of paved trails; spacious, modern rooms. **Cons:** may be too far off the beaten path for some; pricey in summer; sometimes fills up with meetings and conventions. [$] *Rooms from: $179* ✉ *5500 Running Y Rd., 8 miles north of Klamath Falls, Klamath Falls* ☎ *541/850–5500* 🌐 *www.runningy.com* 🛏 *125 units* 🍴 *No meals.*

★ Winchester Inn
$$$$ | **B&B/INN** | You'll find understated elegance and exquisitely comfortable down bedding in this inn's rooms and suites. **Pros:** beautiful tiered gardens; acclaimed restaurant; cushy rooms. **Cons:** not a good choice for small children; about a two-hour drive to Crater Lake; downtown location is handy but not especially serene. [$] *Rooms from: $255* ✉ *35 S. 2nd St., Ashland* ☎ *541/488–1113, 800/972–4991* 🌐 *www.winchesterinn.com* 🛏 *19 rooms* 🍴 *Breakfast.*

Chapter 14

DEATH VALLEY
NATIONAL PARK

Updated by
Deb Hopewell

CALIFORNIA

WELCOME TO DEATH VALLEY NATIONAL PARK

TOP REASONS TO GO

★ **Roving rocks:** Death Valley's Racetrack is home to moving boulders, an unexplained phenomenon that has scientists baffled.

★ **Lowest spot on the continent:** Stand on the lowest spot on the continent at Badwater, 282 feet below sea level.

★ **Wildflower explosion:** During the spring, this desert landscape is ablaze with greenery and colorful flowers, especially between Badwater and Ashford Mill.

★ **Ghost towns:** Death Valley is renowned for its Wild West heritage and is home to dozens of crumbling settlements including Ballarat, Cerro Gordo, Chloride City, Greenwater, Harrisburg, Keeler, Leadfield, Panamint City, Rhyolite, and Skidoo.

★ **Naturally amazing:** From canyons to sand dunes to salt flats and dry lake beds, Death Valley serves up plenty of geological treasures.

1 Central Death Valley. Furnace Creek sits in the heart of Death Valley—if you have only a short time in the park, head here. You can visit gorgeous Golden Canyon, Zabriskie Point, the Salt Creek Interpretive Trail, and Artist's Drive, among other popular points of interest.

2 Northern Death Valley. This region is uphill from Furnace Creek, which means marginally cooler temperatures. Be sure to stop by Rhyolite Ghost Town on Highway 374 before entering the park and exploring colorful Titus Canyon, and jaw-dropping Ubehebe Crater.

3 Southern Death Valley. This is a desolate area, but there are plenty of sights that help convey Death Valley's rich history. Don't miss the Dublin Gulch Caves.

4 Western Death Valley. Panamint Springs Resort is a nice place to grab a meal and get your bearings before moving on to quaint Darwin Falls, smooth rolling sand dunes, beehive-shaped Wildrose Charcoal Kilns, and historic Stovepipe Wells Village.

257

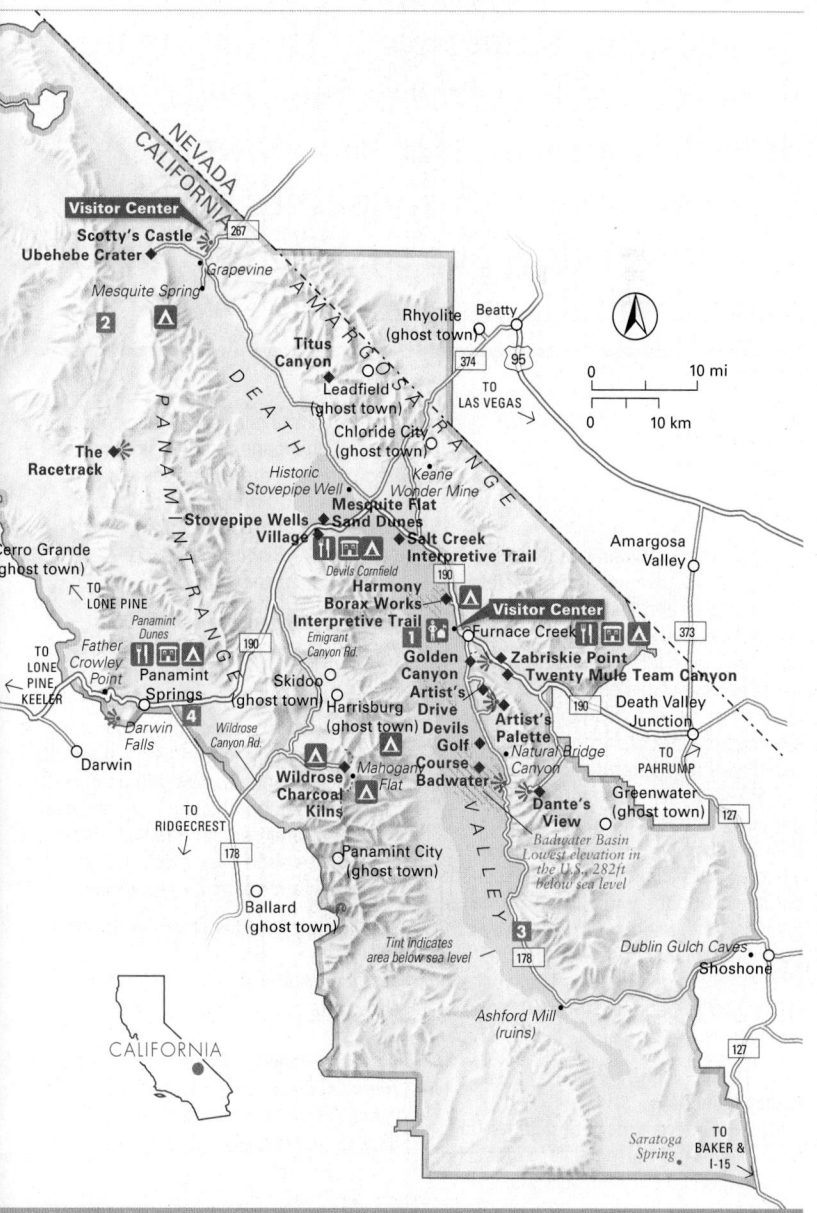

The natural riches of Death Valley—the largest national park outside Alaska—are overwhelming: rolling waves of sand dunes, black cinder cones thrusting up hundreds of feet from a blistered desert floor, riotous sheets of wildflowers, bizarrely shaped Joshua trees basking in the orange glow of a sunset, tiny pupfish, and a dramatic silence.

Planning

WHEN TO GO

Most of the park's one million annual visitors come between late fall and early spring, taking advantage of moderate temperatures and the lack of rainfall. During these cooler months you will need to book a room in advance, but don't worry: the park never feels crowded. If you visit in summer, believe everything you've ever heard about desert heat—it can be brutal, with temperatures often topping 120°F. The dry air wicks moisture from the body without causing a sweat, so drink plenty of water. Bring sunglasses, a hat, and sufficient clothing to block the sun's rays and the wind. Flash floods are fairly common; sections of roadway can be flooded or washed away, as they were after a major flood in 2015. The wettest month is February, when the park receives an average of 0.3 inches of rain.

FESTIVALS AND EVENTS

Bishop Mule Days

FESTIVAL | Entertainment at this five-day festival over the Memorial Day weekend includes top country-music stars, an arts-and-crafts fair, barbecues, country dances, the longest-running nonmotorized parade in the United States, and more than 700 mules competing in 181 events. Admission is free. ⊠ *1141 N. Main St., Bishop* ☎ *760/872–4263* ⊕ *www.muledays.org.*

Death Valley 49er Encampment Days

FESTIVAL | FAMILY | Originally a centennial celebration held in 1949 to honor the area's first European visitors, this five-day event draws thousands of people from around the world to the Ranch at Death Valley for art shows, a wagon train, live music, artisan booths, dancing, and even a poker tournament. ⊠ *Ranch at Death Valley, Greenland Ranch Road, Death Valley* ⊕ *www.deathvalley49ers.org.*

Death Valley Chamber of Commerce Art Show

FESTIVAL | Admission is free for this arts-and-crafts show and sale weekend, held on the lawn of The Ranch at Death Valley (formerly Ranch at Furnace Creek). ⊠ *The Ranch at Death Valley, Greenland Ranch Road, Death Valley* ☎ *760/852–4420* ⊕ *www.deathvalleychamber.org.*

AVERAGE HIGH/LOW TEMPERATURES					
JAN.	FEB.	MAR.	APR.	MAY	JUNE
65/39	72/46	80/53	90/62	99/71	109/80
JULY	AUG.	SEPT.	OCT.	NOV.	DEC.
115/88	113/85	106/75	92/62	76/48	65/39

Lone Pine Film Festival

FESTIVAL | Every Columbus Day weekend, this town pays tribute to its Hollywood history with three days of tours, films, lectures, and celebrity panels. ✉ *701 S. Main St., Lone Pine* ☎ *760/876–9103* ⊕ *www.lonepinefilmfestival.org.*

Shoshone Old West Days

FESTIVAL | Just outside of Death Valley, this annual three-day festival celebrates Wild West heritage with live performances, arts-and-crafts, and deep-pit barbecue. ✉ *Shoshone* ☎ *760/852–4335* ⊕ *www.shoshonevillage.com.*

PLANNING YOUR TIME

DEATH VALLEY IN ONE DAY

If you begin the day in Furnace Creek, you can see several sights without doing much driving. Bring plenty of water with you, and some food, too. Get up early and drive the 20 miles on Badwater Road to **Badwater,** which looks out on the lowest point in the Western Hemisphere and is a dramatic place to watch the sunrise. Returning north, stop at **Natural Bridge,** a medium-size conglomerate rock formation that has been hollowed at its base to form a span across the canyon, and then at the **Devil's Golf Course,** so named because of the large pinnacles of salt present here. Detour to the right onto **Artist's Drive,** a 9-mile one-way, northbound route that passes **Artist's Palette.** The reds, yellows, oranges, and greens come from minerals in the rocks and the earth. Four miles north of Artist's Drive you will come to the **Golden Canyon Interpretive Trail,** a 2-mile round-trip that winds through a canyon with colorful rock walls. Just before Furnace Creek, take Highway 190 3 miles east to **Zabriskie Point,** overlooking dramatic, furrowed red-brown hills and the **Twenty Mule Team Canyon.** Return to Furnace Creek, where you can grab a meal and visit the museum at the Furnace Creek Visitor Center. Heading north from Furnace Creek, pull off the highway and take a look at the **Harmony Borax Works.**

GETTING HERE AND AROUND

AIR TRAVEL

The closest airport to the park with commercial service, Las Vegas McCarren International Airport, is 130 miles away, so you'll still need to drive a couple of hours to reach the park. Roughly 160 miles to the west, Burbank's Bob Hope Airport is the second-closest airport.

CAR TRAVEL

It can take more than three hours to cross from one side of the park to another, so it's important to choose an entrance point that makes sense for what you want to see. If you're driving from Los Angeles, enter through the western portion along Highway 395; if you're coming from Las Vegas, enter from the north at Beatty, Nevada, or via the central entrance at Death Valley Junction. Travelers from Orange County, San Diego, and the Inland Empire should access the park via Interstate 15 North at Baker.

Distances can be deceiving within the park: what seems close can be very far away. Much of the park can be viewed on regularly scheduled bus tours, but these often don't allow time for hikes to sites not seen from the road, such as Salt Creek, Golden Canyon, and Natural Bridge. The best option is to drive to a number of the sites, get out of the car, and walk.

When driving in Death Valley, reliable maps are important, as signage is often limited or, in a few places, nonexistent. Bring a phone but don't rely on cell coverage exclusively in every remote area, and pack plenty of food and water (3 gallons per person per day is recommended). Cars, especially in summer, should be prepared for the hot, dry weather, too. Some of the park's most spectacular canyons are only accessible via four-wheel-drive vehicles but if this is the way you want to travel, make sure the trip is well-planned and use a backcountry map. Be aware of possible winter closures or driving restrictions because of snow. The National Park Service's website (⊕ nps.gov/deva) stays up-to-date on road closures during the wet (and popular) months. ⚠ **One of the park's signature landmarks, Scotty's Castle, and the eight-mile road connecting it to the park border may be closed until 2020 due to damage from a 2015 flood.**

DRIVING INFORMATION California Highway Patrol ☎ 800/427–7623 recorded info from CalTrans, 760/872–5900 live dispatcher at Bishop Communications Center ⊕ www.chp.ca.gov. **California State Department of Transportation Hotline** ☎ 800/427–7623 ⊕ www.dot.ca.gov.

PARK ESSENTIALS
ACCESSIBILITY
All of Death Valley's visitor centers, contact stations, and museums are accessible to all visitors. The campgrounds at Furnace Creek, Sunset, and Stovepipe Wells have wheelchair-accessible sites. Highway 190, Badwater Road, and paved roads to Dante's View and Wildrose provide access to the major scenic viewpoints and historic points of interest.

PARK FEES AND PERMITS
The entrance fee is $30 per vehicle, $25 for motorcycles, and $15 for those entering on foot or bike. The payment, valid for seven consecutive days, is collected at the park's ranger stations, self-serve fee stations, and the visitor center at Furnace Creek. Annual park passes, valid only at Death Valley, are $55.

A permit is not required for groups of 14 or fewer, but if you're planning an overnight visit to the backcountry, complete a registration form at the Furnace Creek Visitor Center. Backcountry camping is allowed in areas that are at least 2 miles from maintained campgrounds and the main paved or unpaved roads and ¼ mile from water sources. Most abandoned mining areas are restricted to day use.

PARK HOURS
The park is open year-round, and can be visited day or night. Most facilities within the park remain open year-round, daily 8–6.

CELL PHONE RECEPTION
Results vary, but in general you should be able to get fairly good cell phone reception on the valley floor. In the surrounding mountains, however, don't count on it.

EDUCATIONAL OFFERINGS
RANGER PROGRAMS
Junior Ranger Program
TOUR—SIGHT | FAMILY | Children can join this program at the Furnace Creek Visitor Center, where they can pick up a workbook and complete activities to earn a souvenir badge. ✉ Death Valley National Park.

RESTAURANTS
Inside the park, if you're looking for a special evening out in Death Valley, head to the Inn at Death Valley Dining Room, where you'll be spoiled with fine wines and juicy steaks. It's also a great spot to start the day with a hearty gourmet breakfast. Most other eateries within the park are mom-and-pop-type places with basic American fare. Outside the park, dining choices are much the same, with little cafés and homey diners serving up coffee shop–style burgers, chicken, and steaks. If you're vegetarian or vegan,

BYOB (bring your own beans). *Restaurant reviews have been shortened. For full information, visit Fodors.com.*

HOTELS

It's difficult to find lodging anywhere in Death Valley that doesn't have breathtaking views of the park and surrounding mountains. Most accommodations, aside from the Inn at Death Valley, are homey and rustic. Rooms fill up quickly during the fall and spring seasons, and reservations are required about three months in advance for the prime weekends.

Outside the park, head to Beatty or Amargosa Valley in Nevada for a bit of nightlife and casino action. The western side of Death Valley, along the eastern Sierra Nevada, is a gorgeous setting, though it's quite a distance from Furnace Creek. Here, you can stay in the historic Dow Villa Motel, where John Wayne spent many a night, or head farther south to the ghost towns of Randsburg or Cerro Gordo for a true Wild West experience. *Hotel reviews have been shortened. For full information, visit Fodors.com.*

What It Costs			
$	$$	$$$	$$$$
RESTAURANTS			
under $12	$12–$20	$21–$30	over $30
HOTELS			
under $100	$100–$150	$151–$200	over $200

TOURS

Death Valley Adventure Tour (*Adventure Motorcycle [AdMo] Tours*)

TOUR—SIGHT | Motorcycle enthusiasts can sign up for a guided Death Valley Adventure Tour that starts and ends in Las Vegas. The five-day tour through Death Valley covers 800 miles. The tours, which run October through May, include hotel accommodations, gasoline, breakfasts, two dinners, snacks, a support vehicle, and a professional guide. To join, you'll need a motorcycle driver's license and experience with off-road and all-terrain riding. ⊠ *Death Valley* ☎ *760/249–1105* ⊕ *www.admotours.com* ☑ *From $3568.*

Furnace Creek Visitor Center programs

GUIDED TOURS | This center has many programs, including ranger-led hikes that explore natural wonders such as Golden Canyon, nighttime stargazing parties with telescopes, and evening ranger talks. Visit the website for a complete list. ⊠ *Furnace Creek Visitor Center, Rte. 190, 30 miles northwest of Death Valley Junction, Death Valley* ☎ *760/786–2331* ⊕ *www.nps.gov/deva/planyourvisit/tours. htm* ☑ *Free.*

Pink Jeep Tours Las Vegas

GUIDED TOURS | A 10-passenger luxury vehicle with oversized viewing windows will pick you up at most Strip hotels for visits to landmarks such as Dante's Peak, Furnace Creek, Devil's Golf Course, Badwater Basin, and Artists Palette. The tours run from about 7 am to 4 pm from September through May, are professionally narrated, and include lunch and bottled water. ⊠ *3629 W. Hacienda Ave., Las Vegas* ☎ *888/900–4480* ⊕ *pinkjeep-tourslasvegas.com* ☑ *From $275.*

VISITOR INFORMATION
MAPS AND INFO

The Death Valley Natural History Association sells a variety of books on the area and publishes a pamphlet outlining a self-guided tour of Golden Canyon, which is available from the association or the bookstore at the visitor center. The association also sells a waterproof, tear-proof topographical map of the entire park. Additional topo maps covering select areas are available at the visitor center or from the **Death Valley Natural History Association** (☎ *760/786–2146 or 800/478–8564* ⊕ *www.dvnha.org*).

PARK CONTACT INFORMATION Death Valley National Park ☎ *760/786–3200* ⊕ *www.nps.gov/deva.*

Plants and Wildlife in Death Valley

There's a general misconception that Death Valley National Park consists of mile upon endless mile of flat desert sands, scattered cacti, and an occasional cow skull. Many people don't realize that across the valley floor from Badwater—the lowest point in the Western Hemisphere—Telescope Peak towers at 11,049 feet above sea level. The extreme topography of Death Valley is a lesson in geology. Two hundred million years ago seas covered the area, depositing layers of sediment and fossils. Between 3.5 million and 5 million years ago faults in the Earth's crust and volcanic activity pushed and folded the ground, causing mountain ranges to rise and the valley floor to drop. The valley was then filled periodically by lakes, which eroded the surrounding rocks into fantastic formations and deposited the salts that now cover the floor of the basin.

Most animal life in Death Valley (51 mammal, 36 reptile, 307 bird, and 3 amphibian species) is found near the limited sources of water. The bighorn sheep spend most of their time in the secluded upper reaches of the park's rugged canyons and ridges. Coyotes often can be seen lazing in the shade next to the golf course and have been known to run onto the fairways to steal a golf ball. The only native fish in the park is the pupfish, which grows to slightly longer than one inch. In winter, when the water is cold, the fish lie dormant in the bottom mud, becoming active again in spring. Because they are wary of large moving shapes, you must stand quietly over a pool at Salt Creek to see them.

Botanists say there are more than 1,000 species of plants here (21 exist nowhere else in the world), though many annual plants lie dormant as seeds for all but a few months in spring, when rains trigger a bloom. The rest congregate around the few water sources. Most of the low-elevation vegetation grows around the oases at Furnace Creek and Scotty's Castle, where oleanders, palms, and salt cedar grow. At higher elevations you will find pinyon, juniper, and bristlecone pine.

VISITOR CENTERS

⚠ The popular visitor center at Scotty's Castle is closed until at least 2020 as a result of a major flash flood in 2015 that damaged the structure and destroyed the access road.

Furnace Creek Visitor Center and Museum

INFO CENTER | The exhibits and artifacts here provide a broad overview of how Death Valley formed; you can pick up maps at the bookstore run by the Death Valley Natural History Association. This is also the place to sign up for ranger-led walks (available November through April) or check out a live presentation about the valley's cultural and natural history. The helpful center offers regular showings of a 20-minute film about the park and children can get their free Junior Ranger booklet here, packed with games and information about the park and its critters. ✉ *Hwy. 190, Death Valley* ✛ *30 miles northwest of Death Valley Junction* ☎ *760/786–3200* ⊕ *www.nps.gov/deva.*

 Sights

SCENIC DRIVE

Artist's Drive

SCENIC DRIVE | This 9-mile, one-way route skirts the foothills of the Black Mountains and provides intimate views of the changing landscape. Once inside the palette, the huge expanses of the valley are replaced by the small-scale natural beauty of pigments created by volcanic deposits or sedimentary layers. It's a quiet, lonely drive, and shouldn't be rushed. Reach Artist's Palette by heading south on Badwater Road from its intersection with Route 190. ⊠ *Death Valley National Park.*

HISTORIC SITES
Charcoal Kilns
MINE | Ten well-preserved stone kilns, each 25 feet high and 30 feet wide, stand as if on parade. The kilns, built by Chinese laborers for a mining company in 1877, were used to burn wood from pinyon pines to turn it into charcoal. The charcoal was then transported over the mountains into Death Valley, where it was used to extract lead and silver from the ore mined there. If you hike nearby Wildrose Peak, you will be rewarded with terrific views of the kilns. ⊠ *Wildrose Canyon Rd., Death Valley* ⊹ *37 miles south of Stovepipe Wells.*

Harmony Borax Works
HISTORIC SITE | Death Valley's mule teams hauled borax from here to the railroad town of Mojave, 165 miles away. The teams plied the route until 1889, when the railroad finally arrived in Zabriskie. Constructed in 1883, one of the oldest buildings in Death Valley houses the Borax Museum, 2 miles south of the borax works at the Ranch at Death Valley (between the restaurants and the post office). Originally a miners' bunkhouse, the building once stood in Twenty Mule Team Canyon. Now it displays mining machinery and historical exhibits. The adjacent structure is the original mule-team barn. ⊠ *Harmony Borax Works Rd., west of Hwy. 190 at Ranch at Death Valley* ⊕ *www.nps.gov/deva/historyculture/ harmony.htm.*

SCENIC STOPS
Artist's Palette
NATURE SITE | So called for the contrasting colors of its volcanic deposits and sedimentary layers, this is one of the signature sights of Death Valley. Artist's Drive, the approach to the area, is one-way heading north off Badwater Road, so if you're visiting Badwater from Furnace Creek, come here on the way back. The drive winds through foothills of sedimentary and volcanic rocks. About 4 miles into the drive, a short side road veers right to a parking lot that's a few hundred feet before the "palette," whose natural colors include shades of green, gold, and pink. ⊠ *Off Badwater Rd., Death Valley* ⊹ *11 miles south of Furnace Creek.*

Badwater
SCENIC DRIVE | At 282 feet below sea level, Badwater is the lowest spot of land in North America—and also one of the hottest. Stairs and wheelchair ramps descend from the parking lot to a wooden platform that overlooks a sodium chloride pool, a small but remarkably persistent reminder that the valley floor used to contain a lake. You can continue past the platform on a broad, white path that peters out after a half mile or so. Badwater is one of the most popular and easily accessible sites within the park. From this lowest point, be sure to look across to Telescope Peak, which towers more than 2 miles above the valley floor. ⊠ *Badwater Rd., Death Valley* ⊹ *19 miles south of Furnace Creek.*

★ Dante's View
VIEWPOINT | This lookout is 5,450 feet above sea level in the Black Mountains. In the dry desert air you can see across most of 160-mile-long Death Valley. The view is astounding. Take a 10-minute, mildly strenuous walk from the parking lot toward a series of rocky overlooks, where with binoculars you can spot some of Death Valley's signature sites. A few interpretive signs point out the highlights below in the valley and across,

in the Sierra. Getting here from Furnace Creek takes about an hour—time well invested. ⊠ *Dante's View Rd., Death Valley* ⊕ *Off Hwy. 190, 35 miles from Badwater, 20 miles south of Twenty Mule Team Canyon.*

Devil's Golf Course

NATURE SITE | Thousands of miniature salt pinnacles carved into surreal shapes by the desert wind dot this wildly varied landscape. The salt was pushed up to the earth's surface by pressure created as underground salt- and water-bearing gravel crystallized. Get out of your vehicle and take a closer look; you'll see perfectly round holes descending into the ground. ⊠ *Badwater Rd., Death Valley* ⊕ *13 miles south of Furnace Creek. Turn right onto dirt road and drive 1 mile.*

Golden Canyon

NATURE SITE | Just South of Furnace Creek, these glimmering mountains are perhaps best known for their role in the original *Star Wars*. The canyon is also a fine hiking spot, with gorgeous views of the Panamint Mountains, ancient dry lake beds, and alluvial fans. ⊠ *Hwy. 178, Death Valley* ⊕ *From Furnace Creek Visitor Center, drive 2 miles south on Hwy. 190, then 2 miles south on Hwy. 178 to parking area; the lot has kiosk with trail guides.*

Racetrack

NATURE SITE | Getting here involves a 28-mile journey over a washboard dirt road, but the reward is well worth the trip. Where else in the world do rocks move on their own? This phenomenon has baffled scientists for years and is perhaps one of the last great natural mysteries. The best research on the rocks shows the movement requires a rare confluence of conditions: rain and then cold to create a layer of ice that becomes a sail for gusty winds that push the rocks along—sometimes for several hundred yards. When the mud dries, a telltale trail remains. The trek to the Racetrack can be made in a sedan, but beware—sharp

rocks can slash tires; a truck or SUV with thick tires, high clearance, and a spare tire are suggested. ⊠ *Death Valley* ⊕ *27 miles west of Ubehebe Crater via rough dirt road.*

Sand Dunes at Mesquite Flat

NATURE SITE | These dunes, made up of minute pieces of quartz and other rock, are ever-changing products of the wind-rippled hills, with curving crests and a sun-bleached hue. The dunes are the most photographed destination in the park, and you can see them at their best at sunrise and sunset. Keep your eyes open for animal tracks—you may even spot a coyote or fox. Bring plenty of water, and note where you parked your car: It's easy to become disoriented in this ocean of sand. If you lose your bearings, climb to the top of a dune and scan the horizon for the parking lot. ⊠ *Death Valley* ⊕ *19 miles north of Hwy. 190, northeast of Stovepipe Wells Village.*

Stovepipe Wells Village

TOWN | This tiny 1926 town, the first resort in Death Valley, takes its name from the stovepipe that an early prospector left to indicate where he found water. The area contains a motel, restaurant, convenience store, gas station, RV hookups, swimming pool, and landing strip, though first-time park visitors are better off staying in Furnace Creek, which is more central. Off Highway 190, on a 3-mile gravel road immediately southwest, are the multicolor walls of Mosaic Canyon. ⊠ *Hwy. 190, Death Valley* ⊕ *2 miles from Sand Dunes, 77 miles east of Lone Pine* ☎ *760/786–2387* ⊕ *www.deathvalleyhotels.com.*

Titus Canyon

SCENIC DRIVE | This popular one-way, 27-mile drive starts at Nevada Highway 374 (Daylight Pass Road), 2 miles from the park's boundary. Along the way you'll see Leadville Ghost Town and finally the spectacular limestone and dolomite narrows. Toward the end, a two-way section of gravel road leads you into the mouth

Footprints along the Mesquite Flat Sand Dunes.

of the canyon from Scotty's Castle Road. This drive is steep, bumpy, and narrow. High-clearance vehicles are strongly recommended. ⊠ *Death Valley National Park* ✛ *Access road off Nevada Hwy. 374, 6 miles west of Beatty, NV.*

Twenty Mule Team Canyon

CANYON | This canyon was named in honor of the 20-mule teams that, between 1883 and 1889, carried 10-ton loads of borax through the burning desert (though they didn't actually pass through this canyon). Along the 2.7-mile, one-way loop road off Highway 190, you'll find the soft rock walls reach high on both sides, making it seem like you're on an amusement-park ride. Remains of prospectors' tunnels are visible here, along with some brilliant rock formations. ⊠ *20 Mule Team Rd.* ✛ *Off Hwy. 190, 4 miles south of Furnace Creek, 20 miles west of Death Valley Junction.*

Ubehebe Crater

VOLCANO | At 500 feet deep and ½ mile across, this crater resulted from underground steam and gas explosions about 3,000 years ago. Volcanic ash spreads out over most of the area, and the cinders lie as deep as 150 feet, near the crater's rim. Trek down to the crater's floor or walk around it on a fairly level path. Either way, you need about an hour and will be treated to fantastic views. The hike from the floor can be strenuous. ⊠ *N. Death Valley Hwy., Death Valley* ✛ *8 miles northwest of Scotty's Castle.*

Zabriskie Point

VIEWPOINT | Although only about 710 feet in elevation, this is one of Death Valley National Park's most scenic spots, overlooking a striking panorama of wrinkled, multicolor hills. It's a great place to watch the sunrise, but it can be bustling any time of day. Pair it with a drive out to magnificent Dante's View. ⊠ *Hwy. 190, Death Valley* ✛ *5 miles south of Furnace Creek.*

 Activities

BICYCLING

Mountain biking is permitted on any of the back roads and roadways open to the public (bikes aren't permitted on hiking trails). Visit ⊕ *www.nps.gov/deva/planyourvisit/bikingandmtbiking.htm* for a list of suggested routes for all levels of ability. Bicycle Path, a 4-mile round-trip trek from the visitor center to Mustard Canyon, is a good place to start. Bike rentals are available at the Oasis at Death Valley, by the hour or by the day.

Escape Adventures (*Escape Adventures*) BICYCLING | Ride into the heart of Death Valley on the Death Valley & Red Rock Mountain Bike Tour, a five-day trip through the national park. The customizable two-day journey (on single-track trails and jeep roads) includes accommodations (both camping and inns). Bikes, tents, sleeping bags, helmets, and other gear may be rented for an additional price. Tours are available February–April and October only. ⊠ *Death Valley National Park* ☏ *800/596–2953, 702/596–2953* ⊕ *www.escapeadventures.com* ✉ *From $1720.*

BIRD-WATCHING

Approximately 350 bird species have been identified in Death Valley. The best place to see the park's birds is along the Salt Creek Interpretive Trail, where you can spot ravens, common snipes, killdeer, spotted sandpipers, and great blue herons. Along the fairways at Furnace Creek Golf Course, you can see kingfishers, peregrine falcons, hawks, Canada geese, yellow warblers, and the occasional golden eagle. Scotty's Castle, closed until at least 2019, draws wintering birds from around the globe that are attracted to its running water, shady trees, and shrubs. Other good spots to find birds are at Saratoga Springs, Mesquite Springs, Travertine Springs, and Grimshaw Lake near Tecopa.

You can download a complete park bird checklist, divided by season, at ⊕ *www.nps.gov/deva/learn/nature/upload/death-valley-bird-checklist.pdf.* Rangers at Furnace Creek Visitor Center often lead birding walks through various locations between November and March.

FOUR-WHEELING

Maps and SUV guidebooks for four-wheel-drive and other backcountry roads (including the popular Cottonwood/Marble canyons, Racetrack, Eureka Dunes, Saratoga Springs, and Warm Springs Canyon) are offered at the Furnace Creek Visitor Center. Remember: never travel alone and be sure to pack plenty of water and snacks. The park recommends checking ⊕ *www.nps.gov/deva/planyourvisit/backcountryroads.htm* for back-road conditions before setting out. Driving off established roads is strictly prohibited in the park.

Butte Valley
TOUR—SPORTS | This 21-mile road in the southwest part of the park climbs from 200 feet below sea level to an elevation of 4,700 feet. The geological formations along the drive reveal the development of Death Valley. High clearance and four-wheel-drive required. If you have a four-wheel-drive high clearance vehicle and nerves of steel, this route takes you past Warm Springs talc mine and through Butte Valley to Geologist's Cabin, a charming and cheery little cabin where you can spend the night, if nobody else beats you to it. The park suggests checking their website or asking a ranger to check current conditions on all backcountry roads. The cabin, which sits under a cottonwood tree, has a fireplace, table and chairs, and a sink. Farther up the road, Stella's Cabin and Russell Camp are also open for public use. Keep the historic cabins clean and restock any items that you use. The road is even rougher if you continue over Mengel Pass. ⊠ *Trailhead on Warm Spring Canyon Rd., Death*

The wildflower "super-bloom," a rare event for Death Valley.

Valley ⊕ 50 miles south of Furnace Creek Visitor Center.

GOLF

Furnace Creek Golf Course at the Oasis at Death Valley

GOLF | Golfers rave about how their drives carry at altitude, so what happens on the lowest golf course in the world (214 feet below sea level)? Its improbably green fairways are lined with date palms and tamarisk trees, and its level of difficulty is rated surprisingly high. You can rent clubs and carts, and there are golf packages available for The Oasis at Death Valley guests. In winter, reservations are essential. ✉ *Hwy. 190, Furnace Creek* ☎ *760/786–2301* ⊕ *www.oasisatdeathvalley.com* 🍽 *From $35* 🏌 *18 holes, 6215 yards, par 70.*

HIKING

Plan to hike before or after midday in the spring, summer, or fall, unless you're in the mood for a masochistic baking. Carry plenty of water, wear protective clothing, and keep an eye out for black widows, scorpions, snakes, and other potentially dangerous creatures. Some of the best trails are unmarked; if the opportunity arises, ask for directions.

★ Darwin Falls

HIKING/WALKING | FAMILY | This lovely 2-mile round-trip hike rewards you with a refreshing year-round waterfall surrounded by thick vegetation and a rocky gorge. No swimming or bathing is allowed, but it's a beautiful place for a picnic. Adventurous hikers can scramble higher toward more rewarding views of the falls. *Easy.* ✉ *Death Valley National Park ⊕ Trailhead: access the 2-mile graded dirt road and parking area off Hwy. 190, 1 mile west of Panamint Springs Resort.*

Fall Canyon

HIKING/WALKING | This is a 3-mile, one-way hike from the Titus canyon parking area. First, walk ½ mile north along the base of the mountains to a large wash, then go 2½ miles up the canyon to a 35-foot dry fall. You can continue by climbing around to the falls on the south side. *Moderate.* ✉ *Death Valley National Park ⊕ Trailhead:*

access road off Scotty's Castle Rd., 33 miles northwest of Furnace Creek.

Keane Wonder Mine

HIKING/WALKING | This fascinating relic of Death Valley's gold-mining past, built in 1907, reopened in November 2017 after 9 years of repair work. Its most unique feature is the mile-long tramway that descends 1,000 vertical feet, which once carried gold ore and still has the original cables attached. From here, a network of trails leads to other old mines. A climb to the uppermost tramway terminal is rewarded by expansive views of the valley. ⊠ Access road off Beatty Cutoff Rd., 17½ miles north of Furnace Creek, Death Valley.

Mosaic Canyon

HIKING/WALKING | **FAMILY** | A gradual uphill trail (4 miles round-trip) winds through the smoothly polished, marbleized limestone walls of this narrow canyon. There are dry falls to climb at the upper end. Moderate. ⊠ Death Valley ✛ Trailhead: access road off Hwy. 190, ½ mile west of Stovepipe Wells Village.

Natural Bridge Canyon

HIKING/WALKING | A rough 2-mile access road from Badwater Road leads to a trailhead. From there, set off to see interesting geological features in addition to the bridge, which is a half-mile away. The one-way trail continues for a few hundred yards, but scenic returns diminish quickly and eventually you're confronted with climbing boulders. Easy. ⊠ Death Valley ✛ Trailhead: access road off Badwater Rd., 15 miles south of Furnace Creek.

Salt Creek Interpretive Trail

HIKING/WALKING | **FAMILY** | This trail, a ½-mile boardwalk circuit, loops through a spring-fed wash. The nearby hills are brown and gray, but the floor of the wash is alive with aquatic plants such as pickleweed and salt grass. The stream and ponds here are among the few places in the park to see the rare pupfish, the only native fish species in Death Valley. The pupfish are most easily observed during their spawning season in February and March. Animals such as bobcats, fox, coyotes, and snakes visit the spring, and you may also see ravens, common snipes, killdeer, and great blue herons. Easy. ⊠ Death Valley ✛ Trailhead: off Hwy. 190, 14 miles north of Furnace Creek.

★ Telescope Peak Trail

HIKING/WALKING | The 14-mile round-trip (with 3,000 feet of elevation gain) begins at Mahogany Flat Campground, which is accessible by a rough dirt road. The steep and at some points treacherous trail winds through pinyon, juniper, and bristlecone pines, with excellent views of Death Valley and Panamint Valley. Ice axes and crampons may be necessary in winter—check at the Furnace Creek Visitor Center. It takes a minimum of six grueling hours to hike to the top of the 11,049-foot peak and then return. Getting to the peak is a strenuous endeavor; take plenty of water and only attempt it in fall unless you're an experienced hiker. Difficult. ⊠ Death Valley ✛ Trailhead: off Wildrose Rd., south of Charcoal Kilns.

HORSEBACK AND CARRIAGE RIDES

Furnace Creek Stables

HORSEBACK RIDING | **FAMILY** | Set off on a one- or two-hour guided horseback, carriage, or haywagon ride from Furnace Creek Stables. The rides traverse trails with views of the surrounding mountains, where multicolor volcanic rock and alluvial fans form a background for date palms and other vegetation. Evening carriage rides take passengers around the golf course and The Ranch at Death Valley. The stables are open October–May only. ⊠ Hwy. 190, Furnace Creek ☎ 760/614–1018 ⊕ www.furnacecreek-stables.net ⧈ From $55.

🛍 Shopping

Experienced desert travelers carry a cooler stocked with food and beverages. You're best off replenishing your food stash in Ridgecrest, Barstow, or Pahrump, larger towns that have a better selection and nontourist prices.

Ranch General Store

CONVENIENCE/GENERAL STORES | This convenience store carries groceries, souvenirs, camping supplies, and other basics. ⊠ Hwy. 190, Furnace Creek ☎ 760/786–2345 ⊕ www.oasisatdeathvalley.com.

Nearby Towns

Founded at the turn of the 20th century, **Beatty** sits 16 miles east of the California-Nevada border on Death Valley's northern side. Named for a single pine tree found at the bottom of the canyon of the same name, **Lone Pine,** on the park's west side, is where you'll find Mount Whitney, the highest peak in the continental United States, at 14,496 feet. The nearby Alabama Hills have been used in many movies and TV scenes, including segments in *The Lone Ranger.* Down south, unincorporated **Shoshone,** a very small town at the edge of Death Valley, started out as a mining town. The area, dotted with tamarisk trees and date palms, is home to a natural warm-springs pool fed by an underwater river.

VISITOR INFORMATION Beatty Chamber of Commerce ⊠ 119 E. Main St., Beatty ☎ 775/553–2424 ⊕ www.beattynevada. org. **Death Valley Chamber of Commerce** ⊠ 860 Tecopa Hot Springs Rd., Tecopa ☎ 888/600–1844 ⊕ www.deathvalleychamber.org. **Lone Pine Chamber of Commerce** ⊠ 120 S. Main St., Lone Pine ☎ 760/876–4444 ⊕ www.lonepinechamber.org.

👁 Sights

Air Force Flight Test Museum at Edwards Air Force Base

MILITARY SITE | This museum, at what many consider to be the birthplace of supersonic flight, chronicles the rich history of flight testing. Numerous airplanes are on exhibit, from the first F-16B to the only remaining YF-22. While those with approved base entry have access to regular museum hours, a general-public tour takes place once a month. The 3½-hour tour includes indoor museum exhibits and driving tours of the base. The tour requires a reservation and you have to provide basic information for a background check at least two weeks in advance (a month for non-U.S. residents), but be aware that slots fill up fast. On the base's website, click Tours for details. ⊠ Edwards Air Force Base Visitor Control Center, 405 S. Rosamond Blvd., Edwards ☎ 661/277–8050, 661/277–3510 ⊕ www. afftcmuseum.org 🎟 Free.

Ancient Bristlecone Pine Forest

FOREST | FAMILY | About an hour's drive from Independence or Bishop you can view some of the oldest living trees on Earth, some of which date back more than 40 centuries. The world's largest bristlecone pine can be found in Patriarch Grove, while the world's oldest known living tree is along Methusula Trail in Schulman Grove. Getting to Patriarch Grove is slow going along the narrow dirt road, especially for sedans with low clearance, but once there you'll find picnic tables, restrooms, and self-guided interpretive trails. ⊠ Schulman Grove Visitor Center, White Mountain Rd., Bishop ✛ From U.S. 395, turn east onto Hwy. 168 and follow signs for 23 miles ⊕ www.fs.usda.gov/main/inyo/home 🎟 $3.

Schulman Grove Visitor Center

INFO CENTER | At this visitor center, open late May–October, you can learn about the bristlecone and take a walk to the 4,700-year-old Methuselah tree. ☎ *760/873–2500* ⊕ *www.bishopvisitor.com* ⊗ *Closed Nov.–mid-May.*

Ballarat Ghost Town

GHOST TOWN | This crusty, dusty town saw its heyday between 1897 and 1917. There's a store-museum where you can grab a cold soda before venturing out to explore the crumbling landscape. For years Ballarat's more infamous draw was **Barker Ranch,** where convicted murderer Charles Manson and his "family" were captured after the 1969 Sharon Tate murder spree; the house burned down in 2009. ⊠ *Death Valley* ✛ *From Hwy. 395, Exit SR-178 and travel 45 miles to historic marker; Ballarat is 3½ miles from pavement.*

★ Manzanar National Historic Site

HISTORIC SITE | A reminder of an ugly episode in U.S. history, the former Manzanar War Relocation Center is where more than 11,000 Japanese-Americans were confined behind barbed-wire fences between 1942 and 1945. A visit here is both deeply moving and inspiring—the former because it's hard to comprehend that the United States was capable of confining its citizens in such a way, the latter because those imprisoned here showed great pluck and perseverance in making the best of a bad situation. Most of the buildings from the 1940s are gone, but two sentry posts, the auditorium, and numerous Japanese rock gardens remain. One of eight guard towers and two barracks have been reconstructed, and a mess hall has been restored. Interactive exhibits inside the barracks include audio and video clips from people who were incarcerated in Manzanar during WWII. You can drive the one-way dirt road on a self-guided tour past various ruins to a small cemetery, where a monument stands. Signs mark where the barracks, a hospital, a school, and the fire station once stood. An outstanding 8,000-square-foot interpretive

center has exhibits and documentary photographs and screens a short film. ⊠ *Independence* ✛ *West side of U.S. 395 between Independence and Lone Pine* ☎ *760/878–2194* ⊕ *www.nps.gov/manz* 🆓 *Free.*

Maturango Museum

CANYON | FAMILY | The museum contains interesting exhibits that survey the Upper Mojave Desert area's art, history, and geology, and sponsors tours of the amazing rock drawings in Petroglyph Canyons. ⊠ *100 E. Las Flores Ave., at Hwy. 178, Ridgecrest* ☎ *760/375–6900* ⊕ *www.maturango.org* 🆓 *$5.*

Mt. Whitney Fish Hatchery

FISH HATCHERY | FAMILY | A delightful place for a family picnic, the hatchery was one of California's first trout farms. The Tudor Revival–style structure, completed in 1917, is an architectural stunner, its walls nearly 3 feet thick with locally quarried granite. Fish production ceased in 2007 after a fire and subsequent mudslide, but dedicated volunteers staff the facility and raise trout for display purposes in a large pond out front. Bring change for the fish-food machines. ⊠ *1 Golden Trout Circle, 2 miles north of town, Independence* ☎ *760/279–1592* ⊕ *www.mtwhitneyfishhatchery.org* 🆓 *Free (donations welcome)* ⊗ *Closed mid-Dec.–mid-Apr. Closed Tues. and Wed.*

★ Petroglyph Canyons

CANYON | FAMILY | Thousands of well-preserved images of animals and humans are scratched or pecked into dark basaltic rocks at Big Petroglyph and Little Petroglyph canyons in the Coso Mountain range, the largest concentration of ancient rock art in the Northern Hemisphere. The canyons lie within the million-acre U.S. Naval Weapons Center at China Lake. Only the drawings of Little Petroglyph can be visited, and only on a guided tour arranged in advance through the Maturango Museum. Tour participants must be U.S. citizens over 10 years of age, and fill out an online application to obtain security clearance. Detailed information about the spring and fall tours, which fill up fast, is provided on the museum's website. ✉ *100 E. Las Flores Ave., Ridgecrest* ☎ *760/375–6900* ⊕ *www.maturango.org* 💲 *$55* ⊙ *Closed Jan. and Feb. and July and Aug.*

★ Randsburg

TOWN | FAMILY | The Rand Mining District first boomed when gold was discovered in the Rand Mountains in 1895. Along with neighboring settlements, it grew further due to the success of the Yellow Aster Mine, which yielded $3 million worth of gold before 1900. Rich tungsten ore, used in World War I to make steel alloy, was discovered in 1907, and silver was found in 1919. Randsburg is one of the few gold-rush communities not to have become a ghost town; the tiny city jail is among the original buildings still standing in this town with a population under 100, and there's a museum that hosts Old West Days the 3rd Saturday in September. In nearby Johannesburg, 1 mile south of Randsburg, spirits are said to dwell in the stunning Old West cemetery in the hills above town. ✉ *Hwy. 395, near the junction with Rte. 14, Death Valley.*

Rhyolite

GHOST TOWN | FAMILY | Though it's not within the boundary of Death Valley National Park, this Nevada ghost town, named for the silica volcanic rock nearby, is still a big draw. Around 1904, Rhyolite's Montgomery Shoshone Mine caused a financial boom, and fancy buildings sprung up all over town. Today you can still explore many of the crumbling edifices. The Bottle House, built by miner Tom Kelly out of almost 50,000 Adolphus Busch beer bottles, is a must-see. ✉ *Hwy. 374* ✛ *35 miles north of Furnace Creek Visitor Center and 5 miles west of Beatty* ⊕ *www.nps.gov/deva/learn/historyculture/rhyolite-ghost-town.htm.*

Shoshone Museum

MUSEUM | This museum chronicles the local history of Death Valley and houses a unique collection of period items, and minerals and rocks from the area. ✉ *Rte. 127, Shoshone* ☎ *760/852–4524* ⊕ *www.shoshonevillage.com/shoshone-museum.html* 💲 *Free.*

Trona Pinnacles National Natural Landmark

ARCHAEOLOGICAL SITE | Fantastic-looking formations of calcium carbonate, known as tufa, were formed underwater along fault lines in the bed of what is now Searles Dry Lake. Some of the more than 500 spires stand as tall as 140 feet, creating a landscape so surreal that it doubled for outer-space terrain in the film *Star Trek V.*

An easy-to-walk ½-mile trail allows you to see the tufa up close, but wear sturdy shoes—tufa cuts like coral. The best road to the area can be impassable after a rainstorm. ✉ *Pinnacle Rd.* ✛ *5 miles south of Hwy. 178, 18 miles east of Ridgecrest* ☎ *760/384–5400 Ridgecrest BLM office* ⊕ *www.recreation.gov.*

🍴 Restaurants

IN THE PARK

★ Inn at Death Valley Dining Room

$$$$ | AMERICAN | Fireplaces, beamed ceilings, and spectacular views provide a visual feast to match this fine-dining restaurant's ambitious menu. Dinner entrées include fare such as salmon, free-range chicken, and filet mignon, and there's a seasonal menu of vegetarian dishes. **Known for:** views of surrounding desert; old-school charm; can be pricey. 💲 *Average main: $38* ✉ *Inn at Death Valley, Hwy. 190, Furnace Creek* ☎ *760/786–3385* ⊕ *www.oasisatdeathvalley.com.*

19th Hole

$ | AMERICAN | Next to the clubhouse of the world's lowest golf course, this open-air spot serves hamburgers, hot dogs, chicken, and sandwiches. The full-service bar has a drive-through service for golfers in carts. **Known for:** kielbasa dog; breakfast burrito; golf cart drive-through. $ *Average main: $8* ✉ *Furnace Creek Golf Course, Hwy. 190, Furnace Creek* ☎ *760/786–2345* ⊕ *www.oasisatdeathvalley.com/dining/* ⊗ *Closed mid-May–mid-Oct. No dinner.*

Panamint Springs Resort Restaurant
$$ | AMERICAN | This is a great place for steak and a beer—choose from more than 150 different beers and ales—or pasta and a salad. In summer, evening meals are served outdoors on the porch, which has spectacular views of Panamint Valley. **Known for:** good burgers; extensive beer selection. $ *Average main: $15* ✉ *Hwy. 190, Death Valley* ✛ *31 miles west of Stovepipe Wells* ☎ *775/482–7680* ⊕ *www.panamintsprings.com/services/dining-bar.*

OUTSIDE THE PARK
Crowbar Café and Saloon
$$ | AMERICAN | FAMILY | In an old wooden building where antique photos adorn the walls and mining equipment stands in the corners, the Crowbar serves enormous helpings of regional dishes such as steak and taco salads. Home-baked fruit pies make fine desserts, and frosty beers are surefire thirst quenchers. **Known for:** home-baked fruit pies; rattlesnake chili; great breakfast spot. $ *Average main: $15* ✉ *Rte. 127, Shoshone* ☎ *760/852–4123* ⊕ *www.shoshonevillage.com/shoshone-crowbar-cafe-saloon.html.*

Mt. Whitney Restaurant
$ | AMERICAN | A boisterous family-friendly restaurant with four flat-screen televisions, this place serves the best burgers in town. In addition to the usual beef variety, you can choose from ostrich, elk, venison, and buffalo burgers. **Known for:** burgers; John Wayne memorabilia. $ *Average main: $10* ✉ *227 S. Main St., Lone Pine* ☎ *760/876–5751.*

Randsburg General Store
$ | AMERICAN | FAMILY | Built as Randsburg's Drug Store in 1896, this popular biker and family spot is one of the area's few surviving ghost-town buildings with original furnishings intact, such as a tin ceiling, light fixtures, and a 1904 marble-and-stained-glass soda fountain. You can still enjoy a phosphate soda from that same fountain, or lunch on slow-roasted barbecue sandwiches and blueberry milk shakes along with chili, hamburgers, and breakfast. **Known for:** friendly service; located in a ghost town;. $ *Average main: $10* ✉ *35 Butte Ave., Randsburg* ☎ *760/374–2143* ⊕ *www.randsburggeneralstore.com* ⊗ *Closed Mon.–Thurs., for extended opening during holiday wks, call ahead.*

Seasons Restaurant
$$$ | AMERICAN | FAMILY | This inviting, country-style diner serves all kinds of traditional American fare. For a special treat, try the medallions of Cervena elk, smothered in port wine, dried cranberries, and toasted walnuts; finish with the Baileys Irish Cream cheesecake or the lemon crème brûlée for dessert. **Known for:** high-end dining in remote area; steaks and wild game; children's menu. $ *Average main: $27* ✉ *206 S. Main St., Lone Pine* ☎ *760/876–8927* ⊕ *www.seasonslonepine.com* ⊗ *No lunch. Closed Mon. Nov.–Mar.*

 Hotels

IN THE PARK
For the busy season (November–March) you should make reservations for lodgings within the park several months in advance.

★ The Inn at Death Valley
$$$$ | HOTEL | Built in 1927, this adobe-brick-and-stone lodge in one of the park's greenest oases reopened in 2018 after an extensive renovation, offering Death Valley's most luxurious accommodations, including 22 brand-new one- and two-bedroom casitas. **Pros:** refined; comfortable; great views. **Cons:** services reduced during low season (July and

Best Campgrounds in Death Valley

You'll need a high-clearance or 4X4 vehicle to reach these locations. To find out where you can camp in the backcountry, pick up a copy of the backcountry map at the visitor center, or check the website ⊕ www.nps.gov/deva/planyourvisit/camping.htm.

You can only build fires in the metal fire grates that are available at most campgrounds, though fires may be restricted in summer (check with rangers about current conditions). Wood gathering is prohibited at all campgrounds. A limited supply of firewood is available at general stores in Furnace Creek and Stovepipe Wells, but because prices are high and supplies limited, you're better off bringing your own if you intend to have a campfire. Camping is prohibited in the historic Inyo, Los Burro, and Ubehebe Crater areas, as well as all day-use spots, including Aguerberry Point Road, Cottonwood Canyon Road, Racetrack Road, Skidoo Road, Titus Canyon Road, Wildrose Road, and West Side Road.

Furnace Creek. This campground, 196 feet below sea level, has some shaded tent sites and is open all year. ⊠ Hwy. 190, Furnace Creek ☎ 760/786–2441.

Mahogany Flat. If you have a four-wheel-drive vehicle and want to scale Telescope Peak, the park's highest mountain, you might want to sleep at one of the few shaded spots in Death Valley, at a cool 8,133 feet. ⊠ Off Wildrose Rd., south of Charcoal Kilns ☎ No phone.

Panamint Springs Resort. Part of a complex that includes a motel and cabin, this campground is surrounded by cottonwoods. The daily fee includes use of the showers and restrooms. ⊠ Hwy. 190, 28 miles west of Stovepipe Wells ☎ 775/482–7680.

Sunset Campground. This first-come, first-served campground is a gravel-and-asphalt RV city. Closed mid-April to mid-October. ⊠ Sunset Campground Rd., 1 mile north of Furnace Creek ☎ 800/365–2267.

Texas Spring. This campsite south of the Furnace Creek Visitor Center has good views and facilities and is a few dollars cheaper than Furnace Creek. Closed mid-May to mid-October. ⊠ Off Badwater Rd., south of Furnace Creek Visitor Center ☎ 800/365–2267.

August); expensive; resort fee. $ Rooms from: $499 ⊠ Furnace Creek Village, near intersection of Hwy. 190 and Badwater Rd., Death Valley ☎ 760/786–2345 ⊕ www.oasisatdeathvalley.com ➥ 88 rooms ⦿ No meals.

Panamint Springs Resort

$ | B&B/INN | Ten miles inside the west entrance of the park, this low-key resort overlooks the sand dunes and peculiar geological formations of the Panamint Valley. **Pros:** slow-paced; friendly;

peaceful and quiet after sundown. **Cons:** far from the park's main attractions; Internet very limited; most rooms don't have TV. $ Rooms from: $94 ⊠ Hwy. 190, Death Valley ⊕ 28 miles west of Stovepipe Wells ☎ 775/482–7680 ⊕ www.panamintsprings.com ➥ 15 rooms, 8 cabins ⦿ No meals.

The Ranch at Death Valley

$$$$ | RESORT | FAMILY | Originally the crew headquarters for the Pacific Coast Borax Company, the four buildings here have motel-style rooms that are a great option

for families. **Pros:** good family atmosphere; central location. **Cons:** rooms can get hot despite air-conditioning; parking near your room can be problematic. [$] *Rooms from: $279* ✉ *Hwy. 190, Furnace Creek* ☎ *760/786–2345, 800/236–7916* 🌐 *www.oasisatdeathvalley.com* 🛏 *224 rooms* 🍴 *No meals.*

Stovepipe Wells Village

$$ | **HOTEL** | If you prefer quiet nights and an unfettered view of the night sky and nearby Mesquite Flat Sand Dunes and Mosaic Canyon, this property is for you. **Pros:** intimate, relaxed; no big-time partying; authentic desert-community ambience. **Cons:** isolated; cheapest patio rooms very small; limited Wi-Fi access. [$] *Rooms from: $140* ✉ *Hwy. 190, Stovepipe Wells* ☎ *760/786–2387* 🌐 *www.escapetodeathvalley.com* 🛏 *83 rooms* 🍴 *No meals.*

OUTSIDE THE PARK

Dow Villa Motel and Dow Hotel

$$ | **HOTEL** | Built in 1923 to cater to the film industry, the Dow Villa Motel and the historic Dow Hotel sit in the center of Lone Pine. **Pros:** clean rooms; great mountain views; in-room whirlpool tubs in some motel rooms. **Cons:** some rooms in hotel share bathrooms. [$] *Rooms from: $119* ✉ *310 S. Main St., Lone Pine* ☎ *760/876–5521, 800/824–9317* 🌐 *www.dowvillamotel.com* 🛏 *92 rooms* 🍴 *No meals.*

Chapter 15

GLACIER AND WATERTON LAKES NATIONAL PARKS

15

Updated by
Debbie Olsen

MONTANA

WELCOME TO GLACIER AND WATERTON LAKES NATIONAL PARKS

TOP REASONS TO GO

★ **Witness the Divide:** The rugged mountains that weave their way through Glacier and Waterton along the Continental Divide seem to have glaciers in every hollow melting into tiny streams, raging rivers, and icy-cold mountain lakes.

★ **Just hike it:** Hundreds of miles of trails of all levels of difficulty lace the park, from flat and easy half-hour strolls to steep, strenuous all-day hikes.

★ **Go to the sun:** Crossing the Continental Divide at the 6,646-foot-high Logan Pass, Glacier's Going-to-the-Sun Road is a spectacular drive.

★ **View the wildlife:** This is one of the few places in North America where all native carnivores, including grizzlies, black bears, coyotes, and wolves, still survive.

★ **See glaciers while you still can:** Approximately 150 glaciers were present in Glacier National Park in 1850; by 2010, there were only 25 left.

In the rocky northwestern corner of Montana, Glacier National Park encompasses 1.2 million acres (1,563 square miles) of untrammeled wilds. Within the park, there are 25 named glaciers, 200 lakes, and 1,000 miles of streams. Neighboring Waterton Lakes National Park, across the border in Alberta, Canada, covers another 124,788 acres (505 square kilometers). In 1932, the parks were unified to form the Waterton-Glacier International Peace Park—the first international peace park in the world—in recognition of the two nations' friendship and dedication to peace.

1 West Glacier. Known to the Kootenai people as "sacred dancing lake," Lake McDonald is the largest glacial water basin lake in Glacier National Park.

2 Logan Pass. At 6,646 feet, the pass is the highest point on the Going-to-the-Sun Road. From mid-June to mid-October, a 1½-mile boardwalk leads to an overlook that crosses an area filled with lush meadows and wildflowers.

3 East Glacier. St. Mary Lake and Many Glacier are the major highlights of the eastern side of Glacier. Services and amenities are located at both sites.

4 Backcountry. This is some of the most incredible terrain in North America and provides the right combination of beautiful scenery and isolation. Although Waterton is a much smaller park, its backcountry trails connect with hiking trails in both Glacier and British Columbia's Akamina-Kishinena Provincial Park.

5 Waterton Lakes. The Canadian national park is the meeting of two worlds: the flatlands of the prairie and the abrupt upthrust of the mountains.

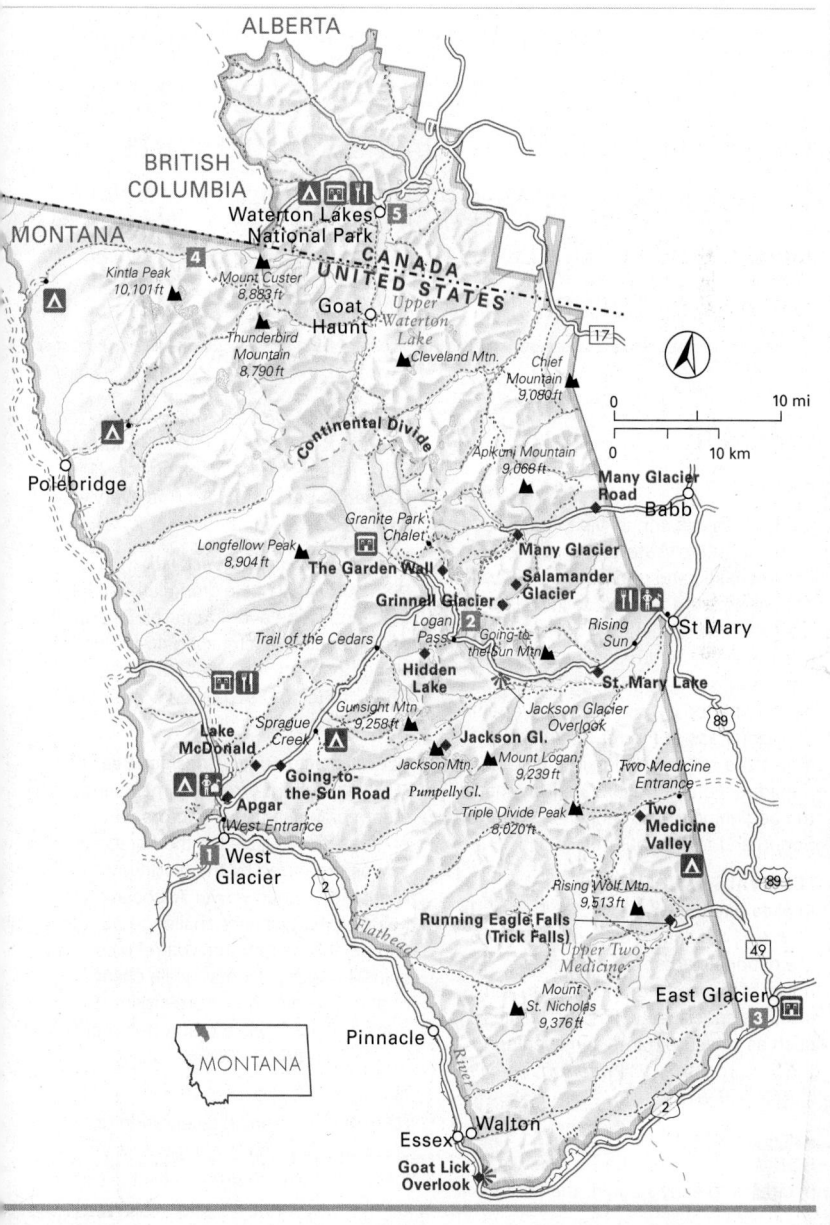

ALBERTA

BRITISH COLUMBIA

MONTANA

Waterton Lakes National Park

Kintla Peak 10,101 ft

Mount Custer 8,883 ft

CANADA
UNITED STATES

Goat Haunt

Upper Waterton Lake

Thunderbird Mountain 8,790 ft

Cleveland Mtn.

Chief Mountain 9,080 ft

17

0   10 mi

0   10 km

Polebridge

Continental Divide

Apikuni Mountain 9,068 ft

Many Glacier Road

Babb

Longfellow Peak 8,904 ft

Granite Park Chalet

Many Glacier

The Garden Wall

Salamander Glacier

Grinnell Glacier

Trail of the Cedars

Logan Pass

Going-to-the-Sun Mtn.

Rising Sun

St Mary

Hidden Lake

Gunsight Mtn. 9,258 ft

St. Mary Lake

Jackson Glacier Overlook

89

Lake McDonald

Sprague Creek

Going-to-the-Sun Road

Jackson Gl.

Jackson Mtn.

Mount Logan 9,239 ft

Two Medicine Entrance

Apgar

West Entrance

Pumpelly Gl.

Triple Divide Peak 8,020 ft

Two Medicine Valley

West Glacier

2

Rising Wolf Mtn. 9,513 ft

89

Flathead

Running Eagle Falls (Trick Falls)

Upper Two Medicine

49

Mount St. Nicholas 9,376 ft

East Glacier

3

MONTANA

Pinnacle

River

Walton

2

Essex

Goat Lick Overlook

The massive peaks of the Continental Divide in northwestern Montana form the backbone of Glacier National Park and its sister park in Canada, Waterton Lakes, which together make up the International Peace Park. Coniferous forests, thickly vegetated stream bottoms, and green-carpeted meadows provide homes for all wildlife.

Planning

WHEN TO GO

Of the 2 million annual visitors to Glacier and 400,000 to Waterton, most come between July and mid-September, when the streams are flowing, wildlife is roaming, and naturalist programs are fully underway. Snow removal on the alpine portion of Going-to-the-Sun Road is usually completed by mid-June; the opening of Logan Pass at the road's summit marks the summer opening of Glacier. Canada's Victoria Day in late May marks the beginning of the season in Waterton. Spring and fall are quieter.

FESTIVALS AND EVENTS

Canada Day

FESTIVAL | On July 1, all guests get into the national parks free of charge in honor of Canada's birthday. Waterton also has special activities for families such as treasure hunts and evening theater programs. ⊠ *Waterton Townsite* ☎ *403/859–5133*.

Summer Concert Series

FESTIVAL | Running each Thursday from mid-June to early August, the series is held in the Don Lawrence Amphitheater at Marantette Park in Columbia Falls. Types of music vary, but the Don Lawrence Big Band performs every year. ☎ *406/892–2072*.

Montana Dragon Boat Festival

FESTIVAL | FAMILY | Held on Flathead Lake, this captivating event features 95 teams of 20 paddlers each racing 46-foot-long Hong Kong–style boats. ☎ *888/888–2308, 406/758–2820* ⊕ *www.montanadragonboat.com*.

NW Montana Antique Threshing Bee

FESTIVAL | Steam threshing machines, steam plows, antique tractors, and engines flex muscles in the Parade of Power, organized by the Northwest Montana Antique Power Association in Kalispell. Participants challenge friends and neighbors to tractor barrel races and shingle-making events, while children of all ages enjoy miniature steam-train rides, music, food, and entertainment. ☎ *406/756–5577, 406/862–0890*.

Ski Fest

FESTIVAL | This annual celebration of cross-country skiing is a great way to introduce newcomers to kick-and-glide skiing. Equipment demonstrations, free ski lessons, and family activities are scheduled at the Izaak Walton Inn in Essex, Montana, and free trail passes are dispensed. ☎ *406/888–5700* ⊕ *www. izaakwaltoninn.com.*

Waterton Wildflower Festival

FESTIVAL | Wildflower walks, horseback rides, hikes, watercolor workshops, photography classes, and family events help visitors and locals celebrate the annual blooming of Waterton's bountiful wildflowers. ✉ *Waterton Lakes National Park* ☎ *800/215–2395* ⊕ *www.waterton-wildflowers.com.*

Waterton Wildlife Weekend

FESTIVAL | Wildlife viewing is at its best in Waterton during the fall. The weekend's events include viewing on foot, on horseback, and by boat. There are also photography, drawing, and sketching courses. ✉ *Waterton Lakes National Park* ☎ *800/215–2395* ⊕ *www.watertonwild-life.com.*

Whitefish Winter Carnival

FESTIVAL | For more than 40 years this February fest has been the scene of lively activities, including a grand parade with more than 100 entries, a torchlight parade on skis, fireworks, a penguin dip, and other family-friendly activities. ✉ *Whitefish* ☎ *406/862–3501* ⊕ *www. whitefishwintercarnival.com.*

PLANNING YOUR TIME
GLACIER IN ONE DAY

It's hard to beat the **Going-to-the-Sun Road** for a one-day trip in Glacier National Park. This itinerary takes you from west to east—if you're starting from St. Mary, take the tour backward. First, however, call the Glacier Park Boat Company (☎ *406/257–2426*) to make a reservation for the **St. Mary Lake** or **Lake McDonald boat tour,** depending on where you end up. Then drive up Going-to-the-Sun Road to **Avalanche Creek Campground,** and take a 30-minute stroll along the fragrant **Trail of the Cedars.** Afterward, continue driving

up—you can see views of waterfalls and wildlife to the left and an awe-inspiring, precipitous drop to the right. At the summit, **Logan Pass,** your arduous climb is rewarded with a gorgeous view of immense peaks, sometimes complemented by the sight of a mountain goat. Stop in at the **Logan Pass Visitor Center,** then take the 1½-mile **Hidden Lake Nature Trail** up to prime wildlife-viewing spots. Have a picnic at the overlook above Hidden Lake. In the afternoon, continue driving east over the mountains. Stop at the **Jackson Glacier Overlook** to view one of the park's largest glaciers. Continue down; eventually the forest thins, the vistas grow broader, and a gradual transition to the high plains begins. When you reach **Rising Sun Campground,** take the one-hour St. Mary Lake boat tour to St. Mary Falls. The Going-to-the-Sun Road is generally closed from mid-September to mid-June.

WATERTON IN ONE DAY

Begin your day with a stop at the **Waterton Information Centre** to pick up free maps and information about interpretive programs and schedules.

Stop at the **Bear's Hump Trailhead,** where you can enjoy a short and invigorating 1.4-km (0.9-mile) hike to a beautiful scenic overlook. After the hike, drive up the hill to the historic **Prince of Wales Hotel** to enjoy the view from the hillside behind the hotel.

Next, visit **Waterton Townsite** for an early lunch. Afterward, walk the easy 3-km (2-mile) **Townsite Loop Trail,** stopping to view **Cameron Falls** and explore the trail behind the falls.

End the day with a scenic two-hour **Waterton Inter-Nation Shoreline Cruise** across the border to **Goat Haunt Ranger Station** and back.

GLACIER AVERAGE HIGH/LOW TEMPERATURES					
JAN.	FEB.	MAR.	APR.	MAY	JUNE
28/15	35/19	42/23	53/30	64/37	71/44
JULY	AUG.	SEPT.	OCT.	NOV.	DEC.
79/47	78/46	67/39	53/32	37/25	30/18

WATERTON LAKES AVERAGE HIGH/LOW TEMPERATURES					
JAN.	FEB.	MAR.	APR.	MAY	JUNE
32/12	34/14	42/22	50/29	59/37	66/43
JULY	AUG.	SEPT.	OCT.	NOV.	DEC.
73/46	72/44	63/38	53/33	38/22	33/15

GETTING HERE AND AROUND

AIR TRAVEL

The nearest airports to Glacier are in Kalispell (25 miles) and Great Falls (157 miles), both in Montana. The nearest airport to Waterton Lakes is in Calgary (271 km [168 miles]).

BUS TRAVEL

Glacier National Park operates a free hop on, hop off shuttle along the Going-to-the-Sun Road from July through early September. The shuttle runs from Apgar to St. Mary Visitor Center; park visitor centers have information about departure times.

CAR TRAVEL

On the east, U.S. 89 accesses Many Glacier and St. Mary, while Highway 49 reaches Two Medicine. On the west, U.S. 2 goes to West Glacier. At the northwestern edge of Glacier, North Fork Road connects to Polebridge. Take the Chief Mountain Highway (Highway 17) to access Waterton Lakes during the summer or U.S. 89 to Alberta Highway 2 through Cardston and then west to the park via Highway 5 any time of the year.

The roads in both parks are either paved or gravel and become deteriorated from freezing and thawing. Drive slowly and anticipate that rocks and wildlife may be around the corner. Road reconstruction is part of the park experience as there are only a few warm months during which road crews can complete projects. Gasoline is available along most paved roads. Scenic pull-outs are frequent; watch for other vehicles pulling in or out, and watch for children in parking areas. Most development and services center on St. Mary Lake in the east and Lake McDonald in the west.

A passport is required of everyone crossing the Canadian/U.S. border. When you arrive at the border crossing, customs officers will ask for information such as where you are going and where you are from. You and your vehicle are subject to random search. Firearms are prohibited, except hunting rifles, which require permission you must obtain in advance. Soil, seeds, meat, and many fruits are also prohibited. Kids traveling with only one parent need a notarized letter from the other parent giving permission to enter Canada or the United States. If you are traveling with pets, you need proof of up-to-date immunizations to cross the border in either direction. Citizens from most countries (Canada, Mexico, and Bermuda are exceptions) entering the United States from Canada must pay $6 (cash only) at the border for a required I–94 or I–94W Arrival-Departure Record form, to be returned to border officials when leaving the United States. Contact United States Customs (☎ *406/335–2611*

⊕ www.cbp.gov) or the Canada Border Services Agency (☎ 403/344–3767 ⊕ www.cbsa-asfc.gc.ca) for more information.

PARK ESSENTIALS
ACCESSIBILITY
All visitor centers are wheelchair accessible, and most of the campgrounds and picnic areas are paved, with extended-length picnic tables and accessible restrooms. Three of Glacier's nature trails are wheelchair accessible: the Trail of the Cedars, Running Eagle Falls, and the Oberlin Bend Trail, just west of Logan Pass. In Waterton, the Linnet Lake Trail, Waterton Townsite Trail, Cameron Lake day-use area, and the International Peace Park Pavilion are wheelchair accessible.

PARK FEES AND PERMITS
Entrance fees for Glacier are $35 per vehicle or $20 for one person on foot or bike. The fee for motorcycles is $30 during peak season and $15 from November 1–April 30. Entrance fees are good for seven days, or you can purchase a Glacier National Park annual pass for $70. An America the Beautiful Pass is $80 and covers entrance to national parks and other federal recreation sites for one year. A day pass to Waterton Lakes costs C$7.80 for an individual or C$15.70 per seven people per vehicle, and a Parks Canada Discovery Pass costs C$67.70 for an individual or C$136.40 for a family and provides unlimited admission to Canada's national parks and historic sites for one year. Youth 17 and under receive free admission to all Canadian national parks and historic sites. *Passes to Glacier and Waterton must be paid separately.*

At Glacier the required backcountry permit is $7 per person per day from the Apgar Backcountry Permit Center after mid-April for the upcoming summer. Reservations cost $40. On the park's official website (⊕ www.nps.gov/glac/planyourvisit/backcountry.htm), you can find the latest backcountry information

and a form that can be faxed to the backcountry office.

Waterton requires backcountry camping permits for use of its backcountry camping spots, with reservations available up to 90 days ahead at the visitor reception center. In 2018, all backcountry campgrounds in the park were closed due to damage from the 2017 Kenow Wildfire. Consult the park website or phone the visitor reception center to find out which campgrounds are open, the condition of camping sites, and the fees for reservations (☎ 403/859–5133).

PARK HOURS
The parks are open year-round, but most roads and facilities close from October through May. The parks are in the Mountain time zone.

CELL PHONE RECEPTION
Cell phone coverage is improving, but in mountainous terrain it is common to have poor reception. Depending on your cell phone carrier, cell service is best available in West Glacier or St. Mary in Glacier National Park and in the Waterton Townsite in Waterton Lakes National Park. Find pay phones at Avalanche Campground, Glacier Highland Motel and Store, Apgar, St. Mary Visitor Center, Two Medicine Camp Store, and all lodges except Granite Park Chalet and Sperry Chalet. Several pay phones are also available in the townsite of Waterton Lakes National Park.

EDUCATIONAL OFFERINGS
Evening interpretive programs at Waterton Lakes National Parks are offered from late June until Labor Day at the Falls Theatre, near Cameron Falls, and the townsite campground. These one-hour sessions begin at 8. A guided International Peace Park hike is held every Wednesday and Saturday in July and August. The 14-km (9-mile) hike begins at the Bertha trailhead, and is led by Canadian and American park interpreters. You take lunch at the International Border before

continuing on to Goat Haunt in Glacier National Park, Montana, and returning to Waterton via boat. A fee is charged for the return boat trip. You must preregister for this hike at the Waterton Information Centre.

CLASSES AND SEMINARS
Glacier Institute
TOUR—SIGHT | FAMILY | Based near West Glacier at the Field Camp and on the remote western boundary at the Big Creek Outdoor Education Center, this learning institute offers more than 75 field courses for kids and adults. Year-round, experts in wildlife biology, native plants, and river ecology lead treks into Glacier's backcountry on daylong and multiday programs. The Youth Adventure Series for children ages 6 to 11 features one-day naturalist courses; preteens and teens can take weeklong trips. Three-day family camps for ages 7 and up are also on offer. ⊠ 137 Main St., Kalispell ☎ 406/755–1211, 406/755–7154 ⊕ www. glacierinstitute.org ☞ From $40.

★ Ranger-led Activities
TOUR—SIGHT | FAMILY | Free ranger-led programs, most of them daily from July to early September, include guided hikes, group walks, evening talks, historical tours, gaze-at-the-stars parties, and naturalist discussions. For the Native America Speaks program, tribal members share their history and culture through stories, poetry, music, and dance. In winter, guided two-hour snowshoe treks take place in the Apgar area. Among the activities for children is the **Junior Ranger Program,** for which children between ages 6 and 12 complete fun educational tasks to become Junior Rangers. To learn more about ranger-led activities, check online or at the visitor centers or refer to the park newspaper. ☎ 406/888–7800 ⊕ www.nps.gov/glac/planyourvisit/rang-er-led-activities.htm ☞ Free.

RESTAURANTS
Steak houses serving certified Angus beef are typical of the region; in recent years, resort communities have diversified their menus to include bison meat, fresh fish, and gluten-free and vegetarian options. Small cafés offer hearty, inexpensive meals and perhaps the chance to chat with locals. Trout, venison, elk, moose, and bison appear on the menus inside the park. In Montana, huckleberries appear on many menus. Attire everywhere is casual.

HOTELS
Lodgings in the parks tend to be rustic and simple, though there are a few grand lodges. Some modern accommodations have swimming pools, hot tubs, boat rentals, guided excursions, and fine dining. The supply of rooms within both parks is limited, but the prices are relatively reasonable. It's best to reserve well in advance, especially for July and August. *Hotel reviews have been shortened. For full information, visit Fodors. com.*

What It Costs			
$	$$	$$$	$$$$
RESTAURANTS			
under $13	$13–$20	$21–$30	over $30
HOTELS			
under $100	$100–$150	$151–$200	over $200

TOURS
Red Jammer Bus Tours
TOUR—SIGHT | Glacier National Park Lodges operates driver-narrated bus tours that cover most of the park accessible by road. The tour of Going-to-the-Sun Road, a favorite, is conducted in "jammers," vintage 1936 red buses with roll-back tops—photo opportunities are plentiful. In addition to tours, which last from a few hours to a full day, hiker shuttles and transfers from the West Glacier train

station to Lake McDonald Lodge or the Village Inn are available. Reservations are essential. ☎ 855/733–4522, 303/265–7010, 303/297–3175 ⊕ www.glacier-nationalparklodges.com/red-bus-tours ✉ From $40 for tours; shuttles from $6.

Sun Tours
TOUR—SIGHT | Tour the park in an air-conditioned coach and learn the Blackfeet perspective from native guides who concentrate on how Glacier's features are relevant to the Blackfeet Nation, past and present. These tours depart from East Glacier and the St. Mary Visitor Center. ✉ 29 Glacier Ave., East Glacier Park ☎ 406/226–9220, 800/786–9220 ⊕ www.glaciersuntours.com ✉ From $50.

VISITOR INFORMATION
PARK CONTACT INFORMATION Glacier National Park ☎ 406/888–7800 ⊕ www.nps.gov/glac. **Waterton Lakes National Park** ☎ 403/859–5133, 403/859–2224 year-round ⊕ www.pc.gc.ca/waterton.

GLACIER VISITOR CENTERS
Apgar Visitor Center
INFO CENTER | FAMILY | This is a great first stop if you're entering the park from the west. Here you can get all kinds of information, including maps, permits, books, and the *Junior Ranger* newspaper, and you can check out displays that will help you plan your tour of the park. In winter, the rangers offer free snowshoe walks. Snowshoes can be rented for $2 at the visitor center. ✉ 2 miles north of West Glacier in Apgar Village, Glacier National Park ☎ 406/888–7800.

Logan Pass Visitor Center
INFO CENTER | Built of stone, this center stands sturdy against the severe weather that forces it to close in winter. When it's open, rangers give 10-minute talks on the alpine environment, and you can get advice from them and buy books and maps. ✉ Going-to-the-Sun Rd., 34 miles east of West Glacier, 18 miles west of St. Mary, Glacier National Park ☎ 406/888–7800.

St. Mary Visitor Center
INFO CENTER | The park's largest visitor complex has a huge relief map of the park's peaks and valleys and screens a 15-minute orientation video. Exhibits are designed to help visitors understand the park from the perspective of its original inhabitants—the Blackfeet, Salish, Kootenai, and Pend d'Orielle tribes. Rangers host evening presentations during the summer. The center has books and maps for sale, backcountry camping permits, and large viewing windows facing the 10-mile-long St. Mary Lake. ✉ Going-to-the-Sun Rd., off U.S. 89, Glacier National Park ☎ 406/732–7750.

WATERTON VISITOR CENTER
Waterton Information Centre
INFO CENTER | The original Waterton Information Centre was destroyed by the Kenow Wildfire in 2017 and plans are underway to construct a new building. Until then, the visitor center is temporarily located in the Lion's Hall in the Waterton Townsite. Stop in to pick up brochures, maps, and books. You can also pick up the booklet for the free Xplorer Program for kids between ages six and 11. Park interpreters are on hand to answer questions and give directions. ✉ Waterton Rd., before townsite, Waterton Lakes National Park ☎ 403/859–5133.

Glacier National Park

 Sights

SCENIC DRIVES
★ Going-to-the-Sun Road
SCENIC DRIVE | This magnificent, 50-mile highway—the only American roadway designated both a National Historic Landmark and a National Civil Engineering Landmark—crosses the crest of the Continental Divide at Logan Pass and traverses the towering Garden Wall. Open from mid-June to mid-September only (due to heavy snowfalls), this is one of the most stunning drives in Glacier National Park. A multiyear Sun Road

Plants and Wildlife in Glacier and Waterton

In summer, a profusion of new flowers, grasses, and budding trees covers the landscape high and low. Spring attracts countless birds, from golden eagles riding thermals north to Canada and Alaska to rare harlequin ducks dipping in creeks. Snow-white mountain goats, with their wispy white beards and curious stares, are seen in alpine areas, and sure-footed bighorn sheep graze the high meadows in the short summers. The largest population of grizzly bears in the lower 48 states lives in the wild in and around the park. Feeding the animals is illegal.

Visiting Glacier in winter makes for easy tracking of many large animals like moose, elk, deer, mountain lions, wolf, lynx, and their smaller neighbors—the snowshoe hare, pine marten, beaver, and muskrat.

In park lakes, sportfishing species include burbot (ling), northern pike, whitefish, grayling, cutthroat, rainbow, lake (Mackinaw), kokanee salmon, and brook trout.

rehabilitation project will result in some driving delays due to reconstruction. The drive is susceptible to frequent delays in summer. To avoid traffic jams and parking problems, take the road early in the morning or in the evening (when the lighting is ideal for photography and wildlife is most likely to appear). Glacier National Park Service operates a free hop on, hop off shuttle service from Apgar Visitor Centre to St. Mary Visitor Centre during the peak season. Vehicle size is restricted to under 21 feet long, 10 feet high, and 8 feet wide, including mirrors, between Avalanche Creek Campground and Sun Point. Cyclists enjoy traveling the open part of the road in early June before it is open to vehicular traffic. ⊠ *Glacier National Park.*

Many Glacier Road

SCENIC DRIVE | This 12-mile drive enters Glacier on the northeast side of the park, west of Babb, and travels along Sherburne Lake for almost 5 miles, penetrating a glacially carved valley surrounded by mountains. It passes through meadows and a scrubby forest of lodgepole pines, aspen, and cottonwood. The farther you travel up the valley, the more clearly you'll be able to see Grinnell and Salamander glaciers. The road, which passes Many Glacier Hotel and ends at the Swiftcurrent Campground, is usually closed from October to May. The road has many potholes and can be extremely rough in places. ⊠ *Glacier National Park.*

HISTORIC SITES

Apgar

TOWN | FAMILY | On the southwest end of Lake McDonald, this tiny hamlet has a few stores, an ice-cream shop, motels, ranger buildings, a campground, and a historic schoolhouse. A store called the Montana House is open year-round in the village, but except for the weekend-only visitor center, no other services remain open from November to mid-May. Across the street from the Apgar visitor center, **Apgar Discovery Cabin** is filled with animal posters, kids' activities, and maps. ⊠ *2 miles north of west entrance, Glacier National Park* ☎ *406/888–7939.*

SCENIC STOPS
ALONG THE GOING-TO-THE-SUN ROAD

The Going-to-the-Sun Road, arguably the most beautiful drive in the country, connects Lake McDonald on the western side of Glacier with St. Mary Lake on the east. Turnoffs provide views of the high country and glacier-carved valleys. If you don't want to drive the Going-to-the-Sun Road, consider making the ride in a "jammer," an antique red bus operated by Glacier National Park Lodges. The drivers double as guides, and they can roll back the tops of the vehicles to give you improved views.

The Garden Wall

NATURE SITE | An abrupt and jagged wall of rock juts above the road and is visible for about 10 miles as it follows Logan Creek from just past Avalanche Creek Campground to Logan Pass. ⊠ *Going-to-the-Sun Rd., 24–34 miles northeast of West Glacier, Glacier National Park.*

Hidden Lake Overlook

BODY OF WATER | Take a walk from Logan Pass up to see the crystalline Hidden Lake, which often still has ice clinging to it in early July. It's a 1½-mile hike on an uphill grade, partially on a boardwalk that protects the abundant wildflowers. ⊠ *Trailhead: behind Logan Pass Visitor Center, Glacier National Park.*

Jackson Glacier Overlook

VIEWPOINT | On the eastern side of the Continental Divide, you come into view of Jackson Glacier looming in a rocky pass across the upper St. Mary River valley. If it isn't covered with snow, you'll see sharp peaks of ice. The glacier is shrinking and may disappear in another 100 years. ⊠ *5 miles east of Logan Pass, Glacier National Park.*

Logan Pass

SCENIC DRIVE | At 6,646 feet, this is the highest point in the park accessible by motor vehicle. Crowded with tourists in July and August, it offers unparalleled views of both sides of the Continental Divide. Mountain goats, bighorn sheep, and grizzly bears frequent the area. The Logan Pass Visitor Center is just east of the pass. ⊠ *34 miles east of West Glacier, 18 miles west of St. Mary, Glacier National Park.*

St. Mary Lake

BODY OF WATER | When the breezes calm, the second-largest lake in Glacier National Park mirrors the snowcapped granite peaks that line the St. Mary Valley. To get a good look at the beautiful scenery, follow the Sun Point Nature Trail (closed for renovation in 2016) along the lake's shore. The hike is 1 mile each way. ⊠ *1 mile west of St. Mary, Glacier National Park.*

OTHER SCENIC STOPS
Goat Lick Overlook

VIEWPOINT | Mountain goats frequent this natural salt lick on a cliff above the Middle Fork of the Flathead River. You can watch the wildlife from an observation stand. ⊠ *U.S. 2, 2½ miles east of Walton Ranger Station, Glacier National Park.*

Grinnell and Salamander Glaciers

NATURE SITE | These glaciers formed as one ice mass, but in 1926 they broke apart and have been shrinking ever since. The best viewpoint is reached by the 5½-mile Grinnell Glacier Trail from Many Glacier. The trailhead is at the far northwestern end of Lake Josephine. You can get there by boat or via the trail behind the Many Glacier Hotel. In summer, rangers lead six-hour hikes to Grinnell Valley that depart each morning from the Many Glacier Picnic Area. ⊠ *Glacier National Park.*

Lake McDonald

BODY OF WATER | This beautiful 10-mile-long lake, the parks' largest lake, is accessible year-round from Going-to-the-Sun Road. Take a boat ride to the middle for a view of the surrounding glacier-clad mountains. You can go fishing and horseback riding at either end, and in winter, snowshoe and cross-country ski. ⊠ *2 miles north of west entrance, Glacier National Park.*

Running Eagle Falls (Trick Falls)

BODY OF WATER | Cascading near Two Medicine, these are actually two different waterfalls from two different sources.

In spring, when the water level is high, the upper falls join the lower falls for a 40-foot drop into Two Medicine River; in summer, the upper falls dry up, revealing the lower 20-foot falls that start midway down the precipice. ⊠ *2 miles east of Two Medicine entrance, Glacier National Park.*

Two Medicine Valley

NATURE SITE | Rugged, often windy, and always beautiful, the valley is a remote 9-mile drive from Highway 49 and is surrounded by some of the park's most stark, rocky peaks. On and around the valley's lake you can rent a canoe, take a narrated boat tour, camp, and hike. Bears frequent the area. The road is closed from late October through late May. ⊠ *Two Medicine entrance, 9 miles east of Hwy. 49, Glacier National Park* ☎ *406/888–7800, 406/257–2426boat tours.*

 Activities

MULTISPORT OUTFITTERS

Glacier Guides and Montana Raft Company

BOATING | Take a raft trip through the Wild-and-Scenic–designated white water of the Middle Fork of the Flathead and combine it with a hike, horseback ride, or a barbecue. Guided hikes, fly-fishing trips, and multiday adventures can also be arranged. ⊠ *11970 U.S. 2 E, 1 mile west of West Glacier, Glacier National Park* ☎ *406/387–5555, 800/521–7238* ⊕ *www.glacierguides.com* ⊠ *From $53.*

Glacier Raft Company and Outdoor Center

BOATING | In addition to running fishing trips, family float rides, saddle and paddle adventures, and high-adrenaline white-water adventure rafting (including multiday excursions), this outfitter will set you up with camping, backpacking, and fishing gear. There's also a full-service fly-fishing shop and outdoor store. You can stay in one of 13 log cabins or a glacier-view home. ⊠ *12400 U.S 2 E, West Glacier* ☎ *406/888–5454,*

800/235–6781 ⊕ *www.glacierraftco.com* ⊠ *From $59.*

Great Northern Whitewater

BOATING | Sign up for daily white-water, kayaking, and fishing trips. Multiday trips can also be arranged. This outfitter also rents Swiss-style chalets with views of Glacier's peaks. ⊠ *12127 U.S. 2 E, 1 mile south of West Glacier, Glacier National Park* ☎ *406/387–5340, 800/735–7897* ⊕ *www.greatnorthernresort.com* ⊠ *From $58.*

Wild River Adventures

BOATING | Brave the white water in an inflatable kayak or a traditional raft or enjoy a scenic float with these guys, who will paddle you over the Middle Fork of the Flathead, and peddle you tall tales all the while. They also conduct trail rides and scenic fishing trips on rivers around Glacier National Park. ⊠ *11900 U.S. 2 E, 1 mile west of West Glacier, Glacier National Park* ☎ *406/387–9453, 800/700–7056* ⊕ *www.riverwild.com* ⊠ *From $58.*

BICYCLING

Cyclists in Glacier must stay on roads or bike routes and are not permitted on hiking trails or in the backcountry. The one-lane, unpaved Inside North Fork Road from Apgar to Polebridge is well suited to mountain bikers. Two Medicine Road is an intermediate paved route, with a mild grade at the beginning, becoming steeper as you approach Two Medicine Campground. Much of the western half of Going-to-the-Sun Road is closed to bikes from 11 am to 4 pm. Other restrictions apply during peak traffic periods and road construction. Many cyclists enjoy the Going-to-the-Sun Road prior to its opening to vehicular traffic in mid-June. You cannot cycle all the way over the pass in early June, but you can cycle as far as the road is plowed and ride back down without encountering much traffic besides a few snowplows and construction vehicles. You can find thrilling off-road trails just outside the park near Whitefish. There are no bike-rental shops

The scenic, 50-mile Going-to-the-Sun Road takes about two hours to drive, depending on how often you stop.

inside the park, but there are two in the town of Whitefish.

Glacier Cyclery

BICYCLING | Daily and weekly bike rentals of touring, road, and mountain bikes for all ages and skill levels are available here. The shop also sells bikes, equipment, and attire, and does repairs. Information about local trails is available on its website and in the store. ✉ *326 2nd St. E., Whitefish* ☎ *406/862–6446* ⊕ *www.glaciercyclery.com* ⌨ *From $30.*

Great Northern Cycle & Ski

BICYCLING | You can rent road bikes and mountain bikes from this outfitter that also services and repairs bikes and sells cycling and skiing attire and gear. ✉ *328 Central Ave., Whitefish* ☎ *406/862–5321* ⊕ *www.gncycleski.com* ⌨ *From $75.*

BOATING AND RAFTING

Glacier has many stunning lakes and rivers, and boating is a popular park activity. Many rafting companies provide adventures along the border of the park on the Middle and North Forks of the Flathead River. The Middle Fork has some excellent white water, while the North Fork has both slow-moving and fast-moving sections. If you bring your own raft or kayak—watercraft such as Sea-Doos or Jet Skis are not allowed in the park—stop at the Hungry Horse Ranger Station in the Flathead National Forest near West Glacier to obtain a permit. Consider starting at Ousel Creek and floating to West Glacier on the Middle Fork of the Flathead River.

Glacier Park Boat Company

BOATING | This company conducts tours of five lakes. A **Lake McDonald cruise** takes you from the dock at Lake McDonald Lodge to the middle of the lake for an unparalleled view of the Continental Divide's Garden Wall. **Many Glacier tours** on Swiftcurrent Lake and Lake Josephine depart from Many Glacier Hotel and provide views of the Continental Divide. **Two Medicine Lake cruises** leave from the dock near the ranger station and lead to several trails. **St. Mary Lake cruises** leave from the launch near Rising Sun Campground

Did You Know?

Grizzly bears can run up to 40 mph and live 30 years in the wild. These 350- to 800-pound omnivores can stretch to 8 feet tall. Here a young grizzly stands on two feet just off the Grinnell Glacier Trail.

and head to Red Eagle Mountain and other spots. The tours last from 45 to 90 minutes. You can rent small watercraft at Apgar, Lake McDonald, Two Medicine, and Many Glacier. ☎ *406/257–2426* ⊕ *www.glacierparkboats.com* ☒ *Tours from $14, rentals from $10.*

FISHING

Within Glacier there's an almost unlimited range of fishing possibilities, with catch-and-release encouraged. You can fish in most waters of the park, but the best fishing is generally in the least accessible spots. A fishing license is not required inside the park, but you must stop by a park office to pick up a copy of the regulations. The fishing season runs from the third Saturday in May through November. Several companies offer guided fishing trips in the area. ■TIP➔ **Fishing on both the North Fork and the Middle Fork of the Flathead River requires a Montana conservation license ($10), an AIS Prevention Pass ($15), and a Montana fishing license ($25 for two consecutive days or $86 for a season). They are available at most convenience stores, sports shops, and from the Montana Department of Fish, Wildlife, and Parks** (☎ *406/752–5501* ⊕ *www.fwp. mt.gov*).

HIKING

With more than 730 miles of marked trails, Glacier is a hiker's paradise. Trail maps are available at all visitor centers and entrance stations. Before hiking, ask about trail closures due to bear or mountain lion activity. Never hike alone. For backcountry hiking, pick up a permit from park headquarters or the Apgar Backcountry Permit Center (☎ *406/888–7939*) near Glacier's west entrance.

Avalanche Lake Trail

HIKING/WALKING | From Avalanche Creek Campground, take this 3-mile trail leading to mountain-ringed Avalanche Lake. The walk is only moderately difficult (it ascends 730 feet), making this one of the park's most accessible backcountry lakes. Crowds fill the parking area and

Shrinking Glaciers

The effects of climate change are on full display at Glacier National Park. In 1850 there were approximately 150 glaciers here; as of 2010, only 25 remained. Some climate scientists predict that by 2050 even these will be gone.

trail during July and August and on sunny weekends in May and June. *Moderate.* ☒ *Glacier National Park* ✛ *Trailhead: across from Avalanche Creek Campground, 15 miles north of Apgar on Going-to-the-Sun Rd.*

Baring Falls

HIKING/WALKING | **FAMILY** | For a nice family hike, try the 1.3-mile path from the Sun Point parking area. It leads to a spruce and Douglas fir woods; cross a log bridge over Baring Creek and you arrive at the base of gushing Baring Falls. *Easy.* ☒ *Glacier National Park* ✛ *Trailhead 11 miles east of Logan Pass on Going-to-the-Sun Rd., at Sun Point parking area.*

Glacier Guides

HIKING/WALKING | The exclusive backpacking guide service in Glacier National Park can arrange guided day hikes or multiday hikes. Guided hiking tours are customized to match the skill level of the hikers, and include stops to identify plants, animals, and habitats. ☒ *11970 U.S. 2 E, West Glacier* ☎ *406/387–5555, 800/521–7238* ⊕ *www.glacierguides.com* ☒ *From $85.*

Grinnell Glacier Trail

HIKING/WALKING | The strenuous 5½-mile hike to Grinnell Glacier, the park's largest and most accessible glacier, is marked by several spectacular viewpoints. You start at Swiftcurrent Lake's picnic area, climb a moraine to Lake Josephine, then climb to the Grinnell Glacier overlook. Halfway up, turn around to see the prairie land to the northeast. You can shortcut the trail by 2 miles each way by taking scenic boat rides across Swiftcurrent Lake and Lake Josephine. From July to mid-September, a ranger-led hike departs from the Many Glacier Hotel boat dock on most mornings at 8:30. *Difficult.* ⊠ *Glacier National Park* ✛ *Trailhead: at Lake Josephine boat dock.*

Hidden Lake Nature Trail

HIKING/WALKING | This uphill, 1½-mile trail runs from Logan Pass southwest to Hidden Lake Overlook, from which you get a beautiful view of the lake and McDonald Valley. In spring, ribbons of water pour off the rocks surrounding the lake. *Easy.* ⊠ *Glacier National Park* ✛ *Trailhead: behind Logan Pass Visitor Center.*

★ Highline Trail

HIKING/WALKING | From the Logan Pass parking lot, hike north along the Garden Wall and just below the craggy Continental Divide. Wildflowers dominate the 7.6 miles to Granite Park Chalet, a National Historic Landmark, where hikers with reservations can overnight. Return to Logan Pass along the same trail or hike down 4½ miles (a 2,500-foot descent) on the Loop Trail. *Moderate.* ⊠ *Glacier National Park* ✛ *Trailhead: at Logan Pass Visitor Center.*

Iceberg Lake Trail

HIKING/WALKING | This moderately strenuous 9-mile round-trip hike passes the gushing Ptarmigan Falls, then climbs to its namesake, where icebergs bob in the chilly mountain loch. Mountain goats hang out on sheer cliffs above, bighorn sheep graze in the high mountain meadows, and grizzly bears dig for glacier lily bulbs, grubs, and other delicacies. Rangers lead hikes here almost daily in summer, leaving at 8:30 am. *Moderate.* ⊠ *Glacier National Park* ✛ *Trailhead: at Swiftcurrent Inn parking lot, off Many Glacier Rd.*

Sun Point Nature Trail

HIKING/WALKING | This 1.3-mile well-groomed trail allows you to walk along the cliffs and shores of picturesque St. Mary Lake. A stunning waterfall awaits at the end of the hike. You can hike one-way and take a boat transfer back. *Easy.* ⊠ *Glacier National Park* ✛ *Trailhead: 11 miles east of Logan Pass on Going-to-the-Sun Rd., at Sun Point parking area.*

Trail of the Cedars

HIKING/WALKING | **FAMILY** | This wheelchair-accessible, ½-mile boardwalk loop through an ancient cedar and hemlock forest is a favorite of families with small children and people with disabilities. Interpretive signs describe the habitat and natural history of the rain forest. *Easy.* ⊠ *Glacier National Park* ✛ *Trailhead: across from Avalanche Creek Campground, 15 miles north of Apgar on Going-to-the-Sun Rd.*

Two Medicine Valley Trails

HIKING/WALKING | One of the least-developed areas of Glacier, the southeastern corner of the park is a good place for a quiet day hike, although you should look out for signs of bears. The trailhead to Upper Two Medicine Lake and Cobalt Lake begins west of the boat dock and camp supply store, where you can make arrangements for a boat pickup or drop-off across the lake. *Difficult.* ⊠ *Glacier National Park* ✛ *Trailhead: west of Two Medicine Campground boat dock, 9 miles west of Hwy. 49.*

HORSEBACK RIDING

Horses are permitted on many trails within the parks; check for seasonal exceptions. Horseback riding is prohibited on paved roads. You can pick up a brochure with suggested routes and lists of outfitters from any visitor center or entrance station. The **Sperry Chalet Trail** to the view of Sperry Glacier above Lake McDonald is a tough 7-mile climb.

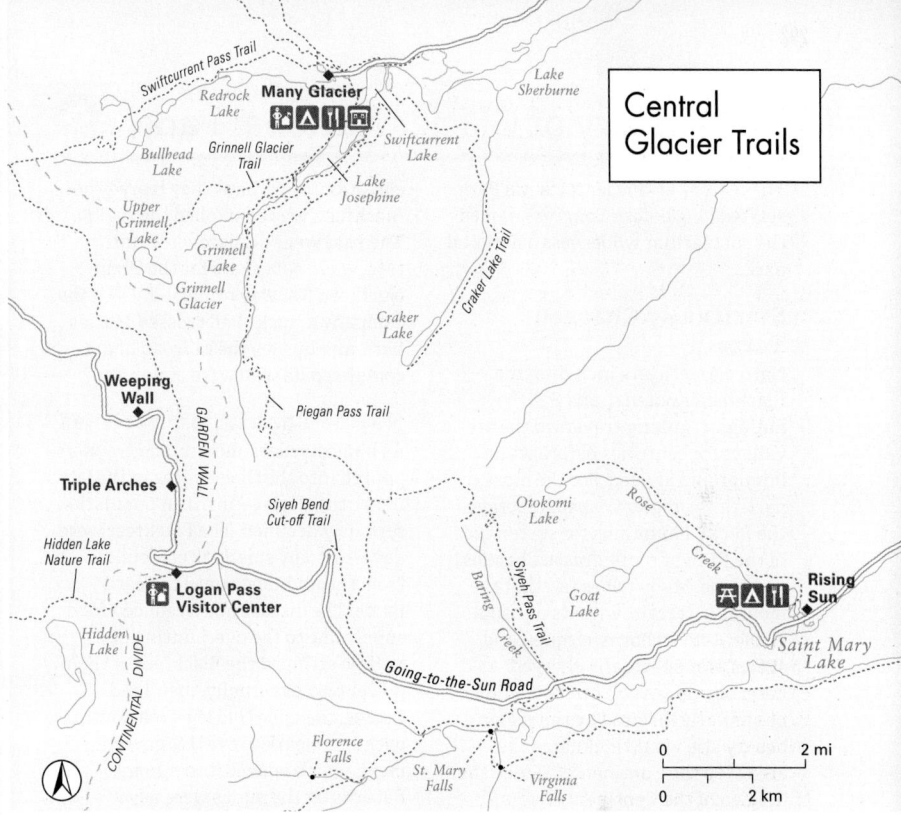

Central
Glacier Trails

Glacier Gateway Outfitters

HORSEBACK RIDING | On this East Glacier company's trips, a Blackfoot cowboy guides riders on Blackfeet Nation land adjacent to the Two Medicine area of Glacier National Park. Rides, from an hour to all day, climb through aspen groves to high-country views of Dancing Lady and Bison mountains. Riders must be seven or older. Reservations are essential. ✉ *East Glacier Park* ☎ *406/226–4408 in season, 406/338–5560 off season* 💲 *From $35.*

Swan Mountain Outfitters

HORSEBACK RIDING | The only outfitter that offers horseback riding inside the park, Swan begins its rides at Apgar, Lake McDonald, Many Glacier, and West Glacier. Trips for beginning to advanced riders cover both flat and mountainous terrain. Fishing can also be included.

Riders must be seven or older and weigh less than 250 pounds. Reservations are essential. ✉ *Coram* ☎ *877/888–5557 central reservations, 406/381–4405 Apgar Corral* ⊕ *www.swanmountainoutfitters. com/glacier* 💲 *From $50.*

SKIING AND SNOWSHOEING

Cross-country skiing and snowshoeing are increasingly popular in the park. Glacier distributes a free pamphlet entitled *Ski Trails of Glacier National Park,* with 16 noted trails. You can start at Lake McDonald Lodge and ski cross-country up Going-to-the-Sun Road. The 2½-mile Apgar Natural Trail is popular with snowshoers. No restaurants are open in winter in Glacier, but you can pop into Montana House (⊕ *montanahouse.info*) for hot cider, coffee, cookies, and a little shopping. The park website (⊕ *home.nps.*

The History of Glacier National Park

The history of Glacier National Park started long before Congress named the spectacular wilderness a national park.

Spiritually Charged Terrain

Native Americans, including the Blackfeet, Kootenai, and Salish nations, regularly traversed the area's valleys for centuries before white immigrants arrived. For the most part, these migratory people foraged the Rocky Mountains for sustenance in the form of roots, grasses, berries, and game. Many tribes felt that the mountain terrain, with its unusual glacier-carved horns, cirques, and arêtes, was spiritually charged. Later, European colonizers would be similarly inspired by the region's beauty and would nickname the area atop the Continental Divide the "Crown of the Continent."

Trappers Arrive

White trappers arrived as early as the 1780s. In 1805, Lewis and Clark passed south of what is now Glacier National Park. Attracted by the expedition's reports of abundant beaver, many more trappers, primarily British, French, and Spanish, migrated to the region. For the next few decades, though, human activity was limited to lone trappers and migrating Native Americans.

Elusive Pass

Lewis and Clark sought but did not find the elusive pass over the Rockies, now known as Marias Pass, on the park's southern edge at elevation 5,200 feet. Their scouts may have been unaware of the relatively low elevation, or perhaps they feared the Blackfeet, who controlled the region. The pass went undiscovered until 1889, when surveyors for the Great Northern Railway found it. By 1891 the company's tracks had crossed Marias Pass, and by 1895 the railroad had completed its westward expansion.

Native Population Declines

As homesteaders, miners, and trappers poured into the Glacier area in the late 1800s, the Native American population seriously declined. The Blackfeet were devastated by smallpox epidemics from the mid-1800s until the early 1900s. The disease and a reduced food supply due to the overhunting of buffalo stripped the Blackfeet of their power and, eventually, their land. In 1895, the tribe sold the area now within the park to the U.S. government, which opened it to miners. Returns on the mines were never substantial, and most were abandoned by 1905.

Protecting the Beauty

Between the late 1880s and 1900, the Great Northern Railway company built seven backcountry chalets to house guests, and promised tourists from the East a back-to-nature experience with daylong hikes and horseback rides between the chalets. Visitors arrived by train at West Glacier, took a stagecoach to Lake McDonald, a boat to the lakeside Snyder Hotel, and began their nature adventures from there. Congress found reason enough to establish Glacier National Park and, in 1910, President William Howard Taft signed the bill that did so.

gov/applications/glac/ski/xcski.htm) has ski trail maps.

Glacier Adventure Guides

CLIMBING/MOUNTAINEERING | This organization leads one-day and multiday guided snowshoe trips on scenic winter trails. On overnight trips, you stay in igloos and snow caves. During the summer, the company conducts guided hiking and rock-climbing adventures outside the park. ⊠ *Glacier National Park* ☎ *877/735–9514, 406/892–2173* ⊕ *www.glacieradventureguides.com* ⧖ *From $180.*

Izaak Walton Inn

SKIING/SNOWBOARDING | Just outside the southern edge of the park, the inn has more than 20 miles of groomed cross-country ski trails on its property. It offers equipment rentals and lessons as well as guided ski and snowshoe tours inside the park. Inn guests can ski for free, but others must purchase a ski pass. The inn is one of the few places in the area that is both open in winter and accessible by Amtrak train, which saves you the worry of driving on icy mountain roads. ⊠ *290 Izaak Walton Inn Rd., off U.S. 2, Essex* ☎ *406/888–5700* ⊕ *www.izaakwaltoninn.com/activities/winter-activities* ⧖ *From $10.*

Waterton Lakes National Park

A World Heritage Site, Waterton Lakes National Park represents the meeting of two worlds—the flatlands of the prairie and the abrupt upthrust of the mountains—squeezing an unusual mix of wildlife, flora, and climate zones into its 505 square km (200 square miles). In September 2017, the Kenow Wildfire burned 19,303 hectares (47,698 acres) in Waterton Lakes National Park. The wildfire had a significant impact on park infrastructure and affected more than 80% of the hiking trail network. Through the efforts of brave fire fighters, the townsite

was virtually untouched. Wildfires play an important role in a forest ecosystem and the park is already recovering. Check the website to learn the status of trails before heading out.

 ## Sights

SCENIC DRIVES

Akamina Parkway

BODY OF WATER | Take this winding 16-km (10-mile) road up to Cameron Lake, but drive slowly and watch for wildlife: it's common to see bears along the way. At the lake you will find a relatively flat, paved, 1.6-km (1-mile) trail that hugs the western shore and makes a nice walk. Bring your binoculars. Grizzly bears are often spotted on the lower slopes of the mountains at the far end of the lake. ⊠ *Waterton Lakes National Park.*

Red Rock Parkway

SCENIC DRIVE | The 15-km (9-mile) route takes you from the prairie up the Blakiston Valley to Red Rock Canyon, where water has cut through the earth, exposing red sedimentary rock. It's common to see bears just off the road, especially in autumn, when the berries are ripe. ⊠ *Waterton Lakes National Park.*

HISTORIC SITES

First Oil Well in Western Canada

HISTORIC SITE | Alberta is known worldwide for its oil and gas production, and the first oil well in western Canada was established in 1902 in what is now the park. Stop at this National Historic Site to explore the wellheads, drilling equipment, and remains of the Oil City boomtown. ⊠ *Waterton Lakes National Park* ⊹ *Watch for sign 7.7 km (4.8 miles) up the Akamina Pkwy.* ⧖ *Free.*

Prince of Wales Hotel

HISTORIC SITE | Named for the prince who later became King Edward VIII, this hotel was constructed between 1926 and 1927 and was designated a National Historic Site in 1995. Stand on the ridge outside the hotel and take in the magnificent view or pop inside and enjoy it from the comfort of the expansive lobby. Tea is served in the lobby in the afternoon. ⊠ *Off Hwy. 5, Waterton Lakes National Park* ☎ *406/892–2525, 403/236–3400 mid-May–late Sept.* ⊕ *www.glacierpark-collection.com/lodging/prince-of-wales-hotel* ⊠ *Free.*

SCENIC STOPS

Cameron Lake

BODY OF WATER | The jewel of Waterton, Cameron Lake sits in a land of glacially carved cirques (steep-walled basins). In summer, hundreds of varieties of alpine wildflowers fill the area, including 22 kinds of wild orchids. Canoes, rowboats, kayaks, and fishing gear can be rented here. ⊠ *Akamina Pkwy., 13 km (8 miles) southwest of Waterton Townsite, Waterton Lakes National Park.*

Goat Haunt Ranger Station

NATURE PRESERVE | Reached only by foot trail or tour boat from Waterton townsite, this spot on the U.S. end of Waterton Lake is the stomping ground for mountain goats, moose, grizzlies, and black bears. The ranger posted at this remote station gives thrice-daily 10-minute overviews of Waterton Valley history. Bring your passport if you want to explore the U.S. side of Waterton Lake beyond the ranger station. The hikes on the U.S. side of the lake were unaffected by the 2017 Kenow Wildfire. ⊠ *Southern end of Waterton Lake, Waterton Lakes National Park* ☎ *403/859–2362* ⊕ *www.watertoncruise.com* ⊠ *Tour boat C$51.*

Waterton Townsite

TOWN | A low-key community in roughly the park's geographical center, the townsite swells with tourists in summer, and restaurants and shops open to serve them. In winter only a few motels are open, and services are limited. ⊠ *Waterton Townsite.*

 Activities

The park contains numerous short hikes for day-trippers and some longer treks for backpackers. Upper and Middle Waterton and Cameron lakes provide peaceful havens for boaters. A tour boat cruises across Upper Waterton Lake, crossing the U.S.–Canada border, and the winds that rake across that lake create an exciting ride for windsurfers—bring a wet suit, though; the water remains numbingly cold throughout summer.

BICYCLING

Bikes are allowed on some trails, such as the 3-km (2-mile) **Townsite Loop Trail.** A great family bike trail is the 6.9-km (4.3-mile) one-way paved **Kootenai Brown Trail,** which leads from the townsite to the park gates along the edges of the lakes. A ride on mildly sloping **Red Rock Canyon Road** isn't too difficult (once you get past the first hill). The **Crandell Loop** trail provides a slightly more challenging ride for mountain bikers.

Pat's Waterton

BICYCLING | **FAMILY** | Choose from surrey bikes, mountain bikes, or motorized scooters at Pat's, which also rents tennis rackets, strollers, and binoculars. ⊠ *224 Mt. View Rd., Waterton Townsite* ☎ *403/859–2266* ⊕ *www.patswaterton.com* ⊠ *From $10.*

BOATING

Nonmotorized boats can be rented at Cameron Lake in summer; private craft can be used on Upper and Middle Waterton lakes.

Waterton Inter-Nation Shoreline Cruise Co.

BOATING | This company's two-hour round-trip boat tour along Upper Waterton Lake from Waterton Townsite to Goat Haunt Ranger Station is one of the most popular activities in Waterton. The narrated tour passes scenic bays, sheer cliffs, and snow-clad peaks. Because Goat Haunt is in the United States, you must clear customs to stay there and hike into Glacier.

✉ *Waterton Townsite Marina, northwest corner of Waterton Lake near Bayshore Inn, Waterton Lakes National Park* ☎ *403/859–2362, 403/859–2362* ⊕ *www.watertoncruise.com* 🎫 *C$51.*

HIKING

There are 225 km (191 miles) of trails in Waterton Lakes that range in difficulty from short strolls to strenuous treks. Some trails connect with the trail systems of Glacier and British Columbia's Akamina-Kishenina Provincial Park. The wildflowers in June are particularly stunning along most trails. In 2017, the Kenow Wildfire damaged more than 80% of the trails in Waterton Lakes National Park. The Crypt Lake and the hikes on the U.S. side of the lake that depart from the Goat Haunt Ranger Station were unaffected by the fire. Trails in other parts of the park received varying amounts of damage. Consult the park website for the latest trail reports. *Hiking Glacier and Waterton National Parks,* by Erik Molvar, has detailed information including pictures and GPS-compatible maps for 60 of the best hiking trails in both parks.

Bear's Hump Trail

HIKING/WALKING | This steep 2.8-km (1.4-mile) trail climbs up the mountainside to an overlook with a great view of Upper Waterton Lake and the townsite. *Moderate.* ✉ *Waterton Lakes National Park* ✛ *Trailhead: across from Prince of Wales access road. Behind site of old visitor information center.*

Bertha Lake Trail

HIKING/WALKING | This 11.4-km (7.1-mile) round-trip trail leads from the Waterton Townsite through a Douglas fir forest to a beautiful overlook of Upper Waterton Lake, then continues on to Lower Bertha Falls. From there, a steeper climb takes you past Upper Bertha Falls to Bertha Lake. In June, the wildflowers along the trail are stunning. *Moderate.* ✉ *Waterton Lakes National Park* ✛ *Trailhead: at parking lot off Evergreen Ave., west of Townsite Campground.*

Cameron Lake Shore Trail

HIKING/WALKING | FAMILY | This relatively flat paved trail, 1.6 km (1 mile) one-way, is a peaceful place for a walk. Look for wildflowers along the shoreline and grizzlies on the lower slopes of the mountains at the far end of the lake. *Easy.* ✉ *Waterton Lakes National Park* ✛ *Trailhead: at lakeshore in front of parking lot, 13 km (8 miles) southwest of Waterton Townsite.*

Crandell Lake Trail

HIKING/WALKING | This 2½-km (1½-mile) trail winds through fragrant pine forest, ending at a popular mountain lake. *Easy.* ✉ *Waterton Lakes National Park* ✛ *Trailhead: about halfway up Akamina Pkwy.*

★ Crypt Lake Trail

HIKING/WALKING | Awe-inspiring and strenuous, this 17.2-km (11-mile) round-trip trail is one of the most stunning hikes in the Canadian Rockies. Conquering the trail involves taking a boat taxi across Waterton Lake, climbing 700 meters (2,300 feet), crawling through a tunnel nearly 30 meters (100 feet) long, and scrambling across a sheer rock face. The reward, and well worth it: views of a 183-meter (600-foot) cascading waterfall and the turquoise waters of Crypt Lake. This hike was completely untouched by the Kenow Wildfire. *Difficult.* ✉ *Waterton Lakes National Park* ✛ *Trailhead: at Crypt Landing, accessed by ferry from Waterton Townsite.*

Waterton Outdoor Adventures

HIKING/WALKING | This is the headquarters for hiker shuttle services that run throughout Waterton to most major trailheads; you can reserve shuttles up to two months ahead. Waterton Outdoor Adventures can also arrange certified hiking guides for groups and individuals and provide lunch for guided excursions. ✉ *Tamarack Outdoor Outfitters, 214 Mt. View Rd., Waterton Townsite* ☎ *403/859–2378* ⊕ *www.hikewaterton.com* 🎫 *From C$30.*

Family Fun

Opportunities for family fun at Glacier and Waterton include canoeing, climbing, hiking, biking, and touring.

Canoe Lake McDonald. Rent a canoe and paddle around the lake. If you work up a sweat, jump in. *Glacier.*

Climb Bear's Hump. This 2.8-km (1.7-mile) trail winds up a mountainside to an overlook with a great view of Upper Waterton Lake and the townsite. *Waterton.*

Hike Hidden Lake Nature Trail. A 2.4-km (1½-mile) trail runs uphill from Logan Pass to the Hidden Lake Overlook, yielding beautiful views of the lake and McDonald Valley. In spring, ribbons of water pour off the rocks surrounding the lake. A boardwalk protects the abundant wildflowers and spongy tundra on the way. *Glacier.*

Surrey Around Town. Rent a surrey bike at Pat's Waterton store and pedal around the townsite. A surrey bike has a flat seat and a canopy and can hold up to three people. *Waterton.*

Tour Going-to-the Sun in a Jammer Bus. With amazing vistas and many stops for photo ops, the Going-to-the-Sun Road tour in a vintage Jammer Bus is a beloved park tradition. *Glacier.*

HORSEBACK RIDING

Rolling hills, grasslands, and rugged mountains make riding in Waterton Lakes a real pleasure. Scenery, wildlife, and wildflowers are easily viewed from the saddle, and horses are permitted on many park trails.

Alpine Stables

HORSEBACK RIDING | At these stables you can arrange hourlong trail rides and full-day guided excursions within the park as well as multiday pack trips through the Rockies foothills. ⊠ *Waterton Lakes National Park* ☎ *403/859–2462 May–Sept., 403/653–2449 Oct.–Apr.* ⊕ *www. alpinestables.com* ✉ *From C$45.*

SWIMMING

Waterton Health Club

SWIMMING | FAMILY | The club has an 18-meter (56-foot) saltwater pool, a hot tub, a sauna, and a gym. Towels are provided. ⊠ *Waterton Lakes Lodge Resort, 101 Clematis Ave., Waterton Townsite* ☎ *403/859–2150, 888/985–6343* ⊕ *watertonlakeslodge.com* ✉ *C$19/wk.*

Waterton Lakes

SWIMMING | FAMILY | The lakes are chilly year-round, but they're a great place to cool off after a long hot day of hiking. Most visitors can only handle dipping in a toe or two, some wade, and a few brave souls join the "polar bear club" and plunge in completely. ⊠ *Waterton Townsite* ✉ *Free.*

Nearby Towns

You could easily spend a week exploring Waterton and Glacier, but you may wish to take in some nearby sights as well. Outside Glacier National Park are the gateway towns of **East Glacier,** 30 miles south of St. Mary Visitor Center; **West Glacier,** 2½ miles south of Apgar Visitor Center; and **Columbia Falls,** 17 miles southwest of West Glacier, where you can find tour operators, accommodations, restaurants, and stores. Not far from Glacier Park are **Essex, Kalispell, Whitefish, Browning,** and **Bigfork,** home to excellent golf courses, world-class cross-country and downhill skiing, summer and winter festivals, diverse recreational opportunities, accommodations, and restaurants. The main attractions in the Canadian town of **Cardston,** east of Waterton Townsite, are an intriguing museum of horse-drawn vehicles and the nearly nightly theater performances in summer.

Bigfork

TOWN | About 45 minutes from Glacier's west entrance on Flathead Lake's pristine northeast shore, Bigfork twinkles with decorative lights that adorn its boutique shops and fine restaurants. Bigfork is a wonderful art community with excellent galleries and one of the finest repertory theaters in the Northwest. ⊠ *Bigfork* ⊕ *www.bigfork.org.*

Browning

TOWN | About 35 miles east of Glacier, Browning is the center of the Blackfeet Nation, whose name is thought to derive from the color of its members' painted or dyed black moccasins. These days there are about 13,000 enrolled tribal members. The city's main attractions are the Museum of the Plains Indian and the Blackfeet Heritage Center and Art Gallery. ⊠ *Browning* ⊕ *www.browning-montana.com.*

Cardston

TOWN | Just 45 km (28 miles) east of Waterton, Cardston is home to the Alberta Temple, built by the Mormon pioneers who established the town. The Remington Carriage Museum contains North America's largest collection of horse-drawn vehicles. The Carriage House Theatre (*www.carriagehouse-theatre.com*) presents entertaining live theatrical performances on most summer evenings. ⊠ *Cardston* ⊕ *cardston.ca.*

Columbia Falls

AMUSEMENT PARK/WATER PARK | This small town 19 miles southwest of the Apgar Visitor Center has restaurants, services, and accommodations. Near the town are two excellent golf courses, a water park, and more than 80 miles of groomed snowmobile trails in winter. ⊠ *Columbia Falls* ⊕ *www.columbiafallschamber.org.*

East Glacier

TOWN | Early tourists to Glacier National Park first stopped in East Glacier, where the Great Northern Railway had established a station. Although most people coming from the east now enter by car through St. Mary, East Glacier, about 30 miles south, U.S. 89 to Highway 49, attracts visitors with its quiet, secluded surroundings and lovely Glacier Park Lodge. ⊠ *East Glacier Park* ⊕ *www.eastglacierpark.info.*

Essex

TOWN | The village of Essex, along U.S. 2, 30 miles southeast of West Glacier, borders the southern tip of the park and is the site of the main rail and bus terminals for park visitors. ⊠ *Essex.*

Fort Macleod

TOWN | Named for its Northwest Mounted Police fort, the town of Fort Macleod is 105 km (65 miles) northwest of Waterton Townsite. You can still explore the old fort, and nearby is Head-Smashed-In Buffalo Jump, a UNESCO World Heritage Site and museum where you can learn about the history of the indigenous people of the North American Plains. ⊠ *Fort Macleod* ⊕ *www.fortmacleod.com.*

West Glacier

TOWN | The green waters of the Flathead River's Middle Fork and several top-notch outfitters make West Glacier, 2½ miles south of the Apgar Visitor Center, an ideal base for river sports such as rafting and fishing. There are several good accommodations and restaurants here. ⊠ *West Glacier.*

Whitefish

TOWN | The best base for the park is Whitefish, 28 miles west of the Apgar Visitor Center. With a population of 6,350, the town has a well-developed nightlife scene and good restaurants, galleries, and shops. ✉ Whitefish ⊕ www.explore-whitefish.com.

VISITOR INFORMATION Bigfork Area Chamber of Commerce ✉ 8155 Hwy. 35, Bigfork ☎ 406/837–5888 ⊕ www.bigfork.org. **East Glacier Chamber of Commerce** ✉ 909 Hwy. 49 N, East Glacier Park ☎ 406/226–4403. **Glacier Country Montana** ✉ 140 N. Higgens Ave., Suite 204, Missoula ☎ 800/338–5072 ⊕ www.glaciermt.com. **Town of Cardston** ✉ 67 3rd Ave. W, Cardston ☎ 403/653–3366, 888/434–3366 ⊕ www.cardston.ca. **Waterton Lakes Chamber of Commerce** ⊕ www.mywaterton.ca. **Whitefish Chamber of Commerce** ✉ 307 Spokane Ave., Suite 103, Whitefish ☎ 406/862–3501 ⊕ www.whitefishchamber.org.

 Sights

Big Sky Waterpark
AMUSEMENT PARK/WATER PARK | FAMILY | During summer, the water park is a popular place. Besides the 10 waterslides and a golf course, there are arcade games, bumper cars, a carousel, barbecue grills, a picnic area, and food service. ✉ 7211 U.S. 2 E, Columbia Falls ✛ at Hwy. 206 ☎ 406/892–5025 ⊕ www.bigskywp.com ⌹ $22.

Museum of the Plains Indian
MUSEUM | The impressive collection of artifacts from the Blackfeet at this museum includes clothing, saddlebags, and artwork. ✉ 19 Museum Loop, Browning ☎ 406/338–2230 ⊕ www.doi.gov/iacb/museum-plains-indian ⌹ $5 June–Sept., free Oct.–May.

 Activities

DOGSLEDDING
Dog Sled Adventures
LOCAL SPORTS | The dogs are raring to run from late November to mid-April at Dog Sled Adventures. Your friendly musher will gear the ride to the passengers, from kids to senior citizens; bundled up in a sled, you'll be whisked through Stillwater State Forest on a 1½-hour ride over a 12-mile trail. Reservations are necessary. ✉ 8400 U.S. 93, Glacier National Park ✛ 20 miles north of Whitefish, 2 miles north of Olney ☎ 406/881–2275 ⊕ www.dogsledadventuresmt.com ⌹ $110.

HIKING
Before lacing up your hiking boots, determine where you want to go, what you need to bring, and what you're likely to encounter on the trail. The book Hiking Montana by Bill Schneider has useful, basic hiking safety information and offers route details from several trailheads. U.S. Forest Service offices have local maps, trail guides, and safety information. If you're new to hiking, you may want to employ an outfitter that offers guided walks.

U.S. Forest Service regional office
HIKING/WALKING | The regional office in Missoula, Montana, is responsible for 12 national forests within Washington, Northern Idaho, and Montana. ✉ Missoula ☎ 406/329–3511 ⊕ www.fs.fed.us/r1.

SKIING AND SNOWBOARDING
Whitefish Mountain Resort
SKIING/SNOWBOARDING | Eight miles from Whitefish, this has been one of Montana's top ski areas since the 1930s, yet it remains comfortably small. The resort is popular among train travelers from the Pacific Northwest and the upper Midwest. Whitefish mountain has good powder skiing, nice glades, and groomed trails for all ski levels. In summer there are bike trails, an alpine slide, an aerial adventure park, and a zip line. The terrain is 25% beginner, 50% intermediate, and 25% advanced; there are two high-speed quad chairs, one quad chair, four triple chairs, one double chair, and three surface lifts. **Facilities:** 105 trails; 3,000 acres; 2,500-foot vertical drop; 11 lifts. ✉ 1015 Glades Dr. ☎ 334/319–9629, 877/754–3474 Toll Free, 406/862–7669 snow report ⊕ www.skiwhitefish.com ⌹ Lift ticket: $79.

🍴 Restaurants

IN THE PARKS

GLACIER

Lake McDonald Lodge Restaurants

$$$ | **AMERICAN** | In Russell's Fireside Dining Room, take in a great view while choosing between standards such as pasta, steak, wild game, and salmon. There are also some delicious salads and other local favorites on the menu such as the huckleberry elk burger or the Montana Rainbow trout. [$] *Average main: $22* ✉ *Glacier National Park* ✣ *Going-to-the-Sun Rd., 10 miles north of Apgar* ☎ *406/888–5431, 406/892–2525* 🌐 *www.glaciernationalparklodges.com* ⏲ *Closed early Oct.–early June.*

Ptarmigan Dining Room

$$$ | **AMERICAN** | The picturesque Ptarmigan's massive windows afford stunning views of Grinnell Point over Swiftcurrent Lake. Known for using regional, sustainably sourced ingredients, the restaurant specializes in dishes such as house smoked Montana trout, bison tenderloin, and roasted duck with Flathead cherry chutney. [$] *Average main: $28* ✉ *Many Glacier Rd., Glacier National Park* ☎ *303/265–7010* 🌐 *www.glaciernationalparklodges.com* ⏲ *Closed late Sept.–early June.*

PICNIC AREAS

There are picnic spots at or near most campgrounds in Glacier National Park. Each has tables, grills, and drinking water in summer. You can get a map at the visitor center that identifies all the picnic sites in the park.

Apgar

RESTAURANT—SIGHT | In a tree-shaded area at the southern end of Lake McDonald, the Apgar Campground has tables, drinking water, and restrooms. ✉ *Glacier National Park* ✣ *Off Going-to-the-Sun Rd., north of campground, 4 km (2½ miles) north of west entrance.*

Fish Creek

RESTAURANT—SIGHT | In a forested area adjacent to Lake McDonald, this picnic area has tables, drinking water, and restrooms. There's a swimming area nearby, and the trailheads for several good hikes. ✉ *Glacier National Park* ✣ *Off Camas Rd. before Fish Creek Campground, 4 miles northwest of west entrance.*

Rising Sun

RESTAURANT—SIGHT | In a cottonwood grove adjacent to St. Mary Lake, this area has tables, restrooms, and drinking water in summer. ✉ *Glacier National Park* ✣ *Off Going-to-the-Sun Rd., 10 km (6 miles) southwest of St. Mary Visitor Center.*

Sprague Creek

RESTAURANT—SIGHT | This picnic site on Lake McDonald's eastern shore has tables, restrooms, and drinking water in summer. ✉ *Glacier National Park* ✣ *Off Going-to-the-Sun Rd., adjacent to Sprague Creek Campground, 15 km (9 miles) northeast of west entrance.*

WATERTON LAKES

Lakeside Chophouse

$$$ | **STEAKHOUSE** | Grab a window seat or a spot on the patio to enjoy the spectacular view from Waterton's only lakefront restaurant. This is the place in the park for a steak dinner—locally produced Alberta beef plays a starring role on the globally inspired menu. **Known for:** great steaks; lakefront views; all-day service. [$] *Average main: C$29* ✉ *111 Waterton Ave., Waterton Townsite* ☎ *888/527–9555, 403/859–2211* 🌐 *www.bayshore-inn.com.*

Red Rock Trattoria

$$$ | **ITALIAN** | There's a large window with lovely mountain views at this intimate Italian restaurant on a quiet side street in the Waterton Townsite. Starters include such classics as Caprese salad, wild mushroom arancini, and fried cauliflower. **Known for:** homemade Italian food; local ingredients; intimate dining. [$] *Average*

main: C$22 ✉ 107 Windflower Ave., Waterton Townsite ☎ 403/859–2004 🌐 www.redrockcafe.ca.

Royal Stewart Dining Room

$$$ | **CANADIAN** | Enjoy Continental Canadian cuisine before a dazzling view of Waterton Lake in the dining room of this century-old chalet high on a hill. Choose from a fine selection of wines to accompany your meal. **Known for:** best view in town; British high tea; local ingredients. [$] *Average main: $27 ✉ Prince of Wales Hotel, off Hwy. 5, outside Waterton Townsite, Glacier National Park ☎ 406/859–2231, 403/236–3400 🌐 www.glacierparkcollection.com/lodging/prince-of-wales-hotel/dining-shopping ⏲ Closed Oct.–May.*

Wieners of Waterton

$ | **HOT DOG** | **FAMILY** | If there is such a thing as a gourmet hot dog, then this is the place to find it. The buns here are baked fresh daily, and the all-beef wieners and smokies are sourced locally with one exception: the genuine Nathan's dogs, which are shipped from New York City. **Known for:** gourmet hot dogs; interesting toppings; fun menu. [$] *Average main: C$9 ✉ 301 Wildflower Ave., Waterton Townsite ☎ 403/859–0007 🌐 www.wienersofwaterton.com ⏲ Closed Oct.–Apr.*

PICNIC AREAS

Waterton has 14 picnic sites in some of the most scenic areas of the park. All sites are equipped with picnic tables and washroom facilities, and most have a water source nearby. Some picnic sites are equipped with barbecues or outdoor fire pits. Firewood is not supplied, but it can be purchased in the village.

OUTSIDE THE PARKS

Backslope Brewing

$ | **AMERICAN** | Pair a great local beer with delicious casual fare at this local brewery. There are always about eight different kinds of house beer on tap as well as kombucha, sparkling water, and nitro iced coffee. **Known for:** local brewery; creative menu; garlic Parmesan fries. [$] *Average main: $12 ✉ 1107 9 St. W, Columbia Falls ☎ 406/897–2850 🌐 backslopebrewing.com ⏲ Closed Sun. Closed nightly at 8 pm.*

★ Belton Chalet Grill Dining Room

$$$$ | **AMERICAN** | The hotel's handsome restaurant still has its original wainscoting and leaded-glass windows, but in fine weather ask to dine on the deck outside to watch the sun set behind the mountains. Bison meat loaf has been a signature dish for years, but you'll also find other unique dishes like pan-seared wild king salmon with locally grown fiddle head ferns, confit duck leg with flathead cherries, and locally produced lamb with huckleberry jus. [$] *Average main: $32 ✉ 12575 U.S. 2 E, next to railroad station, West Glacier ☎ 406/888–5000, 888/235–8665 🌐 www.beltonchalet.com/dining_near_glacier.php ⏲ Closed early Oct.–early Dec. and late Mar.–late May. Closed Mon.–Thurs. early Dec.–late Mar. (brunch only on Sun. Dec.–Mar.). No lunch.*

Great Northern Dining Room

$$$ | **AMERICAN** | A unique natural log dining room made from enormous trees provides a rustic setting for hearty comfort-food classics: slow-roasted prime rib, classic mac and cheese, pan-seared trout, beef pot roast, and butternut squash ravioli. The food goes well with the Montana microbrews available on tap and in the bottle. **Known for:** unique natural log dining room; hearty comfort food; local microbrews on tap. [$] *Average main: $29 ✉ Glacier Park Lodge, Hwy. 49, next to railroad station, East Glacier Park ☎ 406/226–5600 🌐 www.glacierparkcollection.com/lodging/glacier-park-lodge/dining-shopping ⏲ Closed Oct.–May.*

Josephine's Bar & Kitchen

$ | **AMERICAN** | This seasonal restaurant and bar is named for Josephine Doody, "the bootleg lady of Glacier National

Park." The restaurant is affiliated with Glacier Distillery and you'll find some wonderful local cocktails on the menu as well as craft beer and wine. It's very casual; you go to a window beside the bar to order your food, but they bring it to your table. **Known for:** innovative cocktails; fried green tomatoes; casual local hangout. $ *Average main: $12* ✉ *10245 Hwy. 2 E, Coram* 🕿 *406/300–4755* ⊕ *www.josephinesbar.com* ⊘ *Closed mid-Oct.–mid-May.*

Serrano's

$$ | MEXICAN | Mexican food in Montana! After a day on the dusty trail, Serrano's is a treat whether dining inside or on the back patio. **Known for:** excellent Mexican food; fabulous margaritas; huckleberry carrot cake. $ *Average main: $15* ✉ *29 Dawson Ave., East Glacier Park* 🕿 *406/226–9392* ⊕ *www.serranosmexican.com* ⊘ *Closed Oct.–Apr.*

Summit Mountain Steakhouse

$$$ | STEAKHOUSE | The drive to this slightly off-the-beaten-track steak house southwest of East Glacier is well worth the detour. The small dining room seats 30 and has large windows with mountain views shared by an outdoor patio with additional seating. **Known for:** grilled steaks; handmade hamburgers; great views. $ *Average main: $26* ✉ *16900 U.S. 2 W, East Glacier Park* 🕿 *406/226–9319* ⊕ *www.summitmtnlodge.com* ⊘ *Closed Mon. Closed mid-Sept.–mid-June. No lunch* ▭ *No credit cards.*

Three Forks Grille and Deli

$$ | AMERICAN | Italian-influenced classic mountain cuisine is prepared with care at the two-level Grille, which emphasizes local, sustainably produced ingredients. The regional focus extends to the artworks that adorn the walls; many are by area artists. $ *Average main: $19* ✉ *729 Nucleus Ave., Columbia Falls* 🕿 *406/892–2900* ⊕ *threeforksgrille.com* ⊘ *No lunch Sun.*

 Hotels

IN THE PARKS
GLACIER
Granite Park Chalet

$$ | B&B/INN | Early tourists used to ride horses through the park from 7 to 9 miles each day and stay at a different chalet each night. **Pros:** beautiful scenery; secluded. **Cons:** difficult to access; rustic; far from services. $ *Rooms from: $108* ✉ *Going-to-the-Sun Rd., 7.6 miles south of Logan Pass, Glacier National Park* 🕿 *888/345–2649* ⊕ *www.graniteparkchalet.com* ⊘ *Closed mid-Sept.–late June* ⇆ *12 rooms* ❑ *No meals.*

★ Lake McDonald Lodge

$$$ | HOTEL | On the shores of Lake McDonald not far from Apgar and West Glacier, this lodge is an ideal base for exploring the western side of the park and is one of the great historic lodges of the West. **Pros:** lakeside setting; historic property; close to Apgar, West Glacier, and Going-to-the-Sun Road. **Cons:** rustic; no TV (except for in the suites); small bathrooms. $ *Rooms from: $200* ✉ *Going-to-the-Sun Rd., Glacier National Park* 🕿 *855/733–4522, 406/888–5431* ⊕ *www.glaciernationalparklodges.com* ⇆ *32 standard lodge rooms, 36 cabins, 8 hostel dorms, 4 suites* ❑ *No meals.*

Many Glacier Hotel

$$$ | HOTEL | On Swiftcurrent Lake in the park's northeastern section, this is the most isolated of the grand hotels, and—especially if you are able to book a lake-view balcony room—among the most scenic. **Pros:** stunning views from lodge; secluded; good hiking trails nearby. **Cons:** rustic rooms; no TV, limited Internet; the road leading to the lodge is very rough. $ *Rooms from: $207* ✉ *Many Glacier Rd., 12 miles west of Babb, Glacier National Park* 🕿 *855/733–4522, 406/732–4411* ⊕ *www.glaciernationalparklodges.com* ⊘ *Closed mid-Sept.–mid-June* ⇆ *214 rooms* ❑ *No meals.*

Best Campgrounds in Glacier and Waterton

There are 10 major campgrounds in Glacier National Park, and excellent backcountry sites for backpackers. Reservations for St. Mary campground are available through the National Park Reservation Service (☎ *877/444–6777 or 518/885–3639* 🌐 *www.recreation.gov*). Reservations may be made up to five months in advance. Parks Canada operates four campgrounds in Waterton Lakes that range from fully serviced to unserviced sites. There are also some backcountry campsites. Visitors can prebook campsites for a fee of C$11 online or C$13.50 by phone. The reservation service is available at 🌐 *www.reservation.parkscanada.gc.ca* or by phone at ☎ *877/737–3783*.

Best Options in Glacier

Apgar Campground. This popular and large campground on the southern shore of Lake McDonald has many activities and services. ✉ *Apgar Rd.* ☎ *406/888–7800*.

Avalanche Creek Campground. This peaceful campground on Going-to-the-Sun Road is shaded by huge red cedars and bordered by Avalanche Creek. ✉ *25 km (15.7 miles) from west entrance on Going-to-the-Sun Rd.* ☎ *406/888–7800*.

Kintla Lake Campground. Beautiful and remote, this is a trout fisherman's dream. ✉ *23.5 km (14 miles) north of Polebridge Ranger Station on Inside North Fork Rd.*

Many Glacier Campground. One of the most beautiful spots in the park is also a favorite for bears. ✉ *Next to Swiftcurrent Motor Inn on Many Glacier Rd.*

Sprague Creek Campground. This sometimes noisy roadside campground for tents, RVs, and truck campers (no towed units) offers spectacular views of the lake and sunsets, and there's fishing from shore. ✉ *Going-to-the-Sun Rd., 1.6 km (1 mile) south of Lake McDonald Lodge* ☎ *406/888–7800*.

St. Mary Campground. This large, grassy spot alongside the lake and stream has mountain views and cool breezes. ✉ *1.4 km (0.9 mile) from St. Mary entrance to Going-to-the-Sun Rd.* ☎ *406/888–7800*.

Best Options in Waterton

Waterton Townsite Campground. Though the campground is busy and windy, sites here are grassy and flat with access to kitchen shelters and have views down the lake into the U.S. part of the Peace Park. ✉ *Waterton and Vimy Aves.* ☎ *877/737–3783*.

Village Inn

$$$ | **HOTEL** | On the shores of beautiful Lake McDonald, this motel on the National Register of Historic Places was fully renovated in 2015: all rooms have Wi-Fi, new beds, and furnishings that fit with the historic style. **Pros:** great views; convenient Apgar village location; all rooms have Wi-Fi; kitchenettes in some rooms. **Cons:** rustic motel; no air-conditioning; no in-room phones. [$] *Rooms from: $165* ✉ *Apgar Village, Glacier National Park* ☎ *855/733–4522* 🌐 *www.glaciernationalparklodges.com* 🕒 *Closed Oct. 2–late May* 🛏 *36 rooms* 🍴 *No meals.*

WATERTON

Bayshore Inn

$$$ | **HOTEL** | On the shores of Waterton Lake, this inn right in town has a lot going for it: lovely views, the only on-site spa in Waterton, multiple eating establishments on property, and easy access to many services. **Pros:** lakefront views; spa; townsite location; multiple restaurants. **Cons:** older-style rooms; motor inn. [$] *Rooms from: C$154* ✉ *111 Waterton Ave., Waterton Townsite* ☎ *888/527–9555, 403/859–2211, 403/859–2291* 🌐 *www.bayshoreinn.com* 🕒 *Closed mid-Oct.–Apr.* 🛏 *70 rooms* 🍴 *No meals.*

Prince of Wales Hotel

$$$$ | **HOTEL** | Perched between two lakes, with a high mountain backdrop, this hotel has the best view in town and is itself an iconic image of Waterton. **Pros:** spectacular view; historic property; bellmen wear kilts. **Cons:** very rustic rooms; no TVs; no air-conditioning. [$] *Rooms from: C$259* ✉ *Off Hwy. 5, Waterton Lakes National Park* ✥ *Turn left at marked access road at top of hill just before village* ☎ *844/868–7474, 403/859–2231 mid-May–late Sept.* 🌐 *www.glacierparkcollection.com/lodging/prince-of-wales-hotel/* 🕒 *Closed late Sept.–mid-May* 🛏 *86 rooms* 🍴 *No meals.*

Waterton Glacier Suites

$$$$ | **HOTEL** | In the heart of the townsite, this all-suite property is within walking distance of restaurants, shopping, and the dock on beautiful Waterton Lake. **Pros:** modern suites with mini-refrigerators and air-conditioning; open year-round; convenient location. **Cons:** no views; pull-out sofas uncomfortable. [$] *Rooms from: C$309* ✉ *107 Wildflower Ave., Waterton Lakes National Park* ☎ *403/859–2004, 866/621–3330* 🌐 *www.watertonsuites.com* 🛏 *26 rooms* 🍴 *No meals.*

OUTSIDE THE PARKS

Belton Chalet

$$$ | **HOTEL** | This carefully restored 1910 railroad hotel, the original winter headquarters for the park, has a great location just outside the West Glacier entrance and cozy, bright rooms with period furnishings and original woodwork around the windows. **Pros:** excellent restaurant; wraparound decks with lovely views; historic property. **Cons:** train noise; rustic; no air-conditioning or TVs. [$] *Rooms from: $180* ✉ *12575 U.S. 2 E, West Glacier* ☎ *406/888–5000, 888/235–8665, 406/888-5005* 🌐 *www.beltonchalet.com* 🛏 *27 rooms* 🍴 *Breakfast.*

Cedar Creek Lodge

$$$$ | **HOTEL** | If you want the atmosphere of a mountain lodge with modern amenities and good connectivity, this lodge, which opened in 2016, is ideal. **Pros:** mountain lodge atmosphere; modern amenities; great included extras. **Cons:** 18 miles from West Glacier; room price is high during peak season for location; inside a town, so room views are not great. [$] *Rooms from: $350* ✉ *930 2nd Ave. W, Columbia Falls* ☎ *855/733–4542, 406/412–4660* 🌐 *www.glaciernationalparklodges.com/lodging/cedar-creek-lodge/* 🛏 *58 rooms, 6 suites* 🍴 *Free Breakfast.*

Garden Wall Inn B&B

$$$ | **B&B/INN** | This antiques-filled 1923 home has individually decorated guest rooms with down duvets. **Pros:** historic home; nice personal touches; spacious rooms. **Cons:** small property; no view. [$] *Rooms from: $155* ✉ *504 Spokane Ave., Whitefish* ☎ *406/862–3440, 888/530–1700* 🌐 *www.gardenwallinn.com* 🛏 *5 rooms* 🍴 *Breakfast.*

Glacier Guides Lodge

$$$$ | **HOTEL** | Tucked away in a forested canyon, this eco-friendly rustic lodge is walking distance from the restaurants and other amenities of downtown West Glacier. **Pros:** secluded location in West Glacier; delicious included breakfast; mini-refrigerators in rooms. **Cons:** difficult to find; Wi-Fi can be slow; maximum 2 people per guest room. [$] *Rooms from: 229* ✉ *120 Highline Blvd., West*

Glacier ☎ 800/521–7238, 406/412–4545 🌐 https://glacierguides.com/lodging/glacier-guides-lodge/ ⏲ Closed mid-Oct.–Apr. 🛏 12 rooms, 1 guest house 🍴 Free Breakfast.

Glacier Outdoor Center Cabins

$$$$ | RENTAL | FAMILY | Five minutes from the entrance to West Glacier, these cozy cabins with living rooms, barbecues, private decks, and fully equipped kitchens are ideal for families. **Pros:** great for families; can accommodate large groups; kitchens in cabins. **Cons:** outside the townsite; no restaurant. [$] *Rooms from: $235 ✉ 12400 U.S. 2 E, West Glacier ☎ 800/235–6781, 406/888–5454, 🌐 www.glacierraftco.com ⏲ Cabins closed Nov.–Apr., Lodge and Homestead open year-round 🛏 26 accommodations 🍴 No meals.*

Glacier Park Lodge

$$$ | HOTEL | Just east of the park, across from the Amtrak station, this beautiful full-service hotel built in 1913 is supported by 500- to 800-year-old fir and 3-foot-thick cedar logs. **Pros:** golf course; scenic location; lots of activities. **Cons:** small bathrooms; no elevator; no air-conditioning or TV. [$] *Rooms from: $179 ✉ Off U.S. 2, East Glacier Park ☎ 406/892–2525, 844/868–7474 🌐 www.glacierparkcollection.com/lodging/glacier-park-lodge ⏲ Closed late Sept.–May 🛏 161 rooms 🍴 No meals.*

Good Medicine Lodge

$$$$ | B&B/INN | Built of cedar timbers and decorated in a Western style, this lodge-style bed-and-breakfast is warm and inviting. **Pros:** room rate includes a good breakfast; Wi-Fi and many other amenities; one wheelchair-accessible room. **Cons:** no TV in most rooms; small property. [$] *Rooms from: $225 ✉ 537 Wisconsin Ave., Whitefish ☎ 406/862–5489, 800/860–5488 🌐 www.goodmedicinelodge.com 🛏 6 rooms, 3 suites 🍴 Breakfast.*

Great Bear Inn

$$$$ | B&B/INN | This cozy inn has a wraparound deck that provides wonderful mountain views; inside is a comfortable lounge area where guests can relax and mingle. **Pros:** intimate lodge; room rate includes breakfast; close to West Glacier; complimentary laundry facilities. **Cons:** isolated location; cannot accommodate walk-in guests; can be tricky to find. [$] *Rooms from: $235 ✉ 5672 Blankenship Rd., West Glacier ☎ 406/387–9341, 406/250–4220 🌐 www.thegreatbearinn.com 🛏 11 rooms 🍴 Breakfast.*

Izaak Walton Inn

$$$ | HOTEL | This historic railway lodge just south of Glacier National Park is popular with railway buffs: originally built to house railway workers, it is decorated with railroad memorabilia. **Pros:** good location between East and West Glacier; open year-round; fun railway theme. **Cons:** train noise can be a problem; no phones or TVs in rooms; no cell phone access; Wi-Fi signal not always strong. [$] *Rooms from: $159 ✉ 290 Izaak Walton Inn Rd., off U.S. 2, Essex ☎ 406/888–5700, 406/888–5200 🌐 www.izaakwaltoninn.com 🛏 48 rooms 🍴 No meals.*

Chapter 16

GRAND CANYON
NATIONAL PARK

16

Updated by
Elise Riley

ARIZONA

WELCOME TO GRAND CANYON NATIONAL PARK

TOP REASONS TO GO

★ **Awesome vistas:** Painted Desert, sandstone canyon walls, pine and fir forests, mesas, plateaus, volcanic features, the Colorado River, streams, and waterfalls make for some jaw-dropping moments.

★ **Year-round adventure:** Outdoor junkies can bike, boat, camp, fish, hike, ride mules, white-water raft, watch birds and wildlife, cross-country ski, and snowshoe.

★ **Continuing education:** Adults and kids can have fun learning, thanks to free park-sponsored nature walks and interpretive programs.

★ **Sky-high and river-low experiences:** Experience the canyon via plane, train, and automobile, as well as by helicopter, row- or motorboat, bike, mule, or foot.

Grand Canyon National Park is a superstar—biologically, historically, and recreationally. One of the world's best examples of arid-land erosion, the canyon provides a record of three of the four eras of geological time. Almost 2 billion years' worth of Earth's history is written in the colored layers of rock stacked from the river bottom to the top of the plateau. In addition to its diverse fossil record, the park reveals long-ago traces of human adaptation to an unforgiving environment. It's also home to several major ecosystems, five of the world's seven life zones, three of North America's four desert types, and all kinds of rare, endemic, and protected plant and animal species.

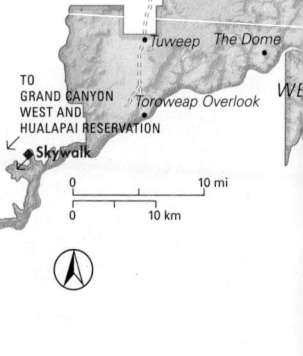

1 South Rim. The South Rim is where the action is: Grand Canyon Village's lodging, camping, eateries, stores, and museums, plus plenty of trailheads into the canyon. Visitor services and facilities are open and available daily, including holidays. Four free shuttle routes cover more than two-dozen stops, and visitors who'd rather relax than rough it can treat themselves to comfy hotel rooms and elegant restaurant meals (lodging and camping reservations are essential).

2 North Rim. Of the nearly 6 million people who visit the park annually, 90% enter at the South Rim, but many consider the North Rim even more gorgeous—and worth the extra effort. Open only from mid-May to the end of October (or the first good snowfall),

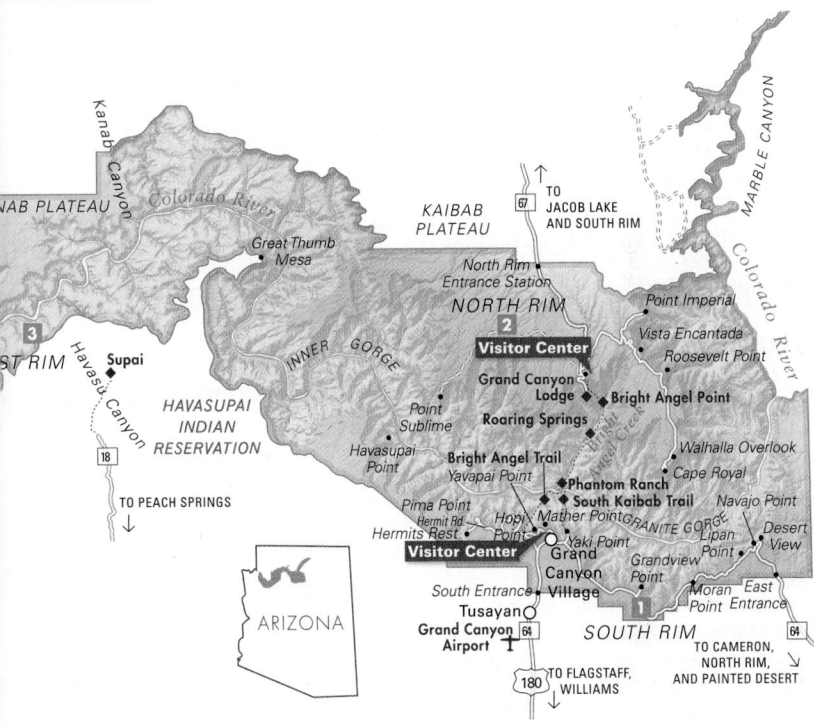

the North Rim has legitimate bragging rights: at more than 8,000 feet above sea level (1,000 feet higher than the South Rim), it has precious solitude and seven developed viewpoints. Rather than staring into the canyon's depths, you get a true sense of its expanse.

3 West Rim. Though not in Grand Canyon National Park, the far-off-the-beaten-path western end of the canyon, often called the West Rim, has some spectacular scenery. On the Hualapai Reservation, the Skywalk has become a major draw. This U-shape glass-floored deck juts out 3,600 feet above the Colorado River and isn't for the faint of heart.

The Grand Canyon measures in at an average width of 10 miles, length of 277 river miles, and depth of 1 mile. Seeing the canyon for the first time is an astounding experience. Hike or ride a trusty mule down into the canyon, bike or ramble along its rim, fly over, or raft through the Colorado River—there are manifold ways to soak up the canyon's magnificence.

Roughly 6 million visitors come to the park each year. You can access the canyon via two main points—the South Rim and the North Rim—but the South Rim is much easier to get to and therefore much more visited. The width from the North Rim to the South Rim varies from 600 feet to 18 miles, but traveling between rims by road requires a 215-mile drive. Hiking arduous trails from rim to rim is a steep and strenuous trek of at least 21 miles, but it's well worth the effort. You'll travel through five of North America's seven life zones. (To do this any other way, you'd have to journey from the Mexican desert to the Canadian woods.) West of Grand Canyon National Park, the tribal lands of the Hualapai and the Havasupai lie along the so-called West Rim of the canyon.

Planning

WHEN TO GO
There's no bad time to visit the canyon, though the busiest times of year are summer and spring break. Visiting during these peak seasons, as well as holidays,

requires patience and a tolerance for crowds. Note that weather changes on a whim in this exposed high-desert region. The North Rim shuts down mid-October through mid-May due to weather conditions and related road closures.

FESTIVALS AND EVENTS
Grand Canyon Music Festival
FESTIVAL | For three weekends in late August–early September, this festival brings mostly chamber music to the Shrine of Ages amphitheater at Grand Canyon Village. In the early 1980s, music aficionados Robert Bonfiglio and Clare Hoffman hiked through the Grand Canyon and decided the stunning spectacle should be accompanied by the strains of a symphony. One of the park rangers agreed, and the wandering musicians performed an impromptu concert. Encouraged by the experience, Bonfiglio and Hoffman started the festival. ☎ 928/638–9215 ⊕ www.grandcanyonmusicfest.org.

PLANNING YOUR TIME
Plan ahead: mule rides require at least a six-month advance reservation, and longer for the busy season (most can be

reserved up to 13 months in advance). Multiday rafting trips should be reserved at least a year in advance.

The park is most crowded on the South Rim, especially near the south entrance and in Grand Canyon Village, as well as on the scenic drives, particularly the 23-mile Desert View Drive.

THE SOUTH RIM IN ONE DAY

Start early, pack a picnic lunch, and drive to the South Rim's **Grand Canyon Visitor Center,** just north of the south entrance, to pick up info and see your first incredible view at **Mather Point.** Continue east along **Desert View Drive** for about 2 miles to **Yaki Point.** Next, continue driving 7 miles east to **Grandview Point** for a good view of the buttes Krishna Shrine and Vishnu Temple. Go 4 miles east and catch the view at **Moran Point,** then 3 miles to the **Tusayan Ruin and Museum,** where a small display is devoted to the history of the Ancestral Puebloans. Continue another mile east to **Lipan Point** to view the Colorado River. In less than a mile, you'll arrive at **Navajo Point,** the highest elevation on the South Rim. **Desert View and Watchtower** is the final attraction along Desert View Drive.

On your return drive, stop off at any of the picnic areas for lunch. Once back at Grand Canyon Village, walk the paved **Rim Trail** to **Maricopa Point.** Along the way, pick up souvenirs in the village and stop at historic **El Tovar Hotel** for dinner (be sure to make reservations well in advance). If you have time, take the shuttle on **Hermit Road** to **Hermits Rest,** 7 miles away. Along that route, Hopi Point and Powell Point are excellent spots to watch the sunset.

GRAND CANYON IN 3 DAYS

On Day 1, follow the one-day itinerary for the morning, but spend more time exploring Desert View Drive and enjoy a leisurely picnic lunch. Later, drive 30 miles beyond Desert View to **Cameron Trading Post,** which has a good restaurant and is an interesting side trip. Travel Hermit Road on your second morning, and drive to Grand Canyon Airport for a late-morning small-plane or helicopter tour. Have lunch in **Tusayan** and cool off at the IMAX film *Grand Canyon: The Hidden Secrets.* Back in the village, take a ranger-led program. On your third day, hike partway down the canyon on **Bright Angel Trail.** It takes twice as long to hike back up, so plan accordingly. Get trail maps at **Grand Canyon Visitor Center,** and bring plenty of water.

Alternatively, spend Days 2 and 3 exploring the remote **West Rim,** 150 miles toward Nevada or California and far away from major highways. Fill the first day with a horseback ride along the rim, a helicopter ride into the canyon, or a pontoon boat ride on the Colorado River. The next day, raft the Class V–VII rapids. Another option is to get a tribal permit and spend Days 2 and 3 in **Havasu Canyon,** a truly spiritual backcountry experience. You can opt to hike, ride horseback, or take a helicopter 8 miles down to the small village of Supai and the Havasupai Lodge.

GETTING HERE AND AROUND
SOUTH RIM

Several carriers fly from North Las Vegas Airport to the **Grand Canyon National Park Airport** in Tusayan (*GCN* ☎ *928/638–2446*) including Grand Canyon Express (☎ *800/940–2550* ⊕ *www.scenic.com*).

The best route into the park from the east or south is from Flagstaff. Take U.S. 180 northwest to the park's southern entrance and Grand Canyon Village. From the west on Interstate 40, the most direct route to the South Rim is taking Highway 64 from Williams to U.S. 180.

The South Rim is open to car traffic year-round, though access to Hermits Rest is limited to shuttle buses part of the year. There are four free shuttle routes: the **Hermits Rest Route** operates March through November, between Grand Canyon Village and Hermits Rest. The **Village Route** operates year-round in

16

Grand Canyon National Park PLANNING

the village area, stopping at lodgings, the general store, and the Grand Canyon Visitor Center. The **Kaibab Rim Route** goes from the visitor center to five viewpoints, including the Yavapai Geology Museum and Yaki Point (where cars are not permitted). The **Hiker's Express** shuttles hikers from the village to the South Kaibab Trailhead each morning. ■TIP➜ **In summer, South Rim roads are congested, and it's easier, and sometimes required, to park your car and take the free shuttle.** Running from one hour before sunrise until one hour after sunset, shuttles arrive every 15 to 30 minutes at 30 clearly marked stops.

Although there's no public transportation into the Grand Canyon, you can hire a taxi to take you to or from the Grand Canyon Airport or any of the Tusayan hotels.

Grand Canyon Railway

There's no need to deal with all of the other drivers racing to the South Rim. Sit back and relax in the comfy train cars of the Grand Canyon Railway. Live music, storytelling, and a pretend train robbery enliven the trip as you journey past the landscape through prairie, ranch, and national park land to the log-cabin train station in Grand Canyon Village. You won't see the Grand Canyon from the train, but you can walk (¼ mile) or catch the shuttle at the restored, historic Grand Canyon Railway Station. The vintage train departs from the Williams Depot every morning and makes the 65-mile journey in 2¼ hours. You can do the round-trip in a single day; however, it's a more relaxing and enjoyable strategy to stay for a night or two at the South Rim before returning to Williams. ☎ 800/843–8724 ⊕ www. thetrain.com ✉ $82–$219 round-trip ☞ Rates do not include $30 park entry fee (for up to 9 persons).

NORTH RIM

The nearest airport to the North Rim is **St. George Municipal Airport** (☎ 435/627–4080 ⊕ www.flysgu.com) in Utah, 164 miles north, with regular service provided by both Delta and United Airlines.

To reach the North Rim by car, take U.S. 89 north from Flagstaff past Cameron, turning left onto U.S. 89A at Bitter Springs. At Jacob Lake, take Highway 67 directly to the Grand Canyon North Rim. You can drive yourself to the scenic viewpoints and trailheads; the only transportation offered in the Park is a shuttle twice each morning that brings eager hikers from Grand Canyon Lodge to the North Kaibab Trailhead (a 2-mile trip). Note that services on the North Rim shut down in mid-October, and the road closes after the first major snowfall (usually the end of October); Highway 67 south of Jacob Lake is closed.

From mid-May to mid-October, the **Trans Canyon Shuttle** (☎ 928/638–2820 ⊕ www. trans-canyonshuttle.com) travels daily between the South and North rims—the ride takes 4½ hours each way. One-way fare is $90, round-trip $170. Reservations are required.

PARK ESSENTIALS
ACCESSIBILITY

Rim Trail and all the viewpoints along the South Rim are accessible to wheelchairs. For detailed information, see the *Grand Canyon Accessibility Guide,* available free at Canyon View Information Plaza, Yavapai Information Station, Tusayan Museum, Desert View Information Center, and all entrance stations. There are free wheelchairs for use inside the park; inquire at one of the information centers. Temporary handicapped parking permits are available at Canyon View Information Plaza, Yavapai Observation Center, and all entrance stations.

PARK FEES AND PERMITS

A fee of $35 per vehicle or $20 per person for pedestrians and cyclists is good for one week's access at both rims.

The $70 Grand Canyon Pass gives unlimited access to the park for 12 months.

No permits are needed for day hikers; but **backcountry permits** (☎ 928/638–7875 ⊕ www.nps.gov/grca, $10, plus $8 per

SOUTH RIM AVERAGE HIGH/LOW TEMPERATURES					
JAN.	**FEB.**	**MAR.**	**APR.**	**MAY**	**JUNE**
41/18	45/21	51/25	60/32	70/39	81/47
JULY	**AUG.**	**SEPT.**	**OCT.**	**NOV.**	**DEC.**
84/54	82/53	76/47	65/36	52/27	43/20

NORTH RIM AVERAGE HIGH/LOW TEMPERATURES					
JAN.	**FEB.**	**MAR.**	**APR.**	**MAY**	**JUNE**
37/16	39/18	44/21	53/29	62/34	73/40
JULY	**AUG.**	**SEPT.**	**OCT.**	**NOV.**	**DEC.**
77/46	75/45	69/39	59/31	46/24	40/20

INNER CANYON AVERAGE HIGH/LOW TEMPERATURES					
JAN.	**FEB.**	**MAR.**	**APR.**	**MAY**	**JUNE**
56/36	62/42	71/48	82/56	92/63	101/72
JULY	**AUG.**	**SEPT.**	**OCT.**	**NOV.**	**DEC.**
106/78	103/75	97/69	84/58	68/46	57/37

16

Grand Canyon National Park **PLANNING**

person per night) are necessary for overnight hikers camping below the rim. Permits are limited, so make your reservation as far in advance as possible—they're taken by fax (☎ *928/638–2125*), by mail (✉ *1824 S. Thompson St., Suite 201, Flagstaff, AZ*), or in person at the Backcountry Information centers (in the village on the South Rim and near the visitor center on the North Rim) up to four months ahead of arrival. **Camping** in the park is restricted to designated campgrounds (☎ *877/444–6777* ⊕ *www. recreation.gov).*

All visitors except Native Americans with a valid tribal ID entering the Havasu Indian Reservation are required to pay an entrance fee ($35) and a $5 per-person environmental care fee, which is refunded to those who carry a bag of garbage back out of the canyon. Entrance fees are to be paid upon arrival at the tribal tourism office. Admission fees to Hualapai Reservation are $29.95 per person plus an $8 impact fee per person.

PARK HOURS

The South Rim is open continuously every day of the year (weather permitting), while the North Rim is open mid-May through October. The park is in the Mountain Standard time zone year-round. Daylight saving time isn't observed.

AUTOMOBILE SERVICE STATIONS

The only gas station inside the national park on the South Rim is at Desert View, and this station operates only from March 31 to September 30, depending on snowfall. Gas is available year-round near the South Entrance at Moqui Lodge (though the lodge itself is now closed), in Tusayan, and at Cameron, to the east.

At the South Rim, in Grand Canyon Village, the **Grand Canyon Garage** (☎ *928/635–0381*) is a fully equipped AAA garage that provides auto repair daily 8 to noon and 1 to 5 as well as 24-hour emergency service. This is a garage for repairs only and does not sell gasoline. There's also a **Conoco Station** (☎ *928/638–2608*) in Tusayan.

Tips for Avoiding Grand Canyon Crowds

It's hard to commune with nature while you're searching for a parking place, dodging video cameras, and stepping away from strollers. However, this scenario is likely only during the peak summer months. One option is to bypass Grand Canyon National Park altogether and head to the West Rim of the canyon, tribal land of the Hualapai and Havasupai. If only the park itself will do, the following tips will help you to keep your distance and your cool.

Take Another Route

Avoid road rage by choosing a different route to the South Rim, forgoing traditional Highway 64 and U.S. 180 from Flagstaff. Take U.S. 89 north from Flagstaff instead, passing near Sunset Crater and Wupatki national monuments. When you reach the junction with Highway 64, take a break at Cameron Trading Post (1 mile north of the junction)—or stay overnight. This is a good place to shop for Native American artifacts, souvenirs, and the usual postcards, dream-catchers, recordings, and T-shirts. There are also high-quality Navajo rugs, jewelry, and other authentic handicrafts, and you can sample Navajo tacos. U.S. 64 to the west takes you directly to the park's east entrance; the scenery along the Little Colorado River gorge en route is eye-popping. It's 23 miles from the east entrance to the visitor center at Grand Canyon Visitor Center.

Explore the North Rim

Although the North Rim is just 10 miles across from the South Rim, the trip to get there by car is a five-hour drive of 215 miles. At first it might not sound like the trip would be worth it, but the payoff is huge. Along the way, you'll travel through some of the prettiest parts of the state and be granted even more stunning views than those on the more easily accessible South Rim. Those who make the North Rim trip often insist it has the canyon's most beautiful views and best hiking. To get to the North Rim from Flagstaff, take U.S. 89 north past Cameron, turning left onto U.S. 89A at Bitter Springs. En route you'll pass the area known as Vermilion Cliffs. At Jacob Lake, take Highway 67 directly to the Grand Canyon North Rim. North Rim services are closed from November through mid-May because of heavy snow, but in summer months and early fall, it's a wonderful way to beat the crowds at the South Rim.

At the North Rim, the Chevron service station, which repairs autos, is inside the park on the access road leading to the North Rim Campground. The station is open daily 7 to 7, mid-May through mid-October. No diesel fuel is available at the North Rim.

CELL PHONE RECEPTION

Cell phone coverage can be spotty at both the South Rim and North Rim—though Verizon customers report better reception at the South Rim. Don't expect a strong signal anywhere in the park.

EMERGENCIES

In case of a fire or medical emergency, dial 911; from in-park lodgings, dial 9–911. To report a security problem, contact the park police (☎ 928/638–7805), stationed at all visitor centers. There are no pharmacies at the North Rim or South Rim. Prescriptions can be delivered daily to the South Rim Clinic from Flagstaff.

A health center is staffed by physicians from 8 to 6, seven days a week (reduced hours in winter). Emergency medical services are available 24 hours a day.

Emergency services ☎ *911, 9–911 from park lodgings* **Grand Canyon Walk-in Clinic** ✉ *Grand Canyon Village* ☎ *928/638–2551.*

EDUCATIONAL OFFERINGS
RANGER PROGRAMS
Interpretive Ranger Programs
TOUR—SIGHT | The National Park Service sponsors all sorts of orientation activities, such as daily guided hikes and talks, which change with the seasons. The focus may be on any aspect of the canyon—from geology and flora and fauna to history and early inhabitants. Schedules are available online. ☎ *928/638–7888* ⊕ *www.nps.gov/grca* ✍ *Free.*

Junior Ranger Program for Families
TOUR—SIGHT | FAMILY | The Junior Ranger Program provides a free, fun way to look at the cultural and natural history of this sublime destination. These hands-on educational activities for children ages four and up, available at the visitor centers, include guided adventure hikes, ranger-led "discovery" talks, and book readings. ☎ *928/638–7888* ⊕ *www.nps. gov/grca/forkids/beajuniorranger.htm* ✍ *Free.*

Discovery Pack Junior Ranger Program
TOUR—SIGHT | FAMILY | In summer, children ages four and up can take part in hands-on educational programs and earn a Junior Ranger certificate and badge. Sign up at the North Rim Visitor Center for these independent and ranger-led activities. ☎ *928/638–7967* ⊕ *www.nps. gov/grca* ✍ *Free.*

Interpretive Ranger Programs
TOUR—SIGHT | Daily guided hikes and talks may focus on any aspect of the canyon—from geology and flora and fauna to history and the canyon's early inhabitants. Schedules are available online. ☎ *928/638–7967* ⊕ *www.nps.gov/ grca* ✍ *Free.*

RESTAURANTS
Within the park on the South Rim, you can find everything from cafeteria food to casual café fare to creatively prepared, Western- and Southwestern-inspired American cuisine—there's even a coffeehouse with organic joe. Reservations are accepted (and recommended) only for dinner at El Tovar Dining Room; they can be made up to six months in advance with El Tovar room reservations, 30 days in advance without. You should also make dinner reservations at the Grand Canyon Lodge Dining Room on the North Rim—as the only "upscale" dining option, the restaurant fills up quickly at dinner throughout the season (the two other choices on the North Rim are a cafeteria and a chuck-wagon-style Grand Cookout experience). The dress code is casual across the board, but El Tovar is your best option if you're looking to dress up a bit and thumb through an extensive wine list. Drinking water and restrooms aren't available at most picnic spots.

Eateries outside the park generally range from mediocre to terrible—you didn't come all the way to the Grand Canyon for the food, did you? Our selections highlight your best options. Of towns near the park, Williams definitely has the leg up on culinary variety and quality, with Tusayan (near the South Rim) and Jacob Lake (the closest town to the North Rim) offering mostly either fast food or merely adequate sit-down restaurants. Near the park, even the priciest places welcome casual dress. On the Hualapai and Havasupai reservations in Havasu Canyon and on the West Rim, dining is limited and basic.

HOTELS
The park's accommodations include three "historic-rustic" facilities and four motel-style lodges, all of which have undergone significant upgrades over the past decade. Of the 922 rooms, cabins, and suites, only 203 are at the North Rim, all at the Grand Canyon Lodge. Outside El Tovar Hotel, the canyon's

architectural highlight, accommodations are relatively basic but comfortable, and the most sought-after rooms have canyon views. Rates vary widely, but most rooms fall in the $100 to $180 range, though the most basic units at the South Rim go for just $89.

Reservations are a must, especially during the busy summer season. ■TIP→ **If you want to get your first choice (especially Bright Angel Lodge or El Tovar), make reservations as far in advance as possible; they're taken up to 13 months ahead. You might find a last-minute cancellation, but you shouldn't count on it.** Although lodging at the South Rim will keep you close to the action, the frenetic activity and crowded facilities are off-putting to some. With short notice, the best time to find a room on the South Rim is in winter. And though the North Rim is less crowded than the South Rim, the only lodging available is at Grand Canyon Lodge.

Just south of the South Rim park boundary, Tusayan's hotels are in a convenient location but without bargains, while Williams (about an hour's drive) can provide price breaks on food and lodging, as well as a respite from the crowds. Extra amenities (e.g., swimming pools and gyms) are also more abundant. Reservations are always a good idea. At Grand Canyon West, lodging options are extremely limited; you can purchase a "package," which includes lodging and a visitation permit, through Hualapai Tourism.

Hotel reviews have been shortened. For full information, visit Fodors.com.

LODGING CONTACTS Xanterra Parks & Resorts ☎ *888/297–2757* ⊕ *www.grand-canyonlodges.com.*

What It Costs

	$	$$	$$$	$$$$
RESTAURANTS				
	under $12	$12–$20	$21–$30	over $30
HOTELS				
	under $101	$101–$175	$176–$250	over $250

TOURS

Grand Canyon Association Field Institute

GUIDED TOURS | Instructors lead guided educational tours, hikes around the canyon, and weekend programs at the South Rim. With more than 200 classes a year, tour topics include everything from archaeology and backcountry medicine to photography and natural history. Contact GCA for a schedule and price list. Private hikes can be arranged. Discounted classes are available for members; annual dues are $35. ✉ *GCA Warehouse, 2–B Albright Ave., Grand Canyon Village* ☎ *928/638–2841, 866/471–4435* ⊕ *www.grandcanyon.org/fieldinstitute* 🔁 *From $235.*

Xanterra Motorcoach Tours

GUIDED TOURS | Narrated by knowledgeable guides, tours include the Hermits Rest Tour, which travels along the old wagon road built by the Santa Fe Railway; the Desert View Tour, which glimpses the Colorado River's rapids and stops at Lipan Point; Sunrise and Sunset Tours; and combination tours. Children 16 and younger are free when accompanied by a paying adult. ☎ *303/297–2757, 888/297–2757* ⊕ *www.grandcanyonlodges.com* 🔁 *From $28.*

VISITOR INFORMATION

PARK CONTACT INFORMATION

Grand Canyon National Park

Before you go, get the complimentary *Trip Planner,* updated regularly, from the Grand Canyon National Park website. At the entrance stations and the visitor centers, pick up a copy of the *Pocket Map and Services Guide,* a weekly listing of ranger talks and other park activities. ☎ *928/638–7888* ⊕ *www.nps.gov/grca.*

SOUTH RIM VISITOR CENTERS
Desert View Information Center
Near the watchtower, at Desert View Point, this nonprofit Grand Canyon Association store and information center has a nice selection of books, park pamphlets, gifts, and educational materials. It's also a handy place to pick up maps and info if you enter the park at the Eastern entrance. All sales from the association stores go to support the park programs. ⊠ *Eastern entrance, Grand Canyon National Park* ☎ *800/858–2808, 928/638–7888.*

Grand Canyon Verkamp's Visitor Center
This small visitor center is named for the Verkamp family, who operated a curios shop on the South Rim for more than a hundred years. The building serves as an official visitor center, ranger station (get your Junior Ranger badges here), bookstore, and museum, with compelling exhibits on the Verkamps and other pioneers in this region. ⊠ *Desert View Dr., Grand Canyon Village* ✛ *Across from El Tovar Hotel* ☎ *928/638–7146.*

Grand Canyon Visitor Center
The park's main orientation center provides pamphlets and resources to help plan your visit. It also holds engaging interpretive exhibits on the park. Rangers are on hand to answer questions and aid in planning canyon excursions. A daily schedule of ranger-led hikes and evening lectures is available, and a 20-minute film about the history, geology, and wildlife of the canyon plays every 30 minutes in the theater. The bicycle rental office, a small café, and a huge gift store are also in this complex. It's a short walk from here to Mather Point, or a short ride on the shuttle bus, which can take you into Grand Canyon Village. The visitor center is also accessible from the village via a leisurely 1-mile walk on the Greenway Trail, a paved pathway that meanders through the forest. ⊠ *East side of Grand Canyon Village, 450 Hwy. 64* ☎ *928/638–7888* ⊕ *www.explorethecanyon.com.*

Yavapai Geology Museum
Learn about the geology of the canyon at this Grand Canyon Association museum and bookstore. You can also catch the park shuttle bus or pick up information for the Rim Trail here. The views of the canyon and Phantom Ranch from inside this historic building are stupendous. ⊠ *1 mile east of Market Plaza, Grand Canyon Village* ☎ *928/638–7888.*

NORTH RIM VISITOR CENTER
North Rim Visitor Center
View exhibits, peruse the bookstore, and pick up useful maps and brochures at this visitor center. Interpretive programs are often scheduled in summer. If you're craving refreshments, it's a short walk from here to the Roughrider Saloon at the Grand Canyon Lodge. ⊠ *Near Grand Canyon Lodge at North Rim, Grand Canyon National Park* ☎ *928/638–7864* ⊕ *www.nps.gov/grca.*

Grand Canyon South Rim

 ## Sights

Visitors to the canyon converge mostly on the South Rim, and mostly in summer. Grand Canyon Village is here, with a majority of the park's lodging and camping, trailheads, restaurants, stores, and museums, along with a nearby airport and railroad depot. Believe it or not, the average stay in the park is a mere half day or so; this is not advised! You need to spend several days to truly appreciate this marvelous place, but at the very least, give it a full day. Hike down into the canyon, or along the rim, to get away from the crowds and experience nature at its finest.

SCENIC DRIVES
Desert View Drive
SCENIC DRIVE | This heavily traveled 25-mile stretch of road follows the rim from the east entrance to Grand Canyon

Village. Starting from the less-congested entry near Desert View, road warriors can get their first glimpse of the canyon from the 70-foot-tall watchtower, the top of which provides the highest viewpoint on the South Rim. Six developed canyon viewpoints in addition to unmarked pullouts, the remains of an Ancestral Puebloan dwelling at the Tusayan Ruin and Museum, and the secluded and lovely Buggeln picnic area make for great stops along the South Rim. The Kaibab Rim Route shuttle bus travels a short section of Desert View Drive and takes 50 minutes to ride round-trip without getting off at any of the stops: Grand Canyon Visitor Center, South Kaibab Trailhead, Yaki Point, Pipe Creek Vista, Mather Point, and Yavapai Geology Museum. ⊠ Grand Canyon National Park.

Hermit Road

SCENIC DRIVE | The Santa Fe Company built Hermit Road, formerly known as West Rim Drive, in 1912 as a scenic tour route. Nine overlooks dot this 7-mile stretch, each worth a visit. The road is filled with hairpin turns, so make sure you adhere to posted speed limits. A 1.5-mile Greenway trail offers easy access to cyclists looking to enjoy the original 1912 Hermit Rim Road. From March through November, Hermit Road is closed to private auto traffic because of congestion; during this period, a free shuttle bus carries visitors to all the overlooks. Riding the bus round-trip without getting off at any of the viewpoints takes 80 minutes; the return trip stops only at Hermits Rest, Pima, Mohave, and Powell points. ⊠ Grand Canyon National Park.

HISTORIC SITES
Tusayan Ruin and Museum

ARCHAEOLOGICAL SITE | This museum offers a quick orientation to the prehistoric and modern Indian populations of the Grand Canyon and the Colorado Plateau, including an excavation of an 800-year-old Pueblo Indian site. Of special interest are split-twig figurines dating back 2,000 to 4,000 years and other artifacts left behind by ancient cultures. A ranger leads daily interpretive tours of the Ancestral Puebloan village. ⊠ Grand Canyon National Park ✛ About 20 miles east of Grand Canyon Village on E. Rim Dr. ☎ 928/638–7888 ◻ Free.

SCENIC STOPS
The Abyss

VIEWPOINT | At an elevation of 6,720 feet, the Abyss is one of the most awesome stops on Hermit Road, revealing a sheer drop of 3,000 feet to the Tonto Platform, a wide terrace of Tapeats sandstone about two-thirds of the way down the canyon. From the Abyss you'll also see several isolated sandstone columns, the largest of which is called the Monument. ⊠ Grand Canyon National Park ✛ About 5 miles west of Hermit Rd. Junction on Hermit Rd.

Desert View and Watchtower

VIEWPOINT | From the top of the 70-foot stone-and-mortar watchtower with its 360-degree views, even the muted hues of the distant Painted Desert to the east and the Vermilion Cliffs rising from a high plateau near the Utah border are visible. In the chasm below, angling to the north toward Marble Canyon, an imposing stretch of the Colorado River reveals itself. Up several flights of stairs, the watchtower houses a glass-enclosed observatory with powerful telescopes. ⊠ Grand Canyon National Park ✛ Just north of East Entrance Station on Desert View Dr. ☎ 928/638–7888 ⊕ www.nps. gov/grca ◻ Free.

Grandview Point

VIEWPOINT | At an elevation of 7,399 feet, the view from here is one of the finest in the canyon. To the northeast is a group of dominant buttes, including Krishna Shrine, Vishnu Temple, Rama Shrine, and Sheba Temple. A short stretch of the Colorado River is also visible. Directly below the point, and accessible by the steep and rugged Grandview Trail, is Horseshoe Mesa, where you can see remnants of Last Chance Copper Mine.

Plants and Wildlife in the Grand Canyon

Eighty-nine mammal species inhabit Grand Canyon National Park, as well as 355 species of birds, 56 kinds of reptiles and amphibians, and 17 kinds of fish. The rare Kaibab squirrel is found only on the North Rim—you can recognize them by their all-white tails and black undersides. The pink Grand Canyon rattlesnake lives at lower elevations within the canyon. Hawks and ravens are visible year-round. The endangered California condor has been reintroduced to the canyon region. Park rangers give daily talks on the magnificent birds, whose wingspan measures 9 feet. In spring, summer, and fall, mule deer, recognizable by their large ears, are abundant at the South Rim. Don't be fooled by gentle appearances; these guys can be aggressive. It's illegal to feed them, as it'll disrupt their natural habitats, and increase your risk of getting bitten or kicked.

The best times to see wildlife are early in the morning and late in the afternoon. Look for out-of-place shapes and motions, keeping in mind that animals occupy all layers in a natural habitat and not just at your eye level. Use binoculars for close-up views. While out and about try to fade into the woodwork by keeping your movements limited and noise at a minimum.

More than 1,700 species of plants color the park. The South Rim's Coconino Plateau is fairly flat, at an elevation of about 7,000 feet, and covered with stands of pinyon and ponderosa pines, junipers, and Gambel's oak trees. On the Kaibab Plateau on the North Rim, Douglas fir, spruce, quaking aspen, and more ponderosas prevail. In spring you're likely to see asters, sunflowers, and lupine in bloom at both rims.

✉ *Grand Canyon National Park* ✛ *About 12 miles east of Grand Canyon Village on Desert View Dr.*

Hermits Rest

VIEWPOINT | This westernmost viewpoint and Hermit Trail, which descends from it, were named for "hermit" Louis Boucher, a 19th-century French-Canadian prospector who had a number of mining claims and a roughly built home down in the canyon. The trail served as the original mule ride down to Hermit Camp beginning in 1914. Views from here include Hermit Rapids and the towering cliffs of the Supai and Redwall formations. You can buy curios and snacks in the stone building at Hermits Rest. ✉ *Grand Canyon National Park* ✛ *About 8 miles west of Hermit Rd. Junction on Hermit Rd.*

★ Hopi Point

VIEWPOINT | From this elevation of 7,071 feet, you can see a large section of the Colorado River; although it appears as a thin line, the river is nearly 350 feet wide. The overlook extends farther into the canyon than any other point on Hermit Road. The incredible unobstructed views make this a popular place to watch the sunrise and sunset.

Across the canyon to the north is Shiva Temple. In 1937 Harold Anthony of the American Museum of Natural History led an expedition to the rock formation in the belief that it supported life that had been cut off from the rest of the canyon. Imagine the expedition members' surprise when they found an empty Kodak film box on top of the temple—it

Best Grand Canyon Views

The best time of day to see the canyon is before 10 and after 4, when the angle of the sun brings out the colors of the rock, and clouds and shadows add dimension. Colors deepen dramatically among the contrasting layers of the canyon walls just before and during sunrise and sunset.

Hopi Point is the top spot on the South Rim to watch the sun set; **Yaki** and **Pima** points also offer vivid views.

For a grand sunrise, try **Mather** or **Yaki Point.**

■ TIP→ Arrive at least 30 minutes early for sunrise views and as much as 90 minutes for sunset views at these points. For another point of view, take a leisurely stroll along the Rim Trail and watch the color change along with the views. Timetables are posted at park visitor centers.

had been left behind by Emery Kolb, who felt slighted for not having been invited to join Anthony's tour.

Directly below Hopi Point lies Dana Butte, named for a prominent 19th-century geologist. In 1919 an entrepreneur proposed connecting Hopi Point, Dana Butte, and the Tower of Set across the river with an aerial tramway, a technically feasible plan that fortunately has not been realized. ⊠ *Grand Canyon National Park* ✛ *About 4 miles west of Hermit Rd. Junction on Hermit Rd.*

Lipan Point

VIEWPOINT | Here, at the canyon's widest point, you can get an astonishing visual profile of the gorge's geologic history, with a view of every eroded layer of the canyon and one of the longest visible stretches of Colorado River. The spacious panorama stretches to the Vermilion Cliffs on the northeastern horizon and features a multitude of imaginatively named spires, buttes, and temples—intriguing rock formations named after their resemblance to ancient pyramids. You can also see Unkar Delta, where a creek joins the Colorado to form powerful rapids and a broad beach. Ancestral Puebloan farmers worked the Unkar Delta for hundreds of years, growing corn, beans, and melons. ⊠ *Grand Canyon*

National Park ✛ *About 25 miles east of Grand Canyon Village on Desert View Dr.*

★ Mather Point

VIEWPOINT | You'll likely get your first glimpse of the canyon from this viewpoint, one of the most impressive and accessible (next to the main visitor center plaza) on the South Rim. Named for the National Park Service's first director, Stephen Mather, this spot yields extraordinary views of the Grand Canyon, including deep into the inner gorge and numerous buttes: Wotans Throne, Brahma Temple, and Zoroaster Temple, among others. The Grand Canyon Lodge, on the North Rim, is almost directly north from Mather Point and only 10 miles away—yet you have to drive 215 miles to get from one spot to the other. ⊠ *Near Grand Canyon Visitor Center, Grand Canyon National Park* ☎ *928/638–7888* ⊕ *www. nps.gov/grca.*

Moran Point

VIEWPOINT | This point was named for American landscape artist Thomas Moran, who was especially fond of the play of light and shadows from this location. He first visited the canyon with John Wesley Powell in 1873. "Thomas Moran's name, more than any other, with the possible exception of Major Powell's, is to be associated with the Grand Canyon," wrote noted canyon photographer

Ellsworth Kolb. It's fitting that Moran Point is a favorite spot of photographers and painters. ✉ *Grand Canyon National Park* ✛ *About 17 miles east of Grand Canyon Village on Desert View Dr.*

Trailview Overlook

VIEWPOINT | Look down on a dramatic view of the Bright Angel and Plateau Point trails as they zigzag down the canyon. In the deep gorge to the north flows Bright Angel Creek, one of the region's few permanent tributary streams of the Colorado River. Toward the south is an unobstructed view of the distant San Francisco Peaks, as well as Bill Williams Mountain (on the horizon) and Red Butte (about 15 miles south of the canyon rim). ✉ *Grand Canyon National Park* ✛ *About 2 miles west of Hermit Rd. Junction on Hermit Rd.*

Yaki Point

NATURE SITE | Stop here for an exceptional view of Wotans Throne, a flat-top butte named by François Matthes, a U.S. Geological Survey scientist who developed the first topographical map of the Grand Canyon. The overlook juts out over the canyon, providing unobstructed views of inner-canyon rock formations, South Rim cliffs, and Clear Creek canyon. About a mile south of Yaki Point is the trailhead for the South Kaibab Trail. **The point is one of the best places on the South Rim to watch the sunset.** ✉ *Grand Canyon National Park* ✛ *2 miles east of Grand Canyon Village on Desert View Dr.*

★ Yavapai Point

MUSEUM | Dominated by the Yavapai Geology Museum and Observation Station, this point displays panoramic views of the mighty gorge through a wall of windows. Exhibits at the museum include videos of the canyon floor and the Colorado River, a scaled diorama of the canyon with national park boundaries, fossils, and rock fragments used to re-create the complex layers of the canyon walls, and a display on the natural forces used to carve the chasm. Dig even

deeper into Grand Canyon geology with free daily ranger programs. This point is also a good location to watch the sunset. ✉ *Grand Canyon Village* ✛ *1 mile east of Market Plaza.*

Activities

AIR TOURS

Flights by plane and helicopter over the canyon are offered by a number of companies, departing from the Grand Canyon Airport at the south end of Tusayan. Though the noise and disruption of so many aircraft buzzing the canyon is controversial, flightseeing remains a popular, if expensive, option. You'll have more visibility from a helicopter but they're louder and more expensive than the fixed-wing planes. Prices and lengths of tours vary, but you can expect to pay about $169 per adult for short plane trips and approximately $179–$250 for brief helicopter tours (and about $500 for tours leaving from Vegas). These companies often have significant discounts in winter—check the company websites to find the best deals.

Grand Canyon Airlines

TOUR—SPORTS | This company offers a variety of plane tours, from a 45-minute fixed-wing tour of the eastern edge of the Grand Canyon, the North Rim, and the Kaibab Plateau to an all-day tour that combines "flightseeing" with four-wheel-drive tours of Antelope Canyon and float trips on the Colorado River. They also schedule combination tours that leave from Las Vegas (plane flight from Las Vegas to Grand Canyon Airport, then helicopter flight into the canyon). ✉ *Grand Canyon Airport, Tusayan* ☎ *928/638–2359, 866/235–9422* ⊕ *www.grandcanyonairlines.com* 🖃 *From $159.*

Maverick Helicopters

TOUR—SPORTS | This company offers 25- and 45-minute tours of the South Rim, North Rim, and Dragon Corridor of the Grand Canyon, and airplane tours out of Las Vegas. A landing tour option for those

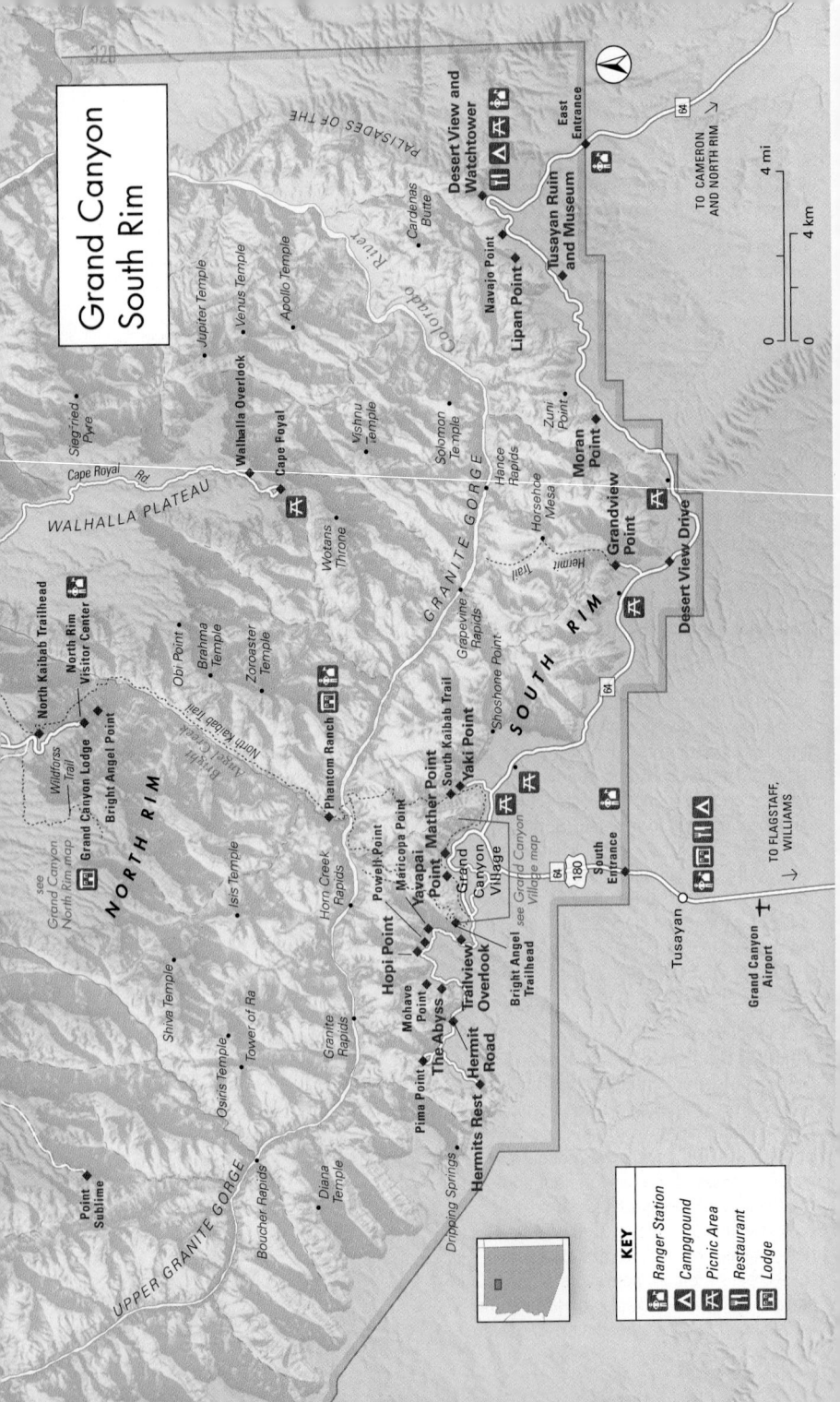

Grand Canyon
South Rim

320

PALISADES OF THE

Desert View and Watchtower

East Entrance

TO CAMERON AND NORTH RIM

Cardenas Butte

Tusayan Ruin and Museum

Navajo Point

Lipan Point

4 mi

4 km

Jupiter Temple

Venus Temple

Apollo Temple

Colorado River

Vishnu Temple

Solomon Temple

Zuni Point

Moran Point

Siegfried Pyre

Walhalla Overlook

Cape Royal

Cape Royal Rd.

WALHALLA PLATEAU

Wotans Throne

GRANITE GORGE

Hance Rapids

Horseshoe Mesa

Grandview Point

Hermit Trail

Desert View Drive

North Kaibab Trailhead

North Rim Visitor Center

Obi Point

Brahma Temple

Zoroaster Temple

Gapewine Rapids

Shoshone Point

SOUTH RIM

Wildforss Trail

Grand Canyon Lodge

Bright Angel Point

Phantom Ranch

North Kaibab Trail

South Kaibab Trail

Yaki Point

Bright Angel Trail

NORTH RIM

see Grand Canyon North Rim map

Isis Temple

Horn Creek Rapids

Powell Point

Maricopa Point

Yavapai Point

Mather Point

Grand Canyon Village

see Grand Canyon Village map

South Entrance

TO FLAGSTAFF, WILLIAMS

Shiva Temple

Tower of Ra

Hopi Point

Mohave Point

Trailview Overlook

Bright Angel Trailhead

Tusayan

Grand Canyon Airport

Granite Rapids

The Abyss

Hermit Road

Pima Point

Hermits Rest

Dripping Springs

Diana Temple

Point Sublime

Osiris Temple

Boucher Rapids

UPPER GRANITE GORGE

KEY

Ranger Station
Campground
Picnic Area
Restaurant
Lodge

flying from Las Vegas to the West Rim sets you down in the canyon for a short snack below the rim. ⊠ *Grand Canyon Airport* ☎ *928/638–2622* ⊕ *www.maverickhelicopter.com* ⊠ *From $175.*

HIKING

Although permits are not required for day hikes, you must have a backcountry permit for longer trips (⇨ *see Park Fees and Permits at the start of this chapter).* Some of the more popular trails are listed here; more detailed information and maps can be obtained from the Backcountry Information centers. Also, rangers can help design a trip to suit your abilities.

Remember that the canyon has significant elevation changes and, in summer, extreme temperature ranges, which can pose problems for people who aren't in good shape or who have heart or respiratory problems. ■**TIP→ Carry plenty of water and energy foods.** The majority of each year's 400 search-and-rescue incidents result from hikers underestimating the size of the canyon, hiking beyond their abilities, or not packing sufficient food and water.

■**TIP→ Under no circumstances should you attempt a day hike from the rim to the river and back.** Remember that when it's 80°F on the South Rim, it's 110°F on the canyon floor. Allow two to four days if you want to hike rim to rim (it's easier to descend from the North Rim, as it's more than 1,000 feet higher than the South Rim). Hiking steep trails from rim to rim is a strenuous trek of at least 21 miles and should only be attempted by experienced canyon hikers.

Bright Angel Trail

HIKING/WALKING | This well-maintained trail is one of the most scenic (and busiest) hiking paths from the South Rim to the bottom of the canyon (9.6 miles each way). Rest houses are equipped with water at the 1.5- and 3-mile points from May through September, and at Indian Garden (4 miles) year-round. Water is also available at Bright Angel Campground, 9¼ miles below the trailhead. Plateau Point, on a spur trail about 1.5 miles below Indian Garden, is as far as you should attempt to go on a day hike; the round-trip will take six to nine hours.

Bright Angel Trail is the easiest of all the footpaths into the canyon, but because the climb out from the bottom is an ascent of 5,510 feet, the trip should be attempted only by those in good physical condition and should be avoided in mid-summer due to extreme heat. The top of the trail can be icy in winter. Originally a bighorn sheep path and later used by the Havasupai, the trail was widened late in the 19th century for prospectors and is now used for both mule and foot traffic. Also note that mule trains have the right-of-way—and sometimes leave unpleasant surprises in your path. *Moderate.* ⊠ *Grand Canyon National Park* ✛ *Trailhead: Kolb Studio, Hermit Rd.*

★ Rim Trail

HIKING/WALKING | The South Rim's most popular walking path is the 12-mile (one-way) Rim Trail, which runs along the edge of the canyon from Pipe Creek Vista (the first overlook on Desert View Drive) to Hermits Rest. This walk, which is paved to Maricopa Point and for the last 1.5 miles to Hermits Rest, visits several of the South Rim's historic landmarks. Allow anywhere from 15 minutes to a full day, depending on how much of the trail you want to cover; the Rim Trail is an ideal day hike, as it varies only a few hundred feet in elevation from Mather Point (7,120 feet) to the trailhead at Hermits Rest (6,650 feet). The trail also can be accessed from several spots in Grand Canyon Village and from the major viewpoints along Hermit Road, which are serviced by shuttle buses during the busy summer months. On the Rim Trail, water is only available in the Grand Canyon Village area and at Hermits Rest. *Easy.* ⊠ *Grand Canyon National Park.*

16

Grand Canyon National Park

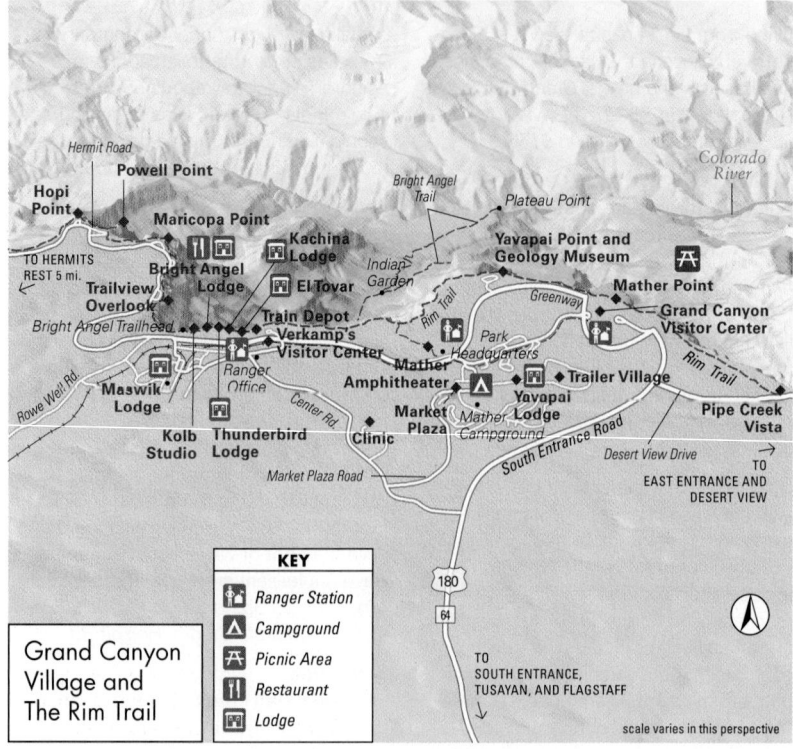

KEY

👫	Ranger Station
⛺	Campground
🌲	Picnic Area
🍴	Restaurant
🏠	Lodge

Grand Canyon Village and The Rim Trail

TO
SOUTH ENTRANCE,
TUSAYAN, AND FLAGSTAFF

scale varies in this perspective

South Kaibab Trail

HIKING/WALKING | This trail starts near Yaki Point, 4 miles east of Grand Canyon Village, and is accessible via the free shuttle bus.

Because the route is so steep (and sometimes icy in winter)—descending from the trailhead at 7,260 feet down to 2,480 feet at the Colorado River—and has no water, many hikers take this trail down, then ascend via the less-demanding Bright Angel Trail. Allow four to six hours to reach the Colorado River on this 6.4-mile trek. At the river, the trail crosses a suspension bridge and runs on to Phantom Ranch. Along the trail there is no water and little shade. There are no campgrounds, though there are portable toilets at Cedar Ridge (6,320 feet), 1.5 miles from the trailhead. An emergency phone is available at the Tipoff, 4.6 miles down the trail (3 miles past Cedar Ridge).

The trail corkscrews down through some spectacular geology. Look for (but don't remove) fossils in the limestone when taking water breaks. *Difficult.* ⊠ *Grand Canyon National Park* ⊹ *Trailhead: Yaki Point Rd., off Desert View Dr.*

MULE RIDES

Mule rides provide an intimate glimpse into the canyon for those who have the time, but not the stamina, to see the canyon on foot. ■TIP➜ **Reservations are essential and are accepted up to 13 months in advance.**

These trips have been conducted since the early 1900s. A comforting fact as you ride the narrow trail: no one's ever been killed while riding a mule that fell off a cliff. (Nevertheless, the treks are not for the faint of heart or people in questionable health.)

★ **Xanterra Parks & Resorts Mule Rides**
TOUR—SPORTS | These trips delve either into the canyon from the South Rim to Phantom Ranch, or east along the canyon's rim. Riders must be at least 57 inches tall, weigh less than 200 pounds (for the Phantom Ranch ride), and understand English. Children under 15 must be accompanied by an adult. Riders must be in fairly good physical condition, and pregnant women are advised not to take these trips.

The three-hour ride along the rim costs $143. An overnight with a stay at Phantom Ranch at the bottom of the canyon, with meals included, is $605 ($1,056 for two riders). Two nights at Phantom Ranch, an option available from November through March, will set you back $875 ($1,440 for two). Meals at Phantom Ranch are included. Reservations (by phone), especially during the busy summer months, are a must, but you can check at the Bright Angel Transportation Desk to see if there's last-minute availability. ☎ *888/297–2757* ⊕ *www. grandcanyonlodges.com* ⚐ *Reservations essential.*

Grand Canyon North Rim

The North Rim stands 1,000 feet higher than the South Rim and has a more alpine climate, with twice as much annual precipitation. Here, in the deep forests of the Kaibab Plateau, the crowds are thinner, the facilities fewer, and the views even more spectacular. Due to snow, the North Rim is off-limits in winter. The buildings and concessions are closed November through mid-May. The road and entrance gate close when the snow makes them impassable—usually by the end of November.

Lodgings are limited in this more remote park, with only one historic lodge (with cabins and hotel-type rooms as well as a restaurant) and a single campground. Dining options have opened up a little

with the addition of the Grand Cookout, offered nightly with live entertainment under the stars. Your best bet may be to pack your camping gear and hiking boots and take several days to explore the lush Kaibab National Forest. The canyon's highest, most dramatic rim views also can be enjoyed on two wheels (via primitive dirt access roads) and on four legs (courtesy of a trusty mule).

 **Sights**

SCENIC DRIVE
★ **Highway 67**
SCENIC DRIVE | Open mid-May to roughly mid-November (or the first big snowfall), this two-lane paved road climbs 1,400 feet in elevation as it passes through the Kaibab National Forest. Also called the North Rim Parkway, this scenic route crosses the limestone-capped Kaibab Plateau—passing broad meadows, sun-dappled forests, and small lakes and springs—before abruptly falling away at the abyss of the Grand Canyon. Wildlife abounds in the thick ponderosa pine forests and lush mountain meadows. It's common to see deer, turkeys, and coyotes as you drive through such a remote region. Point Imperial and Cape Royal branch off this scenic drive, which runs from Jacob Lake to Bright Angel Point. ✉ *Hwy. 67, Grand Canyon National Park.*

HISTORIC SITE
Grand Canyon Lodge
HISTORIC SITE | Built in 1937 by the Union Pacific Railroad (replacing the original 1928 building, which burned in a fire), this massive stone structure is listed on the National Register of Historic Places. Its huge sunroom has hardwood floors, high-beamed ceilings, and a marvelous view of the canyon through plate-glass windows. On warm days, visitors sit in the sun and drink in the surrounding beauty on an outdoor viewing deck, where National Park Service employees deliver free lectures on geology and history. The dining room serves breakfast,

lunch, and dinner; the Roughrider Saloon is a bar by night and a coffee shop in the morning. ☒ *Grand Canyon National Park* ✛ *Off Hwy. 67 near Bright Angel Point* ☏ *928/638–2611 May.–Oct., 928/645–6865 Nov.–Apr.* ⊕ *www.grandcanyonforever.com.*

SCENIC STOPS

★ Bright Angel Point

TRAIL | This trail, which leads to one of the most awe-inspiring overlooks on either rim, starts on the grounds of the Grand Canyon Lodge and runs along the crest of a point of rocks that juts into the canyon for several hundred yards. The walk is only 0.5 mile round-trip, but it's an exciting trek accented by sheer drops on each side of the trail. In a few spots where the route is extremely narrow, metal railings ensure visitors' safety. The temptation to clamber out on precarious perches to have your picture taken should be resisted at all costs. ☒ *North Rim Dr., Grand Canyon National Park* ✛ *Near Grand Canyon Lodge.*

Cape Royal

TRAIL | A popular sunset destination, Cape Royal showcases the canyon's jagged landscape; you'll also get a glimpse of the Colorado River, framed by a natural stone arch called Angels Window. In autumn, the aspens turn a beautiful gold, adding even more color to an already magnificent scene of the forested surroundings. The easy and rewarding 1-mile round-trip hike along **Cliff Springs Trail** starts here; it takes you through a forested ravine and terminates at Cliff Springs, where the forest opens to another impressive view of the canyon walls. ☒ *Cape Royal Scenic Dr., Grand Canyon National Park* ✛ *23 miles southeast of Grand Canyon Lodge.*

Point Imperial

VIEWPOINT | At 8,803 feet, Point Imperial has the highest vista point at either rim; it offers magnificent views of both the canyon and the distant country: the Vermilion Cliffs to the north, the 10,000-foot Navajo Mountain to the northeast in Utah, the Painted Desert to the east, and the Little Colorado River canyon to the southeast. Other prominent points of interest include views of Mount Hayden, Saddle Mountain, and Marble Canyon. ☒ *Point Imperial Rd., Grand Canyon National Park* ✛ *11 miles northeast of Grand Canyon Lodge.*

★ Point Sublime

VIEWPOINT | You can camp within feet of the canyon's edge at this awe-inspiring site. Sunrises and sunsets are spectacular. The winding road, through gorgeous high country, is only 17 miles, but it will take you at least two hours one-way. The road is intended only for vehicles with high road clearance (pickups and four-wheel-drive vehicles). It is also necessary to be properly equipped for wilderness road travel. Check with a park ranger or at the information desk at Grand Canyon Lodge before taking this journey. You may camp here only with a permit from the Backcountry Information Center. ☒ *North Rim Dr., Grand Canyon National Park* ✛ *About 20 miles west of North Rim Visitor Center.*

Roosevelt Point

VIEWPOINT | Named after the president who gave the Grand Canyon its national monument status in 1908 (it was upgraded to national park status in 1919), Roosevelt Point is the best place to see the confluence of the Little Colorado River and the Grand Canyon. The cliffs above the Colorado River south of the junction are known as the Palisades of the Desert. A short woodland loop trail leads to this eastern viewpoint. ☒ *Cape Royal Rd., Grand Canyon National Park* ✛ *18 miles east of Grand Canyon Lodge.*

 **Activities**

HIKING

Cape Final Trail

HIKING/WALKING | This 4-mile (round-trip) gravel path follows an old jeep trail through a ponderosa pine forest to the canyon overlook at Cape Final with panoramic views of the northern canyon, the Palisades of the Desert, and the impressive spectacle of Juno Temple. *Easy. ✉ Grand Canyon National Park ⊕ Trailhead: dirt parking lot 5 miles south of Roosevelt Point on Cape Royal Rd.*

Cape Royal Trail

HIKING/WALKING | FAMILY | Informative signs about vegetation, wildlife, and natural history add to this popular 0.6-mile, round-trip, paved path to Cape Royal; allow 30 minutes round-trip. At an elevation of 7,685 feet on the southern edge of the Walhalla Plateau, this popular viewpoint offers expansive views of Wotans Throne, Vishnu Temple, Freya Castle, Horseshoe Mesa, and the Colorado River. The trail also offers several nice views of Angels Window. *Easy. ✉ Grand Canyon National Park ⊕ Trailhead: end of Cape Royal Rd.*

Cliff Springs Trail

HIKING/WALKING | An easy 1-mile (round-trip), one-hour walk near Cape Royal, Cliff Springs Trail leads through a forested ravine to an excellent view of the canyon. The trailhead begins at the Cape Royal parking lot, across from Angels Window Overlook. Narrow and precarious in spots, it passes ancient dwellings, winds beneath a limestone overhang, and ends at Cliff Springs. *Easy. ✉ Grand Canyon National Park ⊕ Trailhead: end of Cape Royal Rd.*

North Kaibab Trail

HIKING/WALKING | At 8,241 feet, this trail leads into the canyon and down to Phantom Ranch. It is recommended for experienced hikers only, who should allow four days for the round-trip hike. The long, steep path drops 5,840 feet over a distance of 14.5 miles to Phantom Ranch and the Colorado River, so the National Park Service suggests that day hikers not go farther than Roaring Springs (5,020 feet) before turning to hike back up out of the canyon. After about 7 miles, Cottonwood Campground (4,080

feet) has drinking water in summer, restrooms, shade trees, and a ranger. *Difficult.* **A free shuttle takes hikers to the North Kaibab trailhead twice daily from Grand Canyon Lodge; reserve a spot the day before.** *✉ Grand Canyon National Park ⊕ Trailhead: about 2 miles north of Grand Canyon Lodge.*

Roosevelt Point Trail

HIKING/WALKING | FAMILY | This easy 0.2-mile round-trip trail loops through the forest to the scenic viewpoint. Allow 20 minutes for this relaxed, secluded hike. *Easy. ✉ Grand Canyon National Park ⊕ Trailhead: Cape Royal Rd.*

Transept Trail

HIKING/WALKING | FAMILY | This 3-mile-round-trip, 1½-hour trail begins near the Grand Canyon Lodge at 8,255 feet. Well-maintained and well-marked, it has little elevation change, sticking near the rim before reaching a dramatic view of a large stream through Bright Angel Canyon. The trail leads to Transept Canyon, which geologist Clarence Dutton named in 1882, declaring it "far grander than Yosemite." Check the posted schedule to find a ranger talk along this trail; it's also a great place to view fall foliage. Flash floods can occur any time of the year, especially June through September when thunderstorms develop rapidly. *Easy. ✉ Grand Canyon National Park ⊕ Trailhead: near Grand Canyon Lodge east patio.*

Uncle Jim Trail

HIKING/WALKING | This 5-mile, three-hour loop starts at 8,300 feet and winds south through the forest, past Roaring Springs and Bright Angel canyons. The highlight of this rim hike is Uncle Jim Point, which, at 8,244 feet, overlooks the upper sections of the North Kaibab Trail. *Moderate.* ✉ *Grand Canyon National Park ⊕ Trailhead: North Kaibab Trail parking lot.*

Widforss Trail

HIKING/WALKING | Round-trip, Widforss Trail is 9.8 miles, with an elevation change of only 200 feet. Allow five to six hours for

Did You Know?

Sure-footed mules take riders along the rim for half-day trips and down into the canyon for longer excursions. Two-day trips include an overnight stay at Phantom Ranch on the canyon floor.

the hike, which starts at 8,080 feet and passes through shady forests of pine, spruce, fir, and aspen on its way to Widforss Point, at 7,900 feet. Here you'll have good views of five temples: Zoroaster, Brahma, and Deva to the southeast, and Buddha and Manu to the southwest. You are likely to see wildflowers in summer, and this is a good trail for viewing fall foliage. It's named in honor of artist Gunnar M. Widforss, renowned for his paintings of national park landscapes. *Moderate.* ⊠ *Grand Canyon National Park* ✛ *Trailhead: off dirt road about 2 miles north of Grand Canyon Lodge.*

MULE RIDES
Canyon Trail Rides
TOUR—SPORTS | FAMILY | This company leads mule rides on the easier trails of the North Rim. Options include one- to three-hour rides along the rim or three-hour rides down into the canyon (minimum age 7 for one-hour rides, 10 for three-hour rides). The one-hour ride is $45 and the three-hour rides are $90. Weight limits are 200 pounds for canyon rides and 220 pounds for the rim rides. Available daily from May 15 to October 15, these excursions are popular, so make reservations in advance. ☎ *435/679–8665* ⊕ *www.canyonrides. com* ✉ *From $45.*

Grand Canyon West Rim

The West Rim is a 5-hour drive from the South Rim of Grand Canyon National Park or a 2½-hour drive from Las Vegas. From Kingman, drive north 30 miles on U.S. 93, and then turn right onto Pierce Ferry Road and follow it for 28 miles. (A more scenic alternative is to drive 42 miles north on Stockton Hill Road, turning right onto Pierce Ferry Road for 7 miles, but this takes a bit longer because Stockton Hill Road has a lower speed limit than the wide, divided U.S. 93 highway.) Turn right (east) onto Diamond Bar Road and follow for 21 miles to Grand Canyon West entrance.

Visitors aren't allowed to travel in their own vehicles to the viewpoints once they reach the West Rim, and must purchase a tour package—which can range from day use to horseback or helicopter rides to lodging and meals—from Hualapai Tourism.

 ## Sights

Grand Canyon Skywalk
VIEWPOINT | This cantilevered glass terrace is suspended nearly 4,000 feet above the Colorado River and extends 70 feet from the edge of the Grand Canyon. Approximately 10 feet wide, the bridge's deck, made of tempered glass several inches thick, has 5-foot glass railings on each side creating an unobstructed open-air platform. Admission to the skywalk is an add-on to the basic Grand Canyon West admission. Visitors must store personal items, including cameras, cell phones, and video cameras, in lockers before entering. A professional photographer takes photographs of visitors, which can be purchased from the gift shop. ⊕ *www.grandcanyonwest.com* ✉ *$32 (includes lunch).*

Grand Canyon West
CANYON | At the Welcome Center, Grand Canyon West, run by the Hualapai tribe, offers the basic Hualapai Legacy tour package ($50 per person, including taxes and fees), which includes a Hualapai visitation permit and hop-on, hop-off shuttle transportation to three sites. The shuttle will take you to Eagle Point, where the Indian Village walking tour visits authentic dwellings. Educational displays there uncover the culture of five different Native American tribes (Havasupai, Plains, Hopi, Hualapai, and Navajo), and intertribal, powwow-style dance performances entertain visitors at the nearby amphitheater. The shuttle also goes to Hualapai Ranch, site of Western performances, cookouts, horseback and wagon rides, and the only lodging on the West Rim; and Guano Point, where

16

Grand Canyon National Park

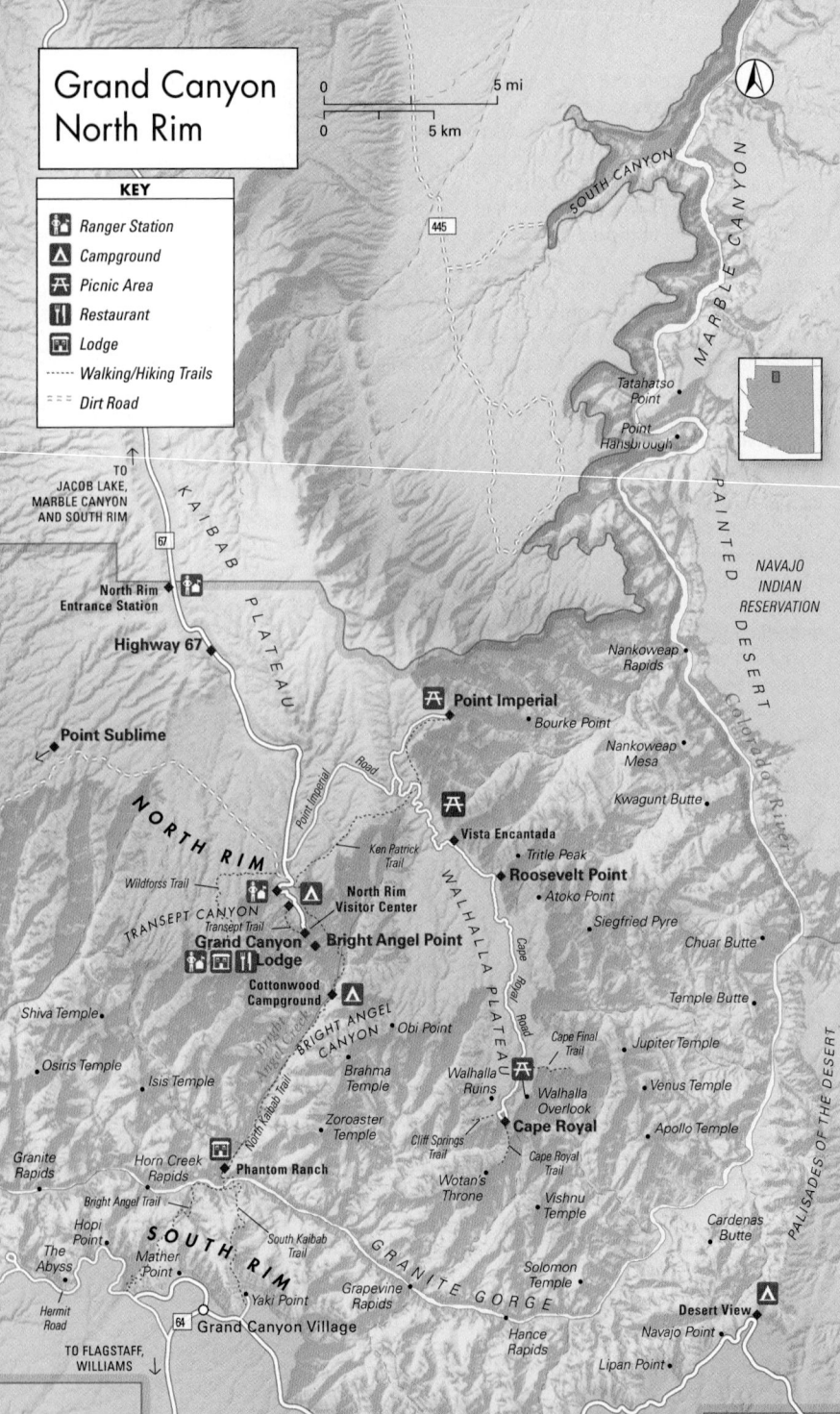

Grand Canyon North Rim

0 — 5 mi
0 — 5 km

KEY

- 🚶 Ranger Station
- 🏕 Campground
- ⛱ Picnic Area
- 🍴 Restaurant
- 🏨 Lodge
- ⋯⋯ Walking/Hiking Trails
- ═══ Dirt Road

SOUTH CANYON

MARBLE CANYON

445

Tatahatso Point

Point Hansbrough

PAINTED DESERT

TO JACOB LAKE, MARBLE CANYON AND SOUTH RIM

67

KAIBAB PLATEAU

North Rim Entrance Station

Highway 67

Point Sublime

NAVAJO INDIAN RESERVATION

Nankoweap Rapids

Point Imperial

Bourke Point

Nankoweap Mesa

NORTH RIM

Point Imperial Road

Vista Encantada

Kwagunt Butte

Tritle Peak

Roosevelt Point

Atoko Point

Colorado River

Wildforss Trail

Ken Patrick Trail

Siegfried Pyre

Chuar Butte

TRANSEPT CANYON

Transept Trail

North Rim Visitor Center

Grand Canyon Lodge

Bright Angel Point

WALHALLA PLATEAU

Cape Royal Road

Temple Butte

Shiva Temple

Cottonwood Campground

Obi Point

BRIGHT ANGEL CANYON

Cape Final Trail

Jupiter Temple

Osiris Temple

Isis Temple

Brahma Temple

Walhalla Ruins

Walhalla Overlook

Venus Temple

North Kaibab Trail

Zoroaster Temple

Cliff Springs Trail

Cape Royal

Apollo Temple

Granite Rapids

Horn Creek Rapids

Phantom Ranch

Cape Royal Trail

Wotan's Throne

PALISADES OF THE DESERT

Bright Angel Trail

SOUTH RIM

Vishnu Temple

Cardenas Butte

Hopi Point

Mather Point

South Kaibab Trail

GRANITE GORGE

The Abyss

Yaki Point

Grapevine Rapids

Solomon Temple

Desert View

Hermit Road

64

Grand Canyon Village

Hance Rapids

Navajo Point

Lipan Point

TO FLAGSTAFF, WILLIAMS

the "High Point Hike" offers panoramic views of the Colorado River. At all three areas, local Hualapai guides and roaming "ambassadors" add a Native American perspective that you won't find on North and South Rim tours.

For extra fees, you can add meals (there are cafés at each of the three stops), overnight lodging at Hualapai Ranch, a helicopter trip into the canyon, a rafting trip on the Colorado, a horseback ride along the canyon rim, or a walk on the Grand Canyon Skywalk. ⊠ *Grand Canyon West* ☎ *928/769–2636, 888/868–9378* ⊕ *www.grandcanyonwest.com* ⊠ *$50.*

 ## Activities

Hualapai River Runners

TOUR—SPORTS | One-day combination river trips are offered by the Hualapai Tribe through the Hualapai River Runners from mid-March through October. The trips leave from Peach Springs (a two-hour drive from the West Rim) and include rafting, a hike, a helicopter ride up to the West Rim, and transport. Lunch, snacks, and beverages are provided. Children must be eight or older to take the trip, which runs several rapids with the most difficult rated as Class VII, depending on the river flow. ⊠ *5001 Buck N Doe Rd., Peach Springs* ☎ *928/769–2636, 888/868–9378* ⊕ *www.grandcanyonwest. com* ⊠ *From $450.*

Nearby Towns

The northwest section of Arizona is geographically fascinating. In addition to the Grand Canyon, it's home to national forests, national monuments, and national recreation areas. Towns, however, are small and scattered. Many of them cater to visiting adventurers, and Native American reservations dot the map.

Towns near the canyon's South Rim include the tiny town of Tusayan, 1 mile south of the entrance station, and

Williams, the "Gateway to the Grand Canyon," 58 miles south.

Tusayan has basic amenities and an airport that serves as a starting point for airplane and helicopter tours of the canyon. The cozy mountain town of **Williams,** founded in 1882 when the railroad passed through, was once a rough-and-tumble joint, replete with saloons and bordellos. Today, it reflects a much milder side of the Wild West, with 3,300 residents and more than 25 motels and hotels. Wander along the main street—part of historic Route 66, but locally named, like the town, after trapper Bill Williams—and indulge in Route 66 nostalgia inside antiques shops or souvenir and T-shirt stores.

The communities closest to the North Rim—all of them tiny and with limited services—include Fredonia, 76 miles north; Marble Canyon, 80 miles northeast; Lees Ferry, 85 miles east; and Jacob Lake, 45 miles north.

Fredonia, a small community of about 1,050, approximately an hour's drive north of the Grand Canyon, is often referred to as the gateway to the North Rim; it's also relatively close to Zion and Bryce Canyon national parks in Utah. **Marble Canyon** marks the geographical beginning of the Grand Canyon at its northeastern tip. It's a good stopping point if you're driving U.S. 89 to the North Rim. En route from the South Rim to the North Rim is **Lees Ferry,** where most of the area's river rafts start their journey. The tiny town of **Jacob Lake,** nestled high in pine country at an elevation of 7,925 feet, was named after Mormon explorer Jacob Hamblin, also known as the "Buckskin Missionary." It has a hotel, café, campground, and lush mountain countryside.

VISITOR INFORMATION
Kaibab National Forest, North Kaibab Ranger District ⊠ *430 S. Main St., Fredonia* ☎ *928/643–7395* ⊕ *www.fs.usda.gov/ kaibab.* **Kaibab National Forest, Tusayan**

Ranger District ⊠ *176 Lincoln Log Loop, Grand Canyon National Park* ☎ *928/638–2443* ⊕ *www.fs.usda.gov/kaibab.* **Kaibab National Forest, Williams Ranger District** ⊠ *742 S. Clover Rd., Williams* ☎ *928/635–5600* ⊕ *www.fs.usda.gov/kaibab.* **Kaibab Plateau Visitor Center** ⊠ *U.S. 89A at Hwy. 67, Jacob Lake* ☎ *928/643–7298* ⊕ *www. fs.usda.gov/kaibab.* **Williams Visitor Center** ⊠ *200 W. Railroad Ave., at Grand Canyon Blvd., Williams* ☎ *928/635–4061* ⊕ *experiencewilliams.com.*

 Sights

National Geographic Visitor Center Grand Canyon

INFO CENTER | Here you can schedule and purchase tickets for air and jeep tours, and buy a national park pass, which enables you to access the park by special entry lanes. Nevertheless, the biggest draw is the six-story IMAX screen that features the short movie *Grand Canyon: The Hidden Secrets.* You can learn about the geologic and natural history of the canyon, soar above stunning rock formations, and ride the rapids through the rocky gorge. The film is shown every hour on the half hour; the adjoining gift store is huge and well stocked. ⊠ *450 Hwy. 64/U.S. 180, Tusayan* ✛ *2 miles south of the Grand Canyon's south entrance* ☎ *928/638–2468* ⊕ *explorethecanyon.com* ⊡ *$13 for IMAX movies.*

Vermilion Cliffs National Monument

NATURE SITE | West of the town of Marble Canyon are these spectacular cliffs, more than 3,000 feet high in many places. Keep an eye out for condors; the giant endangered birds were reintroduced into the area in 1996. Reports suggest that the birds, once in captivity, are surviving well in the wilderness. ☎ *435/688–3200* ⊕ *www.blm.gov/visit/vermilion-cliffs.*

 Activities

FISHING

The stretch of ice-cold, crystal-clear water at Lees Ferry off the North Rim provides arguably the best trout fishing in the Southwest. Many rafters and anglers stay the night in a campground near the river or in nearby Marble Canyon before hitting the river at dawn.

Arizona Game and Fish Department

FISHING | Fish for trout, crappie, catfish, and smallmouth bass at a number of lakes surrounding Williams. To fish on public land, anglers age 10 and older are required to obtain a fishing license from the Arizona Game and Fish Department, available at their office, at stores such as Wal-Mart, or online. ⊠ *Flagstaff* ☎ *928/774–5045* ⊕ *www.azgfd.gov.*

RAFTING

The National Park Service authorizes 16 concessionaires to run rafting trips through the canyon—you can view a full list at the park's website (⊕ *www.nps. gov/grca/planyourvisit/river-concessioners.htm*). Trips run from three to 16 days, depending on whether you opt for the upper canyon, lower canyon, or full canyon. You can also experience a one-day rafting trip, running a few rapids in Grand Canyon West with the Hualapai tribe.

Arizona Raft Adventures

WHITE-WATER RAFTING | This outfitter organizes 6- to 16-day paddle/oar and motor trips through the upper, lower, or full canyon, for all skill levels. Trips depart April through October. ⊠ *4050 E. Huntington Dr., Flagstaff* ☎ *800/786–7238* ⊕ *azraft. com* ⊡ *From $2145.*

Canyoneers

WHITE-WATER RAFTING | With a reputation for high quality and a roster of 3- to 14-day trips, Canyoneers is popular with those who want to do some hiking as well. The five-day "Best of the Grand" trip includes a hike down to Phantom Ranch. Motorized and oar trips are available mid-April through September.

✉ *7195 N. U.S. 89, Flagstaff* ☎ *928/526–0924, 800/525–0924* 🌐 *canyoneers.com* 🎟 *From $1195.*

Grand Canyon Expeditions

WHITE-WATER RAFTING | You can count on Grand Canyon Expeditions to take you down the Colorado River safely and in style: evening meals might include filet mignon, pork chops, or shrimp. The 8-day motorized and 14-day Dory trips range from $2,850 to $4,200, and some trips focus on special interests like archaeology and photography. ☎ *435/644–2691, 800/544–2691* 🌐 *www.gcex.com* 🎟 *From $2850.*

Wilderness River Adventures

WHITE-WATER RAFTING | One of the canyon's larger rafting outfitters, Wilderness River Adventures runs a wide variety of trips from 3 to 16 days, oar or motorized, from April to October. Their most popular trip is the seven-day motor trip. ✉ *2040 E. Frontage Rd., Page* ☎ *928/645–3296, 800/992–8022* 🌐 *www.riveradventures.com* 🎟 *From $1480.*

🍴 Restaurants

IN THE PARK

SOUTH RIM

Arizona Room

$$$ | STEAKHOUSE | The canyon views from this casual Southwestern-style steak house are the best of any restaurant at the South Rim. The dinner menu leans toward steak-house dishes while lunch is primarily salads and sandwiches with a Southwestern twist. **Known for:** views of the Grand Canyon; Southwest fare; local craft beers. [$] *Average main: $24* ✉ *Bright Angel Lodge, Desert View Dr., Grand Canyon Village* ☎ *928/638–2631* 🌐 *www.grandcanyonlodges.com* 🕒 *Closed Jan.; limited service in Feb.*

★ El Tovar Dining Room

$$$ | SOUTHWESTERN | Even at the edge of the Grand Canyon it's possible to find gourmet dining. This cozy room of dark wood beams and stone, nestled in the historic El Tovar Lodge, dates to 1905. **Known for:** historic setting; gourmet fare; local and organic ingredients. [$] *Average main: $28* ✉ *El Tovar Hotel, Desert View Dr., Grand Canyon Village* ☎ *928/638–2631* 🌐 *www.grandcanyonlodges.com.*

Harvey House Café

$$ | SOUTHWESTERN | FAMILY | Open for breakfast, lunch, and dinner, the Harvey House Café at Bright Angel Lodge serves basics like biscuits and gravy, salads, sandwiches, pastas, burgers, and steaks. Or you can step it up a notch and order some of the same selections straight from the neighboring Arizona Room's menu, including prime rib, baby back ribs, and wild salmon. For dessert try the warm bread pudding or fruit cobbler topped with vanilla ice cream. **Known for:** reasonably priced American fare; family-friendly menu and setting. [$] *Average main: $14* ✉ *Bright Angel Lodge, Desert View Dr., Grand Canyon Village* ☎ *928/638–2631* 🌐 *www.grandcanyonlodges.com.*

Maswik Food Court

$ | AMERICAN | You can get a burger, hot sandwich, pasta, or Mexican fare at this food court, as well as pizza by the slice and wine and beer in the adjacent Maswik Pizza Pub. This casual eatery is ¼ mile from the rim, and the Pizza Pub stays open until 11 pm (you can also order pizza to take out). **Known for:** good selection (something for everyone); later hours. [$] *Average main: $8* ✉ *Maswik Lodge, Desert View Dr., Grand Canyon Village* 🌐 *www.grandcanyonlodges.com.*

Yavapai Lodge Restaurant

$$ | AMERICAN | If you don't have time for full-service, the restaurant in Yavapai Lodge offers cafeteria-style dining for breakfast, lunch, and dinner. Offerings include hot and cold sandwiches, pizza, and entrées such as barbecue ribs and rotisserie chicken. **Known for:** quick bites; convenience; beer and wine. [$] *Average main: $14* ✉ *Yavapai Lodge, Desert View Dr., Grand Canyon Village*

Continued on page 340

EXPLORING THE
COLORADO RIVER

High in Colorado's Rocky Mountains, the Colorado River begins as a catch-all for the snowmelt off the mountains west of the Continental Divide. By the time it reaches the Grand Canyon, the Colorado has been joined by multiple tributaries to become a raging river, red with silt as it sculpts spectacular landscapes. A network of dams can only partially tame this mighty river.

Snaking its way through five states, the Colorado River is an essential water source to the arid Southwest. Its natural course runs 1,450 miles from its origin in Colorado's La Poudre Pass Lake in Rocky Mountain National Park to its final destination in the Gulf of California, also called the Sea of Cortez. In northern Arizona, the Colorado River has been a powerful force in shaping the Grand Canyon, where it flows 4,000 to 6,000 feet below the rim. Beyond the canyon, the red river takes a lazy turn at the Arizona–Nevada border, where Hoover Dam creates the reservoir at Lake Mead. The Colorado continues at a relaxed pace along the Arizona–California border, providing energy and irrigation in Arizona, California, and Nevada before draining into northwestern Mexico.

A RIVER RUNS THROUGH IT

Stretching along 277 miles of the Colorado River is one of the seven natural wonders of the world: the Grand Canyon ranges in width from 4 to 18 miles, while the walls around it soar up to a mile high. Nearly 2 billion years of geologic history and majesty are revealed in exposed tiers of rock cut deep in the Colorado Plateau. What caused this incredible marvel of nature? Erosion by water coupled with driving wind are most likely the major culprits: under the sculpting power of wind and water, the shale layers eroded into slopes and the harder sandstone and limestone layers created terraced cliffs. Other forces that may have helped shape the canyon include ice, volcanic activity, continental drift, and earthquakes.

WHO LIVES HERE
Native tribes have lived in the canyon for thousands of years and continue to do so, looking to the river for subsistence. The plateau-dwelling Hualapai ("people of the tall pines") live on a million acres along 108 miles of the Colorado River in the West Rim. The Havasupai ("people of the blue green water") live deep within the walls of the 12-mile-long Havasu Canyon—a major side canyon connected to the Grand Canyon.

ENVIRONMENTAL CONCERNS
When the Grand Canyon achieved national park status in 1919, only 44,173 people made the grueling overland trip to see it—quite a contrast from today's nearly 5 million annual visitors. The tremendous increase in visitation has greatly impacted the fragile ecosystems, as has Lake Powell's Glen Canyon Dam, which was constructed in the 1950s and '60s. The dam has changed the composition of the Colorado River, replacing warm water rich in sediments (nature's way of nourishing the riverbed and banks) with mostly cool, much clearer water. This has introduced non-native plants and animals that threaten the extinction of several native species. Air pollution has also affected visibility and the constant buzz of aerial tours has disturbed the natural solitude.

Above and right, views of Colorado River in the Grand Canyon from Toroweap.

Did You Know?

The North Rim's isolated Toroweap overlook (also called Tuweep) is perched 3,000 feet above the canyon floor: a height equal to stacking the Sears Tower and Empire State Building on top of each other.

RIVER RAFTING THROUGH THE GRAND CANYON

Viewing the Colorado River from a canyon overlook is one thing, but looking up at the canyon from the middle of the river is quite another experience. If you're ready to tackle the churning white water of the Colorado River as it rumbles and hisses its way through the Grand Canyon, take a look at this map of what you might encounter along the way.

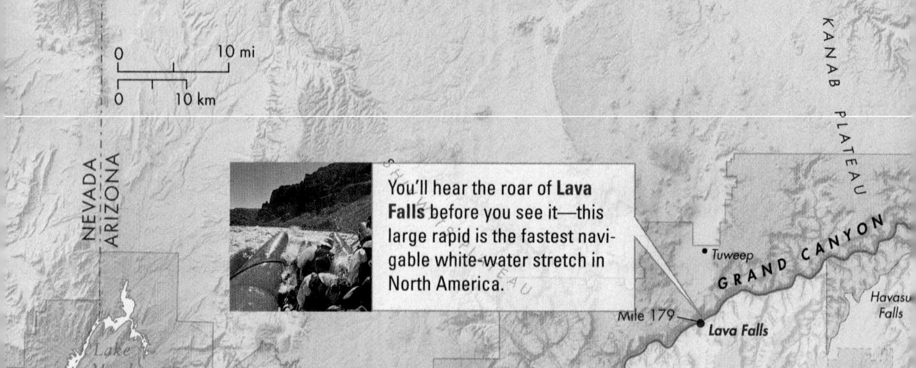

0   10 mi
0   10 km

KANAB PLATEAU

NEVADA
ARIZONA

You'll hear the roar of **Lava Falls** before you see it—this large rapid is the fastest navigable white-water stretch in North America.

• Tuweep

GRAND CANYON

Havasu Falls

Mile 179 — Lava Falls

Lake Mead

Mile 296
South Cove

Kolb Rapid

GRAND CANYON NATIONAL PARK

South Cove, on Lake Mead, is the final destination for many river trips.

Colorado River

Many outfitters end their trips at **Diamond Creek**, where the river begins to slow down.

GRAND WASH CLIFFS

Mile 225 — **Diamond Creek**

Dirt

1

HUALAPAI INDIAN RES.

Dirt

Peach Springs

COLORADO RIVER TRIPS

Time and Length	Entry and Exit points
1 day Float trip	Glen Canyon Dam to Lees Ferry (no rapids)
1 day Combo trip	Diamond Creek, then helicopter to West Rim
3–4 days	Lees Ferry to Phantom Ranch
6 days, 89 miles	Phantom Ranch to Diamond Creek
9–10 days, 136 miles	Lees Ferry to Diamond Creek
14–16 days, 225 miles	Lees Ferry to South Cove

*Trips either begin or end at Phantom Ranch/Bright Angel Beach at the bottom of the Grand Canyon, at river mile 87

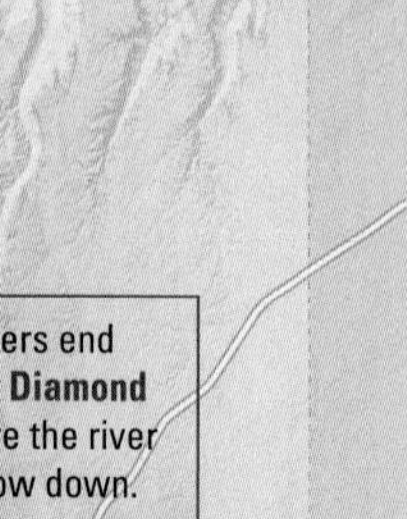

Kanab
89

UTAH
ARIZONA

Lake Powell

Glen Canyon Dam

PARIA CANYON

Direction of Flow

Page
89

Lees Ferry

Marble Canyon

Mile 0

VERMILLION CLIFFS

MARBLE CANYON

ALT 89

Bitter Springs

House Rock Rapids

Colorado River

ECHO CLIFFS

PLATEAU

89

One-day float trips (no white-water) go through beautiful **Glen Canyon.**

Longer trips begin at **Lees Ferry,** a few miles below the Glen Canyon Dam near Page.

⚠ You need to be very fit to hike the arduous 9.6-mile **Bright Angel Trail,** especially if you choose to hike up when departing from Phantom Ranch.

Deer Creek Falls

Great Thumb Mesa

Bedrock Rapid

Fossil Rapid

Forester Rapid

Serpentine Rapid

Sapphire Rapid

Crystal Rapid

Mile 98

Granite Rapid

Mather Pt.

Grand Canyon Village

Tusayan

NORTH RIM

Point Sublime

Bright Angel Point

67

Point Imperial

Mile 61

Phantom Ranch

Mile 87

Bright Angel Trail

Unkar Rapid

Grapevine Rapid

Hance Rapid

Grandview Point

Desert View

64

Little Colorado River

HAVASUPAI INDIAN RES.

HASU CANYON

Phantom Ranch allows you to begin or end your trip in between the scenic North and South Rims.

If you begin at Phantom Ranch, you will soon plunge through the colossal waves of **Granite** and **Crystal Rapids.**

COCONINO PLATEAU

180
64

Cameron

TO FLAGSTAFF, ↓ 49 Miles

NOT JUST RAPIDS

Don't think that your experience will be nonstop white-water adrenaline. Most of the Colorado River features long, relaxing stretches of water, where you drift amid grandiose rock formations. You might even spot a mountain goat or two. Multi-day trips include camping on the shore.

PLANNING YOUR RIVER RAFTING TRIP

OAR, MOTOR, OR HYBRID?

Base the type of trip you choose on the amount of effort you want to put in. Motor rafts, which are the roomiest of the choices, cover the most miles in less time and are the most comfortable. Guides do the rowing on oar boats and these smaller rafts offer a wilder ride. All-paddle trips are the most active and require the most involvement from guests. Hybrid trips are popular because they offer both the opportunity to paddle and to relax.

THE GEAR

Life jackets, beverages, tents, sheets, tarps, sleeping bags, dry bags, first aid, and food are provided—but you'll still need to plan ahead by packing clothing, hats, sunscreen, toiletries, and other sundries. Commercial outfitters allow each river runner two waterproof bags to store items during the day—just keep in mind that one of these will be filled up with the provided sleeping bag and tarp. ■TIP➜ Bring a rain suit: summer thunderstorms are frequent and chilly.

WHEN TO GO

Lots of people book trips for summer's peak period: June through August. If you're flexible, take advantage of the Arizona weather and go from May to early June or in September. ■TIP➜ Seats fill up quickly; make reservations for multiday trips a year or two in advance.

TRIP LENGTH

Rafting options on the Colorado River range from one-day trips at either the east or west end of the Grand Canyon to leisurely, two-week paddle trips through the full length of Grand Canyon National Park. If you're short on time, take a one-day trip near Grand Canyon West, where you'll run several rapids and fly back to the West Rim by helicopter. Another action-packed choice is to raft the river for 3 or 4 days, disembark at Phantom Ranch, then hike up to the Grand Canyon South Rim. "Full Canyon" rafting trips can take 9 to 16 days.

Above, Getting wet—and loving it—on an oar boat.

Did You Know?

As you're hanging on for dear life, consider this: Civil War veteran John Wesley Powell chartered these treacherous rapids in 1869—not only were conditions more dangerous then, but he had only one arm.

Top Picnic Spots 🍴

Bring your picnic basket and enjoy dining alfresco surrounded by some of the most beautiful backdrops in the country. Be sure to bring water, as it's unavailable at many of these spots, as are restrooms.

- **Buggeln,** 15 miles east of Grand Canyon Village on Desert View Drive, has some secluded, shady spots.
- **Cape Royal,** 23 miles south of the North Rim Visitor Center, is the most popular designated picnic area on the North Rim due to its panoramic views.
- **Grandview Point** has, as the name implies, grand vistas; it's 12 miles east of the village on Desert View Drive.
- **Point Imperial,** 11 miles northeast of the North Rim Visitor Center, has shade and some privacy.

☎ *928/638–4001* 🌐 *www.visitgrandcanyon.com.*

NORTH RIM

Deli in the Pines

$ | **AMERICAN** | Dining choices are limited on the North Rim, but this deli next to the lodge is your best bet for a meal on a budget or grabbing a premade sandwich on the go. Selections also include pizza (gluten-free or standard crust), salads, custom-made sandwiches, and soft-serve ice cream. **Known for:** convenient location; sandwiches to take on the trail; outdoor seating. [$] *Average main: $7* ✉ *Grand Canyon Lodge, Bright Angel Point, North Rim* ☎ *928/638–2611* 🌐 *www.grandcanyonforever.com* 🕓 *Closed mid-Oct.–mid-May.*

★ Grand Canyon Lodge Dining Room

$$$ | **SOUTHWESTERN** | The high wood-beamed ceilings, stone walls, and spectacular views in this spacious, historic room are perhaps the biggest draw for the lodge's main restaurant. Dinner includes Southwestern steakhouse fare that would make any cowboy feel at home, including selections such as bison and elk. **Known for:** incredible views; charming, historic room; steaks, fish, game, and vegetarian selections. [$] *Average main: $22* ✉ *Grand Canyon Lodge, Bright Angel Point, North Rim* ☎ *928/638–2611* 🌐 *www.grandcanyonforever.com* 🕓 *Closed mid-Oct.–mid-May.*

OUTSIDE THE PARK

TUSAYAN

Canyon Star Steakhouse and Saloon

$$$ | **AMERICAN** | **FAMILY** | Relax in the rustic timber-and-stone dining room at the Grand Hotel for reliable if uninspired American food, with an emphasis on steaks and barbecue at dinner. Popular options include barbecue chicken and ribs, and Mexican fare. **Known for:** rollicking live music; better-than-average local dining. [$] *Average main: $26* ✉ *Hwy. 64/U.S. 180, Tusayan* ☎ *928/638–3333* 🌐 *www.grandcanyongrandhotel.com* 🕓 *No lunch.*

The Coronado Room

$$$ | **AMERICAN** | Inside the Best Western Grand Canyon Squire Inn is the most sophisticated cuisine in Tusayan. The menu includes well-prepared, hearty American food, with an emphasis on meat (steak, venison, buffalo), plus grilled seafood, escargot, and oversize desserts. **Known for:** Tusayan's finest restaurant; splurge-worthy dining. [$] *Average main: $28* ✉ *100 Hwy. 64/U.S. 180, Tusayan* ☎ *928/638–2681* 🌐 *www.grandcanyonsquire.com* 🕓 *No lunch.*

WILLIAMS
Cruisers Café 66

$$ | **AMERICAN** | **FAMILY** | Patterned after a '50s-style high-school hangout (but with cocktail service), this diner pleases kids and adults with a large menu of family-priced American classics—good burgers and fries, barbecue pork sandwiches, salads, and ribs. A large mural of the town's heyday along the "Mother Road" and historic cars out front make this a Route 66 favorite. **Known for:** burgers and barbecue; nice patio. $ *Average main: $17* ⊠ *233 W. Rte. 66, Williams* ☎ *928/635–2445* ⊕ *www.cruisers66. com.*

★ Red Raven Restaurant

$$$ | **ECLECTIC** | This dapper bistro in the heart of downtown Williams, with warm lighting and romantic booth seating, blends American, Italian, and Asian ingredients into creative and delicious fare. Specialties include a starter of crisp tempura shrimp salad with a ginger-sesame dressing and mains like charbroiled salmon with basil butter over cranberry–pine nut couscous. **Known for:** upscale dining in Williams; good wine list. $ *Average main: $23* ⊠ *135 W. Rte. 66, Williams* ☎ *928/635–4980* ⊕ *www. redravenrestaurant.com.*

 Hotels

IN THE PARK
SOUTH RIM
Bright Angel Lodge

$ | **HOTEL** | Famed architect Mary Jane Colter designed this 1935 log-and-stone structure, which sits within a few yards of the canyon rim and blends superbly with the canyon walls; its location is similar to El Tovar's but for about half the price. **Pros:** some rooms have canyon vistas; steps away from the rim; on-site Internet kiosks and transportation desk for the mule ride; good value for the amazing location. **Cons:** popular lobby is always packed; parking a bit of a hike. $ *Rooms from: $89* ⊠ *Desert View Dr.,* *Grand Canyon Village* ☎ *888/297–2757 reservations only, 928/638–2631* ⊕ *www. grandcanyonlodges.com* ↪ *105 units* ⦿ *No meals.*

★ El Tovar Hotel

$$$ | **HOTEL** | The hotel's proximity to all of the canyon's facilities, European hunting-lodge atmosphere, attractively updated rooms and tile baths, and renowned dining room make it the best place to stay on the South Rim. **Pros:** historic lodging just steps from the South Rim; fabulous lounge with outdoor seating and canyon views; best in-park dining on-site. **Cons:** books up quickly. $ *Rooms from: $249* ⊠ *Desert View Dr., Grand Canyon Village* ☎ *888/297–2757 reservations only, 928/638–2631* ⊕ *www. grandcanyonlodges.com* ↪ *78 rooms* ⦿ *No meals.*

Kachina Lodge

$$$ | **HOTEL** | The well-appointed rooms at this motel-style lodge on the South Rim are a good bet for families and are within easy walking distance of dining facilities at nearby lodges. **Pros:** partial canyon views in half the rooms; family-friendly; steps from the best restaurants in the park. **Cons:** check-in at nearby El Tovar Hotel; limited parking. $ *Rooms from: $234* ⊠ *Desert View Dr., Grand Canyon Village* ☎ *888/297–2757 reservations only, 928/638–2631* ⊕ *www.grand-canyonlodges.com* ↪ *49 rooms* ⦿ *No meals.*

Maswik Lodge

$$ | **HOTEL** | **FAMILY** | Far from the noisy crowds, Maswik accommodations are in two-story motel-style buildings nestled in a shady ponderosa pine forest. **Pros:** north units are well equipped; good for families; affordable dining options. **Cons:** rooms lack historic charm; tucked away from the rim in the forest; no air-conditioning in south units. $ *Rooms from: $116* ⊠ *Grand Canyon Village* ☎ *888/297–2757 reservations only, 928/638–2631* ⊕ *www.grandcanyonlodges.com* ↪ *278 rooms* ⦿ *No meals.*

16

Grand Canyon National Park

Best Campgrounds in the Grand Canyon

Within the national park, camping is permitted only in designated campsites. Some campgrounds charge nightly camping fees in addition to entrance fees, and some accept reservations up to five months in advance through ⊕ *www.recreation.gov*. Others are first-come, first-served.

In-park camping in a spot other than a developed rim campground requires a permit from the Backcountry Information Center, which also serves as your reservation. Permits can be requested by mail or fax only; applying well in advance is recommended. Call ☎ *928/638–7875* between 1 pm and 5 pm weekdays for information.

Outside the park boundaries, there are campgrounds near the South and North rims, and in Havasu Canyon and the Kaibab National Forest. There's no camping on the West Rim, but you can pitch a tent on the beach near the Colorado River.

South Rim

Bright Angel Campground. This backcountry campground is near Phantom Ranch, at the bottom of the canyon. There are toilet facilities and running water, but no showers. ⊠ *Intersection of South and North Kaibab trails* ☎ *928/638–7875*.

Desert View Campground. Popular for spectacular views of the canyon from the nearby watchtower, this campground doesn't take reservations; show up before noon, as it fills up fast in summer. ⊠ *Desert View Dr., 23 miles east of Grand Canyon Village off Hwy. 64.*

Indian Garden. Halfway down the canyon is this backcountry campground, en route to Phantom Ranch on the Bright Angel Trail. Running water and toilet facilities are available, but not showers. ⊠ *Bright Angel Trail* ☎ *928/638–7875*.

North Rim

North Rim Campground. The only designated campground at the North Rim of Grand Canyon National Park sits 3 miles north of the rim, near the general store, and has 84 RV and tent sites (no hookups). ⊠ *Hwy. 67* ☎ *928/638–7888* ⊕ *www.recreation.gov*.

Outside the Park

Diamond Creek. You can camp on the banks of the Colorado River, but your peace might be interrupted by the fact that this smooth beach is a launch point for river runners. The Hualapai permit camping on their tribal lands here, with an overnight camping permit of $32.55 per person per night, which can be purchased at the Hualapai Lodge. ☎ *928/769–2210 or 888/255–9550.*

Havasu Canyon. You can stay in the primitive campgrounds in Havasu Canyon for $17 per person per night (in addition to the $40-per-person entry fee). ☎ *928/448–2174* ⊕ *www.havasupai-tribe.com.*

Kaibab National Forest. Both developed and undeveloped campsites are available on a first-come, first-served basis May through September at this forest that surrounds Williams and extends to the Grand Canyon. ☎ *928/699–1239 or 928/638–2443* ⊕ *www.fs.usda.gov/kaibab.*

Phantom Ranch

$ | **B&B/INN** | In a grove of cottonwood trees on the canyon floor, Phantom Ranch is accessible only to hikers and mule trekkers; there are 40 dormitory beds and 14 beds in cabins, all with shared baths. **Pros:** only inner-canyon lodging option; fabulous canyon views; remote access limits crowds. **Cons:** accessible only by foot or mule; few amenities or means of outside communication. $ *Rooms from: $51* ⊠ *On canyon floor, Grand Canyon National Park* ✢ *At intersection of Bright Angel and Kaibab trails* ☎ *303/297–2757, 888/297–2757* ⊕ *www.grandcanyonlodges.com* ⇆ *54 beds* ⦿ *No meals.*

Thunderbird Lodge

$$$ | **HOTEL** | This motel with comfortable, simple rooms and partial canyon views has all the modern amenities you'd expect at a typical mid-price chain hotel—even pod coffeemakers. **Pros:** canyon views in some rooms; family-friendly. **Cons:** check-in at nearby Bright Angel Lodge; limited parking nearby. $ *Rooms from: $234* ⊠ *Desert View Dr., Grand Canyon Village* ☎ *888/297–2757 reservations only, 928/638–2631* ⊕ *www. grandcanyonlodges.com* ⇆ *55 rooms* ⦿ *No meals.*

Yavapai Lodge

$$ | **HOTEL** | The largest motel-style lodge in the park is tucked in a pinyon-pine and juniper forest at the eastern end of Grand Canyon Village, across from Market Plaza. **Pros:** transportation-activities desk in the lobby; walk to Market Plaza in Grand Canyon Village; forested grounds. **Cons:** farthest in-park lodging from the rim (1 mile); no air-conditioning in west rooms. $ *Rooms from: $158* ⊠ *10 Yavapai Lodge Rd., Grand Canyon Village* ☎ *877/404–4611 reservations only* ⊕ *www.visitgrandcanyon.com* ⇆ *358 rooms* ⦿ *No meals.*

Duffel Service: ◉ Lighten Your Load

Hikers staying at either Phantom Ranch or Bright Angel Campground can also take advantage of the ranch's duffel service: bags or packs weighing 30 pounds or less can be transported to the ranch by mule for a fee of $70 each way. As is true for many desirable things at the canyon, reservations are a must.

NORTH RIM

★ **Grand Canyon Lodge**

$$ | **HOTEL** | This historic property, constructed mainly in the 1920s and '30s, is the only lodging on the North Rim. The main building has locally quarried limestone walls and timbered ceilings. **Pros:** steps away from gorgeous North Rim views; close to several easy hiking trails; historic lodge building a national landmark. **Cons:** fills up fast; limited amenities; most cabins far from main lodge building. $ *Rooms from: $132* ⊠ *Hwy. 67, North Rim* ☎ *877/386–4383 reservations, 928/638–2611 May–Oct., 928/645–6865 Nov.–Apr.* ⊕ *www.grandcanyonforever. com* ◷ *Closed mid-Oct.–mid-May* ⇆ *218 rooms* ⦿ *No meals.*

OUTSIDE THE PARK

TUSAYAN

Best Western Grand Canyon Squire Inn

$$$$ | **HOTEL** | **FAMILY** | About 2 miles from the park's south entrance, this motel lacks the historic charm of the older lodges at the canyon rim, but has more amenities, including a small cowboy museum, an upscale gift shop, and one of the better restaurants in the region. **Pros:** cool pools in summer and a hot tub for cold winter nights; children's activities at the Family Fun Center; close to South Rim. **Cons:** hall noise can be an issue with all of the in-hotel activities. $ *Rooms from: $269* ⊠ *100 Hwy. 64/U.S. 180*

☎ 928/638–2681, 800/622–6966 🌐 www.grandcanyonsquire.com 🛏 254 rooms 🍴 No meals.

The Grand Hotel

$$$ | **HOTEL** | **FAMILY** | At the south end of Tusayan, this popular hotel has bright, clean, and contemporary rooms, a cozy stone-and-timber lobby, and free Wi-Fi. **Pros:** Western entertainment; gift shop stocked with Native American art, outdoor gear, and regional books; indoor pool and hot tub. **Cons:** somewhat generic property. [$] *Rooms from: $179 ✉ 149 Hwy. 64/U.S. 180 ☎ 928/638–3333, 888/634–7263 🌐 www.grandcanyongrandhotel.com 🛏 121 rooms 🍴 No meals.*

WILLIAMS

Canyon Motel and RV Park

$$ | **HOTEL** | **FAMILY** | Railcars, cabooses, and cottages make up this 13-acre property on the outskirts of Williams. **Pros:** family-friendly property with hiking, horseshoes, playground, and indoor swimming pool; general store and Wi-Fi; friendly and helpful owners. **Cons:** short drive to restaurants and shops; RV-park traffic. [$] *Rooms from: $109 ✉ 1900 E. Rodeo Rd., Rte. 66, Williams ☎ 928/635–9371, 800/482–3955 🌐 www.thecanyonmotel.com 🛏 23 units 🍴 No meals.*

Grand Canyon Railway Hotel

$$$ | **HOTEL** | **FAMILY** | Designed to resemble the train depot's original Fray Marcos Hotel, this place features attractive Southwestern-style accommodations with large bathrooms and comfy beds with upscale linens. **Pros:** railway package options; game room and outdoor playground; short walk from historic downtown restaurants and bars. **Cons:** large-scale property. [$] *Rooms from: $229 ✉ 233 N. Grand Canyon Blvd., Williams ☎ 928/635–4010, 800/843–8724 🌐 www.thetrain.com 🛏 298 rooms 🍴 No meals.*

NORTH RIM

Jacob Lake Inn

$$ | **HOTEL** | The bustling lodge at Jacob Lake Inn is a popular stop for those heading to the North Rim, 45 miles south. **Pros:** grocery store, bakery, and restaurant; quiet rooms. **Cons:** only the newer rooms have TVs; old-fashioned key locks. [$] *Rooms from: $110 ✉ U.S. 89A and Hwy. 67, Jacob Lake ☎ 928/643–7232 🌐 www.jacoblake.com 🛏 58 rooms 🍴 No meals.*

Marble Canyon Lodge

$ | **HOTEL** | Popular with anglers and rafters, this Arizona Strip lodge offers two types of accommodations: standard rooms in the original lodge building and two-bedroom apartments in a newer building. **Pros:** convenience store, restaurant, and trading post; great fishing on the Colorado River. **Cons:** no-frills rustic lodging. [$] *Rooms from: $77 ✉ U.S. 89A, Marble Canyon ✥ ¼ mile west of Navajo Bridge ☎ 928/355–2225, 800/726–1789 🌐 www.marblecanyoncompany.com 🛏 54 rooms 🍴 No meals.*

WEST RIM

Hualapai Ranch

$$ | **B&B/INN** | **FAMILY** | The only lodging on the West Rim, the comfortable cabins at Hualapai Ranch are clean and neat, but also small and unassuming. **Pros:** front porches with nice desert views; rustlers tell tall tales while you roast s'mores at campfire programs; dining room meals served all day long. **Cons:** no phones, Internet, or TVs. [$] *Rooms from: $142 ✉ Quartermaster Point Rd., Grand Canyon West ☎ 928/769–2636, 888/868–9378 🌐 www.grandcanyonwest.com 🛏 26 cabins 🍴 Breakfast.*

GRAND TETON NATIONAL PARK

Updated by
Stina Sieg

WYOMING

WELCOME TO
GRAND TETON NATIONAL PARK

TOP REASONS TO GO

★ **Heavenward hikes:** Trek where grizzled frontiersmen roamed. Jackson Hole got its name from mountain man Davey Jackson; now there are hundreds of trails for you to explore.

★ **Wildlife big and small:** Keep an eye out for little fellows like short-tailed weasels and beaver, as well as bison, elk, wolves, and both black and grizzly bears.

★ **Waves to make:** Float the Snake River or take a canoe onto Jackson Lake or Jenny Lake.

★ **Homesteader history:** Visit the 1890s barns and ranch buildings of Mormon Row or Menor's Ferry.

★ **Cycling paradise:** Take to two wheels for safe, speedy transport to and through Grand Teton on miles of pathways and rural roads, then get off the beaten path for spectacular singletrack.

★ **Trout trophies:** Grab your rod and slither over to the Snake River, where cutthroat trout are an angler's delight.

Grand Teton's rugged peaks jut more than a mile above the valley floor in Jackson Hole. Without any foothills as prelude, the sight of these glacier-scoured crags is striking indeed. Several piedmont lakes reflect the mountains, and the winding Snake River cuts south through the expansive sagebrush flats in the heart of the park. The northern portion of the park is outstanding wildlife-watching territory—you can see everything from rare birds to lumbering moose to the big predators (wolves and black and grizzly bears). Two main roads run through the 310,000-acre park; highway U.S. 26/89/191 curves along the eastern or outer side, and Teton Park Road (closed during winter) runs close to the foot of the mountain range.

1 Antelope Flats. Buffalo and antelope frequently roam across this sagebrush-covered area northeast of Moose; it's also where the homesteader barns along Mormon Row dot the landscape. This is a popular place for wildflower viewing and bicycle rides.

2 Jenny Lake. In this developed area, you can go to the visitor center, purchase supplies, and talk to a ranger—plus ride a boat across the lake, hike around it, have a picnic, or camp nearby.

3 Moose. Just north of Craig Thomas Discovery and Visitor Center, this historical area is home to the tranquil Chapel of the Transfiguration and Menor's Ferry, the only way across the Snake until a bridge was built in 1927.

4 Oxbow Bend. At this famously scenic spot, the Snake River, its inhabitants, and the Tetons all converge, especially in early morning or near dusk. You're likely to see moose feeding in willows, elk grazing in aspen stands, and birds such as bald eagles, osprey, sandhill cranes, ducks, and American white pelicans.

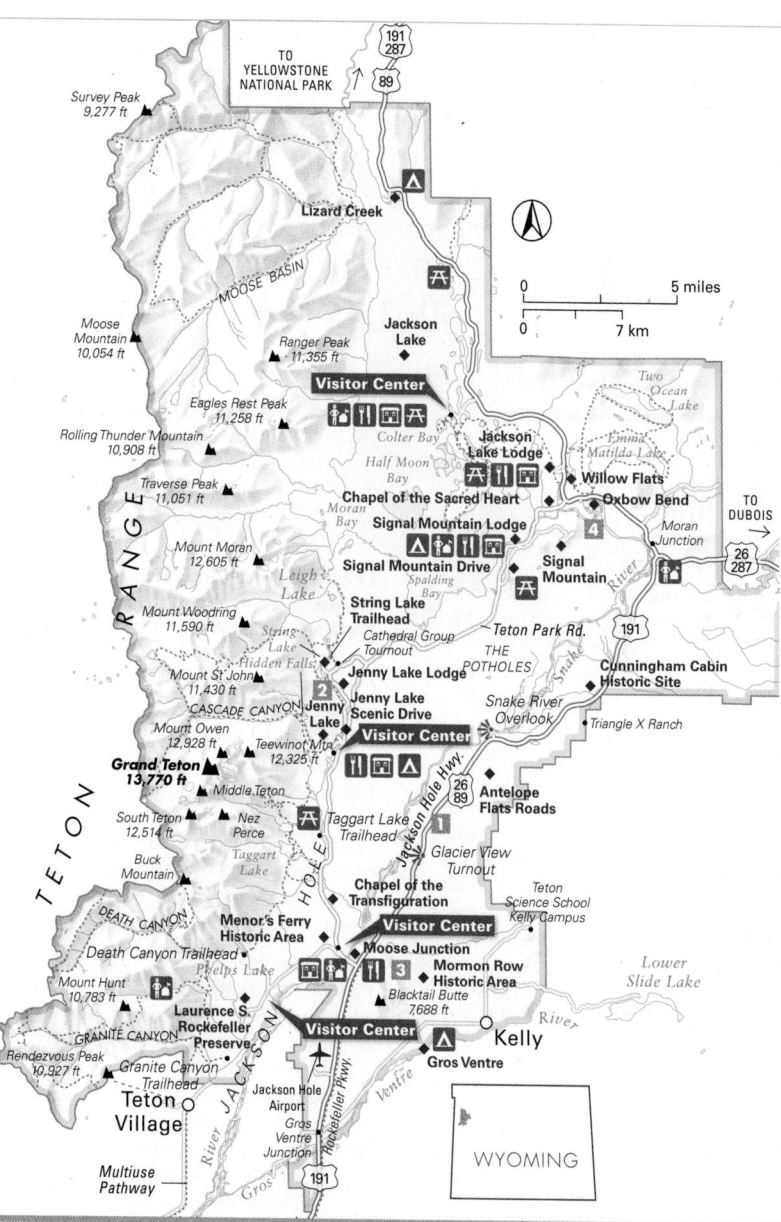

TO
YELLOWSTONE
NATIONAL PARK

191
287
89

Survey Peak
9,277 ft

Lizard Creek

MOOSE BASIN

0   5 miles
0   7 km

Moose
Mountain
10,054 ft

Ranger Peak
11,355 ft

Jackson
Lake

Eagles Rest Peak
11,258 ft

Visitor Center

Two
Ocean
Lake

Colter Bay

Rolling Thunder Mountain
10,908 ft

Half Moon
Bay

**Jackson
Lake Lodge**

Emma
Matilda Lake

Willow Flats

Traverse Peak
11,051 ft

Chapel of the Sacred Heart

Oxbow Bend

TO
DUBOIS

Moran
Bay

Signal Mountain Lodge

Moran
Junction

26
287

Mount Moran
12,605 ft

Signal Mountain Drive

Signal
Mountain

4

R A N G E

Leigh
Lake

Spalding
Bay

**String Lake
Trailhead**

Teton Park Rd.

191

Mount Woodring
11,590 ft

String
Lake

Cathedral Group
Turnout

THE
POTHOLES

Hidden Falls

Jenny Lake Lodge

Mount St John
11,430 ft

2

CASCADE CANYON

Jenny
Lake

**Jenny Lake
Scenic Drive**

Snake River
Overlook

**Cunningham Cabin
Historic Site**

Mount Owen
12,928 ft

Teewinot Mtn
12,325 ft

Visitor Center

Triangle X Ranch

**Grand Teton
13,770 ft**

Middle Teton

T E T O N

South Teton
12,514 ft

Nez
Perce

26
89

Antelope
Flats Roads

1

**Taggart Lake
Trailhead**

Glacier View
Turnout

Teton
Science School
Kelly Campus

Buck
Mountain

Taggart
Lake

**Chapel of the
Transfiguration**

DEATH CANYON

**Menor's Ferry
Historic Area**

Visitor Center

Lower
Slide Lake

Mount Hunt
10,783 ft

Phelps Lake

Moose Junction

Death Canyon Trailhead

3

**Mormon Row
Historic Area**

H O L E

Blacktail Butte
7,688 ft

River

**Laurence S.
Rockefeller
Preserve**

Visitor Center

Kelly

GRANITE CANYON

Rendezvous Peak
10,927 ft

**Granite Canyon
Trailhead**

J A C K S O N

Gros Ventre

Teton
Village

Jackson Hole
Airport

Gros
Ventre
Junction

Ventre

River

Multiuse
Pathway

River

Gros

191

WYOMING

The Teton Range rises above the Jackson Hole valley floor, with unimpeded views of its magnificent, jagged, snowcapped peaks. This massif is dominated by the 13,770-foot Grand Teton. Mountain glaciers creep down 12,605-foot Mount Moran, and large and small lakes gleam along the range's base. Many of the West's animals—elk, bears, bald eagles—call this park home.

Planning

WHEN TO GO

In July and August all the roads, trails, and visitor centers are open, and the Snake River's float season is in full swing. Lower rates and smaller crowds can be found in spring and fall, but some services and roads are limited. Grand Teton Lodge Company, the park's major concessionaire, winds down its activities in late September, and most of Teton Park Road closes from November through April (highway U.S. 26/191/89 stays open all winter). In spring and fall, Teton Park Road is open to pedestrians, cyclists, and in-line skaters; in winter, it's transformed into a cross-country ski trail.
■ TIP→ **To have access to most services without the crowds, plan a trip in late May, June, or September.**

Towns outside the park rev up in winter. Teton Village and Jackson both buzz with the energy of Snow King Resort and Jackson Hole Mountain Resort, the former conveniently in town, the latter an international skiing hot spot 13 miles from Jackson. Prices rise for the peak winter season.

FESTIVALS AND EVENTS

ElkFest

FESTIVAL | FAMILY | More than 50 years old, this popular two-day festival is held the third weekend in May. Its centerpiece is the Jackson Hole Boy Scout Elk Antler Auction, when thousands of pounds of naturally shed antlers are sold to the highest bidder. Pick up some horns for your decor, get a taste of the High Noon Chili Cookoff, or just enjoy the spectacle of khaki-clad lads hauling around massive racks. ⊠ *Jackson* ☎ *307/733–3316* ⊕ *www.elkfest.org.*

Fall Arts Festival

FESTIVAL | More than 50 events celebrate art, music, food, and wine throughout Jackson Hole during the 11-day annual festival, which runs from the first to the second weekend of September. Catch live painting and sculpting demonstrations in the popular quickdraw event, then bid for the spontaneous art. ⊠ *Town Square, Jackson* ☎ *307/733–3316* www.jacksonholechamber.com/fall_arts_festival.

Grand Teton Music Festival

FESTIVAL | Since 1962, these summer symphony concerts have been wowing audiences in the world-renowned Walk Festival Hall in Teton Village. Under the direction of Maestro Donald Runnicles, the festival presents full orchestra concerts on Friday and Saturday in July and the first half of August, and smaller ensembles from Tuesday to Thursday. In winter, concerts take place at least monthly. Tickets cost between $25 and $55, but many performances are free. ⊠ Walk Festival Hall, 3330 West Cody La., Teton Village ☎ 307/733–1128 ⊕ www.gtmf.org.

JH Shootout

FESTIVAL | FAMILY | Following a tradition more than half a century old, gunslingers stage a shootout on summer evenings at 6 pm (except Sunday), at the Town Square's northeastern corner. Don't worry, the bullets aren't real. ⊠ Jackson ☎ 307/733–3316 ⊕ www.jacksonhole-chamber.com/events/jh-shootout.php.

Old West Days

FESTIVAL | FAMILY | This festival's Memorial Day weekend activities include a rodeo, a parade, a brew fest, cowboy music, and the Mountain Man Rendezvous—atlatl (dart-hurling) competition, anyone?—plus the start of the Jackson Hole Shootout's summer performances. The celebration takes place at various spots across town. ⊠ Town Square, Jackson ☎ 307/733–3316 ⊕ www.jacksonholechamber.com/old_west_days.

Pole-Pedal-Paddle

FESTIVAL | Individuals and teams competing seriously or just out for fun participate in this four-part race that has alpine and cross-country skiing segments as well as bicycling and boating legs. Usually held on the last Saturday of March, the race, a fund-raiser, starts at the Jackson Hole Mountain Resort and ends in the Snake River Canyon. ⊠ Jackson ☎ 307/733–6433 ⊕ jhskiclub.org/polepedalpaddle.

Torchlight Parades

FESTIVAL | FAMILY | Skiers celebrate New Year's Eve with torchlight parades at Snow King Mountain in Jackson, Jackson Hole Mountain Resort in Teton Village, and Grand Targhee Resort in Alta. ⊠ Jackson ☎ 800/827–4433, 307/733–5200.

PLANNING YOUR TIME
GRAND TETON IN ONE DAY

Begin the day by packing a picnic lunch or picking one up at a Jackson eatery. Arrive at **Craig Thomas Discovery and Visitor Center** in time for a 9 am, two-hour, guided Snake River scenic float trip (make required reservations with one of the half-dozen outfitters that offer the trip). When you're back on dry ground, drive north on Teton Park Road, stopping at scenic turnouts—don't miss Teton Glacier—until you reach South Jenny Lake Junction.

Park at the Jenny Lake ranger station and take the 20-minute boat ride to the **west shore boat dock** for a short but breathtaking hike to **Hidden Falls** or **Inspiration Point.** Return to your car by mid-afternoon, drive back to Teton Park Road, and head north to Signal Mountain Road to catch an elevated view of the Tetons. In late afternoon descend the mountain and continue north on Teton Park Road.

At Jackson Lake Junction, you can go east to **Oxbow Bend** or north to **Willow Flats,** both excellent spots for wildlife viewing before you head to **Jackson Lake Lodge** for dinner and an evening watching the sun set over the Tetons. Or if you'd like to get back on the water, drive to **Colter Bay Village Marina,** where you can board a 1½-hour sunset cruise across Jackson Lake to Elk Island. You can reverse this route if you're heading south from Yellowstone: start the day with a 7:30 breakfast cruise from Colter Bay and end it with a sunset float down the Snake River.

AVERAGE HIGH/LOW TEMPERATURES					
JAN.	FEB.	MAR.	APR.	MAY	JUNE
28/5	33/8	43/17	53/24	63/31	74/37
JULY	AUG.	SEPT.	OCT.	NOV.	DEC.
82/41	81/39	71/31	59/23	40/16	28/6

GETTING HERE AND AROUND
AIR TRAVEL
Jackson Hole Airport (JAC), the only commercial airport inside a national park, was established before the park opened. Five airlines service the modern airport.

BUS TRAVEL
Grand Teton Lodge Company has shuttle service that makes several trips a day between Colter Bay and Jackson, with several stops in between. It's free for guests of the lodge and $12 for everyone else.

CAR TRAVEL
The best way to see Grand Teton National Park is by car. Unlike Yellowstone's Grand Loop, Grand Teton's road system doesn't allow for easy tour-bus access to the major sights. Only a car will get you close to Jenny Lake, into the remote Gros Ventre Range on the east side of the valley, and to the top of Signal Mountain. You can stop at many points along the roads within the park for a hike or to take in the view. Be extremely cautious in winter when whiteouts and ice are not uncommon. There are adequate road signs throughout the park, but a map is handy to have in the vehicle.

Jackson Hole's main highway (U.S. 89/191) runs the entire length of the park, from Jackson to Yellowstone National Park's south entrance. This highway is also called U.S. 26 south of Moran Junction and U.S. 287 north of Moran Junction. This road is open all year from Jackson to Moran Junction and north to Flagg Ranch, 2 miles south of Yellowstone. In light traffic, the southern (Moose) entrance to Grand Teton is a drive of about 15 minutes from downtown Jackson via the highway. Coming from the opposite direction on the same road, the northern boundary of the park is about 15 minutes south of Yellowstone National Park. Also open year-round, U.S. 26/287 runs east from Dubois over Togwotee Pass to the Moran entrance station, a drive of about one hour.

Two back-road entrances to Grand Teton require high-clearance vehicles. Both roads are closed by snow from November through mid-May and can be heavily rutted through June. Moose-Wilson Road (Wyoming Highway 390) starts at Highway 22 in Wilson (5 miles west of Jackson) and travels 7 miles north past Teton Village to the Granite Canyon entrance station. Of the 9 miles from here to Moose, 1½ are gravel. This route is closed to large trucks, trailers, and RVs. Even rougher is 60-mile Grassy Lake Road, which heads east from Highway 32 in Ashton, Idaho, through Targhee National Forest. It connects with U.S. 89/287 in the John D. Rockefeller Jr. Memorial Parkway, sandwiched between Grand Teton and Yellowstone.

PARK ESSENTIALS
ACCESSIBILITY
The frontcountry portions of Grand Teton are largely accessible to people using wheelchairs. There's designated parking at most sites, and some interpretive trails are easily accessible. There are accessible restrooms at visitor centers. For the *Accessibility* brochure, a guide to accessible trails and facilities, stop by any visitor center.

PARK FEES AND PERMITS

Park entrance costs $35 per car, truck, or RV; $30 per motorcycle; and $20 per person on foot or bicycle, good for seven days in Grand Teton. Annual park passes cost $70. The winter day-use fee is $15.

Backcountry permits, which must be retrieved in person at the Craig Thomas Discovery and Visitor Center, Colter Bay Visitor Center, or Jenny Lake Ranger Station, cost $45. Permits are required for all overnight stays outside designated campgrounds. Reservations are made through ⊕ recreation.gov from early January to mid-May. If you can't snag a permit in advance, you may still have a shot at getting a walk-in permit the day before your trip (with two-thirds of permits designated for this purpose). These are first-come, first-served, and demand can be extremely high. The cost is $35.

For those bringing boats into the park, seven-day permits are available year-round at Craig Thomas Discovery and Visitor Center and in summer at the Jenny Lake and Colter Bay visitor centers. Annual permits cost $40 for motorized craft and $12 for nonmotorized craft, including stand-up paddleboards. State law also requires a special Aquatic Invasive Species decal. Wyoming residents pay $10 for motorized watercraft and $5 for nonmotorized craft; out-of-state visitors pay $30 and $15, respectively.

PARK HOURS

The park is open 24/7 year-round. It's in the Mountain time zone.

CELL PHONE RECEPTION

Cell phones work in most developed areas and occasionally on trails. Public phones are at Dornan's, south Jenny Lake, Signal Mountain Lodge, Moran Entrance Station, Jackson Lake Lodge, Colter Bay Village, Leeks Marina, and Flagg Ranch.

SHOPS AND GROCERS

In the park, there's Dornan's in a pinch, but less expensive and better-stocked stores can be found in Jackson and Wilson.

CONTACTS Dornan's Trading Post & Deli ⊠ Dornan's Rd., off Teton Park Rd., at Moose Junction ☎ 307/733–2415 ⊕ www.dornans.com. **Hungry Jack's General Store** ⊠ 5622 W. Hwy. 22, Wilson ☎ 307/733–3561.

RANGER PROGRAMS

Campfire Programs

TOUR—SIGHT | FAMILY | In summer, park rangers give free slide-show presentations at Colter Bay and sometimes elsewhere. For locations and schedules of topics, check at the visitor centers or in the Grand Teton Guide park newspaper. ⊠ Grand Teton National Park ☎ 307/739–3399, 307/739–3594.

Jackson Hole Historical Society & Museum

Each summer the society sponsors lectures and historic downtown walking tours. The museum itself has exhibits about early homesteaders, dude ranchers, skiers, and the many movies shot in the valley. On the society's website you can download an interactive app with a self-guided tour. ⊠ 225 N. Cache St., Jackson ☎ 307/733–9605 ⊕ www.jacksonholehistory.org.

Junior Ranger Program

TOUR—SIGHT | FAMILY | Children and even adults can earn a Junior Ranger badge or patch by picking up a Junior Ranger booklet at any visitor center in the park. ⊠ Grand Teton National Park ☎ 307/739–3399, 307/739–3594 ⊕ www.nps.gov/kids/jrrangers.cfm.

Nature Explorer's Backpack Program

INFO CENTER | FAMILY | Rangers lend a nature journal and a backpack full of activities to children ages 6 through 12 before sending them out along the trails at the Rockefeller Preserve. ⊠ Laurance S. Rockefeller Preserve Interpretive Center, east side of Moose-Wilson Rd.

✦ *4 miles south of Moose, 3 miles north of Granite Canyon Entrance Station* ☎ *307/739–3654* ⊘ *Closed late Sept.– early June.*

RESTAURANTS

Though the park itself has some excellent restaurants, don't miss dining in Jackson, where chefs apply European and other cooking techniques to game, fowl, and fish dishes and generally include vegetarian entrées. Steaks are usually cut from grass-fed Wyoming or Montana beef, but you'll also find buffalo and elk on the menu; poultry and pasta are offered by most restaurants, as are fresh salads and fish (trout, tilapia, and salmon are most common). Just about everywhere, you can order a burger or a bowl of soup. Casual is the word for most dining within and outside the park. An exception is Jenny Lake Lodge, where jackets and ties for men are required for dinner. Breakfast is big: steak and eggs, pancakes, biscuits and gravy; lunches are lighter, often taken in a sack to enjoy on the trail.

HOTELS

The choice of lodging properties within the park is as diverse as the landscape itself. You'll find simple campgrounds, cabins, and standard motel rooms, but you can also settle into a homey bed-and-breakfast or a luxurious suite in a full-service resort. Between June and August, rates go up and rooms are harder to get unless you make a reservation well ahead of your visit.

For information on lodging and dining in the park, contact the park's largest concessionaire, Grand Teton Lodge Company. ☎ *307/543–2811* ⊕ *www.gtlc.com. Hotel reviews have been shortened. For full information, visit Fodors.com.*

Jackson Hole Central Reservations

You can reserve rooms at Jackson-area hotels and resorts through this service. ☎ *888/838–6606* ⊕ *www.jacksonholewy. com.*

What It Costs

	$	$$	$$$	$$$$
RESTAURANTS				
	under $13	$13–$20	$21–$30	over $30
HOTELS				
	under $100	$100–$150	$151–$200	over $200

TOURS

Alltrans Tours

TOUR—SIGHT | Full-day bus tours from Jackson provide an overview of Grand Teton National Park. You'll learn about the park's geology, history, birds, plants, and wildlife. ⊠ *Jackson* ☎ *307/733–3135, 800/443–6133* ⊕ *www.jacksonholealltrans.com* ☎ *From $245* ⊘ *Closed late Sept.–late May, tours not held on Mon., Wed., Fri., and Sat.*

Grand Teton Lodge Company Bus Tours

TOUR—SIGHT | **FAMILY** | Half-day tours depart from Jackson Lake Lodge and include visits to scenic viewpoints, visitor centers, and other park sites. Guides provide information about park geology, history, wildlife, and ecosystems. Buy tickets in advance at Colter Bay or Jackson Lake Lodge activities desks. Full-day tours continue into Yellowstone. ⊠ *Jackson Lake Lodge* ☎ *307/543–2811, 800/628–9988* ⊕ *www.gtlc.com/activities* ☎ *From $75* ⊘ *Closed early Oct.–late May.*

Jackson Lake Cruises

TOUR—SIGHT | **FAMILY** | Grand Teton Lodge Company runs 1½-hour Jackson Lake cruises from Colter Bay Village Marina throughout the day, as well as three-hour breakfast cruises and sunset cruises. Guides explain how forest fires and glaciers have shaped the Grand Teton landscape. ⊠ *Grand Teton National Park* ✦ *2 miles off U.S. 89/191/287, 5 miles north of Jackson Lake Junction* ☎ *307/543–2811, 800/628–9988* ⊕ *www.*

gtlc.com/activities ✉ *From $34* ⊗ *Closed late Sept.–late May (depending on tour).*

Teton Science School
TOUR—SIGHT | FAMILY | The school conducts wildlife expeditions in Grand Teton, Yellowstone, and surrounding forests—participants see and learn about wolves, bears, bighorn sheep, and other animals. Full-day and half-day excursions are offered, as well as custom trips. The bear and wolf expedition is a thrilling three-day, two-night field adventure during spring and fall. ⊠ *700 Coyote Canyon Rd., Jackson* ☎ *307/733–1313* ⊕ *www. tetonscience.org* ✉ *Tours from $118.*

Teton Wagon Train and Horse Adventures
TOUR—SIGHT | FAMILY | Multiday covered wagon rides and horseback trips follow Grassy Lake Road on the "back side" of the Tetons. You can combine the trip with a river trip and a tour of Yellowstone and Grand Teton. ⊠ *Jackson* ☎ *307/734–6101, 888/734–6101* ⊕ *www.tetonwagontrain. com* ✉ *From about $1100* ⊗ *Closed mid-Aug.–early June.*

VISITOR INFORMATION
PARK CONTACT INFORMATION Grand Teton National Park ☎ *307/739–3300* ⊕ *www.nps.gov/grte.*

VISITOR CENTERS
Colter Bay Visitor Center
INFO CENTER | A small display shows off items from the park's collection of Native American artifacts. (Hundreds more are being conserved and stored for future displays.) In summer, rangers lead daily hikes from here. Nightly ranger talks on various topics are also offered. ⊠ *Colter Bay Marina Rd., off Colter Bay Village Rd., ½ mile west of U.S. 89/191/287, Oxbow Bend* ☎ *307/739–3594* ⊕ *www. nps.gov/grte/planyourvisit/cbvc.htm* ⊗ *Closed early Oct.–Mother's Day.*

Craig Thomas Discovery and Visitor Center
INFO CENTER | This sleek center has interactive and interpretive exhibits dedicated to themes of preservation, mountaineering, and local wildlife. There's also a 3-D map of the park and streaming video along a footpath showing the area's intricate natural features. Dozens of Native American artifacts from the David T. Vernon Collection are housed here. A plush, 155-seat theater shows a nature documentary every half hour. ⊠ *Moose* ⊹ *½ mile west of Moose Junction* ☎ *307/739–3399* ⊕ *www.nps.gov/grte/ planyourvisit/ctdvc.htm* ⊗ *Closed late Oct.–early Mar.*

Jenny Lake Visitor Center
INFO CENTER | The historic cabin that houses this visitor center was once used as a studio by the park's first official park photographer, Harrison Crandall. Today it's filled with exhibits on the history of art and artists in the park. ⊠ *Jenny Lake* ⊹ *S. Jenny Lake Junction, 8 miles north of Moose Junction, off Teton Park Rd.* ☎ *307/739–3392* ⊕ *www.nps.gov/grte/ planyourvisit/jlvc.htm* ⊗ *Closed early Sept.–mid-May.*

Laurance S. Rockefeller Preserve Interpretive Center
INFO CENTER | FAMILY | This contemporary structure feels more like an art gallery than an interpretive facility. The elegant, eco-friendly building is more than just eye candy—you can experience the sounds of the park in a cylindrical audio chamber, and laminated maps in the reading room are great for trip planning. Rangers here promote "contemplative hiking" and are well informed about the many birds around the center's trailheads. It's best to get here in the early morning or late evening because the small parking area fills quickly. A ranger leads a hike to the lake every morning. ⊠ *Grand Teton National Park* ⊹ *East side of Moose-Wilson Rd., about 4 miles south of Moose and 3 miles north of Granite Canyon Entrance Station* ☎ *307/739–3654* ⊕ *www.nps.gov/grte/planyourvisit/lsr. htm* ⊗ *Closed late Sept.–early June* ☞ *Limited group size (no more than 10 to a party); vehicle-size restrictions on Moose-Wilson Rd.*

Plants and Wildlife in Grand Teton

Grand Teton's short growing season and arid climate create a complex ecosystem and hardy plant species. The dominant elements are big sagebrush—which gives the valley its gray-green cast—lodgepole pine trees, quaking aspen, and ground-covering wildflowers such as bluish-purple lupine.

Short Growing Season

In spring and early summer you will see the vibrant yellow arrowleaf balsamroot and low larkspur. Jackson Hole's short growing season gives rise to spectacular if short-lived displays of wildflowers, best seen between mid-June and early July. The changing of the aspen and cottonwood leaves in early fall can be equally dazzling.

Oft and Rarely Seen Wildlife

On almost any trip to Grand Teton, you will see bison, pronghorn antelope, and moose. More rarely you will see a black or grizzly bear, a fox, or a wolf. Watch for elk along the forest edge, and, in the summer, on Teton Park Road. Oxbow Bend and Willow Flats are good places to look for moose, beaver, and otter in twilight hours any time of year. Pronghorn and bison appear in summer along the highway and Antelope Flats Road.

Smaller Animals

The park's smaller animals—yellow-bellied marmots, pikas, and Uinta ground squirrels, as well as a variety of birds and waterfowl—are commonly seen along park trails and waterways. Seek out water sources—the Snake River, the glacial lakes, and marshy areas—to see birds such as bald eagles, ospreys, ducks, and trumpeter swans. Your best chance to see wildlife is at dawn or dusk.

 Sights

SCENIC DRIVES

Antelope Flats Road

SCENIC DRIVE | Off U.S. 191/26/89, about 2 miles north of Moose Junction, this narrow road wanders eastward over sagebrush flats. The road intersects the gravel Mormon Row, where you can turn off to see abandoned homesteaders' barns and houses from the turn of the 20th century. Less than 2 miles past Mormon Row is a three-way intersection where you can turn right to loop around past the town of Kelly and Gros Ventre campground and rejoin U.S. 191/26/89 at Gros Ventre Junction. Keep an eye out for abundant pronghorn, bison, moose, raptors, and cyclists. ⊠ Grand Teton

National Park ⊗ Closed seasonally based on conditions.

★ **Jenny Lake Scenic Drive**

SCENIC DRIVE | This 4-mile, one-way loop provides the park's best roadside close-ups of the Tetons as it winds south through groves of lodgepole pine and open meadows. Roughly 1½ miles off Teton Park Road, the Cathedral Group Turnout faces 13,770-foot Grand Teton (the range's highest peak), flanked by 12,928-foot Mount Owen and 12,325-foot Mount Teewinot. ⊠ Jenny Lake.

Signal Mountain Summit

SCENIC DRIVE | FAMILY | This exciting drive climbs 700 feet along a 4-mile stretch of winding road. As you travel through forest you can catch glimpses of Jackson Lake and Mount Moran. At the top of the road, park and follow the well-marked path to one of the park's best panoramas. From 7,593 feet above sea level your gaze can sweep over all of Jackson Hole and the 40-mile Teton Range. The views are particularly dramatic at sunset. The road is not appropriate for long trailers and is closed in winter. ⊠ *Grand Teton National Park* ⊹ *Off Teton Park Rd., south of Jackson Lake Junction* ⊘ *Closed Nov.–May.*

HISTORIC SITES
Cunningham Cabin Historic Site
HISTORIC SITE | At the end of a gravel spur road, an easy ¾-mile trail runs through sagebrush around Pierce Cunningham's 1888 log-cabin homestead. Although you can peer inside, the building has no furnishings or displays. Watch for badgers, coyotes, and Uinta ground squirrels in the area. ⊠ *Antelope Flats* ⊹ *½ mile off Jackson Hole Hwy., 5 miles south of Moran Junction* ⊕ *www.nps.gov/grte/ learn/historyculture/cunning.htm.*

Menor's Ferry Historic Area
HISTORIC SITE | FAMILY | Down a path from the Chapel of the Transfiguration, the ferry on display here is not the original, but it's an accurate re-creation of the double-pontoon craft built by Bill Menor in 1894. That was how people crossed the Snake River before bridges were installed. While the replica ferry has ceased running, this still makes a worthwhile stop. In the cluster of turn-of-the-20th-century buildings there are displays on historical transportation methods, and in the summer a nearby general store sells candy and soda. Pick up a pamphlet for a self-guided tour. ⊠ *Grand Teton National Park* ⊹ *½ mile off Teton Park Rd., 1 mile north of Moose Junction* ⊕ *www.nps.gov/grte/learn/historyculture/ menors.htm.*

Mormon Row Historic Area
HISTORIC SITE | Settled by homesteaders between 1896 and 1907, this area received its name because many of them were members of the Church of Jesus Christ of Latter-day Saints, also known as Mormons. The remaining barns, homes, and outbuildings are representative of early homesteading in the West. You can wander around, hike the row, and take photographs. The century-old T.A. Moulton Barn is said to be the most-photographed barn in the state. ⊠ *Grand Teton National Park* ⊹ *Off Antelope Flats Rd., 2 miles north of Moose Junction* ⊕ *www.nps.gov/grte/learn/historyculture/ mormon.htm.*

SCENIC STOPS
Chapel of the Sacred Heart
RELIGIOUS SITE | This small log Catholic chapel sits in the pine forest with a view of Jackson Lake. It's open only for services, but you can enjoy the view anytime. ⊠ *Grand Teton National Park* ⊹ *½ mile north of Signal Mountain Lodge, off Teton Park Rd.* ☎ *307/733–2516* ⊕ *olmcatholic. org/about-the-parish/location* ⊘ *Closed Oct.–June.*

Chapel of the Transfiguration
RELIGIOUS SITE | This tiny chapel built in 1925 on land donated by Maud Noble is still a functioning Episcopal church. Couples come here to exchange vows with the Tetons as a backdrop, and tourists snap photos of the small church with its awe-inspiring view. ⊠ *Chapel of the Transfiguration Rd., ½ mile off Teton Park Rd., Moose* ☎ *307/733–2603* ⊕ *www. stjohnsjackson.org/chapel-of-the-transfiguration* ⊘ *Closed Sept.–Memorial Day.*

Jackson Lake
BODY OF WATER | FAMILY | The biggest of Grand Teton's glacier-carved lakes, this body of water in the park's northern reaches was enlarged by construction of the Jackson Lake Dam in 1906. You can fish, sail, and water ski here. Three marinas (Colter Bay, Leeks, and Signal Mountain) provide access for boaters, and several picnic areas, campgrounds, and lodges overlook the lake. ⊠ *Grand Teton National Park* ⊹ *U.S. 89/191/287 from Lizard Creek to Jackson Lake Junction, and Teton Park Rd. from Jackson Lake Junction to Signal Mountain Lodge.*

Jenny Lake

BODY OF WATER | Named for the Shoshone wife of Beaver Dick Leigh, a mountain man, this glacier-carved lake south of Jackson Lake draws paddle-sports enthusiasts to its pristine waters and hikers to its tree-shaded trails. ⊠ *Grand Teton National Park* ✛ *Off Teton Park Rd. midway between Moose and Jackson Lake.*

Laurance S. Rockefeller Preserve

TRAIL | FAMILY | This eco-conscious preserve includes miles of trails. You can access it via the Valley Trail, 1¾ miles north of the Granite Canyon trailhead and ½ mile south of the Death Canyon turnoff. Hikers can admire the Phelps Lake shoreline from a loop trail beginning at the interpretive center, or climb a ridgeline with beautiful views of aspens, wildflowers, and regional birds. ⊠ *Grand Teton National Park* ✛ *East side of Moose-Wilson Rd., about 4 miles south of Moose and 3 miles north of Granite Canyon Entrance Station* ⊕ *www.nps. gov/grte/planyourvisit/lsr.htm* ☞ *Vehicle-size restrictions on Moose-Wilson Rd.*

Oxbow Bend

VIEWPOINT | This peaceful spot overlooks a quiet backwater left by the Snake River when it cut a new southern channel. White pelicans stop here on their spring migration (many stay on through summer), sandhill cranes and trumpeter swans visit frequently, and great blue herons nest amid the cottonwoods along the river. Use binoculars to search for bald eagles, osprey, moose, beaver, and otter. The Oxbow is known for the reflection of Mount Moran that marks its calm waters in early morning. ⊠ *Grand Teton National Park* ✛ *U.S. 89/191/287, 2½ miles east of Jackson Lake Junction.*

Willow Flats

NATURE PRESERVE | You will almost always see moose grazing in this marshy area, in part because of its flourishing willow bushes, where moose both eat and hide. This is also a good place to see birds and waterfowl. ⊠ *Grand Teton National Park* ✛ *U.S. 89/191/287, 1 mile north of Jackson Lake Junction.*

 Activities

BICYCLING

Since the first paved pathways were completed in Jackson Hole in 1996, the valley has become a cyclist's paradise. Almost 60 miles of paved pathways thread through Jackson Hole, with more in the works. Those on two wheels can access Grand Teton on a path that begins at the north end of town and travels 21 miles to South Jenny Lake Junction. A bike lane permits two-way bike traffic along the one-way Jenny Lake Loop Road, a one-hour ride. The River Road, 4 miles north of Moose, is an easy four-hour mountain-bike ride along a ridge above the Snake River on a gravel road. Bicycles are not allowed on trails or in the backcountry.

In the Bridger-Teton National Forest that surrounds Jackson, the Snow King Mountain trail system offers miles of singletrack, from easy to challenging. The Cache Creek to Game Creek loop is a 25-mile ride on dirt roads, trails, and a paved pathway. Roadies can enjoy the rural Fish Creek or Fall Creek roads, and downhillers revel in the Bike Park at Jackson Hole Mountain Resort. Maps can be obtained at the Jackson Hole and Greater Yellowstone Visitor Center at the north end of town on Cache Street.

Hoback Sports

BICYCLING | Get your own bike tuned up or rent one: road, mountain, hybrid, kids', and trailers. The shop also sells bikes, clothing, and mountain sporting accessories, and offers daily mountain-bike tours. ⊠ *520 W. Broadway, Suite 3, Jackson* ☎ *307/733–5335* ⊕ *www.hobacksports. com.*

Teton Mountain Bike Tours

BICYCLING | Mountain bikers of all skill levels can take this company's guided half-, full-, or multiday tours into Grand Teton and Yellowstone national parks, as well as winter tours of Jackson Hole on snow bikes with fat, studded tires. The outfit also rents bikes. ✉ *545 N. Cache St., Jackson* ☎ *307/733–0712, 800/733–0788* ⊕ *www.tetonmtbike.com* ✉ *Half- and full-day trips from $75; from $2850 for 5-day Teton/Yellowstone tour.*

BIRD-WATCHING

With more than 300 species of birds, the Tetons make excellent bird-watching country. Here you might spot both the calliope hummingbird (the smallest North American hummingbird) and the trumpeter swan (the world's largest waterfowl). Birds of prey circle around Antelope Flats Road—the surrounding fields are good hunting turf for red-tailed hawks and prairie falcons. At Taggart Lake you might see woodpeckers, bluebirds, and hummingbirds. Look for songbirds, such as pine and evening grosbeaks and Cassin's finches, in surrounding open pine and aspen forests.

Oxbow Bend

BIRD WATCHING | Impressive birds congregate at this quiet spot. In spring, white pelicans stop by during their northerly migration; in summer, bald eagles, great blue herons, and osprey nest nearby. Year-round, you'll have a good chance of seeing trumpeter swans. Nearby **Willow Flats** has similar bird life, plus sandhill cranes. ✉ *U.S. 89/191/287, 2 miles east of Jackson Lake Junction.*

Phelps Lake

BIRD WATCHING | The moderate, 1.8-mile round-trip Phelps Lake Overlook Trail takes you from the Death Canyon trailhead up conifer- and aspen-lined glacial moraine to a view that's accessible only on foot. Expect abundant bird life: Western tanagers, northern flickers, and ruby-crowned kinglets thrive in the bordering woods, and hummingbirds feed on scarlet gilia beneath the overlook. Don't neglect the Phelps Lake Trail, which circles the lake and is accessible from either Death Canyon or the Rockefeller

Preserve. ✉ *Moose-Wilson Rd., about 3 miles off Teton Park Rd.*

BOATING AND WATER SPORTS

Water sports in Grand Teton are diverse. You can float the Snake River, which runs high and fast early in the season (May and June) and more slowly during the latter part of the summer. Canoes, kayaks, and stand-up paddleboards dominate the smaller lakes and share the water with motorboats on large Jackson Lake. Motorboats also are allowed on Jenny Lake, but there's an engine limit of 10 horsepower. You can launch your boat at Colter Bay, Leek's Marina, Signal Mountain, and Spalding Bay on Jackson Lake.

If you're floating the Snake River on your own, you are required to purchase a permit ($20 per boat for the entire season, or $10 per raft for seven days). Permits are available year-round at Craig Thomas Discovery and Visitor Center and in summer at Colter Bay. Before you set out, check with park rangers about current conditions.

You may prefer to take one of the many guided float trips through calm-water sections of the Snake; outfitters pick you up at the float-trip parking area near Craig Thomas Discovery and Visitor Center for a 15-minute drive to upriver launch sites. Ponchos and life preservers are provided. Early morning and evening floats are your best bets for wildlife viewing. Be sure to carry a jacket or sweater. Float season runs from mid-April to mid-December.

Barker-Ewing Scenic Float Trips

BOATING | FAMILY | Travel the peaceful parts of the Snake River within the park and look for wildlife as knowledgeable guides talk about area history, geology, plants, and animals. ✉ *Moose* ☎ *307/733–1800, 800/365–1800* ⊕ *bark-erewing.com* ✉ *From $80.*

Colter Bay Village Marina

BOATING | FAMILY | You can rent motorboats, kayaks, and canoes at Colter Bay from park concessionaire Grand Teton

Lodge Company. Guided fishing trips are also available. ⊠ *Grand Teton National Park* ✛ *2 miles off U.S. 89/191/287, 5 miles north of Jackson Lake Junction* ☎ *307/543–3100, 800/628–9988* ⊕ *www. gtlc.com/activities/marina* ⊠ *Rentals from $21 for canoes.*

Leek's Marina
BOATING | Parking for boat trailers and other vehicles is available for up to three nights. The marina offers boat rentals, as well as nightly buoys. The pizza restaurant here is superb. Park concessionaire Signal Mountain Lodge operates the marina. ⊠ *U.S. 89/191/287, 6 miles north of Jackson Lake Junction* ☎ *307/543–2831* ⊕ *www.signalmountainlodge.com.*

Mad River Boat Trips
BOATING | FAMILY | Mad River leads a variety of white-water and scenic float trips, some combined with lunch or dinner. The minimum age is four for scenic trips, and six for whitewater trips. ⊠ *Jackson* ☎ *307/733–6203, 800/458–7238* ⊕ *www. mad-river.com* ⊠ *From $72.*

Rendezvous River Sports
BOATING | FAMILY | However you'd like to hit the water, the river rats at Rendezvous are here to help. They offer instruction for stand-up paddleboarding and kayaking, as well as guided trips on area rivers and lakes. Or you could choose a backcountry adventure in the national parks. The shop rents kayaks, canoes, rafts, and paddleboards. ⊠ *945 W. Broadway, Jackson* ☎ *307/733–2471* ⊕ *www. jacksonholekayak.com* ⊠ *From $95.*

Signal Mountain Lodge Marina
BOATING | The marina rents pontoon boats, deck cruisers, motorboats, kayaks, and canoes by the hour or all day; rates run from $25 an hour for a kayak to $139 an hour for a deck cruiser. ⊠ *Teton Park Rd., 3 miles south of Jackson Lake Junction* ☎ *307/543–2831* ⊕ *signalmountainlodge.com.*

Spalding Bay
BOATING | You can launch your boat here and park your trailer and vehicle for the day. No docking or mooring is available. ⊠ *Grand Teton National Park* ✛ *2 miles off Teton Park Rd., 7 miles south of Jackson Lake Junction.*

Triangle X National Park Float Trips
BOATING | FAMILY | The knowledgeable and charismatic Triangle X guides will row you down 10 miles of the Snake River through pristine riparian habitat in Grand Teton National Park. For the best wildlife viewing, book a dawn or evening dinner float. ⊠ *Moose* ☎ *307/733–5500, 888/860–0005* ⊕ *nationalparkfloattrips. com* ⊠ *From $80.*

CLIMBING
The Teton Range has some of the nation's most diverse mountaineering. Excellent rock, snow, and ice routes abound. Unless you're already a pro, it's recommended that you take a course from one of the park's concessionaire climbing schools before tackling the tough terrain. Practice your moves at Teton Boulder Park, a free outdoor artificial climbing wall in Phil Baux Park at the base of Snow King Mountain.

Exum Mountain Guides
CLIMBING/MOUNTAINEERING | The climbing experiences offered by the oldest guide service in North America include one-day mountain climbs, weeklong clinics culminating in a two-day ascent of the Grand Teton, and backcountry adventures on skis and snowboards. ⊠ *Grand Teton National Park* ☎ *307/733–2297* ⊕ *www. exumguides.com* ⊠ *From $180.*

Jackson Hole Mountain Guides
CLIMBING/MOUNTAINEERING | Beginning to advanced climbers can get instruction or explore classic granite routes in the Tetons and beyond. ⊠ *1325 U.S. 89, Suite 104, Jackson* ☎ *307/733–4979* ⊕ *www.jhmg.com.*

FISHING

Rainbow, brook, lake, and native cut-throat trout inhabit the park's waters. The Snake's 75 miles of river and tributary are world-renowned for their fishing. To fish in Grand Teton National Park, you need a Wyoming fishing license, which you can purchase from the state game and fish department or at Colter Bay Village Marina, Dornan's, Signal Mountain Lodge, and area sporting-goods stores. A day permit for nonresidents costs $14, and an annual permit costs $92 plus $12.50 for a conservation stamp; for state residents a license costs $24 per season plus $12.50 for a conservation stamp. Children under age 14 can fish free with an adult who has a license.

Grand Teton Lodge Company

FISHING | The park's major concessionaire operates guided fishing trips on Jackson Lake and guided fly-fishing trips on the Snake River. Make reservations at the activities desks at Colter Bay Village or Jackson Lake Lodge, where trips originate. ⊠ *Grand Teton National Park* ☎ *307/543–3100, 800/628–9988* ⊕ *www. gtlc.com/activities* ⌚ *From $220.*

Signal Mountain Lodge

FISHING | Hourly and half-day Jackson Lake guided fishing trips depart from the marina at Signal Mountain Lodge, weather permitting. The rates include equipment and tackle. ⊠ *Teton Park Rd., 3 miles south of Jackson Lake Junction* ☎ *307/543–2831* ⊕ *www.signalmountain-lodge.com/lodge-services/signal-mountain-fishing* ⌚ *From $115/hr* ⌚ *Minimum age 6.*

Wyoming Game and Fish Department

FISHING | You can purchase a fishing license from the department. ⊠ *420 N. Cache St., Jackson* ☎ *307/733–2321* ⊕ *wgfd.wyo.gov.*

HIKING

Most of Grand Teton's trails are unpaved, with just a few short paved sections in the vicinity of developed areas. You can get trail maps and information about hiking conditions from rangers at the park visitor centers at Moose, Jenny Lake, and Colter Bay, where you will also find bathrooms or outhouses; there are no facilities along trails themselves. Of the more than 250 miles of maintained trails, the most popular are those around Jenny Lake, the Leigh and String lakes area, and Taggart Lake Trail, with views of Avalanche Canyon.

Frontcountry or backcountry you may see moose and bears—keep your distance. Pets are not permitted on trails or in the backcountry, but you can take them along roadsides as long as they are on a leash no more than 6 feet long. Always let someone know where you are going and when you expect to return, and carry plenty of water, snacks, rain gear, warm clothes, bear spray, and a cell phone.

Amphitheater Lake

HIKING/WALKING | A little more than 10 miles round-trip, this hike starts at Lupine Meadows and switches back through steep pines and flowered meadows to Surprise Lake and the regal Amphitheater Lake, tucked away in an expansive rock basin. The strenuous trail weaves out for views of the sprawling valley, while Disappointment Peak looms above. Get to the trail early and allow at least five hours to tackle the 3,000-foot gain. *Difficult.* ⊠ *Jenny Lake* ⊹ *Trailhead: at Lupine Meadows Trailhead, south of Jenny Lake.*

Cascade Canyon Trail

HIKING/WALKING | FAMILY | Take Jenny Lake Boating's 20-minute boat ride from the dock near the Jenny Lake Visitor Center to the start of a gentle, ½-mile climb to 200-foot Hidden Falls, the park's most popular and crowded trail destination. With the 10-minute boat shuttle ($15 round-trip), plan on a couple of hours to experience this trail. Listen here for the distinctive bleating of the rabbit-like pikas among the glacial boulders and pines. The trail continues ½ mile to Inspiration Point over a rocky path that is moderately

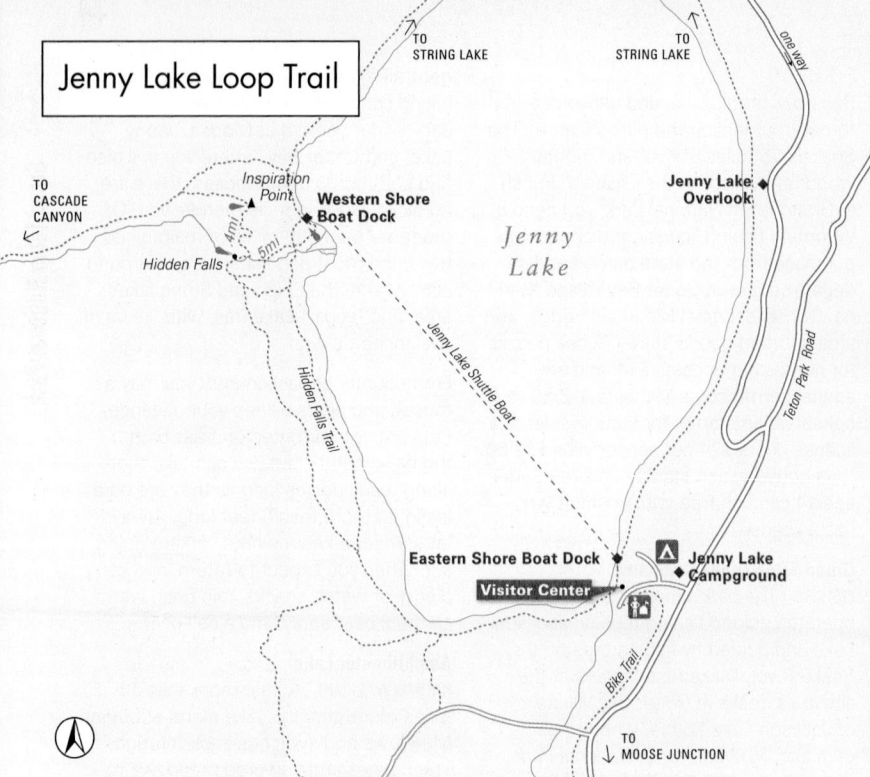

TO
STRING LAKE

TO
STRING LAKE

one way

TO
CASCADE
CANYON

Inspiration
Point

Western Shore
Boat Dock

Jenny Lake
Overlook

*Jenny
Lake*

.4mi

.5mi

Hidden Falls

Hidden Falls Trail

Jenny Lake Shuttle Boat

Teton Park Road

Eastern Shore Boat Dock

Visitor Center

Jenny Lake
Campground

Bike Trail

TO
MOOSE JUNCTION

---

steep. There are two points on the climb that afford good views of Jenny Lake and the surrounding area, but keep climbing; after passing a rock wall you'll finally reach Inspiration Point, with the best views. *Easy.* ☒ *Grand Teton National Park* ⊹ *Trailhead: at Jenny Lake Visitor Center, ¼ mile off Teton Park Rd., 8 miles north of Moose Junction* ⊕ *www.jennylake-boating.com.*

Colter Bay Nature Trail Loop

HIKING/WALKING | This very easy 1¾-mile round-trip excursion treats you to views of Jackson Lake and the Tetons. As you follow the level trail along the forest's edge, you may see moose and bald eagles. Allow two hours to complete the walk. *Easy.* ☒ *Grand Teton National Park* ⊹ *Trailhead: at Colter Bay Visitor Center, 1 mile off U.S. 89/191/287, 5 miles north of Jackson Lake Junction.*

The Hole Hiking Experience

HIKING/WALKING | For more than three decades, guides have led hikes and wildlife tours for all ages and ability levels in the Greater Yellowstone Ecosystem. The trips have an interpretive focus, with information about the history, geology, and ecology of the area. Many excursions incorporate yoga or have a holistic bent. In winter, cross-country tours in Grand Teton National Park are offered. ☒ *Jackson* ☎ *307/690–4453* ⊕ *www.holehike.com.*

Jenny Lake Loop Trail

HIKING/WALKING | FAMILY | You can walk to Hidden Falls from Jenny Lake ranger station by following the mostly level trail around the south shore of the lake to Cascade Canyon Trail. Jenny Lake Trail continues around the lake for 6½ miles. It's an easy trail—classed here as moderate because of its length—that will take you from two to three hours. You'll walk through a lodgepole-pine forest, have expansive views of the lake and the land to the east, and hug the shoulder of the massive Teton range itself. Along the way you are likely to see elk, pikas, golden-mantled ground squirrels, and a variety of ducks and water birds. You may also hear elk bugling, birdsong, and the chatter of squirrels. *Moderate.* ⊠ *Grand Teton National Park* ⊕ *Trailhead: at Jenny Lake Visitor Center, S. Jenny Lake Junction, ½ mile off Teton Park Rd., 8 miles north of Moose Junction.*

Leigh Lake Trail

HIKING/WALKING | This flat trail follows String Lake's northeastern shore to Leigh Lake's southern shore, covering 2 miles in a round-trip of about an hour. You can extend your hike into a moderate 7½-mile, four-hour round-trip by following the forested east shore of Leigh Lake to Bearpaw Lake. Along the way you'll have views of Mount Moran across the lake, and you may be lucky enough to spot a moose or a bear. *Moderate.* ⊠ *Grand Teton National Park* ⊕ *Trailhead: at northwest corner of String Lake Picnic Area, ½ mile west of Jenny Lake Rd., 2 miles off Teton Park Rd., 12 miles north of Moose Junction.*

Lunchtree Hill Trail

HIKING/WALKING | One of the park's easiest trails begins at Jackson Lake Lodge and leads ½ mile to the top of a hill above Willow Flats. The area's willow thickets, beaver ponds, and wet, grassy meadows make it a birder's paradise. Look for sandhill cranes, hummingbirds, and the many types of songbirds described in the free bird guide available at visitor centers. You might also see moose. Round-trip the walk takes no more than half an hour. *Easy.* ⊠ *Grand Teton National Park* ⊕ *Trailhead: at Jackson Lake Lodge, U.S. 89/191/287, ½ mile north of Jackson Lake Junction.*

String Lake Trail

HIKING/WALKING | The 3½-mile loop around String Lake lies in the shadows of 11,144-foot Rockchuck Peak and 11,430-foot Mount Saint John. This is also a good place to see moose and elk, hear songbirds, and view wildflowers. The trail, which takes about three hours to hike, is a bit more difficult than other mid-length trails in the park, which means it's also less crowded. *Moderate.* ⊠ *Grand Teton National Park* ⊕ *Trailhead: ¼ mile west of Jenny Lake Rd., 2 miles off Teton Park Rd., 12 miles north of Moose Junction.*

HORSEBACK RIDING

You can arrange a guided horseback tour at Colter Bay Village and Jackson Lake Lodge corrals or with private outfitters. Most offer rides from an hour or two up to all-day excursions. If you want to spend even more time riding in Grand Teton and the surrounding mountains, consider a stay at a dude ranch. Most shorter rides are appropriate for novice riders. More experienced riders will enjoy the longer journeys where the terrain gets steeper and you may wind through deep forests. For any ride be sure to wear long pants and boots (cowboy boots or hiking boots). Because you may ride through trees, a long-sleeve shirt is also a good idea and a hat is always appropriate, but it should have a stampede string to make sure it stays on your head if the wind comes up.

Grand Teton Lodge Company Horseback Rides

HORSEBACK RIDING | **FAMILY** | Rides start at Jackson Lake Lodge, Colter Bay Village, Headwaters Lodge, and Jenny Lake Lodge corrals. One- and two-hour trips are available, and beginners are welcome, with pony rides for small children. If riding isn't your thing, open-air wagon rides (with breakfast included) depart from Colter Bay Village. Book in advance. ⊠ *Grand Teton National Park* ☎ *307/543–2811, 800/628–9988* ⊕ *www.gtlc.com/activities/horseback-riding* ⌖ *From $45.*

Did You Know?

The Grand Tetons have been called many things—"the three pinnacles," "pilot knobs," and "the hoary brothers" among them. But the name that stuck was given by French fur trappers, who referred to the mountains as *les Trois Tétons* (the Three Breasts).

WINTER ACTIVITES

Grand Teton has some of North America's finest and most varied cross-country skiing. Ski the gentle 3-mile Swan Lake–Heron Pond Loop near Colter Bay, the mostly level 10-mile Jenny Lake Trail, or the moderate 4-mile Taggart Lake–Beaver Creek Loop and 5-mile Phelps Lake Overlook Trail. Teton Park Road is groomed for classic and skate-skiing from early January to mid-March. In winter, overnight backcountry travelers must register or make a reservation at the Craig Thomas Discovery and Visitor Center.

Snowmobiling is permitted on Jackson Lake only for ice fishing. Because snowmobiles must be towed into the park, sledders pay only the regular park entrance fees. Snowmobilers wishing to proceed north from Flagg Ranch into Yellowstone National Park must be with a commercial tour guide.

The Flagg Ranch Information Station is closed in winter but ski and snowshoe trails are open and marked with flagging tape. Pick up a map at the Flagg Ranch convenience store. For information about a free, ranger-guided snowshoe walk, call the Craig Thomas Discovery and Visitor Center.

TOURS AND OUTFITTERS
Skinny Skis
SKIING/SNOWBOARDING | The valley's hub for Nordic skiing sells and rents equipment for snowshoeing, skate-skiing, and classic cross-country skiing. This is the place to find the latest-and-greatest down jackets and wool base layers. Staffers here can give you advice about what trails to explore. ⊠ *65 W. Deloney Ave., Jackson* ☎ *307/733–6094* ⊕ *www.skinnyskis.com.*

Togwotee Mountain Lodge
SKIING/SNOWBOARDING | Here you can rent a snowmobile and explore 600-plus miles of groomed trails and endless powder-filled meadows along the Continental Divide. ⊠ *27655 U.S. 26/287,* *Moran* ☎ *307/543–2847, 800/543–2847, 866/278–4245* ⊕ *www.togwoteelodge. com* ✉ *Snowmobile rentals from $184/ day.*

NEARBY TOWNS

The major gateway to Grand Teton National Park is **Jackson**—but don't confuse this with Jackson Hole. Jackson Hole is the mountain-ringed valley that includes Jackson and much of Grand Teton National Park. The town of Jackson, south of the park, is a small community (roughly 10,000 residents) that gets flooded with 3 to 4 million visitors annually. Expensive homes and fashionable shops have sprung up all over, but with its wooden boardwalks and old-fashioned storefronts, the town center still looks like a Western movie set. There's a lot to do here, both downtown and in the surrounding countryside.

If it's skiing you're after, **Snow King Resort** is the oldest resort in the valley, and its 7,808-foot mountain overlooks the town of Jackson and the National Elk Refuge. It's at the end of Snow King Avenue. **Teton Village,** on the southwestern side of the park, is a cluster of businesses centered around the facilities of the Jackson Hole Mountain Resort. This ski and snowboard area has the longest continuous vertical rise in the U.S. at 4,139 feet, accessed by an aerial tram to the top of Rendezvous Mountain (10,450 feet). A gondola and various other lifts take skiers to other sections of the mountain. There are plenty of places to eat, stay, and shop here.

On the "back side of the Tetons," as eastern Idaho is known, is **Driggs,** the western gateway to Yellowstone and Grand Teton. Easygoing and rural, Driggs resembles the Jackson of a few decades ago. To reach the park from here you have to cross a major mountain pass that is sometimes closed in winter by avalanches. **Dubois,** about 85 miles east of Jackson, is the least known of the gateway communities to Grand Teton and Yellowstone, but this town of 1,000 has all the services of the bigger towns. You can still get a room for the night here during the peak summer travel period without making a reservation weeks or months in advance (though it's a good idea to call a week or so before you intend to arrive).

About an hour to the south is **Pinedale,** another small Wyoming town with lodging, restaurants, and attractions. Energy development has made the area a hopping place these days, so be sure to plan ahead if you want to stay in town.

VISITOR CENTER
Jackson Hole and Greater Yellowstone Visitor Center
Stop at the center for information about area attractions and to see wildlife displays that explain the establishment of the National Elk Refuge, as well as the creatures' migration routes and seasonal range. From early December to late March, buses depart every 20–30 minutes to take visitors 2½ miles north for sleigh rides that glide close to grazing elk on the refuge. ⊠ *532 N. Cache St., Jackson* ☎ *307/733–3316* ⊕ *www.fws.gov/nwrs/threecolumn.aspx?id=2147509813.*

VISITOR INFORMATION Colter Bay Visitor Center ⊠ *U.S. 89/191/287, 6 miles north of Jackson Lake Junction, Moran* ☎ *307/739–3594* ⊕ *www.nps.gov/grte/planyourvisit/cbvc.htm* **Dubois Chamber of Commerce** ⊠ *20 Snalnaker St., Dubois* ☎ *307/455–2556* ⊕ *www.duboiswyomingchamber.org.* **Jackson Hole Chamber of Commerce** ⊠ *260 W. Broadway, Jackson* ☎ *307/733–3316* ⊕ *www.jacksonhole-chamber.com.* **Sublette County Chamber of Commerce** ⊠ *19 E. Pine St., Pinedale* ☎ *307/367–2242* ⊕ *www.sublette-chamber.com.* **Teton Valley Chamber of Commerce** ⊠ *60 S. Main St., Driggs* ☎ *208/354–2500* ⊕ *www.tetonvalley-chamber.com.*

Nearby Towns
 ## Sights

DUBOIS
National Bighorn Sheep Center
NATURE PRESERVE | FAMILY | The local variety is known as the Rocky Mountain bighorn, but you can learn about all kinds of bighorn sheep here. Expect dioramas with full-scale taxidermy mounts that recreate bighorn habitat, as well as interactive exhibits about wildlife management and special adaptations of wild sheep. Reserve ahead for winter wildlife-viewing tours ($100) to Whiskey Mountain. ⊠ *10 Bighorn La., Dubois* ☎ *307/455–3429* ⊕ *www.bighorn.org* ⌨ *$6* ⊙ *Closed Sun. and Mon. late Dec.–Apr.*

JACKSON
Bridger-Teton National Forest
FOREST | This 3.4-million-acre forest has something for everyone: history, hiking, camping, and wildlife. It encompasses the Teton Wilderness east of Grand Teton National Park and south of Yellowstone National Park, the Gros Ventre Wilderness southeast of Jackson, and the Bridger Wilderness farther south and east. No motor vehicles are allowed in the wilderness areas, but between them are many scenic drives, natural springs where you can swim or soak throughout the year, and cultural sights like abandoned lumber camps in the forest. The peaks reach higher than 13,000 feet, and the area is liberally sprinkled with more than a thousand high-mountain lakes, where fishing is generally excellent. ⊠ *Forest headquarters, 340 N. Cache St., Jackson* ☎ *307/739–5500* ⊕ *www.fs.fed.us/r4/btnf* ⌨ *Free.*

Jackson Hole Historical Society & Museum
MUSEUM | FAMILY | At this museum open year-round you can learn about historic homesteaders, dude ranches, and hunters, as well as Jackson's all-female town government of yore—a woman sheriff of that era claimed to have killed

Granite Hot Springs

Soothing thermal baths in pristine outback country await in the heart of the Bridger-Teton National Forest, just a short drive south of Jackson. At Hoback Junction, about 11 miles south of Jackson, head east (toward Pinedale) on U.S. Highway 189/191 and follow the Hoback River through its beautiful canyon. A tributary canyon 10 miles east of the junction is followed by a well-maintained and -marked gravel road to Granite Hot Springs (☎ 307/690–6323), in the Bridger-Teton National Forest. Drive 9 miles off U.S. 189/191 (northeast) on Granite Creek Road to reach the hot springs. The thermal bath at the end of the road, from 93°F to 112°F, is pure bliss, but it's closed from November through early December and from April to late May. The cost is $8 per person, cash or check only. Call for hours, which vary by season.

three men before hanging up her spurs. Native American, ranching, and cowboy artifacts are on display. A free app with a self-guided tour of Jackson is available on the museum's website. ⊠ 225 N. Cache St., Jackson ☎ 307/733–2414 ⊕ www.jacksonholehistory.org ☜ $6 ⊗ Closed Sun. and Mon.

National Elk Refuge
NATURE PRESERVE | FAMILY | Wildlife abounds on this 25,000-acre refuge. From late November to March, more than 7,000 elk, many with enormous antler racks, winter here. Elk can be observed from various pull-outs along U.S. 191 or by slowly driving your car on the refuge's winding, unpaved roads. In winter you can take a horse-drawn sleigh ride for the chance to see the elk up close. Among the other animals that make their home here are buffalo, bighorn sheep, and coyotes, as well as trumpeter swans and other waterfowl. In summer, the refuge is light on big game, but you can tour a historic homestead from June to September. From mid-December to early April, sleigh rides operated by Bar T 5 (www.bart5.com) depart several times a day from the Jackson Hole and Greater Yellowstone Visitor Center. Wear warm clothing, including hats, gloves, boots, long johns, and coats. ⊠ 532 N. Cache, Jackson ☎ 307/733–9212 for refuge ⊕ www.fws.gov/refuge/national_elk_refuge ☜ Sleigh rides $23.

★ National Museum of Wildlife Art of the United States
MUSEUM | See an impressive collection of wildlife art—most of it devoted to North American species—in 14 galleries displaying the work of artists that include Georgia O'Keeffe, John James Audubon, John Clymer, Robert Kuhn, and Carl Rungius. A deck looks out on the National Elk Refuge, where you can see wildlife in a natural habitat. An elaborate ¾-mile outdoor sculpture trail includes a monumental herd of bronze bison by Richard Loffler trudging across the butte. ⊠ 2820 Rungius Rd., Jackson ☎ 307/733–5771 ⊕ www.wildlifeart.org ☜ $14 ⊗ Closed Mon. Nov.–Apr.

Town Square
HISTORIC SITE | You can spend an entire day wandering around Jackson's always-bustling Town Square, crisscrossed with walking paths and bedecked with arches woven from thousands of naturally shed elk antlers. Shops and restaurants surround the square, and there's often entertainment going on in the square itself, including a melodramatic "shoot-out" six nights per week in

summer on the northeastern corner. At the southwestern corner you can board a stagecoach for a ride around the area. ✉ *Cache St. and Broadway, Jackson.*

PINEDALE

Museum of the Mountain Man

MUSEUM | **FAMILY** | Fur trappers were the first non-Native Americans to live in these parts year-round, arriving in the early 19th century when the area was the center of the Rocky Mountain fur trade. The museum celebrates that trapper history, with guns, traps, clothing, and beaver pelts from that time period. In the early summer the museum features living-history demonstrations, children's events, and lectures. In July it hosts reenactment of the Green River Rendezvous, when mountain men, Native Americans, and others got together to barter and socialize. ✉ *700 E. Hennick St., Pinedale* ☎ *307/367–4101* 🌐 *www.museumofthemountainman.com* 🎟 *$10* 🕓 *Closed Nov.–May (except by advance appointment).*

Activities

BOATING

The companies that operate in Grand Teton also generally have trips on other area waters. The Snake River outside the park has spectacular white-water stretches. The rafting season runs from late May through August, with the wildest water during June.

GOLF

Jackson Hole Golf and Tennis Club

GOLF | This 18-hole course redesigned by Robert Trent Jones has views of the Teton Range and an eco-friendly and elegant clubhouse. It has been ranked among Wyoming's top courses. ✉ *5000 Spring Gulch Rd., 9 miles north of Jackson on U.S. 89, then 2 miles west at Gros Ventre Junction* ☎ *307/733–3111* 🌐 *www.jhgtc.com* 🎟 *$65–$190* ⛳ *18 holes, 7409 yards, par 72.*

Teton Pines Resort and Country Tennis Club

GOLF | Arnold Palmer and Ed Seay designed this relatively flat 18-hole course near Teton Village. It has views of the Tetons, abundant wildlife, and is certified as an Audubon course. In winter it becomes a well-groomed cross-country ski track with a full-service shop. The restaurant is excellent. ✉ *3450 N. Clubhouse Dr., Wilson* ☎ *307/733–1005, 800/238–2223* 🌐 *www.tetonpines.com* 🎟 *$130–$175 mid-June–mid-Sept.; from $85 in spring and fall* ⛳ *18 holes, 7402 yards, par 72.*

WINTER ACTIVITIES

Jackson Hole Mountain Resort

SKIING/SNOWBOARDING | Skiers and snowboarders love Jackson Hole, one of the great skiing experiences in America. There are thousands of routes up and down the mountain, and despite Jackson's reputation not all of them are hellishly steep. Early, regular, and peak season prices vary, and some online discounts are available. In the summer, a mountain-bike park takes advantage of the legendary terrain. **Facilities:** 133 trails; 2,500 acres; 4,139-foot vertical drop; 15 lifts. ✉ *Jackson* ☎ *307/733–2292* 🌐 *www.jacksonhole.com* 🎟 *Lift ticket regular season: from $88.*

Performing Arts

★ **Bar J Chuckwagon**

$$$$ | **BARBECUE** | **FAMILY** | This may be the best value in Jackson Hole: you get a complete ranch-style meal plus a rollicking Western show. Served on a tin plate, the food is barbecue beef, chicken, pork ribs, or rib-eye steak with potatoes, beans, biscuits, applesauce, and spice cake, along with lemonade or coffee. [$] *Average main: $31* ✉ *4200 W Bar J Chuckwagon, Wilson* ✥ *Off Moose-Wilson Rd., 1 mile north of Hwy. 22* ☎ *307/733–3370* 🌐 *www.barjchuckwagon.com* 🕓 *Closed Oct.–late May.*

Shopping

ART GALLERIES

Tayloe Piggott Gallery

ART GALLERIES—ARTS | A hot spot for contemporary work, this gallery downplays wildlife and landscape art in favor of hip and bright painting, sculpture, and jewelry. It's a bit of SoHo nestled in the Rockies. ✉ *62 S. Glenwood St., Jackson* ☎ *307/733–0555* 🌐 *www.tayloepiggott-gallery.com* ☞ *Closed Sun.*

Trailside Galleries

ART GALLERIES—ARTS | This gallery's grand selection of traditional Western art includes paintings by the biggest names—Charles M. Russell, John Clymer, and Howard Terpning among them—along with works by talented contemporary artists such as Z.S. Liang, Nancy Glazier, and Morgan Weistling. ✉ *130 E. Broadway St., Jackson* ☎ *307/733–3186* 🌐 *www.trailsidegalleries.com.*

Under the Willow Photo Gallery

ART GALLERIES—ARTS | Abi Garaman has been capturing images of Jackson Hole and Grand Teton National Park on film for more than 50 years. The gallery displays many of his photographs of wildlife, mountains, barns, and other subjects. ✉ *50 S. Cache St., Jackson* ☎ *307/733–6633* 🌐 *www.underthewillow.com.*

★ Wild by Nature Gallery

ART GALLERIES—ARTS | At this bright gallery you'll find wildlife and landscape photography by Henry H. Holdsworth, plus books, note cards, and gifts. Several coffee-table books contain striking Tetons imagery. Wild by Nature offers photography workshops year-round, as well as multiday photo tours in the Greater Yellowstone area alongside the artist himself. ✉ *95 W. Deloney Ave., Jackson* ☎ *307/733–8877* 🌐 *www.wildbynature-gallery.com.*

CLOTHING

Cowboy Shop

CLOTHING | From silk scarves to big shiny buckles, if cowboys wear it, here's the place to get it. Western-style clothing includes hats, boots, and leather goods. This is also a good spot for housewares and souvenirs. ✉ *129 W. Pine St., Pinedale* ☎ *307/367–4300* 🌐 *www.cowboyshop.com* 🕓 *Closed Sun. Oct.–mid-May.*

Hide Out Leathers

CLOTHING | Men's and women's clothing and accessories are the main finds here, including cowboy hats, belts, and deerskin jackets. Regionally made handbags and bison briefcases are other popular purchases. ✉ *40 Center St., Jackson* ✥ *Across Cowboy St.* ☎ *307/733–2422* 🌐 *www.hideoutleathers.com.*

JD High Country Outfitters

SPORTING GOODS | Stocked with the best in outdoor equipment for winter and summer, the shop carries everything from backpacks to skis and hunting rifles, as well as clothing and other supplies. Fishing gear can be rented. ✉ *50 E. Broadway, Jackson* ☎ *307/733–3270* 🌐 *www.jdhcoutfitters.com.*

Restaurants

IN THE PARK

The Cafe Court Pizzeria

$ | AMERICAN | FAMILY | Quick and cheap is the name of the game at this no-frills cafeteria at Colter Bay Village. The menu features pizzas, salads, and toasted subs. **Known for:** big, simple meals to eat in or take out; pizza offered by the slice or whole pie; closes later than fine-dining options. [$] *Average main: $10* ✉ *5 miles north of Jackson Lake Lodge* ☎ *307/543–2811* 🌐 *www.gtlc.com/dining* 🕓 *Closed early Sept.–early June.*

Dornan's Chuck Wagon

$$ | AMERICAN | FAMILY | Hearty portions of beef, beans, potatoes and short ribs, stew, and lemonade or hot coffee are

the dinner standbys at this favorite with locals and families. You can eat your chuck-wagon meal inside the restaurant's teepee if it happens to be raining or windy; otherwise, sit at outdoor picnic tables with views of the Snake River and the Tetons. **Known for:** barbecue cooked over wood fires; good prices, especially for breakfast and lunch; popular with families. $ *Average main: $20* ⊠ *10 Moose Rd., off Teton Park Rd.* ☎ *307/733-2415* ⊕ *www.dornans.com* ☉ *Closed mid-Oct.–mid-June.*

Dornan's Pizza & Pasta Company

$$ | PIZZA | Tasty Italian fare is the draw here, but you'll also find generous margaritas, a diverse wine list, and occasional live music. Place your order at the front counter, then head to a table inside, on the side deck, or upstairs on the roof, which has stunning mountain views. **Known for:** good prices on food and drinks; fast, friendly service; popular with locals and visitors alike. $ *Average main: $14* ⊠ *10 Moose Rd., off Teton Park Rd.* ☎ *307/733-2415* ⊕ *www.dornans.com.*

Jackson Lake Lodge Mural Room

$$$$ | AMERICAN | One of the park's best restaurants gets its name from a 700-square-foot mural painted by the Western artist Carl Roters that details a Wyoming mountain man rendezvous. Select from a menu that features local beef and wild game, as well as sustainable seafood. **Known for:** sumptuous mountain views; upscale lunches, dinners, and buffet breakfasts; regional favorites like bison, elk, and trout. $ *Average main: $34* ⊠ *U.S. 89/191/287, ½ mile north of Jackson Lake Junction* ☎ *307/543-3463, 800/628-9988* ⊕ *www.gtlc.com/dining* ☉ *Closed early Oct.–mid-May.*

Jenny Lake Lodge Dining Room

$$$$ | AMERICAN | Elegant yet rustic, Grand Teton's finest dining space is extremely ambitious for a national park restaurant. For dinner, the prix-fixe, five-course menu features locally sourced ingredients and

an inventive, thoughtfully assembled wine list. **Known for:** jackets encouraged for men and reservations a must; regional meats and fish, like bison, bass, and duck; lovely mountain views. $ *Average main: $94* ⊠ *Jenny Lake Rd., 2 miles off Teton Park Rd., 12 miles north of Moose Junction* ☎ *307/733-4647, 800/628-9988* ⊕ *www.gtlc.com/dining* ☉ *Closed early Oct.–late May.*

Peaks Restaurant

$$$ | AMERICAN | At Signal Mountain Lodge, this casual Western-style bistro offers up delectable fish and meat dishes, as well as views of Jackson Lake and the Tetons. The Trapper Grill next door also serves lunch, and in the adjacent Deadman's Bar, the mountain of nachos and huckleberry margaritas are crowd favorites. **Known for:** regional, and sometimes local, ingredients; seasonal menu; high-end dining at reasonable prices. $ *Average main: $27* ⊠ *Teton Park Rd., 4 miles south of Jackson Lake Junction* ☎ *307/543-2831* ⊕ *www.signalmountainlodge.com* ☉ *Closed mid-Oct.–mid-May.*

Pioneer Grill at Jackson Lake Lodge

$$ | AMERICAN | With an old-fashioned soda fountain, friendly service, and seats along a winding counter, this eatery recalls a 1950s-era luncheonette. Tuck into burgers, sundaes, and other classic American fare. **Known for:** quick, reasonably priced breakfast, lunch, and dinner; seating is along a 200-foot-long counter; huckleberry pancakes and milkshakes. $ *Average main: $14* ⊠ *U.S. 89/191/287, ½ mile north of Jackson Lake Junction* ☎ *307/543-2811* ⊕ *www.gtlc.com/dining* ☉ *Closed early Oct.–mid-May.*

Ranch House at Colter Bay Village

$$$ | AMERICAN | The casual Ranch House offers friendly service and moderate prices, making it a good choice for travelers on a budget or families who can't take another cafeteria meal. Western-style meals—thick steaks, barbecue ribs, rotisserie chicken—dominate the menu. **Known for:** traditional barbecue fare, using

local beef; hearty helpings of pasta; options for gluten-free, vegetarian, and vegan diners. $ *Average main: $22* ⊠ *2 miles off U.S. 89/191/287, 5 miles north of Jackson Lake Junction, Colter Bay* ☎ *307/543–2811* ⊕ *www.gtlc.com/dining* ⊗ *Closed late Sept.–late May.*

PICNIC AREAS

The park has 11 designated picnic areas, each with tables and grills, and most with pit toilets and water pumps or faucets. In addition to those listed here you can find picnic areas at Colter Bay Village Campground, Cottonwood Creek, the east shore of Jackson Lake, and South Jenny Lake and String Lake trailhead.

Chapel of the Sacred Heart

CITY PARK | From this intimate lakeside picnic area you can look across southern Jackson Lake to Mount Moran. ⊠ *Grand Teton National Park* ✛ *¼ mile east of Signal Mountain Lodge, off Teton Park Rd.*

Colter Bay

CITY PARK | This big picnic area, spectacularly located right on the beach at Jackson Lake, gets crowded in July and August. It's close to flush toilets and stores. ⊠ *Grand Teton National Park* ✛ *2 miles off U.S. 89/191/287, 5 miles north of Jackson Lake Junction.*

Jenny Lake

NATIONAL/STATE PARK | Shaded and pine-scented, this picnic site adjacent to the Jenny Lake shuttle boat dock is a good place to have lunch before heading across the lake for the ½-mile hike to Hidden Falls. ⊠ *Grand Teton National Park* ✛ *Near Jenny Lake Visitor Center.*

OUTSIDE THE PARK

The Bunnery Bakery & Restaurant

$ | AMERICAN | Lunch is served year-round and dinner is served in summer, but it's the breakfasts and home-baked pastries that are irresistible here. It's elbow to elbow inside, so you may have to wait to be seated on busy mornings, but any inconvenience is well worth it. **Known for:** incredible baked treats like muffins and danishes; OSM Oatmeal Pancakes with oats sunflower seeds and millet; house-made granola. $ *Average main: $11* ⊠ *Hole-in-the-Wall Mall, 130 N. Cache St., Jackson* ☎ *307/733–5474* ⊕ *www.bunnery.com.*

Il Villaggio Osteria

$$$ | MODERN ITALIAN | Underneath rustic barnwood timbers and columns or on an open-air patio, diners enjoy the flavors of Italy fused with fresh, inventive touches. Try the bone-marrow bruschetta, house-pulled mozzarella figs stuffed with blue cheese, or a generous slice of gooey lasagna. **Known for:** artisan pizza and pasta; hand-crafted cocktails; warm and cozy atmosphere. $ *Average main: $27* ⊠ *3335 W. Village Dr., Teton Village* ☎ *307/739–4100* ⊕ *www.jhosteria.com* ⊗ *No lunch.*

Lift Jackson Hole

$$$ | AMERICAN | Off the beaten path with one of Jackson's best views, this mountain-chic restaurant serves heaping portions of updated pub-style food. From the upper deck you can take in Snow King Mountain vistas, and in winter the après-ski crowd assembles around the stone fireplace to rewarm and refuel. **Known for:** craft beer; higher-end comfort food; rightly popular Jackson Hole Buffalo Burger. $ *Average main: $22* ⊠ *645 S. Cache St., at base of Snow King Resort, Jackson* ☎ *307/733–5438* ⊕ *liftjacksonhole.com* ⊗ *Closed 1st 3 wks in Apr. and 1 wk in late Nov. (Thanksgiving).*

Pica's Taqueria

$ | MEXICAN | FAMILY | A locals favorite a mile from the bustle of Town Square, Pica's serves authentic Mexican dishes at an affordable price. Bright, colorful folk art surrounds the basic counters and tables, and the sunny patio tables are dog-friendly in the summer. **Known for:** strong margaritas; Mexican staples, like fish tacos and wet burritos; a favorite with locals. $ *Average main: $11* ⊠ *1160 Alpine La., Jackson* ☎ *307/734–4457* ⊕ *www.picastaqueria.com.*

★ Snake River Grill

$$$$ | **AMERICAN** | One of Jackson's best restaurants, this sophisticated dining room serves creatively prepared dishes using meats and fish loved across the West. The menu changes seasonally, reflecting what's available in the market, and the extensive wine list seems to pick up another award every year or so. **Known for:** high-end taste of the region; dishes showcase elk, buffalo, venison, and other local favorites. [$] *Average main: $38* ✉ *84 E. Broadway Ave., Jackson* ☎ *307/733–0557* 🌐 *www.snakerivergrill.com* ⏲ *Closed Apr. and Nov. No lunch.*

★ Teton Thai

$$ | **THAI** | By the Ranch Lot at the base of Jackson Hole Mountain Resort, the restaurant is owned by people of Thai heritage, and the cuisine reflects it. The pad thai is the state's finest, and there's a full bar. **Known for:** large portions; updated versions of Thai favorites like curry and pad see ew; lots of spice, though you can request mild. [$] *Average main: $19* ✉ *7342 Granite Loop Rd., Teton Village* ☎ *307/733–0022* 🌐 *www.tetonthai.com* ⏲ *Closed Sun.*

Hotels

IN THE PARK

Colter Bay Village

$$$ | **HOTEL** | Near Jackson Lake, this cluster of Western-style cabins—some with one room, others with two—is within walking distance of the lake. **Pros:** prices are good for what you get; many nearby facilities; close to lake and hiking trails. **Cons:** little sense of privacy; not all cabins have bathrooms; rustic feel won't appeal to everyone. [$] *Rooms from: $179* ✉ *Colter Bay* ✣ *2 miles off U.S. 89/191/287, 10 miles north of Jackson Lake Junction* ☎ *307/543–3100, 800/628–9988* 🌐 *www.gtlc.com/lodges* ⏲ *Closed early Oct.–mid-May* 🛏 *232 cabins* 🍴 *No meals.*

Dornan's Spur Ranch Cabins

$$$$ | **B&B/INN** | Part of Dornan's shopping, dining, and recreation development at Moose, each of these one- and two-bedroom cabins has a great view of meadows, the tops of the Tetons, or the Snake River. **Pros:** cabins are simple but clean; good spot for families and groups; wildlife wander by. **Cons:** not much privacy; rustic interiors not for everyone; no fireplaces. [$] *Rooms from: $275* ✉ *12170 Dornan Rd., off Teton Park Rd. at Moose Junction, Moose* ☎ *307/733–2522* 🌐 *www.dornans.com* ⏲ *Closed Nov. and Apr.* 🛏 *12 cabins* 🍴 *No meals.*

Jackson Lake Lodge

$$$$ | **HOTEL** | This sprawling resort stands on a bluff with spectacular views across Jackson Lake to the Tetons. **Pros:** central location for visiting Grand Teton and Yellowstone; heated outdoor pool; great dining options. **Cons:** rooms without views are pricey for what you get; the hotel hosts many large meetings; limited Wi-Fi. [$] *Rooms from: $330* ✉ *U.S. 89/191/287, ½ mile north of Jackson Lake Junction* ☎ *307/543–3100, 800/628–9988* 🌐 *www.gtlc.com/lodges* ⏲ *Closed early Oct.–mid-May* 🛏 *385 rooms* 🍴 *No meals.*

★ Jenny Lake Lodge

$$$$ | **RESORT** | This lodge, the most expensive and arguably the most elegant in any national park, has been serving travelers since the 1920s. **Pros:** maximum comfort in a pristine setting; perhaps the best hotel in the national park system; homey touches, like furniture and quilts made by hand. **Cons:** very expensive; not suitable for kids under 17; standard rates don't include the lodge's popular activities or meals. [$] *Rooms from: $530* ✉ *Jenny Lake Rd., 2 miles off Teton Park Rd., 12 miles north of Moose Junction* ☎ *307/733–4647, 800/628–9988* 🌐 *www.gtlc.com/lodges* ⏲ *Closed early Oct.–late May* 🛏 *37 cabins* 🍴 *No meals.*

Signal Mountain Lodge

$$$$ | **HOTEL** | The main building of this lodge on Jackson Lake's southern

shoreline has a cozy lounge and a grand pine deck overlooking the lake; stay in a traditional lodge room or a rustic cabin, some with sleek kitchens. **Pros:** popular restaurants and bar; on-site gas station; pets allowed. **Cons:** rustic, motel-like rooms; not all rooms have great views; no TVs or air conditioning, like most area lodges. [$] *Rooms from: $218* ✉ *1 Inner Park Rd.,* ✣ *Teton Park Rd., 3 miles south of Jackson Lake Junction* ☎ *307/543–2831* 🌐 *www.signalmountainlodge.com* ⏲ *Closed mid-Oct.–mid-May* 🛏 *79 rooms* 🍴 *No meals.*

OUTSIDE THE PARK

Alpenhof Lodge

$$$$ | **HOTEL** | With more atmosphere than anywhere else in Teton Village, this Austrian-style hotel sits next to the tram in the heart of Jackson Hole Mountain Resort. **Pros:** quaint feel; great location near slopes; pet-friendly. **Cons:** some rooms are small; dated fixtures and flooring; Austrian-style interiors don't appeal to all travelers. [$] *Rooms from: $219* ✉ *3255 West Village Dr., Teton Village* ☎ *307/733–3242, 800/732–3244* 🌐 *www.alpenhoflodge.com* ⏲ *Hotel closed early Apr.–mid-May; restaurants closed mid-Oct.–Thanksgiving* 🛏 *42 rooms* 🍴 *Breakfast.*

Amangani

$$$$ | **RESORT** | This exclusive resort built of sandstone and redwood blends into the landscape of Gros Ventre Butte, affording beautiful views of the Snake River Range from its cliff-top location. **Pros:** extremely luxurious; impeccable service; extensive amenities. **Cons:** high prices; though the views are wonderful, few rooms can see the Tetons; small gym and spa. [$] *Rooms from: $1295* ✉ *1535 N.E. Butte Rd., Jackson* ☎ *307/734–7333* 🌐 *www.aman.com* 🛏 *40 suites* 🍴 *No meals* ☞ *Rates dependent on season.*

Antler Inn

$$$$ | **HOTEL** | **FAMILY** | No motel in Jackson has a better location than this old-school lodging, a block south of Town Square. **Pros:** restaurants nearby; family-run; good prices in the off-season. **Cons:** frequently booked-up in summer; dated interiors; motel vibe won't appeal to all visitors. [$] *Rooms from: $220* ✉ *43 W. Pearl St., Jackson* ☎ *307/733–2535* 🌐 *www.townsquareinns.com* 🛏 *106 rooms* 🍴 *No meals.*

Hotel Terra Jackson Hole

$$$$ | **HOTEL** | The opulent Hotel Terra takes green hospitality to the next level, but it's also luxe to the core, with a hip, urban feel and all the amenities the price tag suggests. **Pros:** expert staff; delicious restaurant; organic spa. **Cons:** not for budget-conscious; in a crowded corner of Teton Village; a (short) walk to ski slopes. [$] *Rooms from: $399* ✉ *3335 W. Village Dr.* ✣ *West of Mangy Moose* ☎ *307/201–6065* 🌐 *www.hotelterrajacksonhole.com* 🛏 *132 rooms* 🍴 *No meals.*

The Lexington at Jackson Hole

$$$$ | **HOTEL** | Within walking distance of Town Square, this lodging features modern furnishings and lots of light. **Pros:** walking distance to downtown hot spots; small pool and Jacuzzi; friendly and helpful staff. **Cons:** limited views; must drive to mountains; hotel-motel vibe instead of lodge feel. [$] *Rooms from: $299* ✉ *285 N. Cache St., Jackson* ☎ *307/733–2648* 🌐 *www.lexingtonhoteljacksonhole.com* 🛏 *89 rooms* 🍴 *Breakfast.*

R Lazy S Ranch

$$$$ | **RESORT** | **FAMILY** | Jackson Hole, with the spectacle of the Tetons in the background, is true dude-ranch country, and the R Lazy S is one of the finest in the area. **Pros:** authentic all-inclusive dude ranch experience; very popular with kids (7 and older); beautiful setting. **Cons:** no TV; cell service is poor; week minimum stay. [$] *Rooms from: $266* ✉ *7800 Moose-Wilson Rd., Teton Village* ✣ *1 mile north of Teton Village, off Moose-Wilson Rd.* ☎ *307/733–2655* 🌐 *www.rlazys.com* ⏲ *Closed Oct.–mid-June* 🛏 *14 cabins* 🍴 *All meals* ☞ *1-week minimum stay.*

Best Campgrounds in Grand Teton

You'll find a variety of campgrounds, from small areas where only tents are allowed to full RV parks with all services. If you don't have a tent but want to bring your sleeping bags, you can take advantage of the tent cabins at Colter Bay, where you have a hard floor, cots, and canvas walls for shelter. Standard campsites include a place to pitch your tent or park your trailer/camper, a fire pit for cooking, and a picnic table. All developed campgrounds have toilets and water; plan to bring your own firewood. Check in at National Park Service campsites as early as possible—sites are assigned on a first-come, first-served basis.

Developed Sites

Colter Bay Campground. Busy, noisy, and filled by noon, this centrally located campground has tent and trailer or RV sites. ⊠ *2 miles off U.S. 89/191/287, 5 miles north of Jackson Lake Junction, Colter Bay* ☎ *307/543–3100, 800/628–9988.*

Flagg Ranch. In a shady pine grove overlooking the headwaters of the Snake River, these sites provide a great base for exploring Grand Teton or Yellowstone. The showers and laundry facilities are a bonus, and camper cabins are available. ⊠ *U.S. 89/191/287, 20 miles north of Jackson Lake Junction* ☎ *307/543–2861, 800/443–2311.*

Gros Ventre. The park's biggest campground is set in an open, grassy area on the bank of the Gros Ventre River, away from the mountains but not far from the town of Kelly. ⊠ *4½ miles off U.S. 26/89/191, 2½ miles west of Kelly on Gros Ventre Rd., 6 miles south of Moose Junction* ☎ *307/543–3100, 800/628–9988.*

Jenny Lake. Wooded sites and Teton views make this tent-only spot the most desirable campground in the park, and it fills early. ⊠ *Jenny Lake, ½ mile off Teton Park Rd., 8 miles north of Moose Junction* ☎ *307/543–3100, 800/628–9988.*

Lizard Creek. Views of Jackson Lake, wooded sites, and the relative isolation of this campground make it a relaxing choice. ⊠ *U.S. 89/191/287, 13 miles north of Jackson Lake Junction* ☎ *307/543–2831, 800/672–6012.*

Signal Mountain. This campground in a hilly setting on Jackson Lake has boat access to the lake. ⊠ *Teton Park Rd., 3 miles south of Jackson Lake Junction* ☎ *307/543–2831, 800/672–6012.*

Backcountry Permits

You can reserve a backcountry campsite between January 5 and mid-May for a $25 nonrefundable fee using the online reservation system. Two-thirds of all sites are set aside for in-person, day-before permits, so you can also take a chance that the site you want will be open when you arrive. In that case you pay no fee at all, but a trip to Craig Thomas Visitor and Discovery Center or Jenny Lake Ranger Station is still required for a permit and mandatory bear-proof food storage canister. The Jackson Hole Mountain Resort tram provides quick access to the park's backcountry, which can also be reached on foot from various trailheads. ☎ *307/739–3443* ⊕ *www.nps.gov/grte/planyourvisit/bcres.htm.*

Rusty Parrot Lodge & Spa

$$$$ | **HOTEL** | In the heart of Jackson, this small timber inn feels both luxurious and homey, and has the kind of attentive customer service you'd expect from a large resort. **Pros:** family-run; intimate restaurant; great outdoor space with hot tub, fire pits, and sundeck. **Cons:** not geared toward families; limited views; high-end means high prices. [$] *Rooms from: $540* ✉ *175 N. Jackson St., Jackson* ☎ *307/733–2000* 🌐 *www.rustyparrot.com* 🛏 *32 rooms* 🍴 *No meals.*

Snake River Lodge & Spa

$$$$ | **HOTEL** | Anchored by an expansive four-level spa, Snake River combines the best elements of a genteel resort and a large lodge that feels both high-end and folksy. **Pros:** cool public spaces; vast spa menu; great mountain-side location. **Cons:** labyrinthine hallways; most rooms have no real view; like many area lodges, charges a resort fee. [$] *Rooms from: $359* ✉ *7710 Granite Loop Rd., Teton Village* ☎ *307/732–6000, 855/342–4712* 🌐 *www.snakeriverlodge.com* 🕒 *Closed Oct.–mid-Nov. and Apr.–mid-May* 🛏 *146 rooms* 🍴 *No meals.*

Snow King Resort at Jackson Hole

$$$$ | **HOTEL** | At the base of Snow King Mountain and eight blocks from Town Square, this hotel with a modern Western feel has a popular restaurant, a cycling and ski shop, and outdoor fire pits near the beautiful pool. **Pros:** central location; ski-in, ski-out; cycling and ski shop. **Cons:** large groups often dominate the property; somewhat expensive; relatively high daily resort fee. [$] *Rooms from: $295* ✉ *Snow King Resort, 400 E. Snow King Ave., Jackson* ☎ *307/733–5200* 🌐 *www.snowking.com* 🛏 *201 rooms* 🍴 *No meals.*

★ **The Wildflower Lodge At Jackson Hole**

$$$$ | **B&B/INN** | You'll enjoy gourmet breakfasts and an afternoon beverage and snack at this country inn that's surrounded by 3 acres of aspen and pine trees frequented by moose, deer, and other wildlife. **Pros:** excellent views; frequent wildlife sightings; clean and comfortable. **Cons:** books out far in advance; 12 miles from Jackson; high prices to match extreme luxury. [$] *Rooms from: $360* ✉ *3725 Shooting Star La., Jackson* ✣ *Off Moose-Wilson Rd.* ☎ *307/222–4400* 🌐 *www.jhwildflowerlodge.com* 🛏 *5 rooms* 🍴 *Breakfast.*

★ **The Wort Hotel**

$$$$ | **HOTEL** | Built in 1941, this brick Victorian hotel a block from Town Square seems to have been around as long as the Tetons, but its inviting rooms feel up-to-date and feature woodsy, Western-style furnishings made locally. **Pros:** charming old building with lots of history; convenient downtown location; some good package deals, especially in winter/shoulder seasons. **Cons:** limited views; must drive to parks and mountains; in-room air conditioner can be noisy. [$] *Rooms from: $439* ✉ *50 N. Glenwood St., Jackson* ☎ *307/733–2190* 🌐 *www.worthotel.com* 🛏 *55 rooms* 🍴 *No meals.*

Chapter 18

GREAT BASIN
NATIONAL PARK

Updated by
Stina Sieg

NEVADA

WELCOME TO GREAT BASIN NATIONAL PARK

TOP REASONS TO GO

★ **Ancient tree spottings:** The twisting, windswept bristlecone pines in Great Basin are thousands of years old.

★ **Desert skyscraper:** Wheeler Peak rises out of the vast desert basin with summit temperatures often 20–30 degrees below that of the visitor center.

★ **Rare shields:** Look for hundreds of these unique disk-shape formations inside Lehman Caves.

★ **Gather your pine nuts while you may:** Come in the fall and go a little nutty, as you can gather up to three gunnysacks of pinyon pine nuts, found in abundance throughout the park. They're great on salads.

★ **Celestial show:** Pitch-dark nights make for dazzling stars. Gaze on your own or attend a seasonal nighttime talk, led by a park ranger.

One of the smallest (77,180 acres) and one of less-visited national parks in the lower 48 states, Great Basin National Park, on the Nevada–Utah border, occupies only a minute fraction of the almost 200,000 square miles of the Great Basin desert—yet it exemplifies the landscape and ecology of the region. The surrounding high desert (4,500–6,200 feet in elevation) is the largest desert in the United States, bordered by the Sierra Nevada range, the Rocky Mountains, the Columbia Plateau, and the Mojave and Sonoran deserts. It covers 75% of the state of Nevada and extends into California, Oregon, Utah, and Idaho.

1 Lehman Caves. Highlighted by the limestone caverns, this is the primary destination of most Great Basin visitors. It's next to a popular visitor center and the start of Wheeler Peak Scenic Drive.

2 Wheeler Peak. This 13,063-footer is the park's centerpiece, and is especially stunning when capped with snow. Hikers can climb the mountain via day-use-only trails, which also lead to three small alpine lakes, a glacier, and some ancient bristlecone pines.

3 Snake Creek Canyon. This is the less crowded part of an already sparsely visited park. Trails follow a handful of creeks around Pyramid Peak, and six primitive campgrounds line Snake Creek. A bristlecone pine grove is nearby, though far off any beaten path.

4 Arch Canyon. A high-clearance, four-wheel-drive vehicle is recommended, and stout boots are critical if you want to get to Lexington Arch, which is unusual in that it is formed of limestone, not sandstone as most arches are. This is a day-use-only area.

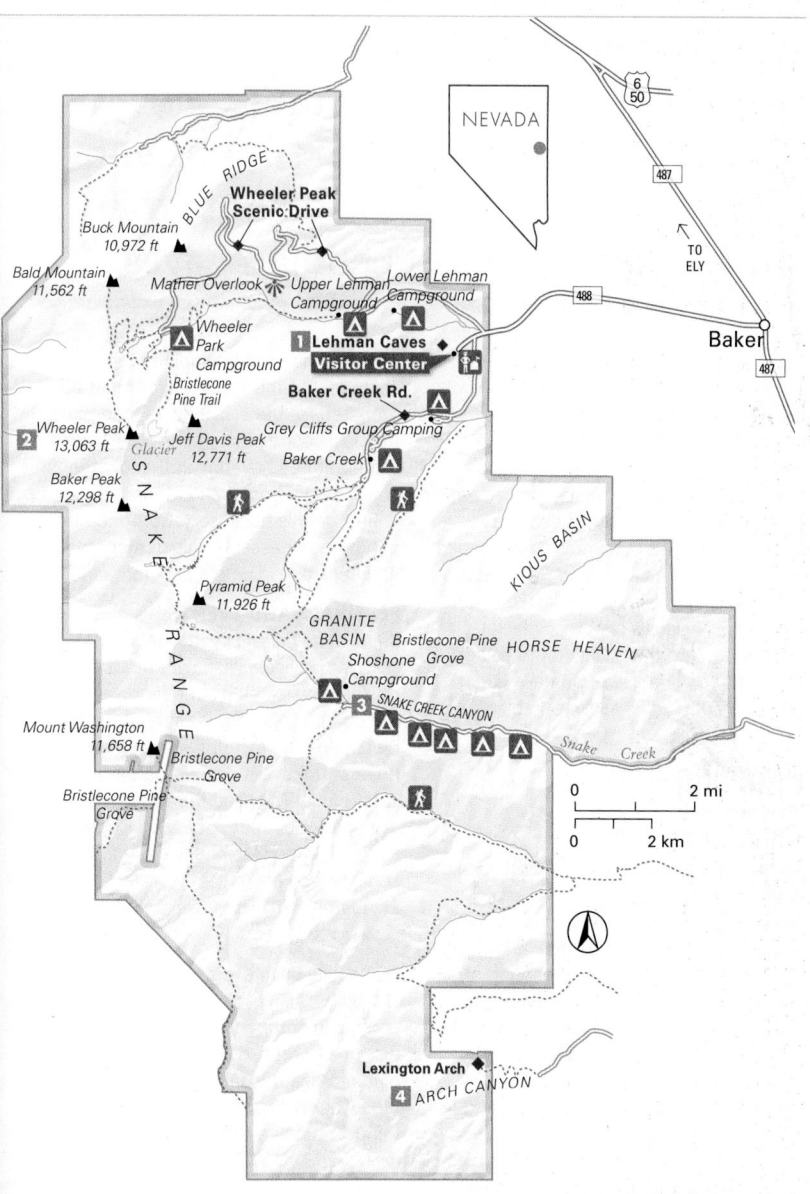

NEVADA

BLUE RIDGE

Buck Mountain
10,972 ft

Bald Mountain
11,562 ft

Wheeler Peak
Scenic Drive

Mather Overlook

Wheeler
Park
Campground

Bristlecone
Pine Trail

Upper Lehman
Campground

Lower Lehman
Campground

1 Lehman Caves
Visitor Center

Baker Creek Rd.

2 Wheeler Peak
13,063 ft

Baker Peak
12,298 ft

Jeff Davis Peak
12,771 ft

Glacier

Grey Cliffs Group Camping

Baker Creek

SNAKE RANGE

Pyramid Peak
11,926 ft

GRANITE
BASIN

Shoshone
Campground

Bristlecone Pine
Grove

HORSE HEAVEN

KIOUS BASIN

3 SNAKE CREEK CANYON

Snake Creek

Mount Washington
11,658 ft

Bristlecone Pine
Grove

Bristlecone Pine
Grove

6
50

487

TO
ELY

488

Baker

487

0   2 mi
0   2 km

Lexington Arch

4 ARCH CANYON

As you drive the straight, desolate road into Great Basin National Park, Wheeler Peak rises up more than 13,000 feet in front of you, as the terrain transitions from dry desert to alpine forest. There's plenty to see, from the ancient, otherworldly bristlecone pines to the surreal formations in Lehman Caves.

No longer a completely undiscovered gem, Great Basin does have a growing number of visitors. Still, its annual visitorship of roughly 170,000 is small compared to, say, the Grand Canyon's 5 million. Even in the high season, it's easy to avoid the crowds. That's especially true on the park's many trails, which take you into lush meadows and up steep mountains, and past alpine lakes, historic ruins, and Nevada's only rock glacier. The farther into the backcountry you go, the more you'll feel like you have Great Basin's 77,000 acres all to yourself.

Planning

WHEN TO GO

As one of the least-visited national parks in the country, Great Basin National Park is never crowded. The small number of visitors ensures that most any time is a fine time to visit this park, though of course much of that number will pass through the entry gates during the warmer months. In summer the high-desert weather here is typically mild, so you'll be comfortable in shorts and T-shirts during the day—though temperatures drop at night, and get colder the higher up you climb, so bring light jackets and pants.

A winter visit can be sublime in its solitude, but the hardy visitor must be prepared for the elements, especially if the backcountry is a destination. With temperatures hovering in the low teens, heavy coats, boots, and other appropriate winter gear is necessary. Some roads might be impassable in inclement weather; check ahead with a park ranger.

FESTIVALS AND EVENTS
Silver State Classic Challenge

FESTIVAL | Twice a year, car enthusiasts of all stripes close a state highway for the country's largest (and most venerable) open-road race for amateur fast-car drivers. The event occurs the third weekend of May and the third weekend of September south of Ely on Route 318, from Lund to Hiko, and is open to just about any four-wheeled vehicle. ⊠ 1139 E. Aultman St., Suite C ☎ 775/289–6900 ⊕ www.sscc.us.

White Pine County Fair

FESTIVAL | FAMILY | Livestock, flower, and vegetable competitions, plus horse races, food booths, dancing, and a barbecue dinner make this fair, held at the White Pine County Fairgrounds in Ely, the real thing. The dates fluctuate every August. ☎ 775/289–4691 ⊕ www.wpcfair.com.

AVERAGE HIGH/LOW TEMPERATURES					
JAN.	FEB.	MAR.	APR.	MAY	JUNE
41/18	44/21	48/24	56/31	66/40	76/48
JULY	AUG.	SEPT.	OCT.	NOV.	DEC.
86/57	83/56	75/47	62/47	49/26	42/20

PLANNING YOUR TIME
GREAT BASIN IN ONE DAY
Start your visit with the 90-minute tour of the fascinating limestone caverns of **Lehman Caves,** the park's most famous attraction (advance reservations heavily encouraged). If you have time before or after the tour, hike the short and family-friendly **Mountain View Nature Trail,** near the Lehman Caves Visitor Center, to get your first taste of the area's pinyon-juniper forests. Stop for lunch at the Lehman Caves Cafe (open mid-April–mid-October) or at least plan on a hand-scooped ice-cream treat—or have a picnic near the visitor center.

In the afternoon, take a leisurely drive up to **Wheeler Peak,** the park's tallest mountain (and the second highest in Nevada) at just over 13,000 feet. You can stop about halfway along your drive to hike the short **Osceola Ditch Trail,** a remnant of the park's gold-mining days, or, alternatively, just enjoy the fantastic views from the two overlooks. If you're feeling energetic when you reach Wheeler Peak, hike into the strange beauty of a bristlecone pine grove on the **Bristlecone Pine Trail.**

GETTING HERE AND AROUND
AIR TRAVEL
The nearest airport is in Cedar City (142 miles) but will likely be pricey. Salt Lake City (234 miles) and Las Vegas (286 miles) are better bets, though you'll probably get the cheapest fares (and might have the most fun) flying into Vegas.

CAR TRAVEL
The entrance to Great Basin is on Route 488, 5 miles west of its junction with Route 487. From Ely, take U.S. 6/50 to Route 487. From Salt Lake City or Cedar City, Utah, take Interstate 15 South to U.S. 6/50 West; from Las Vegas, drive north on Interstate 15 and then north on Route 93 to access U.S. 6/50.

⚠ **Don't rely on GPS to get to the park, as sometimes it sends people up remote dirt roads. The turn-off to the main section of the park is well-marked in the center of Baker.**

In the park, Baker Creek Road and portions of Wheeler Peak Scenic Drive, above Upper Lehman Creek, are closed from November to June. The road to the visitor center and the roads to the developed campgrounds are paved, but two-wheel-drive cars don't do well in winter storms. RVs and trailers over 24 feet aren't allowed above Lower Lehman Creek. With an 8% grade, the road to Wheeler Peak is steep and curvy, but not dangerous if you take it slow. Motorcyclists should watch for gravel on the road's surface.

PARK ESSENTIALS
ACCESSIBILITY
Designated handicap parking spaces are available at both visitor centers. The center itself is all on one level, fully accessible to those with impaired mobility. The park slide show is captioned. At the front desk you can borrow wheelchairs to use in the center and in the first room of Lehman Caves. A cut curb provides access to a table and fire grate at the picnic area near the visitor center, which also has accessible restrooms. Baker Creek Campground, Upper Lehman Creek Campground, and Wheeler Peak Campground are accessible, though the restroom access ramp at Upper Lehman Creek Campground is steep.

PARK FEES AND PERMITS

Admission to the park is free, but if you want to tour Lehman Caves there's a fee ($9–$11, depending on tour length). To fish in Great Basin National Park, those 12 and older need a state fishing license from the Nevada Department of Wildlife (⊕ www.ndow.org). The one-day nonresident license is $18, plus $7 for each additional day at time of purchase. Backcountry hikers do not need permits, but for your own safety you should fill out a form at the visitor center before setting out.

PARK HOURS

The park is open 24/7 year-round; May–August, visitor center hours are 8–5; hours may vary from year to year. It's in the Pacific time zone.

CELL PHONE RECEPTION

There's decent coverage close to Lehman Caves; the more remote you get, the spottier it becomes. The only public phone in the park is at the visitor center.

EDUCATIONAL OFFERINGS
RANGER PROGRAMS
Junior Ranger Program

TOUR—SIGHT | FAMILY | Youngsters answer questions and complete activities related to the park and then are sworn in as Junior Rangers and receive a Great Basin badge. ⊠ Great Basin National Park ☎ 775/234-7331 ⊕ www.nps.gov/grba.

Weekly Astronomy Programs

OBSERVATORY | FAMILY | You'll find some of the country's darkest skies—and brightest stars—at Great Basin. Expect to be dazzled, especially on moonless nights, as you get a chance to see the wild blue yonder through a telescope at these ranger-led events. Expect crowds, especially during the summer, when the program is held several times a week. It drops down to once a week in shoulder seasons. ⊠ Lehman Caves Visitor Center, Baker ۩ Closed Nov.–Mar.

RESTAURANTS

Dining in the park itself is limited to basic but tasty breakfast and lunch fare at the Lehman Caves Cafe and Gift Shop. Nearby, Baker, a town of less than 100 people, has a few good options. Fire grates are available at each campsite in the park's four developed campgrounds for the barbecue fare.

HOTELS

There is no lodging in the park, so unless you're willing and able to snag one of the park's first-come, first-served campsites, or expect to camp in the backcountry, plan on lodging in nearby Baker or in Ely. *Hotel reviews have been shortened. For full information, visit Fodors.com.*

What It Costs			
$	$$	$$$	$$$$
RESTAURANTS			
under $13	$13–$20	$21–$30	over $30
HOTELS			
under $101	$101–$150	$151–$200	over $200

VISITOR INFORMATION

PARK CONTACT INFORMATION Great Basin National Park ⊠ Rte. 488, Baker ☎ 775/234-7331 ⊕ www.nps.gov/grba

VISITOR CENTERS
Great Basin Visitor Center

INFO CENTER | Here you can see exhibits on the flora, fauna, and geology of the park, or ask a ranger to suggest a favorite hike. Books, videos, and souvenirs are for sale; water is available, but for snacks continue up the road to the Lehman Caves Visitor Center. ⊠ Rte. 487, just north of Baker ☎ 775/234-7520 ۩ Closed Oct.–late Apr.

Lehman Caves Visitor Center

INFO CENTER | Regularly scheduled cave tours lasting 60 or 90 minutes depart from here. Mountain View Nature Trail encircles the visitor center and includes

Lehman Caves: It's amazing what a little water and air can do to a room.

Rhodes Cabin and the historic cave entrance. The park is also planning on adding a walk-through replica of its famed caves to this center. Buy gifts for friends and family back home at the bookstore, or just take in the view with a glass of wine at the adjacent café. ✉ *Rte. 488, ½ mile inside park boundary* ☎ *775/234-7331.*

⊙ Sights

SCENIC DRIVES
Baker Creek Road
SCENIC DRIVE | Though less popular than the Wheeler Peak Scenic Drive, this gravel road affords gorgeous views of Wheeler Peak, the Baker Creek Drainage, and Snake Valley. Beautiful wildflowers are an extra treat in spring and early summer. The road is closed in the winter, and there are no pull-outs or scenic overlooks. ✉ *½ mile inside park boundary off Rte. 488* ☾ *Closed Nov.–May.*

★ Wheeler Peak Scenic Drive
SCENIC DRIVE | This is a must for any Great Basin trip. Less than a mile from the visitor center off Route 488, turn onto this paved road that winds its way up to elevations of 10,000 feet. You'll go past pinyon-juniper forest in lower elevations; as you climb, the air cools as much as 20–30 degrees. Along the way, pull off at overlooks for awe-inspiring glimpses of the peaks of the South Snake Range. A short hiking trail leads to views of the Osceola mining site. Turn off at Mather Overlook, elevation 9,000 feet, for the best photo ops. Wheeler Overlook is the best place to see Wheeler Peak, as well as fall colors. Allow 1½ hours for the 24-mile round-trip, not including hikes. ✉ *Just inside park boundary, off Rte. 488 about 5 miles west of Baker, Baker* ⊕ *www.nps.gov/grba/planyourvisit/ wheeler-peak-scenic-drive.htm* ☾ *Closed Nov.–June.*

Plants and Wildlife in Great Basin

Despite the cold, dry conditions in Great Basin, 925 plant species thrive; 13 are considered sensitive species. The region gets less than 10 inches of rain a year, so plants have developed some ingenious methods of dealing with the desert's harshness. For instance, many flowering plants will only grow and produce seeds in a year when there is enough water. Spruces, pines, and junipers have set down roots here, and the bristlecone pine has been doing so for thousands of years.

The park's plants provide a variety of habitats for animals and for more than 230 bird species. In the sagebrush are jackrabbits, ground squirrels, chipmunks, and pronghorn. Mule deer and striped skunks abound in the pygmy forest of pinyon pine and juniper trees. Shrews, ringtail cats, and weasels make their homes around the springs and streams. Mountain lions, bobcats, and sheep live on the rugged slopes and in valleys. The park is also home to coyotes, kit fox, and badgers. Treat the Great Basin rattlesnake with respect. Bites are uncommon and rarely fatal, but if you're bitten, remain calm and call 911.

SCENIC STOPS

★ Lehman Caves

CAVE | FAMILY | In 1885, rancher and miner Absalom Lehman discovered this underground wonder—a single limestone and marble cavern 2½ miles long. Inside, stalactites, stalagmites, helictites, flowstone, popcorn, and other bizarre mineral formations cover almost every surface. Lehman Caves is one of the best places to see rare shield formations, created when calcite-rich water is forced from tiny cracks in a cave wall, ceiling, or floor. Year-round the cave maintains a constant, damp temperature of 50°F, so wear a light jacket and nonskid shoes. Go for the full 90-minute tour if you have time; during summer, it's offered four or five times per day, as is the 60-minute tour. Expect daily tours during the winter. Children under age five are not allowed on the 90-minute tours, except during the winter; those under 16 must be accompanied by an adult. Take the 0.3-mile Mountain View Nature Trail beforehand to see the original cave entrance and **Rhodes Cabin,** where black-and-white photographs of the park's earlier days line the walls. **Get tickets as far in advance as possible at recreation.gov. Tours can sell out quickly.** ✉ *Lehman Caves Visitor Center* ☎ *775/234–7331* 🎟 *From $9.*

🏃 Activities

Great Basin National Park is a great place for experienced outdoor adventurers. The closest outdoor store is an hour away in Ely, so bring everything you might need, and be prepared to go it alone. Permits are not required to go off the beaten path, but if you're planning a multiday hike, register with a ranger just in case. The effort is worth it, as the backcountry is pristine and not at all crowded, no matter the time of year. As is the case in all national parks, bicycling is restricted to existing roads, which can get busy with cars, especially Wheeler Peak Scenic Drive. Always be cautious, and consider biking on less popular roads.

BIRD-WATCHING

An impressive list of bird species have been sighted here—238, according to the National Park Service checklist. Some, such as the common raven and American robin, can be seen at most locations. Others, such as the red-naped sapsucker, are more commonly seen near Lehman Creek. In the higher elevations, listen for the loud shriek of Clark's nutcracker, storing nuts.

CROSS-COUNTRY SKIING
Lehman Creek Trail
SKIING/SNOWBOARDING | In summer, descend 2,050 feet by hiking Lehman Creek Trail one-way (downhill) from Wheeler Peak campground to Upper Lehman Creek campground. In winter, it is the most popular cross-country skiing trail in the park. You may need snowshoes to reach the skiable upper section, with free rentals available at the Lehman Cave Visitor Center.

HIKING
You'll witness beautiful views by driving along the Wheeler Peak Scenic Drive and other park roads, but hiking allows an in-depth experience that just can't be matched. Trails at Great Basin run the gamut from short, wheelchair-accessible paths to multiday backpacking excursions. Destinations include evergreen forest, flowering meadows and an extremely tall mountain peak. When you pick up a trail map at the visitor center, ask about trail conditions and bring appropriate clothing when you set out from any trailhead. No matter the trail length, always carry water, and remember that the trails are at high elevations, so pace yourself accordingly. Never enter abandoned mineshafts or tunnels, because they are unstable and dangerous. Those headed into the backcountry don't need to obtain a permit, but are encouraged to register at either of the two visitor centers. Regardless of the season, inquire about the weather, as it can be harsh and unpredictable.

Alpine Lakes Trail
HIKING/WALKING | This moderate, 2.7-mile trek loops past the beautiful Stella and Teresa lakes from the trailhead near Wheeler Peak Campground. You'll rise and fall about 600 feet in elevation as you pass through subalpine and alpine forest. The views of Wheeler Peak, amid wildflowers (in summer), white fir, twisted aspens, and towering ponderosa pines, make this a memorable hike. The trailhead is at nearly 10,000 feet, so make sure you're adjusted to the altitude and prepared for changing weather. Allow three hours. *Moderate.* ⊠ *Great Basin National Park* ⊕ *Trailhead: at Bristlecone parking area, near end of Wheeler Peak Scenic Dr.*

Baker Lake Trail
HIKING/WALKING | This full-day, 12-mile hike can easily be made into a two-day backpacking trip. You'll gain a total of 2,620 feet in elevation on the way to Baker Lake, a jewel-like alpine lake with a backdrop of impressive cliffs. *Difficult.* ⊠ *Great Basin National Park* ⊕ *Trailhead: Baker Creek Rd., going south from just east of Lehman Caves Visitor Center.*

★ Bristlecone Pine Trail
HIKING/WALKING | FAMILY | Though the park has several bristlecone pine groves, the only way to see the gnarled, ancient trees up close is to hike this trail. From the parking area to the grove, it's a moderate 2.8-mile hike that takes about an hour each way. Rangers offer informative talks in season; inquire at the visitor center. The Bristlecone Pine Trail also leads to the **Glacier Trail,** which skirts the southernmost permanent ice field on the continent and ends with a view of a small rock glacier, the only one in Nevada. From there it's less than 3 miles back to the parking lot. Allow three hours for the moderate hike and remember the trailhead is at 9,800 feet above sea level. *Moderate.* ⊠ *Great Basin National Park* ⊕ *Trailhead: Summit Trail parking area, Wheeler Peak Scenic Dr., 12 miles from Lehman Caves Visitor Center.*

Mountain View Nature Trail
HIKING/WALKING | FAMILY | Just past the Rhodes Cabin on the right side of the visitor center, this short and easy trail (0.3 mile) through pinyon pine and juniper

trees is marked with signs describing the plants. The path passes the original entrance to Lehman Caves and loops back to the visitor center. It's a great way to spend a half hour or so while you wait for your cave tour to start. *Easy.* ✉ *Great Basin National Park* ⊹ *Trailhead: at Lehman Caves Visitor Center.*

Osceola Ditch Trail

HIKING/WALKING | FAMILY | In 1890, at a cost of $108,223, the Osceola Gravel Mining Company constructed an 18-mile-long trench. The ditch was part of an attempt to glean gold from the South Snake Range, but water shortages and the company's failure to find much gold forced the mining operation to shut down in 1905. You can reach portions of the eastern section of the ditch on foot via the Osceola Ditch Trail, which passes through pine and fir trees. Allow 30 minutes for this easy 0.3-mile round-trip hike. *Easy.* ✉ *Great Basin National Park* ⊹ *Trailhead: Wheeler Peak Scenic Dr.*

★ Wheeler Peak Summit Trail

HIKING/WALKING | Begin this full-day, 8.6-mile hike early in the day so as to minimize exposure to afternoon storms. Depart and return to Summit Trailhead near the end of Wheeler Peak Scenic Drive. Most of the route follows a ridge up the mountain to the summit. Elevation gain is 2,900 feet to 13,063 feet above sea level, so hikers should have good stamina and watch for altitude sickness and/or hypothermia due to drastic temperature and weather changes. *Difficult.* ✉ *Great Basin National Park* ⊹ *Trailhead: Wheeler Peak Scenic Dr., Summit Trail parking area.*

Nearby Towns

An hour's drive west of the park, at the intersection of three U.S. highways, **Ely** (population 4,000) is the largest town for hours in every direction. It grew up in the second wave of the early Nevada mining boom, right at the optimistic turn

of the 20th century. For 70 years copper kept the town in business, but when it ran out in the early 1980s, Ely declined fast. Then, in 1986, the National Park Service designated Great Basin National Park, and the town got a boost. Ely has since been rebuilt and revitalized, though it's kept a quirky, faded feel. Take a ride on a vintage locomotive at the railroad museum, or take in a show at the one-screen Art Deco movie theater. If you want to stay much closer to the park, tiny **Baker** (population roughly 75) is slowly reawakening. The cluster of homes and small businesses on Route 487 is 5 miles from the visitor center.

VISITOR INFORMATION Great Basin Business and Tourism Council ⊕ *www.greatbasinpark.com.* **White Pine County Tourism and Recreation Board** ✉ *Bristlecone Convention Center, 150 6th St., Ely* ☎ *800/496–9350, 775/289–3720* ⊕ *www.elynevada.net.*

◉ Sights

Cave Lake State Park

NATIONAL/STATE PARK | FAMILY | This is an idyllic spot 7,350 feet above sea level in the pine and juniper forest of the big Schell Creek Range that borders Ely to the east. You can spend a day fishing for rainbow and brown trout in the reservoir and a night sleeping under the stars. Arrive early; it gets crowded. Access may be restricted in winter. ✉ *15 miles southeast of Ely via U.S. 50/6/93* ☎ *775/296–1505* 🌐 *parks.nv.gov/parks/cave-lake* 🎟 *$5 for Nevada residents, $7 for nonresidents.*

Nevada Northern Railway Museum
HISTORIC SITE | FAMILY | During the mining boom, the Nevada Northern Railroad connected East Ely, Ruth, and McGill to the transcontinental rail line in the northeast corner of the state. The whole operation is now a museum, and the biggest attraction in Ely, open year-round and visited by happy train aficionados from near and far. You can tour the depot, offices, warehouses, yard, engine houses, and repair shops. Catch a ride on one of the vintage locomotives, and get history lessons from enthusiastic guides along the way (check website for times). You can even stay overnight in a caboose or bunkhouse. ✉ *1100 Ave. A, Ely* ☎ *866/407–8326* 🌐 *www.nnry.com* 🎟 *$8 for museum, $31 for train ride (museum included)* 🕒 *Closed Tues. Sept.–June.*

U.S. 93 Scenic Byway
SCENIC DRIVE | The 68 miles between the park and Ely make a beautiful drive with diverse views of Nevada's paradoxical geography: dry deserts and lush mountains. You'll catch an occasional glimpse of a snake, perhaps a rattler, slithering on the road's shoulder, or a lizard sunning on a rock. Watch for deer. A straight drive to Ely takes a little more than an hour; if you have the time to take a dirt-road adventure, don't miss the Ward Charcoal Ovens or a peek at Cave Lake.

Ward Charcoal Ovens State Historic Park
HISTORIC SITE | In the quiet desert south of Ely, this row of six beehive-shaped, 30-foot-tall ovens used to process 35 cords of wood at once. From 1876 to 1879, the ovens turned pinyon, juniper, and mountain mahogany into charcoal, which was used for refining local silver and copper ore. It's a well-preserved piece of unique mining history, and the park includes a campground and hiking trails. ✉ *7 miles south of Ely on U.S. 50/93, and 11 miles southwest on Cave Valley Rd.* ☎ *775/289–1693* 🌐 *http://parks.nv.gov/parks/ward-charcoal-ovens* 🎟 *$5.*

Best Bets for Families

- **Bristlecone Pine Trail.** Enjoy this moderate hike (2.8 miles) to see the park's signature trees in the Wheeler Peak cirque. Bristlecone pines are ancient, often thousands of years old, and gnarled—pretty cool for kids (and adults, too).
- **Lehman Caves.** Explore the array of stalactites, stalagmites, and fantasy-like chambers.
- **Nevada Northern Railway Museum.** Ride the rails year-round at this attraction in Ely.

🍴 Restaurants

IN THE PARK

Lehman Caves Cafe and Gift Shop
$ | AMERICAN | This casual spot is a great place to soak in the vast desert view and offers simple breakfasts and lunches. The sandwiches, filled with meats smoked by the owner, are especially good. **Known for:** a nice place to unwind with a beer or glass of wine; the only restaurant in the park; delicious cookies, baked by a local pastry chef. [$] *Average main: $9* ✉ *Next to visitor center* ☎ *775/234–7200* 🕒 *Closed Nov.–May. No dinner.*

PICNIC AREAS

Lehman Caves Visitor Center Picnic Area
CITY PARK | This picnic site, with tables, fire grills, water, and restrooms (the latter two available during the summer), is a short walk from the visitor center. Summer hours are often extended beyond

the standard 8 am–4:30 pm. ✉ *Just north of Lehman Caves Visitor Center.*

Pole Canyon Trailhead Picnic Area

CITY PARK | Inaccessible when Baker Creek Road is closed in the winter, this picnic area at the mouth of a canyon has a handful of tables and fire grills but no water. It does have a restroom. Access is via a narrow, one-lane road. ✉ *East of entrance to Grey Cliffs Group Camping site, at mouth of Pole Canyon* 🕑 *Closed Nov.–May.*

Upper Lehman Creek Campground

CITY PARK | There are a handful of places here where you can sit down for a bite and a breather. A group picnic site requires advance reservations, but areas near the host site and amphitheater are first come, first served. Water is available. ✉ *4 miles from Lehman Caves Visitor Center on Wheeler Peak Scenic Dr.*

OUTSIDE THE PARK

The Border Inn

$ | **AMERICAN** | This low-key local staple is the place to go for big portions and cold beers every single day of the year except Christmas. There's also a full bar, slot machines and a small grocery store. **Known for:** traditional diner fare like chicken-fried steak and hamburgers; open for breakfast, lunch and dinner; homey feel, with photos of local ranchers adorning the walls. [$] *Average main: $10* ✉ *U.S. 6/50, 13 miles east of Great Basin National Park, Baker* ☎ *775/234–7300* 🌐 *www.borderinncasino.com.*

Cellblock Steakhouse

$$$ | **STEAKHOUSE** | The only fine-dining in Ely, this low-lighted spot comes with a big helping of local color. Each table is its own "cell," complete with metal bars and old-timey photos on the wall—a whimsical spot to eat cowboy-size prime rib or bacon-wrapped filet mignon. **Known for:** all your favorite steak-house staples with cute, jail-themed names; crème brûlée and other desserts worth the calories; the fanciest place in Ely for a fun dinner. [$] *Average main: $24* ✉ *211 5th St., Ely* ☎ *775/289–3033* 🌐 *www.jailhousecasino.com/dining.php* 🕑 *No lunch.*

★ **Kerouac's**

$$ | **AMERICAN** | In an airy, historic building right on the main drag, this is easily the best restaurant and bar in town. Expect the same caliber of burgers, salads, and artisan pizzas you'd get in a hip urban eatery, as well as incredible cocktails and luscious desserts made by a pastry chef. **Known for:** delicious, fresh uncomplicated breakfasts and dinners; the full bar is also a local hangout; friendly, attentive service. [$] *Average main: $14* ✉ *115 S. Baker Ave.* ☎ *775/234–7323* 🌐 *www.stargazernevada.com/eat-drink* 🕑 *Closed Tues. during season, also closed late Oct.–mid-Apr. No lunch.*

T & D's

$ | **AMERICAN** | This casual restaurant offers up burgers, Mexican food, and pasta dishes all year long. A small grocery store stocks some snacks and camping staples, including a good selection of beer and wine. **Known for:** one of very few restaurants close to the park; homemade, signature pasta sauces; comfortable, old-school bar next to dining room. [$] *Average main: $11* ✉ *1 Main St., Baker* ☎ *775/234–7264* 🌐 *www.greatbasinxenman.com* 🕑 *Closed days fluctuate in winter.*

Hotels

OUTSIDE THE PARK

All Aboard Cafe & Inn

$$ | **B&B/INN** | After a dusty journey to far-flung Ely, there may be no better spot to bed down than this charming, early-20th-century house just a block from the historic train station. **Pros:** quiet location; each room has a balcony; busy café serves breakfast, lunch, and dinner. **Cons:** no elevator to second floor; rooms lack some modern conveniences; not in walking distance to downtown. [$] *Rooms from: $119* ✉ *220 E 11th*

Best Campgrounds in Great Basin

Great Basin has four developed campgrounds, all easily accessible by car, but only the Lower Lehman Creek Campground is open year-round. All are first come, first served, and can be paid for on-site with cash, check, or credit card. The campgrounds do fill up, so try to snag your spot early.

Primitive campsites around Snake and Strawberry creeks are open year-round and are free; however, snow and rain can make access to the sites difficult. None have RV hookups (but RVers can stay at Whispering Elms in nearby Baker).

After a few days of roughing it, grab a shower in Baker. Both Stargazer Inn and the Whispering Elms Campground offer them for purchase.

Baker Creek Campground. The turnoff is just past the park entrance, on the left as you approach the Lehman Caves Visitor Center. ✉ *2½ miles south of Rte. 488, 3 miles from visitor center.*

Lower Lehman Creek Campground. Other than Great Basin's primitive sites, this is the only campground in the park that is open year-round. It's the first turnoff past the Lehman Caves Visitor Center. ✉ *2½ miles from visitor center on Wheeler Peak Scenic Dr.*

Upper Lehman Creek Campground. About a mile past the Lower Lehman Creek turnoff, this camp fills up quickly in the summer. ✉ *4 miles from visitor center on Wheeler Peak Scenic Dr.*

Wheeler Park Campground. This cool high-elevation campground at the end of Wheeler Peak Scenic Drive has stunning views and is near trailheads. Many consider it the nicest in the park. ✉ *12 miles from Lehman Caves Visitor Center on Wheeler Peak Scenic Dr.*

Whispering Elms Campground. The largest camping facility close to but not inside the park is also the nearest to offer hookups for RVs. It is open year-round. ✉ *Rte. 487, behind Great Basin Lodge, Baker* ☎ *775/234–9900.*

St., Ely ☎ *775/289–3959* 🛏 *5 rooms* 🍴 *Breakfast.*

The Border Inn

$ | **HOTEL** | Located right on the border between Nevada and Utah on Route 50, the Border Inn is a reliable staple, with air-conditioned rooms, a restaurant, bar, grocery store, gas station, and casino. **Pros:** a great one-stop shop; low prices; open every day of the year but Christmas. **Cons:** gravel parking lot is dusty; Wi-Fi and cell service can be iffy; simple rooms that haven't been updated in years. [$] *Rooms from: $65* ✉ *U.S. 6/50, Baker* ✣ *13 miles east of Great Basin National Park* ☎ *775/234–7300* 🌐 *www.borderinncasino.com* 🛏 *29 rooms* 🍴 *No meals.*

★ **Hidden Canyon Retreat**

$$$ | **B&B/INN** | The most luxurious lodging for hours in any direction, the large rooms here have a modern serenity to them and are surrounded on all sides by hundreds of acres of rugged, high desert beauty. **Pros:** tucked into a canyon, the setting makes this feel like a true retreat; rooms feel modern and inviting; a good place to hike and fish. **Cons:** no cell service or in-room TV and little Wi-Fi; far from services and a 30-minute drive to Great Basin National Park; located down

a dirt road (but it is well-maintained). [$] *Rooms from: $159* ✉ *2000 Hidden Canyon Pkwy., Baker* ☎ *775/234–7172* 🌐 *www.hiddencanyonretreat.com* 🛏 *11 rooms* 🍴 *Breakfast.*

Jailhouse Motel and Casino

$ | **HOTEL** | This motel at Ely's main intersection was built near the town's old-time jail; the rooms are assigned cell numbers and there are prison bars around the booths at its fancy steak house. **Pros:** location in the center of town; on-site casino, two restaurants, and a bar; good value. **Cons:** smoke can waft from the casino adjacent to registration; not as charming as some historic options in the area; rooms are clean but no frills. [$] *Rooms from: $59* ✉ *211 5th St., Ely* ☎ *775/289–3033, 800/841–5430* 🌐 *www.jailhousecasino.com* 🛏 *60 rooms* 🍴 *No meals.*

La Quinta Inn & Suites

$$ | **HOTEL** | One of the newest and largest hotels in Ely, the La Quinta Inn & Suites is a clean, fresh, comfortable stay and offers the dependability of a well-known chain. **Pros:** complimentary hot breakfast; pool; close to train museum and hospital. **Cons:** doesn't have the character of the area's historic options; too far to walk to downtown; no restaurant or bar. [$] *Rooms from: $129* ✉ *1591 Great Basin Blvd., Ely* ☎ *775/289–8833* 🌐 *www.lq.com* 🛏 *100 rooms* 🍴 *Breakfast.*

Prospector Hotel & Gambling Hall

$ | **HOTEL** | One of the best bets in town, this comfortable hotel walks the line between classy and delightfully kitschy, with Western-themed rooms, on-site gambling, and a tasty Mexican restaurant. **Pros:** a good value, with quality that far surpasses many other local options; inviting, modern rooms; friendly staff. **Cons:** can get booked up quickly; not walking distance to downtown; having an in-house casino does not appeal to everyone. [$] *Rooms from: $99* ✉ *1501 E. Aultman St., Ely* ☎ *775/289–8900, 800/750–0557* 🌐 *www.prospectorhotel.us* 🛏 *61 rooms* 🍴 *No meals.*

Stargazer Inn

$ | **HOTEL** | New life has been breathed into this small, quirky roadside motel, with pleasant art and tasteful bedspreads giving the otherwise plain, spotless rooms a rustic elegance. **Pros:** open year-round; fantastic location; delicious restaurant and popular bar. **Cons:** while rooms are comfortable, they are small and older; dated fixtures in bathrooms; swamp cooling means rooms can get hot in the dead of summer. [$] *Rooms from: 75* ✉ *115 S. Baker Ave., Baker* ☎ *775/234–7323* 🌐 *www.stargazernevada.com* 🛏 *9 rooms* 🍴 *No meals.*

Whispering Elms Motel & RV Park

$ | **HOTEL** | The strip of rooms in the back of this friendly RV park may look plain from the outside but are some of the cleanest and best-equipped in town, with microwaves, fridges, and air-conditioning. **Pros:** just 5 miles from the turnoff for Great Basin; bar is a local hangout; good value. **Cons:** no pool or other big-city amenities; gravel parking lot; though rooms are clean and large, they are older. [$] *Rooms from: $67* ✉ *Rte. 487, Baker* ✣ *Just south of Great Basin Visitor Center and north of turnoff for park* ☎ *775/234–9900* 🌐 *www.camptheelms.wix.com/the-elms* 🛏 *6 rooms* 🍴 *No meals.*

GREAT SAND DUNES NATIONAL PARK

Updated by
Whitney Bryen

COLORADO

WELCOME TO GREAT SAND DUNES NATIONAL PARK

TOP REASONS TO GO

★ **Dune climbing:** Trek through the 30 square miles of main dunes in this landlocked dune field.

★ **Unrivaled diversity:** You can see eight completely different life zones in this park, ranging from salty wetlands and lush forests to parched sand sheet and frozen alpine peaks, all in a single day.

★ **Bounty of bison:** Take a ride around the west end of the park, where more than 2,000 bison roam in the grass-lands and wetlands.

★ **Aspens in autumn:** Take a hike—or, if you've got a high-clearance four-wheel-drive vehicle and good driving skills, take the rough road—up to Medano Pass during fall foliage season when the aspens turn gold.

★ **Vigorous hikes:** Pack a picnic lunch and climb up to High Dune, followed by the more strenuous stretch over to Star Dune. Or tackle the dramatic Music Pass Trail, which takes you to the tree line and covers 3.5 miles (and 2,000 feet in eleva-tion change) each way.

1 **Sand dunes.** The 30-square-mile field of sand has no designated trails. The highest dune in the park—and, in fact, in North America—is 750-foot-high Star Dune.

2 **Sangre de Cristo Mountains.** Named the "Blood of Christ" Mountains by Spanish explorers because of their ruddy color—especially at sunrise and sunset—the range contains 10 of Colorado's 54 Fourteeners (mountains taller than 14,000 feet). Six that are more than 13,000 feet tall are within the preserve itself.

3 **Forest.** Ponderosa pines populate the forested areas around the Sangre de Cristo Mountains in the preserve and park's eastern boundaries.

4 **Grasslands.** Wildlife, such as elk and bison, feed on the park's grassy areas, primarily found in the park's southern area and the Great Sand Dunes National Preserve.

5 **Wetlands.** Popular with a variety of birds and amphibians, these seasonal wetlands form in the area around Medano Creek, where cottonwood and willow trees also thrive.

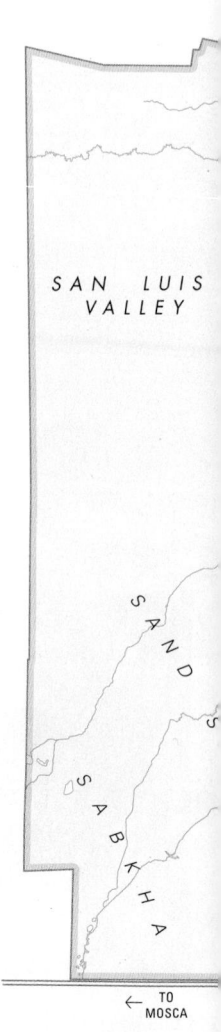

SAN LUIS VALLEY

SAND

SABKHA

← TO MOSCA

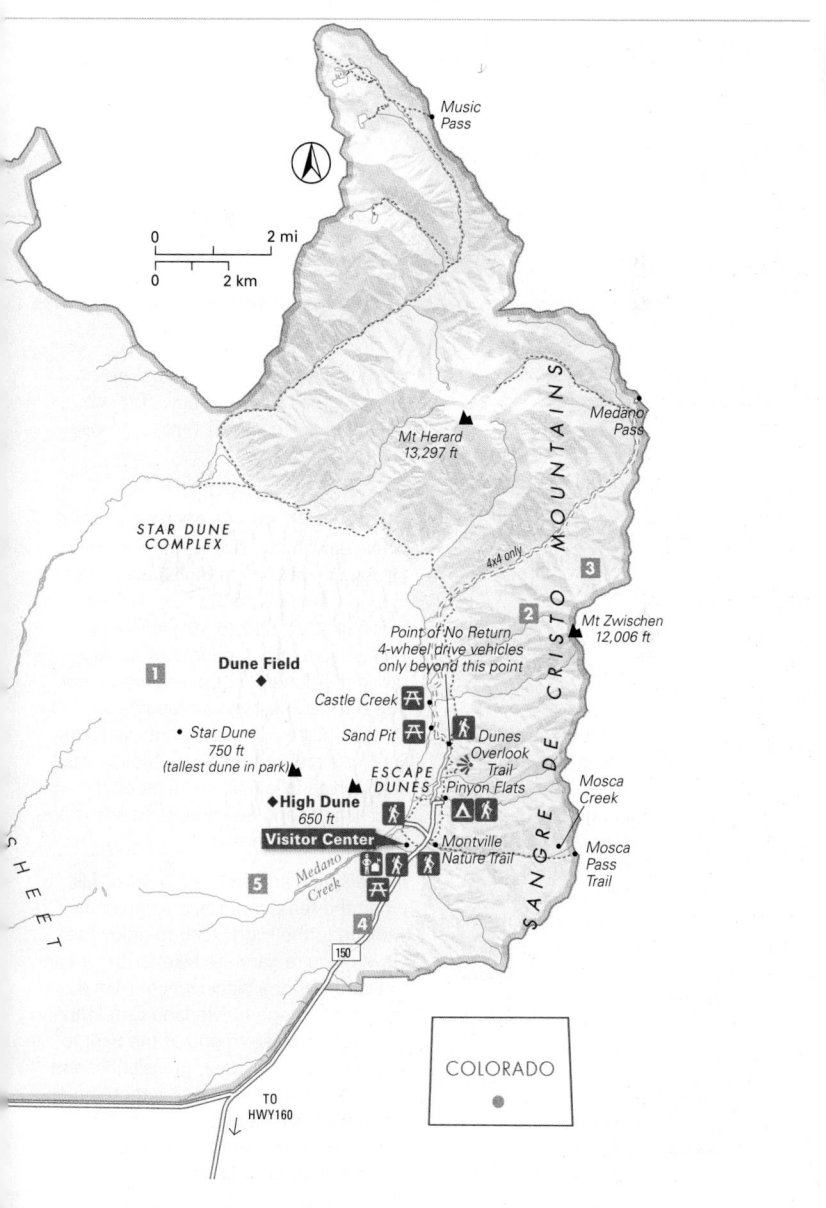

Music Pass

0   2 mi

0   2 km

SANGRE DE CRISTO MOUNTAINS

Medano Pass

Mt Herard
13,297 ft

STAR DUNE
COMPLEX

4x4 only

Point of No Return
4-wheel drive vehicles
only beyond this point

Mt Zwischen
12,006 ft

Dune Field

Castle Creek

Sand Pit

Dunes
Overlook
Trail

Star Dune
750 ft
(tallest dune in park)

Mosca
Creek

ESCAPE
DUNES

Pinyon Flats

High Dune
650 ft

Visitor Center

Montville
Nature Trail

Mosca
Pass
Trail

Medano Creek

SHEET

150

TO
HWY160

COLORADO

Created by winds that sweep the San Luis Valley floor, the enormous sand dunes that form the heart of Great Sand Dunes National Park and Preserve are an improbable, unforgettable sight. The dunes stretch for more than 30 square miles, solid enough to have withstood 440,000 years of Mother Nature.

Planning

WHEN TO GO

About 300,000 visitors come to the park each year, most on summer weekends; they tend to congregate around the main parking area and Medano Creek. To avoid the crowds, hike away from the main area up to the High Dune. Or come in the winter, when the park is a place for contemplation and repose—as well as skiing and sledding.

Fall and spring are the prettiest times to visit, with the surrounding mountains still capped with snow in May, and leaves on the aspen trees turning gold in September and early October. In summer, the surface temperature of the sand can climb to 140°F in the afternoon, so climbing the dunes is best in the morning or late afternoon. Since you're at a high altitude—about 8,200 feet at the visitor center—the air temperatures in the park itself remain in the 70s most of the summer.

FESTIVALS AND EVENTS

Alamosa Round-Up Rodeo

FESTIVAL | FAMILY | The last week in June marks the annual rodeo competition in Alamosa, a genuine Wild West event including barrel racers, bulls, broncos, and bareback riding. ⊕ *www.alamosa-roundup.com* ✉ *$12*.

PLANNING YOUR TIME

GREAT SAND DUNES IN ONE DAY

Arrive early in the day during the summer so you can hike up to **High Dune** and get a view of the entire dune field. Round-trip, the walk itself should take about 1½ to 2 hours (plus time to jump off or slide down the dunes). In the afternoon, hop into the car and head to Zapata Falls, hike on the short-and-shady Montville Nature Trail, or head for the longer Mosca Pass Trail, which follows a small creek through cool aspens and evergreens to one of the lower mountain passes.

In the spring and early summer or fall, when the temperatures are cooler, first walk up to the High Dune to enjoy the view. If you're game to hike farther, head to **Star Dune** for a picnic lunch. Hike down the eastern ridge to Medano Creek, then head to the western end of the park to explore the sand sheet, grasslands, and wetlands. If you're here on a morning when there's a hayride (or four-wheel-drive) tour to see the bison, take it and then head off on your hikes.

AVERAGE HIGH/LOW TEMPERATURES					
JAN.	**FEB.**	**MAR.**	**APR.**	**MAY**	**JUNE**
35/10	39/14	47/21	56/28	66/37	77/45
JULY	**AUG.**	**SEPT.**	**OCT.**	**NOV.**	**DEC.**
81/51	78/49	71/42	60/32	46/20	36/11

19

Great Sand Dunes National Park PLANNING

GETTING HERE AND AROUND
CAR TRAVEL
Great Sand Dunes National Park and Preserve is about 240 miles from both Denver and Albuquerque, and roughly 180 miles from Colorado Springs and Santa Fe. The fastest route from Denver is Interstate 25 south to U.S. 160, heading west to just past Blanca, to Highway 150 north, which goes right to the park's main entrance. For a more scenic route, take U.S. 285 over Kenosha, Red Hill, and Poncha Passes, turn onto Highway 17 just south of Villa Grove, then take County Lane 6 to the park (watch for signs just south of Hooper). From Albuquerque, go north on Interstate 25 to Santa Fe, then north on U.S. 285 to Alamosa, then U.S. 160 east to Highway 150. From the west, Highway 17 and County Lane 6 take you to the park. The park entrance station is about 3 miles from the park boundary, and it's about a mile from there to the visitor center; the main parking lot is about a mile farther.

PARK ESSENTIALS
ACCESSIBILITY
The park has two wheelchairs with balloon tires (for the sand) that can be borrowed; someone must push them. You can reserve one by calling the visitor center. There is one accessible campsite.

PARK FEES AND PERMITS
Entrance fees are $3 per adult above age 15 and are valid for one week from date of purchase. Children are admitted free at all times. Pick up camping permits ($20 per night per site at Pinyon Flats Campground) and backpacking permits (free) at the visitor center.

PARK HOURS
The park is open 24/7. It is in the Mountain time zone.

CELL-PHONE RECEPTION
Cell-phone reception in the park is sporadic. Public telephones are at the visitor center, dunes parking lot, and at the Pinyon Flats campground—you need a calling card (these aren't coin-operated phones).

EDUCATIONAL OFFERINGS
RANGER PROGRAMS
Interpretive Programs
TOUR—SIGHT | FAMILY | Family-friendly nature walks designed to help visitors learn more about the Great Sand Dunes National Park are scheduled most days from late May through September, and sporadically in April and October. Call or drop in to ask about sunset walks, afternoon weekend tours, and evening stargazing programs. The Junior Ranger program is a favorite for children ages 3 to 12 who can earn their badge by completing a booklet of activities. ✉ *Programs begin at the visitor center* ☎ *719/378–6395* 💲 *Free.*

RESTAURANTS
There are no dining establishments in the park. In the visitor center and at the campground there are vending machines with drinks that are stocked mid-spring through mid-fall. There is one picnic area in the park.

HOTELS
There are no hotels, motels, or lodges in the park. The nearest lodge is right outside the park entrance, and there are many hotels in Alamosa and a handful of

Plants and Wildlife in Great Sand Dunes

The salty wetlands are dotted with sedges, rushes, and other plants that are tolerant of changes in water salinity and levels, while the sand sheet and grasslands have prickly pear, rabbit brush, and yucca. The dune field looks barren from afar, but up close you see various grasses have rooted in swales among the dunes. Juniper, pinyon, and ponderosa pine trees grow on the lower portions of the mountain, hardy spruce and fir trees survive in the subalpine forest zone, and lichens and tiny flowers cling to the rock at the top.

Birds inhabit the wetlands; short-horned lizards, elk, and pronghorns live in the sand sheet and grassland; and Great Sand Dunes tiger beetles and Ord's kangaroo rats breed in the dune field. In the forests and on the mountainsides, raptors fly overhead, while mule deer and Rocky Mountain bighorn sheep graze.

them in other surrounding towns including Salida, Walsenburg, and Monte Vista. *Hotel reviews have been shortened. For full information, visit Fodors.com.*

What It Costs

$	$$	$$$	$$$$
RESTAURANTS			
under $13	$13–$18	$19–$25	over $25
HOTELS			
under $121	$121–$170	$171–$230	over $230

VISITOR INFORMATION
PARK CONTACT INFORMATION

VISITOR CENTER
Great Sand Dunes Visitor Center
INFO CENTER | View exhibits and artwork, browse in the bookstore, and watch a 20-minute film with an overview of the dunes. Rangers are on hand to answer questions. Facilities include restrooms and a vending machine stocked with soft drinks and snacks, but no other food. (The Great Sand Dunes Oasis, just outside the park boundary, has a café that is open generally late April through early October.) ⊠ *Near the park entrance* ☎ *719/378–6395* ⊕ *www.nps.gov/grsa/planyourvisit/visitor-center.htm.*

 Sights

Dune Field
NATURE SITE | The more than 30 square miles of big dunes in the heart of the park are the main attraction, although the surrounding sand sheet does have some smaller dunes. You can start putting your feet in the sand 3 miles past the main park entrance. ⊠ *Great Sand Dunes National Park.*

High Dune
VIEWPOINT | This isn't the park's highest dune, but it's high enough in the dune field to provide a view of all the dunes from its summit. It's on the first ridge of dunes you see from the main parking area. ⊠ *Great Sand Dunes National Park.*

 Activities

BIRD-WATCHING

The San Luis Valley is famous for its migratory birds, many of which stop in the park. Great Sand Dunes also has many permanent feathered residents. In the wetlands, you might see American white pelicans and the American avocet. On the forested sections of the mountains there are goshawks, northern harriers, gray jays, and Steller's jays. And in the alpine tundra there are golden eagles, hawks, horned larks, and white-tailed ptarmigan.

HIKING

Visitors can walk just about anywhere on the sand dunes in the heart of the park. The best view of all the dunes is from the top of High Dune. There are no formal trails because the sand keeps shifting, but you don't really need them: It's extremely difficult to get lost out here.

■ TIP➜ **Before taking any of the trails in the preserve, rangers recommend stopping at the visitor center and picking up the handout that lists the trails, including their degree of difficulty.** The dunes can get very hot in the summer, reaching up to 140°F in the afternoon. If you're hiking, carry plenty of water; if you're going into the backcountry to camp overnight, carry even more water and a water filtration system. A free permit is required to backpack in the park. Also, watch for weather changes. If there's a thunderstorm and lightning, get off the dunes or trail immediately, and seek shelter. Before hiking, leave word with someone indicating where you're going to hike and when you expect to be back. Tell that contact to call 911 if you don't show up when expected.

Hike to High Dune

HIKING/WALKING | FAMILY | Get a panoramic view of all the surrounding dunes from the top of High Dune. Since there's no formal path, the smartest approach is to zigzag up the dune ridgelines. High Dune is 699 feet high, and to get there and back takes about two hours, or longer if there's been no rain for some time and the sand is soft. If you add on the walk to the 750-foot Star Dune, plan on another two or three hours and a strenuous workout up and down the dunes. *Easy to moderate.* ⊠ *Great Sand Dunes National Park* ✛ *Start from main dune field.*

★ Mosca Pass Trail

HIKING/WALKING | This moderately challenging route follows the Montville Trail laid out centuries ago by Native Americans, which became the Mosca Pass toll road used in the late 1800s and early 1900s. This is a good afternoon hike, because the trail rises through the trees and subalpine meadows, often following Mosca Creek. It is 3½ miles one-way, with a 1,500-foot gain in elevation. Hiking time is two to three hours each way. *Moderate.* ⊠ *Great Sand Dunes National Park* ✛ *Trailhead: lower end of trail begins at Montville Trailhead, just north of visitor center.*

Music Pass Trail

HIKING/WALKING | This steep trail offers superb views of the glacially carved Upper Sand Creek Basin, ringed by several 13,000-foot peaks and the Wet Mountain Valley to the east. The top of the pass can be covered in snow through midsummer and reaches about 11,000 feet above sea level, surrounded by even higher mountain peaks. It's 3½ miles and a 2,000-foot elevation gain one-way from the lower parking lot on the east side of the preserve, off Forest Service Road 119, and 1 mile from the upper parking lot (reachable only by four-wheel drive). Depending on how fit you are and how often you stop, it can take six hours round-trip from the lower lot. *Difficult.* ⊠ *Great Sand Dunes National Park* ✛ *Trailhead: on eastern side of park, reached via Hwy. 69, 4½ miles south of Westcliffe. Turn off Hwy. 69 to the west at the sign for Music Pass and South Colony Lakes Trails. At the "T" junction, turn left onto South Colony Rd. At the end of the ranch fence on the right you'll see another sign for Music Pass.*

Nearby Towns

The vast expanse one sees from the dunes is the San Luis Valley. Covering 8,000 square miles (and with an average altitude of 7,500 feet), the San Luis Valley is the world's largest alpine valley, sprawling on a broad, flat, dry plain between the San Juan Mountains to the west and the Sangre de Cristo range to the east, and extending south into northern New Mexico. The area is one of the state's major agricultural producers.

Alamosa, the San Luis Valley's major city, is 35 miles southwest of Great Sand Dunes via U.S. 160 and Highway 150. It's a casual, central base for exploring the park and the surrounding region. The rest of the area is dotted with tiny towns, including **Mosca, Blanca, Antonito,** and **Fort Garland,** to the south of the park, and **Monte Vista, Del Norte,** and **Hooper** to the west. They are all within an hour's drive from the park.

VISITOR INFORMATION Alamosa Convention & Visitors Bureau ⊠ *610 State Ave., Alamosa* ☎ *800/258–7597, 719/589–3681* ⊕ *www.alamosa.org.* **Del Norte Chamber of Commerce** ⊠ *505 Grand Ave., Del Norte* ⊕ *www.delnortechamber.org.* **Monte Vista Chamber of Commerce** ⊠ *947 1st Ave., Monte Vista* ☎ *719/852–2731* ⊕ *www. montevistachamber.org.*

 Sights

Alamosa National Wildlife Refuge

NATURE PRESERVE | Less than an hour's drive southwest of Great Sand Dunes is a sanctuary for songbirds, waterbirds, and raptors (it's also home to many other types of birds, along with mule deer, beavers, and coyotes). The Rio Grande runs through the park comprising more than 12,000 acres of natural and man-made wetlands. You can take a 4-mile hike round-trip along the river or a 3½-mile wildlife drive on the park's western side or a drive along Bluff Road to an overlook on the park's eastern side. The refuge office is staffed by volunteers sporadically from March through November and closed in winter—it's wise to call first. ⊠ *9383 El Rancho La., off U.S. 160, Alamosa* ☎ *719/589–4021* ⊕ *www.fws. gov/refuge/alamosa/* 🖼 *Free.*

Cumbres & Toltec Scenic Railroad

TOUR—SIGHT | FAMILY | Take a day trip on the Cumbres & Toltec Scenic Railroad, an 1880s steam locomotive that chugs through portions of Colorado's and northern New Mexico's rugged mountains that you can't reach via roads. It's the country's longest and highest narrow-gauge railroad. The company offers round-trip train routes, several bus-and-train combinations, one-way trips, and themed rides. ⊠ *5234 U.S. 285, Antonito* ☎ *888/286–2737* ⊕ *www.cumbrestoltec. com* 🖼 *$84–$205.*

Fort Garland Museum

MILITARY SITE | Colorado's first military post was established here in 1858 to protect settlers in the San Luis Valley, which was then part of the Territory of New Mexico. The legendary Kit Carson once served here, and the six original adobe structures are still standing. The fort features a re-creation of the commandant's quarters from Carson's era, as well as period military displays, and a rotating local folk-art exhibit. ⊠ *29477 Hwy. 159, Fort Garland* ☎ *719/379–3512* ⊕ *museumtrail.org/fortgarlandmuseum. asp* 🖼 *$5.*

Luther Bean Museum and Art Gallery

ART GALLERIES—ARTS | This Adams State College museum displays American Indian pottery and textiles, European porcelain, photography, and furniture collections in a handsome, wood-paneled 19th-century drawing room, as well as changing exhibits of regional arts and crafts. ⊠ *Richardson Hall, Room 256, 208*

Near water in the park's grasslands area is where you might see elk, mule deer, and lizards.

Edgemont Blvd., Alamosa ☎ 719/587–7827 ⊕ www.adams.edu/lutherbean ✉ Free.

Monte Vista National Wildlife Refuge

NATURE PRESERVE | Just west of the Alamosa wildlife refuge is its sister sanctuary, the Monte Vista National Wildlife Refuge, a 15,000-acre park that's a stopping point for more than 20,000 migrating cranes in the spring and fall. It hosts an annual Crane Festival, held one weekend in mid-March in the nearby town of Monte Vista, and a children's Crane Festival in mid-October at the park with kid-friendly activities. You can see the sanctuary via a 2½-mile driving tour. ⊠ *6120 Hwy. 15, Monte Vista ☎ 719/589–4021 ⊕ www.fws.gov/refuge/monte_vista ✉ Free.*

Rio Grande Scenic Railroad

TRANSPORTATION SITE (AIRPORT/BUS/FERRY/TRAIN) | **FAMILY** | This railroad carries passengers on excursions between Alamosa and La Veta some weekdays. You can also take a weekend ride from Alamosa to the Fir Summit Amphitheater where a wind- and solar-powered performance stage at 9,400 feet attracts regional and national Western and folk artists. The Rio Grande also offers a fall colors trip in September and October. ⊠ *610 State Ave., Alamosa ☎ 877/726–7245, 719/587–0509 ⊕ www.coloradotrain.com ✉ $59–$139.*

Zapata Falls Recreation Area

If it's a hot day, take a drive to the falls section of the Zapata Falls Recreation Area, about 7 miles south of Great Sand Dunes National Park (and about 10 miles north of Alamosa). From the trailhead, it's a ½-mile hike to the 40-foot waterfall and a mildly steep trail, which can include wading in a stream and walking through a narrow gorge to view the falls (depending on water levels). Air temperatures in the gorge are always cool and inviting, and the falls are beautiful, but be careful of the current (and slippery rocks) here. A picnic area and restrooms are at the entrance. The trailhead is 3½ miles off Highway 150, between mile markers 10 and 11. ⊠ *Rio Grande National Forest Supervisor's Office, 1803 W. U.S. 160,*

Monte Vista ☎ *719/852–5941* 🌐 *www.fs.usda.gov/riogrande* 🎟 *Free.*

SCENIC DRIVES

Manassa, San Luis, and Fort Garland Loop

SCENIC DRIVE | To get a real feel for this area, take an easy driving loop from Alamosa through much of the San Luis Valley (the whole trip is about 95 miles). Head east on U.S 160 to Fort Garland, south on Highway 159 to San Luis, west on Highways 159 and 142 to Manassa, then north on U.S. 285 back to Alamosa. More than half of the route is part of the Los Caminos Antiguos Drive, one of Colorado's Scenic Byways.

Activities

FISHING

Colorado fishing license

FISHING | There are plenty of fisheries in the area where you can catch trout, pike, and perch, including the Rio Grande, the Conejos River, and Sanchez, Smith, and Platoro reservoirs. A Colorado fishing license is required ($9 for one day, $21 for five days). ✉ *Colorado Division of Wildlife, SE Region Service Center, 4255 Sinton Rd., Colorado Springs* ☎ *800/244-5613* 🌐 *cpw.state.co.us/thingstodo/Pages/Fishing.aspx.*

EDUCATIONAL OFFERINGS

Colorado Field Institute

COLLEGE | This nonprofit teams up with the experts at the park and other area organizations, such as the Rio Grande National Forest, San Luis Valley National Wildlife Refuges Complex, and the Nature Conservancy's Medano/Zapata Ranch to conduct in-depth outdoor educational programs on the natural and cultural resources of the area. Check its website for the lecture and field-trip schedule. 🌐 *www.coloradofieldinstitute.org.*

Restaurants

IN THE PARK

PICNIC AREAS

Mosca Creek

RESTAURANT—SIGHT | Great Sand Dunes National Park's only picnic area is shaded by cottonwood trees. It has a dozen places where visitors can park a car or small RV near a picnic table and a grill. ✉ *South of the dunes parking lot.*

OUTSIDE THE PARK

Milagros Coffeehouse

$ | CAFÉ | The coffee is full-bodied at this coffeehouse and café where all profits go to local charities. Amish baked goods reign on the menu where local food dominates, which includes plenty of vegetarian and gluten-free options. **Known for:** vegetarian options; charitable donations; excellent coffee. [$] *Average main: $7* ✉ *529 Main St., Alamosa* ☎ *719/589–9299.*

The Oasis Cafe

$ | AMERICAN | The no-frills restaurant in the Great Sand Dunes Oasis (which includes a grocery store and gas station as well as motel rooms and campsites), just outside the park entrance, is open for breakfast, lunch, and dinner. The Navajo taco (served on fry bread) and beef or chicken burritos are among the most popular items, although the menu ranges from grilled-cheese sandwiches to steaks. [$] *Average main: $11* ✉ *5400 Hwy. 150, Mosca* ☎ *719/378–2222* 🌐 *www.greatdunes.com* ⏲ *Closed mid-Sept.–late Apr.*

Best Campgrounds in Great Sand Dunes

Great Sand Dunes has one campground, open year-round. During weekends in the summer, it can fill up with RVs and tents by midafternoon. Black bears live in the preserve, so when camping there, keep your food, trash, and toiletries in the trunk of your car (or use bear-proof containers). There is one campground and RV park near the entrance to Great Sand Dunes, and several others in the area.

Pinyon Flats Campground. Set in a pine forest about a mile past the visitor center, this campground has a trail leading to the dunes. Sites are available on a first-come, first-served basis; RVs are allowed, but there are no hookups. ✉ *On the main park road, near the visitor center* ☎ *719/378–6399.*

Hotels

OUTSIDE THE PARK

Best Western Alamosa Inn

$$ | **HOTEL** | This sprawling, well-maintained complex is your best bet for reasonably priced lodgings. **Pros:** reliable accommodations; easy to find; good base for area activities. **Cons:** noisy street; nothing but fast food nearby; basic rooms. [$] *Rooms from: $145* ✉ *2005 Main St., Alamosa* ☎ *719/589–2567, 800/459–5123* 🌐 *www.bestwestern.com* 🛏 *53 rooms* 🍴 *Free Breakfast.*

Comfort Inn

$$ | **HOTEL** | This property is a few miles west of downtown Alamosa on a strip with other chain hotels and restaurants, several of which will deliver to the hotel. **Pros:** basic accommodations at a reasonable price; pets allowed; hot tub. **Cons:** on a noisy street; a car-ride away from downtown restaurants. [$] *Rooms from: $140* ✉ *6301 W. Hwy. 160, Alamosa* ☎ *800/424–6423, 719/587–9000* 🌐 *www.comfortinn.com* 🛏 *49 rooms, 3 suites* 🍴 *Breakfast.*

Conejos Canyon River Ranch

$ | **HOTEL** | **FAMILY** | Located within the Rio Grande National Forest on the Conejos River, 42 miles southwest of Alamosa, this peaceful, family-friendly retreat is an excellent base for fishing. **Pros:** gorgeous riverfront setting; access to national forest; plenty of activities for adults and kids; on-site gift shop. **Cons:** no amenities nearby; more than an hour from the Great Sand Dunes. [$] *Rooms from: $98* ✉ *25390 Hwy. 17, Antonito* ☎ *719/376–2464* 🌐 *www.conejosranch.com* 🕐 *Limited rooms and cabins available Dec.–Apr.* 🛏 *8 rooms, 8 cabins* 🍴 *Breakfast.*

Mountain View Motor Inn

$ | **HOTEL** | This cheerful, squeaky-clean motel is just a few miles south of the Great Sand Dunes, in the tiny town of Fort Garland, and makes a great base from which to visit the park and other San Luis Valley attractions. **Pros:** spotless, comfortable rooms; 20 minutes from park. **Cons:** no pool or other recreational amenities in hotel; no great eating options nearby. [$] *Rooms from: $94* ✉ *411 U.S. 160, Fort Garland* ☎ *719/379–2993* 🛏 *15 rooms* 🍴 *No meals.*

Great Sand Dunes Lodge

$ | **HOTEL** | Located right at the entrance of the park, behind the Oasis, this simple lodge offers clean, comfortable rooms with private balconies (and great views of the dunes and mountains). **Pros:** closest hotel rooms to the dunes; great views. **Cons:** with the exception of the nearby Oasis Cafe, the nearest restaurants are more than 20 miles away. $ *Rooms from: $95* ⊠ *7900 Hwy. 150 N, Mosca* ☎ *719/378–2900* ⊕ *www.gsdlodge. com* ⊙ *Closed mid-Oct.–mid-Mar.* ⇌ *12 rooms.*

Zapata Ranch

$$$$ | **B&B/INN** | Part of a 103,000-acre working cattle and bison ranch owned by the Nature Conservancy, the Zapata Ranch is focused mainly on all-inclusive, weeklong stays, during which guests learn about bison, land conservation, and renewable ranching practices, and participate in ranch activities (including branding cattle and mending fences).

Pros: beautiful setting among mature cottonwoods; historic lodge buildings; terrific restaurant with indoor and outdoor seating. **Cons:** much pricier than other area accommodations; limited capacity (the ranch rents only those rooms that aren't reserved for guest ranch visitors). $ *Rooms from: $285* ⊠ *5305 State Hwy. 150* ☎ *888/592–7282, 719/378–2356* ⊕ *www.zranch.org* ⇌ *15 rooms* ⦿ *All-inclusive.*

Chapter 20

GUADALUPE MOUNTAINS NATIONAL PARK

Updated by
Andrew Collins

TEXAS

WELCOME TO GUADALUPE MOUNTAINS NATIONAL PARK

TOP REASONS TO GO

★ **Tower over Texas:** This dramatic wilderness that nearly borders New Mexico's Carlsbad Caverns National Park is home to 8,751-foot Guadalupe Peak, the highest point in the state.

★ **Fall for fiery foliage:** Though surrounded by the arid Chihuahuan desert and its forbidding rocky soil, the park has miles of beautiful foliage in McKittrick Canyon. In late October and early November, it bursts with flaming colors.

★ **Hike unhindered:** The main activity at the park is hiking its rugged, remote, and often challenging trails: 80 miles' worth—and they're nearly always free of crowds.

★ **Marvel at wildlife:** A variety of wildlife—including shaggy brown elk, furtive mountain lions, and shy black bears—traipse the mountains, woods, and desert here, and there's fantastic birdwatching, too.

★ **The Old West whispers:** Rock ruins and former homesteads—Frijole Ranch History Museum is a highlight—dot a hardscrabble landscape that pioneers worked hard to tame.

1 **Guadalupe Peak.** This pinnacle tops 8,700 feet. The seven-hour-plus round-trip to the summit offers breathtaking views of New Mexico and southwestern Texas.

2 **McKittrick Canyon.** In fall, the lush green foliage along McKittrick Canyon's trout-filled desert stream bursts into many hues.

3 **El Capitan.** This impressive 3,000-foot cliff dominates the southern skyline of the Guadalupe Range.

4 **Dog Canyon.** Just over the New Mexico border, this tranquil, forested high-desert wilderness contains a scenic campground and trails, including the trek to 7,830-foot Lost Peak.

5 **Frijole Ranch History Museum.** This easily accessible former ranch home is the oldest intact structure in the park, set amid several rock-walled outbuildings and a shaded, landscaped yard.

Butte

TEXAS

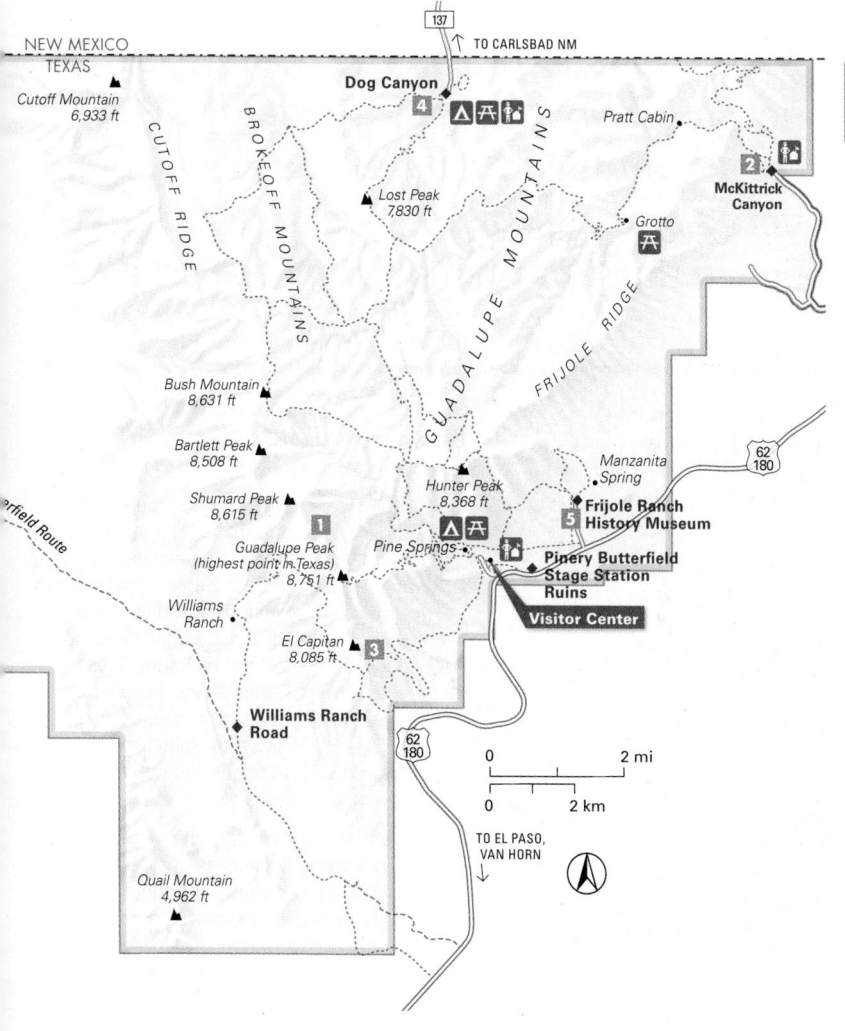

NEW MEXICO
TEXAS

137
↑ TO CARLSBAD NM

Cutoff Mountain
6,933 ft

Dog Canyon
4 ⛺🏕️🚻

Pratt Cabin

CUTOFF RIDGE

BROKEOFF MOUNTAINS

Lost Peak
7,830 ft

2 🚻
McKittrick Canyon

Grotto
🏕️

GUADALUPE MOUNTAINS

FRIJOLE RIDGE

Bush Mountain
8,631 ft

62
180

Bartlett Peak
8,508 ft

Manzanita Spring

Hunter Peak
8,368 ft

Shumard Peak
8,615 ft

5 Frijole Ranch
History Museum

1
Pine Springs
⛺🏕️🚻

Guadalupe Peak
(highest point in Texas)
8,751 ft

**Pinery Butterfield
Stage Station
Ruins**

...erfield Route

Williams Ranch

Visitor Center

El Capitan
8,085 ft
3

**Williams Ranch
Road**

62
180

0   2 mi

0   2 km

Quail Mountain
4,962 ft

TO EL PASO,
VAN HORN
↓

20

Guadalupe Mountains National Park   WELCOME TO GUADALUPE MOUNTAINS NATIONAL PARK

Guadalupe Mountains National Park is a study in extremes: it has mountaintop forests but also rocky canyons, arid desert, and a stream that winds through verdant woods. It also has the loftiest spot in Texas: 8,751-foot Guadalupe Peak. The mountain dominates the view from every approach, but it's just one part of a rugged range carved by wind, water, and time.

Planning

WHEN TO GO

Trails here are rarely crowded, except in fall, when foliage changes colors in McKittrick Canyon, and during spring break in March. Still, this is a very remote area, and you probably won't ever find too much congestion. Hikers are more apt to explore backcountry trails in spring and fall, when it's cooler but not too cold. Snow, not uncommon in winter, can linger in the higher elevations. The windy season is March through May, and the rainy months are July and August.

PLANNING YOUR TIME
GUADALUPE IN ONE DAY

Start your tour at **Pine Springs Visitor Center,** where an exhibit and slide show introduce the park's plants, wildlife, and geology. Nearby is the 0.75-mile, round-trip, wheelchair-accessible **Pinery Trail,** which rambles to the Pinery Butterfield Stage Station ruins. As you take in the sights, do not touch this vulnerable ruins' fragile walls. Next, head to the **Frijole**

Ranch History Museum, housed in a vacated yet well-preserved 1876 ranch home.

After exploring the shaded grounds and admiring the labor that built the compound, turn onto the trailhead behind the ranch house for the 0.2-mile stroll to the calm waters of **Manzanita Spring,** one of two watering holes that gurgle within a couple of miles of the museum. These oases, called riparian zones, supply the fragile wildlife here and can sometimes look like Pre-Raphaelite paintings, with mirrored-surface ponds and delicate flowers and greenery.

Afterward, pay a visit to the famed **McKittrick Canyon.** Regardless of the season, the dense foliage and basin stream are worth the hike—though it's best to visit it in late October and early November when the trees burst into color. Get here quickly by driving northeast from the visitor center on U.S. 62/180 and following McKittrick Road to the contact station and parking area, where you'll find the trailhead. Note that the gate at the McKittrick turnoff is locked at sunset.

AVERAGE HIGH/LOW TEMPERATURES					
JAN.	FEB.	MAR.	APR.	MAY	JUNE
53/30	58/35	63/38	71/46	78/55	88/63
JULY	AUG.	SEPT.	OCT.	NOV.	DEC.
87/63	84/62	78/57	71/49	61/38	57/33

Take your time walking the **McKittrick Canyon Trail,** which leads 2.4 miles to Pratt Lodge, or the strenuous but rewarding 8.4-mile **Permian Reef Trail,** which takes you up thousands of feet, past monumental geological formations. Or traverse the easy, short (less than 1 mile) **McKittrick Canyon Nature Loop.**

GETTING HERE AND AROUND
AIR TRAVEL
To get within striking distance of Guadalupe Mountains National Park by air, Carlsbad's Cavern City Air Terminal, 55 miles northeast, is served by Boutique Air, with regular service from Albuquerque and Dallas/Fort Worth. El Paso International Airport is 105 miles to the west and served by all major carriers.

CAR TRAVEL
About half of the Guadalupe Mountains is a designated wilderness, and few roadways penetrate the park. Most sites are accessible off U.S. 62/180. Dog Canyon, on the north end of the park, is reached via Highway 137 from New Mexico.

PARK ESSENTIALS
ACCESSIBILITY
The wheelchair-accessible Headquarters Visitor Center has a wheelchair available for use. The ¾-mile round-trip Pinery Trail from the visitor center to Butterfield Stage Ruins is wheelchair accessible, as is McKittrick Contact Station.

PARK FEES AND PERMITS
The park fee is $7 ($10 beginning in 2020), good for one week, and can be paid at the visitor center or at major trailheads. Camping is $8 a night per site; pay at the visitor center or at self-registration boards in campgrounds. For overnight backpacking trips, you must get a free permit from either the visitor center or Dog Canyon Office.

PARK HOURS
The park is open 24/7, year-round. It's in the Mountain time zone.

CELL PHONE RECEPTION
Reception in the park is very spotty, but cell phones can sometimes pick up signals along trails. Alternatively, public phones are at the Dog Canyon Office, Pine Springs Visitor Center, and McKittrick Contact Station.

EDUCATIONAL OFFERINGS
RANGER PROGRAMS
Junior Ranger Program
COLLEGE | FAMILY | The park offers a self-guided Junior Ranger Program: kids choose activities from a workbook— including nature hikes and answering questions based on park exhibits—and earn a badge once they've completed four. If they complete six, they earn an additional patch. Workbooks are available at the visitor center or can be downloaded from the park website. ⊠ *Pine Springs Visitor Center* ☎ *915/828–3251* ⊕ *www.nps.gov/gumo.*

RESTAURANTS
Dining in the park is a do-it-yourself affair. There are no restaurants, but the visitor center sells a few drink and snack items, and nearby Whites City has a restaurant and convenience store. You'll find good dining selections in Carlsbad, NM (55 miles), and Van Horn (60 miles).

HOTELS

There are no hotels in or even very near the park. There's one very basic motel in Whites City, NM (35 miles), and several hotels in Carlsbad, NM (55 miles), but these lodgings are astonishingly expensive because of high demand by local oil-industry workers. Many visitors stay in Van Horn (60 miles), which has a cool old historic lodging (Hotel El Capitan), and even farther away in El Paso (115 miles), which is a fairly scenic two-hour drive and has dozens of reasonably priced options. *Hotel reviews have been shortened. For full information, visit Fodors.com.*

VISITOR INFORMATION

VISITOR CENTERS

★ McKittrick Contact Station

ARCHAEOLOGICAL SITE | Poster-size illustrations on a shaded, outdoor patio tell the geological story of the Guadalupe Mountains, believed to have been carved from an ancient sea. You can also hear the recorded memoirs of oilman Wallace Pratt, who donated his ranch and surrounding area to the federal government for preservation. Nearby trailheads access a 1-mile nature loop and lengthier hikes. ⊠ *4 miles off U.S. 62/180* ☎ *915/828–3251* ⊕ *www.nps.gov/gumo.*

★ Pine Springs Visitor Center

INFO CENTER | You can pick up maps, brochures, and hiking permits here at the main visitor center, just off U.S. 62/180. A slide show and a 12-minute movie provide a quick introduction to the park, half of which is protected as a designated wilderness area. Informative exhibits depict geological history, area wildlife, and flora ranging from lowland desert to forested mountaintop. You can access several trails and a lovely picnic area and campground just outside the office. ⊠ *400 Pine Canyon Dr.* ✛ *Just off U.S. 62/180* ☎ *915/828–3251* ⊕ *www.nps.gov/gumo.*

 Sights

SCENIC DRIVES

Williams Ranch Road

ARCHAEOLOGICAL SITE | Take in panoramic views and see limestone cliffs up close on this rough but enjoyable 7¼-mile, one-way drive over what was once the Butterfield Overland Mail Stage Line. Access is from U.S. 62/180, at the park's southeast border, and you must pick up a key at the visitor center to unlock the gate to this road that can be driven only with a high-clearance, four-wheel-drive vehicle. It takes about an hour to reach the old ranch house, at the base of a 3,000-foot cliff. This is a day-trip only; overnight parking prohibited. ✛ *Off U.S. 62/180* ⊕ *www.nps.gov/gumo.*

HISTORIC SITES

★ Frijole Ranch History Museum

COLLEGE | FAMILY | With its grassy, tree-shaded grounds, you could almost imagine this handsome and peaceful little 1876 ranch house somewhere other than the harsh Chihuahuan Desert. Inside what's believed to be the region's oldest intact structure, displays and photographs depict ranch life and early park history. Easy, family-friendly hiking trails lead to wildlife oases at Manzanita Spring and Smith Spring. Hours are sporadic, so call ahead if you wish to go inside. Still, it's good fun just to explore the ranch grounds and outbuildings, orchard, and still-functioning irrigation system. ⊠ *Frijole Ranch Rd.* ✛ *Just off U.S. 62/180* ☎ *915/828–3251* ⊕ *www. nps.gov/gumo.*

Pinery Butterfield Stage Station Ruins

ARCHAEOLOGICAL SITE | FAMILY | In the mid-1800s passengers en route from St. Louis to California on the Butterfield Overland Mail stagecoach route stopped here for rest and refreshment. At more than a mile in elevation, the station was the highest on the journey, but it operated for only about a year. The ruins

Plants and Wildlife in Guadalupe Mountains

Despite the constant wind and the arid conditions, more than a thousand species of plants populate the mountains, chasms, and salt dunes that comprise the park's different geologic zones. Some grow many feet in a single night; others bloom so infrequently they're called "century plants." In fall, McKittrick Canyon's oaks, bigtooth maples, and velvet ashes go Technicolor above the little stream that traverses it. Barren-looking cacti burst into yellow, red, and purple bloom in spring, and wildflowers can carpet the park for thousands of acres after unusually heavy rains.

More than 86,000 acres of mountains, chasms, canyons, woods, and deserts house an incredible diversity of wildlife, including hallmark Southwestern species like roadrunners and long-limbed jackrabbits, which run so fast they appear to float on their enormous, black-tipped ears. Other furry residents include coyotes, black bears, mountain lions, fox, deer, elk, and badgers. You may also spot numerous winged creatures: 300 different bird species, 90 types of butterflies, and 16 species of bats.

Plenty of reptiles and insects make their homes here, too: coachwhip snakes, diamondback rattlers, whiptail lizards, scorpions, and lovelorn tarantulas (the only time you might spy them is in the fall, when they search for mates), to name a few. Texas's famous (and threatened) horned lizards—affectionately called "horny toads"—can also be seen waddling across the soil in search of ants and other insects. Rangers caution parents not to let little ones run too far ahead on the trails. ■ TIP→ Rattlesnakes are common here but they hibernate in winter. In summer, overnight campers should be cautious at dusk and dawn. The snakes are not aggressive, so try to remain calm and give a wide berth to any you spot.

20

Guadalupe Mountains National Park

provide a reasonable peek into the past: the bare remains of a few buildings with rock walls (but no roofs) layered on the desert floor. Do not touch. You can drive here from U.S. 62/180, but it's more interesting to stroll over via the paved ¾-mile round-trip natural trail from the visitor center. ⊠ *U.S. 62/180* ✛ *Just east of visitor center* ⊕ *www.nps.gov/gumo.*

SCENIC STOPS
★ McKittrick Canyon
ARCHAEOLOGICAL SITE | A desert creek flows through this verdant canyon, one of the most wondrous sights of West Texas, lined with walnut, maple, and other trees

that explode into brilliant hues each autumn. Call the visitor center for foliage updates—the spectacular changing of the leaves usually extends into early November. You're likely to spot mule deer heading for the water here. The canyon is ground zero for several hiking trails, including Pratt Cabin (two to three hours) and the Grotto (four hours). ⊠ *McKittrick Canyon Rd.* ✛ *Off U.S. 62/180* ⊕ *www. nps.gov/gumo.*

The sun sets over the desert landscape of west Texas at Guadalupe Mountains National Park.

Activities

BIRD-WATCHING

More than 300 species of birds have been spotted in the park, including the ladder-backed woodpecker, Scott's oriole, Say's phoebe, and white-throated swift. Many migratory birds—such as fleeting hummingbirds and larger but less graceful turkey vultures—stop at Guadalupe during spring and fall migrations. **Manzanita Springs,** near the Frijole Ranch History Museum, is an excellent birding spot. There aren't any local guides, but rangers at the Dog Canyon Office and the Pine Springs Visitor Center can help you spot some native species.

Books on birding are available at the visitor center, and bird lovers will find the park's birding checklist especially helpful. It's easy to spot the larger birds of prey circling overhead, such as keen-beaked golden eagles and swift, red-tailed hawks. Watch for owls in the **Bowl** area and for swift-footed roadrunners in the desert areas (they're quick, but not as speedy as their cartoon counterpart).

HIKING

No matter which trail you select, pack wisely—the visitor center carries only limited supplies. This includes the recommended gallon of water per day per person (there are water-filling stations at the visitor center, McKittrick Canyon Ranger Station, and Dog Canyon Office), as well as sunscreen, sturdy footwear, and hats. The area has a triple-whammy regarding sun ailments: it's very open, very sunny, and has a high altitude (which makes sunburns more likely).

★ The Bowl

HIKING/WALKING | Cutting through forests of pine and Douglas fir, this trail to an aptly named mountaintop valley is considered one of the most gorgeous in the park. The strenuous 9.1-mile round-trip—which can take up to 10 hours—is where rangers go when they want to enjoy themselves. Bring lots of water. *Difficult.*

☒ *Guadalupe Mountains National Park* ⚓ *Trailhead: at Pine Springs Trailhead Campground.*

Devil's Hall Trail

HIKING/WALKING | Wind through Chihuahua Desert habitat thick with spiked agave plants, prickly pear cacti, ponderosa pines, giant boulders, and Devil's Hall, a narrow canyon about 10 feet wide and 100 feet deep. If you travel at a leisurely pace, this 4.2-mile trail will take four or five hours. *Moderate.* ☒ *Guadalupe Mountains National Park* ⚓ *Trailhead: at Pine Springs Campground.*

Dog Canyon Office

HIKING/WALKING | FAMILY | The staff at the Dog Canyon Office can help plan your day hike, horseback ride, or overnight backpacking trip. Dog Canyon is an excellent gateway to the high country of the park's northern boundary. You can reach the office via Hwy.137 off U.S. 285 (12 miles north of Carlsbad, NM) or by Hwy. 408 off U.S. 62/180 (9 miles south of Carlsbad). ☒ *Hwy. 137* ☎ *575/981–2418* ⊕ *www.nps.gov/gumo.*

El Capitan/Salt Basin Overlook Trails

HIKING/WALKING | Several trails combine to form a popular loop through the low desert. El Capitan skirts the base of El Capitan peak for about 3.5 miles, leading to a junction with Salt Basin Overlook. The 4.7-mile Salt Basin Overlook trail begins at the Pine Springs Trailhead and has views of the stark, white salt flat below and loops back onto the El Capitan Trail. The 11.3-mile round-trip is not recommended during the intense heat of summer, because there is absolutely no shade. *Moderate–Difficult.* ☒ *Guadalupe Mountains National Park* ⚓ *Trailhead: at Pine Springs Visitor Center.*

Frijole/Foothills Trail

HIKING/WALKING | FAMILY | Branching off the Frijole Ranch Trail, this hike leads to Pine Springs Campground and Visitor

Center. The 5.5-mile round-trip through desert vistas takes about four hours. *Moderate.* ☒ *Guadalupe Mountains National Park* ⚓ *Trailhead: Frijole Ranch History Museum.*

★ Guadalupe Peak Trail

HIKING/WALKING | An 8.4-mile workout over a steep grade to the top of Texas pays off with a passage through several ecosystems and some great views. The round-trip hike takes six to eight hours, but the trail is clearly defined and doesn't require undue athleticism. The steepest climbs are in the beginning. In summer, start this hike in early morning to allow a descent before afternoon thunderstorms flare up. Lightning targets high peaks. Be alert to changing weather and head for lower ground if conditions worsen. Also, Guadalupe Peak is considered one of the windiest points in the U.S. *Difficult, elevation gain 3,000 feet.* ☒ *Guadalupe Mountains National Park* ⚓ *Trailhead: at Pine Springs Campground* ⊕ *www.nps. gov/gumo.*

Indian Meadow Nature Trail

HIKING/WALKING | FAMILY | A mostly level trail in Dog Canyon, this 0.6-mile hike crosses an arroyo into meadowlands. It's a good way to spend about 45 minutes savoring the countryside. *Easy.* ☒ *Guadalupe Mountains National Park* ⚓ *Trailhead: across from Dog Canyon Office.*

Lost Peak

HIKING/WALKING | The somewhat strenuous trek from Dog Canyon into a coniferous forest is 6.4 miles round-trip and will take about six hours at a fairly slow pace. There is no defined trail the last ¼ mile to the peak, but adventurers are rewarded with terrific views. *Difficult, elevation gain 1,540 feet.* ☒ *Guadalupe Mountains National Park* ⚓ *Trailhead: at Dog Canyon Trailhead* ⊕ *www.nps.gov/gumo.*

Marcus Overlook

HIKING/WALKING | FAMILY | A 4.5-mile round-trip with an 800-foot elevation gain rewards you with a panoramic view of West Dog Canyon. Set aside about half a day for it. *Moderate.* ✉ *Guadalupe Mountains National Park* ✛ *Trailhead: near Dog Canyon Office.*

McKittrick Nature Loop

HIKING/WALKING | FAMILY | Signs along this nearly mile-long loop explain the geological and botanical history of the area, and the views, while not spectacular, are engaging enough to hold your interest. You can take the loop in either of two directions when you come to a fork in the trail. *Easy–Moderate.* ✉ *Guadalupe Mountains National Park* ✛ *Trailhead: at McKittrick Contact Station.*

Permian Reef Geology Trail

HIKING/WALKING | If you're in shape and have a serious geological bent, you may want to hike this approximately 8.5-mile round-trip climb. It heads through open, expansive desert country to a forested ridge with Douglas fir and ponderosa pines. Panoramic views of McKittrick Canyon and the surrounding mountain ranges allow you to observe many rock layers. A geology guidebook coordinated to trail makers is available at the Headquarters Visitor Center. Set aside at least eight hours for this trek. *Difficult, elevation gain 2,000 feet.* ✉ *Guadalupe Mountains National Park* ✛ *Trailhead: accessed via the McKittrick Canyon Trailhead at the northeast corner of the park* 🎫 *A 7-day, $5 hiking permit is available at the trailhead or Headquarters Visitor Center.*

★ Pratt Cabin Trail

HIKING/WALKING | FAMILY | View stream and canyon woodlands along a 4½-mile round-trip excursion that leads to the vacant Pratt Cabin, which was built of stone during the Great Depression in the "most beautiful spot in Texas," according

to its original owner, Wallace Pratt. Perhaps he was enthralled by an oasis of running water carving through the canyon floor or a colorful riot of autumn foliage. Plan on at least two hours if you walk at a brisk pace, but give yourself another hour or two if you want to take your time. *Moderate.* ✉ *Guadalupe Mountains National Park* ✛ *Trailhead: McKittrick Contact Station.*

★ Smith Spring Trail

HIKING/WALKING | FAMILY | Departing from the Frijole Ranch, the trail heads for a shady oasis where you're likely to spot mule deer and elk drawn to the miracle of water in the desert. As a bonus, the route passes Manzanita Spring, another wildlife refuge only 0.2 mile past Frijole Ranch. Allow 1½ hours to complete the 2.2-mile round-trip walk. This is a good hike for older kids whose legs won't tire as easily, but it is not wheelchair accessible past Manzanita Spring. *Easy–Moderate.* ✉ *Guadalupe Mountains National Park* ✛ *Trailhead: Frijole Ranch.*

Best Campgrounds in Guadalupe Mountains

The park has two developed campgrounds that charge fees, and 10 designated primitive, backcountry sites where you can camp for free. First, obtain a permit at Pine Springs Visitor Center or Dog Canyon Office. Visitors haul their supplies for miles to stretch out on the unspoiled land of these backcountry sites. In the backcountry, no restrooms are provided; visitors may dig their own privies, but toilet paper and other waste should be packed out. Wood and charcoal fires are prohibited throughout the park, but you can use a camp stove with containerized fuels at both the developed and backcountry sites.

Dog Canyon Campground. This campground is remote and a little tricky to find, but well worth the effort. The very well-maintained camping area is in a coniferous forest, with nine tent sites and four RV sites (no hookups, 23-foot maximum). ✉ *Hwy. 137, just within park northern entrance* ☎ *575/981–2418.*

Pine Springs Campground. You'll be snuggled amid pinyon and juniper trees near the base of a tall mountain peak at this resting place behind the Pine Springs Visitor Center. It has 19 tent sites, 18 RV sites (no hookups), one wheelchair-accessible site, and two group sites. ✉ *At park east entrance, off U.S. 62/180* ☎ *915/828–3251.*

Trail to Grotto Picnic Area

HIKING/WALKING | FAMILY | The mostly level 6.75-mile round-trip trek to this picnic area affords views of a flowing stream and surface rock that resembles formations in an underground cave with jagged overhangs. Plan on about four to five hours at a leisurely pace. *Moderate.* ✉ *Guadalupe Mountains National Park* ✛ *Trailhead: at McKittrick Contact Station.*

🍴 Restaurants

IN THE PARK

The park has no restaurants but does sell limited snacks in the visitor center, and a few picnic areas are available. Wood and charcoal fires are not allowed anywhere in the park. If you want to cook a hot meal, bring a camp stove.

PICNIC AREAS

★ Dog Canyon Campground

FAMILY | This site at the north end of the park, a two-hour drive from Pine Springs Visitor Center, has 13 campsites with picnic tables, which you can use during the day for free. This is a lovely shaded area with an elevation of 6,300 feet where you're likely to see mule deer. Drinking water and restrooms are available. ✉ *Guadalupe Mountains National Park* ✛ *Rte. 137, just within park northern entrance.*

Frijole Ranch

FAMILY | It's not very secluded, but Frijole sports attractive picnic shelters that can accommodate large groups near the parking area, which also has restrooms. Two picnic tables are also set up under tall trees near Frijole Ranch History Museum. Restrooms are available. ✉ *Guadalupe Mountains National Park* ✛ *1 mile northeast of Pine Springs Visitor Center.*

★ Pine Springs Campground

FAMILY | Drinking water, restrooms, and a picnic area are available at this central campground with sweeping mountain views, near the park's visitor center. Shade, however, can be a bit sparse, and summer heat intense. You can walk off that hearty lunch along one of the several nearby hiking trails. ✉ *Guadalupe Mountains National Park* ✛ *Next to Pine Springs Visitor Center.*

OUTSIDE THE PARK

For dining options near the park, see Restaurants in Big Bend National Park and Carlsbad Caverns National Park.

 Hotels

OUTSIDE THE PARK

For lodging options near the park, see Hotels in Big Bend National Park and Carlsbad Caverns National Park.

Chapter 21

JOSHUA TREE NATIONAL PARK

Updated by
Sarah Amandolare

CALIFORNIA

WELCOME TO JOSHUA TREE NATIONAL PARK

TOP REASONS TO GO

★ **Rock climbing:** Joshua Tree is a world-class site with challenges for climbers of just about every skill level.

★ **Peace and quiet:** Roughly two hours from Los Angeles, this great wilderness is the ultimate escape from technology.

★ **Stargazing:** You'll be mesmerized by the Milky Way flowing across the summer sky. For spectacular natural fireworks, visit in mid-August during the Perseid meteor shower and watch shooting stars streak overhead.

★ **Wildflowers:** In spring, the hillsides explode in a patchwork of yellow, blue, pink, and white.

★ **Sunsets:** Twilight is a magical time here, especially during the winter, when the setting sun casts a golden glow on the mountains.

1 Keys View. This is the most dramatic overlook in the park—on clear days you can see Signal Mountain in Mexico.

2 Hidden Valley. Crawl between the big rocks and you'll understand why this boulder-strewn area was once a cattle rustlers' hideout.

3 Cholla Cactus Garden. Come here in the late afternoon, when the spiky stalks of the bigelow (jumping) cholla cactus are backlit against an intense blue sky.

4 Oasis of Mara. Walk the nature trail around this desert oasis, which the first settlers, the Serrano, dubbed "the place of little springs and much grass."

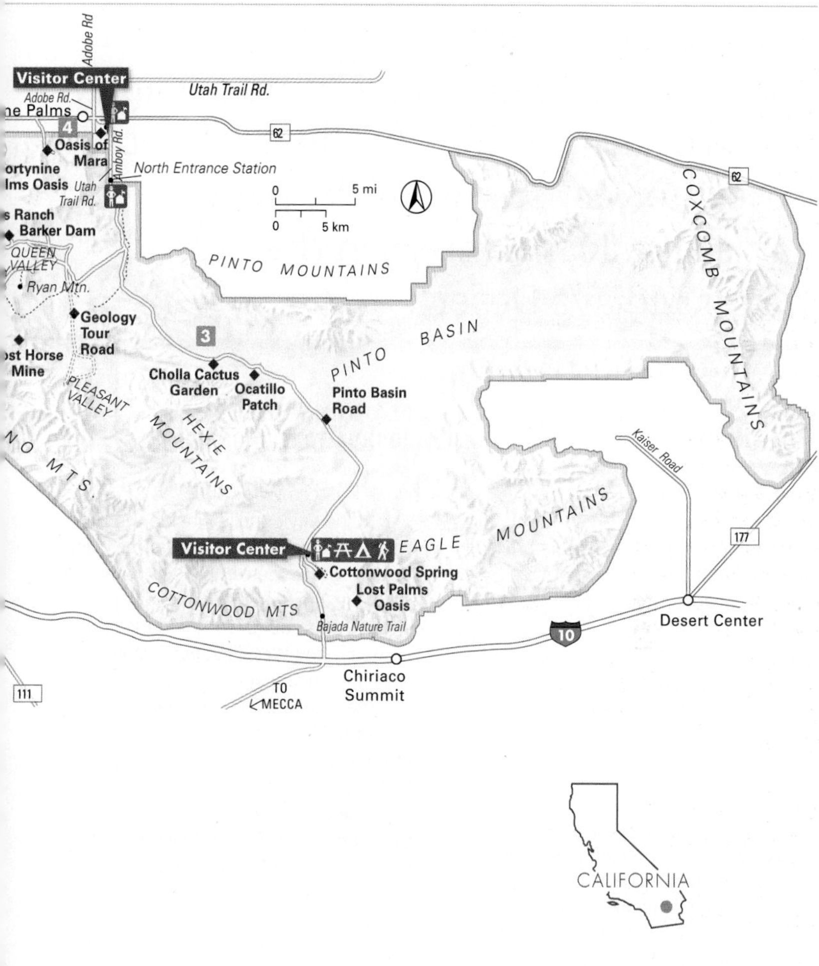

Adobe Rd

Visitor Center
Adobe Rd.
ne Palms
Utah Trail Rd.

Oasis of
Mara
ortynine
lms Oasis
Utah
Trail Rd.

North Entrance Station

0   5 mi

0   5 km

s Ranch
Barker Dam

QUEEN
VALLEY
Ryan Mtn.

PINTO   MOUNTAINS

PINTO   BASIN

COXCOMB MOUNTAINS

Geology
Tour
Road

st Horse
Mine

PLEASANT
VALLEY

Cholla Cactus
Garden   Ocatillo
Patch

PINTO
Pinto Basin
Road

HEXIE
MOUNTAINS

Kaiser Road

177

NO MTS.

EAGLE   MOUNTAINS

Visitor Center
Cottonwood Spring
Lost Palms
Oasis

COTTONWOOD MTS
Bajada Nature Trail

Desert Center

10

111

TO
MECCA

Chiriaco
Summit

CALIFORNIA

Joshua Tree National Park teems with fascinating landscapes and life-forms. It attracts around 1.5 million visitors each year, yet is mysteriously quiet at dawn and dusk. The landscape shifts abruptly from the arid stubble of the low Sonoran Desert to vast stands of the park's namesake Joshua trees in the higher, wetter Mojave Desert.

Planning

WHEN TO GO

October through May, when the desert is cooler, is when most visitors arrive. Daytime temperatures range from the mid-70s in December and January to mid-90s in October and May. Lows can dip to near freezing in midwinter, and you may even encounter snow at the higher elevations. Summers can be torrid, with daytime temperatures reaching 110°F.

FESTIVALS AND EVENTS

Pioneer Days

FESTIVAL | FAMILY | Outhouse races, live music, and arm wrestling mark this celebration held annually, during the third full October weekend, in Twenty-nine Palms. The event also features a parade, carnival, chili dinner, and an old timers' gathering. ⊠ *Twentynine Palms* ☎ *760/367–3445* ⊕ *www.visit29.org.*

Riverside County Fair & National Date Festival

FESTIVAL | FAMILY | Head to Indio for camel and ostrich races. ⊠ *Riverside County Fairgrounds, 82–503 Hwy. 111, Indio* ☎ *800/811–3247* ⊕ *www.datefest.org.*

JOSHUA TREE IN ONE DAY

After stocking up on water, snacks, and lunch in Yucca Valley or Joshua Tree (you won't find any supplies inside the park), begin your visit at the **Joshua Tree Visitor Center,** where you can pick up maps and peruse exhibits to get acquainted with what awaits you. Enter the park itself at the nearby **West Entrance Station** and continue driving along the highly scenic and well-maintained **Park Boulevard.** Stop first at **Hidden Valley,** where you can relax at the picnic area or hike the easy 1-mile loop trail. After a few more miles turn left onto the spur road that takes you to the trailhead for the **Barker Dam Nature Trail.** Walk the easy 1.1-mile loop to view a water tank ranchers built to quench their cattle's thirst; along the way you'll spot birds and a handful of cactus varieties. Return to Park Boulevard and head south; you'll soon leave the main road again for the drive to **Keys View.** The easy loop trail here is only 0.25 mile, but the views extend for miles in every direction—look for the San Andreas Fault, the Salton Sea, and nearby mountains. Return to Park Boulevard, where you'll find **Cap Rock,**

AVERAGE HIGH/LOW TEMPERATURES					
JAN.	FEB.	MAR.	APR.	MAY	JUNE
62/32	65/37	72/40	80/50	90/55	100/65
JULY	AUG.	SEPT.	OCT.	NOV.	DEC.
105/70	101/78	96/62	85/55	72/40	62/31

another short loop trail winding amid rock formations and Joshua trees.

Continuing along Park Boulevard, the start of the 18-mile self-guided **Geology Tour Road** will soon appear on your right. A brochure outlining its 16 stops is available at visitor centers; note that the round-trip will take about two hours, and high-clearance, four-wheel-drive vehicles are recommended after stop 9. ■TIP→ **Do not attempt if it has recently rained.** Back on Park Boulevard, you'll soon arrive at the aptly named **Skull Rock.** This downright spooky formation is next to the parking lot; a nearby trailhead marks the beginning of a 1.7-mile nature trail. End your day with a stop at the **Oasis Visitor Center** in Twentynine Palms, where you can stroll through the historic **Oasis of Mara,** popular with area settlers.

GETTING HERE AND AROUND
AIR TRAVEL
Palm Springs International Airport is the closest major airport to Joshua Tree National Park. It's about 45 miles from the park. The drive from Los Angeles International Airport to Joshua Tree takes about two to three hours.

CAR TRAVEL
An isolated island of pristine wilderness—a rarity these days—Joshua Tree National Park is within a short drive of 11 million Southern California residents. Most visitors, in fact, make the two- to three-hour drive from the Los Angeles area to enjoy a weekend of solitude in 792,726 acres of untouched desert. The urban sprawl of Palm Springs (home to the nearest airport) is 45 miles away, but gateway towns Joshua Tree, Yucca Valley, and Twentynine Palms are just north of the park. If you're staying in the Palm Springs area, you can enjoy the highlights of the park in one day, including a stop for a picnic at a scenic spot.

■TIP→ **If you'd prefer not to drive, most Palm Springs area hotels can arrange a half- or full-day tour that hits the highlights of Joshua Tree National Park.** But you'll need to spend two or three days camping here to truly experience the quiet beauty of the desert.

PARK ESSENTIALS
ACCESSIBILITY
Black Rock Canyon and Jumbo Rocks campgrounds have one accessible campsite each. Nature trails at Oasis of Mara, Bajada, Keys View, and Cap Rock are accessible. Some trails at roadside viewpoints can be negotiated by those with limited mobility.

PARK FEES AND PERMITS
Park admission is $30 per car, $15 per person on foot, bicycle, or horse, and $25 per person by motorcycle. The Joshua Tree Pass, good for one year, is $55.

PARK HOURS
The park is open every day, around the clock, but visitor centers are staffed from approximately 8 am to 5 pm. The park is in the Pacific time zone.

CELL PHONE RECEPTION
Cell phones don't work in most areas of the park. There are no telephones in the interior of the park.

EDUCATIONAL OFFERINGS
LECTURES
The Desert Institute at Joshua Tree National Park

COLLEGE | The nonprofit educational partner of the park offers a full schedule of lectures, classes, and hikes. Class topics include basket making, painting, and photography, while field trips include workshops on cultural history, natural science, and how to survive in the desert. ⊠ *74485 National Park Dr., Twentynine Palms* ☎ *760/367–5525* ⊕ *www.joshuatree.org.*

Stargazing

COLLEGE | At Joshua Tree National Park you can tour the Milky Way on summer evenings using binoculars. Rangers also offer programs on some evenings when the moon isn't visible. Browse the schedule online. ⊠ *Cottonwood Campground Amphitheater and Oasis Visitor Center* ⊕ *www.nps.gov/jotr/planyourvisit/calendar.htm.*

RANGER PROGRAMS
Evening Programs

TOUR—SIGHT | Rangers present 45-minute-long programs, often on Friday or Saturday evening, at Cottonwood Amphitheater, Indian Cove Amphitheater, and Jumbo Rocks Campground. Topics range from natural history to local lore. The schedule is posted online. ⊠ *Joshua Tree National Park* ⊡ *Free.*

★ **Keys Ranch Tour**

HOUSE | A guide takes you through the former home of a family that homesteaded here for 60 years. In addition to the ranch, a workshop, store, and schoolhouse are still standing, and the grounds are strewn with vehicles and mining equipment. The 90-minute tour, which begins at the Keys Ranch gate, tells the history of the family that built the ranch. Tickets are $10, and reservations are required. ⊠ *Keys Ranch gate* ☎ *760/367–5522* ⊕ *www.nps.gov/jotr.*

RESTAURANTS

Dining options in the gateway towns around Joshua Tree National Park are extremely limited—you'll mostly find fast-food outlets and a few casual cafés in Yucca Valley and Twentynine Palms. The exception is the restaurant at 29 Palms Inn, which has an interesting California-cuisine menu that features lots of veggies. Still, you'll have to travel to the Palm Springs desert resort area for a fine-dining experience.

HOTELS

Lodging choices in the Joshua Tree National Park area are limited to a few motels, chain hotels, and a luxury bed-and-breakfast establishment in the gateway towns. In general, most offer few amenities and are modestly priced. Book ahead for the spring wildflower season—reservations may be difficult to obtain then.

For a more extensive range of lodging options, you'll need to head to Palm Springs and the surrounding desert resort communities. *Hotel reviews have been shortened. For full information, visit Fodors.com.*

What It Costs			
$	$$	$$$	$$$$
RESTAURANTS			
under $12	$12–$20	$21–$30	over $30
HOTELS			
under $100	$100–$150	$151–$200	over $200

TOURS
Big Wheel Tours

TOUR—SIGHT | Based in Palm Desert, Big Wheel Tours offers van excursions, Jeep tours, and hiking trips through the park. Bicycle tours (road and mountain bike) are available outside the park boundary. Pickups are available at Palm Springs area hotels. ⊠ *42160 State St., Palm Desert*

☏ 760/779–1837 ⊕ www.bwbtours.com
✉ From $119.

Trail Discovery

TOUR—SIGHT | You can get a full day of exploring Joshua Tree with Trail Discovery, along with information on the park's plants, animals, geography, and history. Sunrise treks are offered in hot, summer months. Park admission, bottled water, hip packs, snacks, and fruit are included. Transportation is not provided. ☏ 760/413–1575 ⊕ www.palmspringshiking.com ✉ From $125.

VISITOR INFORMATION

PARK CONTACT INFORMATION Joshua Tree National Park ✉ 74485 National Park Dr., Twentynine Palms ☏ 760/367–5522 ⊕ www.nps.gov/jotr.

VISITOR CENTERS

Cottonwood Visitor Center

INFO CENTER | The south entrance is the closest to Interstate 10, the east–west highway from Los Angeles to Phoenix. Exhibits in this small center, staffed by rangers and volunteers, illustrate the region's natural history. The center also has restrooms with flush toilets. ✉ Cottonwood Spring, Pinto Basin Rd. ⊕ www.nps.gov/jotr.

Joshua Tree Visitor Center

INFO CENTER | This visitor center has maps and interesting exhibits illustrating park geology, cultural and historic sites, and hiking and rock-climbing activities. There's also a small bookstore and café. Restrooms with flush toilets are on the premises. ✉ 6554 Park Blvd., Joshua Tree ☏ 760/366–1855 ⊕ www.nps.gov/jotr.

Oasis Visitor Center

INFO CENTER | Exhibits here illustrate how Joshua Tree was formed, reveal the differences between the park's two types of desert, and demonstrate how plants and animals eke out an existence in this arid climate. Take the ½-mile nature walk through the nearby Oasis of Mara, which is alive with cottonwood trees, palm trees, and mesquite shrubs. Facilities include picnic tables, restrooms, and a bookstore. ✉ 74485 National Park Dr., Twentynine Palms ☏ 760/367–5500 ⊕ www.nps.gov/jotr.

Plants and Wildlife in Joshua Tree

Joshua Tree will shatter your notions of the desert as a wasteland. Life flourishes here, as flora and fauna have adapted to heat and drought. In most areas you'll be walking among native Joshua trees, ocotillos, and yuccas. One of the best spring desert wildflower displays in Southern California blooms here. You'll see plenty of animals—reptiles such as nocturnal sidewinders, birds like golden eagles or burrowing owls, and occasionally mammals like coyotes and bobcats.

◉ Sights

You can experience Joshua Tree National Park on several levels. Even on a short excursion along Park Boulevard between the Joshua Tree entrance station and Oasis of Mara, you'll see the essence of North American desert scenery—including a staggering abundance of flora visible along a dozen self-guided nature trails. You'll also see remnants of homesteads from a century ago, now mostly abandoned and wind-worn. If rock climbing is your passion, this is the place for you; boulder-strewn mountaintops and slopes beckon. But in the end, Joshua Tree National Park is a pristine wilderness where you can enjoy a solitary stroll along an animal trail and commune with nature. Be sure to take some time to explore on your own and enjoy the peace and quiet.

SCENIC DRIVES

Geology Tour Road

SCENIC DRIVE | Some of the park's most fascinating landscapes can be observed from this 18-mile dirt road. Parts of the journey are rough; a 4X4 vehicle is required after mile marker 9. Sights to see include a 100-year-old stone dam called Squaw Tank, defunct mines, and a large plain with an abundance of Joshua trees. There are 16 stops along the way, so give yourself about two hours to complete the round-trip trek. ⊠ *South of Park Blvd., west of Jumbo Rocks.*

Park Boulevard

SCENIC DRIVE | If you have time only for a short visit, driving Park Boulevard is your best choice. Traversing the most scenic portions of Joshua Tree, this well-paved road connects the north and west entrances in the park's high desert section. Along with some sweeping desert views, you'll see jumbles of splendid boulder formations, stands of Joshua trees, and Hidden Valley and Barker Dam, remnants of the area's wild and woolly past. From the Oasis Visitor Center, drive south. After about 5 miles, the road forks; turn right and head west toward Jumbo Rocks (clearly marked with a road sign). ⊠ *Joshua Tree National Park.*

Pinto Basin Road

SCENIC DRIVE | This paved road takes you from high Mojave desert to low Colorado desert. A long, slow drive, the route runs from the main part of the park to Interstate 10; it can add as much as an hour to and from Palm Springs (round-trip), but the views and roadside exhibits make it worth the extra time. From the Oasis Visitor Center, drive south. After about 5 miles, the road forks; take a left and continue another 9 miles to the Cholla Cactus Garden, where the sun fills the cactus needles with light. Past that is the Ocotillo Patch, filled with spindly plants bearing razor-sharp thorns and, after a rain, bright green leaves and brilliant red

flowers. Side trips from this route require a 4X4. ⊠ *Joshua Tree National Park.*

HISTORIC SITES

Hidden Valley

NATURE SITE | FAMILY | This legendary cattle-rustlers' hideout is set among big boulders along a 1-mile loop trail. Kids love to scramble on and around the rocks. There are shaded picnic tables here. ⊠ *Park Blvd.* ✛ *14 miles south of west entrance.*

★ Keys Ranch

TOUR—SIGHT | This 150-acre ranch, which once belonged to William and Frances Keys and is now on the National Historic Register, illustrates one of the area's most successful attempts at homesteading. The couple raised five children under extreme desert conditions. Most of the original buildings, including the house, school, store, and workshop, have been restored to the way they were when William died in 1969. The only way to see the ranch is on one of the 90-minute walking tours usually offered Friday–Sunday, October–May, and weekends in summer; advance reservations required. ⊠ *Joshua Tree National Park* ✛ *2 miles north of Barker Dam Rd.* ☎ *760/367–5522* ⊕ *www.nps.gov/jotr/planyourvisit/ranchtour.htm* 🎟 *$10, available at Oasis visitor center or reserve by phone.*

Lost Horse Mine

MINE | This historic mine, which produced 10,000 ounces of gold and 16,000 ounces of silver between 1894 and 1931, was among Southern California's most productive mines. The 10-stamp mill is considered one of the best preserved of its type in the park system. The site is accessed via a fairly strenuous 4-mile round-trip hike. Mind the park warnings and don't enter any mine in Joshua Tree. ⊠ *Keys View Rd.* ✛ *About 15 miles south of west entrance.*

SCENIC STOPS
Barker Dam

DAM | Built around 1900 by ranchers and miners to hold water for cattle and mining operations, the dam now collects rainwater and is a good place to spot wildlife such as the elusive bighorn sheep. ⊠ *Barker Dam Rd.* ⊕ *Off Park Blvd., 10 miles south of west entrance.*

Cholla Cactus Garden

GARDEN | This stand of bigelow cholla (sometimes called jumping cholla, because its hooked spines seem to jump at you) is best seen and photographed in late afternoon, when the backlit spiky stalks stand out against a colorful sky. ⊠ *Pinto Basin Rd.* ⊕ *20 miles north of Cottonwood Visitor Center.*

Cottonwood Spring

NATIVE SITE | Home to the native Cahuilla people for centuries, this spring provided water for travelers and early prospectors. The area, which supports a large stand of fan palms and cottonwood trees, is one of the best stops for bird-watching, as migrating birds (and bighorn sheep) rely on the water as well. A number of gold mines were located here, and the area still has some remains, including concrete pillars. ⊠ *Cottonwood Visitor Center.*

Fortynine Palms Oasis

NATIVE SITE | A short drive off Highway 62, this site is a bit of a preview of what the park's interior has to offer: stands of fan palms, interesting petroglyphs, and evidence of fires built by early Native Americans. Because animals frequent this area, you may spot a coyote, bobcat, or roadrunner. ⊠ *End of Canyon Rd.* ⊕ *4 miles west of Twentynine Palms.*

★ Keys View

VIEWPOINT | At 5,185 feet, this point affords a sweeping view of the Santa Rosa Mountains and Coachella Valley, the San Andreas Fault, the peak of 11,500-foot Mt. San Gorgonio, the shimmering surface of Salton Sea, and—on a rare clear day—Signal Mountain in Mexico. Sunrise and sunset are magical times, when the light throws rocks and trees into high relief before bathing the hills in brilliant shades of red, orange, and gold. ⊠ *Keys View Rd.* ⊕ *16 miles south of park's west entrance.*

Lost Palms Oasis

TRAIL | More than 100 fan palms comprise the largest group of the exotic plants in the park. A spring bubbles from between the rocks, but disappears into the sandy, boulder-strewn canyon. The 7.5-mile round-trip hike is not for everyone, and not recommended during summer months. Bring plenty of water! ⊠ *Cottonwood Visitor Center.*

Ocotillo Patch

GARDEN | Stop here for a roadside exhibit on the dramatic display made by the red-tipped succulent after even the shortest rain shower. ⊠ *Pinto Basin Rd.* ⊕ *About 3 miles east of Cholla Cactus Gardens.*

 Activities

BICYCLING

Mountain biking is a great way to see Joshua Tree. Bikers are restricted to roads that are used by motorized vehicles, including the main park roads and a few four-wheel-drive trails. Bicycling on dirt roads is not recommended during the summer. Most scenic stops and picnic areas, and the Wall Street Mill trailhead, have bike racks.

Black Eagle Mine Road

BICYCLING | This 9-mile dead-end road is peppered with defunct mines, the entrances of which should be avoided. It runs along the edge of a former lake bed, then crosses a number of dry washes before navigating several of Eagle Mountain's canyons. ⊠ *Joshua Tree National Park* ⊕ *Trailhead: off Pinto Basin Rd., 6½ miles north of Cottonwood Visitor Center.*

Covington Flats

BICYCLING | This 4-mile route takes you past impressive Joshua trees as well as pinyon pines, junipers, and areas of lush desert vegetation. It's tough going toward the end, but once you reach 5,518-foot Eureka Peak you'll have great views of Palm Springs, the Morongo Basin, and the surrounding mountains. ⊠ *Joshua Tree National Park ✤ Trailhead: at Covington Flats picnic area, La Contenta Rd., 10 miles south of Rte. 62.*

Pinkham Canyon and Thermal Canyon Roads

BICYCLING | This challenging 20-mile route begins at the Cottonwood Visitor Center and loops through the Cottonwood Mountains. The unpaved trail follows Smoke Tree Wash through Pinkham Canyon, rounds Thermal Canyon, and loops back to the beginning. Rough and narrow in places, the road travels through soft sand and rocky floodplains. ⊠ *Joshua Tree National Park ✤ Trailhead: at Cottonwood Visitor Center.*

Queen Valley

BICYCLING | This 13.4-mile network of mostly level roads winds through one of the park's most impressive groves of Joshua trees. You can also leave your bike at one of the racks placed in the area and explore on foot. ⊠ *Joshua Tree National Park ✤ Trailhead: at Hidden Valley Campground, and accessible opposite Geology Tour Rd. at Big Horn Pass.*

BIRD-WATCHING

Joshua Tree, located on the inland portion of the Pacific Flyway, hosts about 240 species of birds, and the park is a popular seasonal location for bird-watching. During the fall migration, which runs mid-September through mid-October, there are several reliable sighting areas. At Barker Dam you might spot white-throated swifts, several types of swallows, or red-tailed hawks. Lucy's warbler, flycatchers, and Anna's hummingbirds cruise around Cottonwood Spring, a serene palm-shaded setting; occasional ducks, herons, and egrets, as well as migrating rufous and calliope hummingbirds, wintering prairie falcons, and a resident barn owl could show up. Black Rock Canyon sees pinyon jays, while Covington Flats reliably gets mountain quail, and you may see La Conte's thrashers, ruby-crowned kinglets, and warbling vireos at either locale. Rufous hummingbirds, Pacific slope flycatchers, and various warblers are frequent visitors to Indian Cove. Lists of birds found in the park, as well as information on recent sightings, are available at visitor centers.

HIKING

There are more than 190 miles of hiking trails in Joshua Tree, ranging from quarter-mile nature trails to 35-mile treks. Some connect with each other, so you can design your own desert maze. Remember that drinking water is hard to come by—you won't find water in the park except at the entrances. Bring along at least a gallon per person for all but the shortest hikes, more if the weather is hot.

Bajada All Access

HIKING/WALKING | Learn all about what plants do to survive in the desert on this wheelchair-accessible ¼-mile loop. *Easy.* ⊠ *Joshua Tree National Park ✤ Trailhead: south of Cottonwood Visitor Center, ½ mile from park entrance.*

Boy Scout Trail

HIKING/WALKING | The moderately strenuous 8-mile trail, suitable for backpackers, extends from Indian Cove to Park Boulevard. It runs through the westernmost edge of the Wonderland of Rocks (where you're likely to see climbers on the outcroppings), passing through a forest of Joshua trees, past granite towers, and around willow-lined pools. Completing the round-trip journey may require camping along the way, so you may want to hike only part of the trail or have a car waiting at the other end. *Difficult.* ⊠ *Joshua Tree National Park ✤ Trailhead: between Quail Springs Picnic Area and Indian Cove Campground.*

Did You Know?

Found only in Arizona, California, Nevada, and Utah, the Joshua tree (*Yucca brevifolia*) is actually a member of the agave family. Native Americans used the Joshua tree's hearty foliage like leather, forming it into everyday items like baskets and shoes. Later, early settlers used its core and limbs for building fences to contain their livestock.

California Riding and Hiking Trail

HIKING/WALKING | You'll need a backcountry camping pass to traverse this 35-mile route between the Black Rock Canyon entrance and the north entrance. You can access the trail for a short or long hike at several points. The visitor centers have trail maps. *Difficult.* ⊠ *Joshua Tree National Park* ✛ *Trailheads: at Upper Covington Flats, Ryan Campground, Twin Tanks, south of north park entrance, and Black Rock Campground.*

Cap Rock

HIKING/WALKING | This ½-mile wheelchair-accessible loop—named after a boulder that sits atop a huge rock formation like a cap—winds through fascinating rock formations and has signs that explain the geology of the Mojave Desert. *Easy.* ⊠ *Joshua Tree National Park* ✛ *Trailhead: Keys View Rd. near junction with Park Blvd.*

Fortynine Palms Oasis Trail

HIKING/WALKING | Allow three hours for this moderately strenuous 3-mile trek. There's no shade, and the trail makes a steep climb in both directions, eventually dropping down into a canyon where you'll find an oasis lined with fan palms, which can be viewed from boulders above, but not accessed. If you look carefully, you'll find evidence of Native Americans in this area, from traces of cooking fires to rocks carved with petroglyphs. *Difficult.* ⊠ *Joshua Tree National Park* ✛ *Trailhead: at end of Canyon Rd., 4 miles west of Twentynine Palms.*

Hidden Valley

HIKING/WALKING | **FAMILY** | Crawl through the rocks surrounding Hidden Valley to see where cattle rustlers supposedly hung out on this 1-mile loop. *Easy.* ⊠ *Joshua Tree National Park* ✛ *Trailhead: at Hidden Valley Picnic Area.*

Hi-View Nature Trail

HIKING/WALKING | This 1.3-mile loop climbs nearly to the top of 4,500-foot Summit Peak. The views of nearby Mt. San Gorgonio (snowcapped in winter) make the moderately steep journey worth the effort. You can pick up a pamphlet describing the vegetation you'll see along the way at any visitor center. *Moderate.* ⊠ *Joshua Tree National Park* ✛ *Trailhead: ½ mile west of Black Rock Canyon Campground.*

Indian Cove Trail

HIKING/WALKING | Look for lizards and roadrunners along this ½-mile loop that follows a desert wash. A walk along this well-signed trail reveals signs of Indian habitation, animals, and flora such as desert willow and yucca. *Easy.* ⊠ *Joshua Tree National Park* ✛ *Trailhead: at west end of Indian Cove Campground.*

Lost Horse Mine Trail

HIKING/WALKING | This fairly strenuous 4-mile round-trip hike follows a former mining road to a well-preserved mill that was used in the 1890s to crush gold-encrusted rock mined from the nearby mountain. The operation was one of the area's most successful, and the mine's cyanide settling tanks and stone buildings are the area's best-preserved structures. From the mill area, a short but steep 10-minute side trip takes you to the top of a 5,278-foot peak with great views of the valley. *Difficult.* ⊠ *Joshua Tree National Park* ✛ *Trailhead: 1¼ miles east of Keys View Rd.*

Lost Palms Oasis Trail

HIKING/WALKING | Allow four to six hours for the moderately strenuous, 7¼-mile round-trip, which leads to the most impressive oasis in the park. It's uphill on the way back to the trailhead. You'll find more than 100 fan palms and an abundance of wildflowers here. *Difficult.* ⊠ *Joshua Tree National Park* ✛ *Trailhead: at Cottonwood Spring Oasis.*

Mastodon Peak Trail

HIKING/WALKING | Some boulder scrambling is optional on this 3-mile hike that loops up to the 3,371-foot Mastodon Peak, and the journey rewards you with stunning views of the Salton Sea. The trail passes through a region where gold was mined from 1919 to 1932, so be on the lookout for open mines. The peak draws its name from a large rock formation that early miners believed looked like the head of a prehistoric behemoth. *Moderate.* ⊠ *Joshua Tree National Park* ⊹ *Trailhead: at Cottonwood Spring Oasis.*

Oasis of Mara

HIKING/WALKING | A stroll along this short, wheelchair-accessible trail, located just outside the visitor center, reveals how early settlers took advantage of this oasis, which was first settled by the Serrano tribe. *Mara* means "place of little springs and much grass" in their language. The Serrano, who farmed the oasis until the mid-1850s, planted one palm tree for each male baby born during the first year of the settlement. *Easy.* ⊠ *Joshua Tree National Park* ⊹ *Trailhead: at Oasis Visitor Center.*

★ Ryan Mountain Trail

HIKING/WALKING | The payoff for hiking to the top of 5,461-foot Ryan Mountain is one of the best panoramic views of Joshua Tree. From here you can see Mt. San Jacinto, Mt. San Gorgonio, Lost Horse Valley, and the Pinto Basin. You'll need two to three hours to complete the 3-mile round-trip with 1,000-plus feet of elevation gain. *Moderate.* ⊠ *Joshua Tree National Park* ⊹ *Trailhead: at Ryan Mountain parking area, 13 miles southeast of park's west entrance, or Sheep Pass, 16 miles southwest of Oasis Visitor Center.*

Skull Rock Trail

HIKING/WALKING | The 1.7-mile loop guides hikers through boulder piles, desert washes, and a rocky alley. It's named for what is perhaps the park's most famous rock formation, which resembles the eye sockets and nasal cavity of a human skull. Access the trail from within Jumbo Rocks Campground or from a small parking area on the highway just east of the campground. *Easy.* ⊠ *Joshua Tree National Park* ⊹ *Trailhead: at Jumbo Rocks Campground.*

ROCK CLIMBING

With an abundance of weathered igneous boulder outcroppings, Joshua Tree is one of the nation's top winter-climbing destinations. There are more than 4,500 established routes offering a full menu of climbing experiences—from bouldering for beginners in the Wonderland of Rocks to multiple-pitch climbs at Echo Rock and Saddle Rock. The best-known climb in the park is Hidden Valley's Sports Challenge Rock. A map inside the *Joshua Tree Guide* shows locations of selected wilderness and nonwilderness climbs.

Joshua Tree Rock Climbing School

CLIMBING/MOUNTAINEERING | The school offers several programs, from one-day introductory classes to multiday programs for experienced climbers, and provides all needed equipment. Beginning classes, offered year-round on most weekends, are limited to six people age eight or older. ⊠ *Joshua Tree National Park* ☎ *760/366–4745* ⊕ *www.joshuatreerockclimbing.com* ✉ *From $195.*

Vertical Adventures Rock Climbing School

CLIMBING/MOUNTAINEERING | About 1,000 climbers each year learn the sport in Joshua Tree National Park through this school. Classes, offered September–May, meet at a designated location in the park, and all equipment is provided. ⊠ *Joshua Tree National Park* ☎ *800/514–8785* ⊕ *www.verticaladventures.com* ✉ *From $155.*

Nearby Towns

Palm Springs, about a 45-minute drive from the North Entrance Station at Joshua Tree, serves as the home base for most park visitors. This city of 46,000 has 95 golf courses, 600 tennis courts, and 50,000 swimming pools. A hideout for Hollywood stars since the 1920s, Palm Springs offers a glittering array of shops, restaurants, and hotels. Stroll down Palm Canyon Drive and you're sure to run into a celebrity or two.

About 9 miles north of Palm Springs and closer to the park is **Desert Hot Springs,** which has more than 1,000 natural hot mineral pools and 40 health spas ranging from low-key to luxurious. **Yucca Valley** is the largest and fastest growing of the communities straddling the park's northern border. The town boasts a handful of motels, supermarkets, and a Walmart. Tiny **Joshua Tree,** the closest community to the park's west entrance, is where the serious rock climbers make their headquarters. **Twentynine Palms,** known as "two-nine" by locals, is sandwiched between the Marine Corps Air Ground Task Force Center to the north and Joshua Tree National Park to the south. Here you'll find a smattering of coffeehouses, antiques shops, and cafés.

VISITOR INFORMATION California Welcome Center Yucca Valley ✉ *56711 Twentynine Palms Hwy., Yucca Valley* ☎ *760/365–5464* ⊕ *www.californiawelcomecenter.com.* **Joshua Tree Chamber of Commerce** ✉ *6448 Hallee Rd., Joshua Tree* ☎ *760/366–3723* ⊕ *www.joshuatreechamber.org.* **Palm Springs Visitor Center** ✉ *2109 N. Palm Canyon Dr., Palm Springs* ☎ *760/778–8415, 800/348–7746* ⊕ *www.visitpalmsprings.com.* **Twentynine Palms Chamber of Commerce** ✉ *73484 Twentynine Palms Hwy., Twentynine Palms* ☎ *760/367–3445* ⊕ *www.29chamber.org.* **Yucca Valley Chamber of Commerce** ✉ *56711 Twentynine Palms Hwy., Yucca Valley* ☎ *760/365–6323* ⊕ *www.yuccavalley.org.*

 **Sights**

Hi-Desert Nature Museum
MUSEUM | FAMILY | Natural and cultural history of the Morongo Basis and High Desert are the focus here. A small live-animal display includes scorpions, snakes, lizards, and small mammals.

You'll also find gems and minerals, fossils from the Paleozoic era, taxidermy, and Native American artifacts. There's also a children's area and art exhibits. ✉ *Yucca Valley Community Center, 57090 Twentynine Palms Hwy., Yucca Valley* ☎ *760/369–7212* ⊕ *hidesertnaturemuseum.org* ✉ *Free* ⊙ *Closed Sun.–Tues.*

Oasis of Murals
PUBLIC ART | Twenty-six murals painted on the sides of buildings depict the history, wildlife, and landscape of Twentynine Palms. If you drive around town you can't miss the murals, but you can also pick up a free map from the Visitor Center. ✉ *Twentynine Palms* ⊕ *www.action-29palmsmurals.com.*

Pioneertown
TOWN | In 1946 Roy Rogers, Gene Autry, the Sons of the Pioneers (the music group for whom the town is named), and Russ Hayden built Pioneertown, an 1880s-style Wild West movie set complete with hitching posts, saloon, and an OK Corral. You can stroll past wooden and adobe storefronts and feel like you're back in the Old West. Pappy and Harriet's Pioneertown Palace, now the town's top draw, has evolved into a hip venue for indie and mainstream performers such as Dengue Fever, Neko Case, and Robert Plant. ✉ *53688 Pioneertown Rd., Pioneertown* ⊹ *4 miles north of Yucca Valley* ⊕ *pappyandharriets.com.*

🍴 **Restaurants**

IN THE PARK
PICNIC AREAS
Black Rock Canyon
CANYON | Set among Joshua trees, pinyon pines, and junipers, this popular picnic area has barbecue grills and drinking water. It's one of the few with flush toilets. ✉ *Joshua Tree National Park* ⊹ *End of Joshua La. at Black Rock Canyon Campground.*

Learn about the park's flora and fauna by attending the ranger programs.

Covington Flats

RESTAURANT—SIGHT | This is a great place to get away from crowds. There's just one table, and it's surrounded by flat, open desert dotted here and there by Joshua trees. ✉ *La Contenta Rd.* ✥ *10 miles from Rte. 62.*

Hidden Valley

RESTAURANT—SIGHT | Set among huge rock formations, with picnic tables shaded by dense trees, this is one of the most pleasant places in the park to stop for lunch. ✉ *Park Blvd.* ✥ *14 miles south of the west entrance.*

OUTSIDE THE PARK

C&S Coffee Shop

$ | **AMERICAN** | If you're yearning for pork chops and gravy for breakfast or eggs over easy for dinner, head to this tidy diner, which has been a local hangout since 1946. The typical diner menu also features soups, salads, and sandwiches, all cooked to order and presented in heaping portions. **Known for:** perfectly-cooked fries; prompt service. [$] *Average main: $8* ✉ *55795 Twentynine Palms Hwy., Yucca Valley* ☎ *760/365–9946.*

Edchada's

$$ | **MEXICAN** | Rock climbers who spend their days in Joshua Tree swear by the margaritas at this Mexican eatery. Specialties include prodigious portions of fajitas, carnitas, seafood enchiladas, and fish tacos. **Known for:** margaritas; large portions. [$] *Average main: $12* ✉ *73502 Twentynine Palms Hwy., Twentynine Palms* ☎ *760/367–2131.*

★ **Pappy & Harriet's Pioneertown Palace**

$$$ | **AMERICAN** | **FAMILY** | Smack in the middle of what looks like the set of a Western is this cozy saloon where you can have dinner, relax over a drink at the bar, and catch some great indie bands or legendary artists—Leon Russell, Lorde, Paul McCartney, and Robert Plant have all played here. Pappy & Harriet's may be in the middle of nowhere, but you'll need reservations for dinner on weekends. **Known for:** live music several days/nights a week; Tex-Mex, Santa Maria–style barbecue; fun and lively atmosphere.

Best Campgrounds in Joshua Tree

Camping is the best way to experience the stark, exquisite beauty of Joshua Tree. You'll also have a rare opportunity to sleep outside in a semi-wilderness setting. The campgrounds, set at elevations from 3,000 to 4,500 feet, have only primitive facilities; few have drinking water. Black Rock, Indian Cove, Jumbo Rocks, and Cottonwood campgrounds accept reservations up to six months in advance, and only for October through Memorial Day. Campsites elsewhere are on a first-come, first-served basis. Belle and White Tank campgrounds, and parts of Black Rock Canyon, Cottonwood, and Indian Cove campgrounds, are closed from the day after Memorial Day to September.

Belle Campground. This small campground is popular with families, as there are a number of boulders kids can scramble over and around. ✉ *9 miles south of Oasis of Mara* ☎ *760/367–5500* 🌐 *www.nps.gov/jotr.*

Black Rock Canyon Campground. Set among juniper bushes, cholla cacti, and other desert shrubs, Black Rock Canyon is one of the prettiest campgrounds in Joshua Tree. ✉ *Joshua La., south of Hwy. 62 and Hwy. 247* ☎ *877/444–6777* 🌐 *www.recreation.gov.*

Cottonwood Campground. In spring this campground, the southernmost one in the park (and therefore often the last to fill up), is surrounded by some of the desert's finest wildflowers and is a great spot to watch the night sky. ✉ *Pinto Basin Rd., 32 miles south of North Entrance Station* ☎ *877/444–6777* 🌐 *www.nps.gov/jotr.*

Hidden Valley Campground. This campground is a favorite with rock climbers, who make their way up valley formations that have names like the Blob, Old Woman, and Chimney Rock. ✉ *Off Park Blvd., 20 miles southwest of Oasis of Mara* ☎ *760/367–5500* 🌐 *www.nps.gov/jotr.*

Indian Cove Campground. This is a sought-after spot for rock climbers, primarily because it lies among the 50 square miles of rugged terrain at the Wonderland of Rocks. ✉ *Indian Cove Rd., south of Hwy. 62* ☎ *877/444–6777* 🌐 *www.nps.gov/jotr.*

Jumbo Rocks. Each campsite at this well-regarded campground tucked among giant boulders has a bit of privacy. It's a good home base for visiting many of Joshua Tree's attractions. ✉ *Park Blvd., 11 miles from Oasis of Mara* ☎ *877/444–6777* 🌐 *www.nps.gov/jotr.*

White Tank. This small, quiet campground is popular with families because a nearby trail leads to a natural arch. ✉ *Pinto Basin Rd., 11 miles south of Oasis of Mara* ☎ *760/367–5500* 🌐 *www.nps.gov/jotr.*

[$] *Average main: $25* ✉ *53688 Pioneertown Rd., Pioneertown* ☎ *760/365–5956* 🌐 *www.pappyandharriets.com* 🕒 *Closed Tues. and Wed.*

Park Rock Café

$ | **CAFÉ** | If you're on your way to the national park on Highway 62, stop in the town of Joshua Tree to grab a hearty breakfast bagel sandwich and order a box lunch to take with you. The café creates some tasty sandwiches, including a healthy option with avocado and pesto mayo. **Known for:** takeout; outdoor dining; lentil barley soup. [$] *Average main: $9* ✉ *6554 Park Blvd., Joshua Tree*

☎ *760/366–8200* 🌐 *jtparkrockcafe.com*
🕑 *No dinner.*

Hotels

OUTSIDE THE PARK

Campbell House

$$ | **B&B/INN** | To the wealthy pioneer who erected the stone mansion now occupied by this bed-and-breakfast, expense was no object, which is evident in the 50-foot-long planked maple floor in the great room, the intricate carpentry, and the huge stone fireplaces that warm the house on the rare cold night. **Pros:** elegant rooms and public spaces; spa services and massage room; great horned owls on property. **Cons:** somewhat isolated location; three-story main building doesn't have an elevator. [$] *Rooms from: $145* ✉ *74744 Joe Davis Dr., Twentynine Palms* ☎ *760/367–3238* 🌐 *www.campbellhouse29palms.com* 🛏 *2 rooms, 10 cottages* 🍴 *Breakfast.*

Casa Cody

$$ | **B&B/INN** | The service is personal and gracious at this historic bed-and-breakfast near the Palm Springs Art Museum; spacious studios and one- and two-bedroom suites hold Santa Fe–style rustic furnishings. **Pros:** former hangout of Charlie Chaplin; friendly ambience; some rooms come with fireplaces, patios, and/or kitchens. **Cons:** old buildings; limited amenities. [$] *Rooms from: $150* ✉ *175 S. Cahuilla Rd., Palm Springs* ☎ *760/320–9346* 🌐 *www.casacody.com* 🛏 *29 rooms* 🍴 *Breakfast.*

★ **Orbit In Hotel**

$$$ | **B&B/INN** | The architectural style of this hip inn on a quiet backstreet dates back to the late 1940s and '50s—nearly flat roofs, wide overhangs, glass everywhere—and the period feel continues inside. **Pros:** saltwater pool; Orbitini cocktail hour. **Cons:** best for couples; style not to everyone's taste; staff not available 24 hours. [$] *Rooms from: $169* ✉ *562 W. Arenas Rd., Palm Springs* ☎ *760/323–3585, 877/996–7248* 🌐 *www.orbitin.com* 🛏 *9 rooms* 🍴 *Breakfast.*

★ **29 Palms Inn**

$$$ | **B&B/INN** | **FAMILY** | The closest lodging to the entrance to Joshua Tree National Park, the funky 29 Palms Inn scatters a collection of adobe and wood-frame cottages, some dating back to the 1920s and 1930s, over 70 acres of grounds that include the ancient Oasis of Mara, a popular destination for birds and bird-watchers year-round. **Pros:** gracious hospitality; exceptional bird-watching; popular with artists. **Cons:** rustic accommodations; limited amenities. [$] *Rooms from: $165* ✉ *73950 Inn Ave., Twentynine Palms* ☎ *760/367–3505* 🌐 *www.29palmsinn.com* 🛏 *20 rooms, 4 guesthouses* 🍴 *Breakfast.*

Chapter 22

LASSEN VOLCANIC
NATIONAL PARK

Updated by
Andrew Collins

CALIFORNIA

WELCOME TO
LASSEN VOLCANIC NATIONAL PARK

TOP REASONS TO GO

★ **Hike a volcano:** The 2½-mile trek up Lassen Peak rewards you with a spectacular view of far northern California.

★ **Spot a rare bloom:** The Lassen Smelowskia, a small white-to-pinkish flower, which grows only in the Cascade Mountains, is especially prolific on Lassen Peak.

★ **View volcano varieties:** All four types of volcanoes found in the world—shield, plug dome, cinder cone, and composite—are represented here.

★ **Listen to the Earth:** The park's thumping mud pots and venting fumaroles roil, gurgle, and belch a raucous symphony, their actions generated by heat from beneath the Earth's crust.

★ **Escape the crowds:** Lassen, in sparsely populated far northern California, is one of the lesser-known national parks.

1 Southwest. Hydrothermal activity is greatest in the southwestern (and Warner Valley) areas; you'll see evidence on hikes to Bumpass Hell and Devils Kitchen. Sidewalks at the Sulphur Works on Lassen Park Highway, just past the Kohm Yah-mah-nee Visitor Center, provide easy access to fumaroles.

2 Middle. Marsh meadows and stunning falls highlight the Kings Creek area in the park's southern midsection. Farther north, Summit Lake—amid a conifer forest at an elevation of about 7,000 feet—has two campgrounds and a trail leading to several smaller lakes.

3 Northwest. Lassen Park Highway winds past Devastated Area, which has slowly returned to a forested landscape, providing stunning views of Lassen Peak and passing Chaos Jumbles before reaching lush, wooded Manzanita Lake.

4 Eastern. Among the delights found in this rugged and less-visited wilderness are Butte and Snag lakes—formed by lava from Cinder Cone—and pristine Horseshoe and Juniper lakes and the many creeks that flow out of them.

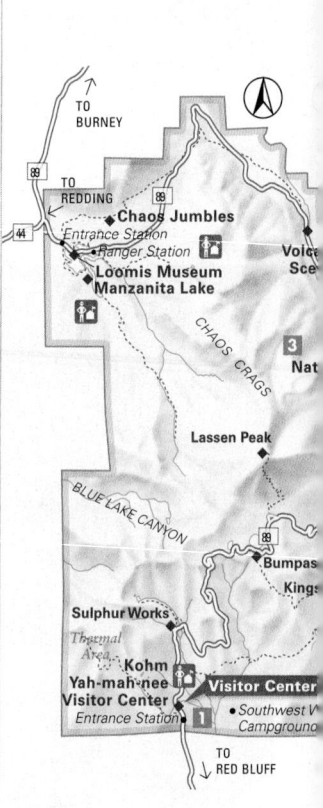

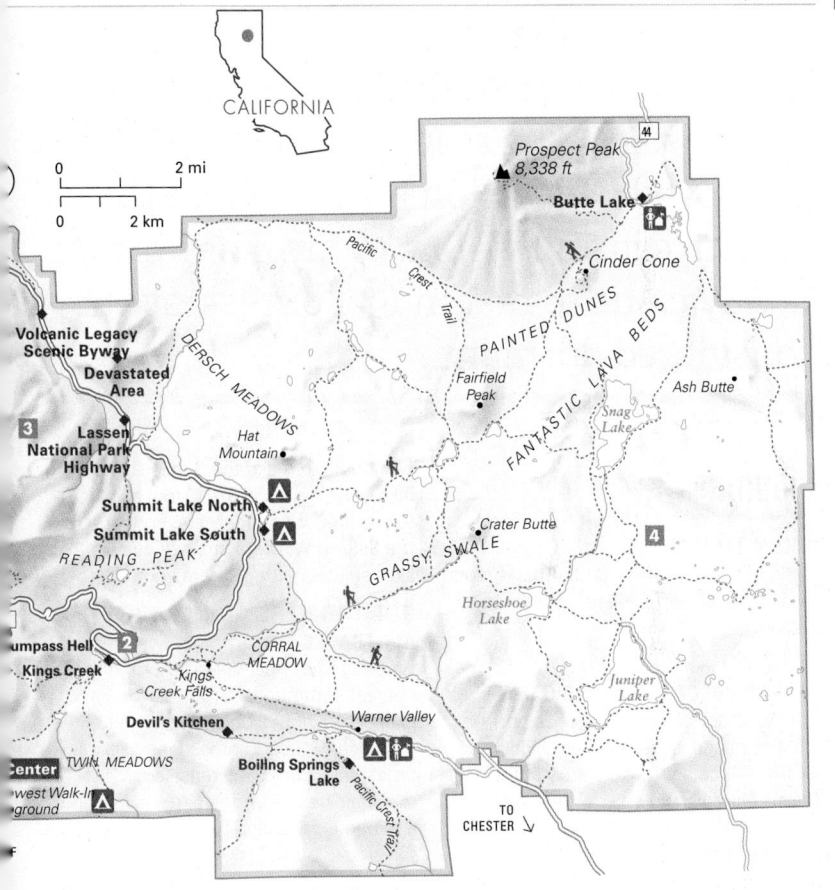

CALIFORNIA

0   2 mi

0   2 km

Prospect Peak
8,338 ft

44

Butte Lake

Cinder Cone

Pacific Crest Trail

PAINTED DUNES

Volcanic Legacy
Scenic Byway

Devastated
Area

DERSCH MEADOWS

Fairfield
Peak

FANTASTIC LAVA BEDS

Ash Butte

Snag
Lake

3

Lassen
National Park
Highway

Hat
Mountain

Summit Lake North

Summit Lake South

READING PEAK

Crater Butte

GRASSY SWALE

4

Horseshoe
Lake

umpass Hell

2

Kings Creek

CORRAL
MEADOW

Kings
Creek Falls

Juniper
Lake

Devil's Kitchen

Warner Valley

Center   TWIN MEADOWS

west Walk-In
ground

Boiling Springs
Lake

Pacific Crest Trail

TO
CHESTER ↓

Lassen Peak, a plug dome, is the main focus of this 165-square-mile tract of dense forests and alpine meadows. Its most spectacular outburst was in 1915, when it blew a cloud of ash almost 6 miles high. The resulting mudflow destroyed vegetation for miles and the evidence is still visible today. The volcano finally came to rest in 1921 but is not yet considered dormant.

Planning

WHEN TO GO

The park is open year-round, though most roads are closed from late October to mid-June due to snow.

PLANNING YOUR TIME

LASSEN VOLCANIC IN ONE DAY

Start your day early at the park's northwest entrance, accessible via Highway 44 from Redding. Make a stop at the **Loomis Museum,** where you can view exhibits before taking the easy, ½-mile loop **Lily Pond Nature Trail.** Back at the museum, drive or walk to **Manzanita Lake.** Take a mid-morning break and pick up supplies at the **Camper Store** for a picnic lunch before taking the park highway toward **Lassen Peak.** As you circle the peak on its northern flank, you come upon **Devastated Area,** testimony to the damage done by the 1915 eruptions. Continue to **Summit Lake,** where you can picnic and swim, or to **Kings Creek,** an area of lush meadows where you can hike to **Kings Creek Falls.** Allow at least two hours to make the 3-mile round-trip hike, which ends in a 700-foot ascent to the falls. If time permits, continue to the **Sulphur Works** to stroll sidewalks that skirt sulfur-emitting steam vents.

GETTING HERE AND AROUND

AIR TRAVEL

Redding Municipal Airport (RDD), the nearest commercial airport to the park, is about an hour's drive west of either entrance. United Express flies a few times daily from San Francisco. Most major airlines serve the airports in Reno, a 2½-hour drive, and Sacramento, a three-hour drive.

CAR TRAVEL

From the north, take the Highway 44 exit off Interstate 5 in Redding and drive east about 50 miles to the park entrance, at the junction with Highway 89. Turn right and drive 1 mile to the northwest entrance station. From the south, take Exit 649 off Interstate 5 and follow Highway 36 northeast 45 miles, turning left onto Highway 89. From here it's about 4 miles to the southwest entrance

AVERAGE HIGH/LOW TEMPERATURES					
JAN.	FEB.	MAR.	APR.	MAY	JUNE
50/13	51/13	53/16	61/23	70/29	79/34
JULY	AUG.	SEPT.	OCT.	NOV.	DEC.
84/40	85/40	78/36	69/30	56/21	50/14

ranger station. The 30-mile main park road, officially called Lassen National Park Highway but often called simply Lassen Park Highway, starts at the southwest entrance. The highway skirts around the southern, eastern, and northern sides of Lassen Peak and exits the park on the northwestern side.

PARK ESSENTIALS
ACCESSIBILITY
Kohm Yah-mah-nee Visitor Center, the Loomis Museum, and the Manzanita Camper Store are fully accessible to those with limited mobility. The Devastated Area Interpretive Trail and the Sulphur Works wayside exhibits are accessible, as are most ranger programs. Butte Lake, Manzanita Lake, and Summit Lake have some campground sites that are accessible.

PARK FEES AND PERMITS
From mid-April through November the fee to enter the park is $25 per car ($20 for motorcycles); the rest of the year the fee is $10 for cars and motorcycles. The fee covers seven consecutive days. Those entering by bus, bicycle, horse, or on foot pay $15. An annual park pass costs $50. For backcountry camping, pick up a free permit at the Loomis Museum or Kohm Yah-mah-nee Visitor Center, or request an application online at ⊕ *www. nps.gov/lavo*.

PARK HOURS
The park is open 24/7 year-round. It is in the Pacific time zone.

CELL PHONE RECEPTION
Cell phones don't work in many parts of the park. There are pay telephones outside the Manzanita Camper Store and the Loomis Museum.

EDUCATIONAL OFFERINGS
If you're wondering why fumaroles fume, how lava is formed, or which critter left those tracks beside the creek, check out the array of ranger-led programs. Most groups meet outside Loomis Museum or near Manzanita Lake. See the park bulletin boards for daily topics and times.

RANGER PROGRAMS
Bear Necessities
TOUR—SIGHT | FAMILY | Learn about black bears at this ranger-led talk, offered mid-June–mid-August, that takes less than an hour. ⊠ *Lassen Volcanic National Park* ⊹ *Outside Loomis Museum, northwest entrance* ☎ *530/595–4480* ⊕ *www.nps. gov/lavo*.

Early Birds
TOUR—SIGHT | Take a morning stroll and learn about the birds of Manzanita Lake. ⊠ *Lassen Volcanic National Park* ⊹ *Meet outside Manzanita Lake Camp Store* ☎ *530/595–4480* ⊕ *www.nps.gov/lavo*.

Inside a Volcano
TOUR—SIGHT | FAMILY | Visit the otherworldly Sulphur Works with a ranger and learn the secrets behind this unique hydrothermal feature. ⊠ *Sulphur Works sidewalk* ☎ *530/595–4480*.

Kids Program
TOUR—SIGHT | FAMILY | Junior Rangers, ages 7 to 12, meet for 45 minutes three times a week with rangers, including for talks about the role wildfires have in

shaping our national parks. Kids unable to attend sessions can earn patches by completing an activity book. Those under 7 can join the Chipmunk Club and earn a sticker by completing an activity card. ⊠ *Lassen Volcanic National Park* ☎ *530/595–4480* ⊕ *www.nps.gov/lavo* ☞ *Call or check at visitor centers for meeting places.*

Pioneers

TOUR—SIGHT | FAMILY | Listen to the fascinating tales of the intrepid travelers who made the journey in 1853 to California via the Nobles Emigrant Trail wagon road. ⊠ *Manzanita Lake Amphitheater* ☎ *530/595–4480.*

RESTAURANTS

Dining options within the park are limited to simple fare at Lassen Café & Gift in Kohm Yah-mah-nee Visitor Center and at the Manzanita Lake Camper Store, and the delicious meals at Drakesbad Guest Ranch, which does offer meals to nonguests by reservation only. The nearest community with a good mix of mostly casual dining options is Chester, about a half-hour drive from the southwest entrance station. About an hour away, the town of Susanville and the small cities of Red Bluff and Redding have more extensive restaurant selections.

HOTELS

Other than the inviting camping cabins at Manzanita Lake, Drakesbad Guest Ranch is the only lodging available inside Lassen. It's rustic (no electricity, just old-fashioned kerosene lamps), expensive, and popular: the ranch is often fully booked a year or more in advance for summer stays. The towns surrounding the park have bed-and-breakfasts, cabin compounds, chain hotels, and budget motels. *Hotel reviews have been shortened. For full information, visit Fodors. com.*

What It Costs			
$	$$	$$$	$$$$
RESTAURANTS			
under $13	$13–$20	$21–$30	over $30
HOTELS			
under $100	$100–$150	$151–$200	over $200

VISITOR INFORMATION

PARK CONTACT INFORMATION Lassen Volcanic National Park ⊠ *Kohm Yah-mah-nee Visitor Center, 21820 Lassen National Park Hwy., Mineral* ☎ *530/595–4480* ⊕ *www.nps.gov/lavo.*

VISITOR CENTER

★ **Kohm Yah-mah-nee Visitor Center**

INFO CENTER | FAMILY | A handsome contemporary structure at the southwest entrance, the center is a helpful stop that's open year-round. You can pick up maps and trail and road guides, inquire about children's activities and ranger-led programs, view an engaging film about the park, and check out the well-conceived interactive exhibits. There are restrooms and first-aid facilities here, and an excellent bookstore. The casual Lassen Café & Gift is a good light-lunch option—the best spot to dine is outdoors at one of the mountain-view picnic tables. Note that in summer, the Loomis Museum by Manzanita Lake is another handy spot for obtaining information on the park. ⊠ *21820 Lassen National Park Hwy.* ☎ *530/595–4480* ⊕ *www.nps.gov/ lavo.*

 **Sights**

SCENIC DRIVES

Lassen National Park Highway

SCENIC DRIVE | The 30-mile two-lane thoroughfare weaves north through the park and passes by such important sites as Lassen Peak, Bumpass Hell, Sulphur Works, Kings Creek, Devastated Area, and Chaos Crags before ending at

Plants and Wildlife in Lassen Volcanic

Because of its varying elevations, Lassen has several different ecological habitats.

Below 6,500 Feet

Below 6,500 feet you can find ponderosa pine, Jeffrey pine, sugar pine, white fir, and several species of manzanita, gooseberry, and Ceanothus. Wildflowers—wild iris, spotted coralroot, pyrola, violets, and lupine—surround the hiking trails in spring and early summer.

Manzanita Lake Area

The Manzanita Lake area has the best bird-watching opportunities, with yellow warblers, pied-billed grebes, white-headed and hairy woodpeckers, golden-crowned kinglets, and Steller's jays. The area is also home to rubber boas, garter snakes, brush rabbits, Sierra Nevada red foxes, black-tailed deer, coyotes, and the occasional mountain lion.

From 6,500 to 8,000 Feet

At elevations of 6,500 to 8,000 feet are red fir forests populated by many of the same wildlife as the lower regions, with the addition of black-backed three-toed woodpeckers, blue grouse, snowshoe hare, pine martens, and the hermit thrush.

Above 8,000 Feet

Above 8,000 feet the environment is harsher, with bare patches of land between subalpine forests. You'll find whitebark pine, groves of mountain hemlock, small pikas, yellow-bellied marmots, and the occasional black bear. Bird-watchers should look for gray-crowned rosy finches, rock wrens, golden eagles, falcons, and hawks. California tortoiseshell butterflies are found on the highest peaks. If you can visit in winter, you'll see one of the park's most magnificent seasonal sights: massive snowdrifts up to 30 and 40 feet high.

Loomis Museum and Manzanita Lake. ⊠ *Lassen Volcanic National Park.*

★ **Volcanic Legacy Scenic Byway**
SCENIC DRIVE | A 500-mile scenic drive that connects Lassen with Oregon's Crater Lake National Park, the byway's southern loop begins in Chester and loops for about 185 miles through the forests, volcanic peaks, hydrothermal springs, and lava fields of Lassen National Forest and Lassen Volcanic National Park, providing an all-day excursion into dramatic wilderness. From Chester, take Highway 36 west to Highway 89 north, which within the park is called Lassen National Park Highway. Upon exiting the park, follow Highway 44 southeast to Highway 36, which leads you back to Chester and around Lake Almanor. Parts of this route are inaccessible in winter and spring. ⊠ *Lassen Volcanic National Park* ☎ *800/474–2782* ⊕ *www.volcaniclegacybyway.org.*

HISTORIC SITES
★ **Loomis Museum**
MUSEUM | FAMILY | Here you can view artifacts from the park's 1914 and 1915 eruptions, including dramatic original photographs taken by Benjamin Loomis, who was instrumental in the park's establishment. The museum also has a bookstore, excellent exhibits about the area's Native American heritage, and a helpful staff who can recommend hikes and points of interest in this side of the park. ⊠ *Lassen Park Hwy.* ⊹ *By Manzanita Lake* ☎ *530/595–6140* ⊠ *Free* ⊗ *Closed late Oct.–late May.*

SCENIC STOPS

Boiling Springs Lake

NATURE SITE | A worthwhile, if occasionally muddy, 3-mile hike leads from the Drakesbad Guest Ranch to Boiling Springs Lake, which is surrounded by steep cliffs topped with trees. Constant bubbles release sulfuric steam into the air. ⊠ Lassen Volcanic National Park ✛ Trailhead: end of Warner Valley Rd., near Drakesbad Guest Ranch.

★ Bumpass Hell

NATURE SITE | This site's quirky name came about when a man with the last name of Bumpass was severely burned after he stepped through brittle ground and into the boiling springs. A scenic but strenuous 3-mile round-trip hike brings you close to hot springs, hissing steam vents, and roiling mud pots. The trail is in the midst of a major rehabilitation and may be fully or partially closed through 2020—check ahead for its current status. ⊠ Lassen Park Hwy. ✛ 6 miles from southwest entrance.

Chaos Jumbles

NATURE SITE | More than 350 years ago, an avalanche from the Chaos Crags lava domes scattered hundreds of thousands of rocks—many of them from 2 to 3 feet in diameter—over a couple of square miles. ⊠ Lassen Park Hwy. ✛ 2 miles east of northwest entrance.

Devastated Area

NATURE SITE | Lassen Peak's 1915 eruptions cleared the area of all vegetation, though after all these years the forest has gradually returned. The easy ½-mile interpretive trail loop is wheelchair accessible. ⊠ Lassen Park Hwy. ✛ 2½ miles northwest of Summit Lake.

Devils Kitchen

NATURE SITE | One of the park's three main hydrothermal areas, this is a great place to view mud pots, steam vents, boiling pools, and even Lassen Peak in the distance. It's much less frequented than Bumpass Hell, so you can expect more wildlife during your moderately difficult 4.2-mile round-trip hike. You need to drive on a partially paved road to reach the trailhead. ⊠ Lassen Volcanic National Park ✛ Trailhead parking near end of Warner Valley Rd., close to Drakesbad Guest Ranch.

★ Lassen Peak

NATURE SITE | When this plug dome volcano erupted in 1915, it spewed a huge mushroom cloud of debris almost 6 miles into the air. A fabulous panoramic view makes the strenuous 2½-mile hike to the 10,457-foot summit worth the effort. ⊠ Lassen Park Hwy. ✛ 7 miles from southwest entrance.

Manzanita Lake

BODY OF WATER | Lassen Peak is reflected in the waters of this rippling lake, which has good catch-and-release trout fishing and a pleasant trail for exploring the area's abundant wildlife. ⊠ Lassen Park Hwy. ✛ Near northwest entrance ranger station.

Sulphur Works Thermal Area

NATURE SITE | FAMILY | Proof of Lassen Peak's volatility becomes evident shortly after you enter the park at the southwest entrance. Sidewalks skirt boiling springs and sulfur-emitting steam vents. This area is usually the last site to close in winter, but even when the road is closed, you can access the area via a 2-mile round-trip hike through the snow. ⊠ Lassen Park Hwy. ✛ 1 mile from southwest entrance.

★ Summit Lake

BODY OF WATER | The midpoint between the northern and southern entrances, Summit Lake is a good place to take an afternoon swim. A trail leads around the lakeshore, and several other trails diverge toward a cluster of smaller lakes in the more remote eastern section of the park. ⊠ Lassen Park Hwy. ✛ 17½ miles from southwest entrance.

Did You Know?

"I took this photo on a camping trip to Lake Manzanita in Lassen Volcanic National Park. The log in the water seemed to point towards the partly snow-covered Lassen Peak." —photo by Shyam Subramanyan, Fodors.com member

⚡ Activities

Lassen is a rugged adventurer's paradise, but be prepared for sudden changes in the weather: fierce thunderstorms sometimes drench the mountains and produce lightning, which poses a threat to hikers above the tree line, and blizzard conditions can develop quickly in winter. In summer, hot temperatures and limited shade can make high-altitude hikers woozy.

BICYCLING

Biking is prohibited on trails and not recommended on park roads due to lack of shoulders, guardrails, and—on the southern half of Lassen Park Highway—steep grades. A better area for cycling near the park is around Lake Almanor in Chester.

FISHING

The best place to fish is in Manzanita Lake, though it's catch and release only. Butte, Snag, and Horseshoe lakes, along with several creeks and streams, are also popular fishing destinations within the park. Anglers will need a California freshwater fishing license; you can pick up an application at most sporting-goods stores or download it from the California Department of Fish and Wildlife's website (⊕ www.dfg.ca.gov). Ask about fishing conditions at bait-and-tackle shops.

The Fly Shop

FISHING | Famous among fly fishers, the Fly Shop carries tackle and equipment and offers guide services. ☒ 4140 Churn Creek Rd., Redding ☎ 530/222–3555, 800/669–3474 ⊕ www.flyshop.com.

HIKING

Of the 150 miles of hiking trails within the park, 17 miles are part of the Pacific Crest Trail through California, Oregon, and Washington. Trails vary greatly, some winding through coniferous forest and others across rocky alpine slopes or along meandering waterways.

★ Bumpass Hell Trail

HIKING/WALKING | Boiling springs, steam vents, and mud pots are the highlights of this 3-mile round-trip hike. Expect the loop to take about two hours. During the first mile there's a slight, gradual climb before a steep 300-foot descent to the basin. You'll encounter rocky patches, so wear hiking boots. Stay on trails and boardwalks near the thermal areas, as what appears to be firm ground may be only a thin crust over scalding mud. Due to ongoing trail rehabilitation, this hike may be fully or partially closed through 2020. *Moderate.* ☒ *Lassen Park Hwy.* ⊹ *Trailhead: 6 miles from southwest entrance.*

Cinder Cone Trail

HIKING/WALKING | Though a little out of the way, this is one of Lassen's most fascinating—and strenuous—trails. It's for more experienced hikers, since the 4-mile round-trip hike to the cone summit includes a steep 800-foot climb over ground that's slippery in parts with loose cinders. Pick up the trail brochure at Loomis Museum or Kohm Yah-mah-nee Visitor Center. *Difficult.* ☒ *Boat ramp at end of Butte Lake Rd.* ⊹ *Trailhead: off Hwy. 44, 33 miles east of Manzanita Lake.*

Crumbaugh Lake Hike

HIKING/WALKING | Taking this 2.6-mile round-trip hike through meadows and forests to Cold Boiling and Crumbaugh lakes is an excellent way to view spring wildflowers. *Moderate.* ☒ *Lassen Park Hwy.* ⊹ *Trailhead: near Kings Creek picnic area, 13 miles north of southwest entrance.*

Kings Creek Falls Hike

HIKING/WALKING | Nature photographers love this 3-mile round-trip hike through forests dotted with wildflowers. A steep 700-foot ascent leads to the spectacular falls. It can be slippery in spots, so watch your step. Be in good shape for this hike. *Moderate.* ☒ *Lassen Park Hwy.* ⊹ *Trailhead: 12 miles from southwest entrance.*

⭐ **Lassen Peak Hike**

HIKING/WALKING | This trail winds 2½ miles to the mountaintop. It's a tough climb—2,000 feet uphill on a steady, steep grade—but the reward is a spectacular view. At the peak you can see into the rim and view the entire park (and much of California's far north). Bring sunscreen, water, snacks, a first-aid kit, and, because it can be windy and cold at the summit, a jacket. *Difficult.* ⊠ *Lassen Park Hwy.* ⊹ *Trailhead: 7 miles north of southwest entrance.*

Lily Pond Nature Trail

HIKING/WALKING | FAMILY | This ½-mile jaunt loops past a small lake and through a wooded area, ending at a pond that is filled with yellow water lilies in summer. Marked with interpretive signs, it's a good choice for families. *Easy.* ⊠ *Lassen Park Hwy.* ⊹ *Trailhead: across road from Loomis Museum.*

Mill Creek Falls

HIKING/WALKING | This 2½-hour 3.8-mile round-trip hike through forests and wildflowers takes you to where East Sulphur and Bumpass creeks merge to create the park's highest waterfall. *Moderate.* ⊠ *Lassen Park Hwy.* ⊹ *Trailhead: east side of Southwest Walk-In Campground parking lot.*

HORSEBACK RIDING

Drakesbad Guest Ranch

HORSEBACK RIDING | FAMILY | This property operated by the park's concessionaire offers guided rides to nonguests who make reservations. Among the options is a two-hour loop to Devils Kitchen. There's also an eight-hour five-lake loop for advanced riders. ⊠ *End of Warner Valley Rd., Chester* ☎ *530/524–2841* ⊕ *www.drakesbad.com* ⊇ *From $39.*

SNOWSHOEING

You can snowshoe anywhere in the park. The gentlest places are in the northern district, while more challenging terrain is in the south.

■TIP→ **Beware of hidden cavities in the snow. Park officials warn that heated sulfur emissions, especially in the Sulphur Works Area, can melt out dangerous snow caverns, which may be camouflaged by thin layers of fresh snow that skiers and snowshoers can easily fall through.**

Bodfish Bicycles & Quiet Mountain Sports

SNOW SPORTS | You can rent snowshoes, skis, boots, and poles at this popular shop 30 miles from the park's Southwest Entrance. ⊠ *149 Main St., Chester* ☎ *530/258–2338* ⊕ *www.bodfishbicycles.com.*

Lassen Mineral Lodge

SNOW SPORTS | This lodge near the park rents snowshoes as well as cross-country skis and poles. ⊠ *38348 Hwy. 36, Mineral* ☎ *530/595–4422* ⊕ *www.minerallodge.com.*

Snowshoe Walks

SNOW SPORTS | On weekends from January through early April, park rangers lead two-hour snowshoe walks that explore the park's geology and winter ecology. The hikes require moderate exertion at an elevation of 7,000 feet; children under age eight are not allowed. If you don't have snowshoes you can borrow a pair; $1 donation suggested. Walks are first come, first served; meet outside Kohm Yah-mah-nee Visitor Center. ⊠ *21820 Lassen National Park Hwy.* ☎ *530/595–4480* ⊕ *www.nps.gov/lavo* ⊇ *Free.*

Nearby Towns

The tiny logging town of **Chester,** 30 miles from the southwest park entrance on Highway 36, serves as the commercial center for the Lake Almanor area. With a population of about 2,100, it contains a handful of accommodations and services and is a good base for exploring the southern half of the park. **Susanville,** population 15,000, a high-desert town 35 miles east of Chester, has some basic motels and a growing selection of restaurants. **Red Bluff,** population 14,000, blends Old West toughness and late-1800s gentility: restored Victorians line the streets west of Main Street, while the downtown looks like a stage set for a Western. Red Bluff is a good place to stock up before heading into the park, as it's just off Interstate 5, about 50 miles from Lassen's southwest entrance via Highway 36.

With a population of 92,000, **Redding** is the largest city in far Northern California and the area's main commercial center. Redding is 32 miles north of Red Bluff via Interstate 5, and 50 miles west of the park's northwest entrance via Highway 44.

Red Bluff and Redding have the most accommodations and services in the area; each is an hour's drive from the park.

VISITOR INFORMATION Lake Almanor Area Chamber of Commerce ☎ 530/258–2426 ⊕ www.lakealmanorarea.com. **Lassen County Chamber of Commerce** ☎ 530/257–4323 ⊕ www.lassencountychamber.org. **Red Bluff–Tehama County Chamber of Commerce** ✉ 100 Main St., Red Bluff ☎ 530/527–6220, 800/655–6225 ⊕ www.redbluffchamber.com. **Redding Convention and Visitors Bureau** ✉ Turtle Bay Store, 844 Sundial Bridge Dr., Redding ☎ 800/874–7562, 530/225–4100 ⊕ www.visitredding.com. **Shasta Cascade Wonderland Association** ✉ 1699 Hwy. 273, Anderson ☎ 530/365–1258 ⊕ www.shastacascade.com.

 Sights

★ Lake Shasta Caverns National Natural Landmark

NATURE SITE | FAMILY | Stalagmites, stalactites, flowstone deposits, and crystals entice visitors to the Lake Shasta Caverns. To see this impressive spectacle, you must take the two-hour tour, which includes a catamaran ride across the McCloud arm of Lake Shasta and a bus ride up North Grey Rocks Mountain to the cavern entrance. The temperature in the caverns is 58°F year-round, making them a cool retreat on a hot summer day. The most awe-inspiring of the limestone rock formations is the glistening Cathedral Room, which appears to be gilded. ✉ 20359 Shasta Caverns Rd., Exit 695 off I–5, 17 miles north of Redding, Lakehead ☎ 530/238–2341, 800/795–2283 ⊕ www.lakeshastacaverns.com ⧉ $28.

★ Turtle Bay Exploration Park

BRIDGE/TUNNEL | FAMILY | This park has walking trails, an aquarium, an arboretum and botanical gardens, and many interactive exhibits for kids. The main draw is the stunning Santiago Calatrava–designed **Sundial Bridge,** a metal and translucent glass pedestrian walkway, suspended by cables from a single tower, spanning a broad bend in the Sacramento River. On sunny days the 217-foot tower lives up to the bridge's name, casting a shadow on the ground below to mark time. Access to the bridge and arboretum is free, but there's a fee for the museum and gardens. ✉ 844 Sundial Bridge Dr., Redding ☎ 530/243–8850, 800/887–8532 ⊕ www.turtlebay.org ⧉ Museum $16 ⊘ Museum closed Mon. and Tues. early Sept.–mid-Mar.

🏃 Activities

Whether you want to camp in national forests, wade in creeks, watch dragonflies dip over meadows thick with wildflowers, or stargaze while listening to a chorus of crickets, the great outdoors is the draw here. When you're ready to merge with civilization, the towns near Lassen Volcanic offer shopping, movies, dining, and a bit of people-watching.

BOATING AND FISHING

Twenty-one types of fish, including rainbow trout and salmon, inhabit Lake Shasta, which is about a 75-minute drive northwest of Lassen Volcanic National Park. The lake area also has one of the state's largest nesting populations of bald eagles. Rent boats, Jet Skis, and windsurfing boards at marinas and resorts along the 370-mile shoreline. The Sacramento River and its numerous creeks and tributaries also attract fishing enthusiasts from across the country.

🍴 Restaurants

IN THE PARK

Lassen Café & Gift

$ | **CAFÉ** | Coffee and hot cocoa, wine and beer (including local brews from Lassen Ale Works), and sandwiches, burgers, soups, salads, bagels, and pizzas are on the menu here. Indoors, there's a fireplace, but if the weather is fine, the patio with its mountain views is the place to be. **Known for:** local beers; stunning mountain views from the outdoor patio; gift shop with local art and crafts. [$] *Average main: $9* ✉ *Kohm Yah-mah-nee Visitor Center, Lassen Park Hwy.* ☎ *530/595–3555* 🌐 *www.lassenrecreation.com* 🕒 *Closed weekdays mid-Oct.–late May.*

Manzanita Lake Camper Store

$ | **CAFÉ** | Pick up simple prepared foods, groceries, and beverages—local wines and beers among them—at the store, which has an ATM and a pay phone. **Known for:** good local craft beer selection; supplies for a picnic by the lake; hearty deli sandwiches. [$] *Average main: $7* ✉ *Manzanita Lake Campground, Lassen Park Hwy.* ☎ *530/335–7557* 🌐 *www.lassenrecreation.com* 🕒 *Closed mid-Oct.–late May.*

PICNIC AREAS

Kings Creek

Trees shade these creekside picnic tables. Vault toilets are the only amenities. ✉ *Lassen Park Hwy.* ✣ *11½ miles north of southwest entrance.*

Lake Helen

This site with picnic tables and vault toilets has views of several summits, including Lassen Peak. ✉ *Lassen Park Hwy.* ✣ *6 miles north of southwest entrance, near Bumpass Hell trailhead.*

OUTSIDE THE PARK

Cravings Cafe

$ | **CAFÉ** | Set in a cheerful 1930s house in downtown Chester that also contains the excellent B&B Booksellers shop and art gallery, this bustling café is one of the best casual breakfast, coffee, and lunch options near the park. The extensive menu lists dozens of savory and sweet egg and griddle options, along with burgers, salads, and sandwiches available after 11 am. **Known for:** breakfast served till closing; waffles with applewood-smoked bacon in the batter; decadent sticky buns and baked sweets. [$] *Average main: $9* ✉ *Stover Landing Commons, 278 Main St., Chester* ☎ *530/258–2229* 🌐 *www.stoverlanding.com* 🕒 *Closed Tues. and Wed. No dinner.*

★ **Highlands Ranch Restaurant and Bar**

$$$ | **AMERICAN** | Dining at the Highlands Ranch Resort's contemporary roadhouse restaurant is in a stained-wood, high-ceilinged room indoors, or out on the deck, which has views of a broad serene meadow and the hillside beyond. Among the few sophisticated eating options within Lassen Volcanic National Park's orbit, the restaurant serves regional American dishes like blackened ahi with carrot-cucumber slaw and classic beef Wellington with a pink-peppercorn bordelaise sauce. **Known for:** striking views inside and out; small plates and burgers in the bar; inventive sauces and preparations. [$] *Average main: $25* ✉ *41515 Hwy. 36 E* ☎ *530/595–3388* 🌐 *www.highlandsranchresort.com/restaurant* 🕒 *Closed Mon.–Wed. Nov.–late May.*

★ **Lassen Ale Works Boardroom**

$$ | **PIZZA** | The newer location of this highly popular craft brewery stands out because of its airy, modern interior and the fact that it turns out some of the best pizzas in the area. But you can also enjoy the same selection of perennial and seasonal ales, from the

Best Campgrounds in Lassen Volcanic

Lassen's seven campgrounds draw a broad range of campers, from large groups singing around a mesmerizing fire to solitary hikers seeking a quiet place under the stars. You can drive a vehicle to all campgrounds except the Southwest Walk-In. This is the only campground open year-round; the others usually open in June and close in early fall. Campfires are restricted to fire rings. Lassen has black bears, so be sure to secure your food and garbage properly by using the bear boxes provided at the park's campsites. For more camping information, go to 🌐 *www.nps.gov/lavo/planyourvisit/camping_in_campgrounds.htm*. For reservations, visit 🌐 *www.recreation.gov*.

Juniper Lake. On the east shore of the park's largest lake, these campsites are close to the water in a wooded area. To reach them, you have to take a rough gravel road 13 miles north of Chester to the park's southeast corner; trailers are not advised. There is no potable water here. ✉ *Chester Juniper Lake Rd.* No reservations.

Manzanita Lake. The largest of Lassen campgrounds accommodates RVs up to 35 feet and has 20 rustic cabins. Many ranger programs begin here, and a trail nearby leads to the crater that holds Crags Lake. ✉ *Off Lassen Park Hwy., near park's northwest entrance* ☎ *530/595–6121, 877/444–6777.*

Southwest Walk-In. Relatively small and Lassen's only campground open year-round, Southwest lies within a conifer forest and has views of Brokeoff Peak. Snow camping is allowed, and drinking water is available at visitor center entryway. ✉ *Near southwest entrance, beside Kohm Yah-mahnee Visitor Center.* No reservations.

Summit Lake North. This completely forested campground has easy access to backcountry trails. You'll likely observe deer grazing. ✉ *Lassen Park Hwy., 17½ miles north of southwest entrance.* ☎ *530/595–6121, 877/444–6777.*

Summit Lake South. Less crowded than its neighbor to the north, this campground has wet meadows where wildflowers grow in the spring. No potable water is available after mid-September. ✉ *Lassen Park Hwy., 17½ miles north of southwest entrance* ☎ *530/595–6121, 877/444–6777.*

Lassen-inspired Volcanic Double IPA to rich Devil's Corral Imperial Stout, at the brewpub inside downtown Susanville's 1860s Pioneer Saloon (724 Main Street), whose kitchen turns out deftly prepared comfort food such as Basque-style fall-off-the-bone lamb stew and beer-braised-sausage sandwiches. **Known for:** ales named for local sites; made-from-scratch pizzas with inventive toppings; chocolate martinis. [$] *Average main: $13* ✉ *702–000 Johnstonville Rd., Susanville* ☎ *530/257–4443* 🌐 *www.lassenaleworks.com* ⏲ *Closed Mon. and Tues. No lunch Wed.–Thurs.*

Ranch House Pub & Grill

$$ | AMERICAN | FAMILY | This convivial neighborhood pub stands out among Chester's eateries because of its abundance of shaded patio seating—and full horseshoes pit—set in the restaurant's landscaped backyard. After a long day of hiking and exploring, the hearty comfort fare, including decadent "loaded" fries with cheese, bacon, and pulled pork, never fails to satisfy. **Known for:** a substantial kids' menu; tasty sides of garlic or sweet potato fries; molten lava chocolate cake. [$] *Average main: $17* ✉ *669 Main St., Chester* ☎ *530/258–4226* 🌐 *www.facebook.com/theranchhouse16* 🕒 *Closed Mon. and Tues.*

White House

$$ | **THAI** | Options for Asian cuisine are quite limited in this part of the world, which makes the consistently tasty cuisine at this homey Thai restaurant on the east side of downtown Susanville all the more surprising—and appreciated. Expect an extensive selection of traditional dishes, including fragrant *tom kha gai* soup, mango curry with chicken and shrimp, and stir-fried rice and noodle dishes.**Known for:** hearty soups large enough to make a meal out of; plenty of vegetarian options; mango sticky rice. [$] *Average main: $15* ✉ *3085 Johnstonville Rd., Susanville* ☎ *530/257–6666* 🌐 *www.whitehousesusanville.com* 🕒 *Closed Sun. and Mon.*

🛏 Hotels

IN THE PARK

★ Drakesbad Guest Ranch

$$$$ | **B&B/INN** | With propane furnaces and kerosene lamps, everything about this century-old property in the park's remote but beautiful southeastern corner harks back to a simpler time. **Pros:** back-to-nature experience; great for family adventures; only full-service lodging inside the park. **Cons:** on a remote partially paved road 45 minutes' drive from nearest town (Chester); rustic, with few in-room frills; not open year-round. [$] *Rooms from: $384* ✉ *14423 Warner Valley Rd., Chester* ☎ *866/999–0914* 🌐 *www.drakesbad.com* 🕒 *Closed mid-Oct.–early June* 🛏 *19 rooms* 🍴 *All meals.*

Manzanita Lake Camping Cabins

$ | **RENTAL** | **FAMILY** | This lakeside compound of 20 rustic but handsomely designed modern cabins provides the only roof-over-your-head lodgings on the main park highway, but this is a camping experience, albeit a nicely outfitted one. **Pros:** only lodgings on Lassen Park Highway; picturesque setting; guests without camping gear can purchase amenity packages, including sleeping bags. **Cons:** guests must supply their own bedding; rustic; open only seasonally. [$] *Rooms from: $72* ✉ *Manzanita Lake, Lassen Park Hwy.* ☎ *530/335–7557 May–Oct., 530/840–6140 Nov.–Apr.* 🌐 *www.lassenrecreation.com* 🕒 *Closed mid-Oct.–late May* 🛏 *20 cabins* 🍴 *No meals.*

OUTSIDE THE PARK

Antlers Motel

$ | **HOTEL** | A spotlessly clean, simple, and affordable option in downtown Chester, this homey two-story 20-room motel is a handy base for exploring both Warner Valley and the southern end of Lassen Park Highway. **Pros:** reasonable rates; coffeemakers and refrigerators in every room; short walk from several restaurants and bars. **Cons:** no on-site breakfast option; pretty basic decor; parking can be a little tight when the motel is fully booked. [$] *Rooms from: $90* ✉ *268 Main St., Chester* ☎ *530/258–2722* 🌐 *www.antlersmotel.com* 🛏 *20 rooms* 🍴 *No meals.*

Best Western Rose Quartz Inn

$$$ | **HOTEL** | Down the road from Lake Almanor and close to Lassen Volcanic National Park, this midrange chain property is basically a motel, but the helpful staff (especially with touring plans) and amenities like good Wi-Fi, comfy bedding, and spacious breakfast area make it a good choice for a short stay. **Pros:** within easy walking distance of town's restaurants; convenient to Lassen Volcanic National Park's southwest entrance; good Wi-Fi and other amenities. **Cons:** a little pricey for what you get; cookie-cutter decor; noise audible between rooms. [$] *Rooms from: $160* ✉ *306 Main St., Chester* ☎ *530/258–2002* 🌐 *www.bestwestern.com* 🛏 *50 rooms* 🍴 *Breakfast.*

Bidwell House

$$$ | B&B/INN | Some guest rooms at this 1901 ranch house near Lake Almanor have wood-burning stoves, claw-foot or Jacuzzi tubs, and antique furnishings; a separate cottage with a kitchen sleeps six. **Pros:** each room is individually decorated; beautiful wooded setting; excellent full breakfast. **Cons:** not ideal for kids; may be too remote for some guests; a little pricey. $ *Rooms from: $155* ✉ *1 Main St., Chester* ☎ *530/258–3338* ⊕ *www.bidwellhouse.com* ⇋ *14 rooms* ⏀ *Breakfast.*

Grace Lake Resort

$$ | B&B/INN | Set in on a grassy plot amid towering shade trees about midway between Redding and Lassen's summer-only northwest entrance, this cluster of individually furnished country cabins—plus one three-bedroom bungalow with a full kitchen—is great for families or groups of friends traveling together. **Pros:** one of the best lodging options near Lassen's northwest (Manzanita Lake) entrance; pretty tree-shaded grounds with an outdoor pool; every unit has charcoal grills, kitchenettes, and picnic tables. **Cons:** a 75-minute drive from park's only winter entrance (in Mineral); need to call or e-mail for rates and availability; few dining options nearby. $ *Rooms from: $130* ✉ *31853 Hwy. 44* ☎ *707/499–3604* ⊕ *www.gracelakeresort.com* ⇋ *7 cabins* ⏀ *No meals.*

★ Highlands Ranch Resort

$$$$ | B&B/INN | On a gorgeous 175-acre alpine meadow 10 miles from Lassen's southwest entrance, this cluster of smartly designed upscale bungalows is peaceful and luxurious. **Pros:** stunning views; most luxurious accommodations near the park; friendly and helpful staff. **Cons:** pricey for the area (but you get a lot for what you pay); remote location 20 miles from Chester, the nearest big town; books up months ahead for summer stays. $ *Rooms from: $249* ✉ *41515 Hwy. 36 E* ☎ *530/595–3388* ⊕ *www. highlandsranchresort.com* ☯ *Closed Mon.–Wed. Nov.–late May* ⇋ *7 cottages* ⏀ *Breakfast.*

Mill Creek Resort

$ | RESORT | FAMILY | Set amid towering evergreens in a tranquil patch of Lassen National Forest, this delightfully unfussy cabin and camping resort feels as though it could be inside the national park, although it's actually about 10 miles south, on a scenic country road. **Pros:** tranquil wooded setting; one of the closest lodging options to Lassen's southwest entrance; old-fashioned, family-friendly summer-camp vibe. **Cons:** remote setting is a bit of a drive from other restaurants and services; bedrooms and bathrooms in each cabin are quite small; a bit too rustic for some tastes. $ *Rooms from: $95* ✉ *40271 Hwy. 172* ☎ *530/595–4449* ⊕ *www.millcreekresort. net* ⇋ *11 cabins* ⏀ *No meals.*

Chapter 23

MESA VERDE
NATIONAL PARK

23

Updated by
Aimee Heckel

COLORADO

WELCOME TO
MESA VERDE NATIONAL PARK

TOP REASONS TO GO

★ **Ancient artifacts:** Mesa Verde is a time capsule for the Ancestral Pueblo culture; more than 4,000 archaeological sites and 3 million objects have been unearthed here.

★ **Bright nights:** Mesa Verde's lack of light and air pollution, along with its high elevation, make for spectacular views of the heavens.

★ **Active adventures:** Get your heart pumping outdoors with hiking, biking, and exploring on trails of varying difficulties.

★ **Cliff dwellings:** Built atop the pinyon-covered mesa tops and hidden in the park's valleys are 600 ancient dwellings, some carved directly into the sandstone cliff faces.

★ **Geological marvels:** View the unique geology that drew the Ancient Pueblo to the area: protected desert canyons, massive alcoves in the cliff walls, thick bands of sandstone, continuous seep springs, and soils that could be used for both agriculture and architecture.

1 Morefield Campground. The only campground in Mesa Verde, Morefield includes a village area with a gas station and store, and is close to some of the best hiking trails in the park.

2 Visitor and Research Center. Buy tickets for the popular ranger-led tours here.

3 Far View. Almost an hour's drive from Mesa Verde's entrance, Far View is the park's epicenter, with several restaurants and the park's only overnight lodge.

4 Chapin Mesa. Home to the park's most famous cliff dwellings and archaeological sites, the Chapin Mesa area includes the famous 150-room Cliff Palace dwelling and other man-made and natural wonders.

5 Wetherill Mesa. See Long House, Two Raven House, Kodak House, and the Badger House Community.

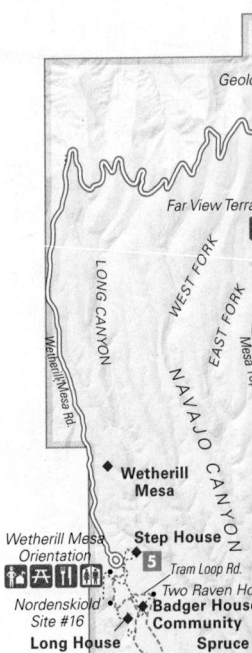

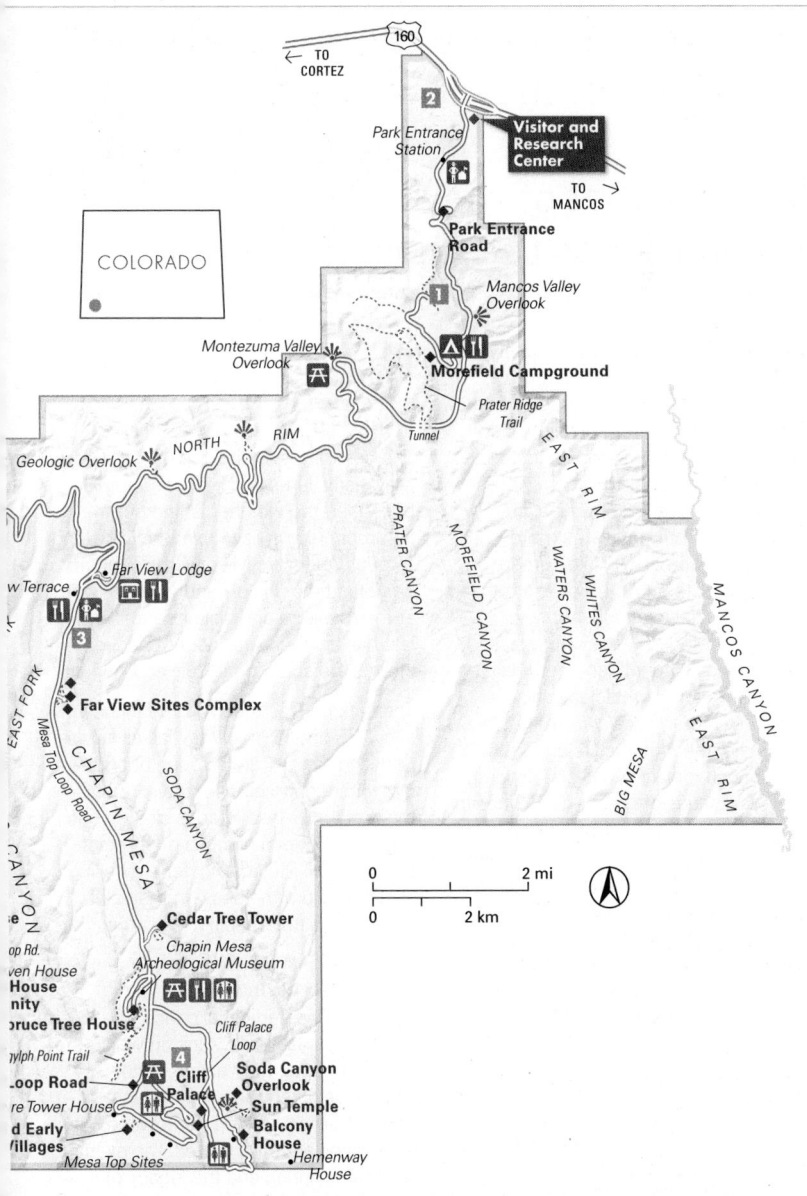

Unlike the other national parks, Mesa Verde earned its status from its ancient cultural history rather than its geological treasures. President Theodore Roosevelt established it in 1906 as the first national park to "preserve the works of man," in this case that of the Ancestral Pueblo, also known as the Anasazi.

They lived in the region from roughly 550 to 1300; they left behind more than 4,000 archaeological sites spread out over 80 square miles. Their ancient dwellings, set high into the sandstone cliffs, are the heart of the park. Mesa Verde (which in Spanish means, literally, "Green Table," but translates more accurately to something like "green flat-topped plateau") is much more than an archaeologist's dreamland, however. It's one of those windswept places where man's footprints and nature's paintbrush—some would say chisel—meet. Rising dramatically from the San Juan Basin, the jutting cliffs are cut by a series of complex canyons and covered in several shades of green, from pines in the higher elevations down to sage and other mountain brush on the desert floor. From the tops of the smaller mesas, you can look across to the cliff dwellings in the opposite rock faces. Dwarfed by the towering cliffs, the sand-color dwellings look almost like a natural occurrence in the midst of the desert's harsh beauty.

Planning

WHEN TO GO
The best times to visit the park are late May, early June, and most of September, when the weather is fine but the summer crowds have thinned. Mid-June through August is Mesa Verde's most crowded time. In July and August, lines at the museum and visitor center may last half an hour. Afternoon thunderstorms are common in July and August.

The park gets as much as 100 inches of snow in winter. Snow may fall as late as May and as early as October, but there's rarely enough to hamper travel. In winter, the Wetherill Mesa Road is closed, but you can still get a glimpse of some of the Wetherill Mesa sandstone dwellings, sheltered from the snow in their cliff coves, from the Chapin Mesa area.

FESTIVALS AND EVENTS
Ute Mountain Ute Bear Dance
FESTIVAL | This traditional dance, the local version of a Sadie Hawkins (in which the women choose their dance partners—and the selected men can't refuse), is held in May or June on the Towaoc Ute reservation south of Cortez. The event celebrates spring and the legacy of a

AVERAGE HIGH/LOW TEMPERATURES

JAN.	FEB.	MAR.	APR.	MAY	JUNE
37/16	41/20	48/26	57/31	67/39	79/49
JULY	AUG.	SEPT.	OCT.	NOV.	DEC.
84/55	81/53	74/46	61/36	47/25	38/18

mythical bear that taught the Ute people her secrets. It's part of a multiday festival that includes music, races, and softball games, and culminates with an hour-long dance that's over when only one couple remains. ⊠ *124 Mike Wash Rd., Towaoc* ☎ *970/565–3751* ⊕ *www.utemountainutetribe.com.*

Durango Fiesta Days

FESTIVAL | FAMILY | A parade, rodeo, barbecue, street dance, cook-offs, live music, and more come to the Durango Fairgrounds in July. ⊠ *La Plata County Fairgrounds, 2500 Main Ave., Durango* ☎ *970/749–4960* ⊕ *www.durangofiestadays.com.*

Durango Cowboy Poetry Gathering

FESTIVAL | FAMILY | A parade accompanies art exhibitions, poetry readings, music, theater, and storytelling in this four-day event run by the Durango Cowboy Poetry Gathering, a nonprofit set up to preserve the traditions of the American West. It's held the first weekend in October. ⊠ *Durango* ☎ *970/749–2995* ⊕ *www.durangocowboypoetrygathering.org.*

PLANNING YOUR TIME
MESA VERDE IN ONE DAY

For a full experience, take at least one ranger-led tour of a major cliff dwelling site, as well as a few self-guided walks. Arrive early and stop first at the Visitor and Research Center, where you can purchase tickets for Cliff Palace and Balcony House tours on Chapin Mesa. If it's going to be a hot day, you might want to take an early-morning or late-afternoon bus tour. Drive to the **Chapin Mesa Museum** to watch a 25-minute film introducing you to the area and its history. Just behind the museum is the trailhead for

the 0.5-mile-long **Spruce Tree House Trail,** which normally leads to the best-preserved cliff dwelling in the park. While the Spruce Tree House is temporarily closed for restabilization, you can still view it from up top. Then drive to **Balcony House** for an hour-long, ranger-led tour.

Have lunch at the Spruce Tree Terrace Café or the Cliff Palace picnic area. Afterward take the ranger-led tour of **Cliff Palace** (one hour). Use the rest of the day to explore the overlooks and trails off the 6-mile loop of **Mesa Top Loop Road.** Or head back to the museum and take **Petroglyph Point Trail** to see a great example of Ancestral Pueblo rock carvings. A leisurely walk along the Mesa Top's **Soda Canyon Overlook Trail** (off Cliff Palace Loop Road) gives you a beautiful bird's-eye view of the canyon below. On the drive back toward the park entrance, be sure to check out the view from **Park Point.**

GETTING HERE AND AROUND
AIR TRAVEL

The cities of Durango (36 miles east of the park entrance) and Cortez (11 miles to the west) have airports.

CAR TRAVEL

The park has just one entrance, off U.S. 160, between Cortez and Durango in what's known as the Four Corners area (which spans the intersection of Colorado, New Mexico, Arizona, and Utah). Most of the roads at Mesa Verde involve steep grades and hairpin turns, particularly on Wetherill Mesa. Vehicles over 8,000 pounds or 25 feet are prohibited on this road. Trailers and towed vehicles are prohibited past Morefield Campground. Check the condition of your vehicle's brakes before driving the road to Wetherill Mesa. For the latest road information, tune to 1610 AM, or call ☎ 970/529–4461. Off-road vehicles are prohibited in the park. At less-visited Wetherill Mesa, you must leave your car behind and hike or bike to the Long House, Kodak House, and Badger House Community.

PARK ESSENTIALS
PARK FEES AND PERMITS
Admission is $25 per vehicle for a seven-day permit. An annual pass is $40. Ranger-led tours of Cliff Palace, Long House, and Balcony House are $5 per person. You can also take ranger-guided bus tours from the Far View Lodge, which last between 3½ and 4 hours and cost $55 ($33 for kids; under 5 free). Backcountry hiking and fishing are not permitted at Mesa Verde.

PARK HOURS
Mesa Verde's facilities each operate on their own schedule, but most are open daily, from Memorial Day through Labor Day, between about 8 am and sunset. The rest of the year, they open at 9. In winter, the Spruce Tree House is open only to offer a few scheduled tours each day. Wetherill Mesa (and all the sites it services) is open from May through October, weather depending. Far View Center, Far View Terrace, and Far View Lodge are open between April and October. Morefield Campground and the sites nearby are open from mid-April through mid-October (and until early November for limited camping with no services). Specific hours are subject to change, so check with the visitor center upon arrival.

CELL-PHONE RECEPTION AND INTERNET
You can get patchy cell service in the park. Best service is typically at the Morefield Campground area, which is the closest to the neighboring towns of Cortez and Mancos. Public telephones can be found at all the major visitor areas (Morefield, Far View, and Spruce Tree). You can get free Wi-Fi throughout the Far View Lodge and at the Morefield Campground store.

EDUCATIONAL OFFERINGS
RANGER PROGRAMS
Evening Ranger Campfire Program
TOUR—SIGHT | FAMILY | Every night in summer at the Morefield Campground Amphitheater, park rangers present a different 45- to 60-minute program on topics such as stargazing, history, wildlife, and archaeology. ⊠ Morefield Campground Amphitheater, 4 miles south of park entrance ☎ 970/529–4465 ⌹ Free ⊙ Closed early Sept.–late May.

Junior Ranger Program
TOUR—SIGHT | FAMILY | Children ages 4 through 12 can earn a certificate and badge for successfully completing at least three activities in the park's Junior Ranger booklet (available at the park or online). ⊠ Mesa Verde Visitor and Research Center or Chapin Mesa Archeological Museum ☎ 970/529–4465 ⊕ www.nps.gov/meve/forkids/beajunior-ranger.htm.

Ranger-Led Tours
ARCHAEOLOGICAL SITE | The cliff dwellings known as Balcony House, Cliff Palace, and Long House can be explored only on ranger-led tours; the first two last about an hour, the third is 90 minutes. Buy tickets at the Mesa Verde Visitor and Research Center. These are active tours and may not be suitable for some children; each requires climbing ladders without handrails and squeezing through tight spaces. Be sure to bring water and sunscreen. Site schedules vary so check ahead. ⊠ Mesa Verde National Park ☎ 970/529–4465 ⊕ www.nps.gov/meve/planyourvisit/visitcliffdwelling.htm ⌹ $5 per site ⊙ Closed: Cliff Palace: Oct./Nov.–late May. Balcony House: early Oct.–late Apr. Long House: mid-Oct.–mid-May.

RESTAURANTS
Dining options in Mesa Verde are limited inside the park, but comparatively plentiful and varied if you're staying in Cortez,

Mancos, or Durango. In surrounding communities, Southwestern restaurants, farm-fresh eateries, and steak houses are common options. *Restaurant reviews have been shortened. For full information, visit Fodors.com.*

HOTELS

All 150 rooms of the park's Far View Lodge, open mid-April through late October, fill up quickly—so reservations are recommended, especially if you plan to visit on a weekend in summer. Options in the surrounding area include chain hotels, cabins, and bed-and-breakfast inns. Although 40 minutes away, Durango in particular has a number of hotels in fine old buildings reminiscent of the Old West. *Hotel reviews have been shortened. For full information, visit Fodors.com.*

What It Costs			
$	$$	$$$	$$$$
RESTAURANTS			
under $13	$13–$18	$19–$25	over $25
HOTELS			
under $121	$121–$170	$171–$230	over $230

TOURS
BUS TOURS
Aramark Tours
ARCHAEOLOGICAL SITE | FAMILY | If you want a well-rounded visit to Mesa Verde's most popular sites, consider a group tour. The park concessionaire provides all-day and half-day guided tours of the Chapin Mesa and Far View sites, departing in buses from either Morefield Campground or Far View Lodge. Tours are led by Aramark guides or park rangers, who share information about the park's history, geology, and excavation processes. Cold water is provided, but you'll need to bring your own snacks. Buy tickets at Far View Lodge, the Morefield Campground, or online. Tours sell out, so reserve in advance. ✉ *Far View Lodge, 1 Navajo Hill, mile marker 15* ☎ *970/529–4422 Far View Lodge, 800/449–2288 Aramark* ⊕ *www.visitmesaverde.com* ✉ *From $41* ⊙ *700 Years Tour closed late Oct.–mid-Apr. Far View Explorer Tour closed mid-Aug.–late May.*

VISITOR INFORMATION
PARK CONTACT INFORMATION Mesa Verde National Park ☎ *970/529–4465* ⊕ *www.nps.gov/meve.*

VISITOR CENTERS
Chapin Mesa Archeological Museum
MUSEUM | This is an excellent first stop for an introduction to Ancestral Pueblo culture, as well as the area's development into a national park. Exhibits showcase original textiles and other artifacts, and a theater plays an informative film every 30 minutes. Rangers are available to answer your questions. The museum sits at the south end of the park entrance road and overlooks Spruce Tree House. Nearby, you'll find park headquarters, a gift shop, a post office, snack bar, and bathrooms. ✉ *Park entrance road, 5 miles south of Far View Center, 20 miles from park entrance* ☎ *970/529–4465 General information line* ⊕ *www.nps.gov/meve/planyourvisit/museum.htm* ✉ *Free.*

Mesa Verde Visitor and Research Center
INFO CENTER | FAMILY | The visitor center is the best place to go to sign up for tours, get the information you need to plan a successful trip, and buy tickets for the Cliff Palace, Balcony House, and Long House ranger-led tours. The sleek, energy-efficient research center is filled with more than 3 million artifacts and archives. The center features indoor and outdoor exhibits, a gift shop, picnic tables, and a museum. Find books, maps, and videos on the history of the park. ✉ *Park entrance on the left, 35853 Rd H.5, Mancos* ☎ *970/529–4465* ⊕ *www.nps.gov/meve/planyourvisit/meve_vc.htm.*

Plants and Wildlife in Mesa Verde

Mesa Verde is home to 640 species of plants, including a number of native plants found nowhere else. Its lower elevations feature many varieties of shrubs, including rabbitbrush and sagebrush. Higher up, you'll find mountain mahogany, yucca, pinyon, juniper, and Douglas fir. During warmer months, brightly colored blossoms, like the yellow perky Sue, blue lupines, and bright-red Indian paintbrushes, are scattered throughout the park.

The park is also home to a variety of migratory and resident animals, including 74 species of mammals. Drive slowly along the park's roads; mule deer are everywhere. You may spot wild turkeys, and black bear encounters are not unheard of on the hiking trails. Bobcats, coyotes, and mountain lions are also around, but they are seen less frequently. About 200 species of birds, including threatened Mexican spotted owls, red-tailed hawks, golden eagles, and noisy ravens, also live here. On the ground, you should keep your eyes and ears open for lizards and snakes, including the poisonous—but shy—prairie rattlesnake. As a general rule, animals are most active in the early morning and at dusk.

Many areas of the park have had extensive fire damage over the years. In fact, wildfires here have been so destructive they are given names, just like hurricanes. For example, the Bircher Fire in 2000 consumed nearly 20,000 acres of brush and forest, much of it covering the eastern half of the park. It will take several centuries for the woodland there to look as verdant as the area atop Chapin Mesa, which escaped the fire. But in the meantime, you'll have a chance to glimpse nature's powerful rejuvenating processes in action; the landscape in the fire-ravaged sections of the park is already filling in with vegetation.

Sights

SCENIC DRIVES

Mesa Top Loop Road

SCENIC DRIVE | This 6-mile drive skirts the scenic rim of Chapin Mesa and takes you to several overlooks and short, paved trails. You'll get great views of Sun Temple and Square Tower, as well as Cliff Palace, Sunset House, and several other cliff dwellings visible from the Sun Point Overlook. ⊠ *Mesa Verde National Park.*

Park Entrance Road

NATIONAL/STATE PARK | The main park road, also known as SH 10, leads you from the entrance off U.S. 160 into the park. As a break from the switchbacks, you can stop at a couple of pretty overlooks along the way, but hold out for Park Point, which, at the mesa's highest elevation (8,572 feet), gives you unobstructed, 360-degree views. Note that trailers and towed vehicles are not permitted beyond Morefield Campground. ⊠ *Mesa Verde National Park.*

Wetherill Mesa Road

SCENIC DRIVE | This 12-mile mountain road, stretching from the Far View Center to the Wetherill Mesa, has sharp curves and steep grades (and is restricted to vehicles less than 25 feet long and 8,000 pounds). Roadside pull-outs offer unobstructed views of the Four Corners region. At the end of the road, you can access Step House, Long House, and Badger House. ⊠ *Mesa Verde National Park* ⊗ *Closed late Oct.–early May.*

HISTORIC SITES

Badger House Community

ARCHAEOLOGICAL SITE | A self-guided walk along paved and gravel trails takes you through a group of four mesa-top dwellings. The community, which covers nearly 7 acres, dates back to the year 650, the Basketmaker Period, and includes a primitive, semisubterranean pit house and what's left of a multistory stone pueblo. Allow about 45 minutes to see the sites. The trail is 2.4 miles round-trip. ⌖ *Wetherill Mesa Rd., 12 miles from Far View Center* ⊕ *www.nps.gov/meve/historyculture/mt_badger_house.htm* ✉ *Free* ⊘ *Closed late Oct.–early May; road closes at 6 pm.*

★ Balcony House

ARCHAEOLOGICAL SITE | The stonework of this 40-room cliff dwelling is impressive, but you're likely to be even more awed by the skill it must have taken to reach this place. Perched in a sandstone cove 600 feet above the floor of Soda Canyon, Balcony House seems suspended in space. Even with modern passageways and trails, today's visitors must climb a 32-foot ladder and crawl through a narrow tunnel. Look for the intact balcony for which the house is named. The dwelling is accessible only on a ranger-led tour. ⌖ *Cliff Palace/Balcony House Rd., 10 miles south of Far View Center, Cliff Palace Loop* ⊕ *www.nps.gov/meve/learn/historyculture/cd_balcony_house.htm* ✉ *$5* ⊘ *Closed early Oct.–late Apr.*

★ Cliff Palace

ARCHAEOLOGICAL SITE | This was the first major Mesa Verde dwelling seen by cowboys Charlie Mason and Richard Wetherill in 1888. It is also the largest, containing about 150 rooms and 23 kivas on three levels. Getting there involves a steep downhill hike and three ladders. **You may enter Balcony House or Cliff Palace by ranger-guided tour only so purchase tickets in advance.** The 90-minute, small-group "twilight tours" at sunset present this archaelogical treasure with dramatic sunset lighting. Tour tickets are only available in advance at ⊕ *www.recreation.gov.* ⌖ *Cliff Palace Overlook, about 2½ miles south of Chapin Mesa Archeological Museum* ⊕ *www.nps.gov/meve/learn/historyculture/cd_cliff_palace.htm* ✉ *Regular tickets $5; twilight tours $20.* ⊘ *Closed Oct./Nov.–late May; loop closes at sunset.*

Far View Sites Complex

ARCHAEOLOGICAL SITE | FAMILY | This was probably one of the most densely populated areas in Mesa Verde, comprising as many as 50 villages in a ½-square-mile area at the top of Chapin Mesa. Most of the sites here were built between 900 and 1300. Begin the self-guided tour at the interpretive panels in the parking lot, then proceed down a ½-mile, level trail. ⌖ *Park entrance road, near the Chapin Mesa area* ⊕ *www.nps.gov/meve* ✉ *Free* ☞ *In winter, access by parking at the gate and walking in.*

Long House

ARCHAEOLOGICAL SITE | This Wetherill Mesa cliff dwelling is the second largest in Mesa Verde. It is believed that about 150 people lived in Long House, so named because of the size of its cliff alcove. The spring at the back of the cave is still active today. The in-depth, ranger-led tour

23

Mesa Verde National Park

Cliff Palace illuminated at night.

begins a short distance from the parking lot and takes about 90 minutes. You hike about two miles, including two 15-foot ladders. ✉ *On Wetherill Mesa, 29 miles past the visitor center, near mile marker 15 ⊕ www.nps.gov/meve/learn/history-culture/cd_long_house.htm ✉ Tours $5 ⊗ Closed mid-Oct.–mid-May.*

Pit Houses and Early Pueblo Villages

ARCHAEOLOGICAL SITE | Three dwellings, built on top of each other from 700 to 950, at first look like a mass of jumbled walls, but an informational panel helps identify the dwellings—and the stories behind them are fascinating. The 325-foot trail from the walking area is paved, wheelchair accessible, and near a restroom. ✉ *Mesa Top Loop Rd., about 2½ miles south of Chapin Mesa Archeological Museum ✉ Free.*

Spruce Tree House

ARCHAEOLOGICAL SITE | FAMILY | This 138-room complex is the best-preserved site in the park, however, the alcove surrounding Spruce Tree House became unstable in 2015 and was closed to visitors. Until alcove arch support is added, visitors can view but not enter this site. You can still hike down a trail that starts behind the Chapin Mesa Archeological Museum and leads you 100 feet down into the canyon to view the site from a distance. Because of its location in the heart of the Chapin Mesa area, the Spruce Tree House trail and area can resemble a crowded playground during busy periods. When allowed inside the site, tours are self-guided (allow 45 minutes to an hour), but a park ranger is on-site to answer questions. ✉ *At the Chapin Mesa Archeological Museum, 5 miles south of Far View Center ⊕ www.nps.gov/meve/learn/historyculture/cd_spruce_tree_house.htm ✉ Free ⊗ Tours closed for reconstruction.*

Step House

ARCHAEOLOGICAL SITE | So named because of a crumbling prehistoric stairway leading up from the dwelling, Step House is reached via a paved (but steep) trail that's ¾ mile long. The house is unique in that it shows clear evidence of two separate occupations: the first around 626, the second a full 600 years later. The self-guided tour takes about 45 minutes. ⊠ *Wetherill Mesa Rd., 12 miles from Far View Center* ⊕ *www.nps.gov/meve/historyculture/cd_step_house.htm* ✉ *Free* ⊙ *Closed mid-May–mid-Oct.; hrs vary seasonally.*

Sun Temple
ARCHAEOLOGICAL SITE | Although researchers assume it was probably a ceremonial structure, they're unsure of the exact purpose of this complex, which has no doors or windows in most of its chambers. Because the building was not quite half-finished when it was left in 1276, some researchers surmise it might have been constructed to stave off whatever disaster caused its builders—and the other inhabitants of Mesa Verde—to leave. ⊠ *Mesa Top Loop Rd., about 2 miles south of Chapin Mesa Archeological Museum* ⊕ *www.nps.gov/meve/historyculture/mt_sun_temple.htm* ✉ *Free.*

SCENIC STOPS
Cedar Tree Tower
ARCHAEOLOGICAL SITE | A self-guided tour takes you to, but not through, a tower and kiva built between 1100 and 1300 and connected by a tunnel. The tower-and-kiva combinations in the park are thought to have been either religious structures or signal towers. ⊠ *Near the four-way intersection on Chapin Mesa; park entrance road, 1½ miles north of Chapin Mesa Archeological Museum* ⊕ *www.nps.gov/meve/learn/historyculture/mt_cedar_tree_tower.htm* ✉ *Free.*

Kodak House Overlook
VIEWPOINT | Get an impressive view into the 60-room Kodak House and its several small kivas from here. The house, closed to the public, was named for a Swedish researcher who absentmindedly left his Kodak camera behind here in 1891. ⊠ *Wetherill Mesa Rd.* ⊕ *www.nps.gov/meve* ⊙ *Closed late Oct.–May.*

Soda Canyon Overlook
CANYON | Get your best view of Balcony House here. You can also read interpretive panels about the site and the surrounding canyon geology. ⊠ *Cliff Palace Loop Rd., about 1 mile north of Balcony House parking area* ☞ *Access in winter by walking the Cliff Palace Loop.*

🏃 Activities

At Mesa Verde, outdoor activities are restricted, due to the fragile nature of the archaeological treasures here. Hiking (allowed on marked trails only) is the best option, especially as a way to view some of the Ancestral Pueblo dwellings.

BICYCLING
Bicycles are allowed on paved roads in the park except the twisty Wetherill Mesa Road, but there are no bike lanes and very narrow shoulders. During periods of low visibility (or when traveling through the tunnel on the main park road), bicycles must be fitted with a white light on the front and a red light (or reflector) on the back. Bikes are not allowed off-road or on trails.

BIRD-WATCHING
Turkey vultures soar between April and October, and large flocks of ravens hang around all summer. Among the park's other large birds are red-tailed hawks, great horned owls, and a few golden eagles. The Steller's jay (the male looks like a blue jay with a dark hat on) frequently pierces the pinyon-juniper forest with its cries, and hummingbirds dart from flower to flower in the summer and fall. Any visit to cliff dwellings late in the day will include frolicking white-throated swifts, which make their home in rock crevices overhead.

Pick up a copy of the park's "Checklist of the Birds" brochure or visit the National Park Service's website (⊕ *www.nps.gov/meve/planyourvisit/birdwatching.htm*) for a detailed listing of the feathered inhabitants here.

23

Mesa Verde National Park

HIKING

A handful of trails lead beyond Mesa Verde's most visited sites and offer more solitude than the often-crowded cliff dwellings. The best canyon vistas can be reached if you're willing to huff and puff your way through elevation changes and switchbacks. Carry more water than you think you'll need, wear sunscreen, and bring rain gear—cloudbursts can come seemingly out of nowhere. Certain trails are open seasonally, so check with a ranger before heading out. No backcountry hiking is permitted in Mesa Verde, and pets are prohibited.

Farming Terrace Trail

HIKING/WALKING | FAMILY | This 30-minute, ½-mile loop begins and ends on the spur road to Cedar Tree Tower, about 1 mile north of the Chapin Mesa area. It meanders through a series of check dams, which the Ancestral Pueblo built to create farming terraces. *Easy.* ⊠ *Mesa Verde National Park* ✛ *Trailhead: park entrance road, 4 miles south of Far View Center.*

Knife Edge Trail

HIKING/WALKING | Perfect for a sunset stroll, this easy 2-mile (round-trip) walk around the north rim of the park leads to an overlook of the Montezuma Valley. If you stop at all the flora identification points that the trail pamphlet suggests, the hike takes about 1½ to 2 hours. The patches of asphalt you spot along the way are leftovers from old Knife Edge Road, built in 1914 as the main entryway into the park. *Easy.* ⊠ *Mesa Verde National Park* ✛ *Trailhead: Morefield Campground, 4 miles from park entrance.*

★ Petroglyph Point Trail

HIKING/WALKING | Scramble along a narrow canyon wall to reach the largest and best-known petroglyphs in Mesa Verde. If you pose for a photo just right, you can just manage to block out the gigantic "don't touch" sign next to the rock art. A map—available at any ranger station—points out three dozen points of interest along the trail. The trail is open even while Spruce Tree House is closed; check with a ranger for times. *Moderate.* ⊠ *Mesa Verde National Park* ✛ *Trailhead: at Spruce Tree House, next to Chapin Mesa Archeological Museum.*

Prater Ridge Trail

HIKING/WALKING | This 7.8-mile round-trip loop, which starts and finishes at Morefield Campground, is the longest hike you can take inside the park. It provides fine views of Morefield Canyon to the south and the San Juan Mountains to the north. About halfway through the hike, you'll see a cut-off trail that you can take, which shortens the trip to 5 miles. *Difficult.* ⊠ *Mesa Verde National Park* ✛ *Trailhead: west end of Morefield Campground, 4 miles from park entrance.*

Soda Canyon Overlook Trail

HIKING/WALKING | FAMILY | One of the easiest and most rewarding hikes in the park, this little trail travels 1½ miles round-trip through the forest on almost completely level ground. The overlook is an excellent point from which to photograph the Chapin Mesa–area cliff dwellings. *Easy.* ⊠ *Mesa Verde National Park* ✛ *Trailhead: Cliff Palace Loop Rd., about 1 mile north of Balcony House parking area* ↗ *Access in winter via Cliff Palace Loop.*

Spruce Canyon Trail

HIKING/WALKING | While Petroglyph Point Trail takes you along the side of the canyon, this trail ventures down into its depths. It's only 2.4 miles long, but you descend about 600 feet in elevation. Remember to save your strength; what goes down must come up again. The trail is open even while Spruce Tree House is closed. Still, check with a ranger. *Moderate.* ⊠ *Mesa Verde National Park* ✛ *Trailhead: at Spruce Tree House, next to Chapin Mesa Archeological Museum* ↗ *Registration required at trailhead.*

STARGAZING
There are no large cities in the Four Corners area, so there is little artificial light to detract from the stars in the night sky. Far View Lodge and Morefield Campground are great for sky watching.

 **Shopping**

Chapin Mesa Archeological Museum Shop
BOOKS/STATIONERY | Books and videos are the primary offering here, with more than 400 titles on Ancestral Pueblo and Southwestern topics. You can also find a selection of touristy T-shirts and hats. Hours vary throughout the year. ⊠ *Spruce Tree Terrace, near Chapin Mesa Archeological Museum, 5 miles from Far View Center* ☎ *970/529–4445* ⊕ *www.nps. gov/meve/planyourvisit/museum.htm.*

Far View Terrace Shop
CLOTHING | In the same building as the Far View Terrace Café, this is the largest gift shop in the park, with gifts, souvenirs, Native American art, toys, and T-shirts galore. ⊠ *Mesa Top Loop Rd., 15 miles south of park entrance* ☎ *800/449–2288 Aramark* ◔ *Hrs vary seasonally.*

Nearby Towns

A onetime market center for cattle and crops, **Cortez,** 11 miles west of the park, is now the largest gateway town to Mesa Verde and a base for tourists visiting the Four Corners region. You can still see a rodeo here at least once a year. **Dolores,** steeped in a rich railroad history, is on the Dolores River, 19 miles north of Mesa Verde. Near both the San Juan National Forest and McPhee Reservoir, Dolores is a favorite of outdoor enthusiasts. East of Mesa Verde by 36 miles, **Durango,** the region's main hub, comes complete with a variety of restaurants and hotels, shopping, and outdoor-equipment shops. Durango became a town in 1881 when the Denver and Rio Grande Railroad pushed its tracks across the neighboring San Juan Mountains.

 **Sights**

★ **Durango & Silverton Narrow Gauge Railroad**
TRANSPORTATION SITE (AIRPORT/BUS/FERRY/TRAIN) | FAMILY | The most entertaining way to relive the Old West is to take a ride on the Durango & Silverton Narrow Gauge Railroad, a nine-hour round-trip journey along the 45-mile railway to Silverton. Travel in comfort in restored coaches or in the open-air cars called gondolas as you listen to the train's shrill whistle. A shorter excursion to Cascade Canyon in heated coaches is available in winter. The train departs from the Durango Depot, constructed in 1882 and beautifully restored. Next door is the Durango & Silverton Narrow Gauge Railroad Museum, which is free and well worth your time. ⊠ *479 Main Ave., Durango* ☎ *970/247–2733, 888/687–2461* ⊕ *www.durangotrain.com* ⊠ *$91–$199.*

Four Corners Monument
LOCAL INTEREST | The Navajo Nation manages this interesting landmark about 65 miles southeast of Bluff and 6 miles north of Teec Nos Pos, Arizona. Primarily a photo op, you'll also find Navajo and Ute artisans selling authentic jewelry and crafts, as well as traditional foods. It's the only place in the United States where four states meet at one single point. Bring plenty of water. ⊠ *Four Corners Monument Rd., off U.S. 160, Teec Nos Pos* ⊕ *www.utah.com/four-corners* ⊠ *$5.*

Ute Mountain Ute Tribal Park
ARCHAEOLOGICAL SITE | The only way to see this spectacular 125,000-acre park, located inside the Ute reservation, is by taking a guided tour. Expert tribal guides lead strenuous daylong hikes into this dazzling repository of Ancestral Pueblo ruins, including beautifully preserved cliff dwellings, pictographs, and petroglyphs. There are also less-demanding half-day

The Four Corners Monument

There's no view to speak of at Four Corners Monument, but it's a popular photo op nonetheless. Set on Navajo land, about one usually dusty mile off U.S. 60, the monument is the only place in the nation where the borders of four states meet. The first permanent marker, a simple "look-what's-here," was erected at the intersection of Colorado, Utah, New Mexico, and Arizona in 1912. As long as there have been cameras, people have gone out of their way just to stand in such a way as to be in four states at once.

The monument was refurbished in 1992, and a larger marker, consisting of a bronze disk embedded in granite, was put in place. Though bigger and more ornate than the first marker, it still seems far too unassuming to have attracted the bazaar that surrounds it. In response to a ready market of tourists and trinket hounds, the main drive is rimmed with plywood booths hawking Ute, Navajo, Apache, and other American Indian artwork, crafts, artifacts, and rugs. You can also buy fry bread and corn on the cob. It's all genuine, but the opportunistic nature of the site—it costs $5 per person just to enter (cash only; kids 6 and under are free)—detracts from what began as the simple fascination of standing at the very point where four southwestern states meet.

No major cities are nearby. Cortez, Colorado, is 40 miles away on U.S. 60; tiny Teec Nos Pos, Arizona, is 6 miles away; Shiprock, New Mexico, is about 27 miles to the east; and Bluff, Utah, is 53 miles distant.

The Navajo Nation Parks and Recreation Department administers the Four Corners Monument, along with numerous natural sites and thousands of square miles of pristine wilderness. For more information, email nslim@navajonationparks.org.

---

tours, as well as private and custom tour options. Tours start at the park's visitor center, off Highway 160. ⊠ *Hwy. 160/491, Cortez* ☎ *970/565–9653* ⊕ *www.utemountaintribalpark.info* ✉ *From $29* ⊗ *Closed Sun.* ☞ *No pets allowed.*

 ## Activities

FISHING
McPhee Reservoir
BODY OF WATER | In 1985, crews completed construction of an irrigation dam across the Dolores River, forming the McPhee Reservoir, the second largest in the state. It draws anglers looking to bag a variety of warm- and cold-water fish along its 50 miles of shoreline, which is surrounded by spectacular specimens of juniper and sage as well as large stands of pinyon pine. There are two boat ramps; the McPhee Boat Ramp also has a marina and convenience store. The area also has camping, hiking, and a relatively easy mountain-bike trail, and the mesa offers panoramic views of the surrounding San Juan National Forest. ⊠ *Forest Service Rd. 271, off State Hwy. 184, Dolores* ✛ *About 9 miles northwest of Dolores* ✉ *Free* ⊗ *Marina closed Nov.–Apr.*

HIKING
Animas Overlook Trail
HIKING/WALKING | If you're looking for a great view without the effort, try the ¾-mile Animas Overlook Trail. It takes you past signs explaining local geology, flora, and fauna before bringing you to a precipice with an unparalleled view of the valley and the surrounding Needle

Mountains. It's the only wheelchair-accessible trail in the area. From town, it's a 45-minute drive up Junction Creek Road. ⊠ *Durango* ✛ *Trailhead: at Forest Rd. 171, milepost 8.*

★ Colorado Trail

HIKING/WALKING | Junction Creek to Gudy's Rest Junction Creek is the southern terminus for the Colorado Trail and one of Durango's best trails for hiking, mountain biking, and trail running. Located just 4 miles or so from downtown, this 8-mile out-and-back day hike rises and falls at a relatively gentle grade, so it's achievable for most hikers. The trail eventually winds it's way up to Gudy's Rest, named after Gudy Gaskill, the "Mother of the Colorado Trail." This high spot is a great place to sit and take in the views of Durango and the San Juan Mountains. Instead of hiking all the way up to Gudy's Rest, you can make the hike a 5-mile round-trip by turning back at the wooden footbridge, which is a great goal for first-timers. ⊠ *Trailhead off County Rd. 204, Durango* ✛ *From town, take 25th St. west; it turns into Junction St. and continues on to the lower parking lot* ⊕ *www.coloradotrail.org.*

RAFTING

Beginning in the San Juan Mountains of southwestern Colorado, the Dolores River runs north for more than 150 miles before joining the Colorado River near Moab, Utah. This is one of those rivers that tends to flow madly in spring and diminish considerably by midsummer, and for that reason rafting trips are usually run in April and May, and occasionally early June.

Durango Rivertrippers

WHITE-WATER RAFTING | This outfitter runs two- and four-hour trips down the Animas River. You can up your adrenaline output by swapping the raft for an inflatable kayak on any of the Animas River trips. Or ask about zipline and rafting packages, or Jeep tours or rentals. ⊠ *724 Main Ave., Durango* ☎ *970/259–0289* ⊕ *www.durangorivertrippers.com.*

 Nightlife

Diamond Belle Saloon

BARS/PUBS | Awash in flocked wallpaper and lace, the Diamond Belle Saloon is dominated by a gilt-and-mahogany bar. With its prime location—on the ground floor of the historic Strater Hotel—and a staff of ragtime piano players, Old West shootout reenactments, and waitresses dressed as saloon girls, the Diamond Belle can really pack them in. Try the Brazilian mint martini; if you're hungry, order the much-hailed Diamond burger. ⊠ *699 Main Ave., Durango* ☎ *970/247–4431 Strater Hotel* ⊕ *www.diamondbelle.com.*

 Performing Arts

Cortez Cultural Center

ART GALLERIES—ARTS | The cultural center has exhibits on regional artists and Ancestral Pueblo culture, as well as events and fairs. Summer evening programs include Native American dances and storytelling. ⊠ *25 N. Market St., Cortez* ☎ *970/565–1151* ⊕ *www.cortezculturalcenter.org* ⊗ *Closed Sun.*

Henry Strater Theatre

THEATER | Boo the villain and cheer the hero at the Henry Strater Theatre's rip-roaring vaudeville and melodrama productions all summer long. Also catch concerts, comedy, and special events at what locals call "the Hank." ⊠ *699 Main Ave., Durango* ☎ *970/375–7160* ⊕ *www.henrystratertheatre.com.*

 Shopping

Notah-Dineh Trading Company and Museum

CRAFTS | This store specializing in Navajo rugs has the largest collection in the area. There are also handmade baskets, beadwork, pottery, and jewelry. If you stop in the free museum you can see relics of the Old West. ⊠ *345 W. Main*

St., Cortez ☎ *800/444–2024* 🌐 *www.notahdineh.com* 🕓 *Closed Sun.*

Toh-Atin Gallery

CRAFTS | Recognized as one of the region's best Native American galleries, Toh-Atin specializes in Navajo rugs and weavings. There's also a wide range of paintings and prints, pottery, baskets, and jewelry made by the artisans of many Southwestern tribes. ✉ *145 W. 9th St., Durango* ☎ *970/247–8277* 🌐 *www.toh-atin.com.*

🍴 Restaurants

IN THE PARK

Far View Terrace Café

$ | **AMERICAN** | This full-service cafeteria offers great views, but it's nothing fancy. Grab a simple coffee here or head across the dining room to Mesa Mocha for a latte. **Known for:** beautiful views; lattes; great gift shop. [$] *Average main: $12* ✉ *Across from Far View Center* ☎ *970/529–4421* 🌐 *www.visitmesaverde.com/lodging-camping/dining/far-view-terrace-cafe* 🕓 *Closed late Oct.–mid-Apr.*

Knife Edge Cafe

$ | **CAFÉ** | **FAMILY** | Located in the Morefield Campground, this simple restaurant in a covered outdoor terrace with picnic tables serves a hearty all-you-can-eat pancake breakfast with sausage every morning. Coffee and beverages are also available. **Known for:** lively gathering spot; breakfast burritos; large coffees with free refills all day. [$] *Average main: $10* ✉ *4 miles south of park entrance* ☎ *970/565–2133* 🌐 *www.nps.gov/meve/planyourvisit/restaurants.htm* 🕓 *Closed mid-Sept.–late Apr.*

★ Metate Room Restaurant

$$$ | **AMERICAN** | The park's rugged terrain contrasts with this relaxing space just off the lobby of the Far View Lodge. The well-regarded dining room is upscale, but the atmosphere remains casual. **Known for:** Native American artwork; cheese and cured meats board; great views. [$] *Average main: $25* ✉ *Far View Lodge, 1 Navajo Rd., across from Far View Center, 15 miles southwest of park entrance* ☎ *970/529–4422* 🌐 *www.visitmesaverde.com/lodging-camping/dining/metate-room-restaurant* 🕓 *Closed late Oct.–mid-Apr. No lunch.*

Spruce Tree Terrace Café

$ | **AMERICAN** | This small cafeteria has a limited selection of hot food, coffee, salads, burgers, and sandwiches. The patio is pleasant, and it's conveniently located across the street from the museum. **Known for:** Southwest specialties; soup of the day specials; Navajo tacos. [$] *Average main: $10* ✉ *Near Chapin Mesa Archeological Museum, 5 miles south of the Far View Center* ☎ *970/529–4465* 🌐 *www.visitmesaverde.com/lodging-camping/dining/spruce-tree-terrace-cafe* 🕓 *No dinner in offseason.*

PICNIC AREAS

Chapin Mesa Picnic Area

RESTAURANT—SIGHT | **FAMILY** | This is the nicest and largest picnic area in the park. It has about 40 tables under shade trees and a great view into Spruce Canyon, as well as flushing toilets. ✉ *Near Chapin Mesa Archeological Museum, 5 miles south of Far View Center.*

Wetherill Mesa Picnic Area

RESTAURANT—SIGHT | **FAMILY** | A handful of benches and tables near drinking water, a covered kiosk, and restrooms make this a pleasant spot for lunch in the Wetherill area. ✉ *12 miles southwest of Far View Center.*

OUTSIDE THE PARK

Ken & Sue's

$$ | **MODERN AMERICAN** | Plates are big and the selection is creative at Ken & Sue's, one of Durango's favorite restaurants. Locals are wild for the contemporary American cuisine with an Asian flair, served in an intimate space. **Known for:** large, pretty patio out back; worth-it desserts; pistachio-crusted grouper with

Best Campgrounds in Mesa Verde

Morefield Campground is the only option within the park, and it's an excellent one. Reservations are accepted; it's open mid-April through mid-October, and through early November with no services. In nearby Mancos, just across the highway from the park entrance, there's a campground with full amenities (but no electrical hookups), while the San Juan National Forest offers backcountry camping.

Morefield Campground and Village. With 267 campsites, including 15 full-hookup RV sites, access to trailheads, a pet kennel, and plenty of amenities, the only campground in the park is an appealing mini-city for campers. It's a 40-minute drive to reach the park's most popular sites. Reservations are recommended, especially for RVs. ⊠ *4 miles south of park entrance* ☎ *970/564–4300, 800/449–2288* ⊕ *www. visitmesaverde.com.*

vanilla-rum butter. $ *Average main: $18* ⊠ *636 Main Ave., Durango* ☎ *970/385–1810* ⊕ *www.kenandsues.com* ⏱ *No lunch weekends.*

★ Ore House

$$$$ | **STEAKHOUSE** | Durango is a meat-and-potatoes kind of town, and the rustic Ore House is a splurge-worthy place to indulge (just ask the locals). The steaks are fantastic, and there are plenty of expertly prepared seafood and vegetarian selections as well. **Known for:** chateaubriand for two; cornbread with bacon butter; deep whiskey and wine lists. $ *Average main: $39* ⊠ *147 E. College Dr., Durango* ☎ *970/247–5707* ⊕ *www.orehouserestaurant.com.*

 Hotels

IN THE PARK
★ Far View Lodge

$$$ | **HOTEL** | Talk about a view—all rooms have a private balcony, from which you can admire views of the neighboring states of Arizona, Utah, and New Mexico up to 100 miles in the distance. **Pros:** close to the key sites; views are spectacular; small on-site fitness center. **Cons:**

simple rooms and amenities, with no TV; walls are thin and less than soundproof; no cell-phone service. $ *Rooms from: $175* ⊠ *Across from Far View Center, 1 Navajo Rd., 15 miles southwest of park entrance* ☎ *800/449–2288* ⊕ *www.visit-mesaverde.com* ⏱ *Closed late Oct.–mid-Apr.* ⤴ *150 rooms* ⦿| *No meals.*

Morefield Campground

$ | **RENTAL** | With 435 campsites, access to trailheads, and plenty of amenities, the only campground in the park is an appealing mini-city for campers. **Pros:** the village has a gas station, grocery store, and café with a great breakfast; inside park boundaries. **Cons:** at the far north end of the park, it's still a long way from key sites. $ *Rooms from: $23* ⊠ *4 mi south of park entrance* ☎ *970/564–4300, 800/449–2288* ⊕ *www.visitmesaverde. com* ⤴ *403 dry tent/RV sites, 17 group sites (tents), 15 full-hookup RV sites.*

OUTSIDE THE PARK
Rochester Hotel

$$$ | **B&B/INN** | The renovated Rochester Hotel is funky yet chic, with colorful photos of local scenery adorning the common areas and Hollywood

Western–themed rooms with steamer trunks and other period pieces. **Pros:** free guest parking; pleasant courtyard; free use of cruiser bikes in town. **Cons:** can be noisy; no counter space in bathrooms; no pool or hot tub. [$] *Rooms from: $199* ✉ *726 E. 2nd Ave., Durango* ☎ *970/385–1920, 800/664–1920* 🌐 *www.rochesterhotel.com* 🛏 *27 rooms* 🍴 *Free Breakfast.*

★ **Strater Hotel**

$$ | **HOTEL** | Still the hottest spot in town, this Western grande dame opened for business in 1887 and has been visited by Butch Cassidy, Louis L'Amour (he wrote many of the *Sacketts* novels here), Francis Ford Coppola, John Kennedy, and Marilyn Monroe (the latter two stayed here at separate times). **Pros:** right in the thick of things; free guest parking; filled with gorgeous antiques. **Cons:** breakfast not included in all rates; noisy bar; Wi-Fi is spotty. [$] *Rooms from: $152* ✉ *699 Main Ave., Durango* ☎ *970/247–4431, 800/247–4431* 🌐 *www.strater.com* 🛏 *93 rooms* 🍴 *No meals.*

Chapter 24

MOUNT RAINIER NATIONAL PARK

24

Updated by
Shelley Arenas

WASHINGTON

WELCOME TO MOUNT RAINIER NATIONAL PARK

TOP REASONS TO GO

★ **The mountain:** Some say Mt. Rainier is the most magical mountain in America. At 14,411 feet, it is a popular peak for climbing, with more than 10,000 attempts per year—nearly half of which are successful.

★ **The glaciers:** About 35 square miles of glaciers and snowfields encircle Mt. Rainier, including Carbon Glacier and Emmons Glacier, the largest glaciers by volume and area, respectively, in the continental United States.

★ **The wildflowers:** More than 100 species of wildflowers bloom in the park's high meadows; the display dazzles from midsummer until the snow flies.

★ **Fabulous hiking:** More than 240 miles of maintained trails provide access to old-growth forest, river valleys, lakes, and rugged ridges.

★ **Unencumbered wilderness:** Under the provisions of the 1964 Wilderness Act and the National Wilderness Preservation System, 97% of the park is preserved as wilderness.

1 Longmire. Inside the Nisqually Gate explore Longmire historic district's museum and visitor center, ruins of the park's first hotel, or the nature loop. Nearby, delicate footbridges span the thundering Christine and Narada falls.

2 Paradise. The park's most popular destination is famous for wildflowers in summer and skiing in winter.

3 Ohanapecosh. Closest to the southeast entrance and the town of Packwood, the giant old-growth trees of the Grove of the Patriarchs are a must-see. Another short trail around nearby Tipsoo Lake has great views.

4 Sunrise and White River. Sunrise is the highest stretch of road in the park and a great place to take in the alpenglow—reddish light on the peak of the mountain near sunrise and sunset. Mt. Rainier's premier mountain-biking area, White River, is also the gateway to more than a dozen hiking trails.

5 Carbon River and Mowich Lake. Near the Carbon River Entrance Station is a swath of temperate forest, but to really get away from it all, follow the windy gravel roads to remote Mowich Lake.

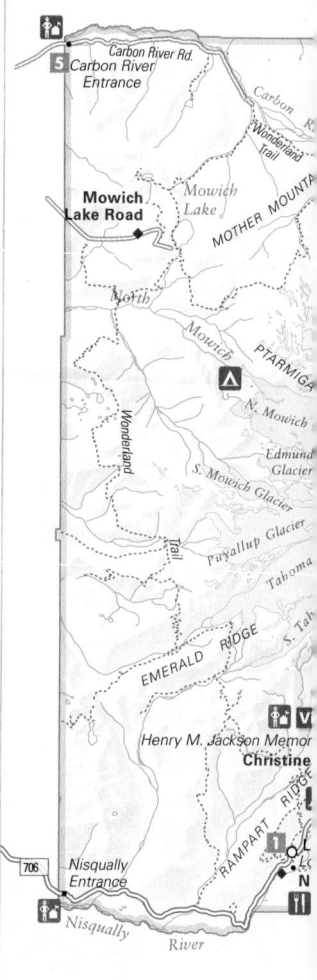

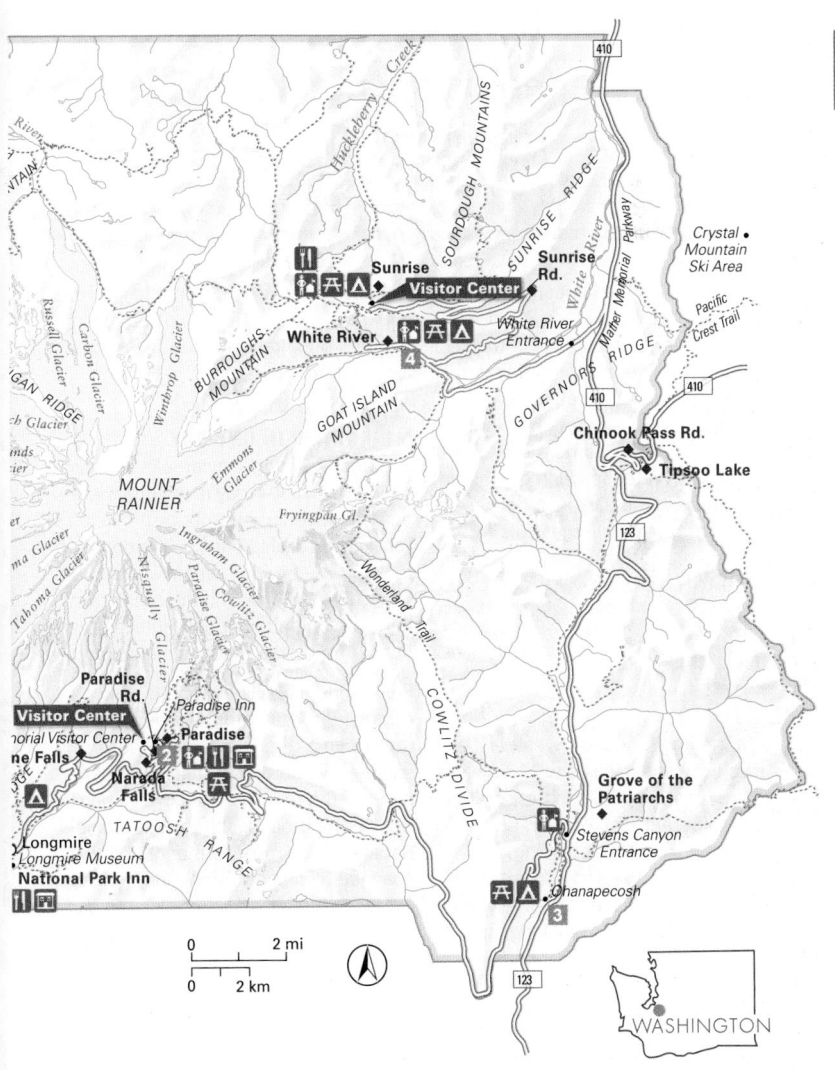

Mt. Rainier is the centerpiece of its namesake park. The impressive volcanic peak stands at an elevation of 14,411 feet, making it the fifth-highest peak in the lower 48 states. Nearly 2 million visitors a year enjoy spectacular views of the mountain and return home with a lifelong memory of its image.

The mountain holds the largest glacial system in the contiguous United States, with more than two dozen major glaciers. On the lower slopes you find silent forests made up of cathedral-like groves of Douglas fir, western hemlock, and western red cedar, some more than 1,000 years old. Water and lush greenery are everywhere in the park, and dozens of thundering waterfalls, accessible from the road or by a short hike, fill the air with mist.

Planning

WHEN TO GO

Rainier is the Puget Sound's weather vane: if you can see it, skies will be clear. Visitors are most likely to see the summit July through September. Crowds are heaviest in summer, too, meaning the parking lots at Paradise and Sunrise often fill before noon, campsites are reserved months in advance, and other lodgings are reserved as much as a year ahead.

True to its name, Paradise is often sunny during periods when the lowlands are under a cloud layer. The rest of the year, Rainier's summit gathers flying-saucer-like lenticular clouds whenever a Pacific storm approaches; once the peak vanishes from view, it's time to haul out rain gear. The rare periods of clear winter weather bring residents up to Paradise for cross-country skiing.

PLANNING YOUR TIME
MT. RAINIER IN ONE DAY

The best way to get a complete overview of Mt. Rainier in a day is to enter via Nisqually and begin your tour by browsing in **Longmire Museum.** When you're done, get to know the environment in and around Longmire Meadow and the overgrown ruins of Longmire Springs Hotel on the ½-mile **Trail of the Shadows** nature loop.

From Longmire, Highway 706 East climbs northeast into the mountains toward Paradise. Take a moment to explore two-tiered **Christine Falls,** just north of the road 1½ miles past Cougar Rock Campground, and the cascading **Narada Falls,** 3 miles farther on; both are spanned by graceful stone footbridges. Fantastic mountain views, alpine meadows crosshatched with nature trails, a welcoming lodge and restaurant, and the excellent **Jackson Memorial Visitor Center** combine to make lofty Paradise the primary goal of most park visitors. One outstanding (but challenging) way to explore the high country is to hike the 5-mile round-trip **Skyline Trail** to

AVERAGE HIGH/LOW TEMPERATURES					
JAN.	**FEB.**	**MAR.**	**APR.**	**MAY**	**JUNE**
36/24	40/26	44/28	53/32	62/37	66/43
JULY	**AUG.**	**SEPT.**	**OCT.**	**NOV.**	**DEC.**
75/47	74/47	68/43	57/38	45/31	39/28

Panorama Point, which rewards you with stunning 360-degree views.

Continue eastward on Highway 706 East for 21 miles and leave your car to explore the incomparable, 1,000-year-old **Grove of the Patriarchs.** Afterward, turn your car north toward White River and **Sunrise Visitor Center,** where you can watch the alpenglow fade from Mt. Rainier's domed summit.

GETTING HERE AND AROUND
AIR TRAVEL
Seattle–Tacoma International Airport, 15 miles south of downtown Seattle, is the nearest airport to the national park.

CAR TRAVEL
The Nisqually entrance is on Highway 706, 14 miles east of Route 7; the Ohanapecosh entrance is on Route 123, 5 miles north of U.S. 12; and the White River entrance is on Route 410, 3 miles north of the Chinook and Cayuse passes. These highways become mountain roads as they reach Rainier, winding up and down many steep slopes, so cautious driving is essential: use a lower gear, especially on downhill sections, and take care not to overheat brakes by constant use. These roads are subject to storms any time of year and are repaired in the summer from winter damage and washouts.

Side roads into the park's western slope are narrower, unpaved, and subject to flooding and washouts. All are closed by snow in winter except Highway 706 to Paradise and Carbon River Road, though the latter tends to flood near the park boundary. (Route 410 is open to the Crystal Mountain access road entrance.)

Park roads have a maximum speed of 35 mph in most places, and you have to watch for pedestrians, cyclists, and wildlife. Parking can be difficult during peak summer season, especially at Paradise, Sunrise, Grove of the Patriarchs, and at the trailheads between Longmire and Paradise; arrive early if you plan to visit these sites. All off-road-vehicle use—4X4 vehicles, ATVs, motorcycles, snowmobiles—is prohibited in Mount Rainier National Park.

PARK ESSENTIALS
ACCESSIBILITY
The only trail in the park that is fully accessible to those with impaired mobility is Kautz Creek Trail, a ½-mile boardwalk that leads to a splendid view of the mountain. Parts of the Trail of the Shadows at Longmire and the Grove of the Patriarchs at Ohanapecosh are also accessible. Campgrounds at Cougar Rock and Ohanapecosh have several accessible sites. All main visitor centers, as well as National Park Inn at Longmire, are accessible. Wheelchairs are available at the Jackson Visitor Center for guests to use in the center.

PARK FEES AND PERMITS
The entrance fee of $30 per vehicle and $15 for those on foot, motorcycle, or bicycle is good for seven days. Annual passes are $55. Climbing permits are $48 per person per climb or glacier trek. Wilderness camping permits must be obtained for all backcountry trips, and advance reservations are highly recommended.

PARK HOURS

Mount Rainier National Park is open 24/7 year-round, but with limited access in winter. Gates at Nisqually (Longmire) are staffed year-round during the day; facilities at Paradise are open daily from late May to mid-October; and Sunrise is open daily July to early September. During off-hours you can buy passes at the gates from machines that accept credit and debit cards. Winter access to the park is limited to the Nisqually entrance, and the Jackson Memorial Visitor Center at Paradise is open on weekends and holidays in winter. The Paradise snow-play area is open when there is sufficient snow.

CELL PHONE RECEPTION

Cell phone reception is unreliable throughout much of the park, although access is clear at Paradise, Sunrise, and Crystal Mountain. Public telephones are at all park visitor centers, at the National Park Inn at Longmire, and at Paradise Inn at Paradise.

EDUCATIONAL OFFERINGS

RANGER PROGRAMS

Junior Ranger Program

NATIONAL/STATE PARK | FAMILY | Youngsters ages 6 to 11 can pick up an activity booklet at a visitor center and fill it out as they explore the park. When they complete it, they can show it to a ranger and receive a Mount Rainier Junior Ranger badge. ⊠ *Visitor centers, Mt. Rainier National Park* ☎ *360/569–2211* ⊕ *www.nps.gov/ mora/learn/kidsyouth* ☑ *Free with park admission.*

Ranger Programs

NATIONAL/STATE PARK | FAMILY | Park ranger-led activities include **guided snow-shoe walks** in the winter (most suitable for those older than eight) as well as **evening programs** during the summer at Longmire/Cougar Rock, Ohanapecosh, and White River campgrounds, and at the Paradise Inn. Evening talks may cover subjects such as park history, its flora and fauna, or interesting facts on climbing Mt. Rainier. There are also daily guided programs that start at the Jackson Visitor Center, including meadow and vista walks, tours of the Paradise Inn, a morning ranger chat, and evening astronomy program. ⊠ *Visitor centers, Mt. Rainier National Park* ☎ *360/569– 2211* ⊕ *www.nps.gov/mora/planyourvisit/ rangerprograms.htm* ☑ *Free with park admission.*

RESTAURANTS

A limited number of restaurants are inside the park, and a few worth checking out lie beyond its borders. Mt. Rainier's picnic areas are justly famous, especially in summer, when wildflowers fill the meadows. Resist the urge to feed the yellow pine chipmunks darting about.

HOTELS

The Mt. Rainier area is remarkably bereft of quality lodging. Rainier's two national park lodges, at Longmire and Paradise, are attractive and well maintained. They exude considerable history and charm, especially Paradise Inn, but unless you've made summer reservations a year in advance, getting a room can be a challenge. Dozens of motels, cabin complexes, and private vacation-home rentals are near the park entrances; while they can be pricey, the latter are convenient for longer stays. *Hotel reviews have been shortened. For full information, visit Fodors.com.*

What It Costs			
$	$$	$$$	$$$$
RESTAURANTS			
under $12	$12–$20	$21–$30	over $30
HOTELS			
under $100	$100– $150	$151– $200	over $200

VISITOR INFORMATION

PARK CONTACT INFORMATION Mount Rainier National Park ⊠ *55210 238th Ave. East, Ashford* ☎ *360/569–2211, 360/569–6575* ⊕ *www.nps.gov/mora.*

VISITOR CENTERS

Jackson Memorial Visitor Center

INFO CENTER | High on the mountain's southern flank, this center houses exhibits on geology, mountaineering, glaciology, and alpine ecology. Multimedia programs are staged in the theater; there's also a snack bar and gift shop. This is the park's most popular visitor destination, and it can be quite crowded in summer. ⊠ *Hwy. 706 E, 19 miles east of Nisqually park entrance, Mt. Rainier National Park* ☎ *360/569–6571* ⊕ *www. nps.gov/mora/planyourvisit/paradise.htm* ☉ *Closed weekdays mid-Oct.–Apr.*

Longmire Museum and Visitor Center

INFO CENTER | Glass cases inside this museum preserve the park's plants and animals, including a stuffed cougar. Historical photographs and geographical displays provide a worthwhile overview of the park's history. The adjacent visitor center has some perfunctory exhibits on the surrounding forest and its inhabitants, as well as pamphlets and information about park activities. ⊠ *Hwy. 706, 10 miles east of Ashford, Longmire* ☎ *360/569–6575* ⊕ *www.nps.gov/mora/ planyourvisit/longmire.htm.*

Sunrise Visitor Center

INFO CENTER | Exhibits at this center explain the region's sparser alpine and subalpine ecology. A network of nearby loop trails leads you through alpine meadows and forest to overlooks that have broad views of the Cascades and Rainier. The visitor center has a snack bar and gift shop. ⊠ *Sunrise Rd., 15 miles from White River park entrance, Mt. Rainier National Park* ☎ *360/663–2425* ⊕ *www.nps.gov/ mora/planyourvisit/sunrise.htm* ☉ *Closed mid-Sept.–June.*

Plants and Wildlife in Mount Rainier

Wildflower season in the meadows at and above timberline is mid-July through August. Large mammals like deer, elk, black bears, and cougars tend to occupy the less accessible wilderness areas of the park and thus elude the average visitor; smaller animals like squirrels and marmots are easier to spot. The best times to see wildlife are at dawn and dusk at the forest's edge. Fawns are born in May, and the bugling of bull elk on the high ridges can be heard in late September and October, especially on the park's eastern side.

◉ Sights

SCENIC DRIVES

Chinook Pass Road

SCENIC DRIVE | Route 410, the highway to Yakima, follows the eastern edge of the park to Chinook Pass, where it climbs the steep, 5,432-foot pass via a series of switchbacks. At its top, take in broad views of Rainier and the east slope of the Cascades. The pass usually closes for the winter in November and re-opens by late May. ⊠ *Mt. Rainier National Park* ⊕ *www.wsdot.wa.gov/traffic/passes/ chinook-cayuse.*

Mowich Lake Road

SCENIC DRIVE | In the northwest corner of the park, this 24-mile mountain road begins in Wilkeson and heads up the Rainier foothills to Mowich Lake, traversing beautiful mountain meadows along the way. Mowich Lake is a pleasant spot for a picnic. The road is open mid-July to mid-October. ⊠ *Mt. Rainier National Park* ⊕ *www.nps.gov/mora/*

24

Mount Rainier National Park

planyourvisit/carbon-and-mowich.htm
🕑 *Closed mid-Oct.–mid-July.*

Paradise Road

SCENIC DRIVE | This 9-mile stretch of Highway 706 winds its way up the mountain's southwest flank from Longmire to Paradise, taking you from lowland forest to the ever-expanding vistas of the mountain above. Visit early on a weekday if possible, especially in peak summer months, when the road is packed with cars. The route is open year-round though there may be some weekday closures in winter. From November through April, all vehicles must carry chains. ✉ *Mt. Rainier National Park* ⊕ *www.nps.gov/mora/planyourvisit/paradise.htm.*

Sunrise Road

SCENIC DRIVE | This popular (and often crowded) scenic road to the highest drivable point at Mt. Rainier carves its way 11 miles up Sunrise Ridge from the White River Valley on the northeast side of the park. As you top the ridge there are sweeping views of the surrounding lowlands. The road is usually open July through September. ✉ *Mt. Rainier National Park* ⊕ *www.nps.gov/mora/planyourvisit/sunrise.htm* 🕑 *Usually closed Oct.–June.*

HISTORIC SITES

National Park Inn

BUILDING | Even if you don't plan to stay overnight, you can stop by year-round to view the architecture of this inn, built in 1917 and on the National Register of Historic Places. While you're here, relax in front of the fireplace in the lounge, stop at the gift shop, or dine at the restaurant. ✉ *Longmire Visitor Complex, Hwy. 706, 10 miles east of Nisqually entrance, Longmire* ☎ *360/569–2411* ⊕ *www.mtrainierguestservices.com/accommodations/national-park-inn.*

SCENIC STOPS

Christine Falls

BODY OF WATER | These two-tiered falls were named in honor of Christine Louise Van Trump, who climbed to the 10,000-foot level on Mt. Rainier in 1889 at the age of nine, despite having a crippling nervous-system disorder. ✉ *Next to Hwy. 706, about 2½ miles east of Cougar Rock Campground, Mt. Rainier National Park* ⊕ *www.nps.gov/mora.*

★ Grove of the Patriarchs

FOREST | Protected from the periodic fires that swept through the surrounding areas, this small island of 1,000-year-old trees is one of Mount Rainier National Park's most memorable features. A 1½-mile loop trail heads through the old-growth forest of Douglas fir, cedar, and hemlock. ✉ *Rte. 123, west of the Stevens Canyon entrance, Mt. Rainier National Park* ⊕ *www.nps.gov/mora/planyourvisit/ohanapecosh.htm.*

Narada Falls

BODY OF WATER | A steep but short trail leads to the viewing area for these spectacular 168-foot falls, which expand to a width of 75 feet during peak flow times. In winter the frozen falls are popular with ice climbers. ✉ *Along Hwy. 706, 1 mile west of turnoff for Paradise, 6 miles east of Cougar Rock Campground, Mt. Rainier National Park* ⊕ *www.nps.gov/mora/planyourvisit/longmire.htm.*

Tipsoo Lake

BODY OF WATER | **FAMILY** | The short, pleasant trail that circles the lake—ideal for families—provides breathtaking views. Enjoy the subalpine wildflower meadows during the summer months; in late summer to early fall there is an abundant supply of huckleberries. ✉ *Off Cayuse Pass east on Hwy. 410, Mt. Rainier National Park* ⊕ *www.nps.gov/mora/planyourvisit/sunrise.htm.*

 Activities

MULTISPORT OUTFITTERS

RMI Expeditions

CLIMBING/MOUNTAINEERING | Reserve a private hiking guide through this highly regarded outfitter, or take part in its one-day mountaineering classes (mid-May through late September), where participants are evaluated on their fitness for the climb and must be able to withstand a 16-mile round-trip hike with a 9,000-foot gain in elevation. The company also arranges private cross-country skiing and snowshoeing guides. ⊠ *30027 Hwy. 706 E, Ashford* ☎ *888/892–5462, 360/569–2227* ⊕ *www.rmiguides.com* ⊠ *From $1118 for 4-day package.*

Whittaker Mountaineering

TOUR—SPORTS | You can rent hiking and climbing gear, cross-country skis, snowshoes, and other outdoor equipment at this all-purpose Rainier Base Camp outfitter, which also arranges for private cross-country skiing and hiking guides. If you forget to bring tire chains (which all vehicles are required to carry in the national park in winter), they rent those too. ⊠ *30027 SR 706E, Ashford* ☎ *800/238–5756, 360/569–2982* ⊕ *www. whittakermountaineering.com.*

BIRD-WATCHING

Be alert for kestrels, red-tailed hawks, and, occasionally, golden eagles on snags in the lowland forests. Also present at Rainier, but rarely seen, are great horned owls, spotted owls, and screech owls. Iridescent rufous hummingbirds flit from blossom to blossom in the drowsy summer lowlands, and sprightly water ouzels flutter in the many forest creeks. Raucous Steller's jays and gray jays scold passersby from trees, often darting boldly down to steal morsels from unguarded picnic tables. At higher elevations, look for the pure white plumage of the white-tailed ptarmigan as it hunts for seeds and insects in winter. Waxwings, vireos, nuthatches, sapsuckers, warblers, flycatchers, larks, thrushes, siskins, tanagers, and finches are common throughout the park.

HIKING

Although the mountain can seem remarkably benign on calm summer days, hiking Rainier is not a city-park stroll. Dozens of hikers and trekkers annually lose their way and must be rescued—and lives are lost on the mountain each year. Weather that approaches cyclonic levels can appear quite suddenly, any month of the year. All visitors venturing far from vehicle access points, with the possible exception of the short loop hikes listed here, should carry day packs with warm clothing, food, and other emergency supplies.

Nisqually Vista Trail

HIKING/WALKING | Equally popular in summer and winter, this trail is a 1¼-mile round-trip through subalpine meadows to an overlook point for Nisqually Glacier. The gradually sloping path is a favorite venue for cross-country skiers in winter; in summer, listen for the shrill alarm calls of the area's marmots. *Easy.* ⊠ *Mt. Rainier National Park* ✛ *Trailhead: at Jackson Memorial Visitor Center, Rte. 123, 1 mile north of Ohanapecosh, at high point of Hwy. 706* ⊕ *www.nps.gov/mora/plan-yourvisit/day-hiking-at-mount-rainier.htm.*

★ Skyline Trail

HIKING/WALKING | This 5-mile loop, one of the highest trails in the park, beckons day-trippers with a vista of alpine ridges and, in summer, meadows filled with brilliant flowers and birds. At 6,800 feet, Panorama Point, the spine of the Cascade Range, spreads away to the east, and Nisqually Glacier tumbles downslope. *Moderate.* ⊠ *Mt. Rainier National Park* ✛ *Trailhead: Jackson Memorial Visitor Center, Rte. 123, 1 mile north of Ohanapecosh at high point of Hwy. 706* ⊕ *www.nps.gov/mora/plan-yourvisit/skyline-trail.htm.*

Sunrise Nature Trail

HIKING/WALKING | The 1½-mile-long loop of this self-guided trail takes you through the delicate subalpine meadows near the Sunrise Visitor Center. A gradual climb to the ridgetop yields magnificent views of Mt. Rainier and the more distant volcanic cones of Mt. Baker, Mt. Adams, and Glacier Peak. *Easy.* ⊠ *Mt. Rainier National*

Park ✛ Trailhead: at Sunrise Visitor Center, Sunrise Rd., 15 miles from White River park entrance ⊕ www.nps.gov/mora/planyourvisit/sunrise.htm.

Trail of the Shadows

HIKING/WALKING | This ¾-mile loop is notable for its glimpses of meadowland ecology, its colorful soda springs (don't drink the water), James Longmire's old homestead cabin, and the foundation of the old Longmire Springs Hotel, which was destroyed by fire around 1900. *Easy.* ✉ Mt. Rainier National Park ✛ Trailhead: at Hwy. 706, 10 miles east of Nisqually entrance ⊕ www.nps.gov/mora/planyourvisit/day-hiking-at-mount-rainier.htm.

Van Trump Park Trail

HIKING/WALKING | You gain an exhilarating 2,200 feet on this route while hiking through a vast expanse of meadow with views of the southern Puget Sound and Mt. Adams and Mt. St. Helens. On the way up is one of the highest water falls in the park, Comet Falls. The 5¾-mile track provides good footing, and the average hiker can make it up and back in five hours. *Moderate.* ✉ Mt. Rainier National Park ✛ Trailhead: Hwy. 706 at Christine Falls, 4½ miles east of Longmire ⊕ www.nps.gov/mora/planyourvisit/van-trump-trail.htm.

★ Wonderland Trail

HIKING/WALKING | All other Mt. Rainier hikes pale in comparison to this stunning 93-mile trek, which completely encircles the mountain. The trail passes through all the major life zones of the park, from the old-growth forests of the lowlands to the alpine meadows and goat-haunted glaciers of the highlands—pick up a mountain-goat sighting card from a ranger station or visitor center if you want to help in the park's effort to learn more about these elusive animals. Wonderland is a rugged trail; elevation gains and losses totaling 3,500 feet are common in a day's hike, which averages 8 miles. Most hikers start out from Longmire or Sunrise and take 10–14 days to cover the 93-mile route. Snow lingers on the high passes well into June (sometimes July); count on rain any time of the year. Campsites are wilderness areas with pit toilets and water that must be purified before drinking. Only hardy, well-equipped, and experienced wilderness trekkers should attempt this trip, but those who do will be amply rewarded. Wilderness permits are required, and reservations are strongly recommended. *Difficult.* ✉ Mt. Rainier National Park ✛ Trailheads: Longmire Visitor Center, Hwy. 706, 17 miles east of Ashford; Sunrise Visitor Center, Sunrise Rd., 15 miles west of White River park entrance ⊕ www.nps.gov/mora/planyourvisit/the-wonderland-trail.htm.

MOUNTAIN CLIMBING

Climbing Mt. Rainier is not for amateurs; each year, adventurers die on the mountain, and many become lost and must be rescued. Near-catastrophic weather can appear quite suddenly, any month of the year. If you're experienced in technical, high-elevation snow, rock, and ice-field adventuring, Mt. Rainier can be a memorable adventure. Climbers can fill out a climbing card at the Paradise, White River, or Carbon River ranger station and lead their own groups of two or more. Climbers must register with a ranger before leaving and check out on return. A $48 annual climbing fee applies to anyone heading above 10,000 feet or onto one of Rainier's glaciers. During peak season it is recommended that climbers make their camping reservations ($20 per site) in advance; reservations are taken by fax and mail beginning in mid-March on a first-come, first-served basis (find the reservation form at ⊕ www.nps.gov/mora/planyourvisit/climbing.htm).

SKIING AND SNOWSHOEING

Mt. Rainier is a major Nordic ski center for cross-country and telemark skiing. Although trails are not groomed, those around Paradise are extremely popular. If you want to ski with fewer people, try the trails in and around the

Ohanapecosh–Stevens Canyon area, which are just as beautiful and, because of their more easterly exposure, slightly less subject to the rains that can douse the Longmire side, even in the dead of winter. Never ski on plowed main roads, especially around Paradise—the snow-plow operator can't see you. Rentals aren't available on the eastern side of the park.

Deep snows make Mt. Rainier a snow-shoeing pleasure. The Paradise area, with its network of trails, is the best choice. The park's east-side roads, Routes 123 and 410, are unplowed and provide other good snowshoeing venues, although you must share the main routes with snowmobilers.

General Store at the National Park Inn

SKIING/SNOWBOARDING | The store at the National Park Inn in Longmire rents cross-country ski equipment and snowshoes. It's open daily in winter, depending on snow conditions. ⊠ *National Park Inn, Longmire* ☎ *360/569–2411* ⊕ *www.mtrainierguestservices.com/ activities-and-events/winter-activities/ cross-country-skiing.*

Paradise Snowplay Area and Nordic Ski Route

SKIING/SNOWBOARDING | Sledding on flexible sleds (no toboggans or runners), inner tubes, and plastic saucers is allowed only in the Paradise snow-play area adjacent to the Jackson Visitor Center. The area is open when there is sufficient snow, usually from late December through mid-March. The easy, 3½-mile Paradise Valley Road Nordic ski route begins at the Paradise parking lot and follows Paradise Valley/Stevens Canyon Road to Reflection Lakes. Equipment rentals are available at Whittaker Mountaineering in Ashford or at the National Park Inn's General Store in Longmire. ⊠ *Adjacent to Jackson Visitor Center at Paradise, Mt. Rainier National Park* ☎ *360/569–2211* ⊕ *www.nps.gov/ mora/planyourvisit/winter-recreation.htm.*

Nearby Towns

Ashford sits astride an ancient trail across the Cascades used by the Yakama Indians to trade with the coastal tribes of western Washington. The town began as a logging railway terminal; today it's the main gateway to Mt. Rainier—and the only year-round access point to the park—with lodges, restaurants, grocery stores, and gift shops. Surrounded by Cascade peaks, **Packwood** is a pretty mountain village on U.S. 12, below White Pass. Between Mt. Rainier and Mt. St. Helens, it's a perfect jumping-off point for exploring local wilderness areas.

VISITOR INFORMATION Destination Packwood Association ⊠ *13011B U.S. Hwy. 12, Packwood* ☎ *360/492–7365* ⊕ *www. destinationpackwood.com.*

 **Sights**

Goat Rocks Wilderness

NATIONAL/STATE PARK | The crags in Gifford Pinchot National Forest, south of Mt. Rainier, are aptly named. You often see mountain goats here, especially when you hike into the backcountry. Goat Lake is a particularly good spot for viewing these elusive creatures. See the goats without backpacking by taking Forest Road 21 to Forest Road 2140, south from U.S. 12. The goats will be on Stonewall Ridge looming up ahead of you. ⊠ *NF-21 and NF-2140, Randle* ☎ *360/891–5000* ⊕ *www.fs.usda.gov/giffordpinchot.*

Johnston Ridge Observatory

INFO CENTER | With the most spectacular views of the crater and lava dome of Mt. St. Helens, this observatory also has exhibits that interpret the geology of the mountain and explain how scientists monitor an active volcano. ⊠ *Rte. 504, 53 miles east of I–5, 24000 Spirit Lake Hwy., Castle Rock* ☎ *360/274–2140* ⊕ *www.fs.usda.gov/recarea/mounts- thelens/recarea/?recid=31562* ⓢ *$8* ⓧ *Closed Nov.–mid-May.*

Mount Rainier, Looking North

MOUNT RAINIER

Little Tahoma Peak 11,138 ft
Disappointment Cleaver
Ingraham Glacier
Anvil Rock 9,584 ft
CATHEDRAL ROCKS
McClure Rock 7,385 ft
Paradise Glaciers
Camp Muir 10,188 ft
Muir Snowfield
Columbia Crest 14,410 ft
Gibraltar Rock 12,660 ft
Nisqually Glacier
Panorama Point 6,800 ft
Point Success 14,153 ft
Liberty Cap 14,122 ft
Skyline Trail
Alta Vista
Paradise
Wilson Glacier
SUNSET AMPHITHEATER
Henry M. Jackson Memorial Visitor Center
Pinnacle Peak 6,562 ft
The Castle
Louise Lake
Reflection Lakes
Unicorn Peak 6,917 ft
St. Andrews Rock 10,992 ft
SUCCESS CLEAVER
Van Trump Glaciers
Kautz Glacier
WAPOWETY CLEAVER
CUSHMAN CREST
Plummer Peak 6,370 ft
Lane Peak 6,012 ft
Wahpenayo Peak 6,231 ft

TATOOSH RANGE

PUYALLUP CLEAVER
Tahoma Glacier
Success Glacier
South Tahoma Glacier
SUCCESS DIVIDE
Pyramid Glaciers
Mildred Point
VAN TRUMP PARK
Chutla Peak

GLACIER ISLAND
Pyramid Peak 6,937 ft
PYRAMID PARK
Eagle Peak 5,958 ft

Tokaloo Rock 7,684 ft
EMERALD RIDGE
Iron Mountain 6,283 ft

Creek

Cougar Rock
RIDGE
Rampart Ridge Trail
RAMPART
THE RAMPARTS
Pyramid
Longmire

KEY
——— Paved Roads
– – – Hiking Trails
· · · · · Climbing Routes

Mt. Rainier Scenic Railroad and Museum

TOUR—SIGHT | **FAMILY** | This trip takes you through lush forests and across scenic bridges, covering 14 miles of incomparable beauty. Trains depart from Elbe, 11 miles west of Ashford, then bring passengers to a lovely picnic area near Mineral Lake before returning. The trains run weekends from mid-May to June, then Friday-Sunday from July through Labor Day weekend, and Saturday through mid-October. They have Halloween special excursions for two weekends in late October. Winter holiday train runs from mid-November to December, Friday through Sunday, and daily during winter break (except Christmas). Prices start at $41 for the basic excursions; special events are more. At Mineral Lake, guests can tour the museum containing old train memorabilia and artifacts, as well as exhibits on the area's old railroad camps, which served as the hub of logging operations by rail. ⊠ *54124 Mountain Hwy. E, Elbe* 🕾 *360/492–6000* ⊕ *www.mtrainier-railroad.com* 🖾 *Rides from $41* ⊙ *Closed Nov.–Apr. (except for holiday excursions).*

Mount St. Helens Science and Learning Center

INFO CENTER | The Mt. St. Helens Institute operates this center, which offers family camps, field trips, and learning experiences throughout the year. It's open to the public on weekends in the off-season when the Johnston Ridge Observatory is closed. Exhibits document the great 1980 blast of Mt. St. Helens and its effects on the surrounding 150,000 acres. A ¼-mile trail leads from the visitor center to Coldwater Lake. ⊠ *Rte. 504, 43 miles east of I–5, 19000 Spirit Lake Hwy., Toutle* 🕾 *360/274–2131* ⊕ *www.mshslc. org* ⊙ *Closed May–Oct. and weekdays except special events.*

Mount St. Helens Visitor Center

INFO CENTER | This facility, one of several visitor centers along Route 504 on the west side of the mountain, has exhibits documenting the eruption, plus a walk-through volcano. ⊠ *Rte. 504, 5 miles east of I–5, 3029 Spirit Lake Hwy., Silver Lake* 🕾 *360/274–0962* ⊕ *parks. state.wa.us/245/Mount-St-Helens* 🖾 *$5* ⊙ *Closed Tues., Wed., and federal holidays during Nov.–Feb.*

Northwest Trek Wildlife Park

NATURE PRESERVE | **FAMILY** | This spectacular, 435-acre wildlife park 35 miles south of Puyallup is devoted to native creatures of the Pacific Northwest. Walking paths wind through natural surroundings—so natural that a cougar once entered the park and started snacking on the deer (it was finally trapped and relocated to the North Cascades). See beavers, otters, and wolverines; get close to wolves, foxes, coyotes; and observe several species of big cats and bears in wild environments. Admission includes a 40-minute tram ride through fields of wandering moose, bighorn sheep, elk, bison, and mountain goats. The most adventurous way to see the park is via one of five ziplines, which traverse the park canopy—rides are available late May through late September. ⊠ *11610 Trek Dr. E, Eatonville* 🕾 *360/832–6117* ⊕ *www. nwtrek.org* 🖾 *From $20* ⊙ *Closed Mon.– Thurs. in Oct.–mid-Mar. (except holidays).*

Activities

Crystal Mountain Ski Area

HIKING/WALKING | Washington State's biggest and best-known ski area has nine lifts (plus a children's lift and a gondola) and 57 runs. In summer, it's open for hiking, rides on the Mt. Rainier Gondola, and meals at the Summit House, all providing sensational views of Rainier and the Cascades. **Facilities:** 57 trails; 2,600 acres; 3,100-foot vertical drop; 11 lifts. ⊠ *33914 Crystal Mountain Blvd., off Rte. 410, Crystal Mountain* 🕾 *360/663–2265* ⊕ *www.crystalmountainresort.com* 🖾 *From $24.*

Did You Know?

Named after British admiral Peter Rainier in the late 18th century, Mt. Rainier had an earlier name. Tahoma (also Takhoma), its Native American name, means "the mountain that was God." Various unsuccessful attempts have been made to restore the indigenous name to the peak. Of course, to most Puget Sound residents, Rainier is simply "the mountain."

🍴 Restaurants

IN THE PARK

National Park Inn Dining Room

$$$ | AMERICAN | Photos of Mt. Rainier taken by top photographers adorn the walls of this inn's large dining room, a bonus on the many days the mountain refuses to show itself. Meals are simple but tasty: rib-eye steak, lamb chops, cedar-plank trout, and blackberry cobbler à la mode. **Known for:** only restaurant open year-round in the park; hearty breakfast options;. $ *Average main: $24 ☒ Hwy. 706, Longmire ☎ 360/569–2411 ⊕ www. mtrainierguestservices.com.*

Paradise Camp Deli

$ | AMERICAN | FAMILY | Grilled meats, sandwiches, salads, and soft drinks are served daily from May through early October and on weekends and holidays during the rest of the year. **Known for:** a quick bite to eat. $ *Average main: $9 ☒ Jackson Visitor Center, Paradise Rd. E, Paradise ☎ 360/569–6571 ⊕ www. mtrainierguestservices.com ⊗ Closed weekdays early Oct.–Apr.*

Paradise Inn

$$$ | AMERICAN | Tall windows in this historic timber lodge provide terrific views of Rainier, and the warm glow of native wood permeates the large dining room, where hearty Pacific Northwest fare is served. Sunday brunch is legendary and served during the summer months; on other days and during the shoulder season there's a breakfast buffet. **Known for:** bourbon buffalo meat loaf; warm liquor drinks;. $ *Average main: $25 ☒ E. Paradise Rd., near Jackson Visitor Center, Paradise ☎ 360/569–2275, 855/755–2275 ⊕ www.mtrainierguestservices.com ⊗ Closed Oct.–mid-May.*

Sunrise Day Lodge Food Service

$ | AMERICAN | FAMILY | A cafeteria and grill serve tasty hamburgers, chili, hot dogs, and soft-serve ice cream from July through September. **Known for:** only food service in this part of the park; often

busy. $ *Average main: $10 ☒ Sunrise Rd., 15 miles from White River park entrance, Mt. Rainier National Park ☎ 360/663–2425 ⊕ www.mtrainierguest-services.com ⊗ Closed Oct.–June.*

PICNIC AREAS

Park picnic areas are usually open only from late May through September.

Sunrise Picnic Area

NATIONAL/STATE PARK | Set in an alpine meadow that's filled with wildflowers in July and August, this picnic area provides expansive views of the mountain and surrounding ranges in good weather. ☒ *Sunrise Rd., 11 miles west of White River entrance, Mt. Rainier National Park ⊕ www.nps.gov/mora/planyourvisit/ sunrise.htm ⊗ Road to Sunrise usually closed Oct.–June.*

OUTSIDE THE PARK

Scaleburgers

$ | BURGER | FAMILY | Once a 1939 logging-truck weigh station, the building is now a popular restaurant serving homemade hamburgers, fries, and shakes. Eat outside on tables overlooking the hills and scenic railroad. **Known for:** views of scenic railroad and surrounding mountains; luscious milkshakes. $ *Average main: $10 ☒ 54109 Mountain Hwy. E, Elbe ✦ 11 miles west of Ashford ☎ 360/569–2247 ▭ No credit cards ⊗ Closed early Sept.–Mar. and weekdays in Apr. and May.*

Summit House

$$$ | PACIFIC NORTHWEST | On top of Crystal Mountain at 6,872 feet is Washington's highest-elevation restaurant with stunning views of Mt. Rainier; the Summit House is a popular stop for skiers, hikers, and summer tourists, too. The menu features Northwest cuisine, including wild Pacific cod fish-and-chips in summer (halibut in winter), elk and bison chili, burgers, and huckleberry ice cream. **Known for:** mountain views; leisurely dining experience; accessible only by gondola (tickets sold separately).

Best Campgrounds in Mount Rainier

Three drive-in campgrounds are in the park—Cougar Rock, Ohanapecosh, and White River—with almost 500 sites for tents and RVs. None has hot water or RV hookups. The nightly fee is $20. The more primitive Mowich Lake Campground has 10 walk-in sites for tents only; no fee is charged. For backcountry camping, get a free wilderness permit at a visitor center on a first-come, first-served basis. Primitive sites are spaced at 7- to 8-mile intervals along the Wonderland Trail.

Cougar Rock Campground. A secluded, heavily wooded campground with an amphitheater, Cougar Rock is one of the first to fill up. Reservations are accepted for summer only. ✉ *2½ miles north of Longmire* ☎ *877/444–6777* ⊕ *www.recreation.gov for reservations.*

Mowich Lake Campground. This is Rainier's only lakeside campground and has just 10 primitive campsites. At 4,959 feet, it's also peaceful and secluded. ✉ *Mowich Lake Rd., 6 miles east of park boundary* ☎ *360/569–2211.*

Ohanapecosh Campground. This lush, green campground in the park's southeast corner has an amphitheater and self-guided trail. It's one of the first campgrounds to open for the season. ✉ *Rte. 123, 1½ miles north of park boundary* ☎ *877/444–6777* ⊕ *www.recreation.gov for reservations.*

White River Campground. At an elevation of 4,400 feet, White River is one of the park's highest and least wooded campgrounds. Here you can enjoy campfire programs, self-guided trails, and partial views of Mt. Rainier's summit. ✉ *5 miles west of White River entrance* ☎ *360/569–2211.*

24

Mount Rainier National Park

$ *Average main: $22* ✉ *33914 Crystal Mountain Blvd., Crystal Mountain* ☎ *360/663–3085* ⊕ *crystalmountainresort.com* ⊙ *Open seasonally during summer and ski season; check website or call for current hrs.*

Wildberry

$$ | **NEPALESE** | Owned and operated by a Himalayan mountain guide, this casual café features the flavors of Nepal as well as more standard American-mountain fare. Nepalese offerings include *thali* (full meals served on metal school-lunch style platters with curry, rice, vegetables, soup, and roti bread).**Known for:** Nepalese-American fusion cuisine; colorful decor; tasty pies. $ *Average main: $15* ✉ *37718 WA-706, Ashford* ☎ *360/569–2277* ⊕ *www.rainierwildberry.com* ⊙ *Closed Oct.–Apr.*

 **Hotels**

IN THE PARK

National Park Inn

$$$ | **B&B/INN** | A large stone fireplace warms the common room of this country inn, the only one of the park's two inns that's open year-round. **Pros:** classic ambience; open all year; friendly atmosphere. **Cons:** jam-packed in summer; must book far in advance; some rooms have shared bath. $ *Rooms from: $187* ✉ *Longmire Visitor Complex, Hwy. 706, 6 miles east of Nisqually entrance, Longmire* ☎ *360/569–2275, 855/755–2275* ⊕ *www.mtrainierguestservices.com* ➶ *25 rooms, 18 with bath* ¶❍¶ *No meals.*

★ **Paradise Inn**

$$$ | **HOTEL** | With its hand-carved Alaskan cedar logs, burnished parquet floors, stone fireplaces, Indian rugs, and glorious

mountain views, this 1917 inn is a classic example of a National Park lodge. **Pros:** central to trails; pristine vistas; nature-inspired details. **Cons:** rooms are small and basic; many rooms have shared bathrooms; no elevators, air-conditioning, cell service, TV, or Wi-Fi. [$] *Rooms from: $182* ✉ *E. Paradise Rd., near Jackson Visitor Center, Paradise* ☎ *360/569–2275, 855/755–2275* 🌐 *www.mtrainierguest-services.com* 🕒 *Closed mid-Oct.–mid-May* 🛏 *121 rooms* 🍴 *No meals.*

OUTSIDE THE PARK

Alexander's Lodge

$$ | **B&B/INN** | At this well-located lodging just a mile from Mt. Rainier's Nisqually entrance, vintage furnishings lend romance to rooms in the main building; there are also two adjacent guesthouses. **Pros:** open since 1912 so plenty of historical character; in-room spa service available; some rooms are pet-friendly. **Cons:** steep stairs to some units; decor is quaint; rooms are small. [$] *Rooms from: $110* ✉ *37515 Hwy. 706 E, Ashford* ✥ *4 miles east of Ashford* ☎ *360/569–2300* 🌐 *www.alexanderslodge.com* 🛏 *21 rooms* 🍴 *Breakfast.*

Alta Crystal Resort

$$$$ | **B&B/INN** | **FAMILY** | In the national forest, this small resort with family-friendly amenities feels remote yet is very close to Mt. Rainier's Sunrise entrance and Crystal Mountain Ski Resort. **Pros:** fun, nightly activities; mini–grocery store and movie library; three standalone cabins for added privacy. **Cons:** not close to restaurants or grocery store; cell phone and Internet can be spotty; pool area gets noisy, especially for first-floor units. [$] *Rooms from: $260* ✉ *68317 SR 410 E, Greenwater* ☎ *360/663–2556, 800/277–6475, 360/663–2500* 🌐 *www.altacrystal-resort.com* 🛏 *26 rooms* 🍴 *No meals.*

Nisqually Lodge

$$$ | **HOTEL** | Crackling flames from the massive stone fireplace lend warmth and cheer to the great room of this hotel, a few miles west of Mount Rainier National Park. **Pros:** breakfast included; central to mountain activities; close to national park entrance. **Cons:** no frills; no elevator; service can be inconsistent. [$] *Rooms from: $190* ✉ *31609 Hwy. 706 E, Ashford* ☎ *360/569–8804, 888/674–3554, 360/569–2435* 🌐 *www.whitepasstravel.com/nisqually/* 🛏 *24 rooms* 🍴 *Breakfast.*

★ Stormking Spa and Cabins

$$$$ | **B&B/INN** | In a forest setting a mile from the Nisqually entrance of Mount Rainier National Park, Stormking features five luxury cabins for adults: four are shaped like yurts, and all have cozy gas fireplaces, hot tubs, private outdoor seating areas, and natural finishes of wood and stone. **Pros:** very romantic and secluded; reasonably priced for special occasion getaways; deer and other wildlife frequent the property. **Cons:** no check-ins on Sunday; Wi-Fi available at spa but not in cabins; two-night minimum stay. [$] *Rooms from: $220* ✉ *37311 SR 706 E, Ashford* ☎ *360/569–2964* 🌐 *www.stormkingspa.com* 🛏 *5 cabins* 🍴 *No meals.*

Wellspring

$$$ | **B&B/INN** | Deep in the woods outside Ashford, the accommodations here include tastefully designed log cabins, a tree house, and a room in a greenhouse. **Pros:** unique lodging with a wide range of prices, depending on the room; some options good for groups and families; relaxing spa and hot soaking tubs. **Cons:** limited amenities; no cell service; no on-site assistance for guests. [$] *Rooms from: $155* ✉ *54922 Kernehan Rd., Ashford* ☎ *360/569–2514* 🌐 *www.wellspring-spa.com* 🛏 *13 rooms* 🍴 *No meals.*

Chapter 25

NORTH CASCADES NATIONAL PARK

Updated by
Shelley Arenas

WELCOME TO
NORTH CASCADES NATIONAL PARK

TOP REASONS TO GO

★ **Pure wilderness:** Spot bald eagles, deer, elk, and other wildlife on nearly 400 miles of mountain and meadow hiking trails.

★ **Majestic glaciers:** The North Cascades are home to several hundred moving ice masses, more than half of the glaciers in the United States.

★ **Splendid flora:** A bright palette of flowers blankets the hillsides in midsummer, while October's colors paint the landscape in vibrant autumn hues.

★ **Thrilling boat rides:** Lake Chelan, Ross Lake, and the Stehekin River are the starting points for kayaking, white-water rafting, and ferry trips.

★ **19th-century history:** Delve into the state's farming, lumber, and logging pasts in clapboard towns and homesteads around the park.

1 North Unit. The park's creek-cut northern wilderness, centered on snowy Mt. Challenger, stretches north from Highway 20 over the Picket Range toward the Canadian border. It's an endless landscape of pine-topped peaks and ridges.

2 South Unit. Hike lake-filled mountain foothills in summer to take in vistas of blue skies and flower-filled meadows. Waterfalls and wildlife are abundant here.

3 Ross Lake National Recreation Area. Drawing a thick line from British Columbia all the way down to the North Cascades Scenic Highway, placid Ross Lake is edged with pretty bays that draw swimmers and boaters.

4 Lake Chelan National Recreation Area. Ferries cruise between small waterfront villages along this pristine waterway, while kayakers and hikers follow quiet trails along its edges. This is one of the Northwest's most popular summer escapes, with nature-bound activities and rustic accommodations.

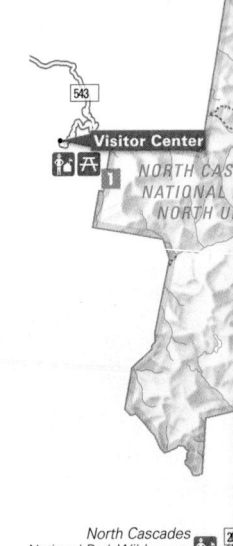

North Cascades
National Park Wilderness
Information Center

Marblemount

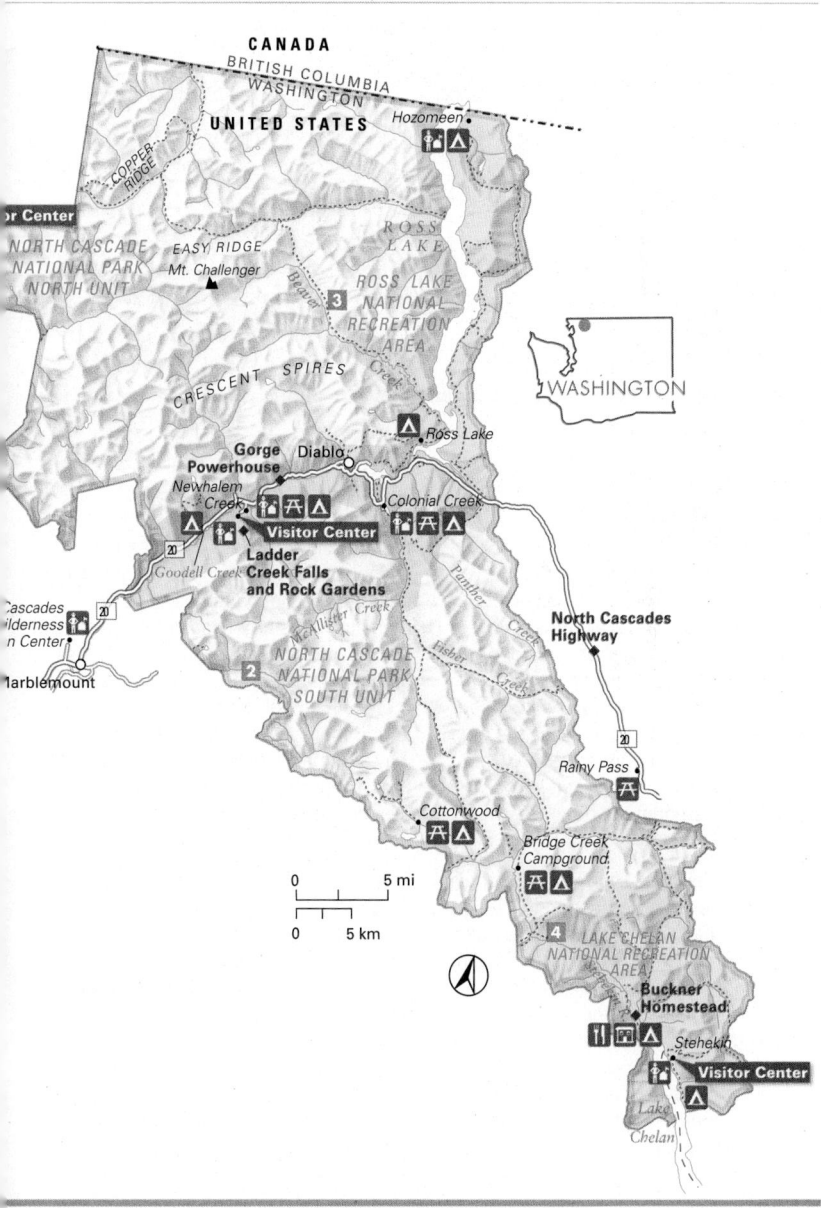

CANADA
BRITISH COLUMBIA
WASHINGTON
UNITED STATES

Hozomeen

COPPER RIDGE

or Center

NORTH CASCADE
NATIONAL PARK
NORTH UNIT

EASY RIDGE
Mt. Challenger

ROSS LAKE

ROSS LAKE
NATIONAL
RECREATION
AREA

CRESCENT SPIRES

WASHINGTON

Ross Lake

Gorge
Powerhouse   Diablo

Newhalem
Creek   Colonial Creek

Visitor Center

20

Ladder
Goodell Creek Creek Falls
and Rock Gardens

Cascades
ilderness
n Center

20

Marblemount

McAllister Creek

NORTH CASCADE
NATIONAL PARK
SOUTH UNIT

Panther Creek

Fisher Creek

North Cascades
Highway

20

Rainy Pass

Cottonwood

Bridge Creek
Campground

0   5 mi

0   5 km

LAKE CHELAN
NATIONAL RECREATION
AREA

Buckner
Homestead

Stehekin

Visitor Center

Lake
Chelan

Countless snow-clad mountain spires dwarf narrow glacial valleys in this 505,000-acre expanse of the North Cascades, which encompasses three diverse natural areas. North Cascades National Park is the core of the region, flanked by Lake Chelan National Recreation Area to the south and Ross Lake National Recreation Area to the north.

Planning

WHEN TO GO

The spectacular, craggy peaks of the North Cascades—often likened to the Alps—are breathtaking anytime. Summer is peak season, especially along the alpine stretches of Highway 20; weekends and holidays can be crowded. Summer is short and glorious in the high country, extending from snowmelt (late May to July, depending on the elevation and the amount of snow) to early September.

The North Cascades Highway is a popular autumn drive in September and October, when the changing leaves put on a colorful show. The lowland forest areas, such as the complex around Newhalem, can be visited almost any time of year. These are wonderfully quiet in early spring or late autumn on mild rainy days. Snow closes the North Cascades Highway from mid-November through mid-April, and sometimes longer.

PLANNING YOUR TIME
NORTH CASCADES IN ONE DAY

The **North Cascades Highway,** with its breathtaking mountain and meadow scenery, is one of the most memorable drives in the United States. Although many travelers first head northeast from Seattle into the park and make this their grand finale, if you start from Winthrop, at the south end of the route, traffic is lighter and there's less morning fog. Either way, the main highlight is **Washington Pass,** the road's highest point, where an overlook affords a sensational panorama of snow-covered peaks.

Rainy Pass, where the road heading north drops into the west slope valleys, is another good vantage point. Old-growth forest begins to appear, and after about an hour you reach **Gorge Creek Falls overlook** with its 242-foot cascade. Continue west to Newhalem and stop for lunch, then take a half-hour stroll along the **Trail of the Cedars.** Later, stop at the **North Cascades Visitor Center** and take another short hike. It's an hour drive down the Skagit Valley to Sedro-Woolley, where

AVERAGE HIGH/LOW TEMPERATURES					
JAN.	FEB.	MAR.	APR.	MAY	JUNE
39/30	43/32	49/34	56/38	64/43	70/49
JULY	AUG.	SEPT.	OCT.	NOV.	DEC.
76/52	76/53	69/49	57/42	45/36	39/31

bald eagles are often seen along the river in winter.

GETTING HERE AND AROUND
AIR TRAVEL
The nearest commercial airports are in Bellingham to the northwest and in Wenatchee south of Chelan.

CAR TRAVEL
Highway 20, the North Cascades Highway, splits the park's north and south sections. The gravel Cascade River Road, which runs southeast from Marblemount, peels off Highway 20; Sibley Creek/Hidden Lake Road (USFS 1540) turns off Cascade River Road to the Cascade Pass trailhead. Thornton Creek Road is another rough four-wheel-drive track. For the Ross Lake area in the north, the unpaved Hozomeen Road (Silver–Skagit Road) provides access between Hope, British Columbia, and Silver Lake and Skagit Valley provincial parks. From Stehekin, the Stehekin Valley Road continues to High Bridge and Car Wash Falls—although seasonal floods may cause washouts. Note that roads are narrow and some are closed seasonally, many sights are off the beaten path, and the scenery is so spectacular that, once you're in it, you'll want to make more than a day trip.

PARK ESSENTIALS
ACCESSIBILITY
Visitor centers along North Cascades Highway are accessible by wheelchair. Hikes include Sterling Munro, Skagit River Loop, and Rock Shelter, three short trails into lowland old-growth forest, all at mile 120 along Highway 20 near Newhalem, and the Happy Creek Forest Trail at mile 134.

PARK FEES AND PERMITS
There are no entrance fees to the national park and no parking fees at trailheads on park land. A Northwest Forest Pass, required for parking at Forest Service trailheads, is $5 per vehicle for a calendar day or $30 for a year. A free wilderness permit is required for all overnight stays in the backcountry; these are available in person only. Dock permits for boat-in campgrounds are also $5 per day. Car camping is $16 per night at Colonial Creek, Goodell Creek, and Newhalem Creek campgrounds during the summer (when water and other services are available) and free off-season; free at the primitive Gorge Lake and Hozomeen campgrounds. Passes and permits are sold at visitor centers and ranger stations around the park area.

PARK HOURS
The park never closes, but access is limited by snow in winter. Highway 20 (North Cascades Highway), the major access to the park, is partially closed from mid-November to mid-April, depending on snow levels.

CELL PHONE RECEPTION
Cell-phone reception in the park is unreliable. Public telephones are found at the North Cascades Visitor Center and Skagit Information Center in Newhalem, and the Golden West Visitor Center and North Cascades Lodge in Stehekin.

EDUCATIONAL OFFERINGS
Seattle City Light Information and Tour Center
DAM | Based at a history museum that has exhibits about the onset of electric power through the Cascade ranges, Seattle's public electric company offers tours

and programs during summer. Several trails start at the building, and the group offers sightseeing excursions on Diablo Lake during the summer in partnership with the North Cascades Institute, Thursday through Monday lunch cruises by advance reservation, and afternoon cruises Friday through Sunday. The boat tour includes a visit to the Diablo Dam. Other tours include a visit to the power-house (with picnic lunch) on weekends, and an evening dinner and guided walk to Ladder Creek Falls on Thursday and Friday. Free 45-minute walking tours through the historic town of Newhalem are offered daily from July through Labor Day. ⊠ *Milepost 120, North Cascades Hwy., Newhalem* ☎ *360/854–2589* ⊕ *www.skagittours.com* ⊠ *Walking tour free, other tours from $19* ⊙ *Closed Oct.–Apr.*

RANGER PROGRAMS

In summer, rangers conduct programs at the visitor centers, where you also can find exhibits and other park information. At the North Cascades Visitor Center (in Newhalem) you can learn about rain-forest ecology, while at the Golden West Visitor Center (in Stehekin) there's an arts-and-crafts gallery as well as audio-visual and children's programs. Check center bulletin boards for schedules.

RESTAURANTS

There are no formal restaurants in North Cascades National Park, just a lakeside café at the North Cascades Environmental Learning Center. The only other place to eat out is in Stehekin, at the Stehekin Valley Ranch dining room, North Cascades Lodge, or the Stehekin Pastry Company; all serve simple, hearty, country-style meals and sweets. Towns within a few hours of the park on either side have a few small eateries, and a few lodgings have small dining rooms with skilled chefs who craft high-end meals of locally grown products, matched with extensive wine lists. Otherwise, don't expect fancy decor or gourmet frills—just

friendly service and generally delicious homemade stews, roasts, grilled fare, soups, salads, and baked goods.

HOTELS

Accommodations in North Cascades National Park are rustic, cozy, and comfortable. Options range from plush Stehekin lodges and homey cabin rentals to spartan Learning Center bunks and campgrounds. Expect to pay roughly $50 to $200 per night, depending on the rental size and the season. Book at least three months in advance, or even a year for popular accommodations in summer. Outside the park are numerous resorts, motels, bed-and-breakfasts, and even overnight boat rentals in Chelan, Con-crete, Glacier, Marblemount, Sedro-Wool-ley, Twisp, and Winthrop. *Hotel reviews have been shortened. For full information, visit Fodors.com.*

What It Costs			
$	$$	$$$	$$$$
RESTAURANTS			
under $12	$12–$20	$21–$30	over $30
HOTELS			
under $100	$100–$150	$151–$200	over $200

TOURS

★ North Cascades Environmental Learning Center

BODY OF WATER | FAMILY | Come here for information on park hiking, wildlife watching, horseback riding, climbing, boat rentals, and fishing, as well as class-room education and hands-on nature experiences. Guided tours staged from the center include lake and dam tours, mountain climbs, pack-train excursions, and guided canoe trips on Diablo Lake. Other choices range from forest ecology and backpacking trips to writing and art retreats. Family getaway weekends in summer are a fun way to unplug from technology and introduce kids to nature.

There's also a research library, a dock on Diablo Lake, an amphitheater, and overnight lodging. The center is operated by the North Cascades Institute, in partnership with the National Parks Service and Seattle City Light. ⊠ *1940 Diablo Dam Rd., Diablo* ☎ *360/854–2599 headquarters, 206/526–2599 environmental learning center* ⊕ *www.ncascades.org* ⊠ *Day programs from $95; overnight lodging (including meals) from $230 per couple.*

VISITOR INFORMATION
PARK CONTACT INFORMATION North
Cascades National Park ⊠ *810 Rte. 20, Sedro-Woolley* ☎ *360/854–7200* ⊕ *www. nps.gov/noca.*

VISITOR CENTERS
Chelan Ranger Station
INFO CENTER | The base for the Chelan National Recreation Area and Wenatchee National Forest has an information desk and a shop selling regional maps and books. ⊠ *428 W. Woodin Ave., Chelan* ☎ *509/682–4900* ⊕ *www.fs.usda.gov/ detail/okawen/about-forest/offices* ⊘ *Closed weekends.*

Glacier Public Service Center
INFO CENTER | This office doubles as a headquarters for the Mount Baker–Snoqualmie National Forest; it has maps, a book and souvenir shop, and a permits desk. The center is also right on the way to some of the park's main trailheads. ⊠ *10091 Mt. Baker Hwy., Glacier* ☎ *360/599–2714* ⊕ *www.nps.gov/noca/ planyourvisit/visitorcenters.htm* ⊘ *Closed Oct.–Apr.; weekdays, early May; Tues. and Wed., mid-May–mid-June.*

Golden West Visitor Center
INFO CENTER | Rangers here offer guidance on hiking, camping, and other activities, as well as audiovisual and children's programs and bike tours. There's also an arts-and-crafts gallery. Maps and concise displays explain the layered ecology of the valley, which encompasses in its length virtually every ecosystem in the Northwest. Campers can pick up free backcountry permits. Note that access to Stehekin is by boat or trail only. ⊠ *Stehekin Valley Rd., Stehekin* ⊕ *¼ mile north of Stehekin Landing* ☎ *509/699–2080* ⊕ *www.nps.gov/noca/planyourvisit/visitorcenters.htm.*

North Cascades Park & Forest Information Center
INFO CENTER | This is the park's major administrative center and the place to pick up passes, permits, and information about current conditions. ⊠ *810 Rte. 20, Sedro-Woolley* ☎ *360/854–7200* ⊕ *www. nps.gov/noca/planyourvisit/visitorcenters. htm* ⊘ *Closed weekends and federal holidays in Oct.–mid-May.*

North Cascades Visitor Center
INFO CENTER | The main visitor facility for the park complex has extensive displays on the surrounding landscape. Learn about the history and value of old-growth trees, the many creatures that depend on the rain-forest ecology, and the effects of human activity on the ecosystem. Park rangers frequently conduct programs; check bulletin boards for schedules. ⊠ *Milepost 120, North Cascades Hwy., Newhalem* ☎ *206/386–4495* ⊕ *www.nps. gov/noca/planyourvisit/visitorcenters.htm* ⊘ *Closed Oct.–mid-May.*

Wilderness Information Center
INFO CENTER | The main stop to secure backcountry and climbing permits for North Cascades National Park and the Lake Chelan and Ross Lake recreational areas, this office has maps, a bookshop, and nature exhibits. If you arrive after hours, there's a self-register permit stop outside. ⊠ *7280 Ranger Station Rd., Marblemount* ⊕ *Off milepost 105.9, N. Cascades Hwy.* ☎ *360/854–7245* ⊕ *www. nps.gov/noca/planyourvisit/visitorcenters. htm* ⊘ *Closed Oct.–Apr.*

 Sights

SCENIC DRIVES

North Cascades Highway

BODY OF WATER | Also known as Highway 20, this classic scenic route first winds through the green pastures and woods of the upper Skagit Valley, the mountains looming in the distance. Beyond Concrete, a former cement-manufacturing town, the highway climbs into the mountains, passes the Ross and Diablo dams, and traverses Ross Lake National Recreation Area. Here several pull-outs offer great views of the lake and the surrounding snowcapped peaks. From June to September, the meadows are covered with wildflowers, and from late September through October, the mountain slopes flame with fall foliage. The pinnacle point of this stretch is 5,477-foot-high Washington Pass: look east, to where the road descends quickly into a series of hairpin curves between Early Winters Creek and the Methow Valley. Remember, this section of the highway is closed from roughly November to April, depending on snowfall, and sometimes closes temporarily during the busy summer season due to mudslides from storms. From the Methow Valley, Highway 153 takes the scenic route along the Methow River's apple, nectarine, and peach orchards to Pateros, on the Columbia River; from here, you can continue east to Grand Coulee or south to Lake Chelan. ⊕ www.cascadeloop.com.

HISTORIC SITES

Buckner Homestead

FESTIVAL | Dating from 1889, this restored pioneer farm includes an apple orchard, farmhouse, barn, and many ranch buildings. You can pick up a self-guided tour booklet from the drop box. Feel free to enjoy apples from the trees in season. A harvest festival is held in October. ⊠ Stehekin Valley Rd., 3½ miles northwest of Stehekin Landing, Stehekin ⊕ www. bucknerhomestead.org.

Plants and Wildlife in North Cascades 👁

Bald eagles are present year-round along the Skagit River and the lakes—in December, hundreds flock to the Skagit to feed on a rare winter salmon run, and remain through January. Spring and early summer bring black bears to the roadsides in the high country. Deer and elk can often be seen in early morning and late evening, grazing and browsing at the forest's edge. Other mountain residents include beaver, marmots, pika, otters, skunks, opossums, and smaller mammals, as well as forest and field birds.

SCENIC STOPS

Gorge Powerhouse/Ladder Creek Falls and Rock Gardens

GARDEN | A powerhouse is just that, but the rock gardens overlooking Ladder Creek Falls, 7 miles west of Diablo, are beautiful and inspiring. In summer, a slide show about the area's history and free guided walking tours to the falls are offered Thursday and Friday evenings at 8; visitors can reserve in advance for a chicken dinner at 7 pm. ⊠ North Cascades Hwy., Newhalem ✛ 2 miles east of North Cascades Visitor Center ☎ 360/854–2589 ⊕ www.seattle.gov/light/tours/skagit ⊠ $19/dinner; walking tour free ⊘ Closed Oct.–Apr.

 Activities

BICYCLING

Mountain bikes are permitted on highways, unpaved back roads, and a few designated tracks around the park; however, there is no biking on footpaths. Ranger stations have details on the best places to ride in each season, as well as notes on spots that are closed due to weather, mud, or other environmental factors. It's $27 round-trip to bring a bike on the Lake Chelan ferry to Stehekin.

Discovery Bikes

BICYCLING | You can rent mountain bikes by the hour at a self-serve rack in front of the Stehekin Log office in Stehekin. Helmets are included. For a longer excursion, meet up at 8 am for a van ride and narrated tour to the Stehekin Valley Ranch, where a full breakfast is served. Then hop on bikes to explore the trails and sites. ⊠ *Stehekin Valley Rd., Stehekin* ✛ *5-min walk from boat landing* ☎ ⊕ *www.stehekindiscoverybikes. com* ⊠ *From $5 per hr; $35 for ranch breakfast ride.*

BOATING

The boundaries of North Cascades National Park touch two long and sinewy expanses: Lake Chelan in the far south, and Ross Lake, which runs toward the Canadian border. Boat ramps, some with speed- and sailboat, paddleboat, kayak, and canoe rentals, can be found all around Lake Chelan, and passenger ferries cross between towns and campgrounds. Hozomeen, accessible via a 39-mile dirt road from Canada, is the boating base for Ross Lake; the site has a large boat ramp, and a boat taxi makes drops at campgrounds all around the shoreline. Diablo Lake, in the center of the park, also has a ramp at Colonial Creek. Gorge Lake has a public ramp near the town of Diablo.

HIKING

⚠ **Black bears are often sighted along trails in the summer; do not approach them. Back away carefully, and report sightings to the Golden West Visitor Center.** Cougars, which are shy of humans and well aware of their presence, are rarely sighted in this region. Still, keep kids close and don't let them run too far ahead or lag behind on a trail. If you do spot a cougar, pick up children, have the whole group

stand close together, and make yourself look as large as possible.

★ Cascade Pass

HIKING/WALKING | This extremely popular 3¾-mile, four-hour trail is known for stunning panoramas from the great mountain divide. Dozens of peaks line the horizon as you make your way up the fairly flat, hairpin-turn track, the scene fronted by a blanket of alpine wildflowers from July to mid-August. Arrive before noon if you want a parking spot at the trailhead. *Moderate.* ⊠ *North Cascades National Park* ✛ *Trailhead: at end of Cascade River Rd., 14 miles from Marblemount* ⊕ *www.nps.gov/noca/planyourvisit/cascade-pass-trail.htm.*

Diablo Lake Trail

HIKING/WALKING | Explore nearly 4 miles of waterside terrain on this route, which is accessed from the Sourdough Creek parking lot. An excellent alternative for parties with small hikers is to take the Seattle City Light Ferry one way. *Moderate.* ⊠ *North Cascades National Park* ✛ *Trailhead: at milepost 135, Hwy. 20* ⊕ *www.nps.gov/noca.*

Happy Creek Forest Walk

HIKING/WALKING | FAMILY | Old-growth forests are the focus of this kid-friendly boardwalk route, which loops just less than a ½ mile through the trees right off the North Cascades Highway. Interpretive signs provide details about flora along the way. *Easy.* ⊠ *North Cascades National Park* ✛ *Trailhead: at milepost 135, North Cascades Hwy.* ⊕ *www.nps. gov/noca.*

Pacific Northwest Trail Association

HIKING/WALKING | Access all sorts of resources here, including advice on tours and independent travel, for hiking the 60 miles of magnificent Pacific Northwest Trail (which links Glacier National Park in Montana to Cape Alava on the Washington coast of Olympic National Park) as it passes through North Cascades National Park and the Ross Lake National

Recreation Area. Sights along the way include Ross Lake, Big Beaver Trail, and the Whatcom and Hannegan passes. ☎ 360/854–9415 ⊕ www.pnt.org.

Rainy Lake Trail

HIKING/WALKING | An easy and accessible 1-mile paved trail leads to Rainy Lake, a waterfall, and glacier-view platform. *Easy.* ✉ North Cascades National Park ⚓ Trailhead: off Hwy. 20, 38 miles east of visitor center at Newhalem ⊕ www.nps.gov/noca.

River Loop Trail

HIKING/WALKING | Take this flat and easy, 1¾-mile, wheelchair-accessible trail down through stands of huge old-growth firs and cedars toward the Skagit River. *Easy.* ✉ North Cascades National Park ⚓ Trailhead: near North Cascades Visitor Center ⊕ www.nps.gov/noca/planyourvisit/newhalem-area-trails.htm.

Rock Shelter Trail

HIKING/WALKING | This short trail—partly boardwalk—leads to a campsite used 1,400 years ago by Native Americans; interpretive signs tell the history of human presence in the region. *Easy.* ✉ North Cascades National Park ⚓ Trailhead: off Hwy. 20 near Newhalem Creek Campground ⊕ www.nps.gov/noca/planyourvisit/newhalem-area-trails.htm.

Sterling Munro Trail

HIKING/WALKING | Starting from the North Cascades Visitor Center, this popular introductory stroll follows a short 300-foot path over a boardwalk to a lookout above the forested Picket Range peaks. *Easy.* ✉ North Cascades National Park ⚓ Trailhead: milepost 120, near Newhalem Creek Campground ⊕ www.nps.gov/noca/planyourvisit/newhalem-area-trails.htm.

Thornton Lakes Trail

HIKING/WALKING | A 5-mile climb into an alpine basin with three pretty lakes, this steep and strenuous hike takes about five to six hours round-trip. *Difficult.* ✉ North Cascades National Park ⚓ Trailhead: off Hwy. 20, 3 miles west of Newhalem, Thornton Lake Rd. and Hwy. 20 ⊕ www.nps.gov/noca/planyourvisit/thornton-lake-trail.htm.

Trail of the Cedars

HIKING/WALKING | Just less than a ½ mile long, this trail winds its way through one of the finest surviving stands of old-growth western red cedar in Washington. Some of the trees on the path are more than 1,000 years old. *Easy.* ✉ Newhalem ⚓ Trailhead: near North Cascades Visitor Center, milepost 120, Hwy. 20 ⊕ www.nps.gov/noca/planyourvisit/newhalem-area-trails.htm.

HORSEBACK RIDING

Many hiking trails and backwoods paths are also popular horseback-riding routes, particularly around the park's southern fringes.

Stehekin Outfitters

HORSEBACK RIDING | Since 1947, the Courtney family has been guiding adventures in the Stehekin Valley. They organize 2½-hour horseback trips to Coon Lake and full-day rides (lunch included) to Bridge Creek. English- and Western-style riding lessons are also available. Rides depart from Stehekin Valley Ranch. Stehekin Outfitters also offers tent rentals at two local campgrounds and multiday hiking adventures. ✉ North Cascades National Park ☎ 509/682–7742 ⊕ stehekinoutfitters.com ⚑ From $65.

KAYAKING

The park's tangles of waterways offer access to remote areas inaccessible by road or trail; here are some of the most pristine and secluded mountain scenes on the continent. Bring your own kayak and you can launch from any boat ramp or beach; otherwise, companies in several nearby towns and Seattle suburbs offer kayak and canoe rentals, portage, and tours. The upper basin of Lake Chelan (at the park's southern end) and Ross Lake (at the top edge of the park) are two well-known kayaking expanses, but there are dozens of smaller lakes and creeks between. The Stehekin River also provides many kayaking possibilities.

Outward Bound
CANOEING/ROWING/SKULLING | Based in the mountain-sports center of Mazama, Outward Bound stages backpacking and mountaineering expeditions for older teens and adults on peaks throughout the park, and offers a variety of special programs for youth, including canoeing and rock climbing. ⊠ *226 Lost River Rd., Mazama* ☎ *866/467–7651 headquarters, 866/404–1512 Pacific Northwest region* ⊕ *www.outwardbound.com, www.nwobs.org.*

Ross Lake Resort
BOATING | The resort, open mid-June–October, rents kayaks, motor boats, canoes, and fishing equipment, and offers portage service for exploring Ross Lake. A water-taxi service is also available; the resort is not accessible by road. ⊠ *503 Diablo St., Rockport* ☎ *206/386–4437* ⊕ *www.rosslakeresort.com.*

Stehekin Valley Ranch
KAYAKING | Kayak tours of the upper estuary of Lake Chelan are offered daily at 8:45 am. ⊠ *Stehekin Valley Rd., Stehekin* ✛ *3½ miles from Stehekin Landing* ☎ *509/682–4677, 800/536–0745* ⊕ *www.stehekinvalleyranch.com* 🖅 *$40.*

RAFTING
June through August is the park's white-water season, and rafting trips run through the lower section of the Stehekin River. Along the way take in views of cottonwood and pine forests, glimpses of Yawning Glacier on Magic Mountain, and placid vistas of Lake Chelan.

North Cascades River Expeditions
WHITE-WATER RAFTING | May through July, North Cascades River Expeditions focuses on regional rivers; trips are offered on the Upper Skagit year-round. ☎ *800/634-8433* ⊕ *www.riverexpeditions.com* 🖅 *From $65.*

Orion River Expeditions
WHITE-WATER RAFTING | FAMILY | Introductory family-oriented floats are offered in August on the Skagit River for ages six and up. More lively white-water tours run on other area rivers April through September. ☎ *509/548–1401, 509/881–9556* ⊕ *www.orionexp.com* 🖅 *From $90.*

Wildwater River Guides
WHITE-WATER RAFTING | FAMILY | Half-day rafting excursions on the Skagit River depart from Goodell Creek Campground near Newhalem, March through September. The mild waters are great for beginners and families. ⊠ *Goodell Creek Campground, Newhalem* ☎ *509/470–8558, 800/522–9453* ⊕ *www.wildwater-river.com* 🖅 *$69.*

WINTER ACTIVITIES
Mt. Baker, just off the park's far northwest corner, is one of the Northwest's premier skiing, snowboarding, and snowshoeing regions—the area set a world record for most snow in a single season during the winter of 1998–99 (1,140 inches). The Mount Baker Highway (Route 542) cuts through the slopes toward state sno-parks; Salmon Ridge Sno-Park, 46 miles east of Bellingham at Exit 255, has groomed trails and parking. Mt. Baker Ski Area, 17 miles east of the town of Glacier, has eight chairlifts and access to backcountry skiing; its season runs roughly from November to April.

Stehekin is another base for winter sports. The Stehekin Valley alone has 20 miles of trails; some of the most popular are around Buckner Orchard, Coon Lake, and the Courtney Ranch (Cascade Corrals).

Mt. Baker
SNOW SPORTS | Off the park's northwest corner, this is the closest winter-sports area, with facilities for downhill and Nordic skiing, snowboarding, and other recreational ventures. The main base is the town of Glacier, 17 miles west of the slopes, where lodging is available.

Equipment rental and food service are on-site. **Facilities:** 38 trails; 1,000 acres; 1,500-foot vertical drop; 10 lifts (8 quad chairs, 2 rope tows). ⌧ *Hwy. 542, Glacier ✛ 52 miles east of Bellingham* ☎ *360/734–6771, 360/671–0211 for snow reports* ⊕ *www.mtbaker.us* ✉ *Lift ticket: weekdays $57, weekends and holidays $62.*

Nearby Towns

Heading into North Cascades National Park from Seattle on Interstate 5 to Highway 2, **Sedro-Woolley** (pronounced "*see*-droh *wool*-lee") is the first main town you encounter. A former logging and steel-mill base settled by North Carolina pioneers, the settlement still has a 19th-century ambience throughout its rustic downtown area. Surrounded by farmlands, it's a pretty spot to stop and has basic visitor services like hotels, gas stations, and groceries. It's also home to the North Cascades National Park Headquarters. From here, it's about 40 miles to the park's western edges. Along the way, you still have a chance to stop for supplies in **Concrete,** about 20 miles from the park along Highway 2.

Marblemount is 10 miles farther east, about 12 miles west of the North Cascades Visitor Center. It's another atmospheric former timber settlement nestled in the mountain foothills, and its growing collection of motels, cafés, and tour outfitters draw outdoors enthusiasts each summer. The park's base town, though, is **Newhalem,** tucked right along the highway between the north and south regions. This is the place to explore the visitor center and its surrounding trails, view exhibits, and pick up maps, permits, and tour information.

Still traveling east on Highway 20, it's about 5 miles from Newhalem to **Diablo,** where the local lake, dam, and overlook are all good reasons to stop. Keep going

until the road turns south along the park's eastern side: this is the famed North Cascades Scenic Highway. From top to bottom, including Rainy Pass and the curve through the chilly Washington Pass overlook, this section is about 20 miles.

Winthrop, a relaxed, riverside rodeo town complete with clapboard cafés and five-and-dime charm, is about a 30-mile drive east of Washington Pass. This is also an outdoor-recreation base, offering activities that range from cross-country skiing to hiking, mountain biking, and white-water rafting. Less than 10 miles southeast of Winthrop, the tiny town of **Twisp** is settled in the farmlands and orchards, its streets lined with a few small lodgings and eateries.

The resort town of **Chelan,** nestled around its serene namesake lake, lies about 60 miles due south of Winthrop along Highway 153. It's a serene summer getaway for boating and swimming, as well as an access point for small villages and campgrounds along the shoreline. **Stehekin,** at the lake's northern end, is a favorite tourist stop for its peaceful isolation; without road connections, your options for getting here are by boat or trail. A ferry runs between Chelan and Stehekin.

VISITOR INFORMATION

Lake Chelan Chamber of Commerce ⌧ *216 E. Woodin Ave., Chelan* ☎ *509/682–3503* ⊕ *www.lakechelan.com.* **Sedro-Woolley Chamber of Commerce** ⌧ *714B Metcalf St., Sedro-Woolley* ☎ *360/855–1841* ⊕ *www. sedro-woolley.com.* **Twisp Visitor Information Center and Chamber of Commerce** ⌧ *118 S. Glover St., Twisp* ☎ *509/997–2020* ⊕ *www.twispinfo.com.* **Winthrop Chamber of Commerce** ⌧ *202 Hwy. 20, Winthrop* ☎ *509/996–2125* ⊕ *www.winthropwashington.com.*

Sights

★ Lake Chelan

BODY OF WATER | Best known as a summer vacation spot, this narrow fjord—Washington's largest natural lake—offers a reason to visit all year: its striking scenery. The views include sparkling blue water with snowcapped peaks in the distance. The lake offers swimming, boating, fishing, and a chance to soak up the sun. Access to the shore is fairly limited, but the lake makes for a beautiful backdrop throughout the region. ✉ *U.S. 97A, Chelan* ☎ *509/682–3503* 🌐 *www.lakechelan.com.*

Lake Chelan Boat Co.

TRANSPORTATION SITE (AIRPORT/BUS/FERRY/TRAIN) | The *Lady of the Lake II* makes journeys from May to October, departing Chelan at 8:30 and returning at 6 ($40.50 round-trip). The *Lady Express,* a speedy catamaran, runs between Stehekin, Holden Village, the national park, and Lake Chelan year-round; schedules vary with the seasons, with daily trips during summer and three to five trips weekly the rest of the year. Tickets are $61 round-trip May to October and $40.50 round-trip the rest of the year. The vessels also can drop off and pick up at lakeshore trailheads. ✉ *1418 Woodin Ave., Chelan* ☎ *509/682–4584, 888/682–4584* 🌐 *ladyofthelake.com.*

Restaurants

IN THE PARK

Restaurant at Stehekin Valley Ranch

$$ | AMERICAN | FAMILY | Meals in the rustic log ranch house, served at polished wood tables, include buffet dinners of steak, ribs, hamburgers, fish, salad, beans, and dessert. Note that breakfast is served 7 to 9, lunch is noon to 1, and dinner is 5:30 to 7; show up later than that and you'll find the kitchen is closed. **Known for:** hearty meals; fresh berries, fruit, and produce; communal dining. [$] *Average main: $20* ✉ *Stehekin Valley Rd., 9 miles north of Stehekin Landing, Stehekin* ☎ *509/682–4677, 800/536–0745* 🌐 *www.stehekinvalleyranch.com* 🕓 *Closed Oct.–mid-June.*

Stehekin Pastry Company

$ | BAKERY | As you enter this lawn-framed timber chalet, you're immersed in the tantalizing aromas of a European bakery. Glassed-in display cases are filled with trays of homemade baked goods, and the pungent espresso is eye-opening. **Known for:** fruit pie; amazing pastries; hearty lunch food. [$] *Average main: $9* ✉ *Stehekin Valley Rd., Stehekin* ✣ *About 2 miles north of Stehekin Landing* ☎ *509/682–7742* 🌐 *www.stehekinpastry.com* 🕓 *Closed mid-Oct.–mid-May.*

Developed picnic areas at both Rainy Pass (Highway 20, 38 miles east of the park visitor center) and Washington Pass (Highway 20, 42 miles east of the visitor center) have a half-dozen picnic tables, drinking water, and pit toilets. The vistas of surrounding peaks are sensational at these two overlooks. More picnic facilities are located near the visitor center in Newhalem and at Colonial Creek Campground, 10 miles east of the visitor center on Highway 20.

OUTSIDE THE PARK

★ Dining Room at Sun Mountain Lodge

$$$$ | PACIFIC NORTHWEST | A sylvan hilltop overlooking the Methow Valley sets the scene for an extraordinary dining experience featuring upscale Pacific Northwest cuisine with local and often organic ingredients. Exquisite flavors match the artful presentation and elegant yet unpretentious lodgelike atmosphere. **Known for:** sophisticated Pacific Northwest fare; sweeping mountain views; extensive wine list. [$] *Average main: $40* ✉ *604 Patterson Lake Rd., Winthrop* ☎ *509/996–4707, 800/572–0493* 🌐 *www.sunmountainlodge.com/dining* 🕓 *Limited hrs in winter and spring; closed 2 wks in Nov. No lunch.*

Best Campgrounds in North Cascades

Tent campers can choose between forest sites, riverside spots, lake grounds, or meadow spreads encircled by mountains. Here camping is as easy or challenging as you want to make it; some campgrounds are a short walk from ranger stations, while others are miles from the highway. Note that many campsites, particularly those around Stehekin, are completely remote and without road access anywhere, so you have to walk, boat, or ride a horse to reach them. Most don't accept reservations, and spots fill up quickly May through September. If there's no ranger on-site, you can often sign yourself in—and always check in at a ranger station before you set out overnight. Note that some areas are occasionally closed due to flooding, forest fires, or other factors.

Lake Chelan National Recreation Area. Many backcountry camping areas are accessible via park shuttles or boat. All require a free backcountry permit. Purple Point, the most popular campground due to its quick access to Stehekin Landing, has six tent sites, bear boxes, and nearby road access. ✉ *Stehekin Landing, Stehekin* ☎ *509/699–2080.*

Hotels

IN THE PARK

North Cascades Lodge at Stehekin

$$$ | **HOTEL** | Crackling fires and Lake Chelan views are provided both in standard rooms in the Alpine House, with its shared lounge and lakeside deck, and in larger rooms in the Swiss Mont building, with private decks overlooking the water. **Pros:** on the water; recreation center with pool table; kayak and canoe rentals. **Cons:** no air-conditioning; TV is only available in the recreation building; limited Internet service and no cell phone service. [$] *Rooms from: $151* ✉ *955 Stehekin Valley Rd., Stehekin* ☎ *509/682–4494, 855/685–4167 reservations* 🌐 *www.lodgeatstehekin.com* 🕒 *General store and all but 7 rooms are closed mid-Oct.–mid-May* 🛏 *28 rooms, 1 house* 🍴 *No meals.*

Stehekin Valley Ranch

$$$$ | **ALL-INCLUSIVE** | **FAMILY** | Alongside pretty meadows at the edge of pine forest, this rustic ranch is a center for hikers and horseback riders, who stay in barnlike cabins with cedar paneling, tile floors, and a private bath, or canvas-roof tent cabins with bunk beds, kerosene lamps, and shared bathrooms. **Pros:** easy access to recreation; playground and outdoor game fields; hearty meals included. **Cons:** no bathrooms in tent cabins; many repeat guests so book early. [$] *Rooms from: $280* ✉ *Stehekin Valley Rd., Stehekin* ✥ *9 miles north of Stehekin Landing* ☎ *509/682–4677, 800/536–0745* 🌐 *stehekinvalleyranch.com* 🕒 *Closed Oct.–mid-June* 🛏 *15 cabins* 🍴 *All meals.*

OUTSIDE THE PARK

Campbell's Resort

$$$$ | **RESORT** | **FAMILY** | More than a century old, this sprawling resort sits on landscaped grounds alongside Lake Chelan; every room has a balcony with mountain and beach views, and some have a kitchen or fireplace. **Pros:** plenty of summer programs to keep kids busy; on-site day spa; great base for winter sports. **Cons:** tour buses, weddings, and conferences bring noisy crowds; some rooms in older building are very worn; service can be inconsistent. [$] *Rooms from: $294* ✉ *104 W. Woodin Ave.,*

Chelan ☎ *509/682–2561, 800/553–8225* 🌐 *www.campbellsresort.com* 🛏 *170 rooms* 🍴 *No meals.*

Chewuch Inn

$$ | **B&B/INN** | Set on 5 acres just south of Winthrop, lodgings at the inn have modern amenities and luxurious touches. **Pros:** free cookies in afternoon; excellent service; short walk to town. **Cons:** basement rooms have no windows; a bit hard to find off the main highway. [$] *Rooms from: $105* ✉ *223 White Ave., Winthrop* ☎ *509/996–3107* 🌐 *www.chewuchinn.com* 🛏 *20 rooms* 🍴 *Breakfast.*

Duck Brand Hotel and Cantina

$$ | **HOTEL** | Named for the town's original 19th-century saloon and retaining its frontier feel, this eclectic, casual and comfortable timber hotel has six small, simple rooms with big wood beams, bright fabrics and walls, and updated bathrooms. **Pros:** small-town charm; fun and friendly; restaurant on-site. **Cons:** a bit rustic for the sophisticated city traveler; limited amenities. [$] *Rooms from: $130* ✉ *248 Riverside Ave., Winthrop* ☎ *509/996–2408* 🌐 *www.duckbrand-winthrop.com* 🛏 *6 rooms* 🍴 *No meals* ☞ *Restaurant on-site.*

★ **Freestone Inn**

$$$$ | **RESORT** | **FAMILY** | At the heart of the 120-acre, historic Wilson Ranch, amid more than 2 million acres of forest, this upscale mountain retreat embraces the pioneer spirit in spacious rooms, suites, and wood-paneled cabins snuggled up to Early Winters Creek. **Pros:** gorgeous scenery; myriad activities; close to North Cascades National Park (17 miles west). **Cons:** limited cell phone and Wi-Fi service ; some resort amenities may be limited in shoulder season; historic cabins are quite rustic. [$] *Rooms from: $259* ✉ *31 Early Winters Dr., Mazama* ✥ *About 14 miles northwest of Winthop* ☎ *509/996–3906, 800/639–3809* 🌐 *www.freestoneinn.com* 🛏 *31 rooms* 🍴 *No meals.*

Lakeside Lodge & Suites

$$$$ | **HOTEL** | **FAMILY** | Adjacent to Lakeside Park, a couple miles from downtown Chelan, this four-story property has all lake-facing rooms to enjoy sunset over the lake, and plenty of family-friendly amenities, including two pools and two hot tubs. **Pros:** lake views; adjacent to park with beach, playground, and sports courts; hot breakfast included. **Cons:** some room views are blocked by a giant tree; rooms open to outside (no halls); no on-site restaurant. [$] *Rooms from: $260* ✉ *2312 W. Woodin Ave., Chelan* ☎ *800/468–2781, 509/682–4396* 🌐 *www.lakesidelodgeandsuites.com* 🛏 *93 rooms* 🍴 *Breakfast.*

Mazama Country Inn

$$ | **B&B/INN** | Ideal as a base for outdoor-recreation enthusiasts, the inn offers clean, no-frills accommodations and nearby access to the Pasayten Wilderness and North Cascades National Park. **Pros:** inclusive meal option available in winter; off-season specials; rooms very clean. **Cons:** no TV; basic rooms are small. [$] *Rooms from: $115* ✉ *15 Country Rd., Mazama* ☎ *800/843–7951, 509/996–2681* 🌐 *www.mazamacountryinn.com* 🛏 *18 rooms* 🍴 *No meals.*

River Run Inn

$$$ | **B&B/INN** | **FAMILY** | The rooms and cabins are comfortable but not fancy here, but the inn's riverfront location and amenities—including picnic tables, hammocks, a playground, lawn games, and an indoor pool—make it a popular place to stay. **Pros:** free use of bikes; serene riverfront setting; free DVD library. **Cons:** hot tub is only big enough for a few people; bathrooms are small; just a few pet-friendly rooms. [$] *Rooms from: $175* ✉ *27 Rader Rd., Winthrop* ☎ *800/757–2709, 509/996–2173* 🌐 *www.riverrun-inn.com* 🛏 *16 rooms (plus 1 house)* 🍴 *No meals.*

★ Sun Mountain Lodge

$$$$ | RESORT | The stunning North Cascades and all its attractions are the stars of this outdoor-oriented resort replete with luxurious accommodations, spectacular mountain views, and a range of activities that make it a year-round destination, whether the peaks are covered in snow or wildflowers. **Pros:** stunning setting; a wide array of outdoor activities year-round; panoramic views; award-winning dining; warm hospitality. **Cons:** limited cell service; roundabout route from Seattle in winter. $ *Rooms from: $265* ✉ *604 Patterson Lake Rd., Winthrop* ☎ *509/996–2211, 800/572–0493* ⊕ *www. sunmountainlodge.com* ⊗ *Closed 2 wks in early Nov.* ⇋ *112 rooms* ⍥ *Breakfast.*

Skagit River Bald Eagle Interpretive Center

TOUR—SIGHT | Open on weekends in December and January to highlight the winter migration of bald eagles, the center offers guided hikes and educational presentations about the Skagit ecosystem. ✉ *52809 Rockport Park Rd., Rockport* ☎ *306/853–7626* ⊕ *www. skagiteagle.org.*

Chapter 26

OLYMPIC NATIONAL PARK

Updated by
Shelley Arenas

WELCOME TO OLYMPIC NATIONAL PARK

TOP REASONS TO GO

★ **Exotic rain forest:** A rain forest in the Pacific Northwest? Indeed, Olympic National Park is one of the few places in the world with this unique temperate landscape.

★ **Beachcombing:** Miles of rugged, spectacular coastline hemmed with sea stacks and tidal pools edge the driftwood-strewn shores of the Olympic Peninsula.

★ **Nature's hot tubs:** A dip in Sol Duc's natural geothermal mineral pools offers a secluded spa experience in the wooded heart of the park.

★ **Lofty vistas:** The hardy can hike up meadowed foothill trails or climb the frosty peaks throughout the Olympics—or just drive up to Hurricane Ridge for endless views.

★ **A sense of history:** Native American history is key to this region, where eight tribes have traditional ties to the park lands—there's 12,000 years of history to explore.

1 Coastal Olympic. Here the Pacific smashes endlessly into the rugged coastline, carving out some of the park's most memorable scenes in the massive, rocky sea stacks and islets just offshore. Back from the water are beaches and tide pools full of sea stars, crabs, and anemones.

2 The Rain Forest. Centered on the Hoh, Queets, and Quinault river valleys, this is the region's most unique landscape. Fog-shrouded Douglas firs and Sitka spruces, some more than 300 feet tall, huddle in this moist, pine-carpeted area, shading fern- and moss-draped cedars, maples, and alders.

3 The Mountains. Craggy gray peaks and snow-covered summits dominate the skyline. Low-level foliage and wildflower meadows make for excellent hiking in the plateaus. Even on the sunniest days, temperatures are brisk. Some roads are closed in winter months.

4 Alpine Meadows. In midsummer, the swath of colors is like a Monet canvas spread over the landscape, and wildlife teems among the honeyed flowers. Trails are never prettier, and views are crisp and vast.

Neah Bay
112
Sekiu
Cla
112
Ozette
113
Lake Ozette
101
SO
Forks
29
La Push Mora
110
Second Third Beach
Beach
101
Kalaloch
Kalaloch Information Station
Queets

0   10 mi
0   10 km

USFS/

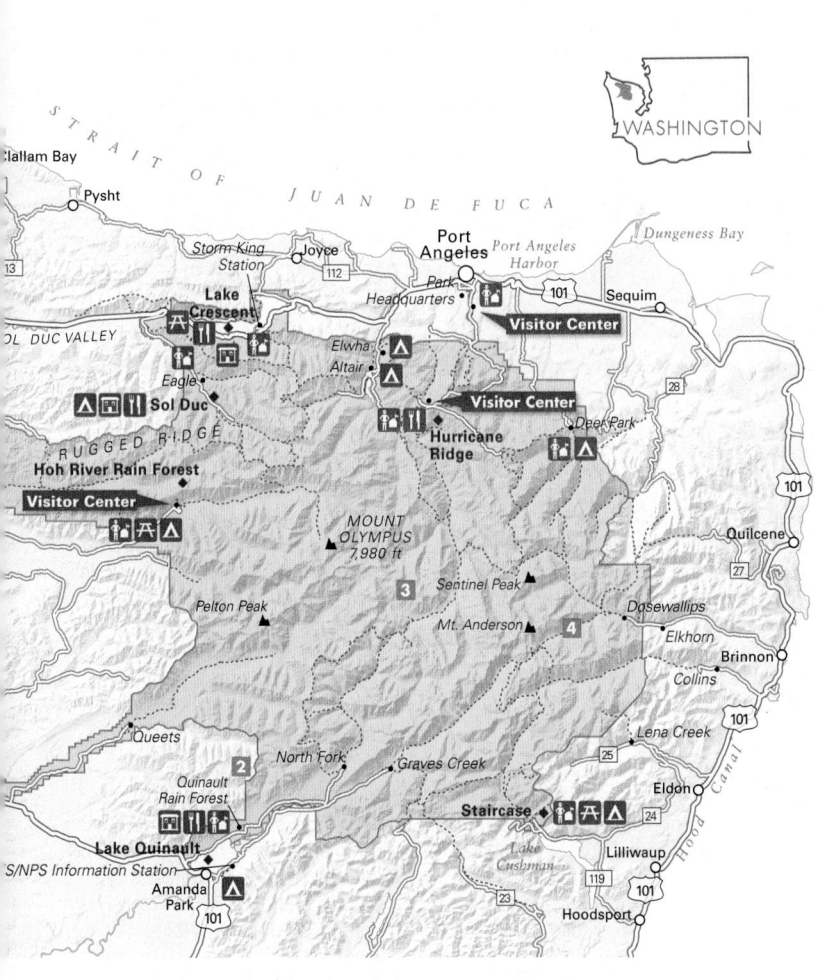

A spellbinding setting is tucked into the country's far northwestern corner, within the heart-shape Olympic Peninsula. Edged on all sides by water, the forested landscape is remote and pristine, and works its way around the sharpened ridges of the snowcapped Olympic Mountains. Big lakes cut pockets of blue in the rugged blanket of pine forests.

Planning

WHEN TO GO

Summer, with its long stretches of sun-filled days, is prime touring time for Olympic National Park. June through September are the peak months; Hurricane Ridge, the Hoh Rain Forest, Lake Crescent, and Ruby Beach are bustling by 10 am.

Late spring and early autumn are also good bets for clear weather; anytime between April and October, you'll have a good chance of fair skies. Between Thanksgiving and Easter, it's a toss-up as to which days will turn out fair; prepare for heavy clouds, rain showers, and chilly temperatures, then hope for the best.

Winter is a great time to visit if you enjoy isolation. Locals are usually the only hardy souls during this time, except for weekend skiers heading to the snowfields around Hurricane Ridge. Many visitor facilities have limited hours or are closed from October to April.

FESTIVALS AND EVENTS
Big Foot Brew Festival

FESTIVAL | The Washington coast's largest brew festival happens on the first Saturday of October in Seabrook. Seasonal craft brews from more than a dozen breweries are featured, along with live music and food vendors; $25 admission includes a logo pint glass and six tasting tickets. ✉ *4275 SR 109, Pacific Beach* ☎ *877/779–9990* ⊕ *www.seabrookwa.com/events/festivals/big-foot-brew-festival.*

Centrum Summer Arts Festival

FESTIVAL | This summer-long lineup of concerts and workshops is held at Fort Worden State Park, a 19th-century Army base near Port Townsend. ✉ *Port Townsend* ☎ *360/385–3102* ⊕ *www.centrum.org.*

Chocolate on the Beach Festival

FESTIVAL | FAMILY | Venues in the North Beach towns of Seabrook, Moclips, and Pacific Beach host this annual celebration of chocolate the last weekend of February. Activities include classes, contests, demonstrations, and dining and sampling events. ✉ *Pacific Beach* ⊕ *www.chocolateonthebeachfestival.com.*

Forks Old-Fashioned Fourth of July

FESTIVAL | A salmon bake, parade, demolition derby, arts-and-crafts exhibits, kids' activities, and plenty of fireworks mark Forks's weekend-long celebration. ✉ *Forks* ☎ *360/374–2531, 800/443–6757* ⊕ *www.forkswa.com.*

Gnome and Fairy Festival

FESTIVAL | FAMILY | The beach resort town of Seabrook hosts this delightful celebration of fairies and gnomes on a mid-August Saturday. Everyone is encouraged to dress up and participate in the parade that kicks off the festivities. Activities include gnome and fairy sand castle building (led by a professional sand carver), a magic show, and live music. Throughout the day, get out in nature and explore Seabrook's Gnome Trail that winds through the town's "enchanted forest" where visitors have been creating whimsical gnome homes and fairy castles throughout the summer to welcome the wee folk. ✉ *4275 SR 109, Pacific Beach* ☎ *877/779–9990* ⊕ *www.seabrookwa.com.*

Irrigation Festival

FESTIVAL | For more than a century, the people of Sequim have been celebrating the irrigation ditches that brought life-giving water here. Highlights of the 10-day festival include a beauty pageant, logging demonstrations, arts and crafts, a classic car show, a strongman competition, parades, and a picnic. ✉ *Sequim* ☎ *360/461–6511* ⊕ *www.irrigationfestival.com.*

Olympic Music Festival

FESTIVAL | A variety of classical concerts are performed in a renovated barn on weekends from July through early September; picnic on the farm while you listen. ☎ *360/385–9699 office, 800/838–3006 tickets* ⊕ *www.olympicmusicfestival.org.*

Sequim Lavender Festival

FESTIVAL | The third weekend in July, a street fair and free self-guided farm tours celebrate Sequim's many fragrant lavender fields. There's also live music outdoors throughout the weekend, and a street dance Saturday night. ✉ *Sequim* ☎ *360/681–3035* ⊕ *www.lavenderfestival.com.*

Wooden Boat Festival

FESTIVAL | Hundreds of antique boats sail into Port Townsend for the weekend; there's also live music, education programs, and demonstrations. ✉ *Port Townsend* ☎ *360/385–3628* ⊕ *www.woodenboat.org.*

PLANNING YOUR TIME
OLYMPIC IN ONE DAY

Start at the **Lake Quinault Lodge** in the park's southwest corner. From here, drive a half hour into the Quinault Valley via **South Shore Road.** Tackle the forested **Graves Creek Trail,** then head up **North Shore Road** to the Quinault Rain Forest Interpretive Trail. Next, head back to U.S. 101 and drive to **Ruby Beach,** where a shoreline walk presents a breathtaking scene of sea stacks and sparkling, pink-hue sands.

Forks and its **Timber Museum** are your next stop; have lunch here, then drive 20 minutes to the beach at **La Push.** Next, head to **Lake Crescent** around the corner to the northeast, where you can rent a boat, take a swim, or enjoy a picnic next to the sparkling teal waters. Drive through **Port Angeles** to **Hurricane Ridge;** count on an hour's drive from bottom to top if there aren't too many visitors. At the ridge, explore the visitor center or hike the 3-mile loop to **Hurricane Hill,** where you can see over the entire park north to Vancouver Island and south past Mt. Olympus.

GETTING HERE AND AROUND

You can enter the park at a number of points, but because the park is 95% wilderness, access roads do not penetrate

AVERAGE HIGH/LOW TEMPERATURES					
JAN.	**FEB.**	**MAR.**	**APR.**	**MAY**	**JUNE**
45/33	48/35	51/36	55/39	60/44	65/48
JULY	**AUG.**	**SEPT.**	**OCT.**	**NOV.**	**DEC.**
68/50	69/51	66/48	58/42	50/37	45/34

far. The best way to get around and to see many of the park's top sites is on foot.

AIR TRAVEL

Seattle–Tacoma International Airport is the nearest airport to Olympic National Park. It's roughly a two-hour drive from the park.

BOAT TRAVEL

Ferries provide another unique (though indirect) link to the Olympic area from Seattle; contact **Washington State Ferries** (☎ 800/843–3779, 206/464–6400 ⊕ www.wsdot.wa.gov/ferries) for information.

BUS TRAVEL

Grays Harbor Transit runs buses Monday through Saturday from Aberdeen and Hoquiam to Amanda Park, on the west end of Lake Quinault. Jefferson Transit operates a Forks–Amanda Park route Monday through Saturday.

BUS CONTACTS Grays Harbor Transit ☎ 360/532–2770, 800/562–9730 ⊕ www.ghtransit.com. **Jefferson Transit** ☎ 800/371–0497, 360/385–4777 ⊕ www.jeffersontransit.com.

CAR TRAVEL

U.S. 101 essentially encircles the main section of Olympic National Park, and a number of roads lead from the highway into the park's mountains and toward its beaches. You can reach U.S. 101 via Interstate 5 at Olympia, via Route 12 at Aberdeen, or via Route 104 from the Washington state ferry terminals at Bainbridge or Kingston.

PARK ESSENTIALS

ACCESSIBILITY

There are wheelchair-accessible facilities—including trails, campgrounds, and visitor centers—throughout the park; contact visitor centers for information.

ADMISSION FEES AND PERMITS

Seven-day vehicle admission is $25; an annual pass is $50. Individuals arriving on foot, bike, or motorcycle pay $10. An overnight wilderness permit, available at visitor centers and ranger stations, is $7 per person per night. An annual wilderness camping permit costs $45. Fishing in freshwater streams and lakes within Olympic National Park does not require a Washington state fishing license; however, anglers must acquire a salmon-on-steelhead catch record card when fishing for those species. Ocean fishing and harvesting shellfish require licenses, which are available at sporting-goods and outdoor-supply stores.

ADMISSION HOURS

Six park entrances are open 24/7; gate kiosk hours (for buying passes) vary according to season and location, but most are staffed during daylight hours. Olympic National Park is in the Pacific time zone.

CELL PHONE RECEPTION

Note that cell reception is sketchy in wilderness areas. There are public telephones at the Olympic National Park Visitor Center, Hoh River Rain Forest Visitor Center, and lodging properties within the park—Lake Crescent, Kalaloch, and Sol Duc Hot Springs. Fairholme General Store also has a phone.

Good Reads

■ Robert L. Wood's *Olympic Mountains Trail Guide* is a great resource for both day hikers and those planning longer excursions.

■ Craig Romano's *Day Hiking Olympic Peninsula: National Park/Coastal Beaches/Southwest Washington* is a detailed guide to day hikes in and around the national park.

■ Stephen Whitney's *A Field Guide to the Cascades and Olympics* is an excellent trailside reference, covering more than 500 plant and animal species found in the park.

■ The park's newspaper, the *Olympic Bugler*, is a seasonal guide for activities and opportunities in the park. You can pick it up at the visitor centers.

■ A handy online catalog of books, maps, and passes for northwest parks is available from Discover Your Northwest (⊕ *www.discovernw.org*).

EDUCATIONAL OFFERINGS
CLASSES AND SEMINARS
NatureBridge

COLLEGE | FAMILY | This rustic educational facility offers talks and excursions focusing on park ecology and history. Trips range from canoe trips to camping excursions, with a strong emphasis on family programs. ✉ *111 Barnes Point Rd., Port Angeles* ☎ *360/928–3720* ⊕ *www. naturebridge.org/olympic.*

RANGER PROGRAMS
Junior Ranger Program

TOUR—SIGHT | FAMILY | Anyone can pick up the booklet at visitor centers and ranger stations and follow this fun program, which includes assignments to discover park flora and fauna, ocean life, and Native American lore. Kids get a badge when they turn in the finished work. Kids can also earn an "Ocean Steward" badge by doing activities in another booklet that teaches about the park's coastal ecosystem. ✉ *Olympic National Park* ☎ *360/565–3130* ⊕ *www.nps.gov/olym/ learn/kidsyouth/beajuniorranger.htm.*

RESTAURANTS
The major resorts are your best bets for eating out in the park. Each has a main restaurant, café, and/or kiosk, as well as casually upscale dinner service, with regional seafood, meat, and produce complemented by a range of microbrews and good Washington and international wines. Reservations are either recommended or required.

Outside the park, small, easygoing cafés and bistros line the main thoroughfares in Sequim, Port Angeles, and Port Townsend, offering cuisine that ranges from hearty American-style fare to more eclectic local flavor.

HOTELS
Major park resorts run from good to terrific, with generally comfortable rooms, excellent facilities, and easy access to trails, beaches, and activity centers. Midsize accommodations, like Sol Duc Hot Springs Resort, are often shockingly rustic—but remember, you're here for the park, not for the rooms.

The towns around the park have motels, hotels, and resorts for every budget. For a full beach-town vacation experience, base yourself in a home or cottage in the coastal community of Seabrook (near Pacific Beach). Sequim and Port Angeles have many attractive, friendly B&Bs, plus lots of inexpensive chain hotels and motels. Forks has mostly motels, with a few guesthouses on the fringes of town.

Hotel reviews have been shortened. For full information, visit Fodors.com.

What It Costs			
$	$$	$$$	$$$$
RESTAURANTS			
under $12	$12–$20	$21–$30	over $30
HOTELS			
under $100	$100–$150	$151–$200	over $200

VISITOR INFORMATION

PARK CONTACT INFORMATION Olympic National Park ⊠ *Olympic National Park Visitor Center, 3002 Mount Angeles Rd., Port Angeles* ☎ *360/565–3130* ⊕ *www. nps.gov/olym.*

VISITOR CENTERS

Hoh Rain Forest Visitor Center
INFO CENTER | Pick up park maps and pamphlets, permits, and activities lists in this busy, woodsy chalet; there's also a shop and exhibits on natural history. Several short interpretive trails and longer wilderness treks start from here. ⊠ *Hoh Valley Rd., Forks* ✛ *31 miles south of Forks* ☎ *360/374–6925* ⊕ *www.nps.gov/olym/ planyourvisit/visitorcenters.htm* ☾ *Closed Jan., Feb., and Mon.–Thurs. off-season.*

Hurricane Ridge Visitor Center
INFO CENTER | The upper level of this visitor center has exhibits and nice views; the lower level has a gift shop and snack bar. Guided walks and programs start in late June. In winter, find details on the surrounding ski and sledding slopes and take guided snowshoe walks. ⊠ *Hurricane Ridge Rd.* ☎ *360/565–3131 for road conditions* ⊕ *www.nps.gov/olym/*

planyourvisit/visitorcenters.htm ☾ *Operating hrs/days vary off-season.*

Olympic National Park Visitor Center
INFO CENTER | This modern, well-organized facility, staffed by park rangers, provides everything: maps, trail brochures, campground advice, weather forecasts, listings of wildlife sightings, educational programs and exhibits, information on road and trail closures, and a gift shop. ⊠ *3002 Mount Angeles Rd., Port Angeles* ☎ *360/565–3130* ⊕ *www.nps.gov/olym/ planyourvisit/visitorcenters.htm.*

South Shore Quinault Ranger Station
INFO CENTER | The National Forest Service's ranger station near the Lake Quinault Lodge has maps, campground information, and program listings. ⊠ *353 S. Shore Rd., Quinault* ☎ *360/288–2525* ⊕ *www.fs.usda.gov/main/olympic/home* ☾ *Closed weekends after Labor Day until Memorial Day weekend.*

Wilderness Information Center (WIC)
INFO CENTER | Located behind Olympic National Park Visitor Center, this facility provides all the information you'll need for a trip in the park, including trail conditions, safety tips, and weather bulletins. The office also issues camping permits, takes campground reservations, and rents bear-proof food canisters. ⊠ *3002 Mount Angeles Rd., Port Angeles* ☎ *360/565–3100* ⊕ *www.nps.gov/olym/ planyourvisit/wic.htm* ☾ *Hrs vary during off-season.*

 Sights

Most of the park's attractions are found either off U.S. 101 or down trails that require hikes of 15 minutes or longer. The west-coast beaches are linked to the highway by downhill tracks; the number of cars parked alongside the road at the start of the paths indicates how crowded the beach will be.

SCENIC DRIVES
★ Port Angeles Visitor Center to Hurricane Ridge
MOUNTAIN—SIGHT | The premier scenic drive in Olympic National Park is a steep ribbon of curves, which climbs from thickly forested foothills and subalpine meadows into the upper stretches of pine-swathed peaks. At the top, the visitor center at Hurricane Ridge has some spectacular views over the heart of the peninsula and across the Strait of Juan de Fuca. A mile past the visitor center, there are picnic tables in open meadows with photo-worthy views of the mountains to the east. Hurricane Ridge also has an uncommonly fine display of wildflowers in spring and summer. In winter, vehicles must carry chains and the road is usually open Friday–Sunday only (call first to check conditions). ⊠ *Olympic National Park* ⊕ *www.nps.gov/olym.*

HISTORIC SITES
La Push
BEACH—SIGHT | At the mouth of Quileute River, La Push is the tribal center of the Quileute Indians. In fact, the town's name is a variation on the French *la bouche,* which means "the mouth." Offshore rock spires known as sea stacks dot the coast here, and you may catch a glimpse of bald eagles nesting in the nearby cliffs. ⊠ *Rte. 110, La Push* ✛ *14 miles west of Forks* ⊕ *www.nps.gov/olym/planyourvisit/upload/mora.pdf.*

Lake Ozette
BEACH—SIGHT | The third-largest glacial impoundment in Washington anchors the coastal strip of Olympic National Park at its north end. The small town of Ozette, home to a coastal tribe, is the trailhead for two of the park's better one-day hikes. Both 3-mile trails lead over boardwalks through swampy wetland and coastal old-growth forest to the ocean shore and uncrowded beaches. ⊠ *Ozette* ✛ *At end of Hoko-Ozette Rd., 26 miles southwest of Hwy. 112 near Sekiu* ☎ *360/565–3130*

Ozette Ranger Station ⊕ *www.nps.gov/olym/planyourvisit/visiting-ozette.htm.*

SCENIC STOPS
★ Hoh River Rain Forest
FOREST | South of Forks, an 18-mile spur road links Highway 101 with this unique temperate rain forest, where spruce and hemlock trees soar to heights of more than 200 feet. Alders and big-leaf maples are so densely covered with mosses they look more like shaggy prehistoric animals than trees, and elk browse in shaded glens. Be prepared for precipitation: the region receives 140 inches or more each year. ⊠ *Olympic National Park* ✛ *From Hwy. 101, at about 20 miles north of Kalaloch, turn onto Upper Hoh Rd. 18 miles east to Hoh Rain Forest Visitor Center* ☎ *360/374–6925* ⊕ *www.nps.gov/olym/planyourvisit/visiting-the-hoh.htm.*

★ Hurricane Ridge
MOUNTAIN—SIGHT | The panoramic view from this 5,200-foot-high ridge encompasses the Olympic range, the Strait of Juan de Fuca, and Vancouver Island. Guided tours are given in summer along the many paved and unpaved trails, where wildflowers and wildlife such as deer and marmots flourish. ⊠ *Hurricane Ridge Rd.* ✛ *17 miles south of Port Angeles* ☎ *360/565–3130 visitor center* ⊕ *www.nps.gov/olym/planyourvisit/visiting-hurricane-ridge.htm* ⊗ *Closed when road is closed.*

Kalaloch
BEACH—SIGHT | With a lodge and restaurant, a huge campground, miles of coastline, and easy access from the highway, this is a popular spot. Keen-eyed beachcombers may spot sea otters just offshore; they were reintroduced here in 1970. ⊠ *Hwy. 101, Kalaloch* ✛ *32 miles northwest of Lake Quinault* ☎ *360/565–3130 visitor center, 360/962–2283 ranger station* ⊕ *www.nps.gov/olym/planyourvisit/visiting-kalaloch-and-ruby-beach.htm.*

Did You Know?

Encompassing more than 70 miles of beachfront, Olympic is one of the few national parks of the West with an ocean beach (Redwood, Channel Islands, and some of the Alaskan parks are the others). The park is therefore home to many marine animals, including sea otters, whales, sea lions, and seals.

Plants and Wildlife in Olympic

Along the high mountain slopes hardy cedar, fir, and hemlock trees stand tough on the rugged land; the lower montane forests are filled with thickets of silver firs; and valleys stream with Douglas firs and western hemlock. The park's famous temperate rain forests are on the peninsula's western side, marked by broad western red cedars, towering red spruces, and ferns festooned with strands of mosses and patchwork lichens. This lower landscape is also home to some of the Northwest's largest trees: massive cedar and Sitka spruce near Lake Quinault can measure more than 700 inches around, and Douglas firs near the Queets and Hoh rivers are nearly as wide.

These landscapes are home to a variety of wildlife, including many large mammals and 15 creatures found nowhere else in the world. Hikers often come across Roosevelt's elk, black-tailed deer, mountain goats, beavers, raccoons, skunks, opossums, and foxes; Douglas squirrels and flying squirrels populate the heights of the forest. Less common are black bears (most prevalent from May through August); wolves, bobcats, and cougar are rarely seen. Birdlife includes bald eagles, red-tailed hawks, osprey, and great horned owls. Rivers and lakes are filled with freshwater fish, while beaches hold crabs, sea stars, anemones, and other shelled creatures. Get out in a boat on the Pacific to spot seals, sea lions, and sea otters—and perhaps a pod of porpoises, orcas, or gray whales.

Beware of jellyfish around the shores—beached jellyfish can still sting. In the woods, check for ticks after every hike and after each shower. Biting nasties include black flies, horseflies, sand fleas, and the ever-present mosquitoes. Yellow-jacket nests populate tree hollows along many trails; signs throughout the Hoh Rain Forest warn hikers to move quickly through these sections. If one or two chase you, remain calm and keep walking; these are just "guards" making sure you're keeping away from the hive. Poison oak is common, so familiarize yourself with its appearance. Bug repellent, sunscreen, and long pants and sleeves will go a long way toward making your experience more comfortable.

Lake Crescent

BODY OF WATER | Visitors see Lake Crescent as Highway 101 winds along its southern shore, giving way to gorgeous views of teal waters rippling in a basin formed by Tuscan-like hills. In the evening, low bands of clouds caught between the surrounding mountains often linger over its reflective surface. ⊠ Hwy. 101 ✛ 16 miles west of Port Angeles and 28 miles northeast of Forks ☎ 360/565–3130 visitor center ⊕ www.nps.gov/olym/planyourvisit/visiting-lake-crescent.htm.

Lake Quinault

BODY OF WATER | This glimmering lake, 4½ miles long and 300 feet deep, is the first landmark you'll reach when driving the west-side loop of U.S. 101. The rain forest is thickest here, with moss-draped maples and alders, and towering spruce, fir, and hemlock. Enchanted Valley, high up near the Quinault River's source, is a deeply glaciated valley that's closer to the Hood Canal than to the Pacific Ocean. A scenic loop drive circles the lake and travels around a section of the Quinault River. ⊠ Hwy. 101 ✛ 38 miles north of

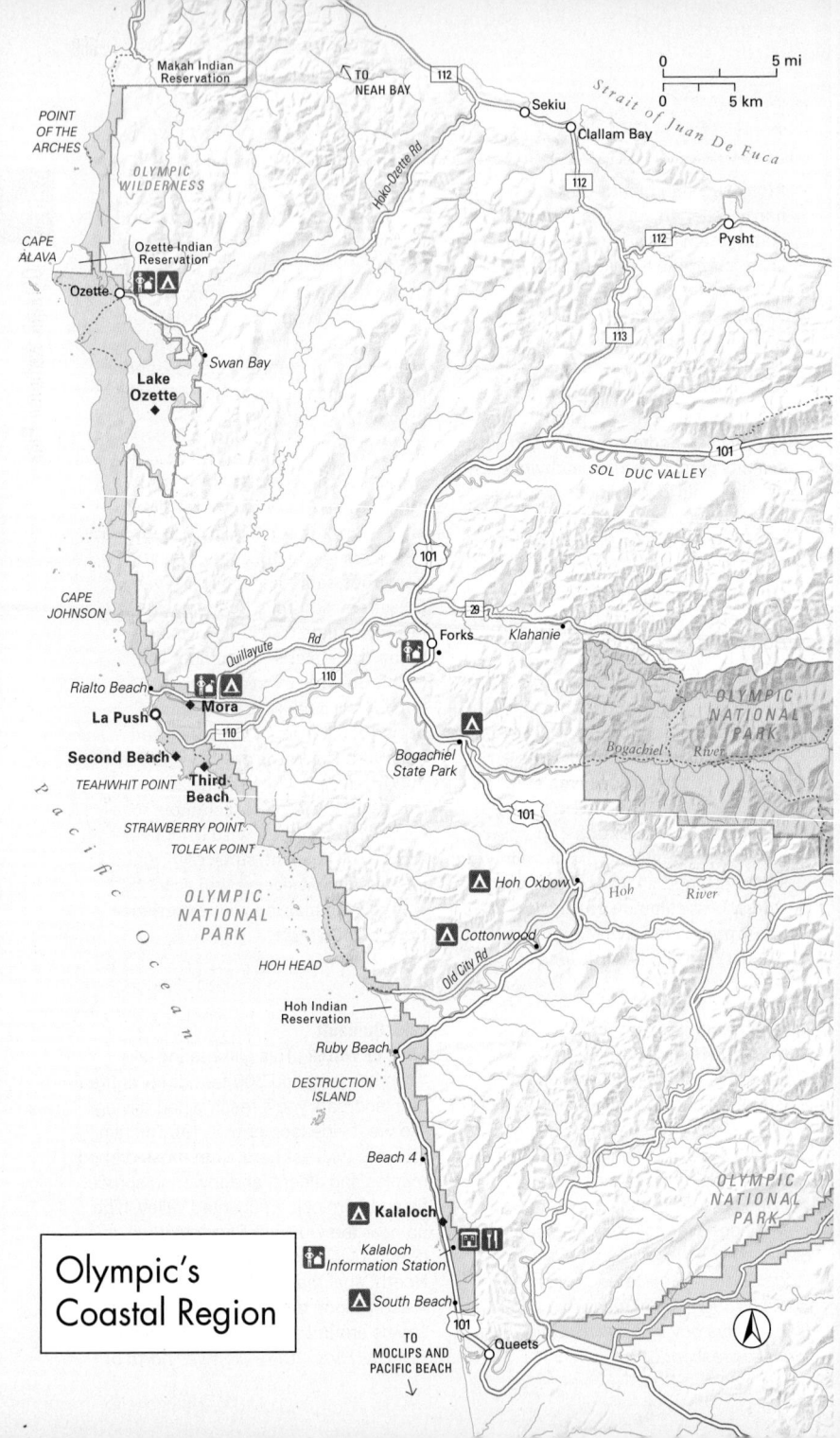

Olympic's Coastal Region

Hoquiam ☎ 360/288–2525 Quinault Rain Forest ranger station ⊕ www.nps.gov/olym/planyourvisit/visiting-quinault.htm.

Second and Third Beaches

BEACH—SIGHT | During low tide these flat, driftwood-strewn expanses are perfect for long afternoon strolls. Second Beach, accessed via an easy forest trail through Quileute lands, opens to a vista of Pacific Ocean and sea stacks. Third Beach offers a 1¼-mile forest hike for a warm-up before reaching the sands. ⊠ Hwy. 101 ✛ 32 miles north of Lake Quinault ☎ 360/565–3130 visitor center ⊕ www.nps.gov/olym.

Sol Duc

BODY OF WATER | Sol Duc Valley is one of those magical places where all the Northwest's virtues seem at hand: lush lowland forests, sparkling river scenes, salmon runs, and serene hiking trails. Here, the popular Sol Duc Hot Springs area includes three attractive sulfuric pools ranging in temperature from 98°F to 104°F. ⊠ Sol Duc Rd. ✛ South of U.S. 101, 12 miles past west end of Lake Crescent ☎ 360/565–3130 visitor center ⊕ www.nps.gov/olym/planyourvisit/visiting-the-sol-duc-valley.htm.

Staircase

INFO CENTER | Unlike the forests of the park's south and west sides, Douglas fir is the dominant tree on the east slope of the Olympic Mountains. Fire has played an important role in creating the majestic forest here, as the Staircase Ranger Station explains in interpretive exhibits. ⊠ Olympic National Park ✛ At end of Rte. 119, 15 miles from U.S. 101 at Hoodsport ☎ 360/565–3130 visitor center ⊕ www.nps.gov/olym/planyourvisit/visiting-staircase.htm.

 ## Activities

BICYCLING

The rough gravel car tracks to some of the park's remote sites were meant for four-wheel-drive vehicles, but can double as mountain-bike routes. The Quinault Valley, Queets River, Hoh River, and Sol Duc River roads have bike paths through old-growth forest. Graves Creek Road, in the southwest, is a mountain-bike path; Lake Crescent's north side is also edged by the bike-friendly Spruce Railroad Trail. More bike tracks run through the adjacent Olympic National Forest. Note that U.S. 101 has heavy traffic and isn't recommended for cycling, although the western side has broad roads with beautiful scenery and can be biked off-season. Bikes are not permitted on foot trails.

Ben's Bikes

BICYCLING | This bike, gear, and repair shop is a great resource for advice on routes around the Olympic Peninsula, including the Olympic Discovery Trail. They can deliver bikes to local lodgings and to the ferry docks in Port Angeles and Port Townsend. They rent a variety of different styles, with rentals starting at $30 per day and $110 per week. ⊠ 1251 W. Washington St., Sequim ☎ 360/683–2666 ⊕ www.bensbikessequim.com.

Sound Bike & Kayak

BICYCLING | This sports outfitter rents and sells bikes, and sells kayaks, climbing gear, and related equipment. They offer several guided mountain climbs, day hikes, and custom trips, and a climbing wall to practice skills. Bike rentals start at $10 per hour and $45 per day. ⊠ 120 E. Front St., Port Angeles ☎ 360/457–1240 ⊕ www.soundbikeskayaks.com.

CLIMBING

At 7,980 feet, Mt. Olympus is the highest peak in the park and the most popular climb in the region. To attempt the summit, climbers must register at the Glacier Meadows Ranger Station. Mt.

Constance, the third-highest Olympic peak at 7,743 feet, has a well-traversed climbing route that requires technical experience; reservations are recommended for the Lake Constance stop, which is limited to 20 campers. Mt. Deception is another possibility, though tricky snows have caused fatalities and injuries in the last decade.

Climbing season runs from late June through September. Note that crevasse skills and self-rescue experience are highly recommended. Climbers must register with park officials and purchase wilderness permits before setting out. The best resource for climbing advice is the Wilderness Information Center in Port Angeles.

Mountain Madness

CLIMBING/MOUNTAINEERING | Adventure through the rain forest to the glaciated summit of Mt. Olympus on a five-day trip, offered several times per year by Mountain Madness. ☎ *800/328–5925, 206/937–8389* ⊕ *www.mountainmadness.com* ✉ *From $1350 for 5-day climb.*

FISHING

There are numerous fishing possibilities throughout the park. Lake Crescent is home to cutthroat and rainbow trout, as well as petite kokanee salmon; Lake Cushman, Lake Quinault, and Ozette Lake have trout, salmon, and steelhead. As for rivers, the Bogachiel and Queets have steelhead salmon in season. The glacier-fed Hoh River is home to chinook salmon April to November, and coho salmon from August through November; the Sol Duc River offers all five species of salmon. The Elwha River has been undergoing restoration since two dams were removed; strong salmon and steelhead runs are expected to return, although a fishing moratorium has been in place for several years. Other places to go after salmon and trout include the Dosewallips, Duckabush, Quillayute, Quinault, Salmon, and Skokomish rivers. A Washington state punch card is required during salmon-spawning months; fishing regulations vary throughout the park and some areas are for catch and release only. Punch cards are available from sporting-goods and outdoor-supply stores.

Bob's Piscatorial Pursuits

FISHING | This company, based in Forks, offers salmon and steelhead fishing trips around the Olympic Peninsula from mid-October through May. ✉ *Forks* ☎ *866/347–4232* ⊕ *www.piscatorialpursuits.com* ✉ *From $225.*

HIKING

Know your tides, or you might be trapped by high water. Tide tables are available at all visitor centers and ranger stations. Remember that a wilderness permit is required for all overnight backcountry visits.

Cape Alava Trail

HIKING/WALKING | Beginning at Ozette, this 3-mile boardwalk trail leads from the forest to wave-tossed headlands. *Moderate.* ✉ *Ozette* ✛ *Trailhead: end of Hoko-Ozette Rd., 26 miles south of Hwy. 112, west of Sekiu* ⊕ *www.nps.gov/olym/planyourvisit/visiting-ozette.htm.*

Graves Creek Trail

HIKING/WALKING | This 6-mile-long moderately strenuous trail climbs from lowland rain forest to alpine territory at Sundown Pass. Due to spring floods, a fjord halfway up is often impassable in May and June. *Moderate.* ✉ *Olympic National Park* ✛ *Trailhead: end of S. Shore Rd., 23 miles east of U.S. 101* ⊕ *www.nps.gov/olym.*

High Divide Trail

HIKING/WALKING | A 9-mile hike in the park's high country defines this trail, which includes some strenuous climbing on its last 4 miles before topping out at a small alpine lake. A return loop along High Divide wends its way an extra mile through alpine territory, with sensational views of Olympic peaks. This trail is only for dedicated, properly equipped hikers who are in good shape. *Difficult.* ⊠ *Olympic National Park* ⊹ *Trailhead: end of Sol Duc River Rd., 13 miles south of U.S. 101* ⊕ *www.nps.gov/olym/planyourvisit/high-divide-loop.htm.*

★ Hoh River Trail

HIKING/WALKING | FAMILY | From the Hoh Visitor Center, this rain-forest jaunt takes you into the Hoh Valley, wending its way for 17½ miles alongside the river, through moss-draped maple and alder trees and past open meadows where elk roam in winter. *Easy.* ⊠ *Olympic National Park* ⊹ *Trailhead: Hoh Visitor Center, 18 miles east of U.S. 101* ⊕ *www.nps.gov/olym/planyourvisit/hoh-river-trail.htm.*

Hurricane Ridge Meadow Trail

HIKING/WALKING | A ¼-mile alpine loop, most of it wheelchair accessible, leads through wildflower meadows overlooking numerous vistas of the interior Olympic peaks to the south and a panorama of the Strait of Juan de Fuca to the north. *Easy.* ⊠ *Olympic National Park* ⊹ *Trailhead: Hurricane Ridge Rd., 17 miles south of Port Angeles* ⊕ *www.nps.gov/olym/planyourvisit/visiting-hurricane-ridge.htm.*

★ Sol Duc River Trail

HIKING/WALKING | FAMILY | The 1½-mile gravel path off Sol Duc Road winds through thick Douglas fir forests toward the thundering, three-chute Sol Duc Falls. Just off the road, below a wooden platform over the Sol Duc River, you'll come across the 70-foot Salmon Cascades. In late summer and autumn, thousands of salmon negotiate 50 miles or more of treacherous waters to reach the cascades and the tamer pools near Sol Duc Hot Springs. The popular 6-mile **Lovers Lane Loop Trail** links the Sol Duc falls with the hot springs. You can continue up from the falls 5 miles to the **Appleton Pass Trail,** at 3,100 feet. From there you can hike on to the 8½-mile mark, where views at the High Divide are from 5,050 feet. *Moderate.* ⊠ *Olympic National Park* ⊹ *Trailhead: Sol Duc Rd., 12 miles south of U.S. 101*

⊕ *www.nps.gov/olym/planyourvisit/sol-duc-river-trail.htm.*

KAYAKING AND CANOEING

Lake Crescent, a serene expanse of teal-color waters surrounded by deep-green pine forests, is one of the park's best boating areas. Note that the west end is for swimming only; no speedboats are allowed here.

Lake Quinault has boating access from a gravel ramp on the north shore. From U.S. 101, take a right on North Shore Road, another right on Hemlock Way, and a left on Lakeview Drive. There are plank ramps at Falls Creek and Willoughby campgrounds on South Shore Drive, 0.1 mile and 0.2 mile past the Quinault Ranger Station, respectively.

Lake Ozette, with just one access road, is a good place for overnight trips. Only experienced canoe and kayak handlers should travel far from the put-in, since fierce storms occasionally strike—even in summer.

Fairholme General Store

CANOEING/ROWING/SKULLING | Kayaks and canoes on Lake Crescent are available to rent from $20 per hour to $60 for eight hours. The store is at the lake's west end, 27 miles west of Port Angeles. Closed after Labor Day until Memorial Day weekend. ⊠ *221121 U.S. 101, Port Angeles* ☎ *360/928–3020* ⊕ *www.olympicnationalparks.com* ⊘ *Closed after Labor Day– Apr. and Mon.–Thurs. in May.*

Lake Crescent Lodge

CANOEING/ROWING/SKULLING | You can rent canoes, kayaks, and paddleboards here for $20 per hour and $60 for a full day. Two-hour guided kayak tours are offered and include instructions; they cost $55 in a single kayak and $75 in a double kayak. ⊠ *416 Lake Crescent Rd.* ☎ *360/928– 3211* ⊕ *www.olympicnationalparks.com* ⊘ *Closed Jan.–Apr.*

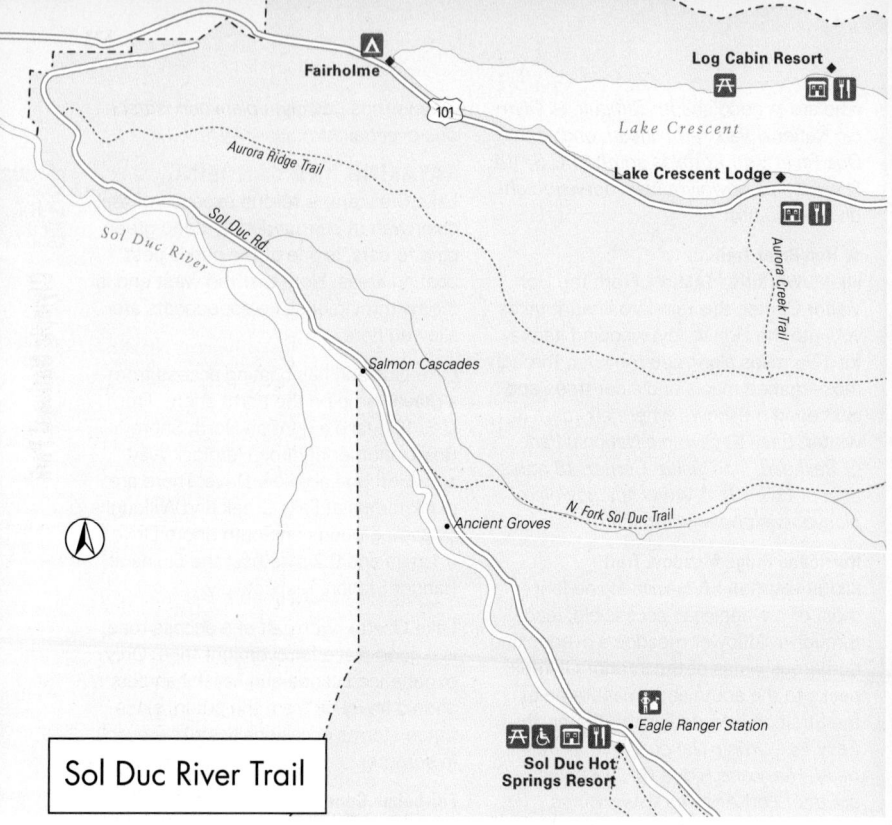

Sol Duc River Trail

Log Cabin Resort
CANOEING/ROWING/SKULLING | This resort, 17 miles west of Port Angeles, has paddle boat, kayak, canoe, and paddleboard rentals for $20 per hour and $60 per day. The dock provides easy access to Lake Crescent's northeast section. ⊠ *3183 E. Beach Rd., Port Angeles* ☎ *360/928–3325* ⊕ *www.olympicnationalparks.com* ⊘ *Closed Oct.–mid-May.*

Rainforest Paddlers
KAYAKING | This company takes kayakers down the Hoh River to explore the rain forest, and down the Quillayute through the estuary to La Push. Rafting trips are offered on both the Hoh and Sol Duc rivers. They also rent kayaks and mountain bikes. ⊠ *4883 Upper Hoh Rd., Forks* ☎ *360/374–5254, 866/457–8398* ⊕ *www. rainforestpaddlers.com* ☝ *Tours from $44; kayak rentals from $11/hr.*

RAFTING
Olympic has excellent rafting rivers, with Class II to Class V rapids. The Elwha River is a popular place to paddle, with some exciting turns. The Hoh is better for those who like a smooth, easy float.

Adventures Through Kayaking
WHITE-WATER RAFTING | This outfitter offers 3½-hour trips twice daily on the Sol Duc River in spring. Cost is $79/person and includes all gear. Beginners are welcome but kids must be 12 or older. Check-in is at the Sol Duc Hatchery. ⊠ *Sol Duc Hatchery, 1423 Pavel Rd., Beaver* ☎ *360/417–3015* ⊕ *www.atkayaking.com.*

WINTER ACTIVITIES
Hurricane Ridge is the central spot for winter sports. Miles of downhill and Nordic ski tracks are open late December through March, and a ski lift, tow-ropes, and ski school are open 10 to 4

weekends and holidays. A snow-play area for children ages eight and younger is near the Hurricane Ridge Visitors Center. Hurricane Ridge Road is open Friday through Sunday in the winter season; all vehicles are required to carry chains.

Hurricane Ridge Visitor Center

SNOW SPORTS | Rent snowshoes and ski equipment here December through March. ✉ *Hurricane Ridge Rd., Port Angeles* ☎ *360/565–3131 road condition information* ⊕ *www.nps.gov/olym/plan-yourvisit/hurricane-ridge-in-winter.htm* ⊘ *Closed Mon.–Thurs.*

Nearby Towns

Although most Olympic Peninsula towns have evolved from their exclusive reliance on timber, **Forks,** outside the national park's northwest tip, remains one of the region's logging capitals. Washington state's wettest town (100 inches or more of rain a year), it's a small, friendly place with just under 3,800 residents and a modicum of visitor facilities. **Port Angeles,** a city of around 20,000, focuses on its status as the main gateway to Olympic National Park and Victoria, British Columbia. Set below the Strait of Juan de Fuca and looking north to Vancouver Island, it's an enviably scenic settlement filled with attractive, Craftsman-style homes.

The Pacific Northwest has its very own "Banana Belt" in the waterfront community of **Sequim,** 15 miles east of Port Angeles along U.S. 101. The town of 6,900 is in the rain shadow of the Olympics and receives only 16 inches of rain per year (compared with the 140-170 inches that drench the Hoh Rain Forest just 40 miles away). The beach community of **Seabrook,** near Pacific Beach, is 25 miles from the southeast corner of the national park via the Moclips Highway. Created in 2004 as a pedestrian-friendly beach town, many of its several hundred Cape Cod-style cottage homes are available for short-term rentals; the community

has parks, swimming pools, bike trails, beach access, special events, and a growing retail district.

VISITOR INFORMATION Forks Chamber of Commerce Visitor Center ✉ *1411 S. Forks Ave. (U.S. 101), Forks* ☎ *800/443–6757, 360/374–2531* ⊕ *www.forkswa.com.* **Port Angeles Chamber of Commerce Visitor Center** ✉ *121 E. Railroad Ave., Port Angeles* ☎ *360/452–2363* ⊕ *www.portangeles.org.* **Sequim-Dungeness Valley Chamber of Commerce** ✉ *1192 E. Washington St., Sequim* ☎ *360/683–6197, 800/737–8462* ⊕ *www.sequimchamber.com.*

◉ Sights

★ Dungeness Spit

BEACH—SIGHT | FAMILY | Curving 5½ miles into the Strait of Juan de Fuca, the longest natural sand spit in the United States is a wild, beautiful section of shoreline. More than 30,000 migratory waterfowl stop here each spring and fall, but you'll see plenty of birdlife any time of year. The entire spit is part of the **Dungeness National Wildlife Refuge.** Access it through the **Dungeness Recreation Area,** which serves as a portal to the shoreline. ✉ *554 Voice of America Rd., Sequim* ✛ *Entrance 3 miles north from U.S. 101, 4 miles west of Sequim* ☎ *360/457–8451 wildlife refuge* ⊕ *www.clallam.net/parks/dungeness.html (recreation area); www.fws.gov/refuge/Dungeness (wildlife refuge)* ▨ *$3 per family.*

New Dungeness Lighthouse

BEACH—SIGHT | At the end of the Dungeness Spit is the towering white 1857 New Dungeness Lighthouse; tours are available, though access is limited to those who can hike or kayak out 5 miles to the end of the spit. Guests also have the opportunity to serve as lighthouse keepers for a week at a time. An adjacent, 66-site camping area, on the bluff above the Strait of Juan de Fuca, is open year-round. ✉ *Sequim* ✛ *Entrance 3 miles north of Hwy. 101 via Kitchen Dick Rd.*

☏ *360/683–6638* ⊕ *www.newdunge-nesslighthouse.com.*

Olympic Discovery Trail

TRAIL | Eventually, 140 miles of nonmotorized trail will lead from Port Townsend west to the Pacific coast. As of this writing, 80 miles of the paved trail are complete and available for use by hikers, bikers, equestrians, and disabled users. The trail has been conceived as the northern portion of a route that will eventually encircle the entire Olympic Peninsula. ⊕ *www.olympicdiscoverytrail. org.*

Port Angeles Fine Arts Center

ARTS VENUE | This small, sophisticated museum is inside the former home of late artist and publisher Esther Barrows Webster, one of Port Angeles's most energetic and cultured citizens; displays are modern, funky, and intriguing. Outside, Webster's Woods Art Park is dotted with oversize sculptures set before a vista of the city and harbor. Exhibitions emphasize the works of emerging and well-established Pacific Northwest artists. ✉ *1203 E. Lauridsen Blvd., Port Angeles* ☏ *360/457–3532* ⊕ *www.pafac. org* ⌕ *Free* ⊗ *Closed Oct.–Mar.*

Timber Museum

MUSEUM | The museum highlights Forks's logging history since the 1870s; a garden and fire tower are also on the grounds. ✉ *1421 S. Forks Ave., Forks* ☏ *360/374–9663* ⊕ *www.forkstimbermuseum.org* ⌕ *$3.*

 Restaurants

IN THE PARK

Creekside Restaurant

$$$ | **AMERICAN** | A tranquil country setting and ocean views at Kalaloch Lodge's restaurant create the perfect backdrop for savoring Pacific Northwest dinner specialties like grilled salmon, fresh shellfish, and elk burgers. Tempting seasonal desserts include local fruit tarts and cobblers in summer and organic winter squash bread pudding in winter; flourless chocolate torte is enjoyed year-round. **Known for:** locally sourced food; Washington wines. $ *Average main: $26* ✉ *157151 Hwy. 101, Forks* ☏ *866/662–9928, 360/962–2271* ⊕ *www. thekalalochlodge.com/dine-and-shop/ creekside-restaurant.*

Lake Crescent Lodge

$$$ | **AMERICAN** | Part of the original 1916 lodge, the fir-paneled dining room overlooks the lake; you won't find a better spot for sunset views. Dinner entrées include wild salmon, brown butter basted halibut, grilled steak, and roasted chicken breast; the lunch menu features elk cheeseburgers, inventive salads, and a variety of sandwiches. **Known for:** award-winning Pacific Northwest wine list; house-made lavender lemonade; certified green restaurant. $ *Average main: $29* ✉ *416 Lake Crescent Rd., Port Angeles* ☏ *360/928–3211* ⊕ *www. olympicnationalparks.com/lodging/dining/ lake-crescent-lodge/* ⊗ *Closed Jan.–Apr.*

The Springs Restaurant

$$$ | **AMERICAN** | The main Sol Duc Hot Springs Resort restaurant is a rustic, fir-and-cedar-paneled dining room surrounded by trees. In summer big breakfasts are turned out daily—hikers can fill up on biscuits and sage pork sausage gravy, Grand Marnier French toast, and omelets before hitting the trails; for lighter fare, there's steel cut oatmeal and yogurt and granola parfaits. **Known for:** three breakfast mimosa choices; boxed lunches. $ *Average main: $22* ✉ *12076 Sol Duc Rd., at U.S. 101, Port Angeles* ☏ *360/327–3583* ⊕ *www.olympicnationalparks.com/stay/dining/sol-duc-hot-springs-resort-.aspx* ⊗ *Closed Nov.–late Mar.*

PICNIC AREAS

All Olympic National Park campgrounds have adjacent picnic areas with tables, some shelters, and restrooms, but no cooking facilities. The same is true for major visitor centers, such as Hoh Rain

Did You Know?

Olympic National Park
is home to 13 species of
amphibians (frogs, toads,
and salamanders), includ-
ing the Pacific Tree Frog.
The park is a rare refuge
for these animals, whose
world populations have
been declining due to
air and water pollution
(amphibians live in both
environments, making
them doubly susceptible).

Forest. Drinking water is available at ranger stations, interpretive centers, and inside campgrounds.

East Beach Picnic Area

Set on a grassy meadow overlooking Lake Crescent, this popular swimming spot has six picnic tables and vault toilets. ✉ *East Beach Rd., Port Angeles* ⊕ *At far east end of Lake Crescent, off Hwy. 101, 17 miles west of Port Angeles.*

La Poel Picnic Area

Tall firs lean over a tiny gravel beach at this small picnic area, which has several picnic tables and a splendid view of Pyramid Mountain across Lake Crescent. It's closed October to April. ✉ *Olympic National Park* ⊕ *Off Hwy. 101, 22 miles west of Port Angeles* ⏲ *Closed mid-Oct.–mid-May.*

Rialto Beach Picnic Area

Relatively secluded at the end of the road from Forks, this is one of the premier day-use areas in the park's Pacific coast segment. This site has 12 picnic tables, fire grills, and vault toilets. ✉ *Rte. 110, 14 miles west of Forks, Forks.*

OUTSIDE THE PARK

Alder Wood Bistro

$$ | **ECLECTIC** | An inventive menu of local and organic dishes makes this one of the most popular restaurants in Sequim. Pizzas from the wood-fired oven include creative combinations, such as pesto, wood-fired vegetables, truffled goat cheese, and picked onions. **Known for:** wood-fired specialties like clams, oysters, mussels, pizza, and apple pie; seasonal dishes; alfresco dining. [$] *Average main: $20* ✉ *139 W. Alder St., Sequim* ☎ *360/683–4321* 🌐 *www.alderwoodbistro.com* ⏲ *Closed Sun.–Tues. in summer, Sun.–Wed. off-season.*

★ **Blondie's Plate**

$$$ | **PACIFIC NORTHWEST** | This Sequim bistro in a former church is a popular spot for both locals and tourists, offering local and Northwest-inspired small plates in categories like garden, surf, pasture, and starch. Many of the small plates are $3 off during happy hour. **Known for:** creative cocktails; small space and popular spot (reserve ahead); happy hour 4–5. [$] *Average main: $25* ✉ *134 S. 2nd Ave., Sequim* ☎ *360/683–2233* 🌐 *www.blondiesplate.com* ⏲ *No lunch; closed Sun.*

C'est Si Bon

$$$$ | **FRENCH** | The interior design as well as the food is far more Euro-savvy than is typical on the Olympic Peninsula. A fanciful dining room is done up in bold red hues, with crisp white linens, huge oil paintings, and glittering chandeliers; the spacious solarium takes an equally formal approach. **Known for:** a little piece of Paris in Port Angeles. [$] *Average main: $32* ✉ *23 Cedar Park Rd., Port Angeles* ☎ *360/452–8888* 🌐 *www.cestsib-on-frenchcuisine.com* ⏲ *Closed Mon. No lunch.*

Dockside Grill

$$$ | **PACIFIC NORTHWEST** | With tremendous views of John Wayne Marina and Sequim Bay, this is a fun place to watch boats placidly sail by. The casual yet elegant menu includes Dungeness crab fritters, steamed clams, cedar-plank salmon, bouillabaisse, cioppino, and pasta. **Known for:** steak and seafood with a spectacular waterfront view. [$] *Average main: $21* ✉ *2577 W. Sequim Bay Rd., Sequim* ☎ *360/683–7510* 🌐 *www.docksidegrill-sequim.com* ⏲ *Closed Mon. and Tues.*

Fountain Café

$$ | **ECLECTIC** | Artwork lines the walls of the small, eclectic café tucked inside a historic clapboard building a block off the main drag, where seafood and pasta dishes carry Mediterranean, Moroccan, Italian, and Pacific Northwest influences. Start with panfried oysters or mussels and clams in a pesto-Chardonnay broth. **Known for:** warm gingerbread with vanilla custard and whipped cream; locally famous clam chowder; buffalo frogs' legs. [$] *Average main: $18* ✉ *920 Washington St., Port Townsend* ☎ *360/385–1364* 🌐 *www.fountaincafept.com.*

★ Oak Table Café

$$ | **AMERICAN** | Carefully crafted breakfasts and lunches are the focus of this well-run, family-friendly eatery, a Sequim institution since 1981. Breakfast is served throughout the day, and on Sunday morning the large, well-lit dining room is especially bustling. **Known for:** the Eggs Nicole with veggies and hollandaise sauce on a croissant; humongous apple pancake filled with fresh fruit. $ *Average main: $13* ✉ *292 W. Bell St., Sequim* ☎ *360/683–2179* ⊕ *www.oaktablecafe. com* ⊗ *No dinner, no lunch Sun.*

Toga's Soup House Deli & Gourmet

$$ | **ECLECTIC** | Toga's serves an eclectic menu of casual fare, ranging from homemade soups and fresh salads to hearty sandwiches. The many windows provide views of the Olympic Mountains, and there's also an open-air patio. $ *Average main: $13* ✉ *122 W. Lauridsen Blvd., Port Angeles* ☎ *360/452–1952* ⊕ *www.togas-souphouse.com* ⊗ *Closed weekends.*

 Hotels

IN THE PARK

★ Kalaloch Lodge

$$$$ | **HOTEL** | **FAMILY** | Overlooking the Pacific, Kalaloch has cozy lodge rooms with sea views, and separate cabins along the bluff. **Pros:** ranger tours; clam digging; supreme storm-watching in winter. **Cons:** no Internet and most units don't have TVs; some rooms are two blocks from main lodge; limited cell phone service. $ *Rooms from: $225* ✉ *157151 U.S. 101, Forks* ☎ *360/962–2271, 866/662–9928* ⊕ *www.thekala-lochlodge.com* ⇲ *64 rooms* ¶⊙¶ *No meals.*

Lake Crescent Lodge

$$$$ | **HOTEL** | Deep in the forest at the foot of Mt. Storm King, this 1916 lodge has a variety of comfortable accommodations, from basic rooms with shared baths to spacious two-bedroom fireplace cottages. **Pros:** gorgeous setting; free wireless access in the lobby; lots of opportunities for off-the-grid fun outdoors. **Cons:** no laundry; Roosevelt Cottages often are booked a year in advance for summer stays. $ *Rooms from: $214* ✉ *416 Lake Crescent Rd., Port Angeles* ☎ *360/928–3211, 888/896–3818* ⊕ *www. olympicnationalparks.com* ⊗ *Closed Jan.–Apr., except Roosevelt fireplace cabins open weekends* ⇲ *52 rooms* ¶⊙¶ *No meals.*

Lake Quinault Lodge

$$$$ | **HOTEL** | On a lovely glacial lake in Olympic National Forest, this beautiful early-20th-century lodge complex is within walking distance of the lakeshore and hiking trails in the spectacular old-growth forest. **Pros:** boat tours of the lake are interesting; family-friendly ambience; year-round pool and sauna. **Cons:** no TV in some rooms; some units are noisy and not very private; service could be friendlier. $ *Rooms from: $249* ✉ *345 South Shore Rd., Quinault* ☎ *360/288–2900, 888/896–3818* ⊕ *www.olympicnational-parks.com* ⇲ *92 rooms* ¶⊙¶ *No meals.*

Log Cabin Resort

$$$ | **HOTEL** | **FAMILY** | This rustic resort has an idyllic setting at the northeast end of Lake Crescent with lodging choices that include A-frame chalet units, standard cabins, small camper cabins, motel units, and RV sites with full hookups. **Pros:** boat rentals available on-site; convenient general store; pets allowed in some cabins. **Cons:** cabins are extremely rustic; no plumbing in the camper cabins; no TVs. $ *Rooms from: $161* ✉ *3183 E. Beach Rd., Port Angeles* ☎ *888/896–3818, 360/928–3325* ⊕ *www.olympicnational-parks.com* ⊗ *Closed Oct.–late May* ⇲ *4 rooms, 20 cabins, 22 RV sites, 4 tent sites* ¶⊙¶ *No meals.*

Sol Duc Hot Springs Resort

$$$$ | **HOTEL** | Deep in the brooding forest along the Sol Duc River and surrounded by 5,000-foot-tall mountains, the main draw of this remote 1910 resort is the pool area, with soothing mineral baths and a freshwater swimming pool. **Pros:**

Best Campgrounds in Olympic

Note that only a few places take reservations; if you can't book in advance, you'll have to arrive early to get a place. Each site usually has a picnic table and grill or fire pit, and most campgrounds have water, toilets, and garbage containers; for hookups, showers, and laundry facilities, you'll have to head into the towns or stay at a privately-owned campground. Firewood is available from camp concessions, but if there's no store you can collect dead wood within 1 mile of your campsite. Dogs are allowed in campgrounds, but not on most trails or in the backcountry. Trailers should be 21 feet long or less (15 feet or less at Queets Campground) though a few campgrounds can accommodate up to 35 feet. There's a camping limit of two weeks. Nightly rates run $15–$22 per site.

If you have a backcountry pass, you can camp virtually anywhere throughout the park's forests and shores. Overnight wilderness permits are $8 per person per night and are available at visitor centers and ranger stations. Note that when you camp in the backcountry, you must choose a site at least ½ mile inside the park boundary.

Kalaloch Campground. Kalaloch is the biggest and most popular Olympic campground, and it's open all year. Its vantage of the Pacific is unmatched on the park's coastal stretch. ⊠ *U.S. 101, ½ mile north of Kalaloch Informa-tion Station, Olympic National Park* ☎ *877/444–6777 or* ⊕ *www.recreation. gov for reservations.*

Lake Quinault Rain Forest Resort Village Campground. Stretch-ing along the south shore of Lake Quinault, this RV campground has many recreation facilities, including beaches, canoes, ball fields, and horse-shoe pits. The 31 RV sites, which rent for $36 per night, are open year-round, but bathrooms are closed in winter. ⊠ *3½ miles east of U.S. 101, South Shore Rd., Lake Quinault* ☎ *360/288–2535, 800/255–6936* ⊕ *www.rainforestresort. com.*

Mora Campground. Along the Quillayute estuary, this campground doubles as a popular staging point for hikes northward along the coast's wilderness stretch. ⊠ *Rte. 110, 13 miles west of Forks* ☎ *No phone.*

Ozette Campground. Hikers heading to Cape Alava, a scenic promontory that is the westernmost point in the lower 48 states, use this lakeshore campground as a jumping-off point. ⊠ *Hoko-Ozette Rd., 26 miles south of Hwy. 112* ☎ *No phone.*

Sol Duc Campground. Sol Duc resembles virtually all Olympic campgrounds save one distinguish-ing feature—the famed hot springs are a short walk away. ⊠ *Sol Duc Rd., 11 miles south of U.S. 101* ☎ *877/444–6777 or* ⊕ *www.recreation.gov for reservations.*

Staircase Campground. In deep woods away from the river, this campground is a popular jumping-off point for hikes into the Skokomish River Valley and the Olympic high country. ⊠ *Rte. 119, 16 miles northwest of U.S. 101* ☎ *No phone.*

nearby trails; peaceful setting; some units are pet-friendly. **Cons:** units are dated; no air-conditioning, TV, or Internet access; pools get crowded. $ *Rooms from: $210* ✉ *12076 Sol Duc Hot Springs Rd.* ☎ *888/896–3818* ⊕ *www.olympicnationalparks.com* ✆ *Closed Nov.–late Mar.* ✆ *32 cabins, 1 suite, 17 RV sites* ¶○¶ *No meals.*

OUTSIDE THE PARK

★ Colette's Bed & Breakfast

$$$$ | **B&B/INN** | A contemporary oceanfront mansion set on a 10-acre sanctuary of gorgeous gardens offers more space, service, and luxury than any other property in the area, with water-view suites that have fireplaces, patios, and two-person spa tubs. **Pros:** water views extend to Victoria, BC; discrete personal service; beautiful setting. **Cons:** like many B&Bs, it's only for adults. $ *Rooms from: $295* ✉ *339 Finn Hall Rd., Port Angeles* ✚ *10 miles east of town* ☎ *360/457–9197, 888/457–9777* ⊕ *www.colettes.com* ✆ *5 suites* ¶○¶ *Breakfast.*

Domaine Madeleine

$$$$ | **B&B/INN** | Perched on a bluff above the Strait of Juan de Fuca, the luxurious accommodations here have updated contemporary decor, colorful murals, fireplaces, and water, mountain, and garden views. **Pros:** colorful waterfront lodgings; abundant wildlife; well-appointed rooms. **Cons:** no children under 10; breakfast costs extra. $ *Rooms from: $329* ✉ *146 Wildflower La., Port Angeles* ✚ *8 miles east of town* ☎ *360/457–4174* ⊕ *www.domainemadeleine.com* ✆ *3 suites, 3 cottages* ¶○¶ *No meals.*

Fort Worden State Park Conference Center

$$$$ | **RENTAL | FAMILY** | The 330-acre Fort Worden, built as a late-19th-century gun emplacement to guard the mouth of the Puget Sound, gained a new purpose when enterprising souls turned the spacious Victorian homes on officer's row into some of the more memorable lodgings on the Olympic Peninsula. **Pros:**

myriad activities; acres of waterfront for play; historic ambience. **Cons:** summer crowds; no TV, Internet, or air-conditioning in the houses. $ *Rooms from: $249* ✉ *200 Battery Way, Port Townsend* ✚ *1 mile north of Port Townsend* ☎ *360/344–4400 for lodging reservations, 888/226–7688 for campsite reservations* ⊕ *www.fortworden.org* ✆ *38 rental homes, 80 camp sites with full hookups* ¶○¶ *No meals.*

Miller Tree Inn Bed and Breakfast

$$$ | **B&B/INN** | This 1916 farmhouse, nicknamed the "Cullen House" for its resemblance to the description in Stephenie Meyer's "Twilight" books, is bordered on two sides by pastures. **Pros:** excellent breakfast; nearby rivers offer prime salmon and steelhead fishing October through April; children are welcome in some rooms. **Cons:** might be too much "Twilight" for nonfans; some rooms are small. $ *Rooms from: $180* ✉ *654 E. Division St., Forks* ☎ *360/374–6806, 800/943–6563* ⊕ *www.millertreeinn.com* ✆ *8 rooms* ¶○¶ *Breakfast.*

Ocean Crest Resort

$ | **RESORT** | Set on a forested bluff above the Pacific Ocean, 30 minutes from Olympic National Park and Lake Quinault, Ocean Crest has small budget studios, large studios with ocean views, and one- and two-bedroom units. **Pros:** windows open to hear the ocean's roar; some rooms are pet-friendly; off-season specials. **Cons:** restaurant prices may be too high for budget travelers; some rooms are very dated. $ *Rooms from: $87* ✉ *4651 Rte. 109, Moclips* ☎ *360/276–4465* ⊕ *www.oceancrestresort.com* ✆ *45 rooms* ¶○¶ *No meals.*

Quality Inn Uptown

$$$ | **HOTEL** | South of Port Angeles, at the green edge of the Olympic Mountain foothills, this no-frills choice has a great thing going for it: a stunning panorama of mountain and harbor views. **Pros:** central location; great views. **Cons:** basic interior design and amenities; somewhat dated;

no elevators. [$] *Rooms from: $180* ✉ *101 E. 2nd St., Port Angeles* ☎ *360/457–9434* 🌐 *www.qualityinnportangeles.com* 🛏 *51 rooms* 🍴 *Breakfast.*

★ Sea Cliff Gardens Bed & Breakfast

$$$$ | **B&B/INN** | A gingerbread-style porch fronts this antiques-furnished waterfront Victorian home on 2 acres of landscaped grounds; all of the exquisitely appointed guest rooms have fireplaces and panoramic water views through large picture windows. **Pros:** sumptuous accommodations with stunning views; gorgeous flower gardens; romantic setting. **Cons:** a bit off the beaten path. [$] *Rooms from: $290* ✉ *397 Monterra Dr., Port Angeles* ☎ *360/452–2322* 🌐 *www.seacliffgardens.com* 🛏 *5 suites* 🍴 *Breakfast.*

★ Seabrook Cottage Rentals

$$$$ | **RENTAL** | **FAMILY** | Crushed seashells line pathways throughout this charming beach resort town that was first established in 2004 and now features a collection of some 350 Cape Cod–style homes, more than half of which are available to rent. **Pros:** recreational activities and beach within walking distance; homes are new with many amenities; some are pet-friendly. **Cons:** ongoing construction; minimum 2-night stay; limited services outside of village. [$] *Rooms from: $259* ✉ *4275 SR 109, Pacific Beach* ☎ *360/276–0265, 877/779–9990* 🌐 *www.seabrookcottagerentals.com* 🛏 *220 cottages* 🍴 *No meals.*

PETRIFIED FOREST NATIONAL PARK

Updated by
Elise Riley

ARIZONA

WELCOME TO PETRIFIED FOREST NATIONAL PARK

TOP REASONS TO GO

★ **Terrific timber:** Be mesmerized by the clusters of petrified (fossilized) wood. The trees look like they're made of colorful stone.

★ **Walls with words:** Don't scratch the surface, but see how others did. Ancestors of the Hopi, Zuni, and Navajo left their mark in petroglyphs cut, scratched, or carved into stone.

★ **Route 66 kicks:** A section of the fabled road is preserved in the park, the only section of the highway protected in a national park.

★ **Triassic treasures:** Find an oasis of water in the desert, or at least evidence that it once existed. Clam fossils in the park indicate that waterways once prevailed where sand, stone, and trees now define the land.

★ **Corps creations:** The Painted Desert Inn, a National Historic Landmark, was modernized by the Civilian Conservation Corps (CCC) during the throes of the Great Depression. It is now a museum and bookstore.

There are few places where the span of geologic and human history is as wide or apparent as it is at Petrified Forest National Park. Fossilized trees and countless other fossils date back to the Triassic Period, while a stretch of the famed Route 66 of more modern lore is protected within park boundaries. Ancestors of the Hopi, Zuni, and Navajo left petroglyphs, pottery, and even structures built of petrified wood. Nine park sites are on the National Register of Historic Places; one, the Painted Desert Inn, is one of only 3% of such sites that are also listed as National Historic Landmarks.

1 Painted Desert. The main area of the park, in the northern section, is where park headquarters, the Painted Desert Inn, and Route 66 are located. It's also the best place for hiking. A permit is required for overnight camping in the wilderness area, but day users need not obtain one. The 28-mile park road begins here, off Interstate 40.

2 Blue Mesa. In the heart of the Painted Desert, this 1-mile loop trail begins off a loop road accessed from the park road. Petrified trees lie among hills of bluish bentonite clay.

3 Rainbow Forest Museum. Get a trail guide here for the short Giant Logs Trail located behind the museum, and keep an eye out for Old Faithful, a log almost 10 feet wide. The southern terminus for the park road is here.

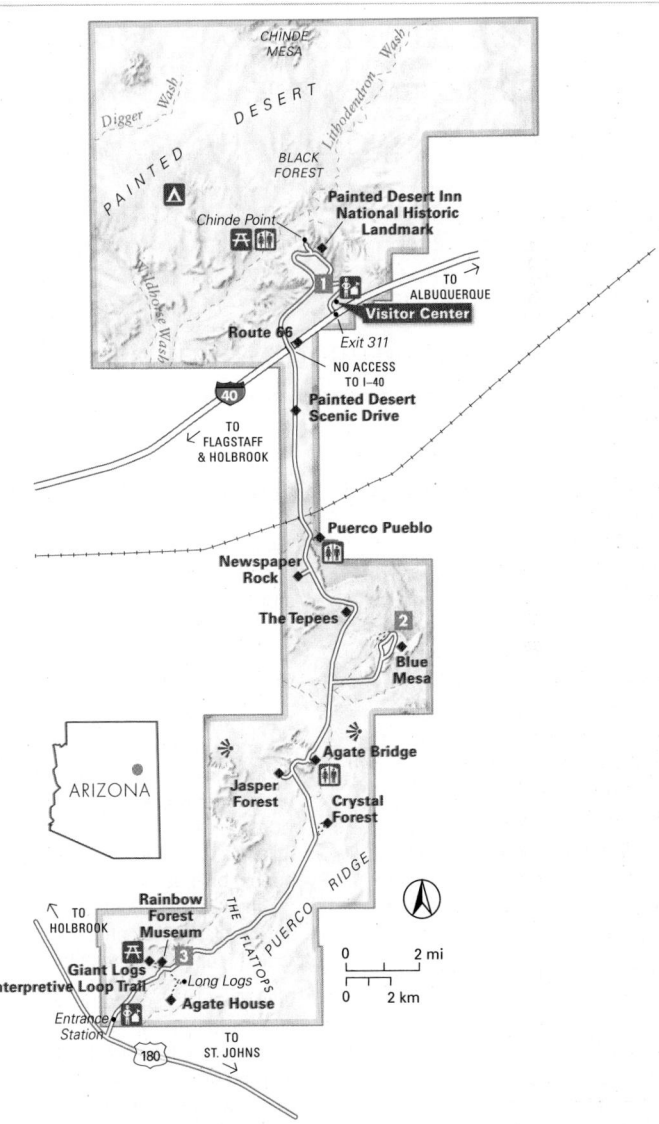

Petrified Forest National Park's 221,390 acres, which include portions of the Painted Desert, are covered with petrified tree trunks whose wood cells were fossilized over centuries by brightly hued mineral deposits—silica, iron oxide, carbon, manganese, aluminum, copper, and lithium. Remnants of humans and their artifacts have been recovered at more than 500 sites in the park.

Planning

WHEN TO GO

The park is rarely crowded. Weather-wise, the best time to visit is autumn, when nights are chilly but daytime temperatures hover near 70°F. Half of all yearly rain falls between June and August, so it's a good time to spot blooming wildflowers. The park is least crowded in winter, because of cold winds and occasional snow, though daytime temperatures are in the 50s and 60s.

FESTIVALS AND EVENTS

National Wildflower Week. Activities include wildflower walks and an interactive wildflower display.

Petrified Forest Park Anniversary. A national monument since 1906 and a national park since 1962, Petrified Forest throws a party for its birthday, with homemade cider, cookies, and cultural demonstrations.

PLANNING YOUR TIME
PETRIFIED FOREST IN ONE DAY

A nonstop drive through the park (28 miles) takes only 45 minutes, but you can spend a half day or more exploring if you stop along the way. From almost any vantage point you can see the multicolored rocks and hills that were home to prehistoric humans and ancient dinosaurs.

Entering from the north, stop at **Painted Desert Visitor Center** for a 20-minute introductory film. Two miles in, the **Painted Desert Inn National Historic Landmark** provides guided ranger tours. Drive south 8 miles to reach **Puerco Pueblo,** a 100-room pueblo built before 1400. Continuing south, you'll find Puebloan petroglyphs at **Newspaper Rock** and, just beyond, the **Tepees,** cone-shape rock formations.

Blue Mesa is roughly the midpoint of the drive, and the start of a 1-mile, moderately steep loop hike that leads you around badland hills made of bentonite clay. Drive on for 5 miles until you come to **Jasper Forest,** just past **Agate Bridge,** with views of the landscape strewn with petrified logs. **Crystal Forest,** about 20 miles

AVERAGE HIGH/LOW TEMPERATURES					
JAN.	FEB.	MAR.	APR.	MAY	JUNE
48/21	54/25	60/29	70/35	79/43	89/52
JULY	AUG.	SEPT.	OCT.	NOV.	DEC.
92/60	89/59	84/52	72/40	59/28	48/22

south of the north entrance, is named for the smoky quartz, amethyst, and citrine along the 0.8-mile loop trail. **Rainbow Forest Museum,** at the park's south entrance, has restrooms, a bookstore, and exhibits. Just behind Rainbow Forest Museum is **Giant Logs,** a 0.4-mile loop that takes you to "Old Faithful," the largest log in the park, estimated to weigh 44 tons.

GETTING HERE AND AROUND
AIR TRAVEL
The nearest major airports are in Phoenix, Arizona (259 miles away via U.S. 17 and U.S. 40), and Albuquerque, New Mexico (204 miles via U.S. 40).

CAR TRAVEL
Holbrook, the nearest large town with services such as gas or food, is on U.S. 40, roughly 30 miles from either of the park's two entrances.

Parking is free, and there's ample space at all trailheads, as well as at the visitor center and the museum. The main park road extends 28 miles from the Painted Desert Visitor Center (north entrance) to the Rainbow Forest Museum (south entrance). For park road conditions, call ☎ *928/524–6228.*

PARK ESSENTIALS
PARK FEES AND PERMITS
Entrance fees are $20 per car for seven consecutive days or $10 per person on foot, bicycle, motorcycle, or bus. Backcountry hiking and camping permits are free (limit of 15 days) at the Painted Desert Visitor Center or the Rainbow Forest Museum before 4 pm.

PARK HOURS
Call ahead or check the website, as the park's hours vary; as a rule of thumb, the park is open daily from sunrise to sunset, and keep in mind that the area does not observe daylight saving time. Hours are approximately: daily 8–5 from November to February, daily 7–6:30 in March and April, daily 7 am–7:30 pm from May to August, and daily 7–6 in September and October.

EDUCATIONAL OFFERINGS
Ask at either park visitor center for the availability of special ranger-led tours, such as the after-hours lantern tour of the Painted Desert Inn Museum.

RANGER PROGRAMS
Junior Ranger
TOUR—SIGHT | FAMILY | Children 12 and younger can learn more about the park's extensive human, animal, and geologic history as they train to become a Junior Ranger. ⊠ *Petrified Forest National Park.*

Ranger Walks and Talks
TOUR—SIGHT | Park rangers lead regular programs along the Great Logs Trail, inside the Painted Desert Inn Museum, and to the Puerco Pueblo. You can view which ranger programs are currently being offered at the visitor centers or online at *www.nps.gov/pefo.* ⊠ *Petrified Forest National Park.*

RESTAURANTS
Dining in the park is limited to a cafeteria in the Painted Desert Visitor Center and snacks in the Rainbow Forest Museum. In and around the Navajo and Hopi reservations, be sure to sample Indian tacos, an authentic treat made with scrumptious fry bread, beans, and chilies. If

you're searching for burger-and-fries fare, Holbrook is your best bet.

HOTELS

There is no lodging within Petrified Forest. Outside the park, lodging choices include modern resorts, rustic cabins, and small bed-and-breakfasts. Note that air-conditioning is not a standard amenity in the mountains, where the nights are cool enough for a blanket even in summer. Closer to the Navajo and Hopi reservations many establishments are run by Native Americans, tribal enterprises intent on offering first-class service and hospitality. Nearby Holbrook offers some national chain motels and comfortable accommodations. *Hotel reviews have been shortened. For full information, visit Fodors.com.*

What It Costs			
$	$$	$$$	$$$$
RESTAURANTS			
under $13	$13–$20	$21–$30	over $30
HOTELS			
under $101	$101–$150	$151–$200	over $200

VISITOR INFORMATION

PARK CONTACT INFORMATION Petrified Forest National Park ⊠ *1 Park Rd.* ☎ *928/524–6228* ⊕ *www.nps.gov/pefo.*

VISITOR CENTERS

Painted Desert Inn National Historic Landmark

INFO CENTER | This visitor center isn't as large as the other two, but here you can get information as well as view cultural history exhibits. ⊠ *Main park road ✛ 2 miles north of Painted Desert Visitor Center* ☎ *928/524–6228.*

Painted Desert Visitor Center

INFO CENTER | This is the place to go for general park information and an informative 20-minute film. Proceeds from books purchased here will fund continued

research and interpretive activities for the park. ⊠ *North entrance ✛ Off I–40, 27 miles east of Holbrook* ☎ *928/524–6228.*

Rainbow Forest Museum and Visitor Center

INFO CENTER | View displays of prehistoric animals, watch an orientation video, and—perhaps most important—use the restroom facilities at this visitor center at the southern end of the park. ⊠ *South entrance ✛ Off U.S. 180, 18 miles southeast of Holbrook* ☎ *928/524–6228.*

 ## Sights

SCENIC DRIVES

Painted Desert Scenic Drive

SCENIC DRIVE | A 28-mile scenic drive takes you through the park from one entrance to the other. If you begin at the north end, the first 5 miles take you along the edge of a high mesa, with spectacular views of the Painted Desert. Beyond lies the desolate Painted Desert Wilderness Area. After the 5-mile point, the road crosses Interstate 40, then swings south toward the Puerco River across a landscape covered with sagebrush, saltbrush, sunflowers, and Apache plume. Past the river, the road climbs onto a narrow mesa leading to Newspaper Rock, a panel of Pueblo Indian rock art. Then the road bends southeast, enters a barren stretch, and passes teepee-shaped buttes in the distance. Next you come to Blue Mesa, roughly the park's midpoint and a good place to stop for views of petrified logs. The next stop on the drive is Agate Bridge, really a 100-foot log over a wide wash. The remaining overlooks are Jasper and Crystal forests, where you can get further glimpses of the accumulated petrified wood. On your way out of the park, stop at the Rainbow Forest Museum for a rest and to shop for a memento. ⊠ *Begins at Painted Desert Visitor Center.*

HISTORIC SITES

Agate House

ARCHAEOLOGICAL SITE | This eight-room pueblo is thought to have been built entirely of petrified wood 700 years ago. Researchers believe it might have been used as a temporary dwelling by seasonal farmers or traders from one of the area tribes. ⊠ *Rainbow Forest Museum parking area.*

Newspaper Rock

ARCHAEOLOGICAL SITE | See huge boulders covered with petroglyphs believed to have been carved by the Pueblo Indians more than 500 years ago. **Look through the binoculars that are provided here—you'll be surprised at what the naked eye misses.** ⊠ *Main park road ✛ 6 miles south of Painted Desert Visitor Center.*

Painted Desert Inn National Historic Landmark

MUSEUM | A nice place to stop and rest in the shade, this site offers vast views of the Painted Desert from several lookouts. Inside, cultural history exhibits, murals, and Native American crafts are on display. ⊠ *Main park road ✛ 2 miles north of Painted Desert Visitor Center.*

Puerco Pueblo

ARCHAEOLOGICAL SITE | This is a 100-room pueblo, built before 1400 and said to have housed Ancestral Puebloan people. Many visitors come to see the petroglyphs, as well as a solar calendar. ⊠ *Main park road ✛ 10 miles south of Painted Desert Visitor Center.*

SCENIC STOPS

Agate Bridge

NATURE SITE | Here you'll see a 100-foot log spanning a 40-foot-wide wash. ⊠ *Main park road ✛ 19 miles south of Painted Desert Visitor Center.*

Crystal Forest

NATURE SITE | The fragments of petrified wood strewn here once held clear quartz and amethyst crystals. ⊠ *Main park road ✛ 20 miles south of Painted Desert Visitor Center.*

Giant Logs Interpretive Loop Trail

NATURE SITE | A short walk leads you past the park's largest log, known as Old Faithful. It's considered the largest

because of its diameter (9 feet 9 inches), as well as how tall it once was. ⊠ *Main park road ✛ 28 miles south of Painted Desert Visitor Center.*

Jasper Forest

VIEWPOINT | More of an overlook than a forest, this spot has a large concentration of petrified trees in jasper or red. ⊠ *Main park road ✛ 17 miles south of Painted Desert Visitor Center.*

The Tepees

NATURE SITE | Witness the effects of time on these cone-shape rock formations colored by iron, manganese, and other minerals. ⊠ *Main park road ✛ 8 miles south of Painted Desert Visitor Center.*

🏃 Activities

Because the park goes to great pains to maintain the integrity of the fossil- and artifact-strewn landscape, sports and outdoor options in the park are limited to on-trail hiking.

HIKING

All trails begin off the main road, with restrooms at or near the trailheads. Most maintained trails are relatively short, paved, clearly marked, and, with a few exceptions, easy to moderate in difficulty. Hikers with greater stamina can make their own trails in the wilderness area, located just north of the Painted Desert Visitor Center. Watch your step for rattlesnakes, which are common in the park—if left alone and given a wide berth, they're passed easily enough.

Agate House

HIKING/WALKING | A fairly flat 1-mile trip takes you to an eight-room pueblo sitting high on a knoll. *Moderate.* ⊠ *Petrified Forest National Park ✛ Trailhead: 26 miles south of Painted Desert Visitor Center.*

★ Blue Mesa

HIKING/WALKING | Although it's only 1 mile long and significantly steeper than the rest, this trail at the park's midway point is one of the most popular and worth

Different minerals in different concentrations cause the rich colors in petrified wood and in the Painted Desert.

the effort. *Moderate.* ⊠ *Petrified Forest National Park* ✛ *Trailhead: 14 miles south of Painted Desert Visitor Center.*

Crystal Forest Trail

HIKING/WALKING | This easy ¾-mile loop leads you past petrified wood that once held quartz crystals and amethyst chips. *Easy.* ⊠ *Petrified Forest National Park* ✛ *Trailhead: 20 miles south of Painted Desert Visitor Center.*

Giant Logs Trail

HIKING/WALKING | At 0.4 mile, Giant Logs is the park's shortest trail. The loop leads you to Old Faithful, the park's largest petrified log—9 feet, 9 inches at its base, weighing an estimated 44 tons. *Easy.* ⊠ *Petrified Forest National Park* ✛ *Trailhead: directly behind Rainbow Forest Museum, 28 miles south of Painted Desert Visitor Center.*

Kachina Point

HIKING/WALKING | This is the trailhead for wilderness hiking at Petrified Forest National Park. A 1-mile trail leads to the Wilderness Area, but from there you're on your own. There are no developed trails, so hiking here is cross-country style. Expect to see strange formations, beautifully colored landscapes, and maybe, just maybe, a pronghorn antelope. *Difficult.* ⊠ *Petrified Forest National Park* ✛ *Trailhead: on northwest side of Painted Desert Inn National Historic Landmark.*

Long Logs Trail

HIKING/WALKING | Although barren, this easy 1.6-mile loop passes the largest concentration of wood in the park. *Easy.* ⊠ *Petrified Forest National Park* ✛ *Trailhead: 26 miles south of Painted Desert Visitor Center.*

Painted Desert Rim

HIKING/WALKING | The 1-mile trail is at its best in early morning or late afternoon, when the sun accentuates the brilliant red, blue, purple, and other hues of the desert and petrified forest landscape. *Moderate.* ⊠ *Petrified Forest National Park* ✛ *Trail runs between Tawa Point and Kachina Point, 1 mile north of Painted Desert Visitor Center; drive to either point from visitor center.*

Plants and Wildlife in Petrified Forest

Engelmann's asters and sunflowers are among the blooms in the park each summer. Juniper trees, cottonwoods, and willows grow along Puerco River wash, providing shelter for all manner of wildlife. You might spot mule deer, coyotes, prairie dogs, and foxes, while other inhabitants, like porcupines and bobcats, tend to hide. Bird-watchers should keep an eye out for mockingbirds, red-tailed and Swainson's hawks, roadrunners, swallows, and hummingbirds. Look for all three kinds of lizards—collared, side-blotched, and southern prairie—in rocks.

Beware of rattlesnakes. They're common but can generally be easily avoided: Watch where you step, and don't step anywhere you can't see. If you do come across a rattler, give it plenty of space, and let it go its way before you continue on yours. Other reptiles are just as common but not as dangerous. The gopher snake looks similar to a rattlesnake, but is nonpoisonous. The collared lizard, with its yellow head, can be seen scurrying out of your way in bursts measured at up to 15 mph. They aren't poisonous, but will bite in the rare instance of being caught.

27

Petrified Forest National Park

Puerco Pueblo Trail
HIKING/WALKING | **FAMILY** | A relatively flat and interesting 0.3-mile trail takes you past remains of a home of the Ancestral Puebloan people, built before 1400. The trail is paved and wheelchair accessible. *Easy.* ⊠ *Petrified Forest National Park* ⊹ *Trailhead: 10 miles south of Painted Desert Visitor Center.*

Nearby Towns

Located in eastern Arizona just off Interstate 40, Petrified Forest National Park is set in an area of grasslands, overlooked by mountains in the distance. At nearly an hour from **American Indian Nations,** nearly two hours from **Flagstaff,** and three hours from the **Grand Canyon,** the park is relatively remote and separated from many comforts of travel. Just a half hour away, **Holbrook,** the nearest town, is the best place to grab a quick bite to eat or take a brief rest.

◉ Sights

★ Canyon de Chelly
ARCHAEOLOGICAL SITE | Home to Ancestral Puebloans from AD 350 to 1300, the nearly 84,000-acre Canyon de Chelly (pronounced d'*shay*) is one of the most spectacular natural wonders in the Southwest. On a smaller scale, it rivals the Grand Canyon for beauty. Its main gorges—the 26-mile-long Canyon de Chelly ("canyon in the rock") and the adjoining 35-mile-long Canyon del Muerto ("canyon of the dead")—comprise sheer, heavily eroded sandstone walls that rise to 1,100 feet over dramatic valleys. Ancient pictographs and petroglyphs decorate some of the cliffs, and within the canyon complex there are more than 7,000 archaeological sites. Stone walls rise hundreds of feet above streams, hogans, tilled fields, and sheep-grazing lands.

You can view prehistoric sites near the base of cliffs and perched on high, sheltering ledges, some of which you can access from the park's two main drives along the canyon rims. The dwellings and cultivated fields of the present-day Navajo lie in the flatlands between the

Petroglyphs: The Writing on the Wall

Like some other historic sites in eastern Arizona, Petrified Forest National Park is a great place to view petroglyphs and pictographs—designs pecked or scratched into the stone are called petroglyphs; those that are painted on the surface are pictographs. Few pictographs remain because of the deleterious effects of weathering, but the more durable petroglyphs number in the thousands.

The rock art of early Native Americans is carved or painted on basalt boulders, on canyon walls, and on the underside of overhangs throughout the area. No one knows the exact meaning of these signs, and interpretations vary; they've been seen as elements in shamanistic or hunting rituals, as clan signs, maps, or even indications of visits by extraterrestrials.

Where to Find It

Susceptible to (and often already damaged by) vandalism, many rock-art sites aren't open to the public. Two good petroglyphs to check out at **Petrified Forest National Park** are Newspaper Rock, an overlook near mile marker 12, and Puerco Pueblo, near mile marker 11. Other sites in Arizona include **Hieroglyphic Point** in Salt River Canyon, and **Five-Mile Canyon** in Snowflake.

Determining Its Age

It's just as difficult to date a "glyph" as it is to understand it. Archaeologists try to determine a general time frame by judging the style, the date of the ruins and pottery in the vicinity, the amount of patination (formation of minerals) on the design, or the superimposition of newer images on top of older ones. Most of eastern Arizona's rock art is estimated to be at least 1,000 years old, and many of the glyphs were created even earlier.

Varied Images

Some glyphs depict animals like bighorn sheep, deer, bear, and mountain lions; others are geometric patterns. The most unusual are the anthropomorphs, strange humanlike figures with elaborate headdresses. Concentric circles are a common design. A few of these circles served as solstice signs, indicating the summer and winter solstice and other important dates. At the solstice, when the angle of the sun is just right, a shaft of light shines through a crack in a nearby rock, illuminating the center of the circle. Archaeologists believe that these solar calendars helped determine the time for ceremonies and planting.

Many solstice signs are in remote regions, but you can visit Petrified Forest National Park around June 20 to see a concentric circle illuminated during the summer solstice. The glyph, reached by a paved trail just a few hundred yards from the parking area, is visible year-round, but light shines directly in the center during the week of the solstice. The phenomenon occurs at 9 am, a reasonable hour for looking at the calendar.

■TIP→ Do not touch petroglyphs or pictographs—the oil from your hands can damage the images.

The stones tell a story with ancient etchings on Newspaper Rock.

cliffs, and those who inhabit the canyon today farm much the way their ancestors did. Most residents leave the canyon in winter but return in early spring to farm.

Canyon de Chelly's South Rim Drive (37 miles round-trip with seven overlooks) starts at the visitor center and ends at **Spider Rock Overlook,** where cliffs plunge nearly 1,000 feet to the canyon floor. The view here is of two pinnacles, Speaking Rock and Spider Rock. Other highlights on the South Rim Drive are Junction Overlook, where Canyon del Muerto joins Canyon de Chelly; White House Overlook, from which a 2½-mile round-trip trail leads to the **White House Ruin,** with remains of nearly 60 rooms and several kivas; and Sliding House Overlook, where you can see dwellings on a narrow, sloped ledge across the canyon. The carved and sometimes narrow trail down the canyon side to White House Ruin is the only access into Canyon de Chelly without a guide—if you have a fear of heights, this may not be the hike for you.

The only slightly less breathtaking **North Rim Drive** (34 miles round-trip with three overlooks) of Canyon del Muerto also begins at the visitor center and continues northeast on Indian Highway 64 toward the town of Tsaile. Major stops include **Antelope House Overlook,** a large site named for the animals painted on an adjacent cliff; **Mummy Cave Overlook,** where two mummies were found inside a remarkably unspoiled pueblo dwelling; and **Massacre Case Overlook,** which marks the spot where an estimated 115 Navajo were killed by the Spanish in 1805. (The rock walls of the cave are still pock-marked by the Spaniards' ricocheting bullets.) ✉ *Indian Hwy. 7, Chinle* ✛ *3 miles east of U.S. 191* ☎ *928/674–5500 visitor center* ⊕ *www.nps.gov/cach* 🎫 *Free.*

Homolovi State Park

ARCHAEOLOGICAL SITE | *Homolovi* is a Hopi word meaning "place of the little hills." The pueblo sites here are thought to have been occupied between AD 1200 and 1425, and include 40 ceremonial kivas and two pueblos containing more than 1,000 rooms each. The Hopi believe their immediate ancestors inhabited this place, and they consider the site sacred. Many rooms have been excavated and recovered for protection. The Homolovi Visitor Center has a small museum with Hopi pottery and Ancestral Puebloan artifacts; it also hosts workshops on native art, ethnobotany, and traditional foods. ✉ *AZ 87, Winslow* ⊕ *3½ miles northeast of Winslow* ☎ *928/289–4106, 520/586–2283 for camping reservations* 🌐 *azstateparks.com/homolovi* 🎫 *$7.*

Rock Art Ranch

ARCHAEOLOGICAL SITE | The Ancestral Puebloan petroglyphs of this working cattle ranch in Chevelon Canyon are startlingly vivid after more than 1,000 years. Ranch owner Brantly Baird will guide you along the ¼-mile trail, explaining Western and archaeological history. Baird houses his Native American artifacts and pioneer farming implements in his own private museum. Reservations are required. ✉ *Off AZ 87, Winslow* ⊕ *13 miles southeast of Winslow* ☎ *928/386–5047* 🎫 *From $35 per person* 🕒 *Closed Sun.*

Restaurants

INSIDE THE PARK

Painted Desert Visitor Center Cafeteria

$ | **AMERICAN** | Serving standard (but pretty decent) cafeteria fare, this is the only place in the park where you can get a full meal. **Known for:** closest restaurant to the park; gift shop; excellent lamb stew and Navajo tacos. [$] *Average main: $7* ✉ *North entrance* ☎ *928/524–6228.*

PICNIC AREAS

Chinde Point Picnic Area

Near the north entrance, this small spot has tables and restrooms. ✉ *Petrified Forest National Park* ⊕ *2 miles north of Painted Desert Visitor Center.*

Rainbow Forest Museum Picnic Area

There are restrooms and tables at this small picnic area near the south entrance. ✉ *Petrified Forest National Park* ⊕ *Off I–40, 27 miles east of Holbrook.*

Hotels

OUTSIDE THE PARK

HOLBROOK

Wigwam Motel

$ | **HOTEL** | On the National Register of Historic Places, the iconic Wigwam consists of 15 bright-white concrete teepees. **Pros:** impeccably kitschy; one of the signature spots along Route 66. **Cons:** very sparse accommodations that can fit no more than two. [$] *Rooms from: $76* ✉ *811 West Hopi Dr., Holbrook* ☎ *928/524–3048* 🌐 *www.sleepinawigwam.com* 🛏 *15 rooms* 🍴 *No meals.*

WINSLOW

★ La Posada Hotel

$$ | **HOTEL** | One of the great railroad hotels, La Posada ("resting place") exudes the charm of an 18th-century Spanish hacienda, and its restoration has been a labor of love. **Pros:** historic charm; unique architecture; impressive restaurant. **Cons:** mazes of staircases aren't wheelchair-friendly (but ground floor rooms and restaurant are). [$] *Rooms from: $139* ✉ *303 E. 2nd St., Winslow* ☎ *928/289–4366* 🌐 *www.laposada.org* 🛏 *51 rooms* 🍴 *No meals.*

Chapter 28

PINNACLES NATIONAL PARK

28

Updated by
Deb Hopewell

CALIFORNIA

WELCOME TO PINNACLES NATIONAL PARK

TOP REASONS TO GO

★ **Condor encounters:** There are only 276 California condors alive in the wild today; Pinnacles has released or hatched 34 of these critically endangered birds and they can be observed anywhere between Pinnacles and the coast.

★ **Cave exploring:** The park contains two talus caves—a unique type of cave formed when boulders fall into narrow canyons, creating ceilings, passageways, and small rooms.

★ **Hiking the pinnacles:** There aren't many roads, so the best way to see the otherworldly rock formations of the ancient volcano found in the middle of the park is to hike the more than 30 miles of trails.

★ **Climbing sans crowds:** Despite achieving National Park status in 2013, Pinnacles is in a remote location, so it gets far fewer visitors than parks like Yosemite, leaving the hundreds of rock-climbing routes crowd-free.

★ **Star appeal:** Far from cities, the park is a popular stargazing destination, especially during the annual Perseid meteor shower.

1 East Entrance. There are only two entrances to Pinnacles, and this is the family-friendly choice. It has the park's only campground—including a visitor center, a small swimming pool that's especially inviting on hot days, and a modest store for food, drinks, and other camping essentials and incidentals—This entrance is also the best access point for Bear Gulch Cave, the most popular hike in the park.

2 West Entrance. The park's western side tends to be quieter than the eastern one, and it has fewer amenities, but coming here is the best way to sneak a peek at the high-peak formations without having to hike. Just drive to the Chaparral Trailhead parking lot, and you can view them from there. The Balconies Cave Trail is also popular on this side of the park. The towering rocks keep the canyon trail shady and relatively cool.

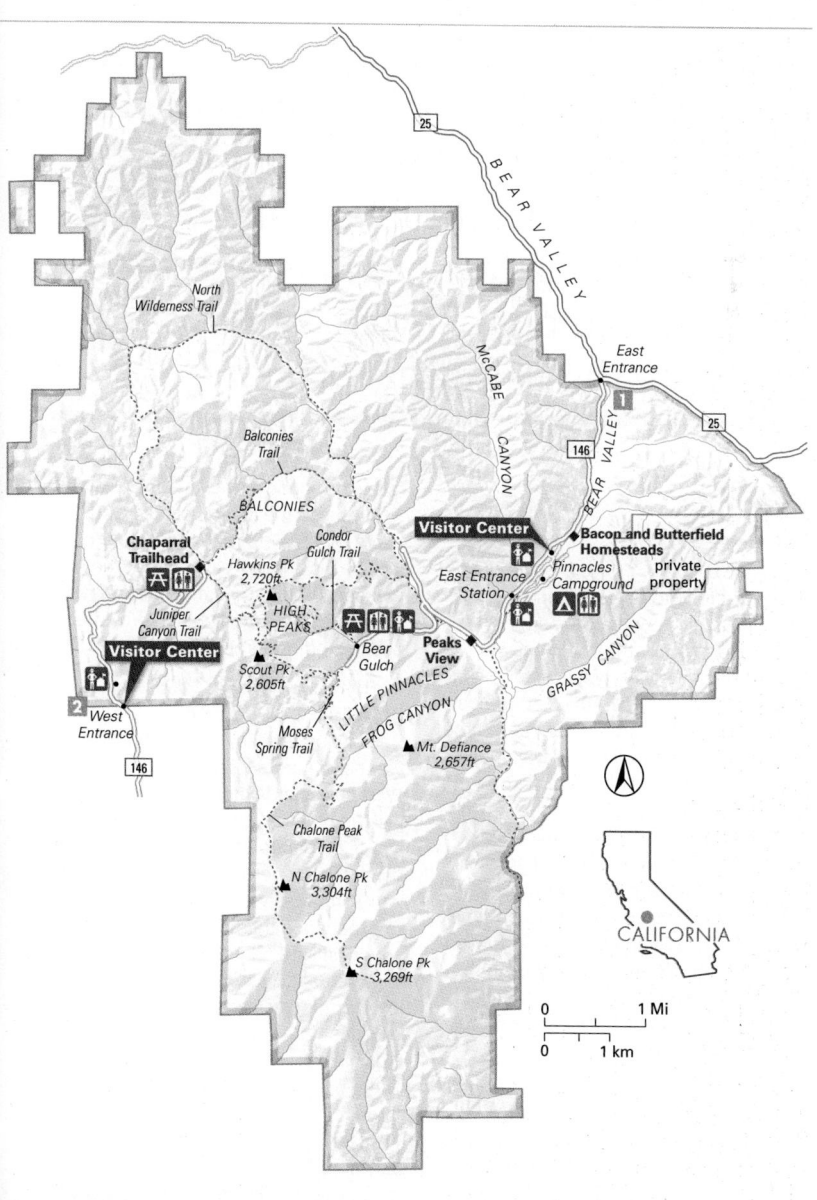

Bear Valley

25

North Wilderness Trail

Balconies Trail

BALCONIES

East Entrance

1

25

146

McCABE CANYON

Chaparral Trailhead

Condor Gulch Trail

Visitor Center

Bacon and Butterfield Homesteads

private property

Hawkins Pk 2,720ft

East Entrance Station

Pinnacles Campground

Juniper Canyon Trail

HIGH PEAKS

Visitor Center

2

West Entrance

146

Scout Pk 2,605ft

Bear Gulch

Peaks View

LITTLE PINNACLES

FROG CANYON

GRASSY CANYON

Moses Spring Trail

Mt. Defiance 2,657ft

Chalone Peak Trail

CALIFORNIA

N Chalone Pk 3,304ft

S Chalone Pk 3,269ft

0   1 Mi

0   1 km

President Theodore Roosevelt recognized the uniqueness of the Pinnacles Volcanic Formation—its jagged spires and monoliths thrusting upward from chaparral-covered mountains—when he made it a national monument in 1908. Legends abound of robbers and banditos who used talus caves as hideouts, though the most famous denizens of the park today are the California condors.

Planning

WHEN TO GO

Summers tend to be very warm, and triple-digit temperatures are not uncommon; luckily this means fewer crowds, especially on weekdays. Spring, particularly March and April, is the most popular season, as this is the prime time for viewing spectacular displays of lupine, poppies, and other wildflowers. Though late September can still be quite warm, fall is a great time to visit if you want to enjoy cooler temperatures and smaller crowds. Winters are cold by California standards, but this is an opportune time to hike, especially the High Peaks, where most of the trails are in the sun. On the other hand, the temperatures in the deeply shaded areas such as the Balconies Trail can reach below freezing.

One thing to keep in mind: Bear Gulch Cave, on the east side, is one of the most popular hikes and attractions, but it's also home to a large colony of Townsend's big-eared bats. This protected species raises its young in the late spring and summer, so the cave is closed from about mid-May to mid-July. If your plans include visiting the cave, check the park's website (⊕ *www.nps.gov/pinn/planyour-visit/cavestatus.htm*), which provides updates on closures.

PLANNING YOUR TIME
PINNACLES IN ONE DAY

Begin your day early by arriving at the west entrance, stopping briefly at the **West Pinnacles Visitor Contact Station** to pick up maps. Continue on Highway 146 about 2 miles to the **Chaparral Trailhead** parking lot, where you can view the park's impressive peaks. The best way to experience them is by hiking, so grab your flashlight and some water and follow the **Balconies Trail** from the parking lot. This mostly level 1-mile hike takes you along the shaded canyon floor to the **Balconies Cave,** where you must duck under boulders and sometimes squeeze through talus passages. From the cave you can hike an extra ½-mile on the **Balconies Cliff Trail,** climbing to fantastic views east to Machete Ridge. Follow the

AVERAGE HIGH/LOW TEMPERATURES					
JAN.	FEB.	MAR.	APR.	MAY	JUNE
62/27	63/30	67/32	72/33	80/37	88/41
JULY	AUG.	SEPT.	OCT.	NOV.	DEC.
95/45	95/45	90/42	81/36	69/31	61/27

trail down to the back side of the caves, and return through the caves to the original trail. Upon returning to your car, head west to Soledad.

From Soledad follow U.S. 101 south about 19 miles to King City, and exit at 1st Street. Follow the East Pinnacles signs to Highway 25 and continue north until you reach Highway 146 and the park's east entrance.

If the store adjacent to the **Pinnacles Visitor Center** is open, pick up a drink or a snack before continuing on Highway 146 a little more than 2 miles to the turnoff for the Bear Gulch Day Use Area. The **Bear Gulch Nature Center** is open seasonally as staffing permits. If the center is open, check out its displays, which include a seismograph (the park lies near the San Andreas Fault). Just past the nature center, there's a small parking lot with shaded tables, a perfect place for a picnic. Make sure you have your water and flashlight with you as you take the **Bear Gulch Trail** from the picnic area to the **Moses Spring Trail** (0.2 mile). Once you get to the caves (about 0.3 mile), you'll scramble through until you come to a long staircase cut into the stone; very shortly the trail will bring you to the **Bear Gulch Reservoir.** Follow the Rim Trail as it leaves the reservoir for views of the peaks to the east and west. After a switchback descent, it connects again with the Moses Spring Trail (0.7 mile), which leads back to the parking lot.

GETTING HERE AND AROUND
AIR TRAVEL
The nearest major airport is Mineta San Jose International Airport (SJC), about 80 miles north of the park. San Francisco International Airport (SFO) is about 100 miles north, and Monterey Regional Airport is 50 miles west.

CAR TRAVEL
One of the first things you need to decide when visiting Pinnacles is which entrance—east or west—you'll use. There is no through road. Entering from Highway 25 on the east side of the park is straightforward. The gate is only a mile or so from the turnoff. From the west, once you head east out of Soledad on Highway 146, the road quickly becomes narrow and hilly, with many blind curves. Park rangers discourage visitors from driving RVs, large vehicles, or vehicles towing trailers on this road. Drive slowly and cautiously along the 11 miles or so before you reach the west entrance.

PARK ESSENTIALS
PARK FEES AND PERMITS
Park admission is $25 per car, $20 for motorcycles, $12 per person on foot or bicycle. The Pinnacles National Park Annual Pass ($50) is valid for one year from the month of purchase.

PARK HOURS
The east entrance is open 24 hours a day, 7 days a week. The west entrance opens daily at 7:30 am and closes at 8 pm. An automatic gate opens for cars leaving the park after closing time.

CELL PHONE RECEPTION
The closer you get to Pinnacles, the less reliable cell phone service will be; it's nearly nonexistent within the park. There's a pay phone at the visitor center at the east entrance and at the Bear Gulch Nature Center. There are no public

28

Pinnacles National Park PLANNING

phones at the west entrance or in the interior of the park.

EDUCATIONAL OFFERINGS

INTERPRETIVE PROGRAMS

Illustrated Ranger Talks

COLLEGE | On some weekend evenings, rangers give free presentations at the east entrance's campground amphitheater. The topics depend on the ranger's particular interests but always relate to the park's main stories and its geology, plants, or wildlife. Times vary, so check the Pinnacles website or the Activity Boards at the east or west entrances or the Bear Gulch Nature Center. ⊠ *5000 Hwy. 146* ☏ *831/389–4486* ⊕ *www.nps. gov/pinn/planyourvisit/programs.htm.*

RANGER PROGRAMS

Junior Ranger Program

LOCAL INTEREST | Kids can pick up a free Junior Ranger booklet at the Bear Gulch Nature Center, Pinnacles Visitor Center, or the West Pinnacles Visitor Contact Station. Once they explore the park and complete the activities in the booklet, they'll earn a Junior Ranger Badge. ⊠ *5000 Hwy. 146* ☏ *831/389–4486* ⊕ *www.nps.gov/pinn/planyourvisit/programs.htm.*

Night Hikes

LOCAL INTEREST | Rangers occasionally lead night hikes, including ones under the full moon or to view stars. Check the park's website to see if any hikes, which are from easy to moderate in difficulty and take between one and two hours, will coincide with your visit. Space is limited, so reservations are recommended. ⊠ *5000 Hwy. 146, Paicines* ☏ *831/389–4486 east side, 831/537–7220 west side* ⊕ *www.nps.gov/pinn/planyourvisit/programs.htm.*

Ranger-Guided Hikes and Activities

LOCAL INTEREST | Ranger programs and guided hikes are offered on the weekends in the fall, winter, and spring. Times and locations vary seasonally, so when you get to the park, ask a ranger about the day's opportunities or consult one of the Ranger Activity Boards outside the Pinnacles Visitor Center, the Bear Gulch Nature Center, or the West Pinnacles Visitor Contact Station. ⊠ *5000 Hwy. 146* ☏ *831/389–4486* ⊕ *www.nps.gov/pinn/planyourvisit/programs.htm.*

RESTAURANTS

The park has no restaurants, so it's a good idea to pack a cooler before you arrive, especially if you plan on staying for more than a day. If coming from the north, you'll find supermarkets and grocery stores in Hollister; at the southern end, King City is the best option. Soledad, the gateway to the park's western entrance, also has a supermarket. The small camp store adjacent to the eastern entrance's visitor center carries mostly canned goods and snacks, as well as bags of ice. Food and drink aren't available at the western entrance. Because you can't drive through to the other entrance, you'll need to come prepared.

HOTELS

There aren't any hotels or lodges within the park, so if you want to stay overnight, camping at the Pinnacles Campground, near the east entrance, is your only option. Outside the park, King City, Hollister, and Soledad have mostly budget-class motels. *Hotel reviews have been shortened. For full information, visit Fodors.com.*

What It Costs			
$	$$	$$$	$$$$
RESTAURANTS			
under $13	$13–$20	$21–$30	over $30
HOTELS			
under $100	$100–$150	$151–$200	over $200

VISITOR INFORMATION

PARK CONTACT INFORMATION Pinnacles National Park ⊠ *5000 Hwy. 146, Paicines* ☎ *831/389–4485, 831/389–4427* ⊕ *www. nps.gov/pinn.*

VISITOR CENTERS
Pinnacles Visitor Center

At the park's main visitor center, located at the eastern entrance, you can purchase admission passes, get maps, browse books, and buy gifts. The adjacent campground store sells snacks and drinks. ⊠ *Hwy. 146, 2 miles west of Hwy. 25, Paicines* ☎ *831/389–4485* ⊕ *www. nps.gov/pinn.*

West Pinnacles Visitor Contact Station

This station is just past the park's western entrance, about 10 miles east of Soledad. Here you can get maps and information, watch a 13-minute film about Pinnacles, and view some displays. Food and drink aren't available here. ⊠ *Hwy. 146, off U.S. 101, Soledad* ☎ *831/389–4427* ⊕ *www.nps.gov/pinn.*

 Sights

HISTORIC SITES
Bacon and Butterfield Homesteads

HISTORIC SITE | On the park's eastern side, these two preserved homesteads in the heart of the 331-acre Ben Bacon Ranch Historic District illustrate what subsistence farming in the area looked like from 1865 to 1941, before large-scale agriculture and ranching became the norm. ⊠ *Pinnacles National Park.*

SCENIC STOPS
Chaparral Trailhead

VIEWPOINT | This is the end of the road on the west side of the park, but it's also the best view of the Peaks you can get without having to hit the trails. Look for knifelike Machete Ridge looming in the distance. ⊠ *Pinnacles National Park* ⊹ *About 2 miles northeast of West Pinnacles Visitor Contact Station on Hwy. 146.*

Peaks View Picnic Area

VIEWPOINT | Short of hiking up to the rugged High Peaks, this east-side viewing area is the best place to catch a glimpse of them (off to the west). You might spot hawks and other birds as well. The area has restrooms and a few picnic tables, and drinking water is available. Here you'll also find the beginning of a section of the Bench Trail that's been recently graded and resurfaced for wheelchair accessibility, winding through shady oak trees. ⊠ *Pinnacles National Park* ⊹ *About 1½ miles west of Pinnacles Visitor Center on Hwy. 146, east side* ⊕ *www.nps.gov/ pinn/planyourvisit/accessibility.htm.*

 Activities

BIRD-WATCHING

You don't have to be an avid bird-watcher to appreciate the diversity of birds at Pinnacles, so don't forget to bring your binoculars, especially for that charged moment when you realize you've spotted a highly rare California condor suspended on a thermal draft. You're most likely to see a condor in the early morning or in the early evening in the relatively remote High Peaks area, or on the Balconies Cliff Trail above the caves as you look toward Machete Ridge. Condors are often seen just southeast of the campground, riding the morning thermals along the ridge, and in the evening coming in to roost on their favorite trees. There are two spotting scopes in the campground (on the Bench Trail near Pinnacles Visitor Center) that may help you get a closer look. If you happen to find yourself especially close to a condor, do not under any circumstances approach it. Condors are a federally protected species, and you can be fined for doing so.

The High Peaks are a good place to spot other raptors, such as prairie and peregrine falcons, golden eagles, red-tailed hawks, and American kestrels. But you don't have to undertake a strenuous uphill hike to catch some of the best

Plants and Wildlife in Pinnacles National Park

Pinnacles doesn't have the wildlife superstars found at other national parks—bison, bear, elk, bighorn sheep. Here, California condors rule the roost.

Magnificent Birds

These magnificent birds, which when fully grown have wingspans approaching 10 feet, were nearly extinct in the 1980s. Only 22 remained in the world just three decades ago, but thanks to an intensive captive breeding program, there are now more than 400, with 240 of them in the wild. Pinnacles is one of the five release locations for California condors, and about 30 make their home in the park. It is also the preferred habitat for prairie falcons, which breed here in one of the highest densities in the world.

From Bobcats to Beetles

Bobcats and cougars also roam Pinnacles, and California quail are abundant. In addition, there are 14 species of bats, including a colony of Townsend's big-eared bats in Bear Gulch Cave, hibernating in winter and raising their young throughout the summer. The park has the most bee species—400 per unit area—of any place ever studied. It's also an essential refuge for native species, among them the big-eared kangaroo rat, the Gabilan slender salamander, the Pinnacles shield-back katydid, and the Pinnacles riffle beetle, that have been challenged by nearby human encroachment.

Wildflowers and Chaparral

Springtime sets the stage for a wildflower extravaganza, especially from March through early May, when more than 80% of the park's plants are in bloom. The most prodigious early bloomers include manzanita, shooting stars, and Indian warriors; by March the park is awash in California poppies, bush poppies, buck brush, fiesta flower, and monkey flower. Late bloomers include suncups, bush lupine, and Johnny-jump-ups. Most of the park is covered in chaparral, which has adapted to the high-heat, low-moisture conditions. This particular plant community is mostly shrubs that grow to around 6 feet tall; the dominant species is chamise, which grows alongside buck brush, manzanita, black sage, and holly-leaved cherry.

bird-watching in the park. The campground and visitor center on the east side lies at the convergence of habitats—riparian, oak/pine trees, chaparral, and human-made. Many species take advantage of water sources provided by the swimming pool and water fountain, and on the paved road past the parking lot, a riparian corridor is the prime habitat for coveys of California quail and wild turkeys.

HIKING

Hiking is the most popular activity at Pinnacles, which has more than 30 miles of trails for every interest and level of fitness. Because there isn't a through road, hiking is the only way to experience the park's interior, including the High Peaks, the talus caves, and the reservoir.

Moses Spring Trail, Bear Gulch Trail, and Balconies Trail are self-guided "interpretive" trails. At the campground store you can purchase trail guides ($.50-1.99) that point out different geological, botanical, and habitat facts of three different trails.

Several trails start near the Bear Gulch Day Use Area. On weekends and holidays year-round, you can catch a shuttle that operates between the east side visitor center and the Bear Gulch parking lot, which sometimes fills up.

Flashlights are required in the Bear Gulch and Balconies cave systems—you won't be able to get through the caves without one. Penlights won't do the job; the best choice is a hands-free, head-mounted light. Also, although the hikes to the caves themselves are easy and short, getting through the caves requires much scrambling, ducking, climbing, and squeezing. Make sure you have suitable, closed-toe shoes.

Balconies Cliffs-Cave Loop
HIKING/WALKING | Grab your flashlight before heading out from the Chaparral Trailhead parking lot for this 2.4-mile loop that takes you through the Balconies Caves. This trail is especially beautiful in spring, when wildflowers carpet the canyon floor. About 0.6 mile from the start of the trail, turn left to begin ascending the Balconies Cliffs Trail, where you'll be rewarded with close-up views of Machete Ridge and other steep, vertical formations; you may run across rock climbers testing their skills before rounding the loop and descending back through the cave. *Easy.* ⊠ *West side of park* ⊹ *Trailhead: from West Pinnacles Visitor Contact Station, drive about 2 miles to Chaparral Trailhead parking lot. Trail picks up on west side of lot.*

Chalone Peak Trail
HIKING/WALKING | If you choose this strenuous 9-mile round-trip hike (2,040 feet of elevation gain), you'll be rewarded with views of the surrounding valleys from the highest point in the park at 3,304 feet (where there are restrooms). If you want to extend the hike, proceed south along the unmaintained portion of the trail for 1.6 miles to South Chalone Peak (3,269 feet). *Difficult.* ⊠ *East side of park* ⊹ *Trailhead: at Bear Gulch Reservoir where Moses Spring, Rim, and Chalone Peak trails meet near caves.*

Condor Gulch Trail
HIKING/WALKING | The trailhead starts at the Bear Gulch Day Use area, and it's a moderately strenuous 1-mile hike uphill to the Condor Gulch Overlook, where you can get a good view of the High Peaks above and look back down to the trail behind you. From the outlook you can turn back the same way you came, or continue another 0.7 mile up to where the Condor Gulch meets the High Peaks Trail and extend your hike by following the High Peaks Trail in either direction. *Moderate–Difficult.* ⊠ *East side of park* ⊹ *Trailhead: opposite Nature Center at Bear Gulch Day Use Area.*

Jawbone Trail
HIKING/WALKING | One of the park's new trails, the easy-to-moderate Jawbone Trail extends from the Prewett Point Trail, starting at the West Pinnacles Visitor Contact Station. It cuts 1.2 miles through the hills to the east of Highway 146, ending at the Jawbone Parking Area, which is overflow parking for the Chaparral Parking Area, another 0.3 miles. ⊠ *Paicines.*

Juniper Canyon Loop
HIKING/WALKING | This steep 4.3-mile loop climbs into the heart of the dramatic High Peaks with a 1,215-foot elevation gain. In summer the temperature can get very high, so be sure to bring plenty of water. From the trailhead follow the switchbacks up for 1.2 miles, where the trail veers right; be sure to stop at Scout Peak, where you'll find restrooms and fantastic views in all directions—keep an eye out for the occasional California condor in flight. From Scout Peak, follow the High Peaks Trail through a steep and narrow section, where you hug the side of rock faces until reaching a short, nearly vertical staircase that has a railing

Did You Know?

The Juniper Canyon Loop trail into the heart of the High Peaks has an elevation gain of 1,215 feet.

to help you up. *Difficult.* ⊠ *West side of park* ⊹ *Trailhead: Chaparral Trailhead parking lot.*

Moses Spring-Rim Trail Loop

HIKING/WALKING | **FAMILY** | Perhaps the most popular hike at Pinnacles, this relatively short (2.2 miles) trail is fun for kids and adults. It leads to the Bear Gulch cave system, and if your timing is right, you'll pass by several seasonal waterfalls inside the caves (flashlights are required). If it has been raining, check with a ranger, as the caves could be flooded. The upper side of the cave is usually closed in spring and early summer to protect the Townsend's big-ear bats and their pups. *Easy.* ⊠ *East side of park* ⊹ *Trailhead: just past Bear Gulch Nature Center, on south side of overflow parking lot.*

Pinnacles Visitor Center to Bear Gulch Day Use Area

HIKING/WALKING | This 4.6-mile round-trip hike (about three hours) follows the Chalone and Bear creeks first along the Bench Trail for about 1½ miles, where it meets up with the Bear Gulch Trail. Purchase an interpretive map at the visitor center and keep your eyes open for signs pointing out where you might be able to spot the rare red-legged frog or the native three-spined stickleback fish. *Moderate.* ⊠ *East side of park* ⊹ *Trailhead: Pinnacles Visitor Center; follow signs to Bench Trail.*

Prewett Point Trail

HIKING/WALKING | This new wheelchair-accessible, 1-mile round-trip trail begins at the West Pinnacles Contact Station, allowing for great panoramic views of the High Peaks, Balconies Cliffs, and Hain Wilderness. It's mostly exposed, so take that into consideration when the weather is hot. ⊠ *Paicines.*

South Wilderness Trail

HIKING/WALKING | This 6½-mile hike with no elevation gain is an easy stroll alongside the Chalone River that eventually reaches the park's eastern boundary.

Listen to birds sing along the creek as you meander among this unmaintained trail's magnificent groves of valley oaks. *Moderate.* ⊠ *East side of park* ⊹ *Trailhead: follow Bench Trail out of Pinnacles Campground for 0.6 mile, then turn left onto fire road to access South Wilderness Trail.*

ROCK CLIMBING

Pinnacles has been a favorite of Bay Area and Central Coast climbers for years, but luckily it remains a relatively quiet spot without the hassle and crowds of better-known parks like Yosemite and Joshua Tree. One important thing to consider is that unlike Yosemite and other granite playgrounds, Pinnacles is largely made of volcanic rock that can be soft and crumbly. The park service suggests that if you have never climbed at Pinnacles before, your first attempts should be well below your usual level to allow you to familiarize yourself with the strength and character of the rocks. In general, the east side of the park has stronger rock, but the west side has much higher peaks.

A good resource for first-time climbers is the Friends of Pinnacles (⊕ *www. pinnacles.org*), a nonprofit that works directly with the park to offer useful tips, guidelines, and updates regarding climbing closures due to nesting raptors. Some formations might also be closed from January through June or July if falcons or eagles are nesting. If you want to know if a specific route is open, check with a ranger or look for the climbing information boards at both the east and west trailheads. Complying with closures is voluntary, but climbers or hikers caught disturbing nesting birds will be fined.

STARGAZING

Though the populous Bay Area is only a couple of hours away, Pinnacles remains nearly untouched by light pollution, making it an outstanding place to watch meteor showers, stars, or the full moon. It's popular with astronomy clubs, whose members occasionally set up their telescopes for public use. Park rangers sometimes lead nighttime activities, usually on the weekends, that include dark-sky and full-moon hikes and "star parties" to watch meteor showers and other celestial phenomena. Campsites often fill up well in advance when meteor showers are expected. These activities are usually limited to 25 or fewer visitors per program, and reservations are required (no more than one week in advance) by calling ☎ 831/389–4485 or visiting the Pinnacles Visitor Center.

Nearby Towns

Soledad, at the park's western entrance, is most famous for being the setting of John Steinbeck's *Of Mice and Men,* but it's also a part of the Monterey County wine region. There are many good wineries with tasting rooms within about 30 miles. Hahn, Scheid, Pessagno, and Ventana, all on the **River Road Wine Trail** (⊕ *www.riverroadwinetrail.com*), are open daily.

To the north in San Benito County is **Hollister,** a farming town that is fast becoming a bedroom community of San Jose. This area is not as well known for wine as is Monterey County, but you can spend a low-key afternoon visiting tasting rooms along the San Benito County Wine Trail. Most are on or near Cienega Road, just south of Hollister off Highway 25. Calera and Léal are among the wineries with tasting rooms open daily.

Popular Monterey and Carmel, on the Monterey Peninsula on the Pacific coast, are a little more than an hour's drive from Pinnacles, yet feel like a world away, with all the amenities a world-class tourist destination has to offer, including an abundance of dining and lodging options.

VISITOR INFORMATION San Benito County Chamber of Commerce ⊠ *243 6th St., Suite 100, Hollister* ☎ *831/637–5315* ⊕ *www.*

sanbenitocountychamber.com. **Soledad-Mission Chamber of Commerce** ⊠ *641 Front St., Soledad* ☎ *831/595–5962* ⊕ *www.soledadchamber.com.*

 Restaurants

IN THE PARK
PICNIC AREAS
Bear Gulch Picnic Area
RESTAURANT—SIGHT | The park's most pleasant picnic area, shaded by live oaks, sits alongside a seasonal creek. It's a convenient spot to picnic before or after a hike to the reservoir via the Moses Spring or Rim trail. The nearby Bear Gulch Day Use Area has bathrooms (across from the Bear Gulch Nature Center) and drinking water. ⊠ *East side of park* ✣ *About 0.3 mile past Bear Gulch Nature Center on Bear Gulch Trail.*

Chaparral Trailhead Picnic Area
RESTAURANT—SIGHT | This is the only designated picnic area on the west side of the park, but there are great views of the nearby High Peaks. There are few trees for shade, however, and it can be quite warm in summer. Restrooms are close by, and drinking water is available. The park has just recently added a nearly 1-mile wheelchair-accessible trail, the Prewett Point Trail, that begins at the West Pinnacles Contact Station and affords views of the High Peaks and Balconies Cliffs. ⊠ *West side of park* ✣ *About 2 miles northeast of West Pinnacles Visitor Contact Station on Hwy. 146.*

East Pinnacles Visitor Center Picnic Area
RESTAURANT—SIGHT | Adjacent to the overflow parking area at the East Pinnacles Visitor Center, there are a number of picnic tables and charcoal grills (allowed only when fire danger is low) that are mostly shaded by trees—a welcome relief in the hot summer months. ⊠ *Paicines.*

Best Campgrounds in Pinnacles

Pinnacles has only one camping option, on the park's eastern side, next to the Pinnacles Visitor Center.

Pinnacles Campground. Set under a canopy of live oaks that provides welcome shade over most of its 134 sites (83 nonelectric tent-only sites, 14 nonelectric group sites, and 37 electric RV sites), this campground is open year-round. The bathrooms, which have flush toilets, are clean if somewhat dated; showers are available for a small fee. Each site has a picnic table and a fire ring, but because of high fire danger, especially in the dry summer and early fall, campfires often aren't allowed. The swimming pool behind the visitor center is open from April through September. Leashed pets are allowed in the campground, but not on trails. The campground store, which shares space next to the visitor center, carries basic food supplies, snacks, soft drinks, beer, and ice. ✉ *5000 Hwy. 146* ☎ *877/444–6777 for reservations, 831/389–4538 for campground store.*

Peaks View Picnic Area

RESTAURANT—SIGHT | A nice spot for a picnic, Peaks View is one of the few places on the east side of the park where you can catch a glimpse of the High Peaks without getting on a trail. Restrooms and drinking water are available. ✉ *East side of park* ✣ *About 1.5 miles west of Pinnacles Visitor Center on Hwy. 146.*

OUTSIDE THE PARK

Cork & Plough

$$ | **CONTEMPORARY** | King City was long overdue for an eatery like Cork & Plough, situated as it is in the southern reaches of Salinas Valley's agricultural bounty. Located on the town's main street, C&P concentrates on contemporary takes on classic fare using seasonal products from the valley and Central Coast. **Known for:** specialty cocktails; wine flights; seasonal fare. [$] *Average main: $16* ✉ *Cork & Plough, 200 Broadway St.* ☎ *831/386–9491* 🌐 *www.thecorkandplough.com.*

Fisher's

$$ | **MODERN AMERICAN** | You won't find a printed menu at Fisher's, because the offerings here can change daily, depending on what's in season at the area's local farms. Le Cordon Bleu Paris-trained chef Mike Fisher returned to Hollister by way of NYC to open a restaurant showcasing the freshest ingredients possible. **Known for:** seasonal produce; menu changes daily; local ingredients. [$] *Average main: $15* ✉ *Fisher's, 650 San Benito St., Hollister* ☎ *831/313–1515* 🌐 *fishershollister.com* 🕒 *Closed Sun. and Mon.*

Steinbeck House Restaurant

$$ | **AMERICAN** | This delightful restaurant, housed in a beautifully restored 1897-era Queen Anne Victorian, was home to author John Steinbeck for the first 17 years of his life. Since 1974, the Steinbeck House, as it's known, has been serving lunch (and monthly Sunday-afternoon teas and Friday-night dinners) thanks to a passionate staff of volunteers who not only manage the restaurant (and gift shop), but serve the guests as well. **Known for:** weekly changing set menu; historic setting; volunteer-run. [$] *Average main: $15* ✉ *Steinbeck House Restaurant, 132 Central Ave., Salinas* ☎ *831/424–2735* 🌐 *steinbeckhouse.com/restaurant* 🕒 *Closed Sun.*

 Hotels

OUTSIDE THE PARK

Casa de Fruta Inn

$$ | HOTEL | FAMILY | You can decide for yourself if the surprisingly pleasant accommodations at one end of a popular fruit stand–cum–amusement park are charming or cheesy, but they're clean and fairly spacious, and the updated fixtures lend the place a fresh, contemporary feel. **Pros:** great for families with young kids; reasonably priced; convenient for travel to or from I–5. **Cons:** location near highway means noise; next door to large RV park. $ *Rooms from: $139* ✉ *10021 Pacheco Pass Hwy., Hollister* ☎ *408/842-9316* ⊕ *www.casadefruta. com/visit/accommodations.php* ⇗ *14 rooms* ❌ *No meals.*

★ Inn at the Pinnacles

$$$$ | B&B/INN | Set amid 160 acres of hilltop vineyards overlooking the Salinas Valley and the coastal Santa Lucia Mountains, this Mediterranean-style bed-and-breakfast is an oasis of comfort just off the winding road leading to the park's western entrance. **Pros:** gorgeous vineyard setting and sunset views; tasty breakfast; close to the park. **Cons:** 20 minutes to closest Soledad restaurants; better for couples than families. $ *Rooms from: $235* ✉ *3025 Stonewall Canyon Rd., Soledad* ☎ *831/678–2400* ⊕ *www.innatthepinnacles.com* ⇗ *6 rooms* ❌ *Breakfast* ⟳ *2-night minimum.*

Paicines Ranch

$$ | RENTAL | Comfortable, somewhat rustic rooms and cottages are tucked into a corner of this 7,000-acre working cattle ranch that's within an easy 30-minute drive of the park's east entrance. **Pros:** easy access to park's east entrance; good for large groups or families; peaceful; cooking facilities available. **Cons:** no amenities outside of rooms; closest restaurants 15 minutes away. $ *Rooms from: $100* ✉ *13388 Old Airline Hwy., Paicines* ☎ *831/688–0288* ⊕ *www. paicinesranch.com/event-center/lodging. php* ⇗ *8 rooms* ❌ *No meals.*

Chapter 29

REDWOOD NATIONAL AND STATE PARKS

Updated by
Andrew Collins

CALIFORNIA

WELCOME TO REDWOOD NATIONAL AND STATE PARKS

TOP REASONS TO GO

★ **Giant trees:** These mature coastal redwoods are the tallest trees in the world.

★ **Hiking to the sea:** The park's trails wind through majestic redwood groves, and many connect to the Coastal Trail, which runs along the western edge of the park.

★ **Rare wildlife:** Mighty Roosevelt elk favor the park's flat prairie and open lands; seldom-seen black bears roam the backcountry; trout and salmon leap through streams; and Pacific gray whales swim along the coast during their spring and fall migrations.

★ **Stepping back in time:** Hike mossy and mysterious Fern Canyon Trail and explore a prehistoric scene of lush vegetation and giant ferns—a memorable scene in Jurassic Park 2 was shot here.

★ **Getting off-the-grid:** Amid the majestic redwoods you're usually out of cell phone range and often free from crowds, offering a rare opportunity to disconnect.

U.S. 101 weaves through the southern portion of Redwood National and State Parks, skirts around the center, and then slips back through redwoods in the north and on to Crescent City. The entire park spans about 50 miles north to south. The Kuchel Visitor Center, Humboldt Lagoons State Park, Prairie Creek Redwoods State Park, Tall Trees Grove, Fern Canyon, and Lady Bird Johnson Grove are in the southern section. In the central section, where the Klamath River Overlook is the dominant feature, the narrow, mostly graveled Coastal Drive loop yields ocean vistas. To the north are Mill Creek Trail, Enderts Beach, and Crescent Beach Overlook in Del Norte Coast Redwoods State Park, as well as Jedediah Smith Redwoods State Park, Stout Grove, Little Bald Hills, and Simpson-Reed Grove.

1 Del Norte Coast Redwoods State Park. The rugged terrain of this far northwestern corner of California combines stretches of treacherous surf, steep cliffs, and forested ridges. On a clear day it's postcard-perfect; with fog, it's mysterious and mesmerizing.

2 Jedediah Smith Redwoods State Park. Gargantuan old-growth redwoods dominate the scenery here. The Smith River cuts through canyons and splits across boulders, carrying salmon to the inland creeks where they spawn.

3 Prairie Creek Redwoods State Park. The forests here give way to spacious, grassy plains where abundant wildlife thrives. Roosevelt elk are a common sight in the meadows and down to Gold Bluffs Beach, where a short trail leads to Fern Canyon.

4 Orick Area. The highlight of the southern portion of Redwood National and State Parks is the Tall Trees Grove. It's difficult to reach and requires a special pass, but it's worth the hassle—this section has some of the tallest coast redwood trees. The current world-record holder, a 379-footer named Hyperion, was discovered outside the grove in 2006.

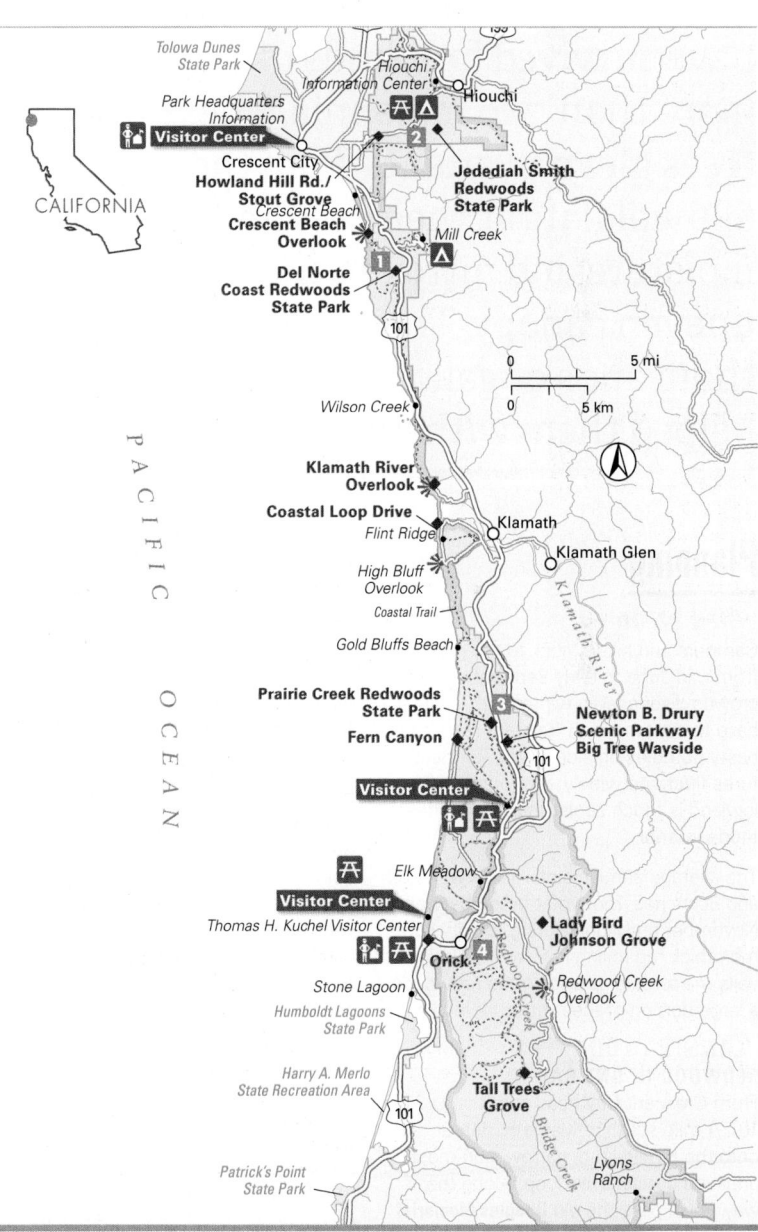

Tolowa Dunes
State Park

Hiouchi
Information Center
Hiouchi

Park Headquarters
Information

Visitor Center

Crescent City

Howland Hill Rd./
Stout Grove

Jedediah Smith
Redwoods
State Park

Crescent Beach
Crescent Beach
Overlook

Mill Creek

Del Norte
Coast Redwoods
State Park

101

CALIFORNIA

PACIFIC OCEAN

Wilson Creek

0   5 mi
0   5 km

Klamath River
Overlook

Coastal Loop Drive
Flint Ridge

Klamath

Klamath Glen

High Bluff
Overlook

Coastal Trail

Gold Bluffs Beach

Klamath River

Prairie Creek Redwoods
State Park

Fern Canyon

Newton B. Drury
Scenic Parkway/
Big Tree Wayside

101

Visitor Center

Elk Meadow

Visitor Center

Thomas H. Kuchel Visitor Center

Lady Bird
Johnson Grove

Orick

Stone Lagoon

Redwood Creek
Overlook

Humboldt Lagoons
State Park

Harry A. Merlo
State Recreation Area

101

Tall Trees
Grove

Redwood Creek

Bridge Creek

Lyons
Ranch

Patrick's Point
State Park

Soaring more than 350 feet high, the coastal redwoods that give this park its name are miracles of efficiency—some have survived hundreds of years, a few more than two millennia. These massive trees glean nutrients from the rich alluvial flats at their feet and from the moisture and nitrogen trapped in their uneven canopy. Their thick bark can hold thousands of gallons of water, which has helped them withstand centuries of fires.

Planning

WHEN TO GO

Campers and hikers flock to the park from mid-June to early September. The crowds disappear in winter, but you'll have to contend with frequent rains and nasty potholes on side roads. Temperatures fluctuate widely: the foggy coastal lowland is much cooler than the higher-altitude interior.

The average annual rainfall is between 60 and 80 inches, most of it falling between November and April. During the dry summer, thick fog rolling in from the Pacific veils the forests, providing the redwoods a large portion of their moisture intake.

PLANNING YOUR TIME
REDWOOD IN ONE DAY

From Crescent City head south on U.S. 101. A mile south of Klamath, detour onto the 8-mile-long, narrow, and mostly unpaved **Coastal Drive** loop. Along the way, you'll pass the old **Douglas Memorial Bridge,** destroyed in the 1964 flood. Coastal Drive turns south above Flint Ridge. In less than a mile you'll reach the **World War II Radar Station,** which looks like a farmhouse, its disguise in the 1940s. Continue south to the intersection with Alder Camp Road, stopping at the **High Bluff Overlook.**

From the Coastal Drive turn left to reconnect with U.S. 101. Head south to reach **Newton B. Drury Scenic Parkway,** a 10-mile drive through an old-growth redwood forest with access to numerous trailheads. This road is open to all noncommercial vehicles. Along the way, stop at **Prairie Creek Visitor Center,** housed in a small redwood lodge. Enjoy a picnic lunch and an engaging tactile walk in a grove behind the lodge on the Revelation Trail, which was designed for vision-impaired visitors. Back on the parkway head north less than a mile and drive out on unpaved **Cal-Barrel Road,** which leads east through redwood forests. Return to the parkway, continue south about 2 miles to reconnect with U.S. 101, and turn west

AVERAGE HIGH/LOW TEMPERATURES					
JAN.	FEB.	MAR.	APR.	MAY	JUNE
54/39	56/41	57/41	59/42	62/45	65/48
JULY	AUG.	SEPT.	OCT.	NOV.	DEC.
67/51	67/51	68/49	64/46	58/43	55/40

on mostly unpaved **Davison Road** (motorhomes/RVs and trailers are prohibited). In about 30 minutes you'll curve right to **Gold Bluffs Beach.** Continue north to the **Fern Canyon** trailhead. Return to U.S. 101, and drive south to the turnoff for the **Thomas H. Kuchel Visitor Center.** Pick up a free permit—a limited number are granted daily—to visit the **Tall Trees Grove** and head north on U.S. 101 to the turnoff for **Bald Hills Road,** a steep route (motorhomes/RVs and trailers are not advised). If you visit the grove, allow at least four hours round-trip from the Kuchel Visitor Center. You could also bypass the turnoff to the grove and continue south on Bald Hills Road to 3,097-foot **Schoolhouse Peak.** For a simpler jaunt, turn onto Bald Hills Road and follow it for 2 miles to the **Lady Bird Johnson Grove Nature Loop Trail.** Take the footbridge to the easy 1-mile loop, which follows an old logging road through a mature redwood forest. ■TIP➜ **Motorhomes/RVs and trailers are not allowed on Coastal Drive, Cal-Barrel Road, and Davison Road, and are not advised on Bald Hills Road. Conditions on these roads can sometimes lead to closures or the requirement of high-clearance vehicles—check with the visitor centers before you set out.**

GETTING HERE AND AROUND
AIR TRAVEL
United Airlines flies a few times daily between San Francisco and the most practical gateway, Arcata/Eureka Airport, between Trinidad and Arcata, about 16 miles north of Eureka. The regional carrier Contour offers daily service from Oakland to Del Norte County Regional Airport in Crescent City. Another option is Oregon's Rogue Valley International Medford Airport, which is served by Alaska, Allegiant, American, Delta, and United, and is about a 2-hour drive from the northern end of the park in Crescent City.

CAR TRAVEL
U.S. 101 runs north–south the entire length of the park. You can access all the main park roads via U.S. 101 and U.S. 199, which runs east–west through the park's northern portion. Many roads within the park aren't paved, and winter rains can turn them into obstacle courses; sometimes they're closed completely. Motorhomes/RVs and trailers aren't permitted on some routes. The drive from San Francisco to the park's southern end takes about six hours via U.S. 101. From Portland it takes roughly the same amount of time to reach the park's northern section via Interstate 5 to U.S. 199. ■TIP➜ **Don't rely solely on GPS, which is inaccurate in parts of the park; closely consult official park maps.**

PARK ESSENTIALS
PARK FEES AND PERMITS
Admission to Redwood National Park is free; several of the state parks collect day-use fees of $8, including the Gold Bluffs Beach and Fern Canyon sections of Prairie Creek Redwoods State Park, and the day-use areas accessed via the campground entrances in Jedediah Smith and Del Norte Coast state parks (the fee for camping overnight is $35). To visit the popular Tall Trees Grove, you must get a free permit at the Kuchel Visitor Center in Orick. Free permits, available at the Kuchel, Crescent City, and (summer only) Hiouchi visitor centers, are needed to stay at all designated backcountry camps.

PARK HOURS

The park is open year-round, 24 hours a day.

CELL PHONE RECEPTION

It's difficult to pick up a signal in much of the park, especially in the camping and hiking areas. If you need a public telephone, go to the Prairie Creek or Jedediah Smith visitor centers.

EDUCATIONAL OFFERINGS

RANGER PROGRAMS

All summer long, ranger-led programs explore the mysteries of both the redwoods and the sea. Topics include how the trees grow from fleck-size seeds to towering giants, what causes those weird fungi on old stumps, why the ocean fog is so important to redwoods, and exactly what those green-tentacled creatures are that float in tide pools. Campfire programs can include slide shows, storytelling, music, and games. Check with visitor centers for offerings and times.

Junior Ranger Program

TOUR—SIGHT | FAMILY | From June to early September, rangers lead one-hour programs for children between ages 7 and 12. Activities include nature walks and lessons in bird identification and outdoor survival. ☎ 707/465–7306 ⊕ www.nps. gov/redw.

Ranger Talks

TOUR—SIGHT | From mid-May through mid-September, state park rangers regularly lead discussions on the redwoods, tide pools, geology, and Native American culture. Check schedules at the visitor centers. ☎ 707/465–7335 ⊕ www.nps. gov/redw.

Redwood EdVentures

TOUR—SIGHT | FAMILY | Fun and engaging nature Redwood EdVentures scavenger hunts for kids, called Quests, include ones in the park. Visit the website for "treasure map" PDFs detailing the Quests, which typically take no more than an hour. Participants receive a patch upon completion. ⊕ www.redwood-edventures.org.

RESTAURANTS

The park has no restaurants, but Eureka and Arcata have diverse dining establishments—everything from hip oyster bars to some surprisingly good ethnic restaurants. The dining options are more limited, though decent, in Crescent City, and there are a few good choices in Klamath, Orick, and Trinidad. Most small-town restaurants close early, around 7:30 or 8 pm.

HOTELS

The only lodgings within park boundaries are the Elk Meadow Cabins, near Prairie Creek Redwoods Visitor Center. Orick, to the south of Elk Meadow, and Klamath, to the north, have basic motels, and in Klamath there's the Requa Inn bed-and-breakfast. Elegant Victorian inns, seaside motels, and fully equipped vacation rentals are among the options in towns north and south of the park. In summer, try to book at least a week ahead at lodgings near the park entrance. *Hotel reviews have been shortened. For full information, visit Fodors.com.*

What It Costs			
$	$$	$$$	$$$$
RESTAURANTS			
under $12	$12–$20	$21–$30	over $30
HOTELS			
under $100	$100–$150	$151–$200	over $200

VISITOR INFORMATION

PARK CONTACT INFORMATION Redwood National and State Parks ✉ 1111 2nd St., Crescent City ☎ 707/465–7335 ⊕ www. nps.gov/redw.

VISITOR CENTERS

Crescent City Information Center

INFO CENTER | At the park's headquarters, this downtown visitor center with a gift shop and picnic area is the main information stop if you're approaching the Redwoods from the north. In winter, hours are limited and dependent on funding; call ahead to confirm. ✉ *1111 2nd St., Crescent City* ☎ *707/465–7335* ⊕ *www. nps.gov/redw.*

Hiouchi Information Center

INFO CENTER | This small center at Jedediah Smith Redwoods State Park has exhibits about the area flora and fauna and screens a 12-minute park film. A starting point for ranger programs, the center has restrooms and a picnic area. ✉ *U.S. 199* ⊕ *Opposite entrance to Jedediah Smith Campground, 9 miles east of Crescent City* ☎ *707/458–3294* ⊕ *www.nps.gov/ redw.*

Jedediah Smith Visitor Center

INFO CENTER | Adjacent to the Jedediah Smith Redwoods State Park main campground, this seasonal center has information about ranger-led walks and evening campfire programs. Also here are nature and history exhibits, a gift shop, and a picnic area. ✉ *U.S. 199, Hiouchi* ⊕ *At Jedediah Smith Campground* ☎ *707/458–3496* ⊕ *www.nps. gov/redw* ⊗ *Closed Oct.–May.*

★ Prairie Creek Visitor Center

INFO CENTER | **FAMILY** | In a small redwood lodge, this center has a massive stone fireplace. The wildlife displays include a section of a tree a young elk died beside. Because of the peculiar way the redwood grew around the elk's skull, the tree appears to have antlers. The center has information about summer programs in Prairie Creek Redwoods State Park, and you'll find a gift shop, a picnic area, restrooms, and exhibits on flora and fauna. Roosevelt elk often roam the vast field adjacent to the center, and several trailheads begin nearby. Stretch your legs with an easy stroll along **Revelation Trail,** a short loop that starts behind the lodge. ✉ *Prairie Creek Rd., Orick* ⊕ *Off southern end of Newton B. Drury Scenic Pkwy.* ☎ *707/488–2039* ⊕ *www.nps.gov/redw.*

★ Thomas H. Kuchel Visitor Center

INFO CENTER | **FAMILY** | The park's southern section contains the largest and best of the Redwoods visitor centers. Rangers here dispense brochures, advice, and free permits to drive up the access road to Tall Trees Grove. Whale-watchers find the center's deck an excellent observation point, and bird-watchers enjoy the nearby Freshwater Lagoon, a popular layover for migrating waterfowl. Many of the center's exhibits are hands-on and kid-friendly. ✉ *U.S. 101, Orick* ⊕ *Redwood Creek Beach County Park* ☎ *707/465– 7765* ⊕ *www.nps.gov/redw.*

◉ Sights

SCENIC DRIVES
★ Coastal Drive Loop

SCENIC DRIVE | The 9-mile, narrow, and partially unpaved Coastal Drive Loop takes about one hour to traverse. Weaving through stands of redwoods, the road yields close-up views of the Klamath River and expansive panoramas of the Pacific. Recurring landslides have closed sections of the original road; this loop, closed to trailers and RVs, is all that remains. Hikers access the Flint Ridge section of the Coastal Trail off the drive. ✉ *Klamath* ⊕ *Off Klamath Beach Rd. exit from U.S. 101.*

Howland Hill Road/Stout Grove

SCENIC DRIVE | Take your time as you drive this 10-mile route along Mill Creek, which winds through old-growth redwoods and past the Smith River. Trailers and RVs are prohibited on this route. ⊕ *Access from Elk Valley Rd., off U.S. 101.*

★ Newton B. Drury Scenic Parkway/Big Tree Wayside

SCENIC DRIVE | This paved 10-mile route threads through Prairie Creek Redwoods State Park and old-growth redwoods. It's open to all noncommercial vehicles. North of the Prairie Creek Visitor Center you can make the 0.8-mile walk to Big Tree Wayside and observe Roosevelt elk in the prairie. ✉ *Orick* ⊕ *Entrances off*

U.S. 101 about 5 miles south of Klamath and 5 miles north of Orick.

SCENIC STOPS

Crescent Beach Overlook

VIEWPOINT | The scenery here includes views of the ocean and, in the distance, Crescent City and its working harbor. In balmy weather this is a great place for a picnic. You may spot migrating gray whales between November and April. ⊠ *Enderts Beach Rd. ✛ 4½ miles south of Crescent City.*

Del Norte Coast Redwoods State Park

BEACH—SIGHT | This park southeast of Crescent City contains 15 memorial redwood groves and 8 miles of pristine coastline, which you can most easily access at Wilson Beach or False Klamath Cove. The old-growth forest extends down steep slopes almost to the shore. ⊠ *U.S. 101, Crescent City ✛ 9 miles southeast of Crescent City* ☎ *707/465–7335* ⊕ *www.parks.ca.gov.*

★ Fern Canyon

CANYON | Enter another world and be surrounded by 50-foot canyon walls covered with sword, deer, and five-finger ferns. Allow an hour to explore the ¼-mile-long vertical garden along a 0.7-mile loop. From the northern end of Gold Bluffs Beach it's an easy walk, although you'll have to wade across or scamper along planks that traverse a small stream several times (in addition to driving across a couple of streams on the way to the parking area). But the lush, otherworldly surroundings, which appeared in *Jurassic Park 2,* are a must-see when creeks aren't running too high. Motorhomes/RVs and all trailers are prohibited. You can also hike to the canyon from Prairie Creek Visitor Center along the moderately challenging West Ridge–Friendship Ridge–James Irvine Loop, 12½ miles round-trip. ⊠ *Orick ✛ 2¾ miles north of Orick, take Davison Rd. northwest off U.S. 101 and follow signs to Gold Bluffs Beach.*

★ Jedediah Smith Redwoods State Park

NATIONAL/STATE PARK | Home to the Stout Memorial Grove, this park with 20 miles of hiking and nature trails is named after a trapper who in 1826 became the first white man to explore northern California's interior. If coming from interior Oregon, this is your first chance to drive and hike among stands of soaring redwoods. ⊠ *U.S. 199, Hiouchi ✛ 9 miles east of Crescent City* ☎ *707/458–4396* ⊕ *www.parks.ca.gov.*

Klamath River Overlook

VIEWPOINT | This grassy, windswept bluff rises 650 feet above the confluence of the Klamath River and the Pacific. It's one of the best spots in the park for spying migratory whales in early winter and late spring, and it accesses a section of the Coastal Trail. Warm days are ideal for picnicking at one of the tables. ⊠ *End of Requa Rd., Klamath ✛ 2¼ miles west of U.S. 101.*

Lady Bird Johnson Grove

FOREST | One of the park's most accessible spots to view big trees, the grove was dedicated by, and named for, the former first lady. An easy 1-mile nature loop follows an old logging road through a redwood forest. ⊠ *Bald Hills Rd., Orick ✛ 2 miles east of U.S. 101.*

★ Prairie Creek Redwoods State Park

NATIONAL/STATE PARK | FAMILY | Spectacular redwoods and lush ferns make up this park traversed by the stunning Newton B. Drury Scenic Parkway. Extra space has been paved alongside the parklands, providing fine places to observe herds of Roosevelt elk, which at one time neared extinction, in adjoining meadows. The park also includes famously spectacular Gold Bluffs Beach and Fern Canyon. If your time is limited, Prairie Creek is one of the best spots for a full day hiking and exploring. ⊠ *Prairie Creek Rd., Orick ✛ Off southern end of Newton B. Drury Scenic Pkwy.* ☎ *707/488–2039* ⊕ *www.parks.ca.gov.*

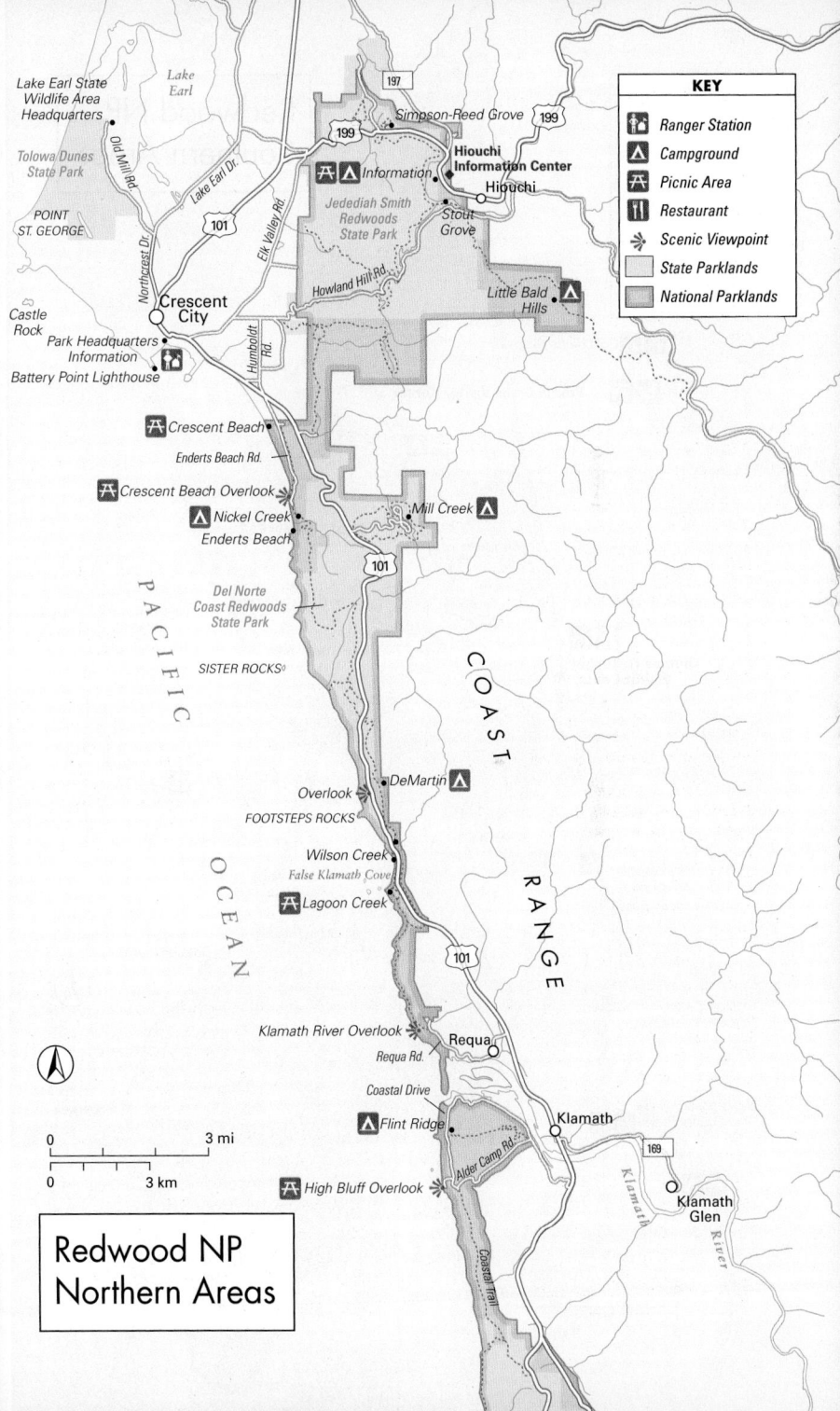

KEY

![Ranger Station]	Ranger Station
![Campground]	Campground
![Picnic Area]	Picnic Area
![Restaurant]	Restaurant
![Scenic Viewpoint]	Scenic Viewpoint
	State Parklands
	National Parklands

Lake Earl State Wildlife Area Headquarters

Lake Earl

Tolowa Dunes State Park

Lake Earl

197

199

Simpson-Reed Grove

199

Old Mill Rd.

Lake Earl Dr.

POINT ST. GEORGE

101

199

Information

Hiouchi Information Center

Hiouchi

Jedediah Smith Redwoods State Park

Stout Grove

Castle Rock

Elk Valley Rd.

Northcrest Dr.

Crescent City

Howland Hill Rd.

Little Bald Hills

Park Headquarters Information

Battery Point Lighthouse

Humboldt Rd.

Crescent Beach

Enderts Beach Rd.

Crescent Beach Overlook

Nickel Creek

Mill Creek

Enderts Beach

101

Del Norte Coast Redwoods State Park

SISTER ROCKS

P A C I F I C

C O A S T

O C E A N

Overlook

DeMartin

FOOTSTEPS ROCKS

Wilson Creek

False Klamath Cove

Lagoon Creek

R A N G E

101

Klamath River Overlook

Requa

Requa Rd.

Coastal Drive

Flint Ridge

Klamath

Alder Camp Rd.

169

High Bluff Overlook

Klamath

Klamath River

Klamath Glen

Coastal Trail

N

0   3 mi

0   3 km

Redwood NP Northern Areas

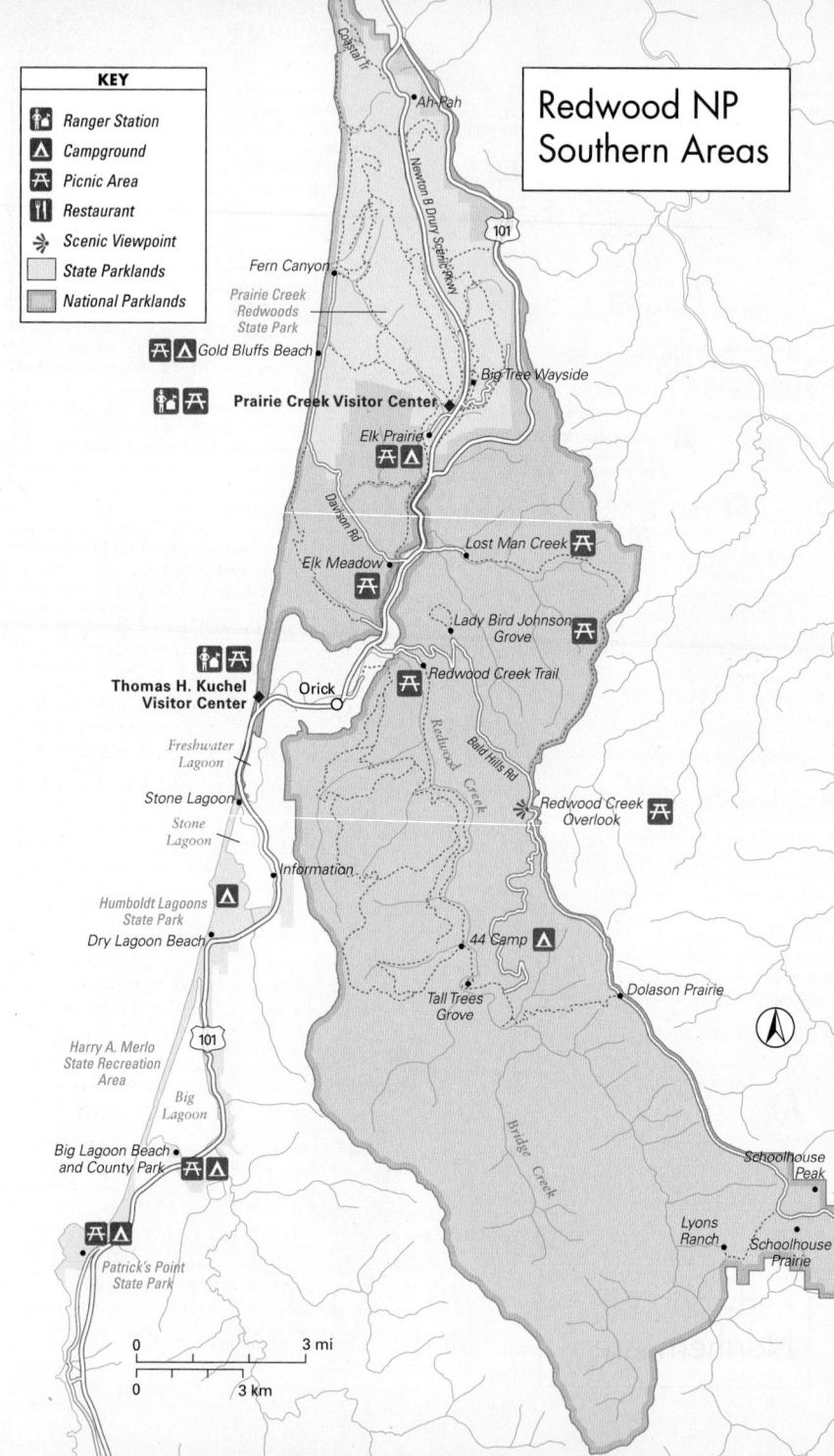

Redwood NP Southern Areas

KEY

- Ranger Station
- Campground
- Picnic Area
- Restaurant
- Scenic Viewpoint
- State Parklands
- National Parklands

Coastal Tr

Ah-Pah

Newton B Drury Scenic Pkwy

101

Fern Canyon

Prairie Creek Redwoods State Park

Gold Bluffs Beach

Big Tree Wayside

Prairie Creek Visitor Center

Elk Prairie

Davison Rd

Elk Meadow

Lost Man Creek

Lady Bird Johnson Grove

Redwood Creek Trail

Thomas H. Kuchel Visitor Center

Orick

Freshwater Lagoon

Stone Lagoon

Stone Lagoon

Redwood Creek

Bald Hills Rd

Redwood Creek Overlook

Information

Humboldt Lagoons State Park

Dry Lagoon Beach

44 Camp

Tall Trees Grove

Dolason Prairie

Harry A. Merlo State Recreation Area

101

Big Lagoon

Bridge Creek

Big Lagoon Beach and County Park

Schoolhouse Peak

Lyons Ranch

Schoolhouse Prairie

Patrick's Point State Park

| 0 | | 3 mi |

| 0 | | 3 km |

Plants and Wildlife in Redwood

Coast redwoods, the world's tallest trees, grow in the moist, temperate climate of California's North Coast. The current record holder, topping out at 379 feet (or 386, depending on who's measuring), was found in the Redwood Creek watershed in 2006. These ancient giants thrive in an environment that exists in only a few hundred coastal miles along the Pacific Ocean. They commonly live 600 years—though some have been around for more than 2,000 years.

Diverse, Complex

A healthy redwood forest is diverse and includes Douglas firs, western hemlocks, tan oaks, and madrone trees. The complex soils of the forest floor support a profusion of ferns, mosses, and fungi, along with numerous shrubs and berry bushes. In spring, California rhododendron bloom all over, providing a dazzling purple and pink contrast to the dense greenery.

Old-Growth Forests

Redwood National and State Parks hold nearly 50% of California's old-growth redwood forests, but only about a third of the forests in the park are old-growth. Of the original 3,125 square miles (2 million acres) in the Redwoods Historic Range, only 4% survived logging that began in 1850. A quarter of these trees are privately owned and on managed land. The rest are on public tracts.

Wildlife Species

In the park's backcountry, you might spot mountain lions, black bears, black-tailed deer, river otters, beavers, and minks. Roosevelt elk roam the flatlands, and the rivers and streams teem with salmon and trout. Gray whales, seals, and sea lions cavort near the coastline. More than 280 species of birds have been recorded in the parks, which are located along the Pacific Flyway.

Tall Trees Grove

FOREST | At the Kuchel Visitor Center you can obtain a free permit to make the steep 14-mile drive to this redwood grove that once contained the world-record holder for tallest tree. Rangers dispense a limited number per day, first come, first served. The hike from the trailhead parking lot is 4 miles round-trip. No trailers or RVs. ⊠ *Tall Trees Access Rd., off Bald Hills Rd., Orick ✛ Off Bald Hills Rd., 7 miles from U.S. 101, then 6½ miles to trailhead.*

 Activities

BICYCLING

Besides the roadways, you can bike on several trails, many of them along former logging roads. Best bets include the 11-mile Lost Man Creek Trail, which begins 3 miles north of Orick; the 12-mile round-trip Coastal Trail (Last Chance Section), which starts at the southern end of Enderts Beach Road and becomes steep and narrow as it travels through dense slopes of foggy redwood forests; and the 19-mile, single-track Ossagon Trail Loop, on which you're likely to see elk as you cruise through redwoods before coasting oceanside toward the end.

BIRD-WATCHING

Many rare and striking winged specimens inhabit the area, including chestnut-backed chickadees, brown pelicans, great blue herons, pileated woodpeckers, northern spotted owls, and marbled murrelets.

FISHING

Deep-sea and freshwater fishing are popular here. Anglers often stake out sections of the Klamath and Smith rivers seeking salmon and trout. A single state license (⊕ *www.wildlife.ca.gov/licensing/ fishing*) covers both ocean and river fishing. A two-day license costs about $24. You can go crabbing and clamming on the coast, but check the tides carefully: rip currents and sneaker waves can be deadly. No license is needed to fish from the long B Street Pier in Crescent City.

HIKING

★ Coastal Trail

HIKING/WALKING | This easy-to-difficult trail, depending on how much of it you tackle, runs most of the park's length; smaller sections that vary in difficulty are accessible at frequent, well-marked trailheads. The moderate-to-difficult **DeMartin section** leads past 6 miles of old-growth redwoods and through prairie. If you're up for a real workout, hike the brutally difficult but stunning **Flint Ridge section,** 4½ miles of steep grades and numerous switchbacks past redwoods and Marshall Pond (check ahead to be sure this section has reopened, following a closure as a result of bridge damage in 2018). The moderate 5½-mile-long **Klamath section,** which connects the Wilson Creek Picnic Area and the Klamath River Overlook, with a short detour to Hidden Beach and its tide pools, provides coastal views and whale-watching opportunities. *Moderate.* ⊠ *Klamath* ⊹ *Trailheads: DeMartin, U.S. 101 mile markers 12.8 (south) and 15.6 (north); Flint Ridge, Alder Camp Rd. at Douglas Bridge parking area, north end of Coastal Dr. (east), and off Klamath Beach Rd. (west); Klamath, Requa Rd. at Klamath River Overlook (south), Wilson Creek Picnic Area, off U.S. 101 (north)* ⊕ *www.nps.gov/redw.*

West Ridge–Friendship Ridge–James Irvine Loop

HIKING/WALKING | For a long, moderately strenuous trek, try this 12½-mile loop. The difficult West Ridge segment passes redwoods looming above a carpet of ferns. The difficult Friendship Ridge portion slopes down toward the coast through forests of spruce and hemlock and accesses iconic Fern Canyon. The moderate James Irvine Trail portion winds along a small creek and amid dense stands of redwoods. *Difficult.* ⊠ *Orick* ⊹ *Trailhead: Prairie Creek Visitor Center* ⊕ *www.nps.gov/redw.*

KAYAKING

With many miles of often shallow rivers, streams, and estuarial lagoons, kayaking is a popular pastime in the park.

Humboats Kayak Adventures

KAYAKING | You can rent kayaks and book kayaking tours that from December to June include whale-watching trips. Half-day river kayaking trips pass beneath massive redwoods; the whale-watching outings get you close enough for good photos. ⊠ *Woodley Island Marina, 601 Startare Dr., Dock A, Eureka* ☏ *707/443– 5157* ⊕ *www.humboats.com* ✉ *From $30 rentals, $55 tours.*

Good Reads

■ The *Redwood Official National and State Parks Handbook,* published by the Redwood Parks Association, covers the area's ecology, botany, natural and cultural history, and wildlife.

■ Richard Preston's *The Wild Trees: A Story of Passion and Daring* chronicles the redwood-climbing exploits of several botanists fiercely passionate about the endangered tall trees and the ecosystem that supports them.

■ If you plan on hiking, stop at one of the visitor centers and purchase the *Redwood National Park Trail Guide,* with details about more than 200 miles of trails.

★ Kayak Zak's

KAYAKING | This outfit rents kayaks and stand-up paddleboards, good for touring the beautiful estuarial and freshwater lagoons of Humboldt Lagoons State Park. You can also book a guided nature paddle. Rentals at the Stone Lagoon Visitor Center take place year-round, and on most summer weekends Kayak Zak's sets up a trailer at nearby Big Lagoon. The lagoons are stunning. Herds of Roosevelt elk sometimes traipse along the shoreline of Big Lagoon; raptors, herons, and waterfowl abound in both lagoons; and you can paddle across Stone Lagoon to a spectacular secluded Pacific-view beach. ⊠ *Humboldt Lagoons State Park Visitor Center, 115336 U.S. 101, about 5½ miles south of Orick, Trinidad* ☎ *707/498– 1130* ⊕ *www.kayakzak.com* ⊠ *From $30.*

WHALE-WATCHING

Good vantage points for whale-watching include Crescent Beach Overlook, the Kuchel Visitor Center in Orick, points along the Coastal Trail, and the Klamath River Overlook. From late November through January is the best time to see their southward migrations; from February through April the whales return, usually passing closer to shore.

Nearby Towns

Crescent City, north of the park, is Del Norte County's largest town (population about 6,700) and home to the Redwood National and State Parks headquarters. Though it curves around a beautiful stretch of ocean, rain and bone-chilling fog often prevail. Very small **Klamath** is outside park boundaries though near to the middle section. The town has a few lodgings but not much dining. Roughly 50 miles south of Crescent City (20 miles north of Eureka), little **Trinidad** has a cove harbor that attracts fishermen and photographers. The picturesque town has a few notable dining and lodging options and is a good base for exploring Prairie Creek Redwoods State Park and other

southerly attractions. Farther south, **Arcata** began life in 1850 as a base camp for miners and lumberjacks and had fewer than 1,000 residents until the early 1900s. Today this artsy, progressive town has about 17,200 citizens, plus another 8,500 students enrolled in Humboldt State University. Activity centers on the grassy Arcata Plaza, which is surrounded by restored buildings containing funky bars, cafés, and indie shops. Nearby **Eureka,** population 27,200 and the Humboldt County seat, was named after a gold miner's hearty exclamation. Its Old Town has an alluring waterfront boardwalk, several excellent restaurants and shops, and the region's largest selection of lodgings. The visitor center here is the area's best overall resource for tourism information. Strip malls dominate the city's outskirts, but the city center has much to recommend it.

VISITOR INFORMATION Arcata Humboldt Visitor Center ⊠ *1635 Heindon Rd., Arcata* ☎ *707/822–3619* ⊕ *www.arcatachamber.com.* **Crescent City/Del Norte County Chamber of Commerce** ⊠ *1001 Front St., Crescent City* ☎ *707/464–3174, 800/343– 8300* ⊕ *www.delnorte.org.* **Eureka-Humboldt Visitors Bureau** ⊠ *322 1st St., Eureka* ☎ *707/443–5097, 800/346–3482* ⊕ *www. visitredwoods.com.*

 Sights

Battery Point Lighthouse

LIGHTHOUSE | Only during low tide, you can walk from the pier across the ocean floor to this working lighthouse, which was built in 1856. It houses a museum with nautical artifacts and photographs of shipwrecks. There's even a resident ghost. ⊠ *Lighthouse parking, 235 Lighthouse Way, Crescent City* ☎ *707/464– 3089, 707/464–3922* ⊕ *www.delnortehistory.org/lighthouse* ⊠ *$5* ☺ *Closed weekdays Oct.–Mar.*

Northcoast Marine Mammal Center

ZOO | The nonprofit center rescues and rehabilitates stranded, sick, and injured

Best Campgrounds in Redwood

Within a 30-minute drive of Redwood National and State Parks are roughly 60 public and private camping facilities. None of the four primitive areas in Redwood—DeMartin, Flint Ridge, Little Bald Hills, and Nickel Creek (which was closed as of this writing due to landslides on the Coastal Trail)—is a drive-in site. You will need to get a free permit from any visitor center except Prairie Creek before camping in these campgrounds, and along Redwood Creek in the backcountry. Bring your own water because drinking water isn't available at any of these sites. These campgrounds, plus Gold Bluffs Beach, are first come, first served.

If you'd rather drive than hike in, Redwood has four developed campgrounds—Elk Prairie, Gold Bluffs Beach, Jedediah Smith, and Mill Creek—that are within the state-park boundaries. None has RV hookups, and some length restrictions apply. Fees are $35 in state park campgrounds.

For details and reservations, contact ☎ 800/444–7275 or ⊕ www.reserveamerica.com.

Elk Prairie Campground. Roosevelt elk frequent this popular campground adjacent to a prairie and old-growth redwoods. ✉ *Newton B. Drury Scenic Pkwy., Prairie Creek Redwoods State Park.*

Gold Bluffs Beach Campground. You can camp in tents right on the beach at this Prairie Creek Redwoods State Park campground near Fern Canyon. ✉ *End of Davison Rd., off U.S. 101.*

Jedediah Smith Campground. This is one of the few places to camp—in tents or RVs—within groves of old-growth redwood forest. ✉ *9 miles east of Crescent City on U.S. 199.*

Mill Creek Campground. Redwoods tower over large Mill Creek, in Del Norte Coast Redwoods State Park. The campground is open mid-May–September. ✉ *U.S. 101, 7 miles southeast of Crescent City.*

---

seals, sea lions, dolphins, and porpoises. Its facility isn't a museum or an aquarium, but placards and kiosks provide information about marine mammals and coastal ecosystems, and even when the place is closed you can observe the rescued animals through a fence enclosing individual pools. The gallery and gift shop is open on most weekends and some weekdays, especially in summer, and volunteers are often on hand to answer questions. It's worth calling the day of your visit to find out when feedings will take place. ✉ *424 Howe Dr., Crescent City* ☎ *707/465–6265* ⊕ *www.northcoastmmc.org* 🖾 *Free.*

Sequoia Park Zoo

ZOO | FAMILY | Animal lovers of all ages appreciate visiting California's oldest zoo (it opened in 1907). A highlight here is strolling high above the forest on the nation's only redwood canopy walk. Although it's a relatively small zoo, it is conservation-focused and fully accredited, and it's developed a number of excellent new exhibits in recent years, Favorite areas for wildlife viewing include the red panda exhibit, a barnyard petting zoo, and a walk-in aviary with both local and exotic birds. ✉ *3414 W St., Eureka* ☎ *707/441–4263* ⊕ *www.sequoiaparkzoo.net* 🖾 *$10.*

Trees of Mystery

FOREST | FAMILY | Since opening in 1946, this unabashedly goofy but endearing roadside attraction has been doling out family fun. From the moment you pull your car up to the 49-foot-tall talking statue of Paul Bunyan (alongside Babe the Blue Ox), the kitschy thrills begin. You can then explore a genuinely informative museum of Native American artifacts, admire intricately carved redwood figures, and browse tacky souvenirs. For a fee you can ride a six-passenger gondola over the redwood treetops for a majestic view of the forest canopy, and stroll along several mostly easy trails through the adjacent forest of redwoods, Sitka spruce, and Douglas firs. ✉ *15500 U.S. 101 N, between Klamath and Del Norte Coast Redwoods State Park, Klamath* ☎ *707/482–2251* 🌐 *www.treesofmystery.net* 🎫 *Museum free, trails and gondola $18.*

🍴 Restaurants

IN THE PARK

PICNIC AREAS

Crescent Beach

RESTAURANT—SIGHT | This beach has a grassy picnic area with tables, fire pits, and restrooms. There's an overlook south of the beach. ✉ *Enderts Beach Rd., Crescent City* ✥ *4 miles south of Crescent City.*

Elk Prairie

RESTAURANT—SIGHT | In addition to many elk, this spot has a campground, a nature trail, and a ranger station. ✉ *Prairie Creek Redwoods State Park, 127011 Newton B. Drury Scenic Pkwy., Orick.*

★ **High Bluff Overlook**

RESTAURANT—SIGHT | This picnic area's sunsets and whale-watching are unequaled. A ½-mile trail leads from here to the beach. ✉ *Coastal Dr. loop, Klamath* ✥ *Off U.S. 1010, via Alder Camp Rd.*

OUTSIDE THE PARK

ARCATA

★ **Cafe Brio**

$$ | **AMERICAN** | With an inviting indoor dining room and outside seating overlooking bustling Arcata Plaza, this artisan bakery and restaurant is known for its savory and sweet breads. Notable noshes include ham-and-cheese breakfast croissants, focaccia sandwiches with avocado and Humboldt Fog goat cheese from Arcata's Cypress Grove creamery, and farm-to-table dinner fare. **Known for:** lemon cream tarts and other pastries available all day; small but terrific wine selection; Blue Bottle coffees. [$] *Average main: $14* ✉ *791 G St., Arcata* ☎ *707/822–5922* 🌐 *www.cafebrioarcata.com* 🕒 *No dinner Sun. and Mon.*

Wildberries Marketplace

$ | **DELI** | This market with juice and salad bars and a small café carries a great selection of deli items, cheeses, and picnic provisions, many of them produced regionally. **Known for:** burgers and jerk chicken sandwiches; organic produce; excellent pizzas, tarts, pies, and other baked goods. [$] *Average main: $8* ✉ *747 13th St., Arcata* ☎ *707/822–0095* 🌐 *www.wildberries.com* 💳 *No credit cards.*

CRESCENT CITY

Good Harvest Cafe

$$ | **AMERICAN** | The café, which serves great breakfasts and espresso drinks, lives up to its name with ample use of locally grown and organic ingredients. For lunch and dinner there are salads, burgers, sandwiches, vegetarian specialties, and several fish entrées, plus a nice range of local beers and West Coast wines. **Known for:** fish-and-chips and other local seafood; hearty, delicious breakfasts; plenty of vegetarian items. [$] *Average main: $16* ✉ *575 U.S. 101 S, Crescent City* ☎ *707/465–6028.*

★ **SeaQuake Brewing**

$$ | **PIZZA** | Water from the cool and clean Smith River goes into the dozen or so beers poured at this microbrewery with a modern-industrial look. They pair well with wood-fired thin-crust pizzas that include one with grilled chicken, bacon, artichoke hearts, garlic cream sauce, and cheeses from the local Rumiano Cheese Company. **Known for:** tacos, wings,

salads, and other starters; well-crafted beers on tap; the caramel stout sundae. ⓢ *Average main: $15* ⊠ *400 Front St., Crescent City* ☎ *707/465–4444* ⊕ *seaquakebrewing.com* ⊘ *Closed Sun. and Mon.*

Vita Cucina
$ | **AMERICAN** | Although set in a nondescript downtown shopping center, this casual café, bakery, and takeout market serves fresh, creative food that's anything but ordinary. Come by in the morning for pastries, eggs, or quiche, or later on for fare that includes Vietnamese *banh mi* and sushi-grade-ahi sandwiches, whole smoked chicken with garlic-mashed potatoes, and barbecue-pork pizzas. **Known for:** great stop for picnic supplies before venturing into the park; daily-changing quiche (always with a vegetarian option); nice selection of fresh salads. ⓢ *Average main: $8* ⊠ *1270 Front St., Crescent City* ☎ *707/464–1076* ⊘ *Closed Sun. No dinner.*

EUREKA
★ Brick & Fire Bistro
$$ | **MODERN AMERICAN** | Just about every seat in the darkly lighted, urbane dining room has a view of this downtown bistro's most important feature, a wood-fired brick oven used to prepare everything from roasted local Kumamoto oysters to a wild-mushroom cobbler topped with a cheesy biscuit—even the "fries," char-roasted potatoes tossed in olive oil and spices, come out of the oven. Creatively topped pizzas, sandwiches, and grilled meats and seafood round out the menu. **Known for:** house-made sausage pizzas; eggplant, brisket, and other sandwich fillings char-grilled in a wood-fired oven; house-made ginger ale. ⓢ *Average main: $19* ⊠ *1630 F St., Eureka* ☎ *707/268–8959* ⊕ *www.brickandfirebistro.com* ⊘ *Closed Tues. No lunch weekends.*

Café Waterfront
$$ | **SEAFOOD** | Amid Old Town's vibrant dining district, this rollicking spot in what

served as a saloon and brothel in the 1950s turns out consistently fresh locally caught seafood. Steamed clams, grilled snapper, oyster burgers, and chowders are all on the menu—one of the West Coast's top oyster beds, in the bay across the street, supplies the oysters on the half shell. **Known for:** historic vibe and Old Town setting; excellent locally sourced oysters (raw and grilled); homemade clam chowder. ⓢ *Average main: $20* ⊠ *102 F St., Eureka* ☎ *707/443–9190* ⊕ *www.cafewaterfronteureka.com.*

TRINIDAD
Beachcomber Cafe
$ | **BAKERY** | Before a day of hiking and exploring, fuel up in downtown Trinidad on organic espresso or coffee drinks, freshly baked breads and pastries, house-made granola, and bagels with lox, chèvre, local jams, poached eggs, and other toppings. The lineup for lunch includes soups, salads, and panini. **Known for:** bagels with creative toppings; strong, organic coffee; vegetarian options. ⓢ *Average main: $7* ⊠ *363 Trinity St., Trinidad* ☎ *707/677–0106* ⊘ *No dinner.*

Trinidad Bay Eatery and Gallery
$$$ | **SEAFOOD** | A short stroll from Trinidad's bay front and near the park's southern end, this unpretentious combination gallery and seafood-oriented restaurant cooks up tasty meals. Buttermilk pancakes and Dungeness crab Benedict are among the favorites for breakfast; at lunchtime burgers, specialty sandwiches, and chowders and solids dominate the menu. **Known for:** well-curated wine list; cioppino in chipotle broth; blackberry cobbler. ⓢ *Average main: $21* ⊠ *607 Parker St., Trinidad* ☎ *707/677–3777* ⊕ *www.trinidadeatery.com.*

 Hotels

IN THE PARK
★ Elk Meadow Cabins
$$$$ | **B&B/INN** | **FAMILY** | From the porches of these beautifully restored 1,200-square-foot former millworkers'

Redwood trees, and the moss that often coats them, grow best in damp, shady environments.

cottages, guests often see Roosevelt elk meandering in the meadows. **Pros:** in a stunning part of Prairie Creek State Park yet conveniently located on U.S. 101; spacious enough for four to six guests; kitchens. **Cons:** a bit of a drive from most area restaurants; expensive for just two occupants, though reasonable for families or groups; furnishings are comfortable but plain. [$] *Rooms from: $299* ✉ *7 Valley Green Camp Rd., off U.S. 101 north of Davison Rd., Orick* ☎ *707/488–2222, 866/733–9637* 🌐 *www.elkmeadowcabins.com* 🛏 *7 cabins* 🍴 *No meals.*

OUTSIDE THE PARK

CRESCENT CITY

Curly Redwood Lodge

$ | **HOTEL** | A single redwood tree produced the 57,000 board feet of lumber used to build this budget 1957 motor lodge. **Pros:** large rooms; several restaurants within walking distance; cool retro furnishings. **Cons:** road noise can be bothersome; very basic amenities; no breakfast. [$] *Rooms from: $79* ✉ *701 U.S. 101 S, Crescent City* ☎ *707/464–2137* 🌐 *www.curlyredwoodlodge.com* 🛏 *36 rooms* 🍴 *No meals.*

Ocean View Inn & Suites

$$ | **HOTEL** | This clean, comfortable, and reasonably priced hotel doesn't have a lot of bells and whistles, but it does enjoy a great location on the edge of downtown Crescent City very close to the water. **Pros:** views of the water; many restaurants nearby; good value. **Cons:** on a busy road; cookie-cutter furnishings; nearby foghorn can be a little noisy. [$] *Rooms from: $125* ✉ *270 U.S. 101, Crescent City* ☎ *707/465–1111, 855/623–2611* 🌐 *www.oceanviewinncrescentcity.com* 🛏 *65 rooms* 🍴 *Free Breakfast.*

EUREKA

★ Carter House Inns

$$$ | **HOTEL** | Owner Mark Carter says he trains his staff always to say yes; whether it's breakfast in bed or an in-room massage, your requests will be accommodated. **Pros:** elegant ambience; every detail in place; aim-to-please service. **Cons:** not suitable for children; restaurant is a bit

pricey; two-night minimum on weekends. $ *Rooms from: $189* ✉ *301 L St., Eureka* ☎ *707/444–8062, 800/404–1390* ⊕ *www.carterhouse.com* ⏎ *32 rooms* ⊚ *Breakfast.*

Inn at 2nd and C

$$ | B&B/INN | By the bustling waterfront and steps from Old Town's inviting shops and restaurants, this towering 1880s Victorian inn exudes character and abounds with opulent architectural details and florid period-style bedding, wallpapers, and furnishings. **Pros:** easy walk to Old Town Eureka dining and shopping; fascinating old building; reasonable rates. **Cons:** thin walls; some rooms don't have flat-screen TVs; least expensive rooms are a little small. $ *Rooms from: $119* ✉ *139 2nd St., Eureka* ☎ *707/444–3344* ⊕ *www. theinnat2ndandc.com* ⏎ *24 rooms* ⊚ *Breakfast.*

KLAMATH

★ Historic Requa Inn

$$ | B&B/INN | This serene 1914 inn overlooks the Klamath River a mile east of where it meets the ocean. **Pros:** serene; relaxing yet central location with river views; excellent restaurant. **Cons:** walls are thin; not a good choice for families with kids; not many dining options in the area. $ *Rooms from: $119* ✉ *451 Requa Rd., Klamath* ☎ *707/482–1425* ⊕ *www. requainn.com* ⏎ *12 rooms* ⊚ *Breakfast.*

Ravenwood Motel

$ | HOTEL | Attentive on-site owners converted a dowdy roadside motel into this class act consisting of 10 rooms and five suites—four with full kitchens—beautifully decorated with different themes. **Pros:** handy to park's central section; exceptionally clean rooms; a bargain. **Cons:** nonsuite rooms small; along a business strip with no view to speak of; no pets. $ *Rooms from: $75* ✉ *151 Klamath Blvd., Klamath* ☎ *707/482–5911, 866/520–9875* ⊕ *www.ravenwoodmotel.com* ⏎ *15 rooms* ⊚ *Breakfast.*

NEAR PARK'S SOUTHERN SECTION

Redwood Coast Vacation Rentals

$$ | RENTAL | Given the relatively limited number of hotels and inns close to the park, renting a vacation home in the area can be a good strategy, especially for groups of friends or families who appreciate kitchen facilities. **Pros:** properties for all budgets; all rentals have kitchens; many rentals have multiple bedrooms and baths. **Cons:** 10 am checkout; one-time cleaning fee adds a lot to the cost for travelers only staying a night or two; quality and furnishings vary from unit to unit. $ *Rooms from: $150* ✉ *McKinleyville* ☎ *707/834–6555* ⊕ *www. redwoodcoastvacationrentals.com* ⏎ *75 units* ⊚ *No meals.*

TRINIDAD

Lost Whale Inn

$$$$ | B&B/INN | For a romantic, special-occasion getaway near the park, look no further than this intimate, luxurious inn perched on a seaside bluff near Patrick's Point State Park in Trinidad. **Pros:** stunning ocean views; elaborate and delicious breakfast spread; spa services, in-room or out on the lawn, are offered. **Cons:** no pets allowed (but you'll find a few adorable pets residing at the inn); two-night minimum on summer weekends; sometimes books up fully for weddings. $ *Rooms from: $295* ✉ *3452 Patrick's Point Dr., Trinidad* ☎ *707/677–3425* ⊕ *www.lostwhaleinn.com* ⏎ *8 rooms* ⊚ *Free Breakfast.*

Trinidad Inn

$$ | HOTEL | FAMILY | These quiet cottage rooms nestled in the evergreens are 2 miles north of Trinidad Bay's harbor, restaurants, and shops. **Pros:** idyllic setting; walking path through adjacent redwood grove; good for kids. **Cons:** older facility. $ *Rooms from: $145* ✉ *1170 Patrick's Point Dr., Trinidad* ☎ *707/677–3349* ⊕ *www.trinidadinn.com* ⏎ *10 rooms* ⊚ *Breakfast.*

Chapter 30

ROCKY MOUNTAIN NATIONAL PARK

Updated by
Lindsey Galloway

COLORADO

WELCOME TO
ROCKY MOUNTAIN NATIONAL PARK

TOP REASONS TO GO

★ **Awesome ascents:** Seasoned climbers can trek to the summit of 14,259-foot Longs Peak or attack the rounded granite domes of Lumpy Ridge. Novices can summit Twin Sisters Peaks or Mount Ida, both reaching more than 11,000 feet.

★ **Continental Divide:** Straddle this great divide, which cuts through the western part of the park, separating water's flow to either the Pacific or Atlantic Ocean.

★ **Gorgeous scenery:** Peer out over more than 100 lakes, gaze up at majestic mountain peaks, and soak in the splendor of lush wetlands, pine-scented woods, forests of spruce and fir, and alpine tundra in the park's four distinct ecosystems.

★ **More than 355 miles of trails:** Hike on dozens of marked trails, from easy lakeside strolls to strenuous mountain climbs.

★ **Wildlife viewing:** Spot elk and bighorn sheep, along with moose, otters, and more than 280 species of birds.

1 Bear Lake. One of the most photographed (and crowded) places in the park, Bear Lake is the hub for many trailheads and a major stop on the park's shuttle service.

2 Longs Peak. The highest peak in the park and the toughest to climb, this Fourteener pops up in many park vistas. A round-trip trek to the top takes 10 to 15 hours, so most visitors forego summit fever and opt for a (still spectacular) partial journey.

3 Trail Ridge Road. The alpine tundra of the park is the highlight here, as the road—the highest continuous highway in the United States—climbs to more than 12,000 feet (almost 700 feet above timberline).

4 Timber Creek Campground. The park's far western area is much less crowded than most other sections, though it has its share of amenities and attractions, including evening programs, 98 camping sites, and a visitor center.

5 Wild Basin Area. Far from the crowds, the park's southeast quadrant consists of lovely expanses of subalpine forest punctuated by streams and lakes.

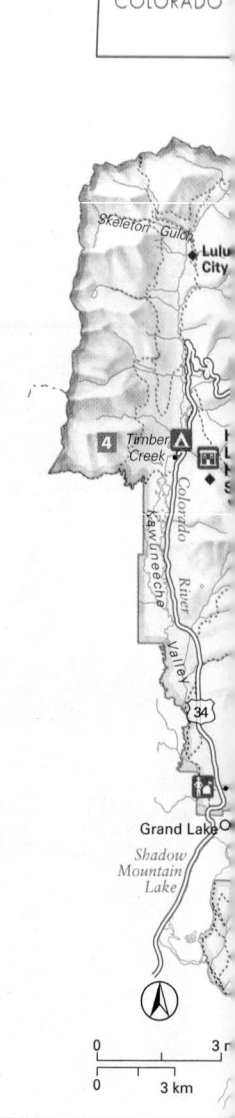

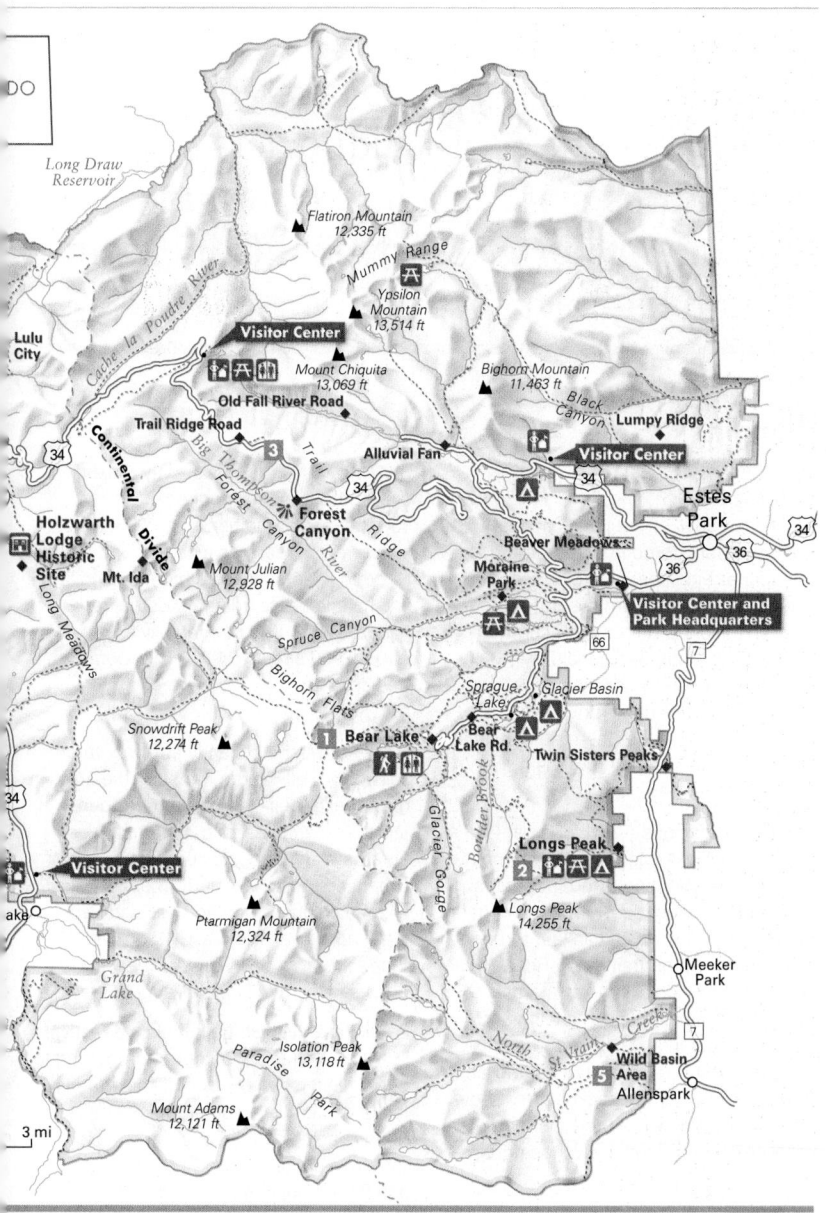

Here, a single hour's drive leads from a 7,800-foot elevation at park headquarters to the 12,183-foot apex of the twisting and turning Trail Ridge Road. More than 355 miles of hiking trails take you to meadows flush with wildflowers, cool dense forests of lodgepole pine and Engelmann spruce, and wildlife including elk and bighorn sheep.

Planning

WHEN TO GO

More than 80% of the park's annual 4.5 million visitors come in summer and fall. For thinner high-season crowds, come in early June or September. But there is a good reason to put up with summer crowds: only from Memorial Day to mid-October will you get the chance to make the unforgettable drive over Trail Ridge Road (note that the road may still be closed during those months if the weather turns bad).

Spring is capricious—75°F one day and a blizzard the next (March sees the most snow). June can range from hot and sunny to cool and rainy. July typically ushers in high summer, which can last through September. Up on Trail Ridge Road, it can be 15°F–20°F cooler than at the park's lower elevations. Wildlife viewing and fishing is best in any season but winter. In early fall, the trees blaze with brilliant foliage. Winter, when backcountry snow can be 4 feet deep, is the time for cross-country skiing, snowshoeing, and ice fishing.

FESTIVALS AND EVENTS

Rooftop Rodeo

FESTIVAL | FAMILY | Consistently ranked one of the top small rodeos in the country (and a tradition since 1908), this six-day event features a parade and nightly rodeo events, such as barrel racing and saddle bronc riding. ⊠ *Estes Park Fairgrounds, 1209 Manford Ave., Estes Park* ☎ *970/586–6104* ⊕ *www.rooftoprodeo.com.*

★ Elk Fest

FESTIVAL | FAMILY | In early autumn, the calls of bull elk fill the forest as the animals make their way down the mountains for mating season. Estes Park celebrates with elk bugle contests, Native American music and performances, and elk educational seminars. ⊠ *Bond Park, E. Elkhorn Ave. and MacGregor Ave., Estes Park* ⊕ *www.visitestespark.com/events-calendar/special-events/elk-fest.*

Longs Peak Scottish-Irish Highland Festival

FESTIVAL | A traditional tattoo (drum- and bugle-filled parade) kicks off this four-day fair of ancient Scottish athletic competitions, including full-armor jousting and throwing contests involving hammers and 20-foot-long, 140-pound wooden

AVERAGE HIGH/LOW TEMPERATURES

JAN.	FEB.	MAR.	APR.	MAY	JUNE
39/16	41/17	45/21	53/27	62/34	73/41
JULY	**AUG.**	**SEPT.**	**OCT.**	**NOV.**	**DEC.**
78/46	76/45	70/38	60/30	46/23	40/18

poles (called cabers). The festival also features Celtic music, Irish dancing, and events for dogs of the British Isles (such as terrier racing and sheepdog demonstrations). ⊠ *Estes Park Fairgrounds, 1209 Manford Ave., Estes Park* ☎ *970/586–6308, 800/903–7837* ⊕ *www.scotfest.com.*

GETTING HERE AND AROUND
AIR TRAVEL
The closest commercial airport is **Denver International Airport** (DEN). Its **Ground Transportation Information Center** (☎ *800/247–2336 or 303/342–4059* ⊕ *www.flydenver.com*) assists visitors with car rentals, door-to-door shuttles, and limousine services. From the airport, the eastern entrance of the park is 80 miles (about two hours). **Estes Park Shuttle** (☎ *970/586–5151* ⊕ *www.estesparkshuttle.com*; reservations essential) serves Estes Park and Rocky Mountain from both Denver International Airport and Longmont/Boulder.

CAR TRAVEL
Estes Park and Grand Lake are the Rocky Mountain's gateway communities; from these you can enter the park via U.S. 34 or 36 (Estes Park) or U.S. 34 (Grand Lake). U.S. 36 runs from Denver through Boulder, Lyons, and Estes Park to the park; the portion between Boulder and Estes Park is heavily traveled—especially on summer weekends. Though less direct, Colorado Routes 119, 72, and 7 have much less traffic (and better scenery). If you're driving directly to Rocky Mountain from the airport, take the E–470 tollway from Peña Boulevard to Interstate 25.

The **Colorado Department of Transportation** (for road conditions ☎ *303/639–1111* ⊕ *www.cotrip.org*) plows roads efficiently, but winter snowstorms can slow traffic and create wet or icy conditions. In summer, the roads into both Grand Lake and Estes Park can see heavy traffic, especially on weekends.

The main thoroughfare in the park is Trail Ridge Road (U.S. 34); in winter, it's closed from the first storm in the fall (typically in October) through the spring (depending on snowpack, this could be at any time between April and June). During that time, it's plowed only up to Many Parks Curve on the east side and the Colorado River trailhead on the west side. (For current road information: ☎ *970/586–1222* ⊕ *www.codot.gov.*)

The spectacular Old Fall River Road runs one-way between the Endovalley Picnic Area on the eastern edge of the park and the Alpine Visitor Center at the summit of Trail Ridge Road, on the western side. It is typically open from July to September, depending on snowfall. It's a steep, narrow road (no wider than 14 feet), and trailers and vehicles longer than 25 feet are prohibited, but a trip on this 90-year-old thoroughfare is well worth the effort. For information on road closures, contact the park: ☎ *970/586–1206* ⊕ *www.nps.gov/romo.*

Rocky Mountain has limited parking, but offers three free shuttle buses, which operate daily from 7 am to 8 pm, late May to early October. All three shuttles can be accessed from a large Park & Ride located within the park, 7 miles from the Beaver Meadows entrance. Visitors who don't want to drive into the park at all can hop on the Hiker Shuttle at the Estes Park Visitor Center. The shuttle, which runs every half hour during peak times, makes stops at the Beaver Meadows Visitor Center and the Park & Ride, where visitors can switch to one of the other two shuttles, which head to various trailheads. The Moraine Park Route shuttle runs every 30 minutes and stops at the Moraine Park Visitor Center and then continues on to the Fern Lake Trailhead. The Bear Lake Route shuttle runs every 10 to 15 minutes from the Park & Ride to the Bear Lake Trailhead.

PARK ESSENTIALS
PARK FEES AND PERMITS

Entrance fees are $25 per automobile for a one-day pass or $35 for a seven-day pass. Those who enter via foot or bicycle can get a seven-day pass for $20. Motorcyclists can get a seven-day pass for $30. An annual pass costs $70.

Backcountry camping requires a permit that's $26 per party from May through October, and free the rest of the year. Visit ⊕ *www.nps.gov/romo/planyourvisit/ wilderness-camping.htm* before you go for a planning guide to backcountry camping. You can get your permit online, by phone (☎ *970/586–1242*), or in person. In person, you can get a day-of-trip permit year-round at one of the park's two backcountry offices, located next to the Beaver Meadows Visitor Center and in the Kawuneeche Visitor Center.

PARK HOURS

The park is open 24/7 year-round; some roads close in winter. It is in the Mountain time zone.

CELL PHONE RECEPTION

Cell phones work in some sections of the park, and free Wi-Fi can be accessed in and around the Beaver Meadows Visitor Center, Fall River, and the Kawuneeche Visitor Center.

EDUCATIONAL OFFERINGS
RANGER PROGRAMS
Ranger Programs

TOUR—SIGHT | FAMILY | Join in on free hikes, talks, and activities about wildlife, geology, vegetation, and park history. In the evening, rangers lead twilight hikes, stargazing sessions, and storytelling around the campfire. Look for the extensive program schedule in the park's newspaper available at the main entrances. ⊠ *Rocky Mountain National Park* ☎ *970/586–1206* ☞ *Free.*

RESTAURANTS

Restaurants in north central Colorado run the gamut from simple diners with tasty, homey basics to elegant establishments with extensive wine lists. Some restaurants take reservations, but many—particularly midrange spots—seat on a first-come, first-served basis. In the park itself, the Trail Ridge Store next to the Alpine Visitor Center has a café and coffee bar open from late May to October. The park also has a handful of scenic picnic areas, all with tables and pit or flush toilets. *Restaurant reviews have been shortened. For full information, visit Fodors.com.*

HOTELS

Bed-and-breakfasts and small inns in north central Colorado vary from old-fashioned fluffy cottages to sleek, modern buildings with understated lodge themes. If you want some pampering, guest ranches and spas will fit the bill.

In Estes Park, Grand Lake, and other nearby towns, the elevation keeps the climate cool, and you'll scarcely need (and you'll have a tough time finding) air-conditioned lodging. For a historic spot, try the Stanley Hotel in Estes Park, which dates to 1909. The park itself has no hotels or lodges. *Hotel reviews have been shortened. For full information, visit Fodors.com.*

Rocky Mountain in One Day

Starting out in Estes Park, begin your day at the **Bighorn Restaurant**, a classic breakfast spot and a local favorite. While you're enjoying your short stack with apple-cinnamon-raisin topping, you can put in an order for a packed lunch (it's a good idea to bring your food with you, as dining options in the park consist of a single, seasonal snack bar at the top of Trail Ridge Road).

Drive west on U.S. 34 into the park, and stop at the **Beaver Meadows Visitor Center** to watch the orientation film and pick up a park map. Also inquire about road conditions on Trail Ridge Road, which you should plan to drive either in the morning or afternoon, depending on the weather. If possible, save the drive for the afternoon, and use the morning to get out on the trails, before the chance of an afternoon lightning storm.

For a beautiful and invigorating hike, head to Bear Lake and follow the route that takes you to **Nymph Lake** (an easy 0.5-mile hike), then onto **Dream Lake** (an additional 0.6 miles with a steeper ascent), and finally to **Emerald Lake** (an additional 0.7 miles of moderate terrain). You can stop at several places along the way. The trek down is much easier, and quicker, than the climb up. ■TIP→ **If you prefer a shorter, simpler (yet still scenic) walk, consider the Bear Lake Nature Trail, a 0.6-mile loop that is wheelchair and stroller accessible.**

You'll need the better part of your afternoon to drive the scenic **Trail Ridge Road.** Start by heading west toward Grand Lake, stop at the lookout at the Alluvial Fan, and consider taking Old Fall River Road the rest of the way across the park. This single-lane dirt road delivers unbeatable views of waterfalls and mountain vistas. You'll take it westbound from Horseshoe Park (the cutoff is near the Endovalley Campground), then rejoin Trail Ridge Road at its summit, near the Alpine Visitor Center. If you're traveling on to Grand Lake or other points west, stay on Trail Ridge Road. If you're heading back to Estes Park, turn around and take Trail Ridge Road back (for a different set of awesome scenery). End your day with a ranger-led talk or evening campfire program.

What It Costs			
$	$$	$$$	$$$$
RESTAURANTS			
under $13	$13–$18	$19–$25	over $25
HOTELS			
under $121	$121–$170	$171–$230	over $230

TOURS

Green Jeep Tours

ADVENTURE TOURS | FAMILY | From the back of an open-air, neon-green Jeep on these tours, you can enjoy the majestic scenery while your experienced guide points out wildlife along the way. Green Jeep Tours also offers a three-hour tour in September and October that focuses on finding elk. Admission includes the cost of the one-day pass into the park. ✉ *157 Moraine Ave., Estes Park* ☎ *970/577–0034* ⌨ *From $80.*

Rocky Mountain Rush

DRIVING TOURS | This company's most popular tour, the "Top of the World," takes visitors in an open-top vehicle all the way to Old Fall River Road and back down Trail Ridge. A waterfall tour and sunset valley tour offer great wildlife spottings at lower elevations. ✉ *212 E. Elkhorn Ave., Estes Park* ☎ *970/586–8687* ⊕ *www.rockymountainrush.com* 🎫 *From $65.*

★ Yellow Wood Guiding

ADVENTURE TOURS | Guided photo safaris, offered year-round, ensure visitors leave the Rocky Mountain National Park with more than just memories. Customized for either beginners or experts, the tours offer the use of professional digital cameras for visitors who don't have their own. ✉ *404 Driftwood Ave., Estes Park* ☎ *970/775–5484* ⊕ *www.ywguiding.com* 🎫 *From $150.*

VISITOR INFORMATION

PARK CONTACT INFORMATION Rocky Mountain National Park ✉ *1000 U.S. 36, Estes Park* ☎ *970/586–1206* ⊕ *www.nps.gov/romo.*

VISITOR CENTERS

Alpine Visitor Center

INFO CENTER | At the top of Trail Ridge Road, this visitor center is open only when that road is navigable. The center also houses the park's only gift shop and snack bar. ✉ *Fall River Pass, at junction of Trail Ridge and Old Fall River Rds., 22 miles from Beaver Meadows entrance* ☎ *970/586–1206.*

Beaver Meadows Visitor Center

INFO CENTER | Housing the park headquarters, this visitor center was designed by students of the Frank Lloyd Wright School of Architecture at Taliesin West using the park's popular rustic style. The center has a terrific 20-minute orientation film and a large relief map of the park. ✉ *U.S. 36, 3 miles west of Estes Park and 1 mile east of Beaver Meadows Entrance Station* ☎ *970/586–1206.*

Fall River Visitor Center

INFO CENTER | FAMILY | The Discovery Room, which houses everything from old ranger outfits to elk antlers, coyote pelts, and bighorn sheep skulls for hands-on exploration, is a favorite with kids at this visitor center. ✉ *U.S. 34, at the Fall River Entrance Station* ☎ *970/586–1206.*

Kawuneeche Visitor Center

INFO CENTER | FAMILY | The only visitor center on the park's far west side, Kawuneeche has exhibits on the plant and animal life of the area, as well as a large three-dimensional map of the park and an orientation film. ✉ *U.S. 34, 1 mile north of Grand Lake and ½ mile south of Grand Lake Entrance Station* ☎ *970/586–1206.*

 Sights

SCENIC DRIVES

Bear Lake Road

SCENIC DRIVE | This 23-mile round-trip drive offers superlative views of Longs Peak (14,259-foot summit) and the glaciers surrounding Bear Lake, winding past shimmering waterfalls shrouded with rainbows. You can either drive the road yourself (open year-round) or hop on one of the park's free shuttle buses. ✉ *Runs from the Beaver Meadow Entrance Station to Bear Lake.*

Old Fall River Road

SCENIC DRIVE | Nearly 100 years old and never more than 14 feet wide, this road stretches from the park's east side to the Fall River Pass (11,796 feet above sea level) on the west. The drive provides a few white-knuckle moments, as the road is steep, serpentine, and lacking in guardrails. Start at West Horseshoe Park, which has the park's largest concentrations of sheep and elk, and head up the gravel road, passing Chasm Falls. ✉ *Runs north of and roughly parallel to Trail Ridge Road, starting near Endovalley Campground (on east) and ending at Fall River Pass/Alpine Visitor Center (on west).*

Plants and Wildlife in Rocky Mountain

Volcanic uplifts and the savage clawing of receding glaciers created Rocky Mountain's majestic landscape. You'll find four distinct ecosystems here—a riparian (wetland) environment with 150 lakes and 450 miles of streams; verdant montane valleys teeming with proud ponderosa pines and lush grasses; higher and colder subalpine mountains with wind-whipped trees (krummholz) that grow at right angles; and harsh, unforgiving alpine tundra with dollhouse-size versions of familiar plants and wildflowers. Alpine tundra is seldom found outside the Arctic, yet it makes up one-third of the park's terrain. Few plants can survive at this elevation of 11,000–11,500 feet, but many beautiful wildflowers—including alpine forget-me-nots—bloom here briefly in late June or early July.

The park has so much wildlife that you can often enjoy prime viewing from the seat of your car. Fall, when many animals begin moving down from higher elevations, is an excellent time to spot some of the park's animal residents. This is also when you'll hear the male elk bugle mating calls (popular spots to see and hear bugling elk are Kawuneeche Valley, Horseshoe Park, Moraine Park, and Upper Beaver Meadows).

May through mid-October is the best time to see the bighorn sheep that congregate in the Horseshoe Park/Sheep Lakes area, just past the Fall River entrance. If you want to glimpse a moose, try Kawuneeche Valley. Other animals in the park include mule deer, squirrels, chipmunks, pikas, beavers, and marmots. Common birds include broad-tailed and rufous hummingbirds, peregrine falcons, woodpeckers, mountain bluebirds, and Clark's nutcracker, as well as the white-tailed ptarmigan, which live year-round on the alpine tundra.

Mountain lions, black bears, and bobcats also inhabit the park but are rarely seen by visitors. Altogether, the park is home to roughly 60 species of mammals and 280 bird species.

★ Trail Ridge Road

SCENIC DRIVE | The park's star attraction and the world's highest continuous paved highway (topping out at 12,183 feet), this 48-mile road connects the park's gateways of Estes Park and Grand Lake. The views around each bend—of moraines and glaciers, and craggy hills framing emerald meadows carpeted with columbine and Indian paintbrush—are truly awesome. As it passes through three ecosystems—montane, subalpine, and arctic tundra—the road climbs 4,300 feet in elevation. You can complete a one-way trip across the park on Trail Ridge Road in two hours, but it's best to give yourself three or four hours to allow for leisurely breaks at the overlooks. Note that the middle part of the road closes with the first big snow (typically by mid-October) and most often reopens around Memorial Day, though you can still drive up about 10 miles from the west and 8 miles from the east. ✉ *Trail Ridge Rd. (U.S. 34), runs between Estes Park and Grand Lake.*

HISTORIC SITES

Rocky Mountain has more than 1,000 archaeological sites and 150 buildings of historic significance; 47 of the buildings are listed in the National Register of Historic Places, which is reserved for structures that tie in strongly to the park's history in terms of architecture, archaeology, engineering, or culture.

Most buildings at Rocky Mountain are done in the rustic style, a design preferred by the National Park Service's first director, Stephen Mather, that works to incorporate nature into these man-made structures.

Holzwarth Historic Site

ARCHAEOLOGICAL SITE | FAMILY | A scenic ½-mile interpretive trail leads you over the Colorado River to the original dude ranch that the Holzwarth family, some of the park's original homesteaders, ran between the 1920s and 1950s. Allow about an hour to view the buildings—including a dozen small guest cabins—and chat with a ranger. Though the site is open year-round, the inside of the buildings can be seen only June through early September. ⊠ *Off U.S. 34, about 8 miles north of Kawuneeche Visitor Center, Estes Park.*

Lulu City

ARCHAEOLOGICAL SITE | The remains of a few cabins are all that's left of this onetime silver-mining town, established around 1880. Reach it by hiking the 3.6-mile Colorado River Trail. Look for wagon ruts from the old Stewart Toll Road and mine tailings in nearby Shipler Park (this is also a good place to spot moose). ⊠ *Off Trail Ridge Rd., 9½ miles north of Grand Lake Entrance Station.*

SCENIC STOPS

Bear Lake

BODY OF WATER | Thanks to its picturesque location, easy accessibility, and the good hiking trails nearby, this small alpine lake below Flattop Mountain and Hallett Peak is one of the most popular destinations in the park. ⊠ *Bear Lake Rd., 7 miles southwest of Moraine Park Visitor Center, off U.S. 36.*

Forest Canyon Overlook

VIEWPOINT | Park at a dedicated lot to disembark on a wildflower-rich, 0.2-mile trail. Easy to access for all skill levels, this glacial valley overlook offers views of ice-blue pools (the Gorge Lakes) framed by

ragged peaks. ⊠ *Trail Ridge Rd., 6 miles east of Alpine Visitor Center.*

Elk Bugling

In September and October, there are traffic jams in the park as people drive up to listen to the elk bugling. Rangers and park volunteers keep track of where the elk are and direct visitors to the mating spots. The bugling is high-pitched, and if it's light enough, you can see the elk put his head in the air.

Activities

BIRD-WATCHING

Spring and summer, early in the morning, are the best times for bird-watching in the park. **Lumpy Ridge** is a nesting ground for several kinds of birds of prey. Migratory songbirds from South America have summer breeding grounds near the **Endovalley Picnic Area.** The **alpine tundra** is habitat for white-tailed ptarmigan. The **Alluvial Fan** is the place for viewing broad-tailed hummingbirds, hairy woodpeckers, ouzels, and the occasional raptor.

FISHING

Rocky Mountain is a wonderful place to fish, especially for trout—German brown, brook, rainbow, cutthroat, and greenback cutthroat—but check at a visitor center about regulations and information on specific closures, catch-and-release areas, and limits on size and possession. No fishing is allowed at Bear Lake. To avoid the crowds, rangers recommend angling in the more-remote backcountry. To fish in the park, anyone 16 and older must have a valid Colorado fishing license, which you can obtain at local sporting-goods stores. See ⊕ *www.cpw.state.co.us* for details.

Did You Know?

A pine beetle epidemic that is affecting forests nationwide has caused some of the Rocky Mountain National Park's trees to turn a reddish color and eventually die. The mitigation efforts of the park service are to remove hazard trees and protect "high value" trees near campgrounds, picnic areas, and visitor centers.

Estes Angler

FISHING | This popular fishing guide arranges fly-fishing trips from two to eight hours into the park's quieter regions, year-round. The best times for fishing are generally from April to mid-November. Equipment is also available for rent. ✉ *338 W. Riverside Dr., Estes Park* ☎ *970/586–2110, 800/586–2110* ⊕ *www. estesangler.com* ✉ *From $125.*

Kirks Fly Shop

CAMPING—SPORTS-OUTDOORS | This Estes Park outfitter offers various guided fly-fishing trips, as well as backpacking, horseback, and llama pack trips. The store also carries fishing and backpacking gear. ✉ *230 E. Elkhorn Ave., Estes Park* ☎ *970/577–0790, 877/669–1859* ⊕ *www. kirksflyshop.com* ✉ *From $50.*

Scot's Sporting Goods

FISHING | This shop rents and sells fishing gear, and provides instruction trips daily from May through mid-October. Clinics, geared toward first-timers, focus on casting, reading the water, identifying insects for flies, and properly presenting natural and artificial flies to the fish. ✉ *870 Moraine Ave., Estes Park* ☎ *970/586–2877 May–Sept., 970/443–4932 Oct.–Apr.* ⊕ *www.scotssportinggoods.com* ✉ *From $210.*

HIKING

Rocky Mountain National Park contains more than 355 miles of hiking trails, so you could theoretically wander the park for weeks. Most visitors explore just a small portion of these trails—those that are closest to the roads and visitor centers—which means that some of the park's most accessible and scenic paths can resemble a backcountry highway on busy summer days. The high-alpine terrain around Bear Lake is the park's most popular hiking area, and although it's well worth exploring, you'll get a more frontierlike experience by hiking one of the trails in the less-explored sections of the park, such as the far northern end or in the Wild Basin area to the south.

Bear Lake Trail

HIKING/WALKING | The virtually flat nature trail around Bear Lake is an easy, 0.6-mile loop that's wheelchair and stroller accessible. Sharing the route with you will likely be plenty of other hikers as well as songbirds and chipmunks. *Easy.* ✉ *Rocky Mountain National Park* ✛ *Trailhead: at Bear Lake, Bear Lake Rd.*

★ Bear Lake to Emerald Lake

HIKING/WALKING | This scenic, calorie-burning hike begins with a moderately level, 0.5-mile journey to **Nymph Lake.** From here, the trail gets steeper, with a 425-foot elevation gain, as it winds around for 0.6 miles to **Dream Lake.** The last stretch is the most arduous part of the hike, an almost all-uphill 0.7-mile trek to lovely **Emerald Lake,** where you can perch on a boulder and enjoy the view. All told, the hike is 3.6 miles, with an elevation gain of 605 feet. Allow two hours or more, depending on stops. *Moderate.* ✉ *Rocky Mountain National Park* ✛ *Trailhead: at Bear Lake, off Bear Lake Rd., 8 miles southwest of the Moraine Park Visitor Center.*

Chasm Lake Trail

HIKING/WALKING | Nestled in the shadow of Longs Peak and Mount Meeker, Chasm Lake offers one of Colorado's most impressive backdrops, which also means you can expect to encounter plenty of other hikers on the way. The 4.2-mile Chasm Lake Trail, reached via the Longs Peak Trail, has a 2,360-foot elevation gain. Just before the lake, you'll need to climb a small rock ledge, which can be a bit of a challenge for the less sure-footed; follow the cairns for the most straightforward route. Once atop the ledge, you'll catch your first memorable view of the lake. *Difficult.* ✉ *Rocky Mountain National Park* ✛ *Trailhead: at Longs Peak Ranger Station, off Rte. 7, 10 miles from the Beaver Meadows Visitor Center.*

Colorado River Trail

HIKING/WALKING | This walk to the ghost town of Lulu City on the west side of the park is excellent for looking for the bighorn sheep, elk, and moose that reside in the area. Part of the former stagecoach route that went from Granby to Walden, the 3.7-mile trail parallels the infant Colorado River to the meadow where Lulu City once stood. The elevation gain is 350 feet. *Moderate.* ⊠ *Rocky Mountain National Park* ✛ *Trailhead: at Colorado River, off Trail Ridge Rd., 1¾ miles north of the Timber Creek Campground.*

Copeland Falls

HIKING/WALKING | **FAMILY** | The 0.3-mile hike to these Wild Basin Area falls is a good option for families, as the terrain is relatively flat (there's only a 15-foot elevation gain). *Easy.* ⊠ *Rocky Mountain National Park* ✛ *Trailhead: at Wild Basin Ranger Station.*

Cub Lake

HIKING/WALKING | This 4.6-mile, three-hour (round-trip) hike takes you through meadows and stands of aspen trees and up 540 feet in elevation to a lake with water lilies. *Moderate.* ⊠ *Rocky Mountain National Park* ✛ *Trailhead: at Cub Lake, about 1¾ miles from Moraine Park Campground.*

Deer Mountain Trail

HIKING/WALKING | This 6-mile round-trip trek to the top of 10,083-foot Deer Mountain is a great way for hikers who don't mind a bit of a climb to enjoy the views from the summit of a more manageable peak. You'll gain more than 1,000 feet in elevation as you follow the switchbacking trail through ponderosa pine, aspen, and fir trees. The reward at the top is a panoramic view of the park's eastern mountains. *Difficult.* ⊠ *Rocky Mountain National Park* ✛ *Trailhead: at Deer Ridge Junction, about 4 miles west of Moraine Park Visitor Center, U.S. 34 at U.S. 36.*

East Inlet Trail

HIKING/WALKING | An easy hike of 0.3 miles from East Inlet trailhead, just outside the park in Grand Lake, will get you to **Adams Falls** in about 15 minutes. The area around the falls is often packed with visitors, so if you have time, continue east to enjoy more solitude, see wildlife, and catch views of **Mount Craig** from near the East Meadow campground. Note, however, that the trail beyond the falls has an elevation gain of between 1,500 and 1,900 feet, making it a more challenging hike. *Easy.* ⊠ *Grand Lake* ✛ *Trailhead: at East Inlet, end of W. Portal Rd. (CO 278) in Grand Lake.*

Fern Lake Trail

HIKING/WALKING | Heading to Odessa Lake from the north involves a steep hike, but on most days you'll encounter fewer other hikers than if you had begun the trip at Bear Lake. Along the way, you'll come to the Arch Rocks; the Pool, an eroded formation in the Big Thompson River; two waterfalls; and Fern Lake (3.8 miles from your starting point). Less than a mile farther, Odessa Lake itself lies at the foot of Tourmaline Gorge, below the craggy summits of Gabletop Mountain, Little Matterhorn, Knobtop Mountain, and Notchtop Mountain. For a full day of spectacular scenery, continue past Odessa to Bear Lake (9 miles total), where you can pick up the shuttle back to the Fern Lake Trailhead. *Moderate.* ⊠ *Rocky Mountain National Park* ✛ *Trailhead: off Fern Lake Rd., about 2½ miles south of Moraine Park Visitor Center.*

★ Glacier Gorge Trail

HIKING/WALKING | The 2.8-mile hike to **Mills Lake** can be crowded, but the reward is one of the park's prettiest lakes, set against the breathtaking backdrop of Longs Peak, Pagoda Mountain, and the Keyboard of the Winds. There's a modest elevation gain of 750 feet. On the way, about 1 mile in, you pass **Alberta Falls,** a popular destination in and of itself. The hike travels along Glacier

Creek, under the shade of a subalpine forest. Give yourself at least four hours for hiking and lingering. *Easy.* ⊠ *Rocky Mountain National Park* ✛ *Trailhead: off Bear Lake Rd., about 1 mile southeast of Bear Lake.*

Longs Peak Trail

HIKING/WALKING | Climbing this 14,259-foot mountain (one of 53 "Fourteeners" in Colorado) is an ambitious goal for almost anyone—but only those who are very fit and acclimated to the altitude should attempt it. The 16-mile round-trip climb requires a predawn start (3 am is ideal), so that you're off the summit before the typical summer afternoon thunderstorm hits. Also, the last 2 miles or so of the trail are very exposed—you have to traverse narrow ledges with vertigo-inducing drop-offs. That said, summiting Longs can be one of the most rewarding experiences you'll ever have. The Keyhole route is the most popular means of ascent, and the number of people going up it on a summer day can be astounding, given the rigors of the climb. Though just as scenic, the Loft route, between Longs and Mount Meeker from Chasm Lake, is less crowded but not as clearly marked and therefore more difficult to navigate. *Difficult.* ⊠ *Rocky Mountain National Park* ✛ *Trailhead: at Longs Peak Ranger Station, off Rte. 7, 10 miles from Beaver Meadows Visitor Center.*

Sprague Lake

HIKING/WALKING | With virtually no elevation gain, this 0.5-mile, pine-lined looped path near a popular backcountry campground is wheelchair accessible and provides views of Hallet Peak and Flattop Mountain. *Easy.* ⊠ *Rocky Mountain National Park* ✛ *Trailhead: at Sprague Lake, Bear Lake Rd., 4½ miles southwest of Moraine Park Visitor Center.*

HORSEBACK RIDING

Horses and riders can access 260 miles of trails in Rocky Mountain National Park.

Glacier Creek Stable

HORSEBACK RIDING | FAMILY | Located within the park near Sprague Lake, Glacier Creek Stable offers two- to 10-hour rides to Glacier Basin, Odessa Lake, and Storm Pass. ⊠ *Glacier Creek Campground, off Bear Lake Rd. near Sprague Lake* ☎ *970/586–3244 stables, 970/586–4577 off-season reservations* ⊕ *sombrero.com* ⌨ *From $55.*

Moraine Park Stable

HORSEBACK RIDING | FAMILY | Located inside the park just before the Cub Lake Trailhead, Moraine Park Stable offers two- to eight-hour trips to Beaver Meadows, Fern Lake, and Tourmaline Gorge. ⊠ *549 Fern Lake Rd* ☎ *970/586–2327 stables, 970/586–4577 off-season reservations* ⊕ *www.sombrero.com* ⌨ *From $55.*

ROCK CLIMBING

Expert rock climbers as well as novices can try hundreds of classic and big-wall climbs here (there's also ample opportunity for bouldering and mountaineering). The burgeoning sport of ice climbing also thrives in the park. The Diamond, Lumpy Ridge, and Petit Grepon are the places for serious rock climbing, while well-known ice-climbing spots include Hidden Falls, Loch Vale, and Emerald and Black lakes.

★ Colorado Mountain School

CLIMBING/MOUNTAINEERING | FAMILY | Guiding climbers since 1877, Colorado Mountain School is the park's only official provider of technical climbing services. They can teach you rock climbing, mountaineering, ice climbing, avalanche survival, and many other skills. Take introductory half-day and one- to five-day courses on climbing and rappelling technique, or sign up for guided introductory trips, full-day climbs, and longer expeditions. Make reservations a month in advance for summer climbs. ⊠ *341 Moraine Ave., Estes Park* ☎ *720/387-8944, 303/447–2804* ⊕ *coloradomountainschool.com* ⌨ *From $90.*

WINTER ACTIVITIES

Each winter, the popularity of snowshoeing in the park increases. It's a wonderful way to experience Rocky Mountain's majestic winter side, when the jagged peaks are softened with a blanket of snow and the summer hordes are nonexistent. You can snowshoe any of the summer hiking trails that are accessible by road; many of them also become well-traveled cross-country ski trails. Two trails to try are Tonahutu Creek Trail (near Kawuneeche Visitor Center) and the Colorado River Trail to Lulu City (start at the Timber Creek Campground).

Backcountry skiing within the park ranges from gentle cross-country outings to full-on, experts-only adventures down steep chutes and open bowls. Ask a ranger about conditions, and gear up as if you were spending the night. If you plan on venturing off trail, take a shovel, probe pole, and avalanche transceiver. Only on the west side of the park are you permitted to snowmobile, and you must register at Kawuneeche Visitor Center before traveling the unplowed section of Trail Ridge Road up to Milner Pass. Check the park newspaper for ranger-guided tours.

Estes Park Mountain Shop

SNOW SPORTS | You can rent or buy snowshoes and skis here, as well as fishing, hiking, and climbing equipment. The store is open year-round and gives four-, six-, and eight-hour guided snowshoeing, fly-fishing, and climbing trips to areas in and around Rocky Mountain National Park. ⊠ *2050 Big Thompson Ave., Estes Park* ☎ *970/586–6548, 866/303–6548* ⊕ *www.estesparkmountainshop.com* ⊠ *From $54.*

Never Summer Mountain Products

CAMPING—SPORTS-OUTDOORS | This well-stocked shop sells and rents all sorts of outdoor equipment, including cross-country skis, hiking gear, kayaks, and camping supplies. ⊠ *919 Grand Ave., Grand Lake* ☎ *970/627–3642* ⊕ *www.neversummer-mtn.com.*

Nearby Towns

Estes Park, 5 miles east of Rocky Mountain, is the park's most popular gateway. The town sits at an altitude of more than 7,500 feet, with 14,259-foot Longs Peak and a legion of surrounding mountains as its stunning backdrop. Many of the small hotels lining the roads are mom-and-pop outfits that have been passed down through several generations.

Estes Park's quieter cousin, **Grand Lake,** 1½ miles outside the park's west entrance, gets busy in summer, but has a low-key, quintessentially Western graciousness. In winter, it's *the* snowmobiling and ice-fishing destination for Front Range Coloradans. At the park's southwestern entrance are the Arapaho and Roosevelt National Forests, Arapaho National Recreational Area, and the small town of **Granby,** the place to go for big-game hunting and mountain biking. There are also skiing and other mountain activities (both summer and winter varieties) at nearby SolVista Basin and the Winter Park/Mary Jane ski areas.

 Sights

SCENIC DRIVES
Peak to Peak Scenic and Historic Byway

SCENIC DRIVE | The byway (highways 119, 72, and 7), a 55-mile stretch that winds from Central City north through Nederland to Estes Park, is not the quickest route to the eastern gateway to Rocky Mountain National Park, but it's certainly the most scenic. You'll pass through the old mining towns of Ward and Allenspark and enjoy spectacular mountain vistas. Mount Meeker and Longs Peak rise magnificently behind every bend in the road. The descent into Estes Park provides grand vistas of snow-covered mountains and green valleys. ⊠ *Nederland* ✛ *From Central City, drive north on Hwy. 119. From Nederland, drive north on Hwy. 72. Turn left at intersection with Hwy. 7 and*

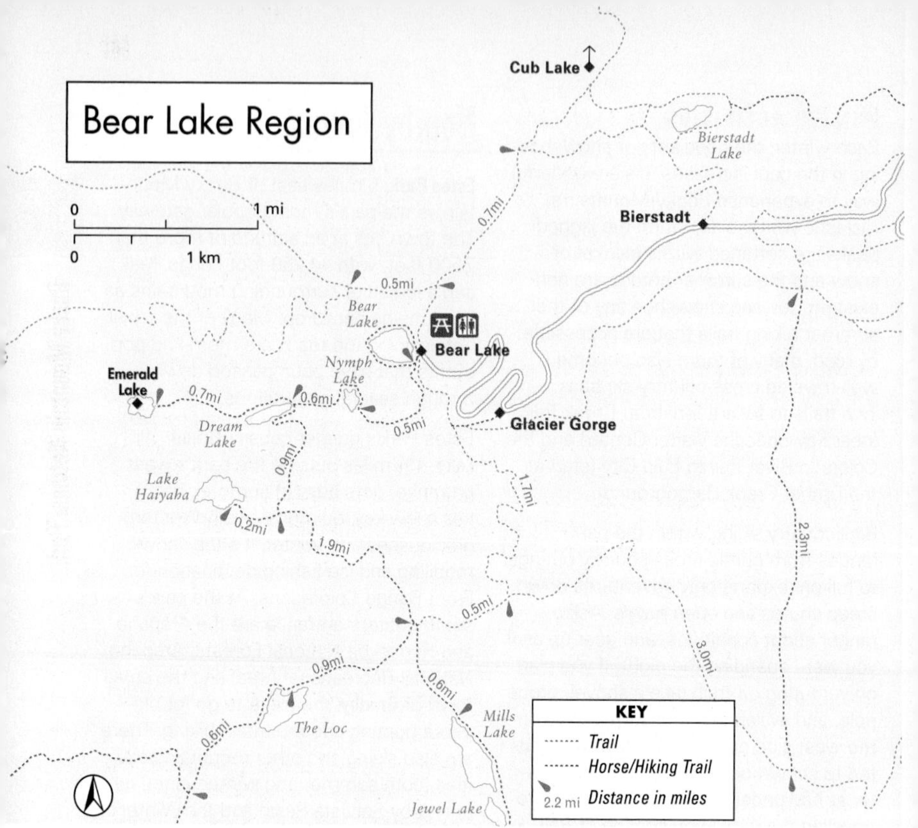

Bear Lake Region

Cub Lake

Bierstadt Lake

0 | 1 mi

0 | 1 km

Bierstadt

0.7mi

0.5mi

Bear Lake

Nymph Lake

◆ Bear Lake

Emerald Lake

0.7mi

0.6mi

0.5mi

Dream Lake

0.9mi

◆ Glacier Gorge

Lake Haiyaha

0.2mi

1.7mi

2.3mi

1.9mi

0.5mi

3.0mi

0.9mi

0.6mi

0.6mi

The Loc

Mills Lake

Jewel Lake

KEY	
┈┈┈	Trail
┈ ┈	Horse/Hiking Trail
2.2 mi	Distance in miles

continue to Estes Park ⊕ *www.codot. gov/travel/scenic-byways.*

Activities

BIRD-WATCHING
Windy Gap Watchable Wildlife Area

BIRD WATCHING | On the path alongside the reservoir at Windy Gap Watchable Wildlife Area, you're likely to spot geese, pelicans, swans, eagles, killdeer, osprey, and more. The park has information kiosks, spotting scopes, viewing areas, covered picnic tables, and a nature trail that's wheelchair accessible. ⊠ *Granby ⊹ 5 miles west of Granby on U.S. 40 where it meets Rte. 125* ☎ *970/725–6200* ⊕ *www.northernwater.org/water-projects/howwindygapworks.aspx.*

FISHING

Anglers in the Grand Lake and Granby area enjoy plentiful trout, mackinaw, and kokanee salmon. Ice fishers will not want to miss the big contest held the first weekend in January on Lake Granby, where winners collect $20,000 in cash and prizes. Anyone older than 16 needs a Colorado fishing license, which you can obtain at local sporting-goods stores. See ⊕ *www.cpw.state.co.us* for more information.

The Big Thompson River, which runs east of Estes Park along U.S. 34, is popular for its good stock of rainbow and brown trout.

TOURS AND OUTFITTERS
Trail Ridge Marina

BOATING | The Trail Ridge Marina is on the western shore of Shadow Mountain Lake, which is connected to Grand Lake by a channel. The marina rents pontoon, pleasure, and fishing boats, as well as kayaks and stand-up paddleboards. ✉ *12634 U.S. 34, Grand Lake* ☎ *970/627–3586* ⊕ *www.trailridgemarina.com* ⊗ *Closed Oct.–Apr.*

GOLF
Grand Elk Golf Club
GOLF | Designed by PGA great Craig Stadler, this challenging mountain course is reminiscent of traditional heathland greens in Britain yet brings its own blend of Colorado style, with expansive views of sagebrush-covered hills, aspen groves, and the Continental Divide. ✉ *1300 Tenmile Dr., Granby* ☎ *970/887–9122* ⊕ *www.grandelk.com* 💲 *$85 weekdays, $95 weekends* 🏌 *18 holes, 7144 yards, par 71* ⊗ *Closed mid-Oct.–mid-May* ♿ *Reservations essential.*

WINTER SPORTS
Many consider Grand Lake to be Colorado's snowmobiling capital, with more than 300 miles of trails (150 miles groomed), many winding through virgin forest. There are several rental and guide companies in the area. If you're visiting during the winter holidays, it's wise to make reservations about three weeks ahead.

Never Summer Mountain Products
SKIING/SNOWBOARDING | Rent skis and snowshoes in the winter, or buy backpacks, tents, and other camping equipment for summer sports. Rocky Mountain National Park requires backpackers to use bear canisters (for overnight food storage), which Never Summer rents for $5 for 24 hours. ✉ *919 Grand Ave., Grand Lake* ☎ *970/627–3642* ⊕ *www.neversummermtn.com.*

 Nightlife

Lariat Saloon
BARS/PUBS | A local hot spot, this rustic bar has pinball, pool, and video games, plus live music on summer weekends. It's also the only spot in town for

---

Longs Peak ⊙

At 14,259 feet above sea level, **Longs Peak** has long fascinated explorers to the region. Longs Peak is the northernmost of the Fourteeners—the 53 mountains in Colorado that reach above the 14,000-foot mark—and one of more than 114 named mountains in the park that are higher than 10,000 feet. The peak, in the park's southeast quadrant, has a distinctive flat-topped, rectangular summit that is visible from many spots on the park's east side and on Trail Ridge Road.

late-night eats. Look for the buffalo and dreadlock-adorned fox amid the eclectic Western decor. ✉ *1121 Grand Ave., Grand Lake* ☎ *970/627–9965.*

Lonigans
BARS/PUBS | This fun Irish pub has karaoke on Wednesday, Friday, and Saturday nights starting at 9 pm, and the occasional theme party like "Freaky Friday" and "International Night," featuring plentiful drink specials. ✉ *110 W. Elkhorn Ave., Estes Park* ☎ *970/586–4346* ⊕ *www.lonigans.com.*

🍴 Restaurants

IN THE PARK
Cafe at Trail Ridge
$ | **AMERICAN** | The park's only source for food, this small café offers snacks, sandwiches, hot dogs, and soups. A coffee bar also serves fair-trade coffee, espresso drinks, and tea, plus water, juice, and salads. **Known for:** quick bite; fair-trade coffee; no-frills food. 💲 *Average main: $7* ✉ *Trail Ridge Rd., at Alpine Visitor Center* ☎ *970/586–3097* ⊕ *www.trailridgegiftstore.com* ⊗ *Closed mid-Oct.–mid-May. No dinner.*

PICNIC AREAS

Endovalley

RESTAURANT—SIGHT | With 32 tables and 30 fire grates, this is the largest picnic area in the park. Here, you'll find aspen groves, nice views of Fall River Pass—and lovely Fan Lake a short hike away. ✉ *Off U.S. 34, at beginning of Old Fall River Rd., about 4½ miles from Fall River Visitor Center.*

Hollowell Park

RESTAURANT—SIGHT | In a meadow near Mill Creek, this lovely spot for a picnic has 10 tables and is open year-round. It's also close to the Hollowell Park and Mill Creek Basin Trailheads. ✉ *Off Bear Lake Rd., about 2½ miles from Moraine Park Visitor Center.*

Sprague Lake

RESTAURANT—SIGHT | **FAMILY** | With 27 tables and 16 pedestal grills, this alfresco dining spot is open year-round, with flush toilets in the summer and vault toilets the rest of the year. ✉ *About ½ mile from intersection of Bear Lake Rd. and U.S. 36, 4 miles from Bear Lake.*

OUTSIDE THE PARK

ESTES PARK

Bighorn Restaurant

$ | **AMERICAN** | **FAMILY** | An Estes Park staple since 1972, this family-run outfit is where the locals go for breakfast. Try a double-cheese omelet, huevos rancheros, or grits before heading into the park in the morning. **Known for:** hearty breakfast; huge portions; picnic lunches to-go. [$] *Average main: $12* ✉ *401 W. Elkhorn Ave., Estes Park* ☎ *970/586–2792* 🌐 *www.estesparkbighorn.com.*

Ed's Cantina & Grill

$$ | **MEXICAN** | **FAMILY** | The fajitas and well-stocked bar make this lively Mexican restaurant popular with locals and visitors alike. The decor is bright, with light woods and large windows. [$] *Average main: $13* ✉ *390 E. Elkhorn Ave., Estes Park* ☎ *970/586–2919.*

Estes Park Brewery

$ | **AMERICAN** | If you want to sample some local brews, check out the Estes Park Brewery, which has been crafting beer since 1993. The food is no-frills (beer chili is the specialty), and the menu includes things like pizza, burgers, sandwiches, and house-made bratwurst. **Known for:** local beer; pool tables; laid-back atmosphere. [$] *Average main: $11* ✉ *470 Prospect Village Dr., Estes Park* ☎ *970/586–5421* 🌐 *www.epbrewery.com.*

Poppy's Pizza & Grill

$ | **PIZZA** | **FAMILY** | This casual riverside eatery serves creative signature pizzas. Try the spinach, artichoke, and feta pie made with sun-dried tomato pesto. **Known for:** create-your-own pizza; riverfront patio; vegan and gluten-free friendly. [$] *Average main: $10* ✉ *342 E. Elkhorn Ave., Estes Park* ☎ *970/586–8282* 🌐 *www.poppyspizzaandgrill.com* ⏲ *Closed Jan.*

GRAND LAKE

★ Fat Cat Cafe

$ | **CAFÉ** | Located on the boardwalk, this cozy family-run café serves up hearty helpings, as well as advice on local sightseeing. The weekend breakfast buffet includes nearly 50 items—including biscuits and gravy, huevos rancheros casserole with house-made green chile sauce, and a wide selection of scones, pastries, and pies that are baked in-house. **Known for:** sprawling brunch buffet; homemade pies; homey decor. [$] *Average main: $10* ✉ *916 Grand Ave., Grand Lake* ☎ *970/627–0900* ⏲ *Closed Tues. No dinner.*

★ Sagebrush BBQ & Grill

$ | **SOUTHERN** | Falling-off-the-bone, melt-in-your-mouth barbecue pork, chicken, and beef draw local and out-of-town attention to this homey café. Munch on peanuts (and toss the shells on the floor) while dining at tables with cowhide-patterned tablecloths set against a backdrop of license plates from across the country. **Known for:** peanut shell-lined floor; wild

Best Campgrounds in Rocky Mountain

The park's five campgrounds accommodate campers looking to stay in a tent, trailer, or RV (only three campgrounds accept reservations—up to six months in advance at 🌐 www. *recreation.gov* or 🌐 *www.reserveamerica.com*; the others fill up on a first-come, first-served basis).

Aspenglen Campground. This quiet, eastside spot near the north entrance is set in open pine woodland along Fall River. There are a few excellent walk-in sites for those who want to pitch a tent away from the crowds but still be close to the car. Reservations are recommended in summer. ✉ *Drive past Fall River Visitor Center on U.S. 34 and turn left at the campground road.*

Backcountry Camping, Rocky Mountain National Park. Experienced hikers can camp at one of the park's many designated backcountry sites with advance reservations or a day-of-trip permit (which comes with a $26 fee in May through October). Contact the Backcountry Permits office before starting out to get a sense of current conditions. ✉ *Beaver Meadows Visitor Center, Kawuneeche Visitor Center* ☎ *970/586–1242.*

Glacier Basin Campground. This spot offers expansive views of the Continental Divide, easy access to the free summer shuttles to Bear Lake and Estes Park, and ranger-led evening programs in the summer. Reservations are essential. ✉ *Drive 5 miles south on Bear Lake Rd. from U.S. 36* ☎ *877/444–6777.*

Longs Peak Campground. Open May to November, this campgound is only a short walk from the Longs Peak trailhead, making it a favorite among hikers looking to get an early start there. The tent-only sites, which are first come, first served, are limited to eight people; firewood, lighting fluid, and charcoal are sold in summer. ✉ *9 miles south of Estes Park on Rte. 7.*

Moraine Park Campground. The only campground in Rocky Mountain open year-round, this spot connects to many hiking trails and has easy access to the free summer shuttles. Rangers lead evening programs in the summer. You'll hear elk bugling if you camp here in September or October. Reservations are essential from mid-May to late September. ✉ *Drive south on Bear Lake Rd. from U.S. 36, 1 mile to campground entrance.*

Timber Creek Campground. Anglers love this spot on the Colorado River, 10 miles from Grand Lake village and the only east-side campground. In the evening you can sit in on ranger-led campfire programs. The 98 campsites are first come, first served. ✉ *1 Trail Ridge Rd., 2 miles west of Alpine Visitor Center.*

game burgers and sausage; rotating daily specials. [$] *Average main: $12* ✉ *1101 Grand Ave., Grand Lake* ☎ *970/627–1404* 🌐 *www.sagebrushbbq.com.*

Hotels

OUTSIDE THE PARK

ESTES PARK

Boulder Brook

$$$$ | **HOTEL** | Watch elk stroll past your spacious luxury suite at this smart, secluded spot on the river amid towering pines. **Pros:** scenic location; quiet area;

attractive grounds. **Cons:** not within walking distance of attractions; no nearby dining. $ *Rooms from: $250* ✉ *1900 Fall River Rd., Estes Park* ☎ *970/586–0910, 800/238–0910* ⊕ *www.boulderbrook.com* ⇆ *20 suites* ⍩⍺ *No meals.*

C Lazy U Guest Ranch

$$$$ | **RESORT** | **FAMILY** | Secluded in a broad, verdant valley, this deluxe dude ranch offers a smorgasbord of activites as well as plush, Western-style accommodations with wood-paneled walls, beautiful furnishings, and bathrooms with copper sinks and custom vanities. **Pros:** kid- and family-friendly; helpful staff; deluxe in every respect. **Cons:** distant from other area attractions; strict meal times; very expensive. $ *Rooms from: $3000* ✉ *3640 Hwy. 125, Granby* ⊹ *3½ miles north on Hwy. 125 from U.S. 40 junction* ☎ *970/887–3344* ⊕ *www.clazyu. com* ⇆ *44 rooms* ⍩⍺ *All-inclusive.*

Glacier Lodge

$$ | **RESORT** | **FAMILY** | Families are the specialty at this secluded, 22-acre guest resort on the banks of the Big Thompson River. **Pros:** great place for families; attractive grounds on the river; on free bus route. **Cons:** not within walking distance of attractions; along rather busy road. $ *Rooms from: $160* ✉ *2166 Hwy. 66, Estes Park* ☎ *800/523–3920* ⊕ *www. glacierlodgeonline.com* ☉ *Closed Nov.– Apr.* ⇆ *26 cabins* ⍩⍺ *No meals.*

★ Stanley Hotel

$$$$ | **HOTEL** | Perched regally on a hill, with a commanding view of town, the Stanley is one of Colorado's great old hotels, featuring Georgian colonial–style architecture and a storied, haunted history, inspiring Stephen King's novel *The Shining* and daily "ghost" tours. **Pros:** historic hotel; many rooms have been updated; good restaurant. **Cons:** some rooms are small and tight; building is old; no air-conditioning. $ *Rooms from: $279* ✉ *333 Wonderview Ave., Estes Park* ☎ *970/577–4000, 800/976–1377* ⊕ *www.stanleyhotel.com* ⇆ *140 rooms* ⍩⍺ *No meals.*

YMCA of the Rockies – Estes Park Center

$$ | **RESORT** | **FAMILY** | Surrounded on three sides by Rocky Mountain National Park, this 860-acre family-friendly property has attractive, clean lodge rooms (with either queen, full, or bunk beds), simple cabins for two to four people, and larger cabins that can sleep as many as 88 people. **Pros:** good value for large groups and longer stays; lots of family-oriented activities and amenities; stunning scenery. **Cons:** very large, busy, and crowded property; fills fast; location requires vehicle to visit town or the national park. $ *Rooms from: $129* ✉ *2515 Tunnel Rd., Estes Park* ☎ *970/586–3341, 888/613–9622 family reservations, 800/777–9622 group reservations* ⊕ *www.ymcarockies.org* ⇆ *770 rooms* ⍩⍺ *Some meals.*

GRAND LAKE

★ Historic Rapids Lodge & Restaurant

$ | **HOTEL** | This handsome lodgepole-pine structure, which dates to 1915, is tucked on the banks of the Tonahutu River and features seven lodge rooms decorated with antique furnishings. **Pros:** in-house restaurant; condos are great for longer stays; quiet area of town. **Cons:** unpaved parking area; lodge rooms are above restaurant; all lodge rooms are on second floor and there's no elevator. $ *Rooms from: $95* ✉ *210 Rapids La., Grand Lake* ☎ *970/627–3707* ⊕ *www.rapidslodge. com* ☉ *Closed Apr. and Nov.* ⇆ *31 rooms* ⍩⍺ *No meals.*

Mountain Lakes Lodge

$ | **HOTEL** | **FAMILY** | Families and dog-lovers enjoy these comfortable, charming, whimsically decorated log cabins, which have such unique touches as cow-spotted walls, canoe-paddle headboards, and wooden ducks swimming on the ceiling. **Pros:** dog-friendly; close to fishing; good value. **Cons:** outside of town (and services); two-night minimum; no daily housekeeping. $ *Rooms from: $99* ✉ *10480 U.S. 34, Grand Lake* ☎ *970/627–8448* ⊕ *www.grandlakelodging.net* ☉ *Closed for 10 days in Apr.* ⇆ *12 rooms* ⍩⍺ *No meals.*

Chapter 31

SAGUARO NATIONAL PARK

Updated by
Elise Riley

ARIZONA

31

WELCOME TO SAGUARO NATIONAL PARK

TOP REASONS TO GO

★ **Saguaro sightseeing:** Hike, bike, or drive through dense saguaro stands for an up-close look at this king of all cacti.

★ **Wildlife watching:** Diverse wildlife roams through the park, including such ground dwellers as javelinas, coyotes, and rattlesnakes, and winged residents ranging from the migratory lesser long-nosed bat to the diminutive elf owl.

★ **Ancient artwork:** Get a glimpse into the past at the numerous petroglyph rock-art sites where ancient peoples etched into the stones as far back as 5000 BC.

★ **Desert hiking:** Take a trek through the undisturbed and magical Sonoran Desert, and discover that it's more than cacti.

★ **Two districts, one park:** Split into two districts, the park offers a duo of separate experiences on opposite sides of Tucson.

1 Saguaro West: Tucson Mountain District. This popular district makes up less than one-third of the park. Here you'll find a Native American video orientation to saguaros at the visitor center, hiking trails, an ancient Hohokam petroglyph site at Signal Hill, and a scenic drive through the park's densest desert growth.

2 Saguaro East: Rincon Mountain District. In the Rincon Mountains, Saguaro East encompasses nearly 60,000 acres of designated wilderness area, an easily accessible scenic loop drive, several easy and intermediate trails through the cactus forest, and opportunities for adventure and backcountry camping at six rustic campgrounds.

3 Rincon Valley Area. This roughly 4,000-acre expansion along the southern border of Saguaro's Rincon Mountain District offers access to the riparian area along Rincon Creek.

4 Saguaro Wilderness Area. In the Rincon Mountain District, this backcountry area travels from desert scrublands at 3,000 feet to mixed conifer forests at 9,000 feet.

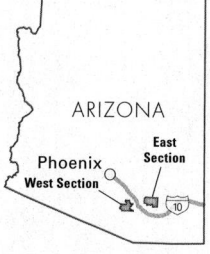

ARIZONA

Phoenix

East Section

West Section

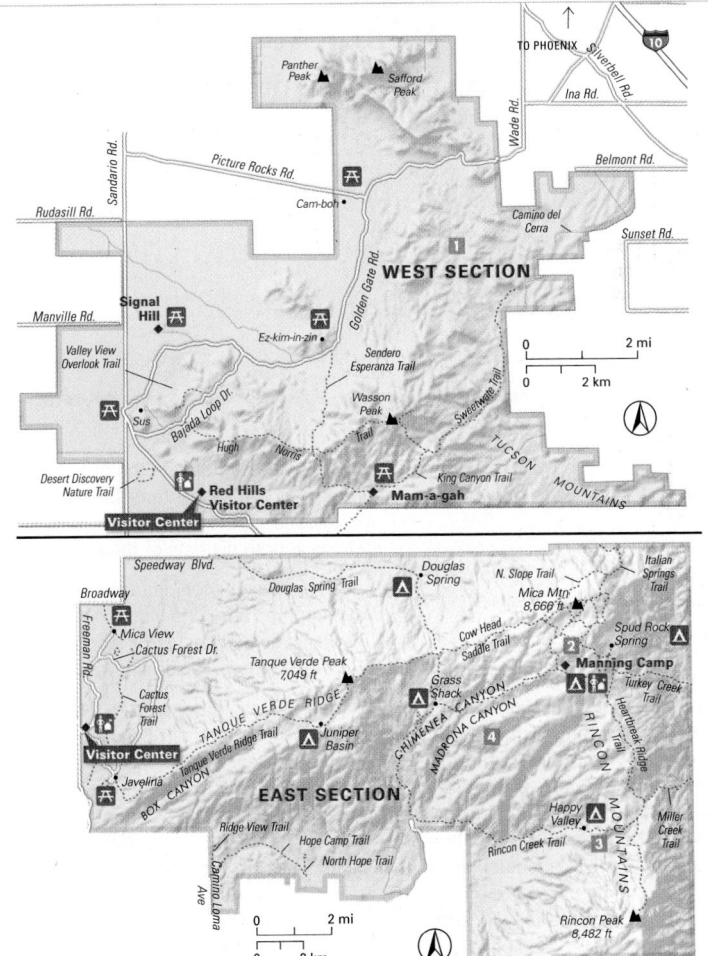

TO PHOENIX

Silverbell Rd.

Ina Rd.

Wade Rd.

Picture Rocks Rd.

Belmont Rd.

Sandario Rd.

Rudasill Rd.

Cam-boh

Camino del Cerra

Sunset Rd.

1

WEST SECTION

Golden Gate Rd.

Manville Rd.

Signal Hill

Valley View Overlook Trail

Ez-kim-in-zin

Sendero Esperanza Trail

Sweetwater Trail

Bajada Loop Dr.

Sus

Wasson Peak

Trail

Hugh

Norris

King Canyon Trail

TUCSON MOUNTAINS

Desert Discovery Nature Trail

Red Hills Visitor Center

Mam-a-gah

Visitor Center

Panther Peak

Safford Peak

0   2 mi
0   2 km

Speedway Blvd.

Broadway

Freeman Rd.

Douglas Spring Trail

Douglas Spring

N. Slope Trail

Italian Springs Trail

Mica Mtn 8,666 ft

Cow Head Saddle Trail

Spud Rock Spring

2

Manning Camp

Mica View

Cactus Forest Dr.

Tanque Verde Peak 7,049 ft

Grass Shack

Turkey Creek Trail

Cactus Forest Trail

TANQUE VERDE RIDGE

Tanque Verde Ridge Trail

Juniper Basin

CHIMENEA CANYON

MADRONA CANYON

4

RINCON

Heartbreak Ridge Trail

Visitor Center

Javelina

BOX CANYON

EAST SECTION

Happy Valley

MOUNTAINS

Miller Creek Trail

Ridge View Trail

Hope Camp Trail

North Hope Trail

Rincon Creek Trail

3

Camino Loma Alta

Rincon Peak 8,482 ft

0   2 mi
0   2 km

Standing sentinel in the desert, the towering saguaro is perhaps the most familiar emblem of the Southwest. Known for their height (often 50 feet) and arms reaching out in weird configurations, a saguaro can survive more than 200 years. They are found only in the Sonoran Desert, and the largest concentration is in Saguaro National Park.

Planning

WHEN TO GO

Saguaro never gets crowded; however, most people visit in milder weather, October through April. December through February can be cool, and are likely to see gentle rain showers. The spring days from March through May are bright and sunny with wildflowers in bloom. Because of high temperatures, from June through September it's best to visit the park in the early morning or late afternoon. The intense summer heat puts off most hikers, at least at lower elevations, but lodging prices are much cheaper—rates at top resorts in Tucson drop by as much as 70%. Cooler temperatures return in October and November, providing perfect weather for hiking and camping throughout the park.

PLANNING YOUR TIME
SAGUARO IN ONE DAY

Before setting off, choose which section of the park to visit and pack a lunch (there's no food service in either park district). Also bring plenty of water—you're likely to get dehydrated in the dry climate—or purchase a reusable bottle at the visitor center (there are water stations in both districts of the park).

In the western section, start out by watching the 15-minute video at the **Red Hills Visitor Center,** then stroll along the 0.5-mile-long **Desert Discovery Trail.**

Drive north along Kinney Road, then turn right onto the graded dirt **Bajada Loop Drive.** Before long you'll see a turnoff for the **Hugh Norris Trail** on your right. If you're game for a steep 45-minute hike uphill, this trail leads to a perfect spot for a picnic. Hike back down and drive along the Bajada Loop Drive until you reach the turnoff for **Signal Hill.** From here it's a short walk to the **Hohokam petroglyphs.**

Alternatively, in the eastern section, pick up a free map of the hiking trails at the **Rincon Mountain Visitor Center.** Drive south along the paved **Cactus Forest Drive** to the Javelina picnic area, where you'll see signs for the **Freeman Homestead Trail,** an easy 1-mile loop that winds through a stand of mesquite as interpretive signs describe early inhabitants in the Tucson

AVERAGE HIGH/LOW TEMPERATURES					
JAN.	**FEB.**	**MAR.**	**APR.**	**MAY**	**JUNE**
63/38	66/40	72/44	80/50	89/57	98/67
JULY	**AUG.**	**SEPT.**	**OCT.**	**NOV.**	**DEC.**
98/73	96/72	93/67	84/57	72/45	65/39

basin. If you're up for more difficult hiking, you might want to tackle part of the **Tanque Verde Ridge Trail,** which affords excellent views of saguaro-studded hillsides.

Along the northern loop of Cactus Forest Drive is **Cactus Forest Trail,** which branches off into several fairly level paths. You can easily spend the rest of the afternoon strolling among the saguaros.

GETTING HERE AND AROUND
AIR TRAVEL
Both districts of Saguaro National Park are approximately a 30-minute drive from the Tucson International Airport.

CAR TRAVEL
Both districts are about a half-hour drive from central Tucson. To reach Rincon Mountain District (east section) from Interstate 10, take Exit 275, then go north on Houghton Road for 10 miles. Turn right on Escalante and left onto Old Spanish Trail, and the park will be on the right side. If you're coming from town, go east on Speedway Boulevard to Houghton Road. Turn right on Houghton and left onto Old Spanish Trail.

To reach the Tucson Mountain District (west section) from Interstate 10, take Exit 242 or Exit 257, then go west on Speedway Boulevard (the name will change to Gates Pass Road), follow it to Kinney Road, and turn right.

As there's no public transportation to or within Saguaro, a car is a necessity. In the western section, Bajada Loop Drive takes you through the park and to various trailheads; Cactus Forest Drive does the same for the eastern section.

PARK ESSENTIALS
PARK FEES AND PERMITS
Admission to Saguaro is $20 per vehicle and $10 for individuals on foot or bicycle; it's good for seven days from purchase at both park districts. Annual passes cost $40. For camping at one of the primitive campsites in the east district (the closest campsite is 6 miles from the trailhead), obtain a required backcountry permit for $8 nightly from the Rincon Mountain Visitor Center up to two months in advance.

PARK HOURS
The park opens at sunrise and closes at sunset every day but Christmas day. It's in the Mountain time zone. Arizona (excluding the Navajo Nation) does not observe Daylight saving time. The visitor center is open daily from 9 am to 5 pm.

CELL PHONE RECEPTION
Cell-phone reception is generally good in the eastern district but is unreliable in the western district. The visitor centers have pay phones.

EDUCATIONAL OFFERINGS
Orientation Programs
TOUR—SIGHT | Daily programs at both park districts introduce visitors to the desert. You might find presentations on bats, birds, or desert blooms, and naturalist-led hikes (including moonlight hikes). Check online or call for the current week's activities. ✉ *Rincon Mountain and Red Hills visitor centers* ☎ *520/733–5100* ⊕ *nps. gov/sagu* ✉ *Free.*

RANGER PROGRAMS
Junior Ranger Program
TOUR—SIGHT | FAMILY | In the Junior Ranger Discovery program, young visitors can pick up an activity pack any time of the year at either visitor center and complete

it within an hour or two. During June, there also are daylong camps for kids ages 5 through 12 in the East district. ✉ *Rincon Mountain and Red Hills visitor centers* ☎ *520/733–5153* ⊕ *nps.gov/ sagu.*

Ranger Talks

TOUR—SIGHT | The assortment of talks by national park rangers are a great way to hear about wildlife, geology, and archaeology. ✉ *Rincon Mountain and Red Hills visitor centers* ☎ *520/733–5100* ✍ *Free.*

RESTAURANTS

At Saguaro, you won't find more than a sampling of Southwest jams, hot sauces, and candy bars at the two visitor centers' gift shops. Vending machines outside sell bottled water and soda, but pack some lunch for a picnic if you don't want to drive all the way back into town. Five picnic areas in the west district, and two in the east, offer scenery and shade. However, the city of Tucson, sandwiched neatly between the two park districts, offers some of the best Mexican cuisine in the country. A genuine college town, Tucson also has excellent upscale Southwestern cuisine, as well as good sushi, Thai, Italian, and Ethiopian food.

HOTELS

Although there are no hotels within the park, its immediate proximity to Tucson makes finding a place to stay easy. A couple of B&Bs are a short drive from the park. Some ranches and smaller accommodations close during the hottest months of summer, but many inexpensive B&Bs and hotels are open year-round, and offer significantly lower rates from late May through August. *Hotel reviews have been shortened. For full information, visit Fodors.com.*

What It Costs

	$	$$	$$$	$$$$
RESTAURANTS				
	under $13	$13–$20	$21–$30	over $30
HOTELS				
	under $101	$101–$150	$151–$200	over $200

VISITOR INFORMATION

PARK CONTACT INFORMATION Saguaro National Park ✉ *3693 S. Old Spanish Trail, Tucson* ☎ *520/733–5158 for Saguaro West, 520/733–5153 for Saguaro East* ⊕ *www.nps.gov/sagu.*

VISITOR CENTERS

The visitor centers in both districts have orientation slide shows and rangers who can answer your questions, as well as loads of books and maps. Both sell bottled water and soda.

Red Hills Visitor Center

INFO CENTER | Take in gorgeous views of nearby mountains and the surrounding desert from the center's large windows and shaded outdoor terrace. A spacious gallery is filled with educational exhibits, and a lifelike display simulates the flora and fauna of the region. A 15-minute slide show, "Voices of the Desert," provides a poetic, Native American perspective on the Saguaro. Park rangers and volunteers hand out maps and suggest hikes to suit your interests. The bookstore sells books, trinkets, a few local items like honey and prickly pear jellies, and reusable water bottles that you can fill at water stations outside. ✉ *2700 N. Kinney Rd., Saguaro West* ☎ *520/733– 5158* ⊕ *www.nps.gov/sagu.*

Rincon Mountain Visitor Center

INFO CENTER | Stop here to pick up free maps and printed materials on various aspects of the park, including maps of hiking trails and backcountry camping permits. Exhibits at the center are comprehensive, and a relief map of the

Plants and Wildlife in Saguaro

The saguaro may be the centerpiece of Saguaro National Park, but more than 1,200 plant species, including 50 types of cactus, thrive in the park. Among the most common cacti here are the prickly pear, barrel cactus, and teddy bear cholla—so named because it appears cuddly, but rangers advise packing a comb to pull its barbed hooks from unwary fingers.

For many of the desert fauna, the saguaro functions as a high-rise hotel. Each spring the Gila woodpecker and gilded flicker create holes in the cactus and then nest there. When they give up their temporary digs, elf owls, cactus wrens, sparrow hawks, and other birds move in, as do dangerous Africanized honeybees.

You may not encounter any of the park's six species of rattlesnake or the Gila monster, a venomous lizard, but avoid sticking your hands or feet under rocks or into crevices. Look where you're walking; if you do get bitten, get to a clinic or hospital as soon as possible. Not all snakes pass on venom; 50% of the time the bite is "dry" (nonpoisonous).

Wildlife, from bobcats to jackrabbits, is most active in early morning and at dusk. In spring and summer, lizards and snakes are out and about but tend to keep a low profile during the midday heat.

---

park lays out the complexities of this protected landscape. Two 20-minute slide shows explain the botanical and cultural history of the region, and there is a short self-guided nature walk along the paved Cactus Garden Trail. A select variety of books and other gift items, along with energy bars, beef jerky, and refillable water bottles, are sold here. ⊠ *3693 S. Old Spanish Trail, Saguaro East* ☎ *520/733–5153* ⊕ *www.nps.gov/sagu.*

◉ Sights

SCENIC DRIVES

Unless you're ready for a long desert hike, the best way to see Saguaro is from the comfort of your car.

★ Bajada Loop Drive

SCENIC DRIVE | This 6-mile drive winds through thick stands of saguaros and past two picnic areas and trailheads to a few short hikes, including one to a petroglyph site. Although the road is unpaved and somewhat bumpy, it's a worthwhile trade-off for access to some of the park's densest desert growth. It's one-way between Hugh Norris Trail and Golden Gate Road, so if you want to make the complete circuit, travel counterclockwise. The road is susceptible to flash floods during the monsoon season (July and August), so check road conditions at the visitor center before proceeding. This loop route is also popular among bicyclists, and dogs on leash are permitted along the road. ⊠ *Saguaro West.*

★ Cactus Forest Drive

SCENIC DRIVE | This paved 8-mile drive provides a great overview of all Saguaro East has to offer. The one-way road, which circles clockwise, has several turnouts with roadside displays that make it easy to pull over and admire the scenery; you can also stop at two picnic areas and three easy nature trails. This is a good bicycling route, but watch out for snakes and javelinas crossing in front of you. ⊠ *Cactus Forest Dr., Saguaro East.*

HISTORIC SITES

Manning Camp

HOUSE | The summer home of Levi Manning, onetime Tucson mayor, was a popular gathering spot for the city's elite in the early 1900s. The cabin can be reached only on foot or horseback via one of several challenging high-country trails: Douglas Spring Trail to Cow Head Saddle Trail (12 miles), Turkey Creek Trail (7.5 miles), or Tanque Verde Ridge Trail (15.4 miles). The cabin itself is not open for viewing. ⊠ *Saguaro East ↔ Douglas Spring Trail (6 miles) to Cow Head Saddle Trail (6 miles).*

SCENIC STOPS

Signal Hill

ARCHAEOLOGICAL SITE | FAMILY | The most impressive petroglyphs, and the only ones with explanatory signs, are on the Bajada Loop Drive in Saguaro West. An easy five-minute stroll from the signposted parking area takes you to one of the largest concentrations of rock carvings in the Southwest. You'll have a close-up view of the designs left by the Hohokam people between AD 900 and 1200, including large spirals some believe are astronomical markers. ⊠ *Bajada Loop Dr., Saguaro West ↔ 4½ miles north of visitor center.*

 Activities

BICYCLING

Fair Wheel Bikes

BICYCLING | Mountain bikes and road bikes can be rented by the day or week here. The company also organizes group rides of varying difficulty. ⊠ *1110 E. 6th St., University* ☎ *520/884–9018* ⊕ *fairwheelbikes.com.*

BIRD-WATCHING

To check out the more than 200 species of birds living in or migrating through the park, begin by focusing your binoculars on the limbs of the saguaros, where many birds make their home. In general, early morning and early evening are the best times for sightings. In winter and spring, volunteer-led birding hikes begin at the visitor centers.

The finest areas to flock to in Saguaro East (the Rincon Mountain District) are the Desert Ecology Trail, where you may find rufous-winged sparrows, verdins, and Cooper's hawks along the washes, and the Javelina picnic area, where you'll most likely spot canyon wrens and black-chinned sparrows. At Saguaro West (the Tucson Mountain District), sit down on one of the visitor center benches and look for ash-throated flycatchers, Say's phoebes, curve-billed thrashers, and Gila woodpeckers. During the cooler months, keep a lookout for wintering neotropical migrants such as hummingbirds, swallows, orioles, and warblers.

Wild Bird Store

BIRD WATCHING | This shop is an excellent resource for birding information, feeders, books, and trail guides. Free bird walks are offered most Sundays October–May. ⊠ *3160 E. Fort Lowell Rd., Central* ☎ *520/322–9466* ⊕ *www.wildbirdsonline.com.*

HIKING

The park has more than 100 miles of trails. The shorter hikes, such as the Desert Discovery and Desert Ecology trails, are perfect for those looking to learn about the desert ecosystem without expending too much energy.

■ **TIP→ Rattlesnakes are commonly seen on trails; so are coyotes, javelinas, roadrunners, Gambel's quail, and desert spiny lizards. Hikers should keep their distance from all wildlife.**

SAGUARO WEST

Desert Discovery Trail

HIKING/WALKING | FAMILY | Learn about plants and animals native to the region on this paved path in Saguaro West. The 0.5-mile loop is wheelchair accessible, and has resting benches and ramadas (wooden shelters that supply shade). Dogs on leash are permitted here. *Easy.* ⊠ *Saguaro West ↔ Trailhead: 1 mile north of Red Hills Visitor Center.*

★ Hugh Norris Trail

HIKING/WALKING | This 10-mile trail through the Tucson Mountains is one of the most impressive in the Southwest. It's full

A saguaro grows under the protection of another tree, such as a paloverde or mesquite, before superseding it.

of switchbacks, and some sections are moderately steep, but the top of 4,687-foot Wasson Peak treats you to views of the saguaro forest spread across the *bajada* (the gently rolling hills at the base of taller mountains). *Difficult.* ⊠ *Saguaro West* ⊹ *Trailhead: 2½ miles north of Red Hills Visitor Center on Bajada Loop Dr.*

King Canyon Trail

HIKING/WALKING | This 3.5-mile trail is the shortest, but steepest, route to the top of Wasson Peak in Saguaro West. It meets the Hugh Norris Trail less than half a mile from the summit. The trail, which begins across from the Arizona–Sonora Desert Museum, is named after the Copper King Mine. It leads past many scars from the search for mineral wealth. **Look for petroglyphs in this area.** *Difficult.* ⊠ *Saguaro West* ⊹ *Trailhead: 2 miles south of Red Hills Visitor Center.*

Signal Hill Trail

HIKING/WALKING | This ¼-mile trail in Saguaro West is a simple, rewarding ascent to ancient petroglyphs carved a millennium ago by the Hohokam people.

Easy. ⊠ *Saguaro West* ⊹ *Trailhead: 4½ miles north of Red Hills Visitor Center on Bajada Loop Dr.*

Sendero Esperanza Trail

HIKING/WALKING | Follow a sandy mine road for the first section of this 6-mile trail in Saguaro West, then ascend via a series of switchbacks to the top of a ridge and cross the Hugh Norris Trail. Descending on the other side, you'll meet up with the King Canyon Trail. The Esperanza ("Hope") Trail is often rocky and sometimes steep, but rewards include ruins of the Gould Mine, dating back to 1907. *Moderate.* ⊠ *Saguaro West* ⊹ *Trailhead: 1½ miles east of the intersection of Bajada Loop Dr. and Golden Gate Rd.*

Sweetwater Trail

HIKING/WALKING | Though technically within Saguaro West, this trail is on the eastern edge of the district, and affords access to Wasson Peak from the eastern side of the Tucson Mountains. After gradually climbing 3.4 miles, it ends at King Canyon Trail (which would then take you on a fairly steep 1.2-mile climb to Wasson Peak). Long and meandering, this little-used trail allows more privacy to enjoy the natural surroundings than some of the more frequently used trails. *Moderate.* ⊠ *Saguaro West* ⊹ *Trailhead: western end of El Camino del Cerro Rd.*

Valley View Overlook Trail

HIKING/WALKING | On clear days you can spot the distinctive slope of Picacho Peak from this 1.5-mile trail in Saguaro West. Even on an overcast day there are splendid vistas of Avra Valley. *Moderate.* ⊠ *Saguaro West* ⊹ *Trailhead: 3 miles north of Red Hills Visitor Center on Bajada Loop Dr.*

SAGUARO EAST
Cactus Forest Trail

HIKING/WALKING | This 2.5-mile one-way loop is a moderately easy walk along a dirt path that passes historic lime kilns and a wide variety of Sonoran Desert vegetation. It's one of the only off-road trails for bicyclists. *Moderate.* ⊠ *Saguaro East* ⊹ *Trailhead: 2 miles south of Rincon Mountain Visitor Center, off Cactus Forest Dr.*

Cactus Garden Trail

HIKING/WALKING | This 100-yard paved trail in front of the Rincon Mountain Visitor Center is wheelchair accessible and has resting benches and interpretive signs about common desert plants. *Easy.* ⊠ *Saguaro East* ⊹ *Trailhead: next to Rincon Mountain Visitor Center.*

Desert Ecology Trail

HIKING/WALKING | FAMILY | Exhibits on this ¼-mile loop near the Mica View picnic area explain how local plants and animals subsist on limited water. Dogs on leash are permitted. *Easy.* ⊠ *Saguaro East* ⊹ *Trailhead: 2 miles north of Rincon Mountain Visitor Center.*

Douglas Spring Trail

HIKING/WALKING | This challenging 6-mile trail, steep in some parts, leads almost due east into the Rincon Mountains. After a half mile through a dense

concentration of saguaros, you reach the open desert. About 3 miles in is Bridal Wreath Falls, worth a slight detour in spring when melting snow creates a larger cascade. *Moderate.* ⊠ *Saguaro East* ⊹ *Trailhead: eastern end of Speedway Blvd.*

Freeman Homestead Trail

HIKING/WALKING | Learn a bit about the history of homesteading in the region on this 1-mile loop. Look for owls living in the cliffs above as you make your way through the lowland vegetation. *Easy.* ⊠ *Saguaro East* ⊹ *Trailhead: next to Javelina picnic area, 2 miles south of Rincon Mountain Visitor Center.*

★ Hope Camp Trail

HIKING/WALKING | Well worth the 5-mile round-trip trek, this Rincon Valley route rewards hikers with gorgeous views of the Tanque Verde Ridge and Rincon Peak. The trail is also open to mountain bicyclists. *Moderate.* ⊠ *Saguaro East* ⊹ *Trailhead: from Camino Loma Alta trailhead to Hope Camp.*

Tanque Verde Ridge Trail

HIKING/WALKING | Be rewarded with spectacular scenery on this 18-mile round-trip trail that takes you through desert scrub, oak, alligator juniper, and pinyon pine at the 6,000-foot peak, where views of the surrounding mountain ranges from both sides of the ridge delight. *Difficult.* ⊠ *Saguaro East* ⊹ *Trailhead: Javelina picnic area, 2 miles south of Red Hills Visitor Center.*

Nearby Towns

Saguaro stands as a protected desert oasis, with metropolitan **Tucson**, Arizona's second-largest city, lying between the two park sections. Spread over 227 miles, and with a population of nearly a half million, Tucson averages 340 days of sunshine a year.

◉ Sights

★ Arizona–Sonora Desert Museum

MUSEUM | FAMILY | The name "museum" is a bit misleading, since this delightful site is actually a zoo, aquarium, and botanical garden featuring the animals, plants, and even fish of the Sonoran Desert. Hummingbirds, coatis, rattlesnakes, scorpions, bighorn sheep, bobcats, and Mexican wolves all busy themselves in ingeniously designed habitats.

An Earth Sciences Center has an artificial limestone cave to climb through and an excellent mineral display. The coyote and javelina (a wild, piglike mammal with an oddly oversize head) exhibits have "invisible" fencing that separates humans from animals, and at the Raptor Free Flight show (October through April, daily at 10 and 2), you can see the powerful birds soar and dive, untethered, inches above your head.

The restaurants are above average, and the gift shop, which carries books, jewelry, and crafts, is outstanding. ■TIP→ **June through August, the museum stays open until 10 pm every Saturday, which provides a great opportunity to see nocturnal critters.** ⊠ *2021 N. Kinney Rd., Westside* ☎ *520/883–2702* ⊕ *www. desertmuseum.org* ⊡ *$22.*

★ Bear Canyon Trail

HIKING/WALKING | FAMILY | Also known as Seven Falls Trail, this route in Sabino Canyon is a three- to four-hour, 7.8-mile round-trip that is moderate and fun, crossing the stream several times on the way up the canyon. Kids enjoy the boulder-hopping, and all hikers are rewarded with pools and waterfalls as well as views at the top. The trailhead can be reached from the parking area by either taking a five-minute Bear Canyon Tram ride ($4) or walking the 1.8-mile tram route. *Moderate.* ⊠ *Sabino Canyon Rd., at Sunrise Dr., Foothills* ☎ *520/749–2861* ⊕ *www.fs.usda.gov/coronado.*

Colossal Cave Mountain Park

CAVE | FAMILY | This limestone grotto 20 miles east of Tucson is the largest dry cavern in the world. Guides discuss the fascinating crystal formations and relate the many romantic tales surrounding the cave, including the legend that an enormous sum of money stolen in a stagecoach robbery is hidden here.

Forty-five-minute cave tours begin every hour on the hour and require a ½-mile walk and a climb of 363 steps. The park includes a ranch area with trail rides (from $38), pony rides ($5), a gemstone-sluicing area, a small museum, nature trails, a butterfly garden, a gift shop, and a café. ⊠ *16721 E. Old Spanish Trail, Eastside* ☎ *520/647–7275* ⊕ *www. colossalcave.com* ⊡ *$18.*

Old Tucson

AMUSEMENT PARK/WATER PARK | FAMILY | This film studio–theme park, originally built for the 1940 motion picture *Arizona,* has been used to shoot countless movies, such as *Rio Bravo* (1959) and *The Quick and the Dead* (1994), and the TV shows *Gunsmoke, Bonanza,* and *Highway to Heaven.* Actors in Western garb perform and roam the streets talking to visitors.

Youngsters enjoy the simulated gunfights, rides, and stunt shows, while adults might appreciate the screenings of old Westerns, guided studio tours, and the little-bit-bawdy Grand Palace Hotel's Dance Hall Revue. There are plenty of places to eat and to buy souvenirs. Horseback riding and stagecoach rides are available for an additional charge. ⊠ *Tucson Mountain Park, 201 S. Kinney Rd., Westside* ☎ *520/883–0100* ⊕ *oldtucson.com* ⊡ *$20* ⊗ *Closed mid-Aug.–Sept. Closed Mon.–Thurs. Oct.–mid-Dec.*

St. Augustine Cathedral

RELIGIOUS SITE | Although the imposing white-and-beige, late-19th-century, Spanish-style building was modeled after the Cathedral of Queretaro in Mexico, a number of its details reflect the desert setting. For instance, above the entryway, next to a bronze statue of St. Augustine, are carvings of local desert scenes with saguaro cacti, yucca, and prickly pears—look closely and you'll find the horned toad. Compared with the magnificent facade, the modernized interior is a bit disappointing. **For a distinctly Southwestern experience, attend the mariachi Mass celebrated Sunday at 8 am.** ✉ *192 S. Stone Ave., Downtown* ☎ *520/623–6351* 🌐 *cathedral-staugustine.org* 🎟 *Free.*

Activities

BALLOONING

Fleur de Tucson Balloon Tours

BALLOONING | Operating out of Northwest Tucson from October through April, this company flies over the Tucson Mountains and Saguaro National Park West. Flights include photos as well as a continental champagne brunch after you arrive back on the ground. ✉ *Northwest* ☎ *520/403–8547* 🌐 *www.fleurdetucson.net* 🎟 *From $250.*

Restaurants

IN THE PARK

PICNIC AREAS

Mam-A-Gah

RESTAURANT—SIGHT | This is the most isolated picnic area in Saguaro West. It's on King Canyon Trail, a good area for birding and wildflower viewing. It's about a mile walk to reach the site, and the undeveloped trail isn't wheelchair accessible. ✉ *King Canyon Trail, Saguaro West* ✣ *1 mile from Kinney Rd.*

Mica View

RESTAURANT—SIGHT | Talk about truth in advertising: this picnic area gives you an eyeful of Mica Mountain, the park's highest peak. None of the tables are in the shade. ✉ *Cactus Forest Dr., Saguaro East* ✣ *2 miles north of Rincon Mountain Visitor Center.*

Signal Hill

RESTAURANT—SIGHT | Because of the nearby petroglyphs, this is the park's most popular picnic site. Its many picnic tables, sprinkled around palo verde and mesquite trees, can accommodate large groups. ✉ *Bajada Loop Dr., Saguaro West* ✣ *4½ miles north of Red Hills Visitor Center.*

OUTSIDE THE PARK

★ Beyond Bread

$ | **CAFÉ** | Twenty-seven varieties of bread are made at this bustling bakery with Central, Eastside, and Northwest locations, and highlights from the menu of generous sandwiches include Annie's Addiction (hummus, tomato, sprouts, red onion, and cucumber) and Brad's Beef (roast beef, provolone, onion, green chiles, and Russian dressing); soups, salads, and desserts are equally scrumptious. Eat inside or on the patio, or order takeout, but either way, splurge on one of the incredible desserts. **Known for:** stellar breads and pastries; large portions; friendliness. [$] *Average main: $9* ✉ *3026 N. Campbell Ave., Central* ☎ *520/322–9965* 🌐 *www.beyondbread.com* 🕒 *No dinner Sun.*

★ Café Poca Cosa

$$ | **MEXICAN** | At what is arguably Tucson's most creative Mexican restaurant, the chef prepares recipes inspired by different regions of her native country in a modern, vibrant setting. The menu, which changes daily, is listed on a chalkboard brought around to each table. **Known for:** innovative Mexican cooking; generous portions; lively energy. [$] *Average main: $18* ✉ *110 E. Pennington St., Downtown* ☎ *520/622–6400* 🌐 *www.cafepocacosatucson.com* 🕒 *Closed Sun. and Mon.*

The Grill at Hacienda del Sol

$$$$ | **SOUTHWESTERN** | Tucked into the foothills and surrounded by spectacular flowers and cactus gardens, this special-occasion restaurant, a favorite among locals hosting out-of-town

visitors, provides an alternative to the chili-laden dishes of most Southwestern nouvelle cuisine. Wild-mushroom bisque, grilled buffalo in dark-chocolate mole, and pan-seared sea bass are among the menu choices at this luxurious guest ranch resort. **Known for:** romantic dining; outstanding wine list; beautiful setting. [$] *Average main: $32* ✉ *Hacienda del Sol Guest Ranch Resort, 5501 N. Hacienda Del Sol Rd., Foothills* ☎ *520/529–3500* 🌐 *www.haciendadelsol.com/dining/the-grill.*

★ Mi Nidito

$ | MEXICAN | A perennial favorite among locals (the wait is worth it), Mi Nidito ("my little nest") has also hosted its share of visiting celebrities: following President Clinton's lunch here, the rather hefty Presidential Plate (bean tostada, taco with barbecued meat, chiles rellenos, chicken enchilada, and beef tamale with rice and beans) was added to the menu. Top that off with the mango chimichangas for dessert, and you're talkin' executive privilege. **Known for:** reliably delicious Mexican food; festive atmosphere. [$] *Average main: $10* ✉ *1813 S. 4th Ave., South* ☎ *520/622–5081* 🌐 *www.minidito.net* ⏲ *Closed Mon. and Tues.*

Vivace

$$$$ | ITALIAN | A nouvelle Italian bistro in a lovely Foothills setting, Vivace has long been a favorite with Tucsonans. Wild mushrooms and goat cheese in puff pastry is hard to resist as a starter, and the fettuccine with grilled salmon is a nice, lighter alternative to such entrées as a rich osso buco. **Known for:** Italian fine dining; lovely patios with mountain and city views. [$] *Average main: $32* ✉ *6440 N. Campbell Ave., Foothills* ☎ *520/795–7221* 🌐 *www.vivacetucson.com* ⏲ *Closed Sun.*

Zinburger

$ | AMERICAN | Have a glass of wine or a cocktail with your gourmet burger and fries at this high-energy, somewhat noisy, and unquestionably hip burger joint. Zinburger delivers tempting burgers—try the Kobe beef with cheddar and wild mushrooms—and decadent milk shakes made of exotic combinations like dates and honey or melted chocolate with praline flakes. **Known for:** gourmet burgers and fries; innovative shakes. [$] *Average main: $10* ✉ *1865 E. River Rd., Foothills* ☎ *520/299–7799* 🌐 *www.zinburgeraz.com.*

Hotels

OUTSIDE THE PARK

★ Arizona Inn

$$$$ | HOTEL | Although near the university and many sights, the beautifully landscaped lawns and gardens of this 1930 inn seem far from the hustle and bustle. **Pros:** unique historical property; emphasis on service. **Cons:** rooms may not be modern enough for some; close to University Medical Center but long walk (1½ miles) from the main campus. [$] *Rooms from: $359* ✉ *2200 E. Elm St., University* ☎ *520/325–1541, 800/933–1093* 🌐 *www.arizonainn.com* 🛏 *94 rooms* 🍴 *No meals.*

Casa Tierra

$$$$ | B&B/INN | For a real desert experience, head to this B&B on 5 acres near the Desert Museum and Saguaro National Park West, the last 1½ miles on a dirt road. **Pros:** peaceful; great Southwest character. **Cons:** far from town (30-minute drive); two-night minimum stay; closed in summer. [$] *Rooms from: $215* ✉ *11155 W. Calle Pima, Westside* ☎ *520/578–3058, 866/254–0006* 🌐 *www.casatierratucson.com* ⏲ *Closed mid-June–mid-Aug.* 🛏 *4 rooms* 🍴 *Breakfast.*

★ Hacienda del Sol Guest Ranch Resort

$$$$ | RESORT | This 32-acre hideaway in the Santa Catalina Foothills is a charming and more intimate alternative to the larger resorts, and is partly a guest ranch, with riding stables down the road. **Pros:** outstanding restaurant and bar; stunningly beautiful buildings and landscaping. **Cons:** golfers must be shuttled to a nearby course. [$] *Rooms from: $225* ✉ *5501 N. Hacienda Del Sol Rd., Foothills*

Best Campgrounds in Saguaro

There's no drive-up camping in the park. All six primitive campgrounds are in the eastern district and require a hike to reach—the shortest hikes are to Douglas Spring Campground (6 miles) and to Happy Valley (5 miles). All are open year-round. Pick up your backcountry camping permit ($6 per night) at the Rincon Mountain Visitor Center. Before choosing a camping destination, look over the relief map of hiking trails and the book of wilderness campground photos taken by park rangers. You can camp in the backcountry for a maximum of 14 days. Each site can accommodate up to six people. Reservations can be made via mail or in person up to two months in advance. Hikers are encouraged to set out before noon. If you haven't the time or the inclination to hike in, several more camping opportunities exist within a few miles of the park.

Douglas Spring. Getting to this 4,800-foot-elevation campground takes a not-too-rough 6-mile hike up the Douglas Spring Trail. ✉ *6 miles on Douglas Spring Trail, off Speedway Blvd.* ☎ *No phone.*

Grass Shack. This pretty campground is among juniper and small oak trees in a transitional area midway up Mica Mountain. ✉ *10.3 miles via Douglas Spring Trail to Manning Camp Trail* ☎ *No phone.*

Juniper Basin. Vegetation here is oak forest, and the expansive views are worth the challenging 7-mile ascent. ✉ *7 miles on Tanque Verde Ridge Trail.* ☎ *No phone.*

☎ *520/299–1501, 800/728–6514* 🌐 *www.haciendadelsol.com* 🛏 *59 rooms* 🍴 *No meals.*

★ Hotel Congress
$$ | HOTEL | This hotel, built in 1919, has been artfully restored to its original Western version of art deco; it's now the center of Tucson's hippest scene and a great place for younger and adventurous travelers to stay. **Pros:** prime location; good restaurant and bars; funky and fun. **Cons:** no elevator to guest rooms; no TVs in rooms (only in common areas); noise from nightclub. [$] *Rooms from: $119* ✉ *311 E. Congress St., Downtown* ☎ *520/622–8848, 800/722–8848* 🌐 *www.hotelcongress.com* 🛏 *40 rooms* 🍴 *No meals.*

Tanque Verde Ranch
$$$$ | RESORT | FAMILY | The most upscale of Tucson's guest ranches and one of the oldest in the country, the Tanque Verde sits on 640 beautiful acres in the Rincon Mountains next to Saguaro National Park East. **Pros:** authentic Western experience; loads of all-inclusive activities; great riding. **Cons:** at the eastern edge of town; all-inclusive package excludes alcohol. [$] *Rooms from: $425* ✉ *14301 E. Speedway Blvd., Eastside* ☎ *520/296–6275, 800/234–3833* 🌐 *www.tanqueverderanch.com* 🛏 *74 rooms* 🍴 *All-inclusive; Breakfast.*

★ White Stallion Ranch
$$$$ | RESORT | FAMILY | A 3,000-acre working cattle ranch run by the hospitable True family since 1965, this place is the real deal, satisfying for families as well as singles or couples. **Pros:** solid dude-ranch experience; charming hosts; airport shuttle. **Cons:** no TV in rooms; alcohol not included in the rate—pay extra or bring your own. [$] *Rooms from: $438* ✉ *9251 W. Twin Peaks Rd., Northwest* ☎ *520/297–0252, 888/977–2624* 🌐 *www.whitestallion.com* 🛏 *41 rooms, 1 house* 🍴 *All-inclusive.*

Chapter 32

SEQUOIA AND KINGS CANYON NATIONAL PARKS

Updated by
Cheryl Crabtree

32

CALIFORNIA

WELCOME TO SEQUOIA AND KINGS CANYON NATIONAL PARKS

TOP REASONS TO GO

★ **Gentle giants:** You'll feel small—in a good way—walking among some of the world's largest living things in Sequoia's Giant Forest and Kings Canyon's Grant Grove.

★ **Because it's there:** You can't even glimpse it from the main part of Sequoia, but the sight of majestic Mount Whitney is worth the trip to the eastern face of the High Sierra.

★ **Underground exploration:** Far older even than the giant sequoias, the gleaming limestone formations in Crystal Cave will draw you along dark, marble passages.

★ **A grander-than-Grand Canyon:** Drive the twisting Kings Canyon Scenic Byway down into the jagged, granite Kings River Canyon, deeper in parts than the Grand Canyon.

★ **Regal solitude:** To spend a day or two hiking in a subalpine world of your own, pick one of the many trailheads at Mineral King.

The two parks comprise 865,964 acres (1,353 square miles), mostly on the western flank of the Sierra. A map of the adjacent parks looks vaguely like a mitten, with the palm of Sequoia National Park south of the north-pointing, skinny thumb and long fingers of Kings Canyon National Park. Between the western thumb and eastern fingers, north of Sequoia, lies part of Sequoia National Forest, which includes Giant Sequoia National Monument.

1 Giant Forest–Lodgepole Village. One of the most heavily visited areas of Sequoia contains major sights such as Giant Forest, General Sherman Tree, Crystal Cave, and Moro Rock.

2 Grant Grove Village–Redwood Canyon. The "thumb" of Kings Canyon National Park is its busiest section, where Grant Grove, General Grant Tree, Panoramic Point, and Big Stump are the main attractions.

3 Cedar Grove. The drive through the high-country portion of Kings Canyon National Park to Cedar Grove Village, on the canyon floor, reveals magnificent granite formations of varied hues. Rock meets river in breathtaking fashion at Zumwalt Meadow.

4 Mineral King. In the southeast section of Sequoia, the highest road-accessible part of the park is a good place to hike, camp, and soak up the unspoiled grandeur of the Sierra Nevada.

5 Mount Whitney. The highest peak in the Lower 48 stands on the eastern edge of Sequoia; to get there from Giant Forest you must either backpack eight days through the mountains or drive nearly 400 miles around the park to its other side.

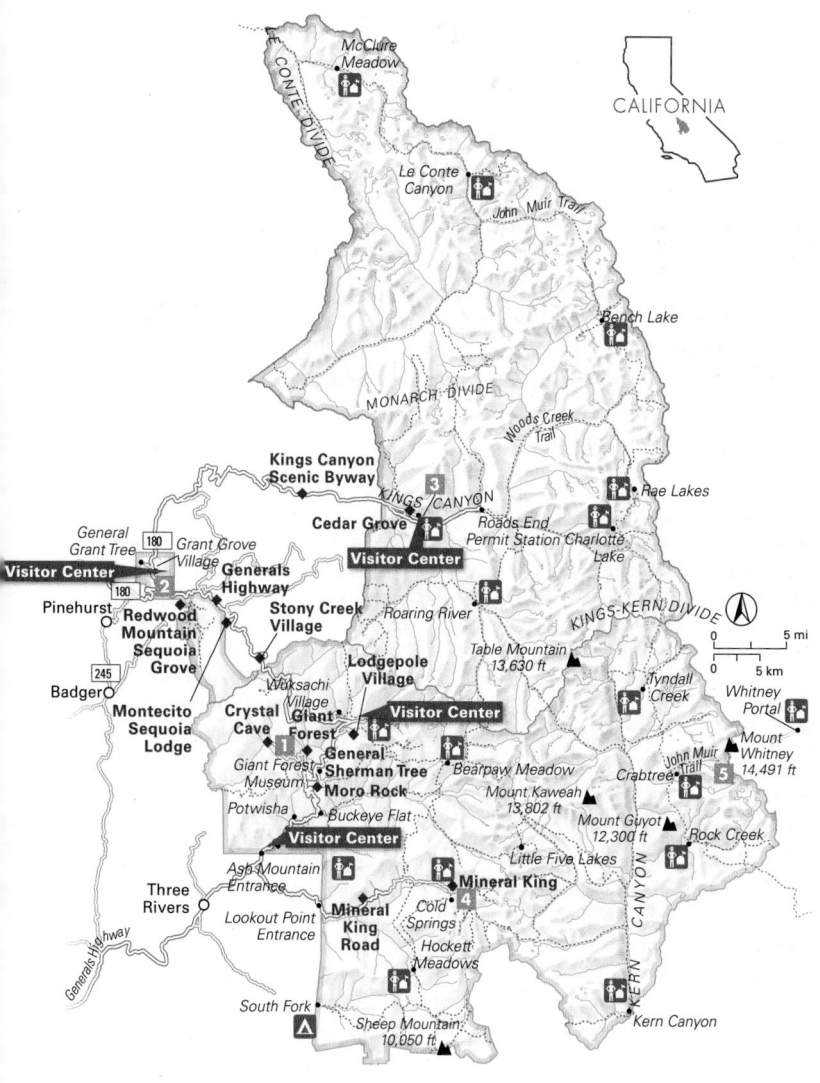

The monstrously thick trunks and branches, remarkably shallow root systems, and neck-craning heights of the Sequoias are almost impossible to believe, as is the fact they can live for more than 2,500 years. Many of these towering marvels are in the Giant Forest stretch of Generals Highway, which connects Sequoia and Kings Canyon national parks.

Next to or a few miles off the 46-mile Generals Highway are most of Sequoia National Park's main attractions and Grant Grove Village, the orientation hub for Kings Canyon National Park. The two parks share a boundary that runs from the Central Valley in the west, where the Sierra Nevada foothills begin, to the range's dramatic eastern ridges. Kings Canyon has two portions: the smaller is shaped like a bent finger and encompasses Grant Grove Village and Redwood Mountain Grove (two of the parks' largest concentration of sequoias), and the larger is home to stunning Kings River Canyon, whose vast, unspoiled peaks and valleys are a backpacker's dream. Sequoia is in one piece and includes Mount Whitney, the highest point in the lower 48 states (although it is impossible to see from the western part of the park and is a chore to ascend from either side).

Planning

WHEN TO GO

The best times to visit are spring and fall, when temperatures are moderate and crowds thin. Summertime can draw hordes of tourists to see the giant sequoias, and the few, narrow roads mean congestion at peak holiday times. If you must visit in summer, go during the week. By contrast, in wintertime you may feel as though you have the parks all to yourself. But because of heavy snows, sections of the main park roads can be closed without warning, and low-hanging clouds can move in and obscure mountains and valleys for days. From early October to late April, check road and weather conditions before venturing out.
■ TIP→ Even in summer, you can escape hordes of people just walking ¼ to ½ mile off the beaten path on a less-used trail.

FESTIVALS AND EVENTS
Annual Trek to the Tree
FESTIVAL | On the second Sunday of December, thousands of carolers gather at the base of General Grant

Tree, the nation's official Christmas tree. ☎ *559/565–3341.*

Big Fresno Fair

FESTIVAL | Over 12 days in October, agricultural, home-arts, and other competitions, plus horse racing and a carnival make for a lively county fair. ✉ *Fresno* ☎ *559/650–3247* ⊕ *www.fresnofair.com.*

Blossom Days Festival

FESTIVAL | On the first Saturday of March, communities along Fresno County's Blossom Trail celebrate the flowering of the area's orchards, citrus groves, and vineyards. ☎ *559/981–5500* ⊕ *www. goblossomtrail.com.*

Jazzaffair

FESTIVAL | On the second weekend of April, a festival of mostly traditional jazz takes place at several venues just south of the parks. ⊕ *sierratraditionaljazzclub. com.*

Woodlake Rodeo

FESTIVAL | The local Lions Club sponsors this rousing rodeo that draws large crowds to Woodlake on Mother's Day weekend. ☎ *559/564–8555* ⊕ *www. woodlakelionsclub.com.*

PLANNING YOUR TIME

SEQUOIA NATIONAL PARK IN ONE DAY

After spending the night in Visalia or Three Rivers—and provided your vehicle's length does not exceed 22 feet—take off early on Route 198 to the **Sequoia National Park entrance.** Pull over at the **Hospital Rock** picnic area to gaze up at the imposing granite formation of Moro Rock, which you later will climb. Heed signs that advise "10 mph" around tight turns as you climb 3,500 feet on **Generals Highway** to the **Giant Forest Museum.** Spend a half hour here, then examine trees firsthand by circling the lovely **Round Meadow** on the **Big Trees Trail,** to which you must walk from the museum or from its parking lot across the road.

Get back in your car and continue a few miles north on Generals Highway to see

the jaw-dropping **General Sherman Tree.** Then set off on the **Congress Trail** so that you can be further awed by the Senate and House big-tree clusters. Buy lunch at the **Lodgepole** complex, 2 miles to the north, and eat at the nearby **Pinewood** picnic area. Now you're ready for the day's big exercise, climbing **Moro Rock.**

You can drive there or, if it is summer, park at the museum lot and take the free shuttle. Count on spending at least an hour for the 350-step ascent and descent, with a pause on top to appreciate the 360-degree view. Get back in the car, or on the shuttle, and proceed past the **Tunnel Log** to **Crescent Meadow.** Spend a relaxing hour or two strolling on the trails that pass by, among other things, **Tharp's Log.** By now you've probably renewed your appetite; head to **Lodgepole Grill & Market** or the restaurant at **Wuksachi Lodge.**

KINGS CANYON NATIONAL PARK IN ONE DAY

Enter the park via the **Kings Canyon Scenic Byway** (Route 180), having spent the night in Fresno or Visalia. Better yet, wake up already in **Grant Grove Village,** perhaps in the **John Muir Lodge.** Stock up for a picnic with takeout food from the **Grant Grove Restaurant,** or purchase prepackaged food from the nearby market. Drive east a mile to see the **General Grant Tree** and compact **Grant Grove's** other sequoias. If it's no later than mid-morning, walk up the short trail at **Panoramic Point,** for a great view of Hume Lake and the High Sierra. Either way, return to Route 180 and continue east. Stop at Junction View to take in several noteworthy peaks that tower over Kings Canyon. From here, visit **Boyden Cavern** or continue to **Cedar Grove Village,** pausing along the way for a gander at **Grizzly Falls.** Eat at a table by the **South Fork of the Kings River,** or on the deck off the Cedar Grove Snack Bar. Now you are ready for the day's highlight, strolling **Zumwalt Meadow,** which lies a few miles past the village.

AVERAGE HIGH/LOW TEMPERATURES					
JAN.	**FEB.**	**MAR.**	**APR.**	**MAY**	**JUNE**
42/24	44/25	46/26	51/30	58/36	68/44
JULY	**AUG.**	**SEPT.**	**OCT.**	**NOV.**	**DEC.**
76/51	76/50	71/45	61/38	50/31	44/27

After you have enjoyed that short trail and the views it offers of **Grand Sentinel** and **North Dome,** you might as well go the extra mile to **Roads End,** where backpackers embark for the High Sierra wilderness. Make the return trip—with a quick stop at **Roaring River Falls**—past Grant Grove and briefly onto southbound **Generals Highway.** Pull over at the **Redwood Mountain Overlook** and use binoculars to look down upon the world's largest sequoia grove, then drive another couple of miles to the **Kings Canyon Overlook,** where you can survey some of what you have done today. Make reservations for a late dinner at **Wuksachi Lodge.**

GETTING HERE AND AROUND
AIR TRAVEL
The closest airport to Sequoia and Kings Canyon national parks is Fresno Yosemite International Airport (FAT).

AIRPORT CONTACTS Fresno Yosemite International Airport (FAT) ✉ 5175 E. Clinton Way, Fresno ☎ 800/244–2359 automated info, 559/454–2052 terminal info desk ⊕ www.flyfresno.com.

CAR TRAVEL
Sequoia is 36 miles east of Visalia on Route 198; Grant Grove Village in Kings Canyon is 56 miles east of Fresno on Route 180. There is no automobile entrance on the eastern side of the Sierra. Routes 180 and 198 are connected by Generals Highway, a paved two-lane road that sometimes sees delays at peak times due to ongoing improvements. The road is extremely narrow and steep from Route 198 to Giant Forest, so keep an eye on your engine temperature gauge, as the incline and congestion can cause vehicles to overheat; to avoid overheated brakes, use low gears on downgrades.

If you are traveling in an RV or with a trailer, study the restrictions on these vehicles. Do not travel beyond Potwisha Campground on Route 198 with an RV longer than 22 feet; take straighter, easier Route 180 instead. Maximum vehicle length on Generals Highway is 40 feet, or 50 feet combined length for vehicles with trailers.

Generals Highway between Lodgepole and Grant Grove is sometimes closed by snow. The Mineral King Road from Route 198 into southern Sequoia National Park is closed 2 miles below Atwell Mill either on November 1 or after the first heavy snow. The Buckeye Flat–Middle Fork Trailhead road is closed from mid-October to mid-April when the Buckeye Flat Campground closes. The lower Crystal Cave Road is closed when the cave closes (typically in November). Its upper 2 miles, as well as the Panoramic Point and Moro Rock–Crescent Meadow roads, close with the first heavy snow. Because of the danger of rockfall, the portion of Kings Canyon Scenic Byway east of Grant Grove closes in winter. For current road and weather conditions, call ☎ 559/565–3341 or visit the park website: ⊕ www.nps.gov/seki.

■ TIP→ **Snowstorms are common from late October through April. Unless you have a four-wheel-drive vehicle with snow tires, you should carry chains and know how to install them.**

PARK ESSENTIALS
ACCESSIBILITY

All the visitor centers, the Giant Forest Museum, and Big Trees Trail are wheelchair accessible, as are some short ranger-led walks and talks. General Sherman Tree can be reached via a paved, level trail near a parking area. None of the caves is accessible, and wilderness areas must be reached by horseback or on foot. Some picnic tables are extended to accommodate wheelchairs. Many of the major sites are in the 6,000-foot range and thin air at high elevations can cause respiratory distress for people with breathing difficulties. Carry oxygen if necessary. Contact the park's main number for more information.

PARK FEES AND PERMITS

The admission fee is $35 per vehicle, $30 per motorcycle, and $20 per person for those who enter by bus, on foot, bicycle, horse, or any other mode of transportation; it is valid for seven days in both parks. U.S. residents over the age of 62 pay $80 for a lifetime pass, and permanently disabled U.S. residents are admitted free.

If you plan to camp in the backcountry, you need a permit, which costs $15 for hikers or $30 for stock users (e.g., horseback riders). One permit covers the group. Availability of permits depends upon trailhead quotas. Reservations are accepted by mail or email for a $15 processing fee, beginning March 1, and must be made at least 14 days in advance (☎ 559/565–3766). Without a reservation, you may still get a permit on a first-come, first-served basis starting at 1 pm the day before you plan to hike. For more information on backcountry camping or travel with pack animals (horses, mules, burros, or llamas), contact the Wilderness Permit Office (☎ 530/565–3766).

PARK HOURS

The parks are open 24/7 year-round. They are in the Pacific time zone.

CELL PHONE RECEPTION

Cell phone reception is poor to nonexistent in the higher elevations and spotty even on portions of Generals Highway, where you can (on rare clear days) see the Central Valley. Public telephones may be found at the visitor centers, ranger stations, some trailheads, and at all restaurants and lodging facilities in the park.

EDUCATIONAL OFFERINGS

Educational programs at the parks include museum-style exhibits, ranger- and naturalist-led talks and walks, film and other programs, and sightseeing tours, most of them conducted by either the park service or the nonprofit Sequoia Parks Conservancy. Exhibits at the visitor centers and the Giant Forest Museum focus on different aspects of the park: its history, wildlife, geology, climate, and vegetation—most notably the giant sequoias. Weekly notices about programs are posted at the visitor centers and elsewhere.

Grant Grove Visitor Center at Kings Canyon National Park has maps of self-guided park tours. Ranger-led walks and programs take place throughout the year in Grant Grove. Cedar Grove and Forest Service campgrounds have activities from Memorial Day to Labor Day. Check bulletin boards or visitor centers for schedules.

EXHIBITS
Giant Forest Museum

MUSEUM | Well-imagined and interactive displays at this worthwhile stop provide the basics about sequoias, of which there are 2,161 with diameters exceeding 10 feet in the approximately 2,000-acre Giant Forest. ⊠ *Sequoia National Park ✛ Generals Hwy., 4 miles south of Lodgepole Visitor Center* ☎ *559/565–4436* 🗐 *Free* ☞ *Shuttle: Giant Forest or Moro Rock–Crescent Meadow.*

PROGRAMS AND SEMINARS

Evening Programs

TOUR—SIGHT | The Sequoia Parks Conservancy presents films, hikes, and evening lectures during the summer and winter. From May through October the popular Wonders of the Night Sky programs celebrate the often stunning views of the heavens experienced at both parks. ⊠ *Sequoia National Park* ☎ *559/565–4251* ⊕ *www.sequoiaparksconservancy.org.*

Free Nature Programs

TOUR—SIGHT | Almost any summer day, ½-hour to 1½-hour ranger talks and walks explore subjects such as the life of the sequoia, the geology of the park, and the habits of bears. Giant Forest, Lodgepole Visitor Center, and Wuksachi Village are frequent starting points. Look for less frequent tours in the winter from Grant Grove. Check bulletin boards throughout the park for the week's offerings. ⊕ *www.sequoiaparksconservancy.org.*

Junior Ranger Program

TOUR—SIGHT | **FAMILY** | Children over age five can earn a patch upon completion of a fun set of age-appropriate tasks outlined in the Junior Ranger booklet. Pick one up at any visitor center. ☎ *559/565–3341.*

Seminars

TOUR—SIGHT | Expert naturalists lead seminars on a range of topics, including birds, wildflowers, geology, botany, photography, park history, backpacking, and pathfinding. Reservations are required. Information about times and prices is available at the visitor centers or through the Sequoia Parks Conservancy. ⊠ *Sequoia National Park* ☎ *559/565–4251* ⊕ *www.sequoiaparksconservancy.org.*

TOURS

★ Sequoia Parks Conservancy Field Institute

TOUR—SIGHT | The Sequoia Parks Conservancy's highly regarded educational division conducts half-day, single-day, and multiday tours that include backpacking hikes, natural-history walks, cross-country skiing, kayaking excursions, and motorcoach tours. ⊠ *47050 Generals Hwy., Unit 10, Three Rivers* ☎ *559/565–4251* ⊕ *www.sequoiaparksconservancy. org* 🖃 *From $40 for ½-day guided tour.*

Sequoia Sightseeing Tours

TOUR—SIGHT | This locally owned operator's friendly, knowledgeable guides conduct daily interpretive sightseeing tours in Sequoia and Kings Canyon. Reservations are essential. The company also offers private tours. ⊠ *Three Rivers* ☎ *559/561–4189* ⊕ *www.sequoiatours. com* 🖃 *From $79 tour of Sequoia; from $139 tour of Kings Canyon.*

RESTAURANTS

In Sequoia and Kings Canyon national parks, you can treat yourself (and the family) to a high-quality meal in a wonderful setting in the Peaks restaurant at Wuksachi Lodge, but otherwise you should keep your expectations modest. You can grab bread, spreads, drinks, and fresh produce at one of several small grocery stores for a picnic, or get take-out food from the Grant Grove Restaurant, the Cedar Grove snack bar, or one of the two small Lodgepole eateries. Between the parks and just off Generals Highway, the Montecito Sequoia Lodge has a year-round buffet. *Restaurant reviews have been shortened. For full information, visit Fodors.com.*

HOTELS

Hotel accommodations in Sequoia and Kings Canyon are limited, and—although they are clean and comfortable—tend to lack much in-room character. Keep in mind, however, that the extra money you spend on lodging here is offset by the time you'll save by being inside the parks. You won't be faced with a 60- to 90-minute commute from the less-expensive motels in Three Rivers (by far the most charming option), Visalia, and Fresno. Reserve as far in advance as you can, especially for summertime stays.

Hotel reviews have been shortened. For full information, visit Fodors.com.

What It Costs

$	$$	$$$	$$$$
RESTAURANTS			
under $12	$12–$20	$21–$30	over $30
HOTELS			
under $100	$100–$150	$151–$200	over $200

VISITOR INFORMATION

NATIONAL PARK SERVICE Sequoia and Kings Canyon National Parks ⊠ *47050 Generals Hwy. (Rte. 198), Three Rivers* ☎ *559/565–3341* ⊕ *nps.gov/seki.*

SEQUOIA VISITOR CENTERS
Foothills Visitor Center

INFO CENTER | Exhibits here focus on the foothills and resource issues facing the parks. You can pick up books, maps, and a list of ranger-led walks, and get wilderness permits. ⊠ *47050 Generals Hwy., Rte. 198, 1 mile north of Ash Mountain entrance, Sequoia National Park* ☎ *559/565–3341.*

Lodgepole Visitor Center

INFO CENTER | Along with exhibits on the area's history, geology, and wildlife, the center screens an outstanding 22-minute film about bears. You can buy books, maps, and tickets to cave tours here. ⊠ *Sequoia National Park* ⊹ *Generals Hwy. (Rte. 198), 21 miles north of Ash Mountain entrance* ☎ *559/565–3341* ⊙ *Closed Oct.–Apr.* ☞ *Shuttle: Giant Forest or Wuksachi-Lodgepole-Dorst.*

KINGS CANYON VISITOR CENTERS
Cedar Grove Visitor Center

INFO CENTER | Off the main road and behind the Sentinel Campground, this small ranger station has books and maps, plus information about hikes and other activities. ⊠ *Kings Canyon National Park* ⊹ *Kings Canyon Scenic Byway, 30 miles east of Rte. 180/198*

junction ☎ *559/565–3341* ⊙ *Closed mid-Sept.–mid-May.*

Kings Canyon Park Visitor Center

INFO CENTER | The center's 15-minute film and various exhibits provide an overview of the park's canyon, sequoias, and human history. Books, maps, and weather advice are dispensed here, as are (if available) free wilderness permits. ⊠ *Kings Canyon National Park* ⊹ *Grant Grove Village, Generals Hwy. (Rte. 198), 3 miles northeast of Rte. 180, Big Stump entrance* ☎ *559/565–3341.*

Sequoia National Park

 Sights

SCENIC DRIVES
★ **Generals Highway**

SCENIC DRIVE | One of California's most scenic drives, this 46-mile road is the main asphalt artery between Sequoia and Kings Canyon national parks. Some portions are also signed as Route 180, others as Route 198. Named after the landmark Grant and Sherman trees that leave so many visitors awestruck, Generals Highway runs from Sequoia's Foothills Visitor Center north to Kings Canyon's Grant Grove Village. Along the way, it passes the turnoff to Crystal Cave, the Giant Forest Museum, Lodgepole Village, and other popular attractions. The lower portion, from Hospital Rock to the Giant Forest, is especially steep and winding. If your vehicle is 22 feet or longer, avoid that stretch by entering the parks via Route 180 (from Fresno) rather than Route 198 (from Visalia or Three Rivers). Take your time on this road—there's a lot to see, and wildlife can scamper across at any time. ⊠ *Sequoia National Park.*

Mineral King Road

SCENIC DRIVE | Vehicles longer than 22 feet are prohibited on this side road into southern Sequoia National Park, and for good reason: it contains 589 twists and

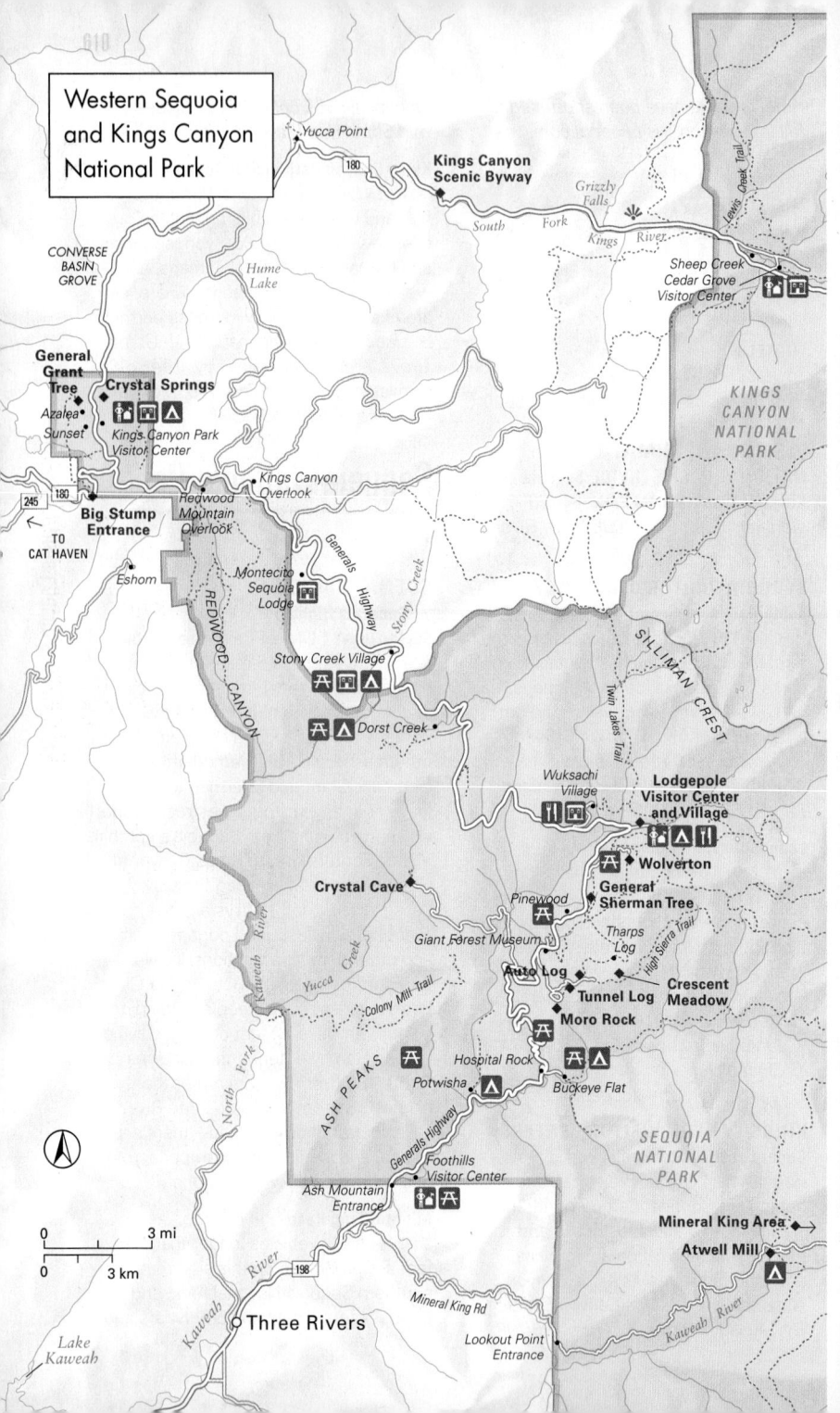

Western Sequoia and Kings Canyon National Park

Yucca Point

Kings Canyon Scenic Byway

180

Grizzly Falls

South Fork *Kings* *River*

Lewis Creek Trail

CONVERSE BASIN GROVE

Hume Lake

Sheep Creek
Cedar Grove Visitor Center

KINGS CANYON NATIONAL PARK

General Grant Tree

Crystal Springs

Azalea
Sunset

King's Canyon Park Visitor Center

Kings Canyon Overlook

180

245

Big Stump Entrance

Redwood Mountain Overlook

↙ TO CAT HAVEN

Eshom

REDWOOD CANYON

Montecito Sequoia Lodge

Generals Highway

Stony Creek

SILLIMAN CREST

Stony Creek Village

Twin Lakes Trail

Dorst Creek

Wuksachi Village

Lodgepole Visitor Center and Village

Wolverton

Crystal Cave

Pinewood

General Sherman Tree

High Sierra Trail

Giant Forest Museum

Tharps Log

Kaweah River

Yucca Creek

Colony Mill Trail

Auto Log

Tunnel Log

Crescent Meadow

Moro Rock

ASH PEAKS

Hospital Rock

Potwisha

Buckeye Flat

SEQUOIA NATIONAL PARK

North Fork

Generals Highway

Foothills Visitor Center

Ash Mountain Entrance

Mineral King Area

Atwell Mill

Mineral King Rd

0   3 mi

0   3 km

○ **Three Rivers**

198

Kaweah River

Lake Kaweah

Lookout Point Entrance

turns. Anticipating an average speed of 20 mph is optimistic. The scenery is splendid as you climb nearly 6,000 feet from Three Rivers to the Mineral King Area. In addition to maneuvering the blind curves and narrow stretches, you might find yourself sharing the pavement with bears, rattlesnakes, and even softball-size spiders. Allow 90 minutes each way. ⊠ *Sequoia National Forest* ✛ *East off Sierra Dr. (Rte. 198), 3.5 miles northeast of Three Rivers* ☉ *Road typically closed Nov.–late May.*

SCENIC STOPS

Sequoia National Park is all about the trees, and to understand the scale of these giants you must walk among them. If you do nothing else, get out of the car for a short stroll through one of the groves. But there is much more to the park than the trees. Try to access one of the vista points that provide a panoramic view over the forested mountains. Generals Highway (on Routes 198 and 180) will be your route to most of the park's sights. A few short spur roads lead from the highway to some sights, and Mineral King Road branches off Route 198 to enter the park at Lookout Point, winding east from there to the park's southernmost section.

Auto Log

FOREST | Before its wood showed signs of severe rot, cars drove right on top of this giant fallen sequoia. Now it's a great place to pose for pictures or shoot a video. ⊠ *Sequoia National Park* ✛ *Moro Rock–Crescent Meadow Rd., 1 mile south of Giant Forest.*

Crescent Meadow

TRAIL | A sea of ferns signals your arrival at what John Muir called the "gem of the Sierra." Walk around for an hour or two and you might decide that the Scotland-born naturalist was exaggerating a bit, but the verdant meadow is quite pleasant and you just might see a bear. Wildflowers bloom here throughout the summer. ⊠ *Sequoia National Park* ✛ *End*

of *Moro Rock–Crescent Meadow Rd., 2.6 miles east off Generals Hwy.* ☞ *Shuttle: Moro Rock–Crescent Meadow.*

★ Crystal Cave

CAVE | One of more than 200 caves in Sequoia and Kings Canyon, Crystal Cave is composed largely of marble, the result of limestone being hardened under heat and pressure. It contains several eye-popping formations. There used to be more, but some were damaged or obliterated by early-20th-century dynamite blasting. You can only see the cave on a tour. The Daily Tour ($16), a great overview, takes about 50 minutes. To immerse yourself in the cave experience—at times you'll be crawling on your belly—book the exhilarating Wild Cave Tour ($135). Availability is limited—reserve tickets at least 48 hours in advance at *www.recreation.gov* or stop by either the Foothills or Lodgepole visitor center first thing in the morning to try to nab a same-day ticket; they're not sold at the cave itself. ⊠ *Crystal Cave Rd., off Generals Hwy.* ☎ *877/444–6777* ⊕ *www.sequoiaparksconservancy.org/ crystalcave.html* ⓓ *$16* ☉ *Closed Oct.– late May.*

★ General Sherman Tree

LOCAL INTEREST | The 274.9-foot-tall General Sherman is one of the world's tallest and oldest sequoias, and it ranks No. 1 in volume, adding the equivalent of a 60-foot-tall tree every year to its approximately 52,500 cubic feet of mass. The tree doesn't grow taller, though—it's dead at the top. A short, wheelchair-accessible trail leads to the tree from Generals Highway, but the main trail (½ mile) winds down from a parking lot off Wolverton Road. The walk back up the main trail is steep, but benches along the way provide rest for the short of breath. ⊠ *Sequoia National Park* ✛ *Main trail Wolverton Rd. off Generals Hwy. (Rte. 198)* ☞ *Shuttle: Giant Forest or Wolverton–Sherman Tree.*

Mineral King Area

NATURE PRESERVE | A subalpine valley of fir, pine, and sequoia trees, Mineral King sits at 7,500 feet at the end of a steep, winding road. This is the highest point to which you can drive in the park. It is open only from Memorial Day through late October. ⊠ *Sequoia National Park* ✛ *Mineral King Rd., 25 miles east of Generals Hwy. (Rte. 198)* ⊘ *Closed late Oct.–May.*

★ Moro Rock

NATURE SITE | This sight offers panoramic views to those fit and determined enough to mount its 350 or so steps. In a case where the journey rivals the destination, Moro's stone stairway is so impressive in its twisty inventiveness that it's on the National Register of Historic Places. The rock's 6,725-foot summit overlooks the Middle Fork Canyon, sculpted by the Kaweah River and approaching the depth of Arizona's Grand Canyon, although smoggy, hazy air often compromises the view. ⊠ *Sequoia National Park* ✛ *Moro Rock–Crescent Meadow Rd., 2 miles east off Generals Hwy. (Rte. 198) to parking area* ☞ *Shuttle: Moro Rock–Crescent Meadow.*

Tunnel Log

LOCAL INTEREST | This 275-foot tree fell in 1937, and soon a 17-foot-wide, 8-foot-high hole was cut through it for vehicular passage (not to mention the irresistible photograph) that continues today. Large vehicles take the nearby bypass. ⊠ *Sequoia National Park* ✛ *Moro Rock–Crescent Meadow Rd., 2 miles east of Generals Hwy. (Rte. 198)* ☞ *Shuttle: Moro Rock–Crescent Meadow.*

🏃 Activities

The best way to see Sequoia is to take a hike. Unless you do so, you'll miss out on the up-close grandeur of mist wafting between deeply scored, red-orange tree trunks bigger than you've ever seen. If it's winter, put on some snowshoes or cross-country skis and plunge into the snow-swaddled woodland. There are not too many other outdoor options: no off-road driving is allowed in the parks, and no special provisions have been made for bicycles. Boating, rafting, and snowmobiling are also prohibited.

BICYCLING

Steep, winding roads and shoulders that are either narrow or nonexistent make bicycling here more of a danger than a pleasure. Outside of campgrounds, you are not allowed to pedal on unpaved roads.

BIRD-WATCHING

More than 200 species of birds inhabit Sequoia and Kings Canyon national parks. Not seen in most parts of the United States, the white-headed woodpecker and the pileated woodpecker are common in most mid-elevation areas here. There are also many hawks and owls, including the renowned spotted owl. Species are diverse in both parks due to the changes in elevation, and range from warblers, kingbirds, thrushes, and sparrows in the foothills to goshawk, blue grouse, red-breasted nuthatch, and brown creeper at the highest elevations. The Sequoia Parks Conservancy (☎ *559/565–4251* ⊕ *www.sequoiaparksconservancy.org*) has information about bird-watching in the southern Sierra.

CROSS-COUNTRY SKIING

For a one-of-a-kind experience, cut through the groves of mammoth sequoias in Giant Forest. Some of the Crescent Meadow trails are suitable for skiing as well; none of the trails is groomed. You can park at Giant Forest. Note that roads can be precarious in bad weather. Some advanced trails begin at Wolverton.

Alta Market and Ski Shop

SKIING/SNOWBOARDING | Rent cross-country skis and snowshoes here. Depending on snowfall amounts, instruction may also be available. Reservations are recommended. Marked trails cut through Giant Forest, about 5 miles south of

Wuksachi Lodge. ☒ *Sequoia National Park* ⊹ *At Lodgepole, off Generals Hwy. (Rte. 198)* ☎ *559/565–3301* ☞ *Shuttle: Wuksachi-Lodgepole-Dorst.*

FISHING

There's limited trout fishing in the creeks and rivers from late April to mid-November. The Kaweah River is a popular spot; check at visitor centers for open and closed waters. Some of the park's secluded backcountry lakes have good fishing. A California fishing license, required for persons 16 and older, costs about $16 for one day, $24 for two days, and $48 for 10 days (discounts are available for state residents and others). For park regulations, closures, and restrictions, call the parks at ☎ *559/565–3341* or stop at a visitor center. Licenses and fishing tackle are usually available at Hume Lake.

California Department of Fish and Game
FISHING | The department supplies fishing licenses and provides a full listing of regulations. ☎ *916/928–5805* ⊕ *www. wildlife.ca.gov.*

HIKING

The best way to see the park is to hike it. The grandeur and majesty of the Sierra is best seen up close. Carry a hiking map and plenty of water. Visitor center gift shops sell maps and trail books and pamphlets. Check with rangers for current trail conditions, and be aware of rapidly changing weather. As a rule of thumb, plan on covering about a mile per hour.

★ Big Trees Trail
HIKING/WALKING | This hike is a must, as it does not take long and the setting is spectacular: beautiful Round Meadow surrounded by many mature sequoias, with well-thought-out interpretive signs along the path that explain the ecology on display. The 0.7-mile Big Trees Trail is wheelchair accessible. Parking at the trailhead lot off Generals Highway is for cars with handicap placards only. The round-trip loop from the Giant Forest

Museum is about a mile long. *Easy.* ☒ *Sequoia National Park* ⊹ *Trailhead: off Generals Hwy. (Rte. 198), near the Giant Forest Museum* ☞ *Shuttle: Giant Forest.*

★ Congress Trail
HIKING/WALKING | This 2-mile trail, arguably the best hike in the parks in terms of natural beauty, is a paved loop that begins near General Sherman Tree. You'll get close-up views of more big trees here than on any other Sequoia hike. Watch for the clusters known as the House and Senate. The President Tree, also on the trail, supplanted the General Grant Tree in 2012 as the world's second largest in volume (behind the General Sherman). An offshoot of the Congress Trail leads to Crescent Meadow, where in summer you can catch a free shuttle back to the Sherman parking lot. *Easy.* ☒ *Sequoia National Park* ⊹ *Trailhead: off Generals Hwy. (Rte. 198), 2 miles north of Giant Forest* ☞ *Shuttle: Giant Forest.*

Crescent Meadow Trails
HIKING/WALKING | A 1-mile trail loops around lush Crescent Meadow to Tharp's Log, a cabin built from a fire-hollowed sequoia. From there you can embark on a 60-mile trek to Mount Whitney, if you're prepared and have the time. Brilliant wildflowers bloom here in midsummer. *Easy.* ☒ *Sequoia National Park* ⊹ *Trailhead: the end of Moro Rock–Crescent Meadow Rd., 2.6 miles east off Generals Hwy. (Rte. 198)* ☞ *Shuttle: Moro Rock–Crescent Meadow.*

Little Baldy Trail
HIKING/WALKING | Climbing 700 vertical feet in 1.75 miles of switchbacking, this trail ends at a granite dome with a great view of the peaks of the Mineral King area and the Great Western Divide. The walk to the summit and back takes about four hours. *Moderate.* ☒ *Sequoia National Park* ⊹ *Trailhead: Little Baldy Saddle, Generals Hwy. (Rte. 198), 9 miles north of General Sherman Tree* ☞ *Shuttle: Lodgepole-Wuksachi-Dorst.*

Marble Falls Trail

HIKING/WALKING | The 3.7-mile trail to Marble Falls crosses through the rugged foothills before reaching the cascading water. Plan on three to four hours one-way. *Moderate.* ⊠ *Sequoia National Park* ⊹ *Trailhead: off dirt road across from concrete ditch near site 17 at Potwisha Campground, off Generals Hwy. (Rte. 198).*

Mineral King Trails

HIKING/WALKING | Many trails to the high country begin at Mineral King. Two popular day hikes are Eagle Lake (6.8 miles round-trip) and Timber Gap (4.4 miles round-trip). At the Mineral King Ranger Station (*559/565–3768*) you can pick up maps and check about conditions from late May to late September. *Difficult.* ⊠ *Sequoia National Park* ⊹ *Trailheads: at end of Mineral King Rd., 25 miles east of Generals Hwy. (Rte. 198).*

Muir Grove Trail

HIKING/WALKING | You will attain solitude and possibly see a bear or two on this unheralded gem of a hike, a 4-mile round-trip from the Dorst Creek Campground. The remote grove is small but lovely, its soundtrack provided solely by nature. The trailhead is subtly marked. In summer, park in the amphitheater lot and walk down toward the group campsite area. *Easy.* ⊠ *Sequoia National Park* ⊹ *Trailhead: Dorst Creek Campground, Generals Hwy. (Rte. 198), 8 miles north of Lodgepole Visitor Center* ☞ *Shuttle: Lodgepole-Wuksachi-Dorst.*

Tokopah Falls Trail

HIKING/WALKING | This trail with a 500-foot elevation gain follows the Marble Fork of the Kaweah River for 1.75 miles one-way and dead-ends below the impressive granite cliffs and cascading waterfall of Tokopah Canyon. The trail passes through a mixed-conifer forest. It takes 2½ to 4 hours to make the round-trip journey. *Moderate.* ⊠ *Sequoia National Park* ⊹ *Trailhead: off Generals Hwy. (Rte. 198),* ¼ mile north of Lodgepole Campground ☞ Shuttle: Lodgepole-Wuksachi-Dorst.

HORSEBACK RIDING

Trips take you through forests and flowering meadows and up mountain slopes.

Grant Grove Stables

HORSEBACK RIDING | Grant Grove Stables isn't too far from parts of Sequoia National Park, and is perfect for short rides from June to September. Reservations are recommended. ☎ *559/335–9292 summer* ⊕ *www.nps.gov/seki/planyourvisit/horseride.htm* ⊠ *From $40.*

Horse Corral Packers

HORSEBACK RIDING | One- and two-hour trips through Sequoia are available for beginning and advanced riders. ⊠ *Big Meadow Rd., 12 miles east of Generals Hwy. (Rte. 198) between Sequoia and Kings Canyon national parks* ☎ *559/565–3404 summer, 559/565–6429 off season,* ⊕ *hcpacker.com* ⊠ *From $45.*

SLEDDING AND SNOWSHOEING

The Wolverton area, on Route 198 near Giant Forest, is a popular sledding spot, where sleds, inner tubes, and platters are allowed. You can buy sleds and saucers, with prices starting at $15, at the Alta Market and Ski Shop (☎ *559/565–3301*), at the Lodgepole Visitor Center.

You can rent snowshoes for $18–$24 at the Alta Market and Ski Shop, at the Lodgepole Visitor Center. Naturalists lead snowshoe walks around Giant Forest and Wuksachi Lodge, conditions permitting, on Saturday and holidays. Make reservations and check schedules at Giant Forest Museum (☎ *559/565–3341*) or Wuksachi Lodge.

SWIMMING

Drowning is the number-one cause of death in both Sequoia and Kings Canyon parks. Though it is sometimes safe to swim in the parks' rivers in the late summer and early fall, it is extremely dangerous to do so in the spring and early summer, when the snowmelt from the high

32

Sequoia and Kings Canyon National Parks

SEQUOIA NATIONAL PARK

country causes swift currents and icy temperatures. Stand clear of the water when the rivers are running, and stay off wet rocks to avoid falling in. Check with rangers for safety information.

Kings Canyon National Park

 **Sights**

SCENIC DRIVES

★ Kings Canyon Scenic Byway

SCENIC DRIVE | The 30-mile stretch of Route 180 between Grant Grove Village and Zumwalt Meadow delivers eye-popping scenery—granite cliffs, a roaring river, waterfalls, and Kings River Canyon itself—much of which you can experience at vista points or on easy walks. The canyon comes into view about 10 miles east of the village at **Junction View.** Five miles beyond, at **Yucca Point,** the canyon is thousands of feet deeper than the more famous Grand Canyon. **Canyon View,** a special spot 1 mile east of the Cedar Grove Village turnoff, showcases evidence of the area's glacial history. Here, perhaps more than anywhere else, you'll understand why John Muir compared Kings Canyon vistas with those in Yosemite. Driving the byway takes about an hour each way without stops. ⊠ *Kings Canyon National Park* ⊕ *Rte. 180 north and east of Grant Grove village.*

HISTORIC SITES

Fallen Monarch

TOUR—SIGHT | This toppled sequoia's hollow base was used in the second half of the 19th century as a home for settlers, a saloon, and even to stable U.S. Cavalry horses. As you walk through it (assuming entry is permitted, which is not always possible), notice how little the wood has decayed, and imagine yourself tucked safely inside, sheltered from a storm or protected from the searing heat. ⊠ *Kings Canyon National Park* ⊕ *Grant Grove Trail,* *1 mile north of Kings Canyon Park Visitor Center.*

Gamlin Cabin

BUILDING | Despite being listed on the National Register of Historic Places, this replica of a modest 1872 pioneer cabin is only borderline historical. The structure, which was moved and rebuilt several times over the years, once served as U.S. Cavalry storage space and, in the early 20th century, a ranger station. ⊠ *Grant Grove Trail.*

SCENIC STOPS

Kings Canyon National Park consists of two sections that adjoin the northern boundary of Sequoia National Park. The western portion, covered with sequoia and pine forest, contains the park's most visited sights, such as Grant Grove. The vast eastern portion is remote high country, slashed across half its southern breadth by the deep, rugged Kings River Canyon. Separating the two is Sequoia National Forest, which encompasses Giant Sequoia National Monument. The Kings Canyon Scenic Byway (Route 180) links the major sights within and between the park's two sections.

General Grant Tree

LOCAL INTEREST | President Coolidge proclaimed this to be the "nation's Christmas tree," and 30 years later President Eisenhower designated it as a living shrine to all Americans who have died in wars. Bigger at its base than the General Sherman Tree, it tapers more quickly. It's estimated to be the world's third-largest sequoia by volume. A spur trail winds behind the tree, where scars from a long-ago fire remain visible. ⊠ *Kings Canyon National Park* ⊕ *Trailhead: 1 mile north of Grant Grove Visitor Center.*

Redwood Mountain Sequoia Grove

FOREST | One of the world's largest sequoia groves, Redwood contains within its 2,078 acres nearly 2,200 sequoias whose diameters exceed 10 feet. You can view the grove from afar at an overlook

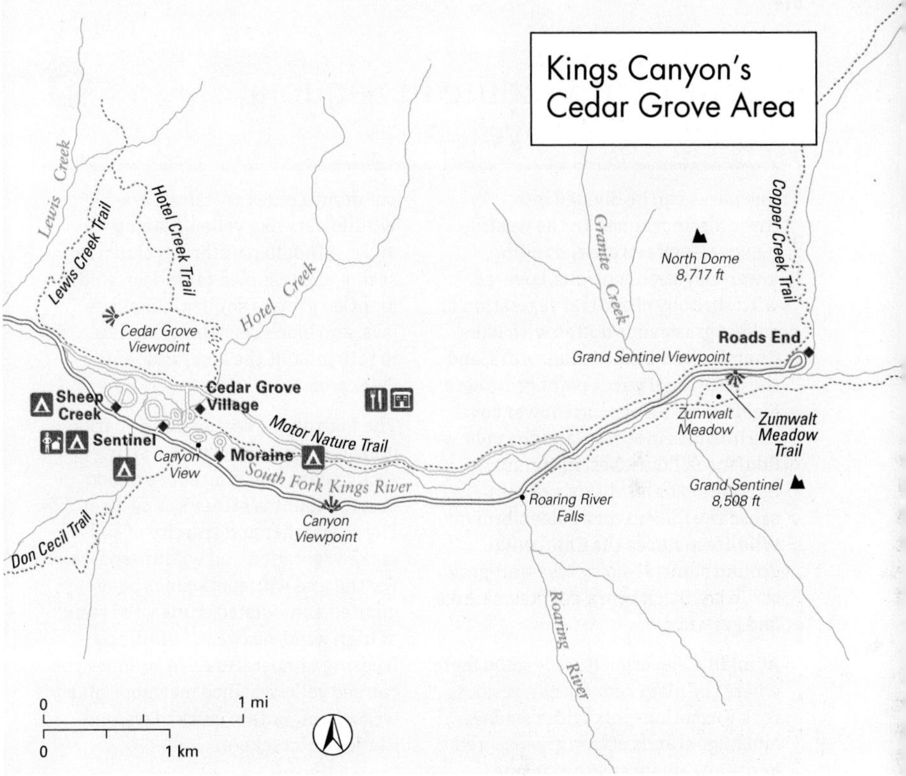

Kings Canyon's Cedar Grove Area

Lewis Creek

Hotel Creek Trail

Lewis Creek Trail

Hotel Creek

Granite Creek

Copper Creek Trail

Cedar Grove Viewpoint

▲ North Dome 8,717 ft

Roads End ◆
Grand Sentinel Viewpoint

▲ **Sheep Creek**

🛉 ▲ **Sentinel**

Cedar Grove Village ◆

🍴 🖼

Motor Nature Trail

▲ Canyon View

◆ **Moraine** ▲

South Fork Kings River

Zumwalt Meadow

Zumwalt Meadow Trail

Grand Sentinel 8,508 ft ▲

Don Cecil Trail

Canyon Viewpoint

◆ Roaring River Falls

Roaring River

0 _____ 1 mi

0 _____ 1 km

---

or hike 6 to 10 miles down into the richest regions, which include two of the world's 25 heaviest trees. ✉ *Kings Canyon National Park* ✛ *Drive 6 miles south of Grant Grove on Generals Hwy. (Rte. 198), then turn right at Quail Flat; follow it 2 miles to the Redwood Canyon trailhead.*

🏃 Activities

The siren song of beauty, challenge, and relative solitude (by national parks standards) draws hard-core outdoors enthusiasts to the Kings River Canyon and the backcountry of the park's eastern section. Backpacking, rock-climbing, and extreme-kayaking opportunities abound, but the park also has day hikes for all ability levels. Winter brings sledding, skiing, and snowshoeing fun. No off-road driving

or bicycling is allowed in the park, and snowmobiling is also prohibited.

BICYCLING

Bicycles are allowed only on the paved roads in Kings Canyon. Cyclists should be extremely cautious along the steep highways and narrow shoulders.

CROSS-COUNTRY SKIING

Roads to Grant Grove are accessible even during heavy snowfall, making the trails here a good choice over Sequoia's Giant Forest when harsh weather hits.

FISHING

There is limited trout fishing in the park from late April to mid-November, and catches are minor. Still, Kings River is a popular spot. Some of the park's secluded backcountry lakes have good fishing. Licenses are available, along with fishing tackle, in Grant Grove and Cedar

Plants and Wildlife in Sequoia and Kings Canyon

The parks can be divided into three distinct zones. In the west (1,500–4,500 feet) are the rolling, lower-elevation foothills, covered with shrubby chaparral vegetation or golden grasslands dotted with oaks. Chamise, red-barked manzanita, and the occasional yucca plant grow here. Fields of white popcorn flower cover the hillsides in spring, and the yellow fiddleneck flourishes. In summer, intense heat and absence of rain cause the hills to turn golden brown. Wildlife includes the California ground squirrel, noisy blue-and-gray scrub jay, black bears, coyotes, skunks, and gray fox.

At middle elevation (5,000–9,000 feet), where the giant sequoia belt resides, rock formations mix with meadows and huge stands of evergreens—red and white fir, incense cedar, and ponderosa pines, to name a few. Wildflowers like yellow blazing star and red Indian paintbrush bloom in spring and summer. Mule deer, golden-mantled ground squirrels, Steller's jays, and black bears (most active in fall) inhabit the area, as does the chickaree.

The high alpine section of the parks is extremely rugged, with a string of rocky peaks reaching above 13,000 feet to Mount Whitney's 14,494 feet. Fierce weather and scarcity of soil make vegetation and wildlife sparse. Foxtail and whitebark pines have gnarled and twisted trunks, the result of high wind, heavy snowfall, and freezing temperatures. In summer you can see yellow-bellied marmots, pikas, weasels, mountain chickadees, and Clark's nutcrackers.

Grove. *See Activities, in Sequoia National Park, above, for more information about licenses.*

HIKING

You can enjoy many of Kings Canyon's sights from your car, but the giant gorge of the Kings River Canyon and the sweeping vistas of some of the highest mountains in the United States are best seen on foot. Carry a hiking map—available at any visitor center—and plenty of water. Check with rangers for current trail conditions, and be aware of rapidly changing weather. Except for one trail to Mount Whitney, permits are not required for day hikes.

Big Baldy

HIKING/WALKING | This hike climbs 600 feet and 2 miles up to the 8,209-foot summit of Big Baldy. Your reward is the view of Redwood Canyon. Round-trip the hike is 4 miles. *Moderate.* ⊠ *Kings Canyon National Park* ✛ *Trailhead: 8 miles south of Grant Grove on Generals Hwy. (Rte. 198).*

Big Stump Trail

HIKING/WALKING | From 1883 until 1890, logging was done here, complete with a mill. The 1-mile loop trail, whose unmarked beginning is a few yards west of the Big Stump entrance, passes by many enormous stumps. *Easy.* ⊠ *Kings Canyon National Park* ✛ *Trailhead: near Big Stump Entrance, Generals Hwy. (Rte. 180).*

Buena Vista Peak

HIKING/WALKING | For a 360-degree view of Redwood Canyon and the High Sierra, make the 2-mile ascent to Buena Vista. *Difficult.* ⊠ *Kings Canyon National Park*

✛ *Trailhead: off Generals Hwy. (Rte. 198), south of Kings Canyon Overlook, 7 miles southeast of Grant Grove.*

★ Grant Grove Trail

HIKING/WALKING | Grant Grove is only 128 acres, but it's a big deal. More than 120 sequoias here have a base diameter that exceeds 10 feet, and the **General Grant Tree** is the world's third-largest sequoia by volume. Nearby, the Confederacy is represented by the **Robert E. Lee Tree,** recognized as the world's 11th-largest sequoia. Also along the easy-to-walk trail are the **Fallen Monarch** and the **Gamlin Cabin,** built by 19th-century pioneers. *Easy.* ✉ *Kings Canyon National Park* ✛ *Trailhead: off Generals Hwy. (Rte. 180), 1 mile north of Kings Canyon Park Visitor Center.*

Hotel Creek Trail

HIKING/WALKING | For gorgeous canyon views, take this trail from Cedar Grove up a series of switchbacks until it splits. Follow the route left through chaparral to the forested ridge and rocky outcrop known as Cedar Grove Overlook, where you can see the Kings River Canyon stretching below. This strenuous 5-mile round-trip hike gains 1,200 feet and takes three to four hours to complete. *Difficult.* ✉ *Kings Canyon National Park* ✛ *Trailhead: at Cedar Grove Pack Station, 1 mile east of Cedar Grove Village.*

Mist Falls Trail

TRAIL | This sandy trail follows the glaciated South Fork Canyon through forest and chaparral, past several rapids and cascades, to one of the largest waterfalls in the two parks. Nine miles round-trip, the hike is relatively flat, but climbs 600 feet in the last 2 miles. It takes from four to five hours to complete. *Moderate.* ✉ *Kings Canyon National Park* ✛ *Trailhead: at end of Kings Canyon Scenic Byway, 5½ miles east of Cedar Grove Village.*

Panoramic Point Trail

HIKING/WALKING | You'll get a nice view of whale-shape Hume Lake from the top of this Grant Grove path, which is paved and only 300 feet long. It's fairly steep—strollers might work here, but not wheelchairs. Trailers and RVs are not permitted on the steep and narrow road that leads to the trailhead parking lot. *Moderate.* ✉ *Kings Canyon National Park* ✛ *Trailhead: at end of Panoramic Point Rd., 2.3 miles from Grant Grove Village.*

Roads End Permit Station

HIKING/WALKING | You can obtain wilderness permits, maps, and information about the backcountry at this station, where bear canisters, a must for campers, can be rented or purchased. When the station is closed (typically October–mid-May), complete a self-service permit form. ✉ *Kings Canyon National Park* ✛ *Eastern end of Kings Canyon Scenic Byway, 6 miles east of Cedar Grove Visitor Center.*

Redwood Canyon Trails

HIKING/WALKING | Two main trails lead into Redwood Canyon Grove, the world's largest sequoia grove. The 6.5-mile **Hart Tree and Fallen Goliath Loop** passes by a 19th-century logging site, pristine Hart Meadow, and the hollowed-out Tunnel Tree before accessing a side trail to the grove's largest sequoia, the 277.9-foot-tall Hart Tree. The 6.4-mile **Sugar Bowl Loop** provides views of Redwood Mountain and Big Baldy before winding down into its namesake, a thick grove of mature and young sequoias. *Moderate.* ✉ *Kings Canyon National Park* ✛ *Trailhead: off Quail Flat. Drive 5 miles south of Grant Grove on Generals Hwy. (Rte. 198), turn right at Quail Flat and proceed 1½ miles to trailhead.*

Roaring River Falls Walk

HIKING/WALKING | Take a shady five-minute walk to this forceful waterfall that rushes through a narrow granite chute. The trail is paved and mostly accessible. *Easy.* ✉ *Kings Canyon National Park*

Mount Whitney

At 14,494 feet, Mount Whitney is the highest point in the contiguous United States and the crown jewel of Sequoia National Park's wild eastern side. The peak looms high above the tiny, high-mountain desert community of Lone Pine, where numerous Hollywood Westerns have been filmed. The high mountain ranges, arid landscape, and scrubby brush of the eastern Sierra are beautiful in their vastness and austerity.

Despite the mountain's scale, you can't see it from the more traveled west side of the park because it is hidden behind the Great Western Divide. The only way to access Mount Whitney from the main part of the park is to circumnavigate the Sierra Nevada via a 10-hour, nearly 400-mile drive outside the park. No road ascends the peak; the best vantage point from which to catch a glimpse of the mountain is at the end of Whitney Portal Road. The 13 miles of winding road leads from

U.S. 395 at Lone Pine to the trailhead for the hiking route to the top of the mountain. Whitney Portal Road is closed in winter.

Mt. Whitney Trail The most popular route to the summit, the Mt. Whitney Trail can be conquered by very fit and experienced hikers. If there's snow on the mountain, this is a challenge for expert mountaineers only. All overnighters must have a permit, as must day hikers on the trail beyond Lone Pine Lake, about 2½ miles from the trailhead. From May through October, permits are distributed via a lottery run each February by *recreation.gov*. The Eastern Sierra Interagency Visitor Center (*760/876–6200*), on Route 136 at U.S. 395 about a mile south of Lone Pine, is a good resource for information about permits and hiking. ✉ *Kings Canyon National Park* ☎ *760/873–2483 trail reservations* ⊕ *www.fs.usda.gov/inyo.*

✛ *Trailhead: 3 miles east of Cedar Grove Village turnoff from Kings Canyon Scenic Byway.*

★ Zumwalt Meadow Trail

HIKING/WALKING | Rangers say this is the best (and most popular) day hike in the Cedar Grove area. Just 1.5 miles long, it offers three visual treats: the South Fork of the Kings River, the lush meadow, and the high granite walls above, including those of Grand Sentinel and North Dome. *Easy.* ✉ *Kings Canyon National Park* ✛ *Trailhead: 4½ miles east of Cedar Grove Village turnoff from Kings Canyon Scenic Byway.*

HORSEBACK RIDING

One-day destinations by horseback out of Cedar Grove include Mist Falls and Upper Bubb's Creek. In the backcountry, many equestrians head for Volcanic Lakes or Granite Basin, ascending trails that reach elevations of 10,000 feet. Costs per person range from $40 for a one-hour guided ride to around $300 per day for fully guided trips for which the packers do all the cooking and camp chores.

Cedar Grove Pack Station

HORSEBACK RIDING | Take a day ride or plan a multiday adventure along the Kings River Canyon with Cedar Grove Pack Station. Popular routes include the Rae Lakes Loop and Monarch Divide. Closed early September–late May. ✉ *Kings Canyon National Park* ✛ *Kings Canyon Scenic*

Byway, 1 mile east of Cedar Grove Village ☎ 559/565–3464 summer, 559/337–2413 off season ⊕ www.nps.gov/seki/plan-yourvisit/horseride.htm ✉ From $40 per hr or $100 per day.

Grant Grove Stables

HORSEBACK RIDING | A one- or two-hour trip through Grant Grove leaving from the stables provides a taste of horseback riding in Kings Canyon. Closed October–early June. ⊠ Kings Canyon National Park ⚓ Rte. 180, ½ mile north of Grant Grove Visitor Center ☎ 559/335–9292 ⊕ www.nps.gov/seki/planyourvisit/horseride.htm ✉ From $40.

SLEDDING AND SNOWSHOEING

In winter, Kings Canyon has a few great places to play in the snow. Sleds, inner tubes, and platters are allowed at both the Azalea Campground area on Grant Tree Road, ¼ mile north of Grant Grove Visitor Center, and at the Big Stump picnic area, 2 miles north of the lower Route 180 entrance to the park.

Snowshoeing is good around Grant Grove, where you can take occasional naturalist-guided snowshoe walks from mid-December through mid-March as conditions permit. Grant Grove Market rents sleds and snowshoes.

Nearby Towns

Numerous towns and cities tout themselves as "gateways" to the parks, with some more deserving of the title than others. One that certainly merits the name is frisky **Three Rivers,** a Sierra foothills hamlet (population 2,200) along the Kaweah River. Close to Sequoia's Ash Mountain and Lookout Point entrances, Three Rivers is a good spot to find a room when park lodgings are full. Either because Three Rivers residents appreciate their idyllic setting or because they know that tourists are their bread and butter, you'll find them almost uniformly pleasant and eager to share tips about

the best spots for "Sierra surfing" the Kaweah's smooth, moss-covered rocks or where to find the best cell phone reception.

Visalia, a Central Valley city of about 128,000 people, lies 58 miles southwest of Sequoia's Wuksachi Village and 56 miles southwest of the Kings Canyon Park Visitor Center. Its vibrant downtown contains several good restaurants. If you're into Victorian and other old houses, drop by the visitor center and pick up a free map of them. A clear day's view of the Sierra from Main Street is spectacular, and even Sunday night can find the streets bustling with pedestrians. Visalia provides easy access to grand Sequoia National Park and the serene Kaweah Oaks Preserve.

Closest to Kings Canyon's Big Stump entrance, **Fresno,** the main gateway to the southern Sierra region, is about 55 miles west of Kings Canyon and about 85 miles northwest of Wuksachi Village. This Central Valley city of nearly a half-million people is sprawling and unglamorous, but it has all the cultural and other amenities you'd expect of a major crossroads.

GETTING HERE AND AROUND
Sequoia Shuttle

In summer the Sequoia Shuttle connects Three Rivers to Visalia and Sequoia National Park. ☎ 877/287–4453 ⊕ www.sequoiashuttle.com ✉ $15 round-trip.

VISITOR INFORMATION Fresno/Clovis Convention & Visitors Bureau ⊠ 1550 E. Shaw Ave., Suite 101, Fresno ☎ 559/981–5500, 800/788–0836 ⊕ www.playfresno.org. **Sequoia Foothills Chamber of Commerce** ⊠ 42268 Sierra Dr., Three Rivers ☎ 559/561–3300. **Visalia Convention & Visitors Bureau** ⊠ Kiosk, 303 E. Acequia Ave., at S. Bridge St., Visalia ☎ 559/334–0141, 800/524–0303 ⊕ www.visitvisalia.org.

 Sights

Exeter Murals More than two dozen murals in the Central Valley city of Exeter's cute-as-a-button downtown make it worth a quick detour if you're traveling on Route 198. Several of the murals, which depict the area's agricultural and social history, are quite good. All adorn buildings within a few blocks of the intersection of Pine and E streets. If you're hungry, the **Wildflower Cafe,** at 121 South E Street, serves inventive salads and sandwiches. Shortly after entering Exeter head west on Pine Street (it's just before the water tower) to reach downtown. ⊠ *Exeter ✛ Rte. 65, 2 miles south of Rte. 198, about 11 miles east of Visalia* ⊕ *cityofexeter.com/galleries/exeter-murals.*

Colonel Allensworth State Historic Park It's worth the slight detour off Highway 99 to learn about and pay homage to the dream of Allen Allensworth and other black pioneers who in 1908 founded Allensworth, the only California town settled, governed, and financed by African Americans. At its height, the town prospered as a key railroad transfer point, but after cars and trucks reduced railroad traffic and water was diverted for Central Valley agriculture, the town declined and was eventually deserted. Today the restored and rebuilt schoolhouse, library, and other structures commemorate Allensworth's heyday, as do festivities that take place each October. ⊠ *4129 Palmer Ave., off Hwy. 43; from Hwy. 99 at Delano, take Garces Hwy. west to Hwy. 43 north; from Earlimart, take County Rd. J22 west to Hwy. 43 south, Allensworth* ☎ *661/849–3433* ⊕ *www.parks.ca.gov* 🖾 *$6 per car.*

★ **Forestiere Underground Gardens**
GARDEN | FAMILY | Sicilian immigrant Baldassare Forestiere spent four decades (1906–46) carving out an odd, subterranean realm of rooms, tunnels, grottoes, alcoves, and arched passageways that once extended for more than 10 acres between Highway 99 and busy, mall-pocked Shaw Avenue. Though not an engineer, Forestiere called on his memories of the ancient Roman structures he saw as a youth and on techniques he learned digging subways in New York and Boston. Only a fraction of his prodigious output is on view, but you can tour his underground living quarters, including bedrooms (one with a fireplace), the kitchen, living room, and bath, as well as a fishpond and auto tunnel. Skylights allow exotic full-grown fruit trees to flourish more than 20 feet belowground. ⊠ *5021 W. Shaw Ave., 2 blocks east of Hwy. 99, Fresno* ☎ *559/271–0734* ⊕ *www.undergroundgardens.com* 🖾 *$17* ⊘ *Closed Dec.–Mar.*

Kaweah Oaks Preserve
NATURE PRESERVE | Trails at this 344-acre wildlife sanctuary off the main road to Sequoia National Park lead past majestic valley oak, sycamore, cottonwood, and willow trees. Among the 134 bird species you might spot are hawks, hummingbirds, and great blue herons. Bobcats, lizards, coyotes, and cottontails also live here. The Sycamore Trail has digital signage with QR codes you can scan with your smartphone to access plant and animal information. ⊠ *Follow Hwy. 198 for 7 miles east of Visalia, turn north on Rd. 182, and proceed ½ mile to gate on left side, Visalia* ☎ *559/738–0211* ⊕ *www.sequoiariverlands.org* 🖾 *Free.*

Project Survival's Cat Haven
ZOO | Take the rare opportunity to glimpse a Siberian lynx, a clouded leopard, a Bengal tiger, and other endangered wild cats at this conservation facility that shelters more than 30 big cats. A guided hour-long tour along a quarter mile of walkway leads to fenced habitat areas shaded by trees and overlooking the Central Valley. ⊠ *38257 E. Kings Canyon Rd. (Rte. 180), 15 miles west of Kings Canyon National Park, Dunlap* ☎ *559/338–3216* ⊕ *www.cathaven.com* 🖾 *$15.*

Sequoia National Forest and Giant Sequoia National Monument

FOREST | Delicate spring wildflowers, cool summer campgrounds, and varied winter-sports opportunities—not to mention more than half of the world's giant sequoia groves—draw outdoorsy types year-round to this sprawling district surrounding the national parks. Together, the forest and monument cover nearly 1,700 square miles, south from the Kings River and east from the foothills along the San Joaquin Valley. The monument's groves are both north and south of Sequoia National Park. One of the most popular is the **Converse Basin Grove,** home of the Boole Tree, the forest's largest sequoia. The grove is accessible by car on an unpaved road.

The Hume Lake Forest Service District Office, at 35860 Kings Canyon Scenic Byway (Route 180), has information about the groves, along with details about recreational activities. In springtime, diversions include hiking among the wildflowers that brighten the foothills. The floral display rises with the heat as the mountain elevations warm up in summer, when hikers, campers, and picnickers become more plentiful. The abundant trout supply attracts anglers to area waters, including 87-acre **Hume Lake,** which is also ideal for swimming and nonmotorized boating. By fall the turning leaves provide the visual delights, particularly in the Western Divide, Indian Basin, and the Kern Plateau. Winter activities include downhill and cross-country skiing, snowshoeing, and snowmobiling. ☒ *Sequoia National Park ✛ Northern Entrances: Generals Hwy. (Rte. 198), 7 miles southeast of Grant Grove; Hume Lake Rd. between Generals Hwy. (Rte. 198) and Kings Canyon Scenic Byway (Rte. 180); Kings Canyon Scenic Byway (Rte. 180) between Grant Grove and Cedar Grove. Southern Entrances: Rte. 190 east of Springville; Rte. 178 east of Bakersfield* ☎ *559/784–1500 forest and monument, 559/338–2251 Hume Lake* ⊕ *www.fs.usda.gov/sequoia.*

 Activities

BOATING AND RAFTING
Hume Lake
BODY OF WATER | This reservoir, built by loggers in the early 1900s, is now the site of several church-affiliated camps, a gas station, and a public campground. Outside Kings Canyon's borders, Hume Lake offers intimate views of the mountains. Summer lodge room rentals start at $160. ☒ *Hume Lake Rd., off Kings Canyon Hwy., 8 miles northeast of Grant Grove, 64144 Hume Lake Rd., Hume* ☎ *559/305–7770* ⊕ *www.humelake.org, visitsequoia.com.*

Kaweah White Water Adventures
BOATING | Kaweah's trips include a two-hour excursion (good for families) through Class III rapids, a longer paddle through Class IV rapids, and an extended trip (typically Class IV and V rapids). ☒ *40443 Sierra Dr., Three Rivers* ☎ *559/740–8251* ⊕ *www.kaweah-white-water.com* 🖅 *From $50 per person.*

Kings River Expeditions
TOUR—SPORTS | This outfit arranges one- and two-day white-water rafting trips on the Kings River. The office is in Clovis, but all trips depart from Twin Pines Camp, 60 miles east of Fresno. ☒ *Twin Pines Camp, Clovis* ☎ *559/233–4881, 800/846–3674* ⊕ *www.kingsriver.com* 🖅 *From $145.*

HORSEBACK RIDING
Wood 'n' Horse Training Stables
HORSEBACK RIDING | For hourly horseback rides, riding lessons, or trail rides in the foothills, contact this outfit. From $45 for lessons; from $65 for trail rides. ☒ *42846 N. Fork Dr., Three Rivers* ☎ *559/561–4268* ⊕ *www.wdnhorse.com.*

PERFORMING ARTS

Fresno Philharmonic Orchestra

CONCERTS | The orchestra performs classical concerts from September through June. ✉ *Saroyan Theatre, 730 M St., near Inyo St., Fresno* ☎ *559/261–0600* 🌐 *fresnophil.org.*

Roger Rocka's Dinner Theater

THEATER | This Tower District venue stages Broadway-style musicals. ✉ *1226 N. Wishon Ave., at E. Olive Ave., Fresno* ☎ *559/266–9494* 🌐 *www.rogerrockas.com.*

SHOPPING

Cedar Grove Gift Shop and Market

GIFTS/SOUVENIRS | This place is small, but it's stocked with the essentials for RV and auto travelers. ✉ *Cedar Grove Village, Kings Canyon National Park* ☎ *559/565–3096* 🕒 *Closed late Oct.–mid-May.*

Grant Grove Gift Shop

GIFTS/SOUVENIRS | This shop sells park-related gifts and souvenirs. ✉ *Grant Grove Village, Kings Canyon National Park* ☎ *559/335–5500.*

Lodgepole Market Center

GIFTS/SOUVENIRS | You'll find gifts, toys, books, souvenirs, and outdoor equipment in Sequoia National Park's largest store. Its grocery department has a fairly wide selection of items, some of them organic, including grab-and-go items for hikes and picnics. Across the hall is a café with various dishes for breakfast, lunch, and dinner. ✉ *63204 Lodgepole Rd., next to Lodgepole Visitor Center, Sequoia National Park* ☎ *559/565–3301* 🌐 *www.visitsequoia.com.*

Wuksachi Gift Shop

GIFTS/SOUVENIRS | Souvenir clothing, Native American crafts, postcards, and snacks are for sale at this tasteful shop off the Wuksachi Lodge lobby. ✉ *Wuksachi Village* ☎ *559/625–7700.*

🍴 Restaurants

IN THE PARKS

SEQUOIA

Lodgepole Market and Grill

$$ | CAFÉ | The choices here run the gamut from simple to very simple, with several counters only a few strides apart in a central eating complex. The café also sells fresh and prepackaged salads, sandwiches, and wraps. **Known for:** quick and convenient dining; many healthful options; grab-and-go items for picnics. [$] *Average main: $12* ✉ *Next to Lodgepole Visitor Center, Sequoia National Park* ☎ *559/565–3301.*

The Peaks

$$$ | MODERN AMERICAN | Huge windows run the length of the Wuksachi Lodge's high-ceilinged dining room, and a large fireplace on the far wall warms both body and soul. The diverse dinner menu—by far the best at both parks—reflects a commitment to locally sourced and sustainable products. **Known for:** seasonal menus with fresh local ingredients; great views of sequoia grove; box lunches. [$] *Average main: $28* ✉ *Wuksachi Lodge, 64740 Wuksachi Way, Wuksachi Village* ☎ *559/625–7700* 🌐 *www.visitsequoia.com/dine/the-peaks-restaurant.*

PICNIC AREAS

Take care to dispose of your food scraps properly (the bears might not appreciate this short-term, but the practice helps ensure their long-term survival).

Crescent Meadow

RESTAURANT—SIGHT | A mile or so past Moro Rock, this comparatively remote picnic area has meadow views and is close to a lovely hiking trail. Tables are under the giant sequoias, off the parking area. There are restrooms and drinking water. Fires are not allowed. ✉ *Sequoia National Park* ✥ *End of Moro Rock–Crescent Rd., 2.6 miles east off Generals Hwy. (Rte. 198).*

Foothills Picnic Area
RESTAURANT—SIGHT | Near the parking lot at the southern entrance of the park, this area has tables, drinking water, and restrooms. ✉ *Sequoia National Park* ✥ *Across Generals Hwy. from Foothills Visitor Center.*

Hospital Rock
RESTAURANT—SIGHT | Native Americans once ground acorns into meal at this site; outdoor exhibits tell the story. The picnic area's name, however, stems from a hunter/trapper who was treated for a leg wound here in 1873. Look up, and you'll see Moro Rock. Grills, drinking water, and restrooms are available. ✉ *Sequoia National Park* ✥ *Generals Hwy. (Rte. 198), 6 miles north of Ash Mountain entrance.*

Pinewood Picnic Area
RESTAURANT—SIGHT | Picnic in Giant Forest, in the vicinity of sequoias if not actually under them. Drinking water, restrooms, grills, and wheelchair-accessible spots are provided in this expansive setting near Sequoia National Park's most popular attractions. ✉ *Sequoia National Park* ✥ *Generals Hwy. (Rte. 198), 2 miles north of Giant Forest Museum, halfway between Giant Forest Museum and General Sherman Tree.*

Wolverton Meadow
RESTAURANT—SIGHT | At a major trailhead to the backcountry, this is a great place to stop for lunch before a hike. The area sits in a mixed-conifer forest adjacent to parking. Drinking water, grills, and restrooms are available. **Known for:** easy access to various trails; good place to grill before and after hiking. ✉ *Sequoia National Park* ✥ *Wolverton Rd., 1½ miles northeast off Generals Hwy. (Rte. 198).*

KINGS CANYON

Cedar Grove Snack Bar
$$ | AMERICAN | The menu here is surprisingly extensive, with dinner entrées such as pasta, pork chops, trout, and steak. For breakfast, try the egg burrito, French toast, or pancakes; sandwiches, wraps, burgers (including vegetarian patties) and hot dogs dominate the lunch and dinner choices. **Known for:** scenic river views; extensive options; alfresco dining on balcony overlooking the Kings River. [$] *Average main: $16* ✉ *Cedar Grove Village, Kings Canyon National Park* ☎ *559/565–3096* 🌐 *www.visitsequoia.com/dine/cedar-grove-snack-bar* ⏲ *Closed Oct.–May.*

Grant Grove Restaurant
$$ | AMERICAN | Gaze at giant sequoias and a verdant meadow while dining in this eco-friendly restaurant's spacious dining room with fireplace, or outdoors on the expansive deck. The menu centers around locally sourced natural and organic ingredients and offers standard American fare. [$] *Average main: $16* ✉ *Grant Grove Village, Kings Canyon National Park* ☎ *559/335–5500.*

PICNIC AREAS

Big Stump
RESTAURANT—SIGHT | Some trees still stand at this site at the edge of a logged sequoia grove. Near the park's entrance, the area is paved and next to the road. It's the only picnic area in either park that is plowed in the wintertime. Restrooms (portable toilets), grills, and drinking water are available, and the area is entirely accessible. ✉ *Kings Canyon National Park* ✥ *Generals Hwy. (Rte. 180), just inside Big Stump entrance.*

Grizzly Falls
RESTAURANT—SIGHT | This little gem is worth a pull-over, if not a picnic at the roadside tables. A less-than-a-minute trek from the parking lot delivers you to the base of the delightful, 100-foot-plus falls. On a hot day, nothing feels better than dipping your feet in the cool water. An outhouse is on-site, but grills are not, and water is not available. ✉ *Kings Canyon National Park* ✥ *Off Rte. 180, 2½ miles west of Cedar Grove entrance.*

OUTSIDE THE PARKS

Antoinette's Coffee and Goodies

$ | **CAFÉ** | For smoothies, well-crafted espresso drinks, breakfast bowls, and pumpkin chocolate-chip muffins and other homemade baked goods, stop for a spell at this convivial coffee shop. Antoinette's is known as the town's hub for vegan and gluten-free items. **Known for:** plentiful vegan and gluten-free items; Wi-Fi on-site; all organic, locally roasted coffee. $ Average main: $7 ✉ 41727 Sierra Dr., Three Rivers ☎ 559/561–2253 ⊕ www.antoinettescoffeeandgoodies. com ⊘ Closed Tues. No dinner.

Buckaroo Diner

$$ | **AMERICAN** | Set on a bluff overlooking the Kaweah River, the boho-chic Buckaroo serves fresh, house-made dishes made with seasonal organic ingredients. The restaurant's main dining room occupies a building that housed the original restaurant ('Ol Buckaroo) for decades; you can also sit in the cozy sun room or outdoor terrace overlooking the river. **Known for:** weekend beer garden; smoked foods; daily specials. $ Average main: $18 ✉ 41695 Sierra Dr., Three Rivers ☎ 559/465–5088 ⊕ theolbuckaroo. com ⊘ No lunch weekdays. Closed Tues. and Wed.

Café 225

$$ | **MODERN AMERICAN** | High ceilings and contemporary decor contribute to the relaxed and sophisticated atmosphere at this popular downtown restaurant. Meats and fish grilled on a wood-fired rotisserie figure prominently on the menu, which also includes pastas and unusual treats such as artichoke fritters and goat cheese and roast lamb pizza. **Known for:** wood-fired rotisserie menu items; fresh local ingredients; sophisticated vibe. $ Average main: $22 ✉ 225 W. Main St., Visalia ☎ 559/733–2967 ⊕ www.cafe225. com ⊘ Closed Sun.

Gateway Restaurant and Lodge

$$$ | **AMERICAN** | The view's the draw at this roadhouse that overlooks the Kaweah River as it plunges out of the high country. The Gateway serves everything from osso buco and steaks to shrimp in Thai chili sauce; dinner reservations are essential on summer weekends. **Known for:** scenic riverside setting; fine dining in otherwise casual town; popular bar. $ Average main: $30 ✉ 45978 Sierra Dr., Three Rivers ☎ 559/561–4133 ⊕ www.gateway-sequoia.com.

School House Restaurant & Tavern

$$$ | **MODERN AMERICAN** | A Wine Country–style establishment that sources ingredients from the on-site gardens and surrounding farms and orchards, this popular restaurant occupies a redbrick 1921 schoolhouse in the town of Sanger. Chef Ryan Jackson, who grew up on local fruit farms, creates seasonal menus from the bounty of familiar backyards, mostly filled with classic American dishes with a contemporary twist. **Known for:** fresh ingredients from neighboring farms and orchards; historic country setting; convenient stop between Kings Canyon and Fresno. $ Average main: $29 ✉ 1018 S. Frankwood Ave., at Hwy. 180 (King's Canyon Rd.), 20 miles east of Fresno, Sanger ☎ 559/787–3271 ⊕ schoolhousesanger.com ⊘ Closed Mon. and Tues.

Sierra Subs and Salads

$ | **AMERICAN** | This well-run sandwich joint satisfies carnivores and vegetarians alike with crispy-fresh ingredients prepared with panache. Depending on your preference, the centerpiece of the Bull's Eye sandwich, for instance, will be roast beef or a portobello mushroom, but whichever you choose, the accompanying flavors— of ciabatta bread, horseradish-and-garlic mayonnaise, roasted red peppers, Havarti cheese, and spinach—will delight your palate. **Known for:** many vegetarian, vegan, and gluten-free options; weekly specials; Wi-Fi. $ Average main: $9 ✉ 41717 Sierra Dr., Three Rivers ☎ 559/561–4810 ⊕ www.sierrasubsandsalads.com ⊘ Closed Mon. No dinner.

★ The Vintage Press

$$$$ | **EUROPEAN** | Built in 1966, this is one of the best restaurants in the Central Valley. The California–Continental cuisine includes dishes such as crispy veal sweetbreads with a port-wine sauce and filet mignon with a cognac-mustard sauce. **Known for:** wine list with more than 900 selections; chocolate Grand Marnier cake and other homemade desserts; sophisticated vibe. [$] *Average main: $32* ✉ *216 N. Willis St., Visalia* ☎ *559/733–3033* 🌐 *www.thevintage-press.com.*

Hotels

IN THE PARKS

SEQUOIA

Silver City Mountain Resort

$$ | **RESORT** | High on Mineral King Road, this privately owned resort has rustic cabins and deluxe chalets—all with a stove, refrigerator, and sink—plus three hotel rooms with private baths. **Pros:** rustic setting; friendly staff; great location for hikers. **Cons:** long, winding road is not for everybody; not much entertainment except hiking; some units have shared baths. [$] *Rooms from: $165* ✉ *Sequoia National Park* ✣ *Mineral King Rd., 21 miles southeast of Rte. 198* ☎ *559/561–3223* 🌐 *www.silvercityresort.com* ⏲ *Closed Nov.–late May* 🛏 *13 cabins, 3 hotel rooms* ☞ *No meals.*

★ Wuksachi Lodge

$$$$ | **HOTEL** | The striking cedar-and-stone main building is a fine example of how a structure can blend effectively with lovely mountain scenery. **Pros:** best place to stay in the parks; lots of wildlife; easy access to hiking and snowshoe/ ski trails. **Cons:** rooms can be small; main lodge is a few-minutes' walk from guest rooms; slow Wi-Fi. [$] *Rooms from: $229* ✉ *64740 Wuksachi Way, Wuksachi Village* ☎ *559/625–7700, 888/252–5757 reservations* 🌐 *www.visitsequoia.com/lodging/wuksachi-lodge* 🛏 *102 rooms* ☞ *No meals.*

KINGS CANYON

Cedar Grove Lodge

$$ | **HOTEL** | Backpackers like to stay here on the eve of long treks into the High Sierra wilderness, so bedtimes tend to be early. **Pros:** a definite step up from camping in terms of comfort; great base camp for outdoor adventures; on-site snack bar. **Cons:** impersonal; not everybody agrees it's clean enough; remote location. [$] *Rooms from: $147* ✉ *Kings Canyon Scenic Byway, Kings Canyon National Park* ☎ *866/807–3598* 🌐 *www.visitsequoia.com/lodging/cedar-grove-lodge* ⏲ *Closed mid-Oct.–mid-May* 🛏 *21 rooms* ☞ *No meals.*

Grant Grove Cabins

$$ | **HOTEL** | Some of the wood-panel cabins here have heaters, electric lights, and private baths, but most have woodstoves, battery lamps, and shared baths. **Pros:** warm, woodsy feel; clean; walk to Grant Grove Restaurant. **Cons:** can be difficult to walk up to if you're not in decent physical shape; costly for what you get; only basic amenities. [$] *Rooms from: $135* ✉ *Kings Canyon Scenic Byway in Grant Grove Village, Kings Canyon National Park* ☎ *866/807–3598* 🌐 *www.visitsequoia.com/Grant-Grove-Cabins.aspx* 🛏 *33 cabins, 9 with bath; 17 tent cabins* ☞ *No meals.*

John Muir Lodge

$$$$ | **HOTEL** | In a wooded area in the hills above Grant Grove Village, this modern, timber-sided lodge has rooms and suites with queen- or king-size beds and private baths. **Pros:** open year-round; common room stays warm; quiet. **Cons:** check-in is down in the village; spotty Wi-Fi; remote location. [$] *Rooms from: $210* ✉ *Kings Canyon Scenic Byway, ¼ mile north of Grant Grove Village, 86728 Hwy. 180, Kings Canyon National Park* ☎ *866/807–3598* 🌐 *www.visitsequoia.com/john-muir-lodge.aspx* 🛏 *36 rooms* ☞ *No meals.*

OUTSIDE THE PARKS

The only lodging immediately outside the parks is in Three Rivers. Options include inns, chain and mom-and-pop motels, and riverside cabins. Numerous chain properties operate in Visalia or Fresno (your favorite is likely represented in one or both cities), about an hour from the south and north entrances, respectively.

Montecito-Sequoia Lodge

$$$$ | **HOTEL** | **FAMILY** | Outdoor activities are what this year-round family resort is all about, including many that are geared toward teenagers and small children. **Pros:** friendly staff; great for kids; lots of fresh air and planned activities. **Cons:** can be noisy with all the activity; no TVs or phones in rooms; not within national park. [$] *Rooms from: $229* ✉ *63410 Generals Hwy., 11 miles south of Grant Grove, Sequoia National Forest* ☎ *559/565–3388, 800/227–9900* 🌐 *www.mslodge.com* 🕒 *Closed 1st 2 wks of Dec.* 🛏 *52 rooms* ☞ *All meals.*

★ Rio Sierra Riverhouse

$$$ | **B&B/INN** | Guests at Rio Sierra come for the river views, the sandy beach, and the proximity to Sequoia National Park (6 miles away), but invariably end up raving equally about the warm, laid-back hospitality of proprietress Mars Roberts. **Pros:** seductive beach; add-on breakfast option; river views from all rooms; contemporary ambience. **Cons:** books up quickly in summer; some road noise audible in rooms; long walk or drive to restaurants. [$] *Rooms from: $200* ✉ *41997 Sierra Dr., Hwy. 198, Three Rivers* ☎ *559/561–4720* 🌐 *www.rio-sierra.com* 🛏 *5 rooms* ☞ *No meals* ☞ *2-night min stay on summer weekends. Closed Jan.–mid-Feb.*

Chapter 33

THEODORE ROOSEVELT NATIONAL PARK

Updated by
Laura M. Kidder

NORTH
DAKOTA

WELCOME TO THEODORE ROOSEVELT NATIONAL PARK

TOP REASONS TO GO

★ **The "Granddaddy Trail":** Hike the Maah Daah Hey Trail, which means "grandfather" or "been here long." It's one of the most popular and well-maintained trails in western North Dakota.

★ **Views from above:** Get an encompassing 360-degree view of the badlands from Buck Hill.

★ **History lessons from the frontier:** View Maltese Cross Ranch Cabin, which once belonged to Theodore Roosevelt.

★ **Badlands Broadway:** Come experience a theatrical tribute to the history and personalities that make up the Old West at the Medora Musical, located in the town, not the park.

★ **Great clubbing—golf, that is:** Perfect your swing at Bully Pulpit Golf Course in Medora, one of America's premier courses near the national park.

★ **Away from it all:** As this is not a heavily visited park, you'll likely encounter more wild horses than people here.

The Little Missouri River winds throughout this western North Dakota park, and plenty of bison, deer, pronghorn, coyote, prairie dogs, and eagles inhabit the land. Climb the peaks and you will get exceptional views of the canyons, caprocks, petrified forest, and other bizarre geological formations that make up the badlands.

1 North Unit. Visitors looking to enjoy the great outdoors should be sure to travel along the 14-mile scenic drive and stop at one of the many hiking trailheads along the way. These trailheads give easy access to the backcountry of the North Unit.

2 South Unit. Often considered the main unit of Theodore Roosevelt National Park and adjacent to the famous town of Medora, the South Unit is home to some of the former president's personal artifacts and even his cabin.

3 Elkhorn Ranch. This area of the park is the actual location of one of T.R.'s ranches in the badlands. None of the ranch buildings are still standing, but signs show their former location.

33

Theodore Roosevelt National Park WELCOME TO THEODORE ROOSEVELT NATIONAL PARK

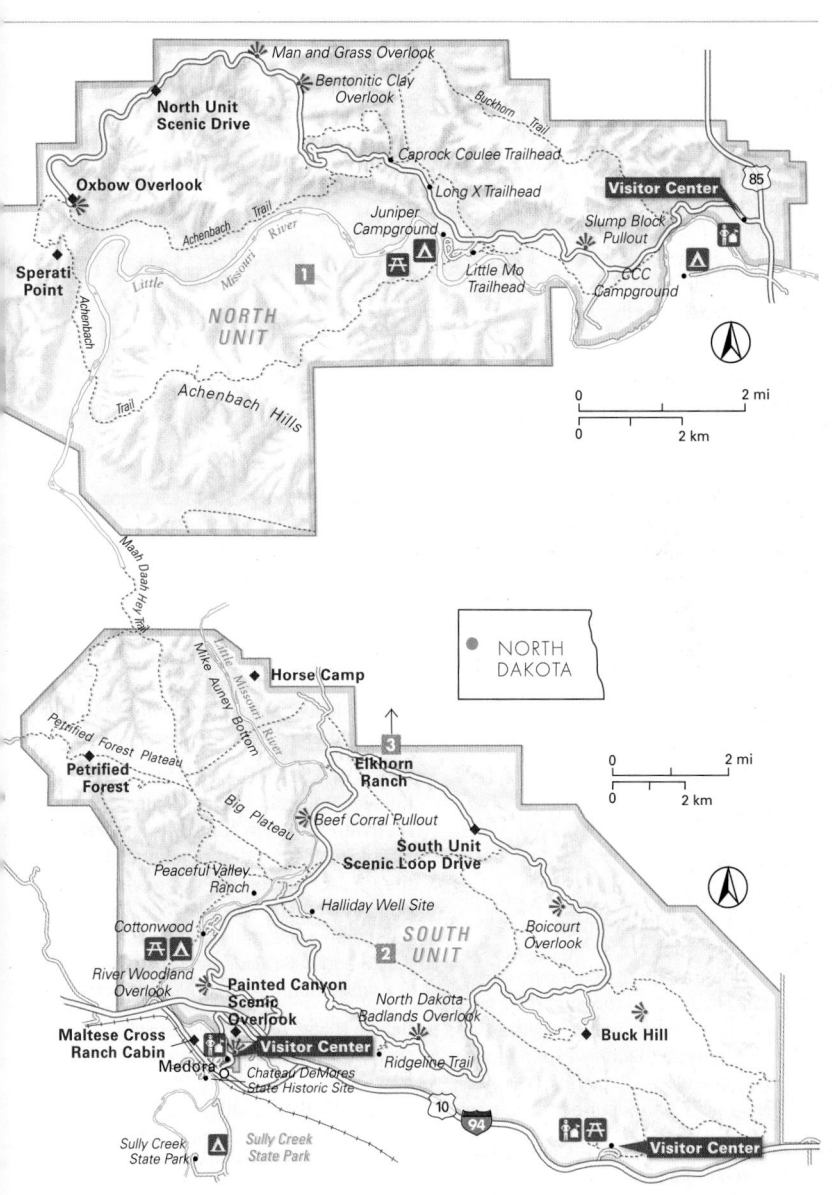

Across much of North Dakota, for a century and a quarter, the terrain remained virtually unchanged from the day Theodore Roosevelt stepped off the train here in 1883, eager to shoot his first bison. Within two weeks, he purchased an open-range cattle ranch, and the following year he returned to establish a second, which is part of the 110-square-mile national park.

Today, some 700,000 annual visitors are attracted to North Dakota's lone national park as much by its namesake as by its vast landscape of craggy ravines, tablelands, and gorges, an otherworldly moonscape that ranks among the least inhabited places in the U.S. For those who seek the road less traveled, a day trekking its backcountry trails or remote gravel roads can be a solitary pursuit, uninterrupted by any other humans.

Planning

WHEN TO GO

The park is open year-round, but North Dakota winters can be extremely cold and windy. Portions of some roads close during winter months, depending on snowfall. Rangers discontinue their outdoor programs when autumn comes, and they recommend that only experienced hikers do any winter explorations. Check the park's website for current conditions.

■TIP→ **Although July and August tend to be the busiest months, the park is rarely**

crowded. About 700,000 people visit each year, with the South Unit receiving the greatest number of visitors. The best times to see wildlife and hike comfortably are May through October. The park is all but desolate December through February, but it's a beautiful time to see the wildlife—also, winter sunsets can be very vivid as the colors reflect off the snow and ice. The park gets an average of 30 inches of snow per year.

FESTIVALS AND EVENTS
Killdeer Mountain Roundup Rodeo
FESTIVAL | Begun in 1923, this is North Dakota's oldest rodeo sanctioned by the PRCA. The community goes all out, hosting a parade, street dance, community barbecue, and fireworks display on July 3 and 4. ⊠ *Killdeer* ☎ *701/590–6820* ⊕ *killdeermountainrounduprodeo.com.*

Dakota Nights Astronomy Festival
FESTIVAL | Without light pollution from nearby towns, Theodore Roosevelt National Park is ideal for astronomical observation any cloudless night of the year. To enjoy the stars with others,

Plants and Wildlife in Theodore Roosevelt

The park's landscape is one of prairies marked by cliffs and rock chasms made of alternating layers of sandstone, siltstone, mudstone, and bentonite clay. In spring the prairies are awash with tall grasses, wildflowers, and shrubs including the ubiquitous poison ivy. The pesky plant also inhabits the forests, where you find box elders, ash, and junipers among the trees. To avoid the rash-inducing plant—and scrapes and bruises that may come from rocks and thick undergrowth—it's always advisable to hike with long pants and sturdy boots.

More than 400 American bison live in the park. These normally docile beasts look tame, but with a set of horns, up to a ton of weight, and legs that will carry them at speeds in excess of 35 mph, they could be the most dangerous animals within park boundaries. Rangers tell visitors repeatedly not to approach them. Some mountain lions also live in the park but are rarely seen. The same goes for prairie rattlers.

On the less threatening side of the park's fauna, a herd of more than 200 to 300 elk live in the South Unit. As many as 150 feral horses are also in the South Unit. The North Unit has some longhorn steers, which are often found in the bison corral area, about 2½ miles west of the visitor center.

come during the annual Dakota Nights Astronomy Festival in September (dates vary). Check the park website for a current schedule, which includes day and evening activities in the park and in the town of Medora. ✉ *Theodore Roosevelt National Park* ☎ *701/623–4466* ⊕ *www.nps.gov/thro* 🎟 *Free.*

PLANNING YOUR TIME
THEODORE ROOSEVELT IN ONE DAY

With just one day, focus on the South Unit. Arrive early at the **Painted Canyon Scenic Overlook,** near the visitor center, for a sweeping and colorful vista of the canyon's rock formations. Stay awhile to watch the effect of the sun's progress across the sky, or come back in the evening to witness the deepening colors and silhouettes in the fading sunlight.

Continue to the **South Unit Visitor Center** in Medora, spending about an hour here touring the Theodore Roosevelt exhibit and the Maltese Cross Ranch Cabin.

Circle the 36-mile **Scenic Loop Drive** twice: once to stop and walk a few trails and visit the overlooks, and once at sundown to watch the wildlife. Your first time around, go counterclockwise. Stop at **Scoria Point Overlook** and hike 0.6 mile on **Ridgeline Nature Trail.** Back on the drive, stop next at the North Dakota Badlands and Boicourt overlooks to gaze at the strange, ever-changing terrain. When you pass through Peaceful Valley, look for prairie dogs. Have a packed lunch at the **Cottonwood picnic area,** then use a couple of hours to hike Jones Creek Trail or Coal Vein Nature Trail.

Return to your car at least an hour before sunset, and drive slowly around Scenic Loop Drive, clockwise this time, to view the wildlife. Plan to be at **Buck Hill** for one of the most spectacular sunsets you'll ever see. Bring a jacket, because it's a bit windy and it gets chilly as the sun sets. After dark, drive carefully out of

AVERAGE HIGH/LOW TEMPERATURES					
JAN.	**FEB.**	**MAR.**	**APR.**	**MAY**	**JUNE**
27/1	34/8	43/18	58/30	71/40	79/50
JULY	**AUG.**	**SEPT.**	**OCT.**	**NOV.**	**DEC.**
87/55	87/52	75/41	62/30	43/17	32/7

the park—elk and other animals may still be on the road.

GETTING HERE AND AROUND
AIR TRAVEL
Planes fly into Bismarck, North Dakota (147 miles east of park's South Unit along Interstate 94), and Billings, Montana (295 miles west). There's also some service to even smaller airports in the North Dakota towns of Dickinson (50 miles east) and Williston (60 miles north of North Unit, 140 miles north of South Unit).

CAR TRAVEL
Despite its somewhat remote location, getting to and from the park is relatively easy. The South Unit entrance and visitor center is just off Interstate 94 in the tiny but lively town of Medora at Exits 24 and 27. The Painted Canyon Visitor Center is 7 miles east of Medora on Interstate 94 at Exit 32. The North Unit entrance is south of Williston and Watford City on U.S. 85 and Interstate 94.

There's ample parking space at all trailheads, and parking is free. Some roads are closed in winter. You may encounter bison and other wildlife on the roadway.

TRAIN TRAVEL
Amtrak serves Williston.

PARK ESSENTIALS
ACCESSIBILITY
The visitor centers, campgrounds, and historic sites such as Roosevelt's cabin, are all wheelchair accessible, and the film at the South Unit Visitor Center is captioned. The first part of the Little Mo Nature Trail in the North Unit and the ¼-mile Skyline Vista Trail in the South Unit are both paved.

PARK FEES AND PERMITS
The entrance pass is $30 per vehicle, $25 per motorcycle, and $15 for an individual, good for seven days. A variety of annual passes are available. A backcountry permit, free from the visitor centers, is required for overnight camping away from campgrounds.

PARK HOURS
The park is open year-round. The North Unit is in the Central time zone. The South Unit and the Painted Canyon Visitor Center are in the Mountain time zone. Keep the locale in mind when checking schedules for park programs, which reflect these time differences. The South Unit Visitor Center is open year-round. The North Unit Contact Station is open daily April through October, and Thursday through Sunday the rest of the year; the Painted Canyon Visitor Center operates from early May through late October. Check the park website for current operating hours.

CELL PHONE RECEPTION
Cell phone reception occurs in some areas of the park, but many places receive no signal. Public telephones can be found at the South Unit's Cottonwood Campground and at the Painted Canyon Visitor Center.

EDUCATIONAL OFFERINGS
RANGER PROGRAMS
Evening Programs
TOUR—SIGHT | FAMILY | Rangers host 45-minute presentations and discussions on such subjects as park history, astronomy, fires, and wildlife. Also check to see if your visit coincides with one of the park's Full Moon hikes, held several evenings each summer. Look for times and

subjects posted at park campgrounds and visitor centers. ⊠ *Cottonwood Campground, South Unit; Juniper Campground, North Unit* ☎ *701/623–4466* ⊕ *www.nps.gov/thro.*

Junior Ranger Adventure

ARTS VENUE | On Saturday from May through August, rangers lead a short hike (just under a mile) from the Old East Entrance. Kids also get an activity book and can earn a badge. Bring water; as the route is dusty, wear closed-toe shoes. ⊠ *Old East Entrance Trailhead* ☎ *701/623–4466* ⊕ *www.nps.gov/thro* 🎫 *Free.*

Ranger-Led Talks and Walks

TOUR—SIGHT | **FAMILY** | Rangers take visitors on the trails of both units and through the backcountry and Elkhorn Ranch, discussing such subjects as geology, paleontology, wildlife, and natural history. There are also tours of Roosevelt's Maltese Cross Cabin and special Bison Chats. Check at campground entrances or at the visitor centers for times, topics, departure points, and destinations. ⊠ *Theodore Roosevelt National Park* ☎ *701/623–4466* ⊕ *www. nps.gov/thro* 🎫 *Free.*

RESTAURANTS

One does not visit Theodore Roosevelt National Park for the fine dining. In fact, the only venues within the park are the picnic areas, and provided you're prepared, this can be a perfectly simple and satisfying way to experience the open spaces and natural wonder of the badlands. In the towns near the park you'll find casual, down-to-earth family establishments that largely cater to the locals. Expect steak and potatoes, and lots of them. Fortunately, the beef here is among the best in the country.

HOTELS

If you're set on sleeping within the park, be sure to pack your tent. Outside the park are mostly small chain hotels catering to interstate travelers—largely retired couples in RVs and young families in minivans. However, there is a handful of historic properties and working ranches that offer guests a truly Western experience. Due to the current oil boom in the region, it's essential to book ahead during summer months. *Hotel reviews have been shortened. For full information, visit Fodors.com.*

What It Costs			
$	**$$**	**$$$**	**$$$$**
RESTAURANTS			
under $13	$13–$20	$21–$30	over $30
HOTELS			
under $101	$101–$150	$151–$200	over $200

VISITOR INFORMATION

PARK CONTACT INFORMATION Theodore Roosevelt National Park ☎ *701/623–4466* South Unit ⊕ *www.nps.gov/thro.*

VISITOR CENTERS
North Unit Contact Station

INFO CENTER | While planning for a new visitor center facility is underway, this unit is being housed in temporary trailers. It still hosts some park programs in addition to offering park information. Amenities include restrooms and a gift shop. It's open daily between April and October and Thursday through Sunday the rest of the year. ⊠ *North Unit entrance, off U.S. 85, North Unit* ☎ *701/623–4466* ⊕ *www. nps.gov/thro* 🎫 *Free.*

Painted Canyon Visitor Center

INFO CENTER | Easily reached off Interstate 94, this South Unit Visitor Center has an information desk, exhibits, a Theodore Roosevelt Nature and History Association bookstore, a picnic area, restrooms, vending machines, water fountains, and public phones. ⊠ *Exit 32 off I–94, South Unit* ☎ *701/575–4020* ⊕ *www.nps.gov/ thro* 🎫 *Free* 🕐 *Closed late Oct.–early May.*

South Unit Visitor Center

INFO CENTER | This building houses a large auditorium screening the 17-minute film, *Refuge of the American Spirit.* There's also an excellent exhibit on Theodore Roosevelt's life with artifacts such as the clothing he wore while ranching in the Dakota Territory, his firearms, and several writings in his own hand reflecting his thoughts on the nation's environmental resources. Be sure to stop in the Theodore Roosevelt Nature and History Association bookstore. Restrooms and a drinking fountain are also available. ⊠ *South Unit entrance, Exits 24 and 27 off I–94* ☎ *701/623–4466* ⊕ *www.nps. gov/thro* 💲 *Free.*

 # Sights

SCENIC DRIVES

North Unit Scenic Drive

SCENIC DRIVE | The 14-mile, two-way drive follows rugged terrain above spectacular views of the canyons, and is flanked by more than a dozen turnouts with interpretive signs. Notice the slump blocks, massive segments of rock that have slipped down the cliff walls over time. Farther along pass through badlands coulees, deep-water clefts that are now dry. There's a good chance of meeting bison, mule deer, and bighorn sheep along the way, also keep an eye out for longhorn steers, just like the ones you would see in Texas. ⊠ *From unit entrance to Oxbow Overlook, North Unit.*

South Unit Scenic Loop Drive

SCENIC DRIVE | A 36-mile, two-way scenic loop takes you past prairie-dog towns, coal veins, trailheads, and panoramic views of the badlands. Information on the park's natural history is posted at the various overlooks—stop at all of the interpretive signs to learn about the park's natural and historical phenomena. Some of the best views can be seen from Scoria Point Overlook, Boicourt Overlook, North Dakota Badlands Overlook, Skyline Vista, and Buck Hill. If you hit the road

at dusk, be prepared to get caught in a buffalo traffic jam, as the huge creatures sometimes block the road and aren't in any hurry to move. Don't get out of your car or honk at them—they don't like it. ⊠ *Loop begins near Peaceful Valley Ranch, South Unit.*

HISTORIC SITES

Elkhorn Ranch

NATURE PRESERVE | This unit of the park is composed of the 218 acres of ranchland where Theodore Roosevelt ran cattle on the open range. Today there are no buildings, but foundation blocks outline the original structures. Check with visitor center staff about road conditions. ⊠ *Theodore Roosevelt National Park ✛ 35 miles north of South Unit Visitor Center* ☎ *701/623–4466 South Unit* 💲 *Free.*

Maltese Cross Ranch Cabin

BUILDING | About 7 miles from its original site in the river bottom sits the cabin Theodore Roosevelt commissioned to be built on his Dakota Territory property. Inside are Roosevelt's original writing table and rocking chair. Interpretive tours are scheduled every day May through August. ⊠ *South Unit entrance, Exits 24 and 27 off I–94* ☎ *701/623–4466 South Unit* 💲 *Free.*

SCENIC STOPS

★ Buck Hill

VIEWPOINT | At 2,855 feet, this is one of the highest points in the park and provides a spectacular 360-degree view of the badlands. Come here for the sunset. ⊠ *Theodore Roosevelt National Park ✛ 17 miles east of South Unit Visitor Center.*

Oxbow Overlook

VIEWPOINT | The view from this spot at the end of the North Unit drive looks over the unit's westerly badlands and the Little Missouri River, where it takes a sharp turn south. This is the place to come for stargazing. ⊠ *Theodore Roosevelt National Park ✛ 14 miles west of North Unit Visitor Center.*

Painted Canyon Scenic Overlook
VIEWPOINT | Catch your first glimpse of badlands majesty here—the South Unit canyon's colors change dramatically with the movement of the sun across the sky. ⊠ *Exit 32 off I–94, South Unit.*

Petrified Forest
NATURE SITE | Although bits of petrified wood have been found all over the park, the densest collection is in the South Unit's west end, accessible via the Petrified Forest Loop Trail from Peaceful Valley Ranch (10 miles round-trip) or from the park's west boundary (3 miles round-trip). ⊠ *Trailheads: Peaceful Valley Ranch, 7 miles north of South Unit Visitor Center; west boundary, 10 miles north of Exit 23 off I–94/U.S. 10.*

Sperati Point
VIEWPOINT | For a great view of the Missouri River's 90-degree angle, hike a 1½-mile round-trip stretch of the much longer Achenbach Trail to this spot 430 feet above the riverbed. ⊠ *Theodore Roosevelt National Park* ✛ *14 miles west of North Unit Visitor Center.*

 Activities

BICYCLING
Bikes are allowed on interior roads but not off-road. On the multiuse Maah Daah Hey Trail you aren't allowed to ride (or even carry or walk your bike) along the portions of the trails within the park. Alternate cycling routes off this trail include the Buffalo Gap Trail near the park's South Unit and existing roadways outside the North Unit.

FISHING
Catfish, little suckers, northern pikes, and goldeyes are among the underwater inhabitants of the Little Missouri River. If you wish to fish in the park or elsewhere in the state and are over age 16, you must obtain a North Dakota fishing license. For out-of-state residents, a three-day permit is $25, a 10-day permit is $25, and a one-year permit is $45. For in-state residents, a one-year permit is $16.

HIKING
During the summer months, the park is best seen by hiking its many trails. Particularly in the South Unit, there are numerous opportunities to jump on a trail right from the park road. The North and South units are connected by the 144-mile Maah Daah Hey Trail. Backcountry hiking is allowed, but you need a permit (free from any visitor center) to camp in the wild. Park maps are available at all three visitor centers. If you plan to camp overnight, let several people know about where you plan to pitch your tent, and inquire about river conditions, maps, regulations, trail updates, and additional water sources before setting out.

NORTH UNIT
Buckhorn Trail
HIKING/WALKING | FAMILY | A thriving prairie-dog town is just 1 mile from the trailhead of this 11.4-mile round-trip North Unit trail. It travels over level grasslands, then it loops back along the banks of Squaw Creek. If you're an experienced hiker, you'll complete the entire trail in about half a day. Novices or families might want to plan on a whole day, however. *Moderate–Difficult.* ⊠ *Theodore Roosevelt National Park* ✛ *Trailhead: Caprock Coulee Nature Trail, 1½ miles west of Juniper Campground.*

Little Mo Nature Trail
HIKING/WALKING | FAMILY | The unpaved but flat lat outer loop of this 1.1-mile trail passes through badlands and woodlands to the river's edge. The trail's paved 0.7-mile inner loop is wheelchair accessible. It's a great way to see the park's diverse terrain and wildlife, and because it shouldn't take you longer than an hour, it's a great trail for families with children. *Easy.* ⊠ *Theodore Roosevelt National Park* ✛ *Trailhead: Juniper Campground in the North Unit.*

Upper Caprock Coulee Trail

HIKING/WALKING | The first 0.75-mile of this 4.3-mile round-trip trail takes you along a nature trail. It then loops around the pockmarked lower-badlands coulees. There's a slow incline that takes you up 300 feet. Portions of the trail are slippery. Beginners should plan a half day for this hike. *Moderate–Difficult.* ⊠ *Theodore Roosevelt National Park* ✛ *Trailhead: 8 miles west of North Unit Visitor Center.*

SOUTH UNIT
★ Maah Daah Hey Trail

HIKING/WALKING | FAMILY | Traversing the full length of the 144-mile Maah Daah Hey Trail is a true multiday wilderness adventure. A popular and well-maintained route, it runs through private and public lands—including the Little Missouri Grasslands and both the North and South units of the national park—with several access points and numerous campgrounds. Maps are available at the park visitor centers and through the U.S. Forest Service and the Maah Daah Hey Trail Association. The 7.1-mile one-way segment that runs through the park's South Unit will take you three or four hours; plan on a full day out and back. *Moderate–Difficult.* ⊠ *Theodore Roosevelt National Park* ✛ *Trailhead: Sully Creek State Park, 3 miles south of South Unit Visitor Center* ⊕ *mdhta.com.*

Ridgeline Nature Trail

HIKING/WALKING | Before heading out along this short (0.6-mile) loop pick up the accompanying map and brochure with information designed to enlighten you on the ecology of the badlands. The first few yards are steep and difficult, and there's a steep descent at the end, but otherwise the trail is even. You'll complete this trail in less than an hour. ⊠ *Trailhead at River Bend Overlook.*

HORSEBACK RIDING

Although there aren't any guided trail rides in the park, you can still see some of its terrain on horseback. If you're traveling with your own animal, the South Unit's Roundup Group Horse Camp has sites that accommodate horse trailers. It's open May through October and reservations (through ⊕ *recreation.gov*) are required. Be sure to bring enough water for the animals and certified weed-free hay. As horses are allowed only on backcountry trails or cross-country, you'll need a backcountry-use permit. Check with the park about routes. In addition to staying off park roadways and nature trails, avoid picnic areas and developed campgrounds (other than the horse camp), and keep your horse tied securely when it's not being ridden.

Nearby Towns

Medora, gateway to the park's South Unit, may have a population of only 96, but it is a walkable town with several museums, tiny shops, and plenty of restaurants and places to stay. Its Wild West history is reenacted in a madcap musical production each night in summer. The town's convention and visitors bureau is a great resource, but you can also book lodgings, show tickets, horseback riding excursions, and other activities through the nonprofit Theodore Roosevelt Medora Foundation. Roughly 50 miles to the east is **Dickinson** (population 28,000), the largest town near the national park. North of Dickinson and about 35 miles east of the park's North Unit, **Killdeer** (pop. about 825) is known for its Roundup Rodeo—North Dakota's oldest—and its gorgeous scenery. Killdeer is the place to fill your tank, because there isn't another gas station around for 40 miles. **Williston** (pop. about 30,000) is 60 miles north of the North Unit (141 miles from the South Unit), just over the Missouri River. The Amtrak stop nearest to the national park is here.

VISITOR INFORMATION

City of Killdeer ⊠ *165 Railroad St., Killdeer* ☎ *701/764–5295* ⊕ *www.killdeer. com.* **Dickinson Convention and Visitors Bureau** ⊠ *72 E. Museum Dr., Dickinson* ☎ *701/483–4988* ⊕ *www.visitdickinson. com.* **Medora Convention & Visitors Bureau** ⊠ *475 4th St., Medora* ☎ *701/623–4830* ⊕ *www.medorand.com.* **Theodore Roosevelt Medora Foundation** ☎ *800/633– 6721, 701/623–4444* ⊕ *medora.com.* **Williston Convention and Visitors Center** ⊠ *212 Airport Rd., Williston* ☎ *701/774–9041, 800/615–9041* ⊕ *www.visitwilliston.com.*

 Sights

Little Missouri National Grasslands

NATURE PRESERVE | This is the largest and most diverse of 19 national grasslands in the western United States, spanning a million acres in western North Dakota. It takes three hours to complete a self-guided 58-mile driving tour known as the Custer Auto Trail, beginning and ending in Medora. The best time to see wildlife is in early morning or late afternoon. Don't forget a camera and binoculars. In addition to stretches of the lengthy Maah Daah Hey Trail, which runs through the grasslands, there are seven designated trails and back-country hiking is permitted. Little Missouri Grassland trails are open to all non-motorized activities, including horseback riding and cycling as well as hiking. For a copy of the driving tour and trail maps, contact the U.S. Forest Service office in Dickinson or the South Unit Visitor Center. ⊠ *U.S. Forest Service, 99 23rd Ave. W, Dickinson* ☎ *701/227–7800* ⊕ *www.fs.usda.gov/dpg* ☜ *Free.*

Little Missouri State Park

NATIONAL/STATE PARK | Called *Makoshika* or "Bad Land" by the Sioux, the Little Missouri State Park has unusual land formations that create the state's most awe-inspiring scenery. The beehive-shaped rock formations resulted from the erosion of sedimentary rock deposited millions of years ago by streams flowing from the Rocky Mountains. Undeveloped and rugged, this wilderness area has both primitive and modern camping and 50 miles of horse trails. ⊠ *Killdeer ✛ Off Rte. 22, 18 miles north and 2 miles east of Killdeer* ☎ *701/764–5256, 701/794–3731 winter* ⊕ *www.parkrec.nd.gov/parks/ lmosp/lmosp.html* ☜ *$7 per vehicle* ☉ *Closed Nov.–Apr.*

North Dakota Cowboy Hall of Fame

MUSEUM | This museum features six galleries and rotating exhibits, hosts special events, and is dedicated to the horse culture of the plains. ⊠ *250 Main St., Medora* ☎ *701/623–2000* ⊕ *www. northdakotacowboy.com* ☜ *$9.*

Roadside Art

PUBLIC ART | Known as the "Enchanted Highway," this self-guided 30-mile driving tour on Route 21 south of Dickinson features seven giant metal sculptures designed by a local artist, including a 51-foot Teddy Roosevelt. Massive sculptures include a deer crossing, grasshopper family, pheasants on the prairie, a 150-foot-long gaggle of geese, and a tin family with a 45-foot father, 44-foot mother, and 23-foot son. ⊠ *Exit 72 off I–94, Rte. 21 between Lefor and Regent, Dickinson* ☎ *701/563–6400, 701/483–4988 to Dickinson Convention and Visitors Bureau* ☜ *Free.*

ACTIVITIES
GOLF
★ Bully Pulpit Golf Course

GOLF | This impressive golf course weaves its way through the badlands buttes, giving players a truly breathtaking backdrop for a round of golf, and some exceptional vertical tee boxes and greens. It's one of the best and most challenging public courses in the United States. ⊠ *3731 Bible Camp Rd., Medora* ☎ *701/623– 4444, 800/633–6721* ⊕ *medora.com* ☜ *$89, includes cart* ⚡ *18 holes, 7166 yards, par 72.*

HORSEBACK RIDING

Medora Stables & Trail Rides

HORSEBACK RIDING | You don't need to be an expert to sign up for these one- or two-hour trail rides through beautiful Badlands scenery outside Theodore Roosevelt National Park. They're offered daily between June and mid-September, departing on the hour between 8 and 3:30 from stables on the east side of Medora. Make reservations (a really good idea) through the Theodore Roosevelt Medora Foundation. Children must be at least 7 years old and at least 45 inches tall to participate. ✉ *Medora* ☎ *800/633–6721, 701/623–4444* 🌐 *medora.com.*

Performing Arts

Medora Musical

THEATER | FAMILY | Well worth your while in summer is this theatrical tribute to the Old West, its history, and its personalities. It's been in operation for five decades and is held nightly early June through early September at the 2,852-seat, open-air Burning Hills Amphitheater. Doors open at 6:45; the show starts at 7:30. Book tickets in advance through the Theodore Roosevelt Medora Foundation, or stop by the Ticket Junction or Medora Musical Welcome Center on the day of the show. ✉ *3422 Chateau Rd., Medora* ☎ *701/623–4444, 800/633–6721* 🌐 *medora.com* 🎟 *From $37.*

Restaurants

IN THE PARK

PICNIC AREAS

Cottonwood

RESTAURANT—SIGHT | This is in a lovely valley near the river. There are fire pits, drinking water, restrooms, eight open tables, and eight covered tables. ✉ *Theodore Roosevelt National Park* ✥ *5½ miles north of South Unit Visitor Center.*

Juniper

RESTAURANT—SIGHT | This area has restrooms, grills, drinking water, and 28 tables (eight with shelter). ✉ *Theodore Roosevelt National Park* ✥ *5 miles west of North Unit Visitor Center.*

Painted Canyon Scenic Overlook

RESTAURANT—SIGHT | This area has eight covered tables, drinking water, restrooms, and a spectacular view. ✉ *Exit 32 off I–94.*

OUTSIDE THE PARK

Boots Bar and Grill

$$ | STEAKHOUSE | FAMILY | This watering hole has Medora's largest tavern, an upstairs dining room, and breezy patios, as well as live music, dancing, and microbrews. Diners feast primarily on pizzas, burgers, and steak and it's kid-friendly until 10 pm. **Known for:** good burgers; lively atmosphere; family-friendly. [$] *Average main: $20* ✉ *300 Pacific Ave., Medora* ☎ *701/623–2668* 🌐 *www.bootsbarmedora.com.*

Buckskin Bar and Grill

$$ | STEAKHOUSE | This steak house, with a saloon and dance hall, was built in 1915. The building has rough-hewn walls, original wood floors, and tin ceilings. **Known for:** cowboy flavor; great steaks; divine desserts. [$] *Average main: $17* ✉ *64 Central Ave. S, Killdeer* ☎ *701/764–5321* 🌐 *www.buckskinbargrill.com.*

Cowboy Cafe

$ | AMERICAN | This locally owned-and-operated café specializes in homemade soups, caramel rolls, and delicious roast beef dishes. Be prepared for a (short) wait, since the cozy dining room is popular with both locals and visitors, particularly at breakfast. **Known for:** great breakfast spot; cash-only; local flavor. [$] *Average main: $10* ✉ *215 4th St., Medora* ☎ *701/623–4343* 💳 *No credit cards* 🕒 *Closed Oct.–Apr.*

Best Campgrounds in Theodore Roosevelt

For the adventurous traveler, camping in Theodore Roosevelt is well worth the effort. The unadulterated isolation, epic views, and relationship with nature afforded by the Spartan campgrounds within the park create an experience you'll be hard-pressed to find elsewhere in the United States. Just remember that the park's campgrounds are relatively undeveloped—you'll have to pack in everything you need. If you pick a campsite in the surrounding wilderness, you must obtain a backcountry camping permit (available free) from a visitor center first.

Cottonwood Campground. Nestled under juniper and cottonwood trees on the bank of the Little Missouri River, this is a wonderful place to watch buffalo, elk, and other wildlife drink from the river at sunrise and just before sunset. ✉ *½ mile north of South Unit Visitor Center* ☎ *701/623–4466.*

Juniper Campground. The sites here are surrounded by junipers, hence the name. Don't be surprised if you see a bison herd wander through on its way to the Little Missouri River. ✉ *5 miles west of North Unit Visitor Center* ☎ *701/842–2333.*

★ Theodore's
$$$$ | **AMERICAN** | Theodore's offers the best fine dining in Medora and, perhaps, in western North Dakota. The lunch menu features salads, prime-rib sandwiches, and buffalo burgers, while dinner fare includes shrimp with lemon risotto, a hickory-seasoned rib eye, and tenderloin with Gorgonzola cream sauce. **Known for:** great service; varied menu; convenient location. [$] *Average main: $35* ✉ *Rough Riders Hotel, 301 3rd Ave., Medora* ☎ *701/623–4433, 800/633–6721* 🌐 *medora.com.*

Hotels

OUTSIDE THE PARK

AmericInn by Wyndham Medora
$$$ | **HOTEL** | A Western theme, complete with mounted animals, dominates the public areas of this contemporary hotel. **Pros:** near shops and restaurants; indoor pool; ideal after long hikes in the park. **Cons:** right on the railroad tracks; on the pricey side; chain-hotel feel. [$] *Rooms from: $190* ✉ *75 E. River Rd. S, Medora* ☎ *701/623–4800, 800/634–3444* 🌐 *www.wyndhamhotels.com/americinn* 🔑 *78 rooms* 🍴 *Free Breakfast.*

Buffalo Gap Guest Ranch
$$ | **RESORT** | Perched on a bluff 8 miles west of Medora, this rustic property commands a view of the Dakota Badlands and has access to the Maah Daah Hey Trail. **Pros:** great prices on lodging and food; exceptional view; large outdoor patio. **Cons:** bar can be smoky; 10 minutes from town. [$] *Rooms from: $150* ✉ *3100 Buffalo Gap Rd., Medora* ☎ *701/623–4200* 🌐 *www.buffalogapguestranch.com* 🔑 *22 cabins, 10 RV sites* 🍴 *No meals.*

Ramada by Wyndham Grand Dakota Hotel Dickinson
$ | **HOTEL** | Across from the Prairie Hills Mall, this three-story motel lets you relax on couches before the fireplace in the huge lobby. **Pros:** full-service restaurant; great customer service. **Cons:** can be busy; pool can be quite popular,

particularly in the summer. [$] *Rooms from: $99* ✉ *532 15th St. W, Dickinson* ☎ *701/483–5600, 800/422–0949* 🌐 *www.wyndhamhotels.com/ramada* 🛏 *192 rooms* 🍴 *No meals.*

★ **Rough Riders Hotel**

$$$$ | **HOTEL** | Renovations over the years have made this place decidedly posh, but it retains the red velvet chairs, antique armoires, and iron-rod and oak bed frames that have made this property a favorite for decades. **Pros:** historic, downtown location; dining on the premises. **Cons:** relatively expensive; occasional railroad noise. [$] *Rooms from: $209* ✉ *301 3rd Ave., Medora* ☎ *701/623–4444, 800/633–6721* 🌐 *medora.com* 🛏 *76 rooms* 🍴 *No meals.*

Chapter 34

WIND CAVE NATIONAL PARK

Updated by
Laura M. Kidder

SOUTH
DAKOTA

WELCOME TO
WIND CAVE NATIONAL PARK

TOP REASONS TO GO

★ **Underground exploring:** Wind Cave offers visitors the chance to get their hands and feet dirty on guided tours through long and complex caves.

★ **The call of the wild:** Wind Cave National Park boasts a wide variety of animals: bison, coyote, deer, antelope, elk, and prairie dogs.

★ **Education by candlelight:** Wind Cave offers numerous educational and interpretive programs, including the Candlelight Cave Tour, which allows guests to explore the cave by candlelight only.

★ **Historic cave:** On January 3, 1903, President Theodore Roosevelt signed a bill that made Wind Cave the first cave in the nation protected by the federal government.

★ **Noteworthy neighbors:** With its proximity to national parks, state parks, and other monuments, Wind Cave is situated perfectly to explore some of America's greatest national treasures.

1 The Surface. Wind Cave lies at the confluence of western mountains and central plains, which blesses the park with a unique landscape. A series of established trails weave in and out of forested hillsides and grassy meadows, providing treks of varying difficulty.

2 The Cave. With an explored maze of caverns totaling 148 miles, Wind Cave is considered one of the longest caves in the world. Notably, scientists estimate that only 5% of the cave has been explored to date. It is also estimated that 95% of the world's boxwork formations are found in Wind Cave, which means that visitors here are treated to some of the rarest geological features on the planet.

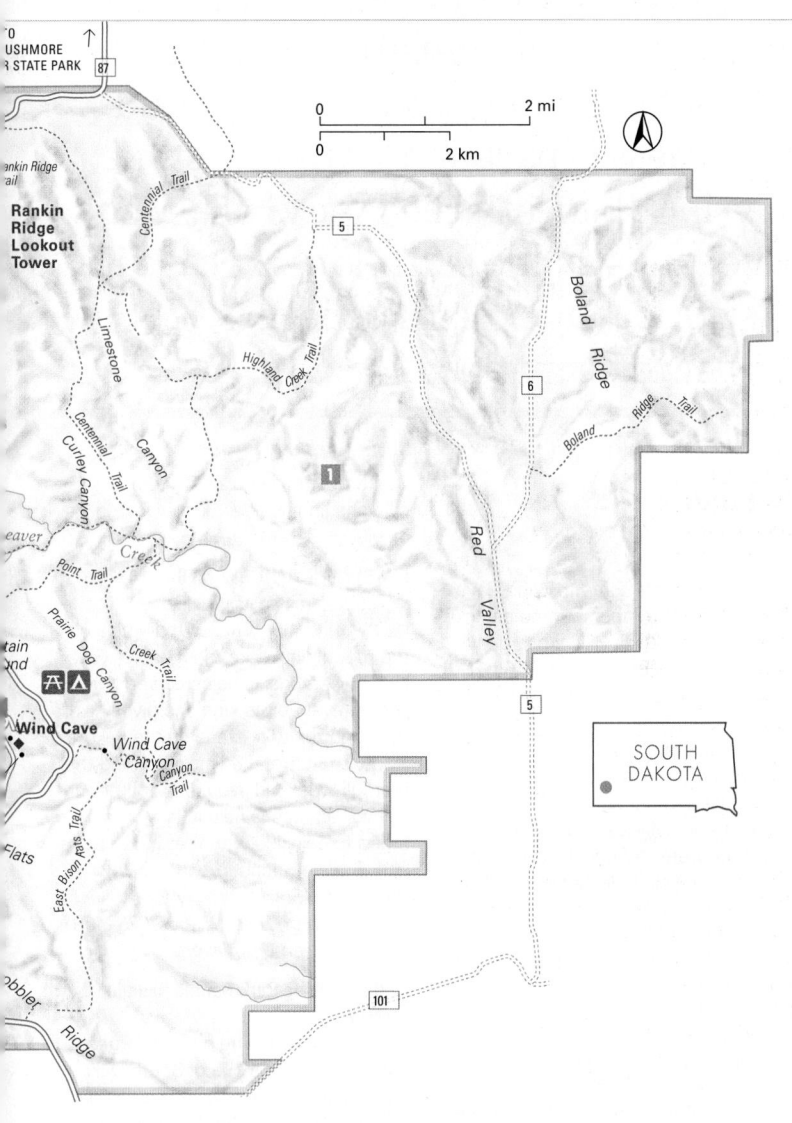

TO
USHMORE
R STATE PARK

87

Rankin Ridge
ail

Rankin
Ridge
Lookout
Tower

Centennial Trail

5

Limestone

Boland Ridge

Centennial Trail

Curley Canyon

Canyon

Highland Creek Trail

6

Boland Ridge Trail

1

eaver

Creek

Point Trail

Prairie Dog Canyon

Creek Trail

Red Valley

tain
nd

Wind Cave

Wind Cave
Canyon

Canyon
Trail

5

East Bison Flats Trail

Flats

bbler

Ridge

101

0 — 2 mi
0 — 2 km

SOUTH
DAKOTA

Wind Cave has 148 miles of underground passageways. Cave formations include 95% of the world's mineral boxwork, and gypsum beard so sensitive it reacts to the heat of a lamp. This underground wilderness is part of a giant limestone labyrinth beneath the Black Hills. Wind Cave ranks as the sixth-longest cave in the world, but experts believe 95% of it has yet to be mapped.

Planning

WHEN TO GO

The biggest crowds come to Wind Cave from June to September, but the park and surrounding Black Hills are large enough to diffuse the masses. Neither the cave nor grounds above are ever too packed, although on busy summer days tours sometimes sell out over an hour ahead of time, so come early in the day and reserve your spot. Park officials contend it's actually less busy during the first full week in August, when the Sturgis Motorcycle Rally brings roughly a half-million bikers to the region, clogging highways for miles around. Most hotels within a 100-mile radius are booked up to a year in advance.

The colder months are the least crowded, though you can still explore underground, thanks to the cave's constant 53°F temperature. The shoulder seasons are also unpopular, though autumn is a perfect time to visit. The days are warm, the nights are cool, and in late September/early October the park's canyons and coulees display incredible colors.

FESTIVALS AND EVENTS

★ Crazy Horse Volksmarch

FESTIVAL | FAMILY | This 6.2-mile hike up the mountain where the massive Crazy Horse Memorial is being carved is the largest event of its kind and gives hikers the opportunity to stand on the Lakota leader's outstretched arm. It's held the first full weekend in June. Another one-day Volksmarch is held in late September, timed to coincide with the Custer State Park Buffalo Roundup. ✉ 12151 Ave. of the Chiefs, Crazy Horse Memorial ✢ 5 miles north of Custer ☎ 605/673–4681 ⊕ crazyhorsememorial.org.

★ Custer State Park Buffalo Roundup & Arts Festival

FESTIVAL | FAMILY | The nation's largest buffalo roundup is one of South Dakota's most exciting events. Early on a Friday morning in late September, cowboys, cowgirls, and rangers saddle up to corral and vaccinate the park's 1,300 head of bison. You'll hear the thunder of more

AVERAGE HIGH/LOW TEMPERATURES					
JAN.	**FEB.**	**MAR.**	**APR.**	**MAY**	**JUNE**
37/8	41/14	49/21	58/30	67/40	77/49
JULY	**AUG.**	**SEPT.**	**OCT.**	**NOV.**	**DEC.**
84/55	84/53	76/44	63/32	46/20	39/12

than 5,000 hooves before you even see the bison. Before, during, and after the roundup, a three-day festival showcases works by South Dakota artists and artisans. ⊠ *Custer State Park, 13329 U.S. Hwy. 16A, Custer ✛ Travel south on Wildlife Loop until you see corrals and crowd* ☎ *605/255–4515* ⊕ *gfp.sd.gov/ parks/detail/custer-state-park.*

Days of '76

FESTIVAL | FAMILY | This award-winning PRCA outdoor rodeo includes the usual riding, roping, and bull riding, two parades with vintage carriages and coaches, and Western arts and crafts. This five-day affair is one of the most popular events in South Dakota, featuring the top cowboys and cowgirls in the sport. ⊠ *Days of '76 Rodeo Grounds, 18 76 Dr., Deadwood ✛ North side of Deadwood across from First Gold Hotel* ☎ *605/578–1876, 800/999–1876* ⊕ *daysof76.com.*

Deadwood Jam

FESTIVAL | A quarter century strong and still filling the streets of Deadwood with live music, the Black Hills' premier music festival showcases an ecelectic collection of country, rock, and blues for two days in mid-September. ⊠ *Deadwood History & Information Center, 3 Siever St., Deadwood* ☎ *605/578–2507, 800/999–1876* ⊕ *www.deadwood.com/ event/deadwood-jam.*

Gold Discovery Days

FESTIVAL | FAMILY | A parade, carnival, car show, stick-horse rodeo, hot-air balloon rally, hunt for gold nuggets, and bed races are all part of the fun at this three-day event in late July in Custer. ⊠ *615 Washington St., Custer*

☎ *605/673–2244* ⊕ *www.visitcuster. com/gold-discovery-days.*

PLANNING YOUR TIME
WIND CAVE IN ONE DAY

Pack a picnic lunch, then head to the visitor center to purchase tickets for a morning tour of Wind Cave. Visit the exhibit rooms in the center afterward. Then drive or walk the quarter mile to the picnic area north of the visitor center. The refreshing air and deep emerald color of the pine woodlands will flavor your meal.

In the afternoon, take a leisurely drive through the parklands south of the visitor center, passing through **Gobbler Pass** and **Bison Flats,** for an archetypal view of the park and to look for wildlife. On the way back north, follow U.S. 385 east toward **Wind Cave Canyon.** If you enjoy bird-watching, park at the turnout and hike the 1.8-mile trail into the canyon, where you can spot swallows and great horned owls in the cliffs and woodpeckers in the trees.

Get back on the highway going north, take a right on Highway 87, and continue a half mile to the turnout for **Centennial Trail.** Hike the trail about 2 miles to the junction with **Lookout Point Trail,** turn right and return to Highway 87. The whole loop is about 4.75 miles. As you continue driving north to the top of Rankin Ridge, a pull-out to the right serves as the starting point for 1.25-mile **Rankin Ridge Trail.** It loops around the ridge, past **Lookout Tower**—the park's highest point—and ends up back at the pull-out. This trail is an excellent opportunity to enjoy the fresh air, open spaces, and diversity of wildlife in the park.

GETTING HERE AND AROUND
AIR TRAVEL
The nearest commercial airport is in Rapid City.

BUS TRAVEL
Bus lines serve Rapid City and Wall.

CAR TRAVEL
Wind Cave is 56 miles from Rapid City, via U.S. 16 and Highway 87, which runs through the park, and 73 miles southwest of Badlands National Park.

U.S. 385 and Highway 87 travel the length of the park on the west side. Additionally, two unpaved roads, NPS Roads 5 and 6, traverse the northeastern part of Wind Cave. NPS Road 5 joins Highway 87 at the park's north border.

PARK ESSENTIALS
ACCESSIBILITY
The visitor center is entirely wheelchair accessible, but only a few areas of the cave itself are navigable by those with limited mobility. Arrangements can be made in advance for a special ranger-assisted tour for a small fee. The Elk Mountain Campground has two accessible sites.

PARK FEES AND PERMITS
There's no fee to enter the park; cave tours cost $10–$30. The requisite backcountry camping and horseback-riding permits are both free from the visitor center. Rates at Elk Mountain Campground are $18 a night per site early spring through late fall (when the water is turned on in the restroom facility); $9 a night per site the rest of the year.

PARK HOURS
The park is open year-round, though visitor center hours and tour schedules vary seasonally. It is in the Mountain time zone.

CELL PHONE RECEPTION
Cell phone reception is hit and miss in the park. You will find a public phone outside the visitor center.

EDUCATIONAL OFFERINGS
RANGER PROGRAMS
Adventures in Nature
TOUR—SIGHT | Although annual themes and invidual program topics vary, nature is always the focus on these seasonlly offered adventures held at the visitor center. They're open to children ages 3 to 12, who are divided into groups that participate in age-appropriate activites. ✉ *26611 Hwy. 385* ☎ *605/745–1134* ⊕ *www.nps.gov/wica.*

Junior Ranger Program
TOUR—SIGHT | FAMILY | Kids 12 and younger can earn a Junior Ranger badge by completing activities that teach them about the park's ecosystems, the cave, the animals, and protecting the environment. Pick up the Junior Ranger guidebook for free at the Wind Cave Visitor Center. ✉ *Wind Cave National Park, 26611 Hwy. 385* ☎ *605/745–4600.*

RESTAURANTS
If you're determined to dine in Wind Cave National Park, be sure to pack your own meal, because other than vending machines, the only dining venues inside park boundaries are the two picnic areas, one near the visitor center and the other at Elk Mountain Campground. The towns beyond the park offer additional options. Deadwood claims some of the best-ranked restaurants in South Dakota. Buffalo, pheasant, and elk are relatively common ingredients in the Black Hills. No matter where you go, beef is king.

HOTELS
While Wind Cave claims a singular campground, you'll have to look outside park boundaries if you want to bed down in something more substantial than a tent. New chain hotels with modern amenities are plentiful in the Black Hills, but when booking accommodations consider a stay at one of the area's historic properties. From grand brick downtown hotels to intimate Queen Anne homes converted to bed-and-breakfasts, historic lodgings are easy to locate. Other distinctive

lodging choices include the region's mountain lodges and forest retreats.

It may be difficult to obtain quality accommodations during summer—and downright impossible during the Sturgis Motorcycle Rally, held the first full week of August every year—so plan ahead and make reservations (three or four months out is a good rule of thumb) if you're going to travel during peak season. To find the best value, choose a hotel far from Interstate 90. *Hotel reviews have been shortened. For full information, visit Fodors.com.*

What It Costs			
$	$$	$$$	$$$$
RESTAURANTS			
under $13	$13–$20	$21–$30	over $30
HOTELS			
under $101	$101–$150	$151–$200	over $200

VISITOR INFORMATION

PARK CONTACT INFORMATION Wind Cave National Park ⊠ *26611 U.S. 385, Hot Springs* ☎ *605/745–4600* ⊕ *www.nps.gov/wica.*

VISITOR CENTERS

Wind Cave Visitor Center
INFO CENTER | The park's sole visitor center is the primary place to get general park information and embark on cave tours. Located on top of the cave, it has three exhibit rooms, with displays on cave exploration, Native American culture, and prairie management. The center also hosts ranger programs and has an auditorium that presents the film, *Wind Cave, Two Worlds.* Other than vending machines, there's no coffee or snacks here or elsewhere in the park. ⊠ *26611 U.S. 385, Hot Springs* ⊕ *Off U.S. 385, 3 miles north of park's southern border* ☎ *605/745–4600* ⊕ *www.nps.gov/wica* ☞ *Free.*

 # Sights

SCENIC DRIVES

Bison Flats Drive (South Entrance)
SCENIC DRIVE | Entering the park from the south on U.S. 385 takes you past Gobbler Ridge and into the hills commonly found in the southern Black Hills region. After a couple of miles, the landscape gently levels onto the Bison Flats, one of the mixed-grass prairies on which the park prides itself. You might see a herd of grazing buffalo (the park has roughly 400 of them) between here and the visitor center. You can also catch panoramic views of the parklands, surrounding hills, and limestone bluffs. ⊠ *Hwy. 385.*

★ **Rankin Ridge Drive (North Entrance)**
SCENIC DRIVE | Entering the park across the north border via Highway 87 is perhaps the most beautiful drive into the park. As you leave behind the grasslands and granite spires of Custer State Park and enter Wind Cave, you see the prairie, forest, and wetland habitats of the backcountry and some of the oldest rock in the Black Hills. The silvery twinkle of mica, quartz, and feldspar crystals dots Rankin Ridge east of Highway 87, and gradually gives way to limestone and sandstone formations. ⊠ *Hwy. 87.*

SCENIC STOPS

Rankin Ridge Lookout Tower
VIEWPOINT | Although some of the best panoramic views of the park and surrounding hills can be seen from this 5,013-foot tower, it's typically not staffed or open to the public. Still, if you want to stretch your legs on a car ride along Rankin Ridge Drive, consider following the 1-mile Rankin Ridge loop to the tower and back. ⊠ *Wind Cave National Park* ⊕ *6 miles north of the visitor center on Hwy. 87.*

★ **Wind Cave**
CAVE | Known to Native Americans for centuries, Wind Cave was named for the strong currents of air that alternately blow in and out of its entrance. The

Plants and Wildlife in Wind Cave

About three-quarters of the park is grassland. The rest is forested, mostly by the ponderosa pine. Poison ivy is common in wetter, shadier areas, so wear long pants and boots when hiking. The convergence of forest and prairies makes an attractive home for bison, elk, coyotes, pronghorn antelope, prairie dogs, and mule deer. Wild turkey and squirrels are less obvious in this landscape, but commonly seen by observant hikers.

Mountain lions also live in the park; although usually shy, they will attack if surprised or threatened. Make noise while hiking to prevent chance encounters. Bison appear docile, but can be dangerous. The largest land mammal in North America, they weigh up to a ton and run at speeds in excess of 35 mph.

cave's winds are related to the difference in atmospheric pressure between the cave and the surface. When the atmospheric pressure is higher outside than inside the cave, the air blows in, and vice versa. With 148 miles of known passageway divided into three different levels, Wind Cave ranks the sixth longest in the world. It's host to an incredibly diverse collection of geologic formations, including more boxwork than any other known cave, plus a series of underground lakes. The cave tours sponsored by the National Park Service allow you to see unusual and beautiful formations with names such as popcorn, frostwork, and boxwork. ⌧ *Wind Cave National Park* ✛ *U.S. 385 to Wind Cave Visitor Center* ⊕ *www.nps.gov/wica/planyourvisit/guidedtours.htm.*

⚡ Activities

Many visitors come to Wind Cave solely to descend into the park's underground passages. While there are great ranger-led tours for casual visitors—and more daring explorations for experienced cavers—the prairie and forest above the cave shouldn't be neglected.

MULTISPORT OUTFITTERS
Granite Sports

HIKING/WALKING | Several miles north of Wind Cave Park in Hill City, Granite Sports sells a wide range of hiking, climbing, and camping apparel and accessories; they also know the best local guides. ⌧ *201 Main St., Hill City* ☎ *605/574–2121* ⊕ *www.granitesports. biz.*

Scheels All Sport

HIKING/WALKING | In the Rushmore Crossing Mall, off Interstate 90 at East-North Street or Lacrosse Street exits, the enormous Scheels All Sport carries a wide selection of all-weather hiking gear, footwear, and clothes, as well as binoculars suitable for bird-watchers. ⌧ *1225 Eglin St., Rapid City* ☎ *605/342–9033* ⊕ *www.scheels.com.*

BIRD-WATCHING
Rankin Ridge

BIRD WATCHING | See large birds of prey here, including turkey vultures, hawks, and golden eagles. ⌧ *Wind Cave National Park* ✛ *6 miles north of the visitor center on Hwy. 87.*

★ Wind Cave Canyon

BIRD WATCHING | Here's one of the best birding areas in the park. The limestone walls of the canyon are ideal nesting grounds for cliff swallows and great horned owls, while the standing dead trees on the canyon floor attract red-headed and Lewis woodpeckers. As you hike down the trail, the steep-sided canyon widens to a panoramic view east across the prairies. ☒ *Wind Cave National Park* ✛ *About ½ mile east of visitor center* ⊕ *www.nps.gov/wica*.

HIKING

There are more than 30 miles of hiking trails within the boundaries of Wind Cave National Park, covering ponderosa forest and mixed-grass prairie. The landscape has changed little over the past century, so a hike through the park is as much a historical snapshot of pioneer life in the 1890s as it is exercise. Be sure to hit the Wind Cave Canyon Trail, where limestone cliffs attract birds like cliff swallows and great horned owls, and the Cold Brook Canyon Trail, a short but fun trip past a prairie-dog town to the park's edge. Besides birds and small animals such as squirrels, you're apt to see deer and pronghorn while hiking, and probably some bison.

Hiking into the wild, untouched backcountry is perfectly safe, provided you have a map (available from the visitor center) and a good sense of direction. Don't expect any developments, however; bathrooms and a water-bottle filling station are available only at the visitor center, and the trails are dirt or gravel. There are no easily accessible sources along the trails, and water from backcountry sources must be treated, so pack your own.

Boland Ridge Trail

HIKING/WALKING | Get away from the crowds for a half day via this strenuous, 2.6-mile (one way) hike. The panorama from the top is well worth it, especially at night. *Difficult.* ☒ *Wind Cave National Park* ✛ *Trailhead: off Park Service Rd. 6, 1 mile north of junction with Park Service Rd. 5*.

Centennial Trail

HIKING/WALKING | Constructed to celebrate South Dakota's centennial in 1989, this trail bisects the Black Hills, covering 111 miles from north to south, from Bear Butte State Park through Black Hills National Forest, Black Elk Wilderness, Custer State Park, and into Wind Cave National Park. Designed for bikers, hikers, and horses, the trail is rugged but accommodating (note, however, that bicycling on the trail is not allowed within park boundaries). It will take you at least a half day to cover the 6-mile Wind Cave segment. *Moderate.* ☒ *Wind Cave National Park* ✛ *Trailhead: off Hwy. 87, 2 miles north of visitor center*.

Cold Brook Canyon Trail

HIKING/WALKING | **FAMILY** | Starting on the west side of U.S. 385, 2 miles south of the visitor center, this 1.4-mile (one way), mildly strenuous hike runs past a former prairie-dog town, the edge of an area burned by a controlled fire in 1986, and through Cold Brook Canyon to the park boundary fence. Experienced hikers can conquer this trail and return to the trailhead in an hour or less, but more leisurely visitors will probably need more time. *Moderate.* ☒ *Wind Cave National Park* ✛ *Trailhead: west side of U.S. 385, 2 miles south of visitor center*.

Highland Creek Trail

HIKING/WALKING | This difficult, roughly 8.6-mile (one way) trail is the longest and most diverse trail within the park, traversing mixed-grass prairies, ponderosa pine forests, and the riparian habitats of Highland Creek, Beaver Creek, and Wind Cave Canyon. Even those in good shape will need a full day to cover this trail round-trip. *Difficult.* ☒ *Wind Cave National Park* ✛ *Southern trailhead stems from Wind Cave Canyon trail 1 mile east of U.S. 385. Northern trailhead on Forest Service Rd. 5*.

Wind Cave Canyon Trail

HIKING/WALKING | This easy 1.8-mile (one way) trail follows Wind Cave Canyon to the park boundary fence. The canyon, with its steep limestone walls and dead trees, provides the best opportunity in the park for bird-watching. Be especially vigilant for cliff swallows, great horned owls, and red-headed and Lewis woodpeckers. Deer, least chipmunks, and other small animals also are attracted to the sheltered environment of the canyon. Even though you could probably do a round-trip tour of this trail in less than an hour and a half, be sure to spend more time here to observe the wildlife. *Easy.* ⊠ *Wind Cave National Park* ⊹ *Trailhead: east side of Hwy. 385, 1 mile north of southern access road to visitor center.*

SPELUNKING

You may not explore the depths of Wind Cave on your own, but you can choose from five ranger-led cave tours, available from June through August; the rest of the year, only one or two tours are available. On each tour you pass incredibly beautiful cave formations, including extremely well-developed boxwork. The least crowded times to visit in summer are mornings and weekends.

The cave is 53°F year-round, so bring a sweater. Note that the uneven passages are often wet and slippery. Rangers discourage those with heart conditions and physical limitations from taking the organized tours. However, with some advance warning (and for a nominal fee) park rangers can arrange private, limited tours for those with physical disabilities. For wild caving tours, the park provides hard hats, knee pads, and gloves, and all cavers are required to have long pants, a long-sleeved shirt, and hiking boots or shoes with nonslip soles. (Note: if you prefer lighted passages and stairways to dark crawl spaces, a tour other than the Wild Caving Tour might appeal to you.) To prevent the spread of white-nose syndrome, a disease that is deadly to bats, don't wear any clothes or shoes or bring any equipment that you might have used to explore other caves (with the exception of the nearby Jewel Cave National Monument).

Tours depart from the visitor center. A schedule can be found online at ⊕ *www. nps.gov/wica.* To make a reservation, call ☎ *605/745–1134.*

Candlelight Cave Tour

SPELUNKING | Available once or twice daily, mid-June through Labor Day, this tour goes into a section of the cave with no paved walks or lighting. Everyone on the tour carries a lantern similar to those used in expeditions in the 1890s. The tour lasts two hours, covers 0.66 mile, and is limited to 10 people, so reservations are essential. Children younger than eight are not admitted. *Moderate.* ⊠ *26611 U.S. 385* ⊹ *Off U.S. 385, 3 miles north of park's southern boundary* ⊕ *www.nps.gov/wica/planyourvisit/ tour-candlelight.htm* ✉ *$12.*

Fairgrounds Cave Tour

SPELUNKING | View examples of nearly every type of calcite formation found in the cave on this 1½-hour, 0.66-mile tour, available three times daily over Memorial Day weekend, eight times daily mid-June through mid-August, and four times daily mid-August through Labor Day. There are some 450 steps, leading up and down. *Moderate.* ⊠ *26611 U.S. 385* ⊹ *Off U.S. 385, 3 miles north of the park's southern boundary* ⊕ *www.nps.gov/wica/planyour- visit/tour-fairgrounds.htm* ✉ *$12.*

Garden of Eden Cave Tour

SPELUNKING | You don't need to go far to see boxwork, popcorn, and flowstone formations. Just take the relatively easy, one-hour tour, which covers 0.33 mile and 150 stairs. It's available one to four times daily, depending on the season; note, though that it's not offered for most of September. *Easy.* ⊠ *26611 U.S. 385* ⊹ *3 miles north of park's southern border* ⊕ *www.nps.gov/wica/planyourvisit/tour- garden-of-eden.htm* ✉ *$10.*

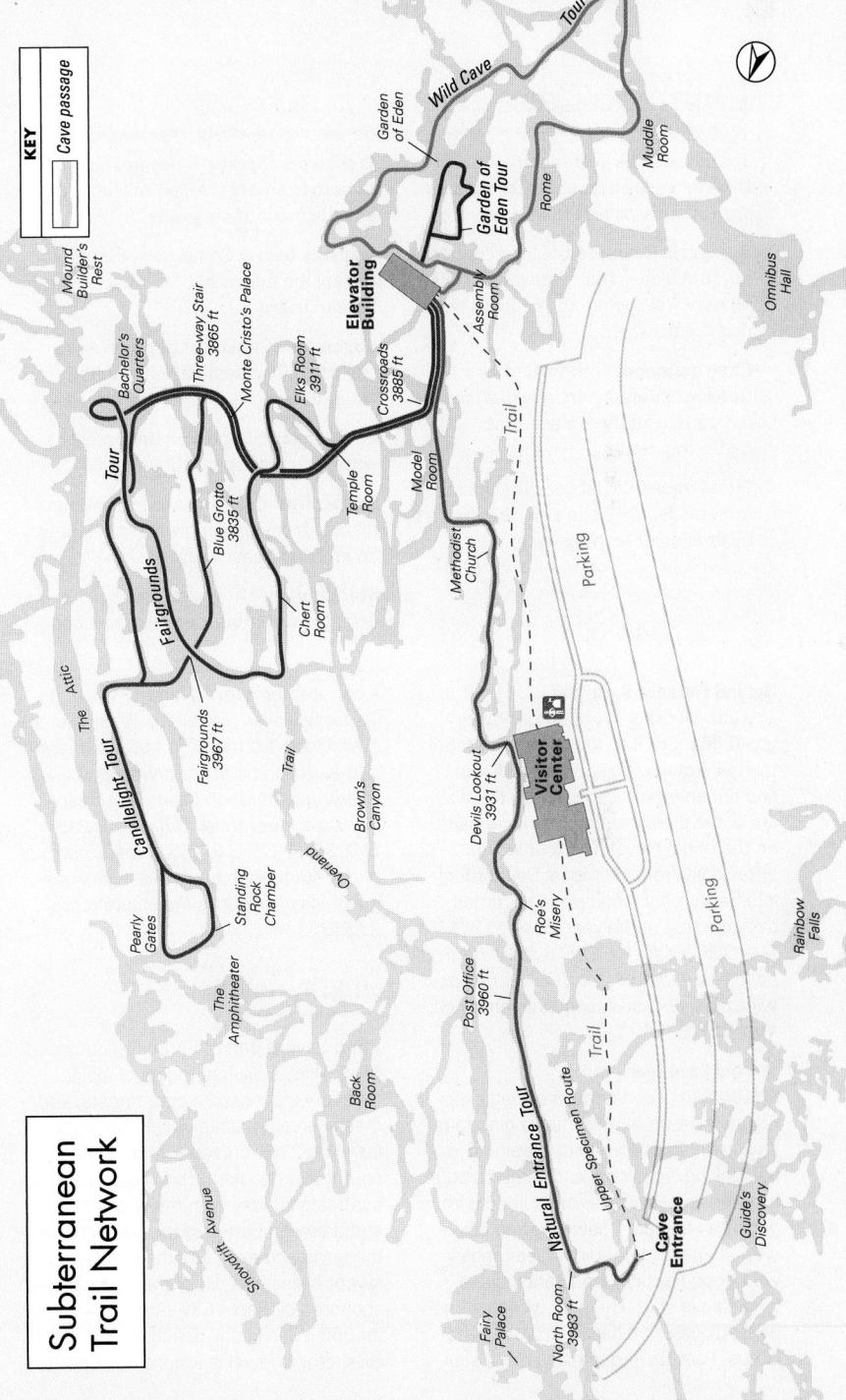

Subterranean Trail Network

KEY

Cave passage

Wild Cave Tour

Garden of Eden

Garden of Eden Tour

Rome

Muddle Room

Omnibus Hall

Mound Builder's Rest

Elevator Building

Assembly Room

Bachelor's Quarters

Three-way Stair 3865 ft

Monte Cristo's Palace

Elks Room 3911 ft

Crossroads 3865 ft

Trail

Fairgrounds Tour

Blue Grotto 3835 ft

Temple Room

Model Room

The Attic

Fairgrounds

Chert Room

Methodist Church

Candlelight Tour

Fairgrounds 3967 ft

Trail

Brown's Canyon

Overland

Parking

Devils Lookout 3931 ft

Visitor Center

Pearly Gates

Standing Rock Chamber

The Amphitheater

Back Room

Roe's Misery

Snowdrift Avenue

Post Office 3960 ft

Natural Entrance Tour

Upper Specimen Route

Parking

Rainbow Falls

Fairy Palace

North Room 3983 ft

Cave Entrance

Trail

Guide's Discovery

Common Cave Terms

Sound like a serious spelunker with this cavemen cheat sheet for various *speleothems* (cave formations).

Boxwork: Composed of interconnecting thin blades that were left in relief on cave walls when the bedrock was dissolved away.

Cave balloons: Thin-walled formations resembling partially deflated balloons, usually composed of hydromagnesite.

Flowstone: Consists of thin layers of a mineral deposited on a sloping surface by flowing or seeping water.

Frostwork: Sprays of needles that radiate from a central point that are usually made of aragonite.

Gypsum beard: Composed of bundles of gypsum fibers that resemble a human beard.

Logomites: Consist of popcorn and superficially resemble hollowed-out stalagmites.

Pool Fingers: Deposited underneath water around organic filaments.

Stalactites: Carrot-shape formations formed from dripping water that hang down from a cave ceiling.

Stalagmites: Mineral deposits from dripping water built up on a cave floor.

Natural Entrance Cave Tour

SPELUNKING | This 1¼-hour tour takes you 0.66 miles into the cave, onto more than 300 stairs (most heading down), and out an elevator exit. Along the way are some significant boxwork deposits on the middle level. The tour leaves 7–12 times daily from Memorial Day through late September, and two to six times daily the rest of the year. *Easy.* ✉ 26611 U.S. 385 ✢ Off U.S. 385, 3 miles north of park's southern border ⊕ www.nps.gov/wica/planyourvisit/tour-natural-entrance.htm ☞ $12.

★ Wild Cave Tour

SPELUNKING | For a serious caving experience, sign up for this challenging four-hour tour. After some basic training in spelunking, you crawl and climb through fissures and corridors, most lined with gypsum needles, frostwork, and boxwork. Expect to get dirty. Wear shoes with good traction, long pants, and a long-sleeve shirt. The park provides knee pads, gloves, and hard hats with headlamps. Parents or guardians must sign a consent form for 16- and 17-year-olds. Tours, which are limited to 10 people, are available at 1 pm daily, mid-June through mid-August, and at 1 pm weekends mid-August through Labor Day. Reservations are essential. *Difficult.* ✉ 26611 U.S. 385 ✢ Off U.S. 385, 3 miles north of park's southern boundary ⊕ www.nps.gov/wica/planyourvisit/tour-caving.htm ☞ $30.

Nearby Towns

Wind Cave is part of South Dakota's Black Hills, a diverse region of alpine meadows, ponderosa pine forests, and creek-carved, granite-walled canyons covering 2 million acres in the state's southwest quadrant. This mountain range contrasts sharply with the sheer cliffs and dramatic buttes of the Badlands to the north and east, and the wide, wind-swept plains of most of the state. Though anchored by Rapid City—the largest city for 350 miles in any direction—the Black Hills' crown jewel is Mount Rushmore

National Memorial, visited by nearly 3 million people each year. U.S. 385 is the backbone of the Black Hills.

Custer

TOWN | About 30 miles north of Hot Springs is the town of Custer, the Mother City of the Black Hills. Near here, George Armstrong Custer and his expedition first discovered gold in 1874, leading to the gold rush of 1875 and '76. ⊠ *605 Washington St., Custer* ☎ *605/673–2244, 800/992–9818* ⊕ *www.visitcuster.com.*

★ Deadwood

TOWN | In one of America's longest ongoing historic preservation projects, you'll discover brick streets fronted by Victorian architecture, with Main Street shops, restaurants, and gaming halls. Deadwood owes its historical character to gold and gaming halls, just as it did in its late-19th-century heyday. You can walk in the footsteps of Wild Bill Hickok and Calamity Jane, who swore she could outdrink, outspit, and outswear any man—and usually did. Both of the Western legends are buried in Deadwood's Boot Hill–Mt. Moriah Cemetery. ⊠ *501 Main St., Deadwood* ☎ *605/578–1876, 800/999–1876* ⊕ *www.deadwood.com.*

Hill City

TOWN | The small, quiet mountain town of Hill City is the gateway to Mount Rushmore. Despite having just 950 residents, the community claims four art galleries, a world-renowned dinosaur research institute, five wineries and craft breweries with tasting rooms, a vintage steam railroad, and a popular visitor center on its eastern flank. ⊠ *23935 Hwy. 385, Hill City* ☎ *800/888–1798* ⊕ *www.hillcitysd. com.*

Hot Springs

TOWN | Noted for its striking sandstone structures, the small and historic community of Hot Springs is the gateway to Wind Cave National Park. It is also the entry point to scores of other natural and historical sites, including Evans Plunge,

a naturally heated indoor-outdoor pool; the Mammoth Site, where more than 50 woolly and Columbian mammoths have been unearthed, the Black Hills Wild Horse Sanctuary, and one of the region's premier golf courses. ⊠ *801 S. 6th St., Hot Springs* ☎ *605/745–4140* ⊕ *www. hotsprings-sd.com.*

Keystone

TOWN | Founded in the 1880s by prospectors searching for gold deposits, the small town of Keystone, 2 miles from Mount Rushmore, has an abundance of restaurants, shops, and attractions, including museums, ziplines, mountain coasters, miniature golf courses, gold-panning experiences, and train or helicopter rides. To serve the millions of visitors passing through the area, there are more than 900 hotel rooms—that's about three times the town's number of permanent residents. ⊠ *110 Swanzey St., Keystone* ☎ *605/666–4896* ⊕ *www. keystonechamber.com.*

Rapid City

INFO CENTER | Called the "City of Presidents" because of the life-size bronze statues of U.S. presidents that adorn virtually every downtown street corner, Rapid City is the largest urban center in a 350-mile radius. The city is the area's cultural, educational, medical, and economic hub, and a good base from which to explore the treasures of the state's southwestern corner, including Mount Rushmore (25 miles south) and Wind Cave National Park (50 miles south). ⊠ *512 Main St., Rapid City* ☎ *605/718–8484, 800/487–3223* ⊕ *www. visitrapidcity.com.*

VISITOR INFORMATION Black Hills, Badlands & Lakes Association ⊠ *1851 Discovery Circle, Rapid City* ☎ *605/355–3700, 888/945–7676* ⊕ *www.blackhills-badlands.com.*

 Sights

SCENIC DRIVES

Peter Norbeck National Scenic Byway

SCENIC DRIVE | Although there are faster ways to get from Mount Rushmore to the southern Black Hills, this scenic drive in the Black Hills is a more stunning route. Take U.S. 16A south into Custer State Park, where bison, bighorn sheep, elk, antelope, and burros roam free. Then drive north on Highway 87 through the Needles, towering granite spires that rise above the forest. A short drive off the highway reaches 7,242-foot Harney Peak, the highest point in North America east of the Rockies. Highway 87 finally brings you to U.S. 16/U.S. 385, where you head south to the Crazy Horse Memorial. Because the scenic byway is a challenging drive (with one-lane tunnels and switchbacks) and because you'll likely want to stop a few times to admire the scenery, plan on spending two to three hours on this drive. Stretches of U.S. 16A and Highway 87 may close in winter. ⊠ *Keystone* ⊕ *www.fhwa.dot. gov/byways.*

Spearfish Canyon Scenic Byway

SCENIC DRIVE | The easiest way to get from Deadwood to Rapid City is east through Boulder Canyon on U.S. 14A. However, it's worth looping north and taking the long way around Spearfish Canyon Scenic Byway, on this 20-mile scenic route past 1,000-foot limestone cliffs and some of the most breathtaking scenery in the region. Cascading waterfalls quench the thirst of quaking aspen, gnarled oaks, sweet-smelling spruce, and the ubiquitous ponderosa pine. The canyon is home to deer, mountain goats, porcupines, and mountain lions. Near its middle is the old sawmill town of Savoy, a jumping-off point for scenic hikes to Spearfish Falls and Roughlock Falls. In fall, changing leaves rival any found in New England. ⊠ *10619 Roughlock Falls Rd.* ⊕ *www. spearfishcanyon.com.*

CUSTER

Crazy Horse Memorial

NATIVE SITE | FAMILY | Designed to be the world's largest work of art, this tribute to the spirit of the North American Native people depicts Crazy Horse, the legendary Lakota leader who helped defeat General Custer at Little Bighorn. A work in progress, thus far the warrior's head has been carved from the mountain, and the colossal head of his horse is beginning to emerge. Self-taught sculptor Korczak Ziolkowski started this memorial in 1948. After his death in 1982, his family carried on the project. Near the work site stands an exceptional orientation center, the Indian Museum of North America, Ziolkowski's home and workshop, and the Indian University of North America. If you're visiting in summer, come in the afternoon, and stick around for the spectacular laser-light show, held nightly from Memorial Day through late September. ⊠ *12151 Ave. of the Chiefs, Crazy Horse Memorial* ⊹ *Hwy. 385, 5 miles north of Custer* ☎ *605/673–4681* ⊕ *crazyhorsememorial.org* ⊠ *$12.*

★ Custer State Park

NATIONAL/STATE PARK | FAMILY | This 71,000-acre park is considered the crown jewel of South Dakota's state park system. Elk, antelope, mountain goats, bighorn sheep, mountain lions, wild turkey, prairie dogs, and the second-largest (behind Yellowstone National Park) publicly owned herd of bison in the world roam this pristine landscape. Scenic drives roll past finger-like granite spires and panoramic views (try the Needles Highway). Take the 18-mile Wildlife Loop Road to see prairies teeming with animals and some of the beautiful backdrops for countless Western films. Accommodations here are outstanding, too, with numerous campgrounds and a resort network that includes five amenities-filled lodges and seven well-appointed vacation cabins. ⊠ *13329 U.S. 16A, Custer* ⊹ *4 miles east of Custer* ☎ *605/255–4515* ⊕ *gfp.sd.gov/*

parks/detail/custer-state-park ✉ From $20.

Jewel Cave National Monument

CAVE | Even though its more than 195 miles of surveyed passages make this cave the country's second largest (after Kentucky's Mammoth Cave), Jewel Cave isn't renowned for its size. Rather, it's the rare crystalline formations that abound in the cave's vast passages. Wander the dark passageways and you'll be rewarded with the sight of tiny crystal Christmas trees, hydromagnesite balloons that would pop if you touched them, and delicate calcite deposits dubbed "cave popcorn." Year-round, you can take ranger-led tours for a fee, from a simple half-hour walk to a lantern-light tour. Surface trails and facilities are free. ✉ 11149 U.S. Hwy. 16, Custer ✛ 15 miles west of Custer ☎ 605/673–8300 ⊕ www.nps.gov/jeca ✉ Tours from $12.

DEADWOOD

Adams Museum

MUSEUM | FAMILY | Between the massive stone-block post office and the old railroad depot, there are three floors of displays at the Adams Museum, including the region's first locomotive, photographs of the town's early days, and an exhibit featuring Potato Creek Johnny's Gold Nugget, the second-largest nugget ever discovered in the Black Hills. The Adams Museum is affiliated with Deadwood History, Inc., which also oversees the Days of 76 Museum, the Historic Adams House, and a cultural center and archives. ✉ 54 Sherman St., Deadwood ☎ 605/578–1714 ⊕ www.deadwoodhistory.com ✉ Free.

Broken Boot Gold Mine

MINE | FAMILY | You're guaranteed to find gold on a panning experience here. If you take the short, guided mine tour, you'll also get a souvenir stock certificate. ✉ U.S. 14A, 1200 Pioneer Way, Deadwood ☎ 605/578–9997 ⊕ www.brokenbootgoldmine.com ✉ Gold panning $8, tour $6 ☉ Closed early Sept.–late May.

HOT SPRINGS

Black Hills Wild Horse Sanctuary

NATURE PRESERVE | More than 600 wild mustangs inhabit this 11,000-acre preserve of rugged canyons, forests, and grasslands along the Cheyenne River. Guided bus tours (no reservations required) take place several times daily June through September; throughout the year, you can also make reservations for photography, custom, and other tours. The drive south from Hot Springs is about 14 miles. This is rattlesnake country, so hiking is not encouraged. ✉ 12165 Highland Rd. (Rte. 71), Hot Springs ☎ 605/745–5955 ⊕ www.wildmustangs.com ✉ From $50.

★ Mammoth Site

ARCHAEOLOGICAL SITE | FAMILY | While building a housing development in the 1970s, workers uncovered this sinkhole where giant mammoths came to drink, got trapped, and died. To date, 61 fossilized woolly beasts have been discovered, and most can still be seen on-site. You can watch the excavation in progress and take guided tours. ✉ 1800 W. Hwy. 18 Bypass, 15 miles south of Wind Cave National Park, Hot Springs ☎ 605/745–6017 ⊕ www.mammothsite.com ✉ $10, with last guided tour at 4 daily.

KEYSTONE

Beautiful Rushmore Cave

CAVE | FAMILY | Stalagmites, stalactites, flowstone, ribbons, columns, helictites, and the "Big Room" are all part of the worthwhile tour into this cave. In 1876, miners found the opening to the cave while digging a flume into the mountainside to carry water to the gold mines below. The cave was opened to the public in 1927, just before the carving of Mount Rushmore began. The attraction also features the Soaring Eagle Zipride, Rushmore Mountain Coaster, and Wingwalker Challenge Course. ✉ 13622 Hwy. 40, Keystone ☎ 605/255–4384 ⊕ www.rushmtn.com ✉ From $16 ☉ Closed Nov.–Feb.

★ Mount Rushmore

MEMORIAL | FAMILY | Abraham Lincoln was tall in real life—6 feet, 4 inches, though add a few more for his hat. But at one of the nation's most famous iconic sights, Honest Abe, along with presidents George Washington, Thomas Jefferson, and Theodore Roosevelt, towers over the Black Hills in a 60-foot-high likeness. The four images look especially spectacular at night, when they're always illuminated.

Follow the Presidential Trail through the forest to gain excellent views of the colossal sculpture, or stroll the Avenue of Flags for a different perspective. Also on-site are an impressive museum, indoor theaters where films are shown, an outdoor amphitheater for live performances, an award-winning audio tour, and concession facilities. The nightly ranger program and special memorial lighting ceremony (June through mid-September) is reportedly the most popular interpretive program in all of the national parks system.

Some of the attractions at Mount Rushmore include:

Avenue of the Flags: Running from the entrance of the memorial to the museum and amphitheater at the base of the mountain, this avenue has the flag of each state, commonwealth, district, and territory—arranged alphabetically—of the United States.

Lakota, Nakota and Dakota Heritage Village: Along the first section of the Presidential Trail, this area focuses on the culture of the region's indigenous tribes. In summer, rangers give twice-daily talks that highlight local Native American traditions.

Lincoln Borglum Museum: This giant granite-and-glass structure underneath the viewing platform has a bookstore; two theaters that show the 14-minute film, *Mount Rushmore, the Shrine* every 20 minutes; and a museum with temporary and permanent exhibits on the carving of the mountain, its history, and its significance. Admission is free.

Presidential Trail: This easy hike along a boardwalk and down some stairs leads to the very base of the mountain. Although the trail is thickly forested, you'll have more than ample opportunity to look straight up the noses of the four giant heads. The trail is open year-round, so long as snow and/or ice don't present a safety hazard.

Sculptor's Studio: Built in 1939 as Gutzon Borglum's on-site workshop, this studio displays tools used by the mountain carvers, a model of the memorial, and a model depicting the unfinished Hall of Records. The studio underwent renovations and was closed throughout 2018 and early 2019; check the park website for the latest on hours and offerings.

Youth Exploration Area: At this stone and wood structure, along the Presidential Trail beneath the towering visage of George Washington, rangers present interactive programs for youngsters. ⊠ *13000 Hwy. 244, Mount Rushmore* ☎ *605/574–2523* ⊕ *www.nps.gov/moru* ⊠ *Free; parking from $10 per vehicle.*

Mount Rushmore Information Center

MEMORIAL | Between the park entrance and the Avenue of Flags, the Mount Rushmore Information Center has a small exhibit of photographs detailing the carving of the presidents' faces. The information desk is staffed by rangers who can answer questions about the area. A nearly identical building across from the information center houses restrooms, telephones, soda machines, and an award-winning audio tour by the nonprofit Mount Rushmore History Association. ⊠ *13000 Hwy. 244, Keystone* ☎ *605/574–2523* ⊕ *www.nps.gov/moru* ⊠ *Free; parking from $10 per vehicle.*

RAPID CITY

★ Bear Country U.S.A.

ZOO | FAMILY | Encounter black bear, elk, sheep, and wolves at this drive-through

In the fall, listen to elk bugling, a high-pitched whistle the animals make as they mate.

wildlife park, which has been entertaining guests for more than 40 years. There's also a walk-through wildlife center with red foxes, porcupines, badgers, bobcats, and lynx. The Babyland area features bear cubs and young otters. ✉ *13820 S. U.S. 16, Rapid City* ☎ *605/343–2290* ⊕ *www. bearcountryusa.com* ✉ *$17, with a maximum per vehicle of $65* ⊗ *Closed late Nov.–late Apr.*

Black Hills Caverns

CAVE | FAMILY | Amethysts, logomites, calcite crystals, and other specimens fill this cave, first discovered by gold-seekers in 1882. Half-hour and hour tours, as well as gemstone and fossil mining, are available. ✉ *2600 Cavern Rd., Rapid City* ☎ *605/343–0542, 800/837–9358* ⊕ *www. blackhillscaverns.com* ✉ *From $16* ⊗ *Closed Nov.–mid-May.*

Reptile Gardens

ZOO | FAMILY | In the valley between Rapid City and Mount Rushmore is western South Dakota's answer to a zoo. In addition to the world's largest private reptile collection, it also has giant tortoises, prairie dogs, and a bald eagle as well as animal presentations and shows. You can also see more than 50,000 orchids, tulips, and banana trees on the grounds and in the giant Sky Dome. ✉ *8955 S. U.S. 16, Rapid City* ☎ *605/342–5873, 800/335–0275* ⊕ *www.reptilegardens. com* ✉ *From $14; $18 in summer* ⊗ *Closed Dec.–Feb.*

SPEARFISH

High Plains Western Heritage Center

MUSEUM | FAMILY | Focusing on a region now covered by five states—the Dakotas, Wyoming, Montana, and Nebraska—this center features artifacts such as a Deadwood-Spearfish stagecoach. Outdoor exhibits include a log cabin, a one-room schoolhouse, and, in summer, an entire farm set up with antique equipment. Often on the calendar are cowboy poetry, a cowboy supper and show, live music, and historical talks. ✉ *825 Heritage Dr., Spearfish* ☎ *605/642–9378* ⊕ *www.westernheritagecenter.com* ✉ *$10.*

Building Mount Rushmore

Like most impressive undertakings, Mount Rushmore's path to realization was one of personalities and perseverance.

When Gutzon Borglum, a talented and patriotic sculptor, was invited to create a giant monument to Confederate soldiers in Georgia in 1915, he jumped at the chance. The son of Danish immigrants, Borglum was raised in California and trained in art in Paris, even studying under Auguste Rodin, who influenced his style. Georgia's Stone Mountain project was to be massive in scope—encompassing the rock face of an entire peak—and would give Borglum the opportunity to exercise his artistic vision on a grand scale.

But the relationship between the project backers and Borglum went sour, causing the sculptor to destroy his models and flee the state. South Dakota state officials had a vision for another mountain memorial, and Borglum was eager to jump on board.

His passion and flamboyant personality were well matched to the project, which involved carving legends of the Wild West on a gigantic scale. In time, Borglum convinced officials to think larger, and the idea of carving a monument to U.S. presidents was born.

On a massive granite cliff, at an elevation of 5,725 feet, Borglum began carving Mount Rushmore in 1927 with the help of some 400 assistants. In consultation with U.S. Senator Peter Norbeck and State Historian Doane Robinson, Borglum chose the four presidents to signify the birth, growth, preservation, and development of the nation. In 6½ years of carving over a 14-year period, the sculptor and his crew drilled and dynamited a masterpiece, the largest work of art on earth. Borglum died in March 1941, leaving his son, Lincoln, to complete the work only a few months later—in the wake of the gathering storm of World War II.

Activities

The Black Hills are a haven for outdoor enthusiasts, and with good reason. The warmer temperatures of spring and summer make for excellent fishing, hiking, mountain climbing, mountain biking, camping, and horseback riding in the national forest. Autumn's cooler weather and changing colors bring out the leaf peepers, and the hunters aren't far behind. Snow can fall as early as October, but really starts coming down in December and January, when snowmobilers and skiers (both downhill and cross-country) come out to play. The northern Black Hills, where there are two ski areas, generally receive the highest

accumulations, and have seen up to 180 inches of annual snowfall.

FISHING
The Black Hills are filled with tiny mountain creeks, especially on the wetter western and northern slopes, that are ideal for fly-fishing. Rapid Creek, which flows down from the Central Hills into Pactola Reservoir and finally into Rapid City, is a favorite fishing venue for the city's anglers, both because of its regularly stocked population of trout and for its easy accessibility.

South Dakota Game, Fish, and Parks
FISHING | Besides the local chambers of commerce, South Dakota Game, Fish, and Parks is your best bet for updated

The colossal Mount Rushmore is one of the United States' most majestic monuments.

information on regional fishing locations and their conditions. ✉ *523 E. Capitol Ave., Pierre* ☎ *605/223–7660* ⊕ *gfp. sd.gov.*

HIKING AND BICYCLING
Mickelson Trail

TRAIL | Beginning in Deadwood and running the length of the Black Hills, the Mickelson Trail incorporates more than 100 converted railroad bridges, four tunnels, and 15 trailheads along its 109-mile-long course. Although the grade is seldom steep, parts of the trail are strenuous. A $4 day pass or $15 annual pass are available at self-service stations along the trail, some state park offices, and from the South Dakota Game, Fish & Parks. A portion of the trail is open for snowmobiling in winter. ✉ *Deadwood* ☎ *605/584–3896* ⊕ *gfp.sd.gov/parks/ detail/george-s–mickelson-trail.*

WATER SPORTS
Angostura Reservoir State Recreation Area

WATER SPORTS | Water-based recreation is the main draw at this park 10 miles south of Hot Springs. Besides a marina,

you'll find a floating convenience store, restaurant, campgrounds, and cabins. Boat rentals are available. ✉ *U.S. 385, off Rte. 79, 13157 N. Angostura Rd., Hot Springs* ☎ *605/745–6996, 800/710–2267 for reservations* ⊕ *gfp.sd.gov/parks/ detail/angostura-recreation-area* 🎟 *From $6 per vehicle.*

WINTER ACTIVITIES

Heavy snowfalls and lovely views make the Black Hills prime cross-country skiing territory. Many trails are open to snowmobilers as well as skiers. Trade and travel magazines consistently rank the Black Hills among the top snowmobiling destinations in the country for two simple reasons: dramatic scenery and an abundance of snow.

Terry Peak Ski Area

SNOW SPORTS | Perched on the sides of a 7,076-foot mountain, Terry Peak claims the Black Hills' second-highest summit and high-speed quad lifts. The runs are challenging for novice and intermediate skiers and should also keep the experts entertained. From the top, on a clear day, you can see Wyoming, Montana, and North Dakota. **Facilities:** 28 trails; 450 acres; 1,100-foot vertical drop; 5 lifts. ⊠ *21120 Stewart Slope Rd., Lead* ✛ *2 miles south of Lead on U.S. 85* ☎ *800/456–0524, 605/584–2165* ⊕ *www. terrypeak.com* ✉ *Lift ticket: $56.*

Trailshead Lodge

SNOW SPORTS | Near the Wyoming border, this lodge has a small restaurant and bar, cabins, a gas station and garage, and dozens of brand-new snowmobiles for rent by the day. This is a favorite pit-stop for snowmobilers exploring the popular Black Hills' 400-mile trail network. ⊠ *22075 U.S. 85 S, Lead* ✛ *21 miles southwest of Lead on U.S. 85* ☎ *605/584–3464* ⊕ *www.trailshead-lodge.com.*

 Performing Arts

Rushmore Plaza Civic Center Fine Arts Theater

THEATER | This is the venue for a half-dozen touring Broadway shows and the Vucurevich Speaker Series, which has attracted prominent names such as the violinist Itzhak Perlman and Apple co-founder Steve Wozniak. There's also an ice rink where the Rush ECHL hockey team plays in winter months. A new, 12,000-capacity arena is also in the works. ⊠ *444 Mt. Rushmore Rd. N, Rapid City* ☎ *800/468–6463, 605/394–4115* ⊕ *www.gotmine.com.*

 Nightlife

★ Old Style Saloon No. 10

BARS/PUBS | Billing itself as "the world's only museum with a bar," the Old Style Saloon No. 10 is where you want to come to drink, listen to music, and socialize. Thousands of artifacts, vintage photos, and a two-headed calf set the scene—plus the chair in which Wild Bill Hickok was supposedly shot. A reenactment of his murder takes place four times daily in summer. Upstairs, there's

an exceptional restaurant, the Deadwood Social Club, with the state's premier wine and martini bar. ⊠ *657 Main St., Deadwood* ☎ *605/578–3346* ⊕ *www. saloon10.com.*

Silverado

BARS/PUBS | Sprawling over half a city block at the top of Main Street, and including the historic Franklin Hotel across the street, the Silverado is among Deadwood's largest gaming establishments. Although the wood paneling and brass accents around the bars recall Deadwood's Wild West past, the red carpets, velvet ropes, and bow-tie-clad staff give the place modern polish. ⊠ *Silverado Franklin Historic Hotel & Gaming Complex, 709 Main St., Deadwood* ☎ *605/578–3670* ⊕ *www.silveradofranklin.com.*

 Shopping

★ Prairie Edge Trading Company and Galleries

CRAFTS | One of the world's top collections of Plains Native American artwork and crafts makes Prairie Edge Trading Company and Galleries seem more like a museum than a store. The collection ranges from books to stunning artwork representing the Lakota, Crow, Cheyenne, Shoshone, Arapaho, and Assiniboine tribes of the Great Plains. ⊠ *6th and Main Sts., Rapid City* ☎ *605/342–3086* ⊕ *www.prairieedge.com.*

 Restaurants

IN THE PARK
PICNIC AREAS
Elk Mountain Campground Picnic Area

RESTAURANT—SIGHT | You don't have to be a camper to use this well-developed picnic spot, with more than 70 tables, fire grates (some of them heightened to accommodate people with disabilities), and restrooms. Some of the tables are on the prairie, others sit amid the pines.

✉ *Wind Cave National Park ✛ ½ mile north of visitor center.*

Wind Cave Picnic Area

$ | **NATIONAL/STATE PARK** | |**NATIONAL/STATE PARK** | On the edge of a prairie and grove of ponderosa, this is a peaceful, pretty place ¼ mile from the visitor center. Small and simple, it's equipped with 12 tables and a potable-water pump. ✉ *Wind Cave National Park ✛ ¼ mile north of visitor center ⊕ www.nps.gov/ wica.*

OUTSIDE THE PARK

Alpine Inn

$$ | **STEAKHOUSE** | With its pastoral paintings, lacy tablecloths, and beer steins, the rustic Alpine Inn brings a version of old-world charm to the Old West. The lunchtime menu changes daily but always has selections of healthful sandwiches and salads—and no fried food. $ *Average main: $12* ✉ *133 Main St., Hill City* ☎ *605/574–2749* ⊕ *www. alpineinnhillcity.com* ▭ *No credit cards* ☽ *Closed Sun.*

Blue Bell Lodge and Resort

$$ | **AMERICAN** | Feast on fresh walleye or buffalo, which you can have as a steak or a stew, in this rustic log building within the boundaries of Custer State Park. There's also a good selection of salads as well as kid-friendly burgers, sandwiches, and wraps. **Known for:** park setting; interesting dining experiences; family-friendly. $ *Average main: $20* ✉ *Custer State Park, 25453 S.D. 87, Custer* ☎ *605/255– 4531* ⊕ *www.custerresorts.com/blue-bell-lodge* ☽ *Closed late Oct.–late Apr.*

Botticelli Ristorante Italiano

$$ | **ITALIAN** | With a wide selection of delectable veal and chicken dishes as well as creamy pastas and a critically acclaimed wine list, this Italian eatery provides a welcome respite from the traditional Midwestern meat and potatoes. The artwork and traditional Italian music in the background give the place a European air. **Known for:** authentic Italian food and atmosphere; terrific wine list; attentive service. $ *Average main: $20* ✉ *523 Main St., Rapid City* ☎ *605/348– 0089* ☽ *No lunch Sun.*

Carvers Cafe

$ | **AMERICAN** | The only restaurant at the Mount Rushmore Memorial affords commanding views of the memorial and the surrounding ponderosa pine forest. It serves exceptional food at reasonable prices. **Known for:** terrific park views; fantastic ice cream; sustainably sourced ingredients. $ *Average main: $8* ✉ *Ave. of Flags, Keystone* ☎ *605/574–2515* ⊕ *www.mtrushmorenationalmemorial. com/dining/carvers-cafe* ☽ *No dinner mid-Oct.–early Mar.*

★ Deadwood Social Club

$$ | **ITALIAN** | On the second floor of historic Saloon No. 10, this warm restaurant surrounds you with wood and old-time photographs of Deadwood. Light jazz and blues play over the sound system. **Known for:** eclectic Italian menu; great martinis; historic setting. $ *Average main: $20* ✉ *657 Main St., Deadwood* ☎ *605/578– 3346* ⊕ *www.saloon10.com.*

Laughing Water

$ | **AMERICAN** | **FAMILY** | With windows facing the mountain sculpture, this airy pine restaurant is noted for its fry bread and buffalo burgers. There's a soup-and-salad bar, but you'd do well to stick to the Native American offerings. **Known for:** monumental views; generous portions; amazing fry bread. $ *Average main: $10* ✉ *12151 Ave. of the Chiefs, Custer* ☎ *605/673–4681* ⊕ *crazyhorsememorial. org/laughing-water-restaurant.html.*

Legends Steakhouse

$$$ | **STEAKHOUSE** | In a place where legends aren't taken lightly, this establishment in the lower level of the historic Franklin Hotel has quickly made a name for itself, beckoning back locals who like its aged beef, moderate prices, and flair. You'll find all the usual suspects on the menu—buffalo, beef, and

Best Campgrounds in Wind Cave

Camping is one of this region's strengths. While there is only one primitive campground within the park, there are countless campgrounds in the Black Hills. The public campgrounds in the national forest are accessible by road but otherwise secluded and undeveloped; private campgrounds typically have more amenities as do some of those in Custer State Park, which has numerous options.

Elk Mountain Campground. If you prefer a relatively developed campsite and relative proximity to civilization, Elk Mountain is an excellent choice. You can experience the peaceful pine forests and wild creatures of the park without straying too far from the safety of the beaten path. ✉ *½ mile north of visitor center* ☎ 605/745–4600.

chicken—but each with a flavorful twist. **Known for:** local hangout; meat-eater's dream; festive ambience. [$] *Average main: $23* ✉ *Silverado Franklin Historic Hotel & Gaming Complex, 709 Main St., Deadwood* ☎ *605/578–3670* 🌐 *www.silveradofranklin.com/food-drink/legends-steakhouse* ⏲ *No lunch.*

Golden Phoenix

$ | **CHINESE** | Great food, low prices, and relaxed, friendly, and quick service make this one of South Dakota's best Chinese restaurants. The chef-owner, who socializes with the locals who frequent his establishment, seasons traditional dishes from all over China with spices from his native Taiwan. **Known for:** efficient service; loved by locals; wallet-friendly prices. [$] *Average main: $10* ✉ *2421 W. Main St., Rapid City* ☎ *605/348–4195* 🌐 *goldenphoenixrc.com.*

Woolly's Western Grill

$$ | **AMERICAN** | **FAMILY** | As it's family-owned and-operated, it's no surprise that this place caters to families. Though it specializes in hand-cut steaks and prime rib, entrées on its modestly priced menu include helpings from the 18-foot salad bar. **Known for:** family-friendly; great value for money; convenient location. [$] *Average main: $15* ✉ *1648 Hwy. 18 Bypass, Hot Springs* ☎ *605/745–6414* 🌐 *www.woollys.com* ⏲ *Closed Nov.–Mar.; no lunch mid-Aug.–Nov. and Mar.–mid-May.*

Hotels

OUTSIDE THE PARK

Americas Best Value Inn by the River

$ | **HOTEL** | This two-story inn is three blocks from downtown and 10 miles south of Wind Cave. **Pros:** convenient location; along the town's River Walk. **Cons:** often busy; rooms look out onto parking lot. [$] *Rooms from: $65* ✉ *602 N.W. River St., Hot Springs* ☎ *605/745–4292, 888/605–4292* 🌐 *www.redlion.com/hot-springs* 🛏 *34 rooms* 🍴 *No meals.*

★ Audrie's and Abend Haus Cottage

$$$$ | **B&B/INN** | Victorian antiques and a hint of romance greet you at this out-of-the-way B&B, set in a thick woods 7 miles west of Rapid City. **Pros:** great antiques; friendly owner; inspiring isolation. **Cons:** fills up fast; cabins lack phones; no restaurant within walking distance. [$] *Rooms from: $205* ✉ *23029 Thunderhead Falls Rd., Rapid City* ☎ *605/342–7788* 🌐 *www.audriesbb.com* 💳 *No credit cards* 🛏 *7 accommodations* 🍴 *No meals.*

Buffalo Rock Lodge B&B
$$$ | **B&B/INN** | A native-rock fireplace surrounded by hefty logs adds to the rustic quality of this lodge. **Pros:** quiet location; exceptional furnishings; view of Mount Rushmore from deck. **Cons:** relatively pricey; drive to shopping and dining; no TVs. [$] *Rooms from: $175* ✉ *24524 Playhouse Rd., Keystone* ☎ *605/666–4781, 888/564–5634* 🌐 *www.buffalorock.net* 🛏 *7 rooms* 🍴 *No meals.*

Bullock Hotel
$$ | **HOTEL** | A casino occupies the main floor of this meticulously restored hotel, a pink granite structure built by Deadwood's first sheriff in 1895. **Pros:** central location; historic property; unusual rooms. **Cons:** some rooms are dated; busy place; some traffic noise. [$] *Rooms from: $139* ✉ *633 Main St., Deadwood* ☎ *605/578–1745, 800/336–1876* 🌐 *www.historicbullock.com* 🛏 *30 rooms* 🍴 *No meals.*

Deadwood Gulch Gaming Resort
$ | **RESORT** | Pine-clad hills, a creek, and a deck from which to view the mountains are at your disposal at this family-style resort about a mile from downtown Deadwood. **Pros:** away from downtown bustle; spacious rooms; attentive staff. **Cons:** more hotel than resort; busy with bus tours. [$] *Rooms from: $99* ✉ *304 Cliff St., Deadwood* ☎ *605/578–1294, 800/695–1876* 🌐 *www.deadwoodgulch.com* 🛏 *87 rooms* 🍴 *Breakfast.*

Holiday Inn Express & Suites
$$ | **HOTEL** | Although the exterior of this four-story hotel resembles the brick facades of Deadwood's Main Street, its interior is contemporary, with guest rooms that have Wi-Fi, free high-speed Internet connection, and other modern amenities. **Pros:** in the heart of town; contemporary comforts; reliable brand. **Cons:** street-facing rooms can be loud; no on-site parking; standard chain decor. [$] *Rooms from: $145* ✉ *22 Lee St., Deadwood* ☎ *605/578–3330, 877/859–5095* 🌐 *www.ihg.com* 🛏 *100 rooms* 🍴 *Breakfast.*

Holiday Inn Rushmore Plaza
$$$ | **HOTEL** | This eight-story hotel has a central lobby with an atrium, glass elevators, and a 60-foot waterfall. **Pros:** excellent atrium and waterfall; good food in restaurant; nice bartenders in lounge. **Cons:** sterile feel; fairly long walk to restaurants; limited parking. [$] *Rooms from: $180* ✉ *505 N. 5th St., Rapid City* ☎ *605/348–4000, 800/315–2621* 🌐 *www.rushmoreplaza.com* 🛏 *205 rooms, 1 suite* 🍴 *Breakfast.*

K Bar S Lodge
$$$ | **HOTEL** | This contemporary lodge on 45 pine-clad acres feels as if it's stood here for a century. **Pros:** excellent staff; exceptional food; amid a wildlife preserve. **Cons:** quite a walk to dining options; pricey rates; often full. [$] *Rooms from: $180* ✉ *434 Old Hill City Rd., Keystone* ☎ *866/522–7724, 605/666–4545* 🌐 *www.kbarslodge.com* 🛏 *96 rooms* 🍴 *Breakfast.*

Silverado Franklin Historic Hotel & Gaming Complex
$ | **HOTEL** | Opened in 1903, this imposing hotel has welcomed many famous guests, including John Wayne, Teddy Roosevelt, and Babe Ruth. **Pros:** at the top of Main Street; spacious rooms; historic. **Cons:** guest rooms are tired and lack amenities; service can be patchy; casino-hotel vibe not for everyone. [$] *Rooms from: $89* ✉ *700 Main St., Deadwood* ☎ *605/578–3670, 800/584–7005* 🌐 *www.silveradofranklin.com* 🛏 *81 rooms* 🍴 *No meals.*

Spearfish Canyon Lodge
$$$ | **RESORT** | Midway between Spearfish and Deadwood, this lodge-style hotel commands some of the best views in the Black Hills. **Pros:** wonderful location; lots of good-value outdoor-activity packages; as pretty as it gets. **Cons:** remote location; half-hour drive to restaurants; standard rooms. [$] *Rooms from: $152*

✉ *10619 Roughlock Falls Rd., Lead* ☎ *877/975–6343, 605/584–3435* ⊕ *www. spfcanyon.com* ⇨ *55 rooms* ⊙ *No meals.*

State Game Lodge and Resort

$$$ | **RESORT** | Once the "Summer White House" for President Calvin Coolidge, this classic stone-and-wood lodge is the largest of Custer State Park's hotels. **Pros:** historic; has the regal feel of some of America's great Western lodges; park location. **Cons:** often booked up; small lobby can get busy; must drive to other restaurants. $ *Rooms from: $180* ✉ *U.S. 16A, Custer* ✛ *16 miles east of Custer* ☎ *605/255–4541, 888/875–0001* ⊕ *www. custerresorts.com* ⇨ *7 lodge rooms, 40 motel rooms, 33 cabins* ⊙ *No meals.*

Sylvan Lake Resort

$$$ | **RESORT** | **FAMILY** | This spacious stone-and-wood lodge in Custer State Park affords fantastic views of pristine Sylvan Lake and Harney Peak, the highest point in the U.S. east of the Rockies. **Pros:** wonderful views; multitude of lodging options; alpine atmosphere. **Cons:** on a winding road; limited dining options;

can be pricey. $ *Rooms from: $160* ✉ *24572 S.D. 87, Custer* ☎ *605/574–2561, 888/875–0001* ⊕ *www.custerresorts. com* ⊙ *Closed Oct.–Mother's Day* ⇨ *66 accommodations* ⊙ *No meals.*

USA Stay Hotel & Suites

$ | **HOTEL** | This independent hotel features standard rooms as well as a spacious breakfast area, indoor hot tub, and convenient location. **Pros:** friendly staff; close to food and attractions. **Cons:** just off a truck route; standard chain rooms. $ *Rooms from: $95* ✉ *1401 Hwy. 18 Bypass, Hot Springs* ☎ *605/745–4411* ⊕ *www.stayusahotel.com* ⇨ *86 rooms* ⊙ *Breakfast.*

Chapter 35

YELLOWSTONE NATIONAL PARK

Updated by
Stina Sieg

WYOMING

WELCOME TO YELLOWSTONE NATIONAL PARK

TOP REASONS TO GO

★ **Hot spots:** Thinner-than-normal crust depth and a huge magma chamber beneath the park explain Yellowstone's abundant geysers, steaming pools, hissing fumaroles, and bubbling mud pots.

★ **Bison:** They're just one of many species that roam freely here. Seemingly docile, the bison make your heart race if you catch them stampeding across Lamar Valley.

★ **Hiking:** Yellowstone has more than 1,000 miles of trails, along which you can summit a 10,000-foot peak, follow a trout-filled creek, or descend into the Grand Canyon of the Yellowstone.

★ **Yellowstone Lake:** Here you can fish, boat, kayak, stargaze, and bird-watch on black obsidian beaches—just don't stray too far into the frigid water.

★ **Canyon:** The Yellowstone River runs through the park, creating a deep yellow-tinged canyon with two impressive waterfalls.

1 Grant Village/West Thumb. Named for President Ulysses S. Grant, Grant Village is on the western edge of Yellowstone Lake.

2 Old Faithful area. Old Faithful erupts every 90 minutes or so. The geyser site is a full-service area with inns, restaurants, and general stores.

3 Madison. Here the Madison River is formed by the joining of the Gibbon and Firehole rivers. Anglers will find healthy stocks of brown and rainbow trout and mountain whitefish.

4 Norris. The Norris area is the hottest and most changeable part of Yellowstone National Park.

5 Mammoth Hot Springs. This full-service fortlike area has an inn, restaurants, campsites, a visitor center, and general stores.

6 Tower-Roosevelt. The least-visited area of the park is the place to go for horseback riding and animal sightings.

7 Canyon area. The Yellowstone River runs through the canyon, exposing geothermally altered rock.

8 Lake area. Yellowstone Lake is the largest body of water within the park. This is a full-service area.

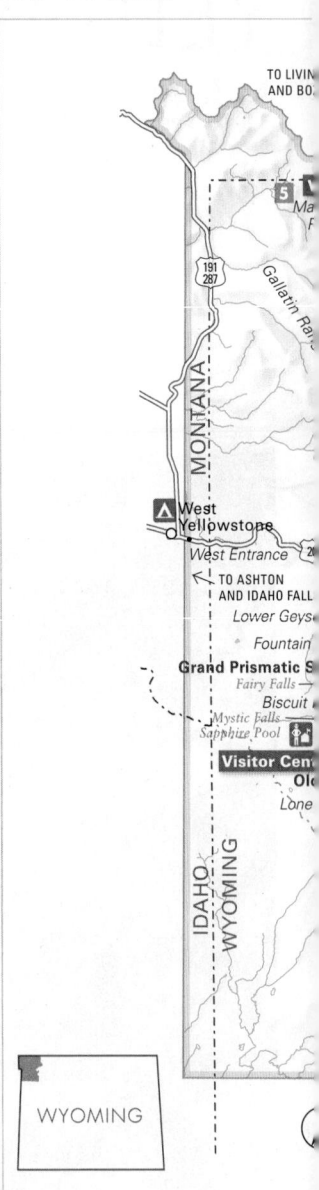

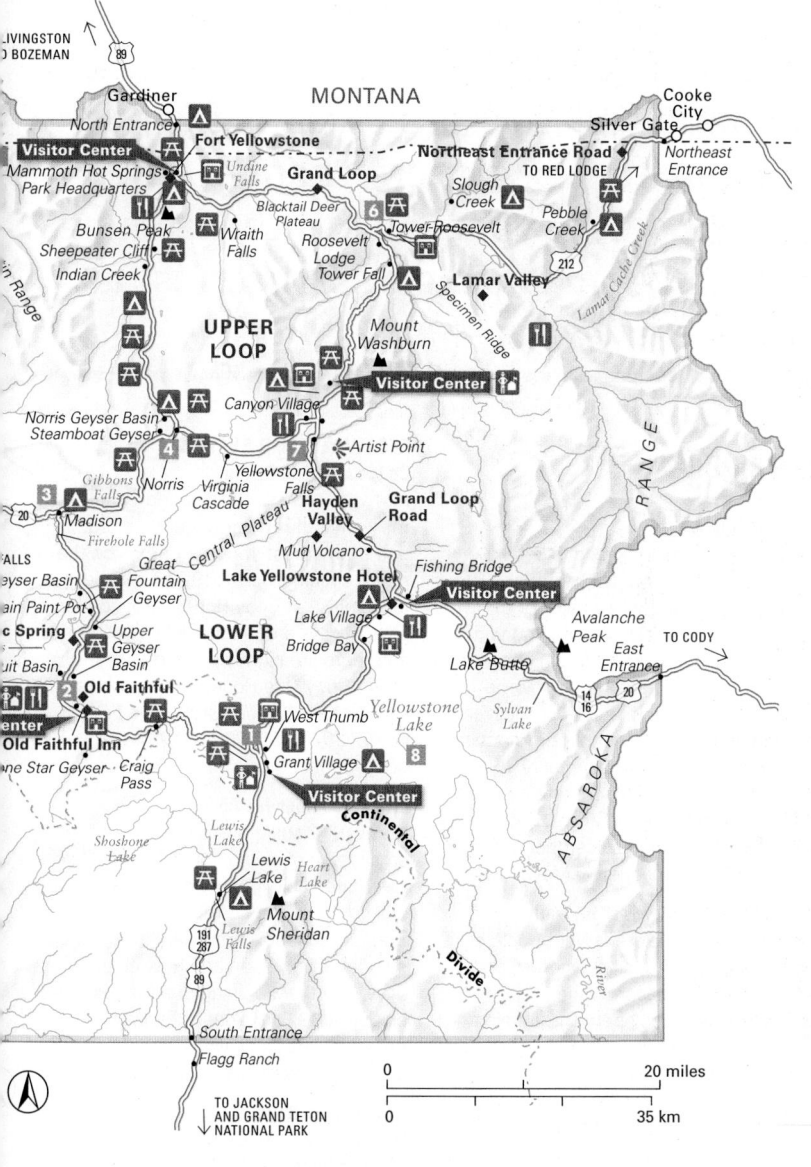

A trip to Yellowstone has been a rich part of the American experience for five generations now. Geysers, mud pots, fumaroles, and hot springs make this magma-filled pressure cooker of a park unlike any place else on Earth. If you're not here for the geysers, chances are that you've come to spot some of the teeming wildlife, from grazing bison to cruising trumpeter swans.

Planning

WHEN TO GO

There are two major seasons in Yellowstone: summer (from May through October), the only time when most of the park's roads are open to cars; and winter (from mid-December through February), when over-snow travel—on snowmobiles, snow coaches, and skis—delivers a fraction of the number of summer visitors to a frigid, bucolic sanctuary. Except for services at park headquarters at Mammoth Hot Springs, the park closes from October to mid-December and from March to late April or early May.

You'll find big crowds from mid-July to mid-August. There are fewer people in the park the month or two before and after this peak season, but there are also fewer facilities open. There's also more rain, especially at lower elevations. Except for holiday weekends, there are few visitors in winter. Snow is possible year-round at high elevations.

FESTIVALS AND EVENTS

Cody Stampede Rodeo

FESTIVAL | FAMILY | The "Rodeo Capital of the World" has hosted the Stampede, one of the most important stops on the rodeo circuit, since 1919. The main event takes place at Cody Rodeo Grounds for several days around the July 4 holiday, and there are nightly performances at the Cody Nite Rodeo. Ticket prices vary. ⊠ *421 W. Yellowstone Ave., Cody* ☎ *307/587–5155, 800/207–0744* ⊕ *www.codystampederodeo.com.*

Livingston Roundup Rodeo

FESTIVAL | FAMILY | Since the 1920s, the small town of Livingston, Montana, has celebrated July 4 with riding, roping, bull-dogging, and barrel racing at the Roundup Rodeo. The revelry includes a parade on July 2, an art show all three days, and the crowning of a rodeo queen on July 4. ⊠ *Park County Fairgrounds, 46 View Vista Dr., Livingston* ☎ *406/222–3199* ⊕ *www.livingstonroundup.com.*

Old Settlers' Days

FESTIVAL | FAMILY | Celebrating Montana's pioneer history, this event in Clyde Park

(75 miles north of Yellowstone's North Entrance) includes a car show, a parade, running races, a quilt display, and entertainment. The family-friendly festival is held on the last full weekend in August. ☎ 406/794–7150 ☞ *Activities in town of Clyde Park at churches, community center, and on Main St.*

Rendezvous Royale

FESTIVAL | FAMILY | Thomas Molesworth and his renowned Western furniture helped put Cody on the map when he moved here in the 1930s. This multiday festival held in late September celebrates his legacy with an art show, auctions, a quick-draw competition, seminars, and a major furniture exhibition. One of the biggest events in Cody, much of it is free. The elegant Patrons Ball, a fundraiser, caps things off. ⌧ *Buffalo Bill Center of the West, 720 Sheridan Ave., Cody* ☎ 307/587–5002 ⊕ *www.rendezvousroyale.org.*

World Snowmobile Expo

FESTIVAL | For more than two decades, this event on the second weekend in March has presented top-notch racing and offered a sneak peek at next year's hot models. The SnowWest SnoCross attracts racers to West Yellowstone from throughout the nation. Races and events are held at various locations. Concerts take place on Friday and Saturday night. ⌧ *West Yellowstone* ☎ 406/646–7701 ⊕ *www.snowmobileexpo.com.*

PLANNING YOUR TIME
YELLOWSTONE IN ONE DAY

If you plan to spend just one full day in the park, your best approach would be to concentrate on one or two of the major areas, such as the two biggest attractions: the famous Old Faithful geyser and the Grand Canyon of the Yellowstone. En route between these attractions, you can see geothermal activity and most likely some wildlife.

Plan on at least two hours for Old Faithful, one of America's most iconic landmarks. Eruptions occur approximately 90 minutes apart, though they can be as close as 60 minutes apart. Check with the visitor center for predicted eruption times. Before and after an eruption you can explore the surrounding geyser basin and Old Faithful Inn. To the north of Old Faithful, make Grand Prismatic Spring in Midway Geyser Basin your can't-miss geothermal stop; farther north, near Madison, veer off the road to the west to do the short Firehole Canyon Drive to see the Firehole River cut a small canyon and waterfall (Firehole Falls).

If you're arriving from the east, start with sunrise at **Lake Butte, Fishing Bridge,** and the wildlife-rich **Hayden Valley** as you cross the park counterclockwise to **Old Faithful.** To try to see wolves or bears, call ahead and ask if rangers will be stationed at roadside turnouts with spotting scopes. Alternatively, hike any trail in the park at least 2 miles. Remember that you're entering the domain of wild and sometimes dangerous animals, so be alert and don't hike alone.

If you're entering through the North or Northeast Entrance, begin at dawn looking for wolves and other animals in Lamar Valley, then head to **Tower-Roosevelt** and take a horseback ride into the surrounding forest. After your ride, continue west to **Mammoth Hot Springs,** where you can hike the **Lower Terrace Interpretive Trail** past Liberty Cap and other strange, brightly colored travertine formations. If you drive 1½ miles south of the visitor center you will reach the **Upper Terrace Drive** for close-ups of hot springs. In the late afternoon, drive south, keeping an eye out for wildlife as you go—you're almost certain to see elk, bison, and possibly a bear. Alternatively, from Tower-Roosevelt you can head south to go through **Canyon Village** to see the north or south rim of the **Grand Canyon of the Yellowstone** and its waterfalls, and then head west through Norris and Madison.

AVERAGE HIGH/LOW TEMPERATURES					
JAN.	**FEB.**	**MAR.**	**APR.**	**MAY**	**JUNE**
30/10	33/12	42/17	49/28	60/32	71/41
JULY	**AUG.**	**SEPT.**	**OCT.**	**NOV.**	**DEC.**
81/45	79/45	67/37	56/30	38/22	30/12

When you reach **Old Faithful,** you can place the famous geyser into context by walking the 1½-mile **Geyser Hill Loop.** Watch the next eruption from the deck of the **Old Faithful Inn.**

GETTING HERE AND AROUND
AIR TRAVEL
Yellowstone National Park is served by airports in nearby communities, including Cody, Wyoming, a one-hour drive east; Jackson, Wyoming, one hour south; Bozeman, Montana, 90 minutes north; and West Yellowstone, Montana, just outside the park's west gate, which has only summer service. The best places to rent cars in the region are at these airports.

BUS TRAVEL
There is no commercial bus service to Yellowstone.

CAR TRAVEL
Yellowstone is well away from the interstates, so drivers make their way here on two-lane highways that are long on miles and scenery. From Interstate 80, take U.S. 191 north from Rock Springs; it's about 177 miles to Jackson, then another 60 miles north to Yellowstone. From Interstate 90, head south at Livingston, Montana, 53 miles to Gardiner and the park's North Entrance. From Bozeman travel south 90 miles to West Yellowstone.

Yellowstone has five primary entrances. Many visitors arrive through the South Entrance, north of Grand Teton National Park and Jackson, Wyoming. Other entrances are the East Entrance, with a main point of origin in Cody, Wyoming; the West Entrance at West Yellowstone, Montana, and the North Entrance at Gardiner, Montana; and the Northeast Entrance at Cooke City, Montana, which can be reached from either Cody, Wyoming, via the Chief Joseph Scenic Highway, or from Red Lodge, Montana, over the Beartooth Pass.

■ TIP➔ The best way to keep your bearings in Yellowstone is to remember that the major roads form a figure eight, known as the Grand Loop, which all entrance roads feed into. It doesn't matter at which point you begin, as you can hit most of the major sights if you follow the entire route.

The 466 miles of public roads in the park used to be riddled with potholes and had narrow shoulders—a bit tight when a motor home was pulled over to the side to capture wildlife or scenery on film. But because of the park's efforts to upgrade its roads, most of them are now smooth, if still narrow. Roadwork is likely every summer in some portion of the park—check the *Yellowstone Today* newspaper or ask a ranger. On holiday weekends road construction usually halts, so there are no construction delays for travelers. Remember, snow is possible at any time of year in almost all areas of the park.

PARK ESSENTIALS
PARK FEES AND PERMITS
Entrance fees of $35 per vehicle, $30 per motorcycle or snowmobile, or $20 per visitor 16 and older entering by foot, bike, ski, and so on, give you access for seven days. An Interagency Pass costs $80.

Fishing permits (available at ranger stations, visitor centers, and Yellowstone general stores) are required if you want to take advantage of Yellowstone's abundant lakes and streams. Live bait is

Plants and Wildlife in Yellowstone

Eighty percent of Yellowstone is forest, and the great majority of it is lodgepole pine. Miles and miles of the "telephone pole" pines were lost in a 1988 fire that burned more than 35% of the park. The fire's heat created the ideal condition for the lodgepole pine's serotinous cones to release their seeds—which now provides a stark juxtaposition between 25-year-old and 100-year-old trees.

Astonishing Scenery

Yellowstone's scenery astonishes at any time of day, though the play of light and shadow makes the visuals most appealing in early morning and late afternoon. That's exactly when you should be looking for wildlife, as most are active around dawn and dusk, moving out of the forest in search of food and water. May and June are the best months for seeing baby bison, moose, and other recent arrivals. Look for glacier lilies among the spring wildflowers and goldenrod amid the changing foliage of fall. Winter visitors see the park at its most magical, with steam billowing from geyser basins to wreath trees in ice, and elk foraging close to roads transformed into ski trails.

Where the Animals Roam

Bison, elk, and coyotes populate virtually all areas; elk and bison particularly like river valleys and the geyser basins. Moose like the marshy areas along Yellowstone Lake and in the park's northeastern corner. Wolves are most common in the Lamar Valley and areas south of Mammoth; bears are most visible in the Pelican Valley–Fishing Bridge area, near Dunraven Pass, and near Mammoth. Watch for trumpeter swans along the Yellowstone River and for sandhill cranes near the Firehole River and in Madison Valley.

not allowed, and for all native species of fish, a catch-and-release policy stands. Anglers 16 and older must purchase an $18 three-day permit, a $25 seven-day permit, or a $40 season permit. Those under 16 need a free permit or must fish under the direct supervision of an adult with a permit. A state license is not needed to fish in Yellowstone National Park.

All camping outside designated campgrounds requires a backcountry permit. For trip dates between late May (Memorial Day) and September 10, the fee is $3 per person per night. The group fee is capped at $15 per night. Day-use horseback riding does not require a permit, but overnight trips with stock are $5 per person per night with no cap. All boats, motorized or nonmotorized, including float tubes, require a permit, which cost $20 (season) or $10 (seven days) for motorized boats and $10 (annual) or $5 (seven days) for nonmotorized vessels. National Park Service rangers inspect all boats for aquatic invasive species before issuing a permit.

PARK HOURS

Depending on the weather, Yellowstone is generally open from late April through November and from mid-December to early March. In winter, only one road, going from the Northeast Entrance at Cooke City to the North Entrance at Gardiner, is open to wheeled vehicles; other roads are used by over-snow vehicles. The park is in the Mountain time zone. Yellowstone is open 24 hours a day, 365 days per year from the North Entrance at Gardiner, Montana, to Mammoth Hot

Springs, and from Mammoth Hot Springs to the Northeast Entrance and the town of Cooke City (with no through-travel beyond Cooke City).

CELL PHONE RECEPTION

There are now cell towers at Mammoth Hot Springs, West Yellowstone, Old Faithful, Grand Village, Lake Village, and Mountain Washington. Limited coverage reaches most developed areas and the North and West entrances. However, don't count on reception, especially in the summer, when the crowds can overwhelm cellular circuits. Texting often works best. Public telephones are near visitor centers and major park attractions. ■ TIP→ Try to use indoor phones rather than outdoor ones so your conversation doesn't distract you from being alert to wildlife that might approach you while you're on the phone.

EDUCATIONAL OFFERINGS

CLASSES AND SEMINARS

Yellowstone Forever

COLLEGE | FAMILY | Learn about the park's ecology, geology, history, and wildlife from park experts, including well-known geologists, biologists, and photographers. Classes last from a few hours to a few days, and rates are reasonable. Some programs are designed specifically for young people and families. ⊠ *308 W. Park St., Gardiner* ☎ *406/848–2400* ⊕ *www.yellowstone.org.*

RANGER PROGRAMS

Yellowstone offers a busy schedule of guided hikes, talks, and campfire programs. For dates and times, check the park's *Yellowstone Today* newsletter, available at all entrances and visitor centers.

Daytime Walks and Talks

NATURE PRESERVE | FAMILY | Ranger-led programs are available during all seasons. Ranger walks are held at various locations throughout the summer. Winter programs and some walks are held at West Yellowstone, Old Faithful, and

Mammoth. Check the website or park newspaper for information. ⊕ *www.nps. gov/yell/planyourvisit/ranger-programs. htm.*

Evening Programs

TOUR—SIGHT | FAMILY | Gather around to hear tales about Yellowstone's fascinating history, with hour-long programs on topics ranging from the return of the bison to 19th-century photographers. Every major area hosts programs during the summer; check visitor centers or campground bulletin boards for updates. Winter programs are held at Mammoth and Old Faithful. ⊕ *www.nps.gov/yell/ planyourvisit/ranger-programs.htm.*

Junior Ranger Program

TOUR—SIGHT | FAMILY | Children ages 4 to 12 are eligible to earn patches and become Junior Rangers. Pick up the Junior Ranger booklet at any visitor center for $3 and start the entertaining self-guided curriculum, or download it for free online. Kids five and older can also participate in the Young Scientist Program. Purchase a self-guiding booklet for $5 at the Canyon or Old Faithful visitor center and solve a science mystery. ⊕ *www.nps.gov/yell/learn/kidsyouth.*

RESTAURANTS

When traveling in Yellowstone it's always a good idea to bring along a cooler—that way you can carry some snacks and lunch items for a picnic or break and not have to worry about making it to one of the more developed areas of the park, where all restaurants and cafeterias are managed by two competing companies (Xanterra and Delaware North). Generally you'll find burgers and sandwiches at cafeterias and full meals at restaurants. The entrée selection includes beef and chicken, game meats such as elk and bison, fish like salmon and trout, and there are kids-oriented offerings. At the several delis and general stores you can purchase picnic items, snacks, sandwiches, and desserts like fudge and ice cream. Considering the park's remoteness, the selection and quality are above average, but expect to pay more as well. Reservations are needed for dinner at the Old Faithful Inn, Lake Yellowstone Hotel, and Grant Village dining rooms; during the summer reservations are recommended for all dining rooms.

HOTELS

Park lodgings range from two magnificent old hotels to simple cabins to bland modern motels. Make reservations at least two months ahead for July and August for all lodgings. Old Faithful Snow Lodge and Mammoth Hot Springs Hotel are the only accommodations open in winter; rates are the same as in summer. Ask about the size of beds, bathrooms, thickness of walls, and room location when you book, especially in the older hotels, where accommodations vary and upgrades are ongoing. Telephones have been put in most rooms, but there are no TVs. There are no roll-away beds available.

Hotel reviews have been shortened. For full information, visit Fodors.com.

What It Costs			
$	**$$**	**$$$**	**$$$$**
RESTAURANTS			
under $13	$13–$20	$21–$30	over $30
HOTELS			
under $100	$100–$150	$151–$200	over $200

TOURS

Historic Yellow Bus Tours

TOUR—SIGHT | FAMILY | Tours on bright yellow buses from as far back as the 1930s, each known as a Historic Yellow Bus, tour Yellowstone on more than a dozen itineraries. Touring in these restored buses is an elegant way to learn about the park. If the weather is warm enough, your driver, who narrates the trip, will roll back the convertible top for you to bask

under the sun. The tour lineup includes Evening Wildlife Encounters, Picture Perfect Photo Safari, and Wake Up to Wildlife, all longtime crowd-pleasers. Other tours, including some all-day ones that efficiently cover huge swaths of the park, are on newer buses. Tours depart from various locations, including the Old Faithful Inn, Mammoth Hotel, and Canyon Lodge in Canyon. ☎ 866/439–7375 ⊕ www.yellowstonenationalparklodges. com ⊠ From $40.

Tour Yellowstone

TOUR—SIGHT | These tours, ranging from half a day to several days in length, focus on topics such as photography, geology, history, and wildlife. The guides have past or current experience as rangers, nature photographers, birders, hikers, and naturalists. ⊠ 1107 Sheridan Ave., Cody ☎ 307/527–6316 ⊕ www.tourtoyellowstone.com ⊠ From $350.

Xanterra Parks & Resorts

TOUR—SIGHT | There are countless corners of the park to explore, and Xanterra, which operates most park lodging and dining, offers tours by boat, bus, horse, stagecoach, and the famed Historic Yellow Bus. In the winter you can head into the park's interior in snow coaches and on skis, snowshoes, and snowmobiles. ⊠ Mammoth Hot Springs, 1 Grand Loop Rd. ☎ 307/344–7901 ⊕ www.yellowstonenationalparklodges.com.

Yellowstone Alpen Guides Co.

SIGHTS OVERVIEW | In summer this company conducts tours that might include day hiking in the backcountry, swimming in a thermally heated river, or embarking on a photo safari. Alpine Guides also leads ski trips and winter park tours, providing a quieter way than snowmobiling to sight buffalo herds, trophy-size bull elk, and moose. ⊠ 555 Yellowstone Ave., West Yellowstone ☎ 406/646–9591, 800/858–3502 ⊕ yellowstoneguides.com ⊠ From $95 in summer; from $145 in winter ☉ Closed when park is closed.

VISITOR INFORMATION

PARK CONTACT INFORMATION Yellowstone National Park ☎ *307/344–7381* ⊕ *www.nps.gov/yell.*

VISITOR CENTERS
Albright Visitor Center

INFO CENTER | FAMILY | Bachelor quarters for U.S. Army cavalry officers from 1909 to 1918, the red-roof visitor center was totally renovated in 2015. In addition to picking up maps, information, advice, and permits inside the hefty stone structure, you can tour the museum, whose exhibits explain the park's history, flora, and fauna. Most kids love the extensive wildlife displays, especially the ones of bears and wolves. Though open year-round, the center's hours are variable, so it's wise to verify them upon entering the park. Enjoy the free Wi-Fi. ⊠ *Mammoth Hot Springs* ☎ *307/344–2263* ⊕ *www.nps.gov/yell/ planyourvisit/visitorcenters.htm.*

Canyon Visitor Center

INFO CENTER | FAMILY | This gleaming visitor center contains elaborate interactive exhibits for adults and kids. The focus here is on volcanoes and earthquakes and includes a room-size relief model of the park that illustrates eruptions, glaciers and seismic activity. There are also exhibits about Native Americans and wildlife, including bison and wolves. As at all visitor centers, you can obtain advice, information, and backcountry camping permits. The adjacent bookstore is the best in the park, with hundreds of books on the park, its history, and related science. ⊠ *Canyon Village* ☎ *307/242– 2550* ⊕ *www.nps.gov/yell/planyourvisit/ visitorcenters.htm* ⊗ *Closed mid-fall–late spring.*

Fishing Bridge Visitor Center

INFO CENTER | FAMILY | This distinctive stone-and-log building, built in 1931, is a National Historic Landmark. If you can't distinguish between a Clark's nuthatch and an ermine (one's a bird, the other a weasel), check out the exhibits here about the park's smaller wildlife. Step out the back door to find yourself on one of the beautiful black obsidian beaches of Yellowstone Lake. Adjacent is one of the park's larger amphitheaters. Ranger presentations take place here nightly in summer. ⊠ *East Entrance Rd., 1 mile from Grand Loop Rd.* ☎ *307/242–2450* ⊕ *www.nps.gov/yell/planyourvisit/visitorcenters.htm* ⊗ *Closed early Sept.–late May.*

Grant Village Visitor Center

INFO CENTER | FAMILY | Exhibits at each visitor center describe a small piece of Yellowstone's history—the ones here provide details about the 1988 fire that burned more than a third of the park's total acreage and forced multiple federal agencies to reevaluate their fire-control policies. Watch an informative video, and learn about the 25,000 firefighters from across the United States who battled the blaze. Bathrooms and a backcountry office are here. ⊠ *2 Grant Village Loop Rd., off U.S. 89/287, Grant Village* ☎ *307/242–2650* ⊕ *www.nps.gov/yell/ planyourvisit/visitorcenters.htm* ⊗ *Closed early Oct.–late May.*

Madison Information Station & Trailside Museum

INFO CENTER | FAMILY | In this stone-and-timber National Historic Landmark, park rangers share the space with a store that sells books, maps, and learning aids. You might find spotting scopes set up for wildlife viewing out the rear window; if this is the case, look for eagles, swans, bison, and elk. Rangers will answer questions about the park, provide basic hiking information, and issue permits for backcountry camping and fishing. Rangers also staff the Junior Ranger Station for kids here. Picnic tables, toilets, and an amphitheater for summer-evening ranger programs are shared with the nearby campground. ⊠ *Grand Loop Rd. at West Entrance Rd.* ☎ *307/344–2876* ⊕ *www. nps.gov/yell/planyourvisit/visitorcenters. htm* ⊗ *Closed early Oct.–late May.*

Old Faithful Visitor Education Center

INFO CENTER | FAMILY | At this $27 million visitor center that's a park-system jewel, you can check out the interactive exhibits and children's area, read about the latest geyser-eruption predictions, and find out the schedules for ranger-led walks and talks. Backcountry and fishing permits are dispensed at the ranger station adjacent to the Old Faithful Snow Lodge. ⊠ *Old Faithful Bypass Rd.* ☎ *307/344–2751* ⊕ *www.nps.gov/yell/planyourvisit/visitorcenters.htm* ⊗ *Closed mid-Nov.–mid-Dec., mid-Mar.–mid-Apr.*

West Thumb Information Station

INFO CENTER | This historic log cabin houses a bookstore and doubles as a warming hut in winter. There are restrooms in the parking area. In summer, check for informal ranger-led discussions beneath the old sequoia tree. ⊠ *Grand Loop Rd., western edge of Yellowstone Lake, West Thumb* ☎ *307/344–2650* ⊕ *www.nps.gov/yell/planyourvisit/visitorcenters.htm* ⊗ *Closed early Oct.–late May.*

 Sights

SCENIC DRIVES

Firehole Canyon Drive

SCENIC DRIVE | The 2-mile narrow asphalt road twists through a deep canyon and passes the 40-foot Firehole Falls. In summer look for a sign marking a pull-out and swimming hole. This is one of only two places in the park (Boiling River on the North Entrance Road is the other) where you can safely and legally swim in the thermally heated waters. Look carefully for osprey and other raptors. ⊠ *Yellowstone National Park ⊹ 1 mile south of Madison junction, off Grand Loop Rd.* ⊗ *Closed early Nov.–early Apr.*

Firehole Lake Drive

SCENIC DRIVE | This one-way, 3-mile-long road takes you past Great Fountain Geyser, which shoots out jets of water reaching as high as 200 feet about twice a day. Rangers' predictions provide a two-hour window of opportunity. Should you witness an eruption, you'll see waves of water cascading down the terraces that form the geyser's edges. This road isn't open to over-snow vehicle traffic in winter, and it's hard to access by foot, snowshoes, or skis. ⊠ *Firehole Lake Dr., 8 miles north of Old Faithful, Old Faithful* ⊗ *Closed early Nov.–early Apr.*

Hayden Valley on Grand Loop Road

SCENIC DRIVE | Bison, bears, coyotes, wolves, and birds of prey all call Hayden Valley home almost year-round. Once part of Yellowstone Lake, the broad valley now contains peaceful meadows, rolling hills, and the placid Yellowstone River. There are multiple turnouts and picnic areas on the 16-mile drive, many with views of the river and valley. Ask a ranger about "Grizzly Overlook," an unofficial site where wildlife watchers, including NPS rangers with spotting scopes for the public to use, congregate in summer. North of Mud Volcano are 11 unsigned turnouts. Look for the telltale timber railings, and be prepared to get caught in a traffic-stopping "bison jam" along the way. ⊠ *Grand Loop Rd. between Canyon and Fishing Bridge* ⊗ *Closed early Nov.–early Apr.*

★ Northeast Entrance Road and Lamar Valley

SCENIC DRIVE | This 29-mile road has the richest landscape diversity of the five entrance roads. Just after you enter the park, you cut between 10,928-foot Abiathar Peak and the 10,404-foot Barronette Peak. Lamar Valley is home to hundreds of bison, and the rugged peaks and ridges adjacent to it shelter some of Yellowstone's most famous wolf packs. (Wolves were reintroduced to the park in the mid-1990s.) This is the park's best place for wolf-watching, especially in the early morning and late evening. As you exit Lamar Valley, the road crosses the Yellowstone River before leading you to the rustic Roosevelt Lodge. ⊠ *From*

Northeast Entrance to junction with Grand Loop Rd.

Northeastern Grand Loop

SCENIC DRIVE | Commonly called Dunraven Pass, this 19-mile segment of Grand Loop Road climbs to nearly 9,000 feet as it passes some of the park's finest scenery, including views of backcountry hot springs and abundant wildflowers. Near Tower Falls, the road twists beneath a series of leaning basalt columns from 40 to 50 feet high. That behemoth to the east is 10,243-foot Mount Washburn. ⊠ *Between Canyon Junction and Tower Falls* ⊙ *Closed early Nov.–early Apr.*

Upper Terrace Drive

SCENIC DRIVE | This popular 1½-mile drive at the top of the Mammoth Terraces will take you back into the woods, where you can see some impressive thermal features, among them White Elephant Back and Orange Spring Mound, that aren't visible from the main road. Park at the top of the Terraces for views of Fort Yellowstone and a short walk along the boardwalk to Canary Springs. RVs, buses, and trailers are not permitted along Upper Terrace Drive. ⊠ *Grand Loop Rd., 2 miles from Mammoth Hot Springs Hotel* ⊙ *Closed Dec.–Apr.*

HISTORIC SITES

OLD FAITHFUL

★ Old Faithful Inn

HOTEL—SIGHT | FAMILY | It's hard to imagine how any work could be accomplished with snow and ice blanketing the region, but this historic hotel was constructed over the course of a single winter. Open since 1904, this massive log structure is an attraction in its own right. Even if you don't spend a night at the Old Faithful Inn, walk through or take the free 45-minute guided tour to admire its massive open-beam lobby and rock fireplace. There are antique writing desks on the second-floor balcony. You can watch Old Faithful geyser from two second-floor outdoor decks. ⊠ *Old Faithful Bypass Rd., Old Faithful* 🕾 *307/344–7311*

⊕ *www.nps.gov/yell/learn/historyculture/ oldfaithfuldistrict.htm* ⊙ *Closed early Oct.–early May.*

MAMMOTH HOT SPRINGS

Fort Yellowstone

MILITARY SITE | The oldest buildings here served as Fort Yellowstone from 1891 to 1918, when the U.S. Army managed the park. The redbrick buildings cluster around an open area reminiscent of a frontier-era parade ground. Pick up a self-guided tour map of the area from the Albright Visitors Center on Officers Row, and start your walking tour there. ⊠ *Mammoth Hot Springs* ⊕ *www.nps. gov/yell/learn/historyculture/fort-yellowstone.htm.*

LAKE AREA

Lake Yellowstone Hotel

HOTEL—SIGHT | Completed in 1891, this structure on the National Register of Historic Places is the oldest lodging in Yellowstone National Park. Casual daytime visitors can lounge in white wicker chairs in the sun room and watch the waters of Yellowstone Lake through massive windows. Robert Reamer, the architect of the Old Faithful Inn, added a columned entrance in 1903 to enhance the original facade of the hotel. A multi-million-dollar renovation in 2014 restored its Colonial Revival heritage. ⊠ *Lake Village Rd., 1 Grand Loop Rd., Lake Village* 🕾 *307/344–7901* ⊕ *www. yellowstonenationalparklodges.com/stay* ⊙ *Closed early Oct.–early May.*

SCENIC STOPS

Along the park's main drive—the Grand Loop (also referred to as Yellowstone's Figure Eight)—are eight primary "communities," or developed areas. On the Western Yellowstone map are five of those communities—Grant Village, Old Faithful, Madison, Norris, and Mammoth Hot Springs—with their respective sights. The Eastern Yellowstone map shows the remaining three—Tower-Roosevelt, Canyon, and Lake (for Yellowstone Lake area)—with their respective sights.

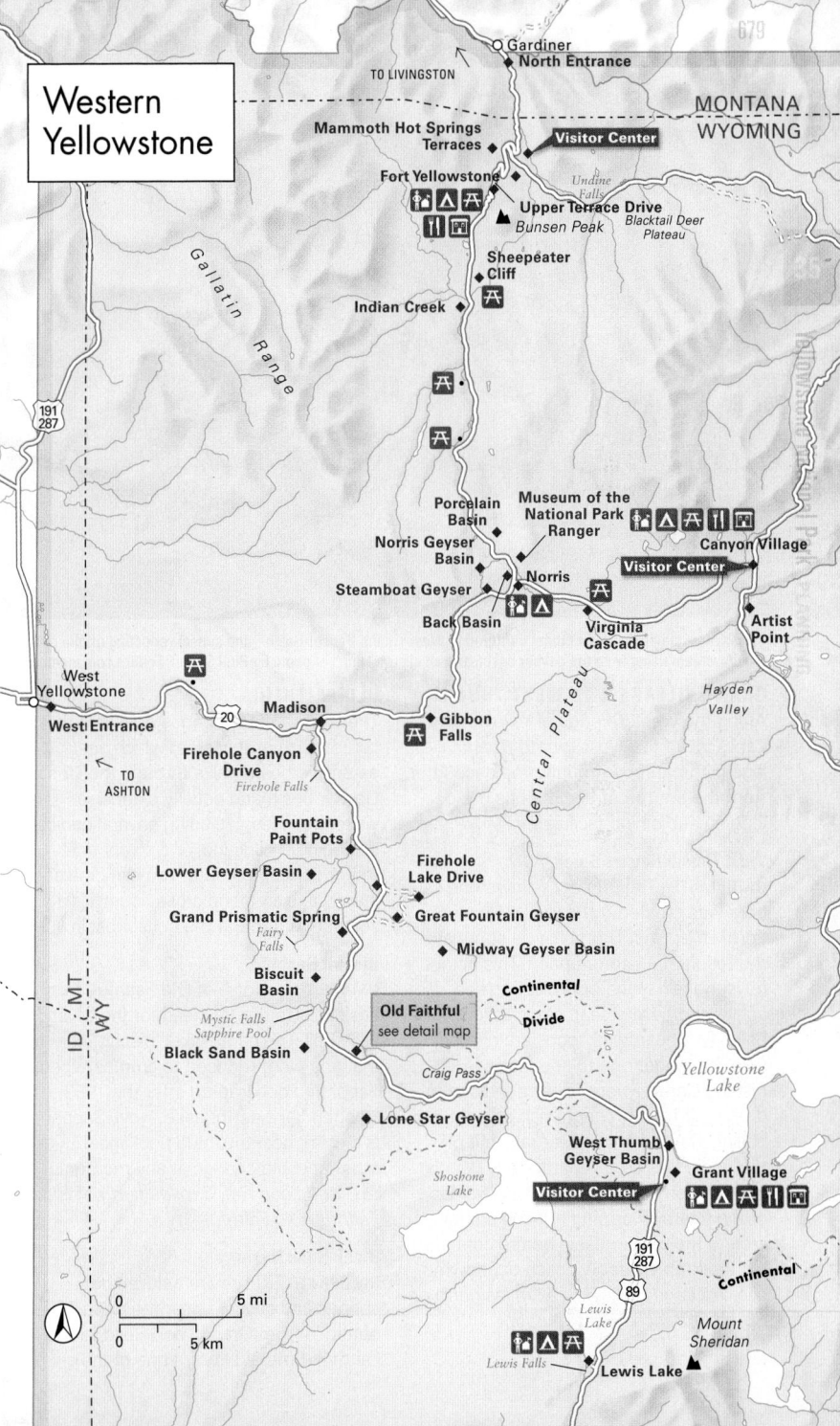

Western Yellowstone

TO LIVINGSTON

Gardiner
North Entrance

MONTANA
WYOMING

Mammoth Hot Springs Terraces

Visitor Center

Undine Falls

Fort Yellowstone

Upper Terrace Drive
Bunsen Peak

Blacktail Deer Plateau

Sheepeater Cliff

Indian Creek

Gallatin Range

Porcelain Basin

Norris Geyser Basin

Museum of the National Park Ranger

Canyon Village

Visitor Center

Steamboat Geyser

Norris

Back Basin

Virginia Cascade

Artist Point

Central Plateau

Hayden Valley

West Yellowstone

West Entrance

20 **Madison**

Gibbon Falls

TO ASHTON

Firehole Canyon Drive
Firehole Falls

Fountain Paint Pots

Lower Geyser Basin

Firehole Lake Drive

Grand Prismatic Spring
Fairy Falls

Great Fountain Geyser

Midway Geyser Basin

Biscuit Basin

Mystic Falls
Sapphire Pool

Continental

Divide

Old Faithful
see detail map

Black Sand Basin

Craig Pass

Yellowstone Lake

Lone Star Geyser

Shoshone Lake

West Thumb Geyser Basin

Visitor Center

Grant Village

ID MT
WY

191
287

89

Continental

Lewis Lake

Lewis Falls

Lewis Lake

Mount Sheridan

0   5 mi

0   5 km

"This was a magical moment that I captured at West Thumb Geyser Basin—the sunset reflecting off the rain clouds, steam rising from the geyser basin, and an elk drinking." —photo by Paul Stoloff, Fodors.com member

GRANT VILLAGE AND WEST THUMB

Along the western edge of Yellowstone Lake, called the West Thumb, Grant Village is the first community you encounter from the South Entrance. It has basic lodging and dining facilities.

West Thumb Geyser Basin

NATURE SITE | The primary Yellowstone caldera was created by one volcanic eruption, while West Thumb came about as the result of a later eruption. This unique geyser basin is the only place to see active geothermal features in Yellowstone Lake. Two boardwalk loops are offered; take the longer one to see features like Fishing Cone, where fishermen used to drop their freshly caught fish straight into boiling water without ever taking it off the hook. This area is particularly popular with winter visitors, who take advantage of the nearby warming hut and a stroll around the geyser basin before continuing their trip via snow coach or snowmobile. ⊠ *Grand Loop Rd., 22 miles north of South Entrance, West Thumb.*

OLD FAITHFUL

The world's most famous geyser is the centerpiece of this area, which has extensive boardwalks through the Upper Geyser Basin and equally extensive visitor services, including several choices in lodging and dining, and a very fine visitor center. In winter you can dine and stay in this area and cross-country ski or snowshoe through the geyser basin.

Biscuit Basin

NATURE SITE | North of Old Faithful, this basin is also the trailhead for the Mystic Falls Trail. The namesake "biscuit" formations were reduced to crumbs when Sapphire Pool erupted after the 1959 Hebgen Lake earthquake. Now, Sapphire is a calm, beautiful blue pool again, but that could change at any moment. ⊠ *Grand Loop Rd., 3 miles north of Old Faithful, Old Faithful.*

Black Sand Basin

NATURE SITE | There are a dozen hot springs and geysers near the cloverleaf entrance from Grand Loop Road to Old Faithful. Emerald Pool is one of the

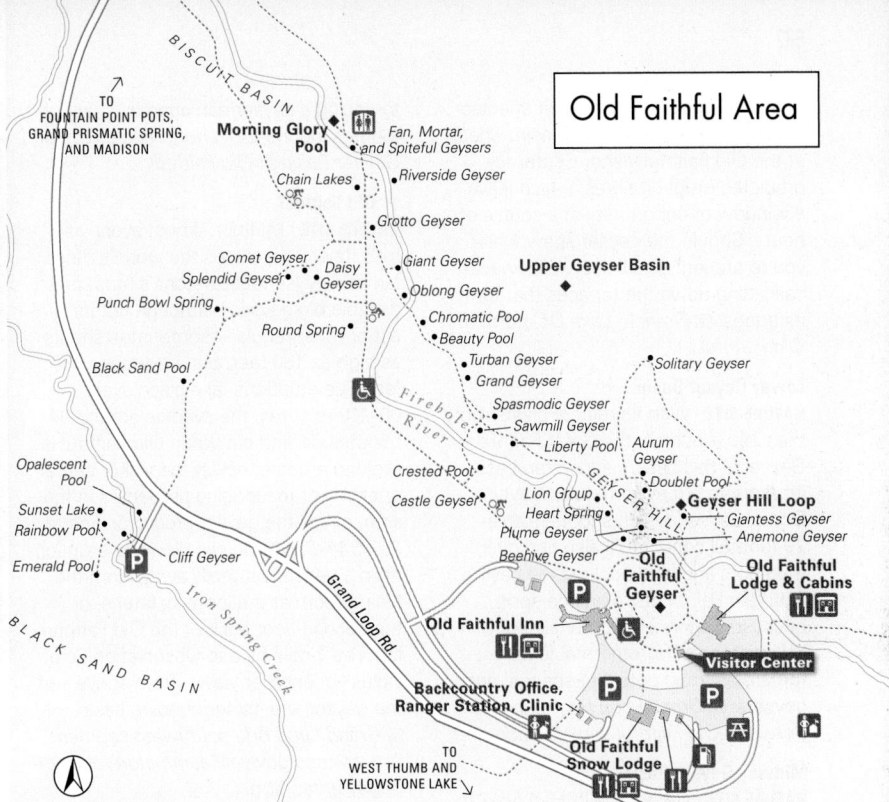

Old Faithful Area

TO FOUNTAIN POINT POTS, GRAND PRISMATIC SPRING, AND MADISON

BISCUIT BASIN

Morning Glory Pool

Fan, Mortar, and Spiteful Geysers

Chain Lakes

Riverside Geyser

Grotto Geyser

Comet Geyser
Splendid Geyser
Daisy Geyser

Giant Geyser

Upper Geyser Basin

Punch Bowl Spring

Oblong Geyser

Round Spring

Chromatic Pool

Beauty Pool

Black Sand Pool

Turban Geyser

Grand Geyser

Solitary Geyser

Firehole River

Spasmodic Geyser

Sawmill Geyser

Liberty Pool

Aurum Geyser

Doublet Pool

Opalescent Pool

Crested Pool

Castle Geyser

Lion Group

Heart Spring

GEYSER HILL

Geyser Hill Loop

Giantess Geyser

Sunset Lake
Rainbow Pool

Plume Geyser

Anemone Geyser

Emerald Pool

Cliff Geyser

Beehive Geyser

Old Faithful Geyser

Old Faithful Lodge & Cabins

Iron Spring Creek

BLACK SAND BASIN

Grand Loop Rd.

Old Faithful Inn

Visitor Center

Backcountry Office, Ranger Station, Clinic

Old Faithful Snow Lodge

TO WEST THUMB AND YELLOWSTONE LAKE

prettiest. It's an easy walk, ski, or bike ride from the Old Faithful area to Black Sand Basin. ⊠ *Grand Loop Rd., north of Old Faithful, Old Faithful.*

Geyser Hill Loop

TRAIL | **FAMILY** | Along the 1.3-mile Geyser Hill Loop boardwalk you will see active thermal features such as violent Giantess Geyser. Erupting only a few times each year, Giantess spouts from 100 to 250 feet in the air for five to eight minutes once or twice hourly for 12 to 43 hours. Nearby Doublet Pool's two adjacent springs have complex ledges and deep blue waters that are highly photogenic. Starting as a gentle pool, Anemone Geyser overflows, bubbles, and finally erupts 10 feet or more, every three to eight minutes. The loop boardwalk brings you close to the action, making it especially appealing to children intrigued by the

basin's sights and sounds. To reach Geyser Hill, head counterclockwise around the Old Faithful boardwalk 0.3 mile from the visitor center, crossing the Firehole River and entering Upper Geyser Basin. ⊠ *Old Faithful, 0.3 mile from Old Faithful Visitor Center, Old Faithful.*

★ Grand Prismatic Spring

NATURE SITE | You can reach Yellowstone's largest hot spring, 370 feet in diameter, by following the boardwalk. The spring, in the Midway Geyser Basin, is deep blue in color, with yellow and orange rings formed by bacteria that give it the effect of a prism. For a stunning perspective, look down on it from the Fairy Falls Trail. ⊠ *Midway Geyser Basin, off Grand Loop Rd.*

Great Fountain Geyser

NATURE SITE | Shooting water from 75 to 200 feet in the air every eight to 15 hours, this geyser is the most spectacular sight in Lower Geyser Basin. Check at the Old Faithful Visitor Center for predicted eruption times, which leave a window of opportunity of a couple of hours. Should the geyser spew while you're present, you'll see water waves cascading down the terraces that form its edges. ⊠ *Firehole Lake Dr., north of Old Faithful.*

Lower Geyser Basin

NATURE SITE | With its mighty blasts more than 150 feet high, the Great Fountain Geyser is this basin's superstar. Less impressive but more regular is White Dome Geyser, which shoots from a 20-foot-tall cone. You'll also find pink mud pots and blue pools at the basin's Fountain Paint Pots, a unique spot because visitors encounter all four of Yellowstone's hydrothermal features: fumaroles, mud pots, hot springs, and geysers. ⊠ *Grand Loop Rd., midway between Old Faithful and Madison.*

Midway Geyser Basin

NATURE SITE | Called "Hell's Half Acre" by writer Rudyard Kipling, Midway Geyser Basin is a more interesting stop than Lower Geyser Basin. Boardwalks wind their way to the Excelsior Geyser, which deposits 4,000 gallons of vivid blue water per minute into the Firehole River. Just above Excelsior is Yellowstone's largest hot spring, Grand Prismatic Spring. ⊠ *Grand Loop Rd., between Old Faithful and Madison.*

Morning Glory Pool

NATURE SITE | Shaped somewhat like a morning glory, this pool once was a deep blue, but the color is no longer as striking as before due to tourists dropping coins and other debris into the hole. To reach the pool, follow the boardwalk past Geyser Hill Loop and stately Castle Geyser, which has the biggest cone in Yellowstone. Morning Glory is the inspiration for popular children's author Jan Brett's story *Hedgie Blasts Off*, in which a hedgehog travels to another planet

to unclog a geyser damaged by space tourists' debris. ⊠ *At north end of Upper Geyser Basin at Old Faithful.*

★ Old Faithful

NATURE SITE | FAMILY | Almost every visitor's itinerary includes the world's most famous geyser. Yellowstone's most predictable big geyser—although not its largest or most regular—sometimes shoots as high as 180 feet, but it averages 130 feet. The eruptions take place every 60–110 minutes, the average around 94 minutes. To find out when Old Faithful is likely to erupt, check at the visitor center or at any of the lodging properties in the area, or call the geyser prediction line at *307/344-2751*. You can view the eruption from a bench just yards away, from the dining room at the lodge cafeteria, or the second-floor deck of the Old Faithful Inn. The 1-mile hike to Observation Point yields yet another view—from above—of the geyser and its surrounding basin. ⊠ *Grand Loop Rd., southwest segment* ⊕ *www.nps.gov/yell/learn/nature/oldfaithfulgeyserfaq.htm.*

Upper Geyser Basin

NATURE SITE | With Old Faithful as its central attraction, this mile-square basin contains about 140 different geysers—one-fifth of the known geysers in the world. It's an excellent place to spend a day or more exploring. You will find a complex system of boardwalks and trails—some of them used as bicycle trails—that take you to the basin's various attractions. ⊠ *Old Faithful.*

MADISON

The area around the junction of the West Entrance Road and the Lower Loop is a good place to take a break as you travel through the park, because you will almost always see bison grazing along the Madison River, and elk are often in the area, too. Limited visitor services are here, and there are no dining facilities.

A Good Tour: Old Faithful Area

Begin your tour at the impressive **Old Faithful Visitor Education Center.** Pick up the Old Faithful–area trail guide and check a bulletin board with the latest predictions for six geyser eruptions.

The Main Attraction

Concentrate first on the main attraction: **Old Faithful** spouts from 130 to 180 feet high approximately every 94 minutes. You don't need to jockey for position on the boardwalk directly in front of the visitor center to enjoy the geyser. It's impressive from any angle on the boardwalk surrounding it. The view from the second-floor deck of the **Old Faithful Inn** is glorious, too. Speaking of that famous, century-old structure, check out its massive log-construction interior.

Exploring the Basins

At Old Faithful Village you're in the heart of the **Upper Geyser Basin,** the densest concentration of geysers on Earth, with about 140 geysers within a square mile. Once you've watched Old Faithful erupt, explore the larger basin with a hike around **Geyser Hill,** where you may see wildlife as well as thermal features. Follow the trail north to the **Morning Glory Pool,** with its unique flower shape. Along this trail are Castle, Grand, and Riverside geysers. Return to the village and continue by car to **Black Sand Basin** or **Biscuit Basin.** At Biscuit Basin, follow the boardwalks to the trailhead for the Mystic Falls Trail, where you can get views of the Upper Geyser Basin.

Paint Pots and a Spring

Take a break from geyser watching with a packed lunch at the Whiskey Flat picnic area. Afterward, continue your drive toward **Lower Geyser Basin,** with its colorful **Fountain Paint Pots.** Then, on the way back to Old Faithful, stop at **Midway Geyser Basin,** where steaming runoff from the colorful 370-foot **Grand Prismatic Spring** crashes continuously into the Firehole River.

Relax and Celebrate

Relax and celebrate your day's accomplishments with dinner (reservations required) at the Old Faithful Inn, or enjoy drinks on the second floor.

Gibbon Falls

BODY OF WATER | The water of this 84-foot fall on the Gibbon River rushes over the caldera rim. Driving east from Madison to Norris, you can see it on your right, but the angle is even better from the paved trail adjacent to the canyon's edge. ⊠ *Grand Loop Rd., 4 miles east of Madison.*

NORRIS

The area at the western junction of the Upper and Lower Loops has the most active geyser basin in the park. The underground plumbing occasionally reaches such high temperatures—the ground itself has heated up in areas to nearly 200°F—that a portion of the basin is periodically closed for safety reasons. There are limited visitor services: two museums, a bookstore, and a picnic area. ■**TIP➜ Ask rangers at the Norris Geyser Basin Museum when different geysers are expected to erupt and plan your walk accordingly.**

Back Basin

NATURE SITE | The trail through Back Basin is a 1½-mile loop guiding you past Steamboat Geyser. When it erupts fully (most recently in 2014), it's the world's largest geyser, climbing 400 feet above

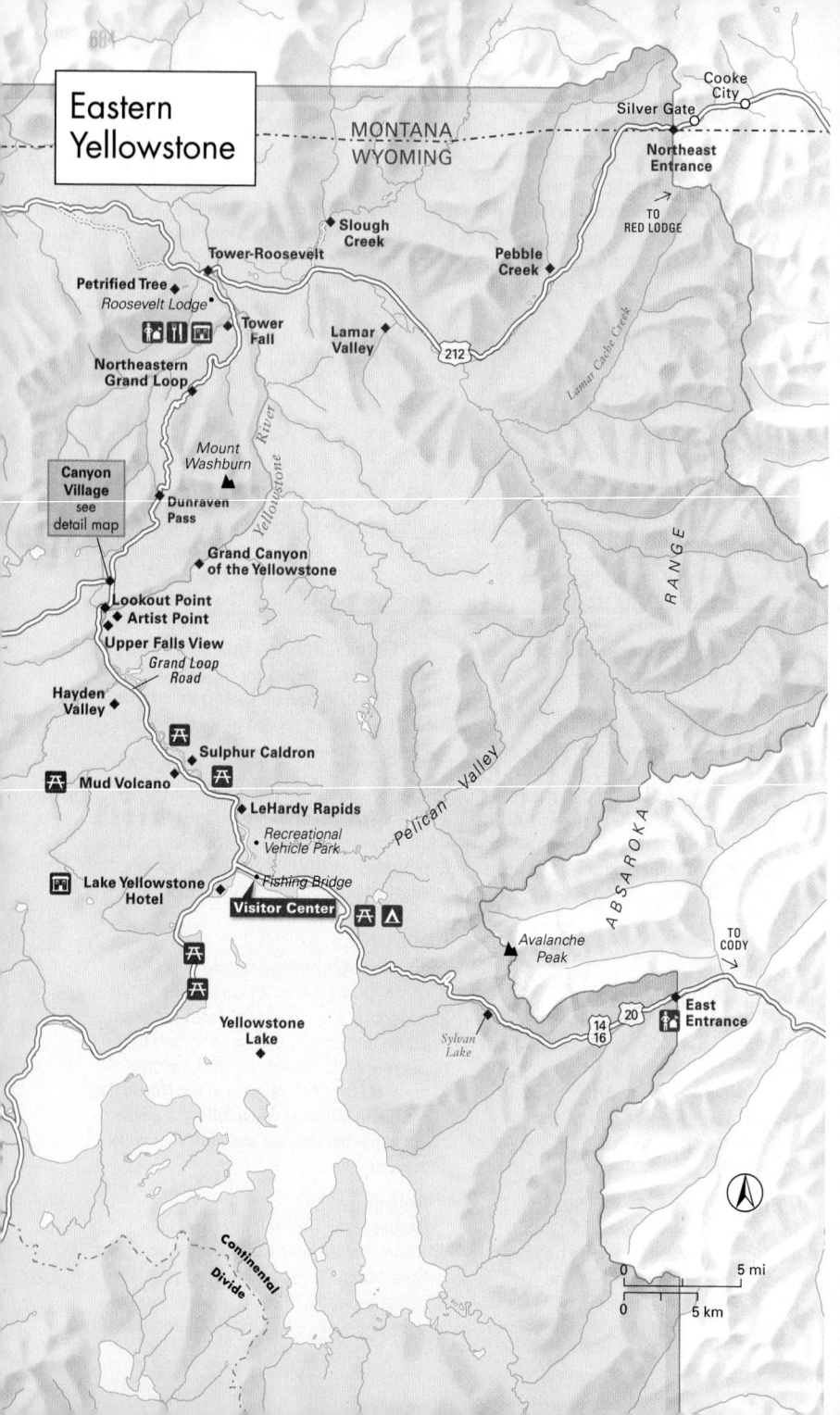

Eastern Yellowstone

Cooke City

Silver Gate

Northeast Entrance

TO RED LODGE →

MONTANA
WYOMING

Slough Creek

Tower-Roosevelt

Pebble Creek

Petrified Tree
Roosevelt Lodge

Tower Fall

Lamar Valley

212

Lamar Cache Creek

Northeastern Grand Loop

Mount Washburn

Canyon Village
see detail map

Dunraven Pass

Grand Canyon of the Yellowstone

Yellowstone River

RANGE

Lookout Point

Artist Point

Upper Falls View

Grand Loop Road

Hayden Valley

Sulphur Caldron

Mud Volcano

LeHardy Rapids

Pelican Valley

Recreational Vehicle Park

ABSAROKA

Lake Yellowstone Hotel

Fishing Bridge

Visitor Center

Avalanche Peak

TO CODY →

East Entrance

14 16

20

Yellowstone Lake

Sylvan Lake

Continental Divide

0   5 mi

0   5 km

the basin. More often, Steamboat growls and spits, sending clouds of steam high above the basin. Kids will love the Puff 'n' Stuff Geyser and the mysterious cavelike Green Dragon Spring. Ask the rangers for an anticipated schedule of geyser eruptions—you might catch the Echinus Geyser, which erupts almost hourly. ⊠ *Grand Loop Rd., at Norris.*

Museum of the National Park Ranger

MUSEUM | FAMILY | This station housed soldiers from 1908 to 1918. The six-room log building is now an engaging museum where you can watch a movie telling the history of the National Park Service and visit with the retired rangers who volunteer here. Other exhibits relate to Army service in Yellowstone and early park rangers. ⊠ *Grand Loop Rd., at Norris Junction* ⊗ *Closed late Sept.–late May.*

Norris Geyser Basin

NATURE SITE | FAMILY | From the Norris Ranger Station, choose Porcelain Basin, Back Basin, or both. These volatile thermal features are constantly changing, although you can expect to find a variety of geysers and springs here at any time. The area is accessible via an extensive system of boardwalks, some of them suitable for people with disabilities. The famous Steamboat Geyser is here, as is a small museum that's a National Historic Landmark. ⊠ *Grand Loop Rd. at Norris* ⊕ *www.nps.gov/yell/planyourvisit/visitorcenters.htm* ⊗ *Museum closed early Oct.–late May.*

Porcelain Basin

NATURE SITE | A ¾-mile partially boardwalk loop from Norris Geyser Basin Museum passes by this thermal area in the Norris basin's eastern portion. In this geothermal field of whitish geyserite stone, the earth bulges and belches from the underground pressure. You'll find bubbling pools, some milky white and others ringed in orange because of the minerals in the water, as well as small geysers such as the extremely active Whirligig. ⊠ *Grand Loop Rd.*

MAMMOTH HOT SPRINGS

This northern community within the park is known for its massive natural terraces, where mineral water flows continuously, building an ever-changing display. Water levels can fluctuate, though, so if it's late in a particularly dry summer, you won't see the terraces in all their glory. You will often see elk grazing here. In the park's early days, this was the site of Fort Yellowstone. The brick buildings constructed during that era are still used for various park activities.

Mammoth Hot Springs Terraces

BODY OF WATER | FAMILY | Multicolor travertine terraces formed by slowly escaping hot mineral water mark this unusual geological formation. You can explore the terraces via an elaborate network of boardwalks, the best of which is the Lower Terrace Interpretive Trail. If you head uphill from Liberty Cap, at the area's northern end, in an hour you'll pass bright and ornately terraced Minerva Spring. Along the way you might spot elk grazing nearby. Alternatively, you can drive up to the Lower Terrace Overlook on Upper Terrace Drive and take the boardwalks down past New Blue Springs to the Lower Terrace. This route, which also takes an hour, works especially well if you can park a second vehicle at the foot of Lower Terrace. There are many steps on the lower terrace boardwalks, so plan to take your time there. The boardwalk routes change as the terraces move and grow. A map and brochure at the boardwalk trailhead has a self-guided tour. ⊠ *Northwest corner of Grand Loop Rd.* ⊕ *www.nps.gov/yell/planyourvisit/explore-mammoth.htm.*

TOWER-ROOSEVELT

The northeastern region of Yellowstone is the least visited part of the park, making it a great place to explore without running into as many people. Packs of wolves may be spotted in the Lamar Valley.

Petrified Tree

NATURE SITE | A century of vandalism has forced park officials to surround this 45-million-year-old petrified redwood tree with high wrought-iron gates. Doing so has protected the geological landmark, but it has utterly ruined the experience of viewing it. ⊠ *Grand Loop Rd., 1 mile west of Tower-Roosevelt.*

Tower Fall

BODY OF WATER | FAMILY | This is one of the easiest waterfalls to see from the roadside; you can also view volcanic pinnacles here. Tower Creek plunges 132 feet at this waterfall to join the Yellowstone River. While a trail that used to go to the base of the falls has washed out, it will take trekkers down to the river. ⊠ *Grand Loop Rd., 2 miles south of Tower-Roosevelt* ⊕ *www.nps.gov/yell/planyourvisit/towerrplan.htm.*

CANYON

The Yellowstone River's source is in the Absaroka Mountains, in the park's southeastern corner. The river winds its way through the heart of the park, entering Yellowstone Lake, then heading northward under Fishing Ridge through Hayden Valley. When it cuts through the multicolor Grand Canyon of the Yellowstone, it creates one of the most spectacular gorges in the world, enticing visitors with its steep canyon walls and waterfalls. All types of visitor services are here, as well as many hiking opportunities.

Artist Point

BODY OF WATER | An impressive view of the Lower Falls of the Yellowstone River can be had from Artist Point, which has two observation platforms, one accessible to wheelchairs. Rangers often give short talks on the lower platform; check the park newspaper for a schedule. The South Rim Trail goes past this point, and the nearby parking area is open year-round. ⊠ *South Rim Rd., east end* ⊕ *www.nps.gov/yell/planyourvisit/canyonplan.htm.*

★ Grand Canyon of the Yellowstone

BODY OF WATER | This stunning canyon is 23 miles long, but there is only one trail from rim to base. As a result, most visitors clog the north and south rims to see Upper and Lower Falls. Unless you're up for the strenuous six-hour hike called Seven Mile Hole, you have no choice but to join the crowds to see this natural wonder. The red-and-ocher canyon walls are topped by emerald-green forest. It's a feast of color. Keep an eye peeled for osprey, which nest in the canyon's spires and precarious trees. ⊠ *Canyon* ⊕ *www.nps.gov/yell/learn/nature/grand-canyon.htm.*

Lookout Point

BODY OF WATER | Midway on the North Rim Trail—also accessible via the one-way North Rim Drive—Lookout Point provides a view of the Grand Canyon of the Yellowstone. Follow the right-hand fork in the path to descend a steep trail, with an approximately 500-foot elevation change, for an eye-to-eye view of the falls from a half mile downstream. The best time to hike the trail is early morning, when sunlight reflects off the mist from the falls to create a rainbow. ⊠ *Off North Rim Dr.* ⊕ *www.nps.gov/yell/planyourvisit/canyonplan.htm.*

Upper Falls View

BODY OF WATER | A spur road off Grand Loop Road south of Canyon accesses the western end of the North Rim Trail and takes you down a fairly steep portion for a view of Upper Falls from almost directly above. ⊠ *Off Grand Loop Rd., ¾ miles south of Canyon* ⊕ *www.nps.gov/yell/planyourvisit/canyonplan.htm.*

LAKE AREA

In the park's southeastern segment, the tranquility of massive Yellowstone Lake sets the mood. Near Fishing Bridge you might see grizzly bears. They like to hunt for fish spawning or swimming near the lake's outlet to the Yellowstone River. Visitor information can be found at Lake Yellowstone Hotel, Fishing Bridge RV

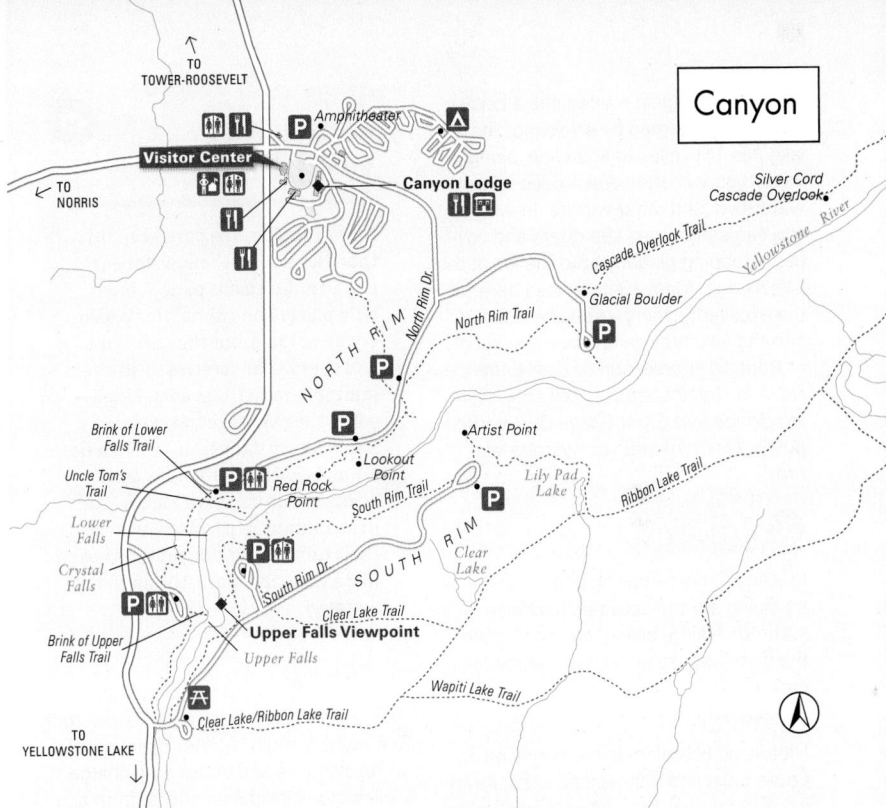

Park (for hard-sided vehicles only), and Bridge Bay Campground, with 432 sites the park's largest campground.

LeHardy Rapids

BODY OF WATER | Witness one of nature's epic battles as cutthroat trout migrate upstream by catapulting themselves out of the water to get over and around obstacles in the Yellowstone River. The ¼-mile forested loop takes you to the river's edge. Look for waterfowl and bears, which feed on the trout. ☒ *Fishing Bridge ✛ 3 miles north of Fishing Bridge* ⊕ *www.nps.gov/yell/learn/nature/yellow-stone-river.htm.*

Mud Volcano

NATURE SITE | **FAMILY** | Gasses hissing from vents underscore the volatile nature of this area's geothermal features. The ¾-mile round-trip Mud Volcano Interpretive Trail loops gently around seething,

sulfuric mud pots with names such as Black Dragon's Cauldron and Sizzling Basin before making its way around Mud Volcano itself, a boiling pot of brown goo. ☒ *Grand Loop Rd., 10 miles south of Canyon, 4 miles north of Fishing Bridge, Fishing Bridge.*

Sulphur Caldron

NATURE SITE | You can smell the sulfur before you even leave your vehicle to walk to the overlook of Sulphur Caldron, where hissing steam escapes from a moonscape-like surface as superheated bubbling mud. ☒ *Grand Loop Rd., 9½ miles south of Canyon, 4½ miles north of Fishing Bridge, Fishing Bridge.*

★ Yellowstone Lake

BODY OF WATER | **FAMILY** | One of the world's largest alpine lakes, the 132-square-mile Yellowstone Lake was formed when the glaciers that once covered the region melted into a caldera—a crater formed by a volcano. The lake has 141 miles of shoreline, along which you will often see moose, elk, waterfowl, and other wildlife. In winter you can sometimes see otters and coyotes stepping gingerly onto the ice at the lake's edge. Many visitors head here for the excellent fishing—streams flowing into the lake provide an abundant supply of trout. ⊠ *Intersection of East Entrance Rd. and Grand Loop Rd., between Fishing Bridge and Grant Village* ⊕ *www.nps. gov/yell/learn/nature/yellowstone-lake. htm.*

 Activities

In winter, snowmobiling and cross-country skiing are the activities of choice. In summer, hiking, biking, and fishing are the best ways to get out and enjoy the park.

BOATING

Motorized boats are allowed only on Lewis Lake and Yellowstone Lake. Kayaking and canoeing are allowed on all lakes except Sylvan Lake, Eleanor Lake, Twin Lakes, and Beach Springs Lagoon. Most lakes are inaccessible by car, though, so accessing them requires long portages. Boating is not allowed on any river except the Lewis between Lewis Lake and Shoshone Lake, where nonmotorized boats are permitted.

You must purchase a seven-day, $5 permit for boats and floatables, or a $10 permit for motorized boats at Bridge Bay Ranger Station, South Entrance Ranger Station, Grant Village Backcountry Office, and Lewis Lake Ranger Station (at the campground). Nonmotorized permits are available at the Northeast Entrance; West Yellowstone Information Center; the backcountry offices at Mammoth, Old Faithful, and Canyon; Bechler Ranger Station; and locations where motorized permits are sold. Annual permits cost $20.

Caution: A Wild Place

As you explore the park keep this thought in mind: Yellowstone is not an amusement park. It is a wild place. The animals may seem docile or tame, but they are wild, and every year careless visitors are injured—sometimes even killed—when they venture too close. Particularly dangerous are female animals with their young, and bison, which can turn and charge in an instant. With bison, watch their tails: if standing up or crooked like a question mark, the animal is agitated.

Boat permits issued in Grand Teton National Park are honored in Yellowstone, but owners must register their vessel in Yellowstone and obtain a no-charge Yellowstone validation sticker from a permit-issuing station.

Bridge Bay Marina

BOATING | FAMILY | Watercraft, from rowboats to powerboats, are available for trips on Yellowstone Lake at Bridge Bay Marina. You also can rent 22- and 34-foot cabin cruisers with a guide. ⊠ *Grand Loop Rd., 2 miles south of Lake Village, Bridge Bay* ☎ *307/344–7311* ⊕ *www. yellowstonenationalparklodges.com/ adventures* ✆ *$10/hr for rowboat; $57/hr for small boat with outboard motor.*

Yellowstone Lake Scenic Cruises

BOATING | FAMILY | This company takes visitors on one-hour cruises aboard the *Lake Queen II.* The vessel makes its way from Bridge Bay to Stevenson Island and back. Reservations are strongly recommended. ⊠ *Bridge Bay Marina, Bridge Bay* ☎ *307/344–7311* ⊕ *www.yellowstonenationalparklodges.com/adventures* ✆ *$18.*

FISHING

Fishing season begins in late May on the Saturday of Memorial Day weekend and ends in November. Native cutthroat trout are among the prize catches, but four other varieties—brown, brook, lake, and rainbow—along with grayling and mountain whitefish inhabit Yellowstone's waters. Popular sportfishing opportunities include the Gardner and Yellowstone rivers as well as Soda Butte Creek, but the top fishing area is Madison River.

Yellowstone fishing permits cost $18 for three days, $25 for seven days, and $40 for the season. Anglers ages 15 and younger must have a (no-fee) permit or fish under direct supervision of an adult with a permit. Permits are available at all ranger stations, visitor centers, and Yellowstone general stores.

Xanterra Parks & Resorts

FISHING | This park concessionaire operates Yellowstone Lake fishing charters between 2 and 12 hours long, for up to six passengers per boat. The fee includes gear. ✉ *Grand Loop Rd., 2 miles south of Lake Village, Bridge Bay* ☎ *307/344–7311* ⊕ *www.yellowstonenationalparklodges. com/adventures* 🖃 *$95/hr.*

HIKING

Your most memorable Yellowstone moments will likely take place along a park hiking trail. Encountering a gang of elk in the woods is unquestionably more exciting than watching them graze on the grasses of Mammoth Hot Springs Hotel. Hearing the creak of lodgepole pines on a breezy afternoon feels more authentic than listening to tourists chatter as you jockey for the best view of Old Faithful.

Even a one-day visitor to Yellowstone can—and should—get off the roads and into the "wilderness." Because the park is a wild place, however, even a half-mile walk on a trail puts you at the mercy of nature, so be sure to prepare yourself accordingly. As a guide on an Old Yellow Bus Tour said, "You don't have to fear the animals—just respect them."

■ TIP➜ **Much of Yellowstone lies more than 7,500 feet above sea level. The most frequent incidents requiring medical attention are respiratory problems, not animal attacks. Be aware of your physical limitations—as well as those of young children or elderly companions.**

Yellowstone Forever Institute

HIKING/WALKING | If you'd like a naturalist, a geologist, a wildlife specialist, or other park expert to accompany you on a hike, book one of the institute's daylong or multiday excursions, which include backcountry trips. In the winter, the institute offers daylong wildlife-watching excursions and multiday skiing and snowshoeing trips. ✉ *308 W. Park St., Gardiner* ☎ *406/848–2400* ⊕ *www.yellowstone. org* 🖃 *From $150 per day.*

OLD FAITHFUL
Biscuit Basin Trail

HIKING/WALKING | FAMILY | This 2½-mile round-trip trail goes via a boardwalk across the Firehole River to colorful Sapphire Pool. *Easy.* ✉ *Old Faithful* ✛ *Trailhead: 3 miles north of Old Faithful Village off Grand Loop Rd.*

Fountain Paint Pots Nature Trail

HIKING/WALKING | FAMILY | Take the ½-mile loop boardwalk to see the fumaroles (steam vents), blue pools, pink mud pots, and mini-geysers in this thermal area. The trail is popular in summer and winter because it's right next to Grand Loop Road. *Easy.* ✉ *Yellowstone National Park* ✛ *Trailhead: at Lower Geyser Basin, between Old Faithful and Madison.*

Mystic Falls Trail

HIKING/WALKING | From the west end of Biscuit Basin boardwalk, this trail climbs gently for 1 mile through heavily burned forest to the lava-rock base of 70-foot Mystic Falls. It then switchbacks up Madison Plateau to a lookout with the park's least-crowded view of Old Faithful

Continued on page 699

35

Yellowstone National Park

YELLOWSTONE'S GEOTHERMAL WONDERS

Steaming, bubbling,
and erupting
throughout the day
like giant teapots.

Yellowstone's geothermal features are constantly putting on a show. The 10,000 hot springs, mud pots, and fumaroles, plus 500 or so active geysers within the park comprise more than half the entire world's thermal features. You'd need to search two or three other continents for as many geysers as you can see during a single afternoon around Old Faithful.

HEATING UP

Past eruptions of cataclysmic volcanoes brought about the steaming, vaporous landscape of Yellowstone today. The heat from the magma (molten rock) under the Yellowstone Caldera, an active volcano, continues to fuel the park's geyser basins, such as the Upper Geyser Basin, where more than 200 spouters cram into less than two square miles; and Norris, where water 1,000 feet below ground is 450° F. The complex underground plumbing in these geyser basins is affected by earthquakes and other subterranean hijinks that geologists are only beginning to understand. Some spouters spring to life, while others fall dormant with little or no warning.

HOT SPOT TIPS

■ **Stay on trails and boardwalks.** In some areas, like in Norris, water boils at temperatures of more than 200°. If you want to venture into the back country, where there are no boardwalks, consult a ranger first.

■ **Leave the area if you feel sick or dizzy.** You might be feeling this way due to overexposure to various thermal gases.

■ **These hot springs aren't for bathing.** The pH levels of some of these features are extremely acidic.

■ **They also aren't wishing wells.** In the past people threw hundreds of coins into the bright blue Morning Glory Pool. The coins clogged the pool's natural water vents, causing it to change to a sickly green color.

(left) Old Faithful. (above) Punch Bowl Spring.

HOW DO GEYSERS WORK?

A few main ingredients make geysers possible: abundant water, a heat source, a certain kind of plumbing system, and rock strong enough to withstand some serious pressure. The layout of any one geyser's underground plumbing may vary, but we know that below each vent is a system of fissures and chambers, with constrictions here and there that prevent hot water from rising to the surface. As the underground water heats up, these constrictions and the cooler surface water "cap" the whole system, keeping it from boiling over and ratcheting up the underground pressure. When a few steam bubbles eventually fight their way through the constrictions, the result is like uncapping a shaken-up soda bottle, when the released pressure causes the soda to spray.

FUN FACTS

■ A cone geyser (like Lone Star Geyser in Yellowstone's backcountry) has a spout-like formation around its vent, formed by silica particles deposited during eruptions.

■ A fountain geyser (like Daisy Geyser in the Old Faithful area) erupts from a vent submerged in a hot spring-like pool. Eruptions tend to be smaller and more sporadic.

■ Yellowstone's tallest geyser is Steamboat, in Norris, shooting up to 350 feet high.

■ When they erupt, geysers sometimes create rainbows amid their spray.

❶ RECHARGE STAGE

Groundwater accumulates in plumbing and is heated by the volcano. Some hot water flashes to steam and bubbles try to rise toward surface.

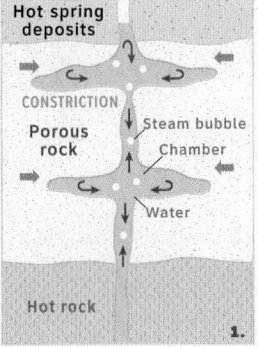

❷ PRELIMINARY ERUPTION STAGE

Pressure builds as steam bubbles clog at constriction. High pressure raises the boiling point, preventing superheated water from becoming steam.

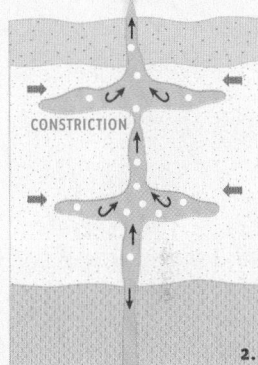

❸ ERUPTION STAGE

Bubbles squeeze through constriction, displacing surface water and relieving pressure. Trapped water flashes to steam, forcing water out of the chambers and causing a chain reaction.

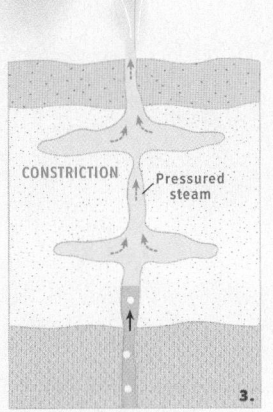

❹ RECOVERY STAGE

Eruption ends when the chambers are emptied or the temperature falls below boiling. Chambers begin to refill with ground water and the process begins again.

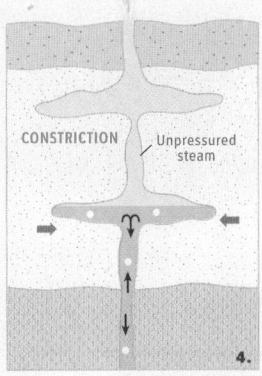

(left) Lone Star Geyser.

HOW DO HOT SPRINGS WORK?

Essentially, what keeps a hot spring from becoming a geyser is a lack of constriction in its underground plumbing. Like their more explosive cousins, hot springs consist of water that seeps into the earth, only to simmer its way back up through fissures after it's heated by hot volcanic rocks. Unlike in constricted geysers, water in a hot spring can circulate by convection. Rising hot water displaces cooling surface water, which then sinks underground to be heated and eventually rise again. Thus the whole mixture keeps itself at a gurgly equilibrium. As it rises, superheated water dissolves some subterranean minerals, depositing them at the surface to form the sculptural terraces that surround many hot springs.

The vivid colors that characterize hot springs and their terraces can be attributed alternately to minerals like sulfur and iron or to thermophiles. Thermophiles are microorganisms that thrive in extremely high temperatures. Blooming in thick bacterial mats, they convert light to energy, like plants, and their bright photosynthetic pigments help give hot springs their rainbow hues. Scientists suppose only a small percentage of Yellowstone's thermophiles have been identified. Still, these microbes have had a big impact on science. In 1965, a microorganism called Thermus aquaticus, or Taq, was discovered in the Lower Geyser Basin. From it, scientists extracted an enzyme that revolutionized molecular biology, ultimately making possible both DNA fingerprinting and the mapping of the human genome. NASA is among those performing research in the park today, studying thermophiles to gain insight on extraterrestrial life.

WHAT'S THAT SMELL?

Most people think hot springs smell like rotten eggs; some even say "burnt gunpowder" and "paper mill smoke-stack." Whatever simile you settle on, there's no question that hot springs and other thermal features stink to high heaven. Sulphur gases escaping from the volcano produce distinctive smells. Other gases are reduced to the stinky chemical hydrogen sulfide, which bubbles up to the surface. In high concentration, hydrogen sulfide can actually kill you, but the small amounts released by thermals can only kill your appetite. It's because hydrogen sulfide is often present in volcanic areas that we associate brimstone (or sulfur) with the underworld.

Did You Know?

Grand Prismatic Spring (pictured here) is the world's third-largest hot spring, at more than 370 feet across. The pool's vivid red and orange colors drizzle down its runoff channels, but from the boardwalk you can only glimpse a portion of these psychedelic tentacles. Thank the little guys: heat-loving microorganisms (bacteria and algae) tint the Grand Prismatic Spring with a rainbow of colors.

THE INNER WORKINGS OF HOT SPRINGS

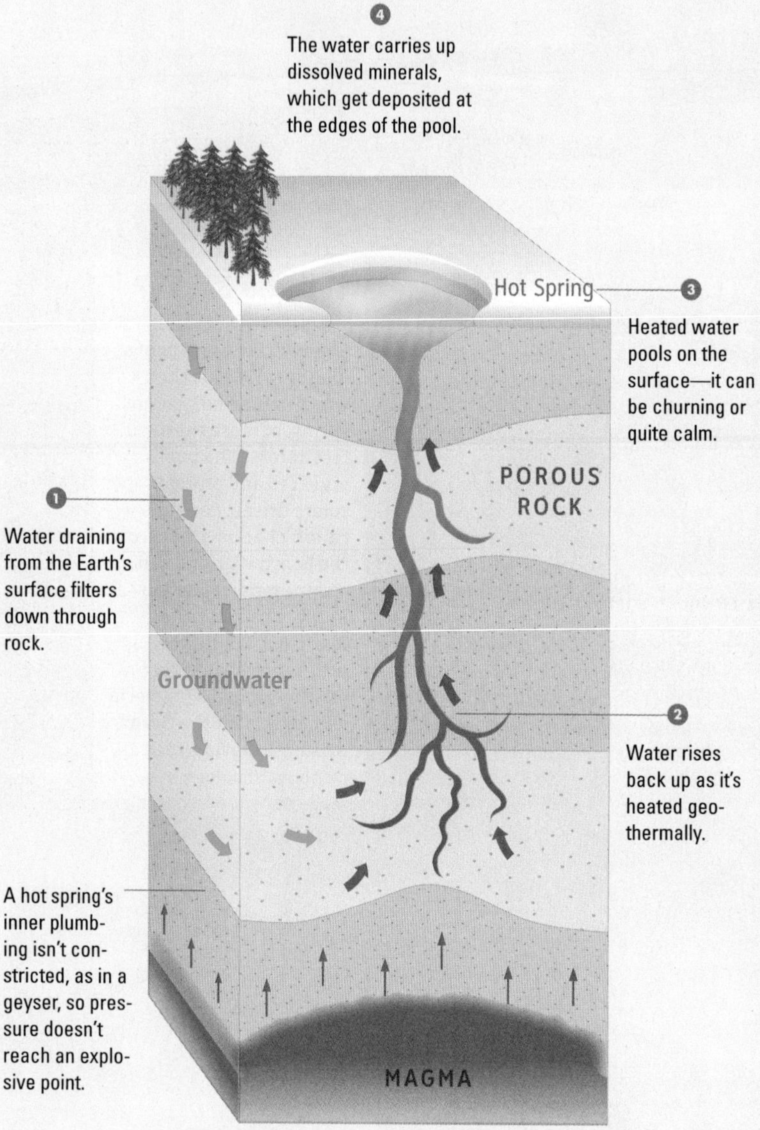

4 The water carries up dissolved minerals, which get deposited at the edges of the pool.

Hot Spring **3**

3 Heated water pools on the surface—it can be churning or quite calm.

POROUS ROCK

1

1 Water draining from the Earth's surface filters down through rock.

Groundwater

2

2 Water rises back up as it's heated geothermally.

A hot spring's inner plumbing isn't constricted, as in a geyser, so pressure doesn't reach an explosive point.

MAGMA

WHAT ARE FUMAROLES?

Take away the water from a hot spring and you're left with steam and other gas, forming a fumarole. Often called steam vents, these noisy thermals occur when available water boils away before reaching the surface. All that escapes the vent is heat, vapor, and the whisper-roar of a giant, menacing teakettle. Fumaroles are often found on high ground. The gases expelled from fumaroles might include carbon dioxide, sulfur dioxide, and hydrogen sulfide. Some hot spots, like Red Spouter in the Lower Geyser Basin, can exhibit different behaviors depending on the seasonal water table, so what's a fumarole today could be a hot spring in a few months.

FUN FACTS

■ The word fumarole comes from the Latin *fumus*, which means "smoke."

■ Fumaroles are also known as steam vents and solfataras, from *sulpha terra*, Latin for "land of sulfur."

■ Yellowstone's hottest fumarole is *Black Growler*, at Norris, which heats up to 280°F.

■ About 4,000 fumaroles are in Yellowstone.

Fumarole

WHAT ARE MUD POTS?

Mud pots in Lower Geyser Basin.

Might as well say it up front: mud pots are great because their thick, bursting bubbles can sound like a chorus of rude noises or "greetings from the interior." That's why the few places they're found in Yellowstone are usually surrounded by gaggles of giggling visitors with video cameras rolling. A mud pot is basically just a hot spring where the water table results in a bubbling broth of water and clay. The acid gases react with surface rocks, breaking them down into silica and clay. As gases escape from below, bubbles swell and pop, flinging mud chunks onto the banks to form gloppy clay mounds. The mud's thickness varies with rainfall through the seasons.

FUN FACTS
■ Mud pots have been nicknamed "paint pots" due to iron and other metals tinting the mud.

■ The biggest cluster of mud pots in the park is in Pocket Basin in Lower Geyser Basin.

■ Before it exploded in 1872, Mud Volcano was 30 feet tall by 30 feet wide.

PHOTOGRAPHY TIPS

■ Set your alarm clock: generally, the best light for shooting the geothermal features is early in the morning. You'll avoid the thickest crowds then, too. The runner-up time is the late afternoon.

■ Breezy days are good for photographing geysers, since the steam will be blown away from the jetting water. But avoid standing downwind or your view can be clouded with steam.

■ If you get water from a thermal feature on your lens, dry it off as quickly as possible, because the water has a high mineral content that can damage your lens.

Thermal pool in the Rabbit Creek Thermal Area.

and the Upper Geyser Basin. *Moderate.* ⊠ *Old Faithful* ⊹ *Trailhead: 3 miles north of Old Faithful Village off Grand Loop Rd.* ⊕ *www.nps.gov/thingstodo/yell-trail-mystic-falls.htm.*

★ Old Faithful Geyser Loop

HIKING/WALKING | FAMILY | The ¾-mile loop departs from Old Faithful's visitor center, circling the geyser's benches, filled nearly all day in summer with tourists. *Easy.* ⊠ *Old Faithful* ⊹ *Trailhead: at Old Faithful Village.*

MAMMOTH HOT SPRINGS
Beaver Ponds Loop Trail

HIKING/WALKING | The hike to Beaver Ponds is a 2½-hour, 5-mile round-trip starting at Liberty Cap in the busy Lower Terrace of Mammoth Hot Springs. You enter Yellowstone backcountry within minutes as you climb 400 feet through spruce and fir, passing several ponds and dams, as well as a glacier-carved moraine, before emerging on a wind-swept plain overlooking the Montana–Wyoming border. Look up to see Everts Peak to the east, Bunsen Peak to the south, and Sepulcher Mountain to the west. Your final descent into Mammoth Springs has great views of Mammoth Springs. *Moderate.* ⊠ *Mammoth Hot Springs* ⊹ *Trailhead: Grand Loop Rd. at Old Gardiner Rd.* ⊕ *www.nps.gov/thingstodo/yell-trail-beaver-ponds.htm.*

Bunsen Peak Trail

HIKING/WALKING | Past the entrance to Bunsen Peak Road, this moderately difficult trail is a 4-mile, three-hour round-trip that climbs 1,300 feet to Bunsen Peak for a panoramic view of Blacktail Plateau, Swan Lake Flats, the Gallatin Mountains, and the Yellowstone River valley. *Moderate.* ⊠ *Yellowstone National Park* ⊹ *Trailhead: Grand Loop Rd., 1½ miles south of Mammoth Hot Springs* ⊕ *www.nps.gov/thingstodo/yell-trail-bunsen-peak.htm.*

TOWER-ROOSEVELT
★ Slough Creek Trail

HIKING/WALKING | Starting at Slough Creek Campground, this trail climbs steeply along a historic wagon trail for the first 1½ miles before reaching expansive meadows and prime fishing spots, where moose are common and grizzlies occasionally wander. From this point the trail, now mostly level, meanders another 9½ miles to the park's northern boundary. Anglers absolutely rave about this trail. *Moderate.* ⊠ *Yellowstone National Park* ⊹ *Trailhead: 7 miles east of Tower-Roosevelt off Northeast Entrance Rd.* ⊕ *www.nps.gov/thingstodo/yell-trail-slough-creek.htm.*

CANYON
Brink of the Lower Falls Trail

HIKING/WALKING | Especially scenic, this trail branches off of the North Rim Trail at the Brink of the Upper Falls parking area. You can also access it from the Brink of the Lower Falls parking area on the North Rim Drive. The steep ½-mile one-way trail switchbacks 600 feet down to within a few yards of the top of the Yellowstone River's 308-foot Lower Falls. *Moderate.* ⊠ *Yellowstone National Park* ⊹ *Trailhead: 300 yards east of Grand Loop Rd. on entrance to North Rim Drive, 1 mile south of Canyon.*

North Rim Trail

HIKING/WALKING | Offering great views of the Grand Canyon of the Yellowstone, the 3-mile North Rim Trail runs from Inspiration Point to Chittenden Bridge. Particularly fetching is the ½-mile section of the North Rim Trail from the Brink of the Upper Falls parking area to Chittenden Bridge that hugs the rushing Yellowstone River as it approaches the canyon. This trail is paved and fully accessible between Lookout Point and Grand View. Note that the North Rim Trail is closed between Cascade Falls and the Brink of Lower Falls, and also between Grandview Point and Inspiration Point. It's expected to reopen in summer of 2019.

Moderate. ⊠ *Yellowstone National Park* ⚓ *Trailhead: 1 mile south of Canyon.*

LAKE AREA
★ Avalanche Peak Trail
HIKING/WALKING | On a busy day in summer, maybe six parties will fill out the trail register at the Avalanche Peak trailhead, so you won't have a lot of company on this hike. Starting across from a parking area on the East Entrance Road, the difficult 4-mile, four-hour round-trip climbs 2,150 feet to the peak's 10,566-foot summit, from which you'll see the rugged Absaroka Mountains running north and south. Look around the talus and tundra near the top of Avalanche Peak for alpine wildflowers and butterflies. Don't try this trail before late June or after early September—it may be covered in deep snow. Rangers discourage hikers from attempting this hike in September or October because of bear activity. *Difficult.* ⊠ *Fishing Bridge* ⚓ *Trailhead: 2 miles east of Sylvan Lake on north side of East Entrance Rd.* ⊕ *www.nps.gov/ thingstodo/yell-trail-avalanche-peak.htm.*

Storm Point Trail
HIKING/WALKING | **FAMILY** | Well marked and mostly flat, this 2.3-mile loop leaves the south side of the road for a perfect beginner's hike out to Yellowstone Lake, particularly with a setting sun. The trail rounds the western edge of Indian Pond, then passes moose habitat on its way to Yellowstone Lake's Storm Point, named for its frequent afternoon windstorms and crashing waves. Heading west along the shore, you're likely to hear the shrill chirping of yellow-bellied marmots, rodents that grow as long as 2 feet. Also look for ducks, pelicans, trumpeter swans, and bison. You will pass several small beaches kids can explore on warm summer mornings. *Easy.* ⊠ *Fishing Bridge* ⚓ *Trailhead: 3 miles east of Lake Junction on East Entrance Rd.* ⊕ *www. nps.gov/thingstodo/yell-trail-storm-point. htm.*

HORSEBACK RIDING
Reservations are recommended for horseback riding in the park. Don't worry about experience, as rangers estimate 90% of riders have not been on a horse in at least 10 years.

About 50 area outfitters lead horse-packing trips and trail rides into Yellowstone. Expect to pay from $250 to $400 per day for a backcountry trip, including meals, accommodations, and guides. A guide must accompany all horseback-riding trips.

Private stock can be brought into the park. Horses are not allowed in front-country campgrounds but are permitted in certain backcountry campsites. For information on planning a backcountry trip with stock, call the Backcountry Office (☏ *307/344–2160*).

Rimrock Dude Ranch
HORSEBACK RIDING | **FAMILY** | Outfitter Gary Fales has been leading multiday pack trips into Yellowstone for decades, operating out of Rimrock Dude Ranch west of Cody. Trips last at least five days and include backcountry camping, fishing, hiking, and horseback activities. All food and camping items are provided. ⊠ *2728 Northfork Hwy., Cody* ☏ *307/587–3970* ⊕ *www.rimrockranch.com* 💲 *From $300 per day.*

★ Wilderness Pack Trips
HORSEBACK RIDING | **FAMILY** | Mike and Erin Thompson at Wilderness Pack Trips have led small group trips exclusively in Yellowstone National Park for many years. Popular destinations include the spectacular remote waterfalls and wildlife-rich regions often closed to the general public. Families are welcome for these excursions. Backcountry fishing trips and other day and overnight adventures are also arranged. ⊠ *172 E. River Rd., Emigrant* ☏ *406/848–9953* ⊕ *www. yellowstonepacktrips.com* 💲 *From $300 per day.*

Yellowstone in Winter

To see a spectacularly different Yellowstone than that experienced by 90% of its visitors, come in winter. Rocky outcroppings are smoothed over. Waterfalls are transformed into jagged sheets of ice.

Crowdless Quiet

The best reason for a visit to Yellowstone between December and March is the opportunity to experience the park without the crowds. The first thing that strikes you during this season is the quiet. The gargantuan snowpack—as many as 200 inches annually at low elevation—seems to muffle the sounds of bison foraging in the geyser basins and of hot springs simmering. Yet even in the depths of a deep freeze, the park is never totally still: the mud pots bubble, geysers shoot skyward, and wind rustles the snow-covered pine trees. Above these sounds, the cry of a hawk, the yip of a coyote, or even on rare occasions the howl of a wolf may pierce the air.

Animals Head Down

Animals in Yellowstone head *down* when the thermometer falls. Herbivores like elk and bison head to the warmer, less snowy valleys to find vegetation; predators like wolves and cougars follow them. As a result, you're more likely to see these animals in the frontcountry in winter. The snow also makes it easier to pick out animal tracks.

Snow Play

Snowmobiling is popular but also controversial (critics cite noise and pollution). At the time of this writing, guided trips with capped speed limits are offered in both Yellowstone and Grand Teton national parks. There are also the options of cross-country skiing and snowshoeing through geyser basins and along the canyon, both excellent ways to see the park. Dogsledding isn't permitted, but outfitters in Jackson lead trips in the nearby national forests.

—Brian Kevin, excerpted from Fodor's *Compass American Guides: Yellowstone and Grand Teton National Parks*

Yellowstone National Park Lodges
HORSEBACK RIDING | FAMILY | Park concessionaire Xanterra offers one-hour horseback rides at Mammoth, and one- and two-hour rides at Tower-Roosevelt and Canyon Village. You can also book an Old West Dinner Cookout which includes a ride. ⊠ *Mammoth Hot Springs, 1 Grand Loop Rd.* ☎ *307/344–7311, 866/439–7375* ⊕ *www.yellowstonenationalparklodges. com/adventure/wild-west-adventures/ saddle-up* 🎟 *From $50.*

SKIING, SNOWSHOEING, AND SNOWMOBILING

Yellowstone can be the coldest place in the continental United States in winter, with temperatures of –30°F not uncommon. Still, winter-sports enthusiasts flock here when the park opens for its winter season on the last week of December. Until early March, the roads teem with over-snow vehicles like snowmobiles and snow coaches, and trails bristle with cross-country skiers and snowshoers.

Snowmobiling is an exhilarating way to experience Yellowstone. It's also controversial: there's heated debate about the pollution and disruption to animal habitats. The number of riders per day is limited, and you must have a reservation, a guide, and a four-stroke engine, less polluting than the more common two-stroke variety. About a dozen companies have been authorized to lead snowmobile excursions. Prices vary, as do itineraries and inclusions: ask about insurance, guides, taxes, park entrance fees, clothing, helmets, and meals.

Lone Star Geyser Trail

SKIING/SNOWBOARDING | The trail is an easy 4.8-mile-roundtrip ski to the Lone Star Geyser, starting south of Kepler Cascades. Ski to Kepler Cascades from Old Faithful Village. You can ski back to the Old Faithful area on the Howard Eaton Trail, or return the way you came. ⊠ *Old Faithful* ⊹ *Start at Bear Den Ski Shop in the Snow Lodge* ⊕ *www.nps.gov/thing-stodo/yell-trail-lone-star-geyser.htm.*

Bear Den Ski Shops

SKIING/SNOWBOARDING | FAMILY | At Mammoth Hot Springs Hotel and Old Faithful Snow Lodge, the park concessionaire rents skis, gear, and snowshoes. Lessons, guided tours, and shuttles to trails are also available. ⊠ *Mammoth Hot Springs, 1 Grand Loop Rd.* ☎ *307/344–7311, 866/439–7375, 307/344–5276* ⊕ *www.yellowstonenationalparklodges. com/shops/bear-den-ski-shops* ⊠ *Ski rental $14/half day, $22/full day; snowshoes $14/half day, $22/full day.*

Free Heel and Wheel

SKIING/SNOWBOARDING | FAMILY | This cross-country boutique outside the West Yellowstone entrance gate rents skis and other equipment and is a source for winter gear, sleds, snowshoes, and advice. Ski lessons and pull sleds for toting children are available. It also rents and repairs bicycles, and has an espresso bar to boot. ⊠ *33 Yellowstone Ave., West Yellowstone* ☎ *406/646–7744* ⊕ *www. freeheelandwheel.com* ⊠ *From $25 for ski rental, from $35 for bikes.*

Togwotee Adventures

SKIING/SNOWBOARDING | This outfit conducts day, overnight, and multiday snowmobile trips in the national forest areas near Yellowstone. Lodging is sometimes within the park, sometimes just outside. In the summer, whitewater trips are offered. ⊠ *1050 S. U.S. 89, Jackson* ☎ *307/733–8800* ⊕ *www.togwoteesnow-mobile.com* ⊠ *Tours start from $250.*

Yellowstone Forever Institute

SKIING/SNOWBOARDING | The institute's winter programs include daylong wildlife-watching excursions and multiday skiing and snowshoeing treks. ⊠ *308 W. Park St., Gardiner* ☎ *406/848–2400* ⊕ *www.yellowstone.org.*

Nearby Towns

Yellowstone National Park is a destination, not something to see as you pass through the area, and it covers a lot of ground. It's easily possible—and sometimes the most convenient strategy—to spend nearly your entire time within the park itself. That said, towns just outside the park contain numerous sights to see and outdoor activities, not to mention upscale resorts and destination restaurants.

Because of its airport and its proximity to both Grand Teton and Yellowstone national parks, **Jackson,** the closest town to Yellowstone's South Entrance, is the region's busiest community in summer and has the widest selection of dining and lodging options. Meanwhile, the least-known gateway, the little town of **Dubois,** southeast of the park, is far from the madding crowds and a good place to stop on the way in or out of the park if you want to visit the National Bighorn Sheep Interpretive Center.

The most popular gateway from Montana, particularly in winter, is **West Yellowstone,** near the park's West Entrance. This is where the open plains of southwestern

Changes in Yellowstone National Park

(Old) Faithful, But Slowing Down

Though Old Faithful continues to spew routinely. The geyser now erupts about every 94 minutes (up from 78 minutes in 1990), and it may look different each time. Monitoring shows that Old Faithful almost always discharges the same amount of water at each eruption, but how it does so varies.

Less Faithful Geysers

The force and nature of the geysers depend on several factors, but the greatest threats to the geyser basin activity are earthquakes (which occur regularly, but they are usually very small tremors) and human impact. In past years people threw hundreds of coins into the bright blue Morning Glory Pool, which clogged the pool's water vents, causing it to turn a green. Though it has been cleaned the pool has never regained its pristine color.

Fossils and Petrified Forests

Besides its unique geology, Yellowstone has many other faces. There are petrified forests and fossil remains of both plants and animals. The ongoing ecological development of the region draws widespread interest.

Bison on the Move

The reintroduction of wolves to the ecosystem and efforts to control the movement of bison—to keep them from wandering out of the park during the winter in search of food—are just two examples of divisive issues regarding the management of Yellowstone.

Bison leave the park in winter—mainly through the North and West entrances—in part because of overpopulation and the need to forage. Their movements are sometimes made easier by the winter grooming of Yellowstone roads for use by over-snow vehicles.

Wolves Return, But Is That Good?

Wolves were brought back to Yellowstone in 1995. They acclimated so well that they quickly formed several packs, some of which have ventured outside the park's boundaries. Wolves from Yellowstone's packs have been spotted as far south as northern Utah and Colorado. The presence of wolves within the park has had a lasting effect on wildlife populations. The wolves feed on elk and buffalo, and researchers have noted a significant decline in elk calf survival as a result of wolf predation. Park rangers have also reported a significant decline in the coyote population. Since the wolves are bigger and stronger than coyotes, they kill coyotes or force them to find a new range.

Fire Takes Its Toll, Helps Park Evolve

When wildfires tore through Yellowstone in 1988, some believed it would take generations for the park to recover. Already, the park has begun to evolve and renew itself. When you visit Yellowstone now you will see scars of the 1988 fires and more recent ones in 2001 and 2002, but you will also see new growth. Pine forests need fire to release their seeds, and once seeds get a start, trees grow quickly. The new growth provides excellent cover for animals, though this does make it harder for visitors to see wildlife.

Montana and northeastern Idaho come together along the Madison River Valley. Affectionately known among winter recreationists as the "snowmobile capital of the world," this town of 1,000 is also a good place to go for fishing, horseback riding, and downhill skiing. Stop by the Grizzly & Wolf Discovery Center and the Yellowstone Historic Center to tap into the area's natural and cultural history.

As the only entrance to Yellowstone open the entire year, **Gardiner,** in Montana, is always bustling. The town's Roosevelt Arch has marked the park's North Entrance since 1903, when President Theodore Roosevelt dedicated it. The Yellowstone River slices through the town, population 800, beckoning fishermen and rafters. Its quaint stores and good restaurants attract shoppers and diners. North of Gardiner, along Interstate 90, is **Livingston,** a town of 7,500 known for its nostalgia-inducing historic district.

With both Yellowstone and the Absaroka-Beartooth Wilderness at its back door, the Montana village of **Cooke City,** at the park's Northeast Entrance, is a good place for hiking, horseback riding, mountain climbing, and other outdoor activities. Some 50 miles to the east of Cooke City and 60 miles southeast of Billings via U.S. 212 is the small resort town of **Red Lodge.** Nestled against the foot of the pine-draped Absaroka-Beartooth Wilderness and edged by the Limestone Palisades, Red Lodge attracts skiers, anglers, golfers, and horseback riders and has more options for dining and lodging than Cooke City. Driving along the Beartooth Scenic Byway between Red Lodge and Cooke City, you'll cross the southern tip of the Beartooth range, literally in the ramparts of the Rockies. From Cooke City, the drive into Yellowstone through the Lamar Valley is one of the prettiest routes in the park.

Named for Pony Express rider, army scout, and entertainer William F. "Buffalo Bill" Cody, the town of **Cody,** in Wyoming,

sits near the park's East Entrance. It is a good base for hiking trips, horseback-riding excursions, and white-water rafting on the North Fork of the Shoshone or the Clarks Fork of the Yellowstone. It also is home to dude ranches and, in season, the nightly rodeo.

VISITOR INFORMATION Cody Country Chamber of Commerce ✉ *836 Sheridan Ave., Cody* ☎ *307/587–2777, 307/587–2777, 800/393–2639* ⊕ *www.codychamber.org.* **Cooke City Chamber of Commerce** ✉ *206 W. Main St.* ☎ *406/838–2495* ⊕ *www.cookecitychamber.org.* **Dubois Chamber of Commerce** ✉ *20 Stalnaker St., Dubois* ☎ *307/455–2556* ⊕ *www.duboiswyomingchamber.org.* **Gardiner Chamber of Commerce** ✉ *222 Park St., Gardiner* ☎ *406/848–7971* ⊕ *www.visitgardinermt.com.* **Jackson Hole Chamber of Commerce** ✉ *250 W. Broadway, Jackson* ☎ *307/733–3316, 307/733–3316* ⊕ *www.jacksonholechamber.com.* **Livingston Area Chamber of Commerce & Visitors Bureau** ✉ *303 E. Park St., Livingston* ☎ *406/222–0850* ⊕ *www.livingston-chamber.com.* **Red Lodge Area Chamber of Commerce** ✉ *701 N. Broadway, Red Lodge* ☎ *406/446–1718* ⊕ *redlodgechamber.org.* **West Yellowstone Chamber of Commerce** ✉ *30 Yellowstone Ave., West Yellowstone* ☎ *406/646–7701* ⊕ *www.destinationyellowstone.com.*

 # Sights

CODY

★ Buffalo Bill Center of the West

MUSEUM | FAMILY | This sprawling "five-in-one" complex, sometimes called the Smithsonian of the West, contains the Buffalo Bill Museum, the Whitney Western Art Museum, the Plains Indian Museum, the Cody Firearms Museum, and the Draper Natural History Museum. All are well organized and mount superb exhibitions in their respective subject areas. The flagship Buffalo Bill Museum puts into context the life, era, and activities of its (and its town's) namesake, William F.

"Buffalo Bill" Cody (1846–1917), whose numerous careers included guide, scout, actor, and entrepreneur. If you want to understand how the myth of the American West developed, this is the place to come. The other four museums—there's also a research library—are equally absorbing. Plan to spend at least four hours here—and to discover that this isn't enough time to take it all in. Luckily, your admission ticket is good for two consecutive days. ⊠ *720 Sheridan Ave., Cody* ☎ *307/587–4771* ⊕ *www.centerofthewest.org* ⊠ *$20, good for 2 consecutive days.*

WEST YELLOWSTONE
Grizzly and Wolf Discovery Center
NATURE PRESERVE | FAMILY | Home to grizzlies and grey wolves, this facility provides an up-close look at Yellowstone's largest and most powerful predators. In summer, birds of prey are also on display. The comprehensive "Bears: Imagination and Reality" exhibit compares myths about bears to what science has revealed about them. This is the only facility that formally tests bear-resistant products such as coolers and canisters in cooperation with state and federal agencies. ⊠ *201 S. Canyon St., West Yellowstone* ☎ *406/646–7001, 800/257–2570* ⊕ *www.grizzlydiscoveryctr.org* ⊠ *$16, good for 2 consecutive days.*

Yellowstone Historic Center
MUSEUM | FAMILY | West Yellowstone's 1909 Union Pacific Depot has been transformed into a museum dedicated to the modes of travel—from stagecoaches to planes—people employed to get to Yellowstone before World War II. Films provide insight on topics such as the fire that devastated Yellowstone in 1988 and the way earthquakes affect the area's hydrothermal features. ⊠ *104 Yellowstone Ave., West Yellowstone* ☎ *406/646–1100* ⊕ *www.yellowstonehistoriccenter.org* ⊠ *$6* ☉ *Closed early Oct.–mid-May.*

 Shopping

Old Faithful Basin Store
FOOD/CANDY | Recognizable by the wooden "Hamilton's Store" sign over the entrance, this shop is the second-oldest building in the park. The old-fashioned soda fountain serves up all your ice-cream favorites. ⊠ *Old Faithful Village, 1 Old Faithful Loop Rd.* ☎ *406/586–7593* ⊕ *www.visityellowstonepark.com/in-park-shopping.*

Sunlight Sports
SPORTING GOODS | This 8,000-square-foot store that stocks major-brand products sells everything from camping gear to downhill and cross-country ski equipment. The staff is friendly and has extensive experience in most outdoor pursuits. ⊠ *1131 Sheridan Ave., Cody* ☎ *307/587–9517* ⊕ *www.sunlightsports.com.*

 Restaurants

IN THE PARK
Bear Paw Deli
$ | FAST FOOD | FAMILY | You can grab a quick bite and not miss a geyser eruption at this snack shop in the Old Faithful Inn. Tasty salads and sandwiches are available throughout the day, as is hand-dipped ice cream. **Known for:** cheap, no-frills meals; opens early, closes late; great location by geyser. $ *Average main: $8* ⊠ *Old Faithful Village, Old Faithful* ☎ *307/344–7311* ⊕ *www.yellowstonenationalparklodges.com/dining* ☉ *Closed early Oct.–early May.*

Canyon Lodge Eatery
$$ | AMERICAN | FAMILY | Diners pack this place for casual breakfasts, as well as lunches and diners that deviate from your standard national park fare. Design your own wok meal with veggies, meat, and toppings, or choose a protein and sauce on a three-item combo plate. **Known for:** more upscale and interesting options than many cafeterias; lets customers customize their breakfasts and lunches;

all-American offerings like barbecue ribs and country fried steak. $ *Average main: $13 ⊠ Canyon Village* ☎ *307/344–7311* ⊕ *www.yellowstonenationalparklodges. com/restaurant/canyon-lodge-eatery* ⊗ *Closed mid-Oct.–mid-May.*

Geyser Grill

$ | FAST FOOD | FAMILY | You're here for the geyser views, not the grub, of this busy grill near Old Faithful. Whimsical carvings fill the walls, and diner favorites like burgers and wraps will fill your plate. **Known for:** convenient stop for a bite or a beer; burgers made from beef, fish and black beans; good kids meals. $ *Average main: $7 ⊠ Snow Lodge at Old Faithful Village* ☎ *307/344–7311* ⊕ *www. yellowstonenationalparklodges.com/ dining* ⊗ *Closed early Nov.–mid-Dec. and mid-Mar.–mid-Apr.*

Grant Village Dining Room

$$$ | AMERICAN | The floor-to-ceiling windows of this waterfront restaurant provide views of Yellowstone Lake through the thick stand of pines. The pine-beam ceilings, cedar-shake walls, and contemporary decor lend the place a homey feel. **Known for:** classic meat, pasta, and fish offerings; signature bison dishes, like meat loaf, bratwurst, and burgers; uses local meat and produce. $ *Average main: $22 ⊠ 1 Grand Loop Rd., 3 miles south of West Thumb Information Station, Grant Village* ☎ *307/344–7311, 866/439–7375* ⊕ *www.yellowstonenationalparklodges.com/dining* ⊗ *Closed Oct.–late May.*

★ Lake Hotel Dining Room

$$$ | AMERICAN | Opened in 1891, this double-colonnaded dining room off the lobby of the Lake Yellowstone Hotel is the park's most elegant dining spot. Arrive early and enjoy a beverage and the view in the airy Reamer Lounge, which debuted as a sunroom in 1928. **Known for:** classic meat and fish dishes; local and regional ingredients; elevated yet casual vibe. $ *Average main: $27 ⊠ Lake Village Rd., 1 mile south of Fishing Bridge, Lake Village* ☎ *307/344–7311, 866/439–7375* ⊕ *www.yellowstonenationalparklodges. com/dining* ⊗ *Closed early Oct.–early May.*

Lake Lodge Cafeteria

$ | AMERICAN | FAMILY | Much of the fare here may be standard cafeteria—roast turkey, pot roast, and the like—but the Yellowstone Lake views are awe-inspiring. The more upscale entrées might include prime rib and poached salmon. **Known for:** casual breakfast, lunch, and dinner; offers both diner favorites and fancier fare; good value. $ *Average main: $12 ⊠ Lake Village Rd., 1 mile south of Fishing Bridge* ☎ *307/344–7311* ⊕ *www. yellowstonenationalparklodges.com/ dining* ⊗ *Closed Oct.–early June.*

Mammoth Hotel Dining Room

$$ | AMERICAN | A wall of windows at the dining room overlooks an expanse of green that was once a military parade and drill field. While enjoying breakfast, lunch, or dinner you might catch a glimpse of elk grazing on the lawn. **Known for:** top-notch bison burgers and elk sliders; appetizers that range from high-end to pub-style; attentive service. $ *Average main: $18 ⊠ Mammoth Hot Springs ✛ 5 miles south of North Entrance* ☎ *307/344–7311, 866/439–7375* ⊕ *www.yellowstonenationalparklodges.com/dining* ⊗ *Closed mid-Oct.–late Apr.*

Mammoth Terrace Grill

$ | FAST FOOD | FAMILY | Although the exterior looks rather elegant, this Mammoth Hot Springs restaurant serves simple fare. Expect hot dogs, hamburgers, and chicken tenders. **Known for:** quick, cheap meals; a few healthier options; beer and wine available. $ *Average main: $8 ⊠ Mammoth Hot Springs ✛ 5 miles south of North Entrance, west of Mammoth Hot Springs Hotel* ☎ *307/344–7311* ⊕ *www.yellowstonenationalparklodges. com/dining* ⊗ *Closed mid-Oct.–late Apr.*

Old Faithful Inn Dining Room

$$$ | AMERICAN | The Old Faithful Inn's original dining room—designed by Robert Reamer in 1903 and expanded by him in 1927—has lodgepole-pine walls and ceiling beams and a giant volcanic rock fireplace. Note the whimsical etched-glass panels that separate the dining room from the Bear Pit Lounge; the images of partying animals were commissioned by Reamer in 1933 to celebrate the end of Prohibition. **Known for:** buffet and à la carte items offered every meal; meat and fish dishes popular in the region; the park's most extensive wine list. $ *Average main: $23* ✉ *Old Faithful* ✛ *Take first left off Old Faithful Bypass Rd.* ☎ *307/344–7311, 866/439–7375* ⊕ *www. yellowstonenationalparklodges.com/ dining* ☉ *Closed early Oct.–early May.*

Old Faithful Lodge Cafeteria & Bake Shop

$ | AMERICAN | FAMILY | This noisy eatery that serves kid-friendly fare like pizza and hamburgers has some of the best views of Old Faithful, and while you eat you can watch it erupt. The cafeteria is not open for breakfast, but the bake shop just outside is, offering a small selection of sweets and ice cream. **Known for:** front-row seat to Old Faithful; economical, filling meals; local favorites like bison meat loaf and trout. $ *Average main: $10* ✉ *Yellowstone National Park* ✛ *End of Old Faithful Bypass Rd.* ☎ *307/344–7311* ⊕ *www.yellowstonenationalparklodges.com/dining* ☉ *Closed mid-Sept.–mid-May.*

★ Old Faithful Snow Lodge Obsidian Dining Room

$$$ | AMERICAN | From the wood-and-leather chairs etched with animal figures to the intricate lighting fixtures that resemble snowcapped trees, there's ample Western atmosphere at this smaller dining room inside the Old Faithful Snow Lodge. The huge windows give you a view of the Old Faithful area, and you can sometimes see the famous geyser as it erupts. **Known for:** Western favorites

like elk, salmon, and prime rib; one of two spots serving full dinners in winter; lounge offering microbrews and appetizers. $ *Average main: $25* ✉ *Old Faithful Snow Lodge, south end of Old Faithful Village* ☎ *307/344–7311, 866/439–7375* ⊕ *www.yellowstonenationalparklodges. com/dining* ☉ *Closed late-Oct.–mid-Dec. and Mar.–late Apr.*

Roosevelt Lodge Dining Room

$$ | AMERICAN | FAMILY | The menu at this log cabin in a pine forest includes appropriately rustic options like sirloin steak and barbecued ribs, but you can also order shrimp tacos or a burger and fries. For a real adventure, make a reservation for the Roosevelt Old West Dinner Cookout, which includes an hour-long trail ride or a stagecoach ride. **Known for:** cowboy favorites like bison burgers and mesquite-smoked chicken; famous beans; ice cream treats for after dinner. $ *Average main: $20* ✉ *Grand Loop Rd. and Northeast Entrance Rd., Tower Junction* ☎ *307/344–7311* ⊕ *www.yellowstonenationalparklodges.com/dining* ☉ *Closed early Sept.–early June.*

PICNIC AREAS

The 49 picnic areas in the park range from secluded spots with a couple of tables to more popular stops with a dozen or more tables. Only nine areas—Snake River, Grant Village, Spring Creek, Nez Perce, Old Faithful East, Bridge Bay, Cascade Lake Trail, Norris Meadows, and Yellowstone River—have fire grates. Gas stoves only may be used in the other areas. None have running water, and all but a few have pit toilets. You can stock up your cooler at any of the park's general stores. It is also possible to purchase from some park restaurants box lunches that include drinks, snacks, sandwiches, and fruit, or vegetarian or cheese-and-crackers selections.

▣ TIP➔ **Keep an eye out for wildlife.** You never know when a herd of bison might decide to march through. If that happens, it's best to leave your food and move a safe distance away from them.

Firehole River

NATIONAL/STATE PARK | **FAMILY** | The Firehole River rolls past this picnic area, and you might see elk grazing along the river's banks. There's one pit toilet here. ✉ *Grand Loop Rd., 3 miles south of Madison, Madison* 🌐 *www.nps.gov/yell/planyourvisit/picnic.htm.*

Gibbon Meadows

NATIONAL/STATE PARK | **FAMILY** | You are likely to see elk or buffalo along the Gibbon River from one of nine tables at this area, which has a wheelchair-accessible pit toilet. ✉ *Grand Loop Rd., 3 miles south of Norris* 🌐 *www.nps.gov/yell/planyourvisit/picnic.htm.*

Sedge Bay

NATIONAL/STATE PARK | **FAMILY** | On the northern end of this volcanic beach, look carefully for the large rock slabs pushed out of the lake bottom. Nearby trees offer shade and a table, or you can hop onto the level rocks for an ideal lakeside picnic. You may see bubbles rising from the clear water around the rocks—these indicate an active underwater thermal feature. The only company you may have here could be crickets, birds, and bison. ✉ *East Entrance Rd., 8 miles east of Fishing Bridge* 🌐 *www.nps.gov/yell/planyourvisit/picnic.htm.*

OUTSIDE THE PARK

Old Piney Dell

$$$ | **AMERICANSTEAKHOUSE** | This small hangout on the banks of Rock Creek has good meat and seafood options, as well as daily pasta specials. Part of the Rock Creek Resort, the restaurant dates to the early 1940s. **Known for:** great schnitzel; calming setting; log-cabin interior. [$] *Average main: $27* ✉ *Rock Creek Resort, 6380 U.S. 212 S, Red Lodge* ☎ *406/446–1111* 🌐 *www.rockcreekresort.com/dining* 🕓 *Closed Sun. and Mon. No lunch.*

Running Bear Pancake House

$ | **AMERICAN** | **FAMILY** | All the pies, muffins, and cinnamon rolls are made on the premises at this eatery. There are a lot of choices, but trust the name and go for the buttermilk or buckwheat pancakes topped with blueberries, strawberries, peaches, coconut, walnuts, or chocolate chips. **Known for:** several varieties of pancakes, plain and topped; espresso drinks using locally roasted beans; woodsy decor. [$] *Average main: $9* ✉ *538 Madison Ave., West Yellowstone* ☎ *406/646–7703* 🌐 *runningbearph.com* 🕓 *No dinner.*

Wild West Pizzeria and Saloon

$$ | **PIZZA** | **FAMILY** | Aaron and Megan Hecht make superb pizzas with crispy crusts, flavorful sauces, and memorable frontier names. Folks also come for the sandwiches, pasta dishes, and the live music hosted at the adjacent saloon. **Known for:** pizza sauce that's a family recipe; the Sitting Bull pie, topped with various meats; the Calamity Jane pie, with a white sauce, mushrooms, and other veggies. [$] *Average main: $16* ✉ *14 Madison Ave., West Yellowstone* ☎ *406/646–4400* 🌐 *www.wildwestpizza.com.*

Wyoming's Rib & Chop House - Cody

$$$ | **AMERICAN** | This place can be packed in the summer with cowboys and tourists enjoying large portions of the succulent steak-house favorites you'd expect. There are gluten-free options, but vegetarians need to make a special request ahead of a visit. **Known for:** delicious baby back ribs; a great place to get a steak of any cut; comprehensive wine list. [$] *Average main: $22* ✉ *1367 Sheridan Ave., Cody* ☎ *307/527–7731* 🌐 *www.ribandchophouse.com.*

Yellowstone Mine & Rusty Rail Lounge

$$ | **STEAKHOUSE** | **FAMILY** | Decorated with picks, shovels, and other mining equipment, this is a place for casual family-style dining. Locals come in for the steaks and seafood. **Known for:**

low-key dining, year-round; steak-house staples; kitchen open later than at other local spots. $ *Average main: $18* ✉ *Best Western by Mammoth Hot Springs, 901 Scott St. W, Gardiner* ☎ *406/848–7336* 🌐 *www.visitgardinermt.com/item/230-yellowstone-mine-restaurant-rusty-rail-lounge.*

Hotels

IN THE PARK

CANYON

Canyon Lodge & Cabins

$$$$ | **HOTEL** | **FAMILY** | A new kind of National Parks lodging, the Canyon Lodges are gorgeous, innovative, and sustainable. **Pros:** central location; new buildings constructed with sustainability in mind; pretty surroundings. **Cons:** you'll likely want to drive to restaurants; park location means top-dollar prices; like most lodgings here, iffy Wi-Fi and no TV. $ *Rooms from: $210* ✉ *North Rim Dr. and Grand Loop Rd., Canyon Village* ☎ *307/344–7311, 866/439–7375* 🌐 *www.yellowstonenationalparklodges.com/stay* 🕒 *Closed mid-Oct.–mid-May* 🛏 *490 rooms, 100 cabins* 🍴 *No meals.*

Canyon Western Cabins

$$$$ | **HOTEL** | **FAMILY** | These recently renovated pine-frame cabins are arranged in clusters of four and six; all have private bathrooms, and the fancier ones also have knotty-pine bed frames and other nice touches. **Pros:** can park close to your cabin; heart-of-the-park location; restaurants and a bar are nearby. **Cons:** busy area; basic, rustic rooms; good location means high prices. $ *Rooms from: $320* ✉ *North Rim Dr. and Grand Loop Rd., Canyon Village* ☎ *307/344–7311, 866/439–7375* 🌐 *www.yellowstonenationalparklodges.com/stay* 🕒 *Closed mid-Oct.–mid-May* 🛏 *100 cabins* 🍴 *No meals.*

Dunraven Lodge

$$$$ | **HOTEL** | This four-story lodge sits amid pine trees that edge the Grand Canyon of the Yellowstone and features simple rooms, almost identical to the adjacent Cascade Lodge. **Pros:** canyon location; well-appointed rooms for people with disabilities; quiet setting. **Cons:** far from dining and other services; park location means high prices; no TV and iffy Wi-Fi. $ *Rooms from: $340* ✉ *1 Grand Loop Rd., at North Rim Dr., Canyon Village* ☎ *307/344–7311, 866/439–7375* 🌐 *www.yellowstonenationalparklodges.com/stay* 🕒 *Closed mid-Oct.–mid-May* 🛏 *44 rooms* 🍴 *No meals.*

GRANT VILLAGE

Grant Village Lodge

$$$$ | **HOTEL** | These six humble lodge buildings have rough pine exteriors painted gray and rust. **Pros:** excellent location; many facilities nearby; closest Yellowstone lodge to Grand Teton National Park. **Cons:** great location means high costs; small rooms without character; slow, expensive Wi-Fi. $ *Rooms from: $270* ✉ *South Entrance Rd., 21 miles north of South Entrance* ☎ *307/344–7311, 866/439–7375* 🌐 *www.yellowstonenationalparklodges.com/stay* 🕒 *Closed late Sept.–late May* 🛏 *300 rooms* 🍴 *No meals.*

MAMMOTH HOT SPRINGS

Mammoth Hot Springs Hotel and Cabins

$$ | **HOTEL** | The rooms at this 1936 lodge are smaller and simpler than those at the park's other historic hotels, but this one is less expensive and often less crowded; the surrounding cabins look like tiny, genteel summer homes. **Pros:** great rates for a historic property; wake up to an elk bugling outside your window; cabins are among the park's nicest. **Cons:** some hotel rooms and cabins lack private bathrooms; like all park lodges, no air-conditioning; no TVs, Wi-Fi is spotty. $ *Rooms from: $109* ✉ *U.S. 89, 2½ miles south of Montana border* ☎ *307/344–7311, 866/439–7375* 🌐 *www.yellowstonenationalparklodges.com/stay* 🕒 *Closed mid-Oct.–mid Dec. and early Mar.–late Apr.* 🛏 *216 rooms* 🍴 *No meals.*

Best Campgrounds in Yellowstone

Yellowstone has a dozen frontcountry campgrounds scattered around the park, in addition to more than 200 backcountry sites. Most campgrounds have flush toilets; some have coin-operated showers and laundry facilities. The campgrounds run by Xanterra Parks & Resorts—Bridge Bay, Canyon, Fishing Bridge RV Park, Grant Village, and Madison—accept bookings in advance. The rest, operated by the National Park Service, are available on a first-come, first-served basis.

Bridge Bay. The park's largest campground, Bridge Bay rests in a wooded grove above Yellowstone Lake and adjacent to the park's major marina. ⊠ *Grand Loop Rd., 3 miles southwest of Lake Village* ☎ *307/344–7311* ⊕ *www.yellowstonenationalpark-lodges.com.*

Canyon. A massive campground with 250-plus sites, Canyon Campground accommodates everyone from hiker/biker tent campers to large RVs. ⊠ *North Rim Dr., ¼ mile east of Grand Loop Rd., Canyon Village* ☎ *307/344–7311* ⊕ *www.yellowstonenationalpark-lodges.com.*

Fishing Bridge RV Park. It's more of a parking lot than a campground, but RV services like tank filling/emptying and hookups are available. ⊠ *Grand Loop Rd., 3 miles southwest of Lake Village* ☎ *307/344–7311* ⊕ *www.yellow-stonenationalparklodges.com.*

Grant Village. The park's second-largest campground, Grant Village has some sites with great views of Yellowstone Lake. Some sites are wheelchair accessible. ⊠ *South Entrance Rd.,* *Grant Village* ☎ *307/344–7311* ⊕ *www. yellowstonenationalparklodges.com.*

Indian Creek. In a picturesque setting next to a creek, this campground is in the middle of a prime wildlife-viewing area. ⊠ *Grand Loop Rd., 8 miles south of Mammoth Hot Springs* ☎ *307/344–2017.*

Madison. The largest National Park Service–operated campground, where no advance reservations are accepted, Madison has eight loops and nearly 300 sites. ⊠ *Grand Loop Rd., Madison* ☎ *307/344–7311* ⊕ *www.yellowstonena-tionalparklodges.com.*

Norris. Straddling the Gibbon River, this is a quiet, popular campground. A few of its "walk-in" sites are among the best in the park. ⊠ *Grand Loop Rd., Norris* ☎ *307/344–2017.*

Pebble Creek. Beneath multiple 10,000-foot peaks (Thunderer, Barronette Peak, and Mount Norris) the park's easternmost campground is set creekside in a forested canopy. ⊠ *Northeast Entrance Rd., 22 miles east of Tower-Roosevelt Junction* ☎ *307/344–2017.*

Slough Creek. Down the park's most rewarding 2 miles of dirt road, Slough Creek is a gem. Nearly every site is adjacent to the creek, which is prized by anglers. ⊠ *Northeast Entrance Rd., 10 miles east of Tower-Roosevelt Junction* ☎ *307/344–2017.*

Tower Falls. It's within hiking distance of the roaring waterfall, so this modest-size campground gets a lot of foot traffic. ⊠ *Grand Loop Rd., 3 miles southeast of Tower-Roosevelt* ☎ *307/344–2017.*

OLD FAITHFUL AREA

★ Old Faithful Inn

$$$$ | **HOTEL** | **FAMILY** | Easily earning its National Historic Landmark status, this lovely lodge has been a favorite of five generations of park visitors. **Pros:** a one-of-a-kind property; rooms at a range of price points; incredible location near geyser. **Cons:** thin walls; waves of tourists in the lobby; some rooms have shared baths. [$] *Rooms from: $260* ✉ *Old Faithful* ✣ *1st left off Bypass Rd.* ☎ *307/344–7311, 866/439–7375* 🌐 *www.yellowstonenationalparklodges.com/stay* 🕒 *Closed mid-Oct.–early May* 🛏 *329 rooms* 🍴 *No meals.*

Old Faithful Lodge Cabins

$$$ | **HOTEL** | There are no rooms inside the Old Faithful Lodge, but close to 100 rustic cabins can be found at the village's northeastern end. **Pros:** good budget-friendly option; stone's throw from Old Faithful; services are within walking distance. **Cons:** some cabins lack private bathrooms; pretty basic; few views from cabins. [$] *Rooms from: $159* ✉ *South end of Old Faithful Bypass Rd.* ☎ *307/344–7311, 866/439–7375* 🌐 *www.yellowstonenationalparklodges.com/stay* 🕒 *Closed late Sept.–mid-May* 🛏 *96 cabins* 🍴 *No meals.*

Old Faithful Snow Lodge

$$$$ | **HOTEL** | This massive modern structure brings back the grand tradition of park lodges by making good use of heavy timber beams and wrought-iron accents in its distinctive facade. **Pros:** the park's most modern hotel; lobby is great for relaxing; one of two park hotels open in the winter. **Cons:** pricey, but you're paying for location; simple rooms without a lot of character; not a lot of frills like air-conditioning or TVs. [$] *Rooms from: $301* ✉ *Far end of Old Faithful Bypass Rd., Old Faithful* ☎ *307/344–7311, 866/439–7375* 🌐 *www.yellowstonenationalparklodges.com/stay* 🕒 *Closed late Oct.–mid-Dec. and mid-Mar.–late Apr.* 🛏 *100 rooms* 🍴 *No meals.*

Old Faithful Snow Lodge Cabins

$$$$ | **HOTEL** | **FAMILY** | Just yards from Old Faithful, the Western Cabins feature bright interiors and a modern motel ambience, while the Frontier Cabins are simple pine structures. **Pros:** affordable; close to geyser; open during winter. **Cons:** no amenities beyond the basics; small rooms; more rustic cabins won't appeal to everyone. [$] *Rooms from: $202* ✉ *Far end of Old Faithful Bypass Rd., Old Faithful* ☎ *307/344–7311, 866/439–7375* 🌐 *www.yellowstonenationalparklodges.com/stay* 🕒 *Closed late Oct.–mid-Dec., early Mar.–late Apr.* 🛏 *100 rooms* 🍴 *No meals.*

LAKE AREA

Lake Lodge Cabins

$$$ | **HOTEL** | **FAMILY** | Located beyond the Lake Yellowstone Hotel, this 1920 lodge is one of the park's homey, hidden treasures. **Pros:** lovely lakeside location; great lobby; good for families. **Cons:** Pioneer cabins are particularly bare bones; few modern conveniences, like microwaves or TVs; Wi-Fi is expensive and only available in lodge. [$] *Rooms from: $158* ✉ *Lake Village Rd., 1 mile south of Fishing Bridge, Lake Village* ☎ *307/344–7311, 866/439–7375* 🌐 *www.yellowstonenationalparklodges.com/stay* 🕒 *Closed late Sept.–early June* 🛏 *186 cabins* 🍴 *No meals.*

Lake Yellowstone Hotel

$$$$ | **HOTEL** | Dating from 1891, the park's oldest lodge maintains an air of refinement; just off the lobby, the spacious sun room offers priceless views of Yellowstone Lake at sunrise or sunset. **Pros:** relaxing atmosphere; the best views of any park lodging; attentive service. **Cons:** the park's most expensive property; wired Internet, but no Wi-Fi; no TVs or air-conditioning. [$] *Rooms from: $320* ✉ *1 Grand Loop Rd., about 1 mile south of Fishing Bridge, Lake Village* ☎ *307/344–7311, 866/439–7375* 🌐 *www.yellowstonenationalparklodges.com*

⏲ *Closed early Oct.–mid-May* 🛏 *194 rooms* 🍴 *No meals.*

OUTSIDE THE PARK

The Cody

$$$$ | **HOTEL** | This all-suites hotel incorporates Western themes into a thoroughly modern and eco-friendly property. **Pros:** shuttle to airport and downtown attractions; pet-friendly rooms available; elegant feel. **Cons:** luxury has its price; not in walking distance to downtown; no bar or restaurant. [$] *Rooms from: $219* ✉ *232 W. Yellowstone Ave., Cody* ☎ *307/587–5915* 🌐 *www.thecody.com* 🛏 *75 rooms* 🍴 *Breakfast.*

Pahaska Tepee Resort

$$$ | **RESORT** | Just 2 miles from Yellowstone's East Entrance, these cabins in a pine forest are a good base for destinations both inside and outside the park. **Pros:** historic property with lots of character; great location on scenic highway; horseback rides available. **Cons:** few services between Cody and Fishing Bridge; small, basic rooms; no TVs or Wi-Fi. [$] *Rooms from: $169* ✉ *183 N. Fork Hwy., Cody* ☎ *307/527–7701, 800/628–7791* 🌐 *www.pahaska.com* 🛏 *43 cabins, 1 lodge* 🍴 *No meals.*

Pollard Hotel

$$$ | **HOTEL** | Guns have been banned in the hotel ever since Harry Longabaugh, aka the Sundance Kid, brandished one when he robbed a bank on the corner. **Pros:** full breakfast discounted; historical property. **Cons:** front-desk service can be erratic. [$] *Rooms from: $165* ✉ *2 N. Broadway, Red Lodge* ☎ *406/446–0001, 406/446–0002* 🌐 *www.thepollard.com* 🛏 *39 rooms* 🍴 *No meals.*

Three Bear Lodge

$$$$ | **HOTEL** | **FAMILY** | A towering stone fireplace and lots of natural wood greet guests in the lobby of this eco-friendly property. **Pros:** family-friendly; a block off the main drag; heated pool. **Cons:** no staff at front desk after 11 pm; older hotel; free breakfast only in high season. [$] *Rooms from: $209* ✉ *217 Yellowstone Ave., West Yellowstone* ☎ *406/646–7353, 800/646–7353* 🌐 *www.threebearlodge.com* 🛏 *70 rooms* 🍴 *No meals.*

Yellowstone Village Inn and Suites

$$$ | **HOTEL** | **FAMILY** | Right in Gardiner across the street from the Yellowstone River, this hotel provides a variety of room types and everything you need between day trips into Yellowstone. **Pros:** great location; homey feel; some suites have full kitchens. **Cons:** like in all of Gardiner, Wi-Fi can be spotty; breakfast is continental; clean but basic rooms. [$] *Rooms from: $159* ✉ *1102 Scott St. W, Gardiner* ☎ *406/848–7417* 🌐 *www.yellowstonevinn.com* 🛏 *45 rooms* 🍴 *Free Breakfast.*

Chapter 36

YOSEMITE NATIONAL PARK

36

Updated by
Cheryl Crabtree

CALIFORNIA

WELCOME TO YOSEMITE NATIONAL PARK

TOP REASONS TO GO

★ **Scenic falls:** An easy stroll brings you to the base of Lower Yosemite Fall, where roaring springtime waters make for misty lens caps and lasting memories.

★ **Tunnel vision:** Approaching Yosemite Valley, Wawona Road passes through a mountainside and emerges before one of the park's most heart-stopping vistas.

★ **Inhale the beauty:** Pause to take in the light, pristine air as you travel about the High Sierra's Tioga Pass and Tuolumne Meadows, where 10,000-foot granite peaks just might take your breath away.

★ **Walk away:** Leave the crowds behind—but do bring along a buddy—and take a hike somewhere along Yosemite's 800 miles of trails.

★ **Winter wonder:** Observe the snowflakes and stillness of winter in the park.

1 Yosemite Valley. At an elevation of 4,000 feet, in roughly the center of the park, beats Yosemite's heart. This is where you'll find the park's most famous sights and biggest crowds.

2 Wawona and Mariposa Grove. The park's southern tip holds Wawona, with its grand old hotel and pioneer history center, and the Mariposa Grove of Giant Sequoias. These are closest to the south entrance, 35 miles (a one-hour drive) south of Yosemite Village.

3 Tuolumne Meadows. The highlight of east-central Yosemite is this wildflower-strewn valley with hiking trails, nestled among sharp, rocky peaks. It's a 1½-hour drive northeast of Yosemite Valley along Tioga Road (closed mid-October–late May).

4 Hetch Hetchy. The most remote, least visited part of Yosemite accessible by automobile, this glacial valley is dominated by a reservoir and veined with wilderness trails. It's near the park's western boundary, about a half-hour drive north of the Big Oak Flat entrance.

El Portal

Pioneer Histo

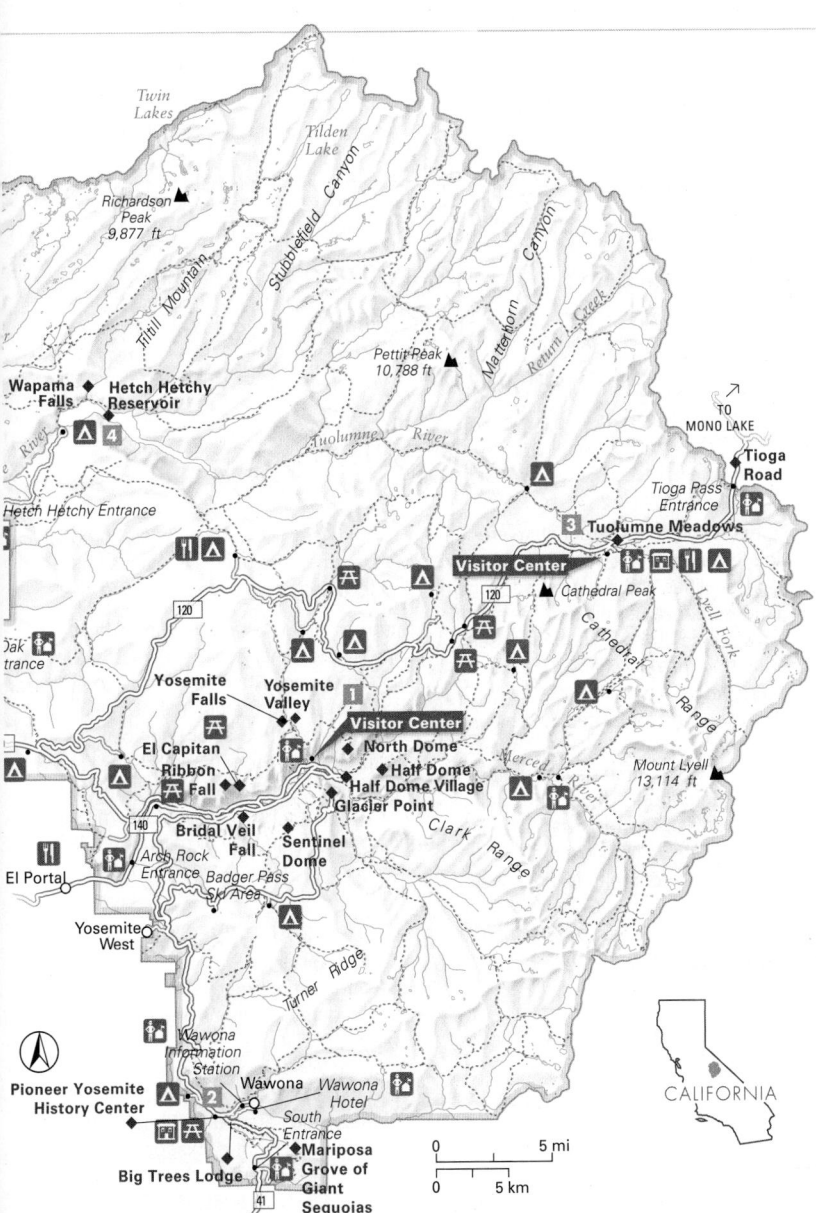

Twin
Lakes

Tilden
Lake

Richardson
Peak
9,877 ft

Stubblefield Canyon

Tiltill Mountain

Matterhorn Canyon

Pettit Peak
10,788 ft

Return Creek

TO
MONO LAKE

Wapama
Falls

Hetch Hetchy
Reservoir

4

Tuolumne   River

River

Tioga
Road

Tioga Pass
Entrance

Hetch Hetchy Entrance

3 Tuolumne Meadows

Visitor Center

Oak
Entrance

120

120

Cathedral Peak

Cathedral   Range

Lyell Fork

Yosemite
Falls

Yosemite
Valley

1

Visitor Center

North Dome

El Capitan

Merced   River

Ribbon
Fall

Half Dome

Half Dome Village

Glacier Point

Mount Lyell
13,114 ft

Bridal Veil
Fall

Sentinel
Dome

Clark   Range

140

Arch Rock
Entrance Badger Pass
Ski Area

El Portal

Yosemite
West

Turner   Ridge

CALIFORNIA

Pioneer Yosemite
History Center

Wawona
Information
Station

2

Wawona

Wawona
Hotel

South
Entrance

0   5 mi

0   5 km

Big Trees Lodge

Mariposa
Grove of
Giant
Sequoias

41

By merely standing in Yosemite Valley and turning in a circle, you can see more natural wonders in a minute than you could in a full day pretty much anywhere else. Half Dome, Yosemite Falls, El Capitan, Bridalveil Fall, Sentinel Dome, the Merced River, white-flowering dogwood trees, maybe even bears ripping into the bark of fallen trees or sticking their snouts into beehives—it's all in Yosemite Valley.

In the mid-1800s, when tourists were arriving to the area, the valley's special geologic qualities and the giant sequoias of Mariposa Grove 30 miles to the south so impressed a group of influential Californians that they persuaded President Abraham Lincoln to grant those two areas to the state for protection on June 30, 1864. On October 1, 1890—thanks largely to lobbying efforts by naturalist John Muir and Robert Underwood Johnson, the editor of *Century Magazine*—Congress set aside an additional 1,500 square miles for Yosemite National Park; the valley and Mariposa Grove remained under state control until 1906, when they merged with the national park.

Planning

WHEN TO GO

During extremely busy periods—such as weekends and holidays throughout the year—you will experience delays at the entrance gates. For smaller crowds, visit midweek. Or come January through March, when the park is a bit less busy and the days usually are sunny and clear.

Summer rainfall is rare. In winter, heavy snows occasionally cause road closures, and tire chains or four-wheel drive may be required on the roads that remain open. The road to Glacier Point beyond the turnoff for Yosemite Ski & Snowboard Area is closed after the first major snowfall; Tioga Road is closed from late October through May or mid-June. Mariposa Grove Road is typically closed for a shorter period in winter.

FESTIVALS AND EVENTS

A Taste of Yosemite

FESTIVAL | Celebrated chefs present cooking demonstrations and multicourse meals at The Majestic Yosemite Hotel in Yosemite Village from mid-January to early February. Dinner-only costs $208. Two-night packages start at $297 per person; three- and four-night packages are also available. Space is limited. ⊠ *Yosemite Village* ☎ *888/413–8869, 602/278–8888* *international* ⊕ *www.travelyosemite. com.*

Bluesapalooza

FESTIVAL | The first weekend of every August, Mammoth Lakes hosts a blues and beer festival—with an emphasis on the beer tasting. ⊠ *Mammoth Lakes* ☎ *888/992–7397* ⊕ *www.mammoth-bluesbrewsfest.com.*

Fireman's Muster

FESTIVAL | North of Sonora in the old mining town of Columbia, history springs to life at this festival of antique fire engines, with hose-spraying contests and a parade of the old pumpers. ⊠ *Columbia* ☎ *209/533–4420,800/446–1333.*

Mammoth Jazzfest

FESTIVAL | This weekend festival funded by the town of Mammoth Lakes features free jazz performances at The Village at Mammoth. ⊠ *Mammoth Lakes* ☎ *760/934–2712, 888/466–2666* ⊕ *www. mammothjazzfest.org.*

Mother Lode Roundup Parade and Rodeo

FESTIVAL | On Mother's Day weekend, the town of Sonora celebrates its gold-mining, agricultural, and lumbering heritage with a parade, rodeo, entertainment, and food. ⊠ *Sonora* ☎ *209/533–4420, 800/446–1333* ⊕ *www.motherloderound-up.com.*

Sierra Art Trails

FESTIVAL | The work of more than 100 artists is on display in studios and galleries throughout eastern Madera and Mariposa counties. Purchase the catalog of locations and hours at area shops. ☎ *559/658–8844* ⊕ *www.sierraarttrails. org.*

The Bracebridge Dinner at Yosemite

Held at The Majestic Yosemite Hotel (formerly The Ahwahnee) in Yosemite Village every Christmas since 1928, this 17th-century-theme madrigal dinner is so popular that most seats are booked months in advance. Dinner costs $380; lodging packages start at $1,019, or

$1,219 if you want to stay at The Majestic Yosemite Hotel. ⊠ *The Majestic Yosemite Hotel, 1 Ahwahnee Dr., Yosemite Village* ☎ *888/413–8869, 602/278–8888 international* ⊕ *www.travelyosemite.com.*

The Grand Grape Celebration

FESTIVAL | Some of California's most prestigious vintners hold two- and three-day midweek seminars in the Great Room of The Majestic Yosemite Hotel (formerly The Ahwahnee) in Yosemite Village. They culminate with an elegant—albeit pricey—banquet dinner. Arrive early for seats; book early for dinner ($208) and lodging and dining packages (from $317). ⊠ *Yosemite Village* ☎ *888/413–8869, 602/278–8888 international* ⊕ *www. travelyosemite.com.*

PLANNING YOUR TIME
YOSEMITE IN ONE DAY

Begin at the **Valley Visitor Center,** where you can watch the documentary *Spirit of Yosemite.* A minute's stroll from there is the **Native American village of the Ahwahnee,** which recalls Native American life circa 1870. Take another 20 minutes to see the **Yosemite Museum.** Then, hop aboard the free shuttle to Yosemite Falls and hike the **Lower Yosemite Fall Trail** to the base of the falls. Have lunch at **Yosemite Valley Lodge,** which you can access by shuttle or walk to from the falls in 20 minutes.

You can either leisurely explore **Half Dome Village (formerly Curry Village)**—by swimming or ice-skating, shopping, renting a bike, or having a beer on the deck; check out family-friendly **Happy Isles Art and Nature Center** and the adjacent nature trail; or hike up the **Mist Trail** to the Vernal Fall footbridge to admire the view.

Hop back on the shuttle, then disembark at **The Majestic Yosemite Hotel (formerly The Ahwahnee).** The Great Lounge here has a magnificent fireplace and Native American artwork; have a meal in the Dining Room if you're up for a splurge. Or, take the shuttle to **Yosemite Village** where you

AVERAGE HIGH/LOW TEMPERATURES

JAN.	FEB.	MAR.	APR.	MAY	JUNE
48/29	53/30	55/32	61/36	69/43	78/49
JULY	**AUG.**	**SEPT.**	**OCT.**	**NOV.**	**DEC.**
85/55	84/55	79/49	70/42	56/34	47/29

can grab some fixings, then drive to **El Capitan picnic area** and enjoy an outdoor evening meal. At this time of day, "El Cap" should be sun-splashed. (You will have also gotten several good looks at world-famous **Half Dome** throughout the day.) If the sun hasn't set yet, drive to the base of **Bridalveil Fall** to take a short hike.

GETTING HERE AND AROUND
AIR TRAVEL
The closest airport to the south and west entrances is Fresno Yosemite International Airport (FAT). Mammoth Yosemite Airport (MMH) is closest to the east entrance. Sacramento International Airport (SMF) is also close to the north and west entrances.

BUS AND TRAIN TRAVEL
Amtrak's daily San Joaquin train stops in Merced and connects with YARTS buses that travel to Yosemite Valley along Highway 140 from Merced. Seasonal YARTS buses (typically mid-May to late September) also travel along Highway 41 from Fresno, Highway 120 from Sonora, and Highway 395 and Tioga Road from Mammoth Lakes with scheduled stops at towns along the way. Once you're in Yosemite Valley you can take advantage of the free shuttle buses, which operate on low emissions, have 21 stops, and run from 7 am to 10 pm year-round. Buses run about every 10 minutes in summer, a bit less frequently in winter. A separate (but also free) summer-only shuttle runs out to El Capitan. Also in summer, you can pay to take the "hikers' bus" from Yosemite Valley to Tuolumne or to ride a tour bus up to Glacier Point. During the snow season, buses run regularly

between Yosemite Valley and Yosemite Ski & Snowboard Area.

CAR TRAVEL
Roughly 200 miles from San Francisco, 300 miles from Los Angeles, and 500 miles from Las Vegas, Yosemite takes a while to reach—and its many sites and attractions merit much more time than what rangers say is the average visit: four hours.

Of the park's four entrances, Arch Rock is the closest to Yosemite Valley. The road that goes through it, Route 140 from Merced and Mariposa, is a scenic western approach that snakes alongside the boulder-packed Merced River. Route 41, through Wawona, is the way to come from Los Angeles (or Fresno, if you've flown in and rented a car). Route 120, through Crane Flat, is the most direct route from San Francisco. The only way in from the east is Tioga Road, which may be the best route in terms of scenery—though due to snow accumulation it's open for a frustratingly short amount of time each year (typically early June through mid-October). Once you enter Yosemite Valley, park your car in one of the two main day parking areas, at Yosemite Village and Yosemite Falls, then visit the sights via the free shuttle bus system. Or walk or bike along the valley's 12 miles of paved paths.

There are few gas stations within Yosemite (Crane Flat and Wawona; none in the valley), so fuel up before you reach the park. From late fall until early spring, the weather is especially unpredictable, and driving can be treacherous. You should carry chains during this period as they are required when roads are icy and when it snows.

PARK ESSENTIALS
ACCESSIBILITY
Yosemite's facilities are continually being upgraded to make them more accessible. Many of the valley floor trails—particularly at Lower Yosemite Fall, Bridalveil Fall, and Mirror Lake—are wheelchair accessible, though some assistance may be required. The Valley Visitor Center is fully accessible, as are the park shuttle buses. A sign-language interpreter is available for ranger programs. Visitors with respiratory difficulties should take note of the park's high elevations—the valley floor is approximately 4,000 feet above sea level, but Tuolumne Meadows and parts of the high country hover around 10,000 feet.

PARK FEES AND PERMITS
The admission fee, valid for seven days, is $35 per vehicle, $30 per motorcycle, or $20 per individual.

If you plan to camp in the backcountry or climb Half Dome, you must have a wilderness permit. Availability of permits depends upon trailhead quotas. It's best to make a reservation, especially if you will be visiting May through September. You can reserve two days to 24 weeks in advance by phone, mail, or fax (preferred method) (⊠ *Box 545, Yosemite, CA* ☎ *209/372–0740* 🖨 *209/372–0739*); you'll pay $5 per person plus $5 per reservation if and when your reservations are confirmed. You can download the reservation forms from ⊕ *www.nps.gov/yose/ planyourvisit/upload/wildpermitform.pdf.* Without a reservation, you may still get a free permit on a first-come, first-served basis at wilderness permit offices at Big Oak Flat, Hetch Hetchy, Tuolumne Meadows, Wawona, the Wilderness Center in Yosemite Village, and Yosemite Valley in summer. From fall to spring, visit the Valley Visitor Center.

PARK HOURS
The park is open 24/7 year-round. All entrances are open at all hours, except for Hetch Hetchy entrance, which is open roughly dawn to dusk. Yosemite is in the Pacific time zone.

CELL PHONE RECEPTION
Cell phone reception depends on the service provider and can be hit or miss everywhere in the park. There are public telephones at park entrance stations, visitor centers, all restaurants and lodging facilities in the park, gas stations, and in Yosemite Village.

EDUCATIONAL OFFERINGS
CLASSES AND SEMINARS
Art Classes
ARTS VENUE | Professional artists conduct workshops in watercolor, etching, drawing, and other mediums. Bring your own materials or purchase the basics at the Happy Isles Art and Nature Center. Children under 12 must be accompanied by an adult. The center also offers beginner art workshops and children's art and family craft programs ($5–$20 per person). ⊠ *Happy Isles Art and Nature Center* ☎ *209/372–1442* ⊕ *www.yosemiteconservancy.org* 🏷 *$20* ⊗ *No classes Sun. Closed Dec.–Feb.*

Yosemite Outdoor Adventures
TOUR—SIGHT | Naturalists, scientists, and park rangers lead multihour to multiday educational outings on topics from woodpeckers to fire management to pastel painting. Most sessions take place spring through fall, but a few focus on winter phenomena. ⊠ *Yosemite National Park* ☎ *209/379–2317* ⊕ *www.yosemiteconservancy.org* 🏷 *From $99.*

MUSEUMS
Happy Isles Art and Nature Center
MUSEUM | FAMILY | This family-focused center has a rotating selection of hands-on, kid-friendly exhibits that teach tykes and their parents about the park's ecosystem. Books, toys, T-shirts, and water bottles are stocked in the small

gift shop. ⊠ *Yosemite National Park* ✛ *Off Southside Dr., about ¾ mile east of Half Dome Village* ☎ *209/372–0631* 🏷 *Free* ⊘ *Closed Oct.–Apr.*

Yosemite Museum

MUSEUM | This small museum consists of a permanent exhibit that focuses on the history of the area and the people who once lived here. An adjacent gallery promotes contemporary and historic Yosemite art in revolving gallery exhibits. A docent demonstrates traditional Native American basket-weaving techniques a few days a week. ⊠ *Yosemite Village* ☎ *209/372–0299* 🏷 *Free.*

RANGER PROGRAMS

Junior Ranger Program

TOUR—SIGHT | **FAMILY** | Children ages seven and up can participate in the informal, self-guided Junior Ranger program. A park activity handbook is available at the Valley Visitor Center, the Happy Isles Art and Nature Center, and the Wawona Visitor Center. Once kids complete the book, rangers present them with a badge and, in some cases, a certificate. ⊠ *Valley Visitor Center or the Happy Isles Art & Nature Center* ☎ *209/372–0299.*

Ranger-Led Programs

TOUR—SIGHT | Rangers lead entertaining walks and give informative talks several times a day from spring to fall. The schedule is more limited in winter, but most days you can find a program somewhere in the park. In the evenings at Yosemite Valley Lodge and Half Dome Village, lectures, slide shows, and documentary films present unique perspectives on Yosemite. On summer weekends, campgrounds at Half Dome Village and Tuolumne Meadows host sing-along campfire programs. Schedules and locations are posted on bulletin boards throughout the park as well as in the indispensable *Yosemite Guide,* which is distributed to visitors as they arrive at the park. ⊠ *Yosemite National Park* ⊕ *nps.gov/yose.*

RESTAURANTS

Yosemite National Park has a couple of moderately priced restaurants in lovely (which almost goes without saying) settings: the Mountain Room at Yosemite Valley Lodge and Wawona Hotel's dining room. The Majestic Yosemite Hotel (formerly The Ahwahnee) provides one of the finest dining experiences in the country.

Otherwise, food service is geared toward satisfying the masses as efficiently as possible. Yosemite Valley Lodge's Base Camp Eatery is the valley's best lower-cost, hot-food option, with Italian, classic American, and world flavor counter options; Half Dome Village Pavilion's offerings are overpriced and usually fairly bland, but you can get decent pizzas on the adjacent outdoor deck. In Yosemite Valley Village, the Village Grill whips up burgers and fries, Degnan's Kitchen has made-to-order sandwiches, and The Loft at Degnan's has a chalet-like open dining area in which you can enjoy pizza, salads, rice bowls, and desserts.

The White Wolf Lodge and Tuolumne Meadows Lodge—both off Tioga Road and therefore guaranteed open only from early June through September—have small restaurants where meals are competently prepared. Tuolumne Meadows also has a grill, and the gift shop at Glacier Point sells premade sandwiches, snacks, and hot dogs. During the ski season you'll also find one at Yosemite Ski & Snowboard Area, off Glacier Point Road.

HOTELS

Indoor lodging options inside the park appear more expensive than initially seems warranted, but that premium pays off big-time in terms of the time you'll save—unless you are bunking within a few miles of a Yosemite entrance, you will face long commutes to the park when you stay outside its borders (though the Yosemite View Lodge, on Route 140, is within a reasonable half-hour's drive of Yosemite Valley).

Because of Yosemite National Park's immense popularity—not just with tourists from around the world but with Northern Californians who make weekend trips here—reservations are all but mandatory. Book up to one year ahead. ■TIP→ **If you're not set on a specific hotel or camp but just want to stay somewhere inside the park, call the main reservation number to check for availability and reserve (888/413–8869 or 602/278–8888 international). Park lodgings have a seven-day cancellation policy, so you may be able to snag last-minute reservations.**

⚠ **A trademark dispute with the former park concessioner, Delaware North, has resulted in Yosemite National Park changing the names of several historic park lodges and properties, including the iconic Ahwahnee. This guide uses the new names: Yosemite Lodge at the Falls is now Yosemite Valley Lodge; The Ahwahnee is now The Majestic Yosemite Hotel; Curry Village is now Half Dome Village; Wawona Hotel is now Big Trees Lodge; and Badger Pass Ski Area is now Yosemite Ski & Snowboard Area. For the latest information visit the Yosemite National Park website.**

Hotel reviews have been shortened. For full information, visit Fodors.com.

What It Costs

	$	$$	$$$	$$$$
RESTAURANTS				
	under $12	$12–$20	$21–$30	over $30
HOTELS				
	under $100	$100–$150	$151–$200	over $200

TOURS

★ Ansel Adams Camera Walks

SPECIAL-INTEREST | Photography enthusiasts shouldn't miss these 90-minute guided camera walks offered four mornings (Monday, Tuesday, Thursday, and Saturday) each week by professional photographers. All are free, but participation is limited to 15 people. Meeting points vary, and advance reservations are essential. ✉ *Yosemite National Park* ☎ *209/372–4413* ⊕ *www.anseladams. com* ✉ *Free.*

Discover Yosemite

GUIDED TOURS | This outfit operates daily tours to Yosemite Valley, Mariposa Grove, and Glacier Point in 14- and 29-passenger vehicles. The tour travels along Highway 41 with stops in Bass Lake, Oakhurst, and Fish Camp; rates include lunch. Sunset tours to Sentinel Dome are additional summer options. ☎ *559/642–4400* ⊕ *www.discoveryosemite.com* ✉ *From $152.*

Glacier Point Tour

GUIDED TOURS | This four-hour trip takes you from Yosemite Valley to the Glacier Point vista, 3,214 feet above the valley floor. Some people buy a $26 one-way ticket and hike down. Shuttles depart from the Yosemite Valley Lodge three times a day. ✉ *Yosemite National Park* ☎ *888/413–8869* ⊕ *www.travelyosemite. com* ✉ *From $52* ⊗ *Closed Nov.–late May* ⚲ *Reservations essential.*

Grand Tour

TOUR—SIGHT | For a full-day tour of Yosemite Valley, the Mariposa Grove of Giant Sequoias and Glacier Point, try the Grand Tour, which departs from the Yosemite Valley Lodge in the valley. The tour stops for a picnic lunch (included) at the historic Big Trees Lodge. ✉ *Yosemite National Park* ☎ *209/372–1240* ⊕ *www. yosemitepark.com* ✉ *$102* ⚲ *Reservations essential.*

Moonlight Tour

TOUR—SIGHT | This after-dark version of the Valley Floor Tour takes place on moonlit nights from June through September, depending on weather conditions. ✉ *Yosemite National Park* ☎ *209/372–4386* ⊕ *www.travelyosemite. com* ✉ *$37.*

Tuolumne Meadows Hikers Bus

BUS TOURS | For a full day's outing to the high country, opt for this ride up Tioga Road to Tuolumne Meadows. You'll stop at several overlooks, and you can connect with another shuttle at Tuolumne Lodge. This service is mostly for hikers and backpackers who want to reach high-country trailheads, but everyone is welcome. ⊠ *Yosemite National Park* ☎ *209/372–1240* ⊕ *www.travelyosemite. com* 🖃 *$15 one-way, $23 round-trip* ⊘ *Closed Labor Day–mid-June* ⚲ *Reservations essential.*

Valley Floor Tour

GUIDED TOURS | Take a two-hour tour of Yosemite Valley's highlights, complete with narration on the area's history, geology, and flora and fauna. Tours are either in trams or enclosed motor coaches, depending on weather conditions. Tours run year-round. ⊠ *Yosemite National Park* ☎ *209/372–1240, 888/413–8869 reservations* ⊕ *www.travelyosemite.com* 🖃 *From $37.*

Wee Wild Ones

TOUR—SIGHT | **FAMILY** | Designed for kids under 10, this 45-minute program includes naturalist-led games, songs, stories, and crafts about Yosemite wildlife, plants, and geology. The event is held outdoors before the regular Yosemite Valley Lodge evening programs in summer and fall. All children must be accompanied by an adult. ⊠ *Yosemite National Park* ☎ *209/372–1153* ⊕ *www. travelyosemite.com* 🖃 *Free.*

VISITOR INFORMATION

PARK CONTACT INFORMATION Yosemite National Park ☎ *209/372–0200* ⊕ *www. nps.gov/yose.*

VISITOR CENTERS

Valley Visitor Center

INFO CENTER | Learn about Yosemite Valley's geology, vegetation, and human inhabitants at this visitor center, which is also staffed with helpful rangers and contains a bookstore with a wide selection

of books and maps. Two films, including one by Ken Burns, alternate on the half hour in the theater behind the visitor center. ⊠ *Yosemite Village* ☎ *209/372–0200* ⊕ *www.nps.gov/yose.*

Yosemite Conservation Heritage Center

INFO CENTER | This small but striking National Historic Landmark (formerly Le Conte Memorial Lodge), with its granite walls and steeply pitched shingle roof, is Yosemite's first permanent public information center. Step inside to see the cathedral-like interior, which contains a library and environmental exhibits. To find out about evening programs, check the kiosk out front. ⊠ *Southside Dr., about ½ mile west of Half Dome Village* ⊕ *sierraclub.org/yosemite-heritage-center* ⊘ *Closed Mon., Tues., and Oct.–Apr.*

 Sights

SCENIC DRIVE

Tioga Road

SCENIC DRIVE | Few mountain drives can compare with this 59-mile road, especially its eastern half between Lee Vining and Olmstead Point. As you climb 3,200 feet to the 9,945-foot summit of Tioga Pass (Yosemite's sole eastern entrance for cars), you'll encounter broad vistas of the granite-splotched High Sierra and its craggy but hearty trees and shrubs. Past the bustling scene at Tuolumne Meadows, you'll see picturesque Tenaya Lake and then Olmstead Point, where you'll get your first peek at Half Dome. Driving Tioga Road one way takes approximately 1½ hours. Wildflowers bloom here in July and August. By November, the high-altitude road closes for the winter; it sometimes doesn't reopen until early June. ⊠ *Yosemite National Park.*

HISTORIC SITES

Big Trees Lodge

HOTEL—SIGHT | Imagine a white-bearded Mark Twain relaxing in a rocking chair on one of the broad verandas of one of the park's first lodges (formerly the Wawona

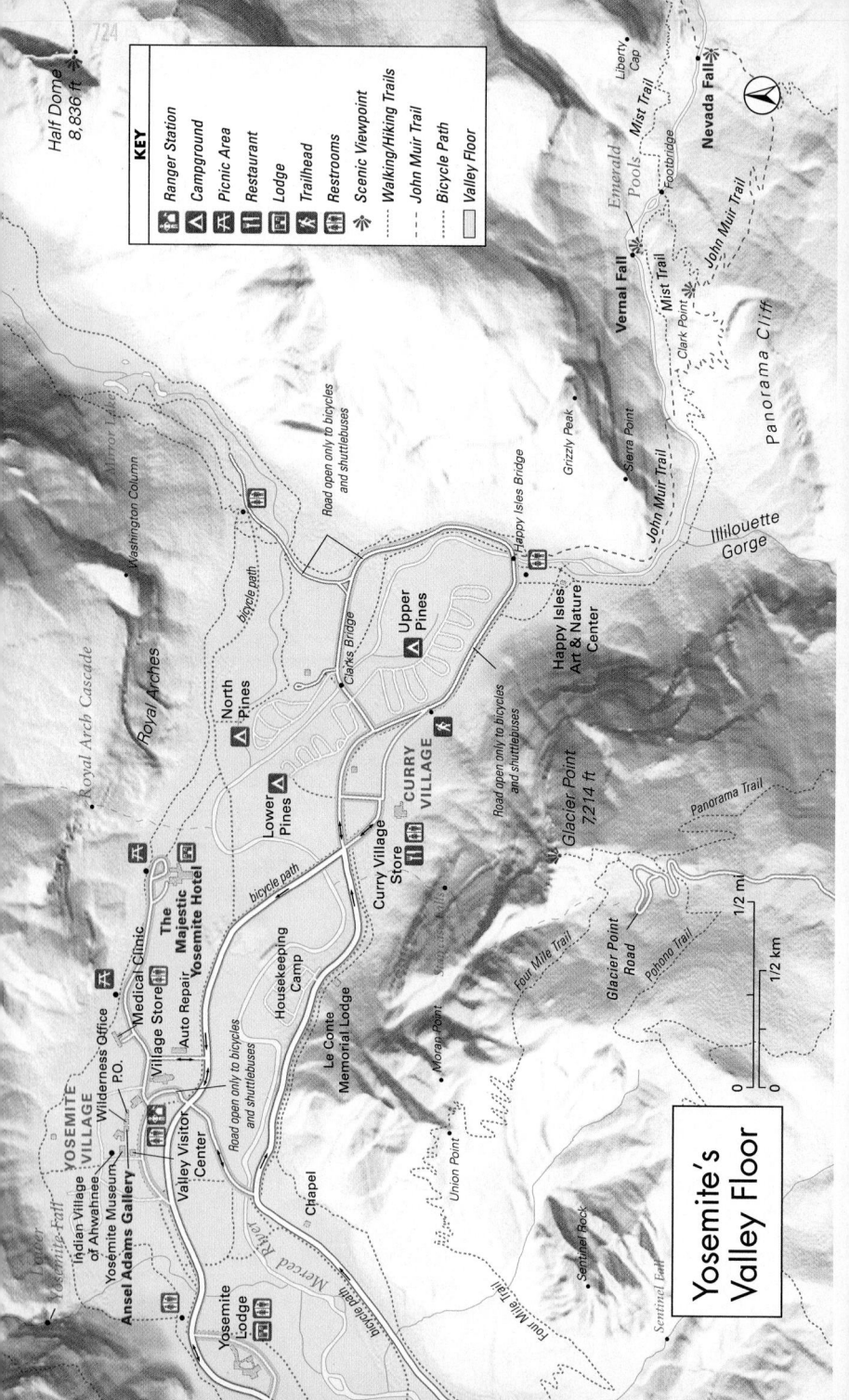

Yosemite's Valley Floor

KEY

- 🏠 Ranger Station
- ⛺ Campground
- 🧺 Picnic Area
- 🍴 Restaurant
- 🏨 Lodge
- 🅿 Trailhead
- 🚻 Restrooms
- ✳ Scenic Viewpoint
- ⋯ Walking/Hiking Trails
- — — John Muir Trail
- ⋯ Bicycle Path
- Valley Floor

724

Half Dome
8,836 ft

Liberty
Cap

Mist Trail

Nevada Fall

Emerald
Pools

Footbridge

Vernal Fall

Mist Trail

John Muir Trail

Clark Point

Panorama Cliff

Grizzly Peak

Sierra Point

Illilouette
Gorge

John Muir Trail

Happy Isles Bridge

Mirror Lake

Washington Column

Road open only to bicycles
and shuttlebuses

bicycle path

Clarks Bridge

Upper
Pines

Happy Isles
Art & Nature
Center

Royal Arch Cascade

Royal Arches

North
Pines

Lower
Pines

CURRY
VILLAGE

Road open only to bicycles
and shuttlebuses

Glacier Point
7214 ft

Panorama Trail

Medical Clinic

The
Majestic
Yosemite Hotel

bicycle path

Curry Village
Store

Glacier Point
Road

Pohono Trail

Village Store

Auto Repair

Wilderness Office

P.O.

YOSEMITE
VILLAGE

Yosemite Museum

Ansel Adams Gallery

Indian Village
of Ahwahnee

Lower Yosemite Fall

Housekeeping
Camp

Le Conte
Memorial Lodge

Four Mile Trail

Moran Point

Road open only to bicycles
and shuttlebuses

Valley Visitor
Center

Chapel

Union Point

Merced River

bicycle path

Yosemite Lodge

Four Mile Trail

Sentinel Rock

Sentinel Fall

0   1/2 mi

0   1/2 km

Hotel), a whitewashed series of two-story buildings from the Victorian era. Plop down in one of the dozens of white Adirondack chairs on the sprawling lawn and look across the road at the area's only golf course, one of the few links in the world that does not employ fertilizers or other chemicals. ✉ *Rte. 41, Wawona* ☎ *209/375–1425* ⊕ *www.travelyosemite. com/lodging/big-trees-lodge/* ⊗ *Closed Dec.–Mar. except 2 wks around Christmas and New Year's.*

Half Dome Village

HOTEL—SIGHT | A couple of schoolteachers from Indiana founded Camp Curry in 1899 as a low-cost option for staying in the valley, which it remains today. Half Dome Village's 400-plus lodging options (formerly Curry Village), many of them tent cabins, are spread over a large chunk of the Valley's southeastern side. This is one family-friendly place, but it's more functional than attractive. ✉ *Southside Dr., about ½ mile east of Yosemite Village.*

Indian Village of Ahwahnee

MUSEUM VILLAGE | This solemn smattering of structures, accessed by a short loop trail behind the Yosemite Valley Visitor Center, is a look at what Native American life might have been like in the 1870s. One interpretive sign points out that the Miwok people referred to the 19th-century newcomers as "Yohemite" or "Yohometuk," which have been translated as meaning "some of them are killers." ✉ *Northside Dr., Yosemite Village* ✉ *Free.*

The Majestic Yosemite Hotel

HOTEL—SIGHT | Gilbert Stanley Underwood, architect of the Grand Canyon Lodge, also designed The Majestic Yosemite Hotel (formerly The Ahwahnee hotel). Opened in 1927, it is generally considered his best work. You can stay here (for about $500 a night), or simply explore the first-floor shops and perhaps have breakfast or lunch in the bustling and beautiful Dining Room or more casual bar. The Great Lounge, 77 feet long with magnificent 24-foot-high ceilings and all manner of artwork on display, beckons with big, comfortable chairs and relative calm. ✉ *Ahwahnee Rd., about ¾ mile east of Yosemite Valley Visitor Center, Yosemite Village* ☎ *209/372–1489* ⊕ *www.travelyosemite.com/lodging/ the-majestic-yosemite-hotel/.*

Pioneer Yosemite History Center

MUSEUM | FAMILY | These historic buildings reflect different eras of Yosemite's history, starting in the 1850s through the early 1900s. They were moved to Wawona (the largest stage stop in Yosemite in the late 1800s) from various areas of Yosemite in the '50s and '60s. There is a self-guided-tour pamphlet available for 50¢. Weekends and some weekdays in the summer, costumed docents conduct free blacksmithing and "wet-plate" photography demonstrations, and for a small fee you can take a stagecoach ride. ✉ *Rte. 41, Wawona* ☎ *209/375–9531* ⊕ *www.nps.gov/yose/planyourvisit/waw. htm* ✉ *Free* ⊗ *Closed Mon., Tues., and mid-Sept.–early June.*

SCENIC STOPS
El Capitan

NATURE SITE | Rising 3,593 feet—more than 350 stories—above the valley, El Capitan is the largest exposed-granite monolith in the world. Since 1958, people have been climbing its entire face, including the famous "nose." You can spot adventurers with your binoculars by scanning the smooth and nearly vertical cliff for specks of color. ✉ *Yosemite National Park* ✛ *Off Northside Dr., about 4 miles west of Valley Visitor Center.*

★ Glacier Point

VIEWPOINT | If you lack the time, desire, or stamina to hike more than 3,200 feet up to Glacier Point from the Yosemite Valley floor, you can drive here—or take a bus from the valley—for a bird's-eye view. You are likely to encounter a lot of day-trippers on the short, paved trail that leads from the parking lot to the main overlook.

Plants and Wildlife in Yosemite

Dense stands of incense cedar and Douglas fir—as well as ponderosa, Jeffrey, lodgepole, and sugar pines—cover much of the park, but the stellar standout, quite literally, is the *Sequoiadendron giganteum*, the giant sequoia. Sequoias grow only along the west slope of the Sierra Nevada between 4,500 and 7,000 feet in elevation. Starting from a seed the size of a rolled-oat flake, each of these ancient monuments assumes remarkable proportions in adulthood; you can see them in the Mariposa Grove of Giant Sequoias. In late May the valley's dogwood trees bloom with white, starlike flowers. Wildflowers, such as black-eyed Susan, bull thistle, cow parsnip, lupine, and meadow goldenrod, peak in June in the valley and in July at higher elevations.

The most visible animals in the park—aside from the omnipresent western gray squirrels, which fearlessly attempt to steal your food at every campground and picnic site—are the mule deer. Though sightings of bighorn sheep are infrequent in the park itself, you can sometimes see them on the eastern side of the Sierra Crest, just off Route 120 in Lee Vining Canyon. You may also see the American black bear, which often has a brown, cinnamon, or blond coat. The Sierra Nevada is home to thousands of bears, and you should take all necessary precautions to keep yourself—and the bears—safe. Bears that acquire a taste for human food can become very aggressive and destructive and often must be destroyed by rangers, so store all your food and even scented toiletries in the bear lockers located at many campgrounds and trailheads, or use bear-resistant canisters if you'll be hiking in the backcountry.

Watch for the blue Steller's jay along trails, near public buildings, and in campgrounds, and look for golden eagles soaring over Tioga Road.

Take a moment to veer off a few yards to the Geology Hut, which succinctly explains and illustrates what the valley looked like 10 million, 3 million, and 20,000 years ago. ⊠ *Yosemite National Park* ✛ *Glacier Point Rd., 16 miles northeast of Rte. 41* ☎ *209/372–0200* ⊗ *Closed late Oct.–mid-May.*

★ Half Dome

NATURE SITE | Visitors' eyes are continually drawn to this remarkable granite formation that tops out at more than 4,700 feet above the valley floor. Despite its name, the dome is actually about three-quarters intact. You can hike to the top of Half Dome on an 8.5-mile (one-way) trail whose last 400 feet must be ascended while holding onto a steel cable. Permits are required (and checked on the trail), and available only by lottery. Call *877/444–6777* or visit *www.recreation.gov* well in advance of your trip for details. Back down in the valley, see Half Dome reflected in the Merced River by heading to Sentinel Bridge just before sundown. The brilliant orange light on Half Dome is a stunning sight. ⊠ *Yosemite National Park* ⊕ *www.nps.gov/yose/planyourvisit/halfdome.htm.*

Hetch Hetchy Reservoir

BODY OF WATER | When Congress approved the O'Shaughnessy Dam in 1913, pragmatism triumphed over aestheticism. Some 2.5 million residents of the San Francisco Bay Area continue to get their water from this 117-billion-gallon reservoir. Although spirited efforts are being made to restore the Hetch Hetchy Valley to its former, pristine glory, three-quarters of San Francisco voters in 2012 ultimately opposed a measure to even consider draining the reservoir. Eight miles long, the reservoir is Yosemite's largest body of water, and one that can be seen up close from several trails. ⊠ *Hetch Hetchy Rd., about 15 miles north of Big Oak Flat entrance station.*

High Country

NATURE PRESERVE | The above-tree-line, high-alpine region east of the valley—a land of alpenglow and top-of-the-world vistas—is often missed by crowds who come to gawk at the more publicized splendors. Summer wildflowers, which usually pop up mid-July through August, carpet the meadows and mountainsides with pink, purple, blue, red, yellow, and orange. On foot or on horseback are the only ways to get here. For information on trails and backcountry permits, check with the visitor center. ⊠ *Yosemite National Park.*

Mariposa Grove of Giant Sequoias

FOREST | Of Yosemite's three sequoia groves—the others being Merced and Tuolumne, both near Crane Flat well to the north—Mariposa is by far the largest and easiest to walk around. Grizzly Giant, whose base measures 96 feet around, has been estimated to be one of the largest in the world. Perhaps more astoundingly, it's about 1,800 years old. Park at the grove's welcome plaza and ride the free shuttle (required most of the year). Summer weekends are usually crowded here. ⊠ *Yosemite National Park ✛ Rte. 41, 2 miles north of south entrance station* ⊕ *www.nps.gov/yose/planyourvisit/mg.htm.*

Sentinel Dome

VIEWPOINT | The view from here is similar to that from Glacier Point, except you can't see the valley floor. A moderately steep 1.1-mile path climbs to the viewpoint from the parking lot. Topping out at an elevation of 8,122 feet, Sentinel is more than 900 feet higher than Glacier Point. ⊠ *Glacier Point Rd., off Rte. 41.*

Tuolumne Meadows

MOUNTAIN—SIGHT | The largest subalpine meadow in the Sierra (at 8,600 feet) is a popular way station for backpack trips along the Pacific Crest and John Muir trails. The setting is not as dramatic as Yosemite Valley, 56 miles away, but the almost perfectly flat basin, about 2½ miles long, is intriguing, and in July it's resplendent with wildflowers. The most popular day hike is up Lembert Dome, atop which you'll have breathtaking views of the basin below. Keep in mind that Tioga Road rarely opens before June and usually closes by mid-October. ⊠ *Tioga Rd. (Rte. 120), about 8 miles west of Tioga Pass entrance station.*

WATERFALLS

Yosemite's waterfalls are at their most spectacular in May and June. When the snow starts to melt (usually peaking in May), streaming snowmelt spills down to meet the Merced River. By summer's end, some falls, including the mighty Yosemite Falls, trickle or dry up. Their flow increases in late fall, and in winter they may be hung dramatically with ice. Even in drier months, the waterfalls can be breathtaking. If you choose to hike any of the trails to or up the falls, be sure to wear shoes with no-slip soles; the rocks can be extremely slick. Stay on trails at all times.

■ **TIP→ Visit the park during a full moon and you can stroll without a flashlight and still make out the ribbons of falling water, as well as silhouettes of the giant granite monoliths.**

Bridalveil Fall

BODY OF WATER | This 620-foot waterfall is often diverted dozens of feet one way or the other by the breeze. It is the first marvelous site you will see up close when you drive into Yosemite Valley.

✉ *Yosemite Valley, access from parking area off Wawona Rd.*

Nevada Fall

BODY OF WATER | Climb Mist Trail from Happy Isles for an up-close view of this 594-foot cascading beauty. If you don't want to hike (the trail's final approach is quite taxing), you can see it—albeit distantly—from Glacier Point. Stay safely on the trail, as there have been fatalities in recent years after visitors have fallen and been swept away by the water. ✉ *Yosemite Valley, access via Mist Trail from Nature Center at Happy Isles.*

Ribbon Fall

BODY OF WATER | At 1,612 feet, this is the highest single fall in North America. It's also the first waterfall to dry up in summer; the rainwater and melted snow that create the slender fall evaporate quickly at this height. Look just west of El Capitan for the best view of the fall from the base of Bridalveil Fall. ✉ *Yosemite Valley, west of El Capitan Meadow.*

Vernal Fall

BODY OF WATER | Fern-covered black rocks frame this 317-foot fall, and rainbows play in the spray at its base. You can get a distant view from Glacier Point, or hike to see it close up. You'll get wet, but the view is worth it. ✉ *Yosemite Valley, access via Mist Trail from Nature Center at Happy Isles.*

★ Yosemite Falls

BODY OF WATER | Actually three falls, they together constitute the highest combined waterfall in North America and the fifth highest in the world. The water from the top descends a total of 2,425 feet, and when the falls run hard, you can hear them thunder across the valley. If they dry up—that sometimes happens in late summer—the valley seems naked without the wavering tower of spray. If you hike the mile-long loop trail (partially paved) to the base of the Lower Fall in spring, prepare to get wet. You can get a good full-length view of the falls from the lawn of Yosemite Chapel, off Southside Drive. ✉ *Yosemite Valley, access from Yosemite Valley Lodge or trail parking area.*

 Activities

BIKING

One enjoyable way to see Yosemite Valley is to ride a bike beneath its lofty granite monoliths. The eastern valley has 12 miles of paved, flat bicycle paths across meadows and through woods, with bike racks at convenient stopping points. For a greater challenge but at no small risk, you can ride on 196 miles of paved park roads—but bicycles are not allowed on hiking trails or in the backcountry. Kids under 18 must wear a helmet.

Yosemite bike rentals

BICYCLING | You can arrange for rentals from Yosemite Valley Lodge and Half Dome Village bike stands. Bikes with child trailers, baby-jogger strollers, and wheelchairs are also available. The cost for bikes is $12 per hour, or $33.50 a day. ✉ *Yosemite Valley Lodge or Half Dome Village* ☎ *209/372–4386* ⊕ *www.travelyosemite.com.*

BIRD-WATCHING

More than 250 bird species have been spotted in the park, including the sage sparrow, pygmy owl, blue grouse, and mountain bluebird. Park rangers lead free bird-watching walks in Yosemite Valley a few days each week in summer; check at a visitor center or information station for times and locations. Binoculars sometimes are available for loan.

Birding seminars

BIRD WATCHING | The Yosemite Conservancy organizes day- and weekend-long seminars for beginner and intermediate birders, as well as bird walks a few times a week. They can also arrange private naturalist-led walks any time of year. ✉ *Yosemite National Park* ☎ *209/379–2321* ⊕ *www.yosemiteconservancy.org* 🎫 *From $99.*

Winter in Yosemite

FISHING

The waters in Yosemite are not stocked; trout, mostly brown and rainbow, live here but are not plentiful. Yosemite's fishing season begins on the last Saturday in April and ends on November 15. Some waterways are off-limits at certain times; be sure to inquire at the visitor center about regulations.

A California fishing license is required; licenses cost around $16 for one day, $24 for two days, and $48 for 10 days. Full-season licenses cost $48 for state residents and $130 for nonresidents (costs fluctuate year to year). Buy your license in season at **Yosemite Mountain Shop in Half Dome Village** (☎ 209/372–1286) or at the **Big Trees General Store** (☎ 209/375–6574).

HIKING

Wilderness Center
HIKING/WALKING | This facility provides free wilderness permits, which are required for overnight camping (advance reservations are available for $5 per person plus $5 per reservation and are highly recommended for popular trailheads in summer and on weekends). The staff here also provides maps and advice to hikers heading into the backcountry, and rents and sells bear-resistant canisters, which are required if you don't have your own. ⊠ *Between Ansel Adams Gallery and post office, Yosemite Village* ☎ *209/372–0308.*

Yosemite Mountaineering School and Guide Service
HIKING/WALKING | From April to November, you can learn to climb, hire a guide, or join a two-hour to full-day trek with Yosemite Mountaineering School. They also rent gear and lead backpacking and overnight excursions. Reservations are recommended. In winter, cross-country ski programs are available at Yosemite Ski & Snowboard Area. ⊠ *Yosemite Mountain Shop, Half Dome Village* ☎ *209/372–8344* ⊕ *yosemitemountaineering.com.*

Cook's Meadow Loop
HIKING/WALKING | **FAMILY** | Take this 1-mile, wheelchair-accessible, looped path around Cook's Meadow to see and learn

the basics about Yosemite Valley's past, present, and future. A self-guiding trail guide (available at a kiosk just outside the entrance) explains how to tell oaks, cedars, and pines apart; how fires help keep the forest floor healthy; and how pollution poses significant challenges to the park's inhabitants. *Easy.* ⊠ *Yosemite National Park* ✛ *Trailhead: across from Valley Visitor Center.*

Chilnualna Falls Trail

HIKING/WALKING | This Wawona-area trail runs 4 miles one way to the top of the falls, then leads into the backcountry, connecting with miles of other trails. This is one of the park's most inspiring and secluded—albeit strenuous—trails. Past the tumbling cascade, and up through forests, you'll emerge before a panoramic vista at the top. *Difficult.* ⊠ *Wawona* ✛ *Trailhead: at Chilnualna Falls Rd., off Rte. 41.*

★ John Muir Trail to Half Dome

HIKING/WALKING | Ardent and courageous trekkers continue on from Nevada Fall to the top of Half Dome. Some hikers attempt this entire 10- to 12-hour, 16¾-mile round-trip trek in one day; if you're planning to do this, remember that the 4,800-foot elevation gain and the 8,842-foot altitude will cause shortness of breath. Another option is to hike to a campground in Little Yosemite Valley near the top of Nevada Fall the first day, then climb to the top of Half Dome and hike out the next day. Get your wilderness permit (required for a one-day hike to Half Dome, too) at least a month in advance. Be sure to wear hiking boots and bring gloves. The last pitch up the back of Half Dome is very steep—the only way to climb this sheer rock face is to pull yourself up using the steel cable handrails, which are in place only from late spring to early fall. Those who brave the ascent will be rewarded with an unbeatable view of Yosemite Valley below and the high country beyond. Only 300 hikers per day are allowed atop Half Dome, and

they all must have permits, which are distributed by lottery, one in the spring before the season starts and another two days before the climb. Contact *www.recreation.gov* for details. *Difficult.* ⊠ *Yosemite National Park* ✛ *Trailhead: at Happy Isles* ⊕ *www.nps.gov/yose/planyourvisit/halfdome.htm.*

Mist Trail

HIKING/WALKING | Except for Lower Yosemite Fall, more visitors take this trail (or portions of it) than any other in the park. The trek up to and back from Vernal Fall is 3 miles. Add another 4 miles total by continuing up to 594-foot Nevada Fall; the trail becomes quite steep and slippery in its final stages. The elevation gain to Vernal Fall is 1,000 feet, and to Nevada Fall an additional 1,000 feet. The Merced River tumbles down both falls on its way to a tranquil flow through the valley. *Moderate.* ⊠ *Yosemite National Park* ✛ *Trailhead: at Happy Isles.*

★ Panorama Trail

HIKING/WALKING | Few hikes come with the visual punch that this 8½-mile trail provides. It starts from Glacier Point and descends to Yosemite Valley. The star attraction is Half Dome, visible from many intriguing angles, but you also see three waterfalls up close and walk through a manzanita grove. *Moderate.* ⊠ *Yosemite National Park* ✛ *Trailhead: at Glacier Point.*

★ Yosemite Falls Trail

HIKING/WALKING | Yosemite Falls is the highest waterfall in North America. The upper fall (1,430 feet), the middle cascades (675 feet), and the lower fall (320 feet) combine for a total of 2,425 feet, and when viewed from the valley appear as a single waterfall. The ¼-mile trail leads from the parking lot to the base of the falls. Upper Yosemite Fall Trail, a strenuous 7.2-mile round-trip climb rising 2,700 feet, takes you above the top of the falls. Lower trail: *Easy.* Upper trail: *Difficult.* ⊠ *Yosemite National*

Ansel Adams's Black-and-White Yosemite

What John Muir did for Yosemite with words, Ansel Adams did with photographs. His photographs have inspired millions of people to visit Yosemite, and his persistent activism helped to ensure the park's conservation.

Born in 1902, Adams first came to the valley when he was 14, photographing it with a Box Brownie camera. He later said his first visit "was a culmination of experience so intense as to be almost painful. From that day in 1916 my life has been colored and modulated by the great earth gesture of the Sierra." By 1919 he was working in the valley, as custodian of LeConte Memorial Lodge (now called Yosemite Conservation Heritage Center), the Sierra Club headquarters in Yosemite National Park.

Adams had harbored dreams of a career as a concert pianist, but the park sealed his fate as a photographer in 1928, the day he shot *Monolith: The Face of Half Dome*, which remains one of his most famous works. Adams also married Virginia Best in 1928, in her father's studio in the valley (now the Ansel Adams Gallery).

As Adams's photographic career took off, Yosemite began to sear itself into the American consciousness. David Brower, first executive director of the Sierra Club, later said of Adams's impact, "That Ansel Adams came to be recognized as one of the great photographers of this century is a tribute to the places that informed him."

In 1934 Adams was elected to the Sierra Club's board of directors; he would serve until 1971. As a representative of the conservation group, he combined his work with the club's mission, showing his photographs of the Sierra to influential officials such as Secretary of the Interior Harold L. Ickes, who showed them to President Franklin Delano Roosevelt. The images were a key factor in the establishment of Kings Canyon National Park.

In 1968, the Department of the Interior granted Adams its highest honor, the Conservation Service Award, and in 1980 he received the Presidential Medal of Freedom in recognition of his conservation work. Until his death in 1984, Adams continued not only to record Yosemite's majesty on film but to urge the federal government and park managers to do right by the park.

In one of his many public pleas on behalf of Yosemite, Adams said, "Yosemite Valley itself is one of the great shrines of the world and—belonging to all our people—must be both protected and appropriately accessible." As an artist and an activist, Adams never gave up on his dream of keeping Yosemite wild yet within reach of every visitor who wants to experience that wildness.

Park ✛ Trailhead: off Camp 4, north of Northside Dr.

HORSEBACK RIDING

Reservations for guided trail rides must be made in advance at the hotel tour desks or by phone. Scenic trail rides range from two hours to a half day; four- and six-day High Sierra saddle trips are also available.

Big Trees Stable

HORSEBACK RIDING | Two-hour rides at these stables start at $67, and a challenging full-day ride to the Mariposa Grove of Giant Sequoias (for experienced riders in good physical condition only) costs $140. Reservations are recommended. ⊠ *Rte. 41, Wawona* ☎ *209/375–6502* ⊕ *www.travelyosemite.com/things-to-do/horseback-mule-riding/* ⌧ *From $67.*

RAFTING

Rafting is permitted only on designated areas of the Middle and South Forks of the Merced River. Check with the Valley Visitor Center for closures and other restrictions.

Half Dome Village Recreation Center

WHITE-WATER RAFTING | The per-person rental fee ($33) at Half Dome Village Recreation Center covers the four- to six-person raft, two paddles, and life jackets, plus a return shuttle at the end of your trip. ⊠ *South side of Southside Dr., Half Dome Village* ☎ *209/372–4386* ⊕ *www.travelyosemite.com/things-to-do/rafting/* ⌧ *From $33.*

ROCK CLIMBING

The granite canyon walls of Yosemite Valley are world-renowned for rock climbing. El Capitan, with its 3,593-foot vertical face, is the most famous, but there are many other options here for all skill levels.

Yosemite Mountaineering School & Guide Service

CLIMBING/MOUNTAINEERING | The one-day basic lesson at Yosemite Mountaineering School and Guide Service includes some bouldering and rappelling, and three or four 60-foot climbs. Climbers must be at least 10 years old and in reasonably good physical condition. Intermediate and advanced classes include instruction in first aid, anchor building, multipitch climbing, summer snow climbing, and big-wall climbing. There's a Nordic program in the winter. ⊠ *Yosemite Mountain Shop, Half Dome Village* ☎ *209/372–8444* ⊕ *www.travelyosemite.com* ⌧ *From $172.*

SWIMMING

The pools at **Half Dome Village** (☎ *209/372–8324* ⊕ *www.travelyosemite.com*) and **Yosemite Valley Lodge** (☎ *209/372–1250* ⊕ *www.travelyosemite.com*) are open to nonguests for $5, late May through early or mid-September. Additionally, several swimming holes with small sandy beaches can be found in midsummer along the Merced River at the eastern end of Yosemite Valley. Find gentle waters to swim; currents are often stronger than they appear, and temperatures are chilling. To conserve riparian habitats, step into the river at sandy beaches and other obvious entry points. ■TIP→ **Do not attempt to swim above or near waterfalls or rapids; people have died trying.**

WINTER ACTIVITIES

The beauty of Yosemite under a blanket of snow has long inspired poets and artists, as well as ordinary folks. Skiing and snowshoeing activities in the park center on Yosemite Ski & Snowboard Area, California's oldest snow-sports resort, which is about 40 minutes away from the valley on Glacier Point Road. Here you can rent equipment, take a lesson, have lunch, join a guided excursion, and take the free shuttle back to the valley after a drink in the lounge.

ICE-SKATING

Half Dome Village Ice Rink

ICE SKATING | Winter visitors have skated at this outdoor rink for decades, and there's no mystery why: it's a kick to glide across the ice while soaking up views of Half Dome and Glacier Point. ⊠ *South side of Southside Dr., Half Dome Village* ☎ *209/372–8319* ⊕ *www.travelyosemite.com* ⚌ *$10 per session, $4 skate rental.*

SKIING AND SNOWSHOEING
Yosemite Ski & Snowboard Area
SKIING/SNOWBOARDING | California's first ski resort has five lifts and 10 downhill runs, as well as 90 miles of groomed cross-country trails. Free shuttle buses from Yosemite Valley operate between December and the end of March, weather permitting. Lessons, backcountry guiding, and cross-country and snowshoeing tours are also available. You can rent downhill, telemark, and cross-country skis, plus snowshoes and snowboards. **Facilities:** 10 trails; 90 acres; 800-foot vertical drop; 5 lifts. ⊠ *Yosemite National Park* ⊹ *Badger Pass Rd., off Glacier Point Rd., 18 miles from Yosemite Valley* ☎ *209/372–8430* ⊕ *www.travelyosemite.com/winter/yosemite-ski-snowboard-area/* ⚌ *Lift ticket: from $55.*

Yosemite Cross-Country Ski School
SKIING/SNOWBOARDING | The highlight of Yosemite's cross-country skiing center is a 21-mile loop from Yosemite Ski & Snowboard Area to Glacier Point. You can rent cross-country skis for $28 per day at the Cross-Country Ski School, which also rents snowshoes ($23 per day) and telemarking equipment ($28). ☎ *209/372–8444* ⊕ *www.travelyosemite.com.*

Yosemite Mountaineering School
SKIING/SNOWBOARDING | This branch of the Yosemite Mountaineering School, open at the Yosemite Ski & Snowboard Area during ski season only, conducts snowshoeing, cross-country skiing, telemarking, and skate-skiing classes starting at $44. ⊠ *Yosemite Ski & Snowboard Area* ☎ *209/372–8444* ⊕ *www.travelyosemite.com.*

Yosemite Ski & Snowboard Area School
SKIING/SNOWBOARDING | The gentle slopes of Yosemite Ski & Snowboard Area make the ski school an ideal spot for children

and beginners to learn downhill skiing or snowboarding for as little as $75 for a group lesson. ☎ *209/372–8430* ⊕ *www.travelyosemite.com.*

 Nightlife

Vintage Music of Yosemite
MUSIC CLUBS | A pianist-singer performs four hours of live old-time music at the Big Trees Lodge (formerly Wawona Hotel); call for schedule of performances. ⊠ *Big Trees Lodge, Rte. 41, Wawona* ☎ *209/375–6556* ⚌ *Free.*

 Performing Arts

Yosemite Theatre
THEATER | Various theater and music programs are held throughout the year, and one of the best loved is Lee Stetson's portrayal of John Muir in *Conversation with a Tramp* and other Muir-theme shows. Purchase tickets in advance at the Conservancy Store at the Valley Visitor Center or the Tour and Activity Desk at Yosemite Valley Lodge. Unsold seats are available at the door at performance time, 7 pm. ⊠ *Valley Visitor Center, Yosemite Village* ☎ *209/372–0299* ⚌ *$10.*

 Shopping

Ansel Adams Gallery
ART GALLERIES | Framed prints of the famed nature photographer's best works are on sale here, as are affordable posters. New works by contemporary artists are available, along with Native American jewelry and handicrafts. The gallery's elegant camera shop conducts photography workshops, from free camera walks a few mornings a week to five-day workshops. ⊠ *Northside Dr., Yosemite Village* ☎ *209/372–4413* ⊕ *anseladams.com/ansel-adams-gallery-in-yosemite/.*

Majestic Hotel Gift Shop
GIFTS/SOUVENIRS | This shop sells more upscale items, such as Native American crafts, photographic prints, handmade

ceramics, and elegant jewelry. For less expensive gift items, browse the small book selection, which includes writings by John Muir. ✉ *The Majestic Yosemite Hotel, Ahwahnee Rd.* ☎ *209/372–1409.*

Yosemite Mountain Shop

A comprehensive selection of camping, hiking, backpacking, and climbing equipment, along with experts who can answer all your questions, make this store a valuable resource for outdoors enthusiasts. This is the best place to ask about climbing conditions and restrictions around the park, as well as purchase almost any kind of climbing gear. ✉ *Half Dome Village* ☎ *209/372–8436.*

Nearby Towns

Marking the southern end of the Sierra's gold-bearing mother lode, **Mariposa** is the last town before you enter Yosemite on Route 140 to the west of the park. In addition to a fine mining museum, Mariposa has numerous shops, restaurants, and service stations.

Motels and restaurants dot both sides of Route 41 as it cuts through the town of **Oakhurst,** a boomtown during the Gold Rush that is now an important regional refueling station in every sense of the word, including organic foods and a full range of lodging options. Oakhurst has a population of about 3,000 and sits 15 miles south of the park.

Almost surrounded by the Sierra National Forest, **Bass Lake** is a warm-water reservoir whose waters can reach 80 degrees F in summer. Created by a dam on a tributary of the San Joaquin River, the lake is owned by Pacific Gas and Electric Company and is used to generate electricity as well as for recreation.

As you climb in elevation along Highway 41 northbound, you see nothing but trees until you get to **Fish Camp,** where there's a post office and general store, but no gasoline. (For gas, head 7 miles north to

Wawona, in Yosemite, or 14 miles south to Oakhurst.)

Near the park's eastern entrance, the tiny town of **Lee Vining** is home to the eerily beautiful, salty Mono Lake, where millions of migratory birds nest. Visit **Mammoth Lakes,** about 40 miles southeast of Yosemite's Tioga Pass entrance, for excellent skiing and snowboarding in winter, with fishing, mountain biking, hiking, and horseback riding in summer. Nine deep-blue lakes form the Mammoth Lakes Basin, and another hundred dot the surrounding countryside. Devils Postpile National Monument sits at the base of Mammoth Mountain.

VISITOR INFORMATION Mammoth Lakes Tourism ✉ *2510 Main St., Mammoth Lakes* ☎ *760/934–2712, 888/466–2666* ⊕ *www.visitmammoth.com.* **Mono Lake Information Center and Bookstore** ☎ *760/647–6595* ⊕ *www.leevining.com.* **Tuolumne County Visitors Bureau** ✉ *193 S. Washington St., Sonora* ☎ *209/533–4420, 800/446–1333* ⊕ *www.visittuolumne. com.* **Visit Yosemite/Madera County** ✉ *40343 Hwy. 41, Oakhurst* ☎ *559/683–4636* ⊕ *www.yosemitethisyear.com.* **Yosemite Mariposa County Tourism Bureau** ✉ *5158 Hwy. 140, Suite E, Mariposa* ☎ *209/742–4567, 866/425–3366 visitor center toll-free, 209/966–7081 visitor center* ⊕ *www.yosemite.com.*

 Sights

★ Bodie Ghost Town

GHOST TOWN | The mining village of Rattlesnake Gulch, abandoned mine shafts, and the remains of a small Chinatown are among the sights at this fascinating ghost town. The town boomed from about 1878 to 1881, but by the late 1940s all its residents had departed. A state park was established here in 1962, with a mandate to preserve everything in a state of "arrested decay." Evidence of Bodie's wild past survives at an excellent museum, and you can tour an old stamp mill where ore was crushed into fine powder to extract gold and silver. Bodie lies 13 miles east of U.S. 395 off Highway 270. The last 3 miles are unpaved, and snow may close the highway from late fall through early spring. No food, drink, or lodging is available in Bodie. ☒ *Bodie Rd., off Hwy. 270, Bodie* ☎ *760/616–5040* ⊕ *www.parks.ca.gov/bodie* ☒ *$8.*

California State Mining and Mineral Museum

MUSEUM | FAMILY | A California state park since 1999, the museum has displays on gold-rush history including a replica hardrock mine shaft to walk through, a miniature stamp mill, and a 13-pound chunk of crystallized gold. ☒ *5005 Fairground Rd., off Hwy. 49, Mariposa* ☎ *209/742–7625* ⊕ *www.parks.ca.gov* ☒ *$4* ☉ *Closed Mon.–Wed.*

★ Devils Postpile National Monument

NATURE SITE | Volcanic and glacial forces sculpted this formation of smooth, vertical basalt columns. For a bird's-eye view, take the short, steep trail to the top of a 60-foot cliff. To see the monument's second scenic wonder, **Rainbow Falls,** hike 2 miles past Devils Postpile. A branch of the San Joaquin River plunges more than 100 feet over a lava ledge here. When the water hits the pool below, sunlight turns the resulting mist into a spray of color. From mid-June to early September, day-use visitors must ride the shuttle bus from the Mammoth Mountain Ski Area to the monument. ☒ *Mammoth Lakes* ✛ *13 miles southwest of Mammoth Lakes off Minaret Rd. (Hwy. 203)* ☎ *760/934–2289, 760/872–1901 shuttle* ⊕ *www.nps.gov/depo* ☒ *$10 per vehicle (allowed when the shuttle isn't running, usually early Sept.–mid-Oct.), $8 per person shuttle.*

Hot Creek Geologic Site

NATURE SITE | Forged by an ancient volcanic eruption, the Hot Creek Geologic Site is a landscape of boiling hot springs, fumaroles, and geysers about 10 miles southeast of the town of Mammoth Lakes. You can stroll along boardwalks through the canyon to view the steaming

volcanic features. Fly-fishing for trout is popular upstream from the springs. ☒ *Hot Creek Hatchery Rd. east of U.S. 395, Mammoth Lakes* ☎ *760/873–2400* ⊕ *www.fs.usda.gov/recarea/inyo/recarea/?recid=20414* ☒ *Free.*

★ Mono Lake

BODY OF WATER | Since the 1940s Los Angeles has diverted water from this lake, exposing striking towers of tufa, or calcium carbonate. Court victories by environmentalists have meant fewer diversions, and the lake is rising again. Although to see the lake from U.S. 395 is stunning, make time to visit South Tufa, whose parking lot is 5 miles east of U.S. 395 off Highway 120. There in summer you can join the naturalist-guided **South Tufa Walk,** which lasts about 90 minutes. The **Scenic Area Visitor Center,** off U.S. 395, is a sensational stop for its interactive exhibits and sweeping Mono Lake views (closed in winter). In town at U.S. 395 and 3rd Street, the **Mono Lake Committee Information Center & Bookstore**, open from 9 to 5 daily (extended hours in summer), has more information about this beautiful area. ☒ *Hwy. 120, east of Lee Vining, Lee Vining* ☎ *760/647–3044 visitor center, 760/647–6595 info center* ⊕ *www.monolake.org* ☒ *Free.*

Yosemite Mountain Sugar Pine Railroad

TRANSPORTATION SITE (AIRPORT/BUS/FERRY/TRAIN) | FAMILY | Travel back to a time when powerful steam locomotives hauled massive log trains through the Sierra. This 4-mile, narrow-gauge railroad excursion takes you near Yosemite's south gate. There's a moonlight special ($58), with dinner and entertainment, and you can pan for gold ($10) and visit the free museum. ☒ *56001 Hwy. 41, 8 miles south of Yosemite, Fish Camp* ☎ *559/683–7273* ⊕ *www.ymsprr.com* ☒ *$24* ☉ *Closed Nov.–Mar. Closed some weekdays Apr. and Oct.*

⚡ Activities

RAFTING
Zephyr Whitewater Expeditions
BOATING | This outfitter conducts half-day to three-day white-water trips on the Tuolumne, Merced, and American rivers for paddlers of all experience levels. ☎ 800/431–3636 reservations, 209/532–6249 ⊕ www.zrafting.com ⌚ From $112.

SKIING
★ Mammoth Mountain Ski Area
SKIING/SNOWBOARDING | One of the West's largest and best ski areas, Mammoth has more than 3,500 acres of skiable terrain and a 3,100-foot vertical drop. The views from the 11,053-foot summit are some of the most stunning in the Sierra. Below, you'll find a 6½-mile-wide swath of groomed boulevards and canyons, as well as pockets of tree-skiing and a dozen vast bowls. Snowboarders are everywhere on the slopes; there are thirteen outstanding freestyle terrain parks of varying difficulty, with jumps, rails, tabletops, and giant super pipes—this is the location of several international snowboarding competitions, and, in summer, mountain-bike meets. Mammoth's season begins in November and often lingers into July. Lessons and equipment are available, and there's a children's ski and snowboard school. Mammoth runs free shuttle-bus routes around town and to the ski area, and the Village Gondola runs from the Village complex to Canyon Lodge. However, only overnight guests are allowed to park at the Village for more than a few hours. **Facilities:** 150 trails; 3,500 acres; 3,100-foot vertical drop; 28 lifts. ✉ Minaret Rd., west of Mammoth Lakes, Rte. 203, off U.S. 395, Mammoth Lakes ☎ 760/934–2571, 800/626–6684, 760/934–0687 shuttle ⊕ www.mammothmountain.com ⌚ From $135.

🍴 Restaurants

IN THE PARK
In addition to the dining options listed here, you'll find fast-food grills and cafeterias, plus temporary snack bars, hamburger stands, and pizza joints lining park roads in summer. Many dining facilities in the park are open summer only.

Base Camp Eatery
$$ | AMERICAN | The design of this modern food court, open for breakfast, lunch, and dinner, honors the history of rock climbing in Yosemite. Choose from a wide range of menu options, from hamburgers, salads, and pizzas, to rice and noodle bowls. **Known for:** grab and go selections; best casual dining venue in the park; automated ordering kiosks to speed up service. $ Average main: $12 ✉ Yosemite Valley Lodge, about ¾ mile west of visitor center, Yosemite Village ☎ 209/372–1265 ⊕ www.travelyosemite.com.

Big Trees Lodge Dining Room
$$$ | AMERICAN | Watch deer graze on the meadow while you dine in the romantic, candlelit dining room of the whitewashed Big Trees Lodge (formerly the Wawona Hotel), which dates from the late 1800s. The American-style cuisine favors fresh ingredients and flavors; trout and flatiron steaks are menu staples. **Known for:** Saturday-night barbecues on the lawn; historic ambience; Mother's Day and other Sunday holiday brunches. $ Average main: $28 ✉ 8308 Wawona Rd., Wawona ☎ 209/375–1425 ⊘ Closed most of Dec., Jan., Feb., and Mar.

Half Dome Village Pavilion
$$ | AMERICAN | Formerly Curry Village Pavilion, this cafeteria-style eatery serves everything from roasted meats and salads to pastas, burritos, and beyond. Alternatively, order a pizza from the stand on the deck, and take in the views of the valley's granite walls. **Known for:** convenient eats; Saturday evening chuckwagon barbecues mid-June–August; additional

venues: Meadow Grill, Pizza Patio, Coffee Corner and Village Bar. $ *Average main: $18* ⊠ *Half Dome Village* ☎ *209/372–8303* ⊙ *Closed mid-Oct.–mid-Apr. No lunch.*

★ The Majestic Yosemite Hotel Dining Room

$$$$ | EUROPEAN | Formerly the Ahwahnee Hotel Dining Room, rave reviews about the dining room's appearance are fully justified—it features towering windows, a 34-foot-high ceiling with interlaced sugar-pine beams, and massive chandeliers. Reservations are always advised, and the attire is "resort casual." **Known for:** lavish $56 Sunday brunch; finest dining in the park; bar menu with lighter lunch and dinner fare at more affordable prices. $ *Average main: $39* ⊠ *The Majestic Yosemite Hotel, Ahwahnee Rd., about ¾ mile east of Yosemite Valley Visitor Center, Yosemite Village* ☎ *209/372–1489* ⊕ *www.travelyosemite.com.*

★ Mountain Room

$$$ | AMERICAN | Gaze at Yosemite Falls through this dining room's wall of windows—almost every table has a view—as you nosh on steaks, seafood, and classic California salads and desserts. The Mountain Room Lounge, a few steps away in the Yosemite Lodge complex, has about 10 beers on tap. **Known for:** locally sourced, organic ingredients; usually there is a wait for a table (no reservations); vegetarian and vegan options. $ *Average main: $29* ⊠ *Yosemite Valley Lodge, Northside Dr., about ¾ mile west of visitor center, Yosemite Village* ☎ *209/372–1403* ⊕ *www.travelyosemite.com* ⊙ *No lunch except Sun. brunch.*

Tuolumne Meadows Grill

$ | FAST FOOD | Serving continuously throughout the day until 5 or 6 pm, this fast-food eatery cooks up basic breakfast, lunch, and snacks. It's possible that ice cream tastes better at this altitude. **Known for:** soft serve ice cream; crowds; fresh local ingredients. $ *Average main: $8* ⊠ *Tioga Rd. (Rte. 120), 1½ miles east*

of *Tuolumne Meadows Visitor Center* ☎ *209/372–8426* ⊕ *www.travelyosemite.com* ⊙ *Closed Oct.–Memorial Day. No dinner.*

Tuolumne Meadows Lodge

$$$ | AMERICAN | In a central dining tent beside the Tuolumne River, this restaurant serves a menu of hearty American fare at breakfast and dinner. The red-and-white-checkered tablecloths and a handful of communal tables give it the feeling of an old-fashioned summer camp. **Known for:** box lunches; communal tables; small menu. $ *Average main: $24* ⊠ *Tioga Rd. (Rte. 120)* ☎ *209/372–8413* ⊕ *www.travelyosemite.com* ⊙ *Closed late Sept.–mid-June. No lunch.*

Village Grill Deck

$$ | FAST FOOD | If a burger joint is what you've been missing, head to this bustling eatery in Yosemite Village that serves veggie, salmon, and a few other burger varieties in addition to the usual beef patties. Order at the counter, then take your tray out to the deck and enjoy your meal under the trees. **Known for:** burgers, sandwiches, and hot dogs; crowds; outdoor seating on expansive deck. $ *Average main: $12* ⊠ *Yosemite Village* ✛ *100 yards east of Yosemite Valley Visitor Center* ☎ *209/372–1207* ⊕ *www.travelyosemite.com* ⊙ *Closed Oct.–May. No dinner.*

PICNIC AREAS

Considering how large the park is and how many visitors come here—some 5 million people every year, most of them just for the day—it is somewhat surprising that Yosemite has few formal picnic areas, though in many places you can find a smooth rock to sit on and enjoy breathtaking views along with your lunch. The convenience stores all sell picnic supplies, and prepackaged sandwiches and salads are widely available. Those options can come in especially handy during the middle of the day, when you might not want to spend precious daylight hours in such a spectacular setting

Did You Know?

In the Sierra's mixed-conifer forests, telling the many types of pines apart can be difficult if you don't know the trick: sizing up the cones and examining the branches to count how many needles are in discrete clusters. If the needles are paired, you're likely looking at a lodgepole pine. If the needles are long and come in threes, chances are you've come upon a ponderosa pine.

sitting in a restaurant for a formal meal. *None of the below options has drinking water available; most have some type of toilet.*

Cathedral Beach. You may have some solitude picnicking here, as this spot usually has fewer people than picnic areas at the eastern end of the valley. *Southside Dr. underneath spirelike Cathedral Rocks.*

Church Bowl. Tucked behind The Majestic Yosemite Hotel, this picnic area nearly abuts the granite walls below the Royal Arches. If you're walking from the village with your supplies, this is the shortest trek to a picnic area. *Behind The Majestic Yosemite Hotel, Yosemite Valley.*

El Capitan. Come here for great views that look straight up the giant granite wall above. *Northside Dr., at western end of valley.*

Sentinel Beach. Usually crowded in season, this area is right alongside a running creek and the Merced River. *Southside Dr., just south of Swinging Bridge.*

Swinging Bridge. This picnic area is just before the little wooden footbridge that crosses the Merced River, which babbles pleasantly by. *Southside Dr., east of Sentinel Beach.*

OUTSIDE THE PARK

Ducey's on the Lake/Ducey's Bar & Grill
$$$$ | **AMERICAN** | With elaborate chandeliers sculpted from deer antlers, the lodge-style restaurant at Ducey's attracts boaters, locals, and tourists with its lake views and standard lamb, beef, seafood, and pasta dishes. It's also open for breakfast: try the Bass Lake seafood omelet, huevos rancheros, or the Rice Krispies–crusted French toast. **Known for:** steaks and fresh fish; lake views; upstairs bar and grill with more affordable eats. [$] *Average main: $32* ✉ *Pines Resort, 54432 Rd. 432, Bass Lake* ☎ *559/642–3131* 🌐 *www.basslake.com.*

★ **Erna's Elderberry House**
$$$$ | **EUROPEAN** | Erna Kubin-Clanin, the grande dame of Château du Sureau, created this culinary oasis, stunning for its understated elegance, gorgeous setting, and impeccable service. Earth-tone walls and wood beams accent the dining room's high ceilings, and arched windows reflect the glow of candles. **Known for:** elite waitstaff; romantic setting; seasonal prix-fixe and à la carte menus. [$] *Average main: $48* ✉ *Château du Sureau, 48688 Victoria La., off Hwy. 41, Oakhurst* ☎ *559/683–6800* 🌐 *www.elderberryhouse.com* 🕒 *No lunch Mon.–Sat.*

The Mogul
$$$ | **STEAKHOUSE** | **FAMILY** | Come here for straightforward steaks—top sirloin, New York, filet mignon, and T-bone. The only catch is that the waiters cook them, and the results vary depending on their skill level; but generally things go well, and kids love the experience. **Known for:** traditional alpine atmosphere; servers custom-grill your order; all-you-can-eat salad bar. [$] *Average main: $30* ✉ *1528 Tavern Rd., off Old Mammoth Rd., Mammoth Lakes* ☎ *760/934–3039* 🌐 *www.themogul.com* 🕒 *No lunch.*

★ **South Gate Brewing Company**
$$ | **AMERICAN** | Locals pack this family-friendly, industrial-chic restaurant to socialize and savor small-lot beers, crafted on-site, along with tasty meals. The creative pub fare runs a wide gamut, from thin-crust brick-oven pizzas to fish tacos, fish-and-chips, and vegan black-bean burgers. **Known for:** craft beer; homemade desserts; live-music calendar. [$] *Average main: $16* ✉ *40233 Enterprise Dr., off Hwy. 49, north of Von's shopping center, Oakhurst* ☎ *559/692–2739* 🌐 *southgatebrewco.com.*

Hotels

At this writing, a still-ongoing trademark dispute with a former park concessioner resulted in Yosemite National Park changing the names of several historic park lodges and properties, including the iconic Ahwahnee. This guide has changed the historic names, with some references to the former. The changes include: Yosemite Lodge at the Falls is Yosemite Valley Lodge, The Ahwahnee is The Majestic Yosemite Hotel, Curry Village is Half Dome Village, Wawona Hotel is Big Trees Lodge, and Badger Pass Ski Area is Yosemite Ski & Snowboard Area.

IN THE PARK
Big Trees Lodge

$$ | **HOTEL** | This 1879 National Historic Landmark at Yosemite's southern end (formerly Wawona Hotel) is a Victorian-era mountain resort, with whitewashed buildings, wraparound verandas, and pleasant, no-frills rooms decorated with period pieces. **Pros:** lovely building; peaceful atmosphere; historic photos in public areas. **Cons:** few modern amenities, such as phones and TVs; an hour's drive from Yosemite Valley; shared bathrooms in half the rooms. $ *Rooms from: $148* ⊠ *8308 Wawona Rd., Wawona* ☎ *888/413–8869* ⊕ *www.travelyosemite.com* ⊗ *Closed Dec.–Mar., except mid-Dec.–Jan. 2* ⇥ *104 rooms, 50 with bath* ❑ *Breakfast.*

Half Dome Village

$$ | **HOTEL** | Opened in 1899 as a place for budget-conscious travelers, Half Dome Village (formerly Curry Village) has plain accommodations: standard motel rooms, simple cabins with either private or shared baths, and tent cabins with shared baths. **Pros:** close to many activities; family-friendly atmosphere; surrounded by iconic valley views. **Cons:** community bathrooms need updating; can be crowded; sometimes a bit noisy. $ *Rooms from: $143* ⊠ *South side of Southside Dr.* ☎ *888/413–8869, 602/278–8888 international* ⊕ *www.travelyosemite.com* ⇥ *583 rooms and cabins* ❑ *No meals.*

★ The Majestic Yosemite Hotel

$$$$ | **HOTEL** | Formerly the Ahwahnee, this National Historic Landmark is constructed of sugar-pine logs and features Native American design motifs; public spaces are enlivened with art deco flourishes, Persian rugs, and elaborate iron- and woodwork. **Pros:** best lodge in Yosemite; helpful concierge; in the historic heart of the valley. **Cons:** expensive rates; some reports that service has slipped in recent years. $ *Rooms from: $581* ⊠ *Ahwahnee Rd., about ¾ mile east of Yosemite Valley Visitor Center, Yosemite Village* ☎ *801/559–4884* ⊕ *www.travelyosemite.com* ⇥ *125 rooms and suites* ❑ *No meals.*

Redwoods in Yosemite

$$$$ | **RENTAL** | This collection of more than 125 homes in the Wawona area is a great alternative to the overcrowded valley. **Pros:** sense of privacy; peaceful setting; full kitchens. **Cons:** 45-minute drive from the valley; some have no air-conditioning; cell phone service can be spotty. $ *Rooms from: $260* ⊠ *8038 Chilnualna Falls Rd., off Rte. 41, Wawona* ☎ *209/375–6666 international, 888/225–6666* ⊕ *www.redwoodsinyosemite.com* ⇥ *125 units* ❑ *No meals.*

White Wolf Lodge

$$ | **HOTEL** | Set in a subalpine meadow, the rustic accommodations at White Wolf Lodge make it an excellent base camp for hiking the backcountry. **Pros:** quiet location; near some of Yosemite's most beautiful, less crowded hikes; good restaurant. **Cons:** far from the valley; tent cabins share bathhouse; remote setting. $ *Rooms from: $138* ⊠ *Yosemite National Park* ✛ *Off Tioga Rd. (Rte. 120), 25 miles west of Tuolumne Meadows and 15 miles east of Crane Flat* ☎ *801/559–4884* ⊗ *Closed mid-Sept.–mid-June* ⇥ *28 cabins* ❑ *No meals.*

Yosemite Valley Lodge

$$$$ | **HOTEL** | This 1915 lodge near Yosemite Falls (formerly Yosemite Lodge at the Falls) is a collection of numerous two-story, glass-and-wood structures tucked beneath the trees. **Pros:** centrally located; dependably clean rooms;

Camping in Bear Country

The national parks' campgrounds and some campgrounds outside the parks provide food-storage boxes that can keep bears from pilfering your edibles (portable canisters for backpackers can be rented in most park stores). It's imperative that you move all food, coolers, and items with a scent (including toiletries, toothpaste, chewing gum, and air fresheners) from your car (including the trunk) to the storage box at your campsite; day-trippers should lock food in bear boxes provided at parking lots. If you don't, a bear may break into your car by literally peeling off the door or ripping open the trunk, or ransack your tent. The familiar tactic of hanging your food from high tree limbs is not an effective deterrent, as bears easily can scale trees. In the southern Sierra, bear canisters are the only effective and proven method for preventing bears from getting human food. Details on bears and food storage are posted on the park website, 🌐 *www.nps.gov/yose/planyourvisit/bears.htm.*

lots of tours leave from out front. **Cons:** can feel impersonal; high prices; no in-room air-conditioning. [$] *Rooms from: $260* ✉ *9006 Yosemite Valley Lodge Dr., Yosemite Village* ☎ *888/413–8869* 🌐 *www.travelyosemite.com* 🛏 *245 rooms* 🍴 *No meals.*

OUTSIDE THE PARK

Best Western Plus Yosemite Gateway Inn

$$$$ | **HOTEL** | **FAMILY** | Perched on 11 hillside acres, Oakhurst's best motel has carefully tended landscaping and rooms with stylish contemporary furnishings and hand-painted murals of Yosemite. **Pros:** close to park's southern entrance; on-site restaurant; indoor and outdoor swimming pools; frequent deer and wildlife sightings. **Cons:** some rooms on the small side; Internet connection can be slow; some rooms need updating. [$] *Rooms from: $249* ✉ *40530 Hwy. 41, Oakhurst* ☎ *559/683–2378* 🌐 *www.yosemitegatewayinn.com* 🛏 *149 rooms* 🍴 *No meals.*

★ **Château du Sureau**

$$$$ | **RESORT** | The inn here is straight out of a children's book: every room is impeccably styled with European antiques, sumptuous fabrics, fresh-cut flowers, and oversize soaking tubs. **Pros:** luxurious; great views; sumptuous spa facility. **Cons:** expensive; cost might not seem worth it to guests not spa-oriented; can seem pretentious to some. [$] *Rooms from: $420* ✉ *48688 Victoria La., Oakhurst* ☎ *559/683–6860* 🌐 *www.chateausureau.com* 🛏 *11 rooms* 🍴 *Breakfast.*

Evergreen Lodge at Yosemite

$$$$ | **RESORT** | **FAMILY** | Amid the trees near Yosemite National Park's Hetch Hetchy entrance, this sprawling property is perfect for families. **Pros:** cabin complex includes amphitheater, pool, and more; guided tours available; great roadhouse-style restaurant. **Cons:** no TVs; long, winding access road; spotty cell service. [$] *Rooms from: $280* ✉ *33160 Evergreen Rd., 30 miles east of town of Groveland, Groveland* ☎ *209/379–2606* 🌐 *www.evergreenlodge.com* 🛏 *88 cabins.*

Homestead Cottages

$$$ | **B&B/INN** | Set on 160 acres of rolling hills that once held a Miwok village, these cottages (the largest sleeps six) have gas fireplaces, fully equipped kitchens, and queen-size beds. **Pros:** remote location; quiet setting; friendly owners.

Best Campgrounds in Yosemite

If you are going to concentrate solely on valley sites and activities, you should endeavor to stay in one of the "Pines" campgrounds, which are clustered near Half Dome Village and within an easy stroll from that busy complex's many facilities. For a more primitive and quiet experience, and to be near many backcountry hikes, try one of the Tioga Road campgrounds.

National Park Service Reservations Office Reservations are required at many of Yosemite's campgrounds. You can book a site up to five months in advance, starting on the 15th of the month. Unless otherwise noted, book your site through the central National Park Service Reservations Office. If you don't have reservations when you arrive, many sites, especially those outside Yosemite Valley, are available on a first-come, first-served basis. ☎ 877/444–6777 reservations, 518/885–3639 international, 888/448–1474 customer service ⊕ www.recreation.gov.

Bridalveil Creek. This campground sits among lodgepole pines at 7,200 feet, above the valley on Glacier Point Road. From here, you can easily drive to Glacier Point's magnificent valley views. ⊠ From Rte. 41 in Wawona, go north to Glacier Point Rd. and turn right; entrance to campground is 25 miles ahead on right side.

Camp 4. Formerly known as Sunnyside Walk-In, and extremely popular with rock climbers, who don't mind that a total of six are assigned to each campsite; no matter how many are in your group, this is the only valley campground available on a first-come, first-served basis. ⊠ Base of Yosemite Falls Trail, just west of Yosemite Valley

Lodge on Northside Dr., Yosemite Village.

Housekeeping Camp. Composed of three concrete walls and covered with two layers of canvas, each unit has an open-ended fourth side that can be closed off with a heavy white canvas curtain. You can rent "bedpacks," consisting of blankets, sheets, and other comforts. ⊠ Southside Dr., ½ mile west of Half Dome Village.

Porcupine Flat. Sixteen miles west of Tuolumne Meadows, this campground sits at 8,100 feet. If you want to be in the high country, this is a good bet. ⊠ Rte. 120, 16 miles west of Tuolumne Meadows.

Tuolumne Meadows. In a wooded area at 8,600 feet, just south of its namesake meadow, this is one of the most spectacular and sought-after campgrounds in Yosemite. ⊠ Rte. 120, 46 miles east of Big Oak Flat entrance station.

Upper Pines. This is one of the valley's largest campgrounds and the closest one to the trailheads. Expect large crowds in the summer—and little privacy. ⊠ At east end of valley, near Half Dome Village.

Wawona. Near the Mariposa Grove, just downstream from a popular fishing spot, this year-round campground has larger, less densely packed sites than campgrounds in the valley. ⊠ Rte. 41, 1 mile north of Wawona.

White Wolf. Set in the beautiful high country at 8,000 feet, this is a prime spot for hikers from early July to mid-September. ⊠ Tioga Rd., 15 miles east of Big Oak Flat entrance.

Cons: 7 miles from center of Oakhurst. [$] *Rooms from: $189* ✉ *41110 Rd. 600, 2½ miles off Hwy. 49, Ahwahnee* ☎ *559/683–0495* 🌐 *www.homesteadcottages.com* 🛏 *7 cottages* 🍴 *Breakfast.*

Narrow Gauge Inn

$$$$ | **HOTEL** | The well-tended rooms at this family-owned property have balconies with views of the surrounding woods and mountains. **Pros:** close to Yosemite's south entrance. **Cons:** rooms can be a bit dark; dining options are limited, especially for vegetarians. [$] *Rooms from: $229* ✉ *48571 Hwy. 41, Fish Camp* ☎ *559/683–7720, 888/644–9050* 🌐 *www.narrowgaugeinn.com* 🛏 *27 rooms* 🍴 *No meals.*

★ **Rush Creek Lodge**

$$$$ | **RESORT** | **FAMILY** | This sleek, nature-inspired complex occupies 20 acres on a wooded hillside and includes a saltwater pool and hot tubs, a restaurant and tavern with indoor/outdoor seating, a guided recreation program, massage studios and wellness program, and a general store. **Pros:** close to Yosemite's Big Oak Flat entrance; YARTS bus stops here and connects with Yosemite Valley and Sonora spring; year-round evening s'mores. **Cons:** no TVs; pricey in high season; spotty cell service. [$] *Rooms from: $410* ✉ *34001 Hwy. 120, Groveland* ✣ *25 miles east of Groveland, 23 miles north of Yosemite Valley* ☎ *209/379–2373* 🌐 *www.rushcreeklodge.com* 🛏 *143 rooms and suites* 🍴 *No meals.*

Sierra Sky Ranch

$$$$ | **HOTEL** | Off Highway 41 just 10 miles south of the Yosemite National Park, this 19th-century cattle ranch near a hidden grove of giant sequoia trees provides a restful, rustic retreat. **Pros:** peaceful setting; historic property; short drive to giant sequoias. **Cons:** some rooms on the small side; not in town; basic breakfast. [$] *Rooms from: $249* ✉ *50552 Rd. 632, Oakhurst* ☎ *559/683–8040* 🌐 *www.sierraskyranch.com* 🛏 *26 rooms* 🍴 *Breakfast.*

Tamarack Lodge Resort

$$$ | **RESORT** | Tucked away on the edge of the John Muir Wilderness Area, where cross-country ski trails loop through the woods, this 1924 lodge looks like something out of a snow globe. **Pros:** rustic but not run-down; tons of nearby outdoor activities; excellent wine list in restaurant. **Cons:** thin walls; some shared bathrooms; some cabins are tiny. [$] *Rooms from: $169* ✉ *Lake Mary Rd., off Rte. 203, Mammoth Lakes* ☎ *760/934–2442, 800/237–6879* 🌐 *www.tamaracklodge.com* 🛏 *45 rooms and cabins* 🍴 *Free Breakfast.*

★ **Tenaya Lodge**

$$$$ | **RESORT** | **FAMILY** | One of the region's largest hotels, Tenaya Lodge is ideal for people who enjoy wilderness treks by day but prefer creature comforts at night. **Pros:** close to Yosemite and Mariposa Grove of Giant Sequoias; exceptional spa and exercise facility, 36 miles of mountain bike trails; activities for all ages. **Cons:** so big it can seem impersonal; pricey during summer; daily resort fee. [$] *Rooms from: $379* ✉ *1122 Hwy. 41, Fish Camp* ☎ *559/683–6555, 888/514–2167* 🌐 *www.tenayalodge.com* 🛏 *352 rooms* 🍴 *No meals.*

Yosemite View Lodge

$$$$ | **HOTEL** | Two miles outside Yosemite's Arch Rock entrance, this modern property is the most convenient place to spend the night if you are unable to secure lodgings in the valley. **Pros:** great location; good views; lots of on-site amenities. **Cons:** somewhat pricey; it can be a challenge to get the dates you want; rooms could use an update. [$] *Rooms from: $239* ✉ *11136 Hwy. 140, El Portal* ☎ *209/379–2681, 888/742–4371* 🌐 *www.stayyosemiteviewlodge.com* 🛏 *335 rooms* 🍴 *No meals.*

Chapter 37

ZION NATIONAL PARK

Updated by
Andrew Collins

UTAH

WELCOME TO ZION NATIONAL PARK

TOP REASONS TO GO

★ **Eye candy:** Pick just about any trail in the park and it's all but guaranteed to culminate in an astounding viewpoint full of pink, orange, and crimson rock formations.

★ **Peace and quiet:** From February through November, cars are generally not allowed on Zion Canyon Scenic Drive, allowing this section of the park to remain relatively quiet and peaceful.

★ **Botanical wonderland:** Zion Canyon is home to approximately 900 species of plants, more than anywhere else in Utah.

★ **Animal tracks:** Zion has expansive hinterlands where furry, scaly, and feathered residents are common. Hike long enough and you'll encounter deer, elk, rare lizards, birds of prey, and other zoological treats.

★ **Unforgettable canyoneering:** Zion's array of rugged slot canyons is the richest place on Earth for scrambling, rappelling, climbing, and descending.

1 Zion Canyon. This area defines Zion National Park for most people. Free shuttle buses are the only vehicles allowed February through November, the busiest months in the park. The backcountry is accessible via the West Rim Trail and the Narrows, and 2,000-foot cliffs rise all around.

2 The Narrows. A quintessential slot canyon, this is one of the national park system's best hiking trails. Following the north fork of the Virgin River, there's something for everyone in the Narrows, whether you're a day-tripper or an overnight explorer.

3 Kolob Canyons. The northwestern corner of Zion is a secluded 30,000-acre wonderland that can be reached only via a special entrance. Don't miss the West Temple and the Kolob Arch, and keep looking up to spot Horse Ranch Mountain, the park's highest point.

4 Lava Point. Infrequently visited, this area has a primitive campground and two nearby reservoirs that offer the only significant fishing opportunities. Lava Point Overlook provides a view of Zion Canyon from the north.

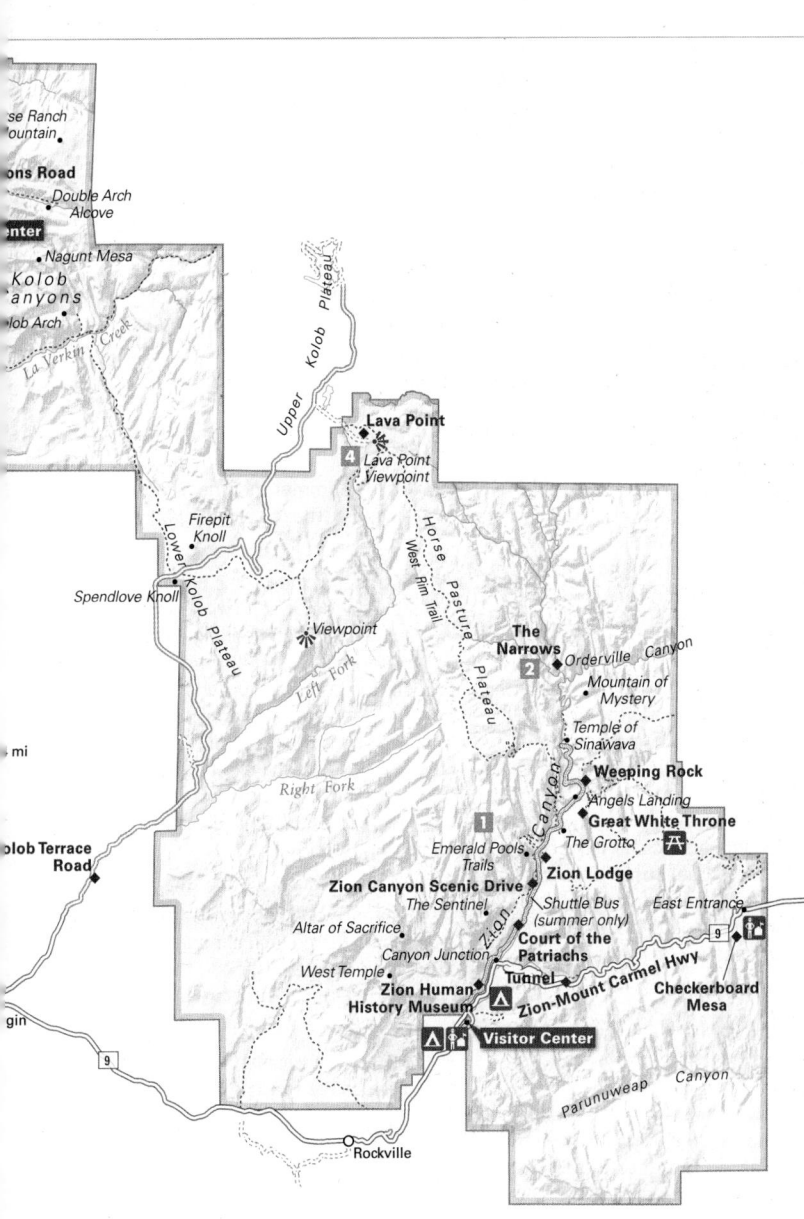

se Ranch
ountain

ons Road
Double Arch
Alcove
enter
Nagunt Mesa
Kolob
anyons
lob Arch

La Verkin Creek

Lower Kolob Plateau

Upper Kolob Plateau

Firepit
Knoll

Spendlove Knoll

Left Fork

mi

Right Fork

olob Terrace
Road

gin

9

Rockville

Lava Point
4 Lava Point
Viewpoint

Viewpoint

Horse Pasture Plateau

West Rim Trail

The
Narrows
2 Orderville Canyon

Mountain of
Mystery

Temple of
Sinawava

Zion Canyon

Weeping Rock

Angels Landing

Great White Throne

The Grotto

1

Emerald Pools
Trails

Zion Canyon Scenic Drive
The Sentinel

Altar of Sacrifice

Canyon Junction

West Temple

Zion Human
History Museum

Zion Lodge

Shuttle Bus
(summer only)

East Entrance

9

Court of the
Patriachs

Tunnel

Zion-Mount Carmel Hwy

Checkerboard
Mesa

Visitor Center

Parunuweap Canyon

The walls of Zion Canyon soar more than 2,000 feet above the valley. Bands of limestone, sandstone, and lava in the strata point to the distant past. Greenery high in the cliff walls indicate the presence of water seepage or a spring. Erosion has left behind a collection of domes, fins, and blocky massifs bearing the names of cathedrals and temples, prophets and angels.

Trails lead deep into side canyons and up narrow ledges to waterfalls, serene spring-fed pools, and shaded spots of solitude. So diverse is this place that 85% of Utah's flora and fauna species are found here. Some, like the tiny Zion snail, appear nowhere else in the world.

The Colorado River helped create the Grand Canyon, while the Virgin River—the Colorado's muddy progeny—carved Zion's features. Because of the park's unique topography, distant storms and spring runoff can transform a tranquil slot canyon into a sluice, and flood damage does sometimes result in extended trail closures, as happened in summer 2018 to three trails near the Grotto and Zion Lodge sections of Zion Canyon.

Planning

WHEN TO GO

Zion is the most heavily visited national park in Utah, receiving 4.5 million visitors each year. Locals used to call the spring and fall the shoulder seasons because traffic would drop off from the highly visited summer months. Not so much anymore. These days the park is busy from March through November.

Summer in the park is hot and dry, punctuated by sudden cloudbursts that can create flash flooding and spectacular waterfalls. Expect afternoon thunderstorms between July and September. Whether the day starts out sunny or not, wear sunscreen and drink lots of water, even if you aren't exerting yourself or spending much time outside. The sun is very powerful at this elevation.

Winters are mild at lower desert elevations. You can expect to encounter winter driving conditions from November to mid-March, and although most park programs are suspended in winter, it is a wonderful and solitary time to see the canyons.

■ TIP→ The temperature in Zion often exceeds 100°F in July and August.

FESTIVALS AND EVENTS
Dixie Roundup
HORSE RACING/SHOW | Dozens of professional rodeo cowboys from across the West take part in this three-day

Plants and Wildlife in Zion

Zion National Park, on the Colorado Plateau and bordered by the Great Basin and Mojave Desert provinces, supports diverse flora and fauna.

Multiple Environments

More than 900 species of plants thrive in environments that range from desert to hanging garden to high plateau. On a visit you might encounter delicate ferns and mosses, hardy cacti and other desert plants, and many trees, grasses, and herbs. Poison ivy, in abundance here, is one species you'll want to avoid. If you're not sure how to recognize it, take a quick lesson from a ranger prior to your first hike.

Wildlife Returns

When car traffic is replaced by a shuttle bus system from February through November, wildlife returns in force to the park. Even in high season you can spot mule deer wandering in shady glens, especially in early morning and near dusk. You'll also see scores of lizards and wild turkeys everywhere you go.

Exotic Fauna

To observe the more exotic fauna, hit the hiking trails. Nearly 300 species of birds reside either full- or part-time in the park, from tiny hummingbirds and chickadees to eagles and even pelicans. Ringtail cats (which are not actually cats but are similar to raccoons) prowl the park. Evening hikes may reveal foxes, but you're more likely to spot their tracks than the elusive animals themselves. All animals, from the smallest chipmunk to the biggest elk, should be given plenty of space, but only the extremely rare mountain lion or black bear poses a threat to humans.

---

mid-September event held since the 1930s. Team roping, saddle-bronc riding, and bull riding are among the main attractions, along with the always entertaining mutton-busting competition for the kids and the rodeo parade. ⊠ *Dixie Sunbowl, 150 S. 400 E, St. George* ☎ *435/703–4779* ⊕ *www.stgeorgelions.com.*

St. George Winter Bird Festival

FESTIVALS | Bird-watchers gather in St. George every January to peep at more than 100 feathered species. Join in three full days of field trips, exhibits, lectures, and activities. ⊠ *Tonaquint Park and Nature Center, 1851 S. Dixie Dr., St. George* ☎ *435/868–8756* ⊕ *www.stgeorgebirdfest.com.*

Western Legends Roundup

FESTIVALS | **FAMILY** | For three days in late August, Kanab plays host to cowboy poets, musicians, and character actors from Old West TV series of yesteryear. A parade, tours to Western movie sites, a dutch-oven dinner, a quilt show, performances by Native American dancers, and a film festival draw visitors from all over. ☎ *435/644–3444* ⊕ *www.westernlegendsroundup.com.*

PLANNING YOUR TIME

ZION IN ONE DAY

Begin your visit at the **Zion Canyon Visitor Center,** where outdoor exhibits inform you about the park's geology, wildlife, history, and trails. Get a taste of what's in store by viewing the far off Towers of the Virgin, then head to the **Court of the Patriarchs** viewpoint to take photos and walk the short path. Take the shuttle (or your car, if it's December or January) to **Zion Lodge,** where you can hike a trail to one of the park's most beautiful spots, the **Emerald Pools.** The Lower Pool Trail is

AVERAGE HIGH/LOW TEMPERATURES.					
JAN.	**FEB.**	**MAR.**	**APR.**	**MAY**	**JUNE**
54/30	59/34	66/39	75/45	86/54	95/63
JULY	**AUG.**	**SEPT.**	**OCT.**	**NOV.**	**DEC.**
100/70	99/68	91/61	79/48	64/37	54/30

the second most popular walk at Zion; the trail branches off into Middle Pool and Upper Pool trails for those with more time (note that Emerald Pools was closed due to storm damage in summer 2018; check for updates before setting out). Ride the next shuttle to the end of the road, where the paved, accessible **Riverside Walk,** Zion's most popular path, will deliver you to the gateway of the canyon's Narrows.

Reboard the shuttle to return to the Zion Canyon Visitor Center to pick up your car (or continue driving December–January). Head out onto the beautiful **Zion–Mount Carmel Highway,** with its long, curving tunnel, keeping your camera at the ready for stops at viewpoints along the road. Once you reach the park's east entrance, turn around, and on your return trip stop to take the short hike up to **Canyon Overlook.** In the evening, you might want to attend a ranger program at one of the campground amphitheaters or at Zion Lodge. Or you can follow a relaxing dinner in **Springdale** with a stroll downtown.

GETTING HERE AND AROUND
AIR TRAVEL
The nearest commercial airport, with direct flights from a number of western U.S. hubs, is an hour away in St. George, Utah. It's about a three-hour drive to the nearest major airport, McCarran in Las Vegas, Nevada, and a 4½-hour drive Salt Lake City's airport.

CAR TRAVEL
Zion National Park lies east of Interstate 15 in southwestern Utah. From the interstate, head east on Highway 9. After 21 miles you'll reach Springdale, which abuts the main entrance.

From February through November, you can drive on Zion Canyon Scenic Drive only if you have reservations at the Zion Lodge. Otherwise, you must park your car in Springdale or at the Zion Canyon Visitor Center and take the shuttle. There are no car restrictions in December and January.

The Zion Canyon Visitor Center parking lot fills up quickly. You can avoid parking heartburn by leaving your car in Springdale and riding the shuttle to the park entrance. Shuttles are accessible for people with disabilities and have plenty of room for gear. Consult the print park guide or check online at ⊕ www.nps.gov/zion/planyourvisit/shuttle-system.htm for the town shuttle schedule.

PARK ESSENTIALS
ACCESSIBILITY
Both visitor centers, all shuttle buses, and Zion Lodge are fully accessible to people in wheelchairs. Several campsites (sites A24 and A25 at Watchman Campground and sites 103, 114, and 115 at South Campground) are reserved for people with disabilities, and two trails— Riverside Walk and Pa'rus Trail—are accessible with some assistance.

PARK FEES AND PERMITS
Entrance to Zion National Park costs $35 per vehicle for a seven-day pass. People entering on foot or by bicycle pay $20 per person for a seven-day pass; those on motorcycle pay $30.

Permits are required for backcountry camping and overnight hikes. Depending on which parts of the trails you intend to explore, you'll need a special permit for the Narrows and Kolob Creek or the Subway slot canyon. Climbing and canyoneering parties need a permit before using technical equipment.

Zion National Park limits the total number of overnight and canyoneering permits issued per day and has a reservation system with most of the permits now issued in an online lottery to apportion them fairly. Permits to the Subway, Mystery Canyon, the Narrows through-hikes, and West Rim are in short supply during high season. The maximum size of a group hiking into the backcountry is 12 people. Permits cost $15 for one or two people; $20 for three to seven; and $25 for eight or more. Permits are available at the visitor centers.

PARK HOURS
The park, open daily year-round, 24 hours a day, is in the Mountain time zone.

CELL PHONE RECEPTION
Cell phone reception is good in Spring-dale but spotty in the park. Public telephones can be found at Zion Canyon Visitor Center, Zion Lodge, and Zion Human History Museum.

EDUCATIONAL OFFERINGS
CLASSES AND SEMINARS
★ **Zion Natl Park Forever Project**
COLLEGE | Formerly known as the Zion Natural History Association, the project conducts workshops about the park's natural and cultural history. Topics can include edible plants, bat biology, river geology, photography, and bird-watching. Most workshops include a hike. For a glimpse of Zion's inner workings, volunteer to assist with one of their ongoing projects. ⊠ *Zion National Park* ☎ *435/772–3264, 800/635–3959* ⊕ *www. zionpark.org* ⊠ *From $45.*

RANGER PROGRAMS
Evening Programs
TOUR—SIGHT | Held each evening May through September in Watchman Campground and at Zion Lodge, these 45-minute ranger-led talks cover geology, biology, and history. You might learn about coyote calls, the night sky, animal hideouts, or observing nature with all your senses. Slide shows and audience participation are often part of the proceedings. Check the visitor center for schedules. ⊠ *Zion National Park.*

★ **Expert Talks**
TOUR—SIGHT | Informal lectures take place on the Zion Human History Museum patio. Past topics have included wildlife, geology, and the stories of early settlers. Talks usually last from 20 to 30 minutes, though some run longer. Check park bulletin boards for schedules. ⊠ *Zion National Park.*

Junior Ranger Program
TOUR—SIGHT | FAMILY | Educational activities aimed at younger visitors include the chance to earn a Junior Ranger badge. Kids do so by attending at least one nature program and completing the free Junior Ranger Handbook, available at visitor centers. ⊠ *Zion National Park.*

★ **Ranger-Led Hike**
TOUR—SIGHT | A daily guided hike along the 2-mile Watchman Trail provides an overview of the park's geology and natural and other history. Groups meet at 8 am at Zion Canyon Visitor Center. Wear sturdy footgear and bring a hat, sunglasses, sunscreen, and water. ⊠ *Zion National Park.*

★ **Ride with a Ranger Shuttle Tours**
TOUR—SIGHT | FAMILY | Once a day from Memorial Day through September, rangers conduct shuttle tours of points of interest along Zion Canyon Scenic Drive. In addition to learning about the canyon's geology, ecology, and history, you'll be treated to some great photo-ops. The 90-minute tour takes place in the morning and departs from the Zion Canyon Visitor Center. Seating is limited to eight people. Make reservations in person at the visitor center up to three days in advance. ⊠ *Zion National Park* ⊠ *Free.*

RESTAURANTS

Only one full-service restaurant operates within the park, at the famed Zion Lodge, but in Springdale, just outside the park's South Entrance, you'll find a growing number of both casual and sophisticated eateries. To the east, options are limited, but there are a handful of options within an hour's drive.

HOTELS

The Zion Lodge is rustic, designed in 1920s period style, and comfortable. Springdale has dozens of lodging options, from quaint bed-and-breakfasts to modest motels to chain hotels with riverside rooms, and farther west you'll find more options (and usually better values) in Hurricane and St. George. To the east and north, you'll find a smaller number of hotels and motels, from Kanab up to Panguitch, both of which are good bases if you're continuing on to Bryce or, in the case of Kanab, the Grand Canyon. *Hotel reviews have been shortened. For full information, visit Fodors.com.*

What It Costs			
$	$$	$$$	$$$$
RESTAURANTS			
under $13	$13–$20	$21–$30	over $30
HOTELS			
under $100	$100–$150	$151–$200	over $200

VISITOR INFORMATION

PARK CONTACT INFORMATION Zion National Park ⊠ *Hwy. 9, Springdale* ☎ *435/772–3256* ⊕ *www.nps.gov/zion.*

VISITOR CENTERS

Kolob Canyons Visitor Center

INFO CENTER | Make this your first stop as you enter this remote section of the park. There are books and maps, a small gift shop, and clean restrooms here, and rangers are on hand to answer questions about Kolob Canyons exploration. ⊠ *3752*

E. Kolob Canyons Rd., Exit 40 off I–15 ☎ *435/772–3256* ⊕ *www.nps.gov/zion.*

Zion Canyon Visitor Center

INFO CENTER | Learn about the area's geology, flora, and fauna at an outdoor exhibit next to a gurgling stream. Inside, a large shop sells everything from field guides to souvenirs. Zion Canyon shuttle buses leave regularly from the center and make several stops along the canyon's beautiful scenic drive; ranger-guided shuttle tours depart once a day from Memorial Day to late September. ⊠ *Zion Park Blvd. at south entrance, Springdale* ☎ *435/772–3256* ⊕ *www.nps.gov/zion.*

 Sights

SCENIC DRIVES

Driving is the only way to easily access Kolob Canyons, and from December through January it's the only way to access the Zion Canyon Scenic Drive.

Kolob Canyons Road

SCENIC DRIVE | The beauty starts modestly at the junction with Interstate 15, but as you move along this 5-mile road the red walls of the Kolob finger canyons rise suddenly and spectacularly out of the earth. With the crowds left behind at Zion Canyon, this drive offers the chance to take in incredible vistas at your leisure. Trails include the short but rugged Middle Fork of Taylor Creek Trail, which passes two 1930s homestead cabins, culminating 2¾ miles later in the Double Arch Alcove. During heavy snowfall Kolob Canyons Road may be closed. ⊠ *I–15, Exit 40.*

Kolob Terrace Road

SCENIC DRIVE | This 21-mile road begins 14 miles west of Springdale at Virgin and winds north to Kolob Reservoir. The drive meanders in and out of the park boundaries, crossing several important trailheads, all the while overlooking the cliffs of North Creek. A popular day-use trail (permit required) leads past fossilized dinosaur tracks to the Subway, a stretch of the stream where the walls of the slot canyon close in so tightly as to form a near tunnel. Farther along the road you reach the Wildcat Canyon trailhead, which connects to the path overlooking the North Guardian Angel. The road terminates at the reservoir, beneath 8,933-foot Kolob Peak. Although paved, this narrow, twisting road is not recommended for RVs. Because of limited winter plowing, the road is closed from November or December through April or May. ⊠ *Zion National Park ✛ Begins in Virgin at Hwy. 9.*

★ Zion Canyon Scenic Drive

SCENIC DRIVE | Vividly colored cliffs tower 2,000 feet above the road that meanders north from Springdale along the floor of Zion Canyon. As you roll through the narrow, steep canyon you'll pass the Court of the Patriarchs, the Sentinel, and the Great White Throne, among other imposing rock formations. From February through November, unless you're staying at the lodge, Zion Canyon Scenic Drive is accessed only by park shuttle. You can drive it yourself at other times. ⊠ *Off Hwy. 9.*

Zion–Mount Carmel Highway and Tunnels

SCENIC DRIVE | Two narrow tunnels as old as the park itself lie between the east entrance and Zion Canyon on this breathtaking 12-mile stretch of Highway 9. One was once the longest man-made tunnel in the world. As you travel the (1.1-mile) passage through solid rock, five arched portals along one side provide fleeting glimpses of cliffs and canyons. When you emerge you'll find that the landscape has changed dramatically. Large vehicles require traffic control and a $15 permit, available at the park entrance, and have restricted hours of travel. This includes nearly all RVs, trailers, dual-wheel trucks, and campers. The Canyon Overlook Trail starts from a parking area between the tunnels. ⊠ *Hwy. 9, 5 miles east of Canyon Junction.*

HISTORIC SITES

Zion Human History Museum

MUSEUM | This informative museum tells the park's story from the perspective of its human inhabitants, among them Ancestral Puebloans and early Mormon settlers. Permanent exhibits illustrate how humans have dealt with wildlife, plants, and natural forces. Temporary exhibits have touched on everything from vintage park employee photography to the history of Union Pacific Railroad hotels. Don't miss the incredible view of Towers of the Virgin from the back patio. ⊠ *Zion Canyon Scenic Dr., ½ mile north of south entrance* ☎ *435/772–3256* 🖅 *Free.*

★ Zion Lodge

HISTORIC SITE | Architect Gilbert Stanley Underwood, responsible for many noteworthy national park lodges, designed the original Zion Lodge, which opened in the 1920s but was destroyed by fire four decades later. In 1990, it was restored to its original rustic style, in some cases down to the very paint color. Natural beauty is on display inside and out, from the lobby's rock columns and exposed wood to the cottonwoods shading the sprawling lawn. The main building includes a gift shop, an upscale restaurant, and an outdoor café with a large patio and beer garden. The lodge has received numerous awards for its eco-friendly practices. Amenities include bike rentals, open-air narrated tram rides, and an electric-vehicle charging station. ⊠ *Zion Canyon Scenic Dr.* ☎ *435/772–7700* ⊕ *www.zionlodge.com.*

SCENIC STOPS

The park comprises two distinct sections, Zion Canyon and the Kolob Plateau and Canyons. Most people visit only the better-known Zion Canyon, but the Kolob area has much to offer and should not be missed if time allows. Though there's little evidence of Kolob's beauty from the entrance point off Interstate 15, once you negotiate the first switchback on the park road, you're hit with a vision of red-rock cliffs shooting out of the earth. As you climb in elevation, you're treated first to a journey through these canyons, then to a view into the chasm. ■ TIP→ **Because you must exit the park to get from Zion Canyon to Kolob Canyons, it is not advisable to explore both sections in one day.**

Checkerboard Mesa

NATURE SITE | It's well worth stopping at the pull-out 1 mile west of Zion's east entrance to observe the distinctive waffle patterns on this huge white mound of sandstone. The stunning crosshatch effect visible today is the result of eons of freeze-and-thaw cycles that caused vertical fractures, combined with erosion that produced horizontal bedding planes. ⊠ *Zion–Mount Carmel Hwy.*

Court of the Patriarchs

NATURE SITE | This trio of peaks bears the names of, from left to right, Abraham, Isaac, and Jacob. Mount Moroni is the reddish peak on the far right that partially blocks the view of Jacob. Hike the trail that leaves from the Court of the Patriarchs Viewpoint, 1½ miles north of Canyon Junction, to get a much better view of the sandstone prophets. ⊠ *Zion Canyon Scenic Dr.*

Great White Throne

NATURE SITE | Dominating the Grotto picnic area near Zion Lodge, this massive Navajo sandstone peak juts 2,000 feet above the valley floor. The popular formation lies about 3 miles north of Canyon Junction. ⊠ *Zion Canyon Scenic Dr.*

★ The Narrows

NATURE SITE | This sinuous 16-mile crack in the earth where the Virgin River flows over gravel and boulders is one of the world's most stunning gorges. If you hike through it, you'll find yourself surrounded—sometimes nearly boxed in—by smooth walls stretching high into the heavens. Plan to get wet, and beware that flash floods can occur here, especially in spring and summer. Check on the weather before you enter. ⊠ *Zion National Park* ⊹ *Begins at Riverside Walk.*

Weeping Rock

NATURE SITE | Surface water from the rim of Echo Canyon spends several thousand years seeping down through the porous sandstone before exiting at this picturesque alcove 4½ miles north of Canyon Junction. A paved walkway climbs ¼ mile to this flowing rock face where wildflowers and delicate ferns grow. In fall, the maples and cottonwoods burst with color, and lizards point the way down the path, which is too steep for wheelchairs or strollers. ⊠ *Zion Canyon Scenic Dr.*

 Activities

Hiking is by far the most popular activity at Zion, with all sorts of trails leading to rewarding hinterland destinations: extreme slot canyons, gorgeous overlooks, verdant meadows, and dripping springs. Some sections of the Virgin River are ideal for canoeing (inner tubes are not allowed). In winter, hiking boots can be exchanged for snowshoes and cross-country skis, but check with a ranger for backcountry snow conditions.

BICYCLING

Zion National Park is a gorgeous destination for road biking, especially along Zion Canyon Scenic Drive and the paved 3½-mile Pa'rus Trail, which winds along the Virgin River in Zion Canyon, but keep in mind that mountain biking is not allowed in the park, and bicycles are not allowed on any trails.

Zion has taken steps to become much more bicycle-friendly, including having bike racks at some of the facilities and on the shuttle buses themselves. If you are renting bikes by the hour from a Springdale outfitter, you can load your bike on the bus, have the shuttle take you to the last stop (Temple of Sinawava), and take an easy one-way pedal back to Springdale. You cannot walk or ride your bicycle through the Zion–Mount Carmel tunnels; the only way to get your bike past this stretch of the highway is to transport it by motor vehicle. ■ TIP→ **When you're on** the park road, shuttle buses and cars have the right of way. You're expected to pull off to the side and let them pass.

Bicycles Unlimited
BICYCLING | A trusted southern Utah biking resource, this shop rents bikes and sells parts, accessories, and guidebooks. ✉ 90 S. 100 E, St. George ☎ 435/673–4492, 888/673–4492 ⊕ www.bicyclesunlimited.com.

Zion Cycles
BICYCLING | This shop just outside the park rents bikes by the hour or longer, sells parts, and has a full-time mechanic on duty. You can pick up trail and other advice from the staff here. They also offer guided road-biking treks in the park and mountain-biking excursions elsewhere in Southern Utah. ✉ 868 Zion Park Blvd., Springdale ☎ 435/772–0400 ⊕ www.zioncycles.com ✉ Guide tours from $150.

BIRD-WATCHING
More than 200 bird species call Zion Canyon home, and scores more pass through the park on their annual migrations. Some species, such as the white-throated swift and ospreys, thrive in the towering cliff walls. Red-tailed and Cooper's hawks are abundant. Closer to the ground you'll doubtless see the bold Steller's jay and scrub jay rustling around the pinyon thickets. The wild turkey population has boomed in recent years; some of the flock might come your way looking for a handout. Five species of hummingbirds reside in the park, with the black-chinned variety being the most common. You might spot members of four transient species as well. Climb to the top of Angel's Landing and you might glimpse a bald eagle. Two of the park's rarest species are the Mexican spotted owl and the enormous California condor. ■TIP➜ Ask for the Zion Bird List brochure at the visitor center or download one. ⊕ www.nps.gov/zion/learn/nature/birds.htm

FISHING
Sitting at over 8,000 feet elevation, Kolob Reservoir offers decent but unspectacular trout angling. Look for the dirt road at the end of Kolob Terrace Road, about 5 miles north of Lava Point. If you do decide to fish in the park, you need to purchase a Utah State Fishing License.

HIKING
The best way to experience Zion Canyon is to walk beneath, between and, if you can bear it (and have good balance), along its towering cliffs. Trails vary, from paved and flat river strolls to precarious cliffside scrambles. Whether you're heading out for a day of rock hopping or an hour of meandering, pack and consume plenty of drinking water to counteract the effects of a high-altitude workout in the arid climate.

Keeping the sun at bay is a real challenge at Zion National Park. Put on sunscreen before you set out, and reapply at regular intervals. Because the park's hikes usually include uneven surfaces and elevation changes, wear sturdy shoes or hiking boots. Many veteran hikers carry good walking sticks, too, as they're invaluable along trails that ford or follow the Virgin River or its tributaries.

Zion is one of the most popular parks in the country, so it can be hard to envision just how alone you'll be on some of the less traveled trails. If you want to do a backcountry hike, make a reservation. Let park rangers know where you're going and when you plan to return.

■TIP➜ Park rangers warn hikers to remain on alert for flash floods; these walls of water can appear out of nowhere, even when the sky above you is clear. You can learn more about hiking safety and obtain a trail map at the visitor centers or online (⊕ www.nps.gov/zion/planyourvisit/hiking-in-zion.htm). A major flood in July 2018 severely damaged the lower West Rim Trail (including Angels Landing), Kayenta Trail, and Upper Emerald Pools Trail. As of this writing, these trails were closed until further notice. Check with the visitor center for updates before attempting to hike any of these trails.

★ Angels Landing Trail

HIKING/WALKING | As much a trial as a trail, this path beneath the Great White Throne, which you access from the Lower West Rim Trail, is one of the park's most challenging hikes. Early on you work your way through Walter's Wiggles, a series of 21 switchbacks built out of sandstone blocks. From there you traverse sheer cliffs that have chains bolted into the rock face to serve as handrails in some (but not all) places. In spite of its hair-raising nature, this trail is popular. Allow 2½ hours round-trip if you stop at Scout's Lookout (2 miles), and four hours if you keep going to where the angels (and birds of prey) play. The trail is 5 miles round-trip and is not appropriate for children or those who are uneasy about heights. Flood damage in July 2018 resulted in the closure of this trail—check with the visitor center for updates. *Difficult.* ⊠ *Zion National Park* ⊹ *Trailhead: off Zion Canyon Scenic Dr. at the Grotto.*

★ Canyon Overlook Trail

HIKING/WALKING | **FAMILY** | The parking area just east of Zion–Mount Carmel tunnel leads to this popular trail, which is about 1 mile round-trip and takes about an hour to finish. From the breathtaking overlook at the trail's end you can see the West and East temples, the Towers of the Virgin, the Streaked Wall, and other Zion Canyon cliffs and peaks. The elevation change is 160 feet. The parking area often fills up—try to come very early or late in the day to avoid crowds. *Moderate.* ⊠ *Zion National Park* ⊹ *Trailhead: off Hwy. 9 just east of Zion–Mount Carmel tunnel.*

Emerald Pools Trail

HIKING/WALKING | **FAMILY** | Multiple waterfalls cascade (or drip, in dry weather) into algae-filled pools along this trail, about 3 miles north of Canyon Junction. The path leading to the lower pool is paved and appropriate for strollers and wheelchairs. If you've got any energy left, keep going past the lower pool. The ¼ mile from there to the middle pool becomes rocky and somewhat steep but offers increasingly scenic views. A less crowded and exceptionally enjoyable return route follows the Kayenta Trail, connecting to the Grotto Trail. Allow 50 minutes for the 1¼-mile round-trip hike to the lower pool, and an hour more each round-trip to the middle (2 miles) and upper pools (3 miles). Flood damage in July 2018 resulted in the closure of this trail—check with the visitor center for updates. *Lower, easy. Upper, moderate.* ⊠ *Zion National Park* ⊹ *Trailhead: off Zion Canyon Scenic Dr., at Zion Lodge or the Grotto.*

Grotto Trail

HIKING/WALKING | **FAMILY** | This flat trail takes you from Zion Lodge, about 3 miles north of Canyon Junction, to the Grotto picnic area, traveling for the most part along the park road. Allow 20 minutes or less for the walk along the ½-mile trail. If you are up for a longer hike and have two or three hours, connect with the Kayenta Trail after you cross the footbridge, and head for the Emerald Pools. You will begin gaining elevation, and it's a steady, steep climb to the pools, which you will begin to see after about 1 mile. The trail to the pools closed in summer 2018 due to storm damage, so check on its status before you attempt it. *Easy.* ⊠ *Zion National Park* ⊹ *Trailhead: off Zion Canyon Scenic Dr. at the Grotto.*

Hidden Canyon Trail

HIKING/WALKING | This steep, 2-mile round-trip hike takes you up 850 feet in elevation. Not too crowded, the trail is paved all the way to Hidden Canyon. Allow about three hours for the round-trip hike. *Moderate–Difficult.* ⊠ *Zion National Park* ⊹ *Trailhead: off Zion Canyon Scenic Dr. at Weeping Rock.*

★ Narrows Trail

HIKING/WALKING | The hike on the Narrows Trail is a stunning and unique nature experience, but it's no picnic. After leaving the paved ease of the Gateway to the Narrows trail behind, the real fun begins. Rather than following a trail or path, you walk on the riverbed itself. In places you'll find a pebbly shingle or dry sandbar path, but when the walls of the canyon close in, you'll be forced into the chilly waters of the Virgin River, walking against the current—tack back and forth, don't fight it head-on. A walking stick and shoes with good tread and ankle support are highly recommended and will make hiking the riverbed much more enjoyable. Be prepared to swim, as chest-deep holes may occur even when water levels are low. Like any narrow desert canyon, this one is famous for sudden flash flooding, even when skies are clear. Before hiking into the Narrows, check with park rangers about the likelihood of flash floods. A day trip up the lower section of the Narrows is 6 miles one-way to the turnaround point. Allow at least five hours round-trip. *Difficult.* ⊠ *Zion National Park* ✛ *Trailhead: off Zion Canyon Scenic Dr., at end of Riverside Walk.*

Pa'rus Trail

HIKING/WALKING | FAMILY | An approximately 1¾-mile, relatively flat paved walking and biking path, Pa'rus parallels and occasionally crosses the Virgin River. Starting at South Campground, ½ mile north of the South Entrance, the walk proceeds north along the river to the beginning of Zion Canyon Scenic Drive. Along the way you'll take in great views of the Watchman, the Sentinel, the East and West temples, and Towers of the Virgin. Leashed dogs are allowed on this trail. Wheelchair users may need assistance. *Easy.* ⊠ *Zion National Park* ✛ *Trailhead: at Canyon Junction.*

Riverside Walk

HIKING/WALKING | FAMILY | This 2.2-mile round-trip hike shadows the Virgin River. In spring, wildflowers bloom on the opposite canyon wall in lovely hanging gardens. The trail, which begins 6½ miles north of Canyon Junction at the end of Zion Canyon Scenic Drive, is the park's most visited trail, so be prepared for crowds in high season. Riverside Walk is paved and suitable for strollers and wheelchairs, though some wheelchair users may need assistance. Round-trip it takes about 90 minutes. At the end, the much more challenging Narrows Trail begins. *Easy.* ⊠ *Zion National Park* ✛ *Trailhead: off Zion Canyon Scenic Dr. at Temple of Sinawava.*

Taylor Creek Trail

HIKING/WALKING | This trail in the Kolob Canyons area descends parallel to Taylor Creek, sometimes crossing it, sometimes shortcutting benches beside it. The historic Larsen Cabin precedes the entrance to the canyon of the Middle Fork, where the trail becomes rougher. After the old Fife Cabin, the canyon bends to the right into Double Arch Alcove, a large, colorful grotto with a high blind arch (or arch "embryo") towering above. To Double Arch it's 2½ miles one-way—about four hours round-trip. The elevation change is 450 feet. *Moderate.* ⊠ *Zion National Park* ✛ *Trailhead: at Kolob Canyons Rd., about 1½ miles east of Kolob Canyons Visitor Center.*

Watchman Trail

HIKING/WALKING | For a dramatic view of Springdale and a look at lower Zion Creek Canyon and the Towers of the Virgin, this strenuous hike begins on a service road east of Watchman Campground. Some springs seep out of the sandstone, nourishing the hanging gardens and attracting wildlife. There are a few sheer cliff edges, so supervise children carefully. Plan on two hours for this 3.3-mile round-trip hike that has a 368-foot elevation change. *Moderate.* ⊠ *Zion National Park* ✛ *Trailhead: at Zion Canyon Visitor Center.*

HORSEBACK RIDING

Canyon Trail Rides

HORSEBACK RIDING | FAMILY | Grab your hat and boots and see Zion Canyon the way the pioneers did—on a horse or mule. Easygoing, one-hour and half-day guided rides are available (minimum age 7 and 10 years, respectively). Maximum weight is 220 pounds. These friendly folks have been around for years, and are the only outfitter for trail rides inside the park. Reservations are recommended and can be made online. ⊠ *Across from Zion Lodge* ☎ *435/679–8665* ⊕ *www.canyon-rides.com* ⊡ *From $45.*

SWIMMING

Swimming is allowed in the Virgin River, but be careful of cold water, slippery rock bottoms, and the occasional flash floods when it rains. Swimming isn't permitted in the Emerald Pools. The use of inner tubes is prohibited within park boundaries, but some companies offer trips on a Virgin River tributary just outside the park.

WINTER ACTIVITIES

Cross-country skiing and snowshoeing are best experienced in the park's higher elevations in winter, where snow stays on the ground longer. Inquire at the Zion Canyon Visitor Center for backcountry conditions.

Nearby Towns

Hotels, restaurants, and shops thrive in steadily growing **Springdale,** population 581, on the southern boundary of Zion National Park, yet the town still manages to maintain its small-town charm. There are plenty of dining and lodging options, and if you take the time to stroll the main drag you can pick up souvenirs. A free shuttle carries you through town and to the park's South Entrance (which is within walking distance of the visitor center), and you can rent bikes in town.

If you have time to explore, there's always **Virgin, La Verkin,** and the ghost town of **Grafton,** which you might recognize from *Butch Cassidy and the Sundance Kid* and other films. Today there's a stone school, a dusty cemetery, and a few other restored buildings. **Hurricane,** population about 16,200, has

experienced much growth since 2000 and keeps sprouting new restaurants and lodgings (many of them chains). (Locals emphasize the first syllable, barely uttering the last.) There are historical sites, a world-class golf course, and the Hurricane Canal, dug by hand and used for 80 years to irrigate fields around town. It's just up Interstate 15 from the largest city in southern Utah, **St. George** (population 82,400), a prosperous and attractive small metropolis with a dramatic red-rock setting.

Heading east from Zion is **Mount Carmel Junction,** an intersection offering a couple of funky small-town lodgings and the studio of American West artist Maynard Dixon. It's a 20-minute drive south from here to funky Kanab, a growing hub of recreation with a handful of excellent restaurants and hotels—it's an excellent base if you'll also be visiting Bryce Canyon, the Grand Canyon, and Grand Staircase–Escalante National Monument.

VISITOR INFORMATION Kane County Office of Tourism ⊠ *78 S. 100 E, Kanab* ☎ *800/733–5263, 435/644–5033* ⊕ *www. visitsouthernutah.com.* **Visit St. George** ☎ *435/634–5747, 800/869–6635* ⊕ *www. visitstgeorge.com.* **Zion Canyon Visitors Bureau** ⊠ *118 Lion Blvd., Springdale* ☎ *435/772–3434* ⊕ *www.zionpark.com.*

 Sights

Coral Pink Sand Dunes State Park
NATIONAL/STATE PARK | Visitors to this sweeping expanse of pink sand about 20 miles west of Kanab enjoy a slice of nature produced by eroding sandstone. Funneled through a notch in the rock, wind picks up speed and carries grains of sand into the area—the undulating formations can move as much as 50 feet per year. Once the wind slows down, the sand is deposited, creating this giant playground for dune buggies, ATVs, and dirt bikes. A small area is fenced off for walking, but the sound of wheeled toys is always with you. Children love to

Did You Know?

With one of the world's largest concentrations of vertical climbing walls exceeding 1,000 feet, Zion National Park is an outstanding spot for climbing. If you are used to the solid granite of Yosemite, you're in for a surprise. Zion's sandstone is much more varied, and can behave unpredictably depending on the weather. Always make sure you're accompanied by someone knowledgeable about the area.

play in the sand, but check the surface temperature; it can get very hot. ⊠ *Coral Sand Dunes Rd./Hwy. 43, Kanab* ✛ *12 miles west of U.S. 89, off Hancock Rd.* ☎ *435/648–2800* ⊕ *www.stateparks. utah.gov* ⊠ *$8.*

Maynard Dixon Living History Museum

MUSEUM | Two miles north of Mount Carmel Junction, this was the final residence of the famous painter of Western life and landscapes. The property and log cabin structure are now maintained by the nonprofit Thunderbird Foundation for the Arts. Tours are self-guided or, from March through November, you can call ahead to arrange a docent tour. ⊠ *2200 U.S. 89, Mount Carmel* ✛ *Near mile marker 84* ☎ *435/648–2653* ⊕ *www.thunderbird-foundation.com* ⊠ *From $10.*

Snow Canyon State Park

NATIONAL/STATE PARK | Named not for winter weather but after a pair of pioneering Utahans named Snow, this gem of a state park is filled with natural wonders. Hiking trails lead to lava cones, sand dunes, cactus gardens, and high-contrast vistas. From the campground you can scramble up huge sandstone mounds and overlook the entire valley. Park staff lead occasional guided hikes. The park is about 10 miles northwest of St. George, and about an hour from Zion. ⊠ *1002 Snow Canyon Dr., Ivins* ☎ *435/628–2255* ⊕ *www.stateparks.utah.gov* ⊠ *$10 per vehicle.*

 ## Activities

BICYCLING
Gooseberry Mesa

BICYCLING | The 28 miles of mountain-biking trails on this mesa southeast of Hurricane are not well traveled, which is good news and bad news. On the plus side, there aren't hordes of fat-tire fanatics to spoil your view of the pristine desert wilderness. However, the trail itself, through gulches and canyons and across slickrock, can be hard to follow. At most major challenges along the path,

there are easier alternatives if you lose your nerve. Come here for solitary and technical single-track challenges. ⊠ *Hurricane* ✛ *Trailhead: off Hwy. 59, 14 miles southeast of Hurricane.*

 ## Nightlife

O.C. Tanner Amphitheater

CONCERTS | Set amid huge sandstone boulders at the base of the stunning red cliffs spilling south from Zion National Park, this amphitheater seats 1,500 people. Summer concerts are held most Fridays and Saturdays in summer, with local and visiting performers in genres from world and classical music to rock and gospel. And the Zion Canyon Music Festival is held here in late September. ⊠ *Dixie State University, 350 W. Lion Blvd., Springdale* ☎ *435/652–7800* ⊕ *www.octannershows.com.*

Zion Canyon Brew Pub

BREWPUBS/BEER GARDENS | Relax after a rugged day of hiking with a flight of ales in the beer garden of southern Utah's first microbrewery, which is just steps from the park's southern entrance. The kitchen turns out decent pub grub, and there's live music most weekend evenings. ⊠ *95 Zion Park Blvd., Springdale* ☎ *435/772–0336* ⊕ *www.zionbrewery. com.*

 ## Shopping

★ Worthington Gallery

ART GALLERIES—ARTS | The emphasis at this superb gallery is on regional art, including pottery, works in glass, jewelry, beguiling copper wind sculptures by Lyman Whitaker, and paintings that capture the dramatic beauty of Southern Utah. ⊠ *789 Zion Park Blvd., Springdale* ☎ *435/772–3446* ⊕ *www.worthingtongallery.com.*

Zion Canyon Offerings

GIFTS/SOUVENIRS | Look for the colorful wind chimes and pinwheels outside this gift shop along Springdale's main street.

Inside you will find handcrafted jewelry and photographs of the local landscape, along with T-shirts, hats, and whimsical crafts. ✉ *933 Zion Park Blvd., Springdale* ☎ *435/772–2443* 🌐 *www.zioncanyonofferings.com.*

🍴 Restaurants

IN THE PARK

Castle Dome Café & Snack Bar

$ | **CAFÉ** | Next to the shuttle stop at Zion Lodge, this small fast-food restaurant is both convenient and enjoys a lovely shaded outdoor patio. You can grab a banana, burger, smoothie, or salad to go, order local brews from the Beer Garden cart, or enjoy a dish of ice cream while soaking up the views of the surrounding geological formations. **Known for:** quick bites; gorgeous views; nice beer selection. [$] *Average main: $6* ✉ *Zion Lodge, Zion Canyon Scenic Dr.* ☎ *435/772–7700* 🌐 *www.zionlodge.com/dining.*

Red Rock Grill

$$$ | **AMERICAN** | The fare at this restaurant at Zion Lodge includes steaks, seafood, and Western specialties such as trout and bison meat loaf headlining the dinner menu. Photos of the surrounding landscape adorn the walls of the spacious dining room, which has enormous windows taking in the scenery, and the large patio has gorgeous views of the real thing. **Known for:** dinner reservations necessary in summer; astounding views inside and out; only full-service restaurant in the park. [$] *Average main: $21* ✉ *Zion Lodge, Zion Canyon Scenic Dr.* ☎ *435/772–7760* 🌐 *www.zionlodge.com/dining.*

PICNIC AREAS

The Grotto

RESTAURANT—SIGHT | **FAMILY** | Get your food to go at the Zion Lodge, take a short walk to this scenic retreat, and dine beneath a shady oak. Amenities include drinking water, picnic tables, and restrooms, but there are no fire grates. A trail from here leads to the Emerald Pools. ✉ *Off Zion Canyon Scenic Dr., at Grotto.*

Kolob Canyons Viewpoint

RESTAURANT—SIGHT | Enjoy a shaded meal with a view at this picnic site 100 yards down the Timber Creek Trail, 5 miles from Kolob Canyons Visitor Center. ✉ *Zion National Park* ✣ *On Timber Creek Trail at end of Kolob Canyons Rd.*

Zion Nature Center

RESTAURANT—SIGHT | **FAMILY** | On your way to or from the Junior Ranger Program you can feed your kids at the center's picnic area. When the center is closed, use the restrooms in South Campground. ✉ *Zion National Park* ✣ *Near entrance to South Campground, ½ mile north of south entrance.*

OUTSIDE THE PARK

Bit & Spur

$$ | **SOUTHWESTERN** | This laid-back Springdale institution has been delighting locals and tourists since the late 1980s, offering a well-rounded menu that includes fresh fish and pasta dishes, but the emphasis is on creative Southwestern fare such as roasted-sweet-potato tamales and chili-rubbed rib-eye steak. Craft beers and the popular house-made sangria complement the zesty cuisine. **Known for:** innovative margaritas; live music; outdoor dining by a fountain beneath shade trees. [$] *Average main: $20* ✉ *1212 Zion Park Blvd., Springdale* ☎ *435/772–3498* 🌐 *www.bitandspur.com* 🕓 *No lunch.*

★ Kanab Creek Bakery

$ | **CAFÉ** | Drop by this urbane little bakery-cafe with an expansive patio for some of the tastiest breakfast and lunch fare for miles, as well as fine espresso drinks, teas, raw juice blends, and a small but well-chosen selection of beer and wine. The Belgian–French-inspired menu features sweet (crepes with jam and delectable pastries) and savory dishes, with croque monsieur, salade Nicoise, and avocado-hummus-tomato panini standing out among the latter. **Known for:** cheerful patio (but limited indoor) seating; heavenly croissants, Belgian chocolate chip cookies, and other sweet treats; fantastic breakfasts. [$] *Average main: $10* ✉ *238 W. Center St., Kanab* ☎ *435/644–5689* 🌐 *www.kanabcreekbakery.com* 🕒 *Closed Mon.*

★ King's Landing Bistro

$$$ | MODERN AMERICAN | If at all possible, sit on the patio—with dramatic views of the area's red rock monoliths—when dining at this casually stylish bistro at the downtown Springdale's popular Driftwood Lodge hotel. The artfully presented cuisine here tends toward creative American—king salmon with saffron couscous, roast chicken with artichoke tapenade—but you'll find some international, mostly Mediterranean, influences in the form of charred Spanish octopus and some one or two outstanding pastas. **Known for:** interesting artisan cocktail list; emphasis on local and seasonal produce and vegetables; rich desserts, including a classic tiramisu. [$] *Average main: $22* ✉ *1515 Zion Park Blvd., Springdale* ☎ *435/772–7422* 🌐 *www.klbzion.com* 🕒 *No lunch.*

Main Street Café

$ | AMERICAN | This colorful storefront eatery in downtown Hurricane pours one of the region's best cups of coffee, a fine prelude or follow-up to the salads, sandwiches, hearty omelets, homemade soups, flavorful pastas, and generous hamburgers on the menu. If you have the time, linger outside on the shaded outdoor patio and watch the hummingbirds. **Known for:** friendly staff; pretty outdoor patio; hefty burgers. [$] *Average main: $12* ✉ *138 S. Main St., Hurricane* ☎ *435/635–9080* 🌐 *www.mainstreetcafeonline.com* 💳 *No credit cards* 🕒 *Closed Sun.*

★ Sego

$$ | CONTEMPORARY | Folks have been known to drive for an hour or more to partake of the outstanding modern American and Asian fare served in this charmingly intimate dining room just off the lobby of the romantic Canyons Boutique Hotel in Kanab, 30 miles from the east entrance of Zion National Park. The menu here changes often according to what's fresh, but recent standouts have included a pork belly and watermelon salad, foraged mushrooms with artichokes and goat cheese, and seared duck-breast lo mein with sambal and jalapeño cream. **Known for:** creative, globally inspired cooking; stellar wine and cocktail list; romantic yet unfussy vibe. [$] *Average main: $20* ✉ *190 N. 300 W, Kanab* ☎ *435/644–5680* 🌐 *www.segokanab.com* 🕒 *Closed Sun. and Mon. No lunch.*

Sol Foods Supermarket

$ | DELI | Stop by this market specializing in healthy, organic foods and check out the premade sandwiches and abundant salad bar, or order a quick sandwich, wrap, or vegetarian snack of your choice. The staff can also prepare a box lunch for your day in the park, and while waiting, you can poke around the affiliated and well-stocked hardware and camping store next door. **Known for:** box lunches; extensive menu; organic snacks, produce, and groceries. [$] *Average main: $8* ✉ *995 Zion Park Blvd., Springdale* ☎ *435/772–3100* 🌐 *www.solfoods.com.*

Spotted Dog Café

$$ | MODERN AMERICAN | Although this restaurant with an eclectic menu that typically includes pastas, lamb, wild-game meat loaf, and rainbow trout is slightly more upscale than most in Springdale, the staff makes you feel right at home even if you saunter in wearing hiking shoes. The exposed wood beams and large windows that frame the surrounding trees and rock cliffs set a Western mood, with tablecloths and original artworks supplying a dash of refinement. **Known for:** impressive but accessible wine list; extensive breakfast buffet; much of the produce is grown on-site. [$] *Average main: $20* ✉ *Flanigan's Inn, 428 Zion Park Blvd., Springdale* ☎ *435/772–0700* 🌐 *www.flanigans.com/dining* 🕒 *Limited hrs Nov.–Mar. No lunch.*

Best Campgrounds in Zion

37

The two campgrounds within Zion National Park—South and Watchman—are family-friendly, convenient, and pleasant, but from early spring through late fall they fill up fast, so book as far ahead as you can. Outside Zion are the park-affiliated Lava Point campground and some private campgrounds.

South Campground. All the sites here are under big cottonwood trees that provide some relief from the summer sun. The campground operates on a reservation system. ✉ *Hwy. 9, ½ mile north of south entrance* ☎ *435/772–3256, 877/444-6777* 🌐 *www.recreation.gov.*

Watchman Campground. This large campground on the Virgin River operates on a reservation system between March and November, but you do not get to choose your site. ✉ *Access road off Zion Canyon Visitor Center parking lot* ☎ *435/772–3256, 877/444–6777* 🌐 *www.recreation.gov.*

Hotels

IN THE PARK

★ Zion Lodge

$$$$ | **HOTEL** | For a dramatic location inside the park, you'd be hard-pressed to improve on a stay at the historic Zion Lodge: the canyon's jaw-dropping beauty surrounds you, access to trailheads is easy, and guests can drive their cars on the lower half of Zion Park Scenic Drive year-round. **Pros:** handsome hotel in the tradition of historic park properties; incredible views; bike rentals on-site. **Cons:** pathways are dimly lit (bring a flashlight); spotty Wi-Fi, poor cell service; books up months ahead. [$] *Rooms from: $217* ✉ *Zion Canyon Scenic Dr.* ☎ *888/297–2757 reservations only, 435/772–7700* 🌐 *www.zionlodge.com* 🛏 *122 rooms* 🍴 *No meals.*

OUTSIDE THE PARK

Best Western East Zion Thunderbird Lodge

$$ | **HOTEL** | **FAMILY** | About 13 miles beyond the east entrance of Zion National Park, this adobe-style motel with clean, spacious rooms is a good option if you also want to be within an hour's drive of Bryce Canyon National Park. **Pros:** restaurant serves great pie; outdoor heated pool, hot tub; well-manicured grounds. **Cons:** no elevator; a bit off the beaten path; standard chain-motel furnishings. [$] *Rooms from: $139* ✉ *U.S. 89 and Hwy. 9, Mount Carmel Junction* ☎ *435/648–2203, 800/780–7234* 🌐 *www.bestwestern.com* 🛏 *61 rooms* 🍴 *No meals.*

★ Cable Mountain Lodge

$$$ | **HOTEL** | With rangy suites with full kitchens and smaller but still generously proportioned studios, this contemporary lodge with a large swimming pool is the closest hotel in Springdale to Zion—it's a scenic five-minute walk over a foot bridge across the Virgin River. **Pros:** steps from Zion National Park's south entrance; many suites have full kitchens; beautiful picnic area along river with gas grills and tables. **Cons:** no breakfast (but a coffeehouse and market steps away); not all rooms have park views; no pets. [$] *Rooms from: $199* ✉ *147 Zion Park Blvd., Springdale* ☎ *435/772–3366, 877/590–3366* 🌐 *www.cablemountainlodge.com* 🛏 *52 rooms* 🍴 *No meals.*

★ Canyon's Lodge

$ | **HOTEL** | With cattle-print throw pillows, papier-mâché mounted deer heads, log walls, and custom beds with rattan headboards or carved-wood headboards, the playful vibe at this quirky 16-room boutique inn sets it apart from the usual budget-friendly lodgings in the Zion and Bryce area. **Pros:** fun and quirky ambience; good base for Zion, Bryce, and the North Rim of the Grand Canyon; there's a small pool. **Cons:** the least expensive rooms are tiny; complimentary breakfast is at nearby sister property; some road noise. $ *Rooms from: $99* ✉ *236 N. 300 W, Kanab* ☎ *435/644–3069* ⊕ *www. canyonslodge.com* ⤴ *16 rooms* ❑ *Free Breakfast.*

Cliffrose Lodge and Gardens

$$$$ | **HOTEL** | The canyon views, acres of lush lawns and flowers, and pool and two-tier waterfall hot tubs at this riverside hotel make it more than a place to rest your head—and you could throw a rock across the river and hit Zion National Park. **Pros:** close to Zion's south entrance; beautiful grounds and views; good restaurant serving breakfast and dinner. **Cons:** pricey during busy times; lots of foot and car traffic nearby; no elevator. $ *Rooms from: $239* ✉ *281 Zion Park Blvd., Springdale* ☎ *435/772–3234, 800/243–8824* ⊕ *www.cliffroselodge. com* ⤴ *52 rooms* ❑ *No meals.*

★ Desert Pearl Inn

$$$$ | **HOTEL** | Offering spacious rooms with vaulted ceilings, oversize windows, sitting areas, small kitchens with wet bars and dishwashers, and a pleasing contemporary decor, this riverside lodge is special. **Pros:** spacious, smartly designed rooms; excellent restaurant adjacent to hotel; rooms facing river have balconies or terraces. **Cons:** often books up well in advance spring through fall; breakfast costs extra; pets not permitted. $ *Rooms from: $255* ✉ *707 Zion Park Blvd., Springdale* ☎ *435/772–8888, 888/828–0898* ⊕ *www.desertpearl.com* ⤴ *73 rooms* ❑ *No meals.*

Flanigan's Inn

$$$ | **HOTEL** | A tranquil, nicely landscaped inn with canyon views and a small pool, Flanigan's has big, comfortable accommodations, including two private villas, and suites that sleep six; some units have a patio or a deck. **Pros:** easy shuttle ride or pleasant walk to Zion Canyon Visitor Center; a meditation maze on the hilltop; great on-site restaurant. **Cons:** not all rooms have views; smaller property that tends to book up quickly; breakfast, though discounted, isn't complimentary. $ *Rooms from: $199* ✉ *428 Zion Park Blvd., Springdale* ☎ *435/772–3244, 800/765–7787* ⊕ *www.flanigans.com* ⤴ *34 rooms* ❑ *No meals.*

Parry Lodge

$$ | **HOTEL** | The simple but clean and comfy rooms at this rambling 1931 hotel in the heart of Kanab are named for the stars—including John Wayne, Lana Turner, Roy Rogers—of the more than two-dozen Hollywood westerns filmed in the area. **Pros:** heated pool; intriguing film history; restaurant on-site serving lunch and complimentary breakfast. **Cons:** some rooms very small; loud air-conditioning; some may find this vintage property a bit too quirky for their tastes. $ *Rooms from: $129* ✉ *89 E. Center St., Kanab* ☎ *435/644–2601, 888/289–1722* ⊕ *www. parrylodge.com* ⤴ *82 rooms* ❑ *Free Breakfast.*

Index

Z

Photo Credits

Front Cover: Aurora Photos / Alamy Stock Photo [Description: Purple Lupin grows in an alpine meadow across from Mount Ranier, WA.] Back cover, from left to right: Lorcel/Shutterstock; David Davis/Shutterstock; NPS. Spine: Francesco R. Lacomino/Shutterstock. Interior, from left to right: Evan Spiler (1). RRuntsch/shutterstock (2-3). Jeff Vanuga (5). Chapter 1: Experience The National Parks of the West: Jeff Vanuga (10-11). cadlikai/Shutterstock (12-13). Tashka | Dreamstime.com (13). Anton Foltin/Shutterstock (13). Ken Wolter/Shutterstock (14). Zack Frank/Shutterstock (14). DnDavis/Shutterstock (14). Oscity/Shutterstock (14). Jill Krueger (15). sumikophoto/Shutterstock (15). Sean Pavone/Shutterstock (15). kan_khampanya/Shutterstock (15). Matthew Connolly/Shutterstock (16). Linda Moon/Shutterstock (16). Mike Brake/Shutterstock (16). Benkrut | Dreamstime.com (16). Charles Haire/Shutterstock (17). Antonel | Dreamstime.com (17). Swdesertlover | Dreamstime.com (17). Anton Foltin/Shutterstock (17). neelsky/Shutterstock (18). Nina B/Shutterstock (18). Sergey Yechikov/Shutterstock (18). kavram/Shutterstock (18). Americanspirit | Dreamstime.com (19). Laurens Hoddenbagh/Shutterstock (19). kojihirano/Shutterstock (19). Sebastien Burel/Shutterstock (19). Gestalt Imagery/Shutterstock (20). Kris Wiktor/Shutterstock (20). Anton Foltin/Shutterstock (20). Checubus/Shutterstock (20). Isu83boo | Dreamstime.com (21). Lorcel/Shutterstock (21). F11photo | Dreamstime.com (21). Hale Kell/Shutterstock (21). Courtesy of Grand Teton Lodge Company (28). 2018 Michel Verdure (28). Roman Khomlyak/Shutterstock (28). Kitleong | Dreamstime.com (29). Asif Islam/Shutterstock (29). Swdesertlover | Dreamstime.com (30). Courtesy Deby Dixon (30). Laurens Hoddenbagh/Shutterstock (30). Edmund Lowe Photography/Shutterstock (31). Steve Lagreca/Shutterstock (31). Andrey Tarantin/Shutterstock (32). NPS (32). Gene Lee/Shutterstock (32). Keifer | Dreamstime.com (33). Jacom Stephens/Avid Creative, Inc./iStockphoto (33). Stephen Fadem (34). Dan King (34). Dan King (34). Erica L. Wainer (34). David Davis/Shutterstock (34). Debbie Bowles (35). BostonGal (35). Roger Bravo (35). Darklich14/Wikimedia Commons (35). Bill Perry/Shutterstock (35). Nate Hovee/Shutterstock (37). ronnybas frimages/Shutterstock (41). Chapter 2: Planning Your Visit: Lorcel/Shutterstock 43). Chapter 3: Great Itineraries: Som Vembar (53). Chapter 4: Arches National Park: Evan Spiler (67). kylepostphotography/Shutterstock (82). Chapter 5: Badlands National Park: Checubus/Shutterstock (91). Chapter 6: Big Bend National Park: Eric Foltz/iStockphoto (109). Chapter 7: Black Canyon of the Gunnison National Park: Tom Till / Alamy (133). Jim Parkin/Shutterstock (141). Chapter 8: Bryce Canyon National Park: Chris Christensen (147). PeteFoley (156). Inc/Shutterstock (160). Chapter 9: Canyonlands National Park: Bryan Brazil/Shutterstock (167). Doug Lemke/Shutterstock (176-177). Chapter 10: Capitol Reef National Park: Luca Moi/Shutterstock (187). 2007 Kerrick James (198). Anton Foltin/Shutterstock (200). Chapter 11: Carlsbad Caverns National Park: Nphoto | Dreamstime.com (205). Doug Meek/Shutterstock (214). Chapter 12: Channel Island National Park: Christopher Russell/iStockphoto (223). Americanspirit | Dreamstime.com (235). Chapter 13: Crater Lake National Park: William A. McConnell (241). Chapter 14: Death Valley National Park: Bryan Brazil/Shutterstock (255). Evan Spiler, Fodors.com member (265). Phitha Tanpairoj/Shutterstock (267). Chapter 15: Glacier and Waterton Lakes National Parks: alfwilde (275). chip phillips/iStockphoto (287). 2008 Kerrick James (288). Chapter 16: Grand Canyon National Park: Courtesy of NPS (305). 2008 Kerrick James (326). Kerrick James (326). Christophe Testi/Shutterstock (332-333). Anton Foltin/Shutterstock (334). Geir Olav Lyngfjell/Shutterstock (335). 2006 Kerrick James (336). 2000 Kerrick James (336). 1995 Kerrick James (337). Grand Canyon NPS/Flickr, [CC BY 2.0] (337). Pacific Northwest Photo | Shutterstock (338). Kerrick James (339). Chapter 17: Grand Teton National Park: Patrick Tr/Shutterstock (345). Courtesy of NPS (362-363). Chapter 18: Great Basin National Park: Dennis Frates / Alamy (375). Heeb Christian / age fotostock (381). Chapter 19: Great Sand Dunes National Park: Andrew Repp/Shutterstock (389). Courtesy of NPS (397). Chapter 20: Guadalupe Mountains National Park: Zack Frank/Shutterstock (401). Michael J Thompson/Shutterstock (408). Chapter 21: Joshua Tree National Park: Eric Foltz/iStockphoto (413). Pixelite/Shutterstock (423). Greg Epperson / age fotostock (427). pmphoto/Shutterstock (428). Chapter 22: Lassen Volcanic National Park: Zack Frank/Shutterstock (431). Shyam Subramanyan (439). Chapter 23: Mesa Verde National Park: Rob Crandall/Shutterstock (447). 2007 Kerrick James (456). Chapter 24: Mount Rainier National Park: chinana, Fodors.com member (465). zschnepf/Shutterstock (478-479). Chapter 25: North Cascades National Park: LoweStock / Getty Images (483). Chapter 26: Olympic National Park: Rita Bellanca (499). Lindsay Douglas/Shutterstock (508). SuperStock/age fotostock (517). Chapter 27: Petrified Forest National Park: Kerrick James (523). Clara/Shutterstock (530). 1995 Kerrick James (533). Chapter 28: Pinnacles National Park: yhelfman/Shutterstock (535). Mike Brake/Shutterstock (544). Chapter 29: Redwoods National and State Parks: iStockphoto (549). Mike Norton/Shutterstock (565). Chapter 30: Rocky Mountain National Park: Stock Connection Distribution / Alamy (567). Harold R. Stinnette Stock Photography / Alamy (577). Chapter 31: Saguaro National Park: Johnny Stockshooter (587). Sasha Buzko/Shutterstock (595). Chapter 32: Sequoia and Kings Canyon National Parks: Robert Holmes (601). urosr/Shutterstock (613). Chapter 33: Theodore Roosevelt National Park: North Dakota Tourism (629). Chapter 34: Wind Cave National Park: South Dakota Tourism (643). South Dakota Tourism (659). Alex Pix/Shutterstock (667). Chapter 35: Yellowstone National Park: funtravlr (667). Paul Stoloff (680). Jeff Vanuga (690-698). Chapter 36: Yosemite National Park: Jill Krueger (713). Nathan Jaskowiak/Shutterstock (723). Katrina Leigh/Shutterstock (738-739). Chapter 37: Zion National Park: John Vaccarelli (745). 2005 Kerrick James (759). About Our Writers: All photos are courtesy of the writers except for the following: Andrew Collins, Courtesy of Fernando Nocedal and Cheryl Crabtree, Courtesy of Bryn Berg.

Notes

Notes

Notes

Notes

Notes

Notes

Notes

Notes

Fodor's THE COMPLETE GUIDE TO THE NATIONAL PARKS OF THE WEST

Editorial: Douglas Stallings, *Editorial Director*; Margaret Kelly, Jacinta O'Halloran, *Senior Editors*; Kayla Becker, Alexis Kelly, Amanda Sadlowski, *Editors*; Teddy Minford, *Content Editor*; Rachael Roth, *Content Manager*

Design: Tina Malaney, *Design and Production Director*; Jessica Gonzalez, *Production Designer*

Photography: Jill Krueger, *Senior Photo Editor*

Maps: Rebecca Baer, *Senior Map Editor*; Mark Stroud (Moon Street Cartography), *Cartographer*

Production: Jennifer DePrima, *Editorial Production Manager*; Carrie Parker, *Senior Production Editor*; Elyse Rozelle, *Production Editor*

Business & Operations: Chuck Hoover, *Chief Marketing Officer*; Robert Ames, *General Manager*; Stephen Horowitz, *Director of Business Development and Revenue Operations*; Tara McCrillis, *Director of Publishing Operations*

Public Relations and Marketing: Joe Ewaskiw, *Manager*; Esther Su, *Marketing Manager*

Writers: Sarah Amandolare, Shelley Arenas, Andrew Collins, Cheryl Crabtree, Deb Hopewell, Laura M. Kidder, Debbie Olsen, Elise Riley, Stina Sieg

Editors: Rachael Roth and Jacinta O'Halloran

Production Editor: Jennifer DePrima

6th Edition

ISBN 978-1-64097-126-4

ISSN 1941–5419

Library of Congress Control Number 2018958614

All details in this book are based on information supplied to us at press time. Always confirm information when it matters, especially if you're making a detour to visit a specific place. Fodor's expressly disclaims any liability, loss, or risk, personal or otherwise, that is incurred as a consequence of the use of any of the contents of this book.

SPECIAL SALES

This book is available at special discounts for bulk purchases for sales promotions or premiums. For more information, e-mail SpecialMarkets@fodors.com.

PRINTED IN THE UNITED STATES OF AMERICA

10 9 8 7 6 5 4 3 2 1